CLASSICAL MYTHOLOGY

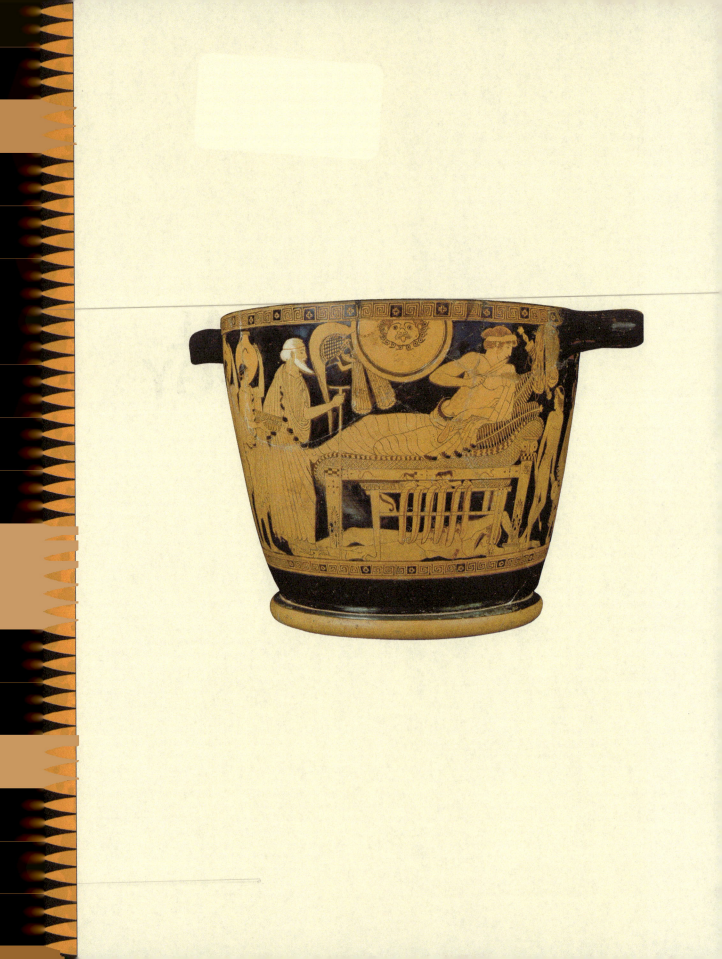

CLASSICAL MYTHOLOGY

TWELFTH EDITION

MARK P. O. MORFORD
University of Virginia, Emeritus

ROBERT J. LENARDON
The Ohio State University, Emeritus

MICHAEL SHAM
Siena College

OXFORD
UNIVERSITY PRESS

IN MEMORIAM

*Since the publication of the eleventh edition of Classical Mythology
we have lost both Robert Lenardon and Mark Morford. It is with deep
sadness that we mark the passing to of two men who were remarkable
scholars, generous colleagues, and gracious mentors. They are missed.*

Dedicated to the memory of

WILLIAM ROBERT JONES

teacher, scholar, friend

OXFORD
UNIVERSITY PRESS

Oxford University Press is a department of the University of Oxford.
It furthers the University's objective of excellence in research, scholarship,
and education by publishing worldwide. Oxford is a registered trade mark
of Oxford University Press in the UK and in certain other countries.

Published in the United States of America by Oxford University Press
198 Madison Avenue, New York, NY 10016, United States of America.

For titles covered by Section 112 of the US Higher Education Opportunity
Act, please visit www.oup.com/us/he for the latest information about
pricing and alternate formats.

Library of Congress Cataloging-in-Publication Data

Names: Morford, Mark P. O., 1929-2019, author. | Lenardon, Robert J., 1928-
author. | Sham, Michael, author.
Title: Classical mythology / Mark P.O. Morford, University of Virginia,
Emeritus; Robert J. Leonardon, The Ohio State University, Emeritus;
Michael Sham, Siena College.
Description: Twelfth edition. | Oxford ; New York : Oxford University
Press, [2023] | Includes bibliographical references and index. |
Summary: "A classical mythology textbook for undergraduate students"—
Provided by publisher.
Identifiers: LCCN 2022041728 (print) | LCCN 2022041729 (ebook) | ISBN
9780197653920 (paperback) | ISBN 9780197653951 (epub)
Subjects: LCSH: Mythology, Classical.
Classification: LCC BL723 .M67 2023 (print) | LCC BL723 (ebook) | DDC
292.1/3—dc23/eng20221031
LC record available at https://lccn.loc.gov/2022041728
LC ebook record available at https://lccn.loc.gov/2022041729

9 8 7 6 5 4 3 2 1
Printed by Marquis, Canada

CONTENTS

PART ONE

The Myths of Creation: The Gods

PREFACE

IT IS NOW OVER FIFTY years since the manuscript of *Classical Mythology* was submitted to the publishers. The original authors have now revised the book through eleven more editions while keeping their research in the field current.

Our work is conceived as a comprehensive source where one may go to explore in depth the nature of the Greek and Roman deities and the heroes and heroines of saga; in a few words, here is a fundamental text for the serious study of the subject of classical mythology. Yet we also have intended to provide a fertile source where one may nourish a sympathetic understanding of the great mythological heritage bestowed by classical antiquity. We also consider the great influence of classical mythology on diverse artistic forms (painting, sculpture, literature, music, opera, dance, theater, and cinema) to be a most enjoyable and rewarding subject, too important to be ignored. The later influence of classical mythology on the arts was originally the subject of Part Four (Chapters 27 and 28), entitled "The Survival of Classical Mythology." This part was removed from the eleventh and subsequent editions, but is still available online in what will hopefully be a more useful format. The subject, however, of the influence of classical mythology permeates all aspects of our presentation throughout. The tenacious persistence of Greek and Roman mythology undeniably remains vital and pervasive in our contemporary world. Greek and Roman myths, of indelible beauty and with great power to inspire, present a particularly fertile and inexhaustible venue for the appreciation of the cultural, intellectual, and artistic history of Western civilization.

Originally, Professor Morford and Professor Lenardon each undertook the major responsibility for certain sections—Professor Lenardon wrote Part One (Chapters 1–16) and Chapter 28 in Part Four (now online), and Professor Morford wrote Parts Two and Three (Chapters 17–26) and Chapter 27 (now online). We have continued to use this approach, although in subsequent revisions all three authors contributed freely throughout the book.

Translations

Successive revisions have been extensive and far-reaching, in grateful response to the many sensitive and appreciative critics over these many years. They have consistently encouraged us to remain firm in our conviction that the literary tradition of Greek and Roman mythology must always remain primary, but they have also confirmed our need and desire to incorporate, insofar as possible, additional comparative and interpretative approaches and more far-reaching evidence from other sources such as archaeology.

Translations of the ancient authors remain extensive, and none has been deleted from this edition. The majority of them throughout the book (except Chapter 26) are by Professor Lenardon, including all thirty-three of the *Homeric Hymns*; all the important passages in Hesiod's *Theogony* and *Works and Days*; and excerpts (many of them substantial) from Homer, Aeschylus, Sophocles, Euripides, Herodotus, Plato, and, in Latin, Ovid and Vergil. These texts are interspersed with interpretative commentary and analysis to elucidate their mythological and literary significance and afford insightful and challenging avenues of interpretation.

Shorter excerpts from many other authors are included, such as the lyric poets, the pre-Socratic philosophers, Pindar, and Lucian; and the Latin authors Statius, Manilius, and Seneca.

All translations are our own.

Spelling

Consistency in spelling has proven impossible to attain. In general, we have adopted Latinized forms (Cronus for Kronos) or spellings generally accepted in English-speaking countries (Heracles, not Herakles). Since non-Latinized spelling of Greek names has become fashionable, we include an appendix listing Greek spellings of important names with their Latinized and English equivalents, which will serve as a paradigm of the principles of transliteration.

Art and Audio Program

Every aspect of *Classical Mythology*'s design and richly rewarding art program has been given great care and attention as we have prepared the twelfth edition.

The illustrations have been an integral part of the work since its inception. Professor Morford was responsible for their selection and for the captions in the first eight editions; for the ninth edition, the first to appear in full color, the opinions of the many colleagues and reviewers also informed our selections. From the ninth to the eleventh editions all three authors took part in the selection of illustrations, a process that often required painful decisions about what to leave out, but one that has also led generally to a consensus about what to include. Professor Morford and Professor Sham divided the responsibility for writing the captions. Professor Sham has been responsible for images and captions new to the twelfth edition.

The visual program is further enriched by the "Myth & Culture" features, all of which were composed by Professor Sham. In twelve illustrated essays throughout the text, this feature allows a close and careful comparative study of the ways in which mythical figures and episodes have been depicted by different artists in a variety of media.

Audio Recordings

Users of *Classical Mythology* consistently praise the book for the quality of the translations of ancient works, all of which were done by the authors. Readers can enjoy listening to many of these translations as streaming audio files in either the enhanced e-book or in Oxford Learning Link: www.oup.com/he/morford12e. The translations that are available in an audio format are indicated in the margin by an icon.

Closer Look Image Analyses

The "Closer Look" image analyses offer the opportunity to examine in detail paintings, frescos, sculpture, mosaics, photographs, and other fine art that represent important episodes from classical myth. Each "Closer Look" includes detailed commentary and guiding questions.

Please visit www.oup.com/he/morford12e for a demo of the audio recordings and Closer Look image analyses.

New to the Twelfth Edition

- **New Artwork**

  The text's rich visual program has been enhanced with a number of new illustrations, each of which includes an informative caption.
- Chapter 25, "Greek Mythology in the Roman World," offers revised coverage of Ovid's *Metamorphoses*.
- **Updated Bibliographies**

  Throughout the text, the end-of-chapter bibliographies have been edited and updated with new material.
- **Improved Organization**

  Every chapter has been edited for greater clarity and accuracy.
- Enhanced e-book. The enhanced e-book, available for purchase at RedShelf, VitalSource, and other vendors, embeds digital resources in line with the text, offering the reader an enhanced learning experience. These resources include note-taking guides, audio flashcards, Closer Look videos, chapter practice questions, audio recordings, and web resources.

Additional Teaching Learning Resources

The twelfth edition of *Classical Mythology* offers a complete suite of classroom resources for both instructors and students, available at Oxford Learning Link (OLL): www.oup.com/he/morford12e. For instructors, these resources include an instructor's manual with chapter outlines, commentaries, translations, and test questions, as well as a computerized test bank and PowerPoint slides. A course cartridge can also be integrated into learning management systems such as Canvas or Blackboard.

For students, resources include commentaries, learning objectives, and chapter activities. In addition, the OLL contains *Now Playing: Learning Classical Mythology through Film*. Designed specifically to accompany *Classical Mythology* and prepared by Professor Sham, this supplement illustrates how classical myths have inspired new adaptations in film, dance, and music, with descriptions from over thirty films and television episodes. Each entry provides a preview of each work, designed to inform an appreciation of the material, an extended treatment of individual scenes, and questions for discussion or written homework assignments.

The OLL also includes two bonus chapters (Chapter 27, "Classical Mythology in Literature," and Chapter 28, "Classical Mythology in Music, Dance, and Film").

Acknowledgments

We have received help and encouragement from many colleagues, students, and friends over the years and generous support from numerous people involved in the editorial development, production, and publication of the twelve editions of this book. To all who have contributed so much, we are deeply grateful.

In particular, for this edition we are thankful to Barbara Polowy, director of the Hillyer Art Library at Smith College, and to the following reviewers for criticism and specific suggestions:

Bart Huelsenbeck,
Ball State University

Robert Carpenter,
University of Missouri

Edmund Cueva,
University of Houston–Downtown

Katrina Dickson,
Emory University

Terri R. Hilgendorf,
Lewis and Clark CC

Salvador Bartrea,
Mississippi State

Debra Trusty,
University of Iowa

This new edition would not have been possible without the enthusiastic and vigorous support of Charles Cavaliere, executive editor; Sukwinder Kaur, editorial assistant; Sheryl Adams, senior marketing manager; and Michele Laseau, art director.

Charles Alton McCloud, through the many editions of the book, generously shared his expertise in music, dance, and theater. His passing in 2014 is still deeply felt.

Mark P. O. Morford
Robert J. Lenardon
Michael Sham

MAPS, FIGURES, AND MYTH & CULTURE

MAPS

FIGURES

MYTH & CULTURE

CLOSER LOOK IMAGES AND AUDIO RECORDINGS

CLOSER LOOK IMAGE ANALYSES

Closer Look

The "Closer Look" image analyses offer the opportunity to examine in detail paintings, frescos, sculpture, mosaics, photographs, and other fine art that represent important episodes from classical myth. Each "Closer Look" includes detailed commentary and guiding questions.

AUDIO RECORDINGS
Audio

Users of *Classical Mythology* consistently praise the book for the quality of the translations of ancient works, all of which were done by the authors. Readers can enjoy listening to many of these translations as streaming audio files in the enhanced e-book or on the book's Learning Link: www.oup.com/he/morford12e. Those translations that are available in an audio format are indicated in the margin by an audio icon.

ABOUT THE AUTHORS

MARK MORFORD was Professor Emeritus of Classics at the University of Virginia, where he joined the faculty in 1984 after teaching at The Ohio State University for twenty-one years and serving as chairman of the Department of Classics. He also served as Kennedy Professor of Renaissance Studies at Smith College, where he held a research appointment in the Mortimer Rare Book Room of the Neilson Library. As vice president for education of the American Philological Association, he actively promoted the cooperation of teachers and scholars in schools and universities. Throughout his fifty years of teaching he was devoted to bringing together teachers of classical subjects and teachers in other disciplines. He has published books on the Roman poets Persius and Lucan and the Renaissance scholar Justus Lipsius (*Stoics and Neostoics: Lipsius and the Circle of Rubens*), as well as many articles on Greek and Roman literature and Renaissance scholarship and art. His book *The Roman Philosophers* was published in 2002, and at his passing he was working on a new book, *The Ancient Romans*.

ROBERT LENARDON was Professor Emeritus of Classics at The Ohio State University, where he was on the faculty for twenty-five years and served as director of graduate studies in classics. He taught at several other universities, including the University of Cincinnati, Columbia University, and the University of British Columbia. He was a visiting fellow at Corpus Christi College, Cambridge University, and has written articles on Greek history and classics and a biography, *The Saga of Themistocles*. He served as book review editor of the *Classical Journal* and presented radio programs about mythology in music, a subject dear to his heart. The afterlife of classical subjects and themes in literature, music, film, and dance was a favorite area of teaching and research. For the fall semester of 2001, he was appointed Visiting Distinguished Scholar in Residence at the University of Louisville, Kentucky. His translations from the *Greek Anthology* have been set to music by Gerald Busby, in a work entitled *Songs from Ancient Greek*, for tenor and piano (premiere, Carnegie Hall, 2005). At his passing he had just completed writing a history, *Hubris: The Persian Wars against the Greeks*.

MICHAEL SHAM is Professor of Classics at Siena College, where for nearly thirty years he has developed a small but vigorous program. He has served as chair of the Department of Modern Languages and Classics at Siena College. Throughout his teaching career he has been dedicated to bringing the value of a classical education to a wider audience. He has worked to bring together scholars, writers, and artists across traditional academic disciplines to explore the continually renewed vitality of the classical tradition. He has written and spoken on a wide range of scholarly interests, including the influence of Ovid's *Metamorphoses* on contemporary American poets and the adaptation and production of Greek tragedy for the contemporary stage. He has himself written an adaption of Euripides' *Iphigenia in Aulis* to some acclaim. He was a contributing author to *A Companion to Classical Mythology* (Longman, 1997). He is responsible for the companion website, the Instructor's Manual for *Classical Mythology,* and the *Now Playing* supplement. He is currently working on a book about the influence of the *Iliad* and the *Odyssey* on contemporary culture.

The Myths of Creation: The Gods

Jean-Auguste-Dominique Ingres, *Jupiter and Thetis*

PART ONE
The Myths of Creation: The Gods

INTERPRETATION AND DEFINITION OF CLASSICAL MYTHOLOGY

PHAEDRUS: Tell me, Socrates, was it not somewhere around here by the stream of Ilissus that Boreas is said to have carried off Oreithyia?

SOCRATES: That's the story.

PHAEDRUS: It *was* around here, wasn't it? At any rate, the stream is beautiful, pure and clear, and perfect for young girls to play along.

SOCRATES: No, it was down farther. . . . There is an altar there to Boreas, I think.

PHAEDRUS: I didn't know that. But tell me, Socrates, by Zeus, do you believe this story is true?

—**PLATO,** *Phaedrus* 229b

Preparation for Sacrifice

THE IMPOSSIBILITY OF ESTABLISHING a satisfactory definition of **myth** has not deterred scholars from developing comprehensive theories on the meaning and interpretation of myth, often to provide bases for a hypothesis about its origins. Useful surveys of the principal theories are readily available, so we shall attempt to touch on only a few theories that are likely to prove especially fruitful or are persistent enough to demand attention. One thing is certain: no single theory of myth can cover all kinds of myths. The variety of traditional tales is matched by the variety of their origins and significance; as a result, no monolithic theory can succeed in achieving universal applicability. Definitions of myth will tend to be either too limiting or so broad as to be virtually useless. In the last analysis, definitions are enlightening because they succeed in identifying particular characteristics of different types of stories and thus provide criteria for classification.

The word *myth* comes from the Greek word *mythos*, which means "word," "speech," "tale," or "story," and that is essentially what a myth is: a story. Some would limit this broad definition by insisting that the story must have proved itself worthy of becoming traditional.[1] A myth may be a story that is narrated orally, but usually it is eventually given written form. A myth also may be told by means of no words at all, for example, through painting, sculpture, music, dance, and mime, or by a combination of various media, as in the case of drama, song, opera, or the movies.

Many specialists in the field of mythology, however, are not satisfied with such broad interpretations of the term *myth*. They attempt to distinguish "true myth" (or "myth proper") from other varieties and seek to draw distinctions in terminology between myth and other words often used synonymously, such as legend, saga, folk tale, and fairy tale.[2]

True Myth or Myth Proper and Saga or Legend

As opposed to an all-encompassing definition for the general term *myth*, **true myth or myth proper** is used for stories primarily concerned with the gods and humankind's relations with them. **Saga or legend** (and we use the words interchangeably) has a perceptible relationship to history; however fanciful and imaginative, it has its roots in historical fact.[3] These two categories underlie the basic division of the first two parts of this book into "The Myths of Creation: The Gods" and "The Greek Sagas."

Folk Tales and Fairy Tales

In addition to these two categories there are **folk tales**, which are often stories of adventure, sometimes peopled with fantastic beings and enlivened by ingenious strategies on the part of the hero or heroine, who will triumph in the end; their goal is primarily, but not necessarily solely, to entertain. Many of the characters and motifs in folk tales are familiar to us all. They are found in both oral and written literature throughout the world, from ancient times to the present, and inevitably will be a source of inspiration for the future, for example, the monstrous giant, the wicked sorceress, the distraught maiden in peril and the special powers of her savior, the wicked sisters, mistaken identity, the imposition of labors, the solving of riddles, the fulfillment of romantic love, and on and on. Among the many folk tales in this book, the tale of Cupid and Psyche (see p. 212) offers a particularly splendid example. It begins with "once upon a time" and ends with "happily ever after."

Fairy tales may be classified as particular kinds of folk tales, defined as "short, imaginative, traditional tales with a high moral and magical content"; a study by Graham Anderson identifying fairy tales in the ancient world is most enlightening.[4] It is impossible to distinguish rigidly between a folk tale and a fairy tale, although perhaps a fairy tale is often created especially for the young.

The Problems Imposed by Rigid Definitions

Rarely, if ever, do we find a pristine, uncontaminated example of any one of these forms. Yet, the traditional categories of myth, saga, and folk tale are useful guides for any attempt to impose some order upon the multitudinous variety of classical tales.[5] How loose these categories are can be seen, for example, in the legends of Odysseus or of the Argonauts, which contain elements of history (saga) but are full of stories that may be designated as myths and folk tales. The criteria for definition merge and the lines of demarcation blur.

Myth and Truth

Since, as we have seen, the Greek word for myth means "word," "speech," or "story," for a critic like Aristotle it became the designation for the plot of a play; thus, it is easy to understand how a popular view would equate myth with fiction. In everyday speech, the most common association of the words *myth* and *mythical* is with what is incredible and fantastic. How often do we hear the expression "It's a myth" uttered in derogatory contrast with such laudable concepts as reality, truth, science, and the facts?

Therefore, important distinctions may be drawn between stories that are perceived as true and those that are not.[6] The contrast between myth and reality has been a major philosophical concern since the time of the early Greek philosophers. Myth is a many-faceted personal and cultural phenomenon created to provide a reality and a unity to what is transitory and fragmented in the world that we experience—the philosophical vision of the afterlife in Plato and any religious conception of a god are mythic, not scientific, concepts. Myth provides us with absolutes in the place of ephemeral values and with a comforting perception of the world that is necessary to make the insecurity and terror of existence bearable.[7]

It is disturbing to realize that our faith in absolutes and factual truth can be easily shattered. "Facts" change in all the sciences; textbooks in chemistry, physics, and medicine are sadly (or happily, for progress) soon out of date. It is embarrassingly banal but fundamentally important to reiterate the platitude that myth, like art, is truth on a quite different plane from that of prosaic and transitory factual knowledge. Yet, myth and factual truth need not be mutually exclusive, as some so emphatically insist. A story embodying eternal values may contain what was imagined, at any one period, to be scientifically correct in every factual detail; and the accuracy of that information may be a vital component of its mythical raison d'être. Indeed, on one hand, one can create a myth out of a factual story, as a great historian must do: any interpretation of the facts, no matter how credible, will inevitably be a mythic invention. On the other hand, a different kind of artist may create a nonhistorical myth for the ages, and whether or not it is factually accurate may be quite beside the point. A case for discussion is presented by the excerpts from the historical myth of Herodotus, which is translated in Chapter 6.

Myth in a sense is the highest reality, and the thoughtless dismissal of myth as untruth, fiction, or a lie is the most barren and misleading definition of all. The dancer and choreographer Martha Graham, sublimely aware of the timeless "blood memory" that binds our human race and that is continually evoked by the archetypal transformations of mythic art, offers a beautifully concise summation: as opposed to the discoveries of science that "will in time change and perhaps grow obsolete . . . art is eternal, for it reveals the inner landscape, which is the soul of man."[8]

Myth and Religion

As we stated earlier, true myth (as distinguished from saga and folk tale) is primarily concerned with the gods, religion, and the supernatural. Most Greek and Roman stories reflect this universal preoccupation with creation, the nature of god and humankind, the afterlife, and other spiritual concerns.

Thus, mythology and religion are inextricably entwined. One tale or another may have been believed at some time by certain people not only factually but also spiritually; specific creation stories and mythical conceptions of deity may still be considered true today and provide the dogma for devout religious belief in a contemporary society. In fact, any collection of material for the comparative study of world mythologies will be dominated by the study of texts that are, by nature, religious. Greek and Roman religious ceremonies and cults were given authority by myths that inspired belief and therefore afford a recurrent theme in the chapters to follow. Among the examples are the worship of Zeus at Olympia, Athena in Athens, and Demeter at Eleusis, as well as the celebration of other mystery religions throughout the ancient world. The ritualist interpretation of the origins of mythology is discussed later in this chapter. Greek religion is discussed in Chapter 6.

Mircea Eliade

Mircea Eliade, one of the most prolific twentieth-century writers on myth, lays great emphasis on the mystical in his conception of myth: he sees myth as a tale satisfying the yearning of human beings for a fundamental orientation rooted in the religious aura of a sacred timelessness. This yearning is fully satisfied only by stories narrating the events surrounding the beginnings and origins of things. Eliade believes that God, once in a holy era, created the world, and this initial cosmogony becomes the origin myth, the model for creations of every kind and stories about them. He conceives, for example, of a ritual or rite having been performed in a sacred place in this sacred timelessness quite beyond the ordinary or profane space in which we live. His concept develops a difficult, complex mysticism. Like a religious sacrament, myth provides in the imagination a spiritual release from historical time. This is the nature of true myths, which are fundamentally paradigms and explanations and most important to the individual and society.[9] This definition, which embraces the explanatory nature of mythology, brings us to another universal theory.

Myth and Etiology

Some maintain that myth should be interpreted narrowly as an explication of the origin of some fact or custom. Hence, the theory is called **etiological**, from the Greek word for cause (*aitia*). In this view, the mythmaker is a kind of primitive scientist, using myths to explain facts that cannot otherwise be explained within the limits of society's knowledge at the time. Again, this theory is adequate for some myths, for example, for those that account for the origin of certain rituals or cosmology; but interpreted literally and narrowly, it does not allow for the imaginative or metaphysical aspects of mythological thought.

Yet, if one does not interpret etiological ("the assignment of causes or origins") too literally and narrowly but defines it by the adjective *explanatory*, interpreted in its most general sense, one perhaps may find at last the most applicable of all the monolithic theories. Myths usually try to explain matters physical, emotional, and spiritual not only literally and realistically but also figuratively and metaphorically. Myths attempt to explain the origin of our physical world: the earth and the heavens, the sun, the moon, and the stars; where human beings came from and the dichotomy between body and soul; the source of beauty and good-ness, and of evil and sin; the nature and meaning of love; and so on. It is difficult to tell a story that does not reveal, and at the same time somehow explain, some-thing; and the imaginative answer usually is in some sense or other scientific or theological. The major problem with this universal etiological approach is that it does nothing to identify a myth specifically and to distinguish it clearly from any other form of expression, whether scientific, religious, or artistic—that is, too many essentially different kinds of story may be basically etiological.

Rationalism versus Metaphor, Allegory, and Symbolism

The desire to rationalize classical mythology arose far back in classical antiqui-ty and is especially associated with the name of Euhemerus (ca. 300 B.C.), who claimed that the gods were men deified for their great deeds (see Chapter 27 on the companion website). The supreme god Zeus, for example, was once a mortal king in Crete who deposed his father, Cronus. At the opposite extreme from **euhemerism** is the metaphorical interpretation of stories. Antirationalists, who favor metaphorical interpretations, believe that traditional tales hide profound meanings. At its best, the metaphorical approach sees myth as allegory (allegory is to be defined as sustained metaphor), where the details of the story are but symbols of universal truths. At its worst, the allegorical approach is a barren exercise in cryptology: to explain the myth of Ixion and the centaurs in terms of clouds and weather phenomena is hardly enlightening and not at all ennobling. (For Ixion and the Centaurs, see pp. 118 and 372.)

Allegorical Nature Myths: Max Müller

An influential nineteenth-century theory was that of Max Müller: myths are nature myths, he said, all referring to meteorological and cosmological phenom-ena. This is, of course, an extreme development of the allegorical approach, and it is hard to see how or why *all* myths can be explained as allegories of, for ex-ample, day replacing night or winter succeeding summer. True, some myths are nature myths, and certain gods, for example, Zeus, represent or control the sky and other parts of the natural order; yet, it is just as true that a great many more myths have no such relationship to nature.[10]

Myth and Psychology: Freud and Jung

Sigmund Freud

The metaphorical approach took many forms in the twentieth century through the theories of the psychologists and psychoanalysts, most especially those of Sigmund Freud and Carl Jung. We need to present at least some of their basic concepts, which have become essential for any understanding of mythic cre-ativity. Freud's views were not completely new, of course (the concept of "deter-minism," for example, "one of the glories of Freudian theory," is to be found in Aristotle),[11] but his formulation and analysis of the inner world of humankind bear the irrevocable stamp of genius.

Certainly, methods and assumptions adopted by comparative mythologists—the formulations of the structuralists and the modern interpretation of mythological tales as imaginative alleviating and directive formulations, created to make existence in this real world tolerable—all these find confirmation and validity in premises formulated by Freud. The endless critical controversy in our post-Freudian world merely confirms his unique contribution.

Among Freud's many important contemporaries and successors, Jung (deeply indebted to the master but a renegade) must be singled out because of the particular relevance of his theories to a fuller appreciation of the deep-rooted recurring patterns of mythology. Among Freud's greatest contributions are his emphasis on sexuality (and in particular infantile sexuality), his theory of the unconscious, his interpretation of dreams, and his identification of the **Oedipus complex** (although the term *complex* belongs to Jung). Freud has this to say about the story of King Oedipus:

> *His fate moves us only because it might have been our own, because the oracle laid upon us before our birth the very curse which rested upon him. It may be that we are all destined to direct our first sexual impulses toward our mothers, and our first impulses of hatred and resistance toward our fathers; our dreams convince us that we were. King Oedipus, who slew his father Laius and wedded his mother Jocasta, is nothing more or less than a wish-fulfillment—the fulfillment of the wish of our childhood. But we, more fortunate than he, in so far as we have not become psychoneurotics, have since our childhood succeeded in withdrawing our sexual impulses from our mothers, and in forgetting the jealousy of our fathers. . . . As the poet brings the guilt of Oedipus to light by his investigation, he forces us to become aware of our own inner selves, in which the same impulses are still extant, even though they are suppressed.*[12]

This Oedipal incest complex is here expressed, in the masculine form, in terms of a man's behavior in relationship to his mother, but it also could be expressed in terms of the relationship between daughter and father; the daughter turns to the father as an object of love and becomes hostile to her mother as her rival. For Jung this is an Electra complex.

Dreams for Freud are the fulfillment of wishes that have been repressed and disguised. To protect sleep and relieve potential anxiety, the mind goes through a process of what is termed **dream-work**, which consists of three primary mental activities: "condensation" of elements (they are abbreviated or compressed); "displacement" of elements (they are changed, particularly in terms of allusion and a difference of emphasis); and "representation," the transmission of elements into imagery or symbols, which are many, varied, and often sexual. Something similar to this process may be discerned in the origin and evolution of myths; it also provides insight into the mind and the methods of the creative artist, as Freud himself was well aware in his studies.[13]

Thus, Freud's discovery of the significance of dream-symbols led him and his followers to analyze the similarity between dreams and myths. Symbols are many and varied and often sexual (e.g., objects like sticks and swords are phallic). Myths, therefore, in the Freudian interpretation, reflect people's waking efforts to systematize the incoherent visions and impulses of their sleep world. The patterns in the imaginative world of children, savages, and neurotics are similar and are revealed in the motifs and symbols of myth.

As can be seen from Freud's description in the earlier quote, one of the basic patterns is that of the Oedipus story, in which the son kills the father in order to possess the mother. From this pattern Freud propounded a theory of our archaic heritage, in which the Oedipal drama was played out by a primal horde in their relationship to a primal father. The murder and the eating of the father led to important tribal and social developments, among them deification of the father figure, the triumph of patriarchy, and the establishment of a totemic system, whereby a totem (i.e., a sacred animal) was chosen as a substitute for the slain father. Most important of all, from the ensuing sense of guilt and sin for parricide emerges the conception of God as Father who must be appeased and to whom atonement must be made. In fact, according to Freud, the Oedipus complex inspired the beginning not only of religion but also of all ethics, art, and society.

It is clear that Freud's connection between dreams and myths is illuminating for many myths, if not for all. In addition to the story of Oedipus one might single out, for example, the legend of the Minotaur or the saga of the House of Atreus, both of which deal with some of the most persistent, if repressed, human fears and emotions and, by their telling, achieve a kind of catharsis.

Carl Jung

Jung went beyond the mere connection of myths and dreams to interpret myths as the projection of what he called the **collective unconscious** of the race, that is, a revelation of the continuing psychic tendencies of society. Jung made a distinction between the personal unconscious and the collective unconscious: the personal concerns matters of an individual's own life, whereas the collective embraces political and social questions involving the group. Dreams therefore may be either personal or collective.

Thus, myths contain images or **archetypes** (to use Jung's term, which embraces Freud's concept of symbols)—traditional expressions of collective dreams, developed over thousands of years, of symbols on which the society as a whole has come to depend. For Jung the Oedipus complex was the first archetype that Freud discovered. There are many such archetypes in Greek mythology and in dreams. Here are some of the ways in which Jung thought about archetypes, the collective unconscious, and mythology. An archetype is a kind of dramatic abbreviation of the patterns involved in a whole story or situation, including the way it develops and how it ends; it is a behavior pattern, an inherited scheme of functioning. Just as a bird has the physical and mental attributes of a bird and builds its nest in a characteristic way, so human beings by nature and by instinct are born with predictable and identifiable characteristics (cf. Xenophanes, translated on p. 138). In the case of human behavior and attitudes, the patterns are expressed in archetypal images or forms. The archetypes of behavior with which human beings are born and which find their expression in mythological tales are called the "collective unconscious." Therefore, "mythology is a pronouncing of a series of images that formulate the life of archetypes."[14] Heroes like Heracles and Theseus are models who teach us how to behave.[15]

The following are a few examples of archetypes. The **anima** is the archetypal image of the female that each man has within him; it is to this concept that he responds (for better or for worse) when he falls in love. Indeed, the force of an archetype may seize a person suddenly, as when one falls in love at first sight. Similarly, the **animus** is the archetypal concept of the male that a woman instinctively harbors within her. The old wise man and the great mother and symbols or signs of various sorts are also among the many Jungian archetypes. These appear in the dreams of individuals or are expressed in the myths of societies.

The great value of Jung's concept is that it emphasizes the psychological dependence of all societies (sophisticated as well as primitive) on their traditional myths, often expressed also in religion and ritual. But Jung's theories, like those we have already examined, have their limitations; they are not the only key to an understanding of mythology.

The Legacy of Freud

Freud's theories about the origin of mythological themes have attracted devotion and criticism in the century since their promulgation—evidence for their undeniable importance. Classical scholars in the English-speaking world have been more dismissive than others: the important book by H. J. Rose on Greek mythology virtually ignores psychological and psychoanalytical approaches to myth, and the former Regius Professor of Greek at the University of Oxford, Hugh Lloyd-Jones, writing toward the end of the twentieth century, is skeptical, yet appreciative, of the work of other Regius professors (Dodds and Kirk), which is based on deep knowledge of Greek language and literatures and some knowledge of comparative sociology, psychology, and religion. Lloyd-Jones is contemptuous of psychoanalytical interpretations of Greek literature and myth by writers unfamiliar with Greek language and history. More gently, Jan Bremmer observes: "Historical and linguistic knowledge remains indispensable."[16]

From the beginning Freud has been under attack from biologists and psychoanalysts. E. O. Wilson, writing in 1998, says that "Freud guessed wrong" with regard to dreams and the unconscious. Wilson embraces the theory of J. A. Hobson that "dreaming is a kind of insanity," which in a way reorganizes information stored in the memory and is not an expression of childhood trauma or repressed desires. For example, in discussing the incest taboo, Wilson prefers "the Westermarck effect" (named after the Finnish anthropologist E. A. Westermarck, who published his theory in 1891 in *The History of Human Marriage*). Westermarck wrote that human avoidance of incest is genetic and that the widespread social taboo comes from this "epigenetic" attribute. In contrast, Freud believed that the desire for incestuous relations (in men directed toward their mothers or sisters) was "the first choice of object in mankind," and therefore its repression was enforced by widespread social taboos. Clearly, very different interpretations of the myth of Oedipus will flow from these competing theories.[17] There will be other theories, and all of them, it can safely be said, will implicitly or explicitly support, attack, or comment on Freud. This is the measure of his genius.

For the purposes of an introduction to Greek mythology, however, arguments in favor of or in opposition to Freud and Jung are ultimately irrelevant. The crucial fact remains that their psychological and psychoanalytical theories permeate most profoundly not only mythological studies but also all literary and artistic pursuits. They are arguably in some ways even more important and pervasive in intellectual fields than they are in the medical. Yet, a recent history of the rise of psychotherapy in the United States reveals how, within some one hundred years, an obscure treatment in Vienna has become "a staple of main-stream America medical practice and a fixture of our modern culture."[18]

Freud's theories have been a springboard for anthropologists and sociologists—most notably Claude Lévi-Strauss, whose theories have been applied to Greek myth with success by the so-called Paris school, namely, Jean-Pierre Vernant, Pierre Vidal-Naquet, and Marcel Detienne.[19] These mythographers combine the study of human societies with psychological theories that explain the origins of myth in terms of the minds of individuals. (Jung was particularly concerned with the collective unconscious of society, as we have seen.) The work of these French scholars is fundamental for any attempt to understand the place of myth in human societies, but, like the theories of Freud and Jung, it overvalues similarities in the minds of individuals and collective rituals and myths of societies while undervaluing variations among individual human societies.

Before we consider Lévi-Strauss and other structural theorists, we begin with earlier mythographers who associated myth with religion and ritual in society.

Myth and Society

Myth and Ritual

J. G. **Frazer** presents a ritualist interpretation of mythology, which has become one of the most influential and enduring points of view. Despite its faults, his work *The Golden Bough* remains a pioneering monument in its attempts to link myth with ritual. It is full of comparative data on kingship and ritual, but its value is lessened by the limitations of the author's ritualist interpretations and by his eagerness to establish dubious analogies between myths of primitive tribes and classical myths.

Similarly, the works of Jane **Harrison**, *Prolegomena to the Study of Greek Religion* and *Themis*, are of seminal importance. Harrison falls in the same tradition as does Frazer, and many of her conclusions about comparative mythology, religion, and ritual are subject to the same critical reservations. Frazer and Harrison established fundamental approaches that were to dominate classical attitudes at the beginning of the twentieth century.

Renowned novelist and poet Robert **Graves** has written an influential treatment of Greek myths that is full of valuable factual information unfortunately embedded in much fascinating but unsubstantiated and idiosyncratic analysis. For him the definition of true myth is "the reduction to narrative shorthand of ritual mime performed in public festivals, and often recorded pictorially on temple walls, vases, seals, bowls, mirrors, chests, shields, tapestries, and the like."[20] He distinguishes this true myth from twelve other categories, such as philosophical allegory, satire or parody, minstrel romance, political propaganda, theatrical melodrama, and realistic fiction. We single out Graves because he was perceptive enough to realize that literary distinctions may be as enlightening as any other type of classification for classical mythology.

Yet, stated most bluntly, this ritualist theory says that "myth implies ritual, ritual implies myth, they are one and the same."[21] True, many myths are closely connected with rituals, and the theory is valuable for the connection it emphasizes between myth and religion; but it is patently untenable to connect *all* true myth with ritual.

Myth as Social Charters

Important in the development of modern theories is the work of Bronislav **Malinowski**, who was stranded among the Trobriand Islanders (off New Guinea) during World War I; he used his enforced leisure to study the Trobrianders.[22] As an anthropologist and ethnographer, he placed a high value on fieldwork in order to reach his final ideological goal: "to grasp the native's point of view, his relation to life, to realize his vision of *his* world."[23]

Malinowski's great discovery was the close connection between myths and social institutions, which led him to explain myths not in cosmic or mysterious terms, but as "charters" of social customs and beliefs. To him myths were related to practical life, and they explained existing facts and institutions by reference to tradition: the myth confirms (i.e., is the "charter" for) the institution, custom, or belief. Clearly, such a theory will be valid only for certain myths (e.g., those involving the establishment of a ritual), but any theory that excludes the speculative element in myth is bound to be too limited.

Structuralist Interpretations of Myth

Structuralism is a theoretical approach to mythology (first developed by Vladimir Propp), which has been explored with different emphases and approaches by various later theorists, among whom we single out Lévi-Strauss and Walter Burkert. Fundamentally, structuralism may be defined as an attempt to analyze myths into their component parts.

Claude Lévi-Strauss

More recently, the structural theories of Claude Lévi-Strauss have enriched the anthropological approach to myth, and they have a connection with Malinowski's most important concept, that is, the link between myth and society.[24]

Lévi-Strauss sees myth as a mode of communication, like language or music. In music it is not the sounds themselves that are important but their *structure*, that is, the relationship of sounds to other sounds. In myth, it is the narrative that takes the part of the sounds of music, and the structure of the narrative can be perceived at various levels and in different codes (e.g., culinary, astronomical, and sociological). From this it follows that no one version of a myth is the "right" one: all versions are valid, for myth, like society, is a living organism in which all the parts contribute to the existence of the whole. As in an orchestral score, certain voices or instruments play some sounds, while the whole score is the sum of the individual parts, so in a myth the different, partial versions combine to reveal its total structure, including the relationship of the different parts to each other and to the whole.

Lévi-Strauss' method is therefore rigorously analytical, breaking down each myth into its component parts. Underlying his analytical approach are basic assumptions, of which the most important is that all human behavior is based on certain unchanging patterns, whose structure is the same in all ages and in all societies. He also assumes that society has a consistent structure and therefore a functional unity in which every component plays a meaningful part. As part of the working of this social machine, myths are derived ultimately from the structure of the mind. And the basic structure of the mind, as of the myths it creates, is *binary*; that is, the mind is constantly dealing with pairs of contradictions or opposites. It is the function of myth to mediate between these opposing extremes—raw/cooked, life/death, hunter/hunted, nature/culture, and so on. "Mythical thought always progresses from the awareness of oppositions towards their resolution."[25] Myth, then, is a mode by which a society communicates and through which it finds a resolution between conflicting opposites. The logical structure of a myth provides a means by which the human mind can avoid unpleasant contradictions and thus, through mediation, reconcile conflicts that would be intolerable if unreconciled. Lévi-Strauss would maintain that all versions of a myth are equally authentic for exploring the myth's structure.

The theories of Lévi-Strauss have aroused passionate controversy among anthropologists and mythographers. His analysis of the Oedipus myth, for example, has been widely criticized. Yet whatever one's judgment may be, there is no doubt that this structural approach can illuminate a number of Greek myths, especially with regard to the function of "mediating." But the approach is open to the same objections as other comprehensive theories: that it establishes too rigid, too universal a concept of the functioning of the human mind. Indeed, the binary functioning of the human mind and of human society may be common, but it has not been proved to be either universal or necessary. Finally, Lévi-Strauss draws most of his evidence from primitive and preliterate cultures, and his theories seem to work more convincingly for them than for the literate mythology of the Greeks. His approach is better applied, for example, to the early Greek succession myths than to the Sophoclean, literate version of the legends of Oedipus and his family. We should all the same be aware of the potential of structuralist theories and should be ready to use them as we seek to make meaningful connections between the different constituent elements of a myth or between different myths that share constituent elements. As we noted earlier, Lévi-Strauss was particularly influential on the Paris school.

Vladimir Propp

The structural interpretation of myth was developed, long before the work of Lévi-Strauss, by Vladimir Propp in his study of the Russian folk tale.[26] Like Lévi-Strauss, Propp analyzed traditional tales into their constituent parts, from which he deduced a single, recurrent structure applicable to all Russian folk tales. Unlike Lévi-Strauss, he described this structure as linear, that is, as having an unchanging temporal sequence, so that one element in the myth always follows another and never occurs out of order. This is significantly different from the pattern in Lévi-Strauss's theory, where the elements may be grouped without regard to time or sequence.

Propp divided his basic structure into thirty-one functions or units of action (which have been defined by others as **motifemes**, on the analogy of morphemes and phonemes in linguistic analysis). These functions are constants in traditional tales: the characters may change, but the functions do not. Further, these functions always occur in an identical sequence, although not all the functions need appear in a particular tale. Those that do, however, will always occur in the same sequence. Finally, Propp states that "all fairy tales are of one type in regard to their structure."[27]

Propp was using a limited number (one hundred) of Russian folk tales of one sort only, that is, the **Quest**. Yet, his apparently strict analysis has proved remarkably adaptable and valid for other sorts of tales in other cultures. The rigid sequence of functions is too inflexible to be fully applicable to Greek myths that have a historical dimension (e.g., some of the tales in the Trojan cycle of saga), where the "facts" of history, as far as they can be established, may have a sequence independent of structures whose origins lie in psychological or cultural needs.

Propp's theories are very helpful, however, in comparing myths that are apparently unrelated, showing, for example, how the same functions appear in the myths, no matter what names are given to the characters who perform them. Mythological names are a strain on the memory. Merely to master them is to achieve very little, unless they can be related in some meaningful way to other tales, including tales from other mythologies. Dreary memorization, however, becomes both easier and purposeful if underlying structures and their constituent units can be perceived and arranged logically and consistently.

A very simple example would be the structural elements common to the myths of Heracles, Theseus, Perseus, and Jason, whose innumerable details can be reduced to a limited sequence of functions. It is more difficult to establish the pattern for, say, a group of stories about the mothers of heroes (e.g., Callisto, Danaë, Io, and Antiope). Yet, as Walter Burkert shows (see the following section), they resolve themselves into a clear sequence of five functions: (1) the girl leaves home; (2) the girl is secluded (beside a river, in a tower, in a forest, etc.); (3) she is made pregnant by a god; (4) she suffers punishment or rejection or a similar unpleasant consequence; and (5) she is rescued, and her son is born.[28]

We can say definitely that in most cases it is helpful to the student to analyze a myth into its constituent parts. There should be four consequences:

1. A perceptible pattern or structure will emerge.
2. It will be possible to find the same structure in other myths, thus making it easier to organize the study of myths.
3. It will be possible to compare the myths of one culture with those of another.
4. As a result of this comparison, it will be easier to appreciate the development of a myth prior to its literary presentation.

Structuralism need not be—indeed, cannot be—applied to all classical mythology, nor need one be enslaved to either Lévi-Strauss or the more rigid but simpler structure of Propp's thirty-one functions. Structuralism basically provides a means toward establishing a rational system for understanding and organizing the study of mythology.

Walter Burkert

Walter Burkert has persuasively attempted a synthesis of structural theories with the more traditional approaches to classical mythology. In defining a theory of myth, he developed four theses, which are in part based on structural theories and in part meet the objection that these theories are not adequate for many Greek myths as they have come down to us after a long period of development. According to Burkert, classical myths have a "historical dimension" with "successive layers" of development, during which the original tale has been modified to fit the cultural or other circumstances of the time of its retelling. This will be less true of a tale that has sacred status, for it will have been "crystallized" in a sacred document—for example, the myth of Demeter in the *Homeric Hymn to Demeter*. In contrast, many Greek myths vary with the time of telling and the teller—for example, the myths of Orestes or Meleager appear differently in Homer from their treatment in fifth-century Athens or in Augustan Rome.

Burkert therefore believes that the structure of traditional tales cannot be discovered without taking into account cultural and historical dimensions. With regard to the cultural dimension, the structure of a tale is shaped by its human creators and by the needs of the culture within which it is developed. Therefore, the structure of a tale is "ineradicably anthropomorphic" and fits the needs and expectations of both the teller and the audience. (Indeed, as Burkert points out, this is why good tales are so easy to remember: "There are not terribly many items to memorize, since the structure has largely been known in advance.") Further—and here we approach the historical dimension—a tale has a use to which it is put, or, expressed in another way, "Myth is traditional tale applied."

This refinement of the structural theory allows for the development of a tale to meet the needs or expectations of the group for whom it is told—family, city, state, or culture group, for example. A myth, in these terms, has reference to "something of collective importance." This further definition meets a fundamental objection to many earlier "unitary" theories of myth. If myth is a sacred tale or a tale about the gods, how do we include, for example, the myths of Oedipus or Achilles? Similar objections can easily be made to other theories that we have been describing. The notions of "myth applied" and "collective importance" avoid the objection of rigid exclusivity, while they allow for the successive stages in the historical development of a myth without the Procrustean mental gymnastics demanded by the theories of Lévi-Strauss.

Here, then, are the four theses of Burkert's modified synthesis of the structural and historical approaches:

1. Myth belongs to the more general class of traditional tale.
2. The identity of a traditional tale is to be found in a structure of sense within the tale itself.
3. Tale structures, as sequences of motifemes, are founded on basic biological or cultural programs of actions.[29]
4. Myth is a traditional tale with secondary, partial reference to something of collective importance.

These theses form a good working basis on which to approach the interpretation of myth. They make use of the significant discoveries of anthropologists and psychologists, while they allow flexibility in exploring the structure of classical myths. Finally, they take account of the historical development of myths and of the culture within which they were told. It will be useful to refer to these theses when studying individual traditional tales.

Comparative Study and Classical Mythology

Comparisons among the various stories told throughout the ages, all over the world, have become influential in establishing definitions and classifications. In the modern study of comparative mythology, much emphasis tends to be placed on stories told by preliterate and primitive societies, and too often the developed literature of the Greeks and Romans has virtually been ignored. It was not always so; for pioneers in the field, such as Frazer (identified earlier), classical mythology was understandably fundamental. Our survey has shown that the comparative study of myths, especially by anthropologists (as opposed to philologically trained classicists), has been one of the most fruitful approaches to the interpretation of myths.

Oral and Literary Myth

The primary reason for the relative neglect of classical mythology is that many insist that a true myth must be oral, and some would add that it also must be anonymous. Today this is certainly the most persistent definition of all, with support from many quarters. Reasons are easy to find in an argument that runs something like this: The tales told in primitive societies, which one may go to hear even today, are the only true myths, pristine and timeless. Such tales represent the poetic vision, the history, the religion, even the science of the tribe, revealing the fascinating early stages of development in the psyche of humankind. The written word brings with it contamination and a specific designation of authorship for what has been passed on by word of mouth for ages, the original creator with no more identity at all. For Malinowski (discussed earlier), myths were synonymous with the tales of the Trobrianders, which they called *lili'u*, the important stories a society has to tell.[30] For those sympathetic to this view, folk tales hold a special place, even those that have become a literary text composed by an author, who has imposed a unity (which may be suspect) upon a multiplicity of oral tales.

What has all this to do with classical mythology?

We do not concur with those who so narrowly define the word *myth*. We would not write a book titled *Classical Mythology* with the conviction that the literary texts that we must deal with are not mythology at all. First of all, myth need not be just a story told orally. It can be danced, painted, and enacted, and this, in fact, is what primitive people do. As we stated at the beginning of this chapter, myth may be expressed in various media, and myth is no less a literary form than it is an oral form. Furthermore, the texts of classical mythology can be linked to the oral and literary themes of other mythologies.

We have established that, over the past few decades, comparative mythology has been used extensively for understanding the myths of any *one* culture. Greek mythology, largely because of the genius of the authors who told the stories in their literary form, has too often in the past been considered as something so unusual that it can be set apart from other mythologies. It is true that Greek and Roman literature has certain characteristics that differentiate it from the many oral preliterate tales gathered from other cultures by anthropologists (discussed at the end of this chapter). Yet, the work of the structuralists has shown that classical myths share fundamental characteristics with traditional tales everywhere. It is important to be aware of this fact and to realize that there were many successive layers in the development of Greek and Roman myths before their crystallization in literary form. The Homeric poems, the *Iliad* and the *Odyssey*, no doubt had oral antecedents.[31] Often, and especially in structural interpretations, the earlier stages of a myth are discovered to have been rooted in another culture, or at least show the influence of other mythologies. For example, there are obvious parallels between the Greek creation and succession myths and the myths of Near Eastern cultures (we explore these parallels in the Appendix to Chapter 4); such structural and thematic similarities do at least show how Greek myths are to be studied in conjunction with those of other cultures.

It is gratifying that comparative studies in the classics are becoming more and more abundant (as is made evident in our bibliographies), the focus being the identification of structures and motifs in Greek and Roman literature that are common to mythologies of the world.

Joseph Campbell

Joseph Campbell is the best known comparative mythologist to the general public, and his body of work embraces mythologies of every sort—oral, literary, whatever—in the world throughout the centuries. In his vast, all-embracing scheme of things, classical mythology is not of major significance, but it easily could be. He has done much to popularize the study of comparative mythology and is to be commended, even though, in his popularizations at least, he has paid less serious attention to the Greeks and the Romans. Perhaps he will appeal most of all to those who seek to recognize the kindred spiritual values that may be found through a comparison of the myths and legends of various peoples over the centuries. Although Jungian archetypes are fundamental to his approach, it is difficult to know how Campbell should be classified under our previous headings: with those who link mythology and society or religion or psychology?[32] His inspiring influence on Martha Graham and her powerful re-creations of mythology in dance is discussed in Chapter 28 (available on the companion website). For a clear and comprehensive introduction to his numerous works, see Robert A. Segal in *Joseph Campbell: An Introduction*.[33]

Gender, Homosexuality, and the Interpretation of Mythology

Feminist Approaches

Feminist critical theories have led to many new, and often controversial, interpretations of classical myths. They approach mythology from the perspective of women and interpret the myths by focusing especially on the psychological and social situation of their female characters. These theories share with structuralism a focus on the binary nature of human society and the human mind, especially in the opposition (or complementary relationship) of female and male. Social criticism of the male-centered world of Greek mythology goes back at least to Sappho, who, in her *Hymn to Aphrodite* (see p. 215), used the image of Homeric warfare to describe her emotions and, in her poem on Anactoria, contrasts what she loves, another human being, with what conventional men love, the panoply of war.[34] In 1942, the French philosopher Simone Weil took basically the same approach in her essay on the *Iliad* (translated by Mary McCarthy as *The Iliad, or the Poem of Force*), focusing on the issues of violence, power, and domination, which are fundamental to Homeric mythology.

More recently, feminist scholars have used the methods of contemporary literary criticism, many of which are outside the scope of this present study (e.g., narratology and deconstruction), to interpret the traditional tales, associating them

Stages in the Development of Feminist Interpretation

Joan Breton Connelly, in her acknowledgments for her book *Portrait of a Priestess*, thanks Mary Lefkowitz (p. ix), "who at Wellesley College, first opened for me the world of ancient women and Greek myth. Her thoughtful insights have informed this book throughout its writing."[37]

In her comments on "Gender, Agency, and Identity" (pp. 21–24), Connelly (following Lynn Meskell) identifies three stages in the development of contemporary feminist analysis, which are presented here essentially in her own words. The so-called first wave of feminism in the 1960s "focused on women's political, social, and economic liberation from and equality with men." A second wave in the 1970s and 1980s brought "new emphasis on the 'inherent' difference between men and women and the special bond between women and Nature . . . and tends to view women as a homogeneous, nomothetic group." A third wave, deconstructive feminism, which arose in the 1980s and continues today, "has focused its energies on difference, plurality, ambiguity, embodiment, the transitory, and the disruptive." Connelly's book finds its roots in the second wave, when women's studies, gender studies, and other newly established fields sought out long-neglected source material, her goal being "to collect and evaluate evidence for ancient women so that they can be reinstated into a long-term cultural history." This worthy goal has been accomplished well, and her research stands as a fertile, seminal resource for future studies.

with the theories of psychologists (especially Freud) and comparative anthropologists. Many feminist interpretations have compelled readers to think critically about the social and psychological assumptions that underlie approaches to mythology. They have led to original and stimulating interpretations of many myths, especially where the central figure is female. The work of feminist scholars has led to greater flexibility and often (although by no means always) greater sensitivity in modern readings of classical literature. Helene P. Foley's edition of *The Homeric Hymn to Demeter* is a good example of how feminist interpretations can be incorporated in an array of varied interpretative viewpoints.[35] Feminist authors, too, are creating new versions of traditional tales designed to illuminate their point of view about political, social, and sexual conflict between men and women in our world today—for example, the two novels (originally in German) by Christa Wolf, *Cassandra* and *Medea*. Nevertheless, some scholars (among them leading classical feminists) have warned against the tendency to interpret classical myths in the light of contemporary social and political concerns. For example, Marilyn Katz criticizes those who object on moral grounds to the apparent infidelity of Odysseus to his wife, saying that "such an interpretation . . . imports into the poem our own squeamish disapproval of the double standard."[36]

Feminist interpretations of mythological stories are often determined by controversial reconstructions of the treatment and position of women in ancient society, often making no distinctions between the Greek version and that of the Roman Ovid and thus embracing two civilizations inhabiting a vast area over a lengthy period of time. We single out two major topics that influence feminist theories of myth: the position of women in Greece and the theme of rape.

Women in Greek Society

Evidence for the position of women in Greek society is meager and conflicting. It is also virtually impossible to make valid broad generalizations, since the situation in sixth-century Lesbos must have been different from that in Athens of the fifth century, and as time went on women in Sparta gained a great deal of power. For a long time, we have been reading the literature and looking at the art, and for us, some of the revisionist histories today depict a civilization that we cannot recognize in terms of what little direct evidence we do possess, controversial as it may be. A good place to begin for one's own control of what little we do know with any kind of certainty is with a study by A. W. Gomme, "The Position of Women at Athens in the Fifth and Fourth Centuries B.C."[38] Following are a few basic observations to give a sense of balance to the controversy.

First, it is sometimes claimed that Greek women, because of their political status, were not citizens in the ancient world. This is not true. Aristotle (*Athenian Constitution*, 42.1) makes it very clear that in Athens citizenship depended on the condition that both parents must be citizens: "Those born of parents who are both citizens share in citizenship, and when they are eighteen years old, they are registered on the rolls." It is evident over and over again that in Greek society the citizens were very much aware of the difference between citizens and noncitizens (resident aliens and slaves) in the structure and benefits of society.[39] Women citizens, however, did not vote; to keep things in perspective, one should remember that women did not win the vote anywhere until the first quarter of the twentieth century. Were there no women citizens in the world before that time? in England? in America? It is only in the first quarter of the last century that women gained not only political but also legal rights equal to those of men, sad as that fact may be in our judgment of humankind. In Athens a woman citizen benefited greatly from the prosperity and the artistic expression and freedom of the democracy and empire. She was very important in religious ceremonies, some of which excluded the participation of males. Women did not always walk outdoors veiled,[40] a few became intoxicated, some had affairs, and many were very outspoken (amazingly so for this period of time in the history of Western civilization) about their own inferior position as citizens in relation to that of males.

Those affluent enough used slaves (both male and female) to do the household chores and take care of the children. It is difficult to believe all women were illiterate. It is likely, however, that their education was different from that of the men. Much would depend on contingencies such as class and individual needs. (The women of Sappho's Lesbos must have been able to read and write.) Athenian women went to the theater, where they saw and heard vivid depictions of the strength of their character and convictions and debates about their rights. They also saw varied portraits, not all evil, but mixed, as it should be, many of great and noble wives such as Alcestis in Euripides and Deïanira in Sophocles' *Women of Trachis*, among others. In art, women appear idealized and beautiful, but not nude (as men could be) until the fourth century B.C. because of Greek mores. The mythological world of goddesses and heroines reflects the real world of Greek women, for whom it had to have some meaning, especially since their devotion and major participation in religious rites and worship were manifestly so fervent.

Joan Connelly (see box on p. 18 and further discussion on pp. 153–155) reveals how "a broadly accepted commonplace that Athenian women held wholly second-class status as silent and submissive figures restricted to the confine of the household where they obediently tended to domestic chores and child-rearing" (pp. 3–4) has been in recent years successfully challenged and proven to be false by an impressive array of scholarly research. There are many reasons for this imposed "invisibility" and oppression: the misreading of well-known literary texts (Greek dramas, Thucydides, Plato, and Xenophon); the failure to distinguish between "separation" and "seclusion" and to understand the contradictions between cultural ideals and real-life social practices; ignorance about the active role of women in the economic sphere and the existence and nature of women's public speech in Athens; and misunderstanding of gendered space and social relations in the household. Connelly convincingly argues that there is more than enough evidence (fragmentary though it may be) to prove that "priestesses spoke before Assemblies; fixed their seals on official documents; and, at least by Hellenistic times, and maybe earlier, took their honored places in the front rows of theaters. Instead of highlighting the women who led public processions, made dedications in sanctuaries, and stepped forward on festal days to perform rituals and initiate sacrifices, the focus has rested on women locked indoors" (p. 276).

Connelly insists that "*all* existing evidence must be considered, and its evaluation must take place independently from the prejudices that privileged texts [such as those mentioned earlier] promote" and warns against "the conscious or unconscious devaluation, even dismissal, of evidence that does not conform to the consensus view." She explains how this consensus view became entrenched: "Nineteenth-century classicists, projecting the gender ideology of the Victorian elite onto the Greek household, ended up in roughly the same place as twentieth-century feminists who employed a 'subordinate theory' construct for managing the material. The result is the widely accepted commonplace of silent, submissive, 'invisible' women, confined to the privacy of their households and wholly dominated by their men" (p. 275). (For an example of the results of "gender ideology" and conformity to the "consensus view," see note 40 at the end of this chapter.)

The Theme of Rape

The theme of rape has become a fertile and seminal topic. What are we today to make of the many classical myths of ardent pursuit as well as those of amorous conquest? Are they religious stories, are they love stories, or are they in the end all fundamentally horrifying tales of victimization? Only a few basic observations about this vast and vital subject can be made here, with the major purpose of insisting that the questions and the answers are complex.

In Ovid's *Metamorphoses*, Apollo's pursuit of Daphne is the first of the love stories in the poem. To some it is a beautiful idyll; to others, it is a glorification of male supremacy and brutality. Quite simply put, it can mean whatever one wants it to mean. Certainly, it has been one of the most popular themes among artists throughout the centuries because it is subject to so many varied overt and subtle interpretations, primary among them not necessarily being that of rape in the sense of the word today. The case is similar in the history of music; the very first opera was *Daphne*, and she has been a profound, spiritual inspiration in the years to follow.

The Greeks and Romans were fascinated with the phenomena of blinding passion and equally compulsive virginity. The passion was usually evoked by the mighty gods Aphrodite and Eros, who could gloriously uplift or pitilessly devastate a human being and a god. The equally ruthless force of chastity was symbolized by devotion to Artemis. Usually, but by no means always, the man defines lust and the woman chastity. In the case of Hippolytus and Phaedra (among others), these roles are reversed.

The motif of pursuit by the lover of the beloved with the implicit imagery of the hunter and the hunted is everywhere and becomes formulaic, with the pursuit ending in a ritualistic acquiescence or the saving of the pursued from a fate worse than death, often through a metamorphosis. The consummation of sex need not be part of the scenario of this ancient motif, played upon with versatile sophistication by a civilized poet such as Ovid.

Many seduction scenes are ultimately religious in nature, and the fact that it is a god who seduces a mortal can make all the difference. Zeus may single out a chosen woman to be the mother of a divine child or hero for a grand purpose intended for the ultimate good of the world, and the woman may or may not be overjoyed. These tales are told from different points of view, sometimes diametrically opposed. For example, Zeus took Io by force, or their son Epaphus was born by the mere touch of the hand of the god.

There is no real distinction between the love, abduction, or rape of a woman by a man and of a man by a woman. Eos is just as relentless in her pursuit of Cephalus or Tithonus as any other god, and they succumb to the goddess. Salmacis attacks innocent and pure Hermaphroditus and wins. Aphrodite seduces Anchises, who does not stand a chance against her devious guile. It is possible, if one so desires, to look beyond the romantic vision of beautiful nymphs in a lovely pool enamored of handsome Hylas to imagine a horrible outrage as the poor lad, outnumbered, is dragged down into the depths.

The title for a famous story that has become traditional may be misleading or false. Paris' wooing of Helen is usually referred to as the Rape of Helen. Yet the ancient accounts generally describe how Helen fell quickly and desperately in love with the exotic foreigner Paris and (despite her complaints about Aphrodite) went with him willingly to Troy. Of course a different version can find its legitimacy, too, if an artist wishes to depict a Helen dragged away, screaming her protests against the savage force of a bestial Paris. The designation of the seduction/abduction of Helen by Paris as the "Rape of Helen" was established at a time when the word *rape* did not necessarily have the narrow, sole connotation it has today, that of a brutal, forceful sexual act against an unwilling partner.

The Rape of Persephone is quite another matter. Hades did brutally abduct Persephone, who did indeed cry out to no avail. Zeus and Hades saw this as the divine right of gods and kings. Demeter and Persephone did not agree. But a religious artist or critic might maintain that god's will is god's will, and it was divinely ordained to have Hades and Persephone as king and queen of the Underworld.

The present book bears testimony again and again in a multitude of ways to the light these Greek and Roman tales have thrown on our civilization. They explored countless issues and emotions (among them passion and lust) that were as burning for them (both men and women) as they are for us, in their own images, just as we explore them in ours. We are no less obsessed with the subject of sex than were the ancients, and our depictions certainly can be much more violent and ugly, yet often not so potent. Critics of classical mythology in previous generations sometimes chose not to see the rape; some critics today choose to see nothing else.

It is fundamental to realize an obvious fact that too often is completely over-looked in our rush to interpretative, righteous judgment about the message of a story. The same tale may embody themes of victimization and rape or sexual love or spiritual salvation, one or all of these issues, or more. Everything depends on the artist and the person responding to the work of art: his or her gender, politics, philosophy, religion, sexual orientation, age, experience or experiences—the list could go on. A major contention of this book is that there is no one "correct" interpretation of a story, just as there is no one "correct" definition of a myth.

Homosexuality

Homosexuality was accepted and accommodated as a part of life in the ancient world. There were no prevailing hostile religious views that condemned it as a sin. Much has been written about this subject in this era of gay liberation, and fundamental works are listed in the bibliography at the end of the chapter. Dover, in his classic study *Greek Homosexuality*, offers a scrupulous analysis of major evidence for ancient Greece, much of which pertains to Athens. This fundamental work is required reading, but his conclusions need to be tempered by other more realistic appreciations of sexuality in the real world, both ancient and modern. Particularly enlightening because of its wider perspective is *Homophobia: A History*, by Byrne Fone. The remarks that follow concentrate on homosexuality in ancient Greece. There were similarities among the Romans but differences as well. The period of time stretches over centuries, and the subject again is vast, complex, and controversial.

A prevailing view persists that Athens (representing a kind of paradigm of the Greco-Roman world) was a paradise for homosexuals, particularly in contrast to the persecution so often found in other societies. There is some truth in this romantic vision, but homosexual activity had to be pursued in accordance with certain unwritten rules, however liberal they may have been. In Athens, a particular respectability was conferred when an older male became the lover of a younger man, and it was important that each play his proper role in the sexual act. The relationship was particularly sanctified by a social code if the primary motive was, at least ostensibly, education of a higher order, the molding of character, and responsible citizenship. Longer homosexual relationships between two mature men, promiscuity, and effeminacy were sometimes not so readily accepted. Some homosexuals were made notorious because of their behavior. Gay pride today could not approve of many attitudes and strictures about sexuality in Athens or for that matter in Greece and Rome generally.

In the mythology, as one would expect, homosexuality may be found as an important theme. Aphrodite and Eros in particular play significant roles as deities particularly concerned about homosexual love. Several important myths have as their major theme male homosexual relationships: Zeus and Ganymede, Poseidon and Pelops, Apollo and Hyacinthus, Apollo and Cyparissus, the friendship of Achilles and Patroclus, Orestes and Pylades (especially in Euripides' *Iphigenia in Tauris*), and Heracles and Hylas. In Roman legend, the love and devotion of Nisus and Euryalus is a particularly moving example. This is not an overwhelming number of such tales in the vast body of classical mythology.

"Our tolerance for explicit descriptions of sexual acts in the post-Kinsey era has encouraged the growth of a minor industry in the study of Greek homosexuality." These are the words of G. W. Bowerstock in his perceptive review of a book by James Davidson (*The Greeks and Greek Love*) and another by Andrew Lear and Eva Cantarella (*Images of Ancient Greek Pederasty*), in which he includes an excellent, brief survey of homosexuality in ancient Greece and important modern works on the subject. He ends with this insightful observation: "The sexual life of the ancient Greeks was as variegated and inventive as its resplendent culture. It was neither consistent nor uniform. To this day it stubbornly resists all modern ideologies and prejudices, and yet had its own principles of decency. In sex as in so much else, the ancient Greeks were unique."[41]

Female homosexuality in Greek and Roman mythology and society is as important a theme as male homosexuality, but it is not nearly as visible. Sappho, a lyric poetess from the island of Lesbos (sixth century B.C.), in the fervent and moving poem (p. 215) mentioned earlier, invokes Aphrodite's help to win back the love of a young woman with whom she has been involved. Her relationships with women are evident both in other poems and in the biographical tradition and have been the subject of endless interpretation. (For those interested in Sappho's biography, the ancient testimony is collected and translated in the Loeb Classical Library, published by Harvard University Press.) From Sappho comes the term *lesbian* and the association of Aphrodite with lesbian love.

Lesbianism is not so readily detectable in the mythology generally. On one hand, sometimes it can be deduced as a subtext here and there; for example, it may be a latent motif in stories about the strong bond of affection among Artemis and her band of female followers and in the depiction of the society and mores of the warlike Amazons. On the other hand, lesbianism in Greek history, while not as well documented as male homosexuality, nevertheless did exist, at Sparta for example, where the position of women was extraordinary in terms of freedom, education, and power, and lesbianism was recognized as a widespread practice. Laws strictly enforced marriage, rewarded childbearing, and promoted the family as the core of the city-state, and anyone who did not comply was stigmatized in various ways. Yet, homosexuality (both male and female), practiced within the bonds of societal demands, was encouraged and respected.

The Mores of Mythological Society

Rather than imagine what Greek and Roman society was like over thousands of years in its feminist and homosexual attitudes and then impose tenuous conclusions on an interpretation of mythological stories treated by many individual artists with different points of view, perhaps it may be more fruitful and fair to look at the mythology itself to determine if there is any consistency in the social values it conveys.

Along with its nonjudgmental acceptance of homosexuality and the beautiful stories it inspires, Greek and Roman mythology overall reflects the point of view of a heterosexual society, from the depiction of the Olympian family of deities on down. Homer's *Odyssey* is the most heterosexual of poems, and one must look long and hard to read any subtext to the contrary. So is the *Iliad* for that matter, although a subtext comes more easily. True, the poem turns upon Achilles' love for Patroclus, but both men are depicted as heterosexuals, leaving the bond between them open for others to read between the lines. Probably Homer takes their bisexuality for granted. Enhancing and illuminating the relationship between Achilles and Patroclus is Achilles' love for Briseïs amid the profound depictions of the couples Priam and Hecuba, Hector and Andromache, and, perhaps the most searching of all, Paris and Helen.

Homer sets the stage for the basic qualities of the literature to follow. The body of Greek drama, as we have it, is shot through with family and religious values, raised to lofty heights by genius. The great families of tragedy, to be sure, are dysfunctional and neurotic, but the ties that bind them together are those of man and woman, husband and wife, father and mother, brother and sister, son and daughter. It would be difficult to imagine more powerful familial and religious bonds than those in the legend of Oedipus. The mutual devotion between Oedipus and his daughters Ismene and, more particularly, Antigone is extreme. Equally powerful is the feud between Oedipus and his sons Eteocles and Polynices. Oedipus dies committed to God, and Antigone remains true to the memory of her brother Polynices because of family and religion. The legend of the *Oresteia* may be an even better example. The criteria by which Herodotus singles out Tellus the Athenian and Cleobis and Biton as the happiest of men are embodied in ennobling tales (translated on pp. 142–148) confirming the fact that marriage and the family were fundamental in the politics and mores of the Greek city-state (*polis*). Roman mythology is possibly even more dominated by religious, familial, and, we may add, patriotic mores, and yet, in Rome too, homosexuality was prevalent, especially in imperial times.

We all read this vast body of classical literature in different ways, and this is how it should be. The texts have something to say to each of us because they spring from a civilization that is all-embracing (not merely bizarre) and all too recognizable and helpful in the face of our own issues and conflicts and their resolution, not least of all those between heterosexuals and homosexuals and men and women.

Some Conclusions and a Definition of Classical Myth

Our survey of some important interpretations of myth is intended to show that something of value can be found in a study of various approaches, and we have included only a selection from a wide range of possibilities. Others might be explored; belief in the importance and validity of diverse interpretations naturally varies from reader to reader. About this conclusion, however, we are convinced: it is impossible to develop any one theory that will be meaningfully applicable to *all* myths; there is no identifiable Platonic Idea or Form of a myth embodying characteristics copied or reflected in the mythologies of the world. The many interpretations of the origin and nature of myths are primarily valuable for highlighting the fact that myths embrace different kinds of stories in different media, which may be classified in numerous ways.

We realize fully the need to study comparative mythology and appreciate its many attractive rewards, but we are also wary of its dangers: oversimplification, distortion, and the reduction of an intricate masterpiece to a chart of leading motifs. Greek and Roman mythology is unique, but not so unique that we can set it apart from other mythologies. In other words, it will illuminate other mythologies drawn from primitive and preliterate societies, just as they will help us understand the origin, development, and meaning of classical literature. We must, however, be aware of the gulf that separates the oral legends from the literary mythological thinking that evolved among the Greeks and Romans and also among their literary antecedents in the Near East. It is misleading, of course, to posit a "primitive" mentality, as some anthropologists and sociologists do, as if it were something childlike and simple, in contrast to the "sophisticated" mentality of more advanced societies such as that of the Greeks.[42] In fact, it has been clearly proved (as attested to earlier) how far the myths of primitive societies reflect the complexities of social family structures, and their tales may be profitably compared to classical literature. Yet, there are important differences, and even our earliest literary sources (Homer, Hesiod, and the lyric poets) provide artistic presentations of intellectual, emotional, and spiritual values and concepts in influential works of the highest order, whatever their debts. Greek and Roman mythology shares similar characteristics with the great literatures of the world, which have evolved mythologies of their own, whether or not they have borrowed thematic material from the ancients. Classical mythology has at least as much (if not more) in common with English and American literature (not to mention French and German, among others)[43] as it does with preliterate comparisons of oral folk tales and the scrutiny of archaic artifacts, however enlightening these studies may be. Greek and Roman mythology and literature look back to an oral and literary past, use it, modify it, and pass on the transformation to the future.

Since the goal of this book is the transmission of the myths themselves as recounted in the Greek and Roman periods, literary myth is inevitably our primary concern. Many of the important myths exist in multiple versions of varying quality, but usually one ancient treatment has been most influential in establishing the prototype or archetype for all subsequent art and thought. Whatever other versions of the Oedipus story exist,[44] the dramatic treatment by Sophocles has established and imposed the mythical pattern for all time—he is the poet who forces us to see and feel the universal implications. Although his art is self-conscious, literary, and aesthetic, nevertheless the myth *is* the play. We cannot provide complete texts of Greek tragedy, but insofar as possible the original text of the dominant version of a myth will be translated in this book. We believe that a faithful translation or even a paraphrase of the sources is far better than a bald and eclectic retelling in which the essential spirit and artistic subtlety of literary myth is obliterated completely for the sake of scientific analysis. It is commonplace to say that myths are by nature good stories, but some are more childish, confused, and repetitious than others; the really good ones are usually good because they have survived in a form molded by an artist. These are the versions to which we may most profitably apply the criteria established by Aristotle in his *Poetics* on the basis of his experience of Greek tragedy. Is the plot (*mythos*) constructed well with a proper beginning, middle, and end? Have the powerful techniques of recognition and reversal been put to the best use? What about the development of characterization—does the protagonist have a tragic flaw? Most important of all, does the work effect a catharsis (an emotional and spiritual purging) involving the emotions of pity and fear, possibly a goal for all serious mythic art?

There are two indisputable characteristics of the literary myths and legends of Greek and Roman mythology: their artistic merit and the inspiration they have afforded to others. To mention only one example, we have from the ancient world touching renditions of the story of Orpheus and Eurydice. The number of retellings of their tale in Western civilization has been legion (in every possible medium), and it seems that the variations will go on forever.[45] Thus, we conclude with a short definition that concentrates on the gratifying tenacity of the classical tradition (in literature and art, but not oral), inextricably woven into the very fabric of our culture:

> A *classical myth* is a story that, through its classical form, has attained a kind of immortality because its inherent archetypal beauty, profundity, and power have inspired rewarding renewal and transformation by successive generations.

The Greeks created a substantial and significant body of myth in various media. The Romans and many subsequent societies have been and continue to be captivated by it. In view of this phenomenal fact, the versions of *Oedipus* by Seneca, Corneille, von Hofmansthal, and Cocteau have equal validity as personal expressions of the authors' own vision of Sophocles and the myth, for their own time and their own culture. The same may be said of the depiction of a myth on a Greek vase and a painting by Picasso, or a frieze of ancient dancers and a reinterpretation by Isadora Duncan, and the music (no longer to be heard) for a fifth-century performance of *Electra* and the opera by Strauss, and so on. This book has been written out of the desire to provide a lucid and comprehensive introduction to Greek mythology, so that the reader may know, appreciate, and enjoy its miraculous afterlife (*Nachleben*, as the Germans call it), which we feel compelled to survey as well because it is integral to the whole continuum. The creation of classical myth has never really stopped, but from the time of Homer it has constantly been reborn and revitalized, expressed in exciting and challenging new ways through literature, art, music, dance, and film.[46]

Appendix to Chapter 1

Sources for Classical Mythology

Traditional tales were handed down orally until they were stabilized in a written form that spread over a wide area. The geography and topography of the Greek world often made communications by land and sea difficult, and these natural tendencies to cultural separatism were enhanced by tribal, ethnic, and linguistic variations. The Greek myths, therefore, varied greatly from place to place, as did the cults of individual gods. With the coming of writing, perhaps in the eighth century, "standard" versions of myths began to be established, but the sophistication of succeeding generations of poets led also to ingenious variations. Even in the central myths of Athenian drama—whose stories were well known to and expected by their audiences—substantial variations are found, as, for example, in the legends of Electra. The problem of variations is especially acute in saga, where differing literary versions and local variations (often based on local pride in the heroic past) make it virtually impossible to identify a "standard" version. This is especially the case with local heroes like Theseus at Athens. Nevertheless, there is a body of recognized principal sources for classical mythology from which major versions may be identified.

To aid the reader, we have included a Timeline of Historical Events and Authors in Chapter 2 (pp. 52–53).

Greek Sources.   Pride of place goes to **Homer** (to use the name of the poet to whom the *Iliad* and the *Odyssey* are ascribed), whose poems stabilized the myths of the Olympian gods and exercised an unparalleled influence on all succeeding

Greek and Roman writers. The *Iliad* is much more than the story of the wrath of Achilles or the record of an episode in the tenth year of the Trojan War, for it incorporates many myths of the Olympian and Mycenaean heroes, while its picture of the gods has ever since been the foundation of literary and artistic representations of the Olympian pantheon. The poems themselves, which developed over centuries of oral tradition, perhaps took something like their final form in the eighth century, the *Iliad* being somewhat earlier than the *Odyssey*. The written text was probably stabilized at Athens under the tyranny of Pisistratus during the second half of the sixth century. Our debt to Homeric mythology and legend will be apparent in this book.

Important also for the Olympian gods and the organization of Olympian theology and theogony are the works of **Hesiod**, the Boeotian poet of the late eighth century, perhaps as late as 700. His *Theogony* is our most important source for the relationship of Zeus and the Olympians to their predecessors, the Titans, and other early divinities; it also records how Zeus became supreme and organized the Olympian pantheon. Hesiod's *Works and Days* also contains important mythology. Thus, substantial portions of these works appear in translation or paraphrase in the earlier chapters.

The thirty-three *Homeric Hymns* are a body of poems composed in honor of Olympian deities, most of which embody at least one myth of the god or goddess. Four (those to Demeter, Apollo, Hermes, and Aphrodite) are several hundred lines long and are the most significant sources for those gods' myths; others are very short indeed and appear to be preludes for longer compositions that have not survived. Because of their importance, we have translated all these hymns in their entirety.[47] The *Homeric Hymns* were composed at widely different times, some perhaps as early as the eighth or seventh century, and some (for example, the *Hymn to Ares*) as late as the fourth century B.C. or Hellenistic times.

Another group of archaic poets whose work is an important source for mythology is the lyric poets, who flourished, especially in the islands of the Aegean Sea, during the seventh and sixth centuries. The lyric tradition was continued in the complex victory *Odes* of the Theban poet **Pindar** during the first half of the fifth century and in the dithyrambs of his rival and contemporary, Bacchylides of Ceos. The lyric choruses of the Athenian dramatists also enshrine important versions of myths.

In the fifth century, the flourishing of the Greek city-states led to the creation of great literature and art, nowhere more impressively than at Athens. Here the three great writers of tragedy, **Aeschylus** (who died in 456), **Sophocles**, and **Euripides** (both of whom died in 406), established the authoritative versions of many myths and sagas: a few examples are the *Oresteia* of Aeschylus for the saga of the House of Atreus; the Theban plays of Sophocles for the saga of the family of Oedipus; and the *Bacchae* of Euripides (translated in large part in Chapter 13) for the myths of Dionysus.

After the fifth century, the creative presentation of myths in Greek literature gave way to more contrived versions, many of which were composed by the Alexandrian poets in the third century. Neither the *Hymns* of **Callimachus** nor the hymn to Zeus of Cleanthes has great value as a source for myth, but the epic *Argonautica*, of Apollonius of Rhodes (ca. 260 B.C.), is the single most important source for the saga of the Argonauts. Other Alexandrian versions of the classical myths are discussed in Chapter 27 (available on the companion website).

The principal Greek prose sources are the historians and the mythographers. Of the former, **Herodotus** is preeminent, although some myths are recorded in

Thucydides (last quarter of the fifth century). Herodotus (born ca. 485) traveled widely, both within the Greek world and to Persia and Egypt, and he recorded traditional tales wherever he went. Some of his stories contain profound and universal truths of the sort we would associate with myth as well as history; his account of the meeting between Solon and Croesus, which we have translated in Chapter 6, is a perfect example of the developed "historical myth," giving us insight into Greek interpretations of god and fate that arose out of their factual and mythical storytelling.

The mythographers were late compilers of handbooks of mythology. Of these, the work ascribed to **Apollodorus** with the title *Bibliotheca* (*Library of Greek Mythology*), which is still valuable, perhaps was composed around A.D. 120. The *Periegesis* (*Description of Greece*) of **Pausanias** (ca. A.D. 150) contains many myths in its accounts of religious sites and their works of art.

The philosophers, most notably **Plato** (fourth century B.C.), used myth for didactic purposes, and Plato himself developed out of the tradition of religious tales the "philosophical myth" as a distinct literary form. His myth of Er, for example, is a philosophical allegory about the soul and its existence after death. It is important as evidence for beliefs about the Underworld, and its religious origins go back to earlier centuries, in particular to the speculations of Pythagorean and Orphic doctrine. The Roman poet Vergil (discussed shortly), in his depiction of the afterlife, combines more traditional mythology developed out of Homer with mythical speculations about rebirth and reincarnation found in philosophers like Plato. Thus, by translating all three authors—Homer, Plato, and Vergil—on the realm of Hades (Chapter 15) we have a composite and virtually complete summary of the major mythical and religious beliefs about the afterlife evolved by the Greeks and Romans.

One late philosopher who retold archaic myths for both philosophical and satirical purposes was the Syrian author **Lucian** (born ca. A.D. 120), who wrote in Greek. His satires, often in dialogue form, present the Olympian gods and the old myths with a good deal of humor and critical insight. His version of the judgment of Paris, found in Chapter 19, is a fine example of his art.

Roman Sources.   The Greek authors are the foundation of our knowledge of classical myth. Nevertheless, the Roman authors were not merely derivative. **Vergil** (70–19 B.C.) developed the myth of the Trojan hero Aeneas in his epic, the *Aeneid*. In so doing, he preserved the saga of the fall of Troy, a part of the Greek epic cycle that is now lost to us. He also developed the legend of the Phoenician queen Dido and told a number of myths and tales associated with particular Italian localities, such as the story of Hercules at Rome. Several passages from Vergil appear in Chapter 26 as well as Chapter 15.

Vergil's younger contemporary, **Ovid** (43 B.C.–A.D. 17), is the single most important source for classical mythology after Homer, and his poem *Metamorphoses* (completed ca. A.D. 8) has probably been more influential even than Homer as a source for representations of the classical myths in literature and art. A kind of epic, the poem includes more than 200 legends arranged in a loose chronological framework from the Creation down to Ovid's own time. Many of the most familiar stories come from Ovid, for example, the stories of Echo and Narcissus, Apollo and Daphne, and Pyramus and Thisbe. Ovid's poem on the Roman religious calendar, *Fasti*, is a unique source for the myths of the Roman gods, although he completed only the first six months of the religious year. We include a great deal from Ovid, in direct translation or in paraphrase.

The historian **Livy** (59 B.C.–A.D. 17) recorded the foundation myths of Rome in the first book of his *Ab urbe condita*. He is the source for many of the legends from Roman history that are closer to myth than history. Other Roman writers had antiquarian interests, but none wrote continuous accounts comparable with those of Livy.

Later in the first century A.D., a literary renaissance took place during the reign of the emperor Nero (54–68). The tragedies of **Seneca** present important versions of several myths, most notably those of Phaedra and Hippolytus, Medea, and Thyestes, the last named being the only surviving full-length version of the myth.

In the generation following Seneca, there was a revival of epic. The *Argonautica* of **Valerius Flaccus** (ca. 80) and the *Thebaid* of **Statius** (d. 96) are important versions of their respective sagas. After this time, there are few original works worth notice. One exception is a novel by the African rhetorician **Apuleius** (b. 123) formally titled *Metamorphoses* but better known to us as *The Golden Ass*. This is our source for the tale of Cupid and Psyche, while its final book is invaluable for its account of the mysteries of Isis.

Interest in mythology continued to be shown in a number of handbooks of uncertain date. We have mentioned the *Bibliotheca* of Apollodorus in Greek; in Latin, compendia were written by **Hyginus** (perhaps in the mid-second century) and Fulgentius (perhaps an African bishop of the sixth century). This tradition was revived during the Renaissance, especially in Italy, and we discuss some of the important handbooks of mythology in Chapter 27 (available on the companion website).

The Eclectic Variety of the Sources.   It is readily apparent that this literary heritage offers infinite variety. The religious tales of Hesiod contrast with the sophisticated stories of Ovid. The historical legend of Herodotus differs in character from the legendary history of Homer. The philosophical myth of Plato and the romantic storytelling of Apuleius reveal contrasting spiritual hues. The dramatic environments of Aeschylus and Seneca are worlds apart. Yet *all* these authors from different periods and with diverse art provide the rich, eclectic heritage from which a survey of Greco-Roman mythology must be drawn.

Translations.   All the Greek and Roman works named here (except for the late Latin handbooks of mythology) are available in inexpensive translations. The Loeb series includes texts with facing translations, the latter of widely varying quality and readability, with improved, new editions made available annually. The translations published by Penguin and by the University of Chicago Press are generally both reliable and in some cases distinguished. But there is considerable choice, and contemporary translations (some of them excellent) of standard works appear with surprising and gratifying frequency. Yet one needs to be wary. Dover Publications offers several Greek and Roman translations that should not be purchased indiscriminately; dramas are available individually, in thrift editions at an extremely modest price, but the poetic translations by Sir George Young (1837–1930), for example, may be a bit more difficult for modern readers than they bargained for; at the same time, the series includes the acceptable *Medea* by Rex Warner. The free translations of the Oresteia and of Ovid's *Metamorphoses* by the distinguished poet Ted Hughes stand as exceptional reinterpretations but can hardly serve as the basis for determining what Sophocles actually said—a vital concern for the student of mythology. Among the translations available for

Homer, Stanley Lombardo's *Iliad* and *Odyssey* deserve special commendation. They bring the poems to life for an audience of today. Richmond Lattimore offers a most faithful and poetic transmission of Homer's *Iliad.* Caveat emptor! Oxford University Press in its series Oxford World's Classics offers attractive paperback volumes of good translations of many works that might supplement our text.

The translations presented in this book are our own, and we attempt to offer accurate and accessible versions for the reader who knows no Greek or Latin and wants to come as close as possible to the original sources.

Select Bibliography

Interpretation, Analysis, and Comparative Studies

Ackerman, Robert. *The Myth and Ritual School: J. G. Frazer and the Cambridge Ritualists.* New York: Routledge, 2002. An examination of works by Frazer, Jane Harrison, Gilbert Murray, F. M. Cornford, and A. B. Cook. The last chapter explores the application of myth and ritual to postclassical literature.

Anderson, Graham. *Fairytale in the Ancient World.* New York: Routledge, 2000.

Burkert, Walter. *Structure and History in Greek Mythology and Ritual.* Berkeley, CA: University of California Press, 1979. By far the best explanation of the significance of structural theories.

Csapo, Eric. *Theories of Mythology.* New York: Blackwell, 2004. A history of theories of myth, with sample readings on how to interpret myths.

Dowden, K. *The Uses of Greek Mythology.* New York: Routledge, 1992. A judicious assessment of psychoanalytical approaches on pp. 32–34 and 180.

———, **and Livingstone, Niall, eds.** *Companion to Greek Mythology.* Hoboken, NJ: Wiley, 2011. An informative and thought-provoking collection of essays on the study of Greek mythology from a wide variety of perspectives.

Dundes, A., ed. *Sacred Narrative: Readings in the Theory of Myth.* Berkeley, CA: University of California Press, 1984. A collection of writing by major interpreters of myth, including Frazer, Eliade, Malinowski, Jung, and Lévi-Strauss.

Edmunds, Lowell, ed. *Approaches to Greek Myth.* Baltimore, MD: Johns Hopkins University Press, 1989.

Eliade, Mircea. *Cosmos and History: The Myth of the Eternal Return.* Princeton, NJ: Princeton University Press, 1954. Perhaps the best among his many works to serve as an introduction.

Ellis, John M. *One Fairy Story Too Many.* Chicago, IL: University of Chicago Press, 1983. A study of the text and history of the work of the brothers Grimm, which, Ellis claims, is a fraud. A warning to those who have too blind a faith in oral myth that has been made literary.

Felton, D. *Haunted Greece and Rome: Ghost Stories from Classical Antiquity.* Austin, TX: University of Texas Press, 1999. A folkloric and literary analysis of ancient ghost stories and the influence and development of themes in modern times.

Frazer, James G. *The New Golden Bough: A New Abridgement of the Classic Work.* Edited by Theodor H. Gaster. New York: Criterion Books, 1959; New York: Mentor Books, 1964.

Graf, Fritz. *Greek Mythology: An Introduction.* Translated by Thomas Marier. Baltimore, MD: Johns Hopkins University Press, 1993 [1987]. A history of the interpretation of the principal Greek myths from the seventeenth century to the present.

Holzberg, Niklas. *The Ancient Fable: An Introduction.* Translated by Christine Jackson-Holzberg. Bloomington, IN: Indiana University Press, 2002.

———. *Ancient Folklore: An Introduction.* Translated by Christine Jackson-Holzberg. Bloomington, IN: Indiana University Press, 2002. A critical study of the fable in the texts of Greek and Roman authors.

Kirk, G. S. *Myth: Its Meaning and Function in Ancient and Other Cultures*. Berkeley, CA: University of California Press, 1970. Valuable for its critical views of comparative studies.

———. *The Nature of Greek Myths*. Baltimore, MD: Penguin Books, 1974. Useful for its treatment of different approaches to myth.

Leach, E. *Claude Lévi-Strauss*. New York: Viking Press, 1970. A good exposition of Lévi-Strauss; in the chapter "The Structure of Myth," Leach offers structural analysis of several Greek myths.

Leeming, David Adams. *Mythology: The Voyage of the Hero*. 3d ed. New York: Oxford University Press, 1998. A comparative study of major themes in various mythologies, including those of Greece and Rome.

Lefkowitz, Mary. *Greek Gods, Human Lives: What We Can Learn from Myths*. New Haven, CT: Yale University Press, 2005.

Lévi-Strauss, Claude. *The Savage Mind*. Chicago, IL: University of Chicago Press, 1966 [1962].

———. *The Raw and the Cooked*. Translated by J. Weightman and D. Weightman. New York: Harper & Row, 1969. Volume 1 of the four volumes of *Mythologiques*; its "Overture" is the best introduction to Lévi-Strauss.

Malinowski, B. *Magic, Science, and Religion*. New York: Doubleday, 1955. Includes "Myth in Primitive Psychology," 1989 [1926].

Propp, Vladimir. *Morphology of the Folktale*. 2d ed. Translated by Lawrence Scott. Austin: University of Texas Press, 1968 [1928]. The pioneer work in the structural theory of myth.

Sebeok, Thomas A., ed. *Myth: A Symposium*. Bloomington, IN: Indiana University Press, 1965.

Segal, Robert A. *Joseph Campbell: An Introduction*. New York: Meridian, 1997 [1987].

———, ed. *Literary Criticism and Myth*. New York: Garland, 1996. A collection in six volumes of important writings by major writers.

Strenski, Ivan. *Four Theories of Myth in Twentieth-Century History: Cassirer, Eliade, Lévi-Strauss and Malinowski*. Iowa City, IA: University of Iowa Press, 1987. An iconoclastic judgment of mythography and mythographers. For Strenski (p. 194), no such thing as *myth* exists: "Rather, what exists is the artifact 'myth' along with the 'industry' manufacturing the concept as it is used here and there."

———, ed. *Malinowski and the Work of Myth*. Princeton, NJ: Princeton University Press, 1992. Collection of central writings by Malinowski.

Struck, Peter T. *Birth of a Symbol: Ancient Readers at the Limit of Their Texts*. Princeton, NJ: Princeton University Press, 2004. An exploration of how the ancient Greek literary critics and theorists invented and developed ideas of symbolism and allegorical interpretation.

Thompson, Stith. *The Folktale*. Berkeley, CA: University of California Press, 1977 [1946].

———. *Motif-Index of Folk-Literature*. 6 vols. Bloomington, IN: Indiana University Press, 1966. The basic reference book for folk tale motifs.

Vernant, J.-P. *Myth and Society in Ancient Greece*. Translated by J. Lloyd. New York: Zone Books, 1990 [1974].

Von Hendy, Andrew. *The Modern Construction of Myth*. Bloomington, IN: Indiana University Press, 2002. A critical account of theorizing about myth from the eighteenth century on.

Myth and Psychology

Bolen, Jean Shinoda. *Goddesses in Everywoman: A New Psychology of Women*. New York: Harper & Row, 1984. A Jungian psychologist provides archetypal descriptions of the Greek and Roman goddesses and shows how they provide meaningful patterns for understanding the character, behavior, and personality of women today. Two sequels followed: *Gods in Everyman* (1989) and *Goddesses in Older Women* (2002).

Eisner, Robert. *The Road to Daulis: Psychoanalysis, Psychology, and Classical Mythology.* Syracuse, NY: Syracuse University Press, 1987. Chapters include "Oedipus and His Kind," "Electra and Other Monsters," and "Apollo and His Boys."

Evans, Richard I. *Dialogue with C. G. Jung.* 2d ed. New York: Praeger, 1981. Basic concepts clearly presented through Jung's own words.

Jung, C. G. *Psyche and Symbol: A Selection from the Writings of C. G. Jung.* Translated by V. S. de Laszlo. Princeton, NJ: Princeton University Press, 1991.

Lloyd-Jones, H. "Psychoanalysis and the Study of the Ancient World," in P. Horden, ed., *Freud and the Humanities.* New York: St. Martin's Press, 1985, pp. 152–180. (Reprinted in *Greek Comedy* [etc.]: *The Academic Papers of Sir Hugh Lloyd-Jones.* New York: Oxford University Press, 1990, pp. 281–305.) Hostile criticism of psychoanalytical theory by an authoritative classical scholar.

Mullahy, Patrick. *Oedipus Myth and Complex: A Review of Psychoanalytic Theory.* New York: Grove Press, 1955. An excellent survey.

Pedrick, Victoria. *Euripides, Freud, and the Romance of Belonging.* Baltimore, MD: Johns Hopkins University Press, 2007. Deals with ancient and modern concerns with origins, identity, parental embrace, and abandonment.

Schneiderman, Leo. *The Psychology of Myth, Folklore, and Religion.* Chicago: Nelson–Hall, 1981. Chapters include "The Mystical Quest," "The Cult of Fertility," and "Jason and the Totem."

Walker, Steven. *Jung and the Jungians on Myth.* New York: Routledge, 2002.

Woolger, Jennifer Barker, and Roger J. Woolger. *The Goddess Within: A Guide to the Eternal Myths That Shape Women's Lives.* New York: Fawcett Columbine, 1987. The major goddesses considered as types, with a bibliography of novels and plays and a list of movies (on video), identifying characters that embody these types.

Gender, Homosexuality, and the Interpretation of Mythology

Two scholarly journals, *Arethusa* and *Helios,* are especially receptive to feminist scholarship. *Arethusa* 6 (1973) and 11 (1978) have been mostly reprinted in J. J. Peradotto and J. P. Sullivan, eds., *Women in the Ancient World: The Arethusa Papers* (Albany: State University of New York, 1984). *Helios* 12, 2 (1985) contains a debate on "Classical Studies vs. Women's Studies," by Marilyn Skinner, Mary Lefkowitz, and Judith Hallett.

Bacchilega, Cristina. *Gender and Narrative Strategies.* University Park, PA: University of Pennsylvania Press, 1997. The representation of women in four classic fairy tales and postmodern revisions in literature and film.

Cantarella, Eva. *Bisexuality in the Ancient World.* Translated by Cormac Ó Cuilleanáin. 2d ed. New Haven, CT: Yale University Press, 2002.

Davidson, James. *The Greeks and Greek Love: A Bold New Exploration of the Ancient World.* New York: Random House, 2009.

Doherty, Lillian E. *Gender and the Interpretation of Classical Myth.* London: Duckworth, 2001.

Dover, K. J. *Greek Homosexuality.* Updated with a new postscript. Cambridge, MA: Harvard University Press, 1989 [1980].

Dynes, Wayne R., and Stephen Donaldson, eds. *Homosexuality in the Ancient World: (Studies in Homosexuality,* vol. 1). New York: Taylor & Francis (Garland), 1992. A collection of papers in their original languages about various aspects of Greek and Roman homosexuality.

Fantham, Elaine, Helene Peet Foley, Natalie Boymel Kampen, Sarah B. Pomeroy, and H. A. Shapiro. *Women in the Classical World: Image and Text.* New York: Oxford University Press, 1994.

Fone, Byrne. *Homophobia: A History.* New York: Metropolitan Books (Henry Holt), 2000. An important study, the first part of which deals with the ancient world.

Gomme, A. W. "The Position of Women at Athens in the Fifth and Fourth Centuries B.C." *Essays in Greek History and Literature*. New York: Essay Index Reprint Series, Books for Libraries Press, 1967.

Halperin, David M. *One Hundred Years of Homosexuality, and Other Essays on Greek Love*. New York: Routledge, 1989. Argues that modern attitudes toward homosexuality are inadequate for an understanding of sexual mores in the ancient world.

Hawley, Richard, and Barbara Levick, eds. *Women in Antiquity: New Assessments*. New York: Routledge, 1995. Includes discussion of women's roles in religious ritual and mythology.

Hubbard, Thomas K., ed. *Homosexuality in Greece and Rome: A Sourcebook of Basic Documents*. Berkeley: University of California Press, 2003. A wide-ranging, invaluable collection from archaic Greek lyric to later Greco-Roman antiquity.

Lear, Andrew, and Eva Cantarella. *Images of Ancient Greek Pederasty*. New York: Routledge, 2008.

Lefkowitz, Mary R. *Women in Greek Myth*. 2d ed. Baltimore, MD: Johns Hopkins University Press, 2007.

Pomeroy, Sarah B. *Goddesses, Whores, Wives, and Slaves*. New York: Schocken, 1975. See especially Chapters 2 and 6.

Sissa, Giulia. *Sex and Sensuality in the Ancient World*. Translated by George Staunton. New Haven, CT: Yale University Press, 2008. A demonstration of how modern concepts of sexuality have emerged from ancient cultures, including portrayals of Medea, Clytemnestra, and Jocasta, with an argument for the centrality of heterosexual desire and against the overemphasis of homosexuality.

Skinner, Marilyn B. *Sexuality in Greek and Roman Culture*. New York: Wiley–Blackwell, 2005. A comprehensive survey based on literary, artistic, and archaeological evidence and covering a variety of subjects, with emphasis on ancient attitudes toward sexual identity and gender as compared with those of contemporary culture.

Thornton, Bruce S. *Eros: The Myth of Ancient Greek Sexuality*. Boulder, CO: Westview Press, 1997. An insightful exploration of the destructiveness of Eros in Greek imagery and metaphor and the links between ancient and present-day attitudes and concerns about sex, love, and family.

Williams, Craig A. *Roman Homosexuality: Ideologies of Masculinity in Classical Antiquity*. New York: Oxford University Press, 1999.

Winkler, John J. *Constraints of Desire: The Anthropology of Sex and Gender in Ancient Greece*. New York: Routledge, 1990. A study of the sexuality of women (e.g., Penelope and Sappho) and the interpretation of rituals (e.g., in honor of Demeter, Aphrodite, and Adonis).

Iconography, Religion, and Feminist Interpretations

Ehrenberg, Margaret. *Women in Prehistory*. Norman, OK: University of Oklahoma Press, 1989. The role of women from the Paleolithic to the Iron Age, with a consideration of matriarchy in Minoan Crete.

Eller, Cynthia. *The Myth of Matriarchal Prehistory: Why an Invented Past Won't Give Women a Future*. New York: Beacon Press, 2000. An argument against the validity of interpretations of feminists such as Marija Gimbutas, who imagine in a time of goddess worship a gynocentric golden age before the onset of patriarchy.

Gimbutas, Marija. *The Language of the Goddesses*. Foreword by Joseph Campbell. New York: Harper & Row, 1989. An analysis of the symbols in the archaeological evidence under the major categories of "Life-Giving," "The Renewing and Eternal Earth," "Death and Regeneration," and "Energy and Unfolding."

Marinatos, Nanno. *The Goddess and the Warrior: The Naked Goddess and Mistress of the Animals in Early Greek Religion.* New York: Routledge, 2000. Traces the origins of concepts of the female goddess in the Bronze Age, with emphasis on Circe, Medusa, and Artemis, who is deemed to have supervised the initiation of males.

Zeitlin, Froma. *Playing the Other: Gender and Society in Classical Greek Literature.* Chicago, IL: University of Chicago Press, 1996. Many of the essays are revisions of previously published material.

Art

Carpenter, T. H. *Art and Myth in Ancient Greece.* New York: Thames & Hudson, 1990.

Condos, Theony. *Star Myths of the Greeks and Romans; A Sourcebook.* Grand Rapids, MI: Phanes, 1997. Includes the only surviving works on the constellation myths from antiquity: an epitome of *The Constellations* of Eratosthenes, never before translated into English, and *The Poetic Astronomy* of Hyginus; also commentaries on each constellation myth.

Freedman, Luba. *The Revival of the Olympian Gods in Renaissance Art.* New York: Cambridge University Press, 2003.

Gantz, Timothy. *Early Greek Myth: A Guide to Literary and Artistic Sources.* 2 vols. Baltimore, MD: Johns Hopkins University Press, 1996. An excellent resource.

Kalil, L., ed. *Lexicon Iconographicum Mythologicae Classicae.* 8 double vols. Zurich: Artemis, 1981–1997. The most complete source for ancient representations of classical myths, with extensive essays (in English, French, German, and Italian), photographs, and bibliography for each entry.

Reid, Jane Davidson. *The Oxford Guide to Classical Mythology in the Arts 1300–1900s.* 2 vols. Oxford: Oxford University Press, 1993. The most comprehensive reference work listing works of art, music, and literature, with bibliography.

Snodgrass, Anthony. *Homer and the Artists: Text and Picture in Early Greek Art.* New York: Cambridge University Press, 1998. Argues that early Greek artists considered Homeric versions not as primary sources but as only one of possible variants.

Torrijos, Rosa López. *Mythology and History in the Great Paintings of the Prado.* London: Scala Books, 1998. The majority of the paintings reproduced and discussed deal with Greek and Roman mythology.

Van Keuren, Frances. *Guide to Research in Classical Art and Mythology.* Chicago, IL: American Library Association, 1991. A bibliographical reference book, clearly arranged by topic and period.

Zajko, Vanda, and Hoyle, Helena, eds. *A Handbook to the Reception of Classical Mythology.* Hoboken, NJ: Wiley, 2017.
A valuable collection of essays on the influence of classical mythology from antiquity to the present day.

The Gods, Religion, and the Occult

See the Select Bibliography at the end of Chapter 6.

Additional Material

Books

Biography: Beard, Mary. *The Invention of Jane Harrison.* Cambridge, MA: Harvard University Press, 2002. A portrayal of anthropologist Jane Ellen Harrison (1850–1928) and her career in the milieu of classical scholarship at Cambridge of the period, along with her younger protégé Eugenie Sellers, virtually forgotten today.

Biography: Robinson, Annabel. *The Life and Work of Jane Ellen Harrison.* New York: Oxford University Press, 2002.

Novel: Calasso, Roberto. The Marriage of Cadmus and Harmony. New York: Knopf, 1993. An idiosyncratic retelling of many ancient myths, but capacious enough to include musings on the interaction of myth and the contemporary world.

Poetry: The following books concern poems in English on mythological subjects.

Bush, Douglas. *Mythology and the Renaissance: Tradition in English Poetry.* New York: Norton, 1963 [1932]. Includes a chronological list of poems on mythological subjects.

De Nicola, Deborah, ed. *Orpheus and Company: Contemporary Poems on Greek Mythology.* Lebanon, NH: University Press of New England, 1999.

Harrison, S. J., ed. *Living Classics: Greece and Rome in Contemporary Poetry in English.* New York: Oxford University Press, 2009. This collection of essays explores the extensive use of Latin and Greek literary texts in a range of recent poetry written in English by scholars and poets, including Tony Harrison, Seamus Heaney, and Michael Longley.

Kossman, Nina, ed. *Gods and Mortals: Modern Poems on Classical Myths.* New York: Oxford University Press, 2001 [1971]. An impressive collection by internationally renowned poets.

Mayerson, Philip. *Classical Mythology in Literature, Art, and Music.* Newburyport, MA: Focus Publishing, 2001. This well-written survey embraces far more than poetry inspired by classical mythology, as its title informs us.

DVDs

Documentary: Joseph Campbell. A Biographical Portrait: The Hero's Journey. Wellspring. A good introduction to Campbell and mythic themes. See also *Sukhavati (Place of Bliss); A Mythic Journey* (the title refers to Campbell's life calling); *Mythos 1: The Shaping of Our Mythic Tradition; Mythos 2: The Shaping of the Eastern Tradition;* and *The Power of Myth* (the PBS series with Bill Moyers). All four Acorn Media.

Notes

1. G. S. Kirk, *The Nature of Greek Myths* (Harmondsworth, UK: Penguin Books, 1974), p. 27. Kirk identifies a "traditional tale" as a myth that has *"succeeded* in becoming traditional . . . [and is] important enough to be passed from generation to generation."
2. See *The Routledge Handbook of Greek Mythology* (New York: Routledge, 2003). This seventh edition is a completely revised version of H. J. Rose's *Handbook of Greek Mythology.*
3. *Legend,* like *myth,* may be used as a general term in its broadest sense. Often, however, it is defined as equivalent to *saga* and refers to stories inspired by actual persons and events. Thus, for us *legend* and *saga* are one and the same. Many prefer the German word *Märchen* for the designation of folk tales because of the pioneering work of the brothers Grimm (1857) in collecting and collating variations of oral tales and publishing their own versions.
4. Graham Anderson, *Fairytales in the Ancient World* (London: Routledge, 2000), p. 1. Anderson has identified several motifs from familiar fairytales in Greek and Roman stories (those of Cinderella, Snow White, Red Riding Hood, and Bluebeard, among many others) and offers a comparison of Cupid and Psyche and Beauty and the Beast.
5. Sometimes *fable* is also applied as a general term, but it is better to restrict its meaning to designate a story in which the characters are animals endowed with human traits, the primary purpose being moral and didactic.
6. Cf. Paul Veyne, *Did the Greeks Believe in Their Myths? An Essay on the Constitutive Imagination* (Chicago, IL: University of Chicago Press, 1988 [1983]), on the creation of truth and history.

7. This has become a commonplace explanation of the human need for mythology; it has been formulated with particular conviction by Leszek Kolakowski in his *The Presence of Myth* (Chicago, IL: University of Chicago Press, 1989 [1972]). Kolakowski frames his discussion in terms of a contrast between myth and science; for him science in its technological aspect represents the truth that is to be distinguished from myth.

8. Martha Graham, *Blood Memory* (New York: Doubleday, 1991), p. 4.

9. Ivan Strenski, *Four Theories of Myth in Twentieth-Century History* (Iowa City, IA: Iowa University Press, 1987), pp. 71–128, provides a clear critique of Eliade's complexity. Among Eliade's many works, we single out in this context *Myths, Dreams, and Mysteries* (London: Harvill, 1960) and *Myth and Reality* (New York: Harper & Row, 1963).

10. See Friedrich Max Müller, *Comparative Mythology: An Essay* (1856; reprint of rev. ed. of 1909, Salem, NH: Ayer, 1977), which includes an "Introductory Preface on Solar Mythology" by Abram Smythe Palmer and a parody by R. F. Littledale, "The Oxford Solar Myth," that is, Müller himself. For an assessment of Müller's theories, see the essay by R. M. Dorson, "The Eclipse of Solar Mythology," in T. A. Sebeok, ed., *Myth: A Symposium* (Bloomington, IN: Indiana University Press), pp. 25–63.

11. Also, "contextualism" or "situationism" and "behaviorism" are to be found in Aristotle's writings, "the first scientific work on bio-social psychology . . . practically unknown to students of human nature today." For these and other observations explaining the profound debt of modern psychology to the perceptions of Greek dramatists and philosophers, see Patrick Mullahy, *Oedipus Myth and Complex: A Review of Psychoanalytic Theory* (New York: Grove Press, 1955), pp. 335–337.

12. "The Interpretation of Dreams," in A. A. Brill, ed., *The Basic Writings of Sigmund Freud* (New York: Random House, Modern Library, 1938), p. 308, quoted at greater length by Mullahy as an introduction to Chapter 1 of *Oedipus Myth*. Plato in his *Republic* (571C) has a famous description of the unbridled nature of dreams that includes the mention of intercourse with one's mother.

13. We do not attempt to summarize a complex and fruitful subject; see Mullahy, *Oedipus Myth*, pp. 102–113. For the beginner, Richard Wollheim, *Freud* (Glasgow: William Collins, 1971), provides a concise introduction to Freudian thought; similarly, one might consult Frieda Fordham, *An Introduction to Jung's Psychology*, 3d ed. (Baltimore: Penguin Books, 1966), with a foreword by Jung. The bibliography for both Freud and Jung is, not surprisingly, voluminous and accessible.

14. Richard I. Evans, *Dialogue with C. G. Jung*, 2d ed. (New York: Praeger, 1981), p. 167.

15. Cf. Joseph Campbell, *Myths to Live By* (New York: Viking Press, 1972). Typically and unfortunately, Campbell does not pay enough attention to the Greeks and the Romans.

16. Jan Bremmer, "Oedipus and the Greek Oedipus Complex," in J. Bremmer, ed., *Interpretations of Greek Mythology* (London: Routledge, 1988), pp. 41–59 (the quotation is from note 42).

17. E. O. Wilson, *Consilience* (New York: Knopf, 1988), pp. 81–85 and 193–196.

18. See Jonathan Engel, *The Rise of Psychotherapy in the United States* (New York: Gotham Books, 2008). The quotation is from the review by Scott Stossel in the *New York Times Book Review* (December 21, 2008).

19. See R. L. Gordon, ed., *Myth, Religion, and Society: Structuralist Essays by M. Detienne, L. Gernet, J.-P. Vernant, and P. Vidal-Naquet* (New York: Cambridge University Press, 1981).

20. Robert Graves, *The Greek Myths* (Baltimore: Penguin Books, 1993 [1955]), vol. 1, p. 10. The basic assumption that permeates his writing has merit: an early matriarchal society once existed in Europe with the worship of a great mother deity, and subsequently there was an invasion of a patriarchal society from the north and east; but many of his detailed arguments are extravagant and rash. This work presents a brilliant mine of information that obscures mythical fact with fictional hypotheses.

21. E. R. Leach, *Political Systems of Highland Burma* (Cambridge, MA: Harvard University Press, 1954), p. 13; quoted in Kirk, *Nature of Greek Myths*, pp. 67 and 226. The best short expositions of the ritualist theory are the essays by Lord Raglan, "Myth and Ritual," and S. E. Hyman, "The Ritual View of Myth and the Mythic," in Sebeok, *Myth*, pp. 122–135 and 136–153.

22. Bronislav Malinowski, "Myth in Primitive Psychology" (1926); reprinted in *Magic, Science and Religion* (New York: Doubleday, 1955).

23. Bronislav Malinowski, *Argonauts of the Western Pacific* (New York: Dutton, 1961 [1922]), p. 25. For a survey of Malinowski's views in a historical context, see Strenski, *Four Theories of Myth*, pp. 42–69.

24. The best introduction to Lévi-Strauss is the "Overture" to *The Raw and the Cooked*, and classicists should read his article "The Structural Study of Myth" (which includes his interpretation of the Oedipus myth), to be found in Sebeok, *Myth*, pp. 81–106.

25. Lévi-Strauss, quoted in G. S. Kirk, *Myth: Its Meaning and Function in Ancient and Other Cultures* (Berkeley: University of California Press, 1971), p. 44.

26. Vladimir Propp, *Morphology of the Folktale*, 2d ed., rev. (Austin: University of Texas Press, 1968 [1928]). Chapter 2 (pp. 19–24) is the essential statement of Propp's methodology.

27. Propp's thirty-one functions are set out in his third chapter, pp. 25–65. The term *motifeme* was coined by the anthropologist Alan Dundes.

28. This sequence of five functions is worked out by Walter Burkert, *Structure and History in Greek Mythology and Ritual* (Berkeley, CA: University of California Press, 1979), n. 22, pp. 6–7. He points out that the metamorphosis of the mother (e.g., Callisto into a bear, Io into a cow) is not part of a fixed sequence of functions.

29. See W. Burkert, *Creation of the Sacred: Tracks of Biology in Early Religion* (Cambridge, MA: Harvard University Press, 1996), especially Chapter 3, "The Core of a Tale."

30. See Strenski, *Four Theories of Myth*, pp. 42–69, for a critical discussion of Malinowski's definition of myth.

31. Some attempt to find the oral antecedent of a literary version of a Greek myth and turn to late compendia of tales such as that of Apollodorus to identify the original version. The original version of a myth (oral or literary and usually hypothetical) is sometimes designated as the Ur-myth. It is difficult and often impossible to ascertain with any certainty the precise details or the date of versions of a classical story told by a deceased author, although the pursuit is interesting and can be rewarding—but it is beyond the scope of this introductory book.

32. Robert A. Segal, *In Quest of the Hero* (Princeton, NJ: Princeton University Press, 1990), pp. xi–xxii, identifies differences among Freud, Jung, and Campbell in their psychological explanations of the hero myth.

33. Robert A. Segal, *Joseph Campbell: An Introduction* (New York: Meridian, 1997 [1987]). The bibliography for Joseph Campbell is considerable. See, for example, *The Hero with a Thousand Faces*, 2d ed., Bollingen Series 17 (Princeton, NJ: Princeton University Press, 1968); and *The Masks of God*, 4 vols. (New York: Viking Press, 1959–1968). These are preferable to his works for a more general audience of television viewers, for whom his approach is exceedingly attractive, but disappointing to the serious classicist who expects a deeper appreciation of Greek and Roman mythology; see *The Power of Myth*, with Bill Moyers (New York: Doubleday, 1988).

34. Numbers 1 and 16 in D. A. Campbell's *Greek Lyric* (New York: St. Martin's Press, 1967), vol. 1.

35. Helene P. Foley, ed., *The Homeric Hymn to Demeter: Translation, Commentary, and Interpretive Essays* (Princeton, NJ: Princeton University Press, 1998).

36. Marilyn Katz, *Penelope's Renown: Meaning and Indeterminacy in the Odyssey* (Princeton, NJ: Princeton University Press, 1991), p. 13. A starting point for the study of feminism and mythology is Mary R. Lefkowitz, *Women in Greek Myth* (Baltimore, MD: Johns Hopkins University Press, 1986). The "moderate" approach of the author, however, is vigorously criticized by some feminists.

37. See Joan Breton Connelly, *Portrait of a Priestess: Women and Ritual in Ancient Greece* (Princeton, NJ: Princeton University Press, 2007).

38. A. W. Gomme, "The Position of Women at Athens in the Fifth and Fourth Centuries B.C.," in A. W. Gomme, ed., *Essays in Greek History and Literature* (Freeport, NY: Essay Index Reprint Series, Books for Libraries Press, 1967 [1925]).

39. Eli Sagan, *The Honey and the Hemlock, Democracy and Paranoia in Ancient Athens and Modern America* (New York: HarperCollins, 1991). This work by a sociologist is all too

typical of many revisionist studies (including some by classicists who should know better) in its blurring of definitions of citizenship and the differing rights and roles of men and women, of different classes, and as citizens, resident aliens, or slaves.

40. A statement that needs no modification, despite the book by Lloyd Llewellyn-Jones, *Aphrodite's Tortoise: The Veiled Women of Ancient Greece* (Swansea: Classical Press of Wales, 2003). There are no sound reasons to concur with his conclusion (p. 1) "that the veiling of the female head or face was part of a male ideology that required women to be silent invisible creatures, like mute tortoises contained and hidden within their shells," since it is based on preconceived misconceptions about Greek society, its customs, and its mores over a long period of time (from 900 B.C. to A.D. 200), concerning which there is abundant testimony to the contrary. His arguments from silence are no real evidence at all.

41. G. W. Bowerstock, "Men and Boys," *The New York Review of Books,* September 24, 2009, pp. 12–14.

42. This was the attitude, for example, of L. Lévy-Bruhl, *Primitive Mentality* (New York: Macmillan, 1923 [1922]).

43. A realization forcefully brought home after a reading of George Steiner, *Antigones* (New York: Oxford University Press, 1984), which discusses treatments of the Antigone theme in European literature; also Ian Donaldson, *The Rapes of Lucretia: A Myth and Its Transformations* (New York: Oxford University Press, 1982). Jane Davidson Reid provides a comprehensive collection of works indebted to Greece and Rome in *The Oxford Guide to Classical Mythology in the Arts, 1300–1990s,* 2 vols. (New York: Oxford University Press, 1991).

44. See Lowell Edmunds, *Oedipus: The Ancient Legend and Its Later Analogues* (Baltimore, MD: Johns Hopkins University Press, 1985), a survey of the many variations in ancient, medieval, and modern versions of this eternal myth.

45. See the bibliography on Orpheus at the end of Chapter 16; and we should not forget the Orpheus of music, theater, and the dance. A most fascinating collection of poetry by internationally acclaimed authors, *Gods and Mortals: Modern Poems on Classical Myths,* edited by Nina Kossman (New York: Oxford University Press, 2001), includes thirty-one works inspired by the theme of Orpheus and Eurydice. See also Deborah DeNicols, ed., *Orpheus and Company: Contemporary Poems on Greek Mythology* (Lebanon, NH: University Press of New England, 1999).

46. *The Classical Tradition,* ed. Anthony Grafton, Glenn W. Most, and Salvatore Settis (Cambridge, MA: Harvard University Press, 2010). Many essays on a wide variety of subjects, arranged alphabetically, for scholars, students, and general readers illustrate how the classical tradition has deeply influenced and shaped civilization.

47. Invaluable is the Greek edition by T. W. Allen, W. R. Halliday, and E. E. Sikes (New York: Oxford University Press, 1963 [1934]). See also J. S. Clay, *The Politics of Olympus: Form and Meaning in the Major Homeric Hymns* (Princeton, NJ: Princeton University Press, 1989).

HISTORICAL BACKGROUND OF GREEK MYTHOLOGY

> At last I was able to realize the dream of my whole life, and to visit at my
> leisure the scene of those events which had such an intense interest for
> me, and the country of the heroes whose adventures had delighted and
> comforted my childhood.
>
> **—HEINRICH SCHLIEMANN**

AS WE HAVE ALREADY seen, the historical dimension is a prominent feature of Greek legend or saga, and an outline of the historical background will be helpful for a fuller understanding.[1] Our knowledge of the early history of Greece and the Aegean is constantly changing, thanks to the fresh discoveries of archaeologists and other scholars. Consequently, our view of Greek religion and mythology has been (and will continue to be) modified by new knowledge, not least in the area of legends that cluster around the sagas of Mycenae and Troy.

The foundations of modern archaeological work in the Mycenaean world were laid by the brilliant pioneer Heinrich **Schliemann** (1822–1890), who, because of his love of Greek antiquity in general and Homer in particular, was inspired by a faith in the ultimate historical authenticity of Greek legend. Although Schliemann's character and achievement have come under vehement attack, it is impossible to deny him pride of place.[2] In the 1870s, he went to Troy, Mycenae, and Tiryns and confirmed the reality of the wealth, grandeur, and power of the cities, kings, and heroes of Minoan-Mycenaean saga. Sir Arthur **Evans** followed at the turn of the century, unearthing the splendid and grand complex of the palace of Minos at Cnossus in Crete. A whole new world had been opened up.

For a long time, it was believed that Greece had not been inhabited before the Neolithic period. But we know today that the country was settled in Paleolithic times (before 70,000 B.C.). With the present state of excavation and study, our knowledge of this early period remains tentative. Evidence for the Neolithic period (ca. 6000–3000 B.C.) is more abundant. Archaeology has revealed settled agricultural communities (i.e., outlines of houses, pottery, tools, and graves). It is conjectured that the Neolithic inhabitants came from the east and the north. For our purposes, it is noteworthy that evidence of religion seems apparent; particularly significant are little female idols, their sexuality exaggerated by the depiction of swollen bellies, buttocks, and full breasts. Male figures (some ithyphallic) also are found, although in far fewer numbers. Was a fertility mother-goddess worshiped in this early period and perhaps already associated with a male consort? The interpretation of prehistoric icons for an understanding of the worship of gods and goddesses in patriarchal and matriarchal societies has become a subject of intense scrutiny.[3]

The Bronze Age

The Stone Age gave way to the Bronze Age in Greece, Crete, and the Islands with a migration from the east (the movement was from Asia Minor across the Aegean to the southern Peloponnesus and up into Greece). These invaders were responsible for building the great Minoan civilization of Crete. The Bronze Age is divided into three major periods: Early, Middle, and Late; these periods are labeled according to geographical areas. Thus, the Bronze Age in Crete is designated as Minoan (from the tradition of King **Minos**); for the Islands the term is Cycladic (the Cyclades are the islands that encircle Delos); in Greece it is called Helladic (Hellas is the Greek name for the country). The Late Bronze Age on the mainland (i.e., the late Helladic period) is also identified as the Mycenaean Age, from the citadel of power (Mycenae) dominant in Greece during this period. The chronology with the terminology is as follows:[4]

3000–2000 B.C.	Early Bronze Age	Early Minoan
		Early Cycladic
		Early Helladic
2000–1600 B.C.	Middle Bronze Age	Middle Minoan
		Middle Cycladic
		Middle Helladic
1600–1100 B.C.	Late Bronze Age	Late Minoan
		Late Cycladic
		Late Helladic; also the Mycenaean Age

Minoan Civilization

The Minoan civilization grew to maturity in the Middle Bronze Age and reached its pinnacle of greatness in the following period (1600–1400 B.C.). The palace at **Cnossus** was particularly splendid (although another at Phaestus is impressive, too). The excavations confirm the tradition (as interpreted later, for example, by Thucydides 1.8.2) that Cnossus was the capital of a great thalassocracy (sea-power) and that Minoan power extended over the islands of the Aegean and even the mainland of Greece. The complex plan of the palace at Cnossus suggests the historical basis for the legend of the **labyrinth** and the slaying of the Minotaur by Theseus. Tribute was in all probability exacted from her allies or her subjects: Cnossus could have won temporary control over Athens, and the monarchy there could have been forced to pay tribute for a time; but subsequently, Athens would have won freedom from Cretan domination. The fact that Cnossus had no walls (unlike the fortress citadels of Hellas) indicates that its confident security depended on ships and the sea. The sophistication of Minoan art and architecture implies much about the civilization, but more particularly

Snake Goddess from the Palace at Cnossos Glazed earthenware figure (faience), ca. 1600 B.C., discovered by Sir Arthur Evans in 1903, now in the Archaeological Museum of Heraklion on Crete. It is representative of so many such figures unearthed at Minoan sites and has become iconic for much of Minoan culture. The statuette depicts a female, like those seen in Minoan frescoes, wearing an elaborate headdress and flounced skirt with open bodice and exposed breasts, holding a pair of snakes. In similar figurines, the snakes curl up the arms and around the ears of the figure. These statuettes have been used to support the still widely held theory that before the coming of the Greeks, the Minoans and early inhabitants of the Greek mainland worshiped a Great Mother Goddess. Since Linear A has yet to be deciphered, the interpretation of the meaning and function of these and other Minoan archaeological remains is elusive without any documentation. The theory that this is a representation of the Earth Mother Goddess herself (or one of her priestesses) is based on the proliferation of the figure, the presumed religious connotations of her ritual posture, her elaborate headdress, her enhanced attributes of fertility (i.e., full breasts and wide hips), and the image of the chthonic (relating to the earth) serpents. (*Anna Pakutina/Shutterstock*)

the painting and the artifacts reflect a highly developed sense of religion, for example, the importance of the bull in ritual, the dominant role of a snake goddess, and the sacred significance of the double ax (**labrys**).[5] The word *labyrinth* may have originally meant "home of the double ax." It seems fairly clear that the worship of a fertility mother-goddess was basic in Minoan religion.

By about 1400 B.C., Cretan power was eclipsed (archaeology reveals signs of fire and destruction), and the focus of civilization shifted to the mainland of Greece. Did the mainland Greeks overthrow Cnossus and usurp the Minoan thalassocracy, with the Athenians playing a significant role? Was an earthquake solely responsible for the eclipse of this island power? Theories abound, but there is no general agreement except insofar as scholars may be divided into two groups: those who stress the dominant influence of the Minoans on the mainland civilization and refuse to attribute the downfall of Crete to a Mycenaean invasion, as against those who argue for Mycenaean (Greek) encroachment and eventual control of the island. We incline to the latter view.

Excavations on the island of **Thera** (modern Santorini, about 70 miles northwest of Crete) have unearthed exciting new finds, among them interesting frescoes, and have indicated clear signs of destruction by earthquakes in the Minoan-Mycenaean period that may be dated ca. 1600 B.C. It had been conjectured that these same earthquakes were responsible for the disintegration of power on the island of Crete, but they now appear to have occurred earlier. At any rate, archaeologists have turned to the mythical tale about Atlantis (recorded by Plato in his *Critias* and *Timaeus*), a great island culture that vanished into the sea; conflict between Atlantis and Attica for control of the sea had broken out when earthquake and flood caused the astonishing disappearance of Atlantis. Does this Platonic legend reflect in any way the actual destruction of Thera, or of Crete itself, and the subsequent encroachment of Mycenaean power?[6] Again no certain answer is forthcoming.

The Mycenaean Age

On the mainland of Greece, the Middle Bronze Age (or Middle Helladic period) was ushered in by an invasion from the north and possibly the east. These Indo-Europeans are the first Greeks (i.e., they spoke the Greek language) to enter the peninsula, and they brought with them the worship of a supreme god of the sky,

THE PALACE AT CNOSSUS

In the *Odyssey*, Odysseus, disguised as a Cretan prince, dissembles about the many cities of his professed homeland, Crete, and says that "among them was Cnossus, a great city, and there Minos, friend of almighty Zeus, ruled for nine years" (*Odyssey* 19.179–180). In 1899, Sir Arthur Evans began his excavations at Cnossus and uncovered a prehistoric civilization previously known only through myth and tradition. Because of the association of the legendary King Minos with Crete (see pp. 582, 589–592), Evans called the civilization that he unearthed "Minoan." The excavations revealed the presence of a prosperous and sophisticated culture on Crete during the Bronze Age and confirmed the tradition of the dominant position of Cnossus. According to Evans, at the center of Minoan civilization was the palace, which was organized around a large, central

Diagram of Palace at Cnossus. This plan of the palace is based on Sir Arthur Evans' original, complex reconstruction of the site. Subsequent archaeologists have argued for modifications. (*GRAHAM, JAMES WALTER; THE PALACES OF CRETE © 1962 Princeton University Press, 1969 revised edition, 1990 renewed PUP Reprinted by permission of Princeton University Press*)

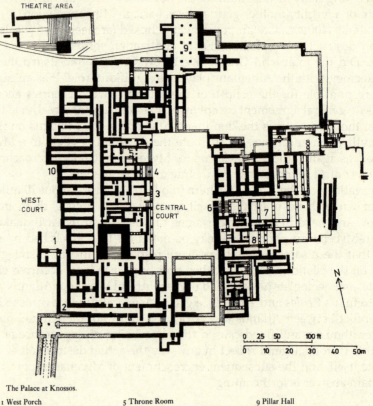

The Palace at Knossos.

1 West Porch
2 Corridor of the Procession
3 Palace Shrine
4 Stepped porch
5 Throne Room
6 Grand Staircase
7 Hall of the Double Axes
8 'Queen's Megaron'
9 Pillar Hall
10 Store-rooms
11 Royal Road, to Little Palace

court surrounded by storerooms, workshops, and living spaces. The palace at Cnossus was begun around 1700 B.C. and grew over the course of many years in a seemingly haphazard fashion, as space was needed. As a result, it is tempting to see in the mazelike complexity of the palace's layout and the ubiquitous bull motif a historical reality behind the legend of the Minotaur in the labyrinth and its link with Theseus.

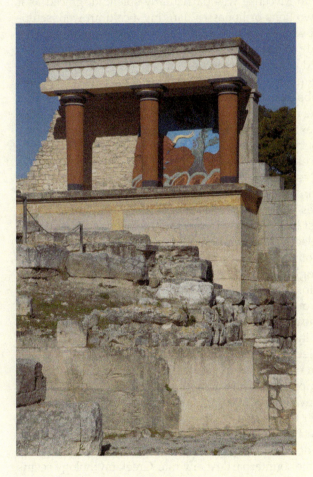

North Entrance Passage, Cnossus. Archaeologists have found in this passage area some of the best-preserved frescoes in the debris at Cnossus. The bull's head, originally part of a more complete scene of a charging bull or a feat of "bull-grappling," is now in the Heraklion Museum. Evans believed the fresco decorated the wall behind the columns. The reconstructed fresco pictured here on site follows Evans' conjecture, though doubt has been cast on the location of the original fresco. (*Carl DeAbreu/Alamy Stock Photo*)

named Zeus. Gradually, they created a civilization (usually called Mycenaean) that reached its culmination in the Late Helladic period (1600–1100 B.C.).[7] They learned much from the Minoans; their painting, palaces, and pottery are strikingly similar, but there are some significant differences. Schliemann was the first to excavate at **Mycenae** (in 1876), the kingdom of the mythological family of Atreus, corroborating the appropriateness of the Homeric epithet, "rich in gold." **Cyclopean** walls (so huge and monumental that they were said to be built by the giant Cyclopes of myth) typically surround the complex palace of the king and the homes of the aristocracy; the entrance to Mycenae was particularly splendid, graced as it was with a relief on which two lions or lionesses flanking a column were sculptured—presumably the relief was of political and religious significance, perhaps the emblem of the royal family. A circle of **shaft graves** within the citadel, set off in ritual splendor, has revealed a hoard of treasures—masks of beaten gold placed on the faces of the corpses, exquisite jewelry, and beautifully decorated weapons. Larger (and later) **tholos tombs** (also typical of Mycenaean civilization elsewhere and confirming a belief in the afterlife), built like huge beehives into the sides of hills below the palace complex, were dramatically and erroneously identified by Schliemann as both the treasury of Atreus and the tomb of Clytemnestra.

Schliemann's discoveries established the certainty of a link between the traditional tales of Greek saga, especially those contained in the Homeric poems, and the actual places named in the poems, for example, Mycenae. Archaeologists have proved that these places were prosperous centers during the Mycenaean Age, and the distinction must be appreciated between the legends of heroes associated with Mycenaean palaces (Agamemnon at Mycenae, Heracles at Tiryns, Oedipus at Thebes, and Nestor at Pylos, to name four such heroes) and the actual world revealed by archaeologists. Carl Blegen's discovery (1939, 1952–1969) of the Mycenaean palace at **Pylos** settled once and for all the controversy over its site and established the plan of the palace, with its well-preserved **megaron** (i.e., central room with an open hearth); and his conclusion that this is the palace of the family of Nestor seems inevitable. It is difficult to imagine to what families, other than those of the legends, these citadels could have belonged. Yet, of course, we must be wary of a naive belief in the details of the poetic tradition.

In religion, there were important differences between the Minoans and the Mycenaeans. The northern invaders of 2000 B.C. worshiped in particular a sky-god, Zeus, and in general their religious attitudes were not unlike those mirrored in the world of Homer's celestial Olympians. How different from the spiritual atmosphere of the Minoans dominated by the conception of a fertility mother-goddess, with or without a male counterpart! At any rate, Greek mythology seems to accommodate and reflect the union of these two cultures, as we shall see in Chapter 3.

Linear B

Clay tablets inscribed with writing have been found on the mainland (an especially rich hoard was found at Pylos, which helped immeasurably in their decipherment). These tablets were baked hard in the conflagrations that destroyed these Mycenaean fortresses when they fell before the onslaught of the invaders.[8] The key to deciphering the Linear B tablets was discovered in 1952 by Michael Ventris, who was killed in 1956 in an accident. His friend and collaborator, John Chadwick, has written for the layperson a fascinating account of their painstaking and exciting work on the tablets, one of the most significant scholastic and

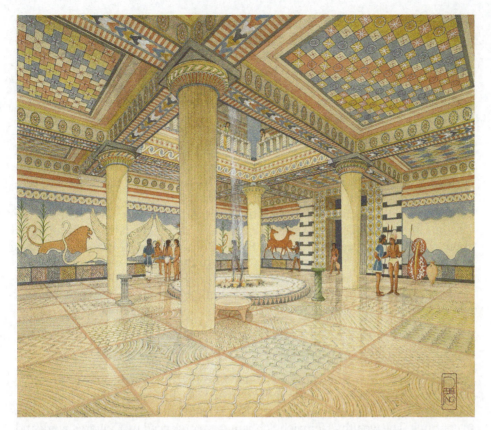

Reconstruction of the Megaron at Pylos, by Piet de Jong; watercolor, originally from the Archaeological Museum in Chora, now in the Ephoreia of Olympia. Before modern color photography and computer-generated imagery became commonplace tools for the archaeologist, Piet de Jong was one of the most prolific archaeology illustrators, and his vision of the reconstruction of Minoan, Mycenaean, and later Greek spaces and art has influenced subsequent generations in terms of how they reimagine these lost worlds. He worked with some of the most famous names in the early days of archaeology, including Carl Blegen (see p. 44), who discovered and excavated the site of the palace of Nestor at Pylos. The megaron is a feature of Mycenaean architecture and is not to be found in Minoan palaces. The floor of the megaron with its central hearth is one of the best preserved of its type. The reconstruction here, except for the details of the floor and the hearth itself, is conjectural; the position of the throne (along the back wall) is based on archaeological evidence. The painted patterns on the hearth, such as tongues of flame, and the linear designs of various colors, set out in squares upon the floor, are still visible today. (*Watercolor by Piet de Jong. Digitally edited by Craig Mauzy. Courtesy of the Department of Classics, University of Cincinnati.*)

linguistic detective stories of this or any other age.[9] It was, however, Emmett L. Bennett Jr. who was the founding father of the study of Mycenaean scripts, and his preliminary work on the Linear B tablets contributed greatly to their final decipherment by Ventris. While working on his PhD (completed in 1947) at the University of Cincinnati with Carl Blegen, who had unearthed hundreds of Linear B tablets in his excavation of Pylos, Bennett was given the golden opportunity to undertake his invaluable, pioneering work. Important for our study is the finding of the names of familiar deities of classical Greece: Zeus and Hera (listed as a pair), Poseidon, Hermes, Athena, Artemis, Eileithyia (Eleuthia in the tablets), and the name of the god Dionysus (a truly startling discovery, since it had usually been assumed that the worship of Dionysus did not come to Greece until after the Mycenaean age); also identified is an early form of the word *paean*, which was later applied as a title or epithet for Apollo. Similarly, Enyalios appears, a name identified in classical times with Ares. The word *potnia* (mistress or lady) is frequent, and thus support is added to the theory that the Mycenaeans as well as the Minoans worshiped a goddess of the mother-fertility type and that the concept of chthonian (i.e., of the earth) deities that this implies was merged with that of the Olympians. The gods are listed in the tablets as the recipients of offerings (i.e., of animals, olive oil, wheat, wine, and honey), which suggests ritual sacrifice and ceremonial banquets.

Linear B tablets have been found in some ten excavations in Mycenaean Greece and Crete. In 1993–1995, a large archive of tablets (over 259) was unearthed in Thebes. Those translated thus far confirm that in the thirteenth century B.C. Thebes controlled a powerful and rich kingdom with an impressive network of relationships. Such was the importance of the place founded by Cadmus and where Dionysus was born, with its many legends including those about the family of Oedipus. Cadmus is actually named by a Mycenaean king as one of that monarch's predecessors (probably in the fifteenth century) in a letter written in Hittite to the Great King of the Hittites. The catalog of the ships in Book 2 of Homer's *Iliad* is historical in the prominent place given to Boeotia, from whose harbor at Aulis the Mycenaean expedition set sail against Troy.

Troy and the Trojan War

Frank Calvert, an amateur archaeologist who had lived for some time in the area of the Dardanelles, was convinced that Hisarlik was the site of Troy. He undertook a preliminary investigation (1863–1868) but did not have the finances to continue. The wealthy Heinrich Schliemann, convinced by Calvert's work and inspired by Homer's *Iliad*, proceeded with a more thorough excavation (1870–1873 and 1879–1890), accompanied by the architect Wilhelm Dörpfeld, who, after Schliemann's death, continued his mission (1882–1890). Carl Blegen was the next archaeologist to provide a significant reexamination of the site, from 1932 to 1938; after Blegen's, excavations have been renewed since 1988 by a team of archaeologists led by Manfred Korfmann from the University of Tübingen (Germany) and C. Brian Rose, who like Blegen before him is from the University of Cincinnati.[10]

Troy I–VI

There were nine settlements on the site of Troy, situated at the hill of Hisarlik. **Troy I** was settled in the Early Bronze Age (ca. 2920–2450 B.C.), and there continued to be successive settlements on the site for a long period of history. It was an important city in the historical Greek period (Troy VIII, Ilion, ca. 700–85 B.C.). The Romans restored the city on a large scale in the first century A.D. (Troy IX, Ilium, 85 B.C.–ca. A.D. 500); the imperial family of Augustus Caesar honored the city as the home of their ancestor Aeneas. It existed in the time of Constantine the Great (in the fourth century) but fell into disuse in the sixth century. Because of Homer and the renowned legend of the Trojan War, which the ancients accepted as historical fact, Troy became a revered site of Greek honor and glory.

Of the seven major settlements in the Minoan-Mycenaean period (Troy I–VII), **Troy II** (ca. 2600–2450 B.C., the citadel contemporary with the Late Troy I settlement) is particularly interesting because of treasure Schliemann claimed to have found at that level and his inaccurate assumption that he had found the city of

Priam and the Trojan War. A picture that has become famous shows Schliemann's wife Sophia decked out in some of the jewelry from this treasure (called "The Gold of Troy" or "Priam's Treasure"), which Schliemann gave to the Berlin Museum. It disappeared during World War II, and not until the 1990s did the world learn that it resided in the Pushkin Museum in Moscow. When the Red Army overran Berlin at the end of World War II, it shipped the valuable treasure off to Russia.[11] **Troy III–V** belong to the Early and Middle Bronze Ages (the period ca. 2450–1700 B.C.). **Troy VI** (Troia or Ilios, ca. 1700–1250 B.C., Middle-Late Bronze Age) was identified by Dörpfeld as the city of the Trojan War. The collapse of Troy VI is dated around 1250 B.C. by the new excavators, who believe that the final building phase was ended by a severe earthquake. The fortification walls of Troy VI are particularly impressive, and Dörpfeld identified this settlement as the great city of King Priam, besieged and taken by the Greeks. According to Blegen, however, Troy VI was devastated by an earthquake, but it was the next city, **Troy VII (Troy VIIa** to be exact), that was the scene of the Trojan War, since for Blegen the evidence seems to provide signs of a siege and fire, indicative of the Trojan War: burned debris and human skeletal remains, amid signs of devastation, wrought by invaders. For him the fall of Troy VIIa (not Troy VI) occurred around 1250. The new excavators date Troy VII at about 1250–1040 B.C., Late Bronze Age–Early Iron Age, its first phase VIIa ending around 1150 B.C. There is a continuity of culture between Troy VI and Troy VIIa; the ruins of houses and citadel walls were reused for repairs; buildings are much smaller, more cramped, and clearly arranged; the style of pottery remains Mycenaean; and the population and number of storage vessels are increased. All signs of a city under siege? After all, both Troy VI and Troy VIIa could be the city of Priam in two different phases. Blegen may, after all, be right, but of course much is in great dispute. Thus far, at any rate, Korfmann's conclusions seem to support Blegen's thesis.

Troy VI–VIIa: The City of Priam

The conclusion seems inevitable that the excavated Troy (whether Troy VI or Troy VIIa, or both) must be the city of Priam that fell to the Greeks; as for chronology, the approximate date of the conflict was 1250–1150 B.C., not too far from the traditionally accepted date of ca. 1184 B.C. for the fall of Troy.[12]

The citadel for Troy VI was newly constructed in eight successive stages, its size greater than any so far found in western Asia Minor, indicating its prestige and power. The fortifications consist of gently sloping walls of ashlar masonry, 4 to 5 meters thick and over 6 meters high, topped by a superstructure of mudbrick, with the inclusion of massive towers. The principal palaces on the summit no longer survive, but remains of large, impressive buildings have been found along the edge of the acropolis within the fortifications. There were several gates leading into the citadel, the principal one to the south, flanked by a tower.

The excavations that are in progress reveal that in Troy VI/VIIa the fortified upper citadel of the king was linked to a lower town by a defensive wall that surrounded it, making the size of the whole settlement approximately 200,000 square meters with a population of roughly 5,000–10,000 inhabitants. A ditch cut in the bedrock defined the outer limit of the inhabited city. This ditch was part of the defensive system, intended as an obstacle to delay attackers before they reached a wall, just north of it, "an arrow's throw" (according to Korfmann), about 90–120 meters from the ditch, on the side of the town.[13] The fortification wall beyond the ditch was of stone, its upper section of mud-brick, enhanced by a wooden palisade with a sentry walk. (Where this wall of the lower town joined up to the northeast bastion of the citadel can be identified.) There are also clear indications of a causeway running through the palisade, in which a double wooden entrance gate was constructed, with a south gate offering controlled access to a major street through the lower town.

Astronomical Evidence in Homer for the Chronology of the Trojan War?

In Book 20 of the *Odyssey*, during a banquet of the suitors (at which Odysseus, disguised as a beggar, is present), the suitor Ageläus claims that Odysseus will never return and urges Telemachus to tell Penelope that she must marry one of them. Telemachus replies that he has told his mother to marry whomever she wishes. Homer describes the scene that follows and foreshadows the death of the suitors (345–358):

> *Thus spoke Telemachus. Then Pallas Athena instilled an unquenchable laughter in the suitors and befuddled their minds and they laughed with lips that seemed not their own. The meat that they were eating became sprinkled with blood, their eyes filled with tears and they thought that they were groaning laments. Among them, the seer Theoclymenus spoke: "Poor wretches, what is this evil you are suffering? Your heads, your faces, your knees, you are completely shrouded in night. Cries of wailing have been aroused. Spattered with blood are the walls and beautiful panels. The entrance and also the courtyard are full of ghosts going below in the dark to the gloom of the Underworld. The sun has been obliterated from the sky and an ill-omened darkness has fallen." These were his words but they all laughed at him happily.*

The allegorist Heraclitus in the first century A.D. and Plutarch both interpreted the last sentence of Theoclymenus' prophecy ("The sun has been obliterated from the sky and an ill-omened darkness has fallen") as a poetic description of a total solar eclipse (when the moon blocks the sun briefly but completely). In 1926, C. Schoch (followed by P. V. Neugebauer) argued that Homer could be referring to a real and specific solar eclipse and identified it as the one that occurred on April 16, 1178 B.C., which would have been visible over the Ionian Islands. If this conclusion is correct, the fall of Troy would then have to be dated ca. 1188, since Odysseus traveled for ten years afterward, before he arrived home in Ithaca. Therefore, this astronomical evidence would provide yet another confirmation of the traditional and archaeological dates for Troy's fall in the period 1250–1150.

In subsequent years, the work of Schoch was evidently too hastily dismissed, and only recently has it found serious support as a result of the research of Marcelo O. Magnasco, head of the Laboratory of Mathematical Physics of the Rockefeller University in New York, and Constantino Baikouzis of the Observatorio Astronómico in La Plata, Argentina. They have scrupulously identified other astronomical indications in the *Odyssey* that may be linked to their argument, among them the presence of a new moon, a prerequisite for a total eclipse. They also readily admit the number of limitations and controversial issues inherent in their analysis, but they hope that other scholars may be inspired to pursue further research. The ingenuity and honesty of this painstaking astronomical scrutiny of Homer's text by two biophysicists of repute make their conclusions provocative.[14]

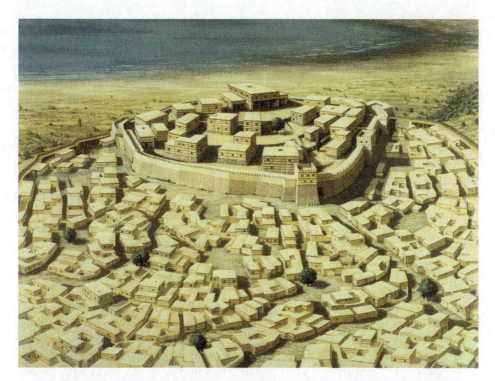

Model of Troy VI, from Joachim Latacz, *Troy and Homer* (*Troia und Homer*), translated by K. Windle and R. Ireland (Oxford: Oxford University Press, 2004), p. 33, fig. 8. The model illustrates the results of the work of Manfred Korfmann (1952–2005) at Troy between 1988 and 2003. It shows the city that was possibly the immediate predecessor of Priam's Troy (Troy VII), destroyed by an earthquake in about 1250 B.C. and soon rebuilt. The citadel, with the royal palace and the houses of the elite Trojans, is at the top center, and below it is the lower town, inhabited by the ordinary citizens. The whole, with an extent of 200,000 square meters, was surrounded by a wall and a ditch. In the distance, about 8 kilometers away, lies the sea. (*Christoph Haussner, Munich*)

The main entrance to the upper citadel of Troy VI/VIIa was from the west, on the seaward side. A broad paved road, affording easy and dangerous access, led gently uphill to the fortress wall and ended at the largest gate in the fortress wall. (There was also a city gate here on the west side, very close, only about 80 meters, to the fortress gate.) Korfmann rightfully sees this topography reflected in the *Iliad*. This most vulnerable section of the fortress wall not only offered a clear view as far as Tenedos over the plain, which the attackers must have crossed, but also it was the only place where these Mycenaean warriors would have come close enough to be identified.

The recent excavations provide greater proof than ever that Troy VI/VIIa was a significant, palatial center, with its fortress citadel and inhabited lower town protected by a ditch and a wall—certainly compatible with the wealth and power of King Priam, celebrated in the heroic tradition.

The excavators have also found, just as Blegen did, indications within the lower town of a violent destruction for the end of Troy VIIa, for example, a hastily buried fifteen-year-old female and "a number of long-range weapons, such as arrowheads and spearheads, and over one hundred stone pellets, probably used for slings, which were piled in heaps. This may indicate defeat in battle because successful defenders usually clean up such piles, whereas victorious aggressors tend not to care about them."

The Luwian Seal from Troy

Perhaps the most exciting find of all is a small, round, bronze seal (biconvex, i.e., convex on both sides) found in a one-room house. This first prehistoric inscription from Troy is to be dated in the second half of the twelfth century. Such seals (which come in various types) are common and abundant because of the need to mark and identify one's own property with a stamp. Biconvex seals are a special type, usually with one side bearing the name of an official and the other the name of his wife. The language of the seal is Luwian, an Indo-European language like Hittite, of which it is a dialect. Traditional cuneiform Hittite (the official language of diplomacy) can be read today, but hieroglyphic Hittite, a complex pictographic script used for Luwian, has only recently been deciphered after prolonged research; complete decipherment has yet to be achieved. The Luwian language became a kind of demotic to high Hittite and was used widely among a multilingual population because it was more easily comprehensible. The text of the Luwian seal from Troy is poorly preserved. The personal names are illegible, but the title of the man is translated as *scribe* or *master-scribe*, and on the other side the word *wife*. Much (indeed, far too much) has been inferred from this one and only seal. That Luwian was a language used in Troy is credible, but there must have been many more languages in this international hub. That it was the major language of the Trojans is a much less likely conjecture. They may have spoken Greek. Perhaps in this case, too, Homer is right. Hector and Achilles could communicate with one another, and so could Paris with Helen. After all, the Trojans were descended from the same Indo-Europeans (identified as ancestors of the Mycenaean Greeks) who around 2000 B.C. came down into Greece from the north and also across the Dardanelles into Asia Minor. There is now real hope that more examples of writing may be found, perhaps in other houses in Troy VI/VIIa or in the tons of rubble that remain from Schliemann's excavations.

Hittite documents have emerged to offer vital new insights into the history of the Bronze Age. These texts "indicate strong connections between the Hittite kingdom and 'Wilusa,' which should probably be identified with Troy." Also, one of the texts (called the Alaksandu treaty) identifies among the deities of Wilusa a deity named Appaliunas, almost certainly the name for Apollo, the great god who took the side of the Trojans in the *Iliad*. The cult of Apollo is believed to be Anatolian or Cypriot in origin; after all, Homer does call him "Lycian-born." There are thousands of other such Hittite texts, which should be so enlightening, but sad to say they remain unread, waiting, waiting for willing scholars trained in the decipherment of cuneiform.

The Greek Armada Lands at Besika Bay

Other excavations under Korfmann's direction in the area of the Troad have unearthed further confirmation for the authenticity of Homeric geography and legend. Five miles southwest of Troy lies Besika Bay, where the original seashore at the time of the Trojan War has been identified; nearby, a cemetery containing about 200 graves surrounded by a single wall has been unearthed; the cremations and burials were accompanied by pottery and funeral offerings that are unmistakably Mycenaean and of the thirteenth century (the period of late Troy VI or Troy VIIa). It is difficult to resist the identification of this cemetery as that of the camp of the invading Greeks and Besika Bay, from which the island of

Tenedos can be seen about 6 miles away, as the harbor where the Greeks anchored and encamped.

The Tomb of Achilles

Nearby is the headland of Yassi Tepe (formerly named Cape Troy) where there rises a great cone-shaped tumulus, Besik Tepe (now called Sivri Tepe), which most certainly goes back to the Bronze Age and very probably is the great tumulus mentioned by Homer. It must also be the mound, believed in classical times to be the tomb of Achilles and visited by Xerxes and Alexander the Great. Alexander, inspired by his love of the *Iliad*, saw himself and his comrade Hephaestion as a second Achilles and Patroclus. Another famous visitor to Troy was Xerxes, king of the Persians. On his march against Greece in 480 B.C., he was anxious to see the ancient and celebrated city of great King Priam. After he made a tour of the citadel and asked about the stirring legends of the Trojan War, he sacrificed oxen to Trojan Athena, and priests poured libations of wine to the heroes of old who had died there.

The Reality of the Trojan War

A detailed examination of abundant evidence confirms that Troy was a major center of commerce and trade in the second millennium. The city held the Hittite Empire at bay and remained relatively independent, eventually becoming a major contender in maritime traffic, with a stronghold on the vital area of the Black Sea, possibly even charging tolls for ships traveling through the Dardanelles. Serious economic reasons can easily be conjured up as legitimate causes for the Trojan War. After the Mycenaeans had conquered Cnossus, they aggressively assumed control of the Aegean and, during the thirteenth century particularly, interfered frequently and significantly in the military and monetary affairs of western Asia Minor, even gaining for a time a foothold in Miletus. It was inevitable that they would finally move against Troy, a most pernicious rival.

In the epic cycle of saga, the great leaders of the Mycenaean kingdoms banded together to sail against Troy, and, even though the historical facts may be a matter of conjecture, the romance of this poetic legend has a reality too. Until it is disproven, we have every right to believe that there once were an Agamemnon and a Clytemnestra, a Hector and an Andromache and an Achilles, who lived and died, no matter how fictitious the details of the story that they inspired; and handsome Paris and beautiful Helen ran away together in the grip of Aphrodite, providing the inciting cause for a great war that has become immortal. The rigorously scientific, contemporary archaeologist and historian will settle for nothing less than written proof for the authenticity of the war and reality of its leaders. Perhaps the time is now here at last for the realization that all sorts of cumulative evidence (not only written records) from recent investigations in support of belief has become overwhelming.[15]

Carl Blegen, on the basis of much good evidence already acquired, wrote in 1963: "It can no longer be doubted, when one surveys the state of our knowledge today, that there really was an actual historical Trojan War in which a coalition of Achaeans, or Mycenaeans, under a king whose overlordship was recognized, fought against the people of Troy and their allies." His conviction gains further substantial support daily, and he would be gratified by the

Timeline of Historical Events and Authors

7000–3000 B.C.	Neolithic Age	
3000–2000 B.C.	Early Greek Bronze Age	*Oral transmission of myth and legend*
2000 B.C.	Greek-speaking peoples enter Greece	
2000–1600 B.C.	Middle Bronze Age	
	The flowering of Minoan civilization and the dominance of Cnossus	
1600–1100 B.C.	Late Bronze Age: The Mycenaean Age	
	Mycenaean dominance over the Minoans	
1250–1150 B.C.	Period of the collapse of Troy VI and VII	
1184 B.C.	A traditional date for the fall of Troy	
1100–800 B.C.	Dark Age	
	The Dorian invasion and the beginning of the Iron Age	
800–480 B.C.	Archaic Period	*Invention of the Greek alphabet*
546 B.C.	Cyrus the Great extends the Persian Empire with the sack of Sardis and the defeat of Croesus, King of Lydia	*Homer (Iliad and Odyssey)*
		Epic cycle
		Hesiod (Theogony and Works and Days)
753–509 B.C.	The founding of Rome by Romulus and the monarchy to the establishment of the Republic	*Homeric Hymns*
		Lyric poets
480–323 B.C.	Classical Period	*Pindar (Victory Odes)*
480 B.C.	The Persians sack Athens and destroy the temples on the Acropolis	*Aeschylus, Sophocles, Euripides (tragedy)*
447–438 B.C.	Construction of the Parthenon as part of Pericles' building program	*Herodotus (history)*
		Thucydides (history)
		Aristophanes (comedy)
		Plato (philosophy)
		Aristotle (philosophy)

323–31 B.C.	Hellenistic period	
323 B.C.	Death of Alexander the Great	*Callimachus (hymns)*
		Apollonius of Rhodes (Argonautica)
1st Century B.C.	Late Roman Republic	*Lucretius (epic)*
		Catullus (lyric)
27 B.C.–A.D. 284	Early Roman Empire	*Vergil (Eclogues, Georgics, and Aeneid)*
27 B.C.–A.D. 14	Rule of Augustus, first emperor of Rome	*Ovid (Metamorphoses, Fasti, etc.)*
		Livy (Ab urbe condita)
		Seneca (tragedy)
		Valerius Flaccus (Argonautica)
		Statius (Thebaid)
		Apollodorus (Library of Greek Mythology)
		Lucian (mythological satire) Apuleius (Metamorphoses or The Golden Ass)
		Pausanias (description of Greece)
		Hyginus (genealogies)
A.D. 284–476	Later Empire to the Fall of Rome	
A.D. 313	Edict of Milan under Constantine establishes religious tolerance for Christianity	
A.D. 361–363	Julian the Apostate, the last non-Christian emperor, attempts to revive pagan worship	
A.D. 380	Theodosius establishes Christianity as the only legitimate religion and closes pagan sanctuaries	
A.D. 476	The fall of Rome	*Fulgentius (mythologies)*

knowledge that Korfmann and many others today confidently use Homer as a secondary source of consequence, with intelligent caution, of course, just the way he did.[16]

End of the Mycenaean Age

The destruction of the later phases of Troy VII (VIIb, to the beginning of the tenth century B.C.) marked the troublesome period of transition from the Late Bronze Age to the Age of Iron. The Greeks, we are to assume, returned from Troy in triumph. Yet not long after their return, the Mycenaean Age in Greece was brought to a violent end, perhaps precipitated by internal dissension. The widely held theory that the destruction was entirely the work of **Dorians** invading from the north and east has been questioned. Some historians not very convincingly associate the destruction of the Mycenaean kingdoms with the "sea peoples" mentioned in an Egyptian inscription put up by the pharaoh Rameses III in the twelfth century B.C., but there is still no certainty about the details of the end of the Bronze Age in Greece.

Homer

A cogent interpretation of the evidence offers answers to some of the many Homeric questions, amid all the controversy. In the *Odyssey* (1.350–351), when the bard Phemius sings of the disasters that the Achaeans suffered upon their return from Troy (so painful for Penelope to hear), Telemachus observes that the audience applauds most for the most recent tales. In a later book (8.487–534), Demodocus at the request of Odysseus (whose identity is not known) sings readily about the wooden horse and the fall of Troy with such art that Odysseus is brought to tears. The recitation of oral poetry to the accompaniment of the lyre (phorminx) was part of the fabric of Mycenaean civilization. (A splendid fresco of a lyre player was found at Pylos.) The story of the Trojan War in all likelihood was first told simultaneous with the event or soon afterward, to be transmitted in a continuous tradition by generations of subsequent poets, with modifications, elaborations, and infinite creative variations. The Dorian invasion bringing an end to Mycenaean civilization (ca. 1100 B.C.) is now believed to have been less disruptive than previously thought. The poetic transmission, however, was in rigidly structured lines (the meter being dactylic hexameter), which was conducive to the retention of historical fact. A large body of repetitive formulaic material of varying types and lengths was crystallized (e.g., "swift-footed Achilles," "rosy-fingered dawn," or the set pattern of sacrificial ritual), to be drawn upon readily and to facilitate impromptu oral recitation before an audience. A highly skilled guild of professional rhapsodists (called Homeridae or Homerids) developed, and by the time of Homer oral epic had reached a pinnacle of artistic perfection. It was Homer who composed the *Iliad* and the *Odyssey* orally and was possibly the one who had the poems set down in writing in the eighth century B.C. Despite the centuries between the time of Homer and the Trojan War, the poet transmits much accurate historical detail that can come only from the period of the Trojan War. The most compelling example (among many others) is the catalog of the ships (2.494–759), which does not fit comfortably in its later context in the *Iliad* and describes an earlier political and geographical world that can only be Mycenaean. Credible is the tradition that a standard text of both poems was established in Athens at the time of the Pisistratid tyranny in the second half of the sixth century B.C.

Darkness descends on the history of Greece, a darkness that is only gradually dispelled with the emergence of the two great Homeric epics, the *Iliad* and the *Odyssey*, in the eighth century B.C. The stories of the earlier period were kept alive by oral recitation, transmitted by bards like those described in the epics themselves. "Homer" almost certainly belongs to Asia Minor or one of the islands (e.g., Chios) off the coast. In the cities of this area in this period, we find that monarchy is the prevailing institution; significantly enough, the social and political environment for the bard of this later age is not unlike that of his predecessors in the great days of Mycenae.

Most important for the appreciation of the cumulative nature of the growth of the legends is the realization that there were two major periods of creative impetus, one before the destruction of Mycenaean civilization and one after. The Homeric poems maintain the fact and fiction of the Bronze Age, but they also portray their own Age of Iron. To mention but one example, archaeology shows us that burial was prevalent in the Mycenaean Age, but in Homer cremation is common. The saga of the Argonauts reflects an interest in the Black Sea that is historical—but was this interest Mycenaean, or do the details belong to the later age of Greek colonization (ca. 800–600 B.C.)? The legend as we have it must be a composite product of both eras. The Theseus story blends, in splendid confusion, Minoan-Mycenaean elements with facts of the later historical period of monarchy in Athens.

The Homeric poems were eventually set down in writing; this was made possible by the invention of an alphabet in the eighth century B.C.[17] The Greeks borrowed the symbols of the Phoenician script and used them to create a true alphabet, distinguishing by each sign individual vowels and consonants, unlike earlier scripts (such as Linear B) in which syllables are the only linguistic units. This stroke of genius, by the way, is typically Greek in its brilliant and inventive simplicity; surely no one of our countless debts to Greek civilization is more fundamental. Is the invention of the Greek alphabet and the setting down of the Homeric epics coincidental? Presumably, the dactylic hexameter of epic poetry cannot be reproduced in the clumsy symbols of Linear B. At any rate, when tradition tells us that the legendary Cadmus of Thebes taught the natives to write, we assume that he instructed them in Mycenaean Linear B rather than in the later Greek alphabet.

Select Bibliography

Bittlestone, Robert, with James Diggle and John Underhill. *Odysseus Unbound: The Search for Homer's Ithaca*. New York: Cambridge University Press, 2005.

Bryce, Trevor. *The Trojans and Their Neighbours*. New York: Routledge, 2005. In addition to a focus on Troy's neighbors, the involvement of Troy in the *Iliad* is explored.

Cambridge Ancient History. 3d ed. Vols. 1 and 2. New York: Cambridge University Press, 1970–1975. The standard work of reference in English, with chapters by various authorities. These volumes cover the early history of the Aegean world and the Near East and Bronze Age Greece, which now needs to be updated.

Castleden, Rodney. *The Attack on Troy*. Barnsley: Pen & Sword, 2006.

———. *Minoans: Life in Bronze Age Crete*. New York: Routledge, 1993. This book follows upon Castleden's previous work, *The Knossos Labyrinth* (1990), in which he postulates a new view about the palace.

Chadwick, John. *The Mycenaean World*. New York: Cambridge University Press, 1976.

Dickinson, Oliver. *The Aegean Bronze Age*. Cambridge World Archaeology. New York: Cambridge University Press, 1994.

Drews, Robert. *The End of the Bronze Age: Changes in Warfare and the Catastrophe ca. 1200 B.C.* Princeton, NJ: Princeton University Press, 1996.

Ellis, Richard. *Imagining Atlantis*. New York: Vintage Books, 1999. Countless and endless are the books about the legendary Atlantis. This one by Ellis is outstanding for its survey of the archaeological evidence and the many theories (fiction and film included) proposed by authors ranging from Plato to Arthur Conan Doyle.

Fields, Nic. *Troy c. 1700–1250 B.C.* New York: Osprey Publishing, 2004. A well-illustrated, up-to-date, and concise discussion.

Fitton, J. Lesley. *The Discovery of the Greek Bronze Age*. Cambridge, MA: Harvard University Press, 1996. An excellent survey of the excavations and their historical interpretation.

Gerster, Georg. *The Sites of Ancient Greece*. London: Phaidon Press, 2012. A beautiful tour of the Greek world using gorgeous aerial photography.

Latacz, Joachim. *Troy and Homer: Towards a Solution of an Old Mystery*. Translated by Kevin Windle and Rosh Ireland. New York: Oxford University Press, 2004. The most up-to-date survey of the continuing excavation, which includes analysis of the most recent important and exciting finds.

Luce, J. V. *Homer's Landscapes: Troy and Ithaca Revisited*. New Haven, CT: Yale University Press, 1998. A gratifying study that restores one's faith in the maligned historicity of Homer. Luce shows the accuracy of Homer's geography of Troy and the Troad in the *Iliad* and convinces us that the modern islands of Lefkas, Itháki, Kephalonia, and Zante, off the Gulf of Corinth, correspond to the descriptions in the *Odyssey* for Doulichion, Ithaca, Samos (Samê), and Zakynthos. Although archaeology confirms Mycenean evidence on the islands, the palace of Odysseus remains to be discovered.

Mellersh, H. E. *The Destruction of Knossos: The Rise and Fall of Minoan Crete*. New York: Weybright & Talley, 1970.

Papadopoulos, John K. *The Art of Antiquity: Piet de Jong and the Athenian Agora*. American School of Classical Studies. New York: David Brown Book Co., 2007. Includes a discussion and illustrations of de Jong's work for the Minoan and Mycenaean periods.

Schofield, Louise. *The Mycenaeans*. New York: Oxford University Press, 2007. Includes one hundred illustrations.

Sowerby, Robin. *The Greeks and Their Culture*. 2d ed. New York: Routledge, 2009. A wide-ranging introductory survey of ancient Greek history, religion, social life, literature, and philosophy.

Vidal-Naquet, Pierre. *A Short History of Plato's Myth of Atlantis*. Exeter: University of Exeter Press, 2007. A reexamination of the different uses made of the myth in different contexts and periods.

Winkler, Martin M., ed. *Troy: From Homer's "Iliad" to Film Epic*. Malden, MA: Blackwell, 2006. Provides an annotated list of films (including television) on the Trojan War, with illustrations.

Wood, Michael. *In Search of the Trojan War*, new ed. Berkeley, CA: University of California Press, 1996. Originally based on the BBC television series and now updated, this is a good survey. It now needs to be updated further, and the reader should consult Latacz (2004) for the most recent finds and interpretations.

Ziolkowski, Theodore. *Minos and the Moderns: Cretan Myth in Twentieth-Century Literature and Art*. New York: Oxford University Press, 2008.

Notes

1. Emily Vermeule, *Greece in the Bronze Age* (Chicago, IL: University of Chicago Press, 1964), offers a survey (now out of date) that contains important earlier bibliography. Vermeule regrettably ignores Homer as evidence; fortunately, however, many archaeologists today have returned to Homer cautiously with important results. See note 15 for Fitton's more recent survey.

2. Schliemann's life and career are the material for a bizarre and exciting success story. He amassed a fortune so that he could prove the validity of his convictions, which he pursued with passion. Earlier biographies tend to be romantically sympathetic: Emil Ludwig, *Schliemann: The Story of a Gold-Seeker* (Boston, MA: Little, Brown, 1931); Robert Payne, *The Gold of Troy* (New York: Funk and Wagnalls, 1959); Lynn and Gray Poole, *One Passion, Two Loves* (New York: Thomas Y. Crowell, 1966); and Irving Stone, *The Greek Treasure* (New York: Doubleday, 1975). More recently, Schliemann has been characterized as a liar and a fraud: David A. Traill, *Schliemann of Troy: Treasure and Deceit* (New York: St. Martin's Press, 1995). Less scholarly, but nevertheless critical and more balanced, is the biography by Caroline Moorehead: *Lost and Found: The 9,000 Treasures of Troy: Heinrich Schliemann and the Gold That Got Away* (New York: Viking Press, 1996 [1994]). Susan Heuck Allen, *Finding the Walls of Troy* (Berkeley, CA: University of California Press, 1999), another detractor, argues that Schliemann obscured his debts to the British archaeologist Frank Calvert for the identification and excavation of the mound of Hisarlik as the site of Troy.

3. See the bibliography for Iconography, Religion, and Feminist Interpretations in Chapter 1, p. 33.

4. The dates for these periods are serviceable. It is rash to insist on greater precision for this early period, for the evidence for it fluctuates daily. The chronology of the Bronze Age is a subject of passionate dispute. Thus, attempts at a more precise chronology with further subdivisions within the periods are not reproduced here. For a scholarly treatment, consult pertinent chapters and charts in *The Cambridge Ancient History*, 3d ed., vol. 2, pt. 1, *The Middle East and the Aegean Region 1800–1380 B.C.*, edited by I. E. S. Edwards, N. G. L. Hammond, and E. Sollberger (New York: Cambridge University Press, 1973); and pt. 2, *The Middle East and the Aegean Region c. 1380–1000 B.C.* (1975).

5. For a more detailed interpretation of the evidence in terms of Minoan-Mycenaean religion, see W. K. C. Guthrie, "The Religion and Mythology of the Greeks," in Edwards et al., eds., *The Cambridge Ancient History*, vol. 2, pt. 2, Chapter 40.

6. For a survey of the excavations at Thera, the relationship to Crete, and theories about Atlantis, see Christos G. Doumas, *Thera: Pompeii of the Ancient Aegean* (London: Thames & Hudson, 1983).

7. Some believe that a later wave of invaders (ca. 1600 B.C.) is to be specifically identified as the Achaeans in Homer; it is better to consider Achaeans as virtually an equivalent term for the Mycenaean Greeks.

8. Linear A tablets (Linear B is derived from the Linear A script), found on Crete, have not yet been deciphered; apparently Minoan Linear A is not Greek. Linear B tablets (written in an early form of Greek) have also been found at Cnossus, with provocative implications for historical reconstruction. Hostile criticism of Evans is offered by Leonard R. Palmer, *Mycenaeans and Minoans*, 2d ed. (New York: Knopf, 1965).

9. John Chadwick, *The Decipherment of Linear B*, 2d ed. (New York: Cambridge University Press, 1958).

10. Blegen's results have been published in a series of highly technical volumes. Like the reports of his excavations at Pylos, they are a monumental testimony to the scientific precision of modern archaeological procedures. Blegen has provided a survey of the excavations at Troy for the general reader: Carl W. Blegen, *Troy and the Trojans* (New York: Praeger, 1963). We are grateful to Manfred Korfmann, C. Brian Rose, and Getzel Cohen for information about the new excavations of Troy.

11. The official catalog of the "Gold of Troy" exhibition at the Pushkin State Museum of Fine Arts, Moscow (with beautiful color illustrations), has been published: Vladimir Tolstikov and Mikhail Treister, *The Gold of Troy: Searching for Homer's Fabled City*. Translated from the Russian by Christina Sever and Mila Bonnichsen (New York: Harry N. Abrams, 1996).

12. Details and quotations about the excavations come from the *Newsletters of the Friends of Troy*, offered by the Institute for Mediterranean Studies in Cincinnati. This information has been updated, with the most recent material from Joachim Latacz, *Troy and Homer: Towards a Solution of an Old Mystery*. Translated by Kevin Windle and Rosh Ireland (New York: Oxford University Press, 2004). Latacz, a friend and colleague of Manfred Korfmann (director of the excavations until his death in 2005), presents the most recent survey (the first edition, 2001, has been revised and expanded). Scholarly annual excavation reports appear in *Studia Troica* (Mainz, Germany: Verlag Philipp von Zabern), published in both German and English, which also includes interdisciplinary research concerning Troy.

13. A second ditch found over 100 meters south of and in front of the first ditch offered another, preliminary obstacle, perhaps against chariot attacks. It is unknown if this measure of redoubled security was backed by a wall.

14. Constantino Baikouzis and Marcelo O. Magnasco, "Is an Eclipse Described in the Odyssey?" *Proceedings of the National Academy of Science* 105, no. 26 (July 2008), pp. 8823–8828.

15. J. Lesley Fitton, in her survey of Bronze Age archaeology, *The Discovery of the Greek Bronze Age* (Cambridge, MA: Harvard University Press, 1996), sensibly observes (p. 203): "It seems a sad decline to our modern recognition that the material remains of a pre-literate society, incompletely recovered, can properly be expected only to answer limited and impersonal questions." Nevertheless, she concludes (p. 197) that "Without writing, 'proof' [of the Trojan War] is well nigh unimaginable."

16. See Carl W. Blegen, *Troy and the Trojans* (New York: Praeger, 1963), p. 20.

17. The argument for connecting Homer with the invention of the alphabet has been cogently made by H. T. Wade-Gery, *The Poet of the Iliad* (New York: Cambridge University Press, 1952). See also Barry B. Powell, *Homer and the Origins of the Greek Alphabet* (New York: Cambridge University Press, 1991).

For additional digital learning resources please go to
www.oup.com/he/morford12e

MYTHS OF CREATION

Now the whole of heaven (uranus)—or let us call it the universe (cosmos) or some other name that it would prefer—regarding it we must consider first that question underlying every investigation which must be sought at the outset. Has it always existed, with no origin from generation, or has it come into being, arising out of some beginning?

—**PLATO**, *Timaeus 28b*

THERE WERE MANY MYTHS about creation among the Greeks and Romans, and these myths have many parallels in other mythologies, such as Egyptian, Sumerian, Babylonian, and Hebraic. Homer (ca. 800 B.C.) has the Titans Oceanus and Tethys (identified later in this chapter) responsible for the origin of the gods (*Iliad* 14.201) and reflects a primitive belief that the universe can be understood in terms of a simple geography. The world is a flat disc with hills, touched at its rim by the vast dome of the heavens. The deity Oceanus is the stream of ocean that encircles the earth (see figure on p. 607). But Homer does not by any means provide a complete account of genesis. Hesiod (ca. 700 B.C.), as far as we can tell, was the first to give literary expression to a systematic explanation of how the gods, the universe, and humankind came into being. At any rate, his account, the earliest to survive, may be considered the classic Greek version. The genealogical scheme is presented in his *Theogony*, while his *Works and Days* adds significant details.

Hesiod

In the opening of the *Theogony*, Hesiod devotes many lines to the beauty and power of the **Muses**, with particular emphasis on their ability to inspire the infallible revelation of the poet. He lovingly describes their graceful dancing and exquisite singing to delight the gods on Olympus. This ardent invocation to the Muses is no mere artistic convention but rather the utterance of a prophetic visionary. Since the Muses are the daughters of Zeus, their revelation comes from the infallible knowledge of the supreme god. Hesiod's vehement sincerity may be illustrated by these lines from the *Theogony* (22–34):

> They, the Muses, once taught Hesiod beautiful song, while he was shepherding his flocks on holy Mount Helicon; these goddesses of Olympus, daughters of aegis-bearing Zeus first of all spoke this word to me, "Oh,

> you shepherds of the fields, base and lowly things, little more than bellies, we know how to tell many falsehoods that seem like truths but we also know, when we so desire, how to utter the absolute truth." (22–28)
>
> Thus they spoke, the fluent daughters of great Zeus. Plucking a branch, to me they gave a staff of laurel, a wondrous thing, and into me they breathed a divine voice, so that I might celebrate both the things that are to be and the things that were before; and they ordered me to honor, in my song, the race of the blessed gods who exist forever, but always to sing of them themselves, the Muses, both first and last. (29–31)   10

Hesiod's attention to the Muses is steeped in a religious aura of divinely inspired revelation. As he begins his genesis, Hesiod asks the Muses, "Tell me how first gods, earth, rivers, the boundless sea . . . the shining stars, and the wide heavens above came into being." This is their answer (*Theogony* 116–125):

> Verily, very first of all Chaos came into being, but then wide-bosomed Gaia, secure foundation of all forever, and dark Tartarus in the depth of the broad land and Eros, the most beautiful of all the immortal gods, who loosens the limbs and overwhelms judgment and wise counsel in the breast of gods and all humans. From Chaos, Erebus [the gloom of Tartarus] and black Night came into being; but from Night were born Aether [the upper atmosphere] and Day, whom Night bore when she became pregnant after mingling in love with Erebus.

The Greek word *chaos* suggests a "yawning void." Exactly what it means to Hesiod, however, is difficult to establish.[1] His account of creation, fraught with problems, begins paratactically; that is, very first of all **Chaos** (not a deity particularly, but a beginning or a first principle, perhaps a void) came into being (or was), but then (next) came **Gaia** (**Gaea** or **Ge**, Earth)[2] and the others. All presumably came out of Chaos, just as Hesiod actually states, as he continues, that "from Chaos" came Erebus and dark Night. **Tartarus** is a place deep in the depths of the earth (*Theogony* 713 ff.); **Erebus** is the gloomy darkness of Tartarus; later it may be equated with Tartarus itself.

The scholarly (sometimes adamant) disagreement that surrounds this passage concerns the interpretation of "then" (i.e., "next"). Do Gaea, Tartarus, and Eros emerge next after Chaos or through generation out of Chaos? It is our conviction that all three arose out of Chaos, as indicated in Figure 3.1 (cf. Ovid's description of Chaos as the primal source of creation, discussed on p. 62).

The Primacy and Mystery of Eros

Love, typically a potent force in tales of creation and procreation, inevitably appears early in the *Theogony*. Hesiod, as we have just seen, describes the most beautiful Eros by one of his characteristically brief touches, which strive to lift his didacticism to the realm of poetry. For the Romans, Eros was called Cupid (or Amor).

Hesiod

The poet Hesiod has a much greater identity than his predecessor Homer, who is more immediately linked to an oral tradition and belongs to the coast of Asia Minor or the adjacent islands. Dates for Hesiod are in much dispute, but he probably composed his two poems, the *Theogony* and *Works and Days*, around 700. Which work was written first also is uncertain, and other works (e.g., the *Catalogs of Women and Heroines* and *Divination by Birds*) are only dubiously to be attributed to him. Certainly, the *Shield of Heracles* belongs to a later period.

As we have seen, in the *Theogony* Hesiod provides some information about his life. More details are to be found in his *Works and Days*, a didactic poem about farming incorporating important mythological stories, which are excerpted in the next chapter. From these two poems, the following biographical sketch may be drawn. Of course, how much of it is true or false, irrefutable fact or fictional literary artifice, is extremely debatable.

Hesiod's father came from Cyme, situated in the larger area of Aeolis in Asia Minor. He eventually crossed the Aegean and settled in Ascra, a town near Mt. Helicon, in Boeotia, where Hesiod was born and lived his life and which he describes with his usual dour outlook as "bad in winter, difficult in summer, and never good at all" (*Works and Days* 640). Hesiod had a son, so we must assume that he got married. Misanthrope that he is, Hesiod still recommends a good marriage, if it can be found. Perhaps he was embittered by his experiences with his wife—an idle conjecture! He does tell us for a fact that his embitterment stems from his brother Perses' betrayal of him.

After the death of their father, Hesiod had a serious dispute with Perses over their inheritance. The case was brought before a court, and the judges, who were bribed by Perses, cheated Hesiod of his fair share. Hesiod composed the *Works and Days* as an admonition to his brother to follow the path of justice and obey the righteous dictates of the one god, Zeus. The *Theogony*, too, is drenched in a similar religious fervor, describing the genesis of the world, mortals, and the gods and tracing the momentous events that led to the supremacy of Zeus.

Hesiod grew up as a farmer and a shepherd and became a poet. He once sailed to Chalcis on the island of Euboea, and there, at the funeral games of Amphidamas, he won the first prize in the poetry contest, a tripod. He dedicated the tripod to the Muses at the very spot on Mt. Helicon where he had received their divine inspiration.

Another myth of creation is found in the *Birds*, a comedy by the playwright Aristophanes (fifth century B.C.). For all its mock heroism and burlesque of religious and philosophical speculation, this account reflects earlier theory and illustrates both the multiplicity of versions and the primacy of Eros. A chorus of birds proves that the birds are much the oldest of all the gods by the following tale (693–702):

> Chaos, Night, black Erebus, and broad Tartarus were first. But Ge, Aer [the lower atmosphere], and Uranus [Sky] did not exist. In the vast hollows of Erebus first of all black-winged Night, alone, brought forth an egg, from which Eros, the desirable,

> burst forth like a swift whirlwind, his back glistening with golden wings. He mingled in broad Tartarus with Chaos, winged and dark as night, and hatched our race of birds and first led it to light. There was no race of immortals before Eros caused all things to mingle. From the mingling of couples, Uranus, Oceanus, Ge, and the immortal race of all the blessed gods came into being.

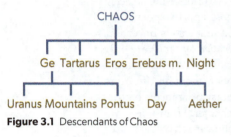

Figure 3.1 Descendants of Chaos

The Eros responsible for this fury of procreation may very well be the same Eros who, in the later tradition, is appropriately called Phanes (the one who first shone forth or gave light to creation) and Protogonus (first-born). If so, we have in Aristophanes a parody of a myth that was the basis of a religion ascribed to Orpheus in which the world-egg was a dominant symbol. Orpheus and Orphism are discussed in Chapter 16 and, with them, other religions similar in nature, designated generically as mystery religions.[3] The link between myth and profound religious thought and experience in the ancient world is a continuing and fascinating theme.

Creation According to Ovid

Ovid, a Roman poet who wrote some 700 years after Hesiod, provides another classic account of genesis, different in important respects from that of Hesiod. Ovid is eclectic in his sources, which include not only Hesiod but also many other writers, in particular, Empedocles, a fifth-century philosopher, who theorized that four basic elements (earth, air, fire, and water) are the primary materials of the universe.

Ovid's Chaos (*Metamorphoses* 1.1–75) is not a gaping void but rather a crude and unformed mass of elements in strife, from which a god (not named) or some higher nature formed the order of the universe.[4] Ovid's poem *Metamorphoses*, which concentrates on stories that involve transformations of various sorts, could very well provide a basic text for a survey of mythology. We shall on occasion reproduce Ovid's versions, since it is often his poetic, sensitive, sophisticated, and at times ironic treatment that has dominated subsequent tradition. But we must remember that Ovid is Roman, and late, and that his mythology is far removed in spirit and belief from that of earlier conceptions. Mythology for him is little more than inspirational, poetic fodder, however successful and attractive the end product may be. Both the poetic and the real worlds of Hesiod and Ovid are poles apart.

The Sacred Marriage of Uranus (Sky) and Gaia (Ge, Earth) and Their Offspring

But let us return to Hesiod's *Theogony* (126–156):

> Gaia first brought forth starry Uranus, equal to herself, so that he might surround and cover her completely and be a secure home for the blessed gods forever. And she brought forth the lofty mountain ranges, charming haunts of the divine nymphs who inhabit the hills and dales. And she also bore, without the sweet union of love, Pontus, the barren deep, with its raging surf. (126–132)

> But then Gaia lay with Uranus and bore the deep-eddying Oceanus, and [the Titans, namely] Coeus, and Crius, and Hyperion, and Iapetus, and Theia, and Rhea, and Themis, and Mnemosyne, and golden-crowned Thebe, and lovely Tethys. After them, she brought forth wily Cronus, the youngest and most terrible of her children and he hated his lusty father. (132–138)   10
>
> Moreover, she bore the **Cyclopes**, insolent at heart, Brontes ("Thunder") and Steropes ("Lightning") and bold Arges ("Bright"), who fashioned and gave to Zeus his bolt of thunder and lightning. They had only one eye, set in the middle of their foreheads but they were like the gods in all other respects. They were given the name Cyclopes ("Orb-eyed") because one single round eye was set in their fore-heads.[5] Might and power and skill were in their works. (139–146)
>
> In turn, Gaia and Uranus were the parents of three other sons, great and un-speakably violent, Cottus, Briareus, and Gyes, arrogant children. A hundred in-vincible arms and hands sprang out of their shoulders and also from out of their shoulders there grew fifty heads, all supported by their strong limbs. Invincible was the powerful strength in these mighty hulks. Of all the children that Gaia and Uranus produced these were the most terrible and they were hated by their father from the very first. (147–156)   20

For Hesiod, it appears, the first deity is female, a basic, matriarchal concept of Mother Earth and her fertility as primary and divine; comparative studies of iconography from primitive societies provide abundant evidence to confirm this archetype of the primacy of the feminine.[6] The male sky-god Uranus (another fundamental conception), produced by Earth herself, emerges, at least in this version, as her equal partner. In matriarchal societies, he is reduced to a subordinate; in patriarchal societies, he becomes the supreme god.

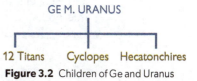

Figure 3.2 Children of Ge and Uranus

So it is, then, that the personification and deification of sky and earth as Uranus and Ge (Gaia) and their physical union represent basic recurring themes in mythology. Uranus is the male principle, a god of the sky, whereas Ge is the female goddess of fertility and the earth. Worship of them may be traced back to very early times; sky and rain, earth and fertility are fundamental concerns and sources of wonder to "primitive" agricultural peoples. The rain of Uranus might, for example, be imagined as his seed that fertilizes the hungry earth and makes her conceive. Thus develops the archetypal concept of a "sacred" or "holy marriage," a translation of the Greek phrase **hieros gamos**. The sky-god and the earth-goddess appear again and again under various names and guises (for example, Uranus and Ge, Cronus and Rhea, and Zeus and Hera) to enact this holy rite.

The worship of the female earth divinity was widespread and diverse, whether or not she assumed the dominant role in the partnership with her male consort. But whatever her name and however varied her worship, she is significant in all periods, either maintaining her own identity or lurking behind, influencing, and coloring more complex and sophisticated concepts of female deity. Ge, Themis, Cybele, Rhea, Hera, Demeter, and Aphrodite are all, either wholly or in part, divinities of fertility.[8] Certainly, the emotional, philosophical, religious, and intellectual range of the worship of the mother-goddess is vast. It may run the gamut from frenzied orgiastic celebrations, with

"For Dust Thou Art, and unto Dust Shalt Thou Return"
(Genesis 3.19)

A Chorus from the lost play of Euripides, *Chrysippus* (fragment 839, Loeb), reads as follows:[7]

Earth, the greatest, and the Aether of Zeus, he who begets human beings and gods and she who receives his moist, nurturing drops and bears mortals, bears vegetation and the families of animals. Therefore she is justly esteemed mother of all. Whatever is born from earth returns to earth but whatever springs from the ethereal seed returns to the vault of heaven. Nothing that has come into being perishes but one is separated from another and exhibits a different form.

In the first line, Aether (the realm of Zeus) and Zeus are essentially one, so that "he" can be interpreted as the rain of Zeus, whose drops fertilize earth. This conception of Zeus as our heavenly father who has given us an immortal soul and Earth, our mother, who is the source of our mortality reflects the mythology of Hesiod and the subsequent development of its profound implications in the sixth and fifth centuries B.C. The succinct and tantalizing utterance of this Chorus about a subject that soon became a major philosophical and religious theme of enormous import was much quoted and its meaning variously interpreted.

the castration of her devoted priests, to a sublime belief in spiritual communion and personal redemption; and from a blatant emphasis on the sexual attributes and potency of the female to an idealized vision of love, motherhood, and virgin birth.[9]

The *Homeric Hymn to Earth, Mother of All* (30), in its invocation of Gaia (Ge), gives us the essentials of her primary archetype:

About Earth, I will sing, all-mother, deep-rooted and eldest, who nourishes all that there is in the world: all that go on the divine land, all that sail on the sea and all that fly—these she nourishes from her bounty. From you, reverend lady, mortal humans have abundance in children and in crops, and it is up to you to give them their livelihood or take it away. Rich and fortunate are those whom you honor with your kind support. To them all things are abundant, their fields are laden with produce, their pastures are covered with herds and flocks, and their homes are filled with plenty. These rule with good laws in cities of beautiful women and much happiness and wealth attend them. Their sons glory in exuberant joy and their daughters, with carefree hearts, play in blossom-laden choruses and dance on the grass over the soft flowers. These are the fortunate whom you honor, holy goddess, bountiful deity. (1–16) [10]

Hail, mother of the gods, wife of starry Uranus. Kindly grant happy sustenance in return for my song and I will remember both you and another song too. (17–19)

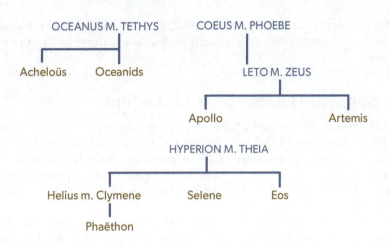

Figure 3.3 Descendants of the Titans

Helius. Red-figure krater by the Darius painter, ca. 330 B.C. Height 13 in. Helius, his head encircled by rays, drives his chariot upward out of the sea. He holds the reins to guide four winged horses. On the extreme left (above the handle) a boy has dived into the sea (his feet are at the top); a second boy stands at the bottom left on a rock, preparing to dive; to his right a third is in mid-flight as he dives in; a fourth, at the bottom center, is already waist deep in the sea, proceeding to the viewer's left but looking back toward Helius and his chariot. A meander design frames the lower edge of the painting, balanced by a laurel wreath around the upper edge. (©*The Trustees of the British Museum*)

The Titans and Their Descendants: Ocean, Sun, Moon, and Dawn

The Titans, children of Uranus and Ge, are twelve in number: Oceanus, Coeus, Crius, Hyperion, Iapetus, Theia, Rhea, Themis, Mnemosyne, Phoebe, Tethys, and "wily Cronus, the youngest and most terrible of these children and he hated his lusty father" (*Theogony* 137–138). They are for the most part deifications of various aspects of nature, and they are important for their progeny, although a few assume some significance in themselves. In the genealogical labyrinth of mythology, all lineage may be traced back to the Titans and to the other powers originating from Chaos. From these beginnings Hesiod creates a universe both real and imagined, physical and spiritual, peopled with gods, demigods, deified or personified abstractions, animals, monsters, and mortals; we cannot list them all here, but we shall select the most important figures. The Titans are best considered in pairs, since there are six males and six females; and the inevitable, incestuous matings of some of these brothers and sisters produce cosmic progeny.

Oceanus and the Oceanids

Oceanus and his mate, Tethys, produced numerous children, the Oceanids, 3,000 daughters, and the same number of sons, spirits of rivers, waters, and springs, many with names and some with mythological personalities.[10] Hesiod provides an impressive list, but he admits (*Theogony* 369–370) that it is difficult for a mortal to name them all, although people know those belonging to their own area.

Hyperion and Helius, Gods of the Sun

The Titan Hyperion is a god of the sun, more important than his sister and mate, Theia. They are the parents of Helius, Selene, and Eos. Helius, like his father, is a sun-god. Duplication of divinities is common in the early scheme of things; they may exist side by side, or their names and personalities may be confused. Very often the younger generation will dominate the older and usurp its power.

The conventional picture of the sun-god is in harmony with the Homeric conception of geography described at the beginning of this chapter. The sun-god dwells in the East, crosses the dome of the sky with his team of horses, descends in the West into the stream of Oceanus, which encircles the earth, and sails back to the East, chariot and all. The *Homeric Hymn to Helius* (31) offers a glowing picture. Euryphaëssa (the word means "widely shining"), given as the wife of Hyperion and the mother of Helius, is probably just another name for Theia.

> Now begin to sing, O Muse Calliope, daughter of Zeus, about shining Helius, whom ox-eyed Euryphaëssa bore to the son of Earth and starry Uranus. For Hyperion married glorious Euryphaëssa, his own sister, who bore him beautiful children: rosy-fingered Eos and Selene of the lovely hair and weariless Helius like the deathless ones, who shines for mortals and immortal gods as he drives his horses. The piercing gaze of his eyes flashes out of his golden helmet. Bright beams radiate brilliantly from his temples and the shining hair of his head frames a gracious countenance seen from afar. The exquisite, finely wrought robe that clothes his body shimmers in the blast of the winds. Mighty stallions are under his control. Then he stays his golden-yoked chariot and horses and stops there at the peak of the heavens, until the time when he again miraculously drives them down through the sky to the Ocean. (1–16)   10
>
> Hail, lord, kindly grant a happy sustenance. From you I have begun and I shall go on to celebrate the race of mortal men, the demigods, whose achievements the Muses have revealed to mortals. (17–19)

Phaëthon, Son of Helius

A well-known story concerns Phaëthon (whose name means "shining"), the son of Helius by one of his mistresses, Clymene. According to Ovid's account (*Metamorphoses* 1.747–779; 2.1–366), Phaëthon was challenged by the accusation that the Sun was not his real father at all. His mother, Clymene, however, swore to him that he was truly the child of Helius and told him that he should, if he so desired, ask his father, the sun-god himself.

Ovid beautifully describes the magnificent palace of the Sun, with its towering columns, gleaming with gold and polished ivory. Phaëthon, awed by the grandeur, is prevented from coming too close to the god because of his radiance; Helius, however, confirms Clymene's account of Phaëthon's parentage, lays aside the rays that shine around his head, and orders his son to approach. He embraces him and promises, on an oath sworn by the Styx (dread river of the Underworld), that the boy may have any gift he likes so that he may dispel his doubts once and for all. Phaëthon quickly and decisively asks that he be allowed to drive his father's chariot for one day.

Helius tries in vain to dissuade Phaëthon, but he must abide by his dread oath. He reluctantly leads the youth to his chariot, fashioned exquisitely by Vulcan,[11] of gold, silver, and jewels that reflect the brilliant light of the god. The chariot is yoked; Helius anoints his son's face as protection against the flames, places the rays on his head, and with heavy heart advises him on his course and the management of the horses.

Phaëthon, young and inexperienced, is unable to control the four-winged horses who speed from their usual path. The chariot races to the heights of heaven, creating havoc by the intensity of the heat, then hurtles down to earth. Ovid delights in his description of the destruction; among the many transformations that result because of the heat, the Ethiopians at this time acquired their dark skins and Libya became a desert. Earth herself is ablaze and unable to endure her fiery anguish any longer.

Jupiter, in answer to Earth's prayer, hurls his thunder and lightning and shatters the car, dashing Phaëthon to his death. The river Eridanus receives and bathes him, and nymphs bury him with the following inscription upon his tomb: "Here is buried Phaëthon, charioteer of his father's car; he could not control it, yet he died after daring great deeds."[12]

Other Loves of Helius

Helius also loved the Eastern princess Leucothoë, daughter of the Persian king Orchamus. Disguising himself as Eurynome, her mother, he seduced her.

Another of the lovers of Helius, the Oceanid Clytië, jealous because Helius preferred Leucothoë to her, told Leucothoë's father of the affair. Orchamus buried Leucothoë, and Helius was too late to save her. He shed drops of nectar on her corpse, which grew into a frankincense tree. Clytië could not persuade Helius to forgive her, nor could she recover his love. She sat, following the Sun's progress with her eyes until she turned into a sunflower, which forever turns its face toward the sun.

The island of Rhodes was sacred to Helius, the Sun. When Zeus was dividing up the lands of the world among the gods, Rhodes had not yet appeared above the surface of the sea. Helius was accidentally not given a share, but he refused Zeus' offer of a redivision, for he could see the future island below the sea, and he took it as his possession when it appeared. There he loved the island's nymph Rhode, and one of her seven sons became the father of the heroes of the three principal cities of Rhodes, Camirus, Ialysus, and Lindos. Even late in historical times, the people of Rhodes threw a chariot and four horses into the sea every October as a replacement for the old chariot and horses of the sun that would be worn out after the labors of the summer.[13]

Selene, Goddess of the Moon, and Endymion

Selene, daughter of Hyperion and Theia, is a goddess of the moon. Like her brother Helius, she drives a chariot, although hers usually has only two horses. The *Homeric Hymn to Selene* (32) presents a picture.

> Tell in song about the moon in her long-winged flight, Muses, skilled in song, sweet-voiced daughters of Zeus, the son of Cronus. The heavenly gleam from her immortal head radiates onto earth. The vast beauty of the cosmos emerges under her shining radiance. The air, unlit before, glistens and the rays from her golden crown offer illumination whenever divine Selene, having bathed her beautiful skin, puts on her far-glistening raiment, and yokes the powerful necks of her shining team, and drives her beautifully maned horses at full speed in the evening; in mid-month brightest are her beams as she waxes and her great orbit is full. From the heavens she is fixed as a sure sign for mortals. (1–13)   10
>
> Once Zeus, the son of Cronus, joined in loving union with her; she became pregnant and bore a daughter, Pandia, who had exceptional loveliness among the immortal gods. (14–16)
>
> Hail, kind queen with beautiful hair, white-armed goddess, divine Selene. From you I have begun and I shall go on to sing of mortal demigods whose achievements minstrels, servants of the Muses, celebrate in songs from loving lips. (17–20)

Only one famous myth is linked with Selene, and that concerns her love for the handsome youth Endymion, who is usually depicted as a shepherd. On a still night, Selene saw Endymion asleep in a cave on Mt. Latmus (in Caria). Night after night, she lay down beside him as he slept. There are many variants to this story, but in all the outcome is the same: Zeus grants Endymion perpetual sleep with perpetual youth. This may be represented as a punishment (although sometimes Endymion is given some choice) because of Selene's continual absence from her duties in the heavens, or it may be the fulfillment of Selene's own wishes for her beloved.

Apollo, Sun-God, and Artemis, Moon-Goddess

Many stories about the god of the sun, whether he be called Hyperion, Helius, or merely the Titan, were transferred to the great god Apollo, who shares with them the same epithet, **Phoebus**, which means "bright." Although Apollo was, in all probability, not originally a sun-god, he came to be considered as such. Thus, Phaëthon may become the son of Apollo, as sun-god. Similarly Apollo's twin sister Artemis became associated with the moon, although originally she probably was not a moon-goddess. Thus, Selene and Artemis merge in identity, just as do Hyperion, Helius, and Apollo; and Selene and Artemis also are described by the adjective "bright," **Phoebe** (the feminine form of Phoebus).[14] Therefore, the lover of Endymion becomes Artemis (or Roman Diana).

The Endymion Sarcophagus. Marble, ca. A.D. 200–220; width 73 in., height 28 in. (with lid). The sarcophagus is shaped like a trough in which grapes were pressed. On the lid is a portrait of its occupant, Arria, with nine reliefs: those on the extreme left and right are of mountain gods, appropriate to the setting of the myth on Mt. Latmos; the next pair represents the seasons, Autumn on the left and Spring on the right; the next pair are Cupid and Psyche on the left and Aphrodite and Eros on the right; the next pair are Ares on the left and his lover, Aphrodite, on the right. Balancing Arria is the union of Selene and Endymion. In the center of the main panel, Selene descends from her chariot, whose horses are held by a nymph, to join Endymion, who lies to the right. Night pours the opiate of sleep over him (note the poppy head between the heads of Night and the lion) and Cupids play around the lovers and beneath the right lion's head. Cupid and Psyche embrace beneath the left lion's head. Oceanus and Ge, respectively, lie to the left and beneath Selene's horses, and the horses of the chariot of Helius can be seen rising at the left, while Selene's chariot disappears to the right. The myth of Endymion was a common subject for Roman sarcophagi (seventy examples are known from the second and third centuries A.D.) because it gave hope that the sleep of death would lead to eternal life. (*Image copyright © The Metropolitan Museum of Art/Art Resource, NY*)

Eos, Goddess of the Dawn, and Tithonus

Eos (the Roman **Aurora**), the third child of Hyperion and Theia, is goddess of the dawn, and like her sister Selene drives a two-horsed chariot. Her epithets in poetry are appropriate: she is called rosy-fingered and saffron-robed. She is an amorous deity. Aphrodite, the goddess of love, caused her to long perpetually for young mortals because she caught her mate Ares in Eos' bed,[15] but her most important mate was Tithonus, a handsome youth of the Trojan royal house. Eos carried off Tithonus; their story is simply and effectively told in the *Homeric Hymn to Aphrodite* (5.220–238), which is translated in its entirety in Chapter 9.

> Eos went to Zeus, the dark-clouded son of Cronus, to ask that Tithonus be immortal and live forever. Zeus nodded his assent and accomplished her wish. Poor goddess, she did not think to ask that her beloved avoid ruinous old age and retain perpetual youth. (220–224)

> Indeed, as long as he kept his desirable youthful bloom, Tithonus took his plea-
> sure with early-born Eos of the golden throne by the stream of Oceanus at the ends
> of the earth. But when the first gray hairs sprouted from his beautiful head and noble
> chin, Eos avoided his bed. But she kept him in her house and tended him, giving
> him food, ambrosia, and lovely garments. When hateful old age oppressed him
> completely and he could not move or raise his limbs, the following plan seemed
> best to her. She laid him in a room and closed the shining doors. From within his
> voice flows faintly and he no longer has the strength that he formerly had in his
> supple limbs. (225–238)   10

These poignant few lines depict simply and powerfully the beauty of youth and the devastation of old age, describe the devotion of love even though sexual attraction has gone, and give a warning to us all: Be care- ful what you pray for, since God may grant your request. Oscar Wilde puts it more cleverly: "When the gods choose to punish us, they merely answer our prayers." Later writers add that eventually Tithonus was turned into a grasshopper.

The Castration of Uranus and the Birth of Aphrodite

We must now return to Hesiod (*Theogony* 156–206) and his account of the birth of the mighty goddess of love, Aphrodite (the Roman Venus). As we learned earlier, the children of Uranus and Ge (the twelve Titans, including the last-born, wily Cronus, who especially hated his father; the Cyclopes; and the Hecatonchires) all were despised by their father from the beginning.

Aurora, by Guido Reni (1575–1642); 112 × 280 in. Reni painted this work in 1614 for the ceiling of the Casino (pavilion) in the gardens of the palace in Rome of Cardinal Scipione Borghese. Aurora (Eos) pre- cedes Apollo (Helius) as she rolls back the curtain of night and scatters flowers. Apollo drives his four- horse chariot accompanied by the Hours. Above the horses flies a winged putto holding a lighted torch symbolic of the dawn. (*Erich Lessing/Art Resource, NY*)

As each of his children was born, Uranus hid them all in the depths of Ge and did not allow them to emerge into the light. And he delighted in his wickedness. But huge Earth in her distress groaned within and devised a crafty and evil scheme. At once she created gray adamant and fashioned a great sickle and confided in her dear children. Sorrowing in her heart, she urged them as follows: "My children born of a presumptuous father, if you are willing to obey, we shall punish his evil insolence. For he was the first to devise shameful actions." (156–166)

Thus she spoke. Fear seized them all and not one answered. But great and wily Cronus took courage and spoke to his dear mother: "I shall undertake and accomplish the deed, since I do not care about our abominable father. For he was the first to devise shameful actions." (167–172)   10

Thus he spoke. And huge Earth rejoiced greatly in her heart. She hid him in an ambush and placed in his hands the sickle with jagged teeth and revealed the whole plot to him. Great Uranus came leading on night, and, desirous of love, lay on Ge, spreading himself over her completely. And his son from his ambush reached out with his left hand and in his right he seized hold of the huge sickle with jagged teeth and swiftly cut off the genitals of his own dear father and threw them so that they fell behind him. And they did not fall from his hand in vain. Earth received all the bloody drops that fell and in the course of the seasons bore the strong Erinyes and the mighty giants (shining in their armor and carrying long spears in their hands) and nymphs of ash trees (called Meliae on the wide earth). (173–187)   20

When first he had cut off the genitals with the adamant and cast them from the land on the swelling sea, they were carried for a long time on the deep. And white foam arose about from the immortal flesh and in it a maiden grew. First she was brought to holy Cythera, and then from there she came to sea-girt Cyprus. And she emerged a dread and beautiful goddess and grass rose under her slender feet. (188–195)

Gods and human beings call her Aphrodite, and the foam-born goddess because she grew amid the foam (*aphros*), and Cytherea of the beautiful crown because she came to Cythera, and Cyprogenes because she arose in Cyprus washed by the waves. She is called too Philommedes (genital-loving) because she arose from the genitals.[16] Eros attended her and beautiful desire followed her when she was born and when she first went into the company of the gods. From the beginning she has this honor, and among human beings and the immortal gods she wins as her due the whispers of girls, smiles, deceits, sweet pleasure, and the gentle delicacy of love. (195–206)   30

The stark power of this passage is felt even in translation. The real, yet anthropomorphic, depiction of the vast earth enveloped sexually by the surrounding sky presents its own kind of poetic power. The transparent illustration of basic motives and forces in human nature, through this brutal allegory of Aphrodite's birth, provides fertile material for modern psychology: the youngest son whose devotion to his mother is used by her against the father, the essentially sexual nature of love, the terror of castration. The castration complex of the Freudians is the male's unconscious fear of being deprived of his sexual potency, which springs from his feeling of guilt because of his unrecognized hatred of his father and his desire for his mother. Hesiod provides literary documentation for the elemental psychic conscience of humankind. Finally, Hesiod, with characteristic simplicity,

SATURN DEVOURING HIS CHILDREN

Francisco Goya was one of the most important Spanish painters of the eighteenth and early nineteenth centuries. The tone of his works darkened with the deteriorating political situation in Spain at the end of the eighteenth century. Spain witnessed the fall of an enlightened monarchy, a devastating invasion by Napoleon in 1808, and the restoration of a monarchy that was oppressive. Savage atrocities suffered during war became one of Goya's major themes, especially as he fell out of court favor and increasingly withdrew from the world. Toward the end of his life, in the seclusion of his country home, he painted on the walls of his retreat a series of dark and disturbing images known collectively as *Las Pinturas Negras* (*The Black Paintings*). *Saturn Devouring His Children* is the most

Saturn Devouring One of His Children, by Francisco Goya y Lucientes (1746–1828); oil on plaster, transferred to canvas, 1820–1822; 57½ × 32½ in. The savagery of Saturn (Cronus) expresses Goya's insight into human cruelty and self-destructiveness, themes that dominated his thoughts in his old age. (*Erich Lessing/Art Resource, NY*)

famous of these paintings. The ancient relief depicts Rhea handing the stone to Cronus to be eaten and shows no hint of the cannibalism in the myth. The tone of the sculpture is restrained and unemotional; the force of the work comes from the stark contrast between this present, sober moment and the future, violent overthrow of Saturn from the throne on which he now sits so securely. Cronus' impending overthrow is foreshadowed in the image of the proffered swaddled stone. In comparison, Goya's painting, concentrating as it does on the act of cannibalism, exists only in a lurid and nightmarish present, with no hint of resolution. It may effectively be compared with Rubens' *Saturn Devouring His Son*, which may have inspired Goya's work. Goya's painting does not make clear whether Cronus is driven to consume his children in madness or whether the savage necessity of the act has driven him mad. It may express the purely personal loss of many of the painter's own children while they were still young or the brutality of war, particularly when a country murders its own children in civil strife; or perhaps it is a more metaphysical portrait of the ravages of the tyrant Chronos (Time), who feeds on us all.

Rhea Offers the Stone to Cronus. Detail of a large relief, a Roman copy from about A.D. 160 of a Greek original from the fourth century B.C. Rhea, with her veil thrown back (appropriate for a wife approaching her husband), has wrapped the stone as if it were a baby in swaddling clothes. Cronus, seated on a throne and nude from the waist up, reaches out to accept the "baby." The hand above the head of Cronus belongs to another figure in the relief, which is not part of this narrative. (*Erich Lessing/Art Resource, NY*)

suggests Aphrodite's powers of fertility by a brief and beautiful image, "and grass rose under her slender feet."

Is it Hesiod's art that gets to the essence of things, or is it that he is close to the primitive expression of the elemental in human nature? It is commonplace to say that, although elements of the more grotesque myths may be detected in Greek literature, they were humanized and refined by the Greeks and transformed by their genius. Yet it is also true that these primitive elements were retained deliberately and consciously because of the horror, shock, and revelation they contain. The Greeks did not suppress the horrible and horrifying; they selected from it and used it boldly with profound insight and sensitivity. Thus, Hesiod's account may reflect a primitive myth, the ultimate origins of which we can never really know, but his version gives it meaning with an artistry that is far from primitive.

Cronus (Sky) and Rhea (Earth) and the Birth of Zeus

Cronus united with his sister Rhea, who gave birth to Hestia, Demeter, Hera, Hades, Poseidon, and Zeus. Cronus devoured all these children, except Zeus, as Hesiod relates (*Theogony* 459–491):

> Great Cronus swallowed his children as each one came from the womb to the knees of their holy mother, with the intent that no other of the illustrious descendants of Uranus should hold kingly power among the immortals. For he learned from Ge and starry Uranus that it was fated that he be overcome by his own child. And so he kept vigilant watch and lying in wait he swallowed his children. (459–467)
>
> A deep and lasting grief took hold of Rhea and when she was about to bring forth Zeus, father of gods and men, then she entreated her own parents, Ge and starry Uranus, to plan with her how she might bring forth her child in secret and how the avenging fury of her father, Uranus, and of her children whom great Cronus of the crooked counsel swallowed, might exact vengeance. And they readily heard their dear daughter and were persuaded, and they counseled her about all that was destined to happen concerning Cronus and his stout-hearted son. And they sent her to the town of Lyctus in the rich land of Crete when she was about to bring forth the youngest of her children, great Zeus. And vast Ge received him from her in wide Crete to nourish and foster. (467–480)   10
>
> Carrying him from Lyctus, Ge came first through the swift black night to Mount Dicte. And taking him in her hands she hid him in the deep cave in the depths of the holy earth on the thickly wooded mountain.[17] And she wrapped up a great stone in infant's coverings and gave it to the son of Uranus, who at that time was the great ruler and king of the gods. Then he took it in his hands, poor wretch, and rammed it down his belly. He did not know in his heart that there was left behind, in the stone's place, his son unconquered and secure, who was soon to overcome him and drive him from his power and rule among the immortals. (481–491)   20

Cronus and Rhea are deities of sky and earth, doublets of Uranus and Gaea, whose power they usurp, and their union represents the reenactment of the

A Cretan Hymn to Dictaean Zeus, Greatest *Kouros* (Youth), Son of Cronus

O Youth, most great,
Hail to you, son of Cronus,
Mighty splendor over all,
Steadfast leader of the gods. . . .

The text goes on to celebrate how the Kouretes (Curetes, Young Men) with their shields received the baby god from Rhea and hid him; the climax of the hymn is a prayer for personal and communal blessings from the young god. The Chorus sings and dances to the sound of lyres and oboes around an altar. In the verses, Dicte (Dikta) is the name of the mountain (now called Petsophas) close to Palaikastro in east Crete, where a Minoan palace has been excavated. Here, remains of a Greek temple from the seventh century B.C. have been found and also an altar and the stone inscribed with this hymn. The inscription derives from the fourth or third centuries B.C. The age of the cult, however, must go back to the second millennium.

A strong tradition existed (as we have seen in Hesiod) that Zeus was born at Mt. Dicte, where this sanctuary of Zeus Dictaeus (Diktaios) was found (but there is no famous Dictaean cave). Mount Dicte was confused with Mt. Ida in central Crete with its famous Idaean cave because of a rival tradition that connected Zeus' birth with Mt. Ida. The two versions were reconciled by claiming that Zeus, born on Mt. Dicte, was taken to the Idaean cave on Mt. Ida to be brought up.

Dominant in the hymn is the depiction of Zeus as a young man (*kouros*). Near the archaic sanctuary of Zeus, with its inscription of the hymn, was found a precious chryselephantine statuette of the Minoan Age, the Palaikastro Kouros. The superb workmanship of this beardless young man wrought in precious materials indicates that he must be a god (his body and face carved in ivory, his eyes of crystal, and his belt of gold). Surely this Kouros from the Bronze Age is an earlier conception of the mighty young Greek Zeus of the hymn.[18]

universal sacred marriage. But in the tradition, Cronus and Rhea have a more specific reality than their parents. Cronus appears in art as a majestic and sad deity, sickle in hand. He rules, as we shall see, in a golden age among mortals; and after he is deposed by Zeus, he retires to some distant realm, sometimes designated as the Islands of the Blessed, one of the Greek conceptions of paradise. Cronus is called Saturn by the Romans.

Rhea, too, has a definite mythical personality, although basically she is yet another mother-goddess of earth and fertility. She sometimes is equated with **Cybele**, a Near Eastern goddess whose worship spread to both Greece and, later, Rome; the worship of Rhea-Cybele involved frenzied devotion and elements of mysticism. Her attendants, **Curetes**, played wild music on drums and cymbals, and she was attended by animals. The *Homeric Hymn to the Mother of the Gods* (14) pays tribute to this aspect of Rhea's nature:

> Through me, clear-voiced Muse, daughter of great Zeus, sing a hymn to the mother of all gods and all mortals too. The din of castanets and drums, along with the shrill-ness of flutes, are your delight, and also the cry of wolves, the roar of glaring lions, the echoing mountains, and the resounding forests.
>
>   So hail to you and, at the same time, all the goddesses in my song.

The Tradition That Zeus Was Born in Greece, Not in Crete

The tradition was also very strong that Zeus was born in Arcadia in Greece. Callimachus in the opening lines of his first *Hymn to Zeus* expresses his quandary: Should he address the supreme god as lord of Mt. Dicte or Ida in Crete or as lord of Mt. Lycaeum (Greek Lykaion) in Arcadia? He believes, however, that the Cretans are always liars, and he affirms that Rhea gave birth to Zeus in Arcadia, on the mountain, in a holy place, sheltered by very dense brush.

In classical times, Mt. Lycaeum in Arcadia (in the southern Peloponnese) became the site of an important Panhellenic sanctuary of Zeus to rival his more famous one at Olympia (see pp. 117–121), only about 22 miles away. Excavations carried out in the early years of the twentieth century revealed a hippodrome, stadium, xenon (guest house), stoa, monuments, and a bath-house, testimony to the importance of the Lycaean games.

The traveler Pausanias visited the site (*Description of Greece*, 8.38.2–7), and he tells us that some Arcadians called Mt. Lycaeum Olympus or Sacred Peak because it was on this mountain that Zeus was born; Pausanias names the three nymphs who brought him up. Furthermore, a specific place on the mountain was called Cretea, and Zeus was born here, not in Crete, as the Cretans claim. Most interesting of all is Pausanias' identification of a mound of earth as an altar of Zeus at the highest peak of the mountain, from which most of the Peloponnesus could be seen. In front of the altar stood two gilded eagles, and on this altar sacrifices were offered, in secret, to Lycaean Zeus. Unfortunately for those of us who would very much like to know, he did not want to inquire into the nature of these sacrifices but preferred to let them continue, as they were and had been from the beginning, without his prying.

New excavations by a team of archaeologists, both Greek and American (from the Universities of Pennsylvania and Arizona), begun in 2004, offer a thorough reexamination of the site, including the altar of Zeus and its sacred area (temenos), 4,500 feet above sea level and presenting a stunning view. The earlier excavators had unearthed material from the altar, dating no earlier than the seventh century B.C. Exciting new finds include objects from earlier periods, for example, the Mycenaean and before, as far back as the early Bronze Age. Of particular interest are a rock crystal seal depicting the image of a bull with a full frontal face, a small bronze hand of Zeus holding a silver lightning bolt, and a piece of fulgurite or petrified lightning (a kind of glass formed when lightning strikes loose earth). Many bones were recovered of both large and small animals but none of humans.

It was only fitting that Zeus as a god of thunder and lightning would be worshiped on this stormy mountain peak.

Religious and Historical Views

Of great mythological significance is Hesiod's account of the birth of Zeus on the island of Crete. In this version, we can detect some of the basic motives in the creation of myth, especially when we take into account later variations and additions. From these we learn that after Rhea brought forth Zeus in a cave on Mt. Dicte, he was fed by bees and nursed by nymphs on the milk of a goat named **Amalthea**. Curetes guarded the infant and clashed their spears on their shields so that his cries would not be heard by his father, Cronus. These attendants and the noise they make suggest the frantic devotees of a mother-goddess: Ge, Rhea, or Cybele. The myth is etiological in its explanation of the origin of the musical din and ritual connected with her worship.

Like many myths, the story of the birth of Zeus on Crete accommodates an actual historical occurrence: the amalgamation of at least two different peoples or cultures in the early period. When the inhabitants of Crete began to build their great civilization and empire (ca. 3000), the religion they developed (insofar as we can ascertain) was Mediterranean in character, looking back to earlier Eastern concepts of a mother-goddess. The northern invaders who entered the peninsula of Greece (ca. 2000 B.C.), bringing with them an early form of Greek and their own gods (chief of whom was Zeus), built a significant Mycenaean civilization on the mainland, but it was strongly influenced by the older, more sophisticated power of Crete. The myth of the birth of Zeus reads very much like an attempt to link by geography and genealogy the religion and deities of both cultures. Zeus, the male god of the Indo-Europeans, is born of Rhea, the Near Eastern goddess of motherhood and fertility.

Two dominant strains in the character of subsequent Greek thought can be understood at least partly in terms of this thesis. W. K. C. Guthrie clearly identifies this dual aspect of the religion of classical Greece in the contrast he makes between the Olympian gods of Homer and the cult of the mother-goddess Demeter at Eleusis:

> The Mother-goddess is the embodiment of the fruitful earth, giver of life and fertility to plants, animals and men. Her cult takes certain forms, involving at least the more elementary kinds of mysticism, that is, the belief in the possibility of a union between the worshipper and the object of his worship. Thus the rites may take the form of adoption as her son or of sexual communion. Orgiastic elements appear, as in the passionate, clashing music and frenzied dancing employed by the followers of Rhea or Cybele. . . . What an essentially different atmosphere we are in from that of the religion of the Achaean heroes described by Homer. There we are in clear daylight, in a world where the gods are simply more powerful persons who might fight for or against one, with whom one made bargains or contracts. The Achaean warrior did not seek to be born again from the bosom of Hera. He was indeed the reverse of a mystic by temperament.[19]

We can detect the ramifications of this paradox again and again in many places in the development of Greek civilization, but perhaps we feel it most clearly in the mysticism and mathematics that permeate Greek philosophical attitudes: the numbers of Pythagoras and the immortality of the soul in Orphic doctrine; the dichotomy of Platonic thought and Socratic character in the search for clarity and definition through rational argument coupled with the sound of an inner voice, the depths of a trance, and divine revelation in terms of the obscure and profound symbols of religious myth. For Plato, God is not only a geometer but also a mystic.[20]

Mythological Interpretations

Ample material is all too apparent for testing the most persistent of interpretative theories discussed in Chapter 1. Here are myths predominantly about nature that accord with the analysis of Max Müller, although we need not, like Müller, argue that all subsequent mythological stories must be interpreted as allegories of cosmological and natural phenomena.

Feminist concerns are addressed prominently: Mother Earth is the first and most fundamental deity, and the feminine will always remain aggressively assertive, if not *always* dominant, in Greco-Roman mythology; but it is encroached upon by masculine conceptions of the divine, as patriarchy in both society and religion gains supremacy, which is not, by any means, always absolute over matriarchy.

Most apparent is the constant interweaving of structuralist motifs. The dualities (binary opposites) of Lévi-Strauss are everywhere: chaos/order, male/female, sky/earth, youth/age, and beauty/ugliness. Psychological and psychoanalytical motifs abound: Freudian sexuality is blatantly manifest in the castration of Uranus, and the subconscious motivations of the psyche reveal themselves in the recurring pattern of the victory of the ambitious son in his battle for power against his ruthless father. The Jungian archetype of the holy marriage that is enacted three times (by Uranus and Gaia, Cronus and Rhea, and finally Zeus and Hera) is equally basic and universal. The characters in these conflicts in the beginning of things are themselves archetypes: earth mother and queen, sky father and king, vying for control and settling for an uneasy and sometimes bitter reconciliation between the sexes.

Above all, these stories are etiological, beautiful and powerful mythical explanations of the origins and nature of the universe and the devastating physical and emotional force of love.

Select Bibliography

See also the Select Bibliography at the end of Chapter 4.

Caldwell, **Richard S.** *Origins of the Gods: A Psychoanalytic Study of Greek Theogonic Myth.* New York: Oxford University Press, 1993. Identifies aspects of psychoanalytic theory relevant for Greek myth and interprets the themes of origin and success, as found in Hesiod's *Theogony.*

Clay, **Jenny Strauss.** *The Politics of Olympus: Form and Meaning in the Major Homeric Hymns.* Princeton, NJ: Princeton University Press, 1989.

Hathorn, **Richmond Y.** *Greek Mythology.* Beirut: American University Press of Beirut, 1977. A good resource for the study not only of creation myths but also of Greek mythology in general.

Kerényi, **Carl.** *The Gods of the Greeks.* London: Thames & Hudson, 1951.

Lamberton, **R.** *Hesiod.* New Haven, CT: Yale University Press, 1988.

Primary Sources

Sources in the Chapter

Euripides	*Chrysippus* fragment 893
Hesiod	*Theogony* (selections)
	Works and Days (selections)
Aristophanes	*Birds* 685–707: Eros and Creation
Homeric Hymn 5	To Aphrodite 220–238
Homeric Hymn 14	To the Mother of the Gods
Homeric Hymn 30	To Earth, Mother of All
Homeric Hymn 31	To Helius
Homeric Hymn 32	To Selene
Ovid	*Metamorphoses* (selections)

Additional Sources

Apollodorus	*Library* 1.1.1–1.1.7: Creation
Pausanias	*Description of Greece* 5.1.3–5.1.5: Endymion
Pindar	*Olympian Ode* 7.54–7.74: Helius and the island of Rhodes
Plato	*Timaeus* 26e–48e: A religious and philosophical discussion of God and the creation of the universe
Strabo	*Geography* 11.4.7: Selene, priests, and human sacrifice

Notes

1. Perhaps Hesiod may anticipate the pre-Socratic philosophers who sought a primal world substance or substances. Thales (ca. 540 B.C.) seems to provide a startling break with mythological and theological concepts when he claims that water is the source of everything, with shattering implications for both science and philosophy.
2. We shall use the names Gaia, Gaea, and Ge, which mean "earth," interchangeably.
3. For the Orphic myth of creation in particular, see pp. 386–387.
4. The concept of god creating something out of nothing is not found in the Greek and Roman tradition.
5. These Cyclopes are distinct from the Cyclops Polyphemus and his fellows.
6. See the bibliography for Iconography, Religion, and Feminist Interpretations in Chaper 1, p. 33. This matriarchal concept belongs to both the matriarchs and the patriarchs; it depends on whose point of view you are talking about.
7. Euripides, *Fragments,* ed. and trans. Christopher Collard and Martin Cropp. Vol. 8 of the Loeb edition of Euripides (Cambridge, MA: Harvard University Press, 2008), pp. 466–467.
8. Cf. Erich Neumann, *The Great Mother: An Analysis of the Archetype,* 2d ed. (Princeton, NJ: Princeton University Press, 1963).
9. Indeed, some scholars are ready to find Ge's presence in every goddess and are deeply suspicious of even the most circumspect virgin deities.
10. Included are many important rivers such as the Nile, Alpheus, and Scamander, to mention only three in this world, and the Styx, an imaginary one in the realm of Hades. The patronymic Oceanid regularly refers to a daughter of Oceanus and not a son.

11. When a Roman version of a myth is recounted, the Roman names of the original text will be used (Vulcan is Hephaestus, Jupiter is Zeus, etc.). For the Roman names of the major Greek deities, see the beginning of Chapter 5, p. 113.

12. His sisters (daughters of the sun), in their mourning for Phaëthon, are turned into trees from whose bark tears flow, which are hardened into amber by the sun and dropped into the river. Away in Liguria his cousin, Cycnus, mourns for him, and he too changes and becomes a swan.

13. Rhodes was associated with several figures of saga. From Egypt came Danaüs, who visited the island on his journey to Argos and there founded the great temple of Athena at Lindos. A son of Heracles, Tlepolemus, murdered his uncle Licymnius at Tiryns and, on the advice of Apollo, fled to Rhodes. He later led the Rhodian contingent in the Trojan War. Rhodes was also the home of the Telchines, who were skilled craftsmen and metal-workers. They were also credited with having the evil eye, and for this reason (says Ovid), Zeus drowned them in the sea.

14. Artemis, like Selene, as a moon-goddess is associated with magic, since there is a close link between magic and worship of the moon. Apollo and Artemis themselves have a close link with the Titans. The Titan Coeus mated with his sister Phoebe, and their daughter Leto bore Artemis and Apollo to Zeus. Coeus and Phoebe are little more than names to us, but Phoebe is the feminine form of Phoebus, and she herself may very well be another moon-goddess. Hecate, goddess of the moon, ghosts, and black magic, is but another aspect of both Selene and Artemis (see pp. 226–227).

15. Orion, Cleitus, and Cephalus were also all beloved by Eos.

16. Perhaps an intentional play on the word *philommeides*, "laughter-loving," a standard epithet of Aphrodite.

17. There is trouble in the text concerning Hesiod's identification of the mountain as Dicte or Aegeum.

18. See William D. Furley and Jan Maarten Bremer, *Greek Hymns: Selected Cult Songs from the Archaic Period to the Hellenistic Period.* Vol. 1: *The Texts in Translation,* pp. 65–76. Vol. 2: *Greek Texts and Commentary,* pp. 1–20. Studies and Texts in Classical Antiquity 9 and 10 (Tübingen: Mohr Siebeck, 2001).

19. W. K. C. Guthrie, *The Greeks and Their Gods* (Boston: Beacon Press, 1955), p. 31.

20. The study of geometry is vital for Plato. In the *Republic* (7.527B), for example, he has Socrates say that geometry is the knowledge of what exists always, and Plutarch (*Quaestionum Convivalium* 8.1 [*Moralia* 718C; Loeb Vol. 9]) quotes Plato as saying that God is always doing geometry (or geometrizes continually, *aei geōmetrein*); that is, God is a geometer. Although Plutarch is not absolutely certain that these actual words are to be attributed to Plato, they accurately represent the essence of the Platonic and Socratic argument. Yet there is also abundant other evidence for the nonmathematical, the spiritual, and the mystical aspects of Plato's philosophy, epitomized in his visionary Myth of Er, narrated by Socrates, which is translated on pages 362–367.

ZEUS' RISE TO POWER: THE CREATION OF MORTALS

My mother Themis or Earth (Ge), if you like, for she has one form but many names, would often foretell the future that would be accomplished saying, "not through strength nor by force, but by guile inevitably will those who are more powerful gain mastery."

—**AESCHYLUS,** *Prometheus Bound* 211–215

The Titanomachy: Zeus Defeats His Father, Cronus

When Zeus had grown to maturity, Cronus was beguiled into bringing up all that he had swallowed, first the stone and then the children.[1] Zeus then waged war against his father with his disgorged brothers and sisters as allies: Hestia, Demeter, Hera, Hades, and Poseidon. Allied with him as well were the **Hecatonchires** and the **Cyclopes**, for he had released them from the depths of the earth, where their father, Uranus, had imprisoned them. The Hecatonchires were invaluable in hurling stones with their hundred-handed dexterity, and the Cyclopes forged for him his mighty thunder and lightning. On the other side, allied with Cronus, were the Titans—with the important exception of Themis and her son Prometheus, both of whom allied with Zeus. (Note that for Hesiod, Clymene is the mother of Prometheus.) Atlas, the brother of Prometheus, was an important leader on the side of Cronus.

This battle, known as the Titanomachy, was of epic proportions, Zeus fighting from Mt. Olympus, Cronus from Mt. Othrys. The struggle is said to have lasted ten years.[2] An excerpt from Hesiod conveys the magnitude and ferocity of the conflict (*Theogony* 678–721):

The boundless sea echoed terribly, earth resounded with the great roar, wide heaven trembled and groaned, and high Olympus was shaken from its base by the onslaught of the immortals; the quakes came thick and fast and, with the dread din of the endless chase and mighty weapons, reached down to gloomy Tartarus. (678–683)

Thus they hurled their deadly weapons against one another. The cries of both sides as they shouted reached up to starry heaven, for they came together with a great clamor. Then Zeus did not hold back his might any longer, but now immediately his heart was filled with strength and he showed clearly all his force. He came direct from heaven and Olympus hurling perpetual lightning, and the bolts with flashes and thunder flew in succession from his stout hand with a dense whirling of holy flame. Earth, the giver of life, roared, everywhere aflame, and on all sides the vast woods crackled loudly with the fire. The whole of the land boiled, and as well the streams of Ocean, and the barren sea. The hot blast engulfed the earth-born Titans and the endless blaze reached the divine aether; the flashing gleam of the thunder and lightning blinded the eyes even of the mighty. Unspeakable heat possessed Chaos. (684–700)   10

The sight seen by the eyes and the sound heard by the ears were as if earth and wide heaven above collided; for the din as the gods met one another in strife was as great as the crash that would have arisen if earth were dashed down by heaven falling on her from above. The winds mingled the confusion of tremor, dust, thunder, and the flashing bolts of lightning (the shafts of great Zeus), and carried the noise and the shouts into the midst of both sides. The terrifying clamor of fearful strife arose, and the might of their deeds was shown forth. They attacked one another and fought relentlessly in mighty encounters until the battle was decided. (700–712)   20

The Hecatonchires (Cottus, Briareus, and Gyes), insatiate of battle, were among the foremost to rouse the bitter strife; they hurled three hundred rocks, one right after another, from their staunch hands and covered the Titans with a cloud of missiles and sent them down far beneath the broad ways of the earth to Tartarus and bound them in harsh bonds, having conquered them with their hands even though they were great of spirit. The distance from earth to gloomy Tartarus is as great as that of heaven from earth. (713–721)   30

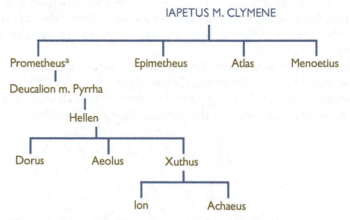

[a]Themis is the mother of Prometheus, according to Aeschylus

Figure 4.1 The Family of Prometheus

The Hecatonchires guarded the Titans imprisoned in Tartarus. Atlas was punished with the task of holding up the sky. In some accounts, when Zeus became secure in power he eventually relented and gave the Titans their freedom.

The Gigantomachy: Zeus Defeats the Giants and Typhoeus

Another threat Zeus had to face came from giants that Earth produced to challenge the new order of the gods or that had been born when the blood from the mutilation of Uranus fell upon the ground. These monstrous creatures are called Gegeneis, which means "earthborn." The many details of this battle, known as the Gigantomachy, vary, but it is generally agreed that the struggle was fierce and ended with the imprisonment of the giants under the earth, usually in volcanic regions where they betray their presence by the violence of their natures. Thus, for example, the giant Enceladus writhes under volcanic Mt. Aetna in Sicily.

One of the most vicious of the monsters who opposed Zeus was the dragon **Typhoeus** (or **Typhaon** or **Typhon**). He sometimes joins others in their conflict with the gods, or he may do battle alone, as in Hesiod's account (*Theogony* 820–880):

> When Zeus had driven the Titans from heaven, vast Gaea brought forth the youngest of her children through the love of Tartarus and the agency of golden Aphrodite. The hands of the mighty god were strong in any undertaking and his feet were weariless. From the shoulders of this frightening dragon a hundred snake heads grew, flickering their dark tongues; fire blazed from the eyes under the brows of all the dreadful heads, and the flames burned as he glared. In all the terrible heads voices emitted all kinds of amazing sounds; for at one time he spoke so that the gods understood, at another his cries were those of a proud bull bellowing in his invincible might; sometimes he produced the pitiless roars of a courageous lion, or again his yelps were like those of puppies, wondrous to hear, or at another time he would hiss; and the great mountains resounded in echo. (820–835)
>
> Now on that day of his birth an irremediable deed would have been accomplished and he would have become the ruler of mortals and immortals, if the father of gods and men had not taken swift notice and thundered loudly and fiercely; the earth resounded terribly on all sides and as well the wide heaven above, the sea, the streams of Ocean, and the depths of Tartarus. Great Olympus shook under the immortal feet of the lord as he rose up and earth gave a groan. The burning heat from them both, with the thunder and lightning, scorching winds, and flaming bolts reached down to seize the dark-colored sea. The whole land was aboil and heaven and the deep; and the huge waves surged around and about the shores at the onslaught of the immortals, and a quake began its tremors without ceasing. Hades who rules over the dead below shook, as did the Titans, the allies of Cronus, in the bottom of Tartarus, from the endless din and terrifying struggle. (836–852)

10

20

Zeus. Bronze, ca. 460 B.C.; height 82 in. The viewer feels awe at the superhuman size, divine nudity, and commanding mien of the god as he hurls his thunderbolt. This statue was found in the sea off Cape Artemisium (at the northern end of Euboea). The identification with Zeus is more likely than with Poseidon hurling his trident. (*Peter Eastland/Alamy Stock Photo*)

When Zeus had lifted up the weapons of his might, thunder and lightning and the blazing bolts, he leaped down from Olympus and struck, and blasted on all sides the marvelous heads of the terrible monster. When he had flogged him with blows, he hurled him down, maimed, and vast earth gave a groan. A flame flared up from the god as he was hit by the bolts in the glens of the dark craggy mountain where he was struck down. A great part of vast earth was burned by the immense conflagration and melted like tin heated by the craft of artisans in open crucibles, or like iron which although the hardest of all is softened by blazing fire and melts in the divine earth through the craft of Hephaestus. Thus the earth melted in the flame of the blazing fire. And Zeus in the rage of his anger hurled him into broad Tartarus. (853–868)   30

From Typhoeus arise the winds that blow the mighty rains; but not Notus, Boreas, and Zephyr[3] who brings good weather, for they are sprung from the gods and a great benefit for mortals. But the others from Typhoeus blow over the sea at random; some fall upon the shadowy deep and do great harm to mortals, raging with their evil blasts. They blow this way and that and scatter ships and destroy sailors. Those who encounter them on the sea have no defense against their evil. Others blowing over the vast blossoming land destroy the lovely works of mortals born on earth, filling them with dust and harsh confusion. (869–880)   40

Gigantomachies and Civic Pride

The battle between the Olympian gods and the giants was often used to represent the triumph of Greek civilization, or of a particular Greek city, over barbarian disorder. In the sculptural program of the Parthenon at Athens (see pp. 174–176), for example, the Gigantomachy was portrayed on the east side of the outer frieze. The most splendid example of this artistic and civic symbolism was the Great Altar of Pergamum (see pp. 88–89), erected during the reign of Eumenes II (181–158 B.C.) to glorify victory over an unknown enemy, probably Gallic invaders. Greek altars were usually erected in the open air in front of the god's temple. Here the altar was independent of the temple, while the chief gods of Pergamum, Zeus and Athena, had their own separate sanctuaries. It was built on a ledge high up on the acropolis of Pergamum: the altar itself stood in an unroofed inner court, surrounded by an Ionic portico and approached by wide steps, on either side of which the north and south wings of the portico were extended. On the outside of the portico was a colossal marble frieze of the Gigantomachy, 100 meters long and 2.5 meters high. The Olympian gods were shown, each vanquishing a giant: the gods' names were painted on the cornice above the frieze and the giants' names were inscribed on the stone course below. The frieze was painted in bright colors and (unlike pedimental sculptures) was designed to be seen by the viewer at close quarters. A second, smaller frieze (58 meters long) of the myth of Telephus (see pp. 478–479) was carved on the inner back wall of the portico. It honored his father, Heracles, whose help was crucial in the victory of the gods over the giants. The altar and its sculptures were excavated between 1878 and 1886 by German archaeologists, who were allowed to take their finds to Berlin and restore them. The subsequent history of the altar in two world wars, including transportation to and from Russia after World War II, is an ironic commentary on the symbolic themes of the friezes. See John Boardman (ed.), *The Oxford History of Classical Art* (New York: Oxford University Press, 1993), pp. 164–166.

Later versions have it that Heracles was an ally of Zeus in the battle; the giants could be defeated only if the gods had a mortal as their ally. In addition, Earth produced a magic plant that would make the giants invincible; Zeus, by a clever stratagem, plucked it for himself.

The attempt of the giants Otus and Ephialtes to storm heaven by piling the mountains Olympus, Ossa, and Pelion upon one another is sometimes linked to the battle of the giants or treated as a separate attack on the power of Zeus. In fact, there is considerable confusion in the tradition concerning details and characters in the battle of the giants (Gigantomachy) and the battle of the Titans (Titanomachy). Both conflicts may be interpreted as reflecting the triumph of the more benign powers of nature over the wilder powers or of civilization over savagery. Historically, it is likely that they represent the fact of conquest and amalgamation when, in about 2000 B.C., the Greek-speaking invaders brought with them their own gods, with Zeus as their chief, and triumphed over the deities of the existing peoples in the peninsula of Greece.

The Creation of Mortals

Various versions of the birth of mortals existed side by side in the ancient world. Very often they are the creation of Zeus alone, or of Zeus and the other gods. Sometimes immortals and mortals spring from the same source. A dominant tradition depicts Prometheus as the creator of man; and sometimes woman is created later and separately through the designs of Zeus.

After describing the creation of the universe and animal life out of the elements of Chaos, Ovid tells about the birth of mortals, depicting the superiority and lofty ambition of this highest creature in the order of things (*Metamorphoses* 1.76–88); Ovid's "man" (*homo*) epitomizes the human race.

> Until now there was no animal more godlike than these and more capable of high intelligence and able to dominate all the rest. Then man was born; either the creator of the universe, originator of a better world, fashioned him from divine seed, or earth, recently formed and separated from the lofty aether, retained seeds from its kindred sky and was mixed with rainwater by Prometheus, the son of Iapetus, and fashioned by him into the likeness of the gods who control all. While other animals look down to the ground, man was given a lofty visage and ordered to look up to the sky and fully erect lift his face to the stars. Thus earth that had been crude and without shape was transformed and took on the figure of man unknown before.   10

A fragment attributed to Hesiod (no. 268 Rzach; no. 382 Merkelbach and West) adds that Athena breathed life into the clay. At Panopea in Boeotia, stones were identified in historical times as solidified remains of the clay used by Prometheus.

The Four or Five Ages

Ovid goes on to describe the four ages: gold, silver, bronze, and iron. We prefer, however, to excerpt Hesiod's earlier account of **the Five Ages of Man**, since he feels compelled to include the historical age of heroes. After he has recounted the story of Pandora and her jar, his introduction to the description of the five ages suggests both the multiplicity of versions of the creation of mortals and the futility of even attempting to reconcile the diverse accounts (*Works and Days* 106–201).

> If you like, I shall offer a fine and skillful summary of another tale and you ponder it in your heart: how gods and mortal humans came into being from the same origin. (106–108)

THE AGE OF GOLD

> At the very first, the immortals who have their homes on Olympus made a golden race of mortal humans. They existed at the time when Cronus was king in heaven, and they lived as gods with carefree hearts completely without toil or trouble. Terrible old age did not come upon them at all, but always with vigor in their hands and their feet they took joy in their banquets removed from all evils. They died as though overcome by sleep. And all good things were theirs; the fertile land of its own accord bore fruit ungrudgingly in abundance. They in harmony and in peace managed their affairs with many good things, rich in flocks and beloved of the blessed gods. But then the earth covered over this race. Yet they inhabit the earth and are called holy spirits, who are good and ward off evils, as the protectors of mortal beings, and are providers of wealth, since they keep watch over judgments and cruel deeds, wandering over the whole earth wrapped in air. For they have these royal prerogatives. (109–126)

10

THE AGE OF SILVER

> Then those who have their home on Olympus next made a second race of silver, far worse than the one of gold and unlike it both physically and mentally. A child was brought up by the side of his dear mother for a hundred years, playing in his house as a mere baby. But when they grew up and reached the measure of their prime they lived for only a short time and in distress because of their senselessness. For they could not restrain their wanton arrogance against one another and they did not wish to worship the blessed immortals or sacrifice at their holy altars, as is customary and right for human beings. Then in his anger, Zeus, the son of Cronus, hid them away because they did not give the blessed gods who inhabit Olympus their due. Then the earth covered over this race too. And they dwell under the earth and are called blessed by mortals, and although second, nevertheless honor attends them also. (127–142)

20

THE AGE OF BRONZE

> Father Zeus made another race of mortal humans, the third, of bronze and not at all like the one of silver; terrible and mighty because of their spears of ash, they pursued the painful and violent deeds of Ares. They did not eat bread at all but were terrifying and had dauntless hearts of adamant. Great was their might, and unconquerable hands grew upon their strong limbs out of their shoulders. Of bronze were their arms, of bronze were their homes, and they worked with bronze implements. Black iron there was not. When they had been destroyed by their own

hands, they went down into the dark house of chill Hades without leaving a name. Black death seized them, although they were terrifying, and they left the bright light of the sun. (143–155)   30

THE AGE OF HEROES

But when the earth covered over this race too, again Zeus, the son of Cronus, made still another, the fourth on the nourishing earth, valiant in war and more just, a god-like race of heroic men, who are called demigods, and who preceded our own race on the vast earth. Evil war and dread battle destroyed some of them under seven-   40 gated Thebes in the land of Cadmus as they battled for the flocks of Oedipus; the end of death closed about others after they had been led in ships over the great depths of the sea to Troy for the sake of Helen of the beautiful hair. Some, father Zeus, the son of Cronus, sent to dwell at the ends of the earth where he has them live their lives; these happy heroes inhabit the Islands of the Blessed with carefree hearts by the deep swirling stream of Ocean. For them the fruitful earth bears honey-sweet fruit that ripens three times a year. Far from the immortals, Cronus rules as king over them; for the father of gods and men released him from his bonds. Honor   50 and glory attend these last in equal measure. (156–173c)

THE AGE OF IRON

Far-seeing Zeus again made still another race who live on the nourishing earth. Oh, would that I were not a man of the fifth generation but either had died before or had been born later. Now indeed the race is of iron. For they never cease from toil and woe by day, nor from being destroyed in the night. The gods will give them difficult troubles, but good will be mingled with their evils. Zeus will destroy this race of mortals too, whenever it comes to pass that they are born with gray hair on their temples. And a father will not be in harmony with his children nor his children with him, nor guest with host, nor friend with friend, and a brother will not be loved as formerly. As they grow old quickly they will dishonor their parents, and they will find fault, blaming them with harsh words and not knowing respect for the gods, since their right is might. They will not sustain their aged parents in repayment for their upbringing. One will destroy the city of another. No esteem will exist for the one who is true to an oath or just or good; rather mortals will praise the arrogance and evil of the wicked. Justice will be might and shame will not exist. The evil person will harm the better, speaking against him unjustly and he will swear an oath besides. Envy, shrill and ugly and with evil delight, will attend all human beings in their woe. Then Aidos and Nemesis both[4] will forsake them and go, their beautiful forms shrouded in white, from the wide earth to Olympus among the company of the gods. For mortals sorry griefs will be left and there will be no defense against evil. (173d–201)   60 70

The bitterness and pessimism of this picture of his own age of iron are typical of Hesiod's generally crabbed, severe, and moral outlook. But his designation of the five ages reflects a curious blend of fact and fiction. Historically his *was* the age of iron, introduced into Greece at the time of the invasions that brought the age of bronze to a close. Hesiod's insertion of an age of heroes reflects the fact of the Trojan War, which he cannot ignore.

THE ALTAR OF ZEUS AT PERGAMON

The kingdom of Pergamon rose to world prominence in the years following Alexander's conquests. After the death of Alexander the Great in 323 B.C. and the subsequent fragmentation of his empire among his successors, Pergamon became an independent kingdom ruled by one family, the Attalids, who would remain in power until the last member of the dynasty, Attalus III, bequeathed the kingdom to Rome in 133 B.C. The kingdom of Pergamon reached the height of its prestige and power under Eumenes II (197–159 B.C.). During this period, the city attained a level of culture and sophistication on a par with Athens and Alexandria. It housed one of the greatest libraries in the ancient world; only the Great Library of Alexandria surpassed its resources. Of the many industries that Pergamon would exploit, the export of parchment became the most lucrative and even came to threaten Egypt's monopoly of the papyrus trade. The word *parchment*, which refers to animal skins treated to be used as a viable alternative to papyrus, is a corruption of the name Pergamon itself.

Athena Defeats Alcyoneus. Detail from the east frieze of the Great Altar of Pergamum, between 180 and 159 B.C.; height of panel 8 ft, 2 in. Athena, shield on her left arm and aegis (with the Gorgon's head) on her breast, strides energetically in the center, as a winged Nike (figure of Victory) flies from the right to place a garland on her head. With her right hand Athena seizes the hair of the giant Alcyoneus, who is helpless to resist despite his massive wings and serpentine legs. To the right, Gaia, mother of Alcyoneus, rises from below, separated by Athena's left leg from her son and so prevented from transferring to him by her touch renewed strength and immortality. (*Erich Lessing/Art Resource, NY*)

Under Eumenes, the city of Pergamon underwent remarkable development and became a center of art and culture. In particular, it came to be in the vanguard of some of the most important developments in Hellenistic sculpture, which can best be appreciated in the remains of the Altar of Zeus, which Eumenes also had constructed. The podium was decorated with relief sculptures depicting the Gigantomachy, the mythic battle between the Olympians and the Gegeneis (Earthborn). The relief is cut very deeply. It is a maelstrom of activity with a profusion of forms and decorative motifs. The melodramatic, emotional intensity of the figures is one of the hallmarks of Hellenistic sculpture, a direct contrast with the classical restraint so evident in earlier works, such as the sculptural decoration on the Parthenon (see pp. 174–176), though there are allusions to the earlier sculptural legacy. For example, the image of Athena victorious in battle (reproduced here), striding to the right, is mirrored by the image of Zeus striding to the left (not shown). The positioning of both Zeus and Athena is meant to recall the positioning of the figures of Athena and Hephaestus on the west pediment of the Parthenon.

The Pergamene Altar. The Great Altar of Zeus, commissioned by Eumenes II, originally stood on the imposing acropolis of Pergamon. Constructed ca. 175 B.C., the structure was composed of an Ionic colonnade with two projecting wings, atop a massive podium. The broad stairway led through the colonnade to the altar. The frieze along the base depicting the Gigantomachy is about 400 feet long and 7 feet in height. For Eumenes, this mythic paradigm memorialized his victories over the invading Gauls, and so, like the sculptural program of the Parthenon (see p. 174), myth is used to prefigure a contemporary reality. (*bpk/ Antikensammlung, SMB/ Johannes Laurentius*)

This conception of the deterioration of the human race has been potent in subsequent literature, both ancient and modern. The vision of a paradise in a golden age when all was well inevitably holds fascination for some, whether imagined as long ago or merely in the good old days of their youth.[5]

It would be wrong to imply that this theory of the degeneration of the human race was the only one current among the Greeks and Romans. Prometheus' eloquent testimony in Aeschylus' play, translated on pages 95–98, listing his gifts to humans, rests on the belief in progressive stages from savagery to civilization.[6]

Atlas and Prometheus. Laconian black-figure cup, ca. 560 B.C. The two Titans endure the punishments of Zeus: Atlas holds up the star-studded heavens and helplessly watches the vulture (or eagle) attack his brother, Prometheus, who is bound to a column. The motif of the column is repeated in the lower register, with lotus-leaf decoration, while the snake on the left seems not to be part of the narrative. (*Photo Copyright ©Government Of The Vatican City State-Directorate of the Vatican Museums*)

Prometheus against Zeus

In the *Theogony* (507–616), Hesiod tells the stories of Prometheus and his conflict with Zeus, with the human race as the pawn in this gigantic clash of divine wills. He begins with the birth of Prometheus and explains how Prometheus tricked Zeus (507–569):

Iapetus led away the girl Clymene, an Oceanid, and they went together in the same bed; and she bore to him a child, stout-hearted Atlas; she also brought forth Menoetius, of very great renown, and devious and clever Prometheus, and **Epimetheus**,[7] who was faulty in judgment and from the beginning was an evil for mortals who work for their bread. For he was the first to accept from Zeus the virgin woman he had formed. Far-seeing Zeus struck arrogant Menoetius with his smoldering bolts and hurled him down into Erebus because of his presumption and excessive pride. Atlas stands and holds the wide heaven with his head and tireless hands through the force of necessity at the edge of the earth, and in the sight of the clear-voiced Hesperides; this fate Zeus in his wisdom allotted him. (507–520)   10

And Zeus bound devious and wily Prometheus with hard and inescapable bonds, after driving a shaft through his middle; and roused up a long-winged eagle against him that used to eat his immortal liver. But all that the long-winged bird would eat during the whole day would be completely restored in equal measure during the night. Heracles, the mighty son of Alcmena of the lovely ankles, killed it and rid the son of Iapetus from this evil plague and released him from his suffering, not against the will of Olympian Zeus who rules from on high, so that the renown of Theban-born Heracles might be still greater than before on the bountiful earth. Thus he respected his famous son with this token of honor. Although he had been enraged, the mighty son of Cronus gave up the anger that he had held previously because Prometheus had matched his wits against him. (521–534)   20

For when the gods and mortals quarreled at Mecone,[8] then Prometheus with quick intelligence divided up a great ox and set the pieces out in an attempt to deceive the mind of Zeus. For the one group in the dispute he placed flesh and the rich and fatty innards on the hide and wrapped them all up in the ox's paunch; for the other group he arranged and set forth with devious art the white bones of the ox, wrapping them up in white fat. (535–541)

Then the father of gods and men spoke to him: "Son of Iapetus, most renowned of all lords, my fine friend, how partisan has been your division of the portions!" Thus Zeus whose wisdom is immortal spoke in derision. Wily Prometheus answered with a gentle smile, as he did not forget his crafty trick. "Most glorious Zeus, greatest of the gods who exist forever, choose whichever of the two the heart in your breast urges." He spoke with crafty intent. (542–549)   30

But Zeus whose wisdom is immortal knew and was not unaware of the trick. And he foresaw in his heart evils for mortals, which would be accomplished. He took up in both his hands the white fat, and his mind was enraged, and anger took hold of his heart as he saw the white bones of the ox arranged with crafty art. For this reason the races of human beings on earth burn the white bones for the immortals on the sacrificial altars. (550–557)   40

Zeus the cloud-gatherer was greatly angered and spoke to him: "Son of Iapetus, my fine friend, who know thoughts that surpass those of everyone, so you have then not yet forgotten your crafty arts." Thus Zeus whose wisdom is immortal spoke in anger. From this time on he always remembered the deceit and did not give the power of weariless fire out of ash trees to mortals who dwell on the earth. (558–564)

But the noble son of Iapetus tricked him by stealing in a hollow fennel stalk the gleam of weariless fire that is seen from afar. High-thundering Zeus was stung to the depths of his being and angered in his heart as he saw among mortals the gleam of fire seen from afar. (565–569)   50

The Creation of Pandora

Hesiod goes on to describe the dread consequence of Zeus' anger at Prometheus for his theft of fire (*Theogony* 570–616):

Immediately he contrived an evil thing for mortals in recompense for the fire. The renowned lame god, Hephaestus, fashioned out of earth the likeness of a modest maiden according to the will of the son of Cronus. Bright-eyed Athena clothed and arrayed her in silvery garments and with her hands arranged on her head an embroidered veil, wondrous to behold. And Pallas Athena put around her head lovely garlands of budding flowers and greenery. And she placed on her head a golden crown that the renowned lame god himself made, fashioning it with his hands as a favor to his father, Zeus. On it he wrought much intricate detail, wondrous to behold, of the countless animals which the land and the sea nourish; many he fixed on it, amazing creations, like living creatures with voices; and its radiant loveliness shone forth in profusion. (570–584)   10

When he had fashioned the beautiful evil in recompense for the blessing of fire, he led her out where the other gods and mortals were, exulting in the raiment provided by the gleaming-eyed daughter of a mighty father. Amazement took hold of the immortal gods and mortals as they saw the sheer trick, from which human beings could not escape. For from her is the race of the female sex, the ruinous tribes of women, a great affliction, who live with mortal men, helpmates not in ruinous poverty but in excessive wealth, just as when in overhanging hives bees feed the drones, conspirators in evil works; the bees each day, the whole time to the setting of the sun, are busy and deposit the white honeycombs, but the drones remain within the covered hives and scrape together the toil of others into their own belly. Thus in the same way high-thundering Zeus made women, conspirators in painful works, for mortal men. (585–602)   20

He also contrived a second evil as recompense for the blessing of fire; whoever flees marriage and the troublesome deeds of women and does not wish to marry comes to ruinous old age destitute of anyone to care for him. He does not lack a livelihood while he is living but, when he has died, distant relatives divide up the inheritance. And again even for the one to whom the fate of acquiring a good and compatible wife in marriage falls as his lot, evil continually contends with good throughout his life. Whoever begets mischievous children lives with a continuous sorrow in his breast; in heart and soul the evil is incurable. Thus it is not possible to go beyond the will of Zeus nor to deceive him. For not even the goodly Prometheus, son of Iapetus, got out from under his heavy wrath and a great bondage held him fast, even though he was very clever. (602–616) 30

Once again Hesiod's dominant note is despair. He provides another dismal account of Prometheus in the *Works and Days* (47–105); despite some minor repetitions, it is worth quoting for its elaboration of the theft of fire and its variations on the creation of woman. The evil is now specifically named; she is Pandora, which means "all gifts," and she has a jar (see figure, p. 93, where she holds a box).[9]

Zeus, angered in his heart, hid the means of human livelihood because Wily Prometheus deceived him. And so he devised for human beings sorrowful troubles. He hid fire. Then the good son of Iapetus, Prometheus, stole it for human beings from wise Zeus in a hollow reed, without Zeus who delights in thunder seeing it. (47–53)

But then Zeus the cloud-gatherer was roused to anger and spoke to him: "Son of Iapetus, who know how to scheme better than all others, you are pleased that you stole fire and outwitted me—a great misery for you and men who are about to be. As recompense for the fire I shall give them an evil in which all may take delight in their hearts as they embrace it." (54–58)   10

Thus he spoke and the father of gods and men burst out laughing. He ordered renowned Hephaestus as quickly as possible to mix earth with water and to implant in it a human voice and strength and to fashion the beautiful and desirable form of a maiden, with a face like that of an immortal goddess. But he ordered Athena to teach her the skills of weaving at the artful loom, and golden Aphrodite to shed grace about her head and painful longing and sorrows that permeate the body. And he commanded the guide Hermes, slayer of Argus, to put in her the mind of a bitch and the character of a thief. (59–68)

Thus he spoke and they obeyed their lord Zeus, son of Cronus. At once the famous lame god molded out of earth the likeness of a modest maiden according to the will of Zeus. Bright-eyed Athena clothed and arrayed her, and the Graces and mistress Persuasion adorned her with golden necklaces. The beautiful-haired Seasons crowned her with spring flowers, and Pallas Athena fitted out her body with every adornment. Then the guide and slayer of Argus contrived in her breast lies and wheedling words and a thievish nature, as loud-thundering Zeus directed. And the herald of the gods put in her a voice, and named this woman Pandora, because all who have their homes on Olympus gave her a gift, a bane to men who work for their bread. (69–82)   20

But when the Father had completed this sheer impossible trick he sent the swift messenger of the gods, the renowned slayer of Argus, to bring it as a gift for Epimetheus.

And Epimetheus did not think about how Prometheus had told him never to accept a gift from Olympian Zeus but to send it back in case that in some way it turned out to be evil for mortals. But he received the gift and when indeed he had the evil he realized. (83–89)

30

Previously the races of human beings used to live completely free from evils and hard work and painful diseases, which hand over mortals to the Fates. For mortals soon grow old amid evil. But the woman removed the great cover of the jar with her hands and scattered the evils within and for mortals devised sorrowful troubles. (90–95)

40

Hope alone remained within there in the unbreakable home under the edge of the jar and did not fly out of doors. For the lid of the jar stopped her before she could, through the will of the cloud-gatherer Zeus who bears the aegis. But the other thousands of sorrows wander among human beings, for the earth and the sea are full of evils. Of their own accord diseases roam among human beings some by day, others by night bringing evils to mortals in silence, since Zeus in his wisdom took away their voice. Thus it is not at all possible to escape the will of Zeus. (96–105)

Interpretations of the Myths of Prometheus and Pandora

The etiology of the myth of Prometheus is perhaps the most obvious of its many fascinating elements. It explains procedure in the ritual of sacrifice and the origin of fire—Promethean fire, the symbol of defiant progress. Prometheus himself is the archetype of the culture god or hero ultimately responsible for all the arts and sciences.[10] Prometheus is also the archetype of the divine or heroic trickster (cf. Hermes and Odysseus).

Other archetypal themes once again abound, and embedded in them is a mythological etiology that provides causes and explanations for various eternal mysteries: What is the nature of god or the gods? Where did we come from? Do we have a dual nature, an earthly, mortal body and a divine, immortal soul? Are human beings the pawns in a war of rivalry between supernatural powers? Did they lose a paradise or evolve from savagery to civilization? What is the source of and reason for evil? In the person of Pandora, the existence of evil and pain in the world is accounted for.

The elements in the myth of the creation of woman reveal attitudes common among early societies. Like Eve, for example, Pandora is created after man and she is responsible for his troubles. Why should this be so? The answer is complex, but inevitably it must lay bare the prejudices and mores inherent in the social structure. But some detect as well the fundamental truths of allegory and see the woman and her jar as symbols of the drive and lure of procreation, the womb and birth and life, the source of all our woes.[11]

The theme of the first woman as the bringer of evil is particularly fraught with social, political, and moral implications. The most obvious interpretation of Hesiod is that Pandora was the first woman (like Eve in the Bible) and

Pandora, by Odilon Redon (1840–1916); oil on canvas, ca. 1910; 56½ × 24½ in. Pandora, holding her box, is framed by jewel-like flowers, but above her is a leafless tree. Redon used symbols "to clothe ideas in a sensuous form" (in the words of the *Symbolist Manifesto* of 1886). This painting is nearly contemporary with Freud's *Interpretation of Dreams* (1900). Like Freud, Redon used the symbols of mythology to express his innermost ideas and emotions. (*Image copyright © The Metropolitan Museum of Art/ Art Resource, NY*)

Pandora's Box

Hesiod identifies the jar that Pandora presents to Epimetheus as a pithos, which usually means a large earthenware container for storing provisions such as wine or oil. It was not until medieval times, it seems, that a pithos became a pyxis, that is, a small portable vessel. Erasmus of Rotterdam has been identified as the one who first translated *pithos* as *pyxis* (in 1508). Ever since, if not before, Pandora's jar has become in art and literature a container of various easily carried shapes, including often that of a box.[12]

responsible for evil. Thus, for the Greeks the world, before Pandora, was populated only by men—an extremely difficult concept. Did Prometheus create only men out of clay? Hesiod's account is riddled with irreconcilable contradictions because various stories have been awkwardly but poetically conflated. In the myth of the Ages of Mankind both men and women are created by Zeus or the gods, and both men and women are held responsible for evil, for which they are punished by the gods. Should we assume that Pandora was sent with her jar of evils (and Hope) to a happy humankind? At any rate, amid all this confusion, Hesiod is more accurately condemned as a misanthropist, rather than only as a misogynist.

Details in the story of Pandora are disturbing in their tantalizing ambiguity. What is Hope doing in the jar along with countless evils? If it is a good, it is a curious inclusion. If it too is an evil, why is it stopped at the rim? What then is its precise nature, whether a blessing or a curse? Is Hope the one thing that enables human beings to survive the terrors of this life and inspires them with lofty ambition? Yet is it also by its very character delusive and blind, luring them on to prolong their misery? It is tempting to see in Aeschylus' play *Prometheus Bound* an interpretation and elaboration: human beings were without hope until Prometheus gave it to them along with the benefit of fire. The hope Prometheus bestows on mortals is both blind and a blessing. The pertinent dialogue between Prometheus and the Chorus of Oceanids runs as follows (248–252):

> PROMETHEUS: I stopped mortals from foreseeing their fate.
> CHORUS: What sort of remedy did you find for this plague?
> PROMETHEUS: I planted in them blind hopes.
> CHORUS: This was a great advantage that you gave mortals.
> PROMETHEUS: And besides I gave them fire.

Fundamental to both Hesiod and Aeschylus is the conception of Zeus as the oppressor of humankind and Prometheus as its benefactor. In Aeschylus the clash of divine wills echoes triumphantly through the ages. His portrait, more than any other, offers the towering image of Prometheus as the Titan, the bringer of fire, the vehement and weariless champion against oppression, the mighty symbol for art, literature, and music of all time.

Aeschylus' *Prometheus Bound*

Aeschylus' play *Prometheus Bound* begins with Strength (Kratos) and Force (Bia), brutish servants of an autocratic Zeus, having brought Prometheus to the remote and uninhabited land of Scythia. Hephaestus accompanies them. Kratos urges the reluctant Hephaestus to obey the commands of Father Zeus and bind Prometheus in bonds of steel and pin him with a stake through his chest to the desolate crags. It was Hephaestus' own brilliant "flower" of fire, deviser of all the arts, that Prometheus stole, and for this error ("sin" is not an inappropriate translation) he must pay to all the gods "so that he might learn to bear the sovereignty of Zeus and abandon his love and championship of mortals" (10–17).

Aeschylus, with great skill and economy, provides us with the essentials for the conflict and the mood of the play. The violent struggle pits a harsh, young, and angry Zeus against the defiant determination of a glorious and philanthropic Prometheus.[13]

Hephaestus, in contrast to savage Strength and Force, is sensitive and humane; he curses his craft, hates the job he has to do, and pities the sleepless torment of Prometheus. Hephaestus also expresses an important theme of the play in his realization that Zeus has only recently seized supreme rule of gods and mortals: "The mind of Zeus is inexorable; and everyone is harsh when he first comes to power." The contrast is presumably intended to foreshadow the later Zeus, who will learn benevolence through experience, wisdom, and maturity. Certainly Zeus, fresh from his triumphant defeat of his father and the Titans, might indeed be uneasy and afraid. He may suffer the same fate as Cronus or Uranus before him; and Prometheus, his adversary, knows the terrifying secret that might lead to Zeus' undoing: Zeus must avoid the sea-nymph Thetis in his amorous pursuits, for she is destined to bear a son mightier than his father. In his knowledge of this lies Prometheus' defiant power and the threat of Zeus' ultimate downfall.

The first utterance of Prometheus after Strength, Force, and Hephaestus have done their work is glorious, perfectly capturing the great and indomitable spirit of the rebel and the oppressed (88–92):

> O divine air and sky and swift-winged breezes, springs of rivers and countless laughter of sea waves, earth, mother of everything, and all-seeing circle of the sun, I call on you. See what I, a god, suffer at the hands of the gods.

In the course of the play, Prometheus expresses his bitterness because, although he with his mother fought on the side of Zeus against the Titans, his only reward is torment. It is typical of the tyrant to forget and turn against his former allies. Prometheus lists the many gifts he has given to humankind for whom he suffers now (442–506):

> PROMETHEUS: Listen to the troubles that there were among mortals and how I gave them sense and mind, which they did not have before. I shall tell you this, not out of any censure of humankind, but to explain the good intention of my gifts. In the beginning they had eyes to look, but looked in vain, and ears to hear, but did not hear, but like the shapes of dreams they wandered in confusion the whole of their long life. They did not know of brick-built houses that face the sun or carpentry, but dwelt beneath the ground like tiny ants in the depths of sunless caves. They did

not have any secure way of distinguishing winter or blossoming spring or fruitful summer, but they did everything without judgment, until I showed them the rising and the setting of the stars, difficult to discern. (442–458)   10

And indeed I discovered for them numbers, a lofty kind of wisdom, and letters and their combination, an art that fosters memory of all things, the mother of the Muses' arts. I first harnessed animals, enslaving them to the yoke to give relief to mortals in their greatest toils, and I made horses docile under the reins of the chariot, the delight of the highest wealth and luxury. No one before me discovered the seamen's vessels which with wings of sail are beaten by the waves. Such are the contrivances I, poor wretch, have found for mortals, but I myself have no device by which I may escape my present pain. (459–471)

CHORUS: You suffer an ill-deserved torment, and confused in mind and heart are all astray; like some bad doctor who has fallen ill, you yourself cannot devise a remedy to effect a cure. (472–475)   20

PROMETHEUS: Listen to the rest, and you will be even more amazed at the kinds of skills and means that I devised; the greatest this: if anyone fell sick, there existed no defense, neither food nor drink nor salve, but through lack of medicines they wasted away until I showed them the mixing of soothing remedies by which they free themselves from all diseases. I set forth the many ways of the prophetic art. I was the first to determine which dreams would of necessity turn out to be true, and I established for them the difficult interpretation of sounds and omens of the road and distinguished the precise meaning of the flight of birds with crooked talons, which ones are by nature lucky and propitious, and what mode of life each had, their mutual likes, dislikes, and association; the smoothness of the innards and the color of the bile that would meet the pleasure of the gods, and the dappled beauty of the liver's lobe. I burned the limbs enwrapped in fat and the long shank and set mortals on the path to this difficult art of sacrifice, and made clear the fiery signs, obscure before. Such were these gifts of mine. And the benefits hidden deep within the earth, copper, iron, silver, and gold—who could claim that he had found them before me? No one, I know full well, unless he wished to babble on in vain.   30

In a brief utterance learn the whole story: all arts come to mortals from Prometheus. (476–506)   40

When Hermes, Zeus' messenger, appears in the last episode, Prometheus is arrogant and insulting in his refusal to bow to the threats of even more terrible suffering and reveal his secret. The play ends with the fulfillment of the promised torment; the earth shakes and cracks, thunder and lightning accompany wind and storm as Prometheus, still pinned to the rock, is plunged beneath the earth by the cataclysm; there he will be plagued by the eagle daily tearing his flesh and gnawing his liver. Prometheus' final utterance echoes and affirms the fiery heat and mighty spirit of his first invocation: "O majesty of earth, my mother, O air and sky whose circling brings light for all to share. You see me, how I suffer unjust torments."

Io, Zeus, and Prometheus

In order to appreciate Aeschylus' depiction of Zeus and his vision of the final outcome of the conflict between Zeus and Prometheus,[14] we must introduce the story of Io, a pivotal figure in *Prometheus Bound*.[15] In the series of exchanges

Mercury and Argus (1659), by Diego Velázquez (1599–1660); oil on canvas, 50 × 97⅝ in. Velázquez fits the two figures, human and divine, and the cow into the rectangular and cave-like space, whose size was dictated by its original placement above a window. Mercury, stealthy and watchful, grasps his sword in his right hand, and his muscular upper torso and arms, with the disreputable felt hat, are quite different from usual and more heroic representations of the god. The light falls on Argus, portrayed as a weary guard, as he begins to fall asleep. The picture is a masterpiece of silence and foreboding. (*Erich Lessing/ Art Resource, NY*)

between Prometheus and the various characters who come to witness his misery, the scene with Io is particularly significant in terms of eventual reconciliation and knowledge.

Io was loved by Zeus; she was a priestess of Hera and could not avoid detection by the goddess. Zeus failed to deceive Hera, who in retaliation turned Io into a white cow,[16] and to guard her new possession, she set Argus over her. Argus, whose parentage is variously given, had many eyes (the number varies from four in Aeschylus to one hundred in Ovid) and was called Argus Panoptes (the "all-seeing"); because his eyes never slept all at once, he could have Io under constant surveillance. Zeus therefore sent Hermes to rescue Io; Hermes lulled Argus to sleep by telling him stories and then cut off his head— hence his title **Argeïphontes**, or "slayer of Argus." Hera set Argus' eyes in the tail of the peacock, the bird with which she is especially associated. Io still could not escape Hera's jealousy; Hera sent a gadfly that so maddened her that she wandered miserably over the whole world until finally she came to Egypt. There, by the Nile, Zeus restored her human form, and she gave birth to a son, Epaphus.[17]

In *Prometheus Bound*, Aeschylus describes Io's sufferings in some detail to illustrate the ultimate wisdom, justice, and mercy of an all-powerful Zeus. In agony because of the stings of the gadfly and tormented by the ghost of Argus, Io flees over the earth in mad frenzy. She asks why Zeus has punished her, an innocent victim of Hera's brutal resentment, and longs for the release of death. This is how the uncomprehending Io tells Prometheus of her anguish (645–682):

> Again and again in the night, visions would appear to me in my room and entice me with seductive words: "O blessed maiden, why do you remain a virgin for so long when it is possible for you to achieve the greatest of marriages? For Zeus is inflamed by the shafts of desire and longs to make love to you. Do not, my child, reject the bed of Zeus but go out to the deep meadow of Lerna where the flocks and herds of your father graze, so that the longing of the eye of Zeus may be requited." I, poor wretch, was troubled every night by such dreams until at last I dared to tell my father

about them. He sent numerous messengers to Delphi and Dodona to find out what he must do or say to appease the gods; and they returned with difficult and obscure answers, cryptically worded. At last an unambiguous injunction was delivered to Inachus, clearly ordering him to evict me from his house and city to wander without a home to the ends of the earth; if he did not comply, the fiery thunderbolt of Zeus would strike and annihilate his whole race. (645–668)   10

In obedience to this oracle of Apollo, my father, unwilling as was I, expelled and drove me from my home; indeed the bridle bit of Zeus forcefully compelled him to do such things. Straightway my body was changed and my mind distorted; with horns, as you can see, and pursued by the sharp stings of a gadfly, I rushed in convulsive leaps to the clear stream of Cerchnea and the spring of Lerna. The giant herdsman Argus, savage in his rage, accompanied me, watching with his countless eyes my every step. A sudden unexpected fate deprived him of his life; but I, driven mad by the stings of the gadfly, wander from land to land under the scourge of god. (669–682)   20

As the scene continues, Prometheus foretells the subsequent course of Io's wanderings. Eventually, she will find peace in Egypt, where (848–851):

Zeus will make you sane by the touch of his fearless hand—the touch alone; and you will bear a son, Epaphus, "Him of the Touch," so named from his begetting at the hand of Zeus.

Aeschylus' version of the conception of **Epaphus** is religious. Io has been chosen by Zeus and has suffered at the hands of Hera for the fulfillment of a destiny, and she will conceive not through rape but by the gentle touch of the hand of god. Prometheus, with the oracular power of his mother, foresees the generations descended from Io, the culmination of his narrative being the birth of the great hero Heracles, who will help Zeus in the final release of Prometheus. Thus, the divine plan is revealed and the absolute power of almighty Zeus is achieved; in mature confidence he will rest secure, without fear of being overthrown, as the supreme and benevolent father of both gods and mortals.

As Aeschylus' other plays on Prometheus survive only as titles and fragments, we do not know how he conceived details in the ultimate resolution. From Hesiod (p. 90) we know that Heracles, through the agency of Zeus, was responsible for killing the eagle and releasing Prometheus—after Prometheus had revealed the fatal secret about mating with Thetis. Conflicting and obscure testimony has Chiron, the centaur, involved in some way, as Aeschylus seems to predict; Chiron, wounded by Heracles, gives up his life and his immortality in a bargain for the release of Prometheus.[18]

Zeus and Lycaon and the Wickedness of Mortals

Prometheus had a son, Deucalion, and Epimetheus had a daughter, Pyrrha. Their story, from Ovid's *Metamorphoses*, involves a great flood sent by Zeus (Jupiter) to punish mortals for their wickedness. In the passage given here, Jupiter tells an assembly of the gods how he, a god, became a man to test the truth of the rumors of human wickedness in the age of iron. There follows an account of Jupiter's anger at the evil of mortals, in particular Lycaon (1.211–252).

Reports of the wickedness of the age had reached my ears; wishing to find them false, I slipped down from high Olympus and I, a god, roamed the earth in the form of a man. Long would be the delay to list the number of evils and where they were found; the iniquitous stories themselves fell short of the truth. I had crossed the mountain Maenalus, bristling with the haunts of animals, and Cyllene, and the forests of cold Lycaeus; from these ridges in Arcadia I entered the realm and inhospitable house of the tyrant Lycaon, as the dusk of evening was leading night on. (211–219)

"I gave signs that a god had come in their midst; the people began to pray but Lycaon first laughed at their piety and then cried: 'I shall test whether this man is a god or a mortal, clearly and decisively.' He planned to kill me unawares in the night while I was deep in sleep. This was the test of truth that suited him best. But he was not content even with this; with a knife he slit the throat of one of the hostages sent to him by the Molossians and, as the limbs were still warm with life, some he boiled until tender and others he roasted over a fire. As soon as he placed them on the table, I with a flame of vengeance brought the home down upon its gods, worthy of such a household and such a master. (220–231)   10

"Lycaon himself fled in terror, and when he reached the silence of the country he howled as in vain he tried to speak. His mouth acquired a mad ferocity arising from his basic nature, and he turned his accustomed lust for slaughter against the flocks and now took joy in their blood. His clothes were changed to hair; his arms to legs; he became a wolf retaining vestiges of his old form. The silver of the hair and the violent countenance were the same; the eyes glowed in the same way; the image of ferocity was the same.[19] (232–239)   20

"One house had fallen but not one house only deserved to perish. Far and wide on the earth the Fury holds power; you would think that an oath had been sworn in the name of crime. Let all quickly suffer the penalties they deserve. Thus my verdict stands." (240–244)

Some cried approval of the words of Jove and added goads to his rage, others signified their assent by applause. But the loss of the human race was grievous to them all and they asked what the nature of the world would be like bereft of mortals, who would bring incense to the altars, and if Jupiter was prepared to give the world over to the ravagings of animals. As they asked these questions the king of the gods ordered them not to be alarmed, for all that would follow would be his deep concern; and he promised a race of wondrous origin unlike the one that had preceded. (245–252)   30

The Flood

Set upon destroying humankind, Jupiter rejects the idea of hurling his thunder-bolts against the world because he fears they may start a great conflagration that could overwhelm the universe. As Ovid continues the story, the god has decided on a different means of punishment: a great flood (260–290). The motif of the Flood is one of the most important and universal in myth and legend.[20]

A different punishment pleased him more: to send down from every region of the sky torrents of rain and destroy the human race under the watery waves. Straightway he imprisoned the North Wind, and such other blasts as put storm clouds to flight in the caves of Aeolus, and let loose the South Wind who flew with drenched wings, his dread countenance cloaked in darkness black as pitch; his beard was heavy with rain, water flowed from his hoary hair, clouds nestled on his brow, and his wings and garments dripped with moisture. And as he pressed the hanging clouds with his broad hand, he made a crash, and out of them thick rains poured down from the upper air. The messenger of Juno, Iris, adorned in varied hues, drew up the waters and brought nourishment to the clouds. The crops were leveled and the farmers' hopeful prayers lay ruined and bemoaned the labor of the long year in vain destroyed. (269–273)   10

Nor was the wrath of Jove content with his realm, the sky. His brother Neptune of the sea gave aid with waves as reinforcements. He called together the rivers and, when they had entered the dwelling of their master, said: "Now I cannot resort to a long exhortation. Pour forth your strength, this is the need—open wide your domains, and all barriers removed, give full rein to your streams." This was his command. They went back home and opened wide their mouths for their waters to roll in their unbridled course over the plains. Neptune himself struck the earth with his trident; it trembled and with the quake laid open paths for the waters. The streams spread from their course and rushed over the open fields and swept away, together and at once, the trees and crops, cattle, human beings, houses, and their inner shrines with sacred statues. If any house remained and was able to withstand being thrown down by so great an evil, yet a wave still higher touched its highest gables, and towers overcome lay submerged in the torrent. (274–290)   20

Deucalion and Pyrrha

Ovid provides further elaborate and poetical description of the ravages of the terrible flood and then concentrates upon the salvation of the pious couple, Deucalion (the Greek Noah) and his wife, Pyrrha, and the repopulation of the world (311–421).

The greatest part of life was swept away by water; those whom the water spared were overcome by slow starvation because of lack of food. (311–312)

The territory of Phocis separates the terrain of Thessaly from that of Boeotia, a fertile area when it was land, but in this crisis it had suddenly become part of the sea and a wide field of water. Here a lofty mountain, Parnassus by name, reaches with its two peaks up to the stars, the heights extending beyond the clouds. When Deucalion with his wife was carried in his little boat to this mountain and ran aground (for the deep waters had covered the rest of the land) they offered worship to the Corycian nymphs,[21] the deities of the mountain, and prophetic Themis, who at that time held oracular power there. No man was better than Deucalion nor more devoted to justice, and no woman more reverent towards the gods than his wife, Pyrrha. (313–323)   10

When Jupiter saw the earth covered with a sea of water and only one man and one woman surviving out of so many thousands of men and women, both innocent and both devout worshipers of deity, he dispelled the clouds, and after the North Wind had cleared the storm, revealed the earth to the sky and the upper air to the world below. The wrath of the sea did not endure and the ruler of the deep laid aside his trident and calmed the waves. He summoned the sea-god Triton, who rose above the waters, his shoulders encrusted with shellfish; he ordered him to blow into his resounding conch shell and by this signal to recall the waves and the rivers. Triton took up the hollow horn which grows from the lowest point of the spiral, coiling in ever widening circles. Whenever he blows into his horn in the middle of the deep, its sounds fill every shore to east and west. Now too, as the god put the horn to his lips moist with his dripping beard and gave it breath, it sounded the orders of retreat and was heard by all the waves on land and on the sea, and as they listened all were checked. (324–342)

Once more the sea had shores and streams were held within their channels, rivers subsided, and hills were seen to rise up. Earth emerged and the land grew in extent as the waves receded. And after a length of time the tops of the woods were uncovered and showed forth, a residue of mud left clinging to the leaves. The world had been restored. (343–348)

When Deucalion saw the earth devoid of life and the profound silence of its desolation, tears welled up in his eyes as he spoke to Pyrrha thus: "O my cousin, and my wife, the only woman left, related to me by family ties of blood, then joined to me in marriage, now danger itself unites us. We two alone are the host of the whole world from east to west; the sea holds all the rest. Besides assurance of our life is not yet completely certain. Even now the clouds above strike terror in my heart. What feelings would you have now, poor dear, if you had been snatched to safety by the Fates without me? In what way could you have been able to bear your fear alone? Who would have consoled you as you grieved? For I, believe me, would have followed, if the sea had taken you, dear wife, and the sea would have taken me with you. How I wish I might be able to repopulate the earth by the arts of my father and infuse the molded clods of earth with life. As it is, the race of mortals rests in just us two—thus have the gods ordained—and we remain the only vestiges of human beings." Thus he spoke and they wept. (348–367)

They decided to pray to the goddess Themis and seek help through her holy oracles with no delay. Together they approached the waves of the river Cephisus, which, although not yet clear, was cutting its accustomed course. When they had drawn water and sprinkled their heads and clothes, they turned their steps from there to the temple of the goddess; its pediments were discolored with vile moss and its altars stood without fire. As they reached the steps of the temple, both fell forward on the ground, and in dread awe implanted kisses on the cold stone. They spoke as follows: "If the divine majesty is won over and made soft by just prayers, if the anger of the gods is turned aside, tell, O Themis, by what art the loss of the human race may be repaired and give help, O most gentle deity, in our drowned world." (367–380)

The goddess was moved and gave her oracle: "Go away from my temple, cover your heads and unloose the fastenings of your garments, and toss the bones of the great mother behind your back." For a long time they were stupefied at this; Pyrrha first broke the silence by uttering her refusal to obey the orders of the goddess; with fearful prayer she begged indulgence, for she feared to hurt the shade of her mother by tossing her bones. But all the while they sought another explanation and mulled over, alone and together, the dark and hidden meaning of the obscure words given by the oracle. Then the son of Prometheus soothed the daughter of Epimetheus with pleasing words: "Unless my ingenuity is wrong, oracles are holy and never urge any evil; the great parent is the earth; I believe that the stones in the body of earth are called her bones. We are ordered to throw these behind our backs." (381–394)

Although the Titan's daughter was moved by the interpretation of her husband, her hope was still in doubt; to this extent they both distrusted heaven's admonitions. But what harm would there be in trying? They left the temple, covered their heads, unloosed their garments, and tossed the stones behind their steps as they were ordered. The stones (who would believe this if the antiquity of tradition did not bear testimony?) began to lose their hardness and rigidity and gradually grew soft and in their softness assumed a shape. Soon as they grew and took on a more pliant nature, the form of a human being could be seen, in outline not distinct, most like crude statues carved in marble, just begun and not sufficiently completed. The part of the stones that was of earth dampened by some moisture was converted into flesh; what was solid and unable to be so transformed was changed into bone; what once had been a vein in the stone remained with the same name; in a short time, through the will of the gods, the stones hurled by the hands of the man assumed the appearance of men, and those cast by the woman were converted into women. Hence we are a hard race and used to toils and offer proof of the origin from which we were sprung. (395–415)

70 80

The earth of her own accord produced other animals of different sorts, after the moisture that remained was heated by the fire of the sun; and the mud and soggy marshes began to swell because of the heat, and fertile seeds of things began to grow nourished by the life-giving earth, as in a mother's womb, and gradually took on a certain form. (416–421)

Deucalion and Pyrrha had a son Hellen, the eponymous ancestor of the Greek people; for the Greeks called themselves Hellenes and their country Hellas.[22]

Succession Myths and Other Motifs

Literature of the ancient Near East has many parallels to Hesiod's account of genesis and the gods. One of the most striking is the archetypal motif known as the Succession Myth. In the Babylonian epic of creation, which begins with the words by which it is entitled (*Enuma Elish*, "When on high"), Marduk plays a role similar to that of Zeus in the conflict for power; and Marduk, like Zeus, attains ultimate control by defeating a monster, Tiamat, who thus resembles Typhoeus. Likewise the epic *Kingship in Heaven* reveals common thematic patterns; especially startling is the episode that tells how Kumarbi defeats Anu by biting off his genitals, a brutal act not unlike the castration of Uranus by Cronus. The flood archetype is particularly fascinating because of its presence worldwide, in virtually all cultures (see note 20). The wickedness of mortals and their punishment, as well as their salvation, are also persistent themes. The appendix at the end of this chapter provides a more detailed identification of parallels between the myths of Greece and those of the ancient Near East.

Among the many themes inherent in the character and career of Zeus himself, the following deserve special emphasis. Even though Zeus was a god, his life illustrates special motifs that appear again and again not only in the lives of other deities but also in the mortal lives of the heroes of saga, to be sure with infinite variations and amplifications. Zeus is the child of extraordinary parents; both of them are gods. The circumstances of his birth are unusual or difficult; he must avoid being swallowed by his father. He must be brought up in secret, and his life as an infant is both precarious and charmed, progressing in accordance with the motif of the Divine Child. He grows up close to nature and the world of animals; and, after an idyllic childhood, with special care and training, upon reaching manhood, he must come into his own by overcoming challenges and adversaries: his father Cronus and the Titans, the Giants, and Prometheus.

Very special on the list of his triumphs is the slaying of a dragon. By killing Typhoeus, Zeus, the supreme god, may be proclaimed as the archetypal dragon slayer—one of the most powerful and symbolic of all divine and heroic achievements.

In the end, as we shall see in the next chapter, Zeus emerges as the ultimate victor and wins a bride, a kingdom, and supreme power. He triumphs to become almighty god, although even then his exploits and trials are by no means over.

Appendix to Chapter 4

Parallels in Myths of Greece and the Ancient Near East

Five basic myths are important for the identification of parallels in the myths of ancient Near Eastern civilizations. These are the myths of Creation, Succession, the Flood, the Descent to the Underworld, and the hero-king Gilgamesh. They have striking parallels in Greek mythology, as we have already observed. "Are there migrating myths?" asks Walter Burkert, and he and others answer that the similarities are undeniable evidence for the influence of Near Eastern cultures on Greek mythology. How this influence traveled cannot be known precisely, but trade is the most likely means, as it has been shown that contacts between the Greek and Near Eastern worlds flourished especially in two periods, the thirteenth and fourteenth centuries and the eighth and seventh centuries B.C.[23] Near Eastern myths appear in the cultures of Sumer and Akkad—southern and northern Mesopotamia, respectively. The Sumerians were the earliest (from the fourth millennium B.C.) to develop a civilization with urban centers, such as Ur and Uruk. They developed *cuneiform* ("wedge-shaped") script on clay tablets, and their religious architecture was distinguished by *ziggurats* (temple towers). They were absorbed by Semitic peoples speaking a different language (Akkadian) but still using cuneiform script. The chief Akkadian urban center (from the late third millennium) was Babylon, which reached its first zenith under King Hammurabi, around 1800 B.C. Babylon was conquered in about 1250 B.C. by the northern Akkadians, who established the Assyrian Empire, with its center at Nineveh.

Among the peoples associated with the Akkadians were the Hurrians of northern Syria, who in their turn were absorbed by the Hittites after about 1400 B.C. The Hittite Empire flourished in Anatolia (the central and eastern area of modern Turkey) during the second millennium B.C., with its center at Hattusas, the modern Boghaz-Köy. Hittite myths absorbed Hurrian themes and the names of Hurrian gods, and several of these myths have themes in common with Greek myth. The same is true of Egyptian, Phoenician, and Hebraic myths, the last named being more familiar to Western readers, especially in the biblical Christian narratives of Genesis (Chapters 1 and 2), Psalms (many references, for example, Psalms 33 and 104), and Job (Chapter 38).

Like Hesiod, the Sumerian, Babylonian, and Akkadian poets do not narrate a myth of creation by an intelligent creator. Their concern, like Hesiod's, is with the bringing of order out of disorder, or, rather, out of a concept similar to the Greek *Chaos* ("Void"). Thus, their myths of creation also involve myths of succession and, to some extent, myths of the Flood and the survival and re-creation of humankind. The best-known myth of creation is in the Babylonian *Epic of*

Creation, usually identified by its opening words, *Enuma Elish* ("When on high . . ."), which was probably composed in the early years of the second millennium B.C. In this version, the gods come into existence from the union of Apsu and Tiamat—the fresh water and saltwater oceans, respectively. From them descend Anu (the sky) and Ea or Enki (the earth-god), who is also the god of wisdom. From Ea, Marduk is born, after Ea has destroyed Apsu. Tiamat then prepares to attack the younger gods, who entrust their defense to Marduk and make him their king, after their leader, Enlil, has proved unequal to the challenge. Armed with bow and arrow, thunderbolt, and storm-winds, Marduk attacks Tiamat, fills her with the winds, and splits her body. The following is part of the battle, which should be compared with Hesiod's account of the battle between Zeus and Typhoeus (see pp. 83–85):

> Face to face they came, Tiamat and Marduk. . . .
> They engaged in combat, they closed for battle.
> The Lord spread his net and made it encircle her,
> To her face he dispatched the *imhullu*-wind. . . .
> Tiamat opened her mouth to swallow it,
> And he forced in the *imhullu*-wind so that she could not close her lips.
> Fierce winds distend her belly. . . .
> He shot an arrow which pierced her belly,
> Split her down the middle and slit her heart,
> Vanquished her and extinguished her life.[24]

After his victory, Marduk places half of Tiamat's body above the earth and there, in the sky, he creates Esharra, the home of the gods, while Tiamat's followers, led by Kingu, are bound. Marduk then organizes the gods and the world and, on the advice of Ea, orders the creation of humankind from the blood of Kingu, who is killed. The work of humankind is to serve the gods, and Marduk's temple of Esagila, with its ziggurat, is built in Babylon. The poem ends with the enumeration of the fifty names of Marduk.

About 200 years later than *Enuma Elish* (ca. 1700 B.C.), the Babylonian epic of *Atrahasis* was written down. Atrahasis is the supremely wise man—his name means "extra-wise," corresponding to Ut-napishtim of the *Gilgamesh Epic*, the Sumerian hero Ziusudra, the Hebrew Noah, and the Greek Prometheus and Deucalion (the former being the pre-Olympian god of wisdom and craftsmanship and the latter the survivor of the Flood). In the myth of Atrahasis, the gods complain of the hard labor that they must perform for Enlil and threaten to rebel against him. Enlil orders the creation of humankind to perform the toil of canal digging and other labors for the gods. Enlil orders the death of the intelligent god Geshtu-e, from whose flesh and blood, mixed with clay, humankind is created, seven males and seven females. After a long period of time Atrahasis, advised by Enki, survives the flood sent by Enlil, who has determined to destroy humankind because their noise disturbs the peace of the gods. Enlil is furious when he sees the boat in which Atrahasis has survived, but the poem ends with a reconciliation between Enlil and Enki, by which the human race is allowed to continue.

The best-known version of the myth of the Flood is narrated in the *Epic of Gilgamesh* by the heroic survivor, Ut-napishtim, whom Gilgamesh visits after a journey through the hitherto impassable "mountains of Mashu" and across the waters of death. Here, too, Enlil is furious at the survival of Ut-napishtim, but again there is a reconciliation. Ut-napishtim lives, immortal, far off "at the mouth of the rivers"; humankind, re-created, cannot escape the evils that occur to the living, nor can they escape death. Gilgamesh ultimately fails in his quest for immortality, and the final tablet (no. xii) of the poem describes the retention of his dead friend, Enkidu, in the world of the dead.[25] Gilgamesh himself was originally a historical figure, ruler of the Sumerian city of Uruk (modern Warka, in central Iraq) ca. 2700 B.C. His legends were incorporated into the Assyrian version of his epic, dating from about 1700 B.C., written on eleven clay tablets, to which a twelfth was added much later. Different versions exist of the epic, the composition of which evolved over a lengthy period. Later tradition claimed that a scholar-priest Sinleqqiunninni was the author.[26]

Gilgamesh, the wise hero and slayer of monstrous beings, has obvious similarities with Greek Odysseus and Heracles (who is also identified with Ninurta, son of Enlil, and with the underworld god, Nergal, consort of Ereshkigal). Like the Babylonian Atrahasis and the Greek Odysseus, he is supremely intelligent. Here are the opening lines of the first tablet of the poem:

> [Of him who] found out all things, I [shall te]ll the land,
> [Of him who] experienced everything, I [shall te]ach the whole.
> He searched [?] lands [?] everywhere.
> He who experienced the whole gained complete wisdom.
> He found out what was secret and uncovered what was hidden.
> He brought back a tale of times before the Flood.
> He had journeyed far and wide, weary and at last resigned.
> He engraved all toils on a memorial monument of stone.[27]

A brief summary of the poem runs as follows. The strong and handsome Gilgamesh is two-thirds divine and one-third human. As king of Uruk, he acts oppressively toward his people, and therefore the gods create a rival for him, valiant Enkidu, a primeval hunter in the forest, quite the opposite of the civilized Gilgamesh. After sexual intercourse with a harlot, Enkidu is depleted of his wild character and eventually challenges Gilgamesh in a wrestling match. Although Gilgamesh defeats Enkidu, they become devoted comrades and their loving friendship now becomes a major theme. They set out together on a quest to cut down the sacred trees in the Pine (or Cedar) Forest in the mountains of southwest Iran, after having killed its guardian Humbaba (or Huwawa), the Terrible. These labors accomplished, upon their return to Uruk, Gilgamesh is confronted by the goddess Ishtar, who desires to marry him. When he rejects her, she sends down the terrifying and destructive Bull of Heaven, which the two heroes kill. Because they have defiled the sacred Forest and killed the Bull of Heaven, the gods decide that one of them, Enkidu, must die. All the long while that Enkidu suffers painfully, Gilgamesh is by his side, and when Enkidu dies, he is overcome with grief. Gilgamesh, horrified by the reality of death and decay, decides to find the secret of immortality. His encounter with Ut-napishtim, the survivor of the Flood, has already been described.

In addition to those mentioned here, many parallels between the Sumerian and Greek heroes and their legends can be found, for example, in the contact of Odysseus with the Underworld and the land of Alcinoüs and the Phaeacians (similar to the realm of Ut-napishtim "at the mouth of the rivers").

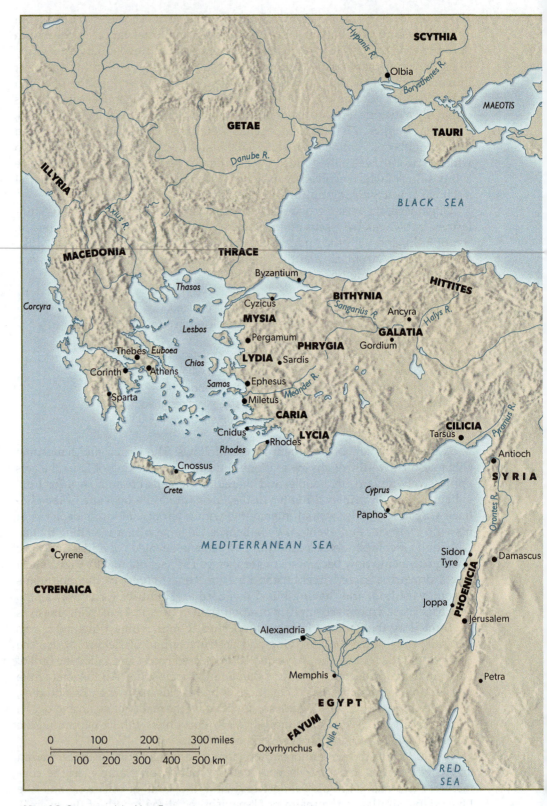

Map 4.1 Greece and the Near East.

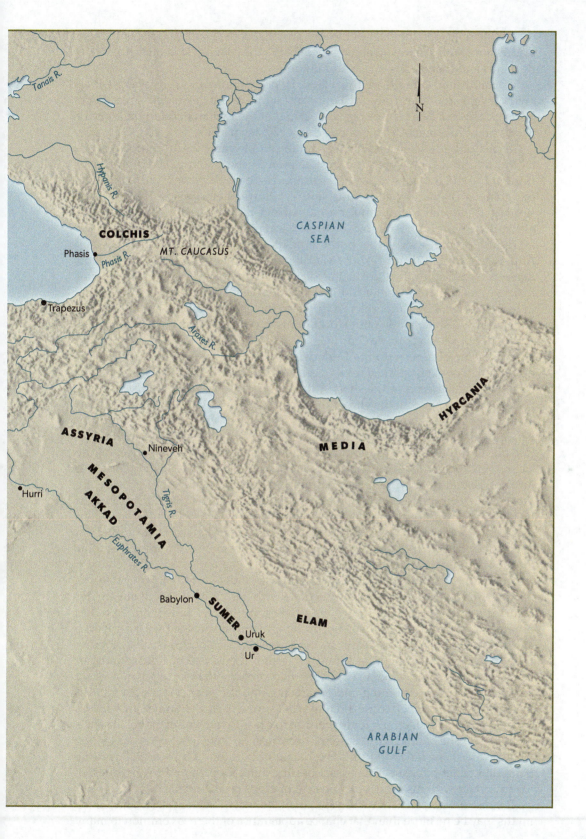

Similarities between the story of the *Iliad* and that of the *Epic of Gilgamesh* are also readily apparent, prominent among them being the comradeship of Achilles and Patroclus and that of Gilgamesh and Enkidu.

In contrast, the myth of the Flood is not prominent in classical Greek myth. It appears more fully (in Latin) in Ovid's narratives of the great flood (*Metamorphoses* 1.260–421: see pp. 98–102) and of the Lydian flood in the story of Baucis and Philemon (*Metamorphoses* 8.689–720: see p. 650).

Myths of succession and the separation of sky and earth appear also in Hittite narratives, of which the best known is the poem called *Kingship in Heaven*, in which Kumarbi (who corresponds to the Sumerian Enlil) bites off the genitals of the sky-god, Anu, and swallows them. Inside Kumarbi the storm-god (Teshub or Tarkhun) develops from the genitals of Anu, and after his birth he plots with Anu to overthrow Kumarbi. The extant poem breaks off as Teshub prepares for battle, but it appears that he defeated Kumarbi. Thus Anu, Kumarbi/Enlil, and Teshub/Marduk are parallel to Uranus, Cronus, and Zeus in Greek myth. In the Hittite *Song of Ullikummis*, Ea cuts off the feet of Ullikummis, a giant made of diorite (a kind of very hard stone), 9,000 leagues in height, created by Kumarbi as a threat to the gods. After his mutilation, the gods, led by Teshub, battle with Ullikummis (the tablet breaks off at this point, but no doubt the gods prevailed).[28]

The theme of descent to the Underworld is also prominent in Near Eastern myth and has many parallels in Greek myth. The most important myth on this theme is narrated in the short Akkadian poem, *The Descent of Ishtar to the Underworld*, dating from the end of the second millennium B.C. It was preceded by a Sumerian version, about three times as long, in which Ishtar is called by her Sumerian name, Inanna.[29] Inanna/Ishtar is daughter of Anu (and therefore one of the earlier generation of gods) and sister of Ereshkigal, queen of the Underworld and wife of Nergal. Ishtar is a goddess of war but also the goddess of love and sexual creation, and thus has much in common with Aphrodite. While Ereshkigal corresponds to the Greek Persephone, Ishtar is like Persephone, in that she returns from the Underworld, and like Eurydice (wife of Orpheus), in that she must return to the Underworld if certain conditions are not fulfilled on her journey back to the upper world. Her consort, Dumuzi (Tammuz), is similar to Adonis and Attis in Greek myth.

In both narratives Ishtar decides to visit the Underworld; knowing that she may be killed there, she leaves instructions with her vizier that will ensure her resurrection if she does not return within a certain time. She is stripped of her ornaments and clothing as she goes through the seven gates of the Underworld, and Ereshkigal orders her death. In the Sumerian version her corpse is hung from a peg. She is brought back to life through the advice of Enki (Sumerian version) or the agency of her vizier (Akkadian version). In the Akkadian version, she receives back her clothing and ornaments, and the poem ends with mourning for the death of her consort, Dumuzi (Tammuz). In the Sumerian version, Ishtar is angry with Dumuzi for his refusal to dress in mourning for her absence, and in anger she hands him over to the demons who were to take her back to the Underworld if she failed to fulfill Ereshkigal's conditions. Only in 1963 was the Sumerian tablet published that describes the annual death and resurrection of Dumuzi, and with his return the renewal of crops on the earth.[30]

It must be stressed that many parallels between Near Eastern and Greek myths may be no more than that chance appearance of themes common to many mythologies, with no direct influence. Yet, in the instances of the succession myth, the Flood, the *Epic of Gilgamesh*, and the myth of Ishtar and Dumuzi, it is most probable that there was some direct contact between Near Eastern and Greek storytellers, in which case we have strong evidence for Eastern sources in early Greek mythography. The Greeks owed many debts to the civilizations with whom they came into contact, not only in the Near East but also in Egypt. They used and transformed what they heard, saw, and read into works of art cast in their own image.[31]

Select Bibliography

Charlesworth, James H. *The Good and Evil Serpent: How a Universal Symbol Became Christianized*. New Haven, CT: Yale University Press, 2009. An exploration of the symbolic meanings of the serpent from 40,000 B.C. to the present.

Dougherty, Carol. *Prometheus*. Gods and Heroes of the Ancient World Series. New York: Routledge, 2005.

Dowden, Ken. *Zeus*. Gods and Heroes of the Ancient World Series. New York: Routledge, 2005.

Griffith, Mark. *Aeschylus: Prometheus Bound*. New York: Cambridge University Press, 1983. An edition of the Greek text, which has an informative introduction.

Kerényi, Carl. *Prometheus: Archetypal Image of Human Existence*. Translated by Ralph Mannheim. Princeton, NJ: Princeton University Press, 1997 [1963].

Greece and the Near East

Burkert, W. "Oriental and Greek Mythology: The Meeting of Parallels," In Jan Bremmer, ed., *Interpretations of Greek Mythology*. New York: Routledge, 1988, pp. 10–40.

Dalley, Stephanie. *Myths from Mesopotamia*. New York: Oxford University Press, 1989. Translations of Akkadian texts, including *Gilgamesh*, *Atrahasis*, and the *Descent of Ishtar*. Especially valuable for the inclusion of recently published texts.

Heidel, A. *The Gilgamesh Epic and Old Testament Parallels*. 2d ed. Chicago, IL: University of Chicago Press, 1946.

Hooke, S. H. *Middle Eastern Mythology*. Baltimore, MD: Penguin, 1963.

Lebrun, R. "From Hittite Mythology: the Kumarbi Cycle," in Sasson (1995), vol. 3, pp. 1971–1980.

López-Ruiz, C. *When the Gods Were Born: Greek Cosmogonies and the Near East*. Cambridge, MA: Harvard University Press, 2010. A comparative study focusing on Hesiod and Orphic texts and Ugaritic, Phoenician, and Hebrew parallels.

McCall, H. *Mesopotamian Myths*. Austin, TX: University of Texas Press, 1991.

Mitchell, Stephen. *Gilgamesh: A New English Version*. New York: Simon & Schuster, 2006. A very readable version by a noted translator, which restores the text with understanding to produce a complete and comprehensible poem.

Moran, W. "The Gilgamesh Epic: A Masterpiece from Ancient Mesopotamia," in *Sasson* (1995), vol. 4, pp. 2327–2336.

Penglase, C. *Greek Myths and Mesopotamia: Parallels and Influence in the Homeric Hymns and Hesiod*. New York: Routledge, 1994.

Pritchard, J. B., ed. *The Ancient Near East*. 2 vols. Princeton, NJ: Princeton University Press, 1958 and 1975. A selection of texts, mostly from Pritchard (1969).

———**, ed.** *Ancient Near Eastern Texts Relating to the Old Testament*. 3d ed. Princeton, NJ: Princeton University Press, 1969. The standard collection of texts in translation and by far the most comprehensive.

Sasson, J. M., ed. *Civilization of the Ancient Near East.* 4 vols. New York: Scribner, 1995. A comprehensive survey of all aspects of the ancient Near East: 189 essays by expert scholars. For students of myth those by Moran and West are especially useful.

West, M. L. "Ancient Near Eastern Myths in Classical Greek Religious Thought," in Sasson (1995), vol. 1, pp. 33–42.

———. *The East Face of Helicon: West Asiatic Elements in Greek Poetry and Myth.* New York: Oxford University Press, 1999. Detailed identification of the links between Hesiod, the Homeric epics, the lyric poets, and Aeschylus and the Near East and possible avenues of transmission.

———. *Hesiod: Theogony, Works and Days.* New York: Oxford University Press, 1988. Valuable introduction by the preeminent scholar on Hesiod.

Primary Sources

Sources in the Chapter

Aeschylus	*Prometheus Bound* (selections)
Hesiod	*Theogony* (selections)
	Works and Days (selections)
Ovid	*Metamorphoses* (selections)

Additional Sources

Aristophanes	*Birds* 1495–1552: Prometheus hides from Zeus using an umbrella.
Herodotus	*History of the Persian Wars* 2.50.1–2.57.3: Names of gods; practices and oracles.
Lucian	*Prometheus* (Loeb vol. 2)
Plato	*Protagoras* 320c–322d: Prometheus and Epimetheus, and the early development of society.

Notes

1. This very stone was exhibited at Delphi in ancient times; it was not large, and oil was poured over it every day. On festival days, unspun wool was placed upon it.
2. Ten years is the traditional length for a serious war, be it this one or the famous conflict of the Greeks against the Trojans.
3. Notus is the South Wind; Boreas, the North Wind; and Zephyr, the West Wind.
4. Aidos is a sense of modesty and shame; Nemesis, righteous indignation against evil.
5. In his fourth *Eclogue*, Vergil celebrates gloriously the return of a new golden age ushered in by the birth of a child. The identity of this child has long been in dispute, but the poem itself was labeled Messianic because of the sublime and solemn nature of its tone, reminiscent of the prophet Isaiah.
6. A similar but more scientific statement of human development, made by some of the Greek philosophers and by Lucretius, the Roman poet of Epicureanism, provides a penetrating account of human evolution that in many of its details is astoundingly modern (*De rerum natura* 5.783–1457).
7. Aeschylus has Themis as the mother of Prometheus, sometimes identified as Ge-Themis, to show that she is a goddess of earth, who possesses oracular power and is associated with justice. The name Prometheus means "forethinker," or "the one who plans ahead"; Epimetheus means "afterthinker," or "the one who plans too late." Prometheus is often called merely "the Titan," since he is the son of the Titan Iapetus.
8. An early name of Sicyon.
9. The name suggests a link with the typical conception of the fertility mother-goddess.
10. He was worshiped by the potters in Athens alongside Hephaestus, with whom he has several attributes in common.

11. For a comparison of Eve with Pandora and female deities throughout the ages, see John A. Phillips, *Eve: The History of an Idea* (New York: Harper & Row, 1984).

12. See Dora and Erwin Panofsky, *Pandora's Box: The Changing Aspects of a Mythical Symbol*, 3d ed. (Princeton, NJ: Princeton University Press, 1991), pp. 14–56.

13. Aeschylus even manages to characterize the brutish Kratos, the unreasonable and monstrous henchman of a tyrannical Zeus. Kratos is the willing and anxious supporter of a new regime rooted in force, the one thing he can understand; to him forceful power is the key to all: "Everything is hard except to rule the gods. For no one except Zeus is free."

14. Any interpretation of Aeschylus' tragedy is difficult since precise details in the outcome as conceived by Aeschylus are unknown. We have the titles and fragments of three additional plays on the Prometheus legend attributed to Aeschylus: *Prometheus the Fire-Bearer*, *Prometheus Unbound*, and *Prometheus the Fire-Kindler*. This last may be merely another title for *Prometheus the Fire-Bearer*, or possibly it was a satyr play belonging either to the Prometheus trilogy itself or to another trilogy on a different theme. We cannot even be sure of the position of the extant *Prometheus Bound* in the sequence.

15. Io is the daughter of Inachus, whose family appears in the legends of Argos; see pp. 539–540.

16. Versions other than that of Aeschylus have Zeus attempt to deceive Hera by transforming Io into a cow, which Hera asked to have for herself.

17. The Egyptians identified Epaphus with Apis, the sacred bull, and Io with their goddess Isis. See p. 539.

18. Chiron possibly dies for Prometheus and bestows his immortality upon Heracles.

19. This is Ovid's version of a tale about a werewolf that appears elsewhere in the Greek and Roman tradition. The name Lycaon was taken to be derived from the Greek word for wolf. The story may reflect primitive rites in honor of Lycaean Zeus performed on Mt. Lycaeus.

20. *The Flood Myth*, edited by Alan Dundes (Berkeley, CA: University of California Press, 1988), provides a fascinating collection of writings by authors in a variety of disciplines who analyze the motif of the flood throughout the world. For parallels in Near Eastern mythology, see the appendix to this chapter.

21. That is, nymphs of the Corycian cave on Mt. Parnassus.

22. Hellen had three sons: Dorus, Aeolus, and Xuthus. Xuthus in turn had two sons: Ion and Achaeus. Thus, eponyms were provided for the four major divisions of the Greeks on the basis of dialect and geography: Dorians, Aeolians, Ionians, and Achaeans. The names *Greeks* and *Greece* came through the Romans, who first met a group of Hellenes called the *Graioi*, participants in the colonization of Cumae just north of Naples.

23. W. Burkert, "Oriental and Greek Mythology: The Meeting of Parallels," in Jan Bremmer, ed., *Interpretations of Greek Mythology* (New York: Routledge, 1988), pp. 10–40 (the quotation is from p. 10). Useful but brief remarks in Ken Dowden, *The Uses of Greek Mythology* (London: Routledge, 1992), pp. 57–60 and 181. Full discussion with bibliography by R. Mondi, "Greek Mythic Thought in the Light of the Near East," in L. Edmunds, ed., *Approaches to Greek Myth* (Baltimore, MD: Johns Hopkins University Press, 1990), pp. 142–198. C. Penglase, *Greek Myths and Mesopotamia* (London: Routledge, 1994), focuses on Hesiod and the *Homeric Hymns* and defines the criteria for influence (as opposed to random similarities) on pp. 5–8.

24. Translated by Stephanie Dalley, from *Myths from Mesopotamia* (New York: Oxford University Press, 1989), p. 253.

25. Tablet xii was composed much later than the rest of the Gilgamesh epic and so was not part of the original poem. The death of Gilgamesh is not part of the Akkadian version of the epic, which is the source of the translation by Stephanie Dalley, but there exists a fragmentary Sumerian version. Gilgamesh's monstrous opponents were Humbaba (or Huwawa), guardian of the Pine Forest in the mountains of southwest Iran (tablet v), and the Bull of Heaven (tablet vi).

26. Maureen Gallery Kovacs provides clear introductory background for the nonspecialist in her translation, *The Epic of Gilgamesh* (Stanford, CA: Stanford University Press, 1989).

27. See Dalley, from *Myths from Mesopotamia*, p. 50.

28. The texts of myths of Kumarbi and Ullikummis are translated by A. Goetze in J. B. Pritchard, ed., *Ancient Near Eastern Texts Relating to the Old Testament*, 3d ed. (Princeton, NJ: Princeton University Press, 1969, previous eds. 1950 and 1955), pp. 120–125. They are not included in Pritchard's selections in paperback, *The Ancient Near East*, 2 vols. (Princeton, NJ: Princeton University Press, 1958 and 1975).

29. Both versions are in Pritchard, *Ancient Near Eastern Texts*, pp. 52–57 (Sumerian version translated by S. N. Kramer) and pp. 106–109 (Akkadian version translated by E. A. Speiser). Stephanie Dalley, see note 24, translates the Akkadian version, pp. 154–162.

30. See Dalley, from *Myths from Mesopotamia*, p. 154.

31. The debts of the Greeks to others have always been recognized and over the years have offered fruitful avenues of research. At times, however, there has been a compulsion to deny the Greeks the credit that is their due for the heritage they have left us. The book by Martin Bernal challenging traditional positions caused quite a stir when it first appeared: *Black Athena: The Afroasiatic Roots of Classical Civilization*, Vol. 1, *The Fabrication of Ancient Greece 1785–1985* (London: Free Association Books; New Brunswick, NJ: Transaction Books, 1987). It has been successfully challenged by many scholars. See in particular a collection of essays edited by Mary R. Lefkowitz and Guy MacLean Rogers, *Black Athena Revisited* (Chapel Hill, NC: University of North Carolina Press, 1996). Mary Lefkowitz offers a refutation accessible to the nonspecialist: *Not out of Africa: How Afrocentrism Became an Excuse to Teach Myth as History* (New York: Basic Books [HarperCollins]), 1996.

THE TWELVE OLYMPIANS: ZEUS, HERA, AND THEIR CHILDREN

First, then, we should define what kind of friendship we are looking for. For there is, some think, a friendship towards God and towards inanimate things, but they are wrong. We believe that friendship exists where there is a reciprocity of friendly affection, but friendship towards God does not admit of such reciprocity, not even of a one-sided friendship on our part. For it would be absurd if someone were to say that he had a friendly love towards Zeus.

—**ARISTOTLE**, *Magna Moralia* 1208 b25–30

THUS ZEUS IS ESTABLISHED as lord of gods and men. He is supreme, but he does share his powers with his brothers. Zeus himself assumes the sky as his special sphere; Poseidon, the sea; and Hades, the Underworld. Homer (*Iliad* 15.187–192) says that they cast lots for their realms. Zeus takes his sister Hera as his wife; she reigns by his side as his queen and subordinate. His sisters Hestia and Demeter share in divine power and functions, as we shall see, and the other major gods and goddesses are also given significant prerogatives and authority as they are born.

And so a circle of major deities (fourteen in number) comes into being; their Greek and Roman names are as follows: Zeus (Jupiter), Hera (Juno), Poseidon (Neptune), Hades (Pluto), Hestia (Vesta), Hephaestus (Vulcan), Ares (Mars), Apollo, Artemis (Diana), Demeter (Ceres), Aphrodite (Venus), Athena (Minerva), Hermes (Mercury), and Dionysus (Bacchus).[1] This list was reduced to a canon of twelve Olympians by omitting Hades (whose specific realm is under the earth) and replacing Hestia with Dionysus, a great deity who comes relatively late to Olympus.

Hestia, Goddess of the Hearth and Its Fire

Although her mythology is meager, Hestia is important. She rejected the advances of both Poseidon and Apollo and vowed to remain a virgin; like Athena and Artemis, then, she is a goddess of chastity.[2] But she is primarily the goddess of the hearth and its sacred fire; her name, Hestia, is the Greek word for "hearth." Among primitive peoples fire was obtained with difficulty, kept alive, and revered for its basic importance in daily needs and religious ceremony. The hearth, too, was the center first of the family and then of the larger political units: the tribe, the city, and the state. Transmission of the sacred fire from one settlement to another represented a continuing bond of affection and kinship. Thus, both the domestic and the communal hearth were designated as holy, and the goddess herself presided over them. Hestia often gained precedence at banquets and in sacrificial ritual, for as the first born of Cronus and Rhea she was considered august, one of the older generation of the gods.

There are two *Homeric Hymns to Hestia.* Number 24 briefly calls on her as the personification of the protecting flame of the sacred hearth in a temple:

> Hestia, you who tend the hallowed house of the far-shooter Apollo in holy Pytho, liquid oil always drips from your hair.[3] Come to this house; enter in sympathetic support, along with Zeus, the wise counselor. Grant as well a pleasing grace to my song.

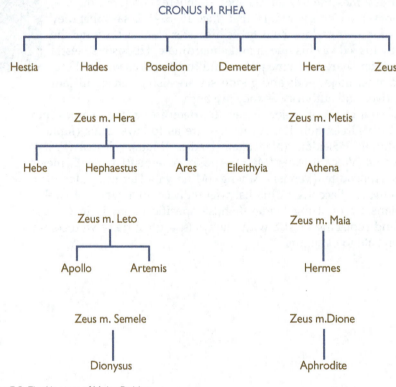

Figure 5.1 The Lineage of Major Deities

In number 29, Hestia is invoked as the protectress of the hearth in the home; the poet appeals to the god Hermes as well, since both deities protect the house and bring good fortune.

> Hestia, you have as your due an everlasting place in the lofty homes of immortal gods and human beings who walk on earth—the highest of honors and a precious right. For without you, there are no banquets for mortals where one does not offer honey-sweet wine as a libation to Hestia, first and last.
>
> And you, Hermes, the slayer of Argus, son of Zeus and Maia, messenger of the blessed gods, bearer of a golden staff and giver of good things, along with revered and beloved Hestia, be kind and help me. Come and inhabit beautiful homes, in loving harmony. For since you both know the splendid achievements of mortals on earth, follow in attendance with intelligence and beauty.   10
>
> Hail, daughter of Cronus, you and Hermes, bearer of a golden staff; yet I shall remember you both and another song too.

The Diverse Character of Zeus

Zeus is a passionately amorous god; he mates with countless goddesses and mortal women, and his offspring are legion. Most genealogies demanded the glory and authority of the supreme god himself as their ultimate progenitor. Along with this necessity emerged the character of a Zeus conceived and readily developed by what might be called a popular mythology. This Zeus belonged to a monogamous society in which the male was dominant; however moral the basic outlook, the standards for the man were different from those for the woman. Illicit affairs were possible and even, if not officially sanctioned, at least condoned for men, but under no circumstances tolerated for women. Thus Zeus is the glorified image not only of the husband and father, but also of the lover. The gamut of Zeus' conquests will provide a recurrent theme.

As the picture evolves, Zeus' behavior may be depicted as amoral or immoral or merely a joke—the supreme god can stand above conventional standards. At other times he will act in harmony with them, and more than once he must face the shrewish harangues of his wife, Hera, and pay at least indirectly through pain and suffering wrought by his promiscuity.

Yet this same Zeus (as we shall see later in his worship at Dodona and Olympia) becomes the one god, and his concerns envelop the whole sphere of morality for both gods and humankind. He is the wrathful god of justice and virtue, upholding all that is sacred and holy in the moral order of the universe. This Zeus we discuss at greater length in Chapter 6. In the literature, the portrayal of Zeus depends on both the period and the intent and purpose of individual authors. The conception of deity is multifaceted, infinitely varied, and wondrously complex.

We are already familiar with Zeus the god of the sky, the cloud-gatherer of epic. The etymological root of his name means "bright" (as does that of Jupiter). His attributes are thunder and lightning, and he is often depicted about to hurl them. The king of gods and men is a regal figure represented as a mature man in his prime, usually bearded. He bears as well the aegis, a word meaning "goatskin" that originally designated merely the cloak of a shepherd. For Zeus it is a shield with wonderful and miraculous protective powers.[4] The majestic eagle and mighty oak were sacred to Zeus.

Finally, it must be fully appreciated that the patriarchy of Zeus was by no means always absolute or supreme. Here are a few examples of his vulnerability. According to some, Zeus' authority was not supreme but always subject to the dictates of fate or the feminine fates (see the final section of this chapter), and the powerful goddess of love, Aphrodite, proclaims in the *Homeric Hymn to Aphrodite* (5) (p. 198) that she is the greatest deity of all, for she can bend not only humans but also even the gods (including almighty Zeus) to her amorous will. Only three goddesses, Athena, Artemis, and Hestia, defy her subjection. Demeter, the greatest matriarch of antiquity with her dominant and universal Eleusinian mysteries (see Chapter 14), refused to submit to the patriarchy of both Zeus and Hades in her grief and outrage over the rape of her daughter Persephone and won. A startling revolution against the power of Zeus is alluded to in the *Iliad* (1.399–401): When Hera, Poseidon, and Athena bound Zeus in chains, it was Thetis, the mother of Achilles, who rescued the supreme god. The most determined critic who constantly challenged the authority of Zeus was his sister and wife Hera.

Zeus and Hera

The union of Zeus and Hera represents yet another enactment of the sacred marriage between the sky-god and earth-goddess; this is made clear in the lines from Homer (*Iliad* 14.346–351) that describe their lovemaking:

> The son of Cronus clasped his wife in his arms and under them the divine earth sprouted forth new grass, dewy clover, crocuses, and hyacinths, thick and soft, to protect them from the ground beneath. On this they lay together and drew around themselves a beautiful golden cloud from which the glistening drops fell away.

Hera has little mythology of her own, being important mainly as Zeus' consort and queen; yet she has great power. The *Homeric Hymn to Hera* (12) makes this power very clear:

> I sing about golden-throned Hera, whom Rhea bore, immortal queen, outstanding in beauty, sister and wife of loud-thundering Zeus; she is the illustrious one whom all the blessed ones throughout high Olympus hold in awe and honor, just as they do Zeus who delights in his lightning and thunder.

Hera consistently appears as the vehement wife and mother who will punish and avenge the sexual escapades of her husband; she consistently acts with a severity befitting her stature as mother, wife, and queen, the fierce champion of morality and marriage.[5] Iris, the fleet-footed and winged goddess of the rainbow (see p. 167), at times a messenger of the gods, often is depicted as the particular servant of Hera. When Iris serves in this capacity, then Hermes performs his role as the messenger of Zeus alone. In art, Hera is depicted as regal and matronly, often with attributes of royalty, such as a crown and a scepter. Homer describes her as ox-eyed and white-armed, both epithets presumably denoting her beauty. If we mistranslate "ox-eyed" as "doe-eyed," perhaps the complimentary nature

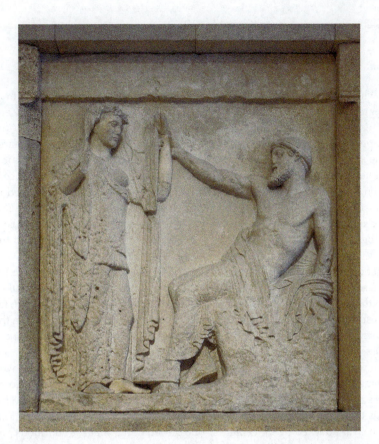

Zeus and Hera, limestone and marble metope from Temple E at Selinus, ca. 470 B.C. Selinus, on the southwestern coast of Sicily, contained many temples, eight of which have been identified, each given an alphabetical letter. Temple E was restored during the twentieth century. It is one of a group of three Doric temples, the exterior decoration of which included metopes. This one portrays the *hieros gamos* of Zeus and Hera. Zeus sits on Mt. Ida and draws Hera toward himself. Hera, whose arms and feet are made of white marble, stands facing Zeus with her veil drawn back to signify her status as his wife. She wears archaic clothing, and her dignified stance contrasts with the relaxed attitude of her husband. (© *Vanni Archive/ Art Resource, NY*)

of that adjective becomes clear. The peacock is associated with Hera; this association is explained by her role in the story of Io (told in Chapter 4). Argos was a special center for her worship, and a great temple was erected there in her honor. Hera was worshiped less as an earth-goddess than as a goddess of women, marriage, and childbirth, functions she shares with other goddesses.

The Sanctuary of Zeus at Olympia

Olympia is a sanctuary beside the river Alpheus, in the territory of the Peloponnesian city of Elis. By the time of the reorganization of the Olympic Games in 776,[6] Zeus had become the principal god of the sanctuary, and his son Heracles was said to have founded the original Olympic Games, one of the principal athletic festivals in the ancient world.[7] An earlier cult of the hero Pelops and his wife, Hippodamia (see p. 431), continued, nevertheless, along with the worship of Zeus and Hera, whose temples were the principal buildings of the sanctuary at the peak of its greatness.

The temple of Hera was older, while the temple of Zeus was built in the fifth century with a monumental statue of Zeus placed inside.[8] The statue and the sculptures on the temple itself together formed a program in which religion, mythology, and local pride were articulated on a scale paralleled only by the sculptures of the Parthenon at Athens.

Centaurs and Lapiths

Ixion, the sinner who was eventually punished by being bound to a wheel in the realm of Hades, had impregnated the Cloud (the Greek word is *Nephele*), a deception placed by Zeus in the likeness of his wife, Hera (see p. 372).

This cloud (Nephele) gave birth to the monster **Centaurus**, which mated with the mares that grazed the slopes of Mt. Pelion and became the father of the Centaurs, creatures with a human head and torso and the legs and body of a horse. The most famous centaur was Chiron, who differs from the others in that he was wise and gentle, skilled in medicine and music. He taught Achilles, Jason, and Asclepius. Pindar calls him the son of Cronus and the nymph Philyra. The other centaurs are generally portrayed as violent beings, and their best-known legend is that of their fight with the Thessalian tribe of the Lapiths.

The Lapith chieftain Pirithoüs was the son of Ixion, and the centaurs were invited to his wedding. At the feast they got drunk and attempted to carry off the bride, Hippodamia, and the other Lapith women. The violent scene was frequently represented in Greek art, for example, in the west pediment of the temple of Zeus at Olympia described earlier and in the metopes of the Parthenon at Athens. The battle is described at length in the twelfth book of Ovid's *Metamorphoses*.

Another Lapith was **Caeneus**. Born a girl, **Caenis**, she was seduced by Poseidon, who then granted her anything she wanted. She asked to be turned into a man and to become invulnerable. As a man, Caeneus set up his spear and ordered people to worship it. This impiety led Zeus to bring about his death. During the battle at the wedding of Pirithoüs and Hippodamia he was attacked by the centaurs, who buried him under the enormous pile of tree trunks they hurled at him. Either his body was driven down into the Underworld by their weight or else a yellow-winged bird emerged from the pile, which the seer Mopsus announced to be Caeneus transformed.

A Centaur and Centauress. These two sculptures come from the Roman villa of Oplontis, southeast of Naples, which was ruined in the eruption of Vesuvius in A.D. 79. They were half of a group of four that made up a fountain. The Centaur carries a boar upside down on his left shoulder; a thin pipe brings water to the fountain through the boar's mouth. His club, ferocious look, and the dead animal are in keeping with the traditional violence of Centaurs (height 35.6 in.). The Centauress is shown as a musician; in her left hand was a lyre (of which part of the tortoise-shaped soundbox is visible) and in her right a *plectrum* with which to pluck the strings of the lyre. Her breasts are naked and over her shoulders is a goatskin (height 36.4 in.). (*Leisure and Luxury in the Age of Nero*)

On the west pediment was displayed the battle of the Greeks and the centaurs at the wedding of a son of Zeus, the Lapith king **Pirithoüs**, a myth that also appears in the metopes of the Parthenon. The central figure in the pediment is another son of Zeus, Apollo, imposing order on the scene of violence and chaos (illustrated on p. 265).

The east pediment shows the scene before the fateful chariot race between **Pelops** and **Hippodamia** and her father Oenomaüs. Zeus himself is the central figure, guaranteeing the success of Pelops in the coming race and the winning of Hippodamia as his wife.

The Twelve Labors of Heracles were carved in the metopes of the Doric frieze (each about 1.6 meters in height), six above the entrance porch to the inner chamber (cella, or naos) at the east end of the temple and six above the corresponding "false" porch on the west end. The climax of the labors, above the east porch, was the local myth of the cleansing of the stables of Augeas, king of Elis (see p. 551). In this labor (and in three others) Athena is shown helping the hero, and in the labors of the Nemean Lion and Cerberus, Hermes is the helper.

The most complex union of myth and religion was in the statue of Zeus, carved by the Athenian sculptor **Pheidias** and the most admired of all ancient statues. It was huge (about 42 feet in height), and its surfaces were made of precious materials, gold (for the clothing and ornaments) and ivory (for the flesh). It inspired awe in those who saw it. Although nothing remains of the statue today, we can reconstruct its appearance.[9] Zeus was seated on his throne, carrying a figure of Nike (Victory) in his right hand and in his left hand a scepter, on which perched his eagle. On the feet of the throne were depicted the myths of the Theban Sphinx and the killing of the children of Niobe by Apollo and Artemis. Also part of the structure of the throne was a representation of Heracles fighting the Amazons, and Heracles appeared again in the paintings on a screen that enclosed the underpart of the throne, performing two of his labors (the Apples of the Hesperides and the Nemean Lion), as well as freeing Prometheus. In the carved reliefs on the base of the throne, the Olympian gods accompanied the miraculous birth of Aphrodite from the sea. In front of the statue was a reflecting pool of olive oil.

Thus, in the temple and its statue, at the heart of the greatest of Panhellenic sanctuaries, myths of human and divine struggle and victory, of destruction and creation, combined to honor Zeus as the supreme god of civilization.[10]

Hera. Roman copy of a Greek original from the second half of the 5th century B.C., perhaps by Alcamenes. Known as the Barberini Hera, the goddess carries a royal scepter and holds a patera (a shallow libation vessel) in her left hand. She wears a crown and a closely clinging chiton, which reveals her body underneath and is falling from her left side. The right arm, nose, and pieces of drapery are restorations. (*Scala/Art Resource, NY/© Artres*)

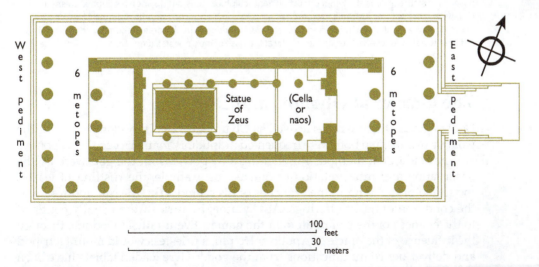

Figure 5.2 Plan of the Temple of Zeus at Olympia (after W. B. Dinsmoor)

Jupiter and Thetis, by J.-A.-D. Ingres (1780–1867); oil on canvas, 1811, 136 × 101 in. In this huge painting, Jupiter is enthroned among the clouds with his attributes, the scepter and the eagle. Thetis kneels and touches Jupiter's chin in a gesture of supplication. To the left, Juno (Hera) appears, though only partially, in a fairly relaxed pose, resting her head on her arms. This work in neoclassical style betrays two influences from antiquity: Homer and Pheidias' monumental, chryselephantine (gold and ivory) statue of Zeus at Olympia. In Book 1 of the *Iliad* Thetis approaches Zeus in the posture of a suppliant, grasping his knees and touching his chin, to request that Zeus aid her in restoring the honor of her son Achilles. The other influence, Pheidias' statue, has not survived, but Pausanias, the second-century A.D. travel writer, in his *Description of Greece* records in some detail the composition of the sculpture. Ingres has inverted the pose of the statue of Zeus at Olympia; in the ancient sculpture, Zeus, sitting upon his throne, grasps in his left hand the scepter with an eagle perched atop, and in his right he holds the figure of Nike (Victory). According to Pausanias, the throne and pedestal were covered with elaborate decoration that Ingres has reduced to a simple relief of the Gigantomachy at the base of the pedestal. (*Erich Lessing/Art Resource, NY*)

The Oracles at Olympia and Dodona

Dodona (in northern Greece) as well as Olympia was an important center for the worship of Zeus, and both were frequented in antiquity for their oracular responses.

The traditional methods for eliciting a response from the god were by the observation and interpretation of omens, for example, the rustling of leaves, the sound of the wind in the branches of his sacred oaks, the call of doves, and the condition of burnt offerings. At Olympia, inquiries were usually confined to the chances of the competitors in the games. Eventually at Dodona, through the influence of the oracle of Apollo at Delphi, a priestess would mount a tripod and deliver her communications from the god.[12] Here leaden tablets have been found inscribed with all kinds of questions posed by the state and the individual. The people of Corcyra ask Zeus to what god or hero they should pray or

Oracles and Prophets

The famous oracles of Zeus at Olympia and Dodona and that of Apollo at Delphi were not the only sources of prophecy in ancient Greece. Here are some others.

The oracle of **Trophonius** was situated at Lebadeia in northern Boeotia. Trophonius is a chthonic hero (his name means "he who fosters growth"), and he was therefore consulted in a subterranean setting with an awesome ritual. His legend is similar to the story of the Egyptian pharaoh Rhampsinitus (Rameses), which Herodotus tells (2.121). Trophonius and his brother Agamedes were skilled builders, sons of Erginus of Orchomenus. They built for King Augeas of Elis (or, as some say, the Boeotian king Hyrieus) a treasury with a movable stone, which they used to steal the king's treasure. In time, the king set a trap for the unknown thief, and Agamedes was caught. At his own suggestion, Agamedes' head was cut off by Trophonius, who then escaped carrying the head. He fled to Lebadeia, where he was swallowed up by the earth and thereafter worshiped as a god.[11] His death is similar to that of Amphiaraüs, one of the Seven against Thebes, whose story is told on p. 422.

Melampus was a seer with the power of understanding the speech of animals. He had honored a pair of snakes killed by his servants by burning their bodies and rearing their young, who later licked his ears and so enabled him to understand the tongues of animals and birds, and from them know what was going to happen. For the story of Melampus and his brother Bias, see p. 552.

The priest and seer Tiresias is a prominent figure in the Theban saga (see pp. 426–428). For the role of historical seers in Greek religion, see p. 155.

sacrifice for their common good; others ask if it is safe to join a federation; a man inquires if it is good for him to marry; another, whether he will have children from his wife. There are questions about purchases, health, and family.

Herodotus (2.55) visited Dodona and was told by three priestesses why the oracle of Zeus was founded; their story was confirmed as true by other servants of the temple. The priestesses' names were Promeneia, the eldest; Timarete, next in age; and Nicandra, the youngest. Two black doves flew from Thebes in Egypt; one came to Libya and the other to Dodona. The latter settled on an oak tree and spoke in human speech, saying that an oracle of Zeus must be established there. The people of Dodona understood that the message was divine and so obeyed the command. The dove that came to Libya ordered the Libyans to establish an oracle there, to the Egyptian god Ammon and also sacred to Zeus.

Children of Zeus and Hera: Eileithyia, Hebe, Hephaestus, and Ares

Eileithyia, Goddess of Childbirth

Zeus and Hera have four children: Eileithyia, Hebe, Hephaestus, and Ares. Eileithyia is a goddess of childbirth, a role she shares with her mother Hera; at times mother and daughter merge in identity. Artemis (as we shall see in Chapter 10) is another important goddess of childbirth.

Hebe and Ganymede, Cupbearers to the Gods

Hebe is the goddess of youthful bloom (the literal meaning of her name). She is a servant of the gods as well.[13] Hebe is primarily known as the cupbearer for the deities on Olympus. When Heracles wins immortality, she becomes his bride. Some versions explain that she resigned from her position to marry. Late authors claim that she was discharged for clumsiness.

The Trojan prince Ganymede shares honors with Hebe as cupbearer of the gods; according to some authors, he replaces her. The *Homeric Hymn to Aphrodite* (5.202–217), translated in its entirety in Chapter 9, tells how Zeus carried off Ganymede, the handsome son of Tros:

> Indeed, Zeus in his wisdom seized and carried off fair-haired Ganymede because of his beauty, so that he might be in the company of the gods and pour wine for them in the house of Zeus, a wonder to behold, esteemed by all the immortals, as he draws the red nectar from a golden bowl. But a lasting sorrow gripped the heart of Tros, for he had no idea where the divine whirlwind had taken his dear son. Indeed he mourned for him unceasingly each and every day; and Zeus took pity on the father and gave him, as recompense for his son, brisk-trotting horses, the kind which carry the gods. These he gave him to have as a gift. (202–212)

10

Interpretations of the Myth of Ganymede

This story indeed illustrates succinctly and powerfully the wide variation of interpretation and reinterpretation that all myths are capable of inspiring—a principal reason for their immortality. The *Homeric Hymn to Aphrodite* tells a simple and beautiful story of how wise Zeus singled out handsome Ganymede to grace Olympus as cupbearer and live there forever, immortal, like a god. Its ecstatic spirituality emerges with sublimity in the poem "Ganymede" by Goethe (especially in its musical settings by Schubert and Wolf). The incident is seen from the point of view of a devoted Ganymede. In a passionate yet spiritual aura, amid the glowing sun, beloved spring, and burning love, Ganymede ecstatically cries to the descending clouds to carry him aloft: "In your lap, upwards, embracing, embraced. Upwards to your breast, loving father." For a different artist, the homosexuality latent in the myth may offer amoral or nonmoral testimony to the fact of a physical relationship, and not a religious calling. Another may tell the story to prove a divine vindication of male relationships. Yet another may vehemently identify the myth as a horrifying Rape of Ganymede by Zeus—accusing God of this brutal sin, an idea inconceivable to the poet and philosopher Xenophanes (see p. 138). The tale may even become (as in the case of the Greek writer Lucian, *Dialogues of the Gods* 4 [10 in the Loeb edition]) a divinely amusing, urbane, satiric jest. So is this a myth about a religious experience, a summoning by God to heaven, a rape, or is it merely a joke? It depends on how the story is told and how it is interpreted; many are the possible variations. There is, of course, no single "correct" interpretation of a great myth. Myth is protean by nature, most gratifying because it forever changes through the personality and genius of each and every artist, in any medium at any time, to provide pleasure and enlightenment in our search for our own individual meaning and enrichment in the work of art.

The myth of Zeus and Ganymede is similar to the story of how Poseidon fell in love with Pelops and brought him up to Olympus (see p. 432).

Zeus and Ganymede. Red-figure kylix, by the Penthesilea painter, ca. 460–440 B.C.; 14.6 in. in diameter. On this vase, the myth of the abduction of Ganymede by Zeus is interpreted in the light of contemporary Athenian sexual mores. Zeus, the mature bearded male, has taken on the role of the active "lover" (*erastes*) and Ganymede that of the passive "beloved" (*eromenos*). With his stylized thunderbolt put by, Zeus, having dropped his scepter, which Ganymede is intently trying to pick up, takes advantage of the young man's momentary distraction to grab hold of the boy's right arm. Ganymede holds a cockerel in his left hand, a typical gift of courtship from an older lover. The kylix is a shallow drinking cup typically used for wine, and so inevitably also at all-male symposia or drinking parties, where such "conquests" might be celebrated, although this vase and its theme need not be linked to any specific occasion. The narrative of the vase highlights the beginning of the "courtship," the moment that Eros has struck the older male but not the younger. In a particularly playful rendering, the artist has made Zeus use the contours of the vase for leverage, as he is about to begin their ascent to the heights of Olympus. (*Scala/Art Resource, NY*)

> And at the command of Zeus, Hermes, the guide and slayer of Argus, told everything and how Ganymede would be immortal and never grow old, just like the gods. When Tros heard this message from Zeus, he no longer continued his mourning but rejoiced within his heart and joyfully was borne by the horses that were as swift as a storm. (212–217)

In some accounts an eagle, not a whirlwind, carries Ganymede away. For some, this myth represents the spiritual calling of a young man by god; others attribute homosexual desire to a bisexual Zeus, thus having the supreme god mirror yet another human trait.[14]

Hephaestus, the Divine Artisan

Hephaestus, the next child of Zeus and Hera to be considered, is a god of creative fire and a divine smith. His divine workshop is often placed in heaven or on Olympus. All that this immortal craftsman produces excites wonder; his major role in mythology is to create things of extraordinary beauty and utility, often elaborately wrought. One of his masterpieces, the shield of Achilles, is described in exquisite detail by Homer (*Iliad* 18.468–617). Hephaestus even has attendants fashioned of gold that look like living young women; these robots can move with intelligence and speak with knowledge. He is indeed the master artisan. Sometimes his forge is under the earth; and as he labors covered with soot and sweat, he may be attended by the three Cyclopes, whom we already know as the ones who create the thunder and lightning of Zeus.[15]

The Return of Hephaestus. Attic red-figure skyphos, by the Kleophon painter, ca. 430-420 B.C.; 11 13/16 × 18 13/16. This unusually large *skyphos* (drinking cup) depicts the return of Hephaestus to Olympus to reconcile with his mother Hera. Hephaestus (left), riding on a mule, is being led back by Dionysus (center) to Hera (right), seated (on the magical chair?). Hephaestus carries tongs and hammer, implements of his craft; Dionysus holds a *kantharos* (a more elaborate drinking cup) and *thyrsos* (staff topped with a pine cone) attended by a young satyr with an *aulos* (double flute); Hera sits with a servant in attendance and holding a fan. (*Image courtesy of Museum of Art, Toledo, Ohio*)

Hephaestus is also a god of fire in general, including destructive fire. When the Scamander (both a river and its god) is about to engulf the hero Achilles during an episode in the Trojan War (*Iliad* 21.324–382), Hera calls upon Hephaestus to raise up his fire and direct it against the raging river, which soon is overcome by the flames.[16]

Hephaestus and the goddess Athena were often linked together as benefactors of wisdom in the arts and crafts and champions of progress and civilization. Their joint worship was particularly significant in Athens. In the *Homeric Hymn to Hephaestus* (20), they are invoked together as archetypal, divine culture figures like Prometheus.

Sing, clear-voiced Muse, about Hephaestus, renowned for his intelligence, who, with bright-eyed Athena, taught splendid arts to human beings on earth. Previously they used to live in mountain caves, like animals, but now, because of Hephaestus, renowned for his skill, they have learned his crafts and live year round with ease and comfort in their own houses.

Be kind, Hephaestus, and give me both excellence and prosperity.

The god Hephaestus was lame from birth. One version of his birth informs us that Hera claimed that Hephaestus was her son alone without Zeus; thus, Hera has her own favorite child, born from herself, just as Zeus has his special daughter, Athena, who was born from his head. In this version too, Hera was ashamed of his deformity and cast him down from Olympus or heaven.[17] Hephaestus refused to listen to any of the other gods, who urged that he return home, except for Dionysus, in whom he had the greatest trust. Dionysus made him drunk and brought him back to Olympus triumphantly. On vases this scene is variously depicted with a tipsy Hephaestus on foot or astride a donkey, led by Dionysus alone or with his retinue.

We are also told that Hephaestus was hurled to earth (presumably on another occasion?), this time by Zeus. Hephaestus landed on the island of Lemnos, was rescued, and eventually returned home. Lemnos in classical times was an important center of his worship. Other volcanic regions (e.g., Sicily and its environs) were also associated with this divine smith; these places bore testimony to the fire and smoke that at times would erupt from his forge.

At the close of Book 1 of the *Iliad*, Hephaestus himself recounts the episode of Zeus' anger against him. We excerpt this passage because it illustrates many things: the character of Hephaestus; his closeness to his mother, Hera; the tone and atmosphere instigated by an episode in the life of the Olympian family; Zeus as the stern father in his house and his difficult relations with his wife; and the uneasy emotions of the children while they witness the quarrel of their parents.

The sea-goddess Thetis has come to Zeus on Olympus to ask that he grant victory to the Trojans until the Achaean Greeks honor her son Achilles and give him recompense for the insult that he has suffered. As Thetis clasps the knees of

Zeus and touches his chin in the traditional posture of a suppliant, Zeus agrees to her wishes with these words (*Iliad* 1.518–611):

"A bad business indeed if you set me at variance with Hera and she reviles me with reproaches. She always abuses me, even as it is, in the presence of the immortal gods and says that I help the Trojans in battle. But you now must withdraw, lest Hera notice anything. These things you have asked for will be my concern until I accomplish them. Come now, I shall nod my assent to you so that you may be convinced. For this from me is the greatest pledge among the immortals; for no promise of mine is revocable or false or unfulfilled to which I give assent with the nod of my head." He spoke and the son of Cronus with his dark brows nodded to her wishes; and the ambrosial locks flowed round the immortal head of the lord and he made great Olympus tremble.[18] (518–530)

After the two had made their plans, they parted; then she leaped into the deep sea from shining Olympus and Zeus returned to his own house. All the gods rose together from their places in the presence of their father and no one dared to remain seated as he entered but all stood before him. Thereupon he sat down on his throne. But Hera did not fail to observe that silver-footed Thetis, daughter of the old man of the sea, had taken counsel with him. Immediately she addressed Zeus, the son of Cronus, with cutting remarks: "Which one of the gods this time has taken counsel with you, crafty rogue? Always it is dear to you to think secret thoughts and to make decisions apart from me and never yet have you dared say a word openly to me about what you are thinking." (531–543)

Then the father of men and gods answered her: "Hera, do not hope to know all that I say; it would be difficult for you even though you are my wife. But whatever is fitting that you should hear, then not anyone either of gods nor of mortals will know it before you. But do not pry or ask questions about each and every thing to which I wish to give thought apart from the gods." (544–550)

And then ox-eyed Hera in her majesty replied: "Most dread son of Cronus, what kind of answer is this you have given? I have not pried too much or asked questions before but completely on your own you plan whatever you wish. Yet now I am terribly afraid in my heart that silver-footed Thetis, daughter of the old man of the sea, has won you over; for early this morning she sat by your side and grasped your knees and I believe that you nodded your oath that you would honor Achilles and destroy many by the ships of the Achaeans." (551–559)

The cloud-gatherer Zeus spoke to her in answer: "You always believe something and I never escape you; nevertheless you will be able to accomplish nothing, but you will be farther removed from my heart; and this will be all the more chill an experience for you. If what you say is so, its fulfillment is what I desire. But sit down in silence, and obey what I say; for now all the gods in Olympus will be of no avail when I come closer and lay my invincible hands upon you." Thus he spoke and ox-eyed lady Hera was afraid, and she sat down in silence wrenching her heart to obedience, and the gods of heaven were troubled in the house of Zeus. (560–570)

But Hephaestus renowned for his art began to make a speech to them showing his concern for his dear mother, Hera of the white arms. "This will be a sorry business indeed and not to be endured any longer, if you two quarrel on account of mortals and bring wrangling among the gods. There will be no further pleasure in

The Forge of Vulcan, by Diego Velázquez (1599–1660); oil on canvas, 1630; 88 in. × 114 in. Velázquez has painted the moment when Helius tells Hephaestus that his wife, Aphrodite, is making love to Ares (Homer, *Odyssey* 8.270–271). At the appearance of Helius in the forge, Hephaestus and his four assistants stop their work on a suit of armor (perhaps for Ares himself), stunned by the news. Helius, whose white flesh, blue-thonged sandals, and orange robe contrast with the burly torsos of the black-smiths, is both sun-god and Apollo, god of poetry (as his laurel wreath indicates). The rays from his head illuminate the dark forge, while the exquisite white jug on the mantelpiece provides another focus of light on the opposite side of the painting. Velázquez catches the intersection of divine omniscience and the blacksmith's toil without diminishing the wit and pathos of Homer's tale. The great anvil in the left foreground, we know, waits for Hephaestus to forge on it the inescapable metal net that will trap the lovers. (*Scala/Art Resource, NY*)

the excellent feast when baser instincts prevail. I advise my mother, even though she is prudent, to act kindly toward my dear father Zeus so that he will not be abusive again and disturb our banquet. Just suppose he, the Olympian hurler of lightning, wishes to blast us from our seats. For he is by far the strongest. But you touch him with gentle words; immediately then the Olympian will be kindly toward us." (571–583)   50

Thus he spoke and springing up he placed a cup with two handles in the hand of his mother and spoke to her: "Bear up, mother dear, and endure, although you are hurt, so that I may not see you struck before my eyes, and then even though you are dear and I am distressed I shall not be able to help. For the Olympian is hard to oppose. Previously on another occasion when I was eager to defend you, he grabbed me by the feet and hurled me from the divine threshold. And I fell the whole day and landed on Lemnos when the sun was setting, and little life was left in me. There Sintian men took care of me at once after my fall." (584–594)   60

Thus he spoke. And the goddess Hera of the white arms smiled and as she smiled she received the cup from his hand. He drew sweet nectar from a mixing bowl and poured it like wine for all the other gods from left to right. Then unquenchable laughter rose up among the blessed gods as they saw Hephaestus bustling about the house. (595–600)

> In this way then the whole day until the sun went down they feasted, nor was anyone's desire for his share of the banquet found wanting nor of the exquisite lyre that Apollo held nor of the Muses, who sang in harmony with beautiful voice. But when the bright light of the sun set they went to bed each to his own home which the renowned lame god Hephaestus had built by his skill and knowledge. Olympian Zeus, the hurler of lightning, went to his own bed where he always lay down until sweet sleep would come to him. There he went and took his rest and beside him was Hera of the golden throne. (601–611)
>
> 70

Hephaestus, Aphrodite, and Ares

Hephaestus is a figure of amusement as he hobbles around acting as the cupbearer to the gods in the previous scene, on Olympus; but he is a deadly serious figure in his art and in his love. His wife is Aphrodite,[19] and theirs is a strange and tempestuous marriage: the union of beauty and deformity, the intellectual and the sensual. Aphrodite is unfaithful to her husband and turns to the virile Ares, handsome and whole, brutal and strong. Homer, with deceptive simplicity, lays bare the psychological implications in a tale about the eternal triangle that remains forever fresh in its humanity and insights.

In Book 8 (266–366) of the *Odyssey*, the bard Demodocus sings of the love affair between Ares and Aphrodite and the suffering of Hephaestus:

> He took up the lyre and began to sing beautifully of the love of Ares and Aphrodite with the fair crown: how first they lay together by stealth in the home of Hephaestus. He gave her many gifts and defiled the marriage bed of lord Hephaestus. But soon Helius, the Sun, came to him as a messenger, for he saw them in the embrace of love, and Hephaestus when he heard the painful tale went straight to his forge planning evil in his heart. He put his great anvil on its stand and hammered out chains that could not be broken or loosened so that they would hold fast on the spot. (266–275)
>
> When he had fashioned this cunning device in his rage against Ares, he went directly to his chamber where the bed was and spread the many shackles all around the bedposts and hung them suspended from the rafters, like a fine spider's web that no one could see, not even the blessed gods, for they were very cunningly made. When he had arranged the whole device all about the bed, he pretended to journey to the well-built citadel of Lemnos, which of all lands was by far the most dear to him. (276–284)
>
> 10
>
> But Ares of the golden reins was not blind in his watch, and as he saw Hephaestus leave he went straight to the house of the craftsman renowned for his art, eager for love with Cytherea of the fair crown. She was sitting, having just come from her mighty father, the son of Cronus, when Ares came into the house; he took her hand and spoke out exclaiming: "My love, come let us go to bed and take our pleasure, for Hephaestus is no longer at home but he has gone now, probably to visit Lemnos and the Sintian inhabitants with their barbarous speech." Thus he spoke and to her the invitation seemed most gratifying; they both went and lay down on the bed. And the bonds fashioned by ingenious Hephaestus poured around them, and they

were not able to raise or move a limb. Then to be sure they knew that there was no longer any escape. (285–299)   20

The renowned lame god came from close by; he had turned back before he had reached the land of Lemnos, for Helius watched from his lookout and told him the story. Hephaestus made for his home, grieving in his heart, and he stood in the doorway and wild rage seized him; he cried out in a loud and terrible voice to all the gods: "Father Zeus and you other blessed gods who live forever, come here so that you may see something that is laughable and cruel: how Aphrodite the daughter of Zeus always holds me in contempt since I am lame and loves the butcher Ares because he is handsome and sound of limb, but I was born a cripple. I am not to blame for this nor is anyone else except both my parents who I wish had never begotten me. You will see how these two went into my bed where they lay down together in love. As I look at them I am overcome by anguish. I do not think that they will still want to lie here in this way for even a brief time, although they are so very much in love, and very quickly they will no longer wish to sleep side by side, for my cunning and my bonds will hold them fast until her father pays back all the gifts that I gave to him for this hussy because she was his daughter and beautiful, but she is wanton in her passion." (300–320)   30   40

Thus he spoke and the gods assembled at his house with the floor of bronze. Poseidon the earthshaker came and Hermes the helpful runner, and lord Apollo the far-shooter. But the goddesses in their modesty stayed at home one and all. The blessed gods, dispensers of good things, stood at the door and unquenchable laughter rose up among them as they saw the skill of ingenious Hephaestus. And one would speak to another who was next to him as follows: "Bad deeds do not prosper; the slow overtakes the swift, since now Hephaestus who is slow and lame has caught by his skill Ares, even though he is the swiftest of the gods who inhabit Olympus. Therefore he must pay the penalty for being caught in adultery." This was the sort of thing that they said to one another. (321–333)   50

And lord Apollo, son of Zeus, spoke to Hermes: "Hermes, son of Zeus, runner and bestower of blessings, would you wish to lie in bed by the side of golden Aphrodite, even though pressed in by mighty shackles?" Then the swift runner Hermes answered: "I only wish it were so, lord Apollo, far-shooter. Let there be three times the number of shackles and you gods looking on and all the goddesses, I still would lie by the side of golden Aphrodite." (334–342)

Thus he spoke and a laugh rose up among the immortal gods. But Poseidon did not laugh; he relentlessly begged Hephaestus, the renowned smith, to release Ares and addressed him with winged words: "Release him. I promise you that he will pay all that is fitting in the presence of the immortal gods, as you demand." Then the renowned lame god answered: "Do not demand this of me, Poseidon, earthshaker; pledges made on behalf of worthless characters are worthless to have and to keep. How could I hold you fast in the presence of the immortal gods, if Ares gets away and escapes both his debt and his chains?" Then Poseidon the earthshaker answered: "Hephaestus, if Ares avoids his debt and escapes and flees, I myself will pay up." Then the renowned lame god replied: "I cannot and I must not deny your request." (343–358)   60

Thus speaking, Hephaestus in his might released the chains. And when they both were freed from the strong bonds, they immediately darted away, the one

Ares. Roman copy of a Greek original (possibly by Skopas) of ca. 340 B.C.; marble, height 61½ in. Known as the *Ludovisi Mars*, this copy (made perhaps in the late second century A.D.) shows Mars, unarmed but holding his sword, with the scabbard-handle turned toward the viewer and with his left foot resting on his helmet. His shield is upright (the inside face turned outward). Is the god simply at rest, or has he been subdued by love, as the cupid (added by the copyist) implies? (*Scala/Art Resource, NY*)

> went to Thrace and the other, laughter-loving Aphrodite, came to Paphos in Cyprus where are her sanctuary and altar fragrant with sacrifices. There the Graces bathed her and anointed her with divine oil, the kind that is used by the immortal gods, and they clothed her in lovely garments, a wonder to behold. (359–366)

70

A funny, yet painful story, glib in its sophisticated and ironic portrayal of the gods, but permeated with a deep and unshakable moral judgment and conviction. The Greeks particularly enjoyed the fact that the lame Hephaestus, by his intelligence and craft, outwits the nimble and powerful Ares.

Ares, God of War

Ares himself, the god of war, is the last child of Zeus and Hera to be considered. His origins probably belong to Thrace, an area with which he is often linked. Aphrodite is usually named as his cult partner; several children are attributed to them, the most important being Eros. Dawn (Eos) was one of his mistresses, and we have already mentioned (in Chapter 3) Aphrodite's jealousy.

In character, Ares is generally depicted as a kind of divine swashbuckler. He is not highly thought of, and at times he appears as little more than a butcher. The more profound moral and theological aspects of war were taken over by other deities, especially Zeus or Athena. Zeus' response to Ares after he has been wounded by Diomedes (Ares sometimes gets the worst of things, even in battle) is typical of the Greek attitude toward him (*Iliad* 5.889–891, 895–898).

> Do not sit beside me and complain, you two-faced rogue. Of all the gods who dwell on Olympus you are the most hateful to me, for strife and wars and battles are always dear to you. … Still I shall not endure any longer that you be in pain, for you are of my blood and your mother bore you to me. But if you were born of some other of the gods, since you are so destructive you would have long since been thrown out of Olympus.

The Greeks felt strongly about the brutality, waste, and folly of war, all of which are personified and deified in the figure of Ares. Yet they inevitably developed an appreciation (if that is the right word) of the harsh realities that Ares could impose and the various aspects of warfare that he might represent. After all, throughout much of their history the Greeks (like us) were plagued by war; and in the pages of the great historian Thucydides we see most clearly of all that despicable war is the harshest of teachers. The Greeks *did* worship Ares, Athena, and Zeus as divine champions in righteous conflict.

The *Homeric Hymn to Ares* (8), a relatively late composition with its astrological reference to the planet Ares (Mars), invokes with more compassion a god of greater complexity who is to provide an intelligent and controlled courage.[20]

> Ares—superior in force, chariot-rider, golden-helmeted, shield-bearer, stalwart in battle, savior of cities, bronze-armored, strong-fisted, unwearyingly relentless, mighty with the spear, defense of Olympus, father of the war-champion Nike [Victory], ally of Themis [Right], tyrant against the rebellious, champion for the righteous, sceptered king of manhood—as you whirl your fiery red sphere among the planets in their seven courses through the air, where your blazing steeds keep you

The Contest between the Muses and the Sirens. Marble sarcophagus, third quarter of the third century A.D.; width 77¼ in.; height 21¾ in. This sarcophagus, dating from the Late Imperial period, depicts a story that perhaps developed sometime during the Hellenistic period. The travel writer Pausanias (second century A.D.) briefly alludes to the tale in his *Description of Greece* (9.34.3), when he describes an image of Hera carrying Sirens. According to Pausanias' account, Hera prevailed on the Sirens to compete with the Muses in song. The Muses won and plucked out the Sirens' feathers and wore them as a memorial of their victory. Here we see the nine Muses, each with a different emblem of her craft and sporting a prominent feather-crown, outdoing six Sirens. Overseeing the competition, on the left, are Athena, Zeus, and Hera. The Muses, the daughters of Mnemosyne (Memory) and Zeus, though here opponents of the Sirens, have much in common with them: both are female beings and gifted singers of song. The Muses live on Olympus and the Sirens, in Homer originally only two in number, dwell on an island in the sea where their song enchants sailors and brings about their death. The Sirens from an early period became associated with death and thus are an appropriate motif for funerary art. Though Homer is not explicit about their appearance, in art and the later literary tradition they are hybrid creatures: heads (and bodies) of women with the feet of birds. (*Metropolitan Museum of Art. Rogers Fund, 1910*)

forever above the third orbit,[21] hear me, helper of mortals, giver of vigorous youth; from above shed upon my life a martial ferocity, so that I may be able to drive off bitter cowardice from my person, and then again a radiant gentleness so that I may be able to bend to my will the treacherous impulse of my spirit to rush to the attack and check the keen fury of my passion which drives me to engage in the chilling din of battle. (1–15)

  You, blessed one, give me the strength to keep within the harmless constraints of peace and flee from the strife of enemies and violence of fateful death. (15–17)

10

Other Children of Zeus: The Muses and the Fates

The Nine Muses, Daughters of Zeus and Memory (Mnemosyne)

We shall conclude this chapter with two of Zeus' many affairs because of the universal significance of the offspring. He mates with the Titaness Mnemosyne (Memory), and she gives birth to the Muses, the patronesses of literature and the arts; thus allegorically Memory with divine help produces inspiration. The home of the Muses is often located in Pieria in northern Thessaly near Mt. Olympus,[22] or about the fountain Hippocrene on Mt. Helicon in Boeotia. The Muses (their name means "the reminders") may originally have been water spirits with the power of prophecy and then inspiration, imagined from the babbling of waters as they flow. They are supreme in their fields, and those who dare to challenge them meet with defeat and punishment. In this respect they resemble Apollo, with whom they are often associated. The number of the Muses is not consistent, but later authors usually identify nine of them, each with a specific function, although assignments will vary. Calliope presides over epic poetry; Clio, history (or lyre playing); Euterpe, lyric poetry (or tragedy and flute playing); Melpomene, tragedy (or lyre playing); Terpsichore, choral dancing (or flute playing); Erato, love poetry (or hymns to the gods and lyre playing); Polyhymnia, sacred music (or dancing); Urania, astronomy; and Thalia, comedy.

In the *Homeric Hymn to the Muses and Apollo* (25), the great deity Apollo is invoked along with them because as god of music, poetry, and the arts he is often their associate.

> With the Muses, let me begin, and with Apollo and Zeus. For through the Muses and far-shooting Apollo, human beings on earth are poets and musicians; but through Zeus, they are kings. Blessed are the ones whom the Muses love; sweet is the sound that flows from their lips. (1–5)
>
> Hail, children of Zeus, and give honor to my song; yet I shall remember you and another song too. (6–7)

The Three Fates, Daughters of Zeus and Themis

Zeus is sometimes said to be the father of the Fates (Greek, *Moirai*; *Parcae* for the Romans) as a result of his union with Themis. Night and Erebus are also said to be their parents. The Fates were originally birth spirits who often came to be depicted as three old women responsible for the destiny of every individual. Clotho (Spinner) spins out the thread of life, which carries with it the fate of each human being from the moment of birth; Lachesis (Apportioner) measures the thread; and Atropos (Inflexible), sometimes characterized as the smallest and most terrible, cuts it off and brings life to an end. On occasion, they can be influenced to alter the fate decreed by their labors, but usually the course of the destiny that they spin is irrevocable.

Fate is often thought of in the singular (Greek, *Moira*), in a conception that is much more abstract and more closely linked to a profound realization of the roles played by Luck or Fortune (Tyche) and Necessity (Ananke) in the scheme of human life. The relation of the gods to destiny is variously depicted and intriguing to analyze in the literature. According to some authors, Zeus is supreme and controls all, but others portray a universe in which even the great and powerful Zeus must bow to the inevitability of Fate's decrees. The depth of the Greeks' feeling for the working of *Moira* or the *Moirai* cannot be overemphasized. It provides a definite and unique tone and color to the bulk of their writing. One thinks immediately of Homer or Herodotus or the tragedians, but no major author was untouched by fascination with the interrelation of god, mortals, and fate and the tantalizing interplay of destiny and free will.[23]

In the brief *Homeric Hymn to the Supreme Son of Cronus* (23), Zeus is invoked as the intimate confidant of Themis; for Zeus and Themis were the parents not only of the Fates but also of the Hours (Horae)[24] and (appropriately for this hymn) of Good Order (Eunomia), Justice (Dike), and Peace (Eirene).

About Zeus, I will sing, the best and greatest of the gods, far-seeing ruler and accomplisher, who confides his words of wisdom to Themis, as she sits and leans close. Be kind, far-seeing son of Cronus, most glorious and most great.

Select Bibliography

Dowden, Ken. *Zeus.* Gods and Heroes of the Ancient World Series. New York: Routledge, 2005.

Gantz, Timothy. *Early Greek Myth: A Guide to Literary and Artistic Sources.* 2 vols. Baltimore, MD: Johns Hopkins University Press, 1996 [1993]. A summary for each myth, tracing its development in literature and art.

Larson, Jennifer. *Ancient Greek Cults.* New York: Routledge, 2007. This study of the deities and heroes and heroines is designed to emphasize a special aspect of the Greek gods.

Miller, Stephen G. *Ancient Greek Athletics.* New Haven, CT: Yale University Press, 2004. A comprehensive and well-illustrated survey of the festivals not only at Olympia but also at Delphi, Isthmia, and Nemea (where Miller himself excavated).

Raschke, Wendy L., ed. *The Archaeology of the Olympics: The Olympics and Other Festivals in Antiquity.* Madison: University of Wisconsin Press, 1988. An informative collection of essays.

Scanlon, Thomas Francis. *Eros and Greek Athletics.* New York: Oxford University Press, 2002.

Slater, Philip E. *The Glory of Hera: Greek Mythology and the Greek Family.* Princeton, NJ: Princeton University Press, 1992.

Stone, Tom. *Zeus: A Journey through Greece in the Footsteps of a God.* New York: Bloomsbury, 2008. An entertaining and unusual biography of Zeus, based on Stone's exploration of the major sites of Greece and their historical and mythological background.

Swaddling, Judith. *The Ancient Olympic Games.* 2d ed. Austin, TX: University of Texas Press, 2000.

Young, David. *A Brief History of the Olympic Games.* London: Blackwell, 2004. A succinct history of the Olympic Games and their modern resurgence.

Primary Sources

Sources in the Chapter

Homeric Hymn 5	*To Aphrodite* 202–217
Homeric Hymn 8	*To Ares*
Homeric Hymn 12	*To Hera*
Homeric Hymn 20	*To Hephaestus*
Homeric Hymn 23	*To the Supreme Son of Cronus*
Homeric Hymn 24	*To Hestia*
Homeric Hymn 25	*To the Muses and Apollo*
Homeric Hymn 29	*To Hestia*
Homer	*Iliad* 1.518–611; 5.889–891, 895–898
Homer	*Odyssey* 8.216–366

Additional Sources

Euripides	*Cyclops* 530–589: The Cyclops imagines Silenus is his Ganymede
Herodotus	*History of the Persian Wars* 2.54.1–2.57.3: Oracle at Dodona
Lucian	*Dialogues of the Gods* 4: "Zeus and Ganymede" (10 in Loeb edition)
Pausanias	*Description of Greece* 5.7.6–5.9.6: History of Olympia and the games

Notes

1. The Roman gods are discussed on pp. 654–671.
2. See the lines (21–32) about Hestia in the *Homeric Hymn to Aphrodite*, translated in Chapter 9, p. 198. Sometimes Hestia does not seem to be conceived fully as an anthropomorphic deity.
3. Pytho is Delphi, the site of Apollo's great temple; oil was used as an ointment for hair, and in religious rites it was poured over the heads of statues.
4. The warrior-goddess Athena will also carry the aegis, on which may be depicted the head of the Gorgon Medusa whom she helped Perseus slay. Athena's aegis may be her own or lent by Zeus to his favorite daughter.
5. Zeus and Hera find their archetypal counterparts in the Wotan and Fricka of Nordic mythology.
6. These games were celebrated every four years after 776; an important system of dating for the Greeks was by Olympiads.
7. Long before 776 B.C., the pre-Olympian deities Cronus and Gaia were worshiped at Olympia. For Heracles at Olympia, see pp. 551, 554–555.
8. The temple was completed in 456 B.C.; the statue, ca. 430 B.C.
9. It was described in detail by the traveler Pausanias (5.11) in the second century A.D.; the Roman Quintilian wrote, "its beauty added something even to the traditional religion."
10. See Bernard Ashmole, N. Yalouris, and Alison Franz, *Olympia: The Sculptures of the Temple of Zeus* (New York: Phaidon, 1967); John Boardman, *Greek Sculpture: The Classical Period* (London: Thames & Hudson, 1985), Chapter 4, "Olympia: The Temple of Zeus," pp. 33–50, includes diagrams, reconstructions, and photographs to illustrate the very brief discussion; Martin Robertson, *A Shorter History of Greek Art* (New York: Cambridge University Press, 1981) (pp. 79–89 for the sculptures of the temple of Zeus at Olympia), is by far the best discussion, distilled from the author's *A History of Greek Art*, 2 vols. (1975), pp. 271–291.
11. Pindar (frags. 2–3), however, has a different story of the brothers' death, one very similar to Herodotus' story of the Argives Cleobis and Biton (see p. 142). In this version, Trophonius and Agamedes built the temple of Apollo at Delphi. When they asked the god for their wages, he said he would pay them on the seventh day. On that day they fell asleep, never to wake. In the *Homeric Hymn to Apollo* the god himself lays the foundations of the temple.
12. Olympia was not as famous for its oracles as was the sanctuary of Apollo at Delphi, another famous Panhellenic festival (i.e., one to which "all Hellenes" came). Delphi was similar to Olympia and is described in Chapter 11 in some detail as representative of this facet of Hellenic worship and life (see pp. 248–250).
13. In the *Iliad* (5.905), Hebe bathes and clothes Ares after he has been healed of the wounds inflicted by the hero Diomedes.
14. For the theme of homosexuality, see Chapter 1, pp. 22–23.
15. Homer (*Iliad* 18) presents a splendid picture of his house on Olympus when Thetis appeals to Hephaestus to forge new armor for her son Achilles. Vergil (*Aeneid* 8) locates Vulcan's workshop in a cave on the island of Vulcania near Sicily. There he fashions magnificent armor for Aeneas, the son of Venus.
16. This scene is not unlike the finale of Act 3 of Richard Wagner's *Die Walküre*, in which Wotan conjures up Loge to surround his Valkyrie daughter Brünnhilde with a ring of magic fire.
17. For this version, see the *Homeric Hymn to Apollo* in the Additional Reading to Chapter 11.
18. Pheidias' majestic statue of the seated figure of Zeus in the temple at Olympia (described earlier) was supposedly inspired by these lines from Homer describing Zeus as he nods.

19. Sometimes Hephaestus' mate is one of the Graces, either the youngest, Aglaea, or Grace herself (Charis), which actually may be but another designation for Aphrodite.

20. This hymn probably belongs to Hellenistic times or even later; some, not very convincingly, associate it with the corpus of Orphic hymns. The richer connotations given to Ares' character and the emphasis on strength in peace as well as war look to Mars, the Roman counterpart of Ares; see p. 657.

21. Ares is in the third planetary zone, if you count from the one that is farthest from Earth.

22. The Muses are sometimes called the Pierides, but Ovid (*Metamorphoses* 5.205–678) tells a story of nine daughters of Pierus of Pella in Macedonia who were also called Pierides. They challenged the Muses to a musical contest, lost, and were changed into magpies, birds that imitate sounds and chatter incessantly.

23. The Romans developed this same tragic view of human existence. For them Fate is personified by the Parcae, or more abstractly conceived as Fatum (Fate).

24. The Horae, Hours, become the Seasons, goddesses who are two, three, or four in number and closely connected with vegetation. They attend the greater deities and provide attractive decoration in literature and art. Zeus and Themis as sky-god and earth-goddess, respectively, enact once again the ritual of the sacred marriage.

THE NATURE OF THE GODS AND GREEK RELIGION

This only is denied to God: the power to undo the past.

—ARISTOTLE,

Nicomachean Ethics 6.2.4 (quoting the playwright Agathon)

Anthropomorphism

By now the nature of the anthropomorphic conception of deity that evolved among the Greeks and the Romans should be evident. The gods are generally depicted as human in form and character; but although they look and act like humans, very often their appearance and their actions are to some extent idealized. Their beauty is beyond that of ordinary mortals, their passions are more grand and intense, their sentiments more praiseworthy and touching; and they can embody and impose the loftiest moral values in the universe. Yet these same gods can mirror the physical and spiritual weaknesses of human counterparts: they can be lame and deformed or vain, petty, and insincere; they can steal, lie, and cheat, sometimes with a finesse that is exquisitely divine.

The gods usually live in houses on Mt. Olympus or in heaven; a very important distinction, however, is to be made between those deities of the upper air and the upper world (the Olympians) and those of the realm below, appropriately named **chthonian** (i.e., of the earth). They eat and drink, but their food is **ambrosia** and their wine **nectar**. **Ichor** (a substance clearer than blood) flows in their veins. Just as they can feel the gamut of human emotion, so too they can suffer physical pain and torment. They are worshiped in shrines, temples, and sanctuaries; they are honored with statues, placated by sacrifices, and invoked by prayers.

In general, the gods are more versatile than mortals. They are able to move with amazing speed and dexterity, appear and disappear in a moment, and change their shape at will, assuming various forms—human, animal, and divine. Their powers also are far greater than those of mortals. Yet gods are seldom omnipotent, except possibly for Zeus himself, and even Zeus may be made subject to Fate or the Fates.

Their knowledge, too, is superhuman, if on occasion limited. Omniscience is most often reserved as a special prerogative of Zeus and Apollo, who communicate their knowledge of the future to mortals. Most important of all, the gods are immortal; in the last analysis, their immortality is the one divine characteristic that most consistently distinguishes them from mortals.

Very often one or more animals are associated with a particular deity. For Zeus, it is the eagle; for Hera, the peacock; for Poseidon, the horse; for Athena, the owl; for Aphrodite, the dove, sparrow, or goose; for Ares, the boar. In addition, a deity who desires to do so can take the form of an animal. There is no concrete evidence, however, to show that the Greeks at an early period ever worshiped animals as sacred.

The Divine Hierarchy

Many of the preceding remarks apply for the most part only to the highest order of divinity in the Greek pantheon. Such wondrous and terrible creations as the Gorgons or Harpies, who populate the universe to the enrichment of mythology and saga, obviously represent a different category of the supernatural. Of a different order, too, are the divine spirits who animate nature. These beings are usually depicted as nymphs—beautiful young girls who love to dance and sing and, in some cases, are extremely amorous. Very often nymphs act as attendants for one or more of the major gods or goddesses. The Muses are a kind of nymph, and so are the Nereids and Oceanids, although some of them assume virtually the stature of deity. More typically, nymphs are rather like fairies, extremely long-lived but not necessarily immortal.[1]

Demigods are another class of superhuman beings, or better, a superior kind of human being—that is, supermen and superwomen. They are the offspring of mixed parentage, the union of a god with a mortal, who may or may not be extraordinary.[2] Demigods are therefore limited in their powers, which are rather less than those of full-fledged gods; and they are mortals, often little more than figures made larger than life because of their tragic and epic environment.

Heroes sometimes are demigods, but the terminology is not easy to define precisely. Mortals like Oedipus and Amphiaraüs are not, strictly speaking, demigods, although they are far from ordinary beings. They may be called heroes, and certainly they become so after death, honored with a cult largely because of the spiritual intensity of their lives and the miraculous nature of their deaths. They thus become associated with chthonic powers of the earth and can exert these powers to bless or curse from beyond the grave. For this reason, where a hero dies becomes a sacred place of cultic ritual in his honor. Heracles, too, is a hero and a demigod, but he is an exception because he joins the company of the immortal gods on Olympus as a reward for his glorious attainments in this world. The difficulty in establishing absolute definitions is complicated further because of the use of the designation "hero" in the vocabulary of literary criticism. Achilles is a demigod, that is, the son of a mortal, Peleus, and the nymph-goddess Thetis. His powers are extraordinary, but it is ultimately as a mortal, the dramatic and epic hero of the *Iliad*, that he is to be judged.

It is apparent that a hierarchy of divinities existed in the Greek pantheon. The Olympians, along with the major deities of the lower world, represent as it were a powerful aristocracy. Although individual gods and goddesses may be especially honored in particular places (e.g., Athena in Athens, Hera in Argos, Hephaestus in Lemnos, Apollo in Delos and Delphi), in general the major divinities were universally recognized throughout the Greek world. At the top is Zeus himself, the king, the father of both gods and mortals, the supreme lord.

Polytheism for the Greeks, however, could also be quite expansive. It usually (though not always) could make room for new divinities without shock or strain. When they encountered foreign divinities, such as in Egypt or the Near East, the Greeks might recognize them as familiar deities and accept them into their pantheon or be willing to import a completely new god or goddess, if they so desired. This is not possible within a purely monotheist religion such as Judaism, Christianity, or Islam.

Zeus and Monotheism

We have already seen the popular anthropomorphic conception of Zeus as the father, husband, and lover; and we know too the primary sphere of his power: the sky and the upper air, with their thunder, lightning, and rain. Zeus also becomes the god who upholds the highest moral values in the order of the universe—values that he absorbs unto himself or that are divided among and shared by other deities. He is the god who protects the family, the clan, and the state, championing the universal moral and ethical responsibilities that these human associations entail. He protects suppliants, imposes ties of hospitality, upholds the sanctity of oaths; in a word, he is the defender of all that is right or just in the mores of advanced civilization.

Thus, within the polytheistic cast of Greek and Roman mythology and religion, a strong element of monotheism emerges from the very beginning. As it evolves, it may be linked closely to the standard depictions of an anthropomorphic Zeus or imagined in terms of more abstract philosophical and religious theories of a supreme power, as philosophical and religious thought becomes more sophisticated.

In Homer and Hesiod, Zeus is unquestionably the sovereign deity, and he is very much concerned with moral values. Yet his monotheism and patriarchy are severely tested by other divinities, especially goddesses. Hera's power is able to thwart Zeus' plans. Aphrodite can bend all the gods to her will, Zeus included, except for the three virgins, Hestia, Athena, and Artemis. Demeter, angry at the rape of her daughter Persephone, forces Zeus and the gods to come to her terms. And Zeus must yield to Fate or the Fates, although this need not always be the case.

At the same time, in the evolution of Zeus as the one supreme god, the almighty god of morality and justice, he could be referred to without a name and simply as god in an abstract, rather than specific, anthropomorphic conception. This greater sophistication in thought, which gave Zeus a more unquestionable, absolute, and spiritual authority, came about through the writings of religious poets and philosophers. Many selections from many authors could be quoted to bear testimony to the variety and complexity of Greek conceptions of the nature of the one god. A few examples must suffice.

Hesiod, who preaches a hard message of righteousness and warns of the terror of Zeus' punishment of the wicked, sounds very much like a severe prophet of the Old Testament. The opening section of his *Works and Days* includes the following lines (3–7):

> Through Zeus, who dwells in a most lofty home and thunders from on high and by his mighty will, mortals are both known and unknown, renowned and unrenowned; for easily he makes them strong and easily he brings them low; easily he makes the overweening humble and champions the obscure; easily he makes the crooked straight and strikes down the haughty.

Xenophanes, a poet and philosopher of the pre-Socratic period, was vehement in his attack on the conventional anthropomorphic depictions of the gods. He argued against the folly of conceiving deities as human beings and insisted that there is one supreme nonanthropomorphic god:

> Homer and Hesiod have ascribed to the gods all that is shameful and reproachful among mortals: stealing, adultery, and deception. [frag. 11]
>
> But mortals think that gods are born and have clothes and a voice and a body just like them. [frag. 14]
>
> The Ethiopians say that their gods are flat-nosed and black and the Thracians that theirs are fair and ruddy. [frag. 16]
>
> But if cattle and horses and lions had hands and could create with their hands and achieve works like those of human beings, horses would render their conceptions of the gods like horses, and cattle like cattle, and each would depict bodies for them just like their own. [frag. 15]
>
> One god, greatest among gods and mortals, not at all like them, either in body or in mind. [frag. 23]

10

The chorus of Aeschylus' *Agamemnon* (160–161) calls upon god by the name of Zeus with words that illustrate beautifully the universality of this supreme deity: "Zeus, whoever he may be, I call on him by this name, if it is pleasing to him to be thus invoked."

It is important to realize that monotheism and polytheism are not mutually exclusive and that human religious experience usually tends (as Xenophanes observes) to be anthropomorphic. It would be absurd to deny that Christianity in its very essence is monotheistic, but its monotheism, too, rests upon a hierarchical conception of the spiritual and physical universe, and its standard images are obviously cast in anthropomorphic molds: for example, there is one God in three divine persons, God the Father, the Son, and the Holy Spirit; there are angels, saints, devils, and so on. This does not mean that the Christian philosopher and layperson view the basic tenets of their religion in exactly the same way; ultimately, each vision of deity is personal, as abstract and sublime for one as it is human and compassionate for another. Among Christian sects alone there are significant variations in dogma and ritual; and of course, there are those who do not believe at all. The range from devout belief to agnosticism and atheism was as diverse and rich in the ancient world as it is in our world. The tendency in a brief survey such as this is to oversimplify and distort.

Greek Humanism

The anthropomorphism of the Greeks is almost invariably linked to their role as the first great humanists. Humanism (the Greek variety or, for that matter, any other kind) can mean many things to many people. Standard interpretations usually evoke a few sublime (though hackneyed) quotations from Greek literature. The fifth-century sophist Protagoras is said to have proclaimed: "Man is the measure of all things." Presumably, he is challenging absolute values by voicing new relativistic attitudes (i.e., mortals, not gods, are individual arbiters of the human condition). The Chorus in Sophocles' *Antigone* sings exultantly: "Wonders are many but none is more wonderful than man"; and Achilles' judgment of the afterlife in Homer's *Odyssey* quoted out of context (translated on p. 354) seems to affirm an unbridled optimism in the boundless hope and achievement possible in this life, as opposed to the dismal gloom and dull inertia of the hereafter. He cries out:

> I should prefer as a slave to serve another man, even if he had no property and little to live on, than to rule all those dead who have done with life.

With words such as these ringing in one's ears, it seems easy to postulate a Greek worship (even idolatry) of the human in a universe where mortals pay the gods the highest (but surely dubious) compliment of casting them in their own image.

Whatever truths this popular view may hold, it is far too one-dimensional and misleading to be genuinely meaningful and fair. In opposition to this myopic, uplifting faith in the potential of human endeavor to triumph against all divine odds, Greek literature and thought are shot through with a somber and awesome reverence for the supremacy of the gods and the inevitability of the Fates. A sense of predetermined destiny for each individual was analyzed in terms of the meaning and possibility of free will and independent action. There also developed a strong and realistic awareness of the miseries, uncertainties, and unpredictability of human life ordained by the gods. If we are lucky, our lives will be more blessed by happiness than doomed to misery. Still, the terrible vicissitudes of life lead to only one conclusion: It is better to be dead than alive. This tragic irony of man's dilemma as both an independent agent and a plaything of fate and the pain and suffering of human existence were pitted against the conviction that mortals may reach glorious and triumphant heights in the face of dreadful uncertainties and terrors. This idealistic optimism and this realistic pessimism, these two seemingly irreconcilable points of view, account for a unique humanism originated by the Greeks, with its emphasis on the beauty and wonder of mortal achievement, despite the horrible disasters that a vindictive god or fate may dispense at any moment.

Myth, Religion, and Philosophy

Another word of caution is in order about generalizations concerning Greek religious attitudes. It has been claimed that the Greeks had no Bible or strict dogma and (incredible as it may seem) no real sense of sin, or that they were innocently free and tolerant in their acceptance of new gods—What difference does one more make to a polytheist? One should not merely repeat stories (many of them from Ovid) and make pronouncements upon the spiritual adequacy or inadequacy of the theological convictions they are supposed to represent. Mythology, philosophy, and religion are inextricably entwined, and one must try to look at all the evidence. Homer offered to the Greeks (as Shakespeare offers to us) a literary bible of humanism that could on occasion be quoted like scripture; the mystery religions provided a dogma and ritual of a more exacting nature. Certainly, Hesiod pronounces his divine revelation with a vehement biblical authority.

Priests and priestesses devoted their lives to the service of the gods. The city-states upheld—by custom, tradition, and law—strict moral and ethical codes of behavior. If the stories of opposition to the new god Dionysus rest upon any stratum of historical truth, a foreign message of salvation was not always readily or easily accommodated, and one could be put to death (in Athens, of all places) on a charge of impiety. The Greeks thought profoundly about god, the immortality of the soul, and the meaning and consequences of vice and virtue. The Platonic myth of Er (translated in Chapter 15) is a terrifying vision of heaven and hell; as such, it is a religious document. Along with much other evidence, it shows that Greek philosophical thought can hold its own with that of any of the so-called higher religions.

The Legendary History of Herodotus

The historian Herodotus (fifth century B.C.) perhaps best represents Greek humanistic and religious attitudes in their clearest and most succinct form when he relates the story of Solon, Croesus, and Cyrus. Fortunately, episodes in this drama may be easily excerpted here, for they illustrate many things. Monotheism and polytheism are shown resting compatibly side by side. The jealous god of Solon is not unlike the wrathful deity of the Old Testament, a god who makes manifest to mortals that it is better to be dead than alive. The divine is able to communicate with mortals in a variety of ways; one can understand the simple and sincere belief in Apollo and Delphi possible in the sixth century B.C. There is a fascinating interplay between the inevitability of fate or destiny and the individuality of human character and free will.

Much that is Homeric has colored the Herodotean view, not least of all a compassion, tinged with a most profound sadness and pity, for the human condition. Homeric and dramatic, too, is the simple elucidation of the dangers of hubris and the irrevocable vengeance of Nemesis—the kernel, as it were, of a theme that dominates Greek tragedy. Herodotus, like most Greek writers, takes his philosophy from Homer. In the last book of the *Iliad* (see pp. 489–492), Priam, great king of Troy, comes alone as a humble suppliant to the Greek hero Achilles to beg for the body of his son Hector, whom Achilles has killed. In the course of their interview, Achilles, who has also suffered much, not least of all because of the death of his beloved Patroclus, divulges his conclusions about human existence:

> No human action is without chilling grief. For thus the gods have spun out for wretched mortals the fate of living in distress, while they live without care. Two jars sit on the doorsill of Zeus, filled with gifts that he bestows, one jar of evils, the other of blessing. When Zeus who delights in the thunder takes from both and mixes the bad with the good, a human being at one time encounters evil, at another good. But the one to whom Zeus gives only troubles from the jar of sorrows, this one he makes an object of abuse, to be driven by cruel misery over the divine earth.

For a translation of Bacchylides, see www.oup.com/us/morford.

The once mighty Priam will soon lose everything and meet a horrifying end, and Achilles himself is destined to die young. His fatalistic words about the uncertainty of human life are mirrored in the sympathetic humanism of Herodotus and echoed again and again by the Greek dramatists, who delight in the interplay of god and fate in human life and the tragic depiction of the mighty fall of those who were once great.

Herodotus' conception of a monotheistic god and his message of knowledge through suffering are strikingly Aeschylean. Herodotean themes *are* the very themes of Greek tragic literature: fate, god, and guilty and misguided mortals, who by their own actions try to avoid their destiny, only to further its fulfillment.

The story of the death of Atys is most Sophoclean in its movement and philosophy, and Croesus, like Oedipus, fulfills his inevitable destinies in terms of his character; each step that he takes in his blind attempts to avoid his fate brings him closer to its embrace. Most significantly, Croesus, again like Oedipus, can learn through sin and suffering to triumph against adversity and win reconciliation with god. There is not a single Greek tragedy that does not echo either implicitly or, in most cases, explicitly, the admonition of Solon, "Never count a person happy, until dead," with its twofold connotation: the happiness of human life cannot be judged until the entire span of that life has been lived, and death is to be preferred to the vicissitudes of life.

Jack Miles, a former Jesuit, provides a Pulitzer Prize–winning study of the anthropomorphic God of the *Tanakh* (the Hebrew Bible).[3] His literary portrait depicts God as a fictional character with many facets. To show that his contention is true, Miles retells the biblical story by presenting "the various personalities fused in the character of the Lord God" as separate characters. The result is a tale that reads very much like Greek and Roman mythology.

Croesus on the Pyre. Attic red-figure amphora by Myson, ca. 500 B.C.; height 23 in. Croesus sits enthroned, wreathed, and holding his scepter. In his right hand he pours a libation from a *phiale*. An attendant, dressed (like Croesus) as a Greek and not as a Persian, lights the pyre. This is the earliest known version, in art or literature, of the story, and its narrative is similar to that of the poet Bacchylides, whose poem was written in 468 B.C., about thirty years before Herodotus' narrative. In this version, Croesus voluntarily erects the pyre to burn himself and his family rather than submit to loss of freedom. This is consistent with his elaborate dress and throne, with the ritual libation to Zeus and Apollo, and with the non-Persian attendant. Like Herodotus' Croesus, he is saved by a rainstorm, but he is then rewarded for his piety toward Apollo by being transported, with his family, to the land of the Hyperboreans. This scene was painted about fifty years after the capture of Sardis in 546 B.C., a remarkable example of the transformation of a historical person into a mythical figure. For additional resources related to this chapter, go to www.oup.com/us/morford. (*Réunion des Musées Nationaux/Art Resource, NY*)

Yet there is no need to retell the story of the Old Testament polytheistically in order to reveal the essential similarity between the God of the Hebrews and the god of the Greeks. It is true that the *Tanakh* illustrates an absolute monotheism that appears more all-pervasive and relentless than that of the Greeks. Yet if we modify the major contention of Miles that for the Hebrews "all depends on a frighteningly unpredictable God" to read "all human happiness and misery depend on a frighteningly unpredictable God," we are describing exactly the god of Homer and Herodotus.

The Tragedy of Croesus

Herodotus presents in the context of his *History of the Persian Wars* a brilliant crystallization of the tragic yet uplifting nature of Greek humanism, which can only be truly understood through the emotional and intellectual experience afforded by great art. He molds the legend of Croesus into a complete and powerful drama, conceived and beautifully executed within the disciplined structure of the short story. Herodotus is neither professional theologian nor philosopher, yet by his molding of traditional tales he sums up the spiritual essence of an age of faith and shows how history, mythology, and religion are for him inextricably one. The story of Solon's meeting with Croesus is found in Book 1 of Herodotus (30.1–45.3):

THE MEETING BETWEEN SOLON AND CROESUS

And so Solon set out to see the world and came to the court of Amasis in Egypt and to Croesus at Sardis. And when he arrived, Croesus received him as a guest in his palace. Three or four days later at the bidding of Croesus, servants took Solon on a tour of his treasuries, pointing out that all of them were large and wealthy. When he had seen and examined them all to suit his convenience, Croesus asked the following question: "My Athenian guest, many stories about you have reached us because of your wisdom and your travels, of how you in your love of knowledge have journeyed to see many lands. And so now the desire has come over me to ask if by this time you have seen anyone who is the happiest." He asked this expecting that he was the happiest of human beings, but Solon did not flatter him at all but following the truth said: "O king, **Tellus the Athenian**." (30.1–30.3)   10

Croesus, amazed at this reply, asked sharply: "How do you judge Tellus to be the most happy?" And Solon said: "First of all he was from a city that was faring well and he had beautiful and good children and to all of them he saw children born and all survive, and secondly his life was prosperous, according to our standards, and the end of his life was most brilliant. When a battle was fought by the Athenians against their neighbors near Eleusis, he went to help and after routing the enemy died most gloriously, and the Athenians buried him at public expense there where he fell and honored him greatly." Thus Solon provoked Croesus as he listed the many good fortunes that befell Tellus, and he asked whom he had seen second to him, thinking   20 certainly that he would at least win second place. (30.4–31.1)

Solon said: "**Cleobis and Biton**. They were Argives by race, and their strength of body was as follows: both similarly carried off prizes at the festivals and as well this story is told. The Argives celebrated a festival to Hera, and it was absolutely necessary that the mother of these boys be brought by chariot to the temple.[4] But the oxen had not come back from the fields in time, and the youths, because it was growing late, yoked themselves to the chariot and conveyed their mother, and after a journey of 5 miles they arrived at the temple. When they had done this deed, witnessed by the whole congregation, the end of life that befell them was the very best. And thereby god showed clearly how it is better for a human being to be dead than alive.[5] For the Argive men crowded around and congratulated the youths for their strength and the women praised their mother for having such fine sons. And the mother was overjoyed at both the deed and the praise and standing in front of the statue prayed to the goddess to give to her sons, Cleobis and Biton, who had honored her greatly, the best thing for a human being to obtain. After this prayer, when they had sacrificed and feasted, the two young men went into the temple itself to sleep and never more woke up, but the end of death held them fast. The Argives had statues made of them and set them up in Delphi since they had been the best of men."[6] (31.1–32.1)   40 30

Thus Solon assigned the second prize of happiness to these two, and Croesus interrupted in anger: "My Athenian guest, is our happiness so dismissed as nothing that you do not even put us on a par with ordinary men?" And he answered: "O Croesus, you ask me about human affairs, who know that all deity is jealous and fond of causing troubles. For in the length of time there is much to see that one does not wish and much to experience. For I set the limit on life at seventy years; these seventy years comprise 25,200 days, if an intercalary month is not inserted. But if one wishes to lengthen every other year by a month, so that the seasons will occur when they should, the months intercalated in the seventy years will number thirty-five and these additional months will add 1,050 days. All the days of the seventy years will total 26,250; and no one of them will bring exactly the same events as another. (32.1–32.4)   50

"And so then, O Croesus, a human being is completely a thing of chance.[7] To me you appear to be wealthy and king of many subjects; but I cannot answer the question that you ask me until I know that you have completed the span of your life well. For the one who has great wealth is not at all more fortunate than the one who has only enough for his daily needs, unless fate attend him and, having everything that is fair, he also end his life well. For many very wealthy men are unfortunate and many with only moderate means of livelihood have good luck. Indeed, the one who is very wealthy but unfortunate surpasses the lucky man in two respects only, but the man of good luck surpasses the wealthy but unlucky man in many. The latter [wealthy but unlucky] is better able to fulfill his desires and to endure a great disaster that might befall him, but the other man [who is lucky] surpasses him in the following ways. Although he is not similarly able to cope with doom and desire, good fortune keeps these things from him, and he is unmaimed, free from disease, does not suffer evils, and has fine children and a fine appearance. If in addition to these things he still ends his life well, this is the one whom you seek who is worthy to be called happy. Before he dies do not yet call him happy, but only fortunate. (32.4–32.8)   60 70

"Now it is impossible that anyone, since he is a man, gather unto himself all these blessings, just as no country is self-sufficient providing of itself all its own needs, but possesses one thing and lacks another. Whichever has the most, this is the best. Thus too no one human person is self-sufficient, for he possesses one thing but lacks another. Whoever continues to have most and then ends his life blessedly, this one justly wins this name from me, O king. One must see how the end of everything turns out. For to be sure, god gives a glimpse of happiness to many and then casts them down headlong." Solon did not find favor with Croesus by his words. He was sent away as one of no account, since Croesus was very much of the opinion that a man must be ignorant who sets aside present goods and bids one look to the end of everything. (32.8–33)   80

ATYS, ADRASTUS, AND THE BOAR HUNT

After the departure of Solon, a great Nemesis from god took hold of Croesus, very likely because he considered himself to be the happiest of all men. Straightway a dream stood before him as he slept, which made clear to him the truth of the evils that were to come about in connection with his son. Croesus had two sons, one of whom was mute, the other by far the first in all respects among youths of his own age. His name was **Atys**. The dream indicated to Croesus that this Atys would die struck by the point of an iron weapon. When he woke up, he thought about the dream and was afraid; he got his son a wife and, although the boy was accustomed to command the Lydian forces, he no longer sent him out on any such mission; and javelins and spears and all such weapons that men use in war he had removed from the men's quarters and piled up in the women's chambers, for fear that any that were hanging might fall on his son. (34.1–35.1)   90

While they had on their hands arrangements for the marriage, there came to Sardis a man seized with misfortune, his hands polluted with blood, a Phrygian by race and of the royal family. This man came to the palace of Croesus, and according to the traditions of the country begged to obtain purification, and Croesus purified him. The ritual of cleansing is similar for the Lydians and the Hellenes.[8] When Croesus had performed the customary rites, he asked from where he came and who he was in the following words: "My fellow, who are you and from where in Phrygia have you come to my hearth? What man or woman have you killed?" And he answered: "O king, I am the son of Gordias, the son of Midas, and I am called **Adrastus**. I killed my brother unintentionally, and I come here driven out by my father and deprived of everything." (35.1–35.4)   100

Croesus answered him with these words: "You happen to be from a family of friends, and you have come to friends where you will want for nothing while you remain with us. It will be most beneficial to you to bear this misfortune as lightly as possible." So Adrastus lived in the palace of Croesus. (35.4–36.1)   110

At this very same time, a great monster of a boar appeared in Mysian Olympus, and he would rush down from this mountain and destroy the lands of the Mysians; often the Mysians went out against him but did him no harm and rather suffered from him. Finally, messengers of the Mysians came to Croesus and spoke as follows: "O king, the greatest monster of a boar has appeared in our country and destroys our lands. We are not able to capture him despite our great effort. Now then we beseech you to send your son to us and with him a picked company of young men and dogs so that we may drive him out of our land." (36.1–36.3)   120

They made this plea, but Croesus remembering the dream spoke the following words: "Do not mention my son further; for I will not send him to you; he is newly married and this now is his concern. I shall, however, send along a select group of Lydians and all my hunting equipment and hounds, and I shall order them as they go to be most zealous in helping you drive the beast from your land." (36.3–37.1)

This was his answer, and the Mysians were satisfied with it when the son of Croesus, who had heard their request, broke in on them. Croesus still refused to send his son along with them, and the young man spoke to him as follows:

"O father, previously the finest and most noble pursuits were mine—to win renown in war and in the hunt. But now you have barred me from both, although you have not seen any lack of spirit or cowardice in me. Now how must I appear in the eyes of others as I go to and from the agora? What sort of man will I seem to my fellow citizens, what sort to my new bride? What kind of husband will she think she has married? So either let me go to the hunt or explain and convince me that it is better for me that things be done as you wish." (37.1–37.3)   130

Croesus answered with these words: "My child, I do not do this because I have seen in you cowardice or any other ugly trait, but the vision of a dream stood over me in sleep and said that your life would be short; for you will die by means of the sharp point of an iron weapon. And so in answer to the vision I urged this marriage on you and do not send you away on the present enterprise, being on my guard if in any way I might be able to steal you from fate for my own lifetime. For you happen to be my one and only child; for the other boy is deaf and I do not count him as mine."[9] (38.1–39.1)   140

The young man answered: "O father, I forgive you for taking precautions for me since you have seen such a vision. But you do not understand; the meaning of the dream has escaped you and it is right for me to explain. You say that the dream said that I would die by the point of an iron weapon. But what sort of hands does a boar have? And what sort of iron point that you fear? For if it said that I would die by a tusk or tooth or some other appropriate attribute, you should do what you are doing. But as it is, the instrument is a weapon's point; and so then let me go since the fight is not against men." (39.1–40)   150

Croesus answered: "My child, you have won me over with your interpretation of the dream; and so since I have been won over by you I reverse my decision and let you go to the hunt." (40–41.1)

After these words, Croesus sent for the Phrygian Adrastus; when he arrived, he spoke as follows to him: "Adrastus, I did not reproach you when you were struck down by an ugly misfortune, I cleansed you, received you in my palace, and offered you every luxury. Now then since you owe me good services in exchange for those that I have done for you, I ask that you be a guardian of my boy while he hastens out to the hunt, in case some malicious robbers turn up on the journey to do you harm. Furthermore, you should go where you will become famous for your deeds, for it is your hereditary duty and you have the strength and prowess besides." (41.1–42.1)   160

Adrastus answered: "Ordinarily I would not go out to this kind of contest, for it is not fitting that one under such a misfortune as mine associate with companions who are faring well, nor do I have the desire and I should hold myself back for many reasons. But now, since you urge me and I must gratify you (for I owe you a return for your good services), I am ready to do this; expect that your boy, whom you order me to guard, will come back home to you unharmed because of his guardian." (42.1–43.1)   170

This was the nature of his answer to Croesus, and afterward they left equipped with a band of picked young men and dogs. When they came to the mountain Olympus, they hunted the wild beast, and after they had found him they stood in a circle round about and hurled their weapons. Then the stranger, the guest and friend who had been cleansed of murder, who was called Adrastus, hurled his javelin at the boar, but missed him, and hit the son of Croesus, who, struck by the point of the weapon, fulfilled the prediction of the dream; someone ran to Croesus, as a messenger of what had happened, and when he came to Sardis he told him of the battle and the fate of his child. (43.1–44.1)   180

Croesus was greatly distressed by the death of his son and was even more disturbed because the very one whom he himself had purified had killed him. Overcome by his misfortune, Croesus called terribly on Zeus the Purifier, invoking him to witness that he had suffered at the hands of the stranger and guest-friend; he called on him too as god of the hearth and as god of friendship, giving this same god these different names: god of the hearth because he did not realize that he received in his palace and nourished as a guest the murderer of his son, and god of friendship because he sent him along as a guardian and found him to be his greatest enemy. (44.1–45.1)   190

Afterward the Lydians arrived with the corpse and the murderer followed behind. He stood before the dead body and stretching forth his hands surrendered himself to Croesus; he bade Croesus slaughter him over the corpse, telling of his former misfortune and how in addition to it he had destroyed the one who had cleansed him, and life for him was not worth living. Croesus heard and took pity on Adrastus, although he was enmeshed in so great a personal evil, and he spoke to him: "I have complete justice from yourself, my guest and friend, since you condemn yourself to death. You are not the one responsible for this evil (except insofar as you did the deed unwillingly), but some one of the gods somewhere who warned me previously of the things that were going to be." (45.1–45.3)   200

Croesus now buried his son as was fitting; and Adrastus, the son of Gordias, the son of Midas, this murderer of his own brother and murderer of the one who purified him, when the people had gone and quietness settled around the grave, conscious that he was the most oppressed by misfortune of mankind, slaughtered himself on the tomb. (45.3)   210

Croesus' personal and domestic tragedy was compounded by his political downfall. Daily the power of **Cyrus the Great** and the Persians was growing; and as they extended their empire to the west, Croesus' own kingdom of Lydia eventually was absorbed. In this crisis, Croesus consulted various oracles and came to believe that the one of Apollo at Delphi alone could speak the truth. He sent magnificent offerings to Delphi and inquired of the oracle whether or not he should go to war with the Persians. The Delphic reply is perhaps the most famous oracle of all time, typically ironic in its simple ambiguity: if Croesus attacked the Persians, he would destroy a mighty empire. Croesus, of course, thought he would destroy the empire of the Persians; instead he brought an end to his own. Through Croesus' suffering, the wisdom of Solon was confirmed. Herodotus tells of the fall of **Sardis** (the capital of Lydia) and the fate of Croesus, its king, and his other son, "a fine boy except that he could not speak" (1.85.3–88.1):

THE DEFEAT OF CROESUS BY CYRUS THE GREAT

When the city was taken, one of the Persians made for Croesus to kill him, not knowing who he was; now Croesus saw the man coming, but he did not care, since in the present misfortune it made no difference to him if he were struck down and died. But the boy, this one who was mute, when he saw the Persian attacking, through fear of the terrible evil that was to happen broke into speech and cried: "Soldier, do not kill Croesus." This was the first time that he had uttered a sound, but afterward he could speak for the rest of his life. (85.3–85.4)

The Persians then held Sardis and took Croesus himself captive after he had ruled for fourteen years and been besieged for fourteen days, and as the oracle predicted, he brought to an end his own mighty empire. The Persians took Croesus and led him to Cyrus, who had a great pyre erected and ordered Croesus bound in fetters to mount it and along with him twice seven children of the Lydians. Cyrus intended either to offer them as the first fruits of the booty to some one of the gods, perhaps in a desire to fulfill a vow, or having learned that Croesus was a god-fearing man placed him on the pyre, wishing to see if any of the gods would save him from being burned alive. At any rate this is what Cyrus did, but to Croesus as he stood on the pyre came the realization (even though he was in such sore distress) that the words of Solon had been spoken under god's inspiration: "No one of the living is happy!" (86.1–86.3)   10 20

As this occurred to him, he sighed and groaned and broke the lengthy silence by calling out three times the name of Solon. When Cyrus heard this, he bade interpreters ask Croesus who this was whom he invoked, and they came up and asked the question. For a time Croesus did not answer, but eventually through compulsion he said: "The man I should like at all costs to converse with every tyrant." (86.3–86.4)

Since his words were unintelligible to them, they asked again and again what he meant; annoyed by their persistence, he told how Solon the Athenian first came to him, and after having beheld all his prosperity made light of it by the nature of his talk, and how everything turned out for him just as Solon had predicted, with words that had no more reference to Croesus himself than to all human beings and especially those who in their own estimation considered themselves to be happy. As Croesus talked, the fire was kindled and began to burn the outer edges of the pyre. (86.4–86.6)   30

When Cyrus heard from his interpreters what Croesus had said, he changed his mind, reflecting that he, too, was a human being who was surrendering another human being while still alive to the fire; besides he feared retribution, and realizing how nothing in human affairs is certain and secure, he ordered the burning fire to be quenched as quickly as possible and Croesus and those with him taken down from the pyre. And they made the attempt but were unable to master the flames. (86.6–87.1)   40

Then, according to the Lydian version of the story, when Croesus learned of Cyrus' change of heart as he saw all the men trying to put out the fire but no longer able to hold it in check, he shouted aloud calling on Apollo, if ever he had received from him any gift that was pleasing, to stand by him and save him from the present evil. In tears he called on the god, and suddenly out of the clear and calm atmosphere storm clouds rushed together, burst forth in violent torrents of rain, and quenched the fire. (87.1–87.2)

Thus Cyrus knew that Croesus was beloved by god and a good man. He brought him down from the pyre and asked: "Croesus, what man persuaded you to march against my land and become my enemy instead of my friend?" And he answered: "O king, these things I have done are to your good fortune but my own misfortune. The god of the Hellenes is responsible since he incited me to war. For no one is so senseless as to prefer war instead of peace. In time of peace sons bury their fathers, but in war fathers bury their sons. But it was somehow the pleasure of the gods that this be so." These were his words, and Cyrus released him and sat by his side and held him in great respect, and both he and all those around him looked on him with wonder. (87.2–88.1)   50

Thus Croesus became the wise and benevolent counselor of Cyrus. In the concluding pages of Herodotus' minisaga, Croesus sends to inquire of the priestess of Apollo why the oracle had misled him. "It is impossible even for god to escape destined fate," the priestess replies and then tells of the ways in which Apollo indeed tried to ameliorate Croesus' fated misfortune (91.1).

> Apollo saved him from burning. And it was not right that Croesus find fault with the oracle that he received. For Apollo warned that if he marched against Persia he would destroy a great empire. He should, if he were going to act wisely with respect to this reply, have sent again to ask whether his own empire or that of Cyrus was meant. If he did not understand the reply and he did not press the question, he should see himself as the one to blame. ... When he [Croesus] heard, he agreed that it was his own fault and not that of the god. (91.3–91.6)

The story of Croesus was also narrated in a poem by the lyric poet Bacchylides of Ceos, written in 468 B.C.. In this version, Croesus himself ordered the pyre to be lit, but Zeus extinguished the fire and Apollo took Croesus to live happily forever among the Hyperboreans as a reward for his piety.

Herodotus as Myth Historian

The Herodotean account gives us a glimpse into the fascinating world of legendary history. How can one possibly with complete confidence isolate the facts from the fiction in the epic context of Herodotus' literary art? The name of Croesus' son Atys means "the one under the influence of Ate" (a goddess of doom and destruction), and he has links, too, in cult and in story, with Attis and Adonis. Adrastus may be connected to the mythological concept of Nemesis or Adrasteia (Necessity), and the name Adrastus can be translated as "the one who cannot escape," that is, "the one who is doomed." Incidents in the tale recall those of the legendary Calydonian boar hunt. Is there anyone today who has enough faith in miracles to believe that Apollo saved Croesus from a fiery death?

Yet there *are* parts of the myth that perhaps may be true. Despite chronological problems, Solon could have met Croesus, although not at the time Herodotus imagines.[10] Croesus may have had a son who died young. But the mythographer and historian Herodotus could never be satisfied with this prosaic truth alone. His stories (wrought with exquisite art) must illustrate a different level of emotional and spiritual truth that illuminates character and elucidates philosophy. The life of Tellus the Athenian, the happiest of men, reveals the character and the values of those Greeks who fought and won in great battles like that of Marathon, defending their country against the Persian invaders in the first quarter of the fifth century B.C.; god will punish their king Xerxes for his sinful hubris, just as he did Croesus, Xerxes' prototype. Herodotus explains through his manipulation of traditional tales (military numbers, strategy, and "facts" will come later) why the Greeks defeated the Persians. These are truths, too, but of another order, and they are the essence of mythic art.

Greek Religion

Our description of the nature of the gods revealed in their mythology and its religious and philosophical ramifications leads inevitably to further consideration (necessarily brief) of the vast and complex subject of Greek religion. It is essential to devote some attention to the role that religion played in the lives of the ancient Greeks and the way that myth and religion converged to give meaning to their world and to establish their proper relationship with the divine. Greek religious observance developed over hundreds of years molded by many diverse influences: the survival of beliefs from their Indo-European forebears, the heritage of Minoan-Mycenaean ideas and practices, the legacy of Near Eastern contact.

Greek Mythology and Religion

Our understanding of the interrelation between Greek mythology and religion has evolved over a long period of time. Up to the end of the nineteenth century, it was assumed that Greek myths presented a largely untrammeled view of ancient religious thought, whether through literal or philosophical and allegorical interpretation. Indeed, similar interpretations can be traced back to antiquity itself. By the end of the nineteenth century, scholarly opinion came to recognize the inadequacy of this approach, and with the rise of modern archaeology, attention shifted to the role of religious ritual and practice as the most fruitful focus of inquiry for understanding ancient Greek religion. What the Greeks actually did in the performance of their worship began to overshadow the significance of the myths they told about their gods. The ability of myths to reveal anything about ancient Greek religious ideas came into serious question. By the beginning of the twenty-first century, the situation had shifted to a much less narrow and dogmatic position. This new appreciation for how Greek myth interacted with ancient Greek religious ideas and practice has become subtler, more complex, and much more sensitive to the interplay of cultural elements within society as a whole through the influence of anthropology and cross-cultural studies, which examine the relationship between myth and religion within societies, both ancient and modern, and through the development of sophisticated literary theories that offer more varied and perhaps more fruitful strategies for teasing out religious symbol and metaphor from literary texts. Jean-Pierre Vernant has eloquently written about this contemporary integration of myth, ritual, and artistic representation.

> *Apart from reverential awe and a diffused feeling of the divine, the Greek religion presents itself as a vast symbolic construction, complex and coherent, that allows room for thought, as well as feeling, on all levels and in all aspects, including the cult. Myth played its part in this system in the same way as ritual practices and representations of the divine. Indeed, myth, rite, and figurative portrayals were the three modes of expression—verbal, gestural, and iconic—by which the Greeks manifested their religious experience. Each constituted a specific language that, even in its association with the two others, responded to particular needs and functioned autonomously.*[11]

We may imagine such an integration of myth, ritual, and image if we consider the religious experience at the Panathenaic festival, celebrated annually to honor Athena Polias, guardian of the city of Athens (see pp. 175–176). The festival would include most of the populace of Athens in procession. The community would ceremonially move through the city toward the Acropolis. The participants would be organized in terms of the various groupings into which the polis was divided, all citizens having their own place, performing their

Other Legendary Folk Tales in Herodotus:
Gyges, Arion, and Polycrates

There are many other important and entertaining mythical legends, with folk tale motifs, in Herodotus' *History*. Although the choice is difficult, we single out three other examples.

Candaules, king of Lydia, continually boasted that his wife was the most beautiful woman in the world. He wanted to convince his favorite bodyguard, Gyges, that this claim was no exaggeration, and so he arranged that Gyges should see his wife naked, without her knowledge. She, however, became aware of the great insult (it is most shameful among the Lydians for even a man to be seen naked). In revenge, she plotted with Gyges, who was forced to kill Candaules and win the throne and the queen for himself (1.10–13).

Herodotus tells the story of the musician Arion of Lesbos. He had traveled around Greece and the Greek cities of Italy teaching the ritual of Dionysus, particularly the singing of the dithyramb, the sacred choral song performed in honor of the god. He was particularly favored by Periander, tyrant of Corinth, and he decided to return to Greece from Italy in a Corinthian ship. Plotting to steal the money Arion had gained from his performances in Italy, the sailors threw him overboard, allowing him first to give a final performance standing on the stern of the ship. When he jumped into the sea, a dolphin saved him and carried him on its back to the sanctuary of Poseidon at Cape Taenarum (the southern cape of the Peloponnese). From there he made his way back to Corinth, where he told Periander what had happened and appeared at Periander's behest to confound the sailors when they told him that Arion was safe in Italy (1.23–24).

Periander was a historical figure who ruled over Corinth around 600 B.C., and Arion was perhaps also historical. He was credited with the invention of the dithyramb. Dionysus is associated with dolphins in the myth of the sailors narrated in the seventh *Homeric Hymn* (see pp. 319–320), and Herodotus tells how there was a statue of a man on a dolphin (said to have been dedicated by Arion himself) in the temple of Poseidon at Taenarum. Thus, the story of Arion is undoubtedly connected with the worship of Poseidon and Dionysus.

Finally, an episode in the life of Polycrates, tyrant of Samos, echoes dramatically the Herodotean philosophy found in the legend of Solon and Croesus. Polycrates, like Croesus, continued to attain vast wealth and great power. His friend, King Amasis of Egypt, expressed troubled concern to Polycrates that his unbridled successes might eventually lead to disaster, since divinity is jealous of prosperity untempered by misfortune. He advised the tyrant to cast far away his most valued and prized possession, so that it might never appear again among human beings. Polycrates chose a beloved work of art, a precious gold ring with an emerald. He himself in a boat threw it way out into the sea and went home to weep at his loss. Five or six days later, a fisherman came proudly to the palace and presented to the tyrant a magnificent fish that he had caught. As the fish was being prepared for dinner, the ring of Polycrates was found in its belly. When Amasis learned what had happened to Polycrates, he realized that one cannot help another avoid what is fated and that Polycrates' life would not end well because he had found what he had tried to cast away forever. Indeed, Polycrates ultimately was murdered by a villainous Persian named Oroetes (3.39–40ff).

For translations of Herodotus' stories about Gyges, Arion, and Polycrates, see www.oup.com/us/morford.

special functions in the ceremony. The central moment of the festival would be the presentation of the ceremonial robe (*peplos*) to deck the old, wooden cult image of Athena. Women of Athens wove the garment anew each year, but it was always embroidered with the same mythic scene, the Gigantomachy. After the presentation, there would be a sacrifice of hecatombs (a hecatomb was a sacrifice of a hundred cattle), and the meat was divided among the populace. Poets would have written hymns to be sung, which reiterated and perhaps re-interpreted the mythic tradition passed down from generation to generation. The citizens, gathered together, would be able to see upon Athena's temple, the Parthenon, artistic treatments of many stories from myth and legend: in the ped-iments, Athena's birth fully grown from the head of Zeus, her father, and the contest she had with Poseidon over the right to be accorded special worship in the city of Athens; on the Ionic frieze, the celebration of the Panathenaea itself, immortalized in stone. The presentation of the robe would serve to underscore that precise and explicit anthropomorphism that characterized the Greek con-ception of deity. In the convergence of myth, art, and ritual, the religious expe-rience would make the multifarious world intelligible: the procession from the periphery of the city to its heart uniting the participants spatially, socially, and politically, orienting the Athenians to their land; the retelling of their myths and traditions, defining them in relation to their gods and their heroic past; the per-formance of sacrifices and ritual offerings, establishing the boundaries between human and god, human and animal, and living and dead.

The Nature of Greek Religion

It is customary to begin a discussion of Greek religion by asserting that the an-cient Greeks as a people possessed no closed priestly caste, no unifying doctrinal creed, no religiously authoritative book or canon that transmitted the essence of one faith, and no fixed and unchanging rite or ritual that was everywhere ob-served. Though perhaps such generalizations are to some extent true, they are extremely misleading. It is more reasonable and accurate to speak of a shared religious viewpoint, a common religious experience that we can intelligibly con-ceptualize under the heading of Greek religion. The reasons for this are many and varied, but the importance of the epic tradition for establishing a shared identity cannot be overstated. The identification of the gods (their names and appearance, their relationships, characteristics, and powers, with Zeus as su-preme) and the elaboration of the genesis of the world of immortals and mortals that was established by Homer and Hesiod became fundamental and pervasive. Here was a fertile reservoir of mythology and legend for the development of re-ligious ideas, affirmations, and practices that were passed down and enhanced by tradition, prized as a common possession that defined what it meant to be Greek, as much as did the acceptance of a common language.

There were, to be sure, a plethora of religious rituals and festivals, a multi-tude of variations on mythical tales, and a profusion of artistic representations of divinity among the hundreds of city-states that existed from the development of the polis in the tenth century B.C. to the end of pagan worship in the Late Roman Empire. Different communities would devote their principal worship to differ-ent gods. At Athens preeminent was Athena, at Argos Hera, and at Ephesus Artemis. Communities would not neglect the other gods in the pantheon, but by their choice of a special patron deity, they would signify their unique relationship with the world beyond the mortal realm. Sometimes even the "pantheon" of gods would itself shift and mutate from polis to polis, with certain gods included and others excluded. In addition, each god could hold within the same community a variety of epithets, could be seen in diverse roles, and could be honored with different rituals. Upon this creative multiplicity, the epic tradition worked as a restraint and set limits on this profusion of belief, expression, and practice, and over time, as might be expected, it imposed a certain homogeneity of religious experience, a familiar and unifying religious landscape beyond the separate and diverse manifestations of religious worship in the individual polis. The decline of the importance of the polis in the fourth century B.C. would have a similar effect. As the Greeks came less and less to identify their uniqueness in terms of the local polis to which they belonged, they appropriated a more cosmopolitan and homogeneous viewpoint.

The Civic Religion of the Polis

The Greeks had many words to express the "sacred," or "holy," or "pious," but no single word that would encompass what we generally mean by "religion," no single term that would take in the broad canvas of beliefs and practices that they associated with worship of their gods. Like all religions, Greek religion had an eminently social function. Nevertheless, it is difficult today to appreciate how deeply ingrained religion was in all facets of ancient life, especially those that we might consider "secular." In fact the Greeks would not have understood such a dichotomy. The power of the sacred permeated almost every aspect of ancient communal life in a Greek city-state. The polis became the center of the Greeks' conception of their identity; it ordered their life socially, politically, militarily, economically, culturally, and, most important for our survey, religiously.

By the sixth century B.C., the main elements of Greek religion (reflected in the epics of Homer and Hesiod) had been set, though diverse developments would continue, as described here. Public, civic worship of the gods would remain the most distinctive feature of religious life in the polis. Let us look at civic worship in Athens as a typical example, since it is so important and so well documented. The Acropolis, with its beautiful buildings and monuments (especially the Parthenon and Erechtheum), was the religious heart of the city. Yet, throughout every part of the community there were temples, sanctuaries, and shrines, some dedicated to the state gods, some to the more localized gods and numinous powers of neighborhoods and homes.

Athenian life, both public and private, was organized around the religious calendar, based on a lunar year, and the most sacred day was at the beginning of the new lunar cycle. Nearly half of the calendar year was devoted to *heortai* (sing., *heorte*), the general Greek term for "festival," derived from the Greek word for "banquet," denoting its primary pleasure. Festivals could take place at the state level or at a much more localized level in various areas or neighborhoods of the city. The first month of the Attic year was named *Hecatombaion*, during which the Hecatombaia (Festival of One Hundred Sacrifices) was held in honor of Apollo. The Panathenaea was also celebrated during this month, and because of its splendor in honor of Athena, the patron goddess of the city, it was appropriately considered the principal festival of the new year (see section Greek Mythology and Religion).

During the month of *Anthesterion*, the Athenians celebrated the Anthesteria. It was the principal spring festival in honor of Dionysus, and for three days it celebrated the opening of the new wine. It was an occasion for great joy, with masked performers entertaining the populace, but it also encompassed darker aspects. Some of the rituals of the Anthesteria were meant to recall a number of unsettling myths: Orestes' arrival in Athens after he had killed his mother (see pp. 437–441), the killing and dismemberment of Dionysus (see p. 318), and the legend of Icarius and his daughter Erigone (see p. 318). In much the same way as an Easter celebration, it incorporated elements of death and rebirth.

Two other festivals of importance are discussed in later chapters: the Brauronia in honor of Artemis (see p. 226) and the Thesmophoria (see p. 346), a women's festival in honor of Demeter, immortalized in Aristophanes' comedy *Thesmophoriazusae*.

Countless festivals were celebrated throughout the year. It has been estimated that some 2,000 cults existed in Attica alone, with about 170 annual festival days in its sacred calendar.

Nowhere is it more evident that for the Greeks the boundary between the religious and the secular was blurred than in the following festivals: the Great Dionysia was established in the sixth century B.C. in Athens, and it was amid the ritual celebrations of this festival that select poets of the city would perform their tragedies and comedies in honor of the god Dionysus; the great Panhellenic festivals, the most famous being at Olympia (in honor of Zeus) and Delphi (in honor of Apollo), included athletic contests amid the religious celebrations.

Heroic Cults of the Dead

In addition to festivals that honored the principal gods of the city, each polis reserved special occasions to honor their great heroes, who were virtually given a divine status after their deaths (see p. 136). The varied, chthonic nature of rituals in heroic cults was meant to differentiate them from the worship of the Olympian gods. For example, in a sacrifice to a chthonic power, the animal's blood was generally not splashed upon the altar but was caught in a pit or poured upon the ground. The animal chosen would more likely be darker in color. The heroes of a community represented more localized traditions and cults. Heroes were like the gods in that they had power to act for good or ill from beyond the grave, especially in favor of the polis where they were honored. Unlike the gods, however, heroes were not immortal and in death lived in the realm of Hades or the Fields of the Blessed.

Two famous legendary heroes honored by chthonic cults were King Oedipus and the seer Amphiaraüs (both from the city of Thebes), who lived extraordinary lives, died mysteriously, and were worshiped as divine. For their legends, see pp. 408–417 and 422.

Priests and Priestesses

Priests belonged to the most important category of religious officials, among many others who were concerned with the performance of rites, especially sacrifice (though generally speaking, anyone could perform a sacrifice), the upkeep of temples and sanctuaries, and the management of accounts. Since civic and religious activities were usually so closely linked, civil magistrates could also be involved, especially in connection with the celebration of the festivals.

Although they represented no official caste or hierarchy and theoretically anyone could officiate at a religious ritual, priests could be elected or appointed by lot and some priesthoods were offered for sale. Others served because of their birth. The observance of the traditions of a particular rite was all that was required, and this was learned by prior participation. The length of service varied considerably, but records show that some served for a very long time. The priesthood for the Eleusinian mysteries was held by only two Athenian families (the Kerkydes and the Eumolpidae) from archaic times throughout its history. Different priesthoods imposed different requirements and rules about marriage or virginity, sexual abstinence, diet, and so on.

It was not a calling that required the devotion of one's entire life, though it could carry great prestige. Important priests were given particular respect because of their special dress and imposing appearance and behavior in the performance of dramatic major rites and rituals and in religious processions. They also were honored by impressive statues of themselves and memorable reliefs on tombstones.

The role of the priestess was also very important, as revealed in the book *Portrait of a Priestess: Women and Ritual in Ancient Greece,* by Joan Breton Connelly. This is required reading for anyone wishing to pursue serious study of both Greek religion and the position of women in antiquity because of Connelly's scrupulous interpretation of a vast amount of evidence ranging from the Archaic through Hellenistic periods and even into Roman imperial times. Even though much of this evidence is fragmentary, elusive, and ambiguous, Connelly is generally able to reconstruct a credible, substantive account embracing "eligibility and acquisition of office, costume and attributes, representations, responsibilities, ritual actions, compensation for service, authority and privileges, and the commemoration of priestesses in death." Her discussion includes not only the life of priestesses but also the religious life of girls, maidens, and women generally, and one of her central themes is "the correlation between domestic ritual, in the care of the house, and public ritual, in the care of the temple." Religion was "the one area in which Greek women assumed roles equal and comparable to those of men." Many of the requirements imposed on priestesses were similar to those imposed on priests—for example, length of service, rules of behavior, and eligibility.

Of particular value is Connelly's concentration on four prominent priesthoods for which there is the most evidence: Athena Polias of Athens; Demeter and Kore (Persephone) at Eleusis; Hera at Argos; and Apollo at Delphi. Her conclusion should carry special weight for the student of religion:

> *For Christianity to truly separate itself from "pagan" cult worship it had to abolish one of the most visible and characteristic pillars of Greek religion, the sacred service of women, maidens, and girls. … In A.D. 503, the emperor Theodosius issued an edict that called not only for the destruction of all temples and images, but also for the cessation of age-old festivals, including the Eleusinian Mysteries, the Panathenaia, and the Olympic Games. With this came the elimination of sacred office and the priestesses who had served the Greek cults for more than a millennium.[12]*

Priestesses tended to have a greater role in cults of female divinities than male divinities, but the relationship between the office of the priest and the official roles of the priestess needs clarification, insofar as the meager, difficult, and controversial evidence may allow.

Seers

A seer was a prophet whose profession was to recognize and interpret signs that were elicited through sacrifice or occurred as a result of unusual portents, which his audience believed were sent explicitly by the gods to inform them about matters of every sort, personal, political, military, financial, and religious. Historical seers wisely modeled themselves on the performances and techniques of legendary ones, such as Calchas, Melampus, and Tiresias, whose pronouncements always came true. Therefore, it was imperative that they perfect their charismatic skills for success in a career that must have been highly competitive.

A successful seer would be much in demand and could earn a great deal of money by traveling extensively to provide personal services to an eager public that would then not have to undergo the inconvenience and expense incurred by a trip to a distant oracular site, such as Delphi. The names of only about seventy historical seers have survived; some female seers (similar to the males) have been identified and are to be distinguished from oracular priestesses, such as the Pythia, the oracular prophetess at Delphi.

The seer's repertoire involved various types of augury, for example, the interpretation of the flight and cries of birds, the behavior of serpents, the content of dreams, and natural portents such as lightning and thunder, earthquakes, and eclipses. In general, it encompassed any occurrence that was sudden and could not be controlled and required explanation. In Homer (*Iliad*, 1.69), the seer Calchas is judged to be the best of bird interpreters by far.

Sacrificial animals were examined for marks and abnormalities that might be signs of divine communication. Prophets would scrutinize the entrails of an animal most intently (extispicy), especially the liver (hepatoscopy). Certain seers could become possessed by the god in the performance of their prophetic skills.

Michael Attyah Flower, in his study *The Seer in Ancient Greece*, concludes:

> *Without divination Greek "religion" itself would have been fundamentally altered, since divination was an integral part of a whole nexus of relationships, rituals, and beliefs that comprised the religious system of the Greeks.*[13]

Mystery Religions

A major religious theme (especially in Part One) and one inextricably bound to the study of mythology concentrates on the vital subject of Mystery Religions, which differ in important respects from the civic religious ceremonies discussed earlier. The important Mysteries (among many) were celebrated in honor of Dionysus, Demeter, and Orpheus and are treated in their respective chapters. Chapter 15, which deals with the Realm of Hades, with a description of its Elysium and Tartarus, highlights the fundamental religious tenets essential to

Mystery Cults: the existence of a soul, the conflict between good and evil, and reward and punishment in the afterlife.

The dogmas on which these religions were based were very different in character and spirit from those of the traditional worship of the Olympians. Whereas the public cults did not demand rigid adherence to a religious dogma, the Mysteries required acceptance of specific doctrine. Sacred texts, written or orally transmitted, laid down the rules for ritual practice and moral behavior. Denial of the divinity of Dionysus, for example, led to disastrous consequences. Those who dared to deny that Zeus was his father, but instead believed that his mortal mother Semele had lied and become pregnant by a mortal and not the god, suffered divine retribution. Rituals in the Eleusinian mysteries were ordained by the goddess Demeter herself for those who wanted to be initiated in order to find redemption, immortality, and joy. A more comprehensive summary of these cults may be found in Chapter 16.

The Sacrifice

The most significant religious act in Greek ritual was the sacrifice. Sacrifices were held at the major festivals that punctuated the religious calendar, as well as at the myriad occasions, both public and private, when the favor of the gods was needed: at the establishment of a colony, at the beginning of a war, at the negotiation of a truce, when an oracle was consulted, when a marriage was celebrated, and so on. The evidence for the elements or stages of the sacrificial ritual comes from the literary record and archaeological remains. The ritual developed over hundreds of years, and local variations existed in every city and sanctuary. There were, however, typical features. Homer is our earliest source; his detailed description indicates the main elements required to conduct a proper sacrifice. Nestor, the king of Pylos, has ordered that a sacrifice be offered to Athena (*Odyssey* 3.430–463):

> Everyone hastened to the task. The cow came from the fields; from the well-balanced ship came the comrades of great-hearted Telemachus; the smith came too with his implements of bronze, the tools of his craft, anvil, and hammer, and well-made tongs, and with these he worked the gold. And Athena came to meet the sacrifice. Nestor, the aged chariot-driver, supplied the gold, which the smith then worked and gilded the horns of the heifer, so that Athena might take delight as she looked upon the offering. Stratios and noble Echephron led the animal by the horns. Aretus came from the storeroom and brought lustral water in a basin adorned with flowers. In his other hand he held a basket of barley-grains. Thrasymedes, steadfast in battle, held a sharp ax and took his position nearby to fell the animal with a blow. Perseus held the bowl that was to receive the blood. Nestor, the aged chariot-driver, began the rite with the ritual purification of the hands and the sprinkling of the barley-groats. He prayed earnestly to Athena, beginning the sacrifice by throwing tufts of hair from the animal's head into the fire. Now when they had prayed and thrown the barley-grains, straightaway Nestor's son, high-spirited Thrasymedes, standing nearby struck the blow. The ax cut through the tendons of the neck and loosened the strength of the heifer. The women delivered the shrill cry: daughters, daughters-in-law, and the noble wife of Nestor, Eurydice, eldest of the daughters of Clymenus. The men lifted the animal up and held it aloft over the

much-traveled earth. Then Peisistratus, best of men, cut its throat. When its black blood had streamed out and its life had left its bones, straightaway they cut the animal up, quickly cut out the thigh bones all in proper fashion, wrapped them round in folds of fat and placed upon them pieces of meat. The old man burned them over a wood fire and poured upon them sparkling wine. Near him the young men held in their hands five-pronged roasting forks. Now after the thigh bones were burned and the inner organs tasted, they cut the rest into pieces and put them on spits and roasted them, holding the pointed spits in their hands … and when they had roasted the outer meat and drawn it off the spits, they sat down and had a feast. Noble men waited on them, pouring wine into golden goblets.   10 20 30

The day of a major sacrificial ceremony was one of religious solemnity, celebration, and rejoicing. Typically, the officiators at the sacrifice would wear white clothes and garland themselves. The animal too, as here, was decked out splendidly. The community as a whole (men and women, old and young) took part, and in a very real sense the sacrifice gave cohesion to the community; it established and sanctified the community and defined who might rightly participate. Certain participants were assigned roles with responsibilities: leading the animal, bringing the basin, providing the ax, felling the animal, cutting up and roasting the parts, and serving the guests. Over time, the further development of the polis, as well as the inherent nature of the sacrifice as drama and performance, fostered a greater elaboration of the rituals and the proliferation of roles assumed by the citizen body: officiating priests, inner-circle attendants, musicians, women carrying baskets, ephebes (young men in military training), the animal herders, political and religious officials, and so on.

Homer gives the essential details of sacrificial procedure. His account is fundamentally important for reconstruction of a typical sacrifice in the classical period. Cattle were the most precious, as well as most prestigious, offering. Since they were the most expensive, they would be used only on special occasions. Sheep were the most common, but goats and pigs and poultry were often used as well. Other animals, like fish, are much rarer. More atypical kinds of sacrifices are attested—for example, the horse-drowning sacrifices in honor of Poseidon. The sex of the animal generally, though by no means always, corresponded to the sex of the divinity honored or propitiated. The animal must be unblemished to serve as a fit offering to the deity. A prominent feature of sacrifice was the fiction that the animal must be a willing victim of the slaughter. Sacrifice specifically included sprinkling the animal with water, which caused it to shake its head as if giving its consent. The presence of water was chiefly for the purification of the participants as an outward sign to god and to the others that those in attendance were clean and pure and rightly present. This ritual action, as a rule, opened the rite of the sacrifice; the use of it is often described as a beginning.

Preparation for Sacrifice. Red-figure krater, attributed to the Kleophon painter or his school, ca. 425 B.C.; height 42.3 cm. The scene depicts a ram led to the sacrifice. In the center is the altar, splashed with blood. The older, bearded male near the altar officiates. He is washing his hands, perhaps in preparation to sprinkle the animal to ensure its consent. The young man opposite him holds the water basin and the *kanoun* (a sacrificial basket to carry grain offerings or other necessary items). Between the two is a *bukranion* (bull skull), a common motif in sacrificial ritual. On the left are an *auletes* (flute player) and a youth leading the animal. To the right another bearded male stands, perhaps another priest or attendant. (© *Catharine Page Perkins Fund, Museum of Fine Arts Boston*)

The animal was brought within the sacred precinct of the god or goddess, called the *temenos* (from the Greek word "to cut") because it has been sanctified, "cut" off from the ordinary, profane world. Then amid much pomp and procession (music was invariably part of the ritual) the animal was led to the altar. The altar typically stood outdoors in front of the temple. For the animal to balk, as we have said, would have been considered a bad omen. At this point, there was the ceremonial washing of hands by the officiators; at this time, water was sprinkled over the animal, as we have said, to ensure its consent. A young maid came forward with a basket on her head and within the basket was the knife, which was covered by the barley grains or barley cakes. The participants would take out handfuls of the grain, and after the priest had uttered a prayer, everyone would throw the grain upon the altar and animal. The priest would remove the knife from the basket and cut tufts of hair from the animal. This was a sign that the animal was no longer inviolable and could fittingly be killed. The hair itself was offered on the flames as an introductory sacrifice.

The larger sacrificial animals would have been given a first, stunning blow with the ax. Smaller animals would be lifted over the altar and have their throat

A Sacrifice to Apollo. Red-figure Attic krater, ca. 430 B.C.; height 33 cm. The vase presents a typical scene after the killing of the sacrificial animal. Parts of the carcass have been cut up and roasted on spits. The altar stands in the center, with logs laid on top for the fire. On the far right stands Apollo, to whom the sacrifice is offered, in which he partakes in some way. He holds a laurel branch. A laurel tree also stands behind the altar. The older, bearded male near the altar officiates. What he is holding is uncertain; it has been identified as one of the internal organs, perhaps the heart. On either side of him is a youth. The one on the left is roasting the *splanchna* (internal organs) on spits held over the fire on the altar. These were cut up, divided among the participants, and eaten immediately. The youth on the right holds in his right hand an *oinochoe* (wine jug) and in his left a *kanoun* (sacrificial basket). (© *RMN-Grand Palais/Art Resource, NY*)

cut. The women would wail the ritual cry (*ololuge*), which was probably understood as expressing joy, an emotional release at the climax of the drama of death. After the stunning blow, the victim was lifted over the altar, so that its neck could be cut. A basin was ready to catch the blood, which was splashed on the altar. The animal was then butchered. The bones, especially the thigh bones, were removed and wrapped in fat and topped with pieces of flesh, to be burned for the god, in the belief that the gods derived pleasure from the savor of the burned fat and thigh bones. After the burning of the thigh bones, the internal organs (*splanchna*) were then spitted, roasted, and eaten by the most important members of the assembly. Wine was poured over the fire, and the roasting for the main meal began. Just what pleasure the gods received from sacrifice was a topic that aroused a great deal of speculation and at times unease among the Greeks. Hesiod's etiological tale in the *Theogony* (see pp. 90–91) of Prometheus' unsuccessful deception of Zeus is a resolution of the problem. Hesiod validates the reality that human beings received the best part of the sacrifice. In fact, the sacrifice provided one of the main opportunities for the eating of meat. After the meal, any meat remaining was distributed and taken home by the participants. The skin belonged to the sanctuary, or, as at Athens, it was sold and the money deposited in the city treasury.

Since antiquity, a great deal of scholarly debate has arisen on the meaning, origin, and development of the sacrifice. In ancient times, Theophrastus (ca. 370–287 B.C.), Greek philosopher and successor of Aristotle, attributed three functions to the sacrifice: to honor the god, to give thanks for a blessing already received, and to persuade the god to grant a blessing in the future. Modern scholars offer various interpretations. Anthropologist Walter Burkert argues that many of the elements of the sacrificial ritual can be traced back to preagricultural hunting practices and that the principal reason for many features of the rite was to allay the fear and anxiety that primitive human beings supposedly felt at the killing of an animal. For Burkert, this was the purpose that lay behind the fiction of the animal's willingness to die. The main features included the shrill cry of the women at the moment of death; the concealment of the knife in the basket of grain; and the gathering of the bones, fat, and flesh in an attempt to reconstitute ritually the animal. Other scholars, for example, Jean-Pierre Vernant, prefer to interpret the meaning of the ritual strictly in terms of a festive celebration, the social and religious hierarchy and cohesion that it established among the participants and between man and god, or as the one vital and essential way to make the community "right" with the gods.

Select Bibliography

The Pre-Socratics and Herodotus

Guthrie, W. K. C. *The Greek Philosophers from Thales to Aristotle*. New York: Harper & Row, 1960. A lucid, introductory survey.

Romm, James. *Herodotus*. New Haven, CT: Yale University Press, 2000. An introduction to the historian that is appreciative of his literary art and the legends that it contains.

Wheelwright, Philip, ed. *The Presocratics*. New York: Odyssey Press, 1966. A helpful collection of English translations of Greek philosophical writings (with pertinent ancient testimony) from the sixth and fifth centuries B.C.

The Gods, Religion, and the Occult

Bremmer, J. N. *Greek Religion.* Greece & Rome New Survey in the Classics, No. 24. New York: Oxford University Press, 1994. A brief survey of modern scholarship on the subject.

Burkert, Walter. *Greek Religion.* Cambridge, MA: Harvard University Press, 1985 [1977]. The most comprehensive modern survey of the subject.

———. *Homo Necans: The Anthropology of Ancient Greek Sacrificial Ritual and Myth.* Berkeley, CA: University of California Press, 1983 [1972].

Connelly, Joan Breton. *Portrait of a Priestess: Women and Ritual in Ancient Greece.* Princeton, NJ: Princeton University Press, 2007.

Detienne, Marcel, and Jean-Pierre Vernant. *The Cuisine of Sacrifice among the Greeks.* Chicago, IL: University of Chicago Press, 1989. Essays on blood sacrifice.

Dodd, David Brooks, and Christopher A. Faraone, eds. *Initiation in Ancient Greek Rituals and Narratives: New Critical Perspectives.* New York: Routledge, 2003. A far-ranging collection of essays on various kinds of initiation in myth and society.

Dowden, Ken. *Death and the Maiden: Girls' Initiation Rites in Greek Mythology.* New York: Routledge, 1989.

Drachmann, A. B. *Atheism in Pagan Antiquity.* Chicago, IL: Ares Publishers, 1977 [1922].

Ferguson, John. *Among the Gods: An Archaeological Exploration of Greek Religion.* New York: Routledge, 1990.

Flower, Michael Attyah. *The Seer in Ancient Greece.* Berkeley, CA: University of California Press, 2008.

Garland, Robert. *Introducing New Gods: The Politics of Athenian Religion.* Ithaca, NY: Cornell University Press, 1992. How the Athenians introduced new gods and cults, through political, economic, and spiritual motives.

Guthrie, W. K. C. *The Greeks and Their Gods.* Boston: Beacon Press, 1955. Still a reliable introductory survey of Greek religion, but without the advantages of Burkert's anthropological and historical research.

Hinnells, John R. *A Handbook of Ancient Religions.* New York: Cambridge University Press, 2007.

Instone, Stephen. *Greek Personal Religion: A Reader.* Oxford: Aris & Phillips, 2009. A selection of Greek texts translated into English with explanatory commentary, illuminating the religious beliefs of individuals.

Johnston, Sarah Iles. *Religions of the Ancient World: A Guide.* Harvard University Press Reference Library. Cambridge, MA: Harvard University Press, 2004.

Larson, Jennifer. *Greek Nymphs: Myth, Cult, Lore.* New York: Oxford University Press, 2001. A comprehensive study from Homer through the Hellenistic period.

Leeming, David, and Jake Page. *Myths of the Male Divine God.* New York: Oxford University Press, 1996. Through a comparative analysis of many mythologies, the authors trace the birth of the archetype (Trickster/Shaman/Animal Master) and its development (Divine Child/Goddess Consort/Dying God/Sky God and Earth Mate/King God) and finally the theologized Creator God and universalized God as Self and God Within. The authors do the same for the archetype of the female divinity in *Goddess: Myths of the Female Divine.* New York: Oxford University Press, 1994.

Luck, Georg, ed. *Arcana Mundi: Magic and the Occult in the Greek and Roman Worlds.* 2d ed. Baltimore, MD: Johns Hopkins University Press, 2006. A collection of ancient texts, translated and annotated.

Marinatos, Nanno, and Robin Hagg, eds. *Greek Sanctuaries: New Approaches.* New York: Routledge, 1995. Deals with origins, historical developments, and social functions of sanctuaries and particular cults in archaic and classical Greece.

Mikalson, Jon. *Ancient Greek Religion*. London: Blackwell, 2004. An introduction to the fundamental beliefs and practices of religious life in a social and political context.

Nilsson, M. P. *A History of Greek Religion*. 2d ed. New York: Norton, 1963. Still the fundamental scholarly introduction.

Ogden, Daniel. *A Companion to Greek Religion*. Blackwell Companions to the Ancient World. Literature and Culture. New York: Blackwell, 2007.

Parker, Robert. *Athenian Religion, a History*. New York: Oxford University Press, 1996.

Pedley, John. *Sanctuaries and the Sacred in the Ancient World*. New York: Cambridge University Press, 2005.

Price, Simon. *Religions of the Ancient Greeks*. New York: Cambridge University Press, 1999. A survey of the religious life of ancient Greece from archaic times to the fifth century A.D., drawn from literary, inscriptional, and archaeological evidence.

Rice, David G., and John E. Stambaugh. *Sources for the Study of Greek Religion*. Atlanta: Scholars Press, 1979. Translations of texts and inscriptions dealing with "The Olympian Gods," "Heroes," "Public Religion," "Private Religion," "Mystery Cults," and "Death and Afterlife."

Sissa, Giulia, and Marcel Detienne. *The Daily Life of the Greek Gods*. Translated by Janet Lloyd. Palo Alto, CA: Stanford University Press, 2000 [1989].

See also the Select Bibliography at the end of Chapter 1 for related comparative studies.

Primary Sources

Sources in the Chapter

Herodotus	*History of the Persian Wars* (selections from Book 1)
Hesiod	*Works and Days* 3–7
Homer	*Iliad* 24.499–502; *Odyssey* 3.430–463
Xenophanes	fragments 11, 14, 15, 16, 23

Additional Sources

Bacchylides	*Ode* 3.15–62: Apollo and Croesus
Hyginus	*Fables (Fabulae)* 194: the story of Arion
Xenophon	*Cryopaedia* 7.2.9–7.2.29: Cyrus and Croesus

Notes

1. Nymphs are sometimes classified as follows: the spirits of waters, springs, lakes, and rivers are called Naiads; Potamiads are specifically the nymphs of rivers; tree-nymphs are generally called Dryads or Hamadryads, although their name means "spirits of oak trees" in particular; Meliae are the nymphs of ash trees.
2. The mortal parent may bask in the grand aura of the great mythological age of saga and boast of a genealogy that in the not too distant past included at least one divine ancestor.
3. Jack Miles, *God: A Biography* (New York: Alfred A. Knopf, 1995), especially pp. 397–408.
4. Her name was Cydippe and she was a priestess of Hera, hence the necessity for her presence at the festival. The temple would be the Argive Heraeum.

5. Herodotus here uses the masculine article with the Greek word for god (not goddess), *ho theos*. He seems to be thinking of one supreme god or more abstractly of a divine power. Significantly, the mother does not refer to Hera specifically, although subsequently it is to the goddess Hera whom she prays on behalf of her sons.

6. These statues have been excavated and do much to tantalize in the quest for precise distinctions between myth and history in Herodotus' account.

7. That is, human beings are entirely at the mercy of what befalls them.

8. The ritual entailed, at least partly, the slaying of a suckling pig and the pouring of the blood over the hands of the guilty murderer, who sat in silence at the hearth while Zeus was invoked as the Purifier.

9. These words of Croesus at first may strike the modern reader as extremely cruel, but he means only that he cannot consider the other boy, who is deaf and mute, as his son in the same way. We are told elsewhere that Croesus did everything for the unfortunate boy, but his hopes, both domestic and political, rested in Atys.

10. Solon held office in Athens as archon extraordinary in 594 B.C., and his travels took place at some time after that date; his death occurred in the years following 560 B.C.. Croesus did not become king of Sardis until ca. 560 B.C., and he was defeated by Cyrus in 546 B.C..

11. J. P. Vernant, "Greek Religion," in Robert M. Seltzer, ed., *Religions of Antiquity* (New York: Collier Macmillan, 1989), p. 167.

12. Joan Breton Connelly, *Portrait of a Priestess: Women and Ritual in Ancient Greece* (Princeton, NJ: Princeton University Press, 2007), p. 279. The earlier quotations come from the introduction, pp. 1–5.

13. Michael Attyah Flower, *The Seer in Ancient Greece* (Berkeley, CA: University of California Press, 2008), p. 245.

POSEIDON, SEA DEITIES, GROUP DIVINITIES, AND MONSTERS

> By the harbor there is a temple of Poseidon and a freestanding statue of stone. In addition to the many names that have been fashioned by the poets for Poseidon as an adornment for their verses, and those names which custom has established for each particular community, the names of the god that all men use are Pelagaios (God of the Sea), Asphaleios (God of Security), and Hippios (God of Horses).
>
> —**PAUSANIAS**, *Description of Greece 7.21.7*

POSEIDON, BEST KNOWN AS the great god of waters in general and of the sea in particular, was by no means the first or only such divinity. As we have seen, Pontus (Sea) was produced by Ge in the initial stages of creation; and two of the Titans, **Oceanus** and Tethys, bore thousands of children, the **Oceanids**. In addition, Pontus mated with his mother, Ge, and begat (among other progeny, discussed later in this chapter) **Nereus**, the eldest of his children, who was gentle, wise, and true, an old man of the sea with the gift of prophecy. Nereus in turn united with Doris (an Oceanid) who bore him fifty daughters, the **Nereids**; three of these mermaids should be singled out: Thetis, Galatea, and Amphitrite.

Peleus and Thetis

We have already mentioned that Thetis was destined to bear a son mightier than his father. Zeus learned this secret from Prometheus and avoided mating with Thetis; she married instead a mortal named Peleus, who was hard pressed to catch his bride. For Thetis possessed the power of changing shape and transformed herself into a variety of states (e.g., a bird, a tree, a tigress) in rapid succession, but eventually she was forced to succumb. Peleus and Thetis celebrated their marriage with great ceremony (although she later left him), and their son Achilles did indeed become mightier than his father (see p. 474).

Acis, Galatea, and the Cyclops Polyphemus

Galatea, another Nereid, was loved by the Cyclops Polyphemus, a son of Poseidon. Ovid's account (*Metamorphoses* 13.750–897) presents a touching rendition of their story, playing upon the incongruity of the passion of the monstrous and boorish giant for the delicate nymph. Repelled by his attentions, she loved Acis, handsome son of Faunus and a sea-nymph, Symaethis, daughter of the river-god, Symaethus, in Sicily. Overcome by emotion, Polyphemus attempted to mend his savage ways; he combed his hair with a rake and cut his beard with a scythe.

Ovid's Galatea tells how the fierce Cyclops would sit on the cliff of a promontory jutting out to the sea, where he would lay down his staff (a huge pine trunk the size of a ship's mast) and take up his pipe of a hundred reeds. Hiding below in the arms of her beloved Acis, Galatea would listen to his song. First, he would extravagantly describe her magnificent beauty, then bitterly lament her adamant rejection of him, and continue with an offer of many rustic gifts. His tragicomic appeal concludes as follows (839–897):

"Now Galatea, come, don't despise my gifts. Certainly I know what I look like; just recently I saw myself in the reflection of a limpid pool, and I was pleased with the figure that I saw. Look at what a size I am! Jupiter in the sky doesn't have a body bigger than mine—you are always telling me that someone or other named Jove reigns up there. An abundance of hair hangs over my rugged features and, like a grove of trees, overshadows my shoulders; and don't think my body ugly because it bristles with the thickest and coarsest of hair. A tree without leaves is ugly; ugly is a horse, if a bushy mane doesn't cover its tawny neck; feathers cover birds, and their own wool is an adornment for sheep; for a man a beard and shaggy hair are only fitting. So there is one eye in the middle of my forehead. What of it? Doesn't   10 the great Sun see all these things here on earth from the sky? Yet the Sun has only a single eye. (839–853)

"Furthermore, my father Neptune rules over your waters, and he is the one I give you as a father-in-law. Only have pity and listen to the prayers of my supplication! I succumb to you alone. I am scornful of Jove, of his sky and his devastating thunder; but I am afraid of you; your wrath is more deadly than his thunderbolt. (854–858)

"I should better endure this contempt of yours, if you would run away from everybody; but why do you reject me and love Acis? Why do you prefer Acis to my   20 embraces? Yet he may be allowed to please himself and you as well—but I don't want him to be pleasing to you! Just let me have the chance. He will know then that my strength is as huge as the size of my body. I'll tear out his living innards, and I'll scatter his dismembered limbs over the land and the waves of your waters—in this way may he mingle in love with you! For I burn with a fiery passion that, upon being rejected, flames up the more fiercely and I seem to carry Mt. Aetna, with all its volcanic force, buried in my breast. And you, Galatea, remain unmoved." (859–869)

After such complaints made all in vain, he rose up (for I saw it all) and was unable to stand still, but wandered the woods and his familiar pastures, like a bull full of fury when his cow has been taken away from him. Then the raging Cyclops saw me   30 and Acis, who were startled by such an unexpected fright. He shouted, "I see you and I'll make this loving union of yours your last." That voice of his was as great as a furious Cyclops ought to have; Aetna trembled at his roar. But I was terrified and dove into the waters nearby. My Symaethian hero, Acis, had turned his back in flight and cried, "Bring help to me, Galatea, help, my parents, and take me, about to die, to your watery kingdom!" (870–881)

The Cyclops, in hot pursuit, hurled a section torn out of the mountain. Although only a mere edge of that jagged mass struck Acis, it buried him completely; but it was through me that Acis appropriated to himself the watery power of his ancestry—the only solution allowed by the Fates. Red blood began to trickle from out the mass that had buried him, and in a short time the red of the blood began to disappear and it became the color of a stream made turbid by an early rain, and in a while the water cleared. Then the mass that had been thrown upon him split open and, through the cleft, a reed, green and slender, rose up and the hollow opening in the rock resounded with the leaping waves. Suddenly a wonderful thing happened—up to his waist in the midst of the waves there stood a youth, the sprouting horns on his brow wreathed with pliant reeds. Except that he was bigger and his whole face the bluish green of water, this was Acis indeed turned into a river-god. (882–897)

40

Poseidon and Amphitrite

The third Nereid, Amphitrite, is important mainly as the wife of Poseidon; like her sister Thetis, she proved a reluctant bride, but Poseidon finally was able to win her. As husband and wife, they play roles very much like those enacted by Zeus and Hera: Poseidon has a weakness for women, and Amphitrite, with good cause, is angry and vengeful. They had a son, Triton, a merman, human above the waist, fish-shaped below. He is often depicted blowing a conch shell, a veritable trumpeter of the sea; he can change shape at will.

Tyro, daughter of Salmoneus, was loved by Poseidon, who disguised himself as the Thessalian river Enipeus (Homer, *Odyssey* 11.245):

> In the form of Enipeus did the Earthshaker lie by her at the mouth of the eddying river. About them rose a crested wave, mountainous in size, which hid both god and mortal woman.

The children born of this union were twins, Neleus and Pelias, notable legendary figures with significant progeny.[1]

Proteus

The sea divinity Proteus, probably another of the older generation of gods, is often named as the attendant of Poseidon or even as his son. Like Nereus, he is an old man of the sea who can foretell the future; he can also change shape. It is easy to see how the identities of Nereus, Proteus, and Triton could be merged. Confusion among sea divinities and duplication of their characteristics are everywhere apparent.

For a translation of the accounts about Proteus by Homer and Vergil, see www.oup.com/us/morford.

There are two classic accounts of Proteus' nature and his powers: those of Homer (*Odyssey* 4.360–570) and Vergil (*Georgics* 4.386–528). In Homer, Menelaüs, on his way home from Troy, was unduly detained off the coast of Egypt; he consulted Proteus, the old man of the sea, with the help of Proteus' daughter Eidothea. Menelaüs explains: "We rushed upon him with a shout and threw our arms about him; but the old man did not forget his devious arts. First off he became a thickly maned lion, and then a serpent, a leopard, and a great boar. And he became liquid water and a tree with lofty branches. But we held on to him firmly with steadfast spirits." Finally, the devious Proteus grew weary and answered Menelaüs' questions about his return home.

The Appearance and Character of Poseidon

Poseidon is similar in appearance to his brother Zeus, a majestic, bearded figure, but he is generally more severe and rough, to illustrate his tempestuous nature; besides, he carries the trident, a three-pronged fork resembling a fisherman's spear. By his very nature, Poseidon is ferocious. He is called the supporter of the earth but the earthshaker as well, and as a god of earthquakes he exhibits his violence by the rending of the land and the surge of the sea. By a mere stroke of his trident, he may destroy and kill. Ovid provides a typical description in his version of the Flood (see p. 99), providing a vivid characterization of Poseidon under his Roman name of Neptune. Poseidon's relentless anger against Odysseus for blinding Polyphemus provides a dominant theme in the Odyssey. The *Homeric Hymn to Poseidon* (22) attempts to appease his anger.

> About Poseidon, a great god, I begin to sing, the shaker of the earth and of the barren sea, ruler of the deep and also over Mt. Helicon and the broad town of Aegae.[2] A double honor, the gods have allotted to you, O Earthshaker—to be both a tamer of horses and a savior of ships. Hail, dark-haired Poseidon, who surrounds the earth and, O blessed god, be of kind heart and protect those who sail your waters. (1–7)

The origins of Poseidon are much disputed. If his trident represents what was once a thunderbolt, then he was in early times a god of the sky. More attractive is the theory that he was once a male spirit of fertility, a god of earth who sent up springs. This theory fits well with his association with horses and bulls (he either creates them or makes them appear) and explains the character of some of his affairs. He mated with Demeter in the form of a stallion; he pursued her while she was searching for her daughter, and her ruse of changing into a

Neptune in His Chariot. Mosaic, mid-second century A.D., diameter 77 in. This is the central panel of a very large square mosaic of *Neptune and the Seasons*, in which female figures representing each of the four seasons occupy the corners. Neptune (Poseidon) dominates the central panel, with four seahorses pulling his chariot: to the viewer's right in the background is a sea-nymph, and on the left is a Triton. The theme was elaborated by Poussin in his *Triumph of Neptune and Amphitrite* (see image on p. 169). (© Gilles Mermet/Art Resource, NY)

mare to escape him was to no avail. Thus, we have the union of the male and female powers of the fertility of the earth.[3] It nevertheless should be remembered that standard epic epithets of the sea are "barren" and "unharvested" as opposed to the fecundity of the land. The suggestion that Poseidon's horses are the mythical depiction of the whitecaps of the waves is not convincing, at least in terms of origins.

The important story of the contest between Poseidon and Athena for control of Athens and its surrounding territory, Attica, is told in Chapter 8 in connection with the sculpture of the west pediment of the Parthenon.

Scylla and Charybdis

Poseidon made advances to Scylla, the daughter of Phorcys and Hecate. Amphitrite became jealous and threw magic herbs into Scylla's bathing place. Thus, Scylla was transformed into a terrifying monster, encircled with a ring of dogs' heads. Ovid's different version of Scylla's transformation (*Metamorphoses* 13.917–968; 14.1–71) is more well known: Glaucus, a mortal who had been changed into a sea-god, fell in love with Scylla; when he was rejected, he turned to the sorceress Circe for help. But Circe fell in love with him and, in her jealousy, poisoned the waters of Scylla's bathing place.

Scylla's home was a cave in the Straits of Messina between Sicily and Italy. With her was Charybdis, the daughter of Poseidon and Ge, a formidable and voracious ally whom Zeus had cast into the sea by his thunderbolt; three times a day she drew in mountains of water and spewed them out again. Scylla and Charybdis have been rationalized into natural terrors faced by mariners when they sailed through the straits. Certainly, many of the tales about the gods of the waters are reminiscent of the yarns spun by fishermen, sailors, and the like, whose lives are involved with the sea and with travel.

The Progeny of Pontus and Ge

Pontus and Ge produced legions of descendants. (Notice how elements of the fantastic and the grotesque appear again and again in the nature of the progeny associated with the sea and the deep.)

In addition to Nereus, Pontus and Ge had two more sons, Thaumas and Phorcys, and two daughters, Ceto and Eurybië. Thaumas mated with Electra (an Oceanid) to produce **Iris** and the **Harpies**. Iris is the goddess of the rainbow (her name means "rainbow"). She is also a messenger of the gods, sometimes the particular servant of Hera, with Hermes' offices then confined to Zeus. She is fleet-footed and winged, as are her sisters, the Harpies, but the Harpies are much more violent in nature. In early sources, they are conceived of as strong winds (their name means "the snatchers"), but later they are depicted in literature and in art as birdlike creatures with the faces of women, often terrifying and a pestilence.[4]

Phorcys and his sister Ceto produce two groups of children, the **Graeae** and the **Gorgons**. The Graeae (Aged Ones) are three sisters, personifications of old age; their hair was gray from birth, but in their general aspect they appeared swan-like and beautiful. They had, however, only one eye and one tooth, which they were forced to share among themselves.

RAPHAËL AND POUSSIN

Raphaël (Raffaello Sanzio or Santi) stands with Leonardo and Michelangelo as one of the great masters of the High Italian Renaissance. He was born in Urbino, and during his early career he worked in Umbria and Tuscany, especially in the city of Florence. He was an accomplished painter and architect. In 1508, at the behest of Pope Julius II, he went to Rome and remained there until his death. One of the first works, if not the first, that Raphael painted in Rome was the *Galatea*.

The most important sources for the story of Galatea are the *Idylls* of the Greek poet Theocritus (third century B.C.) and, of course, the *Metamorphoses* of the Roman poet Ovid (43 B.C.–ca. A.D. 17). In Ovid's version of the tale, the Trojan Aeneas is sailing past Scylla and Charybdis. This encounter leads Ovid to recall that once Scylla had been a beautiful, young woman pursued by many suitors. She would often visit Galatea to gossip about the latest suitor she had rejected. During one of these visits, Galatea contributes her own story at Scylla's urging. Galatea had once been the object of the love of the barbarous Cyclops, Polyphemus. He would often sing to her in an attempt to woo her, but Galatea spurned his advances; she had eyes only for a handsome youth named Acis.

Galatea, by Raphaël (1483–1520); fresco from the *Sala di Galatea* in the Villa Farnesina, ca. 1512; 116 × 88½ in. Galatea, riding in a seashell chariot drawn by dolphins, appears as the image of ideal beauty. Two Tritonesque figures, turning outward on her left and right, are blowing their seashell horns. Two pairs of lovers (one a merman and nymph; the other a centaur and nymph), carefully placed on either side of Galatea, embrace. Beneath her a cupid playfully mirrors Galatea's movements and the direction of her gaze. At the top, three cupids are seen converging their arrows on the scene below, and one cupid in the top left corner is isolated, concealed in a cloud, and keeping a firm grip on his arrows. The emotional tone of the whole is one of exuberant joy. (© *Alinari Archives/Alessandro Angeli/ Art Resource, NY*)

One day, Polyphemus caught them together and buried Acis under a mountain of stone. Galatea, however, had the power to transform her beloved's blood, which was seeping out from between the rocks, into a river, and so Acis became a river-god. (Interestingly, there exists a variant of the tale in which Polyphemus' suit is successful and he wins the hand of Galatea.)

The classical tale was later used in a poem by the famed Italian scholar and poet Angelo Poliziano (1454–1494); his version was one of the main literary influences for Raphaël's fresco. In Raphael's version of the story, neither Polyphemus nor Acis is present, though shortly after Raphaël painted his *Galatea*, another artist, Sebastiano del Piombo, painted to the left of Raphaël's work, on another section of the wall, a fresco of the Cyclops entitled *Polyphemus*. This addition gives Galatea an object for her gaze. If considered alone, Galatea in Raphaël's fresco is neither gazing at anyone nor being gazed upon; she stands strangely isolated amid the activity and amorous pursuits of the other figures. Many have seen in her a symbol of love itself; it is worth noting that she rides on a shell, a symbol that is often associated with Aphrodite (Venus). This vision of the apotheosis of Galatea had a tremendous influence on later artists.

The French painter Nicholas Poussin (1594–1665) was drawn to the past, especially the history and mythology of classical antiquity. Like Raphaël, he was attracted by Rome and spent all of his working life there; Raphaël's work exerted a profound influence on his style and composition. This can certainly be appreciated in *The Triumph of Neptune and Amphitrite*, although the subject matter is different, the color palette darker, and the scene more emotional. Amphitrite occupies the same space as Galatea; she rides in a seashell chariot drawn by dolphins and is the central focus of the surrounding figures. Since both Galatea and Amphitrite were daughters of the sea-god Nereus, this association makes perfect sense. Neptune occupies the same place as the Cyclops Polyphemus in Piombo's fresco; he is the father of the Cyclops and, from the left side, is gazing adoringly at Amphitrite. Although the cupids are multiplied and disposed in various ways at the top, they do correspond to Raphaël's cupids, particularly the one beneath Amphitrite's chariot. The two Triton figures and the amorous couples are also replicated on either side of Neptune's consort. In myth, Amphitrite, like Galatea, spurned the advances of Neptune, at least at first. Poussin's painting reveals the end of the story.

The Triumph of Neptune and Amphitrite, by Nicolas Poussin (1594–1665); oil on canvas, ca. 1637, 45 × 58 in. Amphitrite is at the center, accompanied by Nereids and Tritons as she rides over the sea in her shell drawn by four dolphins. Neptune comes alongside his bride in a chariot drawn by four seahorses. Above, winged cupids (one with butterfly's wings and one with a wedding torch) strew flowers, and in the background to the left ride two cupids, above whom fly the swans of Venus. Poussin exuberantly reinterprets a theme found in Roman floor mosaics and in Raphael's fresco *Galatea* (ca. 1512) in the Villa Farnesina at Rome. (*Philadelphia Museum of Art: The George W. Elkins Collection, 1932. Photo by Graydon Wood*)

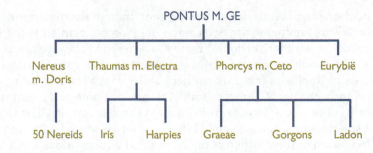

Figure 7.1 Descendants of the Sea

The Graeae knew the way to their sisters, the Gorgons, who were also three in number (Stheno, Euryale, and Medusa) and whose hair writhed with serpents. They were of such terrifying aspect that those who looked upon them turned to stone. Gorgons are a favorite theme in Greek art, especially in the early period; they leer out most disconcertingly with a broad archaic smile, tongue protruding in the midst of a row of bristling teeth. **Medusa** is the most important Gorgon; Poseidon was her lover. She presents the greatest challenge to the hero Perseus (see pp. 534–535), and when he beheaded her, she was pregnant; from her corpse sprang a winged horse, Pegasus, and a son, Chrysaor (He of the Golden Sword).

Phorcys and Ceto also bore a dragon named Ladon; he helped the lovely Hesperides (Daughters of Evening), who guarded a wondrous tree on which grew golden fruit, far away in the West, and passed their time in beautiful singing. Heracles slew Ladon when he stole the Apples of the Hesperides (see p. 553).

Chrysaor mated with an Oceanid, Callirhoë, and produced the monsters Geryon and Echidna (half nymph and half snake). Echidna united with Typhon and bore Orthus (the hound of Geryon), **Cerberus** (the hound of Hades), the Lernaean hydra, and the Chimaera. Echidna and Orthus produced the Theban

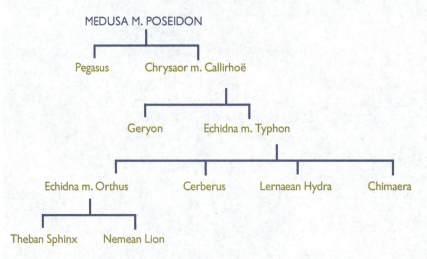

Figure 7.2 Descendants of Medusa

Sphinx and the Nemean lion. These monsters will appear later in saga to be overcome by heroes; many of them are particularly associated with the exploits of Heracles (see Chapter 22).

Interpretative Summary

The stories about waters of all sorts—rivers, lakes, the ocean, and the seas—and the deities associated with them are numerous and revealing. They remind us of how important travel by sea was to the Greeks and Romans and how control of the seas, particularly the Mediterranean, was the key to power. The thalassocracy (sea-power) of Minoan Crete makes this perfectly clear, as does the subsequent dominance of the Mycenaeans, the inheritors of Cretan control. Subsequently, the naval empire of Periclean Athens, in the fifth century B.C., confirms the vital importance of sea-power, and so does the mighty empire acquired by the Romans, for whom their Mediterranean "lake" was the central focus.

That there were two major periods in the initial creation of Greek mythology is made evident by the nature and extent of the travels of the seafarers, Theseus, Jason, Odysseus, and the survivors of the Trojan War in Minoan-Mycenaean times, with the conflation of geographical and historical events belonging to the historical age of colonization after 1100 B.C. From both periods evolved the turbulent and romantic tales about the various facets of waters and their deities and the sea monsters to be overcome by heroes.

We have shown Poseidon, the major god of the sea, to be characterized by ferocity and violence. He is "the earthshaker," a deity of storms and earthquakes. His powers are made evident by his association with bulls and horses. He is the father of the monstrous Cyclops Polyphemus, and his inexorable anger is a major theme of Homer's *Odyssey*. Poseidon lost to the goddess Athena in a contest for control of Athens, as we shall see in the next chapter. Yet the Athenians, great seafarers themselves, continued to give him great honor and linked him particularly to their ancient king Erechtheus and his beautiful temple on the Acropolis. Poseidon was also said to be the true father of Theseus, the great national hero of Athens, through the human figure of Aegeus, an Athenian king, who gives his name to the Aegean Sea.

Tales about waters are often yarns spun by sailors, full of abounding imagination, exciting adventure, and wondrous embellishment, embracing both the beautiful and the grotesque. Witness the fantastic variety in the character and appearance of the progeny of the sea. Poseidon is, like his domain, relentless and prone to stormy violence and anger. Yet gods such as Nereus and Proteus, profoundly wise, appear as ageless as the impenetrable sea itself. Still other deities mirror the unpredictable beauty and fascinating lure of the mysterious deep: the lovely mermaids, who can change shape and mood at will; the beguiling Sirens with their bewitching, lethal song; and monstrous Scylla and Charybdis, who bring terror, destruction, and death.

Neptune and Triton, by Gian-Lorenzo Bernini (1598–1680); marble, 1619, height 71½ in. Neptune (Poseidon) is shown striding forward angrily, supported by Triton blowing his conch. The scene is based on Ovid's description of the Flood (see pp. 99–102: "Neptune struck the earth with his trident"). The statue stood above a pond in the gardens of the Roman villa of Cardinal Montalto, nephew of Pope Sixtus V. (*V & A Images, London/Art Resource, NY*)

Select Bibliography

Barringer, Judith M. *Divine Escorts: Nereids in Archaic and Classical Art.* Ann Arbor, MI: University of Michigan Press, 1995.

Pevnick, Seth D., curator and editor. *Poseidon and the Sea: Myth, Cult, and Daily Life.* London: Tampa Museum of Art, 2014.

Tataki, B. *Sounion: The Temple of Poseidon.* University Park, PA: Museum of the University of Pennsylvania, 1985. Good illustrations of the famous temple of Poseidon at Sunium, at the tip of Attica.

Primary Sources

Sources in the Chapter

Homeric Hymn 22	*To Poseidon*
Ovid	*Metamorphoses* 13.839–897

Additional Sources

Apollodorus	*Library* 3.13.4–3.13.6: Peleus and Thetis
Pausanias	*Description of Greece* 2.1.6–2.1.9: Poseidon's dispute with Helius; depictions of sea deities
Theocritus	*Idylls* 9: In which Theocritus tells a lovesick friend the song the Cyclops sang to his beloved Galatea

Notes

1. Pelias became king of Iolcus (see p. 597) while Neleus founded Pylos (in Messene), which was sacked by Heracles. Neleus and all his sons, save only Nestor, were killed. Homer (*Iliad* 11.682–704) says that Neleus survived into old age. Tyro later married her uncle Cretheus, the founder and king of Iolcus, and by him she became the mother of Aeson, Pheres, and Amythaeon. Aeson was the father of Jason, and Pheres, founder of Pherae, was the father of Admetus, husband of Alcestis. In order to marry Alcestis, Admetus had to perform the task of harnessing a lion and a boar together to a chariot. For the recovery of Alcestis from the Underworld by Heracles, see p. 262.
2. Poseidon Heliconius was worshiped by Ionian Greeks, especially at Mycale in Asia Minor. It is uncertain whether the reference in the hymn to Helicon (from which Heliconius is derived) means Mt. Helicon (in Boeotia) or the town of Helice; Helice and Aegae were both on the Corinthian gulf.
3. The result is the birth both of a daughter and of the wonderful horse Arion, which belonged to the Theban Adrastus. Similarly, Poseidon united with Ge to produce Antaeus, a giant encountered by Heracles.
4. The horrifying Harpies are not unlike the beautiful Sirens, who lure human beings to destruction and death by the enticement of their song.

8

ATHENA

And Athena pitied her companion and said to her: "It was not I who blinded your child Tiresias. It is not sweet for Athena to steal away the eyes of children. But the laws of Cronus decree thus: Whoever sees any of the immortals, when the god himself does not so choose, let him pay a great price for the seeing."

—**CALLIMACHUS,** *On the Bath of Athena*, 95–102

The Birth of Athena

The *Homeric Hymn* (28) tells the story of Athena's birth.

> I begin to sing about Pallas Athena, renowned goddess, with bright eyes, quick mind, and inflexible heart, chaste and mighty virgin, protectress of the city, Tritogeneia. Wise Zeus himself gave birth to her from his holy head, and she was arrayed in her armor of war, all-gleaming in gold, and every one of the immortals was gripped with awe as they watched. She quickly sprang forth from the immortal head in front of aegis-bearing Zeus, brandishing her sharp spear. And great Olympus shook terribly at the might of the bright-eyed goddess, and the earth round about gave a dread groan and the dark waves of the deep seethed. But suddenly the sea became calm, and the glorious son of Hyperion halted his swift-footed horses all the while that the maiden Pallas Athena took the divine armor from her immortal shoulders, and Zeus in his wisdom rejoiced. 10
>
> So hail to you, child of aegis-bearing Zeus; yet I shall remember both you and another song too. (17–18)

Hesiod (*Theogony* 886–898) tells how Zeus had swallowed his consort **Metis** (her name means "wisdom") after he had made her pregnant with Athena; he was afraid that Metis would bear a son who would overthrow him.

> Zeus, king of the gods, first took as his wife Metis, who was very wise indeed among both gods and mortals. But when she was about to give birth to the bright-eyed goddess Athena, then Zeus treacherously deceived her with wheedling words and swallowed her down into his belly at the wise instigations of Gaea and starry Uranus. These two gave Zeus this advice so that no other of the

> eternal gods might rule supreme as king in his place. For Metis was destined to bear exceptional children: first, the keen-eyed maiden Athena, Tritogeneia, the equal of her father in might and good counsel, and then she was to give birth to a son of indomitable spirit who would become the king of both gods and mortals. (886–898)   10

Variations in the story of Athena's birth have Hephaestus split Zeus' head open with an ax to facilitate the birth. Sometimes Prometheus or even Hermes is a helper. Some add to the dread awe of the occasion by having Athena cry out thunderously as she springs to life in full battle dress. This myth (whatever its etiology in terms of the physical manifestations of the thunderstorm) establishes the close bond between Zeus and his favorite daughter and allegorizes the three basic characteristics of the goddess Athena: her prowess, her wisdom, and the masculinity of her virgin nature sprung ultimately not from the female, but from the male.

The Sculpture of the Parthenon

The Parthenon was the great temple to **Athena Parthenos** (*parthenos*, meaning "virgin," was a standard epithet of Athena) on the Acropolis at Athens. It was built between 447 and 438 B.C. and embodied the triumph of Greek (and specifically Athenian) courage and piety over the Persians, who had sacked the Acropolis in 480 and destroyed the Old Parthenon. Like the temple of Zeus at Olympia (described on pp. 117–119), the Parthenon was decorated with a complex program of sculpture in which mythology and religion glorified the city and its gods, above all honoring Athena, whose great statue was housed in the temple. The whole program was directed by **Pheidias**, creator of the statue of Zeus at Olympia.

The **east pediment** of the Parthenon immortalized the dramatic moment of the birth of Athena, who stood in the center before the throne of Zeus, from whose head she had just sprung full grown and fully armed. Hephaestus, who had assisted in the birth, and Hera were probably present, while the announcement of the birth was brought to other divine figures waiting to observe the miracle. At the corners, to set the divine event in cosmic time, were the horses of Helius, rising from the sea, and of Selene, sinking into it.

As at Olympia, the **west pediment** was a scene of violent action, celebrating the victory of Athena in her contest with Poseidon for control of Athens and Attica. The central figures pull away from each other as they produce the gifts with which they vied, and to each side were figures of divinities and heroic kings of early Athens who attended the contest. Athena with her spear created an olive tree; Poseidon with his trident, a salt spring. Athena was proclaimed victor.

Variants are that Poseidon produced the first horse; Athena may plant an olive tree or, more dramatically, as on this pediment, bring one forth by the touch of her spear. The contest took place on the Acropolis with Athena

The Birth of Athena. Athenian black-figure amphora, sixth century B.C.; height 15½ in. Athena emerges fully armed from the head of Zeus, who is seated on his throne holding the thunderbolt. At the left stand Hermes and Apollo (with his kithara), and to the right are Eileithyia, gesturing toward the newborn goddess whose birth she has assisted, and Ares. Beneath the throne is a sphinx. (*Photograph © 2010. Museum of Fine Arts, Boston*)

judged the victor by the gods, or the Athenians, or their king Cecrops. The importance of the olive in Athenian life is symbolized by Athena's victory. Angry at losing, Poseidon flooded the Thriasian plain, but he was appeased. The Athenians were seafarers and Poseidon remained important to them. Poseidon continued to be worshiped (in conjunction with the Athenian hero Erechtheus) in the nearby sanctuary of the **Erechtheum** (described on pp. 572–573). There the marks of Poseidon's trident were enshrined and Athena's olive tree continued to grow.

There were two friezes on the Parthenon. The first, the exterior **Doric frieze**, consisted of ninety-two **metopes** (each 40 inches high), thirty-two on each of the long sides and fourteen on the short ones. On the south were reliefs of the battle of the Lapiths and centaurs, also the subject of the west pediment of the temple of Zeus at Olympia (see p. 118). On the north side the subject was probably the sack of Troy, while on the east it was the Gigantomachy (the battle of the Olympian gods against the giants), and on the west the battle of the Greeks and the Amazons. Thus, the mythical themes of the metopes reinforced the idea of the triumph of Greek courage over the barbarians and of the Greek gods over their predecessors.

The second, an **Ionic frieze**, ran continuously round the outer wall of the cella, or naos (the interior part of the temple that housed the statue of Athena and the treasury). It has been generally thought (at least since the eighteenth century) that this frieze shows the people of Athens moving in procession as they celebrate the festival of the **Panathenaea** in honor of their goddess. Athenian men and women are shown as marshals, attendants, horsemen, hoplites, and assistants in the worship of Athena, along with the animals

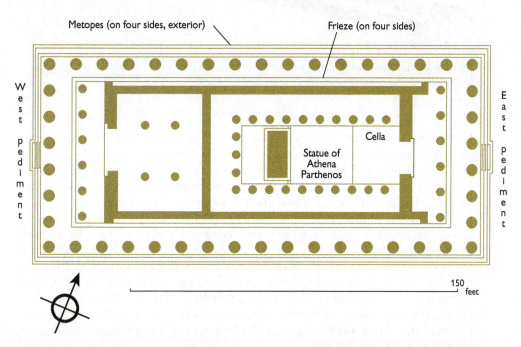

Figure 8.1 Plan of the Parthenon (after J. Travlos)

Figure 8.2 Sectional Drawing of the East End of the Parthenon Showing Relationship of Frieze, Metopes, and Pediment (after N. Yalouris)

for the ritual sacrifice. Games and contests (not on the frieze) were a part of the festivities; the prize awarded was an amphora filled with oil. On it was depicted Athena in her war gear, with an inscription identifying the vase as Panathenaic. At the climax of the procession, on the east side (i.e., over the entrance to the part of the cella housing the statue), the ceremonial robe (*peplos*) was presented to the priestess of Athena. Nearby sat the Olympian immortals enthroned, taking part in the joyous celebration of civic piety. Some parts of the friezes are still in situ, but the major fragments of the pediments and the friezes are in the British Museum in London and are known as the Elgin marbles. The *peplos* was dedicated to the ancient wooden statue of Athena Polias (i.e., "guardian of the city") in the nearby sanctuary of Erechtheus. The old temple was destroyed by the Persians, and the new Erechtheum was completed some thirty years after the Parthenon. For its religious significance, see Chapter 23, pp. 572–574.

Athena Parthenos

In the **cella** of the Parthenon stood a monumental statue, the Athena Parthenos. The original by Pheidias is completely lost, but reconstructions (like the one illustrated on p. 180) may be made with some accuracy.[1] Like Pheidias' later masterpiece at Olympia, the surfaces of the statue were made of gold and ivory, and its decoration, elaborating the themes of the architectural sculptures already described, gave witness to the honor and glory of the goddess and the city she protected. It was nearly 12 meters high, and in front of it was a reflecting pool. The standing goddess held a figure of Nike (Victory) in her right hand, and her armor included a helmet decorated with sphinxes, the **aegis** with the head of Medusa, a shield, and a spear, beside which was a serpent (representing the chthonic divinity Erechtheus). The shield was decorated with the battle of the Amazons on the exterior and the Gigantomachy on the interior; on the rims of her sandals were reliefs of the battle with centaurs (all themes repeated from the metopes). The relief on the base of the statue showed the creation of Pandora. In the sculpture of the Parthenon, mythology and religion combine with local pride to glorify the gods and civilization of the Greeks and to celebrate the city and its citizens under the protection of Athena.[2]

Pallas Athena Tritogeneia

Athena's title, Tritogeneia, is obscure. It seems to refer to a region sometimes associated with her birth, the river or lake Triton, or Tritonis, in Boeotia or in Libya. Some scholars see in this link the possibility that Athena was, at least in her origins, at one time a goddess of waters or of the sea. We are told that soon after her birth Athena was reared by **Triton** (presumably the god of this body of water, wherever it may be). Now Triton had a daughter named Pallas, and Athena and the girl used to practice the arts of war together. But on one occasion they quarreled and, as Pallas was about to strike Athena, Zeus intervened on behalf of his daughter by interposing the aegis. Pallas was startled, and Athena took advantage of her surprise and wounded and killed her. Athena was distraught when she realized what she had done; in her grief she made a wooden image of the girl and decked it with the aegis. Cast down by Zeus, this statue, called the **Palladium**, fell into the territory of the Trojans, who built a temple to house it in honor. The Palladium in saga carries with it the destiny of the city of Troy. In honor of her friend, Athena took the name Pallas for herself. A more likely etiology is that the word Pallas means maiden and is but another designation of Athena's chastity, just as she is called Parthenos (Virgin), or (like Persephone) Kore (Girl).

Athena and Arachne

The famous story of Arachne bears testimony to the importance of Athena as the patroness of women's household arts, especially spinning and weaving. In Ovid's account (*Metamorphoses* 6.5–145) Athena has, of course, become the Roman **Minerva**.

Minerva turned her mind to Arachne's destruction, for she had heard that her fame as a worker in wool equaled her own. Arachne's birth and position brought her no distinction—it was her skill that did. Idmon of Colophon was her father, who dyed the thirsty wool with Ionian purple; her mother, who also was of low birth like her husband, had died. Yet their daughter, Arachne, for all that she was born in a lowly family living at lowly Hypaepa, pursued her quest for fame throughout the cities of Lydia by her work. (5–13)

The nymphs of Tmolus often left their vineyards, the nymphs of Pactolus often left their waters—to see and wonder at Arachne's handiwork. Nor was their pleasure merely in seeing her finished work, but also in observing her at work, such delight was in her skill. Whether at the beginning she gathered the unworked wool into balls, or worked it with her fingers and drew out lengths of fleece like clouds, or with swift-moving thumb turned the smooth spindle, or whether she used her embroidering needle—you would know that Minerva had taught her. Yet she would not admit this; jealous of her great teacher, she said, "Let her compete with me; if she wins I deny her nothing." (14–25)

10

Las Hilanderas (The Weavers), by Diego Velázquez (1599–1660); oil on canvas, ca. 1657; 66½ × 98 in. (as shown); enlarged in the eighteenth century to 87 × 114 in. In the foreground tapestry weavers are at work, with an older woman to the left and a young one to the right as the principal figures. In the background, women view the completed tapestry, in which the helmeted Athena is about to strike Arachne with her shuttle, in anger at her subject, *The Rape of Europa*. Velázquez has thus included a reference to *Titian's Rape of Europa* (see p. 407). (*Erich Lessing/Art Resource, NY*)

Minerva disguised herself as an old woman, white-haired and supporting her-self upon a stick, and spoke as follows: "Not everything that old age brings is to be avoided; experience comes with the passing years. Do not despise my advice! Let your ambition be to excel mortal women at weaving; give place to the god-dess and pray for her forgiveness for your rash words! She will pardon you if you pray." Arachne glowered at her; leaving her half-finished work and with difficulty restraining herself from blows, she openly showed her anger by her expression, as she attacked disguised Minerva with these words: "You old fool, enfeebled by advanced old age. Too long a life has done you no good! Keep your advice for your sons' wives (if you have any) and your daughter. I can think for myself, and you need not think your advice does any good—you will not change my mind. 20 Why does not the goddess herself come? Why does she refuse to compete with 30 me?" (26–42)

Then Minerva cried: "She has come!" and throwing off her disguise she showed herself as she was, the goddess Minerva. The nymphs and women of Lydia worshiped her divine presence; Arachne alone felt no awe. Yet she 40 blushed; a sudden flush stole over her face in spite of herself and as suddenly faded, like the red glow of the sky when Dawn first glows just before the heavens begin to whiten with the sun's rising. Obstinately she held to her course and rushed to destruction in her foolish desire for the prize. Jupiter's daughter resisted no more; she of-fered her no more advice; no more did she put off the competition. (43–52)

Ovid goes on to describe the weaving contest. Each weaves a tapestry at her loom with surpassing skill, depicting scenes from mythology. Minerva displays her contest with Neptune for the lordship of Attica and adds four subor-dinate scenes of mortals who challenged gods and were turned by them into other shapes. The whole was framed by an olive tree motif: "with her own tree she concluded her work."

Heedless of the lessons of Minerva's legends, Arachne depicted scenes of the gods' less honorable amorous con-quests—where Jupiter, Neptune, Apollo, Bacchus, and Saturn deceived goddesses and mortal women. As she completed her tapestry with a design of trailing ivy, Minerva's anger burst forth. Ovid continues:

Minerva could find no fault with the work, not even Envy herself could. Angered by Arachne's success, the golden-haired goddess tore up the embroidered tapestry with its stories of the gods' shameful deeds. With the boxwood shuttle she beat Arachne's face repeatedly. In grief Arachne strangled herself, stopping the passage of life with a noose. Minerva pitied her as she was hanging and raised her up with these words: "Stubborn girl, live, yet hang! And—to make you anxious for the future—may the same punishment be decreed for all your descendants." (129–138)

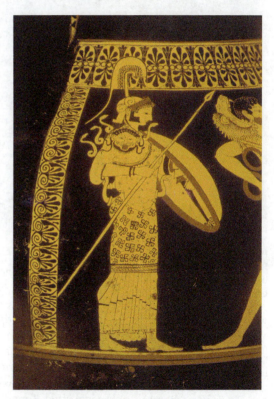

Athena. Detail from an Attic red-figure amphora on p. 562. In the center of the vase, Heracles and Apollo strug-gle for possession of the Delphic tripod. Athena, standing behind Heracles, appears in typical battle dress, wearing a helmet with a prominent crest and holding a spear and shield. She wears an elaborate aegis fringed with snaky tassels with a large *gorgoneion*, a stylized depiction of the Gorgon's head with feral grin and darting tongue. (*bpk Bildagentur/Staatliche Antikensammlung/Ingrid Geske-Heiden /Art Resource, NY*)

ATHENA PARTHENOS AND PALLAS ATHENA

Athena Parthenos. Reconstruction by N. Leipen of the original by Pheidias, 447–438 B.C.; about one-tenth full size. The original cult-statue stood some 38 feet tall, its gold and ivory gleaming in the half-light as the worshiper entered the *cella* with its double row of columns and reflecting pool. Pheidias focused on the majesty of the city's goddess, and the reliefs on her shield, sandals, and statue base all are symbols of the victory of order over disorder in the human and divine spheres. The atmosphere of civic grandeur is far from the intimate emotion of the *Mourning Athena* on p. 183. (*Courtesy of Amanda M. Brown*)

When, in 480 B.C., the Persians crushed the Greek forces holding the pass at Thermopylae, the Great King Darius, with his enormous host, marched without impediment toward Athens. When they arrived, they invaded the city and ravaged it, including its most holy sanctuaries on the Acropolis. In 479 B.C., the Greeks remarkably were able to defeat the Persian fleet at Salamis and the Persian host at Plataea.

In the years after the Persian Wars, Athens became a naval empire and one of the most powerful states of the Greek world under the leadership of her magnetic general and statesman Pericles (ca. 495–429 B.C.). By the middle of the fifth century, Pericles had decided to inaugurate an immense building program that would reflect the increased stature of the city and pay homage to Athena, their patron goddess, for the blessings she had bestowed upon her favored city. Among the projects that resulted from this vast expenditure of funds was the Parthenon. The Greek sculptor Pheidias was commissioned to supervise the work, which was brought to completion between 447 and 438 B.C. He himself produced the chryselephantine (gold and ivory) statue of *Athena Parthenos* that graced the cella of the temple. Gold and ivory seem to have been Pheidias' favored media; he used the same materials for his masterpiece, the statue of Zeus at Olympia.

The *Athena Parthenos* was built around a wooden frame or core and stood almost 40 feet tall. It required more than a ton of gold sheathing. The statue has long since been lost, but a general idea of the conception of the artist and the composition of the figure is preserved through ancient literary sources, like Pausanias, and Roman copies, which do not approach the genius and beauty of the original. Pheidias was a monumental sculptor, and the qualities most admired in the ancient world were the grandeur and beauty of his figures. His *Athena Parthenos* was majestic and awe-inspiring. It was the epitome of the high classical style. Together with the other sculptural decorations on the Parthenon, it expressed the Athenian sense that the Persian Wars, like their mythic analogues, illustrated the triumph of Greek civilization over barbarism.

The Austrian painter Gustav Klimt (1862–1918) was one of the most prominent artists and intellectuals at the forefront of an extraordinary cultural efflorescence in Vienna at the end of the nineteenth and beginning of the twentieth century. During this period, Sigmund Freud and Carl Jung were exposing the darker, sublimated forces at work in the unconscious mind. The German philosopher Friedrich Nietzsche, whose work explored, as he saw it, the opposition of the Apollonian and Dionysian forces in Greek culture, had a profound influence on the intellectual culture of Vienna at the time. For Nietzsche, Greek tragedy, as it developed in the Archaic Age of the sixth century B.C., touched upon the transcendent, liberating spirit of the Dionysian. These Viennese intellectuals, influenced by Nietzsche, rejected the canons of an earlier generation, marred as they were by an unemotional restraint that produced art that was devoid of spirit, passion, and energy.

Klimt, for his part, was a member of a circle of artists who championed the Vienna Secession, a movement that sought to free artistic expression from what they saw as the sterile and lifeless art of the previous generation. The inaugural exhibition for the Secession artists was held in 1898 and included Klimt's *Pallas Athena*. In a real sense, Klimt's vision of Athena became an icon for the Secession movement. His *Pallas Athena* is a remarkably complex and multilayered work. While Klimt, who was a goldsmith, seems to evoke the image of Pheidias' *Athena Parthenos* in the gold-laden head and torso of his Athena and the contrasting white of her face and arm, his work is not an homage. Rather, it bespeaks the illusion of surface and the disquieting depths beneath that surface. Elements of the image belong more properly to the archaic sixth century B.C., not the classical fifth century B.C.: the gorgoneion on her aegis is of an earlier type; her helmet is not the resplendent, ceremonial headdress of Pheidias' image (which allows the viewer to see Athena's whole face), but an earlier Corinthian helmet, which masks the features of the goddess; in the background, Klimt has reproduced a sixth-century B.C. vase depicting Heracles wrestling Triton, who in myth is associated with Athena. The most unsettling features of the image are Athena's eyes; it has been suggested that Klimt was influenced by the Homeric epithet *glaukopis* (see p. 184). Eye motifs are prevalent throughout the entire work, appearing on the circular tassels of her shield, the almost owl-like design on the body of Triton, and even in the decoration on the frame. In fact, Athena's eyes seem to have assumed the terrifying power of the Gorgon; her full-frontal gaze is an assault and a challenge to look upon her and be defeated. Though Klimt's depiction of Athena is very different from his other, more typically erotic *femmes fatales*, an eroticism is channeled into the nude, sexually charged, and triumphant image of Victory that Athena holds.

Pallas Athena, by Gustav Klimt (1862–1918); oil on canvas, 29½ × 29½ in. Klimt focuses on the latent energy of the warrior goddess, while giving a new interpretation to her traditional attributes of helmet, gray eyes, owl, Gorgon and aegis, spear, and Nike (who is painted as a naked woman with red hair). The gold highlights (Klimt was the son of a gold engraver) again reinterpret the gold and ivory of Pheidias' statue. (© RMN-Grand Palais/Art Resource, NY)

> With these words Minerva sprinkled her with the juice of a magic herb. As the fateful liquid touched her, Arachne's hair dropped off; her nose and ears vanished, and her head was shrunken; her whole body was contracted. From her side thin fingers dangled for legs, and the rest became her belly. Yet still from this she lets the thread issue forth and, a spider now, practices her former weaving art. (139–145)

10

This story illustrates the severe, moral earnestness of this warrior maiden that is often only too apparent. Yet, as Ovid tells it, Minerva's punishment of Arachne's hubris is also motivated by jealousy of her success.

The Character and Appearance of Athena

A study of women, cloth, and society in early times presents insights into how women's textile arts function as analogy and metaphor in mythology and illuminates the importance of Athena as the goddess of the "central womanly skill of weaving."[3] Athena represented not only skill but also cunning, and so weaving became a metaphor for human resourcefulness, as illustrated by clever Penelope, a wily wife, just like her wily husband Odysseus. The concept of life as a thread created by women and controlled by the feminine Fates presents a major related theme. Weaving, however necessary, was also revered as a most respected art that belonged to the **arete** (excellence) of a woman as opposed to the different *arete* of a man.

Athena and Heracles. Interior of a kylix by the potter Python and painter Duris, ca. 475 B.C.; diameter 13 in. On the viewer's left Heracles sits on a rock, wearing his lion skin and with his club resting beside him. He is refreshed by Athena, who stands opposite and pours wine from an oinochoe (a jug for wine) into a two-handled kylix. She wears the aegis (note the four snakes on the lower right) and holds an owl in her left hand: her spear is held at rest, and her helmet rests on a plinth. (*bpk Bildagentur/ Staatliche Antikensammlung/ Hermann Buresch/ Art Resource, NY*)

Athena is a goddess of many other specific arts, crafts, and skills (military, political, and domestic), as well as the deification of wisdom and good counsel in a more generic and abstract conception. She is skilled in the taming and training of horses, interested in ships and chariots, and the inventor of the flute. This invention was supposedly inspired by the lamentations (accompanied by the hiss of serpents) uttered by the surviving Gorgons after the death of Medusa. But Athena quickly grew to dislike the new instrument because her beautiful features became distorted when she played, and so she threw it away in disgust. Marsyas, the satyr, picked up the instrument with dire consequences, as we shall see in Chapter 11. In Athens, Athena was worshiped along with Hephaestus as patroness of all arts and crafts.

Athena is often represented in art with her attributes as a war goddess: helmet, spear, and shield (the aegis, on which the head of the Gorgon Medusa may be depicted). Sometimes she is attended by a winged figure (Nike, Victory) bearing a crown or garland of honor and success. Athena herself, as **Athena Nike**, represented victorious achievement in war, and a simple but elegant temple of Athena Nike stood on a bastion to the right of the entrance to the Acropolis. The brief *Homeric Hymn to Athena* (11) invokes her as a deity of war (like Ares).

Mourning Athena. Marble relief from the Acropolis, ca. 460 B.C.; height 21 in. Athena is a young woman, with helmet and spear, but without aegis and shield. She gazes at a stele (an upright stone slab) on which may have been inscribed the names of Athenians killed in the previous year's fighting. The folds of her skirt follow her body and do not fall straight. The title and purpose of the work are unknown, but it shows how closely the goddess was concerned with the life and death of her citizens. (*Scala/ Art Resource, NY*)

> I begin to sing about Pallas Athena, city-guardian, who with Ares is concerned about the deeds of war—the din of fighting and battles and the sacking of cities; she also protects the people as they leave and return. Hail, goddess, give us good luck and good fortune. (1–5)

Pallas Athena is beautiful, with a severe and aloof kind of loveliness that is masculine and striking. One of her standard epithets is *glaukopis*, which may mean gray- or green-eyed, but more probably refers to the bright or keen radiance of her glance rather than to the color of her eyes. Possibly, too, the adjective may be intended to mean owl-eyed, or of owlish aspect or countenance; certainly, Athena is at times closely identified with the owl (particularly on coins). The snake is also associated with her, sometimes appearing coiled at her feet or on her shield. This association (along with those of the owl and the olive tree) suggests that perhaps Athena originally was (like so many others) a fertility goddess, even though her character as a virgin dominates later tradition.

In fact, her character is usually impeccable. Unlike another virgin goddess, Artemis, to whom men made advances (although at their dire peril), Athena remained sexually unapproachable. Hephaestus' attempt on her honor (in the early saga of Athens, p. 571) confirms the purity and integrity of her convictions. It would be a misconception, however, to imagine Athena only as a cold and formidable virago who might easily elicit one's respect but hardly one's love. This Valkyrie-like maiden does have her touching moments, not only in her close and warm relationship with her father, Zeus, but also in her devout loyalty and steadfast protection of more than one hero (e.g., Telemachus and Odysseus, Heracles, Perseus, Jason, and Bellerophon).

Either alone or coupled with Apollo, Athena can be made the representative of a new order of divinity—the younger generation of the gods championing progress and the advanced enlightenment of civilization. As the agent of Zeus, Athena brings the *Odyssey* to a close by answering the primitive demand for blood evoked by the relatives of the suitors and establishing the divine and universal validity of the justice meted out by Odysseus. In Aeschylus' *Oresteia* she is on the side of Apollo for the acquittal of Orestes through the due process of law in Athens before the court of the Areopagus (which the goddess is said to have created), appeasing and silencing, presumably forever, the old social order of family vendetta represented by the Furies.

Select Bibliography

Barber, Elizabeth Wayland. *Women's Work: The First 20,000 Years.* New York: Norton, 1994. An appreciation of the importance and dignity of women's skill in weaving and the worship of Athena.

Beard, Mary. *The Parthenon.* Cambridge, MA: Harvard University Press, 2003. A survey for the general reader and student.

Deacy, Susan. *Athena.* Gods and Heroes of the Ancient World Series. New York: Routledge, 2008.

Hurwit, Jeffrey M. *The Athenian Acropolis, History, Mythology, and Archaeology from the Neolithic Era to the Present.* New York: Cambridge University Press, 2000.

Jenkins, Ian. *The Parthenon Sculptures*. Cambridge, MA: Harvard University Press, 2008. A history of the Parthenon that contains a study of the pediments, metopes, and Ionic frieze, with color illustrations in full and fine detail.

Neils, Jenifer, ed. *Goddess and Polis: The Panathenaic Festival in Ancient Athens*. Princeton, NJ: Princeton University Press, 1992.

————. *Worshipping Athena: Panathenaia & Parthenon*. Madison, WI: University of Wisconsin Press, 1996. A collection of essays divided into three sections: "Myth and Cult," "Contests and Prizes," and "Art and Politics."

Neils, Jenifer, and Stephen V. Tracy. *The Games at Athens: A General Introduction to the Greater Panathenaea*. An Agora Picture Book. Athens: American School of Classical Studies at Athens, 2003.

Robertson, Martin, and Alison Frantz. *The Parthenon Frieze*. New York: Phaidon, 1975. Distinguished by Frantz's photography.

Scheid, John, and Jesper Svenbro. *The Craft of Zeus: Myths of Weaving and Fabric*. Cambridge, MA: Harvard University Press, 1996. The exploration of the metaphor of weaving and its symbolism.

Shearer, Ann. *Athene: Image and Energy*. London: Penguin, 1998 [1996]. Traces, from a feminist perspective, the continuing energy of Athena in literature, art, religion, and psychology.

St. Clair, William. *Lord Elgin and the Marbles. The Controversial History of the Parthenon Sculptures*. New York: Oxford University Press, 1998.

Vrettos, Theodore. *The Elgin Affair*. New York: Arcade, 1997. A detailed re-creation of the history from the beginning to the present day with a scrutiny of interested persons such as **Napoleon, Lord Byron, and Lord Nelson.**

Woodford, Susan. *The Parthenon*. New York: Cambridge University Press, 1981. Brief and basic.

Primary Sources

Sources in the Chapter

Homeric Hymn 11	*To Athena*
Homeric Hymn 28	*To Athena*
Hesiod	*Theogony* 886–898
Homer	*Iliad* 5.733–864
Ovid	*Metamorphoses* 6.5–145

Additional Sources

Callimachus	*On the Bath of Pallas* (Hymn 5)
Pausanias	*Description of Greece* 1.24.5–1.24.7: Sculpture of the Parthenon

Notes

1. There are a number of ancient, miniature replicas and a description by Pausanias (1.24). Copyright permission cannot be obtained to reproduce the most recent full-scale reconstruction in the Parthenon at Nashville, Tennessee.
2. For the Parthenon and its sculpture, see John Travlos, *Pictorial Dictionary of Ancient Athens* (New York: Praeger, 1971), entry for "Parthenon"; Martin Robertson and Alison

Frantz, *The Parthenon Frieze* (New York: Phaidon), distinguished by Frantz's photography; John Boardman, *Greek Sculpture: The Classical Period* (London: Thames & Hudson, 1955), Chapter 10, "The Parthenon," pp. 96–145, includes diagrams, reconstructions, and photographs in his useful, short account; Martin Robertson, *A Shorter History of Greek Art* (New York: Cambridge University Press, 1981), pp. 90–102, for the Parthenon, the best discussion, distilled from the author's *A History of Greek Art*, 2 vols. (1975), Chapter 5, pp. 292–322.

3. Elisabeth Wayland Barber, *Women's Work: The First 20,000 Years* (New York: Norton, 1994), p. 242.

9

APHRODITE AND EROS

> The Babylonians have a most disgraceful custom: a native woman once in her life must sit in the sanctuary of Aphrodite and have sex with a stranger. . . . Those possessed of beauty and stature are quickly released, but those who are unattractive remain for quite a while, since they are unable to fulfill the law. Some wait three or four years.
>
> —HERODOTUS, *History of the Persian Wars* 1.199.1–5

AS WE HAVE SEEN, Hesiod describes the birth of Aphrodite after the castration of Uranus and derives her name from the Greek word *aphros* (foam). Hesiod also links the goddess closely with Cythera (see p. 71) and with Cyprus; the latter was especially associated with her worship, particularly in its city of Paphos. Thus, Aphrodite is called both Cytherea and Cypris. Another version of her birth gives her parents as Zeus and Dione. Dione is little more than a name to us, but a curious one, since it is the feminine form of the name Zeus (which in another form is Dios).

Aphrodite Urania and Aphrodite Pandemos

This double tradition of Aphrodite's birth suggests a basic duality in her character or the existence of two separate goddesses of love: Aphrodite Urania or Celestial Aphrodite, sprung from Uranus alone, is ethereal and sublime; Aphrodite Pandemos (Aphrodite of All the People, or Common Aphrodite), sprung from Zeus and Dione, is essentially physical in nature. Plato's *Symposium* elaborates on this distinction and claims that Aphrodite Urania, the older of the two, is stronger, more intelligent, and spiritual, whereas Aphrodite Pandemos, born from both sexes, is more base and devoted primarily to physical satisfaction.[1] It is imperative to understand that the Aphrodite who sprang from Uranus (despite her sexuality in Hesiod's account) becomes, for philosophy and religion, the celestial goddess of pure and spiritual love and the antithesis of Aphrodite, daughter of Zeus and Dione, the goddess of physical attraction and procreation. This distinction between sacred and profane love is one of the most profound archetypes in the history of civilization.

The Nature and Appearance of Aphrodite

The *Homeric Hymn to Aphrodite* (10), with its brief glimpse of Aphrodite, reminds us of her cult places, Cyprus and Cythera, and the city of Salamis in Cyprus.

> I shall sing about Cyprus-born Cytherea, who gives mortals sweet gifts; on her lovely face, smiles are always suffused with the bloom of love.
>
> Hail, goddess, mistress of well-built Salamis and sea-girt Cyprus. Give me a desirable song. Yet I shall remember you and another song too.

In general, Aphrodite is the goddess of beauty, love, and marriage. Her worship was universal in the ancient world, but its facets were varied. At port cities such as Ephesus, Paphos, and Corinth, temple harlots may have been kept in Aphrodite's honor, but the evidence for widespread temple prostitution is lacking. At Athens this same goddess was the staid and respectable deity of marriage and married love. The seductive allurement of this goddess was very great; she herself possessed a magic girdle with irresistible powers of enticement. In the *Iliad* (14.197–221) Hera borrows it with great effect on her husband, Zeus.

The gamut of the conceptions of the goddess of love is reflected in sculpture as well as literature. Archaic idols, like those of other fertility goddesses, are grotesque in their exaggeration of her sexual attributes. In early Greek art, she is rendered as a beautiful woman, usually clothed. By the fourth century, she is portrayed nude (or nearly so), the idealization of womanhood in all her femininity; the sculptor Praxiteles was mainly responsible for establishing the type—sensuous in its soft curves and voluptuousness.[2] As so often occurred in the ancient world, once a master had captured a universal conception, it was repeated endlessly with or without significant variations. Everyone knows the Venus from Melos or one of the many other extant copies, although Praxiteles' originals have not survived.

The Birth of Aphrodite. Ca. 460 B.C.; marble, height (at corner) 33 in. In this three-sided relief (known as the *Ludovisi Throne*), Aphrodite is shown in the center panel rising from the sea and being clothed by two attendants, who stand on a pebbly beach. On the left panel (not shown) a naked musician plays the double flute, and on the right panel (not shown) a veiled woman burns incense. (*Scala/Ministero per i Beni e le Attività culturali/Art Resource, NY*)

Attendants of Aphrodite

The **Graces** (**Charites**) and the Hours or Seasons (Horae) are often associated with Aphrodite as decorative and appropriate attendants. The Graces, generally three in number, are personifications of aspects of loveliness. The **Horae**, daughters of Zeus and Themis, are sometimes difficult to distinguish from the Graces, but they eventually emerge with clearer identity as the **Seasons**; thus, they usually are thought of as a group of two, three, or four. Horae means "hours" and therefore "time" and thus ultimately "seasons." The *Homeric Hymn to Aphrodite* (6) focuses on the decking out of the goddess by the Horae, whom in this context we call the Hours.

> I shall sing about beautiful and revered Aphrodite of the golden crown, who holds as her domain the battlements of all sea-girt Cyprus. The moist force of the West Wind Zephyrus as he blows brought her there amid the soft foam on the waves of the resounding sea. The gold-bedecked Hours gladly received her and clothed her in divine garments. On her immortal head they placed a finely wrought crown of gold and in her pierced earlobes, flowers of copper and precious gold. About her soft neck and silvery breasts they adorned her with necklaces of gold, the kind that beautify the Hours themselves whenever they go to the lovely dancing choruses of the gods and to the home of their father. Then after they had bedecked her person with every adornment they led her to the immortals, who greeted her when they saw her and took her in their welcoming hands; and each god prayed that she would be his wedded wife and he would bring her home, as he marveled at the beauty of violet-crowned Cytherea. (1–18)
>
> Hail, sweet and winning goddess with your seductive glance; grant that I may win victory in the contest and make my song fitting. Yet I shall remember you and another song too. (19–21)

10

The Phallic Priapus

The more elemental and physical aspects of Aphrodite's nature are seen in her son, Priapus.[3] His father may be Hermes, Dionysus, Pan, Adonis, or even Zeus. Priapus is a fertility god, generally depicted as deformed and bearing a huge and erect phallus. He is found in gardens and at the doors of houses. He is part scarecrow, part bringer of luck, and part guardian against thieves; therefore, he has something in common with Hermes. He also resembles Dionysus and Pan (two of his other reputed fathers) and is sometimes confused with them or their retinues. Whatever the origins of Priapus in terms of sincere and primitive reverence for the male powers of generation, stories about him usually came to be comic and obscene. In the jaded society of later antiquity, his worship meant little more than a cult of sophisticated pornography.

Aphrodite of Melos (Venus de Milo). Late second century B.C.; marble, height 80 in. This is the best known representation of Aphrodite in the Hellenistic age, after Praxiteles had popularized statues of the unclothed female body with his *Aphrodite of Cnidus* (mid-fourth century B.C.): before Praxiteles, Greek convention had limited nudity in statues, with few exceptions, to the male form. Praxiteles' statue survives only in copies dismissed as "lamentable objects" by Martin Robertson. Unlike them, the *Aphrodite of Melos* is unrestored and half draped. It has aroused passionate criticism, favorable and unfavorable. Its sculptor was probably a Greek from Phrygian Antioch, whose name ended in "-andros." See George Curtis, *Disarmed: The Story of the Venus de Milo* (New York: Knopf, 2003). (© *RMN-Grand Palais/Art Resource, NY*)

Pygmalion

Although many stories illustrate the mighty power of Aphrodite, the story of Pygmalion has provided a potent theme (e.g., Shaw's *Pygmalion* and Lerner and Loewe's *My Fair Lady*). Ovid tells how Aphrodite (Venus in his version) was enraged with the women of Cyprus because they dared to deny her divinity; in her wrath, the goddess caused them to be the first women to prostitute themselves, and as they lost all their sense of shame it was easy to turn them into stone. Ovid goes on to relate the story of Pygmalion and the result of his disgust for these women (*Metamorphoses* 10.243–297).

Pygmalion saw these women leading a life of sin and was repelled by the many vices that nature had implanted in the feminine mind. And so he lived alone without a wife for a long time, doing without a woman to share his bed. Meanwhile he fashioned happily a statue of ivory, white as snow, and gave it a beauty surpassing that of any woman born; and he fell in love with what he had made. It looked like a real maiden who you would believe was alive and willing to move, had not modesty prevented her. To such an extent art concealed art; Pygmalion wondered at the body he had fashioned and the flames of passion burned in his breast. He often ran his hands over his creation to test whether it was real flesh and blood or ivory. And he would not go so far as to admit that it was ivory. He gave it kisses and thought that they were returned; he spoke to it and held it and believed that his fingers sank into the limbs that he touched and was afraid that a bruise might appear as he pressed her close. (243–258)   10

Sometimes he enticed her with blandishments, at other times he brought her gifts that please a girl: shells and smooth pebbles, little birds, flowers of a thousand colors, lilies, painted balls, and drops of amber, the tears wept by Phaëthon's sisters who had been changed into trees. He also clothed her limbs with garments, put rings on her fingers, draped long necklaces around her neck, dangled jewelry from her ears, hung adornments on her breast. All was becoming, but she looked no less beautiful naked. He placed her on his bed with covers dyed in Tyrian purple and laid her down, to rest her head on soft pillows of feathers as if she could feel them. (259–269)   20

The most celebrated feast day of Venus in the whole of Cyprus arrived; heifers, their crooked horns adorned with gold, were slaughtered by the blow of the axe on their snowy necks, and incense smoked. When he had made his offering at the altar, Pygmalion stood and timidly prayed: "If you gods are able to grant everything, I desire for my wife. . . ." He did not dare to say "my ivory maiden." Golden Venus herself was present at her festival and understood what his prayers meant. As an omen of her kindly will, a tongue of flame burned bright and flared up in the air. (270–279)   30

When he returned home, Pygmalion grasped the image of his girl and lay beside her on the bed and showered her with kisses. She seemed to be warm. He touched her with his lips again and felt her breasts with his hands. At his touch the ivory grew soft, and its rigidity gave way to the pressure of his fingers; it yielded just as Hymettan wax when melted in the sun is fashioned into many shapes by the working of the hands and made pliable. He is stunned but dubious of his joy and fearful he is wrong. In his love he touches this answer to his prayers. It was a body; the veins throbbed as he felt them with his thumb. Then in truth Pygmalion was full of prayers in which he gave thanks to Venus. At last he presses his lips on lips that are real and

> the maiden feels the kisses she is given and as she raises her eyes to meet his she sees both her lover and the sky. (280–294)   40
>
> The goddess is present at the marriage that she has made, and now when the crescent moon had become full nine times, Pygmalion's wife gave birth to Paphos, and from him the place got its name. (295–297)

Galatea is the name given to Pygmalion's beloved in later versions of the tale.

Aphrodite and Adonis

In the most famous of her myths, Aphrodite is confused with the great Phoenician goddess Astarte; they have in common as their love a young and handsome youth named by the Greeks Adonis.[4] Perhaps the best-known version of the story of Aphrodite and Adonis is told by Ovid. Paphos (the son of Pygmalion and Galatea) had a son, Cinyras. **Myrrha**, the daughter of **Cinyras**, fell desperately in love with her own father. Tormented by her sense of shame and guilt, the poor girl was on the point of suicide, but she was rescued just in time by her faithful nurse, who eventually wrenched the secret from her. Although the old woman was horrified by what she learned, she preferred to help satisfy the girl's passion rather than to see her die.

It was arranged that the daughter should go to the bed of her father without his knowing her identity, and their incestuous relations continued for some time until Cinyras in dismay found out with whom he had been sleeping. In terror, Myrrha fled from the wrath of her father. As he pursued her, she prayed for

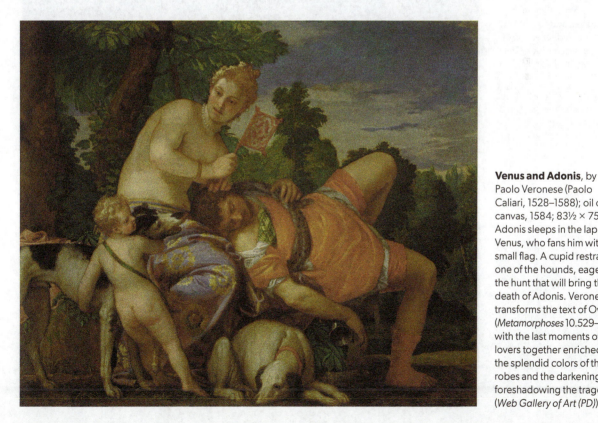

Venus and Adonis, by Paolo Veronese (Paolo Caliari, 1528–1588); oil on canvas, 1584; 83½ × 75 in. Adonis sleeps in the lap of Venus, who fans him with a small flag. A cupid restrains one of the hounds, eager for the hunt that will bring the death of Adonis. Veronese transforms the text of Ovid (*Metamorphoses* 10.529–559), with the last moments of the lovers together enriched by the splendid colors of their robes and the darkening sky foreshadowing the tragedy. (*Web Gallery of Art (PD)*)

PYGMALION AND THE IMAGE

The painter Edward Burne-Jones completed a sequence of paintings (1875–1878) illustrating the myth of the artist Pygmalion sculpting an image of his ideal woman, who through the agency of Venus comes to life. Burne-Jones was one of a group of artists and poets known as the Pre-Raphaelites. Their avowed

The Heart Desires, by Edward Burne-Jones; oil on canvas; 39 × 30 in. The artist Pygmalion stands before a plinth, contemplating the act of creation. He is framed by women in the town, who are seen through the doorway, and a sculpture of the three Graces in traditional pose. The two groups of women suggest a contrast between the real and the ideal, the profane and the sacred. The dichotomy between the two groups of women and the troubled state of Pygmalion's mind is given added intensity by the fractured reflection of the Graces on the floor. (*The Bridgeman Art Library*)

purpose encompassed both a rejection of the rigid, academic, aesthetic canons of their own day and a return to the purity and simplicity of Italian art before the time of the Italian painter and architect Raphael (1483–1520), hence the term *Pre-Raphaelite*. They eschewed long-accepted compositional rules of art and attempted to combine harmoniously an austere realism with a lush symbolism. Both Burne-Jones (1833–1898) and the designer, artist, and writer William Morris (1834–1896), as exponents of the Pre-Raphaelite movement, drew heavily on stories from Greek myth and Arthurian legends. These poets and artists combined a vivid color or sound palette; a highly charged, though sublimated, eroticism;

The Hand Refrains, by Edward Burne-Jones; oil on canvas; 39 × 30 in. The artist Pygmalion has created the perfect realization of his ideal woman. He is caught in a moment of hesitation, yearning to touch the object of his desire. Yet the created image is still not alive. That requires the creative energies of a goddess. (*The Bridgeman Art Library*)

and a tense, hushed, and somber atmosphere. Burne-Jones and Morris met at school and became artistic collaborators. Between 1868 and 1870 Morris published his most famous work *The Earthly Paradise*, a treasury of narrative stories drawn from a variety of sources, including Greek, Norse, and medieval myths and legends. Among the many tales Morris retells is the story of Pygmalion,

The Godhead Fires, by Edward Burne-Jones; oil on canvas; 39 × 30 in. Venus, clothed in a diaphanous garment and holding a sprig of myrtle, appears with her doves and roses and by her touch brings Galatea to life, with the words, "Come down, and learn to love and be alive." Venus extends her arm and with her index finger charges the inert figure with life. Is Venus' gesture meant to suggest a comparison with Michelangelo's fresco on the Sistine Chapel ceiling, in which God with a touch of his finger imbues Adam with life? Galatea reaches down to entwine her arms around the arm of Venus. The entwining of their arms reminds the viewer of the embrace of the two women beyond the door in the first painting. Galatea never looks more alive than in this scene. (*The Bridgeman Art Library*)

entitled "Pygmalion and the Image." Burne-Jones made a number of drawings intended for a lavishly illustrated edition of Morris' *The Earthly Paradise*. The Pygmalion series sprang from those initial drawings. Burne-Jones chose four scenes to delineate the narrative sequence of the tale, with Morris' quatrain lending the titles to each picture in the series.

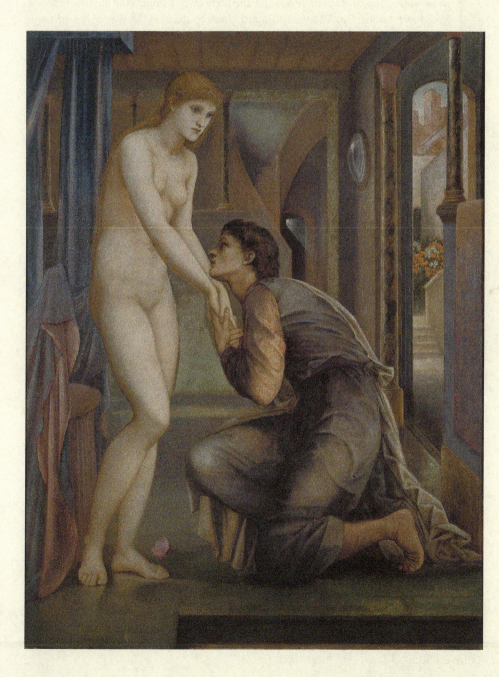

The Soul Attains, by Edward Burne-Jones; oil on canvas; 39 × 30 in. Pygmalion, in the manner of worshipper, reaches up to touch his beloved. He still wears his reticence like a garment. Can he truly love this woman as a woman? His head faces her torso, but his eye seems turned up from under, as if unable or unwilling to gaze upon her naked body. Galatea looks past him and her hands seem more grasped than grasping. The arrangement of the two figures suggests a comparison with Venus and Galatea in the previous painting. Has Galatea become for Pygmalion the goddess of love? The single rose at her feet is suggestive of this transformation. (*The Bridgeman Art Library*)

deliverance and was changed into a myrrh tree, which continually drips with her tears. Myrrha had become pregnant by her father, and from the tree was born a beautiful son named Adonis, who grew up to be a most handsome youth and keen hunter. At the sight of him Aphrodite fell desperately in love. She warned Adonis against the dangers of the hunt, telling him to be especially wary of any wild beasts that would not turn and flee but stood firm. Ovid's story continues as follows (*Metamorphoses* 10.708–739):

> These were the warnings of Venus and she rode away through the air in her chariot yoked with swans. But Adonis' courageous nature stood in the way of her admonitions. By chance his dogs followed the clear tracks of a wild boar and frightened it from its hiding place. As it was ready to come out of the woods, the son of Cinyras hit a glancing blow on its side. With its crooked snout the savage beast immediately dislodged the blood-stained spear and made for the frightened youth as he fled for safety. The boar buried its tusk deep within his groin and brought him down on the yellow sand, dying. (708–716)
>
> As Venus was being borne through the air in her light chariot on the wings of swans (she had not yet reached Cyprus), she heard the groans of the dying boy from afar and turned the course of her white birds toward them. When she saw from the air above his lifeless body lying in his own blood, she rushed down, and rent her bosom and her hair and beat her breast with hands not meant to do such violence. She complained against the Fates, crying: "But still everything will not be subject to your decrees; a memorial of my grief for you, Adonis, will abide forever. The scene of your death will be re-created annually with the ritual of my grief performed. But your blood will be transformed into a flower. O Persephone, you were allowed at one time to change the limbs of the maiden Mentha into the fragrant mint—will I be begrudged then the transformation of my hero, the son of Cinyras?" (717–731)   10
>
> With these words she sprinkled fragrant nectar on his blood which, at the touch of the drops, began to swell just like a gleaming bubble in the rain. In no longer than an hour's time a flower sprang from the blood, red as the thick skin of the fruit of the pomegranate that hides the seeds within. Yet the flower is of brief enjoyment for the winds (which give it its name, anemone) blow upon it; with difficulty it clings to life and falls under the blasts and buffeting. (731–739)   20

Ovid's story predicts the rites associated with the worship of Adonis involving ceremonial wailing and the singing of dirges over the effigy of the dead youth. Obviously, we have here once again a rendition of a recurrent theme: the Great Mother and her lover, who dies as vegetation dies and comes back to life again. Another version of the myth makes this even clearer.

When Adonis was an infant, Aphrodite put him in a chest and gave it to Persephone to keep. Persephone looked inside; and once she saw the beauty of the boy, she refused to give him back. Zeus settled the quarrel that ensued by deciding that Adonis would stay with Persephone below one part of the year and with Aphrodite in the upper world for the other part. It is possible to detect similarities between Easter celebrations of the dead and risen Christ in various parts of the world and those in honor of the dead and risen Adonis. Christianity, too, absorbed and transformed the ancient conception of the sorrowing goddess with her lover dying in her arms to that of the sad Virgin holding in her lap her beloved Son.

Cybele and Attis

Parallels to the figures of Aphrodite and Adonis can readily be found in the Phrygian story of Cybele and Attis, yet another variation of the eternal myth of the Great Mother and her lover that eventually spread throughout the Greco-Roman world.[5] Cybele was sprung from the earth, originally a bisexual deity but then reduced to a female. From the severed organ, an almond tree arose. **Nana**, the daughter of the god of the river Sangarios, picked a blossom from the tree and put it in her bosom; the blossom disappeared, and Nana found herself pregnant. When a son, Attis, was born, he was exposed and left to die, but a he-goat attended him. Attis grew up to be a handsome youth, and Cybele fell in love with him; however, he loved another, and Cybele in her jealousy drove him mad. In his madness, Attis castrated himself and died.[6] Cybele repented and obtained Zeus' promise that the body of Attis would never decay.

In her actual worship, Cybele was followed by a retinue of devotees who worked themselves into a frenzy of devotion that could lead to self-mutilation.[7] The orgiastic nature of her ritual is suggested by the frantic music that accompanied her: the beating of drums, the clashing of cymbals, and the blaring of horns. The myth explains why historically her priests (called **Galli**) were eunuchs. It is also easy to see how the din that attended Cybele could be identified with the ritual connected with another mother-goddess, Rhea, whose attendants long ago hid the cries of the infant Zeus from his father, Cronus, by the clash of their music. So it was that the Curetes became identified with the Galli.

Like Adonis, Attis is another resurrection-god, and their personalities become merged in the tradition. Like Adonis, Attis may die not through his self-inflicted wounds but by the tusk of a boar. Also like Adonis, Attis comes back to life with the rebirth of vegetation.

We have evidence of springtime ceremonies at which the public mourned and rejoiced for the death and rebirth of Attis. We can ascertain, too, the nature of the secret and mystic rites that were also a part of his worship. Frazer provides a compelling reconstruction:

> Our information as to the nature of these mysteries and the date of their celebration is unfortunately very scanty, but they seem to have included a sacramental meal and a baptism of blood. In the sacrament the novice became a partaker of the mysteries by eating out of a drum and drinking out of a cymbal, two instruments of music which figured prominently in the thrilling orchestra of Attis. The fast which accompanied the mourning for the dead god may perhaps have been designed to prepare the body of the communicant for the reception of the blessed sacrament by purging it of all that could defile by contact the sacred elements. In the baptism the devotee, crowned with gold and wreathed with fillets, descended into a pit, the mouth of which was covered with a wooden grating. A bull, adorned with garlands of flowers, its forehead glittering with gold leaf, was then driven on to the grating and there stabbed to death with a consecrated spear. Its hot reeking blood poured in torrents through the apertures, and was received with devout eagerness by the worshipper on every part of his person and garments, till he emerged from the pit, drenched, dripping, and scarlet from head to foot, to receive the homage, nay the adoration of his fellows as one who had been born again to eternal life and had washed away his sins in the blood of the bull. For some time afterwards the fiction of a new birth was kept up by dieting him on milk like a newborn babe. The regeneration of the worshipper took place at the same time as the regeneration of his god, namely, at the vernal equinox.[8]

We are obviously once again in the exotic realm of the mystery religions; this one, like the others, rests on a common fundamental belief in immortality.

The myth of Aphrodite and Adonis, like that of Cybele and Attis, depicts the destruction of the subordinate male in the grip of the eternal and all-powerful Great Goddess, through whom resurrection and new life may be attained.

Aphrodite and Anchises

An important variation on the same theme is illustrated by the story of Aphrodite and Anchises. In this instance, the possibility of the utter debilitation of the male as he fertilizes the female is a key element; Anchises is in dread fear that he will be depleted and exhausted as a man because he has slept with the immortal goddess. As the story is told in the *Homeric Hymn to Aphrodite* (5), we are given ample evidence of the mighty power of the goddess in the universe and a rich and symbolic picture of her devastating beauty. Here Aphrodite is a fertility goddess and mother as well as a divine and enticing woman, epitomizing the lure of sexual and romantic love.

The *Homeric Hymn* begins by telling us that there are only three hearts that the great goddess of love is unable to sway: those of Athena, Artemis, and Hestia. All others, both gods and goddesses, she can bend to her will. So great Zeus caused Aphrodite herself to fall in love with a man because he did not want her to continue her boasts that she in her power had joined the immortal gods and goddesses in love with mortals to beget mortal children but had experienced no such humiliating coupling herself. Although it is this major theme of the union between Aphrodite and Anchises that needs emphasis in this context, the hymn is translated in its entirety, thus preserving its integral beauty and power.

ZEUS' REVENGE ON APHRODITE

Muse, tell me about the deeds of Cyprian Aphrodite, the golden goddess who excites sweet desire in the gods and overcomes the races of mortal humans, the birds of the sky and all animals, as many as are nourished by the land and sea; all these are touched by beautifully crowned Cytherea. (1–6)

Yet she is not able to seduce or ensnare the hearts of three goddesses. First there is the daughter of aegis-bearing Zeus, bright-eyed Athena; for the deeds of golden Aphrodite give her no pleasure. She enjoys the work of Ares—fights, battles, and wars—and splendid achievements. She first taught craftsmen on the earth to make war-chariots and carriages fancy with bronze. She also teaches beautiful arts to soft-skinned maidens in their homes by instilling the proper skill in each of them. (7–15)   10

Next, laughter-loving Aphrodite is never able to subdue in love Artemis, the goddess of the noisy hunt, with shafts of gold; for she enjoys her bow and arrows and killing animals in the mountains, and also the lyre, dancing choruses, thrilling cries, shady groves, and the cities of just mortals. (16–20)

Finally, the deeds of Aphrodite are not pleasing to the modest maiden Hestia, who was the first of the children of crooked-minded Cronus and again the last, by the will of aegis-bearing Zeus.[9] Poseidon and Apollo wooed this revered virgin, but she did not want them at all and firmly said no. She touched the head of father Zeus, who wields the aegis, and swore that she would be a virgin all her days, this goddess of goddesses—and her oath has been fulfilled. Father Zeus has given her

Venus and Anchises. Fresco from the Galleria of the Farnese Palace, Rome, 1597–1600, by Annibale Carracci (1560–1609): dimensions of the Galleria, 66 × 21½ ft. The Farnese Gallery was decorated with Carracci's frescoes of *The Loves of the Gods*, arranged, like Ovid's stories in the *Metamorphoses*, in a complex and logical order. This scene is on the northeast side of the vault, opposite the scene of Zeus making love to Hera. Balancing these two scenes (on the southeast and southwest sides of the vault) are two others of divine lovers, Omphale and Hercules and Diana and Endymion. The Latin inscription on the footstool, on which the smiling Cupid has placed his foot, means "Whence [came] the Roman race," alluding to the birth of Aeneas from the consummation that is about to take place. (*Scala/Art Resource, NY*)

beautiful honor, instead of marriage. In the middle of the home she sits and receives the richest offering, in all the temples of the gods she holds her respected place, and among all mortals she is ordained as the most venerable of deities. (21–32)   20

The hearts of these three goddesses Aphrodite cannot influence or ensnare, but of everyone else there is no one or nothing among blessed gods or human beings that can escape her. She has led astray even the mind of Zeus, who delights in the thunder, the greatest of all, receiving as his due the highest honor. Whenever she wishes, she easily beguiles even his steadfast heart to mate with mortal women, without the knowledge of Hera, his sister and his wife, who in her great beauty is the best among the immortal goddesses. Wily Cronus and her mother Rhea bore her, most glorious, whom Zeus in his eternal wisdom made his august and prudent wife. Yet, into the heart of Aphrodite herself, Zeus instilled sweet desire to have intercourse with a man so that even she would be guilty of love with a mortal and so that laughter-loving Aphrodite could not ever say, smiling sweetly in mockery among all the deities, that she had mated gods with mortal women, who bore mortal sons to deathless gods and mated goddesses with mortal men. (33–52)   30

Yet Zeus put into the heart of Aphrodite herself sweet longing for Anchises, who at that time was tending cattle on the high ranges of Mt. Ida with its many streams. In beauty he was like the immortals; and so when laughter-loving Aphrodite saw him, she fell in love, and a terrible longing seized her being. She went to Paphos in Cyprus and entered her fragrant temple. For her precinct and fragrant altar are there. After she went in, she closed the shining doors; inside the Graces (Charites) bathed her and rubbed her with ambrosial oil, the kind used by the eternal gods, and she emerged perfumed in its heavenly sweetness. (53–63)   40

When she was beautifully clothed in her lovely garments and adorned with gold, laughter-loving Aphrodite left fragrant Cyprus and hastened to Troy, pressing swiftly on her way, high among the clouds. And she came to Ida, the mother of beasts, with its many springs, and crossed the mountain straight for the hut of Anchises. Gray wolves, bright-eyed lions, bears, and swift panthers, ravenous after deer, followed her, fawning. When she saw them, she was delighted within her heart and filled their breasts with desire; and they all went together in pairs to their beds, deep in their shadowy lairs. (64–75)   50

APHRODITE SEDUCES ANCHISES

She came to the well-built shelter and found him in his hut, left alone by the others, the hero Anchises, who had in full measure the beauty of the gods. All the rest were out following the cattle in the grassy pastures, but he, left alone by the others, paced to and fro playing a thrilling melody on his lyre. The daughter of Zeus, Aphrodite, stood before him, assuming the form of a beautiful young virgin, so that Anchises might not be afraid when he caught sight of her with his eyes. After Anchises saw her, he pondered as he marveled at her beautiful form and shining garments. For she wore a robe that was more brilliant than the gleam of fire, and she was adorned with intricate jewelry and radiant flowers, and about her soft throat were exquisite necklaces beautifully ornate and of gold. The raiment about her tender breasts shone like the moon, a wonder to behold. (76–90)   60

Desire gripped Anchises and he addressed her: "Hail to you, O lady, who have come to this dwelling, whoever of the blessed gods you are, Artemis or Leto or golden Aphrodite or well-born Themis or gleaming-eyed Athena; or perhaps you who have come here are one of the Graces, who are the companions of the gods and are called immortal, or one of the nymphs, who haunt the beautiful woods or inhabit this beautiful mountain, the streams of rivers, and the grassy meadows. I shall build an altar for you on a high mound in a conspicuous spot and I shall offer you beautiful sacrifices in all seasons. Be kindly disposed toward me and grant that I be a preeminent hero among the Trojans; make my offspring flourish in the time to come and allow me myself to live well for a long time and see the light of the sun, happy among my people, and reach the threshold of old age." (91–106)   70

Then Aphrodite, the daughter of Zeus, answered him: "Anchises, most renowned of earthborn men, I tell you that I am not any one of the gods. Why do you compare me to the immortals? No, I am a mortal and my mother who bore me was a mortal woman; my father, Otreus, who rules over all Phrygia with its fortresses, has a famous name; perhaps you have heard of him. But I know your language as well as I know our own, for a Trojan nurse reared me in my home in Phrygia; she took me from my mother when I was a very little child and brought me up. And so to be sure I readily understand your language. Now Hermes, the slayer of Argus, with his golden wand, snatched me away from the choral dance in honor of Artemis, the goddess of the golden arrows, who delights in the sounds of the hunt. We were a group of many nymphs and virgins such as suitors pursue, and in a vast throng we circled round about. From here the slayer of Argus with his golden wand snatched me away and whisked me over many places, some cultivated by mortals, others wild and unkempt, through which carnivorous beasts stalk from their shadowy lairs. I thought that I should never set foot again on the life-giving earth. But he told me that I should be called to the bed of Anchises as his lawful wife and that I should bear splendid children to you. And when he had explained and given his directions, then indeed he, the mighty slayer of Argus, went back again among the company of the gods. (107–129)   80 90

"But I have come to you and the force of destiny is upon me. I implore you, by Zeus and by your goodly parents (for they could not be base and have such a son as you), take me, pure and untouched by love, as I am, and present me to your father and devoted mother and to your brothers who are born from the same blood. I shall not be an unseemly bride in their eyes but a fitting addition to your family. And send a messenger quickly to Phrygia, home of swift horses, to tell my father and worried mother. They will send you gold enough and woven raiment; accept their many splendid gifts as their dowry for me. Do these things and prepare the lovely marriage celebration which both mortal human beings and immortal gods cherish." (130–142)   100

As she spoke thus, the goddess struck Anchises with sweet desire and he cried out to her: "If, as you declare, you are mortal, and a mortal woman is your mother, and Otreus is your renowned father, and you have come here through the agency of Hermes and are to be called my wife all our days, then no one of the gods or mortals will restrain me from joining with you in love right here and now, not even if the archer god Apollo himself were to shoot his grief-laden shafts from his silver bow. After I have once gone up into your bed, O maiden, fair as a goddess, I should even be willing to go below into the house of Hades." (143–154)   110

As he spoke he clasped her hand, and laughter-loving Aphrodite turned away and with her beautiful eyes downcast crept into his bed, with its fine coverings, for it had already been made with soft blankets; on it lay the skins of bears and loud-roaring lions that Anchises had slain in the lofty mountains. And then when they went up to his well-wrought bed, Anchises first removed the gleaming ornaments, the intricate brooches and flowers and necklaces; and he loosened the belt about her waist and took off her shining garments and set them down on a silver-studded chair. Then by the will of the gods and of fate he, a mortal man, lay with an immortal goddess, without knowing the truth. (155–167)   120

APHRODITE REVEALS HER TRUE IDENTITY

At the time when herdsmen turn their cattle and staunch sheep back to their shelter from the flowery pastures, Aphrodite poured upon Anchises a sleep that was sound and sweet, and she dressed herself in her lovely raiment. When the goddess of goddesses had clothed her body beautifully, she stood by the couch and her head reached up to the well-wrought beam of the roof, and from her cheeks shone the heavenly beauty that belongs to Cytherea of the beautiful crown. She roused Anchises from sleep and called out to him with the words: "Get up, son of Dardanus; why do you sleep so deeply? Tell me if I appear to you to be like the person whom you first perceived with your eyes." (168–179)   130

Thus she spoke, and he immediately awoke and did as he was told. When he saw the neck and the beautiful eyes of Aphrodite, he was afraid and looked down turning his eyes away, and he hid his handsome face in his cloak and begged her with winged words: "Now from the first moment that I have looked at you with my eyes, O goddess, I know you are divine; and you did not tell me the truth. But I implore you, by aegis-bearing Zeus, do not allow me to continue to dwell among mortals, still alive but enfeebled; have pity, for no man retains his full strength who sleeps with an immortal goddess." (180–190)   140

Then Aphrodite, the daughter of Zeus, replied: "Anchises, most renowned of mortal men, be of good courage and do not be overly frightened in your heart. For you need have no fear that you will suffer evil from me or the other blessed ones; indeed you are beloved by the gods. And you will have a dear son who will rule among the Trojans; and his children will produce children in a continuous family succession. His name will be Aeneas, since I am gripped by a dread anguish[10] because I went into the bed of a man, although among mortals those of your race are always most like the gods in beauty and in stature." (191–201)

Aphrodite is upset because she can no longer taunt the gods with the boast that she has caused them to love mortals while she alone has never succumbed. She continues to try to justify her actions by glorifying the family of Anchises. She tells the story of Ganymede, who was beautiful and made immortal by Zeus, and relates the sad tale of handsome Tithonus, also of the Trojan royal family, who was beloved by Eos and granted immortality. Aphrodite's son Aeneas, of course, emerges eventually as the great hero of the Romans. Here is the conclusion of the *Homeric Hymn to Aphrodite*.

APHRODITE RECALLS THE BEAUTY OF GANYMEDE AND TITHONUS

"Indeed, Zeus in his wisdom seized and carried off fair-haired Ganymede because of his beauty, so that he might be in the company of the gods and pour wine for them in the house of Zeus, a wonder to behold, esteemed by all the immortals, as he draws the red nectar from a golden bowl. But a lasting sorrow gripped the heart of Tros, for he had no idea where the divine whirlwind had taken his dear son. Indeed, he mourned for him unceasingly each and every day, and Zeus took pity on the father and gave him as recompense for his son brisk-trotting horses, the kind which carry the gods. These he gave him to have as a gift. And at the command of Zeus, Hermes, the guide and slayer of Argus, told everything and how Ganymede would be immortal and never grow old, just like the gods. When Tros heard this message from Zeus, he no longer continued his mourning but rejoiced within his heart and joyfully was borne by the horses that were as swift as a storm. (202–217)   10

"So also golden-throned Eos carried off Tithonus, one of your race, and like the immortals. Eos went to Zeus, the dark-clouded son of Cronus, to ask that Tithonus be immortal and live forever. Zeus nodded his assent and accomplished her wish. Poor goddess, she did not think to ask that her beloved avoid ruinous old age and retain perpetual youth. Indeed, as long as he kept his desirable youthful bloom, Tithonus took his pleasure with early-born Eos of the golden throne by the stream of Oceanus at the ends of the earth. But when the first gray hairs sprouted from his beautiful head and noble chin, Eos avoided his bed. But she kept him in her house and tended him, giving him food, ambrosia, and lovely garments. When hateful old age oppressed him completely and he could not move or raise his limbs, the following plan seemed best to her. She laid him in a room and closed the shining doors. From within his voice flows faintly and he no longer has the strength that he formerly had in his supple limbs. (218–238)   20

"I should not choose that you, Anchises, be immortal and live day after day like him; but, if you could live on and on a beautiful man, as you are now, and if you could be called my husband, then grief would not cloud my anxious heart. Now, however, soon you will be enveloped by pitiless old age, which, depleting and destructive, stands beside all human beings and is despised by the gods. (239–246)   30

"Besides, among the immortal gods there will be disgrace for me, continually and forever, because of you. Before this happened, they used to dread the jeers and schemes with which I used to mate all the immortal gods with mortal women at one time or another; for they were all subject to my will. But now no more will I be able to open my mouth about this power of mine among the gods, since driven quite out of my mind, wretched and blameless, I have been utterly insane—I have gone to bed with a mortal and I carry his child in my womb." (247–255)   40

APHRODITE FORETELLS THE BIRTH OF AENEAS

"When our baby first sees the light of the sun, deep-bosomed mountain nymphs who inhabit this great and holy mountain will bring him up. They are not the same as either mortals or immortals; they live a long time and eat ambrosial food and also with the immortals they join in beautiful choruses of dancers. The Sileni and the keen-eyed slayer of Argus make love to them in the depths of desireful caves. When they are born, pines and high-topped oaks are born along with them on the nourishing earth, beautiful and flourishing trees that stand towering on the high mountains; mortals call their groves sacred and do not cut them down with an axe. Yet when the fate of death stands at their side, these trees first begin to wither in the earth, and then their enveloping bark shrivels and their branches fall off. Together with the trees the souls of their nymphs leave the light of the sun. (256–272)   50

"These nymphs will have my son by their side to bring up. When he has first been touched by the enticing bloom of youth, the goddesses will bring the boy here to show you. Yet so that I may go over with you all that I intend, I shall come back again with my son, about the fifth year. Certainly when you first behold with your eyes this flourishing child, you will rejoice at the sight, for he will be very much like a god; and you will bring him to windy Troy. If any mortal person asks who the mother was who carried him under her girdle, remember to say what I tell you. Say she is the daughter of one of the nymphs, beautiful as a flower, who inhabits this forest-covered mountain. If you speak out and boast like a fool that you were joined in love with lovely-crowned Cytherea, Zeus in his anger will strike you with a smoldering thunderbolt. Everything has been told to you; take it all to heart. Refrain from naming me and be intimidated by the anger of the gods." Having spoken thus, she soared upward to windy heaven. (273–291)   60

Hail, goddess, guardian of well-built Cyprus; I began with you and now I shall go on to another hymn.

Amor Vincit Omnia (Love Conquers All), ca. 1601–1602, by Caravaggio (1571–1610); oil on canvas, 75¼ × 58¼ in., also known as *Victorious Cupid* and *Earthly Cupid.* Caravaggio painted this work for Vincenzo Giustiniani, a wealthy Genoese who devoted himself to the refined pursuits of an aristocratic gentleman: music, art, and classical studies. Giustiniani kept it concealed behind a curtain to be unveiled as his crowning possession. At first glance this painting offers an immediate, yet profound, interpretation: the capricious and indifferent destruction of higher, human aspirations by the power of Eros. The more deeply we study it, however, the more striking and unsettling it becomes. Depicted is a wanton, prepubescent Cupid with a mischievous, not to say malicious, grin, decked with dark eagle's wings, treading upon a variety of items: instruments of music and art, armor and a martial baton, an astral globe, laurel leaves, a coronet, manuscript paper, and pen. The viewer has caught the boy in an ungainly pose, as if he has just been discovered in a piece of wickedness but doesn't care. The young boy is not an idealized youth, not comely or attractive, as one would expect a respectable Eros to be, but an individual portrait of a real and dubious youth, namely, Francesco Boneri, nicknamed Cecco da Caravaggio, Cecco being a diminutive of Francesco; he thus became known as "Caravaggio's Cecco." He appears in other Caravaggio works, most notably *St. John the Baptist*. The unusual posture of Eros in Caravaggio's painting is reminiscent of the sculpture of Victory by Michelangelo, his predecessor, who had a profound but ambiguous influence on his work. Michelangelo's male nudes, his Ganymede, and his angelic figures on the Sistine Chapel transform, by their beauty, the erotic into a spiritual symbol or metaphor for human aspirations toward the ultimate, divine love of God. In Platonic terms (see p. 211), profane or sexual love is sublimated into a sacred, intellectual, and sublime passion. Michelangelo's *Victory* idealizes the male form; Caravaggio's Eros portrays a brutally realistic and unashamed portrait of a boy with tarnished wings, raw and animal, who obscenely tramples underfoot the higher ambitions, which for him are nothing more than mere toys to be played with or destroyed at his pleasure. (*Erich Lessing/Art Resource, NY*)

Eros

Eros, the male counterpart of Aphrodite, shares many of her characteristics. He, too, had a dual tradition for his birth. He may be the early cosmic deity in the creation myths of Hesiod and the Orphics or the son of Aphrodite, his father being Ares. At any rate, he is often closely associated with the goddess as her attendant. Eros, like Aphrodite, may represent all facets of love and desire, but often he is the god of male homosexuality, particularly in the Greek classical period. He is depicted as a handsome young man, the embodiment and idealization of masculine beauty.

The *Symposium* of Plato

Plato's *Symposium* provides a most profound analysis of the manifold nature and power of love, especially in terms of a conception of Eros. The dialogue tells of a select gathering at the house of Agathon, a dramatic poet, on the day after the customary celebration with the members of his cast in honor of his victory with his first tragedy. The topic at this most famous of dinner parties is that of love. Each guest in turn is asked to expound on the subject. The speeches of Aristophanes and Socrates, both of whom are present, are by far the most rewarding in their universal implications.[11]

Aristophanes' Speech in the *Symposium*

Aristophanes' speech (*Symposium* 189c2–193d5) follows the speeches of Pausanias and Eryximachus, two of the other guests.

> Men seem to me to have failed completely to comprehend the power of Eros, for if they did comprehend it, they would have built to him the greatest altars and temples and offered the greatest sacrifices, whereas he is given none of these honors, although he should have them most of all. For he is the most friendly to man of all the gods, his helper and physician in those ills, which if cured, would bring about the greatest happiness for the human race. Therefore, I shall try to initiate you into the nature of his power, and you will be the teachers of others. (189c4–189d4)

THE THREE ORIGINAL SEXES

> But first you must understand the nature of mortals and what experiences they have suffered. For our nature long ago was not the same as it is now, but different. In the beginning humankind had three sexes, not two, male and female, as now; but there was in addition, a third, which partook of both the others; now it has vanished and only its name survives. At that time there was a distinct sex, androgynous both in appearance and in name, partaking of the characteristics of both the male and the female, but now it does not exist, except for the name, which is retained as a term of reproach. (189d5–189e5)
>
> Furthermore, every human being was in shape a round entity, with back and sides forming a circle; he had four hands, an equal number of feet, one head, with two faces exactly alike but each looking in opposite directions, set upon a circular neck, four ears, two sets of genitals and everything else as one might imagine from this description. He walked upright just as we do now in whichever direction (backward

10

or forward) he wished. When they were anxious to run, they made use of all their limbs (which were then eight in number) by turning cartwheels, just like acrobats, and quickly carried themselves along by this circular movement. (189e5–190a8)   20

The sexes were three in number and of such a kind for these reasons; originally the male was sprung from the sun, the female from the earth, and the third, partaking of both male and female, from the moon, because the moon partakes of both the sun and the earth; and indeed because they were just like their parents, their shape was spherical and their movement circular. Their strength and might were terrifying; they had great ambitions, and they made an attack on the gods. What Homer relates about Ephialtes and Otus and their attempt to climb up to heaven and assail the gods is told also about these beings as well. (190a8–190c1)   30

ZEUS' PUNISHMENT FOR THEIR HUBRIS

Zeus and the other gods took counsel about what they should do, and they were at a loss. They could not bring themselves to kill them (just as they had obliterated the race of the giants with blasts of thunder and lightning), for they would deprive themselves of the honors and sacrifices which they received from mortals, nor could they allow them to continue in their insolence. After painful deliberation, Zeus declared that he had a plan. "I think that I have a way," he said, "whereby mortals may continue to exist but will cease from their insolence by being made weaker. For I shall cut each of them in two, and they will be at the same time both weaker and more useful to us because of their greater numbers, and they will walk upright on two legs. If they still seem to be insolent and do not wish to be quiet, I shall split them again and they will hop about on one leg." (190c1–190d6)   40

With these words he cut human beings in two, just as one splits fruit which is to be preserved or divides an egg with a hair. As he bisected each one, he ordered Apollo to turn the face with the half of the neck attached around to the side that was cut, so that man, by being able to see the signs of his bisection, might be better behaved; and he ordered him to heal the marks of the cutting. Apollo turned the face around and drew together the skin like a pouch with drawstrings on what is now called the belly and tied it in the middle, making a single knot, which is called the navel. He smoothed out the many other wrinkles and molded the chest using a tool like that of cobblers when they smooth out the wrinkles in the leather on their last. But he left a few on their bellies around their navels as a reminder of their experience of long ago. (190d6–191a5)   50

And so when their original nature had been split in two, each longed for his other half, and when they encountered it they threw their arms about one another and embraced in their desire to grow together again, and they died through hunger and neglect of the other necessities of life because of their wish to do nothing separated from each other. Whenever one of a pair died, the other that was left searched out and embraced another mate, either the half of a whole female (which we now call woman) or of a male. Thus they perished, and Zeus in his pity devised another plan: he transferred their genitals to the front (for until now they had been on the outside, and they begot and bore their offspring not in conjunction with one another but by emission into the earth, like grasshoppers). (191a5–191c1)   60

And so Zeus moved their genitals to the front and thereby had them reproduce by intercourse with one another, the male with the female. He did this for two reasons: if a man united with a woman, they would propagate the race and it would survive, but if a male united with a male, they might find satisfaction and freedom to turn to their pursuits and devote themselves to the other concerns of life. From such early times, then, love for one another has been implanted in the human race, a love that unifies in his attempt to make one out of two and to heal and restore the basic nature of humankind. (191c2–191d3)   70

Each of us therefore is but a broken tally, half a man, since we have been cut just like the side of a flatfish and made two instead of one. All who are a section halved from the beings of the common sex (which was at that time called androgynous) are lovers of women; many adulterers come from this source, including women who love men and are promiscuous. All women who are a section halved from the female do not pay any attention to men but rather turn to women; lesbians come from this source. All who are a section halved from the male pursue males; and all the while they are young, since they are slices, as it were, of the male, they love men and take delight in lying by their side and embracing them; these are the best of boys and youths because they are the most manly in nature. Some say that they are without shame, but they do not tell the truth. For they behave the way they do not through shamelessness but through courage, manliness, and masculinity as they cling to what is similar to them. (191d3–192a5)   80

THE NATURE OF DESIRE

Here is a great proof of what I say. Only men of this sort proceed to politics when they grow up. Once they are men they love boys and do not turn their thoughts to marriage and procreation naturally but are forced to by law or convention; it is enough for them to spend their lives together unmarried. In short, then, a man like this is a lover of men as a boy and a lover of boys as a man, always clinging to what is akin to his nature. Therefore, whenever anyone of this sort and every other kind of person encounters the other half that is actually his, then they are struck in an amazing way with affection, kinship, and love, virtually unwilling to be separated from each other for even a short time. These are the ones who spend their whole life together, although they would not be able to tell what they wish to gain from each other. No one would imagine that it is on account of their sexual association that the one enjoys intensely being with the other; clearly the soul of each desires something else, which it cannot describe but only hint at obscurely. (192a5–192d2)   90 100

Suppose Hephaestus, his tools in hand, were to stand over them as they lay together and ask: "O mortals, what is it that you wish to gain from one another?" Or when they were at a loss for an answer he were to ask again: "Is this what you desire, to be together always as much as possible so as never to be separated from each other night and day? If this is what you desire, I am willing to fuse and weld you together so that the two of you may become one and the same person and as long as you live, you may both live united in one being, and when you die, you may die together as one instead of two, united even in the realms of Hades. Just see if this would be enough to satisfy your longing." We know that there is not one person who, after hearing these words, would deny their truth and say that he wanted something else, but he would believe that he had heard exactly what he had desired for a long time—namely, to be melted in unison with his beloved, and the two of them become one. The reason is that our ancient nature was thus and we were whole. And so love is merely the name for the desire and pursuit of the whole. (192d2–193a1)   110

Previously, as I have said, we were one, but now because of our wickedness we have been split by the god (just as the Arcadians have been split up by the Spartans).[12] There is, too, the fear that if we do not behave properly toward the gods we may again be bisected, just as dice that are divided as tallies, and go around like the figures cut in profile on steles, split right along their noses. For this reason all mortals must be urged to pay reverence to the gods so that we may avoid suffering further bisection and win what Eros has to give as our guide and leader. Let no one act in opposition to him—whoever does incurs the enmity of the gods. For if we are reconciled and friendly to the god of love, we shall find and win our very own beloved, an achievement few today attain. (193a1–193b6)

Eryximachus is not to suppose in ridicule of my speech that I am referring only to Pausanias and Agathon, since they perhaps happen to be of the class of those who love males by nature. I am referring rather to all men and women when I say that the happiness of our race lies in the fulfillment of love; each must find the beloved that is his and be restored to his original nature. If this ancient state was best, of necessity the nearest to it in our present circumstances must be best—namely, to find a beloved who is of one and the same mind and nature. It is right to praise Eros as the god responsible; he helps us most in our present life by bringing us to what is kindred to us and offers us the greatest hopes for the future. If we pay reverence to the gods, he will restore us to our ancient nature and with his cure make us happy and blessed. (193b6–193d5)

Aristophanes concludes by again imploring Eryximachus not to ridicule his speech; and indeed, in the last analysis, we cannot help but take it very seriously. The invention, the wit, and the absurdity are all typical of the comic playwright, but so is the insight that they so brilliantly elucidate. We do not know how much belongs to the genius of Plato, but it would be difficult to imagine anything more in character for Aristophanes. With or without the outspoken glorification of love between males (inspired perhaps by the company present and certainly preliminary to Plato's own message in Socrates' subsequent speech), we have a vision of the basic need of one human being for another that is astonishingly like our own.

Who can ever forget Hephaestus as he stands before the two lovers and asks what they hope to gain from each other? After all, Aristophanes refers to all men and women when he says that happiness lies in the fulfillment of love and that each must find the appropriate beloved. Who can deny that the complex nature of this most fundamental physical and psychological drive is here laid bare, with a ruthless penetration that is disconcertingly familiar to us, however much the scientific quest for precise definition and vocabulary since the time of Freud has replaced the symbols of mythic art?

The archetypal concept of love as a sensual, romantic, and spiritual striving for a blessed completeness, wholeness, and oneness is basic and universal and it is found everywhere. In American literature, the works of Carson McCullers provide affecting examples, especially *Member of the Wedding*. In music, one could find no better illustration of how pervasive the message is than in John Cameron Mitchell's rock musical, *Hedwig and the Angry Inch*. The text of the moving song "Origin of Love" springs directly from Aristophanes, and the visuals that accompany it in the movie version are most touching in their childlike simplicity.

Socrates' Speech in the *Symposium*

In Socrates' speech, which provides the dramatic and philosophical climax of the dialogue, we move from the conception of love that is elemental and essentially physical to a sublime elucidation of the highest spiritual attainments that Eros can inspire. Another myth is evoked, this time to establish the true nature of the divine being, in opposition to the misconceptions of the previous speakers. Socrates tells how he was instructed in the true nature of Eros by a woman of Mantinea called **Diotima**. Although her historical reality is much debated, it is by no means inconceivable that she was a real person. She makes him realize that Eros is neither good and beautiful nor bad and ugly, but in nature lies somewhere between the two. Therefore, he is not a god. Socrates continues his argument quoting from his conversation with Diotima (*Symposium* 201d1–212c3):

DIOTIMA INSTRUCTS SOCRATES ABOUT THE TRUE NATURE OF EROS

"What then might love be," I said, "a mortal?" "Not in the least," she replied. "But what is he then?" "As I told you earlier, he is not mortal or immortal but something between." "What then, O Diotima?" "A great spirit, O Socrates; for every spirit is intermediate between god and human beings." "What power does he have?" I asked. "He interprets and conveys exchanges between gods and human beings, prayers and sacrifices from human beings to gods, and orders and gifts in return from gods to human beings; being intermediate he fills in for both and serves as the bond uniting the two worlds into a whole entity. Through him proceeds the whole art of divination and the skill of priests in sacrifice, ritual, spells, and every kind of sorcery and magic. God does not have dealings with mortals directly, but through Love all association and discourse between the two are carried on, both in the waking hours and in time of sleep. The one who is wise in such matters as these is a spiritual being, and he who is wise in other arts and crafts is his inferior. These spirits are many and of every kind and one of them is Eros." (202d8–203a8)   10

"Who were his father and mother?" I asked. "Although it is a rather long story, I shall tell you," she replied. "When Aphrodite was born, the gods held a feast and among them was **Resourcefulness** (*Poros*), the son of **Cleverness** (*Metis*), and while they were dining, **Poverty** (*Penia*) came and stood about the door to beg, since there was a party.[13] Resourcefulness became intoxicated with nectar (for wine did not yet exist) and went into the garden of Zeus where, overcome by his condition, he fell asleep. Then Poverty, because of her own want and lack of resourcefulness, contrived to have a child by Resourcefulness, and she lay by his side and conceived Eros. And so Eros became the attendant and servant of Aphrodite, for he was begotten on her birthday and he is by nature a lover of beauty and Aphrodite is beautiful. (203a9–203c4)   20

"Since Eros then is the son of Resourcefulness and Poverty, he is fated to have the following kind of character. First of all, he is continually poor, and far from being soft and beautiful as many believe, he is hard and squalid, without shoes, without a home, and without a bed; he always sleeps on the ground, in doorways, and on the street. Thus he has his mother's nature, with want as his constant companion. On the other hand, like his father, he lays his plots to catch the beautiful and the good; being vehement and energetic, he is a dread hunter, always weaving some scheme; full of resource, he has a passion for knowledge and is a lover of wisdom during all his life, a clever wizard, sorcerer, and sophist. He is not immortal nor is he mortal, but at one time he flourishes and lives whenever he is successful, and at another he dies all in the same day, but he will come back to life again because of his nature inherited from his father—what he acquires slips away from him again, and so Eros is never either poor or rich and he is in a state between wisdom and igno-rance. This is the way he is. No one of the gods loves wisdom and longs to become wise, because he is wise; and so with any other who is wise—he does not love wisdom. On the other hand, the ignorant do not love wisdom or long to become wise. Ignorance is a difficult thing for this very reason, that the one who is neither beautiful nor good nor wise is completely satisfied with himself. The one who does not think he is lacking in anything certainly does not desire what he does not think he lacks." (203c5–204a7)   30 40

"O Diotima," I asked, "who are those who love wisdom if not the wise or the ignorant?" "By now certainly it would be clear even to a child," she replied, "that they are those who are in a state between desire and wisdom, one of whom is Eros. To be sure, wisdom is among the most beautiful of things and Eros is love of beauty; and so Eros must be a lover of wisdom, and being a lover of wisdom he lies between wisdom and ignorance. The nature of his birth is the reason for this. He springs from a wise and resourceful father and a mother who is not wise and without re-sources. This then, my dear Socrates, is the nature of this spirit. The conception you had of Eros is not surprising. You believed, to infer from what you said, that Love was the beloved (the one who is loved) and not the lover (the one who loves). For this reason, I think, Love appeared to you to be all beautiful. For that which is loved is that which actually is beautiful and delicate, perfect and most happy, but that which loves has another character, of the kind that I have described." (204a8–204c6)   50

Diotima goes on to explain the function, purpose, and power of Eros in human life. Love and the lover desire what they do not possess, namely, the beautiful and the good, and the ultimate goal of their pursuit is happiness. Love finds particular expression in the procreation of what is beautiful, both physi-cally and spiritually; and all human beings in their quest to bring forth beauty and knowledge are thereby touched by a divine harmony with the immortal. Procreation is the closest means by which the human race can attain to perpetu-ity and immortality; love, then, is a love of immortality as well as of the beautiful and the good.

Animals, as well as human beings, seek to perpetuate themselves and thereby become immortal. But for humans there are various stages in the hierarchy of love. The lowest is that of the animal inspired by the desire for children of the body, but as one ascends, there is the realization of the possibility of producing children of the mind. Who would not prefer the poetic offspring of a Homer or a Hesiod and the more lasting glory and immortality that they have achieved? Just as on the rungs of a ladder we proceed from one step to another, so initiates into the mysteries of love move from the lower to the higher.

Love begins with the physical and sensual desire for the beautiful person or the beautiful thing. From the specific object one moves to the generic conception of beauty, which is wondrous and pure and universal. It is the love of this eternal beauty (and with it the goodness and wisdom it entails) that inspires the pursuit of philosophy in the philosopher.

Diotima describes comprehension of the true nature of love in terms of a philosophical and spiritual journey, not unlike the progressive stages of initia-tion into religious mysteries, culminating in ultimate revelation and knowledge.

THE PLATONIC EROS

> It is necessary for the one proceeding in the right way toward his goal to begin, when he is young, with physical beauty; and first of all, if his guide directs him properly, to love one person, and in his company to beget beautiful ideas and then to observe that the beauty in one person is related to the beauty in another. If he must pursue physical beauty, he would be very foolish not to realize that the beauty in all persons is one and the same. When he has come to this conclusion, he will become the lover of all beautiful bodies and will relax the intensity of his love for one and think the less of it as something of little account. Next he will realize that beauty in the soul is more precious than that in the body, so that if he meets with a person who is beautiful in his soul, even if he has little of the physical bloom of beauty, this will be enough and he will love and cherish him and beget beautiful ideas that make the young better, so that he will in turn be forced to see the beauty in morals and laws and that the beauty in them all is related. (210a4–210c5)   10

This then is the Platonic Eros, a love that inspires the philosopher to self-denial in the cause of humanity and in the pursuit of true wisdom. Presumably, this philosophic Eros can ultimately be aroused from any type of love, heterosexual as well as homosexual (both male and female); the crucial issue is that it be properly directed and become transformed from the erotic to the intellectual. According to Plato in his *Republic*, certain men as well as certain women can attain the highest goals of the true philosopher king. As we have just learned, this cannot be achieved without the sensual and sublime impetus of Eros. Whatever the physical roots, the spiritual import is universal, kindred to the passionate love of God that pervades all serious religious devotion. Aristotle too thinks in Platonic terms when he describes his god as the unmoved mover, the final cause in the universe, who moves as a beloved moves the lover.

Socrates and Eros

Plato's message in the *Symposium* is in accord with his beliefs generally: sexual activity belongs at the lowest level in the ascent to a spiritual, nonsexual, philosophical Eros. In his *Republic*, the highest order of society, the philosopher kings (which include women), engage in sexual activity only at certain times solely for the purpose of procreation. This is impersonal and pragmatic sex. Platonic, true love (which sexual intercourse can endanger and contaminate) inspires their mutual pursuit of knowledge and service to the state. In the *Dialogues* there is ample evidence that Socrates was overwhelmed by the beauty of young men; he is stimulated and inspired, but he presumably never succumbs sexually. At the culmination of the *Symposium* with the dramatic resolution of its mighty themes, Alcibiades (who has never really understood Socrates' philosophical message) tells of his futile attempts to seduce Socrates. His failure is inevitable. Socrates is Plato's exemplar of the way it should be, the philosopher conquering and sublimating lower instincts in the service of his (or her) higher intellect. In his last work, *Laws*, Plato actually condemns homosexual acts. This should not be surprising or judged to be a contradiction of his earlier views. On the contrary, his condemnation represents a logical and final development of his convictions about sex.[14]

How far we have come from the traditional depiction of Eros as the handsome young athlete who attends Aphrodite! Even more remote is the image that later evolved of Eros as Cupid, a chubby mischievous little darling with wings and a bow and arrow. He still attends Aphrodite; and although the wounds he inflicts can inspire a passion that is serious and even deadly, too often he becomes little more than the cute and frivolous deus ex machina of romantic love.

Cupid and Psyche

Finally, the story of Cupid and Psyche remains to be told. It is given its classic form by Apuleius, a Roman author of the second century A.D., in his novel *Metamorphoses*, or *The Golden Ass* (4.28–6.24). One's first impressions about a tale uniting Cupid (or Eros) with Psyche (Soul) should inevitably be Platonic; but whatever philosophical profundities, Platonic or otherwise, have been detected in Apuleius' allegory, popular and universal motifs common to mythology in general and folk tale, fairy tale, and romance in particular emerge with striking clarity: for example, the mysterious bridegroom, the taboo of identification, the hostile mother figure, the jealous sisters, the heroine's forgetfulness, the imposition of impossible labors accomplished with divine assistance—among them descent into the very realm of Hades—and the triumph of romantic love. In this tale, which begins "Once upon a time" and ends "happily ever after," Cupid appears as a handsome young god with wings. Here is a summary of Apuleius' version.[15]

Cupid and Psyche, by Jacques-Louis David (1748–1825); oil on canvas, 1817; 72½ × 95 in. Painted by David in Brussels (where he was exiled for the last nine years of his life), this work has always been controversial and, at the least, disturbing. The focus is on Cupid, while Psyche sleeps on the couch where they have made love, her symbol, a butterfly, hovering above. Cupid's expression is that of a satiated conqueror, an amoral exploiter of the young woman for whom trials and labors lie ahead before she can achieve eternal union with her lover. The landscape, seen through the window in the background, alone gives hope for Psyche's liberation from her oppressive lover. This psychological interpretation of myth was achieved nearly a century before Freud: it confounded David's contemporaries and still discomforts its viewers. (*Leonard C. Hanna, Jr. Fund/ The Cleveland Museum of Art*)

Once upon a time, a certain king and queen had three daughters, of whom Psyche, the youngest, was by far the most fair. In fact, many believed that she was Venus reincarnated and paid her such adulation that the goddess became outraged. And so Venus ordered her son Cupid to make Psyche fall in love with the most base and vile of mankind; instead, Cupid himself fell in love with Psyche. Psyche's inferior sisters had easily found husbands, but Psyche remained unmarried since she was admired by all with the awe that is inspired by divinity. Her father suspected that a god's wrath was responsible. He consulted Apollo, who demanded that Psyche be decked out like a corpse and placed on a mountaintop to be wed by a terrifying serpent.

Therefore, Psyche, amid the rites of a funeral for a living bride, was left on a mountaintop to meet a fate that she finally accepted with resignation. Psyche fell into a deep sleep, and the gentle breezes of Zephyrus wafted her down to a beautiful valley. When she awoke, she entered a magnificent palace, where her every wish was taken care of. And when Psyche went to bed, an anonymous bridegroom visited her, only to depart quickly before sunrise. Thus Psyche spent her days—and her nights—in the palace.

Meanwhile, her sisters set out in search of her; but her mysterious husband continually warned her not to respond to them when they approached. Alone in her prison all day, Psyche besought her husband each night to allow her to see her sisters and give them gold and jewels. He finally consented on the condition that she must not, despite her sisters' urgings, try to learn his identity. When the sisters arrived and interrogated her, Psyche kept her secret—although she did say that her husband was a very handsome young man.

The sisters returned home with the riches that Psyche had given them, but in their hearts they nursed an all-consuming jealousy. The mysterious bridegroom warned Psyche of her sisters' treachery: their purpose was to persuade her to look upon his face; if she did so, she would never see him again. He also told her that she was pregnant, and if she kept their secret, their child would be divine; if she did not, it would be mortal. Nevertheless, he granted Psyche's appeal to see her sisters once again. In answer to their questions, Psyche revealed that she was pregnant. The sisters once again returned home laden with gifts, but more jealous than ever; they now suspected that Psyche's lover must be a god and her expected child divine.

The evil sisters visited Psyche a third time; this time they told her that her husband really was the monstrous serpent of the oracle and that she would be devoured when the time of her pregnancy was completed. Psyche was horrified and, believing that she was sleeping with the monster, forgot the warnings of her husband and took her sisters' advice. She was to hide a sharp knife and a burning lamp; when the monster was asleep, she was to slash it in the neck.

In anguish, Psyche made her preparations; in the night her husband made love to her and then fell asleep. As she raised the lamp, knife in hand, she saw the sweet, gentle, and beautiful Cupid. Overcome by the sight, her first impulse was to take her own life, but this she was unable to do. Spellbound by Cupid's beauty, she gazed at his lovely wings and fondled the bow and quiver that lay at the foot of their bed; she pricked her thumb on one of the arrows and drew blood. Overcome by desire, she kissed her husband passionately. Alas, the lamp dropped oil on the god's right shoulder. Cupid leaped out of bed and attempted to fly away at once; Psyche caught hold of his right leg and soared aloft with him, but her strength gave way and she fell to earth. Before flying away, Cupid admonished her from a nearby cypress: he had ignored Venus' command, he said, and had taken her as his love; he had warned her; his flight was penalty enough; and her sisters would pay for what they had done.

Psyche attempted to commit suicide by throwing herself in a nearby river; but the gentle stream brought her safely to its bank. She was advised by Pan to forget her grief and win back Cupid's love. In her wanderings, she came to the very city where one of her sisters lived. Psyche told her sister what had happened but added that Cupid would marry the sister if she hastened to his side. The sister called on Zephyrus to carry her from a mountaintop to Cupid's palace, but as she leaped into the air she fell and perished on the rocks below. Psyche then found her way to her other sister, who died in the same manner.

Psyche wandered in search of Cupid. He lay in his mother's bedroom, moaning because of his burn; Venus, learning of what had happened, rushed to her son's side, berated him for his behavior, and vowed revenge. In a rage, Venus left to pursue Psyche but eventually abandoned her search. She approached Jupiter, who agreed to send Mercury to make a public proclamation for the capture of Psyche. When she was brought before Venus, the goddess denounced and abused her. In addition, Venus imposed upon the poor girl a series of impossible tasks.

First, Psyche was ordered to sort out before nightfall a vast heap of mixed grains (wheat, barley, and the like). In this endeavor, an ant came to her rescue and summoned his army to isolate each different grain.

The next day Venus ordered Psyche to go to a riverbank where dangerous sheep with thick golden fleeces grazed and to bring back some of their wool. This time, a reed murmured instructions. She was to wait until the sheep had stopped their frenzied wandering under the blazing sun; and when they had lain down to rest, she was to shake from the trees under which they passed the woolly gold clinging richly to the branches. And so she accomplished the task. Still not satisfied, Venus ordered Psyche to go to the top of a high mountain, from which dark water flowed—water that ultimately fed the Underworld stream of Cocytus. Psyche was to bring back a jar filled with this chill water; among the terrors to be faced was a dragon. The eagle of Jupiter swooped down and filled the jar for Psyche.

Angrier now than ever, Venus imposed the ultimate task—descent into the realm of Hades. Psyche was ordered to take a box to Persephone and ask her to send back in it a fragment of her own beauty. In despair, Psyche decided to throw herself off a high tower. But the tower spoke to her and gave her specific directions to the Underworld and instructions about what she was and was not to do. Among the stipulations was that she provide herself with sops to mollify Cerberus and money to pay the ferryman Charon. Most important, the tower warned Psyche not to look into the box. Psyche did everything that she had been told, but she could not resist looking into the box. Inside the box was not beauty but the sleep of the dark night of the Underworld; by this death-like sleep Psyche was enveloped.

By now cured of his burn, Cupid flew to Psyche's rescue. He put sleep back into the box and reminded Psyche that her curiosity once again had gotten the better of her. She was to go and complete her task. Cupid then appealed to Jupiter, who agreed to ratify his marriage with Psyche; since Psyche was made one of the immortals, Venus was appeased. Here is how Apuleius describes the glorious wedding feast on Olympus that marked the happy ending of the story of Cupid and Psyche (*Metamorphoses* 6.23–24):

> Immediately a wedding feast appeared. The bridegroom took the highest place, embracing Psyche. So Jupiter with his own Juno took his place and then, in order, the other gods. Then Jupiter's cupbearer, the shepherd boy Ganymede, brought him a cup of nectar, the wine of the gods, and Bacchus gave nectar to the others. Vulcan cooked the feast; the Hours decorated everything with roses and other flowers. The Graces sprinkled the scent of balsam, and the Muses played and sang. Apollo sang to the cithara and Venus danced in all her beauty to the music; the tableau was so fitting for her that the Muses accompanied her with choral odes or played upon the tibia; a satyr and Pan played the pipes.
>
> So, with all due ceremony, Psyche was married to Cupid and, in due time, a daughter was born to them, whom we call Pleasure (*Voluptas*).

Sappho's Aphrodite

It is impossible to survey the mythological concepts of love without including the poetic vision of Sappho, the lyric poetess[16] of love from the island of Lesbos. Only a little of her work has survived, but the critical acclaim for her artistry glows undiminished. We know practically nothing with certainty about her life and career. She was devoted to Aphrodite and to the young women with whom she was associated. But we cannot even confidently speak about a cult of the goddess, and her relations with her loved ones can legitimately be imagined only from the meager remains of her poetry. Her circle has been interpreted as everything from a finishing school for girls in the Victorian manner to a hotbed of sensuality. From Sappho comes the term *lesbian* and the association of Aphrodite with lesbian love.

In a fervent and moving poem, she calls on Aphrodite for help to win the love of a young woman with whom she has been involved. The literal details of their relationship may be open to endless, subjective interpretation, but Sappho's passionate desperation seems overwhelmingly apparent. Her invocation to Aphrodite has real meaning for us in this context because it illustrates beautifully the intensity that infuses so much of Greek art within the disciplined control of artistic form. It reminds us, too, of the sincerity of the conception of the goddess that was possible in the seventh and sixth centuries B.C. Too often our sensibilities are numbed by the later artificial and conventional stereotypes to which the gods are reduced, once all genuine belief is gone. There can be no question about the reality of Aphrodite in the following lines.

> Exquisitely enthroned, immortal Aphrodite,
> weaver of charms, child of Zeus,
> I beg you, reverend lady,
> do not crush my heart
> with sickness and distress.
> But come to me here,
> if ever once before you heard
> my cry from afar and listened
> and, leaving your father's house,

yoked your chariot of gold. (1.7–8)   10
Beautiful birds drew you swiftly
from heaven over the black earth
through the air between
with the rapid flutter of their downy wings.
Swiftly they came and you,
O blessed goddess,
smiling in your immortal beauty asked
what I wished to happen most
in my frenzied heart. (9–18)
"Who is it this time you desire   20
Persuasion entice to your love?
Who, O Sappho, has wronged you?
For if she runs away now,
soon she will follow;
if she rejects your gifts,
she will bring gifts herself;
if she does not now,
soon she will love,
even though she does not wish it." (18–24)
Come to me now too,   30
free me from my harsh anxieties;
accomplish all that my heart longs for.
You, your very self,
stand with me in my conflict. (25–28)

Select Bibliography

Borgeaud, Philippe. *Mother of the Gods from Cybele to the Virgin Mary*. Translated by Lysa Hochroth. Baltimore, MD: Johns Hopkins University Press, 2004.

Calame, Claude. *The Poetics of Eros in Ancient Greece*. Translated by Janet Lloyd. Princeton, NJ: Princeton University Press, 1999. A comprehensive survey of Eros in poetry, iconography, religion, and society (e.g., initiation rites, celebrations, and education), including the special function of the god in the personal and erotic lives of men and women.

Cavicchioli, Sonia. *The Tale of Cupid & Psyche, An Illustrated History*. Translated from the Italian by Susan Scott. New York: Georges Braziller, 2002. A beautifully illustrated book that traces the history of artistic representations of the myth from ancient times through the nineteenth century.

Cyrino, Monica S. *Aphrodite*. Gods and Heroes of the Ancient World Series. New York: Routledge, 2010.

Ferrari, Franco. *Sappho's Gift: The Poet and Her Community*. Translated by Benjamin Acosta-Hughes and Lucia Prauscello. Ann Arbor, MI: Michigan Classical Press, 2009. New insights into the life and works of Sappho.

Friedrich, Paul. *The Meaning of Aphrodite*. Chicago, IL: University of Chicago Press, 1978.

Greene, Ellen, ed. *Reading Sappho, Contemporary Approaches*. Berkeley, CA: University of California Press, 1997.

———. *Re-Reading Sappho, Reception and Transmission*. Berkeley, CA: University of California Press, 1997. These two anthologies of scholarship on Sappho include contemporary theory about gender. For the ancient biographical tradition about Sappho see the introduction to the translations in the Loeb Classical Library.

Roller, Lynn E. *In Search of God the Mother, The Cult of Anatolian Cybele*. Berkeley, CA: University of California Press, 1999. A comprehensive study of the nature, growth, and evolution of the worship of Cybele.

Rosenzweig, Rachel. *Worshipping Aphrodite: Art and Cult in Classical Athens*. Ann Arbor, MI: University of Michigan Press, 2004.

Snyder, Jane McIntosh. *Lesbian Desire in the Lyrics of Sappho*. New York: Columbia University Press, 1997. Chapters include: "Sappho and Aphrodite," "*Eros* and Reminiscence," "The Aesthetics of Sapphic *Eros*," and "Sappho and Modern American Women Poets."

Thornton, Bruce S. *Eros: The Myth of Ancient Greek Sexuality*. Boulder, CO: Westview Press, 1997.

Primary Sources

Sources in the Chapter

Apuleius	*Metamorphoses* or *The Golden Ass* 4.28–6.24
Homeric Hymn 5	*To Aphrodite*
Homeric Hymn 6	*To Aphrodite*
Homeric Hymn 10	*To Aphrodite*
Ovid	*Metamorphoses* 10.243–297; 10.708–739
Plato	*Symposium* 189c2–193d5; 201d1–212c3
Sappho	Poem 1

Additional Sources

Pausanias	*Description of Greece* 7.17.9–12
Theocritus	*Idyll* 15
Xenophon	*Symposium* 8.9–15

Notes

1. In the speech of Pausanias.
2. His mistress, the courtesan Phryne, was said to be his model, and some claim that Aphrodite herself asked: "Where did Praxiteles see me naked?"
3. Aphrodite's union with Hermes produced Hermaphroditus, whose story is told at the end of Chapter 12.
4. Many of Aphrodite's characteristics are oriental in tone, and specific links can be found that are clearly Phrygian, Syrian, and Semitic in origin.
5. Cf. the Assyro-Babylonian myth of Ishtar and Tammuz.
6. Catullus (63) makes the anguish, love, and remorse of Attis the stuff of great poetry. For a translation, see www.classicalmythology.org.
7. Her worship was introduced into Rome in 205. Lucretius (*De rerum natura* 2.600–651) presents a hostile but vivid account of its orgiastic nature. For Lucretius, the very nature of deity is that it exists forever tranquil and aloof, untouched by the human condition and immune to human prayers. See also p. 672.
8. James G. Frazer, *The Golden Bough: A Study in Magic and Religion*, abridged ed. (New York: Macmillan, 1922), p. 408. One might want to read Theocritus, *Idyll* 15, for a picture of the worship of Adonis in a Hellenistic city.
9. Hestia, the first-born of Cronus, was the first to be swallowed and the last to be brought up.

10. The name Aeneas is here derived from the Greek *ainos*, which means "dread."
11. There has been much discussion about the *Symposium* as a reflection of Athenian views generally about homosexuality. One wonders how typical of the mores of Victorian England would have been the speeches (however profound) of a select group of friends at a dinner party given by Oscar Wilde, who actually does have several things in common with the personality and style of the dramatist Agathon, the host of the *Symposium*. (For more about homosexuality, see pp. 22–23.)
12. This reference to the dispersion of the inhabitants of Mantinea (an Arcadian city) by the Spartans in 385 B.C. is an anachronism since the dramatic date of the speech is purportedly 416 B.C.
13. It is difficult to find one word that expresses adequately the abstract conceptions personified. The name Poros also suggests contrivance; Metis, wisdom or invention; and Penia, need.
14. For more on this subject, see the perceptive discussion by Byrne Fone, *Homophobia: A History* (New York: Metropolitan Books [Henry Holt], 2000), Chapter 1, "Inventing Eros." An aspect of the art of Plato in his complex portrait of Socrates is illuminated by Catherine Osborne, *Eros Unveiled* (New York: Oxford University Press, 1994); in her chapter "Eros the Socratic Spirit," she concludes (p. 100): "The resemblance between Diotima's picture of Eros and Plato's picture of Socrates is remarkable."
15. *Cupid and Psyche* may be compared thematically to *Beauty and the Beast*. See Graham Anderson, *Fairytale in the Ancient World* (London: Routledge, 2000), pp. 61–77.
16. We deliberately use the designation "poetess" rather than "poet" because we concur with the sensible observation of Joan Breton Connelly that "gender differentiation has real meaning in ancient society."

ARTEMIS

Some children—people don't recall the exact number—playing around the sanctuary found some rope, and having tied it round the neck of the statue pretended that Artemis was being hanged. The Caphyans, when they discovered what the children had done, stoned them to death. A sickness then fell upon the wives of those who had done these things and they gave premature birth to stillborn babies. For this reason the Pythia decreed that they bury the children who had been stoned and offer sacrifice to them every year, since they had been unjustly killed. To this day the Caphyans perform this ritual in accordance with the oracle and call Artemis … the Hanged Goddess.

—**PAUSANIAS,** *Description of Greece 8.23.6–7*

THE HOMERIC HYMN TO ARTEMIS (27) draws the essential features of her character and appearance: beautiful virgin of the hunt, armed with bow and arrows.

10

> I sing about Artemis of the golden arrows, chaste virgin of the noisy hunt, who delights in her shafts and strikes down the stag, the very own sister of Apollo of the golden sword. She ranges over shady hills and windy heights, rejoicing in the chase as she draws her bow, made all of silver, and shoots her shafts of woe. The peaks of the lofty mountains tremble, the dark woods echo terribly to the shrieks of wild beasts, and both the earth and fish-filled sea are shaken. But she with dauntless heart looks everywhere to wreak destruction on the brood of animals. But when the huntress, who delights in her arrows, has had her fill of pleasure and cheered her heart, she unstrings her curved bow and makes her way to the great house of her dear brother, Phoebus Apollo, in the rich land of Delphi, where she supervises the lovely dances of the Muses and the Graces. After she has hung up her unstrung bow and arrows, she takes first place and, exquisitely attired, leads the dance. And they join in a heavenly choir to sing how Leto of the beautiful ankles bore two children who are by far the best of the immortals in sagacious thought and action. (1–20)
>
> Hail, children of Zeus and Leto of the lovely hair; yet I shall remember you and another song too.

The shorter *Homeric Hymn to Artemis* (9) dwells upon the closeness of Artemis and Apollo and their cult places in Asia Minor. There was a temple of Artemis where the river Meles flows near Smyrna, and Claros was the site of a temple and oracle of Apollo.

> Sing, O Muse about Artemis, the virgin who delights in arrows, sister of Apollo, the far-shooter, and nursed together with him. She waters her horses at the river Meles, thick with rushes, and swiftly drives her chariot, made all of gold, through Smyrna, to Claros, rich in vines; here Apollo of the silver bow sits and waits for the goddess who shoots from afar and delights in her arrows. (1–6)
>
> So hail to you, Artemis, with my song and at the same time to all the other goddesses as well; yet I begin to sing about you first of all and, after I have made my beginning from you, I shall turn to another hymn.

The Birth of Artemis and Apollo

The goddess **Leto** mated with Zeus and bore the twin deities Artemis and Apollo. The story of Apollo's birth on the island of Delos is recounted in Chapter 11 in the version given by the *Homeric Hymn to Apollo*.[1] Traditionally, Artemis is born first and is able to help with the delivery of her brother, Apollo, thus performing one of her primary functions as a goddess of childbirth early in her career (a role she shares with Hera and Eileithyia, as we have seen). Her birth on Mt. Cynthus in Delos gave her the cult title of **Cynthia**. According to Ovid, after the birth of Artemis and Apollo, Leto was forced by the anger of Hera to wander carrying her two babies. She came to Lycia, where the Lycians refused to allow her to drink water from a marsh. In anger, she changed them into frogs to live their lives in the marsh whose water they had refused to give her.

On other occasions, too, Artemis is closely linked with Apollo, both appearing as vehement and haughty agents of destruction with their shafts of doom. Sudden death (particularly of the young) was often attributed to these two deities, Artemis striking down the girls, Apollo the boys.

Niobe and Her Children

One of the most famous exploits of Artemis and Apollo concerns Niobe and her children, told at length by Ovid (*Metamorphoses* 6.148–315).

The women of Thebes bestowed great honor upon Leto and her twin children, crowning their heads with laurel and offering up incense and prayers in obedience to an injunction by the goddess herself. Niobe, however, was enraged by the whole proceeding and rashly boasted that she was more deserving of

Artemis the Huntress. Roman copy in marble of a Greek bronze of the late fourth century B.C.; height 78 in. Artemis appears both as huntress, taking an arrow from her quiver, and as protectress of animals, as she grasps the leaping stag. Her short skirt, sandals, and loose clothing are appropriate for the activity of the hunt. (*Erich Lessing/Art Resource, NY*)

tribute than Leto. After all, she was rich, beautiful, and the queen of Thebes.[2] Besides, Leto had borne only two children, whereas Niobe was the mother of seven sons and seven daughters. Indeed, Niobe was so confident in the abundance of her blessings that she felt she could afford to lose some of them without serious consequences.

Leto was enraged at such hubris and complained bitterly to Artemis and Apollo. Together the two deities swiftly glided down to the palace of Thebes to avenge the insulted honor of their mother. Apollo struck down all the sons of Niobe with his deadly and unerring arrows, and Artemis in turn killed all her daughters. Just as Artemis was about to shoot the last child, Niobe in desperation shielded the girl and pleaded that this one, her youngest, be spared. While she was uttering this prayer, she was turned to stone, and a whirlwind whisked her away to her homeland, Phrygia, where she was placed on a mountaintop. Tears continue to trickle down from her marble face as she wastes away.[3]

Actaeon

Several stories illustrate the hallowed purity of the goddess Artemis. A famous one concerns Actaeon,[4] an ardent hunter who lost his way and by accident (or was it fate?) had the misfortune to see Artemis (Diana in Ovid's version) naked (*Metamorphoses* 3.138–255):

> Actaeon was the first to tinge with grief the happiness of his grandfather, Cadmus. A stag's horns grew on his head, and his hounds feasted on their master's flesh. Yet, if you look closely, you will find that his guilt was misfortune, not a crime; what crime indeed lies in an innocent mistake? (138–142)
>
> There was a mountain on which had fallen the blood of beasts of many kinds. It was midday, when shadows are at their shortest and the Sun is midway in his course. Young Actaeon calmly called his fellow huntsmen as they tracked the game through the depths of the pathless forest: "My friends, our nets and spears are wet with the blood of our prey; we have had luck enough today! Dawn's saffron-wheeled chariot will bring another day tomorrow and then we will renew the chase. The Sun now stands midway 'twixt east and west and with his hot rays parches the earth. Stop now the hunt, and take in the knotted nets!" His men obeyed and halted from their labors. (143–154)
>
> There was a vale called Gargaphië, sacred to the huntress Diana; clothed with a dense growth of pine and pointed cypress, it had at its far end a woodland cave which no human hand had shaped … on the right from a murmuring spring issued a stream of clearest water, and around the pool was a grassy bank. Here would the woodland goddess rest when weary from the hunt and bathe her virgin body

Death of the Children of Niobe. Attic red-figure krater by the Niobid painter, ca. 460 B.C.; height 21¼ in. The stark cruelty of the gods is shown by the cool detachment of Artemis as she reaches for an arrow out of her quiver, and equally by the restrained energy of Apollo. The Niobids are painted in a rocky landscape (only formally sketched) and disposed on different levels, an unusual technique for vase painters of the time and possibly related to contemporary wall painting: contrast the contemporary *Death of Actaeon*, on page 223. (© *RMN-Grand Palais/ Art Resource, NY*)

10

in the clear water. That day she came there and to one of her nymphs handed her hunting spear, her quiver and bow, and the arrows that were left. Upon another's waiting arms she cast her cloak, and two more took off her sandals. … Other nymphs[5] fetched water and poured it from ample urns. And while Diana thus was being bathed, as she had been many times before, Actaeon, Cadmus' grandson, his labors left unfinished, came to the grotto uncertain of his way and wandering through the unfamiliar wood; so fate carried him along. Into the dripping cave he went, and the nymphs, when they saw a man, beat their breasts and filled the forest with their screams. (155–180)

They surrounded Diana and shielded her with their bodies, but the goddess was taller than they and her head overtopped them all. Just as the clouds are tinged with color when struck by the rays of the setting sun, or like the reddening Dawn, Diana's face flushed when she was spied naked. Surrounded by her nymphs she turned and looked back; wishing that her arrows were at hand, she used what weapons she could and flung water over the young man's face and hair with these words, foretelling his coming doom: "Now you may tell how you saw me naked—if you can tell!" And with this threat she made the horns of a long-lived stag[6] rise on his head where the water had struck him; his neck grew long and his ears pointed, his hands turned to hooves, his arms to legs, and his body she clothed with a spotted deerskin. And she made him timid; Autonoë's valiant son ran away in fear, and as he ran wondered at his speed. He saw his horned head reflected in a pool and tried to say "Alas"—but no words would come. He sobbed; that at least was a sound he uttered, and tears flowed down his new-changed face. (180–203)

Only his mind remained unchanged. What should he do? Go home to the royal palace? Or hide in the woods? Shame prevented him from the one action, fear from the other. While he stood undecided, his hounds saw him. Blackfoot and clever Tracker first raised the hue and cry with their baying, the latter a Cretan hound, the former of Spartan pedigree. Then the rest of the pack rushed up, swifter than the wind, whose names it would take too long to give.[7] Eager for the prey, they hunt him over rocks and cliffs, by rough tracks and trackless ways, through terrain rocky and inaccessible. He fled, by ways where he had often been the pursuer; he fled, pursued by his own hounds! He longed to cry out "I am Actaeon; obey your master!" He longed—but could utter no words; and the heavens echoed to the baying hounds. First Blackie gored his back; then Hunter followed, while Hill-hound gripped Actaeon's shoulder with his teeth. These three had been slower to join the chase but had outstripped the pack along mountain shortcuts; while they held back their master, the pack came up and all sank their teeth into his body. His whole body was torn by the hounds; he groaned, a sound which was not human nor yet such as a stag could make. (203–239)

The hills he knew so well echoed with his screams; falling on his knees, like a man in prayer, he dumbly looked at them in entreaty, for he had no human arms to stretch out to them. But the huntsmen, ignorant of the truth, urge on the pack with their usual cries; they look around for Actaeon and loudly call his name as if he were not there. At the sound of his name he lifts his head; they think it a pity that he is not there, too slow to see the sight of the stag at bay. He could indeed wish he were not there! But he is; he could wish to be the spectator, not the victim, of his hounds' cruel jaws. Completely encircling him, with jaws biting deep, they tear in fact their master's flesh when he seems to be a stag. Only when his life has ebbed out through innumerable wounds, was it said that the vengeance of the huntress Diana was satisfied. (239–252) 70

Opinions varied about the deed. Some thought the goddess had been more cruel than just; others approved and said that her severity was worthy of her virgin chastity. Each view had good reasons to support it.

Callisto and Arcas

The same insistence on purity and chastity and the same vehemence against defilement of any sort appear in the story of Callisto, one of the followers of Artemis (or Diana, as Ovid tells it; *Metamorphoses* 2.409–507):

As Jupiter journeyed back and forth to Arcadia, he saw the Arcadian girl Callisto, and the fires of love were kindled in his bones. She did not care to draw out the unworked wool or to change her hair's style. She would pin her dress with a brooch, keep her hair in place with a white ribbon; with a smooth spear in her hand or a bow, she marched in Diana's troops. No other girl who trod the Arcadian hills was dearer to the goddess—but no one's power can last for long! (409–416)

High in the heaven rode the Sun beyond the middle of his course, when Callisto came to a wood that no one throughout the years had touched. Here she took off the quiver from her shoulder and unstrung the pliant bow; she lay upon the grassy 10 ground, her head resting upon the painted quiver. Jupiter saw her, tired and unprotected. "My wife," said he, "will never discover this affair, and if she does—well, the prize is worth her anger." So he disguised himself to look like Diana and said: "Dear girl, my follower, upon which mountain did you hunt?" Callisto sprang up from the turf. "Hail, goddess," said she, "greater in my opinion than Jupiter—and let him hear my words!" (417–429)

Jupiter smiled as he heard this, glad that Diana was preferred to himself; he kissed the girl, more warmly than a maiden should. He cut short Callisto's tale of the forest hunt with an embrace, and as he forced his advances showed her who he really was. Callisto fought against him with all a woman's strength—Juno's anger 20 would have been lessened could she have seen her—but who is weaker than a girl, and who can overcome Jupiter? He won; to the heavens he flies and she hates the wood that knows her shame; as she fled from it, she almost forgot to take her quiver and arrows and the bow that she had hung up. (429–440)

Diana saw her as she moved with her followers along the heights of Maenalus, flushed with pride at the beasts she had killed, and called her. Callisto hid, afraid at first that Jupiter in disguise was calling her. But as she saw the nymphs and goddess go on together she knew it was no trick and joined the band. Poor Callisto! How hard it is not to show one's guilt in one's face! She could hardly lift her eyes from the ground; no longer did she stay close to Diana's side nor be the first of all her 30 followers. In silence she blushed and showed her shame; if Diana had not been

The Death of Actaeon. Athenian red-figure krater by the Pan painter, ca. 460 B.C.; height 14½ in. Artemis shoots Actaeon, who falls in agony as his hounds tear him. Actaeon is shown in fully human form, and the small size of the hounds compels the viewer to focus on the human figure and his divine antagonist. The scene of the consequences of chastity violated is made the more poignant by the reverse of this vase (on p. 322), which shows the lustful god Pan pursuing a goatherd. (*Photograph © 2010 Museum of Fine Arts, Boston*)

a maiden, she could have known Callisto's guilt by a thousand signs. They say that the nymphs realized it. (441–452)

The horned moon was waxing for the ninth time when Diana, weary from the chase and tired by the sun, her brother's flaming heat, reached a cool wood; here flowed a babbling stream, gliding over its smooth and sandy bed. She praised the place; she dipped her feet into the water and it pleased her. "No man is here to spy on us," she cried: "let us bathe naked in the stream!" Callisto blushed; the others took off their clothes; she alone held back. And as she delayed, they stripped her, and then her naked body and her guilt were plain to see. She stood confused, trying to hide her belly with her hands; but Diana cried: "Be off from here! Do not defile these sacred waters!" and expelled her from her band. (453–465)   40

Long before, Juno had known the truth and put off revenge until the time was ripe. She saw no cause to wait now; Callisto's son, Arcas (his very name caused Juno pain), had been born, and when Juno's cruel gaze fell on him she cried: "So only this was left, you whore; for you to be pregnant and by this birth make known the wrong I suffer and my husband's shameful act! But I will have my revenge! I will take away the beauty that pleases you so much and gives my husband, you flirt, such pleasure." (466–475)   50

And as she spoke she seized Callisto's hair and threw her to the ground. Callisto spread her arms in suppliant prayer; her arms began to bristle with black hair, her hands to be bent with fingers turning to curved claws; she used her hands as feet and the face that once delighted Jupiter grew ugly with grinning jaws. Her power of speech was lost, with no prayers or entreaties could she win pity, and a hoarse and frightening growl was her only utterance. (476–484)

Yet Callisto's human mind remained even when she had become a bear; with never-ceasing moans she made known her suffering; lifting what once had been her hands to heaven, she felt Jupiter's ingratitude, although she could not with words accuse him. Poor thing! How often was she afraid to sleep in the solitary forest, before her former home; how often did she roam in the lands that once were hers! How often was she pursued over the rocky hills by the baying hounds; how often did the huntress run in fear from the hunters! Often she hid herself (forgetting what she was) and though a bear, shrank from the sight of bears; wolves scared her, although her father Lycaon had become one. (485–495)   60

One day Arcas, now nearly fifteen years old and ignorant of his parentage, was out hunting; as he picked a likely covert and crisscrossed the forests of Mt. Erymanthus with knotted nets, he came upon his mother. She saw him and stood still, like one who sees a familiar face. He ran away, afraid of the beast who never took her gaze from him (for he knew not what she was); he was on the point of driving a spear through her body, eager as she was to come close to him. Then almighty Jupiter prevented him; he averted Arcas' crime against his mother and took them both on the wings of the wind to heaven and there made them neighboring stars. (496–507)   70

Callisto became the **Great Bear** (Arctus, or **Ursa Major**) and **Arcas** the Bear Warden (Arctophylax, or Arcturus, or Boötes) or the Little Bear (**Ursa Minor**). Ursa Major was also known as Hamaxa (the Wain). The story of Callisto is typical of myths that provide the etiology of individual stars or constellations. These stories (most of which belong to late antiquity) are told about various figures in mythology, and several of them cluster about Artemis herself.

Orion

One such story concerns Orion, a composite figure about whom many tales are related with multiple and intricate variations.[8] He is traditionally a mighty and amorous hunter and often associated with the island of Chios and its king, Oenopion (the name means "wine-face"; Chios was and still is famous for its wines). The many versions play upon the following themes. Orion woos the daughter of Oenopion, Merope; he becomes drunk and is blinded by the king, but he regains his sight through the rays of the sun-god, Helius. While he is clearing the island of wild beasts as a favor for Oenopion, he encounters Artemis and tries to rape her. In her anger, the goddess produces a scorpion out of the earth that stings Orion to death.[9] Both can be seen in the heavens. Some say that Orion pursued the **Pleiades** (daughters of the Titan Atlas and Pleione, an Oceanid), and they were all transformed into constellations; with Orion was his dog, **Sirius**, who became the **Dog Star**.

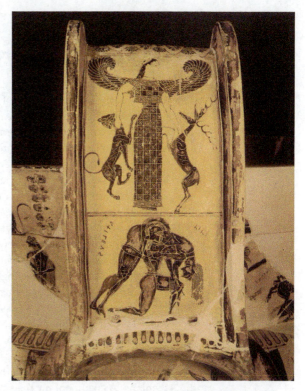

Artemis as Mistress of Animals (*Potnia Theron*). One of the handles of the François vase by the potter Ergotimos and the painter Kleitias, ca. 575 B.C.; height of vase 30 in. (see p. XXX). Artemis is shown in profile, winged and wearing the peplos, an archaic robe folded over the shoulders, belted, and descending to the feet. She is holding a panther and a stag. (© 1994 RMN-Grand Palais (musée du Louvre)/Hervé Lewandowski)

Arethusa

The river-god Alpheus loved the nymph Arethusa, a follower of Artemis or, according to the sixth-century poetess Telesilla, Artemis herself. As he pursued Arethusa along the river bank, she prayed to Artemis, who covered her with a cloud; as the god watched the cloud, both it and the nymph melted into a stream for which Artemis cleft the earth. Flowing underground (where it was united with the waters of Alpheus) and under the sea, it emerged at Syracuse in Sicily, where it is still called by the same name, the fountain Arethusa.

Origins of Artemis

The origins of Artemis are obscure. Although she is predominantly a virgin goddess, certain aspects of her character suggest that originally she may have had connections with fertility.[10] Artemis' interest in childbirth and in the young of both humans and animals seems to betray concerns that are not entirely virginal. Her close association with animals is portrayed on the handle of the François vase. At Ephesus in Asia Minor, a statue of Artemis depicts her in a robe of animal heads, which in its upper part exposes what appears to be (but may not be) a ring of multiple breasts (see p. 228). We should remember, too, that Artemis became a goddess of the moon in classical times. As in the case of other goddesses worshiped by women (e.g., Hera), this link with the moon may be associated with the lunar cycle and women's menstrual period. Thus, the evident duality in Artemis' character and interests definitely links her with the archetypal concept of the virgin/mother.[11]

Artemis Brauronia

The Brauronia, a festival held every four years, was celebrated with a procession from Athens to Brauron. The importance of the cult of Artemis at Brauron (on the eastern coast of Attica) is attested by the archaeological finds, which include a temple of Artemis, a stoa with several dining rooms, which was used to display small marble statues, and reliefs dedicated by parents in gratitude for successful childbirth. Many other types of offering have been found (e.g., ornaments, mirrors, pottery, jewelry). According to Euripides (*Iphigenia in Tauris* 1461–1467), Iphigenia was the first priestess and is buried there.

Lysistrata tells us (Aristophanes, *Lysistrata* 644–655): "I was a bear at the Brauronia and wore and shed the yellow robe" (*krokōtos*). This rite (called the Arcteia) performed at Brauron was also referred to as playing the bear, serving as a bear for Artemis, or dedicating oneself to Artemis. Significant evidence for what is meant are the *krateriskoi*, small cheap bowls of mediocre quality, found also at other shrines of Artemis in Attica (e.g., Munychia in the Piraeus), depicting scenes of girls singing and dancing, holding torches or running in races, dressed in rags or naked, with an altar or a palm tree, or a part of a bear.

Were these girls' initiation or passage rites, a release of their wildness to be restrained by the societal demands of adulthood, marriage, and motherhood, with characteristics of a mystery cult involving secret ceremonies forbidden to the male? The myth behind the ritual explained that once a bear in the region of Brauron, sacred to Artemis, scratched a young girl (*parthenos*) while she played with it. Her brothers killed the bear and a plague befell the Athenians. As payment for the slain bear and release from the plague, Athenians were required to have their maidens do the bear ritual. They also ordained that no woman could marry until she had played the bear for the goddess.

All girls five to ten years of age were required to become "bears" before marriage. They served for a year as attendants in the sanctuary, and together, dressed in yellow robes, they would perform the sacrifice of a goat (a substitute sacrifice for a virgin) to placate the deadly anger of Artemis and ward off, for their community and for themselves, plague, famine, and death, especially in childbirth.[12]

Artemis, Selene, and Hecate

As a moon-goddess, Artemis is sometimes closely identified with Selene and Hecate. Hecate is clearly a fertility deity with definite chthonian characteristics. She can make the earth produce in plenty, and her home is in the depths of the Underworld. She is a descendant of the Titans and in fact a cousin of Artemis.[13] Hecate is a goddess of roads in general and crossroads in particular, the latter being considered the center of ghostly activities, particularly in the dead of night. Thus, the goddess developed a terrifying aspect; triple-faced statues depicted the three manifestations of her multiple character as a deity of the moon: Selene in heaven, Artemis on earth, and Hecate in the realm of Hades. Offerings of food (known as **Hecate's suppers**) were left to placate her, for she was terrible both in her powers and in her person—a veritable Fury, armed with a scourge and blazing torch and accompanied by terrifying hounds. Her skill in the arts of black magic made her the patron deity of sorceresses (like Medea) and witches.

How different is the usual depiction of Artemis, young, vigorous, wholesome, and beautiful! In the costume of the huntress, she is ready for the chase, armed with her bow and arrow; an animal often appears by her side, and crescent moon–like horns rest on her head; the torch she holds burns bright with the light of birth, life, and fertility. Whatever the roots of her fertility connections, the dominant conception of Artemis is that of the virgin huntress. She becomes, as it were, the goddess of nature itself, not always in terms of its teeming procreation, but instead often reflecting its cool, pristine, and virginal aspects. As a moon-goddess too (despite the overtones of fecundity), she can appear as a symbol, cold, white, and chaste.

Artemis versus Aphrodite: Euripides' *Hippolytus*

In her role as a goddess of chastity, Artemis provides a ready foil for Aphrodite's voluptuous sensuality. In this view, Artemis becomes at one and the same time a negative force, representing the utter rejection of love and also a positive compulsion toward purity and asceticism. No one has rendered the psychological and physiological implications of this contrast in more human and meaningful terms than the poet Euripides in his tragedy *Hippolytus.*

As the play begins, Aphrodite is enraged; her power is great and universal, yet she is vehemently spurned by **Hippolytus**, who will have absolutely nothing to do with her. The young man must certainly pay for this hubris, and the goddess uses his stepmother, **Phaedra**, to make certain that he will. Phaedra is the second wife of **Theseus**, the father of Hippolytus (for the saga of Theseus, see Chapter 23). Aphrodite impels the unfortunate Phaedra to fall desperately in love with her stepson. Phaedra's nurse wrests the fatal secret of her guilty love from her sick and distraught mistress and makes the tragic mistake of taking it upon herself to inform the unsuspecting Hippolytus, who is horrified. The thought of physical love for any woman is for him traumatic enough; a sexual relationship with the wife of his father would be an abomination.

In her disgrace, Phaedra commits suicide; but first she leaves a note that falsely incriminates Hippolytus, whose death is brought about by the curse of his enraged father, Theseus, a heroic extrovert who has never really understood the piety of his son. Artemis appears to her beloved follower Hippolytus as he lies dying. She promises him, in return for a lifetime of devotion that has brought about his martyrdom, that she will get even by wreaking vengeance on some favorite of Aphrodite, and she will establish a cult in honor of Hippolytus as well—virgin maidens will pay tribute to him by dedicating their shorn tresses and lamenting his fate by their tears and their songs.[14] Theseus realizes his error too late; he must suffer the consequences of his rash and hasty judgment against Hippolytus; but in the end father and son find understanding and reconciliation.

At the close of the play, we are left with a fascinating chain of enigmas in the Euripidean manner, as the two opposing goddesses—both as real characters and psychological forces—manipulate the action. Is Hippolytus a saint or a foolish and obstinate prig? Has he destroyed himself through the dangerous, if not impossible, rejection of the physical? Are human beings at the mercy of ruthless and irrational compulsions inherent in their very nature, which they deify as ruthless and vindictive women? Certainly, the two goddesses play upon the basic character of the human protagonists. Aphrodite uses the essentially sensual Phaedra, and Artemis responds to the purity of Hippolytus' vision. Each of us is created in the image of a personal and controlling god, or each creates one's own special deity, according to his or her individual nature and character.

Obviously, then, a study of Euripides' *Hippolytus* becomes vital for understanding the nature of both Artemis and Aphrodite. For those who want to study Euripides' play in more detail, the Additional Reading at the end of this chapter offers crucial excerpts with commentary, including the entire final episode in which Artemis herself appears and reveals her essential characteristics. This is one of Euripides' best plays because of its masterful construction and its deceptively transparent simplicity, endlessly revealing intricate subtlety of thought and complexity of characterization. In the context of this and the previous chapter, Euripides' profound and critical scrutiny of the antithetical Artemis and Aphrodite and their worship should be primary.

The Misogyny of Hippolytus

In Euripides' play, after Hippolytus learns from the nurse of Phaedra's desire for him, he bursts out in a tirade against women as vile and evil (p. 233). This reaction has received a great deal of attention and interpretation, particularly today, because of its misogyny. Hippolytus' hatred of women is to be understood, but not necessarily condoned, in the context of his character and the play. This chaste man has suffered the most traumatic shock of his young life. Sex with any woman for him is impossible. The sudden realization of the lust of Phaedra, the wife of his beloved father, strikes him as an abomination. His feelings are in some ways similar to the misogyny of another holy man, John the Baptist, in his outbursts against Salome and her mother, Herodias. Not the least of his psychological problems are his own illegitimacy and the character of his mother, a vehement and chaste Amazon, who succumbed to his father Theseus.

Yet some see in Hippolytus' outcry against women the expression of views generally held in Greek society, particularly in fifth-century Athens, as though somehow Hippolytus himself were a typical ancient Greek male. It is abundantly clear from the play that he is anything but that. Aphrodite herself punishes him for his aberration, and his father hates him for his religious fanaticism and cannot believe his virginal protestations; Theseus hastily convinces

Artemis of Ephesus. Alabaster and bronze, mid-second century A.D. The Ephesian Artemis continues the ancient tradition of the goddess as protectress of nature—seen in the rows of animal heads on her robe, sleeves, breastplate, and head-disk—and revives her original connection with fertility, shown by the multiple breast-like objects (whose identity is much debated). The turreted *polos* (crown) and the figure of Nike (Victory) on her breastplate are symbols of her role as protectress of the city of Ephesus. This Artemis is the "Diana of the Ephesians" at the center of the riot described in the Bible (Acts 19:23–41). (*Scala/Art Resource, NY*)

himself that Hippolytus raped Phaedra because he never could believe that his boy does not like women. Theseus is the archetype of the traditional, extrovert father who loves his wife and is disappointed by his son who has turned out to be an introvert, different from him in almost every way. If one were to pick an average Athenian (a dangerous, if not foolish, game to play), it would be Theseus.

Misandry, Artemis, and the Amazons

Misandry, hatred of men, rather than misogyny, is a more immediate theme in connection with Artemis, where it manifests itself in the close religious bonds of her group, which excludes the male, as made evident in the stories of Actaeon and Callisto. In this connection, the Amazons are relevant, important figures not only in the legends of Theseus, but also in those of Heracles and the Trojan War; the Amazons developed a society not unlike that of Artemis the huntress, which excluded men. The Amazons, however, were devoted to the pursuit of battle and were determined to become invincible warriors. Their *arete* (excellence) was to be the same and in no way different from that of a male.

Lesbian Themes

Lesbianism is a latent motif in stories about the strong bond of affection among Artemis and her band of female followers. The atmosphere is virginal and the relationships pure, although the success of Jupiter with Callisto, when he takes the form of her beloved virgin goddess Diana, is fraught with Freudian overtones and makes one wonder. Athena, another virgin goddess, has close female companions. In Chapter 8, we learned the tragic story of her relationship with Pallas, and she was also closely linked to the nymph Chariclo, who became the mother of Tiresias. Because of the avowed purity of these two virgin goddesses, it seems appropriate that Aphrodite (and not Artemis or Athena) should preside over more sensual female relationships.

The society and mores of the warlike Amazons may also be subjected to lesbian interpretations, if one so desires.

Additional Reading: Euripides' *Hippolytus*

Euripides' *Hippolytus* takes place in front of the palace in Troezen, a city linked to Athens and the hero Theseus. In a typically Euripidean prologue (cf. the opening of the *Bacchae* in Chapter 13), the mighty goddess Aphrodite proclaims the universality of her power and establishes the action of the play. She is outraged because the young and virginal hunter Hippolytus slights her and bestows all his love and attention upon Artemis; she explains how she will exact vengeance (1–28):

> APHRODITE: I am called Cypris, a mighty and renowned goddess both in heaven and among mortals. Everyone who looks upon the light of the sun throughout the whole world (from the eastern boundary of the Black Sea to the western limit of the straits of Gibraltar) is at my mercy; I reward those who celebrate my power, but I destroy all who with arrogant pride oppose me. For gods,

just like mortals, enjoy receiving honor. I will show you the truth of these words directly. (1–9)

Hippolytus, the illegitimate son whom the Amazon woman bore to Theseus, this Hippolytus, brought up by the good Pittheus, is the only citizen of this place Troezen who declares that I am the worst of deities. He renounces sex and rejects marriage, and reveres Artemis, the sister of Apollo and daughter of Zeus, believing her the greatest of deities. Throughout the green woods, he rids the land of wild animals with his swift dogs, always intimate with the virgin goddess and experiencing a greater than mortal relationship. I am not envious. Why should I be? But for his sins against me I will take vengeance upon Hippolytus this very day. I have long since made great progress; I need exert little more effort. For once, when Hippolytus came from the house of Pittheus to Pandion's city of Athens to witness the sacraments of the holy mysteries, Phaedra looked upon him; and she the noble wife of his father was struck to the heart by a terrible desire, in accordance with my plans. (10–28)

These last lines beautifully and succinctly epitomize the tragedy, with their swift series of powerful images. In one fatal moment, sensuous and mature Phaedra glimpses the beautiful, young, chaste, and religious Hippolytus and is overwhelmed by her lust (the Greek word used is *eros*), which is hopeless and impossible and can only lead to catastrophe.

Aphrodite tells us that Theseus is absent from Troezen on a self-imposed exile and that Phaedra, tortured by her guilt, is determined to die without revealing her love for her stepson. She goes on to outline the course of the drama. Although Phaedra, before leaving Athens for Troezen, had built a shrine to Aphrodite on the Acropolis, she must die so that vengeance may be exacted against Hippolytus; Aphrodite is more concerned about punishing her enemy Hippolytus than she is about the suffering and death of the unfortunate Phaedra. As Hippolytus enters with a throng of servants singing the praises of Artemis, "most beautiful of the Olympian deities," Aphrodite withdraws with the dire pronouncement that the joyous youth does not realize that this is the last day of his life.

The prayer with which Euripides introduces us to Hippolytus defines the essential nature of the young man and of Artemis; he stands before a statue of the goddess offering her a diadem of flowers (73–87):

HIPPOLYTUS: For you, my mistress, I bring this garland which I have fashioned of flowers plucked from a virgin meadow untouched by iron implements, where no shepherd has ever presumed to graze his flock—indeed a virgin field which bees frequent in spring. Purity waters it like a river stream for those who have as their lot the knowledge of virtue in everything, not through teaching but by their very nature. These are the ones for whom it is right to pluck these flowers, but those who are evil are forbidden. My dear lady, accept from my holy hand this garland to crown your golden hair. I alone of mortals have this privilege: I am with you and converse with you, for I hear your voice, although I do not see your face. As I have begun life in your grace, may I so keep it to the end. (73–87)

One of the servants warns Hippolytus of the consequences of his hubristic refusal to pay homage to a statue of Aphrodite. Hippolytus avows that since he is pure, he must keep his distance from a goddess who is worshiped in the night, and he bids her a haughty goodbye.

A chorus of women from Troezen expresses concern about Phaedra's mysterious illness and conjectures about its nature. When Phaedra, weak, pale, and wasted, makes her entrance, accompanied by her faithful Nurse, they realize the seriousness of her predicament. In the following scene, only with great difficulty can the Nurse wrest from her distraught mistress the guilty secret that she is in love with her stepson Hippolytus. An anguished Phaedra, whose ravings had been fraught with ambiguous and sexual innuendo, at last explains to the women of Troezen. She begins with some general thoughts (deeply pondered during her tortured, sleepless nights) about how lives of human beings have been destroyed. People are not ruined because they have no moral sense but because they fail to carry out what they know to be right due to inertia or weak submission to temptations and less honorable action. She goes on to explain how her conclusions apply directly to her own behavior and suffering (391–430):

> PHAEDRA: I will tell you the course of my resolves. When *eros* struck me, I thought about how I might best endure the wound. And so I began in this way: to be silent and to hide my affliction. (For one's tongue is not at all trustworthy; it knows how to advise others in a quandary but gets for oneself a multitude of evils.) My second plan was to endure this madness steadfastly, mastering it by self-control. (391–399)
>
> But when I was unable to overcome Cypris by these means, it seemed best to me to die, the most effective of all resolutions—as no one will deny. The good and noble things that I do should be witnessed by all but not my bad and shameful actions. I knew that both my sick passion and its fulfillment were disreputable, and besides, I have learned well the lesson that being a woman and a wife I was open to disgrace. May she die in damnation, that woman, a pollution to us all, who first defiled her marriage bed with other men. This wickedness began in the houses of the nobility to become a defilement on all the female sex. For whenever shameful acts seem right to the aristocrats, most certainly they will seem good to the lower classes. (400–412) 10
>
> I also hate women who say that they are chaste but in secret dare to commit unholy acts. O Lady Cypris, mistress of the sea, how in the world can such women look into the faces of their husbands? How can they help but tremble in the dark, their accomplice, in fear that the walls of the house will utter a sound? (413–418) 20
>
> My friends, I must die for this simple reason: that I may never be found guilty of bringing shame upon my husband and the children whom I bore. Instead may they live and flourish in the renowned city of Athens, free men, open in speech and their good reputation unsullied by their mother. For man is enslaved, even if he is bold of heart, whenever he is conscious of the sins of a mother or a father. (419–425)
>
> They say that to win in life's contest, one needs only this: a good and just character. But the base among mortals are exposed, sooner or later, when Time holds a mirror before them, as before a young girl. Among such as these may I never be discovered. (426–430

Thus the noble Phaedra reveals her character and her motivation. The Nurse, upon first learning of Phaedra's love for Hippolytus, was shocked and horrified. Now, however, in response to her mistress, she offers assurances that Phaedra's experience is nothing unusual. She is the victim of the goddess of love, like many others. Not only mortals but even deities succumb to illicit passions. Phaedra must bear up. The pragmatic Nurse ends her sophistic arguments by claiming that she will find some cure. She is deliberately ambiguous about the precise nature of this cure so that she can win Phaedra's confidence, hinting at some potion or magic that must be employed. She dismisses Phaedra's fear that she will reveal her love for Hippolytus—but this is exactly the cure that she has resolved upon, with the preliminary precaution of exacting from the young man an oath of silence.

From Hippolytus' angry shouts that come from the palace, poor Phaedra learns that her Nurse (in a loving but misguided attempt to help) has indeed approached Hippolytus. She overhears Hippolytus brutally denouncing the Nurse, calling her a procurer of evils, in betrayal of her master's marriage bed. Phaedra, believing that she is now ruined, confides to the Chorus that she is resolved to die. We do not have Euripides' stage directions. Some would have Phaedra exit at this point, but the drama is intensified and her subsequent actions are more comprehensible if she remains, compelled to witness the entire following scene. Hippolytus bursts forth from the palace followed by the Nurse (601–668):

> HIPPOLYTUS: O mother earth and vast reaches of the sun, What unspeakable words have I listened to! (601)
>
> NURSE: Be quiet, my boy, before someone hears you shouting.
>
> HIPPOLYTUS: I have heard such dreadful things that it is impossible for me to be silent.
>
> NURSE: Please, by your strong right hand. (605)
>
> HIPPOLYTUS: Keep your hands off me! Don't touch my cloak!
>
> NURSE: I beseech you, by your knees. Don't ruin me.
>
> HIPPOLYTUS: What do you mean? Didn't you claim that there was nothing wrong in what you said?
>
> NURSE: What I said was by no means intended for all to hear.   10
>
> HIPPOLYTUS: Good words spread among many become even better. (610)
>
> NURSE: My child, do not be untrue to your oath, in any way.
>
> HIPPOLYTUS: My tongue swore but my mind is under no oath.
>
> NURSE: My boy, what will you do? Ruin those near and dear to you?
>
> HIPPOLYTUS: I spit upon them! No evil person is near and dear to me.
>
> NURSE: Be forgiving. To err is human, my son. (615)
>
> HIPPOLYTUS: O Zeus, why did you bring them into the light of this world—women—an ingrained and deceitful evil for mankind? If you wanted to propagate the race, it is not from women that you should have ordained our birth. Instead, men should be able to buy children in your temples, each making a payment of bronze,   20
> iron, or gold, appropriate to his means, and live free in homes without females. (616–624) 20

Hippolytus rages on to show how obvious it is that a woman is a great evil. A father settles on a dowry to be rid of his very own daughter because she is pernicious. A husband takes the woman into his house and enjoys adorning this worthless and ruinous creature with expensive jewelry and fine clothes, little by little squandering his estate, poor fool.

The husband with a wife who is a nonentity has it easiest. Although not without harm, she is kept from folly by her lack of intelligence. "A clever woman, I loathe. May I never have in my house a woman who is more clever than she should be," Hippolytus exclaims, "for Cypris breeds more villainy in the clever ones." Also, a woman should not have access to a servant but instead only wild and dumb animals, so they may not be able to speak to anyone or receive an answer in return. These last admonitions bring Hippolytus back from his wild generalizations to his present trauma, which provoked them. He erroneously thinks that the Nurse has been sent by a wily and evil Phaedra on her abominable mission, and he goes on to denounce her (651–668).

> Thus it is that you, wicked creature, have come to make a deal with me to debauch the sacred bed of my father. I will pour running water into my ears to wash out the pollution of your words. How could I be a sinner, I who feel defiled by just listening to such a vile proposition? Woman, understand this clearly, my piety is your salvation. If I had not been caught off guard and bound by my oath to the gods, I would never keep myself from telling this filthy business to my father. For the time being, as long as Theseus is away from Troezen, I will absent myself from the palace and keep my mouth shut. But I will return when my father does and watch how you face him, both you and your mistress. Having this taste of your effrontery, I will be knowledgeable. (651–663)
>
> May you be damned. I will never have my fill of hatred for women, not even if anyone criticizes me for always declaring it. For they all, like you, are evil in one way or another. Either someone should teach them how to be temperate or allow me to trample them down forever. (664–668)

10

The Greek word translated "to be temperate" is *sophronein*, which has the basic meaning of to show good sense, to exercise self-control and moderation in all things. It is particularly ironic, spoken here by the intemperate and inhumane Hippolytus. The word may in context connote specific restraint, for example, sexual self-control, that is, to be chaste.

The Nurse is overcome with remorse and guilt for the failure of her scheme, but she cannot assuage the fury of Phaedra, whose only recourse now is to end her own life. She confides her decision to the Chorus, whom she has sworn to secrecy (716–721 and 725–731).

> PHAEDRA: I have found a remedy for my misfortune so that I will bequeath to my sons a life of good reputation, and profit from what has now befallen me. For I will never bring shame upon my Cretan home, nor will I go and face Theseus with disgraceful actions for the sake of one life. ... (716–721)
>
> On this day when I have freed myself from life, I will make Cypris happy, the one who destroys me, and I will be defeated by a bitter eros. But after my death, I will become an evil curse for that other person, so that he may understand that he should not exult haughtily over my misfortunes; by sharing in this malady with me, he will learn how to be temperate. (725–731)

Phaedra reaffirms the convictions she revealed earlier. She cannot face either the loss of her reputation or the risk of sullying the reputation of Theseus and her sons, jeopardizing their future. Now she has added another motive for her actions, similar to that of Aphrodite: vengeance against Hippolytus' cruel and arrogant hubris, which she herself has just witnessed, to exacerbate her humiliation and her suffering.

Phaedra echoes Hippolytus' tirade when she promises that he will learn (i.e., she will teach him) how to be temperate (*sophronein*). There is another reminder of Hippolytus and a chilling ambiguity in her earlier assertion: "nor will I go and face Theseus with disgraceful actions for the sake of one life." Does she mean her life or that of Hippolytus?

Phaedra goes into the palace to commit suicide. She hangs herself, and just as she is freed from the noose and her corpse is laid out, Theseus returns. Overcome with grief, he notices a tablet, bearing her seal, dangling from Phaedra's hand. He reads it in horror and cries out for all to hear: "Hippolytus has dared to violate my marriage bed by force, desecrating the holy eye of Zeus." He calls out to his father Poseidon, who has granted Theseus three curses, and asks that with one of them the god kill Hippolytus, who, he prays, may not live out this day. Theseus also pronounces banishment upon his son. Hearing Theseus' cries, a bewildered Hippolytus appears. In the lengthy confrontation between father and son, the following excerpt elucidates the long-standing difficulties in their relationship and the crux of their conflict. To Hippolytus' protestations that he has done nothing wrong, Theseus exclaims (936–980):

> THESEUS: Oh, the human heart, to what lengths will it go? What limit will one set to boldness and audacity? ... (936–937)
>
> Behold this man, who was begotten by me; he has defiled my bed and stands clearly convicted of being the basest of human beings by the woman who is dead. Look at your father directly, face to face; don't be afraid that your gaze will contaminate me, I am already contaminated. Are you the man who consorts with the gods, as though you were superior to everyone else? Are you, the pure virgin, unsullied by sin? I could never be convinced by these boasts of yours and wrongly believe that the gods are fooled by your hypocrisy. Now that you are caught, go ahead and brag, show off with your vegetarian diet, take Orpheus as your lord, celebrate the   10
> mysteries, believing in their many and vacuous writings. I warn everyone to shun men such as these. For they prey upon you with their holy words, while they devise their evil plots. (943–957)
>
> She is dead. Do you imagine that this fact will save you? By this, most of all, O villain, you are convicted. For what kind of oath, what testimony could be more powerful than she to win your acquittal? Will you maintain that she hated you and that it is only natural for a bastard to be in conflict with those who are legitimate? If so, you argue that she made a bad and foolish bargain, if she destroyed what is most precious, her own life, out of hostility to you; but will you claim that folly is an attribute of women and not found in men? I know that young men are no more stable than women, whenever Cypris plays havoc in their young hearts; yet because they are male, they are not discredited. And so now—ah, but why do I wage this contest of words with you, when this corpse lies here, the clearest wit-   20
> ness against you. Get out of this land, go, an exile, as quickly as possible; and stay away from god-built Athens and the borders of any territory ruled by my spear. (958–975)
>
> If I am beaten by you, after these terrible things you have made me suffer, Isthmian Sinis will not bear witness to his defeat at my hands but make it my idle boast, and the Scironian rocks by the sea will refute the fact that I am merciless against those who do evil. (976–980)

Theseus' own boasting about his prowess refers to two of his labors, the killing of the robber Sinis at the Isthmus of Corinth and the brigand Sciron on the cliffs that bear his name. No one would believe his prowess against the wicked if he did not punish Hippolytus.

In his denunciation of Hippolytus, Theseus reveals the long-standing rift that has grown between them. However great his love for Phaedra and the shock of her suicide, how could Theseus so readily accept her accusation of rape if he had any understanding of the nature and character of his son? His suspicions about Hippolytus' avowals of purity, which to him smack of haughty superiority, and his ridicule of mystery religions indicate that Theseus, the hero, has little respect for the beliefs of a son who is so different in temperament. (We cannot help but recall that Phaedra was smitten with desire as she observed the pure Hippolytus participating in the Mysteries. A young and innocent man so unlike his father, her husband!)

Theseus imagines that Hippolytus will argue that Phaedra hated him and that conflict between the two of them was inevitable: he was a bastard, she was a stepmother, and as the wife of Theseus she bore him two legitimate sons, rivals to Hippolytus and heirs to the throne. How much has rejection sullied the relationship between Theseus and Hippolytus? In fact, Hippolytus' fanatical devotion to Artemis and his renunciation of Aphrodite reflect a resentment against his father expressed in his devotion to his real mother, who, as an Amazon, would normally have nothing to do with Aphrodite and heterosexual love, had she not been seduced by Theseus. Later, Hippolytus exclaims (1082–1083): "O my unhappy mother, O my bitter birth, may no one dear to me ever be born a bastard!" At this point in the play, Hippolytus answers his father's accusations as follows (983–1035):

> HIPPOLYTUS: Father, your strength and the intensity of your rage are terrifying. Yet, although your arguments seem just, if one examines the case you present closely, it is not just at all. I am not good at making a speech before many—I am better at talking to a few people of my own age. This is how things go—just as those who are inept among a group of the wise speak more persuasively before a crowd. Be this as it may, since misfortune has befallen me, I must not hold my tongue. (983–991)
>
> First of all, I will begin by answering your first accusation by which you sought to destroy me without a word to say in response. You see the sky and this here earth. There is no one under the sun more righteous than I am, even if you say this is not 10 so. First, I know how to pay reverence to the gods and to pick friends who try to do no wrong and whose sense of decency prevents them from demanding wrong or doing wrong to others. I do not belittle or betray these companions, father, but am the same to them, whether they are with me or not. I am innocent of the one charge, of which you now think you have convicted me. To this very moment, my body is chaste. I have never had sex but only heard about it, or seen depictions of it which I do not like to look at because I am a virgin, pure in heart and soul. (991–1006)
>
> Suppose you are not convinced about my chastity. So be it. You must then show in what way I was corrupted. Was her body more beautiful than that of any other woman? Or did I hope to become an heir in your palace, by taking her to bed? If so, 20 I was a fool, completely out of my mind. Will you argue that to be a king is a sweet temptation for a man in his right senses? Not in the least, because all those who love the power of a king have been corrupted. No, I would like to win first place in the Greek Games but in the city to be second and always to enjoy good fortune with the best people for friends; this allows for achievement, and the absence of danger affords more pleasure than kingship. (1007–1020)
>
> You have all my arguments, except for one thing. If I had a truthful witness like myself to testify to what kind of man I am, and if I were pleading my case while Phaedra were still alive to see and hear me, you would know the guilty ones by a

careful scrutiny of the evidence. As it is, now I swear to you by Zeus, god of oaths   30
and by vast earth that I never touched your wife, never wanted to, nor ever even
had the thought. May I die without a name or reputation, without a city or a home,
wandering the earth as an exile, and after my death, may neither sea nor land accept
my corpse, if I have done any wrong. (1021–1031)

Why and through what fear she took her own life, I do not know, since it is not
right for me to speak further. She acted virtuously, when she could not be virtuous.
I am virtuous but I have not used my virtue well.

Hippolytus' last words present Theseus with a riddle. The message he conveys is that Phaedra, when she could not control her passion (she could not be
temperate; the verb *sophronein* is used again), was not virtuous. When she committed suicide to ensure that she would not commit adultery, this virtuous act
absolved her of guilt. Hippolytus, however, is virtu-
ous and chaste, but his behavior has led to disaster.
Hippolytus does not break his oath and reveal the truth
but, from many of his words, a less hot-tempered and
more sympathetic Theseus would have suspected that
his son knows more than he has revealed. For example,
Hippolytus picks friends and associates who in character and behavior are the antithesis of Phaedra.

In the heated exchange that follows, the father banishes
his son from the land. Hippolytus leaves driving his four-
horsed chariot. A messenger comes to report to Theseus
the terrible fate of Hippolytus, brought about by the curse
that Theseus had evoked through the god Poseidon. His dramatic speech vividly describes how, amid a terrifying surge
of the sea, a huge wave brought forth a monstrous bull,
bellowing savagely, which made directly for Hippolytus
as he was driving his chariot along the sea coast. The four
horses were seized by such a panic that even the experienced Hippolytus was not able to control them. In the horrible crash that ensued, Hippolytus was caught in the leather
reins and brutally dragged along the rocks. Finally, he was

The Death of Hippolytus. Lower register of an Apulian volute-krater (a large
vase with elaborate handles) by the Darius painter, ca. 340 B.C. The painter illustrates the opening scene described in the messenger's speech from Euripides'
Hippolytus. To the right an old retainer runs behind the chariot, with a gesture
of horror. *Hippolytus*, dressed as a charioteer, begins to lose control as the four
horses panic at the sight of the bull emerging from the sea. To the left a Fury (not
mentioned in the messenger's speech) holds a flaming torch with her right hand,
while an animal skin is draped over her left arm. The painter chooses the precise
moment at which the disaster begins and, with great economy, reduces the messenger's elaborate description to a vivid prelude to the breakup of the chariot
and the mutilation of Hippolytus. In the upper register is an array of six gods, only
three of whom (Aphrodite, Artemis, Poseidon) are involved in the tragedy. (© *The
Trustees of the British Museum*)

cut loose; and Theseus, upon learning that his son is still alive, orders that he be brought to face him once again. At this juncture, Artemis appears, a veritable deus ex machina, to set things right, serving as the counterpart to Aphrodite who had opened the play (1283–1466):

ARTEMIS: I command you, royal son of Aegeus, to listen; for I address you, I, Artemis, the daughter of Leto. Why, Theseus, poor wretch, do you take pleasure in these things? You have murdered your son, persuaded to commit this unholy act by the false accusations of your wife, with no clear evidence. Clear, however, is the ruin you have earned. In shame you should hide yourself in the depths of the earth or escape from this misery by exchanging your life for that of a bird above, since you do not deserve to share in the lives of good men. (1283–1295)

Listen, Theseus, to the extent of your evils. Although I will accomplish nothing, yet I will cause you pain. I have come for this purpose, to disclose the righteous nature of your son so that he may die with a good name and the frenzied passion of   10
your wife or, from another point of view, her nobility. For stung by the goads of the goddess most hateful to all of us whose joy is in chastity, she fell in love with your son. (1296–1303)

She tried to overcome Cypris by reason, but she was ruined unwittingly by the machinations of her Nurse, who revealed her malady to your son sworn to secrecy. He did not give in to her entreaties, as was right, and again, being virtuous, he did not break the bond of his oath, although you wronged him so. Phaedra, terrified that she would be exposed, wrote a false letter and destroyed your son by her lies, but nevertheless she convinced you to believe them. (1304–1312)

THESEUS: Woe is me!   20

ARTEMIS: Do my words sting you? Yet be quiet and listen to the rest so that you may lament all the more. Didn't you know that the three curses you got from your father were bound to be fulfilled? You are a most base man to use one of them against your own son, when you could have used it against any of your enemies. The god of the sea, your father and kindly disposed toward you, fulfilled your curse; he had to, since he had promised. Yet both in his eyes and in mine you appear base, you who did not wait either for proof or the guidance of prophets; you did not put the accusation to the test nor allow a lengthy time for scrutiny but, more quickly than you should have, you hurled a curse against your son and killed him. (1313–1324)

THESEUS: My lady, let me die!   30

ARTEMIS: You have done terrible things, but nevertheless it is still possible, even for you, to find pardon for your actions. For it was Aphrodite who wished that these things should come about to satisfy her anger. There is a law for the gods as follows: no one of us wishes to thwart the will of another, but we always stand aside. (1325–1330)

For understand me clearly—If I were not in fear of Zeus' retaliation, I would never have sunk to such a depth of shame as to allow the death of the man dearest to me of all mortals. Ignorance, first of all, acquits you of evil; and besides, your wife by dying prevented your testing the truth of her accusations and so she made you believe her. As it is, these misfortunes have burst upon you most of all; but I too feel pain. The   40
gods have no joy in the deaths of the good and reverent, but those who are wicked we destroy, children, house and all. (1331–1341)

(Hippolytus is brought in by servants.)

CHORUS: Here comes the poor fellow, his young flesh mutilated, his fair hair befouled. Oh, the suffering of this house. What grief—not once but now a second time—has been brought down upon it by the gods! (1342–1346)

HIPPOLYTUS: Ah, what pain. I, unfortunate, destroyed by the unjust curse of an unjust father. Alas, wretched, I am done for, woe is me. Pains shoot through my head, spasms dart around my brain. Stop, servants, let me rest my exhausted body. Oh, what pain! O hateful chariot, drawn by horses fed by my own hand. You have destroyed me, you have killed me. Ah what agony! Servants, by the gods, place your hands lightly on my lacerated flesh. Who stands at my right side? Lift me gently; take me along carefully, me the ill-fated one, cursed by my father's wrongdoing. Zeus, Zeus, do you see what is happening? Here I am, a holy and god-revering man, one who surpassed all others in virtue going to my inevitable death. My life is utterly destroyed, and I have performed my labors of piety on behalf of mortals, all for nothing. (1347–1369)   10

Ah, ah, the pain, the pain which now overwhelms me. Let go of me in my misery and may death come as my healer. Kill me, destroy me and my pain, doomed as I am. I long for the thrust of a two-edged sword to end my life and bring peaceful rest. Oh, unfortunate curse of my father. Some bloodstained evil, inherited from my ancestors long ago, rises up and does not stay dormant but has come against me. Why, oh why, when I am guilty of no evil myself? Woe is me, alas! What am I to say? How will I turn my life of pain into painlessness? If only the inevitable fate of death would transport me, one doomed to suffer so, into the night of Hades' realm. (1370–1388)   20

ARTEMIS: O poor, wretched fellow, how great is the yoke of your misfortune! The nobility of your nature has destroyed you.

HIPPOLYTUS: Ah, what a breath of divine fragrance! Even amid my misfortunes, I feel your presence, and the pain in my body is lifted. The goddess Artemis is present in this place.

ARTEMIS: Gallant sufferer, yes, she is most dear to you of all the gods.

HIPPOLYTUS: Do you see me, my Lady, how wretched I am? (1395)

ARTEMIS: I see your misery but it is not right for my eyes to shed a tear.   30

HIPPOLYTUS: Your huntsman and your servant is no more.

ARTEMIS: No, indeed, but you die most dear to me.

HIPPOLYTUS: No longer the keeper of your horses or the attendant of your statues.

ARTEMIS: Because the evil-schemer Cypris planned it so. (1400)

HIPPOLYTUS: Alas, I understand what goddess has destroyed me.

ARTEMIS: She resented your slights to her honor and hated you for being chaste.

HIPPOLYTUS: This one goddess has destroyed the three of us, I realize now.

ARTEMIS: Your father and you, and his wife, the third.   40

HIPPOLYTUS: And so I bemoan the misfortunes of my father as well as my own. (1405)

ARTEMIS: He was deceived by the designs of a god.

HIPPOLYTUS: Oh, how unhappy you must be, father, because of your great misfortune!

THESEUS: I am done for, my son, and for me there remains no joy in life.

HIPPOLYTUS: I pity you more than I pity myself for mistaken wrongdoing.

THESEUS: If only I could die, my son, instead of you. (1410)

HIPPOLYTUS: How bitter the gifts of your father, Poseidon!

THESEUS: That curse should never have come to my lips.   50

HIPPOLYTUS: Why not? You would have killed me anyway, you were in such a state of anger.

THESEUS: Because the gods had taken away my good sense.

HIPPOLYTUS: Oh, if only mortals could send a curse upon the gods! (1415)

ARTEMIS: No need of a curse. Even though you are in the dark depths of the earth, the rage that has been leveled against your very being through the zealous will of the goddess Cypris will not go unavenged, so that your piety and goodness of heart may be rewarded. For I will punish a lover of hers, the one mortal who is especially the dearest, by this unfailing bow of mine. To you, poor sufferer, I will bestow the greatest of honors in the city of Troezen in recompense for these evil   60 torments of yours. Unmarried girls, before their marriage, will cut off their hair in dedication to you, the one who will reap the rich harvest of their mourning and tears through the span of the ages. The songs of maidens inspired by the Muses will keep your memory alive forever, and Phaedra's passion for you will not be left unsung and become forgotten. (1416–1480)

You, son of revered Aegeus, take your son in your arms and embrace him; for you destroyed him unwittingly, and it is to be expected for human beings to err, when the gods so ordain. I advise you, Hippolytus, not to hate your father. You have been destroyed by the destiny that is yours. (1431–1436)

Farewell. It is not right for me to look upon the dead or to defile my sight with   70 the last gasps of the dying; and I see that you are now near that terrible state. (1437–1439)

HIPPOLYTUS: Go as I bid you farewell, blessed virgin; how easily you leave behind our long relationship. Yet I put an end to my conflict with my father, since you so desire. For, in the past, indeed, I was persuaded by your words.

Ah, darkness is now closing over my eyes. Take hold of me, father, and lay out my body in death. (1440–1445)

THESEUS: Alas, my son, what terrible thing are you doing to me, one so ill-fated?

HIPPOLYTUS: I am done for; indeed, I see the gates of the Underworld.

THESEUS: And will you leave me with my hands defiled?   80

HIPPOLYTUS: No, not at all, since I acquit you of this murder.

THESEUS: What are you saying? Do you free me from blood-guilt? (1450)

HIPPOLYTUS: I invoke Artemis with her indomitable bow as my witness.

THESEUS: O dearest son, what nobility you show toward your father!

HIPPOLYTUS: Farewell to you, father, I wish you much happiness.

THESEUS: Alas for me to lose a son of such piety and goodness!

HIPPOLYTUS: Pray that your true-born sons may be like me. (1455)

THESEUS: Do not forsake me now, my son, but hold on courageously.

HIPPOLYTUS: I can hold on to life no longer. It is over, father. Cover my face—quickly.

THESEUS: O renowned land of Erechtheus and Pallas, what a man you have   90 lost. I, in my wretchedness, will remember all too well, Cypris, the evils you have wrought. (1459–1461)

CHORUS: This unexpected sorrow has come for all the citizens to share. There will be a flood of many tears. For lamentable stories about those who are great can inspire a more intense grief. (1462–1466)

Although Artemis declares her love for Hippolytus, she remains cool and aloof, as antiseptic in some respects as her fanatical follower. The rites she predicts in honor of Hippolytus were celebrated in Troezen, and the beloved of Cypris whom she will kill has been specifically identified as Adonis (who in some versions of his death is killed by Artemis' arrows).

Hippolytus' farewell to Artemis is a beautiful example of Euripides' succinct and profound irony. The sad ambiguity of Hippolytus' words may be highlighted by a different but not unfaithful translation with interpretation: "You, go without any pain, fortunate lady! [I am in pain, unfortunate, and dying.] How readily (or lightly) you abandon my deep devotion. I will become reconciled to my father since you want me to. I will obey you now, as I have done in the past [through the ingrained conviction of a religious habit, which not even my disappointment in your present behavior can dispel. My worship and obedience end like this]."

In their final reconciliation, the theme of Theseus' recognition of the true nobility of his bastard son, and Hippolytus' hope for Theseus that his true-born sons by Phaedra may turn out as worthy, underlines the psychological importance of this basic motif of legitimacy in the play.

Later Adaptations of the Legend

There have been many subsequent dramatic versions of the legend. The treatment by the Roman Seneca (A.D. 65) in his *Phaedra* is well worth studying for its own dramatic merit and as a contrast to Euripides' extant version. There are many differences, both in plot and in characterization, and he explores the psychological tensions of the myth without the goddesses Aphrodite or Artemis appearing as actual figures in the play. Seneca has Phaedra herself (not her Nurse) confront Hippolytus with her lust as she attempts to seduce him. Euripides wrote two dramas about Hippolytus, and Seneca, in this scene, was probably inspired by the earlier version; this first *Hippolytus* of Euripides was not a success and no longer survives. The second version (named *Hippolytos Stephanephoros* to distinguish it from the first), which Euripides produced in 428 B.C., is the one that we know today.

Other later plays on the theme are Jean Racine's *Phèdre* (1677); Eugene O'Neill's *Desire under the Elms* (1924), also influenced by *Medea*; and Robinson Jeffers' *The Cretan Woman* (1954). The manipulation of the character of Hippolytus is illuminating. For example, Racine, by giving Hippolytus a girlfriend in his version, drastically changes the configuration of the Euripidean archetype. Jeffers is closer to Euripides by keeping Hippolytus' abhorrence of sex; but when he introduces a companion for Hippolytus who is "slender and rather effeminate," he suggests another shifting of the archetype of the holy man. At any rate, once Hippolytus' sexual orientation is made too explicit, the mystery of his psyche is diminished. Euripides gets everything right, a judgment made with due respect for the masterpieces that he has inspired. The twentieth-century novel *The Bull from the Sea*, by Mary Renault, is yet another rewarding reinterpretation of the myth. The movie adaptation, *Phaedra* (see Chapter 28 on the companion website), is of some interest.

The attempted seduction of a holy man and its dire consequences represent familiar motifs in literature (in the Bible, for example, see the stories of Joseph and Potiphar's wife and of John the Baptist and Salome).

Select Bibliography

Glinister, Fay. *Diana*. Gods and Heroes of the Ancient World Series. New York: Routledge, 2010.

Marinatos, Nanno. *The Goddess and the Warrior: The Naked Goddess and Mistress of the Animals in Early Greek Religion*. New York: Routledge, 2000.

Wall, Kathleen. *The Callisto Myth from Ovid to Atwood: Initiation and Rape in Literature*. Kingston: McGill–Queen's University Press, 1988.

Primary Sources

Sources in the Chapter

Euripides	*Hippolytus* (selections)
Homeric Hymn 9	*To Artemis*
Homeric Hymn 27	*To Artemis*
Ovid	*Metamorphoses* 2.409–507; 3.138–255

Additional Sources

Callimachus	*To Artemis* (Hymn 3)
Ovid	*Heroides 4*: Phaedra to Hippolytus
Seneca	*Phaedra*
Theocritus	*Idyll* 2

Notes

1. Sometimes the place of birth is called Ortygia (the name means "quail island"), which cannot be identified with certainty. In some accounts, it is clearly not merely another name for Delos; in others, it is.
2. Niobe was the wife of Amphion, ruling by his side in the royal palace of Cadmus. As the daughter of Tantalus and the granddaughter of Atlas, her lineage was much more splendid than that of Leto, the daughter of an obscure Titan, Coeus.
3. A rock on Mt. Sipylus in Asia Minor was identified in antiquity as the figure of Niobe.
4. Actaeon was the son of Aristaeus and Autonoë.
5. The nymphs' names, which are omitted in the translation, are Greek words suggestive of cool, crystal-clear water.
6. A stag was commonly believed to live nine times as long as a man.
7. Still Ovid goes on to give thirty-one more names, which are omitted in the translation.
8. Orion sometimes appears as the son of Earth; in other accounts, his father is Poseidon.
9. Or Orion was run through by Artemis' arrows. Orion also attempted to rape Opis, a follower of Artemis, if indeed she is not the goddess herself.
10. Several of the nymphs associated with her (e.g., Callisto and Opis) were probably once goddesses in their own right and may actually represent various manifestations of Artemis' own complex nature. One of them, Britomartis, is closely linked to Crete and perhaps was once a traditional mother-goddess.
11. Cf. Michael P. Carroll, *The Cult of the Virgin Mary: Psychological Origins* (Princeton, NJ: Princeton University Press, 1986). Carroll ignores the aspects of Artemis as a mother figure when he states (p. 8): "There is little or no basis in Graeco-Roman mythology for portraying either [Artemis or Athena] as a mother figure." He has, however, very perceptive analogies to make with the worship of Cybele (pp. 197–198, 389).
12. See John M. Camp, *The Archaeology of Athens* (New Haven, CT: Yale University Press, 2001); Ken Dowden, *Death and the Maiden: Girls' Initiation Rites in Greek Mythology* (New York: Routledge, 1989), pp. 20–47; and Christopher Faraone, "Playing the Bear

and the Fawn for Artemis: Female Initiation or Substitute Sacrifice?" in *Initiation in Ancient Greek Rituals and Narratives: New Critical Perspectives,* ed. David B. Dodd and Christopher A. Faraone (New York: Routledge, 2003), pp. 43–68.

13. Hecate's mother, Asterie, is Leto's sister; her father is Perses.

14. For more on the legend of Hippolytus and his cult-sites, see pp. 598 and 667.

For additional digital learning resources please go to
www.oup.com/he/morford12e

11

APOLLO

Now the sun, the brilliant four-horsed chariot, shines down upon the earth and at the sky's fire the stars withdraw into holy night. The shining, untrodden crests of Parnassus receive for mortals the day's wheel. The smoke of dried myrrh wafts gently to Phoebus' roof. The Delphic woman sits on the sacred tripod, singing to the Greeks the cries which Apollo sounds.

—EURIPIDES, *Ion* 82–94

The Birth of Apollo

As has been told in the preceding chapter, Zeus mated with **Leto**, and she conceived the twin gods, Artemis and Apollo. The *Homeric Hymn to Apollo* (3) concentrates in its first part (1–178: To Delian Apollo) on the story of how Delos became the site of Apollo's birth. The hymn begins with a scene of the gods in the home of Zeus (1–29):

> I shall not forget far-shooting Apollo but remember him before whom the gods tremble when he comes to the home of Zeus. They all spring up from their seats as he approaches and draws his shining bow, and Leto alone remains beside Zeus, who delights in thunder. But then she unstrings his bow and closes his quiver and, taking them from his mighty shoulders, hangs them on a column of his father's house from a golden peg. She leads him to a chair and sits him down, and his father welcomes his dear son by giving him nectar in a gold cup. Then the other deities sit down in their places and the lady Leto rejoices because she has borne a son who is a mighty archer. Rejoice, O blessed Leto, since you have borne splendid children, lord Apollo and Artemis, who take delight in arrows; Artemis you bore in Ortygia and Apollo in rocky Delos as you leaned against the great and massive Cynthian hill, right next to the palm tree near the stream of the Inopus. (1–18)   10
>
> How then shall I celebrate you in my song—you who are in all ways the worthy subject of many hymns? For everywhere, O Phoebus, music is sung in your honor, both on the mainland where heifers are bred and on the islands. All mountaintops give you pleasure and the lofty ridges of high hills, rivers flowing to the sea, beaches sloping to the water, and harbors of the deep. Shall I sing about how Leto gave you birth against Mt. Cynthus on the rocky island, on sea-girt Delos? On either side a dark wave was driven towards the land by shrill winds. From your beginning here, you rule over all mortals [including those to whom Leto came when she was in labor]. (19–29)   20

243

Leto had roamed far and wide in her search for a refuge where she might give birth to Apollo. The hymn continues with a long and impressive list of cities and islands to emphasize the extent of her wanderings; she visited all those who lived in these places (30–139):[1]

Crete and the land of Athens, the islands of Aegina and Euboea famous for its ships, and Aegae, Eiresiae, and Peparethus by the sea, Thracian Athos, the tall peaks of Pelion, Thracian Samos, the shady hills of Ida, and Scyros, Phocaea, the sheer mountain of Autocane, well-built Imbros, hazy Lemnos, and holy Lesbos, seat of Macar, the son of Aeolus, and Chios, most shimmering of the islands that lie in the sea, craggy Mimas, the tall peaks of Corycus, gleaming Claros, the steep mountain of Aesagea, rainy Samos, the sheer heights of Mycale, Miletus and Cos, the city of Meropian mortals, and steep Cnidos, windy Carpathos, Naxos, Paros, and rocky Rhenaea. (30–44)

DELOS ACCEPTS LETO

Leto approached these many places in labor with the far-shooting god in the hope that some land might want to make a home for her son. But they all trembled and were very much afraid; and not one of them, even the more rich, dared to receive the god Phoebus, until lady Leto came to Delos[2] and asked with winged words: "Delos, if you would like to be the home of my son, Phoebus Apollo, and to establish for him a rich temple—do not refuse, for no one else will come near you, as you will find out, and I do not think that you will be rich in cattle and sheep or bear harvests or grow plants in abundance—if you would then have a temple of Apollo, the far-shooter, all people will congregate here and bring hecatombs, and the aroma of rich sacrifices will rise up incessantly and your inhabitants will be nourished by the hands of foreigners."(45–60)   20

Thus she spoke; Delos rejoiced and said to her in answer: "Leto, most renowned daughter of great Coeus, I should receive your son, the lord who shoots from afar, with joy, for the terrible truth is that I have a bad reputation among human beings, and in this way I should become greatly esteemed. But I fear this prediction (and I shall not keep it from you): they say that Apollo will be someone of uncontrollable power, who will mightily lord it over both immortal gods and mortal humans on the fruitful earth. And so I am dreadfully afraid in the depths of my heart and soul that when he first looks upon the light of the sun he will be contemptuous of me (since I am an island that is rocky and barren) and overturn me with his feet and push me down into the depths of the sea where the surge of the great waves will rise mightily   30
above me. And he will come to another land that pleases him, where he will build his temple amid groves of trees. But sea monsters will find their dens in me, and black seals will make me their home without being disturbed, since I will be without human inhabitants. But if, O goddess, you would dare to swear to me a great oath that he will build here first of all a very beautiful temple to be an oracle for men; then after he has done this, let him proceed to extend his prestige and build his sanctuaries among all people; for to be sure his wide renown will be great." (61–82)

Thus Delos spoke. And Leto swore the great oath of the gods: "Now let Gaea and wide Uranus above bear witness and the flowing waters of the Styx (this is the greatest and most dread oath that there is for the blessed gods), in truth a fragrant   40
altar and sacred precinct of Apollo will be established here forever, and he will honor you above all." (83–88)

LETO GIVES BIRTH TO APOLLO

When she had ended and sworn her oath, Delos rejoiced greatly in the birth of the lord who shoots from afar. But Leto for nine days and nine nights was racked by desperate pains in her labor. All the greatest of the goddesses were with her—Dione, Rhea, righteous Themis, and sea-moaning Amphitrite—and others too, except for white-armed Hera; for she sat at home in the house of Zeus the cloud-gatherer. Eileithyia, the goddess of pangs of childbirth, was the only one who had not heard of Leto's distress, for she sat on the heights of Olympus beneath golden clouds through the wiles of white-armed Hera, who kept her there because she was jealous that Leto of the beautiful hair was about to bear a strong and noble son. (89–101)   50

But the goddesses on the well-inhabited island sent Iris away to fetch Eileithyia, promising her a great necklace strung with golden threads, over 13 feet long. They ordered her to call Eileithyia away from white-armed Hera so that Hera might not be able to dissuade the goddess of childbirth from going. When Iris, swift-footed as the wind, heard their instructions, she ran on her way and quickly traversed all the distance between. And when she came to sheer Olympus, home of the gods, immediately she called Eileithyia out of the house to the door and addressed her with winged words, telling her everything just as the goddesses who have their homes on Olympus had directed. (102–112)   60

EILEITHYIA ASSISTS LETO

Thus she moved Eileithyia to the depths of the heart in her breast, and like timid doves they proceeded on their journey. As soon as Eileithyia, goddess of the pangs of childbirth, came to Delos, the pains of labor took hold of Leto, and she was anxious to give birth. And she threw her arms about the palm tree and sank on her knees in the soft meadow, and the earth beneath her smiled. The baby sprang forth to the light, and all the goddesses gave a cry. There, O mighty Phoebus, the goddesses washed you with lovely water, holily and purely, and wrapped you in white swaddling clothes, splendid and new, fastened round about with a golden cord. And his mother did not nurse Apollo of the gold sword, but Themis from her immortal hands gave him nectar and delicious ambrosia. And Leto rejoiced because she had borne a strong son who carries a bow. (113–126)   70

But after you had tasted the divine food, O Phoebus, then no longer could golden cords hold you in your restlessness or bonds keep you confined, but they all were undone. And straightway Phoebus Apollo exclaimed to the immortal goddesses: "Let the lyre and curved bow be dear to my heart, and I shall prophesy to human beings the unerring will of Zeus." With these words Phoebus, the far-shooter with unshorn hair, strode on the ground that stretches far and wide; all the goddesses were amazed, and the whole of Delos blossomed, laden with gold like the top of a mountain with woodland flowers, as she beheld the son of Zeus and Leto,   80 in her joy that the god had chosen her among all islands and mainland sites to be his home, and loved her most of all in his heart. (127–139)

The conclusion of this first part of the *Homeric Hymn to Apollo* tells about the great festival to Apollo at Delos, the amazing chorus of maidens, the **Deliades**, who can sing in all dialects, and about the poet himself, the blind bard from the island of Chios (140–178):

And you yourself, O lord Apollo, far-shooter of the silver bow, come at times to the steep Cynthian hill of Delos, and on other occasions you wander among other islands and other peoples; indeed many are your temples and wooded groves, and every vantage point, highest peak of lofty mountains and river flowing to the sea, is dear to you. But, O Phoebus, your heart is delighted most of all with Delos, where the long-robed Ionians gather with their children and their revered wives. In commemoration of you they will take pleasure in boxing and dancing and song when they celebrate your festival. And anyone who might encounter the Ionians while they are thus assembled together would say that they were immortal and ageless, for he would perceive grace in them all and be delighted in his heart as he beheld the men and the beautifully robed women, the swift ships, and the abundant possessions. (140–155)   10

In addition to this, there would be the maidens who serve the far-shooting god, the Deliades, a great and wondrous sight, whose renown will never perish. They sing their hymn to Apollo first of all and then to Leto and Artemis, who delights in her arrows, and they remember the men and women of old and enchant the assembled throng with their songs. They know how to imitate the sounds and sing in the dialects of all human beings. So well does their beautiful song match the speech of each person that one would say he himself were singing. (156–164)   20

But come now Apollo with Artemis, and be propitious. Farewell, all you Delian maidens. Remember me hereafter when someone of earthborn mortals, a stranger who has suffered, comes here and asks: "Maidens, what man do you think is the sweetest of the singers who frequent this place and in whom do you delight most of all?" Then all of you answer that I am the one: "A blind man who lives in rocky Chios; all his songs are the best forevermore."[3] (165–173)

I will bring your renown wherever I roam over the earth to the well-inhabited cities of humans; and they will believe since it is true. Yet I shall never cease to hymn the praises of Apollo, god of the silver bow, whom Leto of the beautiful hair bore. (174–178)   30

Apollo and Delos

It is most evident from the *Homeric Hymn* that the island of Delos was sacred to Apollo and the location of one of his most important sanctuaries, as the impressive remains today confirm. The following story was told about Anius, the son of Apollo.

Delos was the home of Anius, who was both his father's priest and king of the island at the time of the Trojan War. He had three daughters, Elaïs (Olive Girl), Spermo (Seed Girl), and Oeno (Wine Girl), who received from Dionysus the power of producing, respectively, oil, grain, and wine. Agamemnon attempted to compel them to go to Troy with the Greeks to supply the army with these provisions. As they resisted and tried to escape, Dionysus turned them into white doves; ever after, doves were sacrosanct at Delos.

Apollo and Delphi

Some believe that the first part of the lengthy *Hymn to Apollo* was originally a separate composition, a hymn to Delian Apollo. The second part of the hymn, which is translated in the Additional Reading at the end of this chapter, would have been recited as a song to **Pythian Apollo**, the god of Delphi.[4] Filled with a wealth of mythological information, it tells how Apollo descended from Mt. Olympus and made his way through northern and central Greece, finally discovering the proper spot for the foundation of his oracle among humankind at Crisa under snow-capped **Parnassus**. Apollo laid out his temple and then slew a she-dragon by the fair-flowing stream nearby. The name of the site was henceforth called Pytho (and Apollo, the Pythian) because the rays of the sun made the monster rot. (The Greek verb *pytho* means "I rot.")[5]

A cogent historical reconstruction of the conflicting evidence[6] suggests that originally the site was occupied by an oracle of the great mother-goddess of the Minoan-Mycenaean period, sometimes known as Ge-Themis. The slaying of the dragon (the traditional manifestation of a deity of earth), therefore, represents the subsequent conquest by Hellenic or Hellenized Apollo. For murdering the dragon, Zeus sent Apollo into exile in Thessaly for nine years (his punishment presumably mirrors the religious dictates of ancient society).[7]

The **omphalos**, an archaic stone shaped like an egg, which was kept in the temple during the classical period, seems to confirm an early habitation of the site.[8] Legend has it that this omphalos (the word means "navel") signified that Delphi actually occupied the physical center of the earth (certainly it was in many ways the spiritual center of the ancient world). Zeus was said to have released two eagles who flew from opposite ends of the earth and met exactly at the site of Apollo's sanctuary—a spot marked out for all to see by the stone omphalos with two birds perched on either side.

The hymn to Pythian Apollo concludes with a curious and interesting story. After he had established his sanctuary at Crisa, Apollo was concerned about recruiting attendants to his service. He noticed a ship passing, manned by Cretans from Cnossus, on its way to sandy Pylos. Phoebus Apollo transformed himself into a dolphin and immediately sprang aboard. At first, the men tried to throw the monster into the sea, but such was the havoc it created that they were awed to fearful submission. Speeded on by a divine wind, the ship would not obey the efforts of the crew to bring it to land. Finally, after a lengthy course, Apollo led them to Crisa, where he leaped ashore and revealed himself as a god amid a blaze of fiery brightness and splendor. He addressed the Cretan men, ordering them to perform sacrifices and pray to him as **Apollo Delphinius**. Then he led them to his sanctuary, accompanying them on the lyre as they chanted a paean in his honor. The hymn ends with the god's instruction to the Cretan band, who are placed in his charge, and his prediction of the prestige and wealth that is to come to his sanctuary.

The story links the early cult of Apollo with Crete, explains the epithet Delphinius in terms of the Greek word for dolphin, and provides an etymology for Delphi as the name of the sanctuary. As god of sailors and of colonization (his oracle was consulted to give religious sanction for the establishment of colonies), Apollo was worshiped under the title Delphinius. The hymn as a whole confirms the universality of the worship of Apollo and the importance of his outstanding cult centers, certainly at Delos but above all at Delphi.

The sanctuary of Apollo at Delphi is representative of the nature and character of other Panhellenic sites elsewhere.[9] The sacred area was built on the lower slopes of Mt. Parnassus, about 2,000 feet above the Corinthian Gulf. It is an awe-inspiring spot to this day. For anyone walking along the Sacred Way up to the great temple of the god, it is not difficult to sense the feelings of reverence and exaltation that filled the heart and soul of the ancient believer. The excavations have laid bare the foundations of the many and varied types of monuments along the winding path that were set up by individuals and city-states in honor and gratitude. Small temples (called treasuries) were a particularly imposing type of dedication, erected to house expensive and precious offerings. Among the major buildings of the sanctuary were a stadium, a theater, and of course the great temple of Apollo himself.

The **Pythian Games**, which were celebrated every four years, included (after 582 B.C.) both physical and intellectual competitions. Footraces, chariot races, and musical, literary, and dramatic presentations were among the events that combined to make the festival second only to that of Zeus at Olympia. The sanctuary and the celebrations reflect much that is characteristic of Greek life and thought. The numerous triumphant dedications of victory in war mirror the narrow particularism and vehement rivalry among individual city-states, while the fact of the festivals themselves, to which *all* Greeks might come to honor gods common to their race, reveals the strivings toward a wider and more humane vision. Certainly, the sense of competition in both athletics and the arts was vital to the Greek spirit. The importance of both the physical and the aesthetic also suggests a fundamental duality made one and whole in the prowess and intellectuality of the god Apollo himself. The *Odes* of **Pindar**, written to celebrate the glorious victors in the athletic competitions, are among the most sublime lyrical outpourings of the human spirit. Physical excellence intensified a sense of physical beauty that inspired Greek artists to capture in sculpture and in painting the realism and idealism of the human form. The development of the Doric, Ionic, and Corinthian orders and the construction of magnificent architectural buildings were also inspired by religious as well as civic devotion. The spiritual and human impetus to great feats of body and mind is among the most wondrous achievements of the Greek religious experience.

The Oracle and the Pythia at Delphi

The Panhellenic sanctuary of Delphi was above all an oracle.[10] People from all over the Greek world (and even beyond) came to Apollo with questions of every sort, both personal and political. Herodotus' story of Solon and Croesus, translated in Chapter 6, testifies to the prestige of the god, already well established in the sixth century B.C., and provides primary evidence for the nature and form of his responses as well.

The exact oracular procedures followed cannot be determined precisely because our sources are inadequate. The Pythia (prophetess of Apollo) uttered the responses of the god. Her seat of prophecy was the tripod, a bowl supported by three metal legs. A tripod was a utensil of everyday life; a fire could be lit beneath or inside the bowl, and it could be used for many obvious practical purposes. The tripod at Delphi was both a symbol and a source of divine prophetic power. Ancient pottery depicts Apollo himself seated on the bowl; his Pythian priestess, who does likewise, becomes his mouthpiece. In a frenzy of inspiration, she utters her incoherent ravings. A priest or prophet nearby will transcribe them into intelligible prose or verse (usually dactylic hexameters) to be communicated to the inquirer (see box on p. 250).

The Pythia prophesied in the inner sanctuary of the temple, the adyton (in which there was placed a stone omphalos, the navel marking the center of the earth), where vaporous gases could have emerged from a cleft below to enhance her inspiration. The exact location of the adyton cannot be located in the ruins of the excavated temple. The Pythia herself underwent certain initial ceremonies to ensure purification— among them a ritual drinking of the sacred water from the famous Castalian spring.

The inquirer who came to the temple with his question for the god had to go through certain prescribed ceremonies that were in the nature of a fee.[11] First he had to offer an expensive sacred cake on the altar outside the temple; and once he had entered, he was required to sacrifice a sheep or goat, a portion of which went to the Delphians. After these preliminaries, he could enter the adyton, the holy of holies, the innermost shrine of the temple, where he took his seat to wait for his turn to make his inquiry.[12]

In early times, according to tradition, the Pythia was a young virgin. On one occasion, an inquirer fell in love with one and seduced her. From then on, only mature women (probably over fifty years old, who dressed in the costume of a maiden) could become priestesses; whatever the nature of their previous lives (they could have been married), purity was required once they had been appointed to serve the god for life. At times, one from among at least three women could be called upon to prophesy, and there were probably more in reserve.[13] During the winter, when Apollo left for the land of the Hyperboreans, as was believed, the oracle was closed; thus, the Pythia prophesied for only nine months of the year.

Inevitably, one must wonder about the religious sincerity of the priests and priestesses at Delphi. Was it all a fraud? There is no good reason to think so. Many people have believed in the possibility of god communicating with mortals in marvelous ways. And belief in a medium, a person with special mantic gifts, is by no means unique to the Greeks. The Pythia presumably was chosen because of her special nature and religious character—she was susceptible to supernatural callings. It is true that the oracle was often on the side of political expediency and that the ambiguity of the responses was notorious. Apollo's obscure epithet, Loxias, was thought to bear testimony to the difficult and devious nature of his replies. But only a glance at the life and career of Socrates shows the sincere and inner religious meaning that an intellectually devout person is able to wrest from the material trappings of established institutions in any society. According to Plato's *Apology*, Socrates' friend Chaerephon went to Delphi to ask who was the wisest of men. The answer was "Socrates." When the philosopher learned this, he could not rest until he had determined the meaning of the response and proved the god right. If we are to take the *Apology* at all literally and historically (and why not?), this message from Apollo provided a turning point for Socrates in his missionary-like zeal to make men and women think of eternal moral and ethical values because of a belief in their immortal souls.

Aegeus before Themis. Red-figure kylix, by the Codrus painter, ca. 440 B.C.; 12.8 in. in diameter. Aegeus, crowned with laurel, is seen consulting Themis about why he cannot have children (see p. 579). In the opening lines of Aeschylus' *Eumenides*, the priestess gives a genealogy in which Ge is the first Pythia, followed by her daughter Themis. She holds a phiale or libation vessel in her left hand, into which she seems to be gazing intently; it is unclear whether it is an instrument of prophecy. She holds in her right hand a laurel branch, sacred to Apollo, and the tripod she is sitting on makes clear that the scene is at Delphi. The Doric column indicates that we are within the temple of Apollo. (*Bildarchiv Preussischer Kulturbesitz/Art Resource, NY*)

The Controversy About the Pythia and Her Prophecies

Ancient sources attest that after hallucinogenic effects caused by gases were observed in the behavior of goats and shepherds, a tripod was set up over the chasm for a priestess to breathe the vapors and, under their intoxicating influence, utter her oracles.[14] Archaeological and geological investigations at the site of the temple of Apollo have revealed that the Pythia actually could have inhaled narcotic fumes (from such gases as methane, ethane, and especially ethylene), created in the highly volcanic region of Delphi. Two faults were identified that meet directly under the temple.[15] As a result, much debate has been aroused about the nature and procedure of the Pythia in particular and prophets and prophecy in general, with the challenging of traditional theories.

A persistent consensus may be emerging (especially as a result of a reexamination of procedure described in Herodotus) in support of the argument that the Pythia herself gave her oracles in comprehensible verses, in dactylic hexameter, directly to the inquirer, who could then write them down and take them home, with absolutely no priestly intervention. If intoxicating vapors or any other hallucinatory drugs were used to enhance communication with Apollo, the priestess was not reduced to incoherent ravings that needed to be interpreted by a priest.

It is impossible to debate the problems here, and so we can pose only a few of the many troubling questions. Final answers must, however, remain elusive because of the inadequate and conflicting evidence, much of which comes from later sources, especially Plutarch, a Delphic priest to be sure, but in the second century A.D., when practices at Delphi must have changed significantly.

It is perfectly credible that a priestess could improvise dactylic verses on the spot, but would she not have needed, to some degree, special qualifications or training? How deep could her communication with Apollo go, and how could a Pythia control possession by the god? Could an inquirer easily copy down her recitation of verses for retention, without some help? Many oracles quoted by Herodotus are by no means simple. How did these oracles survive as many most certainly did? Are the some 600 that have come down to us today merely frauds? The male temple hierarchy at Delphi was large. How was the priesthood (both male and female) organized? Is it conceivable that the Pythia herself would be solely and primarily responsible for creating pronouncements about important political affairs, including issues of war and peace, with great consequences not only for Delphi but also the entire Greek world and beyond? There are examples of Pythias acting like crazed mediums, raving like the Cumaean Sibyl, as described by Vergil, presumably accurately, even allowing for poetic license. Was oracular procedure generally the same throughout the Greek and Roman world and similar for both female and male prophets (those originally at Dodona, for example)?

Jelle Z. De Boer, a principal researcher in the investigation at Delphi, concludes that ethylene did "not much" for the Pythias. It was only "one of many stimuli to a deeply religious state of mind." These were inspired women, "a sisterhood of mystics," and not druggies "in a narcotic haze." The team's discoveries "did little to explain or diminish the Oracle's possibilities, even otherworldly ones" and "said nothing about a range of oracular feats that were indisputably real." Michael Attyah Flower draws a modern parallel with the Chief State Oracle of Tibet, located at the monastery of Nechung in Northern India: "The Nechung oracle, a male priest, is called the Kuden (which means "receiving body") and acts as the mouthpiece of the counseling spirit Dorje Drakden (the Renowned Immutable One)." His inspired prophecies are intelligible and believed today.[16]

The Cumaean Sibyl

The Pythia is the specific title given to the priestess of Apollo at Delphi. A more generic term for prophetess was Sibyl, and many Sibyls were found at various places in various periods in the ancient world. Originally, the title was probably the proper name (Sibylla) of an early prophetess. At any rate, the Sibyls at Cumae were among the most famous seers of antiquity.[17] The description of the Cumaean Sibyl acting like a medium as she prophesies to Aeneas helps us understand the nature of the communication of a prophetess with her god, even though we must allow for poetic imagination.[18] The innermost shrine of the temple is a cavern from which the responses issue (Vergil, *Aeneid* 6.42–51):

> The vast end of the temple, built of Euboean stone, is cut out into a cavern; here are a hundred perforations in the rock, a hundred mouths from which the many utterances rush, the answers of the Sibyl. They had come to the threshold, when the virgin cried: "Now is the time to demand the oracles, the god, behold, the god!" She spoke these words in front of the doors, and her countenance and color changed; her hair shook free, her bosom heaved, and her heart swelled in wild fury; she seemed of greater stature, and her cries were not mortal as she was inspired by the breath of the god drawing nearer.

Later follows the metaphor of a wild horse trying to throw its rider (77–82, 98–101):

> Not yet willing to endure Apollo, the prophetess raged within the cavern in her frenzy, trying to shake the mighty god from her breast; all the more he wore out her ravings, mastering her wild heart and fashioning her to his will by constraint. Now the hundred mouths of the cavern opened wide of their own accord and bore the responses of the prophetess to the breezes. . . . The Cumaean Sibyl chants her terrifying riddles and, from the innermost shrine of the cavern, truth resounded, enveloped in obscurity, as Apollo applied the reins to her raving and twisted the goad in her breast.

Earlier in the *Aeneid* (3.445), the seer Helenus warned Aeneas that the Sibyl wrote her prophecies on leaves that were carefully arranged. But when the doors of the cavern were opened, these leaves were scattered by the wind so that those who had come for advice left without help and hated the dwelling of the Sibyl. Thus, Aeneas asks (6.74–76) that the Sibyl utter the prophecies herself and not entrust them to the leaves. All this may be an oblique reference to some characteristic of the **Sibylline books** (collections of prophecies of the Sibyls often consulted by the Romans) and the way in which they were interpreted.[19]

Ovid has the Sibyl tell Aeneas the story of her fate (*Metamorphoses* 14.132–153):

> Eternal life without end would have been given me if I had yielded my virginity to Phoebus Apollo who loved me. He hoped that I would and desired to bribe me with gifts, so he said: "Virgin maid of Cumae, choose what you desire; you will attain whatever it is." I picked up a heap of sand, showed it to him and asked for the vain wish that I might have as many birthdays as the individual grains in my hand. I forgot to ask for continuous youth along with the years. He would have given me both, long life and eternal youth, if I had succumbed to his love. But I despised Phoebus' gift, and I remain unmarried. And now the happier time of youth is gone, and sick old age has come with its feeble steps; and I must endure it for a long time. (132–144)

> For now, as you see, I have lived through seven generations; there remain for me to witness 300 harvests, 300 hundred vintages in order to equal in years the number of grains of sand.[20] The time will come when length of days will have reduced me from my former stature and make me small, and my limbs consumed by age will be diminished to the tiniest weight. And I shall not seem like one who was pleasing to a god and loved by him. Perhaps even Phoebus himself either will not recognize me or will deny that he once desired me; I shall be changed to such an extent that I shall be visible to no one, but I shall be recognized by my voice; the Fates will leave me my voice. (144–153)

10

In another version, the Sibyl became a tiny thing suspended in a bottle. Boys asked: "Sibyl, what do you want?" Her answer was: "I want to die."[21]

Other Loves of Apollo

Apollo, just as many a god or goddess, has sexual or emotional appetites that he desires to be fulfilled. It is worth noting that Apollo, unlike his father Zeus, is sometimes quite unsuccessful.

Apollo and Cassandra

Priam's daughter Cassandra, a pathetic figure in the Trojan saga, was another of Apollo's loves and another prophetess. When she agreed to give herself to Apollo, as a reward the god bestowed upon her the power of prophecy. But Cassandra then changed her mind and rejected his advances. Apollo asked for one kiss and spat into her mouth. Although he did not revoke his gift, Cassandra was thereafter doomed to prophesy in vain, for no one would believe her.

Apollo and Marpessa

Apollo also attempted to win Marpessa, daughter of Evenus, a son of Ares. She was also wooed by Idas, one of the Argonauts, who carried her off in his chariot against the will of her father. Evenus unsuccessfully pursued the pair, and then in his anger and heartbreak committed suicide. Subsequently Apollo, who had also been a suitor for Marpessa's hand, stole her away from Idas in similar fashion. Ultimately the two rivals met face to face in conflict over the girl. At this point, Zeus intervened and ordered Marpessa to choose between her lovers. She chose Idas because he was a mortal, for she was afraid that the undying and eternally handsome god Apollo would abandon her when she grew old.

Apollo and Cyrene

Nearly all of Apollo's numerous affairs are tragic; he is perhaps the most touchingly human and the most terrifyingly sublime of all the Greek gods. A notable exception is his success with Cyrene, an athletic nymph, with whom he fell in love as he watched her wrestling with a lion. He whisked her away to Libya in his golden chariot, to the very site of the city that would be given her name, and she bore him a son, Aristaeus.[22]

Apollo and Daphne

The story of Apollo's love for Daphne explains why the laurel (the Greek word *daphne* means "laurel") was sacred to him. Ovid's version is the best known (*Metamorphoses* 1.452–567):

> Daphne, daughter of Peneus, was the first object of Apollo's love. It was not blind fate that brought this about, but Cupid's cruel anger. Apollo, flushed with pride at his victory over Python, had seen Cupid drawing his bow and taunted him: "What business of yours are brave men's arms, young fellow? The bow suits *my* shoulder; I can take unerring aim at wild animals or at my enemies. I it was who laid low proud Python, with uncounted arrows, though he stretched over wide acres of ground. You should be content with kindling the fires of love in some mortal with your torch; do not try to share my glory!" (452–462)
>
> To him Cupid replied: "Although your arrows pierce every target, Apollo, mine will pierce you. Just as all animals yield to you, so your glory is inferior to mine." And as he spoke, he quickly flew to the peak of shady Parnassus and from his quiver drew two arrows. Different were their functions, for the one, whose point was dull and leaden, repelled love; the other—golden, bright, and sharp—aroused it. Cupid shot the leaden arrow at Peneus' daughter, while he pierced Apollo's inmost heart with the golden one. (463–473)
>
> Straightway Apollo fell in love, and Daphne ran even from the name of "lover." As a companion of Diana, her joy was in the depths of the forests and the spoils of the chase; a headband kept her flowing hair in place. Many suitors courted her, while she cared not for love or marriage; a virgin, she roamed the pathless woods. Her father often said, "My daughter, you owe me a son-in-law and grandchildren"; she, hating the marriage torch as if it were a disgrace, blushed and embraced her father saying, "Allow me, dearest father, always to be a virgin. Jupiter granted this to Diana." Peneus granted her prayer; but Daphne's beauty allowed her not to be as she desired and her loveliness ran counter to her wish. (474–489)
>
> Apollo loved her; he saw her and desired to marry her. He hoped to achieve his desire, misled by his own oracle. Even as the stubble burns after the harvest, or a hedge catches fire from a careless traveler's embers, so the god burned with all-consuming fire and fueled his love with fruitless hope. He sees her hair lying unadorned upon her neck and says, "What if it were adorned?" He sees her flashing eyes like stars; he sees her lips—and merely to see is not enough. He praises her fingers, hands, arms, and shoulders half-bared; those parts which are covered he thinks more beautiful. (490–502)
>
> Swifter than the wind, Daphne runs from him and stays not to hear him call her back: "Stay, nymph! Stay, daughter of Peneus, I pray! I am not an enemy who pursues you. Stay, nymph! A lamb runs like this from the wolf, a hind from the lion, doves with fluttering wings from the eagle. Each kind runs from its enemy; love makes me pursue! Oh, take care you do not fall; let not the thorns scratch those legs that never should be marred and I be the cause of your hurt! Rough is the place where you run; run more slowly, I beg, and I will pursue more slowly. Yet consider who loves you; I am not a mountain peasant; I am not an uncouth shepherd who watches here his flocks and herds. Unheeding, you know not whom you try to escape, and therefore do you run. I am lord of Delphi, of Claros, Tenedos, and royal Patara; Jupiter is my father! I show the future, the past, the present; through me came the harmony

Apollo and Daphne, by Gian-Lorenzo Bernini (1598–1680); marble, 1624; height 96 in. Bernini has chosen the moment when swift movement is stopped. The sculptor brilliantly incorporates the psychological tensions of Ovid's narrative, frozen in the moment of metamorphosis. The contrast between Apollo, adapted from the famous *Apollo Belvedere*, and the agitated emotions of Daphne serves to heighten the tragedy. On the base (not shown) are inscribed Ovid's description of the metamorphosis (*Metamorphoses* 1.519–521) and two Latin lines by the future Pope Urban VIII: "Every lover who pursues the joys of fleeing beauty fills his hands with leaves or plucks bitter berries." (*Scala/Art Resource, NY*)

of lyre and song! Unerring are my arrows, yet one arrow is yet more unerring and has wounded my heart, before untouched. The healing art is mine; throughout the world am I called the Bringer of Help; the power of herbs is mine to command. Ah me! for no herb can remedy love; the art which heals all cannot heal its master!" (502–524)

Even as he spoke, Daphne fled from him and ran on in fear; then too she seemed   50 lovely—the wind laid bare her body, and her clothes fluttered as she ran and her hair streamed out behind. In flight, she was yet more beautiful. Yet the young god could not bear to have his words of love go for nothing; driven on by love, he followed at full speed. Even as a Gallic hound sees a hare in an empty field and pursues its prey as it runs for safety—the one seems just to be catching the quarry and expects each moment to have gripped it; with muzzle at full stretch, it is hot on the other's tracks; the other hardly knows if it has been caught and avoids the snapping jaws—so the god chased the virgin: hope gave him speed; her speed came from fear. Yet the pursuer gains, helped by the wings of love; he gives her no respite; he presses hard upon her and his breath ruffles the hair upon her neck.   60 (525–542)

Now Daphne's strength was gone, drained by the effort of her flight, and pale she saw Peneus' waters. "Help me, Father," she cried, "if a river has power; change me and destroy my beauty which has proved too attractive!" Hardly had she finished her prayer when her limbs grew heavy and sluggish; thin bark enveloped her soft breasts; her hair grew into leaves, her arms into branches. Her feet, which until now had run so swiftly, held fast with clinging roots. Her face was the tree's top; only her beauty remains. (543–552)

Even in this form Apollo loves her; placing his hand on the trunk he felt the heart beating beneath the new-formed bark. Embracing the branches, as if they were   70 human limbs, he kisses the wood; yet the wood shrinks from his kisses. "Since you cannot be my wife," said he, "you shall be my tree. Always you shall wreathe my hair, my lyre, my quiver. You shall accompany the Roman generals when the joyous triumph hymn is sung and the long procession climbs the Capitol . . . and as my young locks have never been shorn, so may you forever be honored with green leaves!" Apollo's speech was done: the new-made laurel nodded her assent and like a head bowed her topmost branches. (553–567)

As discussed in Chapter 1 (on p. 20), Ovid's artistry has created a tale of passion that has inspired artists throughout the centuries.

Apollo and Hyacinthus

Apollo was also susceptible to the love of young men.[23] His devotion to Hyacinthus, a handsome Spartan youth from Amyclae, is well known from Ovid's account; the great god neglected his other duties in order to be in the company of his beloved (*Metamorphoses* 10.174–219):

The Titan sun was almost midway between the night that had passed and the one to come—equidistant from both—when Apollo and the boy took off their garments and glistening with olive oil began to compete with the broad discus. Phoebus made the first throw. He poised the discus and hurled it so far into the air that the clouds were scattered by its course, and only after a long time, because of its own sheer weight, did it fall back again to solid earth. His throw exhibited great skill combined with great strength. Straightway Hyacinthus under the impulse of his enthusiasm, heedless of all but the game, made a dash to pick up the discus. But it bounced back, O Hyacinthus, as it hit the hard earth and struck you full in the face.[24] The god turned as pale as the boy himself. He took up the limp body in his attempt to revive him, frantically staying the flow of blood from the sad wound and applying herbs to sustain the life that was ebbing away. His arts were to no avail; the wound was incurable. Just as when someone in a garden breaks off violets or brittle poppies or lilies that cling to their tawny stems, and suddenly these flowers droop and fade and cannot support the tops of their heavy heads which look down to the ground, so dropped the head of the dying boy and his neck, once strength was gone, gave way to the burden of its weight and sank on his shoulder. (174–195)

Phoebus cried: "You slip away, cheated of your youthful prime. Your wound that I look upon accuses me. You are my grief and my guilt—my own hand is branded with your death! I am the one who is responsible. But what fault was mine? Can it be called a fault to have played a game with you, to have loved you? O that I could give you my life as you deserve or die along with you. But we are bound by fate's decree. Yet you will always be with me, your name will cling to my lips, forever remembering. You will be my theme as I pluck my lyre and sing my songs and you, a new flower, will bear markings in imitation of my grief; and there will come a time when the bravest of heroes will be linked to this same flower and his name will be read on its petals." (196–208)

While Apollo spoke these words from his unerring lips, lo and behold, the blood that had poured upon the ground and stained the grass ceased to be blood and a flower arose, of a purple more brilliant than Tyrian dye; it took the shape of a lily and differed only in color, for lilies are silvery white. Apollo, though responsible for so honoring Hyacinthus, was not yet satisfied. The god himself inscribed his laments upon the petals, and the flower bears the markings of the mournful letters *AI AI*.[25] Sparta was proud to claim Hyacinthus as her son, and his glory endures to this day; every year a festival, the Hyacinthia, is celebrated in his honor with ceremonies ancient in their traditions. (209–219)

Apollo and Cyparissus

Cyparissus, from Ceos, was another youth loved by Apollo. His sad story is told by Ovid (*Metamorphoses* 10.106–142). On the island was a very beautiful stag, sacred to the nymphs. He had no fear of human beings and was befriended by all. But the stag was especially dear to the most handsome of Ceans, Cyparissus. He would lovingly lead the animal to fresh pastures and clear springs, weave flowers for his horns, and joyfully ride like a horseman on his back.

Unfortunately, one summer day, Cyparissus accidentally killed his beloved stag, and when he saw him dying from the cruel wound he had himself inflicted, he wanted to die too. Apollo tried in vain to comfort him. The lad only renewed his sobs and begged that the gods would grant him his ultimate wish that he might continue his mourning forever. Exhausted by grief and endless tears, his life ebbed away and he was transformed into a tree, the cypress, ever after called by his name and associated with mourning, as Apollo predicted in anguish: "You will be mourned by me, you will mourn for others and you always will be there, where others grieve."

Apollo and Coronis

Several stories emphasize Apollo's role as a god of medicine, which is taken over in large part by his son Asclepius. And this brings us to Apollo's affair with Coronis, the last we shall tell. Coronis (in Ovid's version) was a lovely maiden from Larissa in Thessaly whom Apollo loved; in fact, she was pregnant with his child. Unfortunately, the raven, Apollo's bird, saw Coronis lying with a young Thessalian and told all to the god (*Metamorphoses* 2.600–634):

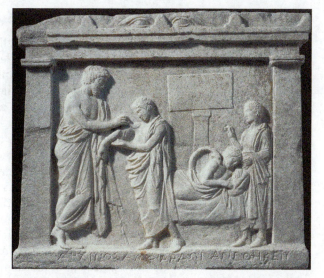

> When Apollo heard this charge against Coronis, the laurel wreath slipped from his head, his expression changed, and the color drained from his cheeks. As his heart burned with swollen rage, he took up his accustomed weapons and bent his bow to string it; with his unerring arrow he pierced the breast which he had so often embraced. She gave a groan as she was struck; and when she drew the shaft from her body, red blood welled up over her white limbs. She spoke: "You could 10 have exacted this punishment and I have paid with my life, after I had borne your child; as it is, two of us die in one." With these words her life drained away with her blood; the chill of death crept over her lifeless corpse. (600–611)
>
> Too late, alas, the lover repented of his cruel punishment. He hated himself because he had listened to the charge against her and had been so inflamed. He hated his bow and his arrows and his hands that had so rashly shot them. He fondled her limp body and strove to thwart the Fates; but his efforts came too late, and he applied his arts of healing to no avail. When he saw that his attempts were in vain 20 and that the pyre was being built and saw her limbs about to be burned in the last flames, then truly (for it is forbidden that the cheeks of the gods be touched by tears) Apollo uttered groans that issued from the very depths of his heart, just as when a young cow sees the mallet poised above the right ear of her suckling calf to shatter the hollow temples with a crashing blow. He poured perfumes upon her unfeeling breast, clasped her in his embrace, and performed the proper rites so just and yet unjust. Phoebus could not bear that his own seed be reduced to the same ashes, but he snatched his son out of the flames from the womb of his mother and brought him to the cave of the centaur Chiron. The 30 raven, who hoped for a reward for the truth of his utterances, Apollo forbade evermore to be counted among white birds. Meanwhile, the centaur was happy to have the divine infant as a foster child and delighted in such an honorable task. (612–634)

Amphiaraüs as Healer. Votive relief from Oropus, first quarter of the fourth century B.C. Amphiaraüs was one of the Seven against Thebes. Oropus, a city on the border between Attica and Boeotia, was the site of his famous oracle (p. 422) and a center for his healing art. At the sanctuary of Amphiaraüs (the Amphiareion), archaeologists have uncovered remains of the temple, altar, incubation hall, sacred spring, stoa, and stadium. Numerous inscriptions and votive objects, like the one shown here, have been found as well. As in the worship of Asclepius at Epidaurus, incubation was practiced. The inscription at the base of the relief records that it was dedicated by a man named Archinus to Amphiaraüs. The relief narrates the healing process. On the right, in the background, Archinus is asleep. As he sleeps, a snake, often present during incubations, appears to be biting his right shoulder. Perhaps Archinus is being visited by a divinely sent dream. In the left foreground, Amphiaraüs is personally tending to the same shoulder of Archinus. The figure on the far right may be yet another portrayal of Archinus, healed, or perhaps an attendant of the sanctuary. The relief makes the observer privy to the divine action, perhaps as envisioned by Archinus in his dream, at work behind the visible reality. (*DeAgostini/Superstock*)

Asclepius, the God of Healing

Thus, like many another mythological figure, Asclepius was trained by the wise and gentle Chiron, and he learned his lessons well, particularly in the field of medicine. In the *Iliad*, Asclepius is a heroic physician, and his two sons, Machaon and Podalirius, are also skilled in medicinal practice, learned from their father. Hygeia or Hygieia (Health) and Panacea, personifications of abstract concepts, are reputed to be his children as well. As the son of Apollo, the god of medicine, Asclepius himself was transformed into a god, and his birthplace became Epidaurus, the major center of his worship. He exemplified the divine ideal of the kindly physician who restores the sick to health, a blessed savior, and a spiritual worker of miracles. As such, he became a most serious rival to Jesus of Nazareth for several centuries, and therefore Christian apologists and church fathers had good reason to fear and attack him.

After drinking the hemlock and on the point of death, Socrates spoke these last words in Plato's *Phaedo*: "Crito, we owe a cock to Asclepius. Pay it and do not neglect it." This demand by a pious man was to fulfill a vow he had forgotten or a debt of gratitude just now incurred for a good end of life, for

Asclepius' Staff or Hermes' Caduceus as a Medical Emblem?

The staff of Asclepius, entwined by a single serpent, has been considered the true symbol for the medical profession since the second century A.D. It is derived from a walking stick, which Asclepius himself and his peripatetic followers, the Asclepiads, used in their profession as physicians. A snake (identified as the common species *Elaphe longissima*) appropriately surrounds the staff, since its shedding of its skin every year symbolizes rejuvenation, and it was thought by the ancients to be a practical healer of the sick (as we have seen). How could the single-serpent staff of the Greek god of medicine, Asclepius, clearly a symbol uniquely medical, become confused with the authoritative winged caduceus (with its two coiled serpents) of the herald and messenger Hermes, a god of multiple unmedical concerns, among them money and commerce, especially as Mercury for the Romans?

The caduceus came late as the usurper in medical symbolism. The confusion arose when the caduceus was used by publishers of books (including medical texts) as a symbol of their business. An early American dentist, Josiah Flagg, used in an advertisement a caduceus embellished with crossed toothbrushes—a splendid juxtaposition of the medical and commercial. Then, some medical associations actually adopted the caduceus officially, and in 1902 it became the symbol of the US Army Medical Corps. It appears today in the logo of many associations connected with health.

Some are outraged that the caduceus as a symbol of commerce and even worse should be associated with medicine. (Hermes was also a god of dishonest eloquence and thievery.) Others suggest that Hermes' caduceus may today be as appropriate an emblem for medicine as the staff of Asclepius. After all, the important business of medicine grows ever more complex, with advertising essential for competitive marketing. So one medical doctor, Glenn W. Geelhoed, poses the dilemma: "Each of us physicians may choose what the profession should mean, and [between two serpent symbols representing very competitive ideals] adopt a symbol that is appropriate to the heritage of the professional healing art."[26]

making the soul sound and pure again, before its escape from the contaminated prison of the body.

Asclepius' chief method of healing in his sanctuaries was by **incubation** (i.e., sleeping in a holy place). After preparatory rites, patients went to sleep at night in a special building, where they were to dream, in hope of seeing an oracular vision of Asclepius, who would heal them immediately or prescribe cures (e.g., magical incantations, drinking potions, bandaging wounds with soothing remedies). Stories were told that surgical operations were magically performed on sleeping patients. After the vision of the god, snakes would move freely among patients to provide healing by licking the afflicted. Excavations reveal the importance of running spring water for curative baths and ritual purity. One should read Aristophanes' *Plutus (Wealth)* for the curing of Plutus' blindness by incubation—very funny, yet important evidence, just as the *Frogs* is for the celebration of the mysteries at Eleusis.

Asclepius gave his name to a guild of physicians, called Asclepiadae or Asclepiads, who considered themselves his spiritual children. Among them was **Hippocrates**, a great physician of the fifth century B.C., who founded a renowned medical school at Cos. He moved medicine out of the temples and established rational principles of therapy that raised the profession into a scientific art.[27]

The *Homeric Hymn to Asclepius* (16) is a short and direct appeal to the mythical physician:

> About the healer of sicknesses, Asclepius, son of Apollo, I begin to sing. In the Dotian plain of Argos, goddess-like Coronis, daughter of King Phlegyas, bore him, a great joy to mortals, a soother of evil pains. (1–4)
> So hail to you, lord; I pray to you with my song.

Asclepius was so skilled a physician that when Hippolytus died, Artemis appealed to him to restore her devoted follower to life. Asclepius agreed and succeeded in his attempt; but he thus incurred the wrath of Zeus, who hurled him into the lower world with a thunderbolt for such a disruption of nature.

Apollo's Musical Contest with Marsyas

Apollo's skill as a musician has already been attested. Two additional stories concentrate more exclusively on the divine excellence of his art and the folly of inferiors who challenged it. The first concerns Marsyas, the satyr (as we previously mentioned in Chapter 8) who picked up the flute after it had been invented and then discarded by Athena. Although the goddess gave Marsyas a thrashing for taking up her instrument, he was not deterred and became so proficient that he dared to challenge Apollo himself to a contest. The condition imposed by the god was that the victor could do what he liked with the vanquished. Of course, Apollo won, and he decided to flay Marsyas alive. Ovid describes the anguish of the satyr (*Metamorphoses* 6.385–400):

> Marsyas cried out: "Why are you stripping me of my very self? Oh no, I am sorry; the flute is not worth this torture!" As he screamed, his skin was ripped off all his body, and he was nothing but a gaping wound. Blood ran everywhere, his nerves were laid bare and exposed, and the pulse of his veins throbbed without any covering. One could make out clearly his pulsating entrails and the vital organs in his chest

Apollo Flaying Marsyas, by Jusepe (or José) de Ribera (1591–1652); 72 × 91 in. Ribera was a Spanish painter of the baroque period, who spent most of his working life in Italy. He was called "Lo Spagnoletto" (the Little Spaniard) by his peers and was determined to maintain his Spanish identity by signing his works "Jusepe de Ribera, español." His work shows a wide influence from artists like Caravaggio, Raphael, and Guido Reni. His style, imbued with an unsettling realism and marked by a pervading gloom, is called *tenebrism*, from the Latin *tenebrae*, which means "darkness." It employs a sharp and dramatic contrast of light and dark in figural composition. His subjects, drawn from the tradition of Catholic martyrology and Greek myth, frequently present an individual enduring physical and psychological suffering, in scenes of horrific and realistically rendered depictions of torture. Apollo has bound the offending satyr at the wrists and hung him by his feet where the skinning commences. But Apollo seems to pause and insert his hand into the wound, while looking rather dispassionately at the response of Marsyas, who is screaming in utter agony. In the background are what appear to be fellow satyrs expressing their pity or fear at the treatment of one of their own. Note the musical instruments, which remind us of the contest: one hanging from the tree and one at the bottom left. The meaning of this unnerving painting remains mysterious and ambiguous. The two main figures are clearly drawn in opposition to one another in almost every particular detail, but on whose side is the viewer? (*National Museum of Capodimonte, Naples, Italy*)

that lay revealed. The spirits of the countryside and the fauns who haunt the woods wept for him; and so did his brothers, the satyrs and nymphs and all who tended woolly sheep and horned cattle on those mountains—and Olympus, dear to him now, wept as well. The fertile earth grew wet as she received and drank up the tears that fell and became soaked to the veins in her depths. She formed of them a stream which she sent up into the open air. From this source a river, the clearest in all Phrygia, rushes down between its sloping banks into the sea. And it bears the name of Marsyas.

10

Apollo's Musical Contest with Pan

Apollo was involved in another musical contest, this time with the god Pan, and King Midas of Phrygia acted as one of the judges (Ovid, *Metamorphoses* 11.146–193):

> Midas, in his loathing for riches,[28] found a retreat in the woods and the country and worshiped Pan, the god who always inhabits mountain caves. But his intelligence still remained limited, and his own foolish stupidity was going to harm him once again as it had before. There is a mountain, Tmolus, that rises high in its steep ascent with a lofty view to the sea; on one side it slopes down to Sardis, on another to the little town of Hypaepa. Here, while he was singing his songs to his gentle nymphs and playing a dainty tune on his pipes made of reeds and wax, Pan dared to belittle the music of Apollo compared to his own. (146–155)
>
> And so he engaged in an unequal contest, with Tmolus as judge. This elderly judge took his seat on his own mountain and freed his ears of trees; only the oak remained to wreathe his dark hair, and acorns hung down around his hollow temples. He turned his gaze upon the god of flocks and said: "Now the judge is ready." Pan began to blow on his rustic pipes; and Midas, who happened to be nearby as he played, was charmed by the tune. When Pan had finished, Tmolus, the sacred god of the mountain, turned around to face Phoebus, and his forests followed the swing of his gaze. The golden head of Apollo was crowned with laurel from Parnassus, and his robe, dyed in Tyrian purple, trailed along the ground. His lyre was inlaid with precious stones and Indian ivory; he held it in his left hand with the plectrum in his right. His very stance was the stance of an artist. Then he played the strings with knowing hand; Tmolus was captivated by their sweetness and ordered Pan to concede that his pipes were inferior to the lyre. (156–171)
>
> The judgment of the sacred mountain pleased everyone except Midas; he alone challenged the verdict and called it unjust. At this the god of Delos could not bear that such stupid ears retain their human shape. He made them longer, covered them with white shaggy hair, and made them flexible at their base so that they could be twitched. As for the rest of him, he remained human; in this one respect alone he was changed, condemned to be endowed with the ears of a lumbering ass. (172–179)
>
> Midas of course wanted to hide his vile shame, and he attempted to do so by covering his head with a purple turban. But his barber, who regularly trimmed his long hair, saw his secret. He wanted to tell about what he had seen, but he did not dare reveal Midas' disgrace. Yet it was impossible for him to keep quiet, and so he stole away and dug a hole in the ground. Into it, with the earth removed, he murmured in a low whisper that his master had ass's ears. Then he filled the hole up again, covering up the indictment he had uttered, and silently stole away from the scene. But a thick cluster of trembling reeds began to grow on the spot; in a year's time, as soon as they were full grown, they betrayed the barber's secret. For, as they swayed in the gentle south wind, they echoed the words that he had buried and revealed the truth about his master's ears. (180–193)

Thus, if one listened carefully to the wind whistling in the reeds, he could hear the murmur of a whisper: "King Midas has ass's ears."[29]

The *Alcestis* of Euripides

Apollo was enraged by the death of his son Asclepius; he did not, of course, turn against Zeus, but he killed the Cyclopes who had forged the lethal thunderbolt. Because of his crime, he was sentenced (following once again the pattern of the human social order and its codes concerning blood-guilt) to live in exile for a year under the rule of Admetus, the beneficent king of Pherae in Thessaly. Apollo felt kindly toward his master, and when he found out that Admetus had only a short time to live, he went to the Moirai and induced them, with the help of wine, to allow the king a longer life. But they imposed the condition that someone must die in his place. Admetus, however, could find no one willing to give up his or her life on his behalf (not even his aged parents) except his devoted wife, Alcestis; and he accepted her sacrifice. She is, however, rescued from the tomb in the nick of time by the good services of Heracles, who happens to be a visitor in the home of Admetus and wrestles with Death himself (*Thanatos*) for the life of Alcestis.

In his fascinating and puzzling play *Alcestis* (it is difficult to find general agreement on the interpretation of this tragicomedy), Euripides presents a touching and ironic portrait of the devoted wife and an ambiguous depiction of her distraught husband.

The Nature of Apollo

The facets of Apollo's character are many and complex. His complex nature sums up the many contradictions in the tragic dilemma of human existence. He is gentle and vehement, compassionate and ruthless, guilty and guiltless, healer and destroyer. The extremes of his emotion are everywhere apparent. He acts swiftly and surely against Tityus, who dared to attempt the rape of Leto, and for this crime he is punished (as we see later) in the realm of Hades. As he shot down Tityus with his arrows, Apollo acted the same way against Niobe, this time in conjunction with his sister, Artemis (see pp. 220–221). Can one ever forget Homer's terrifying picture of the god as he lays low the Greek forces at Troy with a plague in response to the appeal of his priest Chryses (*Iliad* 1.43–52)?

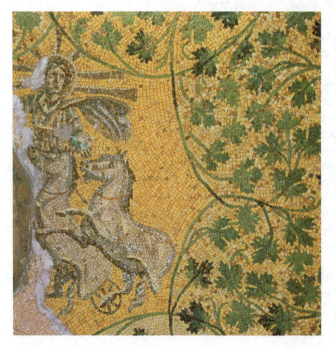

Christus Apollo. Vault mosaic, third century A.D.; height of vault 72 in. Christ is shown with the attributes of the sun-god (Apollo or Helius), ascending into the vault of the sky on a chariot drawn by four white horses (two are missing from the damaged part). The rays emanating from his head form a cross. Across the background trails the ivy of Dionysus, another pagan symbol of immortality used in early Christian art. This vault mosaic is in a Christian tomb in the cemetery beneath the basilica of St. Peter's in the Vatican. (*Scala/Art Resource, NY*)

> Phoebus Apollo . . . came down from the peaks of Olympus, angered in his heart, wearing on his shoulders his bow and closed quiver. The arrows clashed on his shoulders as he moved in his rage, and he descended just like night. Then he sat down apart from the ships and shot one of his arrows; terrible was the clang made by his silver bow. First he attacked the mules and the swift hounds, but then he let go his piercing shafts against the men themselves and struck them down. The funeral pyres with their corpses burned thick and fast.

Yet this same god is the epitome of Greek classical restraint, championing the proverbial Greek maxims: "Know thyself" and "Nothing too much." He knows by experience the dangers of excess. From a sea of blood and guilt, Apollo brings enlightenment, atonement, and purification wherever he may be, but especially in his sanctuary at Delphi.

The origins of Apollo are obscure. He may have been one of the gods brought into Greece by the northern invaders of 2000 B.C.; if not, he was probably soon absorbed by them in the period 2000–1500. Some scholars imagine Apollo as originally the prototype of the Good Shepherd, with his many protective powers and skills, especially those of music and medicine.[30] As we have seen in Chapter 3, he becomes a sun-god and usurps the power of Hyperion and of Helius.

For many, Apollo appears to be the most characteristically Greek god in the whole pantheon—a gloriously conceived anthropomorphic figure, perhaps epitomized best of all in the splendid depiction of the west pediment of the great temple of Zeus at Olympia (see p. 265). Here Apollo stood with calm intelligent strength, his head turned to one side, his arm upraised against the raging turmoil of the battle between the Centaurs and Lapiths by which he is surrounded.

By stressing his disciplined control and intellectuality and ignoring his tumultuous extremes of passion, Apollo may be presented as the direct antithesis of the god Dionysus. In the persons of these two deities, the rational (Apollonian) and irrational (Dionysiac) forces in human psychology, philosophy, and religion are dramatically pitted against one another. Some scholars maintain that Apollo represents the true and essential nature of the Greek spirit, as reflected in the poetry of Homer, in contrast to the later, foreign intrusion of the mysticism of Dionysus. Whatever kernel of truth this view may hold, it must be realized that by the sixth and fifth centuries B.C., Dionysus had become an integral part of Greek civilization. By the classical period, he was as characteristically Greek as Apollo, and *both* deities actually reflect a basic duality inherent in the Greek conception of things. We have already detected in Chapter 3 this same dichotomy in the union of the mystical and mathematical that was mirrored in the amalgamation of two cultures (the Nordic and the Mediterranean) in the Minoan and Mycenaean periods.

Just as Apollo may be made a foil for the mystical Dionysus, so he may be used as a meaningful contrast to the figure of the spiritual Christ. Each in his person and his life represents, physically and spiritually, different concepts of meaning and purpose in both this world and the next. Apollo and Christ do indeed afford a startling and revealing antithesis.

Here now is the brief *Homeric Hymn to Apollo* (21):

IMAGES OF APOLLO

The statue of Apollo is the highest ideal of art among all the works of antiquity that have escaped its destruction. . . . This Apollo surpasses all other images of him as much as the Apollo of Homer surpasses those portrayed by later poets. His build is elevated above the human, and his stance bears witness to the fullness of his grandeur. An eternal springtime, like that of the blissful Elysian Fields, clothes the alluring virility of mature years with a pleasing youth and plays with soft tenderness upon the lofty structure of his limb. . . . In gazing upon this masterpiece of art, I forget all else, and I myself adopt an elevated stance, in order to be worthy of gazing upon it. My chest seems to expand with veneration and to leave like those I have seen swollen as if by the spirit of prophecy, and I feel myself transported to Delos and to the Lycian groves, places Apollo honored with his presence—for my figure seems to take on life and movement, like Pygmalion's beauty. How is it possible to paint and describe it![31]

To many, the effusiveness that the art historian Johann Joachim Winckelmann (1717–1768) lavishes upon the Apollo Belvedere is difficult now to appreciate. The statue no longer holds its once august position in the Western canon of art. And yet Winckelmann's aesthetic taste left such an indelible mark on the centuries that followed and contributed so much to the enshrinement of this statue, at least in the eighteenth and nineteenth centuries, as one of the highest expressions of Greek art, that it is a bit sobering to reflect that he wrote at a time when the remarkable statues that graced the Parthenon had not yet filtered more broadly into European consciousness. As a result of this early reception, the Apollo Belvedere has had a profound influence on some of the greatest artists and most iconic art since its discovery in the late fifteenth or early sixteenth century.

The Apollo Belvedere has proven to be both a battleground of scholarly debate, as to its origin, history, and artistic appreciation, and a mirror reflecting the viewer's relationship to the Greek past, that is, what he or she wishes to see in it. Because of

Apollo Belvedere. Roman marble copy, possibly of the second century A.D., of a fourth-century B.C. Greek bronze; height 94½ in. Apollo strides ahead just as the *Homeric Hymn to Delian Apollo* describes. His left hand would have held his bow: the tree trunk was added by the copyist to support the weight of the marble on the right ankle and foot. This has been the most famous statue of Apollo since its discovery in Rome in or before 1509, and its stance has been copied in innumerable works of art. It takes its name from the courtyard in the Vatican Palace where it stands in its own niche. (*androver/Shutterstock*)

this dual nature, it is nearly impossible to see it afresh. A comparison of the two works of art presented here is instructive.

The severe angularity, commanding stillness, and strength of the Apollo from the west pediment of the temple of Zeus at Olympia does indeed contrast with what some have called the "effeminate" softness and awkward movement of the Belvedere, whose head, glance, and upper torso are directed toward his left, while his stride carries him to the right. In general terms, the Belvedere seems to be an inversion of the Olympian Apollo; the figures are gazing and gesturing in opposite directions. If the Belvedere is a Roman copy of a fourth-century Greek original (and certainty eludes us), then perhaps it is a deliberate rejection of the classical ideals represented in the pedimental Apollo.

The Apollo at Olympia is the calm focal point within a narrative of violence (the assault upon the Lapith women by centaurs); the composition is thereby made coherent and gains in intensity by the contrast of the god with the other figures. The Belvedere is unmoored from any such context. Though some, like Winckelmann, have argued that he has just triumphed over the Python and taken possession of Delphi, this is far from certain. Without that strong narrative context, the Belvedere seems somehow detached, bestriding the world, indifferent to where he is going.

Apollo. From the west pediment of the temple of Zeus at Olympia, ca. 460 B.C.; height of complete figure ca. 120 in. This is the central figure in the pediment (see p. 118). Son of Zeus, he imposes peace on the drunken brawl of the Lapiths and centaurs at the wedding of Pirithoüs (also the subject of the metopes on the south side of the Parthenon). The ancient traveler Pausanias thought that the figure was Pirithoüs, but no modern scholars accept his interpretation. (*Alinari/Art Resource, NY*)

Phoebus, about you even the swan sings clearly as it wings its way and alights on the bank along the swirling river, Peneus; and about you the sweet-voiced minstrel with his lovely sounding lyre always sings both first and last. (1–4)

So hail to you, lord; I propitiate you with my song.

Additional Reading: *Homeric Hymn to Pythian Apollo*

THE *HOMERIC HYMN TO APOLLO (3.179–546: TO PYTHIAN APOLLO)*

O lord, you hold Lycia and charming Maeonia and Miletus, desirable city on the sea; but you yourself rule mightily over Delos, washed by the waves. (179–180)

The renowned son of Leto, dressed in divine and fragrant garments, goes to rocky Pytho, as he plays upon his hollow lyre; at the touch of his golden pick, the lyre makes a lovely sound. From there, as swift as thought, he soars from earth to Olympus, to the house of Zeus and the company of the other gods. Immediately the immortals are obsessed with the lyre and song. The Muses, all together, harmonize with their charming voices and celebrate the endless gifts enjoyed by the gods and the sufferings inflicted by these immortals that human beings must bear, as they live foolish and helpless lives, unable to find a defense against old age and a cure for death. (181–193)   10

Also, the Graces with beautiful hair, and the cheerful Hours, and Harmonia, Hebe, and Aphrodite, daughter of Zeus, dance together, holding hands at the wrist; and with them sings a goddess who is not slight or homely but awesome to behold and wondrously beautiful, Artemis, who delights in her arrows, sister to Apollo. Among them too, Ares and the keen-eyed slayer of Argus join in the merriment, and Apollo continues to play his beautiful music on the lyre, as he steps high and stately. The radiance from his glittering feet and glistening robe envelops him in splendor. Both golden-haired Leto and wise Zeus watch their dear son playing his music among the immortal gods and rejoice in their mighty hearts. (194–206)   20

Shall I sing about you as a suitor in your love affairs? How you went to woo the daughter of Azan along with godlike Ischys, the son of Elatus famous for his horses, or with Phorbas, the son of Triops, or with Ereuthus or with Leucippus for the wife [to be] of Leucippus, you on foot and he from his chariot; indeed he was not a rival inferior to Triops.[32] (207–213)

APOLLO SEEKS A SITE FOR HIS ORACLE

Or shall I sing about how at first you went over all the earth, seeking a location for your oracle for the human race, O far-shooting Apollo?[33] First, you came down from Olympus to Pieria and went past sandy Lectus and Enienae and through the territory of the Perrhaebi. Soon you came to Iolcus and entered Cenaeum in Euboea, famous for its ships, and you stood on the Lelantine plain; but it did not please your heart to   30
build a temple amid forest groves. From there you crossed the Euripus, far-shooting Apollo, and made your way along the holy green mountains, and quickly you went on from here to Mycalessus and grassy Teumessus and reached the forest-covered home of Thebe; for no one of mortals as yet lived in holy Thebes, nor were there yet at that time paths or roads running through the wheat-bearing plain of Thebes; but it was overgrown with trees. (214–228)

From there you went further, O far-shooting Apollo, and came to Onchestus, with its splendid grove of Poseidon. Here, while the newly broken colt, worn out with drawing the beautiful chariot, slows down to get its wind, the noble driver springs out of his seat to the ground and makes his own way. Without guidance, the horses for a time knock about the empty chariot; and, if they smash it in the forest grove, the horses are taken care of but the chariot is put at a tilt and left there. For in this way from the very first the holy rite was enacted. They pray to the god, lord of the shrine, who then keeps the chariot as his allotted portion.[34] From there you went further, far-shooting Apollo, and then you came upon the beautifully flowing river, Cephisus, which pours its sweet-running water from Lilaea; you crossed it, and from many-towered Ocalea you arrived at grassy Haliartus. Then you went to Telphusa; here was a propitious place that you found pleasing for making a forest grove and a temple. You stood very near her and spoke these words: "Telphusa, here I intend to build a very beautiful temple, an oracle for mortals. Here all those who live in the rich Peloponnesus, in Europe, and on the sea-girt islands will bring perfect hecatombs and consult the oracle. To them I shall deliver my answers and ordain infallible counsel in my wealthy temple." (229–253)

Thus, Phoebus Apollo spoke and laid out the foundations, wide and very long overall. But Telphusa, upon seeing his actions, became deeply incensed and spoke: "Phoebus, lord and far-worker, I shall give you this warning to think about. Since you intend to build a very beautiful temple here, to be an oracle for mortals, who will always bring perfect hecatombs, I will speak out and you take my words to heart. The clatter of swift horses and the sounds of mules being watered at my holy spring will always annoy you; here any person will prefer to look at the well-made chariots and the noisy swift-footed horses rather than at your great temple and the many treasures inside. But if you were to listen to me (you are better and stronger than I am and your might is the greatest), build in Crisa, beneath the slopes of Mt. Parnassus, where beautiful chariots will not clatter and no noise will be made by swift-footed horses around your well-built altar. So there hordes of renowned mortals will bring gifts to you as Ie Paean,[35] and you will rejoice greatly in your heart to receive the beautiful sacrifices of the people living roundabout." Thus, Telphusa spoke and convinced the far-shooter, so that renown in her land should go to Telphusa herself and not to Apollo. (254–275)

APOLLO BUILDS HIS TEMPLE AT THE SITE OF DELPHI

From there you went further, far-shooting Apollo, and you reached the town of the hubristic people, the Phlegyae, who have no concern for Zeus and live on earth in a beautiful glen near the Cephisean lake. You darted away from here quickly and came to mountain ridges and arrived at Crisa beneath snowy Mt. Parnassus. Its foothills turn toward the west, and its rocky cliffs hang from above over the hollow glade that stretches below. Here the lord Phoebus Apollo decreed that he would make his lovely temple and he said: "Here I intend to build a very beautiful temple, an oracle for mortals. Here all those who live in the rich Peloponnesus, in Europe, and on the sea-girt islands will bring perfect hecatombs and consult the oracle. To them I shall deliver my answers and ordain infallible counsel in my wealthy temple." (276–293)

Thus, Phoebus Apollo spoke and laid out the foundations, wide and very long overall. On these foundations Trophonius and Agamedes, the sons of Erginus, both dear to the immortal gods, placed a threshold of stone; and countless numbers of men built up with finished blocks of stone the temple, to sing about forever. There was a beautifully flowing spring nearby, where the lord, son of Zeus, killed with his mighty bow a she-dragon, a huge, bloated, and fierce monster who had done many evils to mortals on earth, to mortals themselves and to their thin-shanked flocks; for she was a bloodthirsty scourge. (294–304)

HERA GIVES BIRTH TO THE MONSTER TYPHAON

Once this she-dragon received, from golden-throned Hera to bring up, Typhaon, another terrible and cruel scourge for mortals;[36] this was when Hera became angry with father Zeus and gave birth to the monster because the son of Cronus bore renowned Athena from his head. Lady Hera was quickly enraged, and she spoke among the immortals: "Hear from me, all you gods and all you goddesses, how Zeus, the cloud-gatherer, first begins to dishonor me, when he has made me his dear and trusting wife. Apart from me, just now, he has given birth to keen-eyed Athena, who is outstanding among all the blessed immortals. But my son, Hephaestus, whom I myself bore, with his withered feet, was a weakling among the immortals—a shame to me and a disgrace on Olympus. I grabbed him myself with my own hands and threw him out, and he fell into the wide sea. But silver-footed Thetis, daughter of Nereus, accepted him and with her sisters took care of him. (How I wish that she had done some other favor for the blessed gods!) Villain, crafty deceiver, what other scheme will you devise now? How do you dare, all alone, to give birth to keen-eyed Athena? Would I not have borne a child by you? To be sure I was the one called your very own among the immortals who hold the wide heaven. Watch out now that I don't devise some evil for you in the future. Indeed, I will contrive how a son of mine will be born, who will be outstanding among the immortals, without any shame to our sacred marriage vow, either yours or mine. I shall not go near your bed, but separated from you I shall associate with the immortal gods." (305–330)

Thus she spoke and went apart from the gods, angered in her heart. Then straightway ox-eyed lady Hera prayed and struck the ground with the flat of her hand and uttered this invocation: "Earth and wide Heaven, hear me now, and you, Titan gods dwelling beneath the earth in vast Tartarus, from whom both mortals and gods are descended—all of you listen to me and give me, without Zeus as father, a child in no way inferior to him in might. But let him be as much stronger than Zeus as all-seeing Zeus is stronger than Cronus." Thus, she called out and lashed the ground with her mighty hand. The life-giving Earth was moved; and, when Hera saw this, she rejoiced in her heart. For she believed that her prayer would be answered. (331–342)

From this time then, for a whole year, Hera never approached the bed of wise Zeus, nor did she ever, as before, sit on her intricate throne and by his side devise shrewd plans. But ox-eyed lady Hera remained in her temples, filled with her worshipers, and took delight in their offerings. Yet when the months and days were completed and the seasons had passed as the full year came round, she gave birth to a terrible scourge for mortals, cruel Typhaon, like neither a god nor a human being. Ox-eyed lady Hera at once took and gave him, an evil, to the

90

100

110

120

evil she-dragon, who accepted him, Typhaon, who used to inflict many sufferings on the renowned tribes of human beings. (343–355)

APOLLO VAUNTS OVER THE SHE-DRAGON HE HAS SLAIN

As for the she-dragon, whoever opposed her met the fatal day of death, until lord Apollo, the far-shooter, struck her with a mighty arrow. Racked by bitter pain, she lay gasping frantically for breath and writhing on the ground. An unspeakable and terrifying sound arose as she twisted and rolled in the forest; breathing out blood, she gave up her life, and Phoebus Apollo vaunted over her: (356–362)

"Now rot here on the ground that nourishes mortals. You shall not live any longer to be the evil ruin of human beings who eat the fruit of the all-fostering earth and who will bring perfect hecatombs to his place." Thus he spoke, boasting; and darkness covered her eyes and the holy might of Helius caused her to rot there. Because of this, now the place is named Pytho, and they call its lord by the title, Pythian, since the mighty glare of the burning sun made the monster rot on the very spot. (363–374)

Then Phoebus Apollo knew in his heart why the beautifully flowing spring, Telphusa, had tricked him. In anger, he went to her and quickly he was there; standing very near her, he said: "Telphusa, you were not about to deceive my intelligence and keep this desirable place for you to put forth your beautifully flowing water. Here, to be sure, will be my glory, and not only yours." He spoke and lord Apollo, the far-worker, pushed on top of her a massive shower of rocks and hid her flowing stream; and he built an altar in the forest grove very near her beautifully flowing fountain. There all pray to Apollo under the name Telphusian because he shamed the stream of holy Telphusa. (375–387)

APOLLO RECRUITS CRETANS TO SERVE AS HIS PRIESTS

Then Phoebus Apollo thought deeply about what people he would bring in as his priests who would serve him in rocky Pytho. While he was thinking this over, he noticed a swift ship on the wine-dark sea. On it were many fine men, Cretans from Minoan Cnossus, who perform sacrifices to their lord and make known the pronouncements of Phoebus Apollo of the golden sword, whatever oracle he gives from his laurel beneath the slopes of Parnassus. These men were sailing in their black ship to sandy Pylos and the people in Pylos for trade and profit. But Phoebus Apollo intercepted them on the sea and leaped onto their swift ship in the shape of a dolphin and lay there, a huge and dread monster. None of the men understood, nor did they recognize the dolphin as the god, and they wanted to throw it overboard. But he kept making the entire ship quake and its timbers quiver. They were afraid and sat in silence on the hollow black ship; and they did not slacken the ropes or the sail of their dark-prowed ship. But as they had fixed their course by the ox-hide ropes, so they sailed on, and a fierce south wind drove the swift ship from behind. (388–409)

130

140

150

160

170

Apollo Delphinius. Attic red-figure hydria by the Berlin painter, ca. 480 B.C.; height 20½ in. Apollo rides over the sea in a winged tripod, as dolphins leap above the waves and fishes and an octopus swims below. He wears the laurel wreath and plays the lyre, while his bow and quiver are slung on his back. The artist brilliantly combines three aspects of Apollo, as prophet (symbolized by the Delphic tripod and the dolphins, associated with Delphi), musician, and archer. (*Photo Copyright © Government Of The Vatican City State-Directorate of the Vatican Museums.*)

First, they sailed by Malia and the coast of Laconia and came to Taenarum, a sea-crowned town, and the land of Helius, who makes mortals glad, where the thick-fleeced sheep of lord Helius pasture always and inhabit a pleasurable country.[37] They wanted to bring the ship ashore, disembark, and study the great marvel and watch with their own eyes whether the monster would remain on the deck of the hollow ship or leap back into the swell of the sea, full of fish. But the well-built ship did not obey their directions but made its way along the fertile Peloponnesus; lord Apollo, the far-worker, easily directed it with a breeze. The ship, continuing its course, came to Arena, lovely Argyphea, and Thryon, the ford of the river Alpheus, and well-built Aepy and Pylos and the inhabitants of Pylos;   180
and it went past Cruini and Chalcis and past Dyme and splendid Elis, where the Epei hold power. When it was sailing toward Pherae, jaunty in a wind from Zeus, beneath the clouds appeared the steep mountain of Ithaca and Dulichium and Same and wooded Zacynthus. But when it had passed the whole coast of the Peloponnesus, then to be sure, as they turned toward Crisa, there loomed before them the vast gulf whose length cuts off the rich Peloponnesus. A west wind, strong, clear, and vehement, came out of the sky by Zeus' decree and speeded the ship along so that it might complete its fast course over the briny water of the sea as quickly as possible. Then indeed they were sailing back toward the dawn and the sun. Lord Apollo, son of Zeus, was their guide, and they came to the   190
conspicuous harbor of vine-clad Crisa, where the seafaring ship was grounded on the sands. (409–439)

There lord Apollo, the far-worker, leaped out of the ship like a star at midday. His person was engulfed by a shooting fiery shower, and his splendor reached to the heavens. He made his way, amid precious tripods, to his innermost sanctuary. Then he caused a blaze to flare up and his arrows were bathed in a brilliance that encompassed the whole of Crisa. The wives and the lovely-dressed daughters of the Crisaeans cried out in amazement at the spectacular sight of Apollo; for the god instilled an awesome fear in each of them. Thereupon, swift as thought, he made a flying leap back onto the ship, in the form of a man in his prime, strong and vigorous,   200
with his hair flowing about his broad shoulders. Uttering winged words, he spoke to them. (440–451)

"Strangers, who are you? From where do you sail the watery paths? Is barter your goal, or do you roam recklessly, like pirates over the deep, who hazard their lives as they wander bringing evil to strangers? Why do you sit this way, despondent? Why don't you disembark and take your gear from your black ship to land? This is the right thing for enterprising men to do whenever they come from the sea to shore in their black ship; they are worn out and weary and straightway overcome by the desire for luscious food." (452–461)

Thus he spoke and put spirit in their breasts, and the leader of the Cretans said   210
in answer: "Stranger, indeed you do not look at all like mortals in your appearance and stature, but like the immortal gods. Good health and all hail, may the gods give you prosperity! Tell me this truly so that I may understand fully: What territory, what land is this? What people live here? For we were sailing the great seas, with other intentions, bound for Pylos from Crete, where we are proud to have been born; yet now we have arrived here with our ship, in a different way and by another course, not at all willingly, and anxious to return; but someone of the immortals has taken us here, against our wishes." (462–473)

Then Apollo, the far-worker, spoke in answer: "Strangers, who used to live in wooded Cnossus before, now no longer will you return again to your lovely city,   220 beautiful homes, and dear wives; but each of you here will keep my rich temple, honored by many mortals. I say proudly that I am Apollo, son of Zeus, and I took you to this place over the wide expanse of the sea. I intend you no harm, but you will keep my rich temple here, greatly esteemed and honored by all human beings; and you will know the counsels of the immortals, by whose will you always will be honored continually all your days. But come, as quickly as possible obey me in what I say. First let down the sails and loosen the ropes of ox-hide; then draw the swift ship up from the water onto dry land and remove your posses-sions and gear from the well-balanced ship; and build an altar on the shore of the sea; and, kindling a fire, make an offering of white barley. Then pray, standing around the altar. As I first leaped aboard your swift ship on the hazy sea in the form of a dolphin, so pray to me as Delphinius; furthermore, the altar itself will be Delphinius and overlooking[38] forever. Next, take your meal by the swift black ship and make a libation to the blessed gods who hold Olympus. But when you have satisfied your desire for luscious food, come with me and sing the Ie Paean (Hail Healer) until the time when you arrive at the place where you will keep my rich temple." (474–501)

So Apollo spoke, and they readily listened to him and obeyed. First, they let down the sails and loosened the ropes of ox-hide; and, lowering the mast by the forestays, they brought it to rest on the mast-holder. They themselves disembarked on the seashore and drew the swift ship up from the water onto dry land. They built an altar on the shore of the sea; and, kindling a fire, they made an offering of white barley; and they prayed, as he ordered, standing around the altar. Then they took their meal by the swift black ship and made a libation to the blessed gods who hold Olympus. But when they had satisfied their desire for food and drink, they got up and went with their leader, lord Apollo the son of Zeus, who held his lyre in his hands and played a lovely tune, as he stepped high and stately. The Cretans followed, marching to his rhythm, and they sang the Ie Paean, like the Cretan paean singers and those in whose breasts the divine Muse has placed sweet song. (502–519)

With weariless feet, they reached the mountain ridge and quickly arrived at Parnassus itself and the desirable place where they were going to live, honored by human beings. Apollo, who had led them there, pointed out his sacred sanctuary and rich temple. And the spirit was aroused in their dear breasts; and the leader of the Cretans questioned him with these words: "O lord, since you have brought us far from our loved ones and our fatherland—so was it somehow your wish—how then shall we live now? This we ask you to explain. This place is desirable neither as a vineyard nor as a pasture." (520–530)

And Apollo, the son of Zeus, smiling upon them, said: "Foolish, wretched mor-tals, who prefer heartfelt care, hard work, and trouble; I shall give you a message of comfort, and take it in earnest. Even if each of you, holding a knife in his right hand, were to slaughter sheep continuously, still the supply would not be exhausted with all that the renowned tribes of human beings bring to me here. Guard my temple and receive the human hordes who gather here, and above all point out to them my directions and keep my ordinances in your hearts. But if anyone is foolish enough to pay no heed and disobey, if there will be any idle word or deed or hubris, which is usually the case among mortal humans, then other men will be masters over you and you will be forced to submit to their might all your days. Everything has been told to you; store it in your hearts." (531–544)

So farewell, son of Zeus and Leto. Yet I shall remember you and another song too.

230

240

250

260

270

Select Bibliography

Barnard, Mary E. *The Myth of Apollo and Daphne from Ovid to Quevedo: Love, Agon and the Grotesque.* Durham, NC: Duke University Press, 1987.

Broad, W. J. *The Oracle: The Lost Secrets and Hidden Message of Ancient Delphi.* New York: Penguin Press, 2006.

Edelstein, Emma J., and Ludwig Edelstein. *Asclepius: A Collection and Interpretation of the Testimonies.* Baltimore, MD: Johns Hopkins University Press, 1998 [1945].

Fontenrose, Joseph. *The Delphic Oracle: Its Responses and Operations.* Berkeley, CA: University of California Press, 1978.

Graf, Fritz. *Apollo.* Gods and Heroes of the Ancient World Series. New York: Routledge, 2008.

———. *Python: a Study of Delphic Myth and Its Origins.* New York: Biblio & Tannen, 1974.

Parke, H. W. *Sibyls and Sibylline Prophecy in Classical Antiquity.* Edited by Brian C. McGing. Croom Helm Classical Studies. New York: Routledge, 1988.

Petrakos, Basil. *Delphi.* Athens: Clio Editions, 1977. A brief, well-illustrated introduction to the site of Delphi.

Stoneman, Richard. *The Ancient Oracles: Making the Gods Speak.* New Haven, CT: Yale University Press, 2011. A history of Greek oracles until they were silenced by the Christians.

Wickiser, Bronwen L. *Asklepios, Medicine, and the Politics of Healing in Fifth-Century Greece.* Baltimore, MD: Johns Hopkins University Press, 2008. An exploration of the early development and later spread of the cult of Asclepius.

Wood, Michael. *The Road to Delphi.* New York: Farrar, Straus and Giroux, 2003. A lively, entertaining interpretation of oracular phenomena from ancient times to the present.

Primary Sources

Sources in the Chapter

Homer	*Iliad* 1.43–52
Homeric Hymn 3a	*To Delian Apollo*
Homeric Hymn 3b	*To Pythian Apollo*
Homeric Hymn 16	*To Ascelpius*
Homeric Hymn 21	*To Apollo*
Ovid	*Metamorphoses* 1.452–567; 2.600–634; 6.385–400; 10.174–219; 11.146–193; 14.132–153
Vergil	*Aeneid* 6.42–51; 77–82; 98–101

Additional Sources

Aristophanes	*Plutus* (Wealth, a blind beggar, is healed through incubation)
Asclepius	*Alcestis*
Euripides	*Ion*
Lucian	*of the Gods: Hermes and Apollo*
Pausanias	*Description of Greece* 2.26.1–2.29.1: Epidaurus and Asclepius; 5.10.8: The Olympia pediment: Battle between Lapiths and Centaurs (Note that Pausanias identifies Apollo as Pirithoüs)

DVDs

Opera: Strauss, Richard (1864–1949). *Daphne.* Anderson et al. Venice Teatro la Fenice Orchestra, cond. Reck. Strauss' dynamic operatic version of the myth is an amalgamation of Ovid and Pausanias. The ecstatic final scene brilliantly evokes Daphne's transformation into a laurel tree. Some, however, may find the staging and direction of this production disappointing. The final scene is available on CD performed by many singers, including Renée Fleming, who also has made a recording of the complete opera.

Opera: Gluck, Christoph Willibald (1718–1787). *Alceste.* von Otter et al. English Baroque soloists, cond. Gardiner. Image Entertainment. Also Naglestad et al. Staatsoper Stuttgart, cond. Carydis. Arthaus Musik. Both of these modern productions are very controversial in their theatrical presentations of this most beautiful but static opera, the first staged by Robert Wilson, the second updated to modern times by Jossi Wieler. Both use the French (Paris) extensively revised version (1776), much preferred to the original (1767), which has no scene with Hercules. There are many recorded performances on CD with notable singers (e.g., Flagstad, Callas, Norman, and Baker, not to mention the tenors).

Ballet: Apollo. Choreography by George Balanchine. Music by Igor Stravinsky. In *Jacques D'Amboise: Portrait of a Great American Dancer.* VAI. At last, a complete performance on DVD. Among the other ballets D'Amboise performs is *Afternoon of a Faun,* choreographed by Jerome Robbins, with music by Debussy. See Chapter 28 on the companion website.

Song: Strauss, Richard (1864–1949). "Gesang der Apollopriesterin" ("Song of the Priestess of Apollo"). Text by Emanuel von Bodman. On *Renée Fleming: Lieder.* Wiener Philharmoniker, cond. Thielemann. Opus Arte. Also included are two other selections by Strauss: *An Alpine Symphony* (*Eine Alpensimphonie*) and the last scene from his opera *Arabella.* This is one of Strauss' best songs and is not as performed or recorded as often as it should be. On CD, the "Song of the Priestess of Apollo" is included on recordings of recitals by Evelyn Lear, Karita Mattila, Adrienne Pieczonka, Michaela Kaune, and Rose Pauly.

Documentary: Delphi Center of the World. A film by Frieder Käsmann, Kultur. Excellent, interesting photography of the site itself and its architecture and sculpture.

Notes

1. Many had cults of Apollo. Leto's wanderings are at times geographically erratic. Most of the places mentioned are familiar enough, but some names are problematic. Any attempt to trace Leto's wanderings precisely should begin with the notes in *The Homeric Hymns,* ed. T. W. Allen, W. R. Halliday, and E. E. Sikes, 2d ed. (New York: Oxford University Press, 1963).

2. In later accounts, Hera employs various schemes to prevent Leto from finding a place to bear her children, and through fear of Hera the whole earth rejects Leto's pleas. Hera also is said to have decreed that Leto's children could not be born in any place where the sun shone, so Poseidon kept the island of Delos (which in this early time was afloat) covered by his waves from the sun's rays during the birth of the twins.

3. These lines were thought to refer to Homer, who, among the many traditions, becomes a blind bard from the island of Chios. It is extremely unlikely that the Homer associated with the *Iliad* and *Odyssey* wrote this hymn or any of the others. Bards are

archetypically blind as opposed to the hale and hearty politicians and warriors; in terms of another fundamental motif, blind poets see the Muses' truth.

4. It is not difficult to imagine a fluid bardic tradition in which hymns could vary in length and be presented in diverse combinations.

5. In later accounts, the dragon or serpent is sometimes masculine with the name Python (as in Ovid's story of Apollo and Daphne, translated later in this chapter). It may also be described as the hostile opponent of Leto before the birth of her children. Some versions stress the great prowess of Apollo early in his life and career (as in the case of the wondrous childhood of Hermes and Heracles) to the extent of having him kill the dragon while still a child.

6. Aeschylus in the prologue to his *Eumenides* and Euripides in a chorus from his *Iphigenia in Tauris*. A scholarly survey of the problems, with a reconstruction of the origins and procedures of the oracle, is provided by H. W. Parke and D. E. W. Wormell, *The Delphic Oracle*, 2 vols. (Oxford: Blackwell, 1956).

7. A festival (called the Stepteria) was celebrated every ninth year at Delphi to commemorate these events in the early history of the sanctuary.

8. The omphalos found in the excavations and originally identified as the archaic sacred stone has subsequently been labeled a fraud.

9. The other major Panhellenic festivals were those at Olympia and Nemea, both in honor of Zeus, and the Isthmian Games at Corinth, dedicated to Poseidon.

10. For the oracular Apollo elsewhere, see H. W. Parke, *The Oracles of Apollo in Asia Minor* (London: Croom Helm, 1985); also Joseph Fontenrose, *Didyma: Apollo's Oracle, Cult, and Companions* (Berkeley, CA: University of California Press, 1988), who is overly skeptical in his scholarly treatment of evidence.

11. One could inquire on one's own behalf or on the behalf of someone else. Inquiries often came from state representatives. Both the question and the answer were usually set down in writing. See Joseph Fontenrose, *The Delphic Oracle: Its Responses and Operations* (Berkeley, CA: University of California Press, 1978).

12. Among the religious objects that decked the temple was the tomb of Dionysus. The god Dionysus was worshiped alongside Apollo in the sanctuary (perhaps as early as the sixth century B.C.). The prophetic trance of the Pythia has something in common with Dionysiac frenzy. See Walter Burkert, *Ancient Mystery Cults* (Cambridge, MA: Harvard University Press, 1987), p. 108.

13. The first Pythia, who is named Phemonoë (Prophetic Mind), is a poetic figure; we have from Herodotus the names of later ones (Aristonice and Perallus), historically much more real.

14. Diodorus Siculus, 16.26; Plutarch *Moralia*, "Oracles in Decline," 435d; and Pausanias 10.5.7.

15. J. Z. De Boer and J. R. Hale, "The Geological Origins of the Oracle at Delphi, Greece," in *The Archaeology of Geological Catastrophies*, W. G. McGuire et al., eds., *Geological Society Special Publication* no. 171 (London 2000), pp. 399–412; J. Z. De Boer, J. R. Hale, and J. Chanton, "New Evidence of Geological Origins of the Ancient Delphic Oracle (Greece)," *Geology* 29 (2001), pp. 707–710. J. Z. De Boer and J. R. Hale, "Was She Really Stoned? The Oracle of Delphi," *Archaeological Odyssey* 5 (Nov./Dec. 2002), pp. 46–53, 58–59.

16. W. J. Broad, *The Oracle: The Lost Secrets and Hidden Message of Ancient Delphi* (New York: Penguin Press, 2006), pp. 240–241; and Michael Attyah Flower, *The Seer in Ancient Greece* (Berkeley: University of California Press, 2008), pp. 227–230. See also Joan Breton Connelly, *Portrait of a Priestess: Women and Ritual in Ancient Greece* (Princeton, NJ: Princeton University Press), pp. 72–81.

17. See H. W. Parke, *Sibyls and Sibylline Prophecy in Classical Antiquity*, ed. Brian C. McGing, Croom Helm Classical Studies (New York: Routledge, 1988).

18. This Sibyl is Deïphobe, daughter of Glaucus, priestess of the temple of Phoebus Apollo and Diana.

19. Vergil's works themselves were consulted as oracles in later times as the *sortes Vergilianae*.

20. A total of 1,000 years, counting the generations (*saecula*) as one hundred years each.

21. Petronius, *Satyricon* 48.8. The Sibyl's story appears to be late in its reminiscences of Cassandra and Tithonus.

22. This is the Aristaeus who will become the husband of Autonoë and father of Actaeon; he, too, is the one who made advances to Eurydice. He is particularly linked with agricultural pursuits, especially beekeeping.

23. For the theme of homosexuality, see pp. 22–23.

24. Ovid puts the story in the mouth of Orpheus. Other accounts have Zephyrus (the West Wind) deliberately divert the course of the discus because of his jealous love for Hyacinthus.

25. These marks not only reproduce Apollo's moans of grief, they are also the initial letters of the name of the hero of the Trojan saga, the great Ajax (Greek *Aias*), son of Telamon, as Apollo indicates in his prophetic words. When Ajax committed suicide, the same flower, the hyacinth, sprang from his blood (Ovid, *Metamorphoses* 13.391–398).

26. See Glenn W. Geelhoed, "The Caduceus as a Medical Emblem: Heritage or Heresy?" *Southern Medical Journal* 81, no. 9 (September 1988), pp. 1155–1161. See also by an account executive (not a doctor), Paul T. Frett, "Medicine's Identity Crisis Revealed: The Asclepius vs. the Caduceus," *Minnesota Medicine* 77 (October 1994), pp. 48–50. He argues for the Asclepius staff.

27. See Emma J. Edelstein and Ludwig Edelstein, *Asclepius: A Collection and Interpretation of the Testimonies* (Baltimore, MD: Johns Hopkins University Press, 1998 [1945]) and E. R. Dodds, *The Greeks and the Irrational* (Berkeley, CA: University of California Press, 1951).

28. This is the famous Midas of the golden touch (Ovid's version of his story, *Metamorphoses* 11.85–145, is well known). His story is told in Chapter 13, pp. 318–319.

29. Elements of folk tale appear dominant in this story, particularly in the traditional depiction of the garrulous barber. In some versions, Midas plays this same role in the contest between Apollo and Marsyas. Thus, he favors the satyr against Apollo and suffers the same humiliation.

30. Apollo's epithet Lykios was believed by the Greeks to mean "wolf-god," whatever this may signify—that he was a hunter like a wolf? That he was the protector against the wolf? Perhaps Lykios is to be derived from Lycia, a district in southwestern Asia Minor.

31. Johann Joachim Winckelmann, *History of the Art of Antiquity*, trans. Harry Francis Mallgrave (Los Angeles, CA: Getty Research Institute, 2006), pp. 333–334.

32. These lines about Apollo as a suitor are full of problems; the text seems to be corrupt. Ischys and Apollo vied for Coronis, and Leucippus and Apollo vied for Daphne (in a version given by Pausanias, 8.20.3). Nothing much can be made of the other rivals.

33. Apollo's itinerary offers some geographical problems, but in general he goes from Olympus through Larissa (the home of the Perrhaebi) to Iolcus and eventually crosses to the Lelantine plain (between Chalcis and Eretria) on the island of Euboea, and then back again to the mainland and Onchestus, Thebes, Lake Copais, and the Cephisus River—all in Boeotia. Next, continuing westward, Apollo comes to the spring Telphusa in the region of Mt. Helicon, and from there finally to Crisa, the site of his Delphi.

34. This is our only evidence for this ritual in honor of Poseidon at his famous precinct in Onchestus, and the numerous conjectures made by scholars about its meaning and purpose are not at all convincing.

35. Some etymologists do not agree with the ancients, who thought this name was derived from the cry *Ie* and *Paean*, meaning "healer." Later in this hymn, it is the name of a song.

36. *Typhaon* is also the name of the monster killed by Zeus, that is, Typhoeus or Typhaon or Typhon; see p. 83.
37. The ship sails along the south coast of the Peloponnesus, then up the north coast until it turns into the Corinthian gulf and makes for Crisa.
38. The Greek word translated as "overlooking" is *epopsios* and may refer to another epithet of Apollo (and Zeus) as "overseers" of everything; or the adjective may only mean that the altar is "conspicuous."

HERMES

The messenger, the slayer of Argos, did not disobey. He immediately put on his feet the beautiful sandals, immortal and golden, which carried him upon the waters and over the boundless earth swift as a breath of wind. He took his staff with which he enchants the eyes of those whom he wishes and rouses those who slumber.

—**HOMER**, *Odyssey* 5.43–48

The Birth and Childhood of Hermes

The *Homeric Hymn to Hermes* (18) concentrates on the story (repeated at the beginning of the much more lengthy and important hymn that follows) of how Zeus became the father of Hermes as the result of his union with **Maia**, one of the Pleiades, the daughters of Atlas and Pleione.

> I sing about Hermes, the Cyllenian slayer of Argus, lord of Mt. Cyllene and Arcadia rich in flocks, the messenger of the gods and bringer of luck, whom Maia, the daughter of Atlas, bore, after uniting in love with Zeus. She in her modesty shunned the company of the blessed gods and lived in a shadowy cave; here the son of Cronus used to make love to this nymph of the beautiful hair in the dark of night, without the knowledge of immortal gods and mortal humans, when sweet sleep held white-armed Hera fast. (1–9)
>
> So hail to you, son of Zeus and Maia. After beginning with you, I shall turn to another hymn. Hail, Hermes, guide and giver of grace and other good things. 10

The more famous *Homeric Hymn to Hermes* (4) tells the story of the god's birth and childhood with delightful charm and disarming candor. Here is a most artful depiction of this mischievous divine child, who invents the lyre and steals Apollo's cattle:

> Sing, O Muse, of the son of Zeus and Maia, lord of Mt. Cyllene and Arcadia rich in flocks, the messenger of the gods and bringer of luck, whom Maia of the beautiful hair bore after uniting in love with Zeus. She in her modesty shunned the company of the blessed gods and lived within a shadowy cave; here the son of Cronus joined in love with this nymph of the beautiful hair in the dark of night, without the knowledge of immortal gods and mortal humans, while sweet sleep held white-armed

Hermes and the Infant Dionysus, by Praxiteles, ca. 340 B.C.; height 82 in. The Greek author Pausanias saw this statue in the temple of Hera at Olympia in the mid-second century A.D. and named its sculptor. It is possible that the present statue is an ancient copy of the one that Pausanias saw, which may have been damaged and replaced. The infant Dionysus is reaching for a bunch of grapes held in the (missing) right hand of Hermes, whose left had originally held his caduceus. The white Parian marble is highly polished, and the off-center weight of the figures is supported by the tree trunk, which is largely concealed by Hermes' cloak. (*Vanni/Art Resource, NY*)

Hera fast. But when the will of Zeus had been accomplished and her tenth month was fixed in the heavens, she brought forth to the light a child, and a remarkable thing was accomplished; for the child whom she bore was devious, winning in his cleverness, a robber, a driver of cattle, a guide of dreams, a spy in the night, a watcher at the door, who soon was about to manifest renowned deeds among the immortal gods. (1–16)   10

Maia bore him on the fourth day of the month. He was born at dawn, by midday he was playing the lyre, and in the evening he stole the cattle of far-shooting Apollo. After he leaped forth from the immortal limbs of his mother, he did not remain lying in his sacred cradle; but he sprang up and looked for the cattle of Apollo. When he crossed the threshold of the high-roofed cave, he found a tortoise and obtained boundless pleasure from it. (17–24)   20

HERMES INVENTS THE LYRE

Indeed, Hermes was the very first to make the tortoise a minstrel. He happened to meet it in the very entranceway, waddling along as it ate the luxurious grass in front of the dwelling. When Zeus' son, the bringer of luck, saw it, he laughed and said at once: "Already a very good omen for me; I shall not be scornful. Greetings; what a delight you appear to me, lovely in shape, graceful in movement and a good dinner companion. Where did you, a tortoise living in the mountains, get this speckled shell that you have on, a beautiful plaything? Come, I shall take you and bring you inside. You will be of some use to me, and I shall do you no dishonor. You will be the very first to be an advantage to me, but a better one inside, since the   30 out-of-doors is dangerous for you. To be sure, while you are alive you will continue to be a charm against evil witchcraft, but if you were dead, then you would make very beautiful music."[1] (25–38)

Thus he spoke and lifted the tortoise in both hands and went back into his dwelling carrying the lovely plaything. Then he cut up the mountain-dwelling tortoise and scooped out its life-marrow with a knife of gray iron. As swiftly as a thought darts through the mind of a man whose cares come thick and fast or as a twinkle flashes from the eye, thus glorious Hermes devised his plan and carried it out simultaneously. He cut to size stocks of reeds, extended them across the back and through the tortoise shell and   40 fastened them securely. In his ingenuity, he stretched the hide of an ox all around and affixed two arms to which he attached a bridge, and then he extended seven tuneful strings of sheep gut. (39–51)

When he had finished, he took up the lovely plaything and tried it by striking successive notes. It resounded in startling fashion under his hand, and the god accompanied his playing with a beautiful song, improvising at random just as young men exchange banter on a festive occasion. He sang about Zeus, the son of Cronus, Maia with the beautiful sandals, and their talk in the intimacy of their love, and proclaimed aloud the renown of his birth. He honored, too, the handmaids of the nymph, her splendid   50 home, and the tripods and the ample cauldrons it contained. He sang of these things, but his heart was set on other pursuits. He took the hollow lyre and set it down in his sacred cradle; for he craved for meat and leaped out of the fragrant hall to a place where he could watch, since he was devising in his heart sheer trickery such as men who are thieves plan in the dead of black night. (52–67)

HERMES STEALS APOLLO'S CATTLE

Helius, the Sun, with his horses and chariot was descending to earth and the stream of Ocean, when Hermes came hurrying to the shady mountains of Pieria[2] where the immortal cattle of the blessed gods have their home, grazing on the lovely untouched meadows. The sharp-sighted son of Maia, the slayer of Argus, cut off 60 from the herd fifty loud-bellowing cattle and drove them over sandy ground, reversing their tracks as they wandered. For he did not forget his skill at trickery, and he made their hoofs go backward, the front ones last and the back ones first; he himself walked straight ahead. For quickly, by the sandy seashore, he wove sandals of wicker, a wonderful achievement, beyond description and belief; he combined twigs of myrtle and tamarisk and fastened together bundles of the freshly sprouting wood which he bound, leaves and all, under his feet as light sandals. The glorious slayer of Argus made them so, as he left Pieria, improvising since he was hastening over a long journey.[3] (68–86)

But an old man, who was working in a luxuriant vineyard, noticed him coming 70 to the plain through Onchestus with its beds of grass. The renowned son of Maia spoke to him first: "Old man, digging about with stooped shoulders, you will indeed have much wine when all these vines bear fruit, if you listen to me and earnestly remember in your heart to be blind to what you have seen and deaf to what you have heard and to keep silent, since nothing of your own has been harmed in any way." He said only this much and pushed the sturdy head of cattle on together. Glorious Hermes drove them over many shady mountains, echoing hollows, and flowery plains. (87–96)

The greater part of divine night, his dark helper, was over; and the break of day that calls men to work was soon coming on, and bright Selene, daughter of lord 80 Pallas, the son of Megamedes,[4] had climbed to a new watchpost, when the strong son of Zeus drove the broad-browed cattle of Phoebus Apollo to the river Alpheus. They were unwearied when they came to the lofty shelter and the watering places that faced the splendid meadow. Then, when he had fed the loud-bellowing cattle well on fodder, he drove them all together into the shelter, as they ate lotus and marsh plants covered with dew. He gathered together a quantity of wood and pursued, with diligent passion, the skill of producing fire. He took a good branch of laurel and trimmed it with his knife, and in the palm of his hand he grasped a piece of wood; and the hot breath of fire rose up.[5] Indeed, Hermes was the very first to invent fire sticks and fire. He took many dry sticks which he left as they were and 90 heaped them up together in a pit in the ground. The flame shone forth, sending afar a great blaze of burning fire. (97–114)

While the power of renowned Hephaestus was kindling the fire, Hermes dragged outside near the blaze two horned cattle, bellowing, for much strength went with him. He threw them both, panting upon their backs, onto the ground and bore down upon them. Rolling them over, he pierced through their life's marrow; he followed up this work with more, cutting the meat rich in fat and spearing the pieces with wooden spits, and roasted all together the flesh, choice parts from the back, and the bowels that enclosed the black blood. He laid these pieces on the ground and stretched the hides on a rugged rock, and thus still even now they are 100 there continually long afterward, despite the interval of time. Next Hermes in the joy of his heart whisked the rich bundles away to a smooth flat rock and divided them into twelve portions that he allotted, adding a choice piece to each, making it wholly an honorable offering. (115–129)

Then glorious Hermes longed for the sacred meat of the sacrifice, for the sweet aroma made him weak, even though he was an immortal. But his noble heart did not yield, although his desire was overwhelming to gulp the offering down his holy throat.[6] But he quickly put the fat and all the meat away in the cave with its lofty roof, setting them up high as a testimony of his recent childhood theft, and he gathered up wood for the fire and destroyed all the hoofs and the heads in the blaze. When the god had accomplished all that he had to do, he threw his sandals into the deep-eddying stream of the Alpheus; he put out the embers and hid the black ashes in the sand. Thus he spent the whole night as the beautiful light of Selene shone down on him. Swiftly then he went back to the divine peaks of Cyllene and encountered no one at all (neither blessed gods nor mortal humans) on his long journey, and dogs did not bark. (130–145)

Hermes, the luck-bringer, son of Zeus, slipped sideways past the lock into his house, like the gust of a breeze in autumn, and went directly through the cave to his luxurious inner chamber, stepping gently on his feet, for he did not make a sound as one would walking upon the floor. Glorious Hermes quickly got into his cradle and wrapped the blankets about his shoulders like a helpless baby and lay toying with his fingers at the covers on his knees; at his left side he kept his beloved lyre close by his hand. (145–154)

But the god did not escape the notice of his goddess mother, who spoke to him: "You devious rogue, in your cloak of shameless guile, where in the world have you come from in the nighttime? Now I am convinced that either Apollo, son of Leto, by his own hands will drag you with your sides bound fast right out the door, or you will prowl about the valleys, a robber and a cheat. Be gone then! Your father begat you as a great trouble for mortals and immortal gods!" (155–161)

Hermes answered her with clever words: "Mother, why do you throw this up at me, as to a helpless child who knows in his heart very little of evil, a fearful baby, frightened of his mother's chiding? But I shall set upon whatever work is best to provide for me and you together. We two shall not endure to stay here in this place alone, as you bid, apart from the immortals without gifts and prayers. Better all our days to live among the gods, rich and full in wealth and plenty, than to sit at home in the shadows of this cave! And I shall go after divine honor just as Apollo has. And if my father does not give it to me, to be sure I shall take my honor myself (and I can do it) which is to be the prince of thieves. And if the glorious son of Leto search me out, I think he will meet with another even greater loss. For I shall go to Pytho and break right into his great house, and I shall seize from within plenty of very beautiful tripods and bowls and gold and gleaming iron and an abundance of clothing. You will be able to see it all, if you like." Thus they conversed with each other, the son of aegis-bearing Zeus and the lady Maia. (162–183)

APOLLO CONFRONTS HERMES

As Eos, the early-born, sprang up from the deep-flowing waters of Ocean, bringing light to mortals, Apollo was on his way and came to Onchestus, a very lovely grove sacred to loud-roaring Poseidon, who surrounds the earth. There he found the old man, who on the path within was feeding the animal that guarded his vineyard. The glorious son of Leto spoke to him first: "Old man, who pulls the weeds and briars of grassy Onchestus, I have come here from Pieria looking for some cattle from my herd—all cows, all with curved horns. The bull, which was black, fed alone away 150 from the others; keen-eyed dogs followed behind, four of them, of one mind like humans. They were left behind, both the dogs and the bull—a truly amazing feat. But just as the sun had set, the cows went out of the soft meadow away from the sweet pasture. Tell me this, old fellow, have you seen a man passing along the road with these cows?" (184–200)

The old man spoke to him in answer: "My friend, it is hard to tell everything that one sees with one's eyes. For many wayfarers pass along the road; some travel intent on much evil, others on much good. To know each of them is difficult. But, good sir, the whole day long until the sun set I was digging about in my fruitful vine-yard and I thought that I noticed a child, I do not know for sure; whoever the child 160 was, he, an infant, tended the fine-horned cattle and he had a stick. He walked from side to side as he drove them backward and kept their heads facing him." (201–211)

Thus the old man spoke; after Apollo had heard his tale, he went more quickly on his way. He noticed a bird with its wings extended, and from this sign he knew at once that the thief was a child born of Zeus, the son of Cronus. So lord Apollo, the son of Zeus, eagerly hastened to holy Pylos in search of his shambling cows, his broad shoulders enshrouded in a dark cloud. When the archer-god spied the tracks, he cried out: "Why, indeed, here is a great marvel that I see with my eyes. These are definitely the tracks of straight-horned cows, but they are turned back-ward toward the asphodel meadow. And these here are not the prints of a man or 170

Hermes in Crib with Zeus, Apollo, and Maia. Black-figure hydria, from Caere (Cerveteri), ca. 500 B.C.; 17 in. in height. This vase is one of a number of vases known as *Caeretan Hydrias*, which represent a similar style of treatment and craftsmanship. Most of these vases have been discovered at Caere in southern Eturia in Italy, hence the name. One of the marked features of the style is a playful sense of humor, which is perfectly suited to recount the exploits of the infant Hermes. Just behind Apollo are the stolen cattle, shielded from the main scene by a tree with luxuriant foliage. Apollo delivers his accusations against the baby Hermes, snugly nestled in his crib, to an indulgent Zeus and Maia, who defend him. (*Left: Réunion des Musées Nationaux/Art Resource, NY*) (*Right: Erich Lessing/Art Resource, NY*)

a woman or gray wolves or bears or lions; nor are they, I expect, those of a shaggy-maned centaur or whoever makes such monstrous strides with its swift feet. On this side of the road the tracks are strange, but on the other side they are even stranger." (212–226)

With these words lord Apollo, the son of Zeus, hurried on and came to the forest-clad mountain of Cyllene and the deeply shaded cave in the rock where the immortal nymph bore the child of Zeus, the son of Cronus. A lovely odor pervaded the sacred mountain, and many sheep ranged about grazing on the grass. Then the archer-god, Apollo himself, hurried over the stone threshold down into the shadowy cave. (227–234)   180

When the son of Zeus and Maia perceived that far-shooting Apollo was in a rage about his cattle, he sank down into his fragrant blankets. As ashes hide a bed of embers on logs of wood, so Hermes buried himself in his covers when he saw the archer-god. He huddled head and hands and feet tightly together as though just bathed and ready for sweet sleep, but he was really wide awake, and under his arm he held his lyre. The son of Zeus and Leto knew both the beautiful mountain nymph and her dear son, the little boy enveloped in craft and deceit, and he was not fooled. He looked in every corner of the great house. He took a shining key and opened three chambers full of nectar and lovely ambrosia, and in them, too, lay stored much silver and gold and many of the nymph's garments, rich in their hues of purple and silver, such as are found in the sacred dwellings of the blessed gods. (235–251)   190

Then, when the son of Leto had searched every nook in the great house, he addressed glorious Hermes with these words: "You, O child, lying in the cradle, inform me about my cattle and be quick, or soon the two of us will be at variance and it will not be nice. For I shall take hold of you and hurl you down into the terrible and irrevocable darkness of murky Tartarus; neither your mother nor your father will release you to the light above, but you will wander under the earth, a leader among little people." (252–259)

Hermes answered him craftily: "Son of Leto, what are these harsh words you have spoken? Have you come here looking for cattle of the field? I have not seen   200 a thing, I do not know a thing, I have not heard a word from anyone. I cannot give information nor can I win the reward. Do I look like a man of brawn, a cattle rustler? That is not my line; I am interested rather in other things: sleep, milk from my mother's breast, baby blankets about my shoulders and warm baths. Do not let anyone find out how this dispute came about. It would indeed be a source of great amazement among the immortals that a newborn child should bring cattle of the field right through the front door of his house. What you say is pretty unlikely. I was born yesterday, my feet are tender and the ground is rough beneath them. If you wish, I shall swear a great oath by the head of my father; I pledge a vow that I am not guilty myself and that I have not seen anyone else who might be the one who stole your   210 cows—whatever cows are, for I have only heard about them now for the first time." (260–277)

Thus Hermes spoke, his eyes twinkling and his brows raised as he looked all about, and gave a long whistle to show how fruitless he considered Apollo's quest. But far-shooting Apollo laughed softly and spoke to him: "Oh splendid, you sly-hearted cheat; from the way that you talk I am sure that many a time you have broken into the better homes during the night and reduced more than one poor fellow to extremities by grabbing everything in the house without a sound. And you will distress many a shepherd in the mountain glens, when greedy after meat you come upon their herds of cattle and their woolly sheep. But come on now, if you do not   220 want to sleep your last and longest sleep, get down out of your cradle, you comrade of black night. For this then you will have as your prerogative hereafter among the gods: you will be called forevermore the prince of thieves." (278–292)

Thus Phoebus Apollo spoke and took hold of the child to carry him away. At that very moment, the mighty slayer of Argus had an idea; as he was being lifted in Apollo's hands he let go an omen, a bold and servile messenger from his belly, a hearty blast, and right after it he gave a violent sneeze. And when Apollo heard, he dropped glorious Hermes out of his hands to the ground and sat in front of him; even though he was eager to be on his way he spoke with taunting words: "Rest assured, son of Zeus and Maia, in your swaddling clothes, with these omens I shall   230 find my sturdy head of cattle by and by, and furthermore you will lead the way." Thus he spoke. (293–304)

HERMES AND APOLLO BRING THEIR CASE BEFORE ZEUS

And Cyllenian Hermes gave a start and jumped up pushing the blanket away from both his ears with his hands, and clutching it around his shoulders he cried out: "Where are you taking me, O far-shooter, most vehement of all the gods? Is it because of the cows that you are so angry and assault me? Oh, oh, how I wish the whole breed of cattle might perish! For I did not steal your cows and I have not seen anyone else who has—whatever cows are, for I have only heard about them now for the first time. Let us have the case decided before Zeus, the son of Cronus." (304–312)   240

Thus, as they quarreled over each and every point, Hermes, the shepherd, and the splendid son of Leto remained divided. The latter spoke the truth and not without justice seized upon glorious Hermes because of the cattle; on the other hand, the Cyllenian wished to deceive the god of the silver bow by tricks and by arguments. But when he in his ingenuity found his opponent equally resourceful, he hastened to walk over the sandy plain in front with the son of Zeus and Leto behind. Quickly these two very beautiful children of Zeus came to their father, the son of Cronus, on the top of fragrant Olympus. For there the scales of justice lay ready for them both. (313–324)

A happy throng occupied snow-capped Olympus, for the deathless gods had   250 assembled with the coming of golden-throned Dawn. Hermes and Apollo of the silver bow stood before the knees of Zeus, and he who thunders from on high spoke to his glorious son with the question: "Phoebus, where did you capture this delightful booty, a child newly born who has the appearance of a herald? This is a serious business that has come before the assembly of the gods." (325–332)

Then lord Apollo, the archer, replied: "O father, you, who scoff at me for being the only one who is fond of booty, are now going to hear a tale that is irrefutable. After journeying for a long time in the mountains of Cyllene I found a child, this out-and-out robber here; as sharp a rogue I have not seen either among gods or mortals who cheat their fellows on earth. He stole my cows from the meadow in the   260 evening and proceeded to drive them along the shore of the loud-sounding sea making directly for Pylos. The tracks were of two kinds, strange and marvelous, the work of a clever spirit. The black dust retained the prints of the cattle and showed them leading into the asphodel meadow. But this rogue I have here, an inexplicable wonder, did not cross the sandy ground on his feet or on his hands; but by some other means he smeared the marks of his amazing course as though someone had walked on oak saplings. As long as he followed the cattle across the sandy ground, the tracks stood out very clearly in the dust. But when he had covered the great stretch of sand, his own course and that of the cows quickly became imperceptible on the hard ground. But a mortal man noticed him driving the herd of cattle straight for Pylos. When he had quietly penned up the cows and slyly confused his homeward trail by zigzagging this way and that, he nestled down in his cradle, obscure as the black night, within the darkness of the gloomy cave, and not even the keen eye of an eagle would have spied him. He kept rubbing his eyes with his hands as he devised his subtle wiles, and he himself immediately maintained without a qualm: 'I have not seen a thing, I do not know a thing and I have not heard a word from anyone. I cannot give information nor can I win the reward.'" Thus Phoebus Apollo spoke and then sat down. (333–365) 270

And Hermes in answer told his side of the story, directing his words pointedly to Zeus, the ruler of all the gods. "Father Zeus, I shall indeed tell you the truth. For I am honest and I do not know how to lie. He came to our house today as the sun was just rising, in search of his shambling cattle. He brought none of the blessed gods as witnesses or observers and with great violence ordered me to confess; he made many threats of hurling me down into wide Tartarus, since he is in the full bloom of his glorious prime, while I was born only yesterday (as he too well knows himself) and do not look at all like a cattle rustler or a man of brawn. Believe me (for you claim to be my own dear father too) that I did not drive his cows home nor even cross the threshold—so may I prosper, what I tell you is the truth. I deeply revere Helius and the other gods; I love you and I am in dread of this fellow here. You know yourself that I am not guilty—I shall swear a great oath besides—no, by these beautifully ornate portals of the gods. Somehow, someday, I will pay him back, even though he is mighty, for his ruthless behavior. Be on the side of a defenseless baby." Thus the Cyllenian slayer of Argus spoke, blinking in innocence, and he held his baby blanket on his shoulder and would not let it go. (366–388) 280 290

Zeus gave a great laugh as he saw the devious child knowingly and cleverly make his denials about the cattle. He ordered the two of them to act in accord and make a search; Hermes, in his role of guide, was to lead without any malicious intent and point out the spot where he had hidden away the mighty herd of cattle. The son of Cronus nodded his head and splendid Hermes obeyed, for the will of aegis-bearing Zeus easily persuaded him. (389–396) 300

THE RECONCILIATION BETWEEN HERMES AND APOLLO

The two very beautiful sons of Zeus hastened together to sandy Pylos, crossed the river Alpheus, and came to the lofty cave where the animals were sheltered in the nighttime. Then, while Hermes went into the rocky cavern and drove the mighty head of cattle out into the light, the son of Leto looked away and noticed the cowhides on the steep rock and immediately asked glorious Hermes: "O sly rogue, how were you, a newborn infant, able to skin two cows? I do indeed wonder at the strength that will be yours in the future; there is no need to wait for you to grow up, O Cyllenian, son of Maia." (397–408)

Thus he spoke and fashioned with his hands strong bonds out of willow.[7] But they grew up in that very spot on the ground under their feet; and twisting and twining together, they readily covered over all the cattle of the field at the will of the trickster Hermes, while Apollo watched in wonder. Then the mighty slayer of Argus looked away to the ground, fire flashing from his eyes, in his desire to get out of his predicament. But it was very easy for him, just as he wished, to soften the far-shooting son of Leto, even though he was strong; he took up the lyre in his left 310 hand and tried it by striking successive notes. The instrument resounded in star-tling fashion, and Phoebus Apollo laughed with delight as the lovely strains of the heavenly music pierced his being, and sweet yearning took hold of his heart while he listened. (409–423)

The son of Maia, growing bold as he played so beautifully, took his stand on the left side of Phoebus Apollo and began to sing a song—and lovely was the ensu-ing sound of his voice—fashioned on the theme of the immortal gods and the dark earth and how in the beginning they came into being and how each was allotted his due. Of the gods he honored first of all Mnemosyne, mother of the Muses, for she honored him, the son of Maia, as one of her own. The splendid son of Zeus paid tribute to each of the other immortal gods according to age and birth, mentioning all in the proper order, as he played the lyre on his arm. (423–433)

But an irresistible desire took hold of Apollo, heart and soul, and he spoke up, interrupting with winged words: "Cattle slayer, contriver, busy worker, good com-panion at a feast, this skill of yours is worth fifty cows—I think that we soon will be peacefully reconciled. Come now, tell me, ingenious son of Maia, was this wonder-ful achievement yours from birth, or did one of the gods or mortal humans give you this noble gift and teach you inspired song? For this newly uttered sound I hear is wonderful, and I tell you that no one, either mortal or god who dwells on Olympus, has ever before known it, except you, you trickster, son of Zeus and Maia. What skill! What Muse's art! What salve for sorrow and despair! It gives the choice of three blessings together all at once: joy and love and sweet sleep. I follow the Olympian Muses who delight in dancing, the swelling beat of music, and the lovely tune of flutes, yet never have I been as thrilled at young men's feasts by such clever delights as these. I marvel, O son of Zeus, at your charming playing. Since you know such a glorious skill, even though you are little, sit down, my boy, and listen to what I intend. For you yourself and your mother will have renown among the immortal gods. And I shall vow this to you truly: By this spear of cornel wood, I shall make you a renowned and prosperous guide among the immortal gods, and I shall give you splendid gifts and to the end I shall not deceive you." (434–462)

Hermes answered him with clever words: "Archer-god, your questions are well considered; I do not begrudge your taking up my art. You will know it this very day. I want us to be friends, alike in what we think and what we say. You know all things in your heart, for you, son of Zeus, sit in the first place among the immortals, brave and strong. Zeus in his wisdom loves you as he rightly should and has granted you splen-did gifts. And they say that you have acquired from the mouth of Zeus honors and, O archer-god, from him too every kind of divine oracular power. I know then that you are very rich in these gifts and you have only to make the choice of whatever you desire to learn. So, since your heart is set on playing the lyre, sing and play and be merry; accept this gift from me; and you, my dear friend, bestow glory upon me. With this clear-voiced companion in your hands,[8] sing beautifully and well, knowing the art of proper presentation. Then with confidence take it to a luxurious feast and lovely dance and splendid revel, a thing of joy both night and day. Whoever makes demands of it after acquiring skill and knowledge is informed with sounds of every sort to delight the mind, for it is played by gentle familiarity and refuses to respond to toilsome drudgery. And whoever through lack of skill is from the first vehement in his demands is answered in return with wild and empty notes that clang upon the air. But you have only to make the choice of learning whatever you desire. To you I give this gift, splendid son of Zeus, and we both shall feed the cattle of the field on the pastures in the mountain and the plain where horses also graze. Even you, shrewd bargainer that you are, ought not to be violently angry." (463–495)

Hermes Weighing Lives. Attic red-figure stamnos attributed to Hermonax, ca. 470 B.C.; height 15 in. On one side of this vase (unseen here), Achilles and Memnon face each other on the battle-field at Troy. The mother of each stands behind her son in support: Thetis for Achilles and Eos for Memnon. On the other side (seen here), Hermes (with petasus slung on his back, caduceus and talaria) is holding the pans of the scale that will determine the fate of the two heroes. He stands between Zeus and Hera. This story was depicted in a lost tragedy by Aeschylus entitled *Psychostasia* (*Weighing of Souls*). The scene inevitably recalls two passages in the *Iliad* in which Zeus uses scales to determine the fate (*kēr* in Greek) of a group or individual (a *kerostasia* or "weighing of fates"). In *Iliad* 8.70 Zeus decides to favor the Trojans over the Greeks and so he puts the fate of each in the pans of the scale; the fate of the Greeks goes down, indicating their impending losses. Later, in 22.210, when Achilles confronts Hector, Zeus weighs the fate of the two heroes; Hector's fate sinks down, which indicates his imminent death. From the 6th century B.C. onward, scenes of such a weighing are represented in art, though Hermes is usually depicted holding the scales, perhaps because of his role generally as a god of boundaries, or more specifically as *psychopompos* (guide of souls to the Underworld). By the fifth century the practice is referred to as *psychostasia*, or "weighing of souls." (*National Gallery of Victoria, Melbourne Purchased through The Art Foundation of Victoria with the assistance of the National Bank of Australasia Limited, Governor, 1980 © Public Domain*)

With these words he held out the lyre, and Phoebus Apollo accepted it. And he entrusted to Hermes the shining whip that he had and put him in charge of cattle herds. The son of Maia accepted this with joy. The far-shooting lord Apollo, the glorious son of Leto, took the lyre in his left hand and tried it by striking successive   370
notes. It sounded in startling fashion at his touch, and the god sang a beautiful song in accompaniment. (496–502)

Afterward the two of them turned the cows out into the sacred meadow, and they, the very beautiful sons of Zeus, hastened back to snow-capped Olympus, all the while taking delight in the lyre. Zeus in his wisdom was pleased and united them both in friendship; Hermes has loved the son of Leto steadfastly, and he still does even now, as is evident from the pledges made when Hermes entrusted his lovely lyre to the archer-god and Apollo took it on his arm and learned how to play. But Hermes himself fashioned another instrument and learned another art, producing the sound of pipes that are heard from afar.[9] (503–512)   380

Then the son of Leto said to Hermes, "I fear, cunning guide, that you may steal my lyre and my curved bow; for you have from Zeus the prerogative of establishing the business of barter among people on the nourishing earth. Yet if, for my sake, you would deign to swear the great oath of the gods, either by a nod of your head or by the mighty waters of the river Styx, you would do everything that would satisfy my heart's desire." Then the son of Maia nodded and promised that he would never steal a thing from all that the far-shooter possessed and that he would never come near his mighty house. In turn Apollo, the son of Leto, nodded in loving friendship that no one else among mortals would be more dear, neither god nor mortal sprung from Zeus, and said, "I shall pledge that this bond between us will be trusted and   390
honored both in my heart and that of all the gods. Besides, I will give you in addition a very beautiful golden staff of prosperity and wealth, three-branched and protec-tive; it will keep you safe while, in the name of all the gods, you accomplish by word

and by deed the good things which I declare that I learn from the divine voice of Zeus. (513–532)

"As for this gift of prophecy which you mention, O best of Zeus' sons, it is not allowed by god that you or any other of the immortals learn what the mind of Zeus knows; but I have pledged, vowed, and sworn a mighty oath that no other one of the eternal gods (apart from me) should know the infinite wisdom of Zeus. You, my brother, with your rod of gold, do not bid me reveal any of the divine plans which far-seeing Zeus is devising. I shall hurt some and help others, as I cause great perplexity for the masses of unhappy human beings. The person will profit from my utterance who comes under the guidance of the flight and the cry of my birds of true omen. This is the one who will profit from my utterance and whom I will not deceive; but the one who trusts the birds of meaningless chatter will seek to find out my prophecies and to know more than the eternal gods, quite against my will. I declare that for this one the journey will be in vain, but I would take his gifts anyway. (533–549)

"I shall tell you another thing, son of illustrious Maia and aegis-bearing Zeus, O divine luck-bringer of the gods: indeed, certain holy sisters have been born, three virgins, glorying in their swift wings and having on their heads a sprinkling of white barley, and they live under a ridge of Mt. Parnassus;[10] set apart, they are masters of divination, an art I practiced while still a lad tending cattle and my father did not mind. Then from their home they fly from one place to another and feed from every honeycomb until it is empty. When they have eaten the yellow honey, they become inspired and willingly desire to speak the truth; but if they are deprived of the sweet food of the gods, they gather in a swarm and tell lies. These sisters I give to you; inquire of them carefully and take pleasure in your heart. If then you inform mortal persons, they will listen to what you say often, if they are fortunate. Have these things, son of Maia, and care for the horned oxen of the field, the toiling mules and the horses." (550–568)

Thus he spoke, and from heaven father Zeus himself added a final pledge to his words: he ordered that glorious Hermes be the lord of all birds of good omen, fierce-eyed lions, boars with gleaming tusks, dogs, and every flock and herd that the wide earth nourishes; and that he alone would be the ordained messenger to Hades, who, although he accepts no gifts, will grant this, by no means the least of honors. (569–573)

So lord Apollo loved the son of Maia in an all-encompassing friendship; and Zeus, the son of Cronus, bestowed on him a beguiling charm. He associates with mortals and immortals. On occasion he gives profit or help to a few, but for the most part he continually deceives human beings by the horde in the blackness of night. (574–578)

So hail to you, son of Zeus and Maia; yet I shall remember both you and another song too.

400

410

420

430

Mercury, by Giovanni Bologna (known as Giambologna, 1529–1608); bronze, 1576; height 25 in. Giambologna has taken the classical attributes of Hermes—the petasus, caduceus, and winged sandals—and combined them with the nude figure of a running man to create a masterpiece of Late Renaissance Mannerism. (© *Alinari Archives/George Tatge /Art Resource, NY*)

440

This artful hymn to Hermes has been much admired; the English poet Percy Bysshe Shelley (1792–1822) himself was one of its translators. The glib and playful treatment of both Hermes and Apollo is often labeled typically Greek.[11] It is typically Greek only if we mean by typical *one* of the many brilliant facets of Hellenic genius and a suggestion of the wide variety and scope in the conception of deity. Sincere profundity in religion and philosophy are as typically Greek as wit and facetious sophistication.

The Nature of Hermes and His Worship

Many of Hermes' characteristics and powers are evident from the poem. The Greek admiration for cleverness is readily apparent; it is this same admiration that condones the more dubious traits of the hero Odysseus. Anthropomorphism and liberalism are both pushed to their extreme in the depiction of the god Hermes as a thief and in the implication that thieves too must have their patron deity. Divine Hermes, like Prometheus, represents another (albeit extreme) example of the **archetypal trickster**. Yet in delightful, archetypal variations, the major quest of this charming young rogue is extremely dubious—a robbery— and, moreover, is accomplished when he is only a little baby!

The similarities between Hermes and Apollo are equally apparent. They share pastoral and musical characteristics, and the origins of both were probably rooted in the same pastoral society of shepherds with their interest in flocks, music, and fertility. The Sicilian shepherd **Daphnis** was the son of Hermes and a nymph and became the inventor of pastoral music and a leading character in the pastoral poetry of Theocritus. Hermes and Apollo are alike in appearance, splendid examples of vigorous and handsome masculinity. But Hermes is the younger and more boyish, the idealization and patron of youths in their late teens; his statue belonged in every gymnasium. Hermes is perhaps best known as the divine messenger, often delivering the dictates of Zeus himself; as such he wears a traveler's hat (**petasus**) and sandals (**talaria**) and carries a herald's wand (**caduceus**), which sometimes bears two snakes entwined. The entwined snakes may be a symbol for Hermes as a fertility god, connected with the Underworld. The staff of Hermes became confused with the staff of the physician Asclepius, for whom serpents represented new life, since they could slough their old skins (see p. 258). Wings may be depicted on Hermes' hat, his sandals, and even his wand. Thus he is also the god of travelers and roads. As the guide of souls (**psychopompos**) to the realm of Hades under the earth, he provides another important function, which reminds us once again of his fertility connections.

Statues of Hermes, called herms (singular, herm), were common in the ancient world and were symbols of fertility. They were intended to bring prosperity and luck. In the classical period, a herm might be found outside any house; and these herms could be taken very seriously. In appearance, they were square pillars equipped with male genitals; on top of each was the head of Hermes. These phallic statues probably marked areas regarded as sacred or designated, at least originally, the bounds of one's home or property.

Nilsson's theory about the origins of Hermes and his depiction as a herm is of interest.[12] There were various stone cults in Greece such as the one at Delphi in connection with the omphalos. It was believed that a divine power (*daimon*) resided in the stone, which was anointed and covered with sacred

The Mutilation of the Herms

Many ancient Greeks did believe in their gods. A historical incident concerning herms warns us to be wary of facile generalizations about Greek religious attitudes. In 415 B.C., on the eve of the great Athenian expedition against Sicily, the herms in the city of Athens were mutilated during the night. The religious scandal that ensued became a political football; the general Alcibiades was charged, and the consequences were serious—quite a fuss over phallic statues of a god in a period fraught with sophistic skepticism, agnosticism, and atheism. Alcibiades was also charged with the parody and desecration of the Eleusinian mysteries of Demeter in a private home; he called himself Hierophant and wore a robe like that of the high priest when he shows the holy secrets to the initiates (Plutarch, *Alcibiades* 22.3; see also Thucydides 6.27–29).

Herm with Bird. Attic red-figure pelike by the Perseus painter (left) and red-figure amphora by the Pan painter (right), both 470–460 B.C. These images illustrate the importance of Hermes and his phallic statues in the life of the ordinary citizens of Athens, as well as the disparate tonal treatment Hermes and his herms might receive: one light and irreverent, the other serious and sober. On the left, a bird has perched on the oversized phallos to kiss the statue; in front, an altar burns. On the right, a young man, standing between two herms and touching the god's beard in a traditional gesture of supplication, offers a garland and a prayer, perhaps before going on a journey. The god is the object of humble prayers for success, be it in love or business or travel. (*Left: bpk Bildagentur/Antikensammlung, Staatliche Museen, Berlin, Germany/Johannes Laurentius/Art Resource, NY*) (*Right: Musée d'Art et d'Archéologie de Laon*)

Hermes Trismegistus

Hermes came to be equated with the Egyptian god Thoth and thus began to acquire some of his attributes as a god of magic, knowledgeable in things mystic and occult. In this transformation, he was given the epithet Trismegistus, which means thrice great (an appellation denoting a superlative, "great, great, great"). Hermes Trismegistus (supposedly the grandson of Hermes the god and not the god himself) is said to have composed many books on various aspects of Egyptian religion. The extant corpus of works attributed to him is referred to as the *Hermetica* (*Discourses of Hermes*) or *Hermetic Writings*. Topics deal with philosophy, astrology, and alchemy and despite some Egyptian influence are essentially Greek in character. These texts belong to the Hellenistic period (in the fourth century B.C.) after the time of Plato, whose influence is evident.

wool (see p. 247). On the top of a grave mound, which was often composed of lesser stones, a tall stone was erected. Passersby would add their stones to the mound, making it a guiding landmark. The god Hermes, whose name means "he from the stone-heap," was believed to live in this landmark grave-mound, and so he became the guide and protector of travelers and also of souls on their way to the Underworld. Subsequently, his abode, a monumental stone on a stone heap, was regarded as his image (a herm) and given a human head. A herm never became fully anthropomorphic, and it continued to offer guidance for travelers and protection for graves, roads, and streets, and also to provide many blessings for homes.

To sum up, many of the functions of Hermes can be characterized by his role as a creator and crosser of boundaries and an intermediary between two different worlds. His herms served to mark the boundaries between one's property and that of another and what has to be bridged. As a messenger of the gods, Hermes joins the human with the divine realm of the Olympians; as psychopompos, he brings mortals across the barriers of the Underworld. As a god of young men, Hermes stands as an exemplar of the critical rite of passage between youth and adulthood. Finally, in relation to Hermes and the crossing of established boundaries, consider the story of Hermaphroditus, a figure who unites the attributes of both sexes but transgresses the limitations of gender.

Hermaphroditus and Salmacis

Among the adventures and affairs of Hermes, his union with Aphrodite is important because of their offspring, Hermaphroditus, whose story is told by Ovid (*Metamorphoses* 4.285–388):

> Let me tell you how the fountain Salmacis got its bad reputation and why it weakens and softens limbs touched by its enervating waters.[13] This power of the fountain is very well known; the reason for it lies hidden. A son was born to Mercury and Venus, and Naiads brought him up in the cave of Mt. Ida. You could recognize his mother and father in his beauty, and his name also came from them. As soon as he

reached the age of fifteen, he left the hills of his homeland. When he had departed from Ida, the mountain that had nurtured him, he took delight in wandering over unknown lands and in seeing unknown rivers; his zeal made the hardships easy. (285–295)

Then he came to the cities of the Lycians and their neighbors the Carians. There   10 he saw a pool of water that was clear to the very bottom with no marsh reeds, barren sedge, or sharp-pointed rushes to be seen. The water was transparent in its clarity, and the edge of the pool was surrounded by fresh turf and grass that was always green. (296–301)

A nymph lived here; but one who was not inclined to hunt and not in the habit of bending the bow or contending in the chase. She alone of the Naiads was unknown to swift Diana. It is told that her sisters often said to her: "Salmacis, take up a javelin or a lovely painted quiver; vary the routine of your idleness with the strenuous exercise of the hunt." She did not take up the javelin or the lovely painted quiver and did not vary the routine of her idleness with the strenuous exercise of the hunt. Instead   20 she would only bathe her beautiful limbs in her fountain and often comb out her hair with a comb of boxwood and look into the water to see what suited her best; and then she would clothe her body in a transparent garment and recline on the soft leaves or the soft grass. Often she picked flowers. (302–315)

Salmacis was picking flowers as it happened when she saw the boy Hermaphroditus. As soon as she saw him, she desired to have him. Although she was anxious to hasten to him, she did not approach until she had composed herself, arranged her garment, and assumed a beautiful countenance. When she looked as attractive as she ought, she began to speak as follows: "Lovely boy, most worthy to be believed a god; if you are a god, you could be Cupid; if a mortal, blessed   30 are your parents, and happy your brother and fortunate indeed your sister, if you have one, and the nurse who gave you her breast. But by far the most blessed of all is your betrothed, if she exists, whom you will consider worthy of marriage. If you have such a beloved, let my passion be satisfied in secret, but if you do not, let me be the one and let us go together to our marriage bed." With this the nymph was silent. (315–329)

A blush flared up in the boy's face, for he did not know what love was. But the flush of red was becoming; his was the color of apples hanging in a sunny orchard or of tinted marble or of the moon, a reddish glow suffusing its whiteness. … To the nymph, as she demanded without end at least the kisses of a sister and brought her   40 hand to touch his ivory neck, he exclaimed: "Are you going to stop, or am I to flee and leave you and your abode?" Salmacis was frightened and replied: "I give over to you free access to this place, my guest and friend." She turned her step away and pretended to depart, though still with a glance back. She concealed herself in a hidden grove of bushes, dropping on bended knees. But he moved on the deserted grass from one spot to another, confident that he was not being watched and gradually dipped his feet as far as the ankles in the playful waves. (329–343)

Taken by the feel of the captivating waters, with no delay he threw off the soft clothes from his body. Then, to be sure, Salmacis was transfixed, enflamed with desire for his naked form. Her eyes, too, were ablaze just as if the radiant orb of the   50 glowing sun were reflected in their mirror. With difficulty she endured the agony of waiting, with difficulty she held off the attainment of her joy. Now she longed to embrace him, now in her frenzy she could hardly contain herself. He swiftly struck his hollow palms against his sides and plunged into the pool, and as he moved one arm and then the other he glistened in the limpid water like an ivory statue or

Sleeping Hermaphrodite. Roman marble copy of a Greek bronze by Polycles of the mid-second century B.C.: marble mattress added by Gian-Lorenzo Bernini in 1620. Length 58 in. Hermaphrodites were popular from the fourth century onward in the Greek and (later) Roman worlds. The discovery of this one in Rome in 1608 led to fascination with the subject and the manufacture of many copies in the seventeenth and eighteenth centuries. It was presented to Cardinal Scipione Borghese, for whom Bernini made the mattress. The room in which it was displayed in his villa at Rome was later decorated with a fresco of the legend of Salmacis and Hermaphroditus. Napoleon (whose brother-in-law was a Borghese) bought the statue in 1807, and by 1811 it was on display in Paris, where it has remained. The male and female sexual attributes in the same figure have always intrigued viewers, while in the eighteenth century a cynical English tourist remarked that it was "the only happy couple that she ever saw." (*Erich Lessing/Art Resource, NY*)

a lily that one has encased within clear glass. The nymph cried out: "I have won, he is mine!" And she flung off all her clothes and threw herself into the middle of the waves. She held him as he fought and snatched kisses as he struggled; she grasped him with her hands and touched his chest and now from this side and now from that enveloped the youth. (344–360)

  Finally, she encircled him as he strove against her in his desire to escape, like a serpent which the king of birds has seized and carried aloft, and which as it hangs binds the eagle's head and feet and with its tail enfolds the spreading wings, even as ivy is wont to weave around tall trunks of trees or as the octopus grabs and holds fast its enemy in the deep with tentacles let loose on every side. Hermaphroditus,

60

the descendant of Atlas, endured and denied the nymph the joys that she had hoped for. She continued her efforts, and her whole body clung to him as though they were glued together. She cried: "You may fight, cruel villain, but you will not escape. May the gods so ordain and may we never be separated in future time, you from me or me from you." The gods accepted her prayer. (361–373)   70

For their two bodies were joined together as they entwined, and in appearance they were made one, just as when one grafts branches on a tree and sees them unite in their growth and become mature together; thus, when their limbs united in their close embrace, they were no longer two but a single form that could not be called girl or boy and appeared at the same time neither one, but both. And so, when he saw that the limpid waters into which he had gone as a man had made him half a man and in them his limbs had become enfeebled, Hermaphroditus stretched out his hands and prayed in a voice that was no longer masculine: "Father and mother, grant this gift to your son who bears both your names. Let whatever man who enters this pool come out half a man and let him suddenly become soft   80 when touched by its waves." Both parents were moved and granted the wish of their child, who was now of a double nature, and they tainted the waters with this foul power. (373–388)

Hermaphroditus

Ovid's narrative of Salmacis and Hermaphroditus has dominated the literary and artistic tradition, obscuring the factual account of the first-century B.C. author Vitruvius, who explained the weakness caused by the pool of Salmacis as an allegory for the civilizing of local tribes by Greek settlers. Ovid's source was a collection of tales from Asia Minor, one of them concerning Salmacis, a pool near Halicarnassus in Caria, beside which was a temple dedicated to Hermes and Aphrodite. The name Hermaphroditus was first used by the philosopher Theophrastus in about 320 B.C., describing how on the fourth and seventh days of the month (the fourth day was sacred to Hermes and Aphrodite) the superstitious man "spends all day putting wreaths on the Hermaphrodites." By this time Hermaphroditus was worshiped as a god embodying the union of Hermes, with his erect phallus (see p. 289), and Aphrodite, as the physical expression of female fertility. He was, then, a minor fertility god, described by the historian Diodorus Siculus in the first century B.C. as "very like Priapus" (see p. 189), but his reputation received a boost from Polycles' statue (which was said to have "made him noble"). Nevertheless, Ovid's story, with its explicit focus on emasculation and physical weakness, has concealed whatever divine authority Hermaphroditus may once have held, and at Rome hermaphrodites were considered to be ill-omened prodigies and were drowned. Bisexuality is significant in Greek mythology and philosophy, as it is in nature. In the Orphic hymns Phanes, the original creator of everything, is bisexual. In Plato's *Symposium*, Aristophanes explains how Zeus divided human beings into three sexes, with each individual seeking its other half (see pp. 205–207). These serious religious and philosophical allegories gave way to voyeuristic interest in bisexual human beings, furthered in literature by Ovid's tale and in art by such works as the sculpture on p. 292. From Ovid came countless poetic elaborations from Spenser to Swinburne, while eighty artistic representations survive from the ancient world. Essential reading for Hermaphroditus is the article (in English) by Aileen Ajootian in *Lexikon Iconographicum Mythologiae Classicae*, Vol. 1, pp. 269–285.

Statues of Hermaphroditus and hermaphrodites became common in the fourth century B.C. and in the following Hellenistic period, when Greek masters strove to vary their repertoires with fascinating and brilliantly executed studies in the realistic, erotic, and unusual.

Select Bibliography

Delcourt, Marie. *Figure in Classical Antiquity.* London: Studio Books, 1961.
Fowden, Garth. *The Egyptian Hermes: A Historical Approach to the Late Pagan Mind.* New York: Cambridge University Press, 1986.
Hermetica: The Greek Corpus Hermeticum and the Latin Asclepius. New English translation, with notes and introduction by Brian P. Copenhaver. New York: Cambridge University Press, 1992.
Hyde, Lewis. *Trickster Makes This World: Mischief, Myth, and Art.* New York: Farrar, Straus and Giroux, 1998. A comparative study of tricksters: Hermes, Coyote (North American), Eshu (West African), Loki (Norse), and others, with analogies among many artists, including Picasso, John Cage, and Allen Ginsberg.
Kerényi, Karl. *Hermes Guide of Souls: The Mythologem of the Masculine Source of Life.* Translated from German by Murray Stein. Zurich: Spring Publications, 1976.
Mead, G. R. S. *Hymns of Hermes.* Hermetic Ecstatic Hymns. York Beach, ME: Red Wheel/Weiser, 2006.

Primary Sources

Sources in the Chapter

Homeric Hymn 4	*To Hermes*
Homeric Hymn 18	*To Hermes*
Ovid	*Metamorphoses* 4.285–388

Additional Sources

Lucian	*Dialogues of the Gods: Hermes and Maia*

The following are ancient sources for the historical incidents of the mutilation of the Herms, the desecration of the Mysteries, and the charges against Alcibiades and others.

Andocides	*On the Mysteries*
Thucydides	*History of the Peloponnesian War* 6.27.1–6.29.3

Notes

1. The live tortoise was believed to be a taboo against harm and sorcery.
2. This is probably the well-known Pieria near Mt. Olympus in northern Thessaly. On his journey from Pieria, Hermes passes through Onchestus, situated between Thebes and Orchomenus, and brings the cattle to the river Alpheus, which flows near Olympia in the western Peloponnesus.
3. As he walks along, Hermes makes the cattle walk backward. Thus the hoofprints of the cattle will seem to be going toward the meadow and not out of it. Hermes' own tracks will be obscured by his sandals.

4. As we have seen, according to Hesiod (*Theogony* 387), Selene is the daughter of Hyperion and Theia; Pallas (*Theogony* 375, 377, 409) was the son of the Titan Crius; and his brother Perses was the father of Hecate. Megamedes is not found elsewhere.

5. The text is corrupt at this point; apparently, Hermes used the laurel branch to rub against a piece of wood grasped in the palm of his hand, thus creating the friction to produce fire.

6. Hermes offers a portion to each of the twelve gods. According to sacrificial ritual, he (as one of them) must not eat his portion or those of the other gods but merely savor the aroma.

7. Presumably Apollo intends to bind either Hermes or the cows.

8. The lyre is mentioned as a beloved companion, that is, a girlfriend, and in the next few lines Hermes sustains the metaphor, which reads naturally in Greek but is difficult to render in English. Thus she will accompany Apollo to the feast and the dance, and she will behave and respond as a beloved should, if only she is treated in the right way.

9. These are shepherds' pipes of reed, also called panpipes since they are often said to be the invention of the god Pan. Hermes sometimes is named as the father of Pan, whom he resembles in certain respects.

10. These are identified as the Thriae; their name means "pebbles." Thus they are the eponymous nymphs of divining pebbles, that is, pebbles used for divination. They appear to be women with wings. Probably their hair is literally powdered with white flour; some suggest that they are meant to be white-haired and old or that the image intended is that of bees covered with pollen.

11. In tone and mood, this story is not unlike that of Aphrodite, Ares, and Hephaestus in Homer (*Odyssey* 8.266–366, translated in Chapter 5, pp. 127–129).

12. See Martin P. Nilsson, *A History of Greek Religion,* translated by F. J. Fielden, 2d ed. (New York: W. W. Norton, 1952 [1964]), pp. 109–110.

13. In context, Alcithoë is telling the story to her sisters. The spring Salmacis was located at Halicarnassus.

For additional digital learning resources please go to
www.oup.com/he/morford12e

DIONYSUS, PAN, ECHO, AND NARCISSUS

Reenactment of the Marriage of Dionysus and Ariadne When Dionysus cast his eyes upon her, he danced over to her and like a lover sat upon her lap. He took her in his arms and kissed her. Ariadne behaved modestly, but nevertheless she lovingly embraced him. When the party-guests beheld this, they kept applauding and shouting for an encore. And when Dionysus got up and drew Ariadne up with him, then you could see a real performance, as they proceeded to kiss and fondle one another. The audience saw a very good-looking Dionysus and a gorgeous Ariadne not playing a role but truly kissing each other and they all watched with great excitement. … In the end the dinner guests seeing the couple embracing and moving off to their marriage bed, the unmarried ones vowed to get married, those who were already married got on their horses and rode off to visit their wives.

—XENOPHON, *Symposium* 9.4–7

The Birth, Childhood, and Origins of Dionysus

The traditional account of the birth of Dionysus (Bacchus)[1] runs as follows. Disguised as a mortal, Zeus was having an affair with **Semele**, a daughter of **Cadmus**. When Hera found out, her jealousy led her to get even. She appeared to Semele disguised as an old woman and convinced her rival that she should ask her lover to appear in the full magnificence of his divinity. Semele first persuaded Zeus to swear that he would grant whatever she might ask of him, and then she revealed her demand. Zeus was unwilling but was obliged to comply, and Semele was burned to a cinder by the splendor of his person and the fire of his lightning flash. The unborn child, being divine, was not destroyed in the conflagration; Zeus saved his son from the ashes of his mother and sewed him up in his own thigh, from which he was born again at the proper time.[2]

Various nurses are associated with the infant Dionysus, in particular certain nymphs of Nysa, a mountain of legendary fame located in various parts of the ancient world. Hermes, who had rescued Dionysus from Semele's ashes, carried the baby to the nymphs of Nysa. **Ino**, Semele's sister, is traditionally singled out as one who cared for the god when he was a baby.[3] When Dionysus reached manhood, he carried the message of his worship far and wide, bringing happiness and prosperity to those who would listen and madness and death to those who dared oppose. The tradition of his arrival in Greece stresses the belief that he is a latecomer to the Olympian pantheon and that his origins lie in Thrace and ultimately Phrygia.[4] Since the name Dionysus (clearly that of the god) appears in the Linear B tablets, his worship must have been introduced into Greece in the Bronze Age, earlier than previously conjectured by scholars, probably in the Mycenaean period and perhaps in the time of the legendary Cadmus, as Euripides assumes.

The *Bacchae* of Euripides

Dionysus is basically a god of vegetation in general, and in particular of the vine, the grape, and the making and drinking of wine. But his person and his teaching eventually embrace very much more. The best source for the profound meaning of his worship and its most universal implications is found in Euripides' *Bacchae* (*The Bacchic Women*). Whatever one makes of the playwright's depiction of the rites in a literal sense, the sublimity and terror of the spiritual message are inescapable and timeless. The *Bacchae* is essential for understanding the complex nature of Dionysus and his worship.

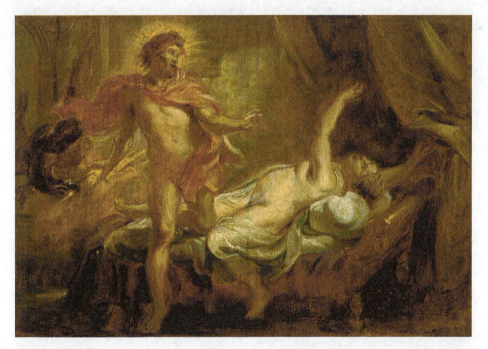

The Death of Semele, by Peter Paul Rubens (1577–1640); oil on panel, 1636, 10½ × 15½ in. Both Semele and Zeus are shown under extreme emotion—she, as death approaches, and he, rising from her couch with pity and horror, knowing her coming agony. He holds the thunderbolt back in his right hand, and his eagle grips it in its beak. (*The Picture Art Collection/Alamy Stock Photo*)

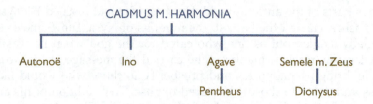

Figure 13.1 The Children of Cadmus. (A fuller genealogy for the House of Cadmus is given on p. 409)

The play opens with Dionysus himself, who has come in anger to Thebes; his mother's integrity has been questioned by her own relatives, and the magnitude and power of his very godhead have been challenged and repudiated; the sisters of Semele claim (and **Pentheus**, grandson of Cadmus and now king of Thebes, agrees) that she became pregnant because she slept with a mortal and that Cadmus was responsible for the story that Zeus was the father of her child; as a result, Zeus killed her with a blast of lightning (1–63):

The Indian Triumph of Dionysus. Roman marble sarcophagus, mid-second century A.D.; width (without lid) 92 in., height 39 in., lid, width 93 in., height 12½ in. Dionysus rides on a chariot drawn by panthers. He is preceded by satyrs, maenads, sileni, and animals, among which elephants and lions are prominent. He has come from India, bringing happiness and fertility to the Greek world. On the lid are reliefs of the death of Semele, the birth of Dionysus from the thigh of Zeus, and his nurture by the nymphs of Nysa. Hermes appears in each of the three scenes on the lid—rescuing the infant from the dying Semele in the left panel; taking him to the nymphs in the center panel after his birth from the thigh of Zeus; and pointing toward the scene of his nurture by the nymphs in the right panel. The sarcophagus is one of seven found in the tomb of the family of the Calpurnii Pisones in Rome. (*Sarcophagus with the Triumph of Dionysus, Anonymous, Roman, ca. 190, Thasian marble, 47½ × 92½ × 40 × 35¹³⁄₁₆ in [120.7 × 234.9 × 101.6 × 90.96 cm]; Photo © The Walters Museum, Baltimore*)

DIONYSUS: I, Dionysus, the son of Zeus, have come to this land of the Thebans; my mother Semele, the daughter of Cadmus, gave birth to me, delivered by a fiery blast of lightning. I am here by the stream of Dirce and the waters of the Ismenus, not as a god but in disguise as a man. I see here near the palace the shrine that commemorates my mother, who was struck dead by the lightning blast, and the ruins of her home, smoldering yet from the flame of Zeus' fire that still lives—the everlasting evidence of Hera's outrage against my mother. I am pleased with Cadmus for setting this area off as a holy sanctuary dedicated to his daughter, and I have enclosed it round about with the fresh greenery of the clustering vine. (1–12)

I left the fertile plains of gold in Lydia and Phrygia and made my   10
way across the sunny plateaus of Persia, the walled towns of Bactria, the grim land of the Medes, rich Arabia, and the entire coast of Asia Minor, where Hellenes and non-Hellenes live together in teeming cities with beautiful towers. After having led my Bacchic dance and established my mysteries in these places, I have come to this city of the Hellenes first. (13–22)

I have raised the Bacchic cry and clothed my followers in the fawnskin and put into their hands the thyrsus—my ivy-covered shaft—here in Thebes first of all Greece, because my mother's sisters claim (as least of all they should) that I, Dionysus, was not begotten of Zeus but that Semele became pregnant by some mortal man and through the clever instigations of Cadmus laid the blame on Zeus; they gloatingly proclaim that Zeus because of her deception struck her dead. (23–31)

And so these same sisters I have stung with madness, driving them from their homes, and they inhabit Mt. Cithaeron, bereft of sense; I have compelled them to take up the symbols of my rituals, and all the women of Thebes—the entire female population—I have driven from their homes in frenzy. Together with the daughters of Cadmus they sit out in the open air on rocks under the evergreens.   30
For although it does not wish to, this city must learn full well that it is still not completely schooled in my Bacchic mysteries and I must defend the reputation of my mother Semele by showing myself to mortals as the god whom she bore to Zeus. (32–42)

Cadmus has handed over the prerogatives of his royal power to his daughter's son, Pentheus, who fights against my godhead, thrusting me aside in sacrifices and never mentioning my name in prayers. Therefore I shall show myself as a god to him and all the Thebans. And when I have settled matters here, I shall move on to

The Birth of Dionysus. Attic red-figure lekythos, by the Alkimachos painter, ca. 460 B.C. The birth of Dionysus is not a very common subject on ancient vases. The artist of this vase has rendered the scene with sensitivity. It conveys the moment of the birth of this powerful god with stillness and a strangely detached curiosity on the part of Zeus and Hermes. Zeus, with a wreath on his head, long locks, and beard, sits naked upon a rock, covered with the garments he has just removed. Hermes, garbed in his traveling hat and winged sandals, stands waiting, intent upon the birth, dutifully holding his father's scepter in one hand and his caduceus in the other. Hermes will take the child to the nymphs of Nysa to be raised. Zeus attends to his own delivery, as his newborn son just begins to push his head out of his father's thigh. (*Photograph* © 2010. Museum of Fine Arts, Boston)

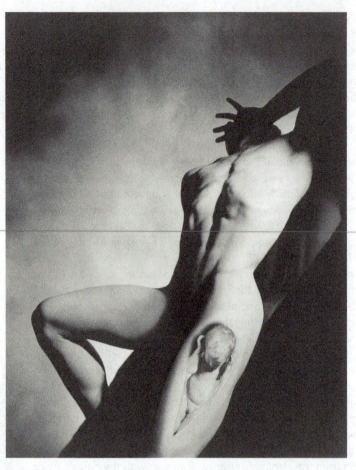

The Second Birth of Dionysus, by George Platt Lynes (1907–1955), 3 11/16 × 3 in. Photographer George Platt Lynes worked within a surrealist-inspired aesthetic and was particularly influential in the development of the homoerotic representation of the male nude. In his early travels abroad, particularly in France of the expatriate era (1920s and 1930s), he developed close friendships with a number of in-fluential artists, such as Gertrude Stein, Jean Cocteau, and Monroe Wheeler (affiliated with the Museum of Modern Art in New York). In the early 1930s, he worked as a photographer for such magazines as *Harper's Bazaar* and *Vogue*. The fame of his fashion photography soon led to work as a documentary photographer for dance companies, especially George Balanchine's American Ballet Company (now the New York City Ballet), which included the ballet *Orpheus*. From 1937 to 1940, Lynes began a series of works based on Greek myth, including Endymion, Narcissus, Danaë, and the birth of Dionysus shown here. In his last years, he began an association with noted sex researcher Alfred Kinsey. Lynes himself was afraid of the reception his homoerotic images, which included some of his most creative output, would receive and had many of them destroyed. He died in poverty and almost forgotten. Subsequent exhibi-tions of his work since his death have re-established him as a major photographer of the twentieth cen-tury. In the work shown here he displays a characteristic virtuosity in his use of light and shadow, together with an uncanny and unsettling focus on the pose of the figures. The naked figure of Zeus, here erotically charged, in contrast to his representation in the vase depicting the birth of Dionysus, is frozen in the moment of the agonizing pain, not to say horror, of the birth, which itself is represented in a disconcert-ingly and clinically realistic fashion. (*Image copyright © Estate George Platt Lynes and The Metropolitan Museum of Art. Image source: Art Resource, NY*)

another place and reveal myself. If the city of Thebes in anger tries by force to drive   40
the Bacchae down from the mountains, I shall join them in their madness as their
war commander. This then is why I have assumed a mortal form and changed myself
into the likeness of a man. (43–54)

O you women whom I have taken as companions of my journey from foreign
lands, leaving the Lydian mountain Tmolus far behind, come raise the tambourines,
invented by the great mother Rhea, and by me, and native to the land of Phrygia.
Come and surround the royal palace of Pentheus and beat out your din so that the
city of Cadmus may see. I will go to my Bacchae on the slopes of Cithaeron, where
they are, and join with them in their dances. (55–63)

The chorus of women that follows reveals the exultant spirit and mystic aura
surrounding the celebration of their god's mysteries (64–167):

CHORUS: Leaving Asia and holy Mt. Tmolus, we run in sweet pain and lovely weariness with ecstatic Bacchic cries in the wake of the roaring god Dionysus. Let everyone, indoors or out, keep their respectful distance and hold their tongue in sacred
silence as we sing the appointed hymn to Bacchus. (64–72)

Happy is the one who, blessed with the knowledge of the divine mysteries,
leads a life of ritual purity and joins the holy group of revelers, heart and soul, as they
honor their god Bacchus in the mountains with holy ceremonies of purification. He
participates in mysteries ordained by the great mother, Cybele herself, as he follows
his god, Dionysus, brandishing a thyrsus. (73–82)

Run, run, Bacchae, bringing the roaring god, Dionysus, son of a god, out of the   10
Phrygian mountains to the spacious streets of Hellas. (83–87)

Once when his mother carried him in her womb, the lightning bolt flew from the
hand of Zeus and she brought the child forth prematurely with the pains of a labor
forced on her too soon, and she gave up her life in the fiery blast. Immediately Zeus,
the son of Cronus, took up the child and enclosed him in the secret recess of his
thigh with fastenings of gold, and hid him from Hera thus in a second womb. When
the Fates had so decreed, Zeus bore the bull-horned god and wreathed his head
with a crown of serpents, and so the Maenads hunt and catch wild snakes and twine
them in their hair. (88–104)

O Thebes, crown yourself with ivy, burst forth luxuriant in verdant leaves and   20
lovely berries; join the Bacchic frenzy with branches torn from trees of oak or fir and
consecrate your cloak of dappled fawnskin with white tufts of purest wool. Be reverent with the violent powers of the thyrsus. Straightway the whole land will dance
its way (whoever leads the sacred group represents the roaring god himself) to
the mountain, to the mountain where the crowd of women waits, driven from their
labors at the loom by the maddening sting of Dionysus. (105–119)

O secret chamber on Crete, holy cavern where Zeus was born, attended by the
Curetes![5] Here the Corybantes with their three-crested helmets invented for us this
drum of hide stretched tight and their ecstatic revels mingled its tense beat with
the sweet alluring breath of the Phrygian flutes, and they put it into the hand of   30
mother Rhea, so that she might beat an accompaniment to the cries of her Bacchic
women. The satyrs in their frenzy took up the drum from the mother-goddess and
added it to the music of their dances during the festivities in which Dionysus delights. (120–134)

How sweet it is in the mountains when, out of the rushing throng, the priest of the
roaring god falls to the ground in his quest for blood and with a joyful cry devours

the raw flesh of the slaughtered goat. The plain flows with milk and wine and the nectar of bees; but the Bacchic celebrant runs on, brandishing his pine torch, and the flame streams behind with smoke as sweet as Syrian frankincense. He urges on the wandering band with shouts and renews their frenzied dancing, as his delicate 40 locks toss in the breeze. (135–150)

Amid the frantic shouts is heard his thunderous cry: "Run, run, Bacchae, you the pride of Tmolus with its streams of gold. Celebrate the god Dionysus on your thundering drums, honoring this deity of joy with Phrygian cries and shouts of ecstasy, while the melodious and holy flute sounds its sacred accompaniment as you throng, to the mountain, to the mountain." (151–165)

Every Bacchanal runs and leaps in joy, just like a foal that frisks beside her mother in the pasture.

The scene that follows (170–313) is fraught with tragic humor and bitter irony. Cadmus (retired king) and Tiresias (priest of the traditional religion) welcome

Dionysus and Maenads. Attic red-figure amphora, by the Kleophrades painter, ca. 490 B.C.; height 56 cm. Dionysus, bearded and with long hair in ringlets down his neck, is moving to the right, though his head is turned to the left, perhaps to indicate an inebriated state. He holds a kantharos (wine cup) in his right hand and a vine branch in his left. He is wearing a dappled animal skin around his shoulders and a garland of ivy on his head. On either side of Dionysus, maenads are being assailed by satyrs. Each of the maenads is mimicking the posture of Dionysus, moving in one direction toward the god while facing the other. Both maenads carry the thyrsus, and the maenad on the left is also holding a serpent. On the neck, three athletes are seen with discus and spear. (*Staaliche Antikensammlungen und Glyptothek München. Photograph by Renate Kühling*)

the new god with motives that are startling in their blatant pragmatism. Each of them sees personal advantage in accepting the rites of the new god. In their joyous rejuvenation, these two old men, experienced realists, present just the right foil for the introduction of the doomed Pentheus, who, in his mortal blindness, dares to challenge the god, his cousin, Dionysus.

TIRESIAS: Who attends at the gate? Summon Cadmus from the house, the son of Agenor, who came from Sidonia and fortified the city of the Thebans. Let someone go and announce that Tiresias wants to see him. He already knows for what reason I have come. I made an agreement with him, even though I am old and he is even older, to make myself a thyrsus, wear a fawnskin, and crown my head with shoots of ivy. (170–177)

CADMUS: My dearest friend, I knew your voice from inside the palace, and recognized the wise words of a wise man. I have come ready with the paraphernalia of the god. For since Dionysus, who has revealed himself to mortals as a god, is the son of my daughter, I must do everything in my power to magnify his greatness. Where 10 should we go to join the others in the dance, shaking our gray heads in ecstasy? Tell me, an old man, Tiresias, for you are old too and wise. I shall never grow tired by night or by day as I strike the ground with my thyrsus. It will be a sweet pleasure to forget that we are old. (178–188)

TIRESIAS: You experience the same sensations as I do, for I feel young again and I shall attempt the dance.

CADMUS: Shall we not proceed to the mountain by chariot?

TIRESIAS: No, the god would not have as appropriate an honor.

CADMUS: I will lead the way for you, two old men together.

TIRESIAS: The god will lead the two of us there without any difficulty.   20

CADMUS: Are we to be the only men of the city to dance in honor of Bacchus? (195)

TIRESIAS: We are the only ones who think the way one should; the others are wrong and perverse.

CADMUS: We delay too long; give me your hand.

TIRESIAS: Here it is, take hold and join our hands together.

CADMUS: Being a mere mortal, I am not scornful of the gods.

TIRESIAS: About the gods we have no new wise speculations. The ancestral beliefs that we hold are as old as time, and they cannot be destroyed by any argument or clever subtlety invented by profound minds. How could I help being ashamed, 30 one will ask, as I am about to join in the dance, at my age, with an ivy wreath on my head? The god does not discriminate whether young or old must dance in his honor, but he desires to be esteemed by all alike and wishes his glory to be magnified, making no distinctions whatsoever. (200–209)

CADMUS: Since you are blind, Tiresias, I shall be a prophet for you, and tell you what I see. Pentheus, the son of Echion, to whom I have given my royal power in Thebes, comes in haste to this palace. How excited he is; what news has he to tell us? (210–214)

PENTHEUS: Although I happened to have been away from Thebes, I have heard of the new evils that beset the city; the women have abandoned our homes on the 40 pretense of Bacchic rites and gad about on the dark mountainside honoring by their dances the new god, Dionysus, whoever he is. Bowls full of wine stand in the midst of each group, and they sneak away one by one to solitary places where they satisfy the lust of males. Their pretext is that they are Maenad priestesses, but they put

Aphrodite ahead of Bacchus. All those I have caught are kept safe with their hands tied by guards in the state prison. The others, who still roam on the mountain, I shall hunt out, including my own mother, Agave, and her sisters, Ino and Autonoë, the mother of Actaeon. And when I have bound them fast in iron chains, I shall soon put an end to this evil Bacchism. (215–232)

They say too that a stranger has come here from Lydia, some wizard and sorcerer, with scented hair and golden curls, who has the wine-dark charms of Aphrodite in his eyes. He spends both night and day in the company of young girls, enticing them with his Bacchic mysteries. If I catch him here in my palace, I'll cut off his head and put a stop to his thyrsus-pounding and head-tossing. That fellow is the one who claims that Dionysus is a god, who was once sewn up in the thigh of Zeus, when he was in fact destroyed by the fiery blast of lightning along with his mother, because she lied and said that Zeus had been her husband. Whoever this stranger may be, does he not deserve to hang for such hubris? (233–247)

But here is another miracle—I see the prophet Tiresias in a dappled fawnskin, and my mother's father, a very funny sight, playing the Bacchant with a wand of fennel reed. I refuse, sir, to stand by and see you behave so senselessly in your old age. You are my grandfather; won't you toss away your garland of ivy and rid your hand of the thyrsus? (248–254)

You persuaded him, Tiresias. Why? By introducing this new divinity among people do you hope that he will afford you an additional source of income from your omens and your sacrifices? If it were not for your gray hairs, you would not escape being bound and imprisoned along with the Bacchae for initiating evil rites. As far as women are concerned, I maintain that whenever the gleam of wine is in their feasts, there can be nothing further that is wholesome in their ceremonies. (255–262)

CHORUS: What sacrilege, sir! Do you not have respect for the gods and Cadmus, who sowed the seeds from which the earthborn men arose; are you, the son of Echion, who was one of them, bringing shame on your own family? (262–265)

TIRESIAS: Whenever a wise man takes a good theme for his argument, it is no great task to speak well. You seem to be a man of intelligence from the glibness of your tongue, but there is no good sense in your words. A headstrong man who is powerful and eloquent proves to be a bad citizen because he is wanting in intelligence. This new divinity whom you laugh at—I could not begin to tell you how great he will become throughout Hellas. …6 (266–274)

Pentheus, believe me; do not be overly confident that force is all-powerful in human affairs, and do not think that you are wise when the attitude that you hold is sick. Receive the god into the city, pour him libations, crown your head, and celebrate his worship. (309–313)

Tiresias goes on to argue that self-control is a question of one's own nature and character. Dionysus is not immoral; he cannot corrupt a chaste woman or restrain a promiscuous one. Besides, the god (just like Pentheus himself) is happy to receive the homage of his people.

Cadmus reinforces Tiresias' appeal for reason and control. Pentheus must be sick to defy the god; and even if he were right and Dionysus were an impostor, he should be willing to compromise and lie in order to save the honor of Semele and the whole family. But Pentheus is young and adamant; he accuses his peers of folly and madness and directs one of his henchmen to smash Tiresias' place of augury (after all, has he not himself desecrated his own priestly office?) and to hunt down the effeminate foreigner who has corrupted the women of Thebes.

A guard brings in the exotic stranger who has come with his new religion (in reality, he is Dionysus himself), and Euripides presents the first of three interviews between the god and the man which turn upon the ironic reversal of their positions. Pentheus, believing himself triumphant, is gradually but inevitably caught in the net prepared for him by Dionysus. The calm and sure strength of the god plays beautifully upon the neurotic impulsiveness of the mortal (434–518):

GUARD: Pentheus, here we are, having hunted the quarry you sent us after, and our efforts have not been unsuccessful. But we found this wild beast tame—he did not attempt to flee but gave me his hands willingly; he did not even turn pale but kept the flush of wine in his cheeks. With a smile he bade me tie him up and lead him away and waited for me, thus making my task easy. I was taken aback and said: "O stranger, I do not arrest you of my own free will but at the orders of Pentheus who has sent me." (434–442)

About the Bacchae whom you seized and bound and imprisoned—they are freed and have gone and dance about the glens calling on their god, Bacchus. The bonds fell from their feet of their own accord, and the locks on the door gave way 10 untouched by mortal hands. This man who has come to our city of Thebes is full of many miraculous wonders—and what else will happen is your concern, not mine. (443–450)

PENTHEUS: Untie his hands. Now that he is in my trap, he is not nimble enough to escape me. Well, stranger, you are not unattractive physically—at least to women— and, after all, your purpose in Thebes is to lure them. Your flowing locks that ripple down your cheeks so seductively prove that you are no wrestler. Your fair complexion too is cultivated by avoiding the rays of the sun and by keeping in the shade so that you may ensnare Aphrodite with your beauty. But first tell me where you come from. (451–460)   20

DIONYSUS: I can answer your question easily and simply. I am sure you have heard of the mountain of Tmolus with its flowers.

PENTHEUS: I have; its range encircles the city of Sardis.

DIONYSUS: I am from there; Lydia is my fatherland.

PENTHEUS: How is it that you bring these mysteries of yours to Hellas? (465)

DIONYSUS: Dionysus, the son of Zeus, has directed me.

PENTHEUS: Is there a Zeus in Lydia who begets new gods?

DIONYSUS: No, he is the same Zeus who wedded Semele here in Thebes.

PENTHEUS: Did he bend you to his service, an apparition in the night, or did you really see him with your own eyes?   30

DIONYSUS: We saw each other face to face, and he gave me his secrets. (470)

PENTHEUS: What is the nature of these secrets of yours?

DIONYSUS: It is not lawful for the uninitiated to know them.

PENTHEUS: What advantage is there for those who do participate?

DIONYSUS: It is not right for you to learn this, but the knowledge is worth much.

PENTHEUS: Your answer is clever, designed to make me want to hear more. (475)

DIONYSUS: An impious man is abhorred by the god and his mysteries.

PENTHEUS: You say that you saw the god clearly; well then, what did he look like?

DIONYSUS: He looked as he wished; I had no control over his appearance. 40

PENTHEUS: Once again you have sidetracked me cleverly with an answer that says nothing.

DIONYSUS: The words of the wise seem foolish to the ignorant. (480)

PENTHEUS: Have you come here first of all to introduce your god?

DIONYSUS: Every foreigner already dances his rituals.

PENTHEUS: Yes, of course, for they are far inferior to Hellenes.

DIONYSUS: Customs differ, but in these rituals the foreigners are superior.

PENTHEUS: Do you perform your holy rites by night or by day? (485)

DIONYSUS: By night for the most part; darkness adds to the solemnity.

PENTHEUS: For women it is treacherous and corrupt. 50

DIONYSUS: One may find, if one looks for it, shameful behavior by daylight too.

PENTHEUS: You must be punished for your evil sophistries.

DIONYSUS: And you for your ignorance and blasphemy against the god. (490)

PENTHEUS: How bold our Bacchant is and how facile his retorts.

DIONYSUS: What punishment must I suffer? What terrible thing will you do to me?

PENTHEUS: First I shall cut your pretty locks.

DIONYSUS: My hair is sacred; it belongs to the god.

PENTHEUS: Hand over your thyrsus then. (495)

DIONYSUS: Take it away from me yourself. I carry it for Dionysus; it really belongs to him. 60

PENTHEUS: I shall close you up in a prison.

DIONYSUS: The god himself will free me, whenever I wish.

PENTHEUS: As you call on him when you take your stand amid your Bacchic women, I suppose.

DIONYSUS: Even now he is near at hand and sees what I endure. (500)

PENTHEUS: Where is he? My eyes cannot see him.

DIONYSUS: Here with me. But you in your blasphemy cannot perceive him for yourself.

PENTHEUS: Guards, seize him; he is making a fool of me and of all Thebes.

DIONYSUS: I tell you not to bind me—I am the sane one, not you. 70

PENTHEUS: My orders are to bind you, and I have the upper hand. (505)

DIONYSUS: You do not know what life you live, what you do, or who you are.

PENTHEUS: I am Pentheus, the son of Agave; my father is Echion.

DIONYSUS: Your name, Pentheus, which means sorrow, is appropriate for the doom that will be yours.

PENTHEUS: Get out of here—Guards, imprison him in the neighboring stables where he may find his secret darkness—do your mystic dances there. And the women you have brought with you as accomplices in your evil I shall either keep as slaves myself to work the loom or sell them to others—this will stop their hands from beating out their din on tambourines. (509–514) 80

DIONYSUS: I will go, since what is not destined to be, I am not destined to suffer. But Dionysus, who you say does not exist, will exact vengeance for your insolence. For as you do me wrong and imprison me, you do the same to him. (515–518)

Pentheus confidently follows Dionysus into the prison. But the god miraculously frees himself amid fire, earthquake, and the destruction of the entire palace. He explains to the Chorus how he has escaped from Pentheus' evil clutches, maintaining throughout the fiction of his role as the god's disciple. Quite typically Dionysus is associated with or transformed into an animal (616–636):

> DIONYSUS: I have made a fool of Pentheus—he thought that he was tying me up, yet he did not so much as lay a finger on me but fed on empty hopes. In the chamber where he led me a prisoner, he found a bull. It was the knees and hoofs of this animal that he tried to bind, fuming and raging, biting his lips, and dripping with sweat, while I sat calmly close by his side and watched. In this crisis Bacchus arrived and made the building shake and raised a flame up from the tomb of his mother. When Pentheus saw it, he thought that the palace was on fire and rushed this way and that, calling on the servants to bring water. The entire household joined in the work, but their toil was for nothing. Pentheus, thinking that I had got away, abandoned his efforts and seized a dark sword and rushed inside the palace in pursuit.   10 (616–628)
>
> Then Dionysus created an illusion in the courtyard (I am telling you what I believe happened), and Pentheus made a dash for it, jabbing and stabbing at the sunny air, imagining he was butchering me. Bacchus had even greater humiliation for him than this. He razed the whole palace to the ground; all lies shattered for him as he beholds the most bitter results of my imprisonment. Worn out and exhausted, he has dropped his sword; a mere mortal, he dared to go to battle against a god. (629–636)

As Dionysus coolly finishes his account, Pentheus appears, bewildered, angry, and, despite his experience, still relentlessly aggressive. A brief exchange between the two is interrupted by the arrival of a messenger, who reports what he and others have seen of the Bacchic women and their worship in the mountains; at first a calm, peaceful scene full of miracles, then madness and bloodshed when the interlopers are detected—a grim foreshadowing of what is in store for Pentheus (677–774):

> MESSENGER: I had just reached the hill country with my pasturing herds by the time that the sun had risen and was warming the earth with its rays. And I saw the women, who had arranged themselves in three groups; Autonoë led one, your mother, Agave, the second, and Ino, the third. All were stretched out asleep, some reclined on beds of fir, others rested their heads on oak leaves, having flung themselves down at random but with modesty; and they were not, as you said they would be, intoxicated with wine and the music of the flute, bent on satisfying their lust in solitary places. (677–688)
>
> When your mother heard the sounds of our horned cattle, she stood up in the midst of the Bacchae, and cried out to rouse them from their sleep, and they threw   10 off the heavy slumber from their eyes and jumped up—amazing in their orderliness, young and old (many still unwed). The first thing they did was to loosen their hair to their shoulders and tie up their fawnskins if any of the fastenings had come loose; and they made a belt for the dappled fur with snakes that licked their cheeks. Some held in their arms the young of the wild, a gazelle or wolf cubs, and those who had left their newborn babes at home gave them white milk from breasts that were still full. (689–702)

And they put on crowns of ivy, oak, and flowering vine. One took her thyrsus and struck it against a rock, and from it a gush of dewy water welled up; another hit the solid earth with her wand, and from the spot the god sent forth a spring of wine. Those who thirsted for milk scraped the earth with their fingertips and produced white streams; and from each thyrsus, wreathed in ivy, dripped sweet drops of honey. And so, if you had been there to see these things, you would have invoked with prayers the god whom you now blame. (702–713)

We herdsmen and shepherds gathered together to discuss and argue about the strange and wondrous actions. One of the group, who always goes into town and has a way with words, spoke to us all: "You who inhabit the sacred mountain heights, how would you like to hunt down Agave, the mother of Pentheus, in her revels and do the king a favor?" What he said seemed good to us, so we hid ourselves in a leafy thicket and waited in ambush. At the appointed time they began their Bacchic revels, shaking their thyrsus and calling on the god, the son of Zeus, with one voice "Iacchus, Bromius!" The whole mountain and animals joined in their ecstasy and there was nothing that remained unmoved by the dance. (714–727)

It happened that Agave, as she leaped and ran, came close to me, and I leaped out of the ambush where I had hidden myself, bent on seizing her. But she cried

Dionysus, Maenads, and Satyrs. Attic black-figure kylix by Nikosthenes, ca. 520 B.C. Dionysus sits on a square chair on the right, holding a rhyton (a drinking horn with a hole in the narrow end through which the wine flowed) in his right hand, with a stylized crown or garland on his head. Around the kylix are dancing ithyphallic satyrs and maenads. Note the double "flute" (a reed instrument) played by the satyr to the left of Dionysus and the wine jug in the left hand of the maenad to the right of Dionysus. The scene is decorated with trailing vine leaves and clusters of grapes: in the center is a running winged Gorgon. (©RMN (Musée du Louvre)/Hervé Lewandowski)

aloud: "O my swift-running hounds, we are being hunted by these men; so follow me, follow, armed with your thyrsus in your hands." (728–733)

And so we fled and escaped being torn into pieces by the Bacchae, but with their bare hands they attacked our cattle grazing on the grass. You could see one of them wrenching apart a bellowing cow, its udders full. Others ripped apart the 40 calves, and you could see ribs and cloven hoofs being scattered high and low, and from the pines the pieces hung dripping with blood. Bulls, arrogant before as they raged with their horns, were laid low, dragged bodily to the ground by the countless hands of girls; and their flesh was stripped from their bodies more quickly than you, O king, could wink your eyes. (734–747)

Like birds propelled aloft by the speed of their course, the Bacchae ranged across the stretch of plain along the stream of the Asopus, which affords the Thebans a rich harvest. Like a hostile army they descended upon the villages of Hysiae and Erythrae, nestled low on the slopes of Cithaeron, and devastated them. They snatched children from their homes, and all the booty (including bronze and 50 iron) that they carried off on their shoulders did not fall onto the dark earth, although it was not fastened. They bore fire on their hair and it did not burn. The villagers, enraged by the plundering of the Bacchae, rushed to arms. (748–759)

Then, my king, there was a terrifying sight to behold. The weapons that the villagers threw did not draw any blood, but when the Bacchae hurled the thyrsus from their hands they inflicted wounds on many. Women routed men—a feat not to be accomplished without the power of some god. Back they came to where they sallied forth, to the very streams which the god made gush for them. They washed their hands of blood, and snakes licked the stains from their cheeks. (760–768)   60

And so, my lord, receive into the city this god, whoever he is. He is great in many respects but especially in his reputed gift to mortals, about which I have heard, the grape, our remedy for pain and sorrow. With no more wine, there could be no more love and no other pleasure for humankind besides. (769–774)

Pentheus refuses to listen to the pleas of the messenger. He is determined to make an armed assault on the Bacchae. But the stranger, Dionysus, finds a way to restrain him by appealing to Pentheus' basic nature and psychology—in general, the complex neurosis that stems from his repressions; in particular, his prurient preoccupation with sex and his desire to see the orgies that he insists are taking place (811–861):

DIONYSUS: Would you like to see the women banded together in the mountains? (811)
PENTHEUS: Yes, indeed. I would give a ton of gold for that.
DIONYSUS: Why are you driven by such a great desire to see them?
PENTHEUS: Actually, it would pain me to see them drunk.
DIONYSUS: Nevertheless, you would be pleased to see what is painful to you? (815)
PENTHEUS: To be sure, if I watched in silence crouched beneath the firs.
DIONYSUS: But they will track you down, even if you go in secret.
PENTHEUS: Then I shall go openly; what you say is right.   10
DIONYSUS: You will undergo the journey then? Let me lead you.
PENTHEUS: Come, as quickly as possible; I begrudge you this delay. (820)
DIONYSUS: Then dress up in a fine linen robe.
PENTHEUS: What is this? Am I to change from a man to a woman?

DIONYSUS: If you are seen there as a man, they will kill you.
PENTHEUS: Again, what you say is right. You are like some sage of long ago.
DIONYSUS: Dionysus gives me this inspiration. (825)
PENTHEUS: How may what you advise best be accomplished?
DIONYSUS: I will go inside and dress you up there.
PENTHEUS: In the garb of a woman? But shame holds me back!   20
DIONYSUS: You are no longer interested in watching the Maenads?
PENTHEUS: What dress did you say that you would put on me? (830)
DIONYSUS: I shall set on your head a long flowing wig.
PENTHEUS: And what is the next feature of my outfit?
DIONYSUS: A robe that falls to your feet and a band around your head.
PENTHEUS: What else will you give me?
DIONYSUS: A thyrsus in your hand and a dappled fawnskin cloak. (835)
PENTHEUS: I cannot bring myself to put on the costume of a woman.
DIONYSUS: But if you attack the Bacchae in battle, you will shed blood.
PENTHEUS: This is true; I must first go as a spy.   30
DIONYSUS: To be sure, it is wiser than to hunt out evil by evil.
PENTHEUS: How shall I get out of the city without being seen? (840)
DIONYSUS: We shall take a deserted route, and I shall lead the way.
PENTHEUS: Anything, rather than have the Bacchae laugh at me. I shall go into
the house and make preparations that are for the best.
DIONYSUS: So be it, and I am at your side ready for everything.
PENTHEUS: I am going inside; I shall either proceed with arms or follow your in-
structions. (845–846)
DIONYSUS: Women, this man is ready to be caught in the net. He will go to the
Bacchae, and he will pay the penalty with his life. Dionysus, now do your work; for   40
you are not far away. We shall exact our retribution. First we shall inflict upon him
delirious madness and drive him out of his wits; in his right mind, he would not want
to dress up in the costume of a woman; but once driven from reason he will put it
on. My desire is to make him the laughingstock of the Thebans as they see him led
in a woman's garb through the city in return for the terrible threats that he uttered
before. I go now to deck out Pentheus in the dress with which he will go down to
the realm of Hades, slaughtered by the hands of his mother. He will know Dionysus
as the son of Zeus and a deity of his own right, among humankind most dread and
most gentle. (847–861)

The dressing of Pentheus in the garb of the Bacchae suggests the ceremonial decking out of the sacrificial victim. By the ritual of donning his costume,
Pentheus falls under the spell and the power of the god, eventually to be offered
up to him. The Chorus sings of the joys of their worship and the justice of their
triumph over impiety; and at the end of their song, Dionysus exerts final and
complete mastery over Pentheus, who is delirious (912–970):

DIONYSUS: Pentheus, I call on you, the one who desires to see what he should
not see and hastens upon what he should not do. Come forward out of the house,
let me behold you dressed in the garb of a woman, a Bacchic Maenad, about to go
as a spy on your mother and her group. (912–917)
PENTHEUS: I think that I see two suns, and the image of Thebes with its seven
gates appears double. You look like a bull as you lead me forward, with horns growing out of your head. Were you then an animal? Now, indeed, you have become a
bull. (918–922)

DIONYSUS: The god walks with us; he is on our side, although he was not kindly
disposed before. Now you see what you should see.   10
PENTHEUS: Tell me how I look. Do I not have the bearing of Ino or my mother, Agave?
DIONYSUS: Looking at you, I seem to see those very two. But this lock here that I
had fixed under your hairband has fallen out of place. (927–929)
PENTHEUS: I shook it loose indoors while I was tossing my head back and forth
like a Bacchic reveler.
DIONYSUS: Well we, whose concern is to serve you, shall put it back in place.
Bend your head. (932–933)
PENTHEUS: Fine, you deck me out properly, for I am now dedicated to you.
DIONYSUS: Your belt is loose and the folds of your dress do not hang straight to
your ankles.   20
PENTHEUS: They are not straight at the right foot, but here on the left the dress
hangs well at the heel. (937–938)
DIONYSUS: You will, I am sure, consider me the best of your friends, when con-
trary to your expectation you witness the temperance of the Bacchae.
PENTHEUS: Shall I be more like one of the Bacchae if I hold my thyrsus in my right
or my left hand? (941–942)
DIONYSUS: You should hold it in your right hand, and raise it and your right foot
at the same time.
PENTHEUS: Will I be able to lift up on my shoulders Mt. Cithaeron with its glens   30
full of Bacchae? (945–946)
DIONYSUS: You will, if you wish; before your mind was not sound, but now it is
as it ought to be.
PENTHEUS: Let us take crowbars, or shall I thrust my shoulder or my arm under the
peaks and crush them with my hands?
DIONYSUS: Do not destroy the haunts of the nymphs and the places where Pan
does his piping. (951–952)
PENTHEUS: Your words are right; women must not be overcome by force; I will
hide myself among the firs.
DIONYSUS: You will find the hiding place that you should, coming upon the
Maenads as a crafty spy. (955–956)   40
PENTHEUS: Indeed, I can see them now in the bushes like birds held fast in the
enticing coils of love.
DIONYSUS: Yes, of course, you go on a mission to guard against this very thing.
Maybe you will catch them, if you yourself are not caught first.
PENTHEUS: Take me through the middle of Thebes, for I am the only man among
them who dares this deed. (961–962)

DIONYSUS: You alone bear the burden of toil for this city—you alone. And so the
struggle which must be awaits you. Follow me; I shall lead you there in safety, but
another will lead you back.
PENTHEUS: My mother. (966)   50
DIONYSUS: A spectacle for all.
PENTHEUS: It is for this I am going.
DIONYSUS: You will be carried home.
PENTHEUS: What luxury you are suggesting.
DIONYSUS: In the hands of your mother. (969)
PENTHEUS: You insist upon pampering me.
DIONYSUS: Pampering of sorts.
PENTHEUS: Worthy of such rewards, I follow you. (970)

Pentheus imagines he will return in a splendid carriage, with his mother by his side. This terrifying scene is built on more than this one irony and is laden with a multiplicity of ambiguities. Pentheus the transvestite imagines, like a child, loving care at the hands of his mother. How bitter now appear the earlier taunts of Pentheus against Cadmus and Tiresias! In his delirium, does Pentheus really see the god in his true and basic character—a beast? Or does his vision spring from his own warped interpretation of the bestial nature of the worship?

Ambiguity, very much a part of the Dionysian experience, runs throughout the play. In the description of the Bacchae we hear two stories, one of serenity and tranquility on the mountains, where man and nature are in harmony, another of unnatural acts and violent and bloody sacrifice. Dionysus himself is both gentle and terrifying, powerless and potent, a giver of joy and pain. Pentheus' vision is confused, when he sees within the same person a bull and the smiling figure of a man. In the end, Pentheus becomes the hunter and the hunted, an adversary of the god and a devotee, concerned with the proper dress and carriage of a bacchant. He who wanted to see will be seen. He who wanted to battle a god will be possessed by him and become his sacrificial victim.

A messenger arrives to tell of Pentheus' horrifying death (1043–1152):

> MESSENGER: When we had left the town of Thebes behind and crossed the stream of the Asopus, we made our way up the slopes of Cithaeron, Pentheus and I (for I followed with my master) and the stranger who led us to the scene. (1043–1047)
>
> First we took a position in a grassy glen, with silent footsteps and not a word, so that we might see and not be seen. It was a valley surrounded by cliffs, watered by streams, and shaded by pines; here Maenads sat, their hands occupied in their joyous tasks. Some were restoring a crown of ivy on a thyrsus that had lost its foliage; others, happy as fillies let loose from their painted yokes, were singing Bacchic hymns in answering refrains. (1048–1057)   10
>
> But poor Pentheus, who could not see this crowd of women, said: "My friend, from where I stand I am too far away to see these counterfeit Maenads clearly, but if I climbed up a towering pine on the hillside, I could properly behold the orgies of the Maenads." Then and there I saw the stranger do wondrous things. He took hold of the very top branch of a pine that reached up to the sky and pulled it down, down, down to the black earth. And it was bent like a bow or the curving line of the circle of a wheel. Thus the stranger grabbed the mountain pine with his hands and bent it to the ground, a feat no mortal could accomplish. (1058–1069)
>
> He sat Pentheus on the topmost branches and let the tree go, sliding it through   20 his hands until it was upright again, slowly and carefully so that he might not dislodge him. It towered straight to towering heaven, with our king perched on top. He could be seen more clearly by the Maenads than he could see them. He was just becoming visible, seated aloft, when the stranger was no longer to be seen, and from heaven a voice (I imagine that of Dionysus) cried aloud: "O women, I bring the man who made a mockery of you and me and our mysteries; now take vengeance on him." (1070–1081)
>
> As the voice spoke these words, a blaze of holy fire flashed between heaven and earth. The air grew still, every leaf in the wooded glen stood silent, and no sound of a beast was to be heard. The women had not made out the voice clearly, and they   30 stood up straight and looked around. He called again, and when the daughters of Cadmus understood the clear command of Bacchus, they rushed forth as swift as doves in their relentless course, his mother, Agave, her sisters, and all the Bacchae.

With a madness inspired by the breath of the god, they darted over the glen with its streams and rocks. When they saw the king seated in the pine tree, they first climbed on the rock cliff that towered opposite and hurled stones at him with all their might and pelted him with branches of pines. Others hurled the thyrsus through the air at Pentheus, a pitiable target. (1082–1100)

But they were unsuccessful, for the poor wretch sat trapped and helpless, too 40 high for even their fanaticism. Finally, with a lightning force they ripped off oak branches and tried to use them as levers to uproot the tree. But when these efforts too were all in vain, Agave exclaimed: "Come, O Maenads, stand around the tree in a circle and grab hold of it, so that we may catch the climbing beast and prevent him from revealing the secret revels of the god." And they applied a thousand hands and tore up the tree out of the earth. And from his lofty seat, Pentheus fell hurtling to the ground with endless cries; for he knew what evil fate was near. (1100–1113)

His mother as priestess was the first to begin the slaughter. She fell on him, and he ripped off the band from his hair so that poor Agave might recognize him and not 50 kill him, and he cried out as he touched her cheek: "Mother, it is your son, Pentheus, whom you bore in the home of Echion. Have pity on me for my sins and do not kill me, your son." (1114–1121)

But Agave was not in her right senses; her mouth foamed, and her eyes rolled madly as the god Bacchus held her in his power. And Pentheus could not reach her.

Pentheus. Attic red-figure kylix by Douris, ca. 480 B.C. This drinking cup graphically depicts the dismemberment of Pentheus. The maenads on either side of Pentheus, wearing spotted animal skins, are wrenching his body apart. The maenad at which Pentheus seems to be gazing pleadingly has been identified as Agave. Others have been identified as Autonoë and Ino. The maenad at the far left is holding one of his limbs. At the right, a satyr, with arms raised in excitement, is observing the sparagmos (the sacrificial rending of the victim). On the opposite side of the vase, between two maenads holding parts of Pentheus' body and unnervingly staring directly out at the viewer, sits Dionysus, enjoying his wine to the music of another satyr playing a double flute. On the tondo (within the center of the cup) is a swaying maenad holding a live leopard in one hand and a thrysos in the other. (*Kimbell Art Museum, Fort Worth, Texas/Art Resource, NY*)

> She seized his left arm below the elbow and placing her foot against the ribs of her ill-fated son, wrenched his arm out of his shoulder. It was not done through her own strength, but the god made it easy for her hands. From the other side, Ino clawed and tore at his flesh, and Autonoë and the whole pack converged on him. All shouted together, he moaning with what breath remained, they scream- 60
> ing in triumph. One carried an arm, another a foot with the boot still on; his ribs were stripped clean, and they all with blood-drenched hands tossed the flesh of Pentheus among them like a ball. His body lies scattered, some pieces under hard rocks, others in the shady depths of the woods—not easy to find. (1122–1139)
>
> His mother has taken his poor head and affixed it on the point of her thyrsus; she carries it like that of a mountain lion through the depths of Cithaeron, leaving her sisters and their Maenad bands. She comes within these walls, exulting in her ill-fated prey and calling on Bacchus, her partner in the hunt, her comrade in the chase, her champion of victory, who gave her tears as her reward. And so I am leaving now, 70
> before Agave reaches the palace, to get away from this misfortune. Temperance and reverence for the gods are best, the wisest possessions, I believe, that exist for mortals who will use them. (1139–1152)

Agave returns and in a terrifying scene with her father Cadmus, she awakens from her madness to recognize the horror of her deed; it is the head of her son Pentheus, not that of a mountain lion that she holds in her hands. The conclusion of the play affirms the divine power of Dionysus. He appears now as god, the deus ex machina, to mete out his harsh justice against those who have denied his godhead and blasphemed his religion.

Pentheus has already died for his crimes; the other principal sinners must go into exile. Cadmus and Harmonia will experience much war and suffering in their wanderings and will be turned into serpents; but eventually they will be saved by Ares (the father of Harmonia) and transported to the Islands of the Blessed. Agave and her sisters must leave Thebes immediately. In her anguished farewell to her father, she utters this provocative commentary on her bitter and tragic experience with the religion of Dionysus.

> May I reach a place where Cithaeron, that mountain polluted by blood, may never see me or I lay eyes upon it, where any record of the thyrsus is unknown. Let Cithaeron and the thyrsus be the concern of other Bacchic women, not me. (1383–1387)

There are serious textual problems in the last section of the play. A medieval work, the *Christus Patiens*, which drew upon Euripides, is of some help—an interesting fact that rivets our attention to the parallels between Dionysus and Christ.

The pathos and horror of the butchering of Pentheus have led some to advance a sympathetic view of the rash king as an ascetic martyr, killed in his crusade against the irrational tide of religious fanaticism. But too much in the makeup of this young man suggests the myopic psychopath who is unable to accept human nature as it is and foolishly tries to suppress it. The basic impulses toward both the bestial and the sublime are terrifyingly and wondrously interrelated; Dionysus is, after all, the god of mob fury and religious ecstasy and anything in between. Was the celebration of his worship a cry for release from the restraints of civilized society and a return to the mystic purity and abounding

Harry Partch's American Bacchae

Harry Partch, the American composer, offers enlightening insights into elements of Dionysiac worship in his elucidation of his musical and theatrical Americanization of Euripides' tragedy, *Revelation in the Courthouse Park* (1960):

> *I first decided that I would bodily transfer Euripides'* The Bacchae *to an American setting. But in the end the better solution seemed to be to alternate scenes between an American courthouse park and the area before the palace of the city of Thebes. … I was determined to make this an American here-and-now drama, which, tragically, it truly is. … Many years ago I was struck by a strong and strange similarity between the basic situation in the Euripides play and at least two phenomena of present-day America. Religious rituals with a strong sexual element are not unknown to our culture, nor are sex rituals with a strong religious element. (I assume that the mobbing of young male singers by semihysterical women is recognizable as a sex ritual for a godhead.) And these separate phenomena, after years of observing them, have become synthesized as a single kind of ritual with religion and sex in equal parts, and with deep roots in an earlier period of evolution.*[7]

The equation of the idolization of Elvis Presley with the worship of Dionysus has turned out to be more apt than Partch might even suspect. For the devout, Elvis either has never really died or has been resurrected, and he is still very much with us. Pilgrimages to his temple in Graceland are legion. The Dionysiac experience in relation to singers of popular music and rock has spanned more than one generation. It can be recognized in the bobby-soxers who swooned at the feet of Frank Sinatra and in the androgynous cults of Michael Jackson and Boy George, and it afflicts both sexes with equal passion. The furor aroused by the female singer Madonna or the rock group the Beatles devastates men and women equally, sometimes enhanced by the Dionysiac use of intoxicating drugs (see also the section on Harry Partch in Chapter 28 on the companion website). Every generation has its new idols.

freedom of nature, or was it merely a deceptive excuse for self-indulgence in an orgy of undisciplined passion?

Other Opponents of Dionysus

At Tiryns in Argos the **daughters of King Proetus** resisted Dionysus, who caused them to rush over the countryside, leaving their homes and killing their children. In return for half of the kingdom, the famous seer **Melampus**, who, according to Herodotus (2.29) introduced the rituals of Dionysus to Greece, cured the madness of the daughters of Proetus by means of herbs and therapeutic dances.[8] He joined a group of strong young men in performing a kind of war dance, although one daughter, Iphinoë, died during the pursuit. This myth was connected with the festival of the Agriania, which involved a ritual pursuit of women by night and a return the next day to the normal order of society. It was celebrated at Orchomenus and at many other places in Greece.

In Orchomenus, a city of Boeotia, the **daughters of Minyas** refused to participate in Bacchic worship but remained at home to weave. Dionysus, in the guise of a girl, warned them of their folly to no avail, and they were driven mad. One of them, Leucippe, bore a son named Hippasus, who (like Pentheus) was torn to pieces. Unlike the daughters of Proetus, the Minyads did not return to normal life. They became winged creatures of the night, either owls or bats. Clymene, however, one of the daughters of Minyas, appears as the wife of five different husbands and thus becomes both the aunt of Jason (through her marriage to Pheres) and the mother (by Iasus) of Atalanta. She also was loved by Helius to become the mother of Phaëthon.

Lycurgus of Thrace pursued the nurses of Dionysus with an ox goad, and Dionysus himself in terror jumped into the sea and was rescued and comforted by Thetis. The gods became angry with Lycurgus, and Zeus struck him with blindness and he died soon afterward.

The Nature of Dionysus, His Retinue, and His Religion

The *Homeric Hymn to Dionysus* (1)[9] gives some variant information about Dionysus' birth, derives his name from Zeus (Dios) and the mountain Nysa (which is here placed in Egypt), and establishes the universal power of his worship.

> O divinely born god, sewn in Zeus' thigh,[10] some say it was on Dracanum, some in windy Icarus, some at the deep flowing Alpheus,[11] where Semele, made pregnant by Zeus who delights in the lightning, gave birth to you. Others say, O lord, that you were born in Thebes. They are all wrong; the father of both gods and men gave you birth, away from people and hidden from white-armed Hera.   10
>
> There is a certain mountain, Nysa, very high and with verdant forests, far from Phoenicia, near the streams of Egypt.[12] (8–9)
>
> "… and they will set up many statues in temples; and as things are three, mortals always, everywhere, will sacrifice perfect hecatombs to you in triennial festivals."[13] The son of Cronus spoke and nodded with his dark brows; and the divine hair   10 of our lord flowed down around his immortal head and he made great Olympus shake. Thus speaking, wise Zeus nodded confirmation with his head. (10–16)
>
> Be kind, you, sewn in Zeus' thigh, who drive women mad. We bards sing of you as we begin and end our song. It is utterly impossible for anyone who is forgetful of you to remember how to sing his holy song. (17–19)
>
> So hail to you, Dionysus, sewn in Zeus' thigh, along with your mother, Semele, whom indeed they call Thyone. (20–21)

Another *Homeric Hymn to Dionysus* (26) tells us more about the god:

> I begin to sing about ivy-crowned, loud-crying Dionysus, glorious son of Zeus and renowned Semele. The nymphs with beautiful hair took him to their bosoms from the lord his father and nurtured him tenderly in the vales of Mt. Nysa. By the grace of his father, he grew up in a fragrant cave, to be counted among the immortals. But when the goddesses had brought up this much-hymned god, then indeed he used to wander, heavily wreathed in ivy and laurel, among the woodland haunts of the forest. The nymphs followed along, with him as leader, and the sound of their cries filled the vast forest. (1–10)

> So hail to you, Dionysus, rich in grape clusters; grant that we may in our joy go through these seasons again and again for many years.   10

The essential characteristics of Dionysiac religion are an ecstatic spiritual release through music and dance,[14] the possession by the god of his followers, the rending apart of the sacrificial animal, and the eating of the raw flesh (**omophagy**, a kind of ritual communion, since the god was believed to be present in the victim). The religious congregation (the holy **thiasus**) was divided into groups, often with a male leader for each, who played the role of the god. The Bacchae, or **maenads**, are the female devotees, mortal women who become possessed. In mythology they are more than human, nymphs rather than mere mortals.

Their mythological male counterparts are **satyrs**, who, like them, are spirits of nature; they, however, are not completely human but part man and part animal, possessing various attributes of a horse or a goat—a horse's tail and ears, a goat's beard and horns—although in the later periods they are often depicted as considerably more humanized. Satyrs dance and sing and love music; they make wine and drink it, and they are perpetually in a state of sexual excitement. One of their favorite sports is to chase maenads through the woods. Animal skins and garlands are traditional attributes of Bacchic revelers (although satyrs are usually nude); maenads, in particular, carry the thyrsus, a pole wreathed with ivy or vine leaves, pointed at the top to receive a pine cone. As we have seen, it is a magic wand that evokes miracles, but if necessary it can be converted into a deadly weapon.

Sileni also attend Dionysus; they often cannot be distinguished from satyrs, although some of them are older (*papposileni*) and even more lecherous. Yet others are old and wise, like **Silenus** himself, the tutor of Dionysus. A story tells how once one of them was made drunk by drinking water from a spring laced with wine; when he was brought to **King Midas**, this Silenus philosophized that the best fate for human beings was not to be born at all and that the next best was to die as soon as possible after birth, providing a typical example of Greek pessimism and wisdom reminiscent of Solon and Herodotus.[15] Dionysus and his retinue are favorite subjects in Greek art.

As the male god of vegetation, Dionysus was, as we should expect, associated with a fertility goddess; his mother, Semele, was a full-fledged earth deity in her own right before she became Hellenized. The story of Zeus' birth on Crete, with the attendants who drowned out his infant cries by their frenzied music, suggests contamination with Dionysiac ritual. Certainly, Euripides associates Bacchic mysticism with the ritual worship of both Rhea and Cybele. Dionysus' "marriage" with Ariadne, saving her after she was deserted by Theseus on the island of Naxos (see pp. 583–585), not only provides an example of the union of the male and female powers of vegetation but also illustrates allegorically his powers of redemption. Dionysus represents the sap of life, the coursing of the blood through the veins, the throbbing excitement and mystery of sex and of nature; thus he is a god of ecstasy and mysticism.

Dionysus and Satyrs. Red-figure kylix, by the Brygos painter, ca. 480 B.C. Some 200 vases have been attributed to this painter, who is best known for the liveliness of the poses and the exquisite rendering of the figures, particularly their faces. Here we see a Bacchic revel with Dionysus, wreathed with ivy, playing a lyre and throwing his head back with remarkable abandon. He is flanked by two typically Attic satyrs: balding, snub nosed, with goat's beard, but with the tail and ears of a horse. The satyr on the right wears the familiar dappled leopard skin. The satyr on the left holds a vine branch with leaves, forming the background. Both satyrs are dancing around the god with castanets.

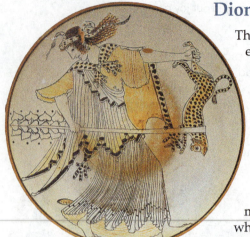

Maenad. Interior of an Attic kylix by the Brygos painter, ca. 480 B.C.; diameter 11¼ in. This lively white-ground painting (the cup is signed by the potter Brygos) shows a maenad in violent motion, holding a thyrsus in her right hand and a small leopard in her left. A leopard skin is fastened over her dress, and a wreath of serpents encircles her head. (*Erich Lessing/Art Resource, NY*)

Dionysus Spiritualized as Zagreus

The essence and spirit of Greek drama are to be found in the emotional environment of Dionysiac ecstasy. Theories concerning the origins of this genre in its relationship to Dionysus are legion. But it is a fact that tragedy and comedy were performed at Athens in a festival in his honor. It is difficult to agree with those who feel that this connection was purely accidental. Certainly, Aristotle's treatise dealing with the nature of tragedy in terms of a catharsis of pity and fear takes for granted emotions and excitement that are essentially Bacchic.[16]

Another myth told about his birth even more clearly established Dionysus in this role as a god of the mysteries. Zeus mated with his daughter Persephone, who bore a son, Zagreus, which is another name for Dionysus. In her jealousy, Hera then aroused the Titans to attack the child. These monstrous beings, their faces whitened with chalk, attacked the infant as he was looking in a mirror (in another version, they beguiled him with toys and cut him to pieces with knives). After the murder, the Titans devoured the dismembered corpse.[17] But the heart of the infant god was saved and brought to Zeus by Athena, and Dionysus was born again—swallowed by Zeus and begotten on Semele. Zeus was angry with the Titans and destroyed them with his thunder and lightning; but from their ashes humankind was born.

Surely, this is one of the most significant myths in terms of the religious dogma that it provides. By this myth human beings are endowed with a dual nature—a body gross and evil (since we are sprung from the Titans) and a soul that is pure and divine (for after all the Titans had devoured the god). Thus basic religious concepts (which lie at the root of all mystery religions) are accounted for: sin, immortality, resurrection, life after death, reward, and punishment. It is no accident that Dionysus is linked with Orpheus and Demeter and the message they preached. He is in his person a resurrection-god; the story is told that he went down into the realm of the dead and brought back his mother, who in this account is usually given the name Thyone.

Dionysus, Icarius, and Erigone

Dionysus, however, can be received amid peace and joy, although even then tragedy might result. In Attica, in the days of King Pandion, a man named Icarius was most hospitable to the god, and as a reward he was given the gift of wine. But when the people first felt the effects of this blessing, they thought they had been poisoned, and they turned upon Icarius and killed him. Erigone, his devoted daughter, accompanied by her dog Maira, searched everywhere for her father. When she found him, she hanged herself in grief. Suffering and plague ensued for the people until, upon Apollo's advice, they initiated a festival in honor of Icarius and Erigone.

Dionysus' Gift to Midas of the Golden Touch

We have learned how the philosophical Silenus was captured and brought to King Midas.[18] Midas at once recognized the satyr as a follower of Dionysus and returned him to Dionysus. The god was so delighted that he gave the king the right to choose any gift he would like for himself. Midas foolishly asked that whatever he should touch might be turned into gold. At first, Midas was delighted with his new power, when he saw that he could transform everything into gleaming riches by the mere touch of his hand. But the blessing quickly became a curse, for he could no longer eat or drink; any morsel or drop that he brought to his lips became a solid mass of gold. Midas' greed turned to loathing; in some accounts, even his beloved daughter was transformed. He begged the god's forgiveness for his sin and release from his accursed power. Dionysus took pity and ordered the king to cleanse himself of the remaining traces of his guilt in the source of the river Pactolus, near Sardis. Midas obeyed, and the power of transforming things into gold passed from his person into the stream, whose sands forevermore were sands of gold.

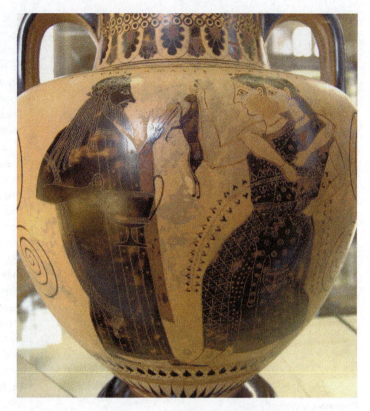

Dionysus and Maenads. Black-figure amphora by the Amasis painter, ca. 530 B.C. Dionysus, clothed in a chiton (a kind of long shirt) and himation (cloak) and holding a kantharos (cup) of wine, salutes two maenads, each clothed in a patterned peplos, who link arms and dance. They hold tendrils of ivy, and the one on the right holds a small deer by its ears. (*Bibliothèque nationale de France*)

Dionysus and the Pirates

In the *Homeric Hymn to Dionysus* (7), the god is abducted by pirates who mistake him for a mortal. The ensuing events aboard ship offer a splendid picture of Dionysus' power and majesty and remind us of fundamental elements in the nature of his character and worship: miracles, bestial transformation, violence to enemies, and pity and salvation for those who understand.[19]

> I shall sing of how Dionysus, the son of renowned Semele, appeared as a man in the first bloom of youth on a projecting stretch of shore by the sea that bears no harvest. His hair, beautiful and dark, flowed thickly about his head, and he wore on his strong shoulders a purple cloak. Before long, foreign pirates, led on by evil fate, appeared swiftly over the sea, dark as wine, in a ship with fine benches of oars. As soon as they saw him, they nodded one to the other and, quickly jumping out, seized him at once and put him on board ship, delighted in their hearts. For they thought that he was the son of kings, who are cherished by Zeus, and wanted to bind him in harsh bonds. But the bonds fell far from his hands and feet and did not hold him as he sat with a smile in his dark eyes. (1–15)
>
> When the helmsman saw this, he called aloud to his comrades: "Madmen, who is this mighty god whom you have seized and attempt to bind? Not even our strong ship can carry him, for this is either Zeus or Apollo of the silver bow or Poseidon, since he is not like mortal men but like the gods who have their homes on Olympus. But come, let us immediately set him free on the dark shore; do not lay hands on him for fear that he become angered in some way and rouse up violent winds and a great storm." (15–24)
>
> So he spoke, but the commander of the ship rebuked him scornfully: "Madman, check the wind, and while you are at it seize the tackle and hoist the sail. I expect

10

Dionysus. Kylix by Exekias, ca. 530 B.C.; diameter 4½ in. The scene depicts the story told in the *Homeric Hymn to Dionysus*. The god reclines on the pirates' ship, round whose mast a grape-laden vine entwines itself. The crew have leaped overboard and have been transformed into dolphins. (*bpk Bildagentur/ Staatliche Antikensammlung/ Art Resource, NY*)

that he will come with us to Egypt or Cyprus or the northern Hyperboreans or farther. But at his destination he will eventually tell us about his friends and all his possessions and his brothers, since a divine power has put him in our hands." When he had spoken, the mast and sail were hoisted on the ship; the wind breathed into the midst of the sail and the men made the ropes tight all around. (25–34)

But soon deeds full of wonder appeared in their midst. First of all, a sweet and fragrant wine flowed through the black ship, and a divine ambrosial odor arose. Amazement took hold of all the sailors as they looked, and immediately a vine spread in all directions up along the very top of the sail, with many clusters hanging down; dark ivy, luxuriant with flowers, entwined about the mast, and lovely fruit burst forth, and all the oar pins bore garlands. When they saw this, they ordered the helmsman to bring the ship to land. But then the god became a terrifying lion in the upper part of the ship and roared loudly, and in the middle of the ship he created a shaggy-necked bear, thus manifesting his divinity. The bear stood up raging, while on the upper deck the lion glared and scowled. (34–48)

The sailors fled into the stern and stood in panic around the helmsman, who had shown his good sense. The lion sprang up suddenly and seized the commander of the ship, but the sailors when they saw this escaped an evil fate and leaped all together into the shining sea and became dolphins. (48–53)

The god took pity on the helmsman and saved him and made him happy and fortunate in every way, saying: "Be of good courage, you who have become dear to my heart. I am loud-crying Dionysus, whom my mother, Semele, daughter of Cadmus, bore after uniting in love with Zeus." (53–57)

Hail, son of Semele of the beautiful countenance; it is not at all possible to forget you and compose sweet song.

Pan

The god Pan has much in common with the satyrs and sileni of Dionysus.[20] He is not completely human in form but part man and part goat—he has the horns, ears, and legs of a goat; he will join in Bacchic revels, and he is full of spirit, impulsive, and amorous. His parents are variously named: his mother is usually some nymph or other; his father is very often Hermes or Apollo. Like them, he is a god of shepherds and a musician.

Pan is credited with the invention of his own instrument, the **panpipe** (or in Greek, **syrinx**); Ovid tells the story with brevity and charm (*Metamorphoses* 1.689–712). Syrinx was once a lovely nymph, devoted to Artemis, who rejected the advances of predatory satyrs and woodland spirits. Pan caught sight of her, and as he pursued her, she was transformed into a bed of marsh reeds.

The wind blowing through them produced a sad and beautiful sound, and Pan was inspired to cut two of the reeds, fasten them together with wax, and thus fashion a pipe on which he could play.

Pan's haunts are the hills and the mountains, particularly those of his homeland, **Arcadia**, and he came to be especially honored in Athens. According to Herodotus (6.106), Pan was encountered by the runner Phidippides, who had been sent to Sparta by the Athenians to ask for help when they were about to fight the Persians at Marathon in 490 B.C.. Phidippides claimed that Pan called him by name and asked why the Athenians ignored him although he was a deity friendly to them. The Athenians believed Phidippides and later built a shrine to Pan, honoring him with annual sacrifices and torch races.

Pan had other loves besides Syrinx.[21] His passion for the nymph **Echo** also ended tragically. She fled from his advances, and Pan spread such madness and "panic" among a group of shepherds (a particular feat to which he was prone) that they tore her to pieces. All that remained was her voice.

The *Homeric Hymn to Pan* (19) presents a memorable account of his birth and his revels; in this case, his father is Hermes and his mother Dryope, the daughter of Dryops.

> Tell me, O Muse, about the dear son of Hermes—Pan, goat-footed, two-horned, lover of musical clangor—who wanders through wooded meadows together with a chorus of nymphs dancing along the heights of sheer rock. They call upon Pan, the splendid shaggy-haired god of shepherds, who has for his domain every snowy ridge, and mountaintops and rocky summits. He roams this place and that through

The *Dionysiaca* of Nonnus

Nonnus, a poet from Panopolis in Egypt, composed in the fifth century A.D. a Greek epic poem in forty-eight books on the theme of Dionysus and his exploits. In the "Mythical Introduction" to the three-volume Loeb text, H. J. Rose begins with this arresting statement: "The mythology of the *Dionysiaca* is interesting as being the longest and most elaborate example we have of Greek myths in their final stage of degeneracy."[22] Full of learned information, this work does have its moments (often more academic than poetic) that justify proclaiming Nonnus "the last great epic poet of antiquity."

Book 1 begins with Zeus carrying off Europa, and Book 48 concludes with Dionysus' final return to Olympus, where he places the crown of his beloved Ariadne. Nonnus, in his varied and crammed tapestry of countless events, gives us information that is to be found nowhere else—for example, the fight between Dionysus and Perseus and the myth of Beroë, a child of Aphrodite, invented to afford Berytus, the site of a great Roman school of law, its very own foundation myth. One should single out as well Nonnus' wealth of knowledge of astronomy, astrology, and religious doctrine, especially that of the Orphics. The amorous exploits of Dionysus seem endless, and a whole group of his lovers are all metamorphosized into various plants. Most interesting and bizarre of all Nonnus' excesses is the lengthy account of Dionysus as world conqueror, whose military conquests are obviously inspired by the legendary career of Alexander the Great. This same author Nonnus is credited with a poetic paraphrase of the Gospel of John.

Pan Pursuing a Goatherd, by the Pan painter, Attic red-figure krater, ca. 460 B.C.; height 14½ in. Pan pursues a herdsman, possibly Daphnis, son of Hermes. Pan's intentions are clear, and his lust is wittily echoed by the herm (or, more likely, the figure of Priapus) in the rocky background. This is the reverse of the vase illustrated in Chapter 10 on page 223, which depicts the mortal Actaeon punished by the goddess Artemis. The impunity of divine lust contrasts with the tragic consequences of divine anger for human error. (*Museum of Fine Arts Boston. Julia Bradford Huntington James Fund and Museum purchase with funds donated by contribution*)

dense thickets; sometimes he is tempted by soft streams, and then again he passes among sheer rocks and climbs up to the highest peak that overlooks the flocks. Often he moves across gleaming high mountains; often, among the slopes, he presses on and, sharply on the outlook, kills animals. (1–14)

Then, in the evening only, returning from the chase, he plays a lovely tune on his pipe of reeds. Not even the nightingale, the bird that pours forth her sad lament in honeyed song amid the petals of flower-laden spring, could surpass him in melody. With him then the clear-voiced mountain nymphs, moving on nimble feet, sing by a dark-watered spring; and Echo's wails reverberate around the mountaintop. The god Pan dances readily here and there among the chorus and then slips easily into their midst. He wears a spotted pelt of a lynx on his back, and his heart is delighted by his piercing tunes in a soft meadow where the crocus and fragrant hyacinth blooming at random mingle in the grass. (14–26)   10

They sing hymns about the blessed gods and high Olympus, and, above the rest, they single out Hermes, the bringer of luck. They sing how he is the swift messenger for all the gods and how he came into Arcadia, full of springs and mother of flocks, the place where his sacred precinct is located. There, even though he was a god, he tended the shaggy-fleeced sheep, in the service of a mortal. For a melting longing seized Hermes, and his passion to make love to the daughter of Dryops,[23] the nymph with the beautiful hair, intensified; and he brought to its fulfillment a fruitful marriage. (27–35)   20

Dryope bore to Hermes in their house a dear son, a marvel to behold right from his birth, a goat-footed, two-horned baby who loved music and laughter. But his mother was startled and fled, and she abandoned the child, for she was frightened when she saw his coarse features and full beard. Hermes, the luck-bringer, took him at once and clasped him in his arms; and the god felt extremely happy. Quickly, he covered the child in the thick skin of a mountain hare and went to the homes of the immortals and sat him down beside Zeus and the other gods and showed them the boy. All the immortals were delighted in their hearts, and especially Bacchic Dionysus; and they called him Pan because he delighted the hearts of them all.[24]   30

So hail to you, lord. I pray to you with my song, and I shall remember both you and another song too. (35–49)

Echo and Narcissus

We know that because she rejected him, Pan caused Echo to be torn to pieces so that only her voice remained. A more famous story about Echo concerns her love for Narcissus. Ovid's version is as follows (*Metamorphoses* 3.342–510):

> The river-god Cephisus once embraced the nymph Liriope in his winding stream and, enveloping her in his waves, took her by force. When her time had come, the beautiful Liriope bore a child with whom even as a baby the nymphs might have fallen in love. And she called him Narcissus. She consulted the seer Tiresias, asking whether her son would live a long time to a ripe old age; his answer was: "Yes, if he will not have come to know himself." For a long time this response seemed to be an empty prophecy, but as things turned out, its truth was proven by the unusual nature of the boy's madness and death. (342–350)
>
> The son of Cephisus had reached his sixteenth year and could be looked upon as both a boy and a young man. Many youths and many maidens desired him, but such a firm pride was coupled with his soft beauty that no one (either boy or girl) dared to touch him. He was seen once as he was driving the timid deer into his nets by the talkative nymph, who had learned neither to be silent when another is speaking nor to be the first to speak herself, namely, the mimic Echo. (351–358)
>
> At that time, Echo was a person and not only a voice; but just as now, she was garrulous and was able to use her voice in her customary way of repeating from a flood of words only the very last. Juno brought this about because, when she might have been able to catch the nymphs lying on the mountain with her Jove, Echo knowingly detained the goddess by talking at length until the nymphs could run away. When Juno realized the truth, she exclaimed: "The power of that tongue of yours, by which I have been tricked, will be limited; and most brief will be the use of your voice." She made good her threats; Echo only gives back the words she has heard and repeats the final phrases of utterances. (359–369)

ECHO'S PASSION FOR NARCISSUS

> And so she saw Narcissus wandering through the secluded countryside and burned with passion; she followed his footsteps furtively, and the closer she pursued him, the nearer was the fire that consumed her, just like the tops of torches, smeared with sulfur, that catch fire and blaze up when a flame is brought near. O how often she wanted to approach him with blandishments and tender appeals! Her very nature made this impossible, for she was not allowed to speak first. But she was prepared to wait for his utterances and to echo them with her own words—this she could do. (370–378)
>
> By chance, the boy became separated from his faithful band of companions, and he cried out: "Is there anyone there?" Echo replied "There!" He was dumbfounded and glanced about in all directions; then he shouted at full voice: "Come!" She called back to him with the same word. He looked around but saw no one approaching; "Why do you run away from me?" he asked. She echoed his words just as he spoke them. He was persistent, beguiled by the reflection of the other's voice, and exclaimed: "Come here and let us get together!" Echo replied, "Let us get together," and never would she answer any other sound more willingly. She emerged from the woods, making good her very words and rushed to throw her arms about the neck of her beloved. But he

Echo and Narcissus, by Nicolas Poussin (1594–1665); oil on canvas, ca. 1630, 29¼ × 39½ in. Narcissus lies along the edge of the pool with flowers growing near his head, while Echo, waiflike, fades away in the background. The cupid's burning torch is more fitting for a funeral than for a celebration of love. (*Erich Lessing/Art Resource, NY*)

fled and in his flight exclaimed, "Take your hands off me; I would die before I let you possess me." She replied with only the last words "Possess me." (379–392)

Thus spurned, Echo hid herself in the woods where the trees hid her blushes; and from that time on she has lived in solitary caves. Nevertheless, her love clung fast and grew with the pain of rejection. Wakeful cares wasted away her wretched body, her skin became emaciated, and the bloom and vigor of her whole being slipped away on the air. Her voice and her bones were all that was left. Then only her voice remained; her bones, they say, were turned into stone. From that time on, she has remained hidden in the woods; she is never seen on the mountains, but she is heard by everyone. The sound of her echo is all of her that still lives. (393–401)

Narcissus had played with her so, just as he had previously rejected other nymphs sprung from the waves or the mountains, and as well males who had approached him. Thereupon one of those scorned raised up his hands to the heavens and cried: "So may he himself fall in love, so may he not be able to possess his beloved!" The prayer was a just one, and Nemesis heard it. (402–406)

NARCISSUS' PASSION FOR HIS OWN REFLECTION

There was a spring, its clear waters glistening like silver, untouched by shepherds, mountain goats, and other animals, and undisturbed by birds, wild beasts, and falling tree branches. Grass grew round about, nourished by the water nearby, and the woods protected the spot from the heat of the sun. Here the boy lay down, tired out by the heat and his quest for game and attracted by the pool and the beauty of the place. While he was trying to quench his thirst, another desire grew, and as he continued to drink, he was captivated by the reflection of the beauty that he saw. (407–416)

He fell in love with a hope insubstantial, believing what was only an image to be real and corporeal. He gazed in wonder at himself, clinging transfixed and emotionless to what he saw, just like a statue formed from Parian marble. From his position on the ground he looked at his eyes, twin stars, and his hair, worthy of both Bacchus and Apollo, and his smooth cheeks, his ivory neck, and the beauty of his face, a flush of red amid snowy whiteness. He marveled at all the things that others had marveled at in him. Unwise and unheeding, he desired his very self, one and the same person approving and being approved, seeking and being sought, inflaming and being inflamed. How many times he bestowed vain kisses on the deceptive pool! How many times he plunged his arms into the midst of the waters to grasp the neck that he saw! But he could not catch hold of himself in their embrace. He did not understand what he was looking at, but was inflamed by what he saw, and the same illusion that deceived his eyes aroused his passion. (417–431)

Poor deluded boy, why do you grasp at your fleeting reflection to no avail? What you seek is not real; just turn away and you will lose what you love. What you perceive is but the reflection of your own image; it has no substance of its own. With you it comes and stays, and with you it will go, if you can bear to go. No concern for food or rest could drag him away from his post, but stretched out on the shady grass he looks at this deceptive beauty with insatiable gaze and destroys himself through his own eyes. He raised himself up a little and stretching out his arms to the surrounding woods exclaimed: (432–441)

"Has there ever been anyone smitten by more cruel a love? Tell me, O trees, for you know since you have provided opportune haunts for countless lovers. In the length of your years, in the many ages you have lived, can you remember anyone who has wasted away like me? I behold my beloved, but what I see and love I cannot have; such is the frustration of my unrequited passion. And I am all the more wretched because it is not a vast sea or lengthy road or impregnable fortress that separates us. Only a little water keeps us from each other. My beloved desires to be held, for each time that I bend down to kiss the limpid waters, he in return strains upward with his eager lips. You would think that he could be touched; it is such a little thing that prevents the consummation of our love. Whoever you are, come out to me here. Why, incomparable boy, do you deceive me? When I pursue you, where do you go? Certainly you do not flee from my youthful beauty, for nymphs loved me too. You promise me some kind of hope by your sympathetic looks of friendship. When I stretch forth my arms to you, you do the same in return. When I laugh, you laugh back, and I have often noted your tears in response to my weeping. And as well you return my every gesture and nod; and, as far as I can surmise from movements of your lovely mouth, you answer me with words that never reach my ears. I am you! I realize it; my reflection does not deceive me; I burn with love for myself, I am the one who fans the flame and bears the torture. What am I to do? Should I be the one to be asked or to ask? What then shall I ask for? What I desire is with me; all that I have makes me poor. O how I wish that I could escape from my body! A strange prayer for one in love, to wish away what he loves! And now grief consumes my strength; the time remaining for me is short, and my life will be snuffed out in its prime. Death does not weigh heavily upon me, for death will bring an end to my misery. I only wish that he whom I cherish could live a longer time. As it is, we two who are one in life shall die together!" (442–473)

THE METAMORPHOSIS OF NARCISSUS

He finished speaking and, sick with longing, turned back again to his own reflection. His tears disturbed the waters and caused the image in the pool to grow less distinct. When he saw it disappearing, he screamed: "Where are you going? Stay here, do not desert me, your lover. I cannot touch you—let me look at you, give me this nourishment at least in my misery and madness." As he grieved, he tore his garment in its upper part and beat his bare chest with his marble-white hands. And 120 his chest when struck took on a rosy tinge, as apples usually have their whiteness streaked with red, or grapes in various clusters when not yet ripe are stained with purple. As soon as he beheld himself thus in the water that was once again calm, he could endure it no further; but, as yellow wax is wont to melt under the touch of fire and the gentle frost under the warmth of the sun, so he was weakened and destroyed by love, gradually being consumed in its hidden flame. His beautiful complexion, white touched with red, no longer remained nor his youthful strength, nor all that he had formerly looked upon with such pleasure. Not even his body, which Echo had once loved, was left. (474–493)

When Echo saw what he had become, she felt sorry, even though she had been 130 angry and resentful. Each time that the poor boy exclaimed "Alas," she repeated in return an echoing "Alas." And as he struck his shoulders with his hands, she gave back too the same sounds of his grief. This was his last cry as he gazed into the familiar waters: "Alas for the boy I cherished in vain!" The place repeated these very same words. And when he said "Farewell," Echo repeated "Farewell" too. He relaxed his weary head on the green grass; night closed those eyes that had so admired the beauty of their owner. Then too, after he had been received in the home of the dead below, he gazed at himself in the waters of the Styx. His sister Naiads wept and cut off their hair and offered it to their brother; the Dryads wept, and Echo sounded their laments. Now the pyre and streaming torches and the bier 140 were being prepared, but the corpse was nowhere to be seen. They found instead a yellow flower with white petals encircling the center. (494–510)

Narcissism

This tragic story of self-love and self-destruction has cast a particularly potent spell on subsequent literature and thought, not least of all because of Ovid's perceptive and moving tale. The fact that it was a male lover's prayer for just retribution that was answered defines the homoerotic nature of Narcissus' self-love and self-destruction.[25] We do believe that Ovid intends us to understand that a male lover (*aliquis*) was rejected because then Narcissus' affliction becomes so ironic and so just: "Let the punishment fit the crime." The ominous words of Tiresias predict the tragedy in a fascinating variation of the most Greek of themes, "Know thyself," preached by Apollo and learned by Oedipus and Socrates. "When his mother inquired if Narcissus would live to a ripe old age, the seer Tiresias answered, "Yes, if he will not have come to know himself." We should not be surprised that Ovid is so profound.

"Narcissism" and "narcissistic" have been technical psychological terms and part of our everyday vocabulary since 1914, the year of Freud's paper "On Narcissism: An Introduction."[26]

Select Bibliography

Bloom, Harold. *Euripides*. New York: Chelsea House, 2003.

Carpenter, Thomas. *Dionysian Imagery in Fifth Century Athens*. New York: Oxford University Press, 1997.

———, and C. A. Faraone, eds. *Masks of Dionysus*. Ithaca, NY: Cornell University Press, 1993. Essays about the influence of Dionysus and tragedy.

Dodds, E. R. *The Greeks and the Irrational*. Berkeley, CA: University of California Press, 1951.

Kerényi, Carl. *Dionysos: Archetypal Image of Indestructible Life*. Translated by Ralph Mannheim. Princeton, NJ: Princeton University Press, 1996 [1976].

Merivale, Patricia. *Pan the Goat-God, His Myth in Modern Times*. New York: Cambridge University Press, 1969.

Otto, Walter F. *Dionysus: Myth and Cult*. Bloomington, IN: Indiana University Press, 1965.

Seaford, Richard. *Dionysos*. Gods and Heroes of the Ancient World Series. New York: Routledge, 2006.

Primary Sources

Sources in the Chapter

Euripides	*Bacchae*
Homeric Hymn 1	*To Dionysus*
Homeric Hymn 7	*To Dionysus*
Homeric Hymn 19	*To Pan*
Homeric Hymn 26	*To Dionysus*
Ovid	*Metamorphoses* 3.342–510

Additional Sources

Apollodorus	*Library* 3.4.3–3.5.1
Bacchylides	*Ode* 11.39–112 (How Hera drove the daughters of Proetus mad)
Euripides	*Cyclops* (Silenus and his satyr sons must serve the Cyclops Polyphemus)
Nonnus	*Dionysiaca*

Notes

1. Bacchus, the name for the god preferred by the Romans, is often used by the Greeks as well.
2. The word *dithyrambos*, an epithet of Dionysus and the name of a type of choral poetry that included hymns sung in the god's honor, was in ancient times believed to refer etymologically to his double birth.

3. The career of Ino is extremely confusing because of the multiple versions of her story. She was the second wife of Athamas (whom we shall meet again in the Argonautic saga), and they had two sons, Learchus and Melicertes. Angry with Ino because of her care for Dionysus, Hera drove both Ino and her husband mad. Athamas killed his son Learchus and pursued Ino, who escaped with Melicertes in her arms. She leaped from a cliff into the sea and was transformed into the sea-goddess Leucothea; Melicertes also became deified under the new name of Palaemon.

4. Note the Dionysiac aspects of Orpheus' missionary zeal in Thrace, which establish the influence of the god there.

5. The Curetes, as we have seen, are the attendants of Rhea, who hid the cries of the infant Zeus from his father Cronus (see box, p. 75). In this passage, Euripides associates them with the Corybantes, the ministers of Cybele.

6. We have translated only the beginning and end of Tiresias' lengthy and learned sermon on the great power of Dionysus.

7. Harry Partch, *Bitter Music, Collected Journals, Essays, Introductions, and Librettos,* ed. Thomas McGeary (Urbana, IL: University of Illinois Press, 1991), pp. 244–246. Reprinted from his *Genesis of Music,* 2d ed. (New York: Da Capo Press, 1974 [1949]).

8. Amphiaraüs, a seer and one of the Seven against Thebes, was a descendant of Melampus. The wife of Proetus, Stheneboea, is prominent in the myth of Bellerophon (see pp. 541–543).

9. The initial nine lines, quoted by Diodorus Siculus (3.66.3), are probably not a separate hymn but should in some way be joined to the fragmentary last section of this first hymn, which is found in manuscript.

10. The epithet *eiraphiotes* is of uncertain derivation. It may mean "insewn," but it may instead refer to Dionysus' connection with the ivy plant or the goat or the bull.

11. Dracanum is a cape on the island of Cos; Icarus and Naxos are islands, and the Alpheus is a river in Elis.

12. There must be a lacuna after these lines from Diodorus and before the next section from the manuscript text.

13. The reference to three things is unclear; it may refer to the ritual of dismemberment.

14. E. R. Dodds' helpful edition of the Greek text of the *Bacchae,* 2d ed. (New York: Oxford University Press, 1960), includes an enlightening introduction. He notes that Dionysiac religion shares a belief, found universally, that musical rhythms and ritual dances lead to the most satisfying and highest religious experiences. See also Walter F. Otto, *Dionysus: Myth and Cult* (Bloomington, IN: Indiana University Press, 1965 [1933]); M. Detienne, *Dionysos at Large* (Cambridge, MA: Harvard University Press, 1989 [1986]); Carl Kerényi, *Dionysos: Archetypal Image of Indestructible Life,* translated from the German by Ralph Mannheim, Bollingen Series LXV.2 (Princeton, NJ: Princeton University Press, 1976); and Thomas H. Carpenter and Christopher A. Faraone, eds., *Masks of Dionysus,* Myth and Poetics Series (Ithaca, NY: Cornell University Press, 1993), a collection of essays about various aspects of Dionysus and his worship.

15. Vergil wrote a famous adaptation of this legend in his sixth *Eclogue,* in which the utterance of the silenus is cosmogonical and mythological.

16. Friedrich Nietzsche has provided the most imaginative and influential modern analysis of the Dionysiac experience, particularly in enunciating its antithetical relationship to the Apollonian. See M. S. Silk and J. P. Stern, *Nietzsche on Tragedy* (New York: Cambridge University Press, 1981), a study of Nietzsche's first book, *The Birth of Tragedy.*

17. Variations in the story are obviously etiological attempts to account for elements of Bacchic ritual. Later ceremonies enacted the passion, death, and resurrection of the god in all their details.

18. Ovid's version of Midas' story (*Metamorphoses* 11.85–145) is well known. This is the same Midas whose ears were turned into those of an ass as a result of his preference for the music of Pan over that of Apollo (see p. 261).

19. The same story is told by Ovid (*Metamorphoses* 3.597–691), who provides an interesting comparison in artistic method and purpose.

20. See Philippe Borgeaud, *The Cult of Pan in Ancient Greece* (Chicago: University of Chicago Press, 1988) for a study of changing representations of Pan. See also Patricia Merivale, *Pan the Goat-God: His Myth in Modern Times* (Cambridge, MA: Harvard University Press, 1969).

21. Another nymph he pursued was turned into a tree that bore her name, Pitys (the Greek word for "pine").

22. Nonnos, *Dionysiaca*, translated by W. H. D. Rouse (New York: Harvard University Press, 1934), vol. 1, p. x.

23. This is Dryope; Ovid (*Metamorphoses* 9.325 ff.) has a different version.

24. The Greek word *pan* means "all."

25. See Louise Vinge, *The Narcissus Theme in Western European Literature up to the Early 19th Century* (Lund, Sweden: Gleerups, 1967); also Gerasimos Santas, *Plato and Freud: Two Theories of Love* (Oxford: Blackwell, 1988). Freud believed (and of course many disagree) that an individual's sexual development as an infant may determine his or her choices as an adult concerning the object and nature of love. Thus the theory of narcissism had a great impact on his conviction that, for some, relationships in love may stem not from their primal attachment to their mothers but from infantile self-love.

26. See *The Standard Edition of the Complete Psychological Works of Sigmund Freud*, edited by James Strachey, vol. 14 (London: Hogarth Press, 1957), pp. 69–129. Of great interest is a biography of the psychoanalyst Heinz Kohut by Charles B. Strozier, *Heinz Kohut: The Making of a Psychoanalyst* (New York: Farrar, Straus and Giroux, 2001). Kohut became famous through his profound exploration of narcissism in papers such as "Forms and Transformations of Narcissism" (1966) and "The Analysis of the Self" (1971).

DEMETER AND THE ELEUSINIAN MYSTERIES

But Jupiter mediated between his brother and his sorrowful sister and divided the rolling year equally. Now the goddess, her divinity shared between two realms, lives with her mother for as many months as she lives with her husband. And suddenly the cast of her mind and face changed. For now her countenance, which could seem mournful even to Dis, is radiant as the sun, emerging from the dark clouds that had concealed it.

—OVID, *Metamorphoses* 5.564–571

The Myth of Demeter and Persephone

There are two *Homeric Hymns to Demeter*. Number 13 is a very short prelude.

> I begin to sing about the holy goddess Demeter of the beautiful hair, about her and her very lovely daughter Persephone. Hail, goddess; preserve this city and lead my song.

The lengthy and powerful *Homeric Hymn to Demeter* (2), by contrast, is of the utmost importance; it begins with Hades' abduction of Persephone at the will of Zeus:

> I begin to sing about the holy goddess, Demeter of the beautiful hair, about her and her daughter, Persephone of the lovely ankles, whom Hades snatched away; loud-thundering Zeus, who sees all, gave her to him. (1–3)
>
> Alone, away from Demeter of the golden scepter and goodly crops, Persephone was playing with the deep-bosomed daughters of Oceanus and picking flowers along a soft meadow: beautiful roses, crocuses, violets, irises, and hyacinths; and Earth in accordance with the will of Zeus to please Hades, the host of many, produced as a snare for the fair maiden a wonderful and radiant narcissus, an awesome sight to all, both 10 immortal gods and mortal humans. From its stem a hundred blossoms sprouted forth, and their odor was most sweet. All wide heaven above, the whole earth below, and the swell of the salt sea laughed. The girl was

astounded and reached out with both her hands together to pluck the beautiful delight. And the wide-pathed Earth yawned in the Nysaean plain, and the lord and host of many, who goes by many names, the son of Cronus, rushed at her with his immortal horses. And he snatched her up in his golden chariot and carried her away in tears. (4–20)

She shouted with shrill cries and called on father Zeus, the son of Cronus, the highest and the best, but no one of the immortals or of mortals—not even the olive trees laden with their fruit—heard her voice except for the daughter of Persaeus [Perses], Hecate, her hair brightly adorned, who listened from her cave as she thought kindly thoughts, and lord Helius, the splendid son of Hyperion. These two heard the maid call on the son of Cronus, father Zeus; but he sat apart, away from the gods, in his temple with its many suppliants, receiving beautiful holy offerings from mortals. By the counsel of Zeus, his brother and her uncle Hades, the son of Cronus, who bears many names, the lord and host of many, led her off with his immortal horses against her will. (20–32)

As long as the goddess could behold the earth, starry heaven, the deep flowing sea full of fish, the rays of the sun, and still hoped to see her dear mother and the race of everlasting gods, hope soothed her great heart, although she was distressed. But the peaks of the mountains and the depths of the sea echoed with her immortal voice, and her lady mother heard her. (33–39)

DEMETER'S GRIEF, ANGER, AND RETALIATION

Sharp pain seized Demeter's heart, and she tore the headdress about her ambrosial hair with her own dear hands and threw off the dark covering from both her shoulders; and she rushed in pursuit, just like a bird, over land and water. But no one—either of gods or mortals—wished to tell what had really happened—not even a bird came to her as a messenger of truth. For nine days, then, lady Demeter roamed over the earth holding burning torches in her hands and in her grief did not eat any ambrosia or drink sweet nectar, nor did she bathe her body. But when dawn brought on the light of the tenth day, Hecate, a torch in hand, met her and gave her some news as she exclaimed: "Lady Demeter, bringer of goodly gifts in season, who of the heavenly gods or mortals carried off Persephone and troubled your dear heart? For I heard her voice but did not see with my eyes who it was. I am telling you the whole truth quickly." (40–58)

Thus Hecate spoke, and the daughter of Rhea of the beautiful hair did not answer but swiftly rushed away with her, holding burning torches in her hands. They came to Helius, the lookout for both gods and human beings, and stood before his horses, and the goddess of goddesses spoke: "Helius, do at least have respect for me, a goddess, if I have ever by word or by deed gladdened your heart and your spirits. Through the barren air I heard the piercing cry of the girl whom I bore, a sweet daughter, illustrious in her beauty, as though she were being violated; yet I saw nothing with my eyes. But since you look down from the divine aether with your rays on all the earth and sea, tell me truthfully if you have seen my dear child at all and who, either of gods or mortals, has seized her alone, away from me, by force against her will and made away." (59–73)

Thus she spoke. And the son of Hyperion answered her: "Demeter, regal daughter of Rhea of the beautiful hair, you will know the truth. For indeed I revere you greatly and I pity you in your grief for your daughter of the lovely ankles. No other of

the immortals is to blame except the cloud-gatherer Zeus, who gave her to his own 60
brother Hades to be called his lovely wife. And he seized her and with his horses
carried her away to the gloomy depths below as she cried aloud. But, O goddess,
desist from your great lament; you should not thus bear an unrelenting anger to
no avail. Indeed Hades, the ruler over many, is not an unseemly husband for your
daughter; he is your own brother and born from the same blood; and as for honor,
when in the beginning power was divided three ways, his lot was to be made lord
of all those with whom he dwelt." (74–87)

Thus he spoke and called out to his horses. And at his cry they nimbly bore the
swift chariot, just like long-winged birds. But a more dread and terrible grief possessed Demeter's heart, and thereafter she was angry with the son of Cronus, Zeus, 70
enwrapped in clouds; she kept away from the gatherings of the gods and high
Olympus; and for a long time she went among the cities and rich fields of human
beings, disguising her beautiful form. (88–94)

DEMETER COMES TO ELEUSIS AND THE PALACE OF CELEUS

No one of men or deep-bosomed women who saw her recognized her until she
came to the home of wise Celeus, who at that time was ruler of fragrant Eleusis.
Grieving in her dear heart, she sat near the road by the Maiden Well, from which
the people drew their water; she was in the shade, for an olive tree grew over-
head. Her appearance resembled that of a very old woman long past her days for
childbearing and the gifts of garland-loving Aphrodite; she was like the nurses
for the children of law-pronouncing kings or the housekeepers in their echoing 80
halls. (94–104)

The daughters of Celeus, of the family of Eleusis, saw her there as they came
after the easily drawn water so that they might bring it in their bronze pitchers to
the dear home of their father. There were four of them, just like goddesses in their
youthful bloom, Callidice and Cleisidice and lovely Demo and Callithoë, who was
the oldest of them all. They did not know Demeter, for it is difficult for mortals to
recognize the gods; and standing near they spoke winged words: "Who are you,
old woman, of those born long ago? Where are you from? Why have you come
away from the city and not approached the houses there, in whose shadowy halls
dwell women just like you and younger, who would welcome you in word as well 90
as in deed?" (105–117)

Thus they spoke. And she, the queenly goddess, answered with these words:
"Dear children, whoever you are of women, I bid you greeting, and I shall tell you
my tale. To be sure, it is not inappropriate to relate the truth to you who have asked.
My name is Doso, for my lady mother gave it to me. Now then, I have come from
Crete over the broad back of the sea—not willingly but against my wishes, for by
force pirates carried me away. Then they put in at Thoricus, where the women and
the men together disembarked; they were busy with their meal beside the cables
of the ship, but my heart had no desire for the delicious food. I hastened away over
the black land and escaped from my overbearing masters so that they might not 100
sell me, whom they had not bought, and reap a profit from me. And so I have come
here after my wanderings, and I have no idea at all what land this is or who inhabit
it. But may all those who dwell in homes on Olympus grant that you have husbands
and bear children just as parents desire. But you maidens pity me now and show

concern until, dear children, I come to the home of a man and woman to perform for them zealously the tasks appropriate for an elderly woman like me; I could hold a newborn child in my arms and care for him well, make my master's bed in the recess of his well-built chambers, and teach the women their tasks." (118–144)

Thus spoke the goddess, and at once the virgin maiden 110 Callidice, the most beautiful of the daughters of Celeus, answered: "Good woman, we mortals, even though we suffer, must bear what the gods bestow, for indeed they are much the stronger. I shall help you with the following advice, and I shall tell you the names of the men who have great honor and power here and who are foremost among the people and guard the battlements of our city by their counsels and firm judgments. There is clever Triptolemus and Dioclus and Polyxeinus and noble Eumolpus and Dolichus and our own brave father. All of these have wives who take care of their homes, and no one of them at the very first sight of your person 120 would dishonor you or turn you out of his house, but they will welcome you, for to be sure you are like one of the gods. But if you wish, stay here, so that we may go to our father's house and tell our mother, the deep-bosomed Metaneira, the whole story in the hope that she will bid you come to our place and not search for the homes of the others. She cherishes in our well-built house an only son, born late, a darling long prayed for. If you were to bring him up and he attained the measure of his youth, you would easily be the envy of any woman who saw you. Such are the great rewards that would be yours for your care." (145–168)   130

Thus she spoke, and Demeter nodded her head in agreement. And the girls filled their shining pitchers with water and carried them away happy. Quickly, they came to the great house of their father and told their mother at once what they had seen and heard. She enjoined them to go with all speed and to hire the woman at any price. Just as deer or heifers bound along the meadow when in the springtime they have had their fill of pasture, thus they hurried along the hollow wagon path, holding up the folds of their lovely garments, and their hair, which was like the flower of the crocus, danced about their shoulders. And they found the illustrious goddess where they had left her earlier and thereupon led her to the dear house of their father; she followed behind with her head veiled, distressed at heart, and the 140 dark robe grazed the slender feet of the goddess. (169–183)

Soon they arrived at the house of Celeus, a man cherished by Zeus, and passed through the vestibule to where their lady mother sat by the pillar that supported the sturdy roof, holding her son, just a baby, in her lap. Her daughters ran to her, but the goddess stood at the threshold; her head reached up to the beams and she filled the doorway with a divine radiance. Then awe and reverence and fear seized Metaneira, and she sprang up from her couch and bade her guest be seated, but Demeter, the giver of goodly gifts in season, did not wish to sit on the splendid couch but waited in silence with her beautiful eyes downcast, until [the servant] Iambe in her wisdom set out for her a chair, artfully made, and threw a silvery fleece over it; then Demeter sat down, holding her veil over her face with 150 her hands. (184–197)

Demeter. Marble, second half of the fourth century B.C.; height 58 in. This is the cult-statue from the sanctuary of Demeter at Cnidus in Asia Minor. She is shown seated and heavily draped. Her solemn gaze and matronly clothing are consistent with the Demeter of the *Homeric Hymn to Demeter.* (© *The Trustees of the British Museum*)

Hades and Persephone, by Gian-Lorenzo Bernini (1598–1680); marble, 1621–1622; height 87 in. Bernini carved this statue for Cardinal Scipione Borghese; it was meant to be seen from the front, for it was placed against a wall. Hades has just seized Persephone and is entering his kingdom, indicated by its guardian, Cerberus, who is seen at the lower right. Persephone twists and cries out as she vainly attempts to escape the clutches of the god. Seen from the right side, the statue is yet more dramatic, for the impression of Hades' fingers sinking into Persephone's thigh and the open jaws of Cerberus (not shown here) heighten the viewer's pity and horror at the violence of the cruel god. (*Scala/ Ministero per i Beni e le Attività culturali/Art Resource, NY*)

For a long time she remained seated without a sound, grieving; she did not by word or action acknowledge anyone; but without a smile, not touching food or drink, she sat wasted with longing for her deep-bosomed daughter, until Iambe in her wisdom resorted to many jests and jokes and brought the holy lady around to smile and laugh and bear a happy heart (thereafter, too, Iambe was to cheer her in her anguish). And Metaneira filled a cup with wine as sweet as honey and offered it, but she refused saying that it was not right for her to drink red wine. But she ordered them to mix meal and water with tender mint and give it to her to drink. Metaneira mixed the 160 potion and gave it to the goddess as she had ordered. And the great lady Demeter took it for the sake of the holy rite.[1] (198–211)

DEMETER NURSES DEMOPHOÖN

Beautifully robed Metaneira was the first to speak among them: "Greetings, O lady, I expect that you are not born of base parents but of noble ones. Majesty and grace shine clearly in your eyes as though from the eyes of royalty who mete out justice. But we mortals, even though we suffer, must bear what the gods bestow, for the yoke lies on our necks. Yet now since you have come here, as much as I have will be yours. Nurse this child, whom the immortals gave me late in life, fulfilling my desperate hopes and endless prayers. If 170 you were to bring him up and he attained the measure of his youth, you would easily be the envy of any woman who saw you. Such are the great rewards that would be yours for your care." Then Demeter of the beautiful crown replied to her: "Sincere greetings to you, also, O lady, and may the gods afford you only good. I shall take the boy gladly, as you bid, and tend to him, and I have good hopes that he will not be harmed or destroyed by any evil charms, for I know much more potent remedies and effective antidotes for harmful spells." (212–230)

Thus she spoke, and with her immortal hands she took the child to her fragrant bosom. And his mother rejoiced in her heart. Thus she nursed in the house the 180 splendid son of wise Celeus, Demophoön, whom beautifully robed Metaneira bore. And he grew like a god, not nourished on mortal food but anointed by Demeter with ambrosia, just as though sprung from the gods, and she breathed sweetness upon him as she held him to her bosom. At night she would hide him in the might of the fire, like a brand, without the knowledge of his dear parents. It was a source of great wonder to them that he grew and flourished before his time, for he was like the gods to look upon. And she would have made him immortal and never to grow old if beautifully robed Metaneira in her foolishness had not seen what was happening, as she watched in the night from her fragrant chamber. Great was her dismay, and she gave a shriek and struck both her thighs, terrified for her child. Amid her groans she uttered winged words: "Demophoön, my 190 child, this stranger buries you within the blazing fire to my anguish and grievous pain." (231–249)

Thus she spoke in agony, and the goddess of goddesses, Demeter of the beautiful crown, grew angry as she listened; with her immortal hands she snatched from the fire the dear son whom Metaneira had borne in her house, blessing beyond hope, and threw him down on the floor. Demeter was dreadfully angry in

Pluto and Proserpina by Jeff Koons; stainless steel brushed with yellow-gold paint; decorated with live flowering plants; height 129 in. Koons based his design on an eighteenth-century porcelain figurine. Using twentieth-century materials on a huge scale and twisting them to focus on the violence and speed of Pluto's (Hades') seizure of Proserpina (Persephone), he illuminates the mythical figures by the skillful use of gold color. (*Jeff Koons, Pluto and Proserpina, 2010–2013 © Jeff Koons, Photo: Tom Powel Imaging mirror-polished stainless steel with transparent color coating and live flowering plants 129 x 65¾ x 56⅝ inches, 327.7 x 167 x 143.8 cm*)

her heart as she spoke to beautifully robed Metaneira: "Mortals are ignorant and stupid who cannot foresee the fate both good and bad that is in store. Thus you in your foolishness have done a thing that cannot be remedied. I call to witness by the relentless waters of the river Styx, the oath of the gods, that I would have made 200 your dear child immortal and never to grow old all his days, and I would have granted him imperishable honor; but now, as it is, he will not be able to escape death and the Fates. Yet imperishable honor will always be his because he has lain on my knees and slept in my arms. But when the years go by and he has reached his prime, the new generation of Eleusinians will continually engage in dread wars and battles all their days. I am Demeter, esteemed and honored as the greatest benefit and joy to mortals and immortals. Now then, let all the people build to me a great temple and an altar with it, below the town and its steep wall, on the rising hill above the well, Kallichoron. And I myself shall teach my rites, so that performing them with reverence you may propitiate my heart." (250–274)   210

Thus the goddess spoke and cast aside her old age, transforming her size and appearance. Beauty breathed around and about her, and a delicious odor was wafted from her fragrant garments. The radiance from the immortal person of the goddess shone far and wide, and her golden hair flowed down on her shoulders. The sturdy house was filled with her brilliance as though with a lightning flash. She disappeared from the room, and at once Metaneira's knees gave way; for a long time she was speechless and did not even remember at all to pick up her late-born son from the floor. But his sisters heard his pitiful cries and sprang down from their beds, spread well with covers; one of them then picked up the child in her arms and   220
took him to her bosom, another stirred the fire, and a third hastened on her delicate feet to rouse their mother from her fragrant chamber. They gathered around the frantic child and bathed him with loving care. But his spirits were not soothed, for the nurses who tended him now were indeed inferior. (275–291)

The whole night long, trembling with fear, they made their supplication to the illustrious goddess, and as soon as dawn appeared they told the truth to Celeus, whose power was great, just as Demeter the goddess of the beautiful crown had commanded. Then Celeus called the many people to an assembly and bade them build a splendid temple to Demeter of the lovely hair and an altar on the rising hill.   230
They listened to him as he spoke and immediately complied and did as they were told. And the child flourished by divine destiny. (292–300)

HADES AND PERSEPHONE AND HER EATING OF THE POMEGRANATE

When they had finished and ceased from their labor, each made his way homeward. But golden Demeter remained sitting there quite apart from all the blessed gods, wasted with longing for her deep-bosomed daughter. And she caused human beings a most terrible and devastating year on the fruitful land. The earth would not send up a single sprout, for Demeter of the lovely crown kept the seed covered. In vain the oxen dragged the many curved ploughs through the fields, and much white barley was sown in the earth to no avail. Now she would have destroyed the entire human race by cruel famine and deprived   240
those who have their homes on Olympus of their glorious prestige from their gifts and sacrifices, if Zeus had not noticed and taken thought in his heart. First, he roused golden-winged Iris to summon Demeter of the lovely hair, desirable in her beauty. (301–315)

Thus he ordered. And Iris obeyed Zeus, the dark-clouded son of Cronus, and on swift feet traversed the interval between. She came to the citadel of fragrant Eleusis and found dark-robed Demeter in her temple. She spoke to her, uttering winged words: "Demeter, father Zeus, whose knowledge is imperishable, commands you to join the company of the eternal gods. Come now, let not the word I bring from Zeus be unaccomplished." (316–323)   250

Thus she spoke in supplication, but Demeter's heart was unswayed. Thereupon father Zeus sent down to her all the blessed gods who exist forever; and they came one by one, calling out her name and offering her many very beautiful gifts and whatever honors she would like to choose for herself among the immortals. But no one was able to sway her mind and her heart from her anger, and she stubbornly rejected all appeals. She maintained that she would never set foot on fragrant

Olympus or allow fruit to sprout from the earth until she saw with her own eyes her lovely daughter. (324–333)

Then loud-thundering Zeus, who sees all, sent the slayer of Argus, Hermes, with his golden wand to Erebus to appeal to Hades with gentle words and bring chaste Persephone up from the murky depths to the light, so that her mother might desist from anger when she saw her daughter with her own eyes. Hermes did not disobey, and straightway he left the realms of Olympus and swiftly rushed down to the depths of the earth. He encountered the lord Hades within his house, sitting on a couch with his modest wife, who was very reluctant because of her longing for her mother. And Demeter, far away, brooded over her designs to thwart the actions of the blessed gods. (334–345)

The mighty slayer of Argus stood near and said: "Hades of the dark hair, ruler of the dead, father Zeus has ordered me to bring to him from Erebus august Persephone, so that her mother may see her with her own eyes and desist from her wrath and dread anger against the immortals. For she is devising a great scheme to destroy the feeble tribes of earthborn men by keeping the seed hidden under earth and ruining the honors that are bestowed on the immortals. She clings to her dire wrath and does not associate with the gods but remains on the rocky citadel of Eleusis sitting apart within her fragrant temple." (346–357)

Thus he spoke. And Hades, the lord of those below, smiled with furrowed brows and did not disobey the commands of Zeus the king; and he hastily ordered wise Persephone: "Go, Persephone, to the side of your dark-robed mother, with a gentle and loving heart in your breast. Be not distraught. I among the immortals shall not be an unworthy husband for you, since I am the full brother of your father, Zeus. While you are here with me you will rule over all that lives and moves, and you will hold the greatest honors among the immortals. Those who wrong you and do not propitiate your power by performing holy rites and sacrifices and offering appropriate gifts will find eternal retribution." (357–369)

Thus he spoke. And wise Persephone was delighted and jumped up quickly in her joy. But her husband secretly gave her the honey-sweet fruit of the pomegranate to eat, taking thought for himself that she should not remain all her days above with august, dark-robed Demeter. Hades, host of many, then yoked his immortal horses to the front of his golden chariot, which Persephone mounted; the mighty slayer of Argus, Hermes, took the reins and whip in his hands and drove them up and away from the palace; the pair of horses readily sped along and easily covered their long journey. Neither the sea nor streams of rivers nor grassy glens nor mountaintops impeded the onrush of the immortal horses as they cut through the deep air above them in their course. The charioteer brought them to a halt in front of the fragrant temple where Demeter of the lovely crown waited. (370–385)

DEMETER'S ECSTATIC REUNION WITH PERSEPHONE

At the sight of her daughter, she rushed out like a maenad down a mountain thick with woods. When Persephone on the other side saw the beautiful eyes of her mother, she leaped down from the chariot with its horses and ran, throwing her arms about her neck in an embrace. But while Demeter still had her dear child in her arms, suddenly her heart sensed some treachery; trembling with dread she let go her loving embrace and asked quickly: "My child, have you eaten any food while you were below? Speak up, do not hide anything so that we both may know. If you have not, even though you have been in the company of loathsome Hades, you will live with me and your father, Zeus the cloud-gatherer, son of Cronus, in honor among all the immortals. But if you have eaten anything, you will return again beneath the depths of the earth and live there a third part of each year; the other two-thirds of the time you will spend with me and the other immortals. When the spring blooms with all sorts of sweet-smelling flowers, then again you will rise from the gloomy region below, a great wonder for gods 310 and mortals. But tell me, too, by what trick the strong host of many deceived you?" (385–404)

The very beautiful Persephone then said in answer: "To be sure, mother, I shall tell you the whole truth. When Hermes, the bringer of luck and swift messenger, came from my father, the son of Cronus, and the other gods of the sky, saying that I was to come up from Erebus in order that you might see me with your own eyes and desist from your wrath and dread anger against the immortals, I immediately jumped up in my joy. But Hades swiftly put in my mouth the fruit of the pomegranate, a honey-sweet morsel, and compelled me to eat it by force against my will. I shall tell you too how he came and carried me down to the depths of the earth 320 through the shrewd plan of my father, the son of Cronus, going through it all as you ask. (405–416)

"We were all playing in a lovely meadow: Leucippe, Phaeno, Electra, Ianthe, Melite, Iache, Rhodeia, Callirhoë, Melobosis, Tyche, Ocyrhoë beautiful as a flower, Chryseïs, Ianeira, Acaste, Admete, Rhodope, Pluto, lovely Calypso, Styx and Urania, charming Galaxaura,[2] and Pallas the battle-rouser and Artemis delighting in arrows. (417–424)

"We were playing and gathering lovely flowers in our hands, a mixed array of soft crocuses, irises, hyacinths, roses in full bloom, and lilies, wonderful to behold, and a narcissus, which the wide earth produced, in color yellow of a crocus. I plucked 330 it joyously, but the earth beneath opened wide and thereupon the mighty lord, the host of many, leaped up and carried me away in his golden chariot beneath the earth despite my violent protests—my cries were loud and shrill. I tell you the whole truth, although the story gives me pain." (425–433)

Thus they then in mutual love and tender embraces greatly cheered each other's heart and soul the whole long day. Their grief was assuaged as they exchanged their joys. Hecate, her hair brilliantly arrayed, approached them and frequently embraced the holy daughter of Demeter. From that time on, regal Hecate became the lady and attendant of Persephone. (434–440)

DEMETER RESTORES FERTILITY AND ESTABLISHES THE MYSTERIES

Loud-thundering Zeus, who sees far and wide, sent as a messenger to them 340 Rhea of the lovely hair to lead dark-robed Demeter among the company of the gods, and he promised to grant her the honors that she would choose among the immortal gods, and he consented that her daughter live a third part of the revolving year in the gloomy depths below and the other two-thirds by the side of her mother and the other immortals. Thus he ordered, and the goddess Rhea did not disobey the message of Zeus. She quickly rushed down from the heights of Olympus and came to the Rharian plain, previously very fertile, but now not fertile at all, standing leafless and barren. The white seed was hidden through the machinations of Demeter of the lovely ankles. But soon thereafter, with the burgeoning of spring, long ears of grain would be luxuriant, and the rich 350

Hades and Persephone. Terra cotta plaque, ca. 460 B.C.; height 10¼ in. This is one of a series of small votive reliefs from the sanctuary of Persephone at Locri (in southern Italy). The divinities of the Underworld sit enthroned, holding emblems connected with their worship—grain, parsley, a cock, a bowl. In front stands a lamp with a tiny cock on it, and another cock stands beneath Persephone's throne. (*Scala/Art Resource, NY*)

furrows too along the ground would be laden with grain, some already bound in sheaves. (441–456)

Rhea came from the barren air to this place first of all, and the goddesses beheld each other gladly and rejoiced in their hearts. Rhea, her hair brilliantly arrayed, spoke to Demeter thus: "Come here, my daughter; loud-thundering Zeus, who sees far and wide, summons you to join the company of the gods, and he has promised to grant you whatever honors you would like among the immortals, and he has consented that your daughter live a third part of the revolving year in the gloomy depths below and the other two-thirds with you and the other gods. Thus he said it would be accomplished and nodded his head in assent. But come, my child, and be obedient; do not persist in your relentless anger against Zeus, the dark-clouded son of Cronus. But quickly make grow for human beings the life-bringing fruit in abundance." (457–469)

Thus she spoke, and Demeter of the lovely crown obeyed. Quickly, she caused fruit to spring up from the fertile plains, and the whole wide land was laden with leaves and flowers. She went to the kings who minister justice (Triptolemus, Diocles, the rider of horses, the mighty Eumolpus, and Celeus, the leader of the people) and showed them the performance of her holy rites and taught her mysteries to them all, Triptolemus and Polyxeinus and Diocles besides—holy mysteries that one may not by any means violate or question or express. For the great reverence due to the gods restrains one's voice.

Happy is the one of mortals on earth who has seen these things. But those who are uninitiated into the holy rites and have no part never are destined to a similar joy when they are dead in the gloomy realm below. (470–482)

But when the goddess of goddesses had ordained all these things, they made their way to Olympus among the company of the other gods. There they dwell

360

380

beside Zeus, who delights in the thunder, august and holy goddesses. Greatly happy is the one of mortals on earth whom they dearly love; straightway they send, as a guest to his great house, Plutus, who gives wealth to human beings. (483–489)   380

Come now you who hold power over the land of fragrant Eleusis, sea-girt Paros, and rocky Antron, lady and queen Demeter, the giver of good things in season, both yourself and your daughter, very beautiful Persephone, kindly grant me a pleasing substance in reward for my song. Yet I shall remember both you and another song too. (490–495).

Interpretations of the Hymn

The myth of Demeter and Persephone represents another variation of a fundamental and recurring theme—the death and rebirth of vegetation as a metaphor or allegory for spiritual resurrection. In the New Testament (John 12:24), this archetype is expressed in this way: "Unless a grain of wheat falls into the earth and dies, it remains alone; but if it dies it bears much fruit." In this Greek hymn, the allegory is rendered in terms of the touching emotions of mother and daughter; more often the symbols and metaphors involve the relationship between a fertility goddess and her male partner, either lover or son (e.g., Aphrodite and Adonis, Cybele and Attis, Semele and Dionysus). Demeter is often imagined as the goddess of the ripe grain; Persephone then is the deity of the budding tender shoots. They are invoked together as the "two goddesses." Persephone (who is often called merely *Kore*, a name meaning "girl") is the daughter of Demeter and Zeus, who enact once again the sacred marriage between earth-goddess and sky-god.

This is a hymn permeated by emotional longings and religious allegories about death and rebirth, resurrection, and salvation. The parable of the infant **Demophoön** is particularly revealing. Nursed and cherished by Demeter, he flourished like a god and would have become immortal, his impure mortality cleansed away in the fire, if only the unfortunate Metaneira, who did not understand the rituals, had not interfered. If we are nourished like this child by Demeter's truth and become initiated into her mysteries, we too shall find redemption, immortality, and joy through the same love and devotion of this holy mother, lavished not only upon Demophoön but also upon her lovely daughter.

The *Homeric Hymn to Demeter* also illustrates the grim character of Hades in his method of obtaining a wife and provides the mythological reasons

Persephone, Hermes, and Hecate. Athenian red-figure krater, ca. 440 B.C. Persephone emerges from the Underworld under the protection of Hermes *psychopompos*, who looks directly at the viewer. He is dressed as a traveler and wears the *petasus* and *chlamys* (traveler's cloak), while the caduceus in his left hand points toward the ground. To the right, Hecate, looking back at Persephone and with a torch in each hand, lights the way. (*Image copyright © The Metropolitan Museum of Art/Art Resource, NY*)

for Hecate's prominence as a goddess of the Underworld. Hades' basic character as a fertility god is evident from the location of his realm, the violence of his nature, and his link with horses. He is thus a god of agricultural wealth (compare his names, Pluto or Dis, among the Romans); but he should not be confused with Plutus (Wealth) mentioned in the last lines of the hymn, another deity of agricultural plenty and prosperity (and thus wealth in general), the offspring of Demeter and Iasion.

The Departure of Triptolemus. Attic red-figure cup by Makron, ca. 480 B.C.; height 8¼ in. Triptolemus holds stalks of grain in his left hand and in his right hand a dish (*phiale*), into which Persephone pours liquid from the jug in her right hand; she holds a torch in her left hand. The libation is a necessary ritual before departure on a journey. To the left stands Demeter, holding a torch and grain stalks, and the personification of Eleusis stands behind Persephone. Triptolemus sits in a throne-like wheeled vehicle, whose wings symbolize the speed and extent of his travels, while the serpent indicates his association with the grain-bearing earth. (© *The Trustees of the British Museum*)

Triptolemus

Triptolemus, who also appears in the concluding lines of the hymn, is generally depicted as the messenger of Demeter when she restored fertility to the ground. He is the one who taught and spread her arts of agriculture to new lands at that time and later, often traveling in a magical car drawn by winged dragons, a gift of Demeter. He is sometimes either merged in identity with the infant Demophoön (variant spelling is Demophon) of the hymn or said to be his brother; in Plato, Triptolemus is a judge of the dead.

The Eleusinian Mysteries

This hymn to Demeter is of major importance because it provides the most significant evidence that we have for the nature of the worship of Demeter at **Eleusis**. The town of Eleusis is about 14 miles west of Athens; the religion and ceremony that developed in honor of Demeter and her daughter had its center here, but the city of Athens, too, was intimately involved. This religious observance was of a special kind, not the general prerogative of everyone but open only to those who wished to become initiates. These devotees were sworn to absolute secrecy and faced dire punishments if they revealed the secret rites.[3] This does not imply that initiation was confined to a select few. In early times, membership was inevitably limited to the people of Eleusis and Athens; but soon participants came from all areas of the Hellenic world and eventually from the Roman Empire as well.

This worship of Demeter was not restricted to men; women, children, and even slaves could participate. Appropriately, the religious celebration that evolved was given the name of the Eleusinian Mysteries. Demeter, then, along with other Hellenic deities, is the inspiration for a kind of worship that is generally designated as the mystery religions (compare elements in the worship of Dionysus and aspects of the devotion to Aphrodite and Adonis or Cybele and Attis). Orpheus is credited with originating the Mysteries, and the nature of Orphism and kindred mystery religions will be considered in Chapter 16. Although there must have been differences among the various mystery religions (some of them probably quite marked) obvious to the ancient world, today we have difficulty distinguishing precisely among them. It seems certain that the major common denominator is a belief in the immortality of the soul and a future life.

The Mysteries at Eleusis were kept secret so successfully that scholars are by no means agreed about what can be said with any certainty, particularly about the highest and most profound elements of the worship. The sanctuary at Eleusis has been excavated,[4] and buildings connected with the ceremonies have been found; most important among them is the temple of Demeter, where the final revelation of the Mysteries was celebrated.[5] But no evidence has been unearthed that might dispel the secrecy with absolute certainty once and for all. The priests in charge of the rites presumably transmitted orally what Demeter was said to have taught.

It is impossible to know just how much of the ritual is revealed in the *Hymn to Demeter*. It would be presumptuous to imagine that the most profound secrets are here for all to read, and we cannot be sure how much may be inferred from what is directly stated. That elements of the ceremonies are indicated cannot be denied, but presumably these are only the elements that were witnessed or revealed to all, not only to the initiated. Thus the text prescribes such details as an interval of nine days, fasting, the carrying of torches, the exchange of jests, the partaking of the drink **Kykeon**, the wearing of a special dress (e.g., the veil of Demeter); even precise geographical indications (e.g., the Maiden Well and the site of the temple) are designated.

The emotional tone of the poem, too, might hold the key for a mystic performance in connection with the celebrations. The anguish of Demeter, her frantic wanderings and search, the traumatic episode with Demophoön, the miraculous transformation of the goddess, the thrilling reunion between mother and daughter, the blessed return of vegetation to a barren earth—these are some of the obvious emotional and dramatic highlights.

The Greater and Lesser Mysteries

On the basis of our inadequate evidence, we present the following tentative outline of basic procedures in the celebration of the Eleusinian Mysteries; ultimate revelation and meaning are matters of more tenuous conjecture. Two major compulsory stages had to be undertaken: (1) participation in the Lesser Mysteries, involving preliminary steps in initiation; (2) advancement to the Greater Mysteries, which entailed full initiation into the cult. A third stage, not required but possible, entailed participation in the highest rites.[6] It is immediately apparent that these mysteries are basically different from the festivals celebrated in the Panhellenic sanctuaries at Olympia and Delphi, which were open to all, without secrecy or initiation or a fundamental mystic philosophy, however religious the tone that oracular response and devotion to a god might set.

Two major priestly families were connected with Eleusis.[7] Among the many important priesthoods and assistant officials, the highest was that of the **Hierophant**. This priest alone could reveal to the worshipers the ultimate mysteries that entailed the showing of the **Hiera**, the sacred objects—his title means "he who reveals the Hiera." Prominent too was the priestess of Demeter, who lived in a sacred house. Many of the priests received a fixed sum of money from each initiate as a fee for their services. The initiate was sponsored and directed by a patron.[8]

The Lesser Mysteries were held in Athens, usually once a year in early spring. Precise details are unknown, but the general purpose was certainly the preliminary preparation of the initiates for subsequent advancement to higher things.

Ceremonies probably focused on ritual purification, involving sacrifices, prayer, fasting, and cleansing by water.

The Greater Mysteries were held annually during the months of September and October. A holy truce was declared for a period of fifty-five days, and heralds were sent to issue invitations to states. Both Athens and Eleusis were involved in the festivities. Preliminary to the festival proper was the day on which the Hiera were taken out of the temple of Demeter in Eleusis and brought to Athens amid great pomp and ceremony. The splendid procession, headed by the priests and priestesses who carried the Hiera in sacred caskets bound by ribbons, was met officially in Athens and escorted in state to the sanctuary of Demeter in the city (the Eleusinion). The next day began the formal celebration of the Greater Mysteries, which continued through eight days, the ceremonies culminating in Eleusis, with a return to Athens on the ninth. The first day saw the people summoned to an assembly in the Athenian agora; those who were pure and knew Greek were invited by proclamation to participate in the Mysteries. On the second day, all participants were ordered to cleanse themselves in the sea. The third day was devoted to sacrifices and prayers. The fourth day was spent honoring the god of healing, Asclepius, who according to tradition had in previous times arrived late for initiation. So on this day other latecomers could enroll.

The festivities in Athens culminated on the fifth day in a brilliant procession back to Eleusis. Priests and laymen wended their prescribed way, crowned with myrtle and carrying mystic branches of myrtle tied with wool strands.[9] Heading the procession was a wooden statue of Iacchus (very likely another name for the god Dionysus) escorted in a carriage. At some stages of the journey, abuse, jest, and insults in scurrilous language were exchanged, perhaps in part to instill humility in the throng. Prayers were chanted and hymns sung; torches were carried and lit as night fell, and the sacred procession reached the sanctuary of Demeter in Eleusis.

The sixth and seventh days brought the initiates to the secret core of the Mysteries, and it seems safe to assume that much of the ritual was performed in remembrance of the episodes described in the *Hymn to Demeter*. Thus there was a fast (certain foods, such as pomegranates and beans, were prohibited) and a vigil; the fast was probably ended by the drinking of the prescribed drink, the Kykeon, whatever its significance.

Conjectures About the Revelation

The heart of the ceremonies, which were celebrated in Demeter's temple, apparently involved three stages: a dramatic enactment, the revelation of sacred objects, and the uttering of certain words. What were the themes of the dramatic pageant? Probably it focused on incidents from the story of Demeter and her wanderings and other episodes recorded in the hymn, all designed to elicit a religious catharsis. Some have suggested scenes of an Orphic character involving a simulated trip to the Underworld, with fabricated apparitions of terror and sublimity as the action moved from Hell (Tartarus) to Paradise (Elysium). That no underground chambers have been found in the excavations does not necessarily invalidate this theory. We do not know whether the initiates merely witnessed the drama or actually participated in it. Eventually, the culmination was the awe-inspiring exhibition by the Hierophant himself of the holy objects, bathed

THE NIINNION PINAX AND THE CELEBRATION OF THE MYSTERIES AT ELEUSIS

This clay tablet is a *pinax* (a votive plaque set up in a sanctuary to honor a god or goddess). This particular pinax has the name of the woman who dedicated it, Niinnion, inscribed along the bottom, and indicates that it was dedicated to "the two goddesses," Demeter and Persephone. It is in the shape of a temple with a pediment. It was discovered, broken into nine pieces, at Eleusis in 1895. It is now in the National Archaeological Museum in Athens.

There are many questions about what this plaque is intended to illustrate: does it represent the celebration of the Mysteries or another festival associated with Attica and Eleusis? Who precisely are the individual figures, and what are the other objects in the scene? Does it represent one single, discrete incident in a ritual, or is it a composite? Although absolute certainty is elusive, the plaque

Niinion Pinax. Red-figure clay votive tablet, ca. 370 B.C.; height: 0.44 m.; width: 0.32 m. (*akg-images/De Agostini Picture Lib./G. Nimatallah*)

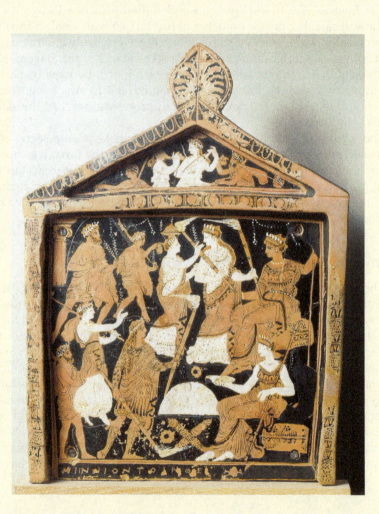

remains a provocative and compelling reminder of how difficult it can be to interpret a work that is so highly allusive and suggestive.

The great majority of scholars interpret the plaque as representing scenes associated with the Mysteries. The column in the upper left corner may indicate that we are within a sanctuary. A thin, white line curls through the center of the plaque and might indicate that the figures are to be understood as representing two groups. Perhaps the scene is depicting two processions, with the one in the upper part of the panel being the procession during the celebration of the Greater Mysteries and the one in the lower part of the panel being the procession of the Lesser Mysteries.

The lower scene, starting from the left, shows a mature, bearded male, crowned in myrtle and carrying over his shoulder a staff, which has a pouch tied to it. A woman precedes him, holding a staff with a pouch in one hand and a sprig of myrtle in the other. Myrtle had sacred associations in the rites of both Demeter and Dionysus. The gesture she makes signifies an attitude of reverence or adoration. This woman has been identified by some as Niinnion herself, taking part in the procession from Athens to Eleusis in preparation for the celebration of the Greater Mysteries proper. Upon her head she is carrying a *kernos* (a sacred vessel for offerings), which was used in the rites of Eleusis. The *Kernophoria* (Bearing of the Kernoi) was indeed part of the Greater and Lesser Mysteries. She stands on her toes and appears to be dancing. In front of her stands a figure, whose size seems to indicate that he is not a mortal but a god. He, too, wears a myrtle wreath upon his head and is leading the two *mystai* (initiates). He carries two torches, one pointed up and the other down. This may suggest the divergent existence of Persephone in the upper and lower worlds. This figure has been identified as Iacchus, an avatar of Dionysus, who is associated with the Mysteries of Eleusis. During the procession to Eleusis, preceded by a statue of Iacchus, the initiates would utter the cry "Iacche! Iacche!" signaling their excitement and anticipation. The figures in the lower panel make their procession to a seated goddess, who has been identified as Demeter. She is holding a *phiale* (libation vessel) and a staff. Between Iacchus and Demeter are depicted objects associated with Eleusis. The two crossing rods may be *bacchoi*, the sacred wands carried in the torch-lit procession to Eleusis. The white semicircular object is a bit harder to explain. Scholars have variously interpreted it: an *omphalos* (navel-stone); the rock left exposed within the *anaktoron* (the enclosed structure within the Telesterion); the *pelanos* (sacred cake offering of barley and wheat); or perhaps the *kiste* (covered basket), symbolizing the secrecy at the heart of the ritual.

In the upper register, from the left, we see a bearded male, crowned with a myrtle wreath and holding two sprigs of myrtle (the same man as below?); a garlanded youth who holds a cup in one hand and a staff in the other; and another woman bearing a kernos on her head. This woman has also been identified as Niinnion, depicted at a different moment in the ritual. A much larger figure, a goddess, precedes her, bearing torches, both of which point upward. Some have taken her to be Persephone leading the initiates toward her mother, Demeter, who is seated and holding a scepter. Others have understood the torch-bearing woman to be Hecate, who would certainly not be out of place in the scene. The coloring of the seated goddess is problematic. All the other female figures, whether mortal or divine, are depicted in white. Might she be Persephone, darkened to represent her chthonic existence?

The triangular pediment depicts the *Pannychis*, the nighttime celebration that followed the arrival of the initiates in Eleusis.

in a radiant light as he delivered his mystic utterances. The highest stage of all, which was not required for full initiation, entailed further revelation of some sort. The eighth day concluded the ceremonies; the ninth brought the return to Athens, this time with no organized procession. The following day the Athenian council heard a full report on the conduct of the ceremonies.

Conjectures about the exact nature of the highest Mysteries have been legion. Comments by the fathers of the Christian church have been brought to witness, but their testimony has been rightly viewed with grave suspicion because it was probably rooted in prejudice, stemming from ignorance and hostility. No one of them had ever been initiated into the Mysteries, and surprisingly enough, those Christian converts who had been initiated seem to have continued to take their pledges of secrecy very seriously. It has been claimed that the ultimate revelation was connected with the transformation of the Eleusinian plain into a field of golden grain (as in the hymn). The heart of the Mysteries consisted of no more than showing an ear of grain to the worshipers. Thus we actually *do* know the secrets; or, if you like, they are really not worth knowing at all in terms of serious religious thought. Yet this ear of grain may, after all, realistically and allegorically represent the enigma of the mystery itself. Others insist on an enactment of the holy marriage in connection with the ceremonies, imagining not a spiritual but a literal sexual union between the Hierophant and the Priestess of Demeter. The Hiera too might be a representation of the female genitalia and, since Dionysus may be linked with Demeter and Kore, the male phallus as well. These holy objects were witnessed, or even manipulated, by the initiates in the course of the ritual. But there is no good evidence to argue with any certainty for such orgiastic procedures. The Hiera, as has been conjectured, could have been merely sacred and antique relics handed down from the Mycenaean Age.

It is difficult to agree with those who assert that Dionysus was completely excluded from the worship of Demeter at Eleusis. Iacchus has good claims to be Dionysus. And the myth of Zagreus-Dionysus, which provides the authority

The Festival of the Thesmophoria

Women generally played a dominant role in the religion of the ancient world. Only women were permitted to participate in the celebration of some of these rites, and not only men but also virgins and children were excluded. One of the most famous of these women's festivals was the Thesmophoria, common to all Greece. The rites as performed in Athens became the subject of Aristophanes' comedy *Thesmophoriazusae*, which focused on the doings of the feminine participants and the dire consequences for any male who dared to intrude. The festival, lasting five days, took place in the fall, and its purpose was to ensure fertility, especially that of the crops to be sowed. Important in the ceremonies was the throwing of piglets into subterranean pits; after three days, their remains were recovered and mixed with the seed to be planted in hopes of a good harvest. The etiology for this practice was provided by the myth of Eubouleus, a swineherd, who was swallowed up with his swine by the earth at the very time Persephone was taken by Pluto. Celebrations also included sexual abstinence, a procession, sacrifices, fasting and feasting, and even ribald jests.[10]

for Orphism (see pp. 318 and 385), makes Persephone his mother. Any spiritual message in the cult at Eleusis must have, in common with Dionysiac cults, a belief in the immortality of the soul and in redemption. If a doctrine similar to that of Orphism is also involved, it need not spring directly from Orphism. The confusion arises because all the mystery religions (whatever their precise inter-relation)[11] did in fact preach certain things in common.

The death and rebirth of vegetation as deified in Demeter and Kore surely suggest a belief in the afterlife. After all, this is the promise of the hymn: "But the one who is not initiated into the holy rites and has no part never is destined to a similar joy when he is dead in the gloomy realm below." If at some future time only obscure evidence remained for the ritual of the Christian Mass, scholars might imagine all sorts of things and miss completely the religious and spiritual doctrine on which it rests. The words uttered by the Hierophant could have ordained spiritual direction and hope. But there was no church body as such for the followers of Demeter, in the sense that they were required to return each year; we know of no sacred writings like those, say, of Orphism. George Mylonas' conclusions affirm the universal power of the matriarchal cult of Demeter in the Greco-Roman world:

Whatever the substance and meaning of the Mysteries was, the fact remains that the cult of Eleusis satisfied the most sincere yearnings and the deepest longings of the human heart. The initiates returned from their pilgrimage to Eleusis full of joy and happiness, with the fear of death diminished and the strengthened hope of a better life in the world of shadows: "Thrice happy are those of mortals, who having seen those rites depart for Hades; for to them alone is it granted to have true life there; to the rest all there is evil," Sophocles cries out exultantly. And to this Pindar with equal exultation answers: "Happy is he who, having seen these rites goes below the hollow earth; for he knows the end of life and he knows its god-sent beginning." When we read these and other similar statements written by the great or nearly great of the ancient world, by the dramatists and the thinkers, when we picture the magnificent buildings and monuments constructed at Eleusis by great political figures like Peisistratos, Kimon, Perikles, Hadrian, Marcus Aurelius and others, we cannot help but believe that the Mysteries of Eleusis were not an empty, childish affair devised by shrewd priests to fool the peasant and the ignorant, but a philosophy of life that possessed substance and meaning and imparted a modicum of truth to the yearning human soul. That belief is strengthened when we read in Cicero that Athens has given nothing to the world more excellent or divine than the Eleusinian Mysteries. Let us recall again that the rites of Eleusis were held for some two thousand years; that for two thousand years civilized humanity was sustained and ennobled by those rites. Then we shall be able to appreciate the meaning and importance of Eleusis and of the cult of Demeter in the pre-Christian era. When Christianity conquered the Mediterranean world, the rites of Demeter, having perhaps fulfilled their mission to humanity, came to an end. The "bubbling spring" of hope and inspiration that once existed by the Kallichoron well became dry and the world turned to other living sources for sustenance. The cult that inspired the world for so long was gradually forgotten, and its secrets were buried with its last Hierophant.[12]

Finally, a word of caution about the usual generalizations put forth concerning the dichotomy between the mystery religions and the state religions (see pp. 152–153) of antiquity. The argument runs something like this. The formal state religions were sterile or very soon became so; people's hope and faith lay only in the vivid experience offered by the Mysteries. Whatever the general truth of this view, it must be noted that for classical Greece, at any rate, the lines are not so distinct. Ceremonies connected with Demeter at Eleusis are tied securely to the policies of the Athenian state. The *archon basileus* (an Athenian official in charge of religious matters in general) directed the celebrations for Demeter in Athens. The Athenian council as a political body was very much concerned about the festival. The pomp and procession involved are startlingly similar to the pageant connected with the Panathenaic festival in honor of Athena, a civic function, whatever its spiritual import. The "church" at Eleusis and the Athenian state were, to all intents and purposes, one.

The Triumph of Matriarchy

Again and again there appear in mythology variations on the theme of the dominant earth-goddess and her subordinate male lover, who dies and is reborn to ensure the resurrection of the crops and of the souls of mortals. Demeter's name may mean "earth mother," but her myth and that of Persephone introduce a startling and drastic variation of this eternal and universal archetype. The myth's blatant sexuality is replaced by a more refined and purer concept of motherhood and the love between a mother and daughter. In this guise, with nobility and humanity, the mother-goddess and matriarchy sustained their dominance in the ancient world.

Details of the myth continually challenge Zeus' patriarchal power. The abduction of Persephone ordained by the supreme god so that Hades might have a wife and the Underworld might have a queen is depicted not as a divine right but as a brutal rape, seen from the point of view of Demeter, who will not accept the status quo and is mighty enough to modify it. Through compromise, both the will of Zeus and the will of Demeter are fulfilled. Demeter shares the love and the person of her daughter with Hades; Hades has his wife; and Persephone attains honor as queen of the Underworld: the mystic cycle of death and rebirth is explained by a myth accommodating a specific matriarchal religious ritual, promising joy in this life and the next.

As we have seen, the Eleusinian Mysteries were an inspiring spiritual force and became the one universal mystery religion of the ancient world before Christianity. Indeed, matriarchy was very much alive and well in the patriarchal world of the Greeks and the Romans.

Select Bibliography

Dillon, Matthew. *Girls and Women in Classical Greek Religion.* New York: Routledge, 2002.

Foley, Helene P., ed. *The Homeric Hymn to Demeter: Translation, Commentary, and Interpretive Essays.* Princeton, NJ: Princeton University Press, 1998. A wealth of material, with contributions by several scholars, on all sorts of subjects related to the *Hymn*, for example, religion, psychology, politics, variants of the myth, archetypal themes, female experience, and manifold influences on literature and thought.

Hinds, S. *The Metamorphosis of Persephone: Ovid and the Self-Conscious Muse.* New York: Cambridge University Press, 1987. Deals with Ovid's treatment of the rape of Persephone in *Metamorphoses* 5 and *Fasti* 4.

Jung, C. G., and Kerényi, C. *Essays on a Science of Mythology: The Myth of the Divine Child and the Mysteries of Eleusis.* Princeton, NJ: Princeton University Press, 1963. Jung provides a psychological commentary for Kerényi's essays on the Divine Child and the Kore (the maiden).

Kerényi, C. *Archetypal Image of Mother and Daughter.* New York: Schocken, 1977.

Mylonas, George E. *Eleusis and the Eleusinian Mysteries.* Princeton, NJ: Princeton University Press, 1961.

Spaeth, Barbette Stanley. *The Roman Goddess Ceres.* Austin, TX: University of Texas Press, 1995. This study of the Roman counterpart of Demeter challenges the interpretation of goddesses as archetypes for feminist liberation.

Primary Sources

Sources in the Chapter

Homeric Hymn 2	*To Demeter*
Homeric Hymn 13	*To Demeter*

Additional Sources

Aristophanes	*Thesmophoriazuse*
Herodotus	*History of the Persian Wars* 8.65.1–6 (a mysterious cloud comes from Eleusis)
Ovid	*Metamorphoses* 5.341–571

Notes

1. That is, "to initiate and observe the holy rite or sacrament." There appears to be a lacuna after this sentence. The words translated "for the sake of the holy rite" are difficult, and their precise meaning is disputed. The reference must be to an important part of the ceremony of the Eleusinian mysteries, namely, the partaking of a drink called the *Kykeon*. But the nature and significance of the ritual are unknown: was this in any real sense the sharing of a sacrament, an act of communion fraught with mystic significance, or was it merely a token remembrance of these hallowed actions of the goddess?
2. Sixteen of these names are listed among the daughters of Oceanus and Tethys by Hesiod (*Theogony* 346–361); and Melite is a Nereid (246). The poet adds Leucippe, Phaeno, Iache, and Rhodope.
3. The charges against Alcibiades mentioned in the box on p. 289 are indicative of the seriousness of the consequences if the sacred ceremonies were divulged or desecrated in any way.
4. See in particular George E. Mylonas, *Eleusis and the Eleusinian Mysteries* (Princeton, NJ: Princeton University Press, 1961); this remains the best general survey of all the evidence and the inherent archaeological, historical, religious, and philosophical problems. For the priestess of Demeter and Kore at Eleusis, see Joan Breton Connelly, *Portrait of a Priestess* (Princeton, NJ: Princeton University Press, 2007), pp. 64–69.
5. As a place for the celebration of the mysteries (the Greek word is *teletai*), the temple of Demeter is called a *telesterion*.
6. Known as the *Epopteia*.
7. The Eumolpids (whose ancestor Eumolpus, according to the hymn, received the mysteries from Demeter herself) and the Kerykes.
8. The initiate was the *mystes* and his patron the *mystagogos*.
9. Aristophanes' *Frogs*, 340 ff., gives us some idea of this procession.

10. Another important woman's festival in honor of Demeter, the Haloa, during the season of wine making, celebrated Dionysus as well. There was an abundance of food and drink, and the worshipers were particularly raucous and ribald. See Matthew Dillon, *Girls and Women in Classical Greek Religion* (New York: Routledge, 2002). For a survey of festivals, see H. W. Parke, *Festivals of the Athenians* (Ithaca, NY: Cornell University Press, 1977); also Erika Simon, *Festivals of Attica: An Archaeological Commentary* (Madison, WI: University of Wisconsin Press, 1983).

11. Herodotus (8.65) tells a tale about a mysterious cloud (arising from Eleusis amid the strains of the mystic hymn to Iacchus) that provided a true omen of future events; in the context, the worship of the mother and the maiden is mentioned. This miracle sets the right tone for elements common to the worship and myths of both Demeter and Dionysus. It is not impossible that the passion of this resurrection-god played some role in the mysteries; Dionysus, too, is close to drama, and drama lies at the essence of the emotional aspects of Eleusinian ritual.

12. Mylonas, *Eleusis and the Eleusinian Mysteries,* pp. 284–285; footnotes are omitted.

15

VIEWS OF THE AFTERLIFE: THE REALM OF HADES

An Ancient Painting of the Underworld

The water appears to be a river, clearly representing Acheron, and there are reeds growing in it and fish. The shapes of the fish are so faintly drawn you would guess they were shadows rather than fish. And on the river there is a boat and at the oars the ferryman.

—PAUSANIAS, *Description of Greece* 10.28.1

Homer's Book of the Dead

The earliest surviving account of the realm of Hades appears in Book 11 of the *Odyssey*. Homer's geographical and spiritual depiction is fundamental to subsequent elaborations and thus deserves to be excerpted at some length. Odysseus is telling the Phaeacians and their king Alcinoüs of his visit to the Underworld, where he must consult the seer Tiresias about how to reach Ithaca, his homeland (12–99):

> Our ship came to the farthest realm of deep-flowing Oceanus, where the country of the Cimmerians lies shrouded in cloud and mist. Bright Helius never looks down on them with his rays, either when he ascends to starry heaven or returns to earth; but dire night covers these poor mortals. Here we beached our ship, and after putting the animals ashore, we went along the stream of Oceanus until we came to the place that Circe had indicated. Here two of my men, Perimedes and Eurylochus, held the sacrificial victims, and I drew my sharp sword from my side and dug a pit about 18 inches square. Around it I poured a libation to all the dead, first with a mixture of honey and milk, then with sweet wine, and a third 10 time with water; over this I sprinkled white barley. I then supplicated the many strengthless spirits of the dead, promising that once I had come to Ithaca I should sacrifice, in my own halls, a barren heifer, the very best I had, and heap the sacrificial pyre with the finest things and offer separately to Tiresias alone a jet-black sheep that was outstanding among my flocks.[1] (12–33)
>
> When I had finished entreating the host of the dead with prayers and supplications, I seized the victims and cut their throats, and their dark

blood flowed into the pit. Then the souls of the dead who had departed swarmed up from Erebus:[2] young brides, unmarried boys, old men having suffered much, 20 tender maidens whose hearts were new to sorrow, and many men wounded by bronze-tipped spears and wearing armor stained with blood. From one side and another they gathered about the pit in a multitude with frightening cries. Pale fear took hold of me, and then I urgently ordered my companions to flay the animals which lay slaughtered by the pitiless bronze and burn them and pray to the gods, to mighty Hades and dread Persephone. But I myself drew my sword from my side and took my post and did not allow the strengthless spirits of the dead to come near the blood before I had questioned Tiresias. (34–50)

But first the soul of my comrade Elpenor came up, for he had not yet been buried in the wide earth.[3] We had left his body in Circe's palace, unwept and 30 unburied, since other toil had oppressed us. I wept at seeing him and pitied him and calling out addressed him with winged words: "Elpenor, how have you come in this gloomy realm? You arrived on foot sooner than I in my black ship." (51–58)

Thus I spoke; and he replied with a groan: "Royal son of Laërtes, clever Odysseus, a divine and evil destiny and too much wine were my undoing. When I went to sleep in Circe's palace, I forgot to climb down the long ladder and fell headlong from the roof; my neck was severed from my spine and my soul came down to the realm of Hades.[4] Since I know that when you leave this house of Hades you will stop with your fine ship at Circe's island of Aeaea, I beseech you by those whom you left 40 behind far away, by your wife and father who took care of you as a child, and by Telemachus, your only son whom you left at home in your palace, do not turn away and go back leaving me unwept and unburied for future time, or I may become the cause of wrathful vengeance from the gods upon you. But burn my body with all the armor that I have and pile up a mound for me on the shore of the gray sea, the grave of an unfortunate man, so that posterity too may know. Do these things for me and plant on the mound the oar with which I rowed alongside my companions while I was alive." (59–78)

Thus he spoke. And I addressed him in answer: "My poor friend, I shall accomplish to the full all your wishes." So we two faced each other in sad conver- 50 sation, I holding my sword over the blood and on the other side the shade of my companion recounting many things. The soul of my dead mother came up next, daughter of great-hearted Autolycus, she who was alive when I went to sacred Ilium. I cried when I saw her and pitied her in my heart. Still, even though I was deeply moved I did not allow her to come near the blood before I had questioned Tiresias. (79–89)

Then the soul of Theban Tiresias came up, bearing a golden scepter. He knew me and spoke: "Royal son of Laërtes, clever Odysseus, why, why, my poor fellow, have you left the light of the sun and come to see the dead and their joyless land? But step back from the pit, and hold aside your sharp sword so that I may drink the 60 blood and speak the truth to you." So he spoke; and I drew back my silver-studded sword and thrust it into its sheath. After he had drunk the dark blood, then the noble seer spoke to me.[5] (90–99)

Tiresias then tells Odysseus what destiny has in store for him; after the seer has prophesied, Odysseus asks how he can enable his mother, Anticlea, to recognize him (141–159):

"I see there the soul of my dead mother, and she stays near the blood in silence and has not dared to look at her own son face to face nor speak to him. Tell me, O prince, how may she recognize that I am her son?" Thus I spoke. And he addressed me at once with the answer: "I shall tell you simple directions which you must follow. Any one of the dead you allow to come near the blood will speak to you clearly, but anyone you refuse will go back away from you." With these words the soul of Prince Tiresias went into the home of Hades, after he had uttered his prophecies. (141–151)

But I remained steadfast where I was until my mother came up and drank the dark blood. Immediately then she knew me and in her sorrow spoke winged words: "My son, how have you come, while still alive, below to this gloomy realm which is difficult for the living to behold? For great rivers and terrible waters lie between, first Oceanus which, if one does not have a sturdy ship, he cannot in any way cross on foot." (152–159)

Anticlea and Odysseus continue their conversation, questioning each other. Finally, she reveals to her son that it was heartache and longing for him that brought her life to an end. At this Odysseus cannot restrain himself (204–234):

Troubled in spirit I wished to embrace the soul of my dead mother; three times I made the attempt, as desire compelled me, three times she slipped through my hands like a shadow or a dream. Sharp pain welled up from the depths of my heart, and speaking I addressed her with winged words: "O my mother, why do you not stay for me so eager to embrace you, so that we both may throw our arms about each other, even in Hades' realm, and take comfort in chill lamentation? Or has august Persephone conjured up this phantom for me so that I may groan still more in my grief?" (204–214)

Thus I spoke, and she, my lady mother, answered at once: "O my poor child, ill-fated beyond all men; Persephone, daughter of Zeus, does not trick you at all; but this is the doom of mortals when they die, for no longer do sinews hold bones and flesh together, but the mighty power of blazing fire consumes all, as soon as the life breath leaves our white bones and the soul like a dream flutters and flies away. But as quickly as possible make your way back to the light, but understand all these things so that you may in the future tell them to your wife." Thus we two exchanged words; then women came up (for august Persephone compelled them), all of whom were the wives or daughters of noble men. And they gathered all together about the dark blood. But I deliberated how I might speak to each one individually, and upon reflection this seemed to me the best plan. I drew my sharp sword from my sturdy side and did not allow them to drink the dark blood all at the same time. And they came up one by one and each explained her lineage and I questioned them all. (215–234)

The parade of beautiful women that follows is packed with mythological and genealogical information that has little meaning for us in this context. At the end, Persephone drives away the souls of these illustrious ladies. A lengthy interview follows between Odysseus and Agamemnon, who tells bitterly of his murder at the hands of his wife, Clytemnestra, and her lover, Aegisthus, and remains suspicious and hostile toward all women. Then the souls of Achilles and Patroclus and

The Underworld, Apulian red-figure krater by the Underworld painter, ca. 320 B.C.; dimensions not given. This large vase represents many of the myths of the Underworld. In the center, Hades sits enthroned facing Persephone in a small temple. She is crowned and holds a staff; chariot wheels hang from the ceiling, probably the wheels of the chariot in which Hades abducted Persephone. To the left Orpheus plays his lyre, and behind him may be Megara and the children of Heracles. To the right a Fury stands next to a seated judge of the Underworld, before whom is the soul of an old man. In the bottom register Heracles drags off Cerberus, while Hermes points the way. To the left a Fury lashes Sisyphus, and to the right Tantalus, wearing a Phrygian cap, reaches up toward an overhanging cliff. In the upper register appear to be scenes of initiation, and on the neck are the chariots of Helius and Selene, beneath which fishes symbolize the Ocean in which their daily (or nightly) journeys begin and end. (*Carole Raddato/Flickr (CC BY-SA 2.0)*)

the greater Ajax appear. The soul of Achilles addresses Odysseus next (Patroclus does not speak). We must excerpt two portions of their conversation to establish more completely the tone and humanity of Homer's conception. The first reveals Achilles' despair (473–491):

"Royal son of Laërtes, clever and indomitable Odysseus, what still greater exploit have you ingeniously devised? How have you dared to come down to Hades' realm where spirits without body or sense dwell, shadows of mortals worn out by life?" Thus he spoke, and I addressed him in answer, "O Achilles, son of Peleus, by far the mightiest of the Achaeans, I came down to Hades' realm to ask the seer Tiresias if he might tell me some way by which I might return to rocky Ithaca. For I have not yet come near Achaea ⟨10⟩ nor yet reached my homeland, but I always have misfortunes. But no man either before or after is more fortunate than you, Achilles. Previously while you lived, we Argives heaped honors on you equal to those of the gods, and now being in this place you have great power among these shades. So, Achilles, do not be at all distressed, even though you are dead." (473–486)

Thus I spoke, and he at once addressed me in answer: "Do not speak to me soothingly about ⟨20⟩ death, glorious Odysseus; I should prefer as a slave to serve another man, even if he had no property and little to live on, than to rule over all these dead who have done with life." (487–491)

Achilles goes on to inquire about his son, Neoptolemus; and when Odysseus has given details of how the boy has proven himself a man worthy of his father, Achilles in his pride feels a surge of joy illumine his gloomy existence (538–544):

The soul of swift-footed Achilles [Odysseus goes on to relate] made its way in great strides over the plain full of asphodel, rejoicing because I said that his son was a renowned hero. Other souls of the dead stood grieving, and each recounted his sorrows. Only the soul of Ajax, son of Telamon, stood apart. (538–544)

Ajax, who committed suicide because Odysseus was awarded the armor of Achilles rather than he, will not respond to Odysseus' appeals (563–600):

Instead he followed the dead spirits into Erebus, where perhaps he might have spoken to me or I to him. But desire in my breast wished to see the souls of the other dead. (563–567)

There I saw Minos, the splendid son of Zeus, sitting with a gold scepter in his hand and pronouncing judgments for the dead, and they sitting and standing asked the king for his decisions within the wide gates of Hades' house. And I saw next the giant hunter Orion, driving together on the plain of asphodel the wild beasts which he himself had killed on the lonely mountains, having in his hand a bronze club that was always unbreakable. And I saw Tityus, son of revered Earth, lying on the ground covering a vast area. Two vultures sitting on either side of him tore into his body and   10
ate at his liver, and his hands could not keep them off. For he had assaulted Leto, the renowned consort of Zeus, as she was going through Panopeus, a city of beautiful dancing places, to Pytho.[6] (568–581)

And also I saw Tantalus enduring harsh sufferings as he stood in a pool that splashed to his chin. He strained to quench his thirst but was not able; for every time the old man leaned eagerly to take a drink, the water was swallowed up and gone and about his feet there was black earth, dried up by some divine power. Tall and leafy trees dangled fruit above his head: pears, pomegranates, apples, sweet figs, and olives, growing in luxuriant profusion. But whenever he reached out to grasp them in his hands, the wind snatched them away to the shadowy clouds.[7]   20
(582–592)

And also I saw Sisyphus enduring hard sufferings as he pushed a huge stone; exerting all his weight with both his hands and feet, he kept shoving it up to the top of the hill. But just when he was about to thrust it over the crest, then its own weight forced it back, and once again the pitiless stone rolled down to the plain. Yet again he put forth his strength and pushed it up; sweat poured from his limbs and dust rose up high about his head. (593–600)

Sisyphus

The greatest exploit of Sisyphus, the son of Aeolus, was outwitting Death (Thanatos) himself. In its simplest form, it is alluded to by the seventh-century poet Alcaeus of Lesbos (frag. 110. 5–10):

For Sisyphus also, the son of Aeolus, thought that he was the cleverest of men to overpower Death. Yet, although he was crafty and crossed swirling Acheron twice (avoiding his destiny), the King [Zeus], son of Cronus, devised labor for him beneath the black earth.

Sisyphus aroused the anger of Zeus by telling the river-god Asopus that Zeus had carried off his daughter Aegina, and Zeus sent Death to carry Sisyphus off. Sisyphus chained Death, and as long as he was bound, no mortals could die. Eventually, Ares freed Death and handed Sisyphus over to him, but before he went down to the Underworld, Sisyphus left instructions with his wife, Merope, not to make the customary sacrifices after his death. When Hades found that no sacrifices were being made, he sent Sisyphus back to remonstrate with Merope. So Sisyphus returned to Corinth and stayed there until he died in advanced old age. It was for his revelation of Zeus' secret that he was punished in the Underworld by having to roll a huge rock uphill only to have it roll down again.

Odysseus next sees the phantom of Heracles—the real Heracles is with his wife, Hebe, among the immortal gods. Heracles tells how he, too, was ill-fated while he lived, performing labors for an inferior master.

Homer's Book of the Dead ends when hordes of the shrieking dead swarm up and Odysseus in fright makes for his ship to resume his journey.

Interpretations of the Homeric Underworld

Countless difficulties beset any interpretation of the Homeric view of the afterlife, many of them linked to the nature of the composition of the *Odyssey* as a whole and of this book in particular. Discrepancies are apparent, and explanations must finally hinge on one's views on the much wider problems of the Homeric question. Does the Book of the Dead reflect different attitudes and concepts put together by one man or by several, at one time or over a period of years—even centuries? Basic to the account, perhaps, is a cult of the dead—seen in the sacrificial ceremonies performed at the trench and in the serious note of moral compulsion to provide burial for one who has died. But as the description proceeds, there is much that is puzzling. Odysseus apparently remains at his post while the souls come up; if so, how does he witness the torments of the sinners and the activities of the heroes described? Are they visions from the pit of blood, or is this episode an awkward addition from a different treatment that had Odysseus actually tour the realm of Hades? Certainly, the section listing the women who come up in a group conveys strongly the feelings of an insertion, written in the style of the Boeotian epic of Hesiod. As the book begins, the stream of Oceanus seems to be the only barrier, but later Anticlea speaks of other rivers to be crossed.

Thus the geography of the Homeric Underworld is vague, and similarly the classification of those who inhabit it is obscurely defined, particularly in terms of the precision that is evident in subsequent literature. Elpenor, among those who first swarm up, may belong to a special group in a special area, but we cannot be sure. Heroes like Agamemnon and Achilles are together, but they do not clearly occupy a separate paradise; the meadow of asphodel they inhabit seems to refer to the whole realm, not to an Elysium such as we find described by Vergil. One senses, rather, that all mortals end up together pretty much in the same place, without distinction. Since Odysseus thinks that Achilles has power among the shades as great as that which he had among the living, perhaps some prerogatives are assigned or taken for granted. A special hell for sinners may be implied (at least they are listed in a group), but it is noteworthy that these sinners are extraordinary indeed, great figures of mythological antiquity who dared great crimes against the gods. Apparently, ordinary mortals do not suffer so for their sins. Homer does not seem to present an afterlife of judgment and reward and punishment, and Minos presumably acts as a judge among the dead, settling their disputes there very much as he did in real life.

The tone and mood of the Homeric afterlife are generally more consistent. Vague and fluttering spirits, with all the pursuits, passions, and prejudices they had while alive, drift aimlessly and joylessly in the gloom; the light and hope and vigor of the upper world are gone. Philosophical and religious thought, shot through with moral earnestness and righteous indignation, will soon bring about sublime and terrifying variations in this picture.

Depicting the Underworld

The Underworld of the ancient Greeks from Homer to the time of Plato was a dim and shadowy place, best described in words. Precise pictures on vases and reliefs were rare, and the Underworld vase, painted some fifty years after Plato's *Republic* and illustrated on p. 354, is an unusually precise image, focusing on the myths of Orpheus, Heracles, and the sinners against the gods. Plato's word-picture gave new definition to the shadows of the Homeric Underworld, preparing the way for Vergil's detailed picture. Only with the Christian expansion of the ancient doctrines of justice and retribution, allied to the ideas of sin and punishment, were artists free to depict an underworld of fire and ice, of devils and exquisite punishments. The *Inferno* of Dante, composed early in the fourteenth century, changed the picture forever, combining the classical myths with medieval doctrines and preparing the way for the great representations of the Last Judgment, such as the fresco by Michelangelo in the Sistine Chapel and innumerable medieval stained-glass windows in French and English churches. Their creators would be surprised, and perhaps shocked, to realize that their Christian interpretations were ultimately founded on the pagan myths.

The Last Judgment, by Luca Signorelli (1450–1523); fresco, 1499–1502. In the chapel of San Brizio within the cathedral at Orvieto, Signorelli created his masterpiece, a fresco cycle depicting the end of the world. His work had a profound influence on Michelangelo's *Last Judgment* in the Sistine Chapel. This section of the work depicts the assembly of the damned as they are brought to hell to be tormented by demons. The decorations on the lower sections of the walls, beneath the larger frescoes such as this one, include portraits of famous poets, including Dante, Vergil, and Ovid, surrounded by grisaille (monochromatic painting using shades of gray) roundels, illustrating stories from their works that touch upon the Underworld—for example, Aeneas, the Sibyl, and the golden bough; Orpheus playing before Pluto and Proserpina; and Heracles capturing Cerberus. When seen in the context of the chapel, these classical poets with their vision of the Underworld appear as the literal foundation of later Christian thinking about the afterlife. (*Scala/Art Resource, NY*)

Plato's Myth of Er

Plato concludes the last book of his great dialogue, *The Republic*, with the myth of Er. This vision of the afterlife is steeped in religious and philosophical concepts; and although figures from mythology are incorporated, the symbolic and spiritual world depicted is far removed from that of Homer. Addressing Glaucon, Socrates makes this clear as he begins (614b2–616b1):

I shall not tell a tale like that of Odysseus to Alcinoüs, but instead my story is of a brave man, Er, the son of Armenius, a Pamphylian, who at one time died in war; after ten days, when the bodies—by now decayed—were taken up, his alone was uncorrupted. He was brought home, and on the twelfth day after his death placed on a funeral pyre in preparation for burial. But he came back to life and told what he had seen in the other world. He said that, after his soul had departed, it traveled with many and came to a divine place, in which there were two openings in the earth next to each other, and opposite were two others in the upper region of the sky. (614b2–614c3)

In the space between these four openings sat judges who passed sentence: the just they ordered to go to the right through one of the openings upward in the sky, after they had affixed their judgments in front of them; the unjust they sent to the left through one of the downward openings, bearing on their backs indications of all that they had done; to Er, when he approached, they said that he must be a messenger to human beings about the afterlife and commanded him to listen and watch everything in this place. (614c3–614d3)

To be sure, he saw there the souls, after they had been judged, going away through the opening either in the heaven or in the earth, but from the remaining two openings he saw some souls coming up out of the earth, covered with dust and dirt, and others descending from the second opening in the sky, pure and shining. And they kept arriving and appeared as if they were happy indeed to return after a long journey to the plain that lay between. Here they encamped as though for a festival, and mutual acquaintances exchanged greetings; those who had come from the earth and those from the sky questioned one another. The first group recounted their experiences, weeping and wailing as they recalled all the various things they had suffered and seen in their journey under the earth, which had lasted one thousand years; the others from the sky told in turn of the happiness they had felt and sights of indescribable beauty. (614d3–615a4)

O Glaucon, it would take a long time to relate everything. But he did say that the essential significance was this: everyone had to suffer an appropriate penalty for each and every sin ten times over, in retribution for the number of times and the number of persons he had wronged; that is, he must make one full payment once every hundred years (since this is considered the span of human life) so that he might pay in full for all his wrongs, tenfold in one thousand years. For example, if any were responsible for the deaths of many or betrayed and enslaved cities or armies or were guilty of any other crime, they would suffer torments ten times over for all these sins individually; but on the other hand, if they had done good deeds and were just and holy, in the same proportion they were given a worthy reward. About those who died immediately after birth and those who had lived a short time he said other things not worth mentioning. (615a4–615c2)

He described still greater retribution for honor or dishonor toward gods and parents and for murder. He told how he was near one spirit who asked another where Ardiaeus the Great was. This Ardiaeus had been tyrant in a city of Pamphylia a thousand years before this time, and he was said to have killed his aged parents and older brother and to have committed many other unholy deeds. The reply was that he had not come and would not come back to the plain. For to be sure this was one of the terrifying sights that we witnessed. (615c2–615d4)   50

When we were near the mouth and about to come up, after experiencing everything else, we suddenly saw Ardiaeus and others, most of whom were tyrants, but there were also some ordinary persons who had committed great wrongs. They all thought that they would at last ascend upward, but the mouth would not let them; instead it gave forth a roar, whenever any who were so incurable in their wickedness or had not paid sufficient penalty attempted to come up. Then indeed wild men, fiery of aspect, who stood by and understood the roar, seized some of them and led them away, but they bound Ardiaeus and the others, head, hand, and foot, threw them down, and flayed them; they dragged them along the road outside the mouth combing their flesh like wool with thorns, making clear to others as they passed the reason for the punishment and that they were being led away to be   60
hurled down to Tartarus. (615d4–616a4)

Of all the many and varied terrors that happened to them there, by far the greatest for each was that he might hear the roar as he came up, and when there was silence each ascended with the utmost joy. The judgments then were such as these: punishments for some and again rewards for others in due proportion.

The souls who have completed their cycle of 1,000 years spend seven days on the plain and then proceed on another journey, accompanied by Er. Four days later they arrive at a place from which they behold a beam of light that extends like a pillar through all of heaven and earth. After another day's journey, they can see that this light provides as it were a bond or chain to hold the universe together; from this chain of light extends the spindle of Necessity (*Ananke*) by which all the revolving spheres are turned. The next section of the myth presents a difficult, cosmological explanation of the universe, with its circles of fixed stars and revolving planets, the earth being at the center.[8]

Then Plato's account of Er, as Socrates relates it, continues with a description of the harmony of the spheres (617b4–621d3):

The spindle turned on the knees of Necessity. A Siren was perched aloft each of the circles and borne along with it, uttering a single sound on one musical note; from all eight came a unified harmony. Round about at equal distances sat three others, each on a throne, the Fates (*Moirai*), daughters of Necessity, in white robes with garlands on their heads, Lachesis, Clotho, and Atropos, singing to the music of the Sirens: Lachesis of the past, Clotho of the present, and Atropos of the future. Clotho touches with her right hand the outside circle of the spindle and helps turn it; with her left Atropos moves the inner circles in the same way, and Lachesis touches and moves both, alternating with each hand. (617b4–617d1)   10

Immediately after the souls arrived, they had to approach Lachesis. First of all, a prophet arranged them in order; and then, after taking from the knees of

Lachesis lots and examples of lives, he mounted a lofty platform and spoke: "Hear the word of Lachesis, maiden daughter of Necessity. Ephemeral souls, this is the beginning of another cycle of mortal life fraught with death. A divinity will not allot himself to you, but you will choose your divinity.[9] Let one who has drawn the first lot choose a life, which will be his by necessity. Virtue is without master; each man has a greater or lesser share, insofar as he honors or dishonors her. The blame belongs to the one who makes the choice; god is blameless." (617d1–617e5)   20

With these words, he cast the lots among them all, and each picked up the one that fell near him. Only Er was not allowed to participate. It was clear to each when he had picked up his lot what number he had drawn. Next he placed the examples of lives on the ground in front of them, many more than those present and of every kind; lives of all living creatures and all human beings. Among them lives of tyrants, some complete, others cut short and ending in poverty, exile, and destitution. There were lives of illustrious men, renowned for form and beauty or strength and physical achievement, others for family and the virtues of their ancestors; in the same way were lives of unknown or disreputable men; and so it was for women. But the disposition of the soul was not included because with its choice of another   30 life it too of necessity became different, but the other qualities were mixed with one another, wealth and poverty, sickness and health, and intermediate states. (617e6–618b6)

REINCARNATION IMPOSES A DIFFICULT CHOICE

Herein to be sure, as it seems, my dear Glaucon, lies all the risk; therefore each one of us must seek to find and understand this crucial knowledge; he must search if he can hear of and discover one who will make him capable of knowing; he must distinguish the good life from the wicked and choose always in every situation from the possibilities the better course, taking into account all that has now been said. He must know how these qualities, individually or combined, affect virtue in a life; what beauty mixed with poverty or wealth achieves in terms of good and   40 evil, along with the kind of state of soul that it inspires; and what high and low birth, private status, public office, strength, weakness, intelligence, stupidity, and all such qualities, inherent or acquired, achieve in combination with one another, so that after deliberation he may be able to choose from all of these between the worse and better life, looking only to the effect upon the nature of his soul. (618b6–618d7)

By the worse life I mean that leading the soul to become more unjust; by the better, that leading it to become more just. All other considerations he will ignore. For we have seen that this is the most crucial choice for a human being living or dead. Indeed, one must cling to this conviction even when he comes to the realm   50 of Hades, so that here, just as in the other world, he may not be overwhelmed by wealth and similar evils and succumb to acts like those of a tyrant, committing many incurable evils, and besides suffering still greater ones himself, and so that he may know how to choose a life that follows the mean in such circumstances, and to avoid the excess in either direction, both in this life and in every future life, as far as he is able. For in this way a person becomes most fortunate and blessed. (618d7–619b1)

Then indeed Er, the messenger from the afterlife, reported that the prophet spoke as follows: "Even for the one who comes last, there lies a life that is desirable

and not evil, if he chooses intelligently and lives it unflinchingly. Let not the one 60
who chooses first be careless, nor the last discouraged." After he had spoken, the
one who had drawn the first lot immediately went up and chose the most extreme
tyranny, and he made his choice out of senselessness and greed and did not look
closely at everything, and he did not notice that his life entailed the fate of eating
his own children and other evils. And when he examined his choice at leisure,
he beat his breast and lamented that he had not abided by the warnings of the
prophet. For he did not accept the responsibility for these evils, but he blamed
fate and the gods and everything rather than himself. He was one of those who
had come down from the sky and had lived his previous life in a city with an orderly political constitution and adopted virtue through habit rather than wisdom. 70
(619b2–619d1)

Generally speaking, the number of those who came down from the sky and
were caught in this kind of predicament was not small, since they were un-
trained in suffering. But many of those from earth, since they had themselves suffered and seen others suffer, did not make their choice on impulse. Because of
this and because of the chance of the lot, for many souls there occurred a change
from an evil to a good fate or the reverse. For if one always pursues wisdom with
all his strength each time he takes a life in the world, and if the lot of choosing
does not fall to him among the last, it is likely, from all that has been reported,
that not only will he be happy in life but also his journey after death from the plain 80
and back will not be under the earth and hard, but easy and upward to the sky.
(619d1–619e5)

Er said that to watch each soul as he chose his life was a worthwhile sight,
piteous, laughable, and wondrous. For the most part, they made their choices
on the basis of their experiences in their previous lives. He saw the soul that
had been that of Orpheus choose the life of a swan through hatred of the
female sex because of his death at their hands, not wishing to be born again of
woman. And he saw the soul of Thamyras select the life of a nightingale, and
a swan decide to change to the life of a human, and other musical creatures
make similar decisions. The soul that drew the twentieth lot chose the life of a 90
lion; this was the soul of Ajax, son of Telamon, avoiding a human life because
he remembered the judgment concerning Achilles' armor. After him came the
soul of Agamemnon; he too through hatred of the human race because of his
sufferings changed to the life of an eagle. The choice of the soul of Atalanta fell
in the middle of the proceedings; she saw great honors attached to the life of a
male athlete and took it, not being able to pass it by. He saw after her the soul
of Epeus, the son of Panopeus, assuming the nature of a craftswoman, and far
away among the last the soul of the ridiculous Thersites taking the form of an
ape. (619e6–620c3)

In his fated turn, the soul of Odysseus, who had drawn the last lot, went to 100
choose; remembering his former toils, he sought to be free from ambition; he
looked a long time and with difficulty found the quiet life of an ordinary man lying
somewhere disregarded by the others and, when he saw it, he made his choice
gladly and said that he would have done the same thing even if the first lot had fallen
to him. In the same way, souls of wild animals exchanged forms or entered human
beings, the unjust changing to savage beasts, the just to tame ones; and all kinds of
combinations occurred. (620c3–620d5)

When all the souls had chosen lives, they proceeded in order according to
their lots to Lachesis. She gave to each the divinity (*daimon*) he had chosen to

accompany him as a guardian for his life and to fulfill his choices. This divinity first   110
led the soul to Clotho, under her hand as it turned the revolving spindle, to ratify
the fate each had chosen after drawing his lot. He touched her and then led the
soul to the spinning of Atropos, thus making the events on the thread of destiny un-
alterable. From here without turning back they went under the throne of Necessity
and passed beyond it. When all the souls and their guardian divinities had done
this, they proceeded together to the plain of the river of forgetfulness (Lethe)
through a terrible and stifling heat. For it was devoid of trees and all that the earth
grows. (620d6–621a4)

Now that it was evening, they encamped by the river of forgetfulness, whose
water no container can hold. It is necessary for all to drink a fixed amount of the   120
water, but some do not have the wisdom to keep from drinking more than this
amount. As one drinks, one becomes forgetful of everything. In the middle of the
night when they were asleep, there was thunder and an earthquake, and then suddenly just like shooting stars they were borne upward, each in a different direction
to his birth. Er himself was prevented from drinking the water. He does not know
where and how he returned to his body, but suddenly opening his eyes he saw that
he was lying on the funeral pyre at dawn. (621a4–621b7)

Thus, O Glaucon, the myth has been preserved and has not perished. We
should be saved if we heed it, and we shall cross the river of forgetfulness well
and not contaminate our souls. But if we all agree in believing the soul is immor-   130
tal and capable of enduring all evils and all good, we shall always cling to the
upward path and in every way pursue justice with wisdom, so that we may be in
loving reconciliation with ourselves and the gods, and so that when we carry off
the prizes of justice, just like victors in the games collecting their rewards, both
while we are here and in the thousand-year journey we have described, we may
fare well. (621b8–621d3)

This vision of an afterlife, written in the fourth century B.C., comes from various sources about which we can only conjecture. We must also allow for the
inventive genius of Plato himself in terms of his own philosophy. The numeric
intervals (e.g., the journey of a thousand years) are reminiscent of Pythagoras
and the belief in the transmigration of the soul; reward and punishment, with
ultimate purification, is usually identified as Orphic. Since this myth of revelation concludes *The Republic* with proof of divine immortality, problems abound
in connection with its precise interpretation. How much was intended to be accepted literally? Is Er's story an allegory filled with profound symbols hiding the
universal truths it wishes to disclose?

In his *Phaedo*, Plato provides another vision of the afterlife in which he
explains (114b–c) how true philosophers eventually are released from the
cycle of reincarnation. Those who have lived a life of exceptional holiness
and purify themselves sufficiently through their pursuit of philosophy live
entirely as souls in the hereafter in beautiful dwellings, which are not easy
to describe.

For the purposes of our sketch of the development of the Greek and Roman
concept of the afterlife, it is important to stress that a heaven and a hell are
clearly depicted for the soul of every mortal; and in addition to the upward
and downward paths that must be traversed, special tormentors exist, as does a
special place of torment (Tartarus) in which the greatest sinners are placed forever.[10] In such a conception lies the mythical and biblical basis for the mystery

religions of antiquity, whether their god be Demeter or Dionysus and their prophet Orpheus or Plato.[11] Ties with Christian sentiments are not hard to see, despite the obvious differences. More specific links are provided by the early Christian identification of Er as an ancestor of St. Joseph and by the fact that these early Christians, in their championship of free will, seized upon the admonition of Lachesis: "This blame belongs to him who makes the choice; god is blameless."

Vergil's Book of the Dead

In Book 6 of the *Aeneid*, Vergil paints his sad and prophetic picture of the Underworld in shadowy halftones fraught with tears and pathos. His sources are eclectic, but his poetic vision is personal and unique. Despite the centuries of oral and written tradition and the Roman chauvinism of his depiction, Homeric and Platonic elements are often still distinctly evident. At Cumae, in Italy, the Sibyl, prophetess of Apollo, tells Aeneas what the requirements are to visit his father in the realm of Hades. He must get a golden bough, sacred to Proserpine (i.e., Persephone), and bury his comrade, Misenus. It is easy to descend to the Underworld; the task is to retrace one's steps to the upper air, which only a special few have managed. While his men are preparing a funeral pyre for Misenus, Aeneas goes in search of the bough (186–204):

> As Aeneas gazed at the vast woods, it happened that he uttered a prayer: "If only the golden bough would show itself to me in so immense a forest. For the priestess told all that was true—alas, too true—about your need for burial, Misenus." At that moment, as it happened, twin doves came flying from the sky under his very eyes and settled on the green ground. Then the great hero recognized his mother's birds and in his joy prayed: "Be leaders, if there is some way, and direct your course to the grove where the branch rich in gold shades the fertile earth; O goddess mother do not fail me in this crisis." (186–197)
>
> Thus he spoke and stopped in his tracks, watching what sign they gave and what course they took. They would stop to feed and then fly ahead, always permitting Aeneas to keep them in sight as he followed. When they approached the foul odor coming up from Lake Avernus, they quickly flew higher; and gliding through the liquid air the doves settled down together on the longed-for tree, where the tawny gleam of gold flickered through the branches. (197–204)

10

Aeneas eagerly breaks off the golden bough; after the funeral rites for Misenus have been completed, he takes the bough to the Sibyl (237–332):

> There was a deep and rocky cave with a huge yawning mouth sheltered by the black lake and the darkness of the forest; no birds at all were able to wing their way overhead, so great and foul an exhalation poured up to the vault of heaven from the lake. Its name, Avernus, deriving from the Greek, means "birdless." Here first of all the priestess set four black bullocks and poured wine over their heads; between their horns she cut the tips of bristles and placed them on the sacred fire as first libations, calling aloud on Hecate, who holds power both in the sky above and in the depths of Erebus. Attendants applied their knives and caught the warm blood in bowls. Aeneas himself slaughtered with his sword a black-fleeced lamb for Night,

Aeneas and the Sibyl in the Underworld (1600), by Jan Brueghel the Elder (1568–1625); oil on canvas, 14¼ × 10½ in. Aeneas strides along holding his sword (useless against the powers of the Underworld) and the golden bough, which he must offer to Persephone before he can enter the Elysian Fields. Behind are the lurid fires of Tartarus, and on either side are monsters and sinners enduring or awaiting punishment. (*Szépmüsésti Museum, Budapest, Hungary*)

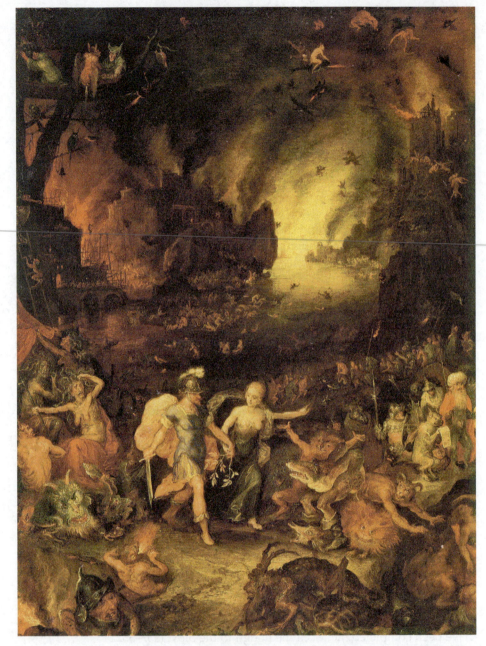

the mother of the Eumenides, and her great sister, Earth; and for you, Proserpine, a   10
barren cow; then he built an altar in the night for the Stygian king and placed on the
flames the whole carcasses of bulls, pouring rich oil over their entrails. Lo, at the first
rays of the rising sun, the ground rumbled and the wooded ridges began to move
and she-dogs appeared howling through the gloom as the goddess approached
from the Underworld. (237–258)

The Sibyl cried: "Keep back, keep back, you who are unhallowed; withdraw completely from this grove. But you, Aeneas, enter the path and seize your sword from its sheath. Now there is need for courage and a stout heart." This much she spoke and threw herself furiously into the cave. Aeneas, without fear, matched the   20 steps of his leader as she went. (258–263)

You gods who rule over spirits, silent shades, depths of Chaos, Phlegethon, and vast realms of night and silence, let it be right for me to speak what I have heard; by your divine will let me reveal things buried deep in earth and blackness.

They went, dim figures in the shadows of the lonely night, through the empty homes and vacant realms of Dis, as though along a road in woods by the dim and treacherous light of the moon, when Jupiter has clouded the sky in darkness, and black night has robbed objects of their color. At the entrance itself, in the very jaws of Orcus, Grief and avenging Cares have placed their beds; here dwell pale   30 Diseases, sad Old Age, Fear, evil-counseling Hunger, foul Need, forms terrible to behold, and Death and Toil; then Sleep, the brother of Death, and Joys evil even to think about, and opposite on the threshold, death-dealing War, the iron chambers of the Eumenides, and insane Discord, her hair entwined with snakes and wreaths of blood. (268–281)

In the middle, a huge and shady elm spreads its boughs, aged arms in which empty Dreams are said to throng and cling beneath all the leaves. There were also many different forms of beasts and monsters: Centaurs had their haunt in the doorway, Scyllas with twofold form, hundred-handed Briareus, the creature of Lerna hissing dreadfully, the Chimaera armed with flames, Gorgons, Harpies, and the   40 shade of triple-bodied Geryon. Suddenly Aeneas, startled by fear, snatched his sword and threatened them with his drawn blade as they approached. If his wise companion had not warned that these insubstantial lives without body flitted about with but the empty shadow of a form, he would have rushed in and smitten the shades with his weapon for nothing. (282–294)

From here is a path that leads to the waters of Acheron, a river of Tartarus, whose seething flood boils turbid with mud in vast eddies and pours all its sand into the stream of Cocytus.[12] A ferryman guards these waters, Charon, horrifying in his terrible squalor; a mass of white beard lies unkempt on his chin, his eyes glow with a steady flame, and a dirty cloak hangs from his shoulders by a knot. He pushes his   50 boat himself by a pole, tends to the sails, and conveys the bodies across in his rusty craft; he is now older, but for a god old age is vigorous and green. Here a whole crowd poured forth and rushed down to the bank: mothers and men, the bodies of great-souled heroes finished with life, boys and unmarried girls, young men placed on the pyres before the eyes of their parents, as many as the leaves that drop and fall in the forest at the first cold of autumn or as the birds that flock to land from the stormy deep, when winter puts them to flight across the sea and sends them to sunny lands. They stood pleading to be the first to cross and stretched out their hands in longing for the farther shore. The grim boatman accepted now these and now those, but he drove others back and kept them at a distance from the sandy   60 shore. (295–316)

Aeneas, who was moved by the tumult, asked in wonder: "Tell me, O virgin Sibyl, the meaning of this gathering at the river. What do these souls seek? By what distinction do some retire from the bank, while others are taken across the murky stream?" The aged priestess answered him briefly as follows: "Son of Anchises, and

Cerberus (1825–1827), by William Blake (1757–1827); watercolor on board, 9½ × 13 in. Blake worked on his illustrations of Dante's *Divine Comedy* for the last two years of his life, leaving 102 drawings at his death, of which 72 were for *Inferno*. This is the first of his two drawings of Cerberus, the guardian of the third circle of Hell, the place of the gluttons, in the sixth canto of *Inferno*. Blake represents Dante's description of the fist-like paws of Cerberus, with which he seizes sinners. Cerberus' middle head looks toward Vergil on the right, behind whom the faint figure of Dante waits to throw handfuls of earth into the monster's mouth. (© *Tate, London/Art Resource, NY*)

most certainly a descendant of the gods, you see the deep pools of Cocytus and the marshes of the Styx, the river by which the gods fear to swear falsely. This one group here consists of those who are poor and unburied.[13] The ferryman is Charon. The others whom he takes across are those who have been buried. Charon is not allowed to transport them over the hoarse-sounding waters to the dread shore if their bones have not found rest in proper burial; but a hundred years they wander and flit about this bank before they come back at last to the longed-for waters to be admitted to the boat." The son of Anchises stopped in his tracks and stood thinking many thoughts, pitying in his heart the inequity of the fate of human beings. (317–332)

Among those who have not received burial, Aeneas sees his helmsman Palinurus, who had fallen overboard on their voyage from Africa; he managed to reach the coast of Italy, but once he came ashore tribesmen killed him. The interview is reminiscent of the exchange between Odysseus and Elpenor in human emotion and religious sentiment. The Sibyl comforts Palinurus with the prediction that he will be buried by a neighboring tribe. The book continues (384–449):

Aeneas and the Sibyl proceed on their way and approach the river. When the ferryman spied them from his post by the river Styx, coming through the silent grove and turning their steps toward the bank, he challenged them first with unprovoked abuse: "Whoever you are who approach our river in arms, explain why you have come but answer from there, do not take another step. This is the place of the shades, of sleep and drowsy night; it is forbidden to carry living bodies in my Stygian boat. To be sure, I was not happy to accept Heracles and Theseus and Pirithoüs when they came to these waters, although they were of divine descent and invincible strength. Heracles by his own hand sought and bound in chains the guardian dog of Tartarus and dragged it away trembling from the throne of the king himself. The other two attempted to abduct the queen from the chamber of Dis." (384–397)

The priestess of Apollo answered briefly: "No such plots this time; be not dismayed; our weapons bear no violence; let the huge doorkeeper howl forever and strike terror into the bloodless shades; let Proserpine remain safe and pure within the house of Pluto, her uncle. Trojan Aeneas, outstanding in goodness and valor, descends to the shades below to his father. If the sight of such great virtue and devotion does not move you, at least recognize this bough." (398–406)

She revealed the bough that lay hidden in her robe, and at this his heart that was swollen with anger subsided. Not a word more was uttered. He marveled at the hallowed gift of the fateful branch, which he had not seen for a long time, and turned his dark-colored boat around to approach the shore. Then he drove away the souls that were sitting on the long benches, cleared the gangway, and at the same time took the mighty Aeneas aboard; the leaky seams groaned under his weight and let in much of the swampy water. At last Charon disembarked the seer and the hero safe and sound on the further shore amid shapeless mud and slimy sedge. (406–416)

Huge Cerberus, sprawling in a cave facing them, made these regions echo with the howling from his three throats. When the prophetess saw his necks bristling with serpents she threw him a cake of meal and honey drugged to make him sleep. He opened wide his three throats in ravenous hunger and snatched the sop; his immense bulk went limp and spread out on the ground, filling the whole of the vast cavern. With the guard now buried in sleep, Aeneas made his way quickly over the bank of the river of no return. (417–425)0

Immediately, on the very threshold, voices were heard and a great wailing and the souls of infants weeping who did not have a full share of sweet life but a black day snatched them from the breast and plunged them into bitter death. Next to them were those who had been condemned to die by a false accusation. To be sure, their abode has not been assigned without an allotted jury, and a judge, Minos, is the magistrate; he shakes the urn and draws lots for the jury, summons the silent court, and reviews the lives and the charges. Right next is an area occupied by an unhappy group who were guiltless but sought death by their own hand and hating the light abandoned their lives. How they wished now even for poverty and hard labor in the air above! But fate stands in the way and the hateful marsh binds them with its gloomy waters, and the Styx flowing round nine times imprisons them. (426–439)

Not far from here spread out in all directions were the fields of Mourning, as they are named. Here those whom relentless and cruel love had wasted and consumed hide themselves in secret paths in the woods of myrtle; even in death itself their anguish does not leave them. In this place he saw Phaedra, Procris, and unhappy Eriphyle displaying the wounds inflicted by a cruel son, and Evadne, Pasiphaë, and with them Laodamia and Caeneus, who had been changed into a boy and now once again was a woman. (440–449)

Here Aeneas meets Dido, queen of Carthage, who has recently committed suicide because of her love for Aeneas and his betrayal. He addresses her in sad, piteous, and uncomprehending tones; but she refuses to answer and turns away to join the shade of her former husband, Sychaeus.

From here Aeneas and his guide move on to the last group and farthest fields, reserved for those renowned in war, who had been doomed to die in battle and were much lamented by those on earth. Tydeus, Parthenopaeus, Adrastus, and many, many others come to meet Aeneas. Trojan heroes crowd around him, but the Greek warriors from Troy flee in terror. Aeneas converses with Deïphobus, the son of Priam who married Helen after the death of Paris. Deïphobus tells the story of his death at the hands of Menelaüs and Odysseus through the treachery of Helen. Their talk is interrupted by the Sibyl, who complains that they are wasting what brief time they have; it is now already past midday on earth and night is coming on (540–543):

> This is the place where the road divides and leads in two directions: our way is to the right and extends under the ramparts of Dis to Elysium, but the left path leads to the evil realms of Tartarus, where penalties for sin are exacted.

We must look at Vergil's comprehensive and profound conception of Hell, Tartarus, and Paradise, Elysium or the Elysian Fields (548–579):

> Suddenly Aeneas looked back to the left and saw under a cliff lofty fortifications enclosed by a triple wall around which flowed Phlegethon, the swift stream of Tartarus, seething with flames and rolling clashing rocks in its torrent. He saw in front of him a huge door, with columns of solid adamant that no human force nor even the gods who dwell in the sky would have the power to attack and break through. Its tower of iron stood high against the winds; and one of the Furies, Tisiphone, clothed in a bloody robe, sat guarding the entrance, sleepless day and night. From within he heard groans and the sound of savage lashes, then the grating of iron and the dragging of chains. Aeneas stood in terror, absorbed by the din. "Tell me, virgin prophetess, what is the nature of their crimes? What penalties are imposed? What is this   10
> great wail rising upward on the air?" (548–561)
>
> Then she began to speak: "Renowned leader of the Trojans, it is not permitted for anyone who is pure to cross the threshold of the wicked. But when Hecate put me in charge of the groves of Avernus, she herself taught me the penalties exacted by the gods and went through them all. Cretan Rhadamanthus presides over this pitiless kingdom; he punishes crimes and recognizes treachery, forcing each to confess the sins committed in the world above, atonement for which each had postponed too long, happy in his futile stealth, until death. At once the avenging fury, Tisiphone, armed with a whip, leaps on the guilty and drives them with blows; as she threatens with her fierce serpents in her left hand, she   20
> summons the phalanx, her savage sisters. Then at last the sacred gates open wide, turning with strident horror on their creaking hinges. Do you see what kind of sentry sits at the entrance? What forms are watching in the threshold? The monstrous Hydra, more fierce than the Furies with its fifty black and gaping throats, has its home within. Then Tartarus itself yawns deep under the shades, extending straight down twice as far as the view upward to the sky and celestial Olympus." (562–579)

In Tartarus Vergil places the Homeric sinners Tityus, Sisyphus, and possibly Tantalus; but there is difficulty in the text and its interpretation. Tityus, the son of universal Mother Earth, is the only one of the three named directly, and here is how the Sibyl describes his punishment (596–600):

> His body is stretched over nine whole acres and a huge vulture with its crooked beak tears at his immortal liver, forever renewed for the penalty of suffering. It digs deep within his breast to probe for the feast, giving no respite. As Tityus' liver is restored, it is immediately devoured.

Other criminals identified by Vergil are the Titans, who were hurled to the very bottom of Tartarus by the thunderbolts of Jupiter; the sons of Aloeus, Otus, and Ephialtes,[14] who tried to storm heaven and seize Jupiter himself; Theseus and Pirithoüs; Phlegyas;[15] and also Salmoneus, a son of Aeolus, who left Thessaly and founded Salmone in Elis. Salmoneus dressed himself as Zeus and imitated the god's thunder and lightning by driving in a chariot with brazen vessels attached to it and hurling lighted torches until Zeus killed him with his thunderbolt. The Sibyl describes his crime and fate (585–594):

> I saw Salmoneus also being cruelly punished, who imitated the flames of Jupiter and the thunder of Olympus. He drove arrogantly through the Greek states and the city in the middle of Elis, riding in a chariot drawn by four horses, and he demanded that he be honored like a god. He was mad, because he tried to imitate the storm-clouds and the lightning that cannot be imitated with bronze and the clatter of horses' hooves. But Jupiter, all-powerful, hurled his thunderbolt through the thick clouds and cast him headlong down with a violent whirlwind.

Vergil only mentions Ixion. He is one of the more famous sinners condemned to Tartarus, who in other sources is punished by being bound to a fiery wheel that eternally revolves.

Vergil's Tartarus is not a hell just for heroic sinners of mythological antiquity; in it all who are guilty suffer punishment. It is important to realize fully the ethical standards he applies. The nature of sin is clearly summed up by the Sibyl as she continues; just as clear is the moral conviction that assigns happiness to the good in the paradise of Elysium (608–751):

> "Here are imprisoned and await punishment those who hated their brothers while they were alive or struck a parent and devised guile against a dependent or who hovered over their acquired wealth all alone and did not share it with their relatives (these misers were the greatest throng), and those who were killed for adultery or took up arms in an impious cause and were not afraid to betray the pledges made to their masters. Do not seek to learn the nature of the crime and fate of each and every sinner and the punishment in which he is submerged. Some roll a huge rock, others hang stretched on the spokes of a wheel; Theseus sits in his misery and will remain sitting forever; wretched Phlegyas admonishes all as he bears testimony in a loud voice among the shades: 'Be warned! Learn justice and not to despise the gods.' This one sold his country for gold, set up a tyrannical despot, made laws and revoked them for a price. This one invaded the bedroom of his daughter in forbidden incestuous marriage. (608–623)

"All dared enormous crime and were successful in the attainment of their daring. I should not be able to recount all the forms of wickedness or enumerate all the names of the punishments if I had a hundred tongues and a hundred mouths." (624–627)

After the aged priestess of Phoebus had uttered these words, she continued: "But come now, proceed on your way and accomplish the task you have undertaken. Let us hurry. I see opposite fortifications of Pluto's palace erected by the forges of the Cyclopes and the vaulted arch of its door where we have been ordered to lay down this gift!" She had spoken, and making their way together through the gloom of the path, they hurried over the space between and approached the gates. Aeneas reached the entrance, sprinkled himself with fresh water, and placed the bough on the threshold. (628–636)

When this had been done and the gift had been given to the goddess, then at last they came to the happy places, the pleasant green glades of the Woods of the Fortunate, the home of the blessed. Here air that is more pure and abundant clothes the plains in soft-colored light and they have their own sun and their own stars. Some exercise their limbs on the grassy wrestling grounds, vie in sport, and grapple on the yellow sand. Others dance in a chorus and sing songs; and the Thracian priest, Orpheus, in his long robe, accompanies their measures on the seven strings of his lyre, plucking them now with his fingers, now with an ivory quill. Here is the ancient Trojan line of King Teucer, a most beautiful race, great-souled heroes born in better years, and Ilus, Assaracus, and Dardanus, the founder of Troy. (637–650)

Aeneas marvels at the unreal arms of the heroes and their chariots nearby. The spears stand fixed in the ground, and horses browse freely everywhere on the plain. The same pleasure that they had in their chariots and arms and in tending their sleek horses follows them after they have been laid in the earth. Behold he sees others feasting to the right and to the left on the grass and singing a happy paean in a chorus amidst a fragrant grove of laurel, from which the full stream of the Eridanus River rolls through the woods in the upper world.[16] (651–659)

Here in a group were those who suffered wounds while fighting for their country, and the priests who remained pure while they lived, and the poets who were devout in their art and whose words were worthy of their god, Phoebus Apollo, or those who made life better by their discoveries in the arts and the sciences and who through merit made others remember them. All of these wore around their temples a snowy white garland; the Sibyl spoke to them as they surrounded her, singling out Musaeus especially: "Tell me, happy souls and you, O illustrious poet, what region, what place does Anchises inhabit? We crossed the great rivers of Erebus and have come on his account." Musaeus replied in these few words: "No one has a fixed abode; we inhabit shady groves, living in meadows fresh with streams along whose banks we recline. But if the desire in your heart so impels you, cross over this ridge; I shall show you an easy path." He spoke and walked ahead of them pointing out the shining fields below; then they made their way down from the height. (660–678)

Father Anchises was eagerly contemplating and surveying souls that were secluded in the depths of a green valley and about to enter upon the light of the upper air. It happened that he was reviewing the whole number of his own dear descendants; the fate, fortune, character, and exploits of Roman heroes. When he saw Aeneas coming toward him over the grass, he quickly extended both his hands and a cry escaped his lips as the tears poured down his cheeks: "At last you have come, and your long-awaited devotion to your father has overcome the hard journey. Is it granted to me to see your face, to hear your voice, to speak to you as of old? I have been pondering your visit, thinking about when it would be, counting out the time, and my anxiety has not gone unrewarded. I receive you here after your travels over so many lands and so many seas, harried by so many dangers! How much I feared that Dido in her African kingdom might do you some   70 harm!" (679–694)

Aeneas replied: "The vision of you in your sadness appearing to me again and again compelled me to pursue my way to this realm. My ships are moored on the Italian shore. Give me, give me your right hand, father, do not shrink from my embrace." As he was speaking, his face was moist with many tears. Three times he attempted to put his arms around his father's neck, three times he reached in vain as the phantom escaped his hands as light as a breeze, like a fleeting vision of the night.[17] Meanwhile, Aeneas saw in this valley set apart, a secluded grove and the rustling thickets of a wood and the stream of Lethe, which flowed by the serene abodes. Around the river countless tribes and peoples were flitting, just as   80 when bees settle on different flowers in a meadow in the calm heat of summer and swarm about the white lilies; the whole plain was filled with a murmuring sound. (695–709)

Aeneas, who did not understand, gave a sudden shudder at the sight; and seeking reasons for it all, he asked what the river was in the distance and what crowd of men filled its banks. Then father Anchises replied: "The souls to which bodies are owed by Fate at the stream of the river Lethe drink waters that release them from previous cares and bring everlasting forgetfulness. Indeed, I have desired for a long time to tell you about these souls, to show them before your very eyes, and to list the number of my descendants; now all the more may you rejoice   90 with me that you have found Italy." "O father, am I to think that some souls go from here to the upper air and enter sluggish bodies again? What is this dread desire of these poor souls for light?" "To be sure I shall tell you and not hold you in suspense." Thus Anchises replied and proceeded step by step to reveal the details in order. (710–723)

"In the first place, a spirit within sustains the sky, the earth, the waters, the shining globe of the moon, and the Titan sun and stars; this spirit moves the whole mass of the universe, a mind, as it were, infusing its limbs and mingled with its huge body. From this arises all life, the race of mortals, animals, and birds, and the monsters that the sea bears under its marble surface. The seeds of this mind and spirit have   100 a fiery power and celestial origin, insofar as the limbs and joints of the body, which is of earth, harmful, and subject to death, do not make them dull and slow them down. Thus the souls, shut up in the gloomy darkness of the prison of their bodies, experience fear, desire, joy, and sorrow, and do not see clearly the essence of their celestial nature. (724–734)

"Moreover, when the last glimmer of life has gone, all the evils and all the diseases of the body do not yet completely depart from these poor souls; and it is inevitable that many ills, for a long time encrusted, become deeply ingrained in an amazing way. Therefore they are plied with punishments, and they pay the penalties of their

Ixion

Originally, the punishment of Ixion, son of Phlegyas, king of the Lapiths, was in the sky. He was the first to shed kindred blood. He invited his father-in-law Eïoneus to come and collect the price that Ixion was to pay for his bride, Dia. Eïoneus came but fell into a pit of burning coals that Ixion had dug and camouflaged. Since this was a new crime, no mortal was able to purify Ixion, and Zeus himself purified him, receiving him as a guest at his own hearth. Yet Ixion repaid him with a second crime, the attempt to violate Hera. Pindar describes the deception practiced by Zeus and the punishment of Ixion, bound to the wheel (*Pythian Odes* 2.21–48):

They say that Ixion, upon the winged wheel that rolls in every direction, by the orders of the gods says this to mortals: "Pay back the one who does you good with gentle recompense." He learned this clearly. For he obtained a sweet life among the children of Cronus, yet he did not long enjoy happiness. For with mad thoughts he loved Hera, whom the bed of Zeus with its many pleasures had as his portion. But Pride urged him on to overbearing folly, and soon the man obtained a special woe, suffering what was reasonable. Two crimes bring him lasting labor: the first, because he was the first hero to shed kindred blood among mortals, not without clever planning; the second, that he made trial of the wife of Zeus in the deeply hidden marriage chamber. But his unlawful passion cast him into overwhelming evil when he approached the bed, since he lay beside a cloud, ignorant man, a sweet deception. For in appearance it was like the daughter of Cronus, the greatest of the daughters of the son of Uranus. The hands of Zeus put it there to deceive him, a beautiful cause of suffering. And he accomplished his own destruction, bound to the four spokes. Cast down in ineluctable fetters he proclaims his message to all. To him she [i.e., the cloud, Nephele] bore a monstrous child, alone, without the Graces, a solitary child that had no honor amongst human beings nor in the homes of the gods. This she nursed and named it Centaurus. And it mated with the mares in Magnesia, in the foothills of Pelion, and from them sprung a wondrous host, like both parents, below like their mother, above like their father.

Ixion. Attic red-figure vase by the Amphitrite painter, ca. 460 B.C. Ixion is naked, looking toward Hera (on the viewer's left), who is seated on her throne. Athena is on the right, holding the winged wheel on which Ixion will be bound. Ixion's left wrist is held by Hermes and his right wrist by Ares. (© *The Trustees of the British Museum/Art Resource, NY*)

> former wickedness. Some spirits are hung suspended to the winds; for others the   110
> infection of crime is washed by a vast whirlpool or burned out by fire. Each of us
> suffers his own shade.[18] (735–743)
>
> "Then we are sent to Elysium, and we few occupy these happy fields, until a long
> period of the circle of time has been completed and has removed the ingrown cor-
> ruption and has left a pure ethereal spirit and the fire of the original essence. When
> they have completed the cycle of one thousand years, the god calls all these in a
> great throng to the river Lethe, where, of course, they are made to forget so that
> they might begin to wish to return to bodies and see again the vault of heaven."
> (743–751)

Anchises then leads Aeneas and the Sibyl to a mound from which they can view the souls as they come up, and he points out to them, with affection and pride, a long array of great and illustrious Romans who are to be born. The book ends with Aeneas and his guide leaving by the gate of ivory; why Vergil has it so, no one knows for sure:

> "There are twin gates of Sleep; one is said to be of horn, through which easy exit
> is given to the true shades. The other is gleamingly wrought in shining ivory, but
> through it the spirits send false dreams up to the sky." After he had spoken, Anchises
> escorted his son and the Sibyl and sent them out by the gate of ivory. Aeneas made
> his way to his ships and rejoined his companions. (893–899)

Vergil's Vision of the Afterlife

Vergil wrote in the second half of the first century B.C., and variations and additions are apparent when his depiction is compared to the earlier ones of Homer
and Plato. There are, of course, many other sources for the Greek and Roman
conception of the afterlife, but none is more complete or more profound than the
representative visions of these authors. A comparison of them gives the best possible insight into the general nature and development of the ancient conception
both spiritually and physically.

Vergil's geography of Hades is quite precise. First of all, a neutral zone contains those who met an untimely death (infants, suicides, and persons condemned
unjustly); next the Fields of Mourning are inhabited by victims of unrequited
love and warriors who fell in battle. The logic of these allocations is not entirely
clear. Is a full term of life necessary for complete admission to the Underworld?
Then appear the crossroads to Tartarus and the Fields of Elysium. The criteria
for judgment are interesting; like many another religious philosopher and poet,
Vergil must decide who will merit the tortures of his hell or the rewards of his
heaven on the basis both of tradition and of personal conviction. Other writers
vary the list. The Danaids, the forty-nine daughters of Danaüs who killed their
husbands on their wedding night, are frequently added to the group in Tartarus;
their punishment is that they must attempt in vain to carry water in containers that have no real bottoms. Some have observed that the tortures inflicted
are often imaginative and ingenious, involving vain and frustrating effort of
mind and body, and therefore characteristically Greek in their sly inventiveness.
Perhaps so, but depicted as well is sheer physical agony through scourging and
fire. Attempts made to find a logic in the meting out of a punishment to fit the

crime are only sometimes successful. Thus, for example, Tityus has his liver devoured because he attempted to violate Leto, since the liver was believed to be the seat of the passions.

Vergil's Paradise is very much an idealization of the life led by Greek and Roman gentlemen; and the values illustrated in the assignment of its inhabitants are typical of ancient ethics: devotion to humankind, to country, to family, and to the gods. In Elysium, too, details supplement the religious philosophy of Plato, which has been labeled Orphic and Pythagorean in particular and mystic in general. The human body is of earth—evil and mortal; the soul is of the divine upper ether—pure and immortal. It must be cleansed from contamination and sin. Once again we are reminded of the myth of Dionysus, which explains the dual nature of human beings in terms of their birth from the ashes of the wicked Titans (the children of Earth) who had devoured the heavenly god Dionysus. Presumably in the cycle of rebirth and reincarnation, the weary chain is ultimately broken; and we are no longer reborn into this world, but join the oneness of divinity in the pure spirit of the upper air.

Traditional Elements of Hades' Realm

Some identification and clarification of the various names and terminology linked with the Underworld are in order. The realm as a whole may be called **Tartarus** or **Erebus**, although these are also the names given solely to the region of torment, as opposed to **Elysium** or the **Elysian Fields**. Sometimes the realm of Paradise is located elsewhere in some remote place of the upper world, such as the **Islands of the Blessed**.

There are usually three judges of the Underworld: **Minos**, **Rhadamanthys** (or Rhadamanthus), and **Aeacus.** Their duties are variously assigned. Aeacus is sometimes relegated to more menial tasks; in comedy he appears as the gatekeeper. The rivers are generally five in number, with appropriate names: **Styx** (the river of hate); **Acheron** (of woe); **Lethe** (of forgetfulness); **Cocytus** (of wailing); and **Pyriphlegethon** or **Phlegethon** (of fire). Acheron came to be used as a synonym for "hell" or "death." For philosophical and religious conceptions of the afterlife and the belief in the transmigration of souls and rebirth, the River of Forgetfulness (Lethe) assumes great importance. It was a custom to bury the dead with a coin in the mouth to provide the ferryman **Charon** with his fare.[19] **Hermes Psychopompos** often plays the role of guide for the souls from this world to the next. The ferocious dog **Cerberus**, usually depicted with three heads, guards the entrance to the realm of the dead (see image on p. 366).

Hades, king of the Underworld, is also called **Pluto** or (in Latin) **Dis**, which means "the wealthy one." He is referred to either as a god of earth and fertility or as a deity rich in the numbers of those who are with him. The Romans called him and his realm **Orcus**, which probably means "the one or the place that constrains or confines." Sometimes Hades (this word may mean "the unseen one") is given no name at all or is addressed by some complimentary epithet, as is the custom with all dreadful deities or spirits—including the devil. Hades and his realm and its inhabitants are in general called *chthonian*, that is, of the earth, as opposed to the bright world of the Olympian gods of the upper air; Hades himself may even be addressed as Chthonian Zeus. His queen is **Persephone**.

In Hades' realm, we may find either our heaven (Elysium) or our hell (Tartarus). Tradition developed a canon of mythological sinners who suffer there forever:

Tityus, with vultures tearing at his liver; **Ixion**, bound to a revolving wheel; the **Danaids**, vainly trying to carry water in sieve-like containers; **Sisyphus**, continually rolling a rock up a hill; and **Tantalus**, tantalized by food and drink. Tantalus' misery is vividly described in Seneca's play *Thyestes* (152–175).

The **Furies** (**Erinyes**) usually have their home in the realm of Hades; so does **Hecate**, who sometimes resembles them in appearance and in character. Hesiod, as we have seen, tells how the Furies were born from the blood that fell onto the earth after the castration of Uranus; according to others, they are the offspring of Night. Both versions are appropriate in terms of their sphere and their powers. They vary in number, but they may be reduced to three with specific names: Allecto, Megaera, and Tisiphone. In literature and art, they are depicted as formidable, bearing serpents in their hands or hair and carrying torches and scourges. They are the pitiless and just avengers of crime, especially murder; blood guilt within the family is their particular concern, and they may relentlessly pursue anyone who has killed a parent or close relative. It has been conjectured that

The Universality of Greek and Roman Concepts

A consideration of how different societies and peoples at various times have viewed the afterlife cannot help but be fascinating. We all must die, and what will happen after death is a question that each of us has pondered deeply. Whatever our beliefs, the Greco-Roman view must stand as one of the most philosophically profound and religiously archetypal, with themes that find parallels not only with religions of the West (such as Judaism and Christianity) but also with those of the East (Buddhism and Platonism share basic concepts).[20] For those who dismiss any certain knowledge of death's aftermath as futile, the artistic bequest of the ancient world can offer its own rewards.

The profundity and intensity of the Greek and Roman visions of an afterlife have been all-pervasive in the art and literature of Western civilization. The most explicit literary description is that of Vergil, and this has been the most potent inspiration for postclassical artists and writers. The great Italian poet Dante (1265–1321) was steeped in its radiance, which he suffused with Christian imagination and dogma. Dante takes Vergil as his guide through the *Inferno*, in which many of the classical features of Hades are to be found. In Canto 1, Dante, terrified and lost in a wilderness, encounters Vergil, who becomes his guide through Christian Hell; lines 82–87 express Dante's intense devotion to the Roman poet, inherent in the poem.

> O, honor and light of all the other poets,
> May the long study and great love
> which made me pore over your tome
> help me now.
> You are my master and my authority,
> You are the only one from whom
> I drew and cultivated the noble style
> which has brought me honor.

Many excerpts from Dante could be offered to show the myriad debts to the *Aeneid*. The depiction of Cerberus in Canto 6 is a particularly famous example (see image on p. 366).

originally they were thought of as the ghosts of the murdered seeking vengeance on the murderer or as the embodiment of curses called down upon the guilty.

The Furies definitely represent the old moral order of justice within the framework of primitive society, where the code of "an eye for an eye and a tooth for a tooth" is meted out by the personal vendetta of the family or the clan. This is Aeschylus' conception of them in his dramatic trilogy, the *Oresteia*. The Furies persecute Orestes after he murders his mother (who has murdered his father), but eventually their role is taken over by a new regime of right: the Areopagus, the court of Athens, decides Orestes' case through the due process of law; and it is significant that Apollo and Athena (the new generation of progressive deities) join forces with the justice of advanced civilization. The last play in the trilogy is called the *Eumenides*, which means the "kindly ones"; this is the name for the Furies as they were worshiped in Athens, after having finally been appeased and put to rest once and for all. The Furies also may be called the **Eumenides** in an attempt to ward off their hostility by a euphemistic appellation, as in the case of Hades.

The Christian concept of Satan should not be confused with the ancient portrayal of Hades, who is not fighting with his brother Zeus for our immortal souls. We all end up in his realm, where we may or may not find our heaven or our hell. The only exceptions are those who (like Heracles) are specifically made divinities and therefore allowed to join the gods in heaven or on Olympus. Hades, to be sure, is terrible and inexorable in his severity, but he is not in himself evil or our tormentor; we may fear him as we fear death and its possible consequences, which we cannot avoid. But he does have assistants, such as the Furies, who persecute with devilish and fiendish torments.[21] Hades' wife and queen of his realm, Persephone, is considered in Chapter 14.

It would be misleading, however, to conclude our survey of the Underworld with the impression that all Greek and Roman literature treats the realm of Hades and the afterlife so seriously. One thinks immediately of Aristophanes' play *The Frogs*, in which the god Dionysus rows across the Styx to the accompaniment of a chorus croaking *brekekekex koax koax*; his tour of the Underworld is quite different from Aeneas' and is at times hilarious.

The brilliant, satiric *Dialogues of the Dead* (e.g., nos. 18 and 22) by Lucian also illustrates the varied moods of the Greek and Roman portrayal of the Underworld.

Select Bibliography

Bernstein, Alan E. *The Formation of Hell, Death and Retribution in the Ancient and Early Christian Worlds*. Ithaca, NY: Cornell University Press, 1993.

Bremmer, Jan. *The Early Greek Concept of the Soul*. Princeton, NJ: Princeton University Press, 1983.

Dietrich, B. C. *Death, Fate and the Gods: The Development of a Religious Idea in Greek Popular Belief and in Homer*. London: Athlone Press, 1965.

Garland, Robert. *The Greek Way of Death*. London: Duckworth, 1985.

Nasser, Eugene P. *Illustrations to Dante's Inferno*. Rutherford, NJ: Fairleigh Dickinson University Press, 1994.

Russell, Jeffrey Burton. *The History of Heaven*. Princeton, NJ: Princeton University Press, 1997.

Vermeule, Emily. *Aspects of Death in Early Greek Art and Poetry*. Berkeley, CA: University of California Press, 1979. Death as depicted in literature, vase painting, myth, and artifacts found in graves.

Wright, J. Edward. *The Early History of Heaven*. New York: Oxford University Press, 1999. A study of the origin of concepts of heaven from Egypt, Mesopotamia, Persia, Greece, and Rome in the context of Hebrew biblical texts and developments in Jewish and Christian belief.

Primary Sources

Sources in the Chapter

Homer	*Odyssey* 11 (selections)
Plato	*Republic* 10.614b–end (the myth of Er)
Vergil	*Aeneid* 6

Additional Sources

Aristophanes	*Frogs*
Homer	*Odyssey* 24.1–24.204 (the shades of Penelope's suitors in the Underworld)
Lucian	*Dialogues of the Dead* (Loeb vol. 7)
Pausanias	*Description of Greece* 10.28.1–10.31.12: A lengthy description of Polygnotus' painting of the Underworld

In addition to the myth of Er, Plato presents several other visions of the afterlife and much discussion about the immortality of the soul.

Plato	*Apology* 40c–end
	Gorgias 522e–527e
	Phaedo 110b–115a
	Phaedrus 245c–257a
	Republic 386a–387d

Notes

1. Tiresias is the famous seer of the Theban cycle, who holds special prerogatives in the world of the dead. His wits are intact, and to him alone in death Persephone has left a mind for reasoning; all others are mere shadows (*Odyssey* 10.492–495).
2. Another name for Hades' realm or part of it.
3. Elpenor can address Odysseus first without drinking the blood because his corpse has not yet been cremated.
4. As we learn in Book 10 (551–560), Elpenor got drunk and, wanting fresh air, left his companions in Circe's palace. He fell asleep on the roof; in the morning he was awakened suddenly and forgot where he was.
5. Tiresias does not have to drink the blood before he can speak, but he needs to drink it in order to express his prophetic powers to the full. He may also be drinking it as a mortal would drink wine, for refreshment, and thus he establishes ties of hospitality and friendship with Odysseus.
6. An early name of Delphi.
7. Tantalus' crime is variously described by later writers; whatever its specific nature, it is a crime against the gods, often identified as some abuse of their trust or hospitality. The verb *tantalize* comes from his name and his punishment. For Pindar's version, see pp. 431–432.
8. Plato's image is of a spindle with its shaft at one end and a fly or whorl at the other. We may liken this to an open umbrella held upside down and filled with eight concentric circular rings, which revolve and carry with them the stars and the planets.

9. This divinity (*daimon*) is the destiny that accompanies each soul through its life on earth, its good or bad *genius*.

10. In Hesiod (*Theogony* 713–814), Tartarus is a dark place in the depths of the earth into which Zeus hurled the Titans after he defeated them. It is surrounded by a fortification of bronze, and inside dwell Night and her children, Sleep and Death. The house of Hades and Persephone is guarded by a terrifying hound. The river of Tartarus is the Styx, by whose water the gods swear dread oaths; if they break these oaths, they must suffer terrible penalties for a full nine years.

11. In graves in southern Italy and Crete have been found thin plates of gold inscribed with religious verses that were presumably intended to help the mystic believer in the afterlife. Some of the sentiments reflect the eschatology found in Plato, especially concerning the drinking of the waters of Lethe.

12. Vergil's conception of the rivers of the Underworld is far from clear. Charon seems to ferry the souls across Acheron, although Cocytus is mentioned in the immediate context; the Styx is identified by Vergil later. Tradition often has Charon cross the river Styx.

13. By poor, Vergil probably means that they do not have the fare to pay Charon. A coin was traditionally placed between the lips of the dead for passage to the Underworld.

14. The mother of the Aloadae was Iphimedeia, who said that their real father was Poseidon, according to the Greek version. These twins grew to be giants, and their attack on Zeus was made by piling Mt. Ossa upon Olympus and then Mt. Pelion upon Ossa. For this presumption, both were killed by Apollo while they were still young.

15. In some accounts Phlegyas is the father of Ixion; he burned the temple of Apollo at Delphi because of Apollo's affair with his daughter Coronis.

16. Near its source, the Po River flowed for some distance underground, and the legendary river of the Underworld, Eridanus, was identified with it.

17. Vergil echoes Homer's lines about Odysseus trying to embrace the shade of his mother.

18. That is, each of us has a soul that must bear the consequences of its life on earth.

19. For Charon in the Western tradition, see R. H. Terpening, *Charon and the Crossing: Ancient, Medieval and Renaissance Transformations of a Myth* (Lewisburg, PA: Bucknell University Press, 1985).

20. For the development of concepts of reward and punishment, see Jeffrey Burton Russell, *A History of Heaven* (Princeton, NJ: Princeton University Press, 1997), and, by the same author, *The Devil: Perceptions of Evil from Antiquity to Primitive Christianity* (Ithaca, NY: Cornell University Press, 1977). See also Alice K. Turner, *History of Hell* (Orlando, FL: Harcourt Brace, 1993). Alan E. Bernstein, *The Formation of Hell: Death and Retribution in the Ancient and Early Christian Worlds* (Ithaca, NY: Cornell University Press, 1995), reveals how Christianity, in developing its own particular views, chose between the two options offered by the Greco-Roman and Judaic conceptions: all the dead live on with no distinction made between the good and the wicked, or the good are rewarded and the wicked punished. Bernstein's discussion of "Christ's Descent into Hades" is relevant for its theme of the Harrowing of Hell or the Conquest of Death by both resurrection-god and hero, an archetype with which we have already become very familiar.

21. Zeus and the gods may destroy human beings and punish evil in this life, at times in opposition to one another. And the justice of the moral order of the Olympian gods and the Fates is the same as that of the realm of Hades. It is Prometheus who champions the human race as a whole against the antagonism of Zeus, but this is a quite different story.

16

ORPHEUS AND ORPHISM: MYSTERY RELIGIONS IN ROMAN TIMES

A sudden madness took hold of the incautious lover—certainly forgivable, if the infernal world knew how to forgive. He stopped, unmindful of the condition, and overwhelmed by emotion he looked back at his Eurydice, who was at that very moment verging on the light. There all his labor was wasted and the agreement of the pitiless tyrant broken. Three times a shattering was heard throughout the Avernian fens . . . and Eurydice disappeared from before his eyes, scattered in different directions, like smoke caught in a gentle breeze.

—VERGIL, *Georgics* 4.488–500

Orpheus and Eurydice

Ovid tells the story of how Orpheus lost his new bride Eurydice (*Metamorphoses* 10.1–85; 11.1–66).

> Hymen, god of marriage, wrapped in his saffron-colored cloak, left the wedding of Iphis and Ianthe and made his way through the vast tracts of air to the shores of the Thracian Cicones; he came at the call of Orpheus, but in vain, for although he was certainly present at the marriage of Orpheus to Eurydice, he did not smile or bless the pair or give good omens. Even the torch he held kept sputtering with smoke that drew tears and would not burn despite vigorous shaking. The outcome was even more serious than this ominous beginning. For while the new bride was wandering through the grass accompanied by a band of Naiads, she was bitten on the ankle by a serpent and collapsed in death. (10.1–10)   10

ORPHEUS' DESCENT TO THE UNDERWORLD

> After Orpheus, the bard of the Thracian mountains, had wept his fill to the breezes of the upper world, he dared to descend to the Styx by the entrance near Taenarus so that he might rouse even the shades.[1] Past the

insubstantial multitudes of ghosts beyond the grave, he approached Persephone and her lord, who rule this unlovely realm of shadows, and sang his song as he plucked the strings of his lyre: "O deities of the world below the earth, into which all of us who are mortal return, if it is right and you allow me to utter the truth, laying aside evasion and falsehood, I did not come down to see the realms of Tartarus or to bind the triple neck, bristling with serpents, of the monstrous hound descended from Medusa; the cause of my journey is my wife; she stepped on a snake, and its venom coursing through her veins stole from her the bloom of her years. I wanted to be able to endure, and I admit that I have tried; but Love has conquered. He is a god who is well known in the world above; I suspect that he is famous even here as well (although I do not know for sure); if the story of the abduction of long ago is not a lie, Love also brought you two together. (10.11–29)　20

Spring: Orpheus and Eurydice, by Eugène Delacroix (1798–1863); oil on canvas, 1863; 78 × 65¼ in. Eurydice falls as a companion holds her and looks in horror at the snake gliding into the undergrowth at the bottom right corner. Orpheus with his lyre approaches from the left, and another nymph looks on in fear on the right, kneeling like the figure of Eurydice in Poussin's painting of the same subject. This painting, left unfinished at the artist's death, is one of a series of the four seasons with mythological subjects. (*São Paulo Museum of Art, photo by João Musa*)

"By these places full of fear, by this yawning Chaos, and by the silent vastness of this kingdom, reweave I pray the thread of Eurydice's destiny cut off too soon! We pay everything to you, and after tarrying but a little while, we hasten more slowly or more quickly to this one abode. All of us direct our course here, this is our very last home, and you hold the longest sway over the human race. Eurydice too, when she in her ripe age has gone through the just allotment of her years, will fall under your power; I ask as a gift her return to me. If the Fates refuse this reprieve for my wife, it is sure that I do not wish to return either. Take joy in the death of us both!" (10.29–39) 30

As he made this plea and sang his words to the tune of his lyre, the bloodless spirits wept; Tantalus stopped reaching for the receding waters, the wheel of Ixion stopped in wonder, the vultures ceased tearing at the liver of Tityus, the Danaid descendants of Belus left their urns empty, and you, O Sisyphus, sat on your stone. Then for the first time, the story has it, the cheeks of the Eumenides were moist with tears as they were overcome by his song, and the king who rules these lower

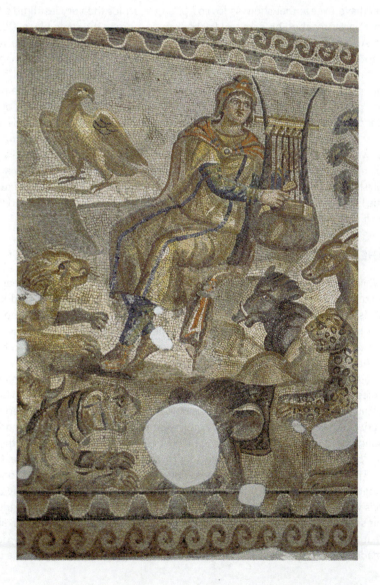

Orpheus Charms the Wild Animals. Mosaic from Antioch (Antakya), second century A.D. Orpheus, dressed as a Thracian, sitting on a rock, plucks the lyre and by his music pacifies the ferocious beasts and birds. The forest landscape is indicated by the formal tree in the upper right. (© *Vanni Archive/Art Resource, NY*)

regions and his regal wife could not endure his pleas or their refusal. They called Eurydice; she was among the more recent shades, and she approached, her step slow because of her wound. Thracian Orpheus took her and with her the command that he not turn back his gaze until he had left the groves of Avernus, or the gift would be revoked. (10.40–52)   40

ORPHEUS LOSES EURYDICE AGAIN

Through the mute silence, they wrest their steep way, arduous, dark, and thick with black vapors. They were not far from the border of the world above; here frightened that she might not be well and yearning to see her with his own eyes, through love he turned and looked, and with his gaze she slipped away and down. He stretched out his arms, struggling to embrace and be embraced, but unlucky and unhappy he grasped nothing but the limp and yielding breezes. Now as Eurydice was dying for a second time, she did not reproach her husband; for what complaint should she have except that she was loved? She uttered for the very last time a farewell that barely reached his ears and fell back once more to the same place. (10.53–63) 50

At the second death of his wife, Orpheus was stunned. . . . The ferryman kept Orpheus back as he begged in vain, wishing to cross over once again; yet he remained seated on the bank for seven days, unkempt and without food, the gift of Ceres; anxiety, deep grief, and tears were his nourishment as he bewailed the cruelty of the gods of Erebus. He then withdrew to the mountains of Thrace, Rhodope, and windswept Haemus. Three times the Titan sun had rounded out the year with the sign of watery Pisces, and Orpheus the while had fled from love with all women, either because of his previous woe or because he had made a pledge. Many women were seized with passion for union with the bard, and many in anguish were repulsed. He was the originator for the Thracian peoples of turning to the love of young men and of enjoying the brief spring of their youth and plucking 60
its first flowers. . . . (10.64; 10.72–85)   70

THE DISMEMBERMENT OF ORPHEUS

While the Thracian bard was inducing the woods, the rocks, and the hearts of the wild beasts to follow him, Ciconian women, their frenzied breasts clad in animal skins, spied Orpheus from the top of a hill as he was singing to his lyre. One of them, her hair tossing in the light breeze, exclaimed: "Ah look, here is the one who despises us." And she hurled her weapon, wreathed with foliage, straight at the face of Apollo's son as he sang, and it made its mark but did not wound. The weapon of another was a stone, which as it hurtled was overcome in midair by the harmony of voice and lyre and fell prone at his feet like a suppliant apologizing for so furious an assault. But their hostility grew more bold, and restraint was abandoned until the Fury of madness held absolute sway. All weapons would have been softened by his song, but the great clamor, the Phrygian flutes with their curved pipes, the drums, the pounding, and the Bacchic shrieks drowned out the sound of his lyre. (11.1–18) 80

Then at the last the stones that could not hear grew red with the blood of the poet. But first the maenads seized the hordes of birds still spellbound by the singer's voice, the serpents, and the throng of beasts, all testimonies to the triumph of his song. And then they turned with bloody hands on Orpheus himself, like birds that throng together if at any time they see the owl of night abroad by day. They made for the bard, just as the stag about to die is prey for the dogs in the morning sand of the amphitheater, and they flung the verdant leafy thyrsus, not made for such deadly purpose. Some hurled clods of earth, others branches ripped from trees, still others stones. (11.18–30)   90

So that weapons might not be wanting for their fury, it happened that oxen were working the earth, yoked to the ploughshare; and nearby sturdy farmers were digging the hard fields with much sweat preparing for the harvest. When they saw the throng, they fled leaving behind the tools with which they worked. Hoes, heavy mattocks, and long rakes lay scattered through the empty fields. The madwomen snatched them up; and after they had torn apart the oxen that threatened with their horns, they rushed back again to mete out the poet's fate. In their sacrilege, they destroyed him as he stretched out his hands and spoke then for the first time in vain with a voice that touched no one. And through that mouth, which was heard, god knows, by stones and understood by bestial senses, his soul breathed forth receding on the winds. (11.30–43)   100

For you, O Orpheus, for you the trees let fall their leaves and shorn of foliage made lament. They say too that rivers swelled with their own tears, and the Naiads and Dryads changed their robes to black and wore their hair disheveled. His limbs lie scattered in various places; his head and lyre you got, O river Hebrus; and—O wonder—while they floated in midstream, the lyre made some plaintive lamentation, I know not what; the lifeless tongue murmured laments too, and the banks lamented in reply. And then they left his native Thracian river and were carried out to sea, until they reached Methymna on the island of Lesbos. Here they were washed ashore on foreign sands, and a savage snake made for the mouth and hair soaked with the dripping foam. At last Phoebus Apollo appeared and stopped the serpent as it prepared to make its bite and froze hard its open mouth and gaping jaws, just as they were, in stone. (11.44–60)   110

The shade of Orpheus went down below the earth and recognized all the places he had seen before; he looked amid the fields of the pious and found Eurydice, and clasped her in his eager arms. Here now they walk together side by side, sometimes he follows her as she precedes, sometimes he goes ahead and safely now looks back at his Eurydice. (11.61–66)   120

As Ovid continues the story, we learn that Bacchus was distressed at the loss of the poet who sang his mysteries; he punished the Thracian women by turning them into trees and then abandoned Thrace all together.

For a translation of Vergil, see www.oup.com/us/morford.

The other major classical version of the story of Orpheus and Eurydice is Vergil's (*Georgics* 4.452–526). Most, but not all, of the details are similar, although the poetic timbre is different. According to Vergil, Eurydice stepped on the snake while running away from the unwelcome advances of Aristaeus, son of Apollo and Cyrene.[2] Thus Ovid and Vergil represent the tradition for the tragic love story of Orpheus and Eurydice: a paean to the devotion of lover and beloved, husband and wife. Their eternal myth has been re-created again and again with imagination, beauty, and profundity, whether it be in an opera by Gluck or a movie by Cocteau. Orpheus has become the archetype of the poet and musician and of the great and universal power of art.

A burning question fascinates us all: "Why did Orpheus look back?" Ovid is quite explicit as we have just seen: "Frightened that she might not be well and yearning to see her with his own eyes, through love he turned and looked, and with his gaze she slipped away and down." In Vergil's poetry (*Georgics* 4.486–492), similarly

Orpheus, Eurydice, and Hermes. Marble relief, Roman copy of a Greek original of the fifth century B.C.; height 46½ in. This panel was originally part of a parapet placed around the Altar of the Twelve Gods in the Agora at Athens. It shows the moment when Orpheus has looked back at Eurydice and they part forever. Hermes Psychopompos has his hand on Eurydice's wrist, ready to lead her back to the Underworld—a poignant contrast with the tender placement of Eurydice's left hand on her husband's shoulder. The names of the figures appear above them, Orpheus' being written right to left. (*Erich Lessing/Art Resource, NY*)

at the verge of reaching the upper air, "a sudden frenzy seized the unwary lover—worthy of pardon, except by the pitiless Underworld—he stopped, and unmindful, alas, and overcome in spirit, looked back at his own Eurydice. Then and there all his labor was spent in vain." To explore the variations wrought by countless artists over the centuries in their interpretation of Orpheus' tragic decision is fascinating. In many subsequent versions, Eurydice herself, unaware of the pact that Orpheus has sworn and unable to understand the cold cruelty of her beloved husband who will not turn to give her comfort, assails him with desperate and anguished pleas. Overcome by her remorse, Orpheus relents. As some believe, at that dread and irrevocable moment, the master musician lost faith in the power of his art. Had the gods imposed a condition that they knew he could never fulfill?

Life of Orpheus, Religious Poet and Musician

There is another very important side to Orpheus' character, of which we can only catch glimpses today because of the inadequacy of our evidence. He was considered the founder of a religion, a prophet, who with his priests and disciples committed to writing holy words that provided a bible for dogma, ritual, and behavior. Variations and inconsistencies in the tradition make it difficult to know this Orpheus and his religion precisely, but the general nature of their character and development can be discerned, despite the frustrating contradictions and obscurities.[3] Some of the significant "facts" that can be isolated from the diverse accounts are as follows.

Orpheus' home was in Thrace; his mother was one of the Muses, usually said to be Calliope; his father was either Oeagrus, a Thracian river-god, or the great god Apollo, whom he followed. He wooed and won Eurydice, a Dryad, by the charm of his music. When she died, he went to Hades to fetch her but failed. Orpheus was one of the members of Jason's Argonautic expedition.[4] He had a son or a pupil, **Musaeus**, who assumed many of the characteristics of Orpheus himself. Among the versions of his death, several prove interesting in the quest for the historical religious teacher. He is said to have been struck down by the thunderbolt of Zeus because in his mysteries he taught things unknown before; he also is said to have died through a conspiracy of his countrymen, who would not accept his teachings.

The common tradition (which both Ovid and Vergil reflect) makes the women of Thrace responsible for his death. But the reasons for their hostility vary: they were angry because he neglected them after the death of Eurydice, or refused to initiate them into his mysteries, or enticed their husbands away from them. Sometimes the women are followers of Dionysus, expressly directed against Orpheus by their god: Dionysus, in his attempts to convert Thrace to his religion, met the opposition of Orpheus, a devoted follower of Apollo the sun-god, and so sent his maenads to tear the bard to pieces. According to some, the fragments of his body were buried by his mother and sister Muses in Thrace or in the region of Mt. Olympus. His head and lyre were claimed by Lesbos (as already explained by Ovid), where a shrine was erected in his honor. His head became an oracular source, but its prophecies were suppressed by Apollo. A temple of Bacchus was built over the spot where the head was buried.[5]

In these conflicting speculations, a fundamental and puzzling duality is evident. Orpheus is linked in one way or another to both Apollo and Dionysus. Was there a *real* Orpheus, a missionary in Thrace who met his death violently? Did he champion Apollo against Dionysus or Dionysus against Apollo? Did he compromise and adapt the religion of the Near Eastern Dionysus to that of the Hellenic Apollo, taking from both and preaching a message that was new and convincing, at least to some?

However one would like to interpret the evidence, this duality cannot be ignored. On one hand, the music, magic, and prophecy suggest Apollo, as does the championship of civilization, but Orpheus' sermon of gentleness and peace has none of the violence of the archer-god. On the other hand, Orpheus' music is the antithesis of the clashing din of Bacchus; and the tales of his misogyny could imply a religion that at some period was confined to men, in contrast to the worship of Dionysus with its appeal to women. At the same time, Orphic initiation and mysteries are by their very nature Dionysiac. Other elements in the legends of both Orpheus and Dionysus are strikingly parallel: Orpheus is torn to pieces like Dionysus himself (at the hands of the Titans), or like Pentheus, who also opposed the god and met destruction at the hands of his maenads. Like Orpheus, Dionysus descended to the Underworld, in his case to fetch his mother, Semele. Indeed, a less common variant has Orpheus successful (like Dionysus) in his pursuit of Eurydice.[6]

There is nevertheless a well-established tradition that the historic Orpheus was not a god but a hero who lived, suffered, and died; his tomb was sacred, and he had a cult. He was in this view a prophet, a priest, or, if you like, a saint, whose god was Apollo or Dionysus, or both. Such a belief is ultimately subjective; but by the fifth century B.C., he *was* accepted as a human religious teacher, whose doctrine was communicated in sacred writings attributed to him and believed to be much earlier in time. Tablets were said to be found in the mountains of Thrace inscribed with his writing, prescribing potent charms, incantations, and spells. In the fourth century B.C., Plato quotes hexameter lines of Orpheus and tells of priests who preached his message of salvation. Later, Orpheus is credited with songs about the gods and the origin of all things. The hymns that have come down to us under Orpheus' name were given their present form in

Orpheus among the Thracians. Athenian red-figure krater by the Orpheus painter, ca. 440 B.C. Orpheus, seated on a rock and garlanded with ivy, sings with the accompaniment of his seven-stringed lyre to a group of four Thracians, dressed in their native cloaks and fox-skin headwear. They are enchanted. (*bpk Bildagentur/Staatliche Antikensammlung/Johannes Laurentius /Art Resource, NY*)

Orpheus—The Immortal Artist

Orpheus exemplifies the universal power of the artist and in particular music and poetry. Art eases care, makes life meaningful and beautiful, and can instruct. Orpheus is also the archetypal religious teacher, illustrating the omnipotence of the word in music. Orpheus suffers and dies the martyr's death of a prophet and a savior. Just as potent are the eternal elements in the romance of Orpheus and Eurydice. Theirs is a moving and tragic love story that, in its endless metamorphoses, never fails to touch the hearts and minds of human beings of all times.

There is a wondrous duality of religion and music in the archetype that illuminates the uplifting and informing spiritual power of his gift. "Indeed, what then is music? Music is a sacred art, which brings together all who have spirit, like cherubim around a radiant throne, and that is why it is the holiest among the arts, sacred music."[9]

The following simple but sublime verses from Shakespeare's *Henry VIII*, act 3, scene 3, which also sum up the spiritual power of Orpheus, have often been set to music. A beautiful version is that of William Schuman:

Orpheus with his lute made trees,
And the mountains that freeze
Bow themselves when he did sing.
To his music plants and flowers
Ever sprung, as sun and showers
There had made a lasting spring.
Every thing that heard him,
Even the billows of the sea,
Hung their heads and then lay by.
In sweet music is such art,
Killing care and grief of heart.
Fall asleep, or hearing, die.

the early centuries of our era;[7] in fact, this corpus of *Orphic Hymns* may have been composed (rather than compiled) in the second or third century A.D. It is of little help for reconstructing early Orphic doctrine.[8]

In music, art, and poetry, Orpheus has been a source of inspiration for thousands of works. His myths address several of the most profound of human concerns: the power of music over animals and inanimate nature, over human discord, and over death itself; the pain of bereavement and the hope of reunion after the loss of one's beloved.

The Orphic Bible

Dominant in the pantheon of Orphism was Dionysus, very often under the name of **Zagreus**. Although we hear about initiation into mysteries and a ritual life of purity demanded by the Orphics, we do not know their details. The shedding of blood and the eating of flesh seem to have been important prohibitions inspired by a fundamental belief in the transmigration of the soul and the sanctity of all life.

It is possible to reconstruct the basic themes of the Orphic theogony, with its myth of Dionysus crucial to the doctrine. Although parallels to the *Theogony* of Hesiod are apparent, there are meaningful differences and variations. The major stages in the Orphic theogony run as follows, although there are many versions and contradictions in the tradition.

The first principle was **Chronus** (Time), sometimes described as a monstrous serpent having the heads of a bull and a lion with a god's face between. Chronus was accompanied by brooding Adrasteia (Necessity), and from Chronus came Aether, Chaos, and Erebus. In Aether (the bright upper air), Chronus fashioned an egg that split in two; and from this appeared the first born of all the gods, **Phanes**, the creator of everything, called by many names, among them Eros.[10] He was a bisexual deity, with gleaming golden wings and four eyes, described as possessing the appearance of various animals. Phanes bore a daughter, Night, who became his partner in creation and eventually his successor in power. Night then bore Gaea (Earth) and Uranus (Heaven), and they produced the Titans. Next Cronus succeeded to the rule of Night, and subsequently (as in the Hesiodic account) Zeus wrested power from his father, Cronus.

Then Zeus swallowed Phanes, and with him all previous creation (including a special race of human beings of a golden age); Zeus now created everything anew, with the help of Night. As a second creator, Zeus became the beginning and middle and end of all things. Eventually, Zeus mated with Kore (Persephone), and Dionysus was born. This myth of the birth of Dionysus is most potent for the dogma it provides, and we have related it in connection with Dionysus himself (p. 318). Its essential features are that the infant god was dismembered and devoured by the monstrous Titans, who were then struck down in punishment by the thunderbolt of Zeus. From the ashes of the Titans came mortals; thus humans are partly evil and mortal but also partly pure and divine, since the wicked Titans had consumed the god, although not completely. The heart of Dionysus was saved and he was born again.

In this way, the Orphic bible provided the divine authority for belief in an immortal soul; the necessity for keeping this soul pure despite the contamination and degradation of the body; the concept of a kind of original sin; the transmigration of the soul to an afterlife of reward or punishment; and finally, after various stages of purification, an apotheosis, a union with the divine spirit in the realms of the upper aether. The seeds of everything came from Phanes or Zeus; out of the One, all things come to be, and into the One they are once again resolved.

Plato's myth of Er and Vergil's vision of the afterlife are, as far as we can tell, strongly influenced by Orphic concepts; a reading of both, translated in Chapter 15, conveys most simply and directly a feeling for the basic tenets of Orphism. The ritual purification and catharsis of the great god Apollo are mingled with the Dionysiac belief in the ultimate immortality of the human soul to provide a discipline and control of the ecstatic passion of his Bacchic mysteries.

There are parallels between characteristics of Orpheus and his religion and that of a **shaman** and **shamanism**. Shamanism is a religious belief system of great antiquity and was practiced in many northern Asian and native North American cultures. A shaman is one who has been called to a spiritual life and who undergoes a period of solitary training and fasting to emerge as a mystical figure with supernatural powers. Shamans are said to enter trance-like states, which include the undertaking of journeys into the spirit realm. Through this unique access to the spirit world, a shaman claims to return from his spirit journey with special powers of divination and healing. He becomes the wise teacher, revealing his wisdom in religious poetry, and a man of god, preaching doctrine and worship. Orpheus shares many traits with traditional shamans, including such attributes as the ability to bewitch birds and beasts, to travel to the Underworld, and to deliver oracles after his death, through his magical, singing head.[11]

Mystery religions have been a persistent theme; their spiritual essence has been associated with Eros, Rhea, Cybele and Attis, Aphrodite and Adonis, Dionysus, Demeter, and Orpheus. We cannot distinguish with clear precision among the many different mystery religions and philosophies of the ancient world. It is possible, for example, to argue that the mysteries of Demeter, with their emphasis on participation in certain dramatic rites, lacked the spiritual depth of Orphism, with its insistence on the good life as well as mere initiation and ritual. In any comparison or contrast for the greater glory or detriment of one god or goddess and one religion as opposed to another, it must be remembered that we know practically nothing about the Greek and Roman mysteries. In contrast, our knowledge, say, of Christianity, particularly in its full development, is infinitely greater.

The correspondences between Christianity and the other mystery religions of antiquity are perhaps more startling than the differences. Orpheus and Christ share attributes in the early centuries of our era;[12] and of all the major ancient deities, Dionysus has most in common with the figure of Christ. It was the son of Apollo, however, Asclepius, the kindly healer and miracle worker, who posed the greatest threat to early Christianity (see pp. 258–259).

Mystery Religions in Roman Times

Indeed, the association of Christ with the vine frequently led to the use of the myths and attributes of Dionysus in early Christian iconography. We can see this influence in a wall mosaic (third century A.D.) in the cemetery beneath St. Peter's Basilica in the Vatican (see the image on p. 262). In both cases, the vine of Dionysus, the symbol of new life after release from the old life, is associated with the Christian resurrection and the words of Jesus in John 15:1, "I am the true vine." In the same cemetery, there is a tomb containing both pagan and Christian burials, one of which is a second-century A.D. sarcophagus decorated with a relief showing Dionysus finding Ariadne (see p. 586). Whether or not the occupant of the sarcophagus was Christian, the finding of Ariadne as she wakes from sleep, by the god of life renewed, is an allegory of the soul waking from death equally applicable to the Christian doctrine of the resurrection or to pagan beliefs in an afterlife. The mysteries of Dionysus were widely practiced, and the similarities between them and the Christian *mythoi* made the process of **syncretism** inevitable. The term *syncretism* literally means "growing together," and in the context of religion and mythology it describes the harmonizing of different cults and their myths into some sort of unity. You can clearly see this process in our discussion of the worship of Isis later in this chapter.

Mystery religions were widely practiced in the Roman Empire during the first four centuries of the Christian era.[13] Like Christianity, they gave the individual worshiper hope for a better life in an uncertain world and frequently the expectation of a new life after death. Since mystery religions involved initiation into secret knowledge, our information about them is at best partial and generally inadequate. We can say with certainty that the mysteries involved a sense of belonging to a group and that initiation preceded some sort of revelation, which resulted in a sense of release and joy, with hope for a better future in this life and in the life after death. Often the initiate submitted to the discipline of a rule of life, so that morality and religion were closely associated.

The mysteries of Demeter at Eleusis (discussed at length in Chapter 14) attracted initiates from all classes all over the empire and continued to be practiced down into late antiquity. The sanctuary was destroyed by the Huns in A.D. 395, and the Christians saw to it that it was never rebuilt.

Other Mystery Religions

Cybele and Attis.   The mysteries of Cybele and Attis continued to be important throughout the Roman world, but their violent elements, especially the self-mutilation of the Galli (i.e., priests), made the cult less attractive than other cults with central resurrection myths (see pp. 672–673). Shedding the blood of a bull came to be a spectacular feature of the rite of initiation into these mysteries. It was called the **taurobolium**, and the initiate stood in a pit under the bull, so that its blood poured down upon him.[14] This baptism symbolized purification, the washing away of the old life, and resurrection to a new one; and the rebirth was further symbolized by the drinking of milk, the drink of a newborn child, while the ancient musical instruments of Cybele's worship became part of a kind of communion: "I have eaten from the tambourine, I have drunk from the cymbal, I have become a mystic of Attis," are the words of one hymn. Like the Eleusinian mysteries, the mysteries of Cybele ceased to be practiced after the fourth century A.D..

The Cabiri.   The oldest of the Greek mysteries after those of Demeter were those of the **Cabiri**, whose cult center was associated with the island of Samothrace and the city of Pergamum. The Cabiri themselves were usually referred to as *theoi megaloi*, the "great gods." Sometimes they were identified with the Dioscuri, Castor and Pollux, and thus offered protection from the dangers of seafaring. The Argonauts were said to have been initiated, and there are innumerable records of actual initiations in the Greek and Roman world right down until the end of the fourth century A.D..[15]

The Persian Mithras.   Three Eastern mystery religions widely practiced in the Roman Empire were sometimes assimilated to Greek and Roman mythology. From Persia came the mysteries of Mithras (or Mithra), the god of light and truth and righteous champion of good against evil. His myth included a miraculous birth from a rock and the slaying of a bull, from whose blood sprang the fertility of the earth. Mithraism was practiced in underground chapels or *Mithraea*. More than 400 of these have been found all over the Roman world, wherever Roman soldiers and merchants traveled. Basic to the iconography of a Mithraeum was a **tauroctony**, a scene depicting Mithras, amid other figures, killing a bull, presumably a ritualistic sacrifice by which the god ensured beneficence and rebirth for his initiates.[16] The cult appealed especially to officers, soldiers, and sailors;

Mithras Killing the Bull. Marble relief, second century A.D. In this side of the double-sided relief, Mithras plunges his long dagger into the bull's throat. The bull's tail changes into ears of wheat, and below are a scorpion, a snake, and a dog. In the medallions above are the sun (to the left) and the moon. (*Erich Lessing/Art Resource, NY*)

and only men could be initiated. We do not know the details of the initiation rituals, but we do know that there were seven grades of initiation and that the cult demanded a high level of self-discipline from its initiates. Its ceremonies also involved a communal meal. Mithraism was a major rival to Christianity; and, like the other mystery religions we have mentioned, it continued to be practiced widely until the end of the fourth century A.D..

Dea Syria and Other Syrian Cults. The second Eastern religion, which was not strictly a mystery religion with the usual elements of secrecy and revelation, was the worship of Atargatis, known to the Romans simply as Dea Syria, the Syrian goddess. She was originally an earth mother, like Cybele and Demeter, whose cult was spread through the Roman world, especially by soldiers. Shrines have been found at Rome itself and as far away as Hadrian's Wall, which the Romans built in northern England. Her consort was variously called Tammuz or Dushara, but her sacred marriage to the Semitic god of the thunder, Hadad, led to her association with the other sky-gods, the Syrian Baal, the Greek Zeus, and the Roman Jupiter. She was worshiped in wild rituals with self-flagellation by ecstatic priests.[17] Among Romans, her consort was usually called Jupiter Dolichenus, who was portrayed holding an axe and a thunderbolt and standing on the back of a bull.[18]

The Egyptian Isis. The third Eastern mystery religion is the worship of the Egyptian goddess Isis, and we have a full account of an initiate's conversion. Like Demeter and Cybele, Isis was a goddess of fertility, bringer of new life and hope. Her myth involved a search, in this case for her husband and brother, **Osiris** (dismembered by the evil power, Seth),[19] and for a child, Horus (also known as Harpocrates). Her attributes included a musical instrument (the *sistrum*, a kind of rattle), a breast-shaped container (the *situla*) for milk, and a jug for the holy water of the Nile. Her cult was associated with the god **Serapis**, whose origin is quite obscure; temples to Isis and Serapis are found all over the Roman world. Isis herself, however, as mother and nurturer, appealed to multitudes of men and women, who found in her a less terrible presence than that of Cybele or the Syrian goddess. Lucius, the hero of Apuleius' novel *Metamorphoses* (or *The Golden Ass*), appealed to her for help in becoming a human being again and shedding his form as a donkey. She appeared to him in a dream and instructed him to take the garland of roses from the hand of a priest, who would be taking part in the procession in her honor the next day. When Lucius did this, he resumed his human form, and the miracle was greeted with the praise of the crowd (*Metamorphoses* 11.16):

> The august divinity of the all-powerful goddess today has restored this man to human form. Fortunate indeed and thrice blessed is he who has deserved such glorious protection from heaven because of the innocence of his earlier life and faith.

The Syncretism of the Goddesses

When Isis first appeared to Lucius in answer to his prayer, she described herself in terms that perfectly illustrate the meaning of syncretism, expressed with a power and enthusiasm that even translation cannot totally obliterate (*Metamorphoses* 11.5):

> Behold, Lucius, I have come, moved by your prayers. I am the mother of things in nature, the mistress of all the elements, the firstborn of the ages, the sum of the divine powers, queen of the souls of the dead, first of the heavenly powers, the single form of the gods and goddesses, who by my nod control the bright heights of heaven, the health-bringing winds of the sea, the grievous silence of the gods of the Underworld. My name, one with many forms, varied rituals, and many names, is revered by the whole world. Thus the firstborn Phrygians call me Pessinuntia, the Mother of the Gods; the autochthonous people of Attica call me Cecropian Minerva; the Cyprians, tossed by the waves, call me Paphian Venus; the archer Cretans call me Dictynna Diana; the Sicilians of three languages call me Stygian Proserpina; the Eleusinians the ancient goddess Ceres; some call me Juno, others Bellona, some Hecate, others Rhamnusia [i.e., Nemesis]; the . . . Ethiopians . . . and the . . . Egyptians, who worship me with proper ceremonies, call me by my true name, Queen Isis.   10

Cybele, Athena, Aphrodite, Artemis, Demeter, Persephone, Hera—the ancient Queens of Heaven and Earth—are here, through the process of syncretism, included in the great Egyptian goddess, Isis. Apuleius, whose evidence is almost certainly reliable, shows us how in the second century (he was born about A.D. 120) the figures of Greek and Roman mythology had given way to the idea of a single divine power. Her devotees experienced a sense of liberation, of hope and joy. Lucius (through whom Apuleius is evidently describing his own experience) was initiated three times into the mysteries of Isis and Serapis; his life was consecrated to Isis. In this experience, we can see how the mythology of the gods of the Greek city-state became incorporated in the mysteries that brought hope of salvation to the individual worshiper. The power of that experience is revealed in Lucius' description, with which we end our survey of the mystery religions (*Metamorphoses* 11.23):

> Perhaps you may ask, studious reader, what then was said, what was done. I would tell you, if it were lawful to speak; and you would know, if it were lawful to hear. . . . I do not wish to torture you . . . with the pain of long suspense. Therefore hear, but believe, because these things are true. I approached the boundaries of death; I trod the entrance of Proserpina and, carried through all the elements, I returned. At midnight I saw the sun shining with brilliant light, I came into the presence of the gods below and the gods above, and close by I worshiped them. Behold, I have told you that about which, although you have heard, you must remain ignorant.

Select Bibliography

Orpheus

Athanassakis, Apostolos N. *The Orphic Hymns.* Text, translation, and notes. Atlanta, GA: Scholars Press, 1977.

Bernstock, Judith E. *Under the Spell of Orpheus: The Persistence of a Myth in Twentieth-Century Art.* Carbondale, IL: Southern Illinois University Press, 1991. The three parts of the book examine the different ways in which various artists have identified themselves with the paradoxical aspects of the Orpheus myth: 1. Paul Klee, Carl Milles, and Barbara Hepworth; 2. Max Bechmann, Oskar Kokoschka, and Isamu Noguchi; 3. Pablo Picasso, Jacques Lipchitz, Ethel Schwabacher, and Cy Twombly.

Detienne, Marcel. *The Writing of Orpheus: Greek Myth in Cultural Context*. Translated by Janet Lloyd. Baltimore, MD: Johns Hopkins University Press, 2002. A study of the far-reaching influence of the Orphic myth.

Friedman, John Block. *Orpheus in the Middle Ages*. Cambridge, MA: Harvard University Press, 1970.

Graf, Fritz, and Sarah Iles Johnston. *Ritual Texts for the Afterlife: Orpheus and the Gold Tablets*. New York: Routledge, 2007. Texts on small gold tablets (from the late fifth century B.C. to the second century A.D.) found in graves reveal information about beliefs concerning life after death.

Guthrie, W. K. C. *Orpheus and Greek Religion: A Study in the Orphic Movement*. Princeton, NJ: Princeton University Press, 1993 [1966]. The best introductory survey.

Segal, Charles. *Orpheus: The Myth of the Poet*. Baltimore, MD: Johns Hopkins University Press, 1989. Chapters deal with various aspects of the subject. Vergil, Ovid, Seneca, H. D., Rukeyser, Rich, Ashbery, and Rilke are among the authors treated. A concluding chapter is called "Orpheus from Antiquity to Today."

Warden, J., ed. *Orpheus: The Metamorphoses of a Myth*. Toronto: University of Toronto Press, 1985.

West, M. L. *The Orphic Poems*. New York: Oxford University Press, 1983.

Mystery Religions

Burkert, Walter. *Ancient Mystery Cults*. Cambridge, MA: Harvard University Press, 1987.

Clauss, Manfred, *The Roman Cult of Mithras: The God and His Mysteries*. New York: Routledge, 2001.

Cole, Susan. *Theoi Megaloi: The Cult of the Great Gods of Samothrace*. Leiden: Brill, 1984.

Cosmopoulos, Michael R. *Greek Mysteries: The Archaeology of Ancient Greek Secret Cults*. New York: Routledge, 2003. Essays on the major cults from the Bronze Age to the Roman imperial period in Greece and Asia Minor.

Ferguson, John. *The Religions of the Roman Empire*. Ithaca, NY: Cornell University Press, 1970. See especially Chapter 7.

Godwin, Joscelyn. *Mystery Religions in the Ancient World*. Ithaca, NY: Cornell University Press, 1971.

Meyer, Marvin W., ed. *Sacred Texts of the Mystery Religions: A Sourcebook*. Philadelphia, PA: University of Pennsylvania Press, 1999 [1987]. The translated texts relate to the following mysteries: of the Grain Mother and Daughter; of Andania in Messenia; of Dionysus; of the Great Mother and her Lover and the Syrian Goddess; of Isis and Osiris; of Mithras; and those within Judaism and Christianity.

Mojsov, Bojana. *Osiris*. Malden, MA: Blackwell, 2005. A survey of the development of the cult and its influences on Christianity and Western mystical traditions, such as the Alchemists, Rosicrucians, and Freemasons.

Mylonas, George E. *Eleusis and the Eleusinian Mysteries*. Princeton, NJ: Princeton University Press, 1961.

Nabarz, Payam. *The Mysteries of Mithras: The Pagan Belief That Shaped the Christian World*. Rochester, VT: Inner Traditions, 2005. A history of Mithraism that also includes its connections to Islam, Freemasonry, and modern neopagan practices today.

Rahner, Hugo. *Greek Myths and Christian Mystery*. Foreword by E. O. James. New York: Harper & Row, 1963.

Schroeder, John, and Michael Jordan. *Cults, from Bacchus to Heaven's Gate.* London: Carlton, 2002. Brief but informative surveys of ancient and modern cults for our own age of religious fanaticism.

Turcan, Robert. *The Cults of the Roman Empire.* Translated by Antonia Nevill. Oxford: Blackwell, 1996 [1989].

Ulansey, David. *The Origins of the Mithraic Mysteries: Cosmology and Salvation in the Ancient World.* New York: Oxford University Press, 1989.

Vermaseren, Maarten J. *Cybele and Attis: The Myth and the Cult.* London: Thames & Hudson, 1977.

Primary Sources

Sources in the Chapter

Ovid	*Metamorphoses* 10.1.85; 11.1–66

Additional Sources

Pausanias	*Description of Greece* 9.30.4–12
Strabo	*Geography* 10.3.1–10.3.23 (a lengthy discussion of the Curetes and various mystery religions)
Vergil	*Georgics* 4.315–566 (Aristaeus and his bees)

Notes

1. One of the many places identified as an entrance to the Underworld was a cave near Taenarus, a town in Laconia.

2. Aristaeus, the son of Apollo and Cyrene, is the traditional hero or deity of rustic pursuits, especially beekeeping. When Eurydice died, her sister Dryads in their grief and anger caused all the bees of Aristaeus to die. Perplexed by this action, he eventually consulted the wise old man of the sea, Proteus. Aristaeus appeased the nymphs, and a new swarm of bees was created. Through the role of Aristaeus, Vergil artfully introduces the touching account of Orpheus and Eurydice in the last book of his didactic poem on farming.

3. An important survey offers the general reader a scholarly examination of the whole question: W. K. C. Guthrie, *Orpheus and Greek Religion: A Study of the Orphic Movement* (New York: Norton, 1966).

4. He does not seem really to belong, but the gentle bard was placed among the brawny heroes because of his prestige and the magical powers of his song, which saved them all in more than one crisis. Orpheus appropriately was the leader in religious matters. The chronology also seems wrong for our historical Orpheus, if we must put him back in the heroic age in the generation before the Trojan War.

5. The chronological tradition for Orpheus is equally muddled. Those who connect his dates with Homer's deserve the most credibility. Thus either he was the inventor of writing and his works immediately preceded the Homeric epics, or Homer was the first poet and Orpheus followed shortly after.

6. This link with Dionysus may mean that Orpheus is yet another god (however faded) of the death and rebirth of vegetation; Eurydice, too, has some of the chthonian characteristics of Semele and Persephone. These parallels could likewise have been added to the legend that grew up about a historical prophet. Some of the themes also look like motifs common to folk tale: conjugal devotion, the journey to Hades' realm, the taboo of looking back.

7. The words of the Composer, yet another Orpheus (*Musik ist eine heilige Kunst . . .*), in the opera *Ariadne auf Naxos*, by Richard Strauss and Hugo von Hofmannsthal, which

epitomizes the profundity of Orpheus' art in one of the most beautiful of all musical motifs.

8. The date and authorship of these hymns are not securely established; perhaps at least some of them are earlier. See Apostolos N. Athanassakis, *The Orphic Hymns*, text, translation, and notes (Atlanta, GA: Scholars Press, 1977); Athanassakis (pp. viii–ix) inclines to accept the theories of Otto Kern that the hymns belong to the city of Pergamum for use in the celebration of the mysteries of Dionysus, third century A.D.

9. An attractive thesis claims that the religion attributed to the legendary musician was formulated in large part by philosophers in southern Italy and Sicily (although not necessarily confined to this region) in the sixth century B.C. Thus we can explain the elements identified as Orphic in the philosophy of Empedocles and in the religious sect of Pythagoras and thereby account for the Orphic–Pythagorean thought transmitted by Plato.

10. See Aristophanes' parody translated on pp. 61–62.

11. See E. R. Dodds, *The Greeks and the Irrational* (Berkeley, CA: University of California Press, 1951), and I. Lewis, *Ecstatic Religion, a Study of Shamanism and Spirit Possession,* 3d ed. (New York: Routledge, 2003 [1971]).

12. For the archetypal Orpheus and subsequent motifs, including that of the Good Shepherd, see John Block Friedman, *Orpheus in the Middle Ages* (Cambridge, MA: Harvard University Press, 1970).

13. The Roman emperor Augustus himself was initiated, while Nero, according to his biographer Suetonius, did not dare to become a candidate because of his guilty conscience. In the third century A.D., Gallienus (253–268) commemorated his initiation by issuing a coin with his name and title in the feminine gender (*Galliena Augusta*) in honor of the goddess.

14. The *taurobolium* is described in detail by the fourth-century A.D. Christian poet Prudentius in the tenth of his hymns about martyrs, *Peri Stephanon* (*On Crowns*). The most vivid details are translated in John Ferguson, *Religions of the Roman Empire* (Ithaca, NY: Cornell University Press, 1970), pp. 104–105. The *taurobolium*, which is recorded in many inscriptions, the first being in A.D. 105, was practiced by initiates of Mithraism and even of Demeter; for a description by Frazer in connection with the worship of Attis, see p. 197.

15. See Susan Cole, *Theoi Megaloi: The Cult of the Great Gods of Samothrace* (Leiden: Brill, 1984).

16. This interpretation, advocated by Franz Cumont, *The Mysteries of Mithra* (New York: Dover, 1956 [1903]), has been challenged. David Ulansey, *The Origins of the Mithraic Mysteries* (New York: Oxford University Press, 1989), follows those scholars who believe the tauroctony represents a series of stars and constellations, and in this kind of star map, the figure of Mithras is to be equated with the Greek and Roman Perseus.

17. Vividly described by Apuleius, *Metamorphoses* 8.27–29.

18. To this Jupiter, the Romans assimilated the dedications of the great temples of Baal at Baalbek (in modern Lebanon), usually referred to as the temple of Jupiter and of Bel at Palmyra.

19. See R. E. Witt, *Isis in the Greek and Roman World* (Baltimore, MD: Johns Hopkins University Press, 1997 [1971]). For Io, who came to be worshiped as Isis, see pp. 97–98 and 539.

The Greek Sagas

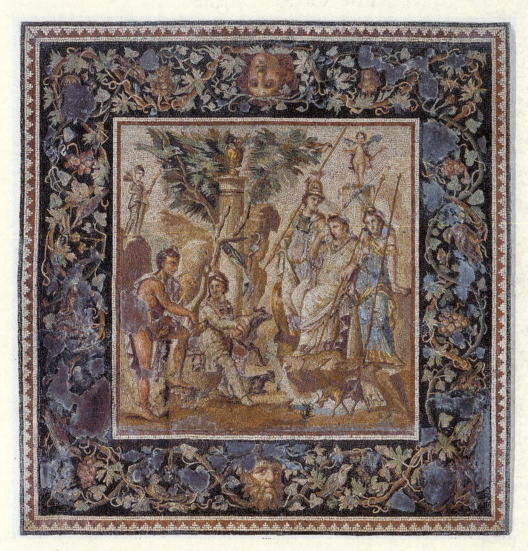

The Judgment of Paris, mosaic from Antioch

PART TWO

The Greek Sagas

Introduction to the Greek Sagas

Introduction to the Greek Sagas

Universal themes are persistent in the myths of Greek gods, who present archetypal images of fundamental human traits—the passions, psychology, and mores of mortal men and women writ large—and basic familial relationships, social ties, and political aspirations. Variations of these recurring themes are equally prominent in saga (or legend) and folk tale. These classes of myth have been discussed in Chapter 1 (p. 4), and saga will be the principal focus of the chapters in this part. Although saga has a relationship (however tenuous) to history, it often includes elements of folk tale that are common to other legends, and its heroes are descended from gods and often associate with divine beings. A defining feature of saga is the focus upon the deeds of one or more heroes.

The Hero and Heroine in Saga and Folk Tale

We have seen (pp. 13–14) how the Russian scholar Vladimir Propp has demonstrated how one particular kind of folk tale (the Quest) has a universal structure, in which the elements always appear in the same sequence. In Greek saga, as in folk tales, we find many recurring motifs, though not always as predictably as in Propp's structural theory. Ten motifs frequently appear: (1) The hero usually has elements of the extraordinary linked to his birth and his childhood. (2) He inevitably faces opposition of one sort or another from the beginning, and as a result he must prove his inherent worth by surmounting challenges of every kind. (3) His enemy or enemies usually instigate his achievement, and (4) he is helped by at least one ally, divine or human. (5) He faces apparently insuperable obstacles, often labors that must be accomplished or a quest that must be completed. (6) Adventurous conflicts with divine, human, or monstrous opponents present him with physical, sexual, and spiritual challenges. (7) He may also have to observe taboos—he must not, for example, look back, eat of a forbidden fruit, or be too inquisitive. (8) Death itself is the ultimate conquest, usually achieved by going to and returning from the Underworld. (9) The hero's success may be rewarded with marriage, political security, or wealth and power. (10) But knowledge through suffering and more lasting spiritual enlightenment (literal or symbolic)—entailing purification, rebirth, redemption, and even deification—are also part of a hero's attainment. These and other motifs recur with seemingly infinite variation, and they will continue to do so as long as human nature remains the same. Refined by artistic experience, they delight and inform, while they touch the very depths of the human spirit.

Propp's analysis of structure is very helpful for the scientific mythographer interested in structural analysis and similarities in the patterns of comparative mythology. It can be very misleading, however, for those who delight in the study of the subtle differences in the manipulation of motifs and the diverse characterization of heroes in all periods of mythological creation. The quests of Perseus, Odysseus, and Aeneas, to name only three, are to some degree alike, but they are all the more fascinating because of their differences. Achilles and Ajax represent two very different personalities in their response to the thematic code of heroic *arete* (excellence). Hector and Paris are not simple reflections of the pattern of brotherly opposites; instead, emotionally and psychologically they are worlds apart, and their feelings about war, life and death, and love and marriage

Greece and the Near East.

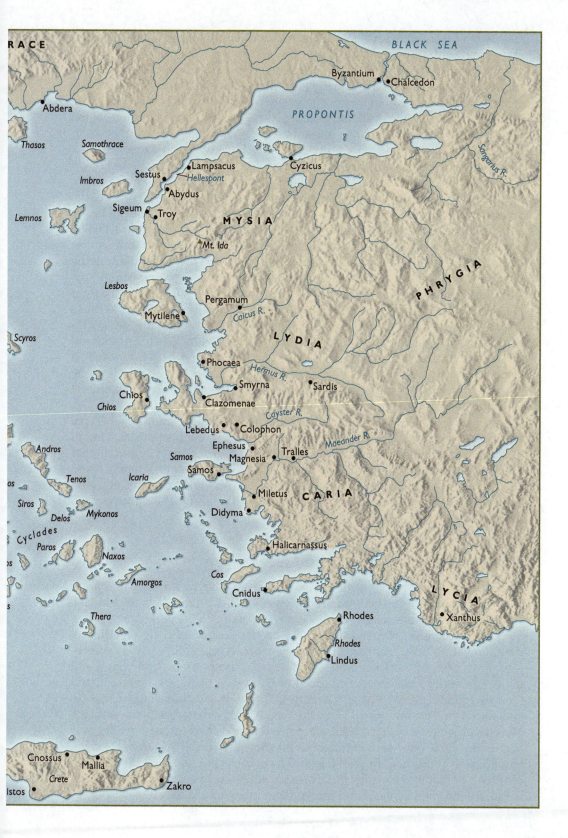

RACE

BLACK SEA

Byzantium
•Chalcedon

•Abdera

PROPONTIS

Thasos   Samothrace

Sangarius R.

Imbros

Sestus   •Lampsacus
Hellespont   •Cyzicus

•Abydus

Lemnos

Sigeum   •Troy

MYSIA

▲Mt. Ida

PHRYGIA

Lesbos

Pergamum
•   Caicus R.
Mytilene•

LYDIA

Scyros

•Phocaea   Hermus R.

•Smyrna   •Sardis

Chios•   Clazomenae
Chios   Cayster R.

Andros   Lebedus•   •Colophon

Samos   Ephesus•   Maeander R.
Samos•   Magnesia•   •Tralles

Tenos   Icaria

Siros   CARIA

Delos   Mykonos   •Miletus

Cyclades   Didyma•

Paros

Naxos   Halicarnassus•

Amorgos   Cos

Thera   •Cnidus   LYCIA

•Rhodes   •Xanthus

Rhodes
•Lindus

Cnossus•   •Mallia
Crete
istos•   •Zakro

may be most intricately juxtaposed. The rich and illuminating examples of complexity and profundity in heroic portraits make up the substance of our text.

Some heroes do not always act as heroes and reveal their feet of clay, and all heroes, to be sure, do not live happily ever after; a few of them are even undone by the heroines with whom they are associated. Witness the life and humiliating demise of Jason and the death of Heracles, both excruciating and glorious at the same time; Theseus too suffers a miserable end as a dishonored exile.

Heroines also provide motifs that are just as intriguing and varied as those of the heroes. They usually are of royal or divine stature, are possessed of extraordinary beauty, wield great power, and become the mothers of heroes. Like Propp in his analysis of the hero, Burkert (as we have seen, pp. 14–15) reduces the diverse lives of heroines into a clear sequence of five functions: (1) The girl leaves home. (2) The girl is secluded (beside a river, in a tower, in a forest, etc.). (3) She is made pregnant by a god. (4) She suffers punishment or rejection or a similar unpleasant consequence. (5) She is rescued, and her son is born. Yet, just as in the case of heroes, the lives of heroines reveal astonishing variety and complexity, which are not easy to summarize.

As the lover or the wife of a hero, a heroine can perform great feats because of passionate devotion. Ariadne helps Theseus kill the Minotaur, and without Medea, Jason never could have won the Golden Fleece. When heroines are abandoned or betrayed, they can be driven by despair and hatred to wreak a terrifying revenge or, like Ariadne, find salvation. Heroes can be destroyed by heroines through cleverness or guile, for example, the murder of Agamemnon by Clytemnestra or the ruin of Jason by Medea.

Helen of Troy, alluring in her multifaceted nature, has become an archetypal image. Antigone, devoted daughter and loving sister, by contrast presents for all time brave and righteous defiance against tyranny. Penelope as wife and mother offers us a paradigm of intelligence, integrity, and loyalty, her *arete* a match and a foil for that of her husband Odysseus. Then there are the Amazons, every bit like men in their *arete*, heroes and not heroines with respect to their prowess and courage in war.

The Mycenaean World and Greek Saga

The cycles of Greek saga are for the most part connected with cities and areas that were important in the later Bronze Age—that is, from about 1600 to 1100 B.C. The richest of these cities, Mycenae, gave its name to the period, and it was the king of Mycenae who led the Greeks on the greatest of their expeditions, the war against Troy. There are three major geographical groups in the cycles of saga: first, cities of the Peloponnese—Mycenae, Tiryns, Argos, and Sparta and the rural area of Arcadia; second, cities of the rest of the Greek mainland and their surrounding areas—Athens in Attica, Thebes and Orchomenus in Boeotia, and Iolcus in Thessaly; third, Troy in Asia Minor, whose relations with the Mycenaean cities may have been extensive. Beyond these groups are legends connected with Crete, whose Minoan civilization preceded Mycenae as the dominant power in the Aegean world, before its collapse at the end of the fifteenth century B.C. Finally, the story of Odysseus, although based in the Mycenaean world, extends far beyond it and incorporates many folk tales.

There is a historical dimension to Greek saga that archaeological discoveries have confirmed. It is important therefore to keep in mind our review of the historical background given in Chapter 2. Many Minoan and Mycenaean sites that can be linked to the legends of the Greek and Roman heroes and heroines have been and are being excavated: Cnossus, Troy, Mycenae, Tiryns, Pylos, Thebes, and Athens, to name some of the more important. How to distinguish historical fact from romantic fiction affords endless and exciting debate.

The sequence of these chapters from Greek saga is quite deliberate. We begin with Thebes and Oedipus because the treatment by Sophocles is so uniquely religious that it should follow closely upon a study of the gods. The spiritual intensity of *Oedipus at Colonus*, for example, provides concrete and sublime evidence for how the Greeks could actually use their myths for moral edification, and Sophocles makes us understand more clearly how they might have actually believed them, whether as reality or metaphor. Following this premise, Mycenaean legend comes next, which leads directly into the events of the Trojan War. We know that a different order, along legendary, chronological lines, may seem more logical. The chapters, however, are designed so that they can be read with profit in any order that one wishes.

Select Bibliography

Campbell, Joseph. *The Hero with a Thousand Faces.* Princeton, NJ: Princeton University Press, 1949. A classic overview of mythology, identifying the archetype of the hero as fundamental.

Kerényi, C. *The Heroes of the Greeks.* New York: Grove Press, 1960.

Larson, Jennifer. *Greek Heroine Cults.* Madison: University of Wisconsin Press, 1995. A counterpart to the study of male heroic cults.

Lyons, Deborah. *Gender and Immortality: Heroines in Ancient Greek Myth and Cult.* Princeton, NJ: Princeton University Press, 1997. An extensive and probing exploration of the multifaceted nature of the heroine.

Miller, Dean A. *The Epic Hero.* Baltimore: Johns Hopkins University Press, 2000. This study shows why the hero presented in the genre of epic is so compelling.

Segal, Robert A., ed. *In Quest of the Hero.* Princeton, NJ: Princeton University Press, 1990. Contains writings by Otto Rank, Lord Raglan, and Alan Dundes on the myth of the hero.

THE THEBAN SAGA

I see the ancient woes of the dead falling on the family of Labdacus, woe upon woe. No generation liberates the next, but some god shatters it. There is no release.

—SOPHOCLES, *Antigone* 594–598

The Founding of Thebes

The historical Thebes was the leading city of Boeotia, the plainland area of central Greece, ringed by the mountain ranges of Parnes, Cithaeron, Helicon, and Parnassus and bounded on the east by the Straits of Euboea. Thebes was situated on the low ridge that separates the two chief plains of Boeotia; its citadel was called the Cadmeia, preserving the name of Cadmus, legendary founder of the city. Cadmus was son of Agenor, king of Tyre, and brother of Europa. Agenor sent him to find Europa, whose abduction from Tyre is one of several myths in which a woman was taken against her will from Asia to Europe or vice versa. Herodotus narrates these legends at the beginning of his *History* in order to underline the difference between mythology and history. In these myths the opposition of the Greek and Asiatic worlds, which came to a historical climax in the Persian Wars of 494–479 B.C., began when Phoenician traders kidnapped the Argive princess Io and took her to Egypt. The Greeks (whom Herodotus calls "Cretans") in return seized the Phoenician princess Europa and took her to Crete. The pattern was then reversed: the Greeks took Medea from Colchis, and in return the Trojan Alexander (Paris) took Helen from Sparta. Herodotus explained that the Persians, reasoning from these myths, believed that Europe and Asia were permanently divided and hostile. As a historian, he was skeptical about these tales, for he could not vouch for their truth, whereas he could report things of which he had knowledge: "About these things I am not going to come and say that they happened in this way or in another, but the man who I myself know was the beginner of unjust works against the Greeks, this man I will point out and advance with my story. . . ." (1.5). So for the Greek historian of the Persian Wars the distinction between myth and history was evident.

402

Europa

The story of Europa is the first in which the Asiatic figure makes her way to the Greek world. In the usual version of the myth (which is different from the skeptical account of Herodotus), Zeus, disguised as a bull, took Europa to Crete. Here is Ovid's description of the abduction (*Metamorphoses* 2.846–3. 2), which should be compared with the nearby illustrations.

> Majesty and love are not well joined, nor do they sit well together. Abandoning the dignity of his royal office, the father and ruler of the gods took on the appearance of a bull, and as a beautiful animal shambled over the tender grass. Agenor's daughter [Europa] wondered at the bull's beauty, amazed that he did not threaten to attack, yet, gentle as he seemed, she at first was afraid to touch him. After a while she came up close and offered flowers to his white face. The young princess even dared to sit upon the bull's back. Then the god little by little began to take his deceptive steps further from the dry land into the sea, then he went further and carried his prey across the central waters of the sea. At length he laid aside the disguise of the deceiving bull and revealed who he was and reached the shores of Crete.
>   10

In Crete, Europa became the mother of Minos by Zeus.

Cadmus, Founder of Thebes

Meanwhile Cadmus, Europa's brother, set out to find her and came to Delphi, where he asked the oracle for advice. Apollo told him not to worry about Europa any more but to follow a certain cow until she lay down out of weariness and there to found a city. Cadmus found the cow in Phocis (the district of Greece in which Delphi is situated), and she led him to **Boeotia**, where he founded his city, **Cadmeia**, later called Thebes. As for the divinely sent cow, it was Cadmus' duty to sacrifice her; to perform the ceremony, he needed water, which he sent his companions to draw from the nearby spring sacred to Ares. A serpent, a child of Ares, guarded the spring; it killed most of Cadmus' men and in return was itself killed by Cadmus. Ovid relates that Cadmus then heard a voice saying: "Why, son of Agenor, do you look at the dead serpent? You too will be looked at as a serpent." Thus the final episode in the life of Cadmus was prophesied.

Athena, to whom Cadmus had been sacrificing the cow, now advised Cadmus to take the serpent's teeth and sow them; from the ground sprang up armed men, who fought and killed each other until only five were left. From these five survivors, who were called **Spartoi** (i.e., sown men), descended the noble families of Thebes.

Euripides recounts Cadmus' achievement as follows (*Phoenissae* [*The Phoenician Women*] 639–675):

> Tyrian Cadmus came to this land where the cow fell down on all fours, providing irrevocable fulfillment of the oracle by which god had ordained that he was to make his home amid the fertile plains—here where the beautiful stream of Dirce waters the rich and green fields. . . . In this place the bloodthirsty serpent

1. Cadmus	6. Laius
2. Pentheus	7. Oedipus (regency of Creon)
3. Labdacus	8. Eteocles
4. Lycus	9. Creon
5. Zethus and Amphion	10. Laodamas

Figure 17.1 The Kings of Thebes. (According to Sophocles, Polydorus became king after Pentheus; see genealogy, p. 409.)

of Ares kept his savage guard over the freshly flowing waters, looking far and wide with his swiftly darting glances. Cadmus came for sacrificial water and destroyed him, wielding a stone by the might of his arm and showering deadly blows upon the monster's head. At the bidding of Pallas Athena, he sowed its teeth in the bountiful ground; and in their place Earth sent up onto its surface the spectacle of armored men. Iron-willed Slaughter sent them back to Mother Earth; and she who had presented them to the bright breezes of the upper air was steeped in their blood.   10

Now Cadmus had to appease Ares for the death of the serpent; he therefore became his slave for a year (which was the equivalent of eight of our years). At the end of this time, he was freed and given **Harmonia**, daughter of Ares and Aphrodite, as his wife. The marriage was celebrated on the Cadmeia, and all the gods came as guests. Among the gifts for the bride were a robe and a necklace from her husband; the necklace was made by Hephaestus and given by him to Cadmus; it came to play an important part in the Theban saga. Cadmus and Harmonia had four daughters—Ino, Semele, Autonoë, and Agave—whose stories, with those of their husbands and sons, are told in Chapters 10 and 13.

Despite the misfortunes of their daughters, Cadmus and Harmonia reigned a long time, civilizing their people and introducing knowledge of writing. Eventually, they went away to northwest Greece, where Cadmus became king of the Illyrians; at the end of their lives, they both were turned into great harmless serpents (according to Euripides and Ovid; Apollodorus says that Zeus sent them to Elysium). They were worshiped by their descendants, and their departure from Cadmeia was not the outcome of any misdeed or grief, but a symbol of their change from mortal to heroic or divine status.

The Families of Labdacus and Lycus

Cadmus' successor as king was his grandson Pentheus, son of Agave, whose misfortunes are dealt with in Chapter 13. After his death, a new dynasty was founded by Labdacus, possibly a grandson of Cadmus. He is said to have perished while pursuing the same policy as Pentheus, leaving as his successor an infant son, Laius. Lycus, a great-great-uncle of Laius, first assumed the regency and then made himself king, reigning for twenty years. He was the son of

The Abduction of Chrysippus. Apulian bell-krater by the Darius painter, ca. 340 B.C. This illustrates a scene (probably part of the messenger's speech) from Euripides' lost tragedy, *Chrysippus*. In the lower register, Laius drives off in his four-horse chariot with Chrysippus, who reaches out to his father, Pelops. Pelops is dressed in oriental clothing and vainly stretches out his right hand. On the left, two naked men with spears (possibly Atreus and Thyestes) appear to be trying to stop the chariot. In the upper register four gods are seated: from the left, Pan, Apollo, Athena, and Aphrodite, who is approached by a winged Eros. To the right is the old tutor (Paidagogos) of Chrysippus. (*Bildarchiv Preussischer Kulturbesitz/Art Resource, NY*)

Chthonius, one of the five Spartoi, and his family has an important legend. His brother's daughter **Antiope** was loved by Zeus; while she was pregnant, she fled to Sicyon (a city in the northern Peloponnese) to escape from the anger of her father, Nycteus. In despair Nycteus killed himself, and his brother (Lycus) then attacked Sicyon and recovered Antiope.

Somewhere in Boeotia, Antiope gave birth to twin sons, who were left to die. A shepherd found them and named them **Amphion** and **Zethus**. Zethus became a skilled herdsman, while Amphion became a musician, playing on a lyre given him by the god Hermes. Many years later, Amphion and Zethus met and recognized their mother, who had escaped from the imprisonment in which she was kept by Lycus and his wife, Dirce. They avenged Antiope by killing Lycus and tying Dirce to the horns of a bull that dragged her to her death. From Dirce's blood sprang the fountain at Thebes that is called by her name.

OVID AND THE ICONOGRAPHY OF THE RAPE OF EUROPA

She is afraid, and as she is borne away she gazes back at the receding shore. She grasps a horn with her right hand; her left rests upon its back. Her billowing garments flutter in the breeze.

METAMORPHOSES 2.872–875

She grabbed his mane with her right hand, and with her left her clothes. Her very fear was an added adornment.

FASTI 5.607–608

The iconography of the Rape of Europa has proven tenacious, from one of the earliest depictions of the story in the metope from Selinus, through Ovid's treatment of the tale in his *Metamorphoses* and *Fasti*, to the masterpiece created by Titian. Artistic representations both in antiquity and later typically isolate one of two moments in the story: either the scene of Europa among her companions as she approaches the bull and garlands its head with flowers or that of Europa on the back of the bull as it careers through the sea. In the metope, Europa, riding sidesaddle, grasps a horn with her left hand, which seems the obvious choice,

The Rape of Europa. Limestone metope from Selinus, ca. 540 B.C.; height 58 in. Europa rides over the sea, represented by the dolphins, upon the bull, which looks frontally at the viewer. The formality and restraint of the relief contrast with the swirling motion of Titian's painting. (*Scala/Art Resource, NY*)

since in most visual representations of the story in antiquity, the movement is generally from left to right. Europa appears rather calm as she steadies herself with a hand (her right) on the bull's back. The movement of the bull across the waters is suggested by the positioning of the forelegs and the dolphins beneath. The frontal gaze of the bull (characteristic of Greek Archaic art; see p. 537) is meant perhaps to suggest that the bull is not what it appears to be.

In Ovid's *Metamorphoses*, the positioning of the hands is reversed, but special attention is given to her garments and her alarm. Indeed, the motion of her clothes (*tremulae vestes*) mirrors her own movements, her gaze, and the state of her mind; she is gripped by a restless panic, the effect of which the poet enhances by focusing first on her being carried away and then on her looking back at a shore that is fast moving away from her. In the *Fasti*, Ovid has altered one detail: he now has one of her hands grab at her clothes, and the association of her fear with her garments is further underscored by describing her terror as an adornment.

Titian's treatment, one of a series of what he termed *poesie*, since they treated erotic myths selected from Ovid's *Metamorphoses*, was painted for Philip II of Spain. The composition reflects a number of features of both the metope and Ovid's description. The bull has launched himself into the sea and, as in the metope, gazes out at the viewer. The garland on its head alludes to the earlier incident onshore. The scene moves from left to right, one of Europa's hands (her left) grasps a horn, and, as in Ovid's *Fasti*, the other grasps her fluttering wrap. Her alarm, as in Ovid, is highlighted. The awkward diagonal movement across the canvas, which has brought the pair closer to the viewer; the distant shore, which appears so remote; and the contrast between Europa's gaze and the bull's wonderfully represent the tension of movement in Ovid's account (2.872).

The Rape of Europa, by Titian (ca. 1487–1576); oil on canvas, 1559–1562; 73 × 81 in. Titian relies on Ovid's narratives (*Fasti* 5.605–614 and *Metamorphoses* 2.843–875). As in the Selinus metope, dolphins swim near the bull (one in the right foreground and one supporting a cupid), and Europa grasps the bull's horn. Her windblown drapery and desperate gestures, and the cupids flying through the air, impart an air of agitated movement in keeping with the mixed emotions, fear and anticipation, of the principal figures. In the distant background, Europa's companions vainly call her back to the shore. (*Credit: Europa, 1559–62 (oil on canvas) by Titian [Tiziano Vecellio] [c.1488–1576] © Isabella Stewart Gardner Museum, Boston, MA, USA/ The Bridgeman Art Library Nationality/copyright status: Italian/out of copyright*)

Amphion and Zethus now became rulers of Cadmeia and drove Laius into exile. They built walls for the city, whose stones were moved into place by the music of Amphion's lyre. Amphion married Niobe (whose story is told on pp. 220–221), and Zethus married Thebe, in whose honor the newly walled city was renamed Thebes.

The story of the family of Lycus repeats motifs from the story of Cadmus. The walling of Cadmeia and its renaming is a doublet of the founding of the city by Cadmus, and just as Cadmus and Harmonia civilized their people, so Amphion's music demonstrated the power of harmony and beauty over the disunited and inanimate stones.

Laius

After a reign of many years, Amphion and Zethus died, after which Laius returned from exile and resumed the kingship of which he had been deprived as an infant. In exile, he had been hospitably received by **Pelops**, king of Elis. The ties of guest and host were among the most sacred of human relationships, and Laius brought upon himself and his descendants a curse by abducting **Chrysippus**, the son of Pelops, with whom he had fallen in love. In his lost tragedy *Chrysippus*, Euripides made Laius "the first of the Hellenes to practice love for men," an accepted practice among Athenian men in Euripides' time. The scene in the Darius painter's vase shows the violence of Laius and the dismay of Pelops and Chrysippus, who committed suicide after the rape. Apollo foretold the working out of the curse in the first generation when Laius (now king of Thebes) consulted the Delphic oracle about the children who should be born to him and his wife, Jocasta. This is the reply of the oracle (Sophocles, Argument to *Oedipus Tyrannus*):

> I will give you a son, but you are destined to die at his hands. This is the decision of Zeus, in answer to the bitter curses of Pelops, whose son you abducted; all this did Pelops call down upon you.

Oedipus, Son of Laius and Jocasta

When a son was born, Laius attempted to avoid the fate foretold by the oracle by ordering the infant to be exposed upon **Mt. Cithaeron**, with a spike driven through his ankles. The servant entrusted with the task pitied the baby and instead gave him to a Corinthian shepherd (for the Theban and Corinthian summer pastures were adjacent on Cithaeron). The shepherd in turn brought the infant to his master, **Polybus**, king of Corinth. The child was brought up as the son of Polybus and his queen, **Merope**, and was called Oedipus (which means "swellfoot") from the injury to his ankles.

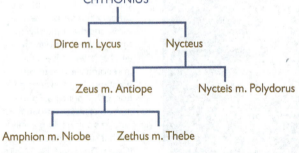

Figure 17.2 Descendants of Chthonius

Years later, a drunken companion jeered at Oedipus during a feast at Corinth and said that he was not Polybus' natural son. In alarm and shame at the taunt (which soon spread through the city), Oedipus left Corinth to ask the oracle at Delphi who his parents were. The oracle warned him in reply to avoid his homeland, since he must murder his father and marry his mother. So he determined not to return to Corinth and took the road from Delphi that led to Thebes. What happened then, Oedipus himself relates to Jocasta (Sophocles, *Oedipus Tyrannus* 800–813):

> As I came on my journey to this junction of three roads, a herald and a man (like him whom you described) riding in a horse-drawn chariot blocked my way; they violently drove me off the road. In anger I struck the driver, who was pushing me aside; and when the old man saw me passing by him, he took aim at the middle of my head and struck me with the two-pronged goad. But he paid for this with interest; struck promptly by the staff in this hand of mine, he quickly tumbled out of the chariot. I killed them all.[1]

The old man, whom Oedipus did not recognize, was Laius. The curse of Pelops was being fulfilled.

Oedipus and the Sphinx. Interior of Attic red-figure cup by the Oedipus painter, ca. 470 B.C. Oedipus, dressed as a traveler, ponders the riddle of the Sphinx, who sits on an Ionic column. The Sphinx is winged, with a woman's head and a lion's body and tail. (*Photo Copyright © Government Of The Vatican City State-Directorate of the Vatican Museums.*)

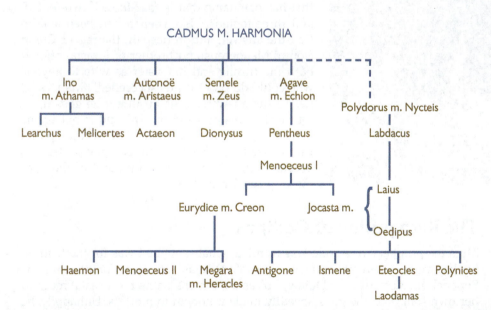

Figure 17.3 The Dynasties of Thebes

Oedipus and the Sphinx, by Gustave Moreau (1826–1898); oil on canvas, 1864, 81¼ × 41¼ in. The Sphinx clutches Oedipus, ready to tear him to pieces (like his predecessors whose remains lie in the foreground), while Oedipus gazes at her intensely. Like Ingres (*Oedipus and the Sphinx*, 1808), Moreau sets the scene in the mountains outside Thebes (faintly seen in the background of both paintings), but he paints the whole of the monster's body and includes a column with a serpent, topped by an ancient vase with griffins' heads, copied from an engraving by Piranesi. The close physical contact of man and monster heightens the intensity of Oedipus' encounter. This was Moreau's best-known work, and it drew the attention of critics (favorable and unfavorable) and cartoonists (Daumier's caption read in part: "A bare-shouldered cat with the head of a woman, so that's called a sphinx?"). (*Image copyright © The Metropolitan Museum of Art/Art Resource, NY*)

Oedipus and the Sphinx

So Oedipus came to Thebes, a city in distress; not only was the king dead, but also the city was plagued by a monster sent by Hera, called Sphinx (which means "strangler"). This creature had the face of a woman, the body of a lion, and the wings of a bird. It had learned a riddle from the Muses, which it asked the Thebans. Those who could not answer the riddle, it ate; and it was prophesied that Thebes would be free of the Sphinx only when the riddle was answered. The riddle was: "What is it that has one name that is four-footed, two-footed, and three-footed?"[2] No Theban had been able to find the answer; and in despair, the regent **Creon** (son of Menoeceus and brother of Jocasta) offered both the throne and his sister as wife to anyone who could do so. Oedipus succeeded. "Man," said he, "is the answer: for as an infant he goes upon four feet; in his prime upon two; and in old age he takes a stick as a third foot." And so the Sphinx threw itself off the Theban acropolis; Oedipus became king of Thebes and husband of the widowed queen, his mother.

The Recognition of Oedipus

Thus the prophecy of Apollo was fulfilled; what remained was for the truth to be discovered. There are three versions of Oedipus' fate, two Homeric and one Sophoclean. According to Homer, Epicasta (Homer's name for Jocasta) married her own son, "and the gods speedily made it known to mortals. Unhappily, he reigned on at Thebes, but she went down to the house of Hades, fastening a noose to the roof of the lofty hall" (*Odyssey* 11.271). In the *Iliad*, Oedipus is spoken of as having fallen in battle. In this version, another wife is the mother of the children of Oedipus.

The most widely accepted story, however, is the later version, that of Sophocles. Oedipus and Jocasta lived happily together, and she bore him two sons, **Polynices** and **Eteocles**, and two daughters, **Antigone** and **Ismene**. After many years, a plague afflicted Thebes, and the oracle of Apollo advised the Thebans that it was the result of a pollution on their state, for the murderer of Laius was in their midst. At this point, Polybus died, and the messenger who brought the news also brought the invitation to Oedipus from the people of Corinth to become their king. Oedipus, still thinking that Merope was his mother, refused to return to Corinth; but the messenger—who was the same shepherd to whom the infant exposed on Cithaeron had been given—tried to reassure him by telling him that he was not in fact the son of Merope and Polybus. Oedipus then sent for the servant to whom Laius had given his infant son to be exposed on Mt. Cithaeron. This man was also the sole survivor of the incident in which Laius died. Now the truth came out. This is how Sophocles describes the moment of Oedipus' discovery. He is questioning the servant (who already knows the truth) in the presence of the messenger (*Oedipus Tyrannus* 1164–1185):

> OEDIPUS: Which of these citizens [gave you the baby] and from what house [did it come]?
> SERVANT: Do not, I beg you by the gods, master, do not question me any more. (1165)
> OEDIPUS: You will be killed if I have to ask you this question again.
> SERVANT: Well, it was one of the children of Laius.
> OEDIPUS: A slave? Or one of his own children?
> SERVANT: Alas! I am on the point of revealing a terrible secret!
> OEDIPUS: And I of hearing it. Yet hear it I must. (1170)
> SERVANT: Well, it was called the son of Laius. The woman inside the palace best would tell—your wife—the facts.   10
> OEDIPUS: So she it was who gave you the baby?
> SERVANT: Yes, my lord.
> OEDIPUS: For what purpose?
> SERVANT: That I might kill him.
> OEDIPUS: Was she his mother, unhappy woman?
> SERVANT: Yes, and she was afraid of the harm that had been foretold by the oracle. (1175)
> OEDIPUS: And what was that?
> SERVANT: The prophecy was that he would kill his parents.   20
> OEDIPUS: How then did you give him up to this old man, how did you?
> SERVANT: I was sorry for him, master, and I thought this man would carry him to another country, from which he came himself. But he saved him for evils much worse. For if *you* are the person this man says you are, then, I tell you, you were born to a wretched destiny. (1178–1181)
> OEDIPUS: Alas! Alas! All is revealed! O light, may this be the last time I look upon you, I who have been shown to be born from those from whom I should not have been born, to be living with those with whom I should not live, and to have killed those whom I should not have killed! (1182–1185)

The horror of Oedipus' predicament is powerfully expressed in the stark dialogue, and it is no wonder that Sophocles' version of the myth has swept aside all other versions.[3] While Oedipus was questioning the servant, Jocasta, who already knew the truth, had gone into the palace and hanged herself. Oedipus rushed into the palace and, when he saw her corpse, blinded himself with the brooches from her robe. Creon became regent again, and Oedipus was banished, in accordance with a curse he himself earlier pronounced on the (as yet unknown) killer of Laius and in obedience to an oracle of Apollo.

The End of the *Oedipus Tyrannus*

Modern readers and viewers of Sophocles' tragedy are likely to find the 234 lines (15 percent of the whole) that are spoken after the entry of the blind Oedipus an anticlimax after the discovery of his identity. This would be a mistake. Oedipus establishes the true measure of his heroic stature in his lament and dialogue with the Chorus and with Creon. The central themes of the tragedy are the relationship of the human to the divine and, as a consequence, the way in which human beings react to or control events brought about by the divine will. The audience knows the end result of Oedipus' search for the killer before he begins the process of discovery. Part of the suspense lies in our not knowing how he will react to the discovery. His self-blinding cannot be the end of the story: Sophocles shows how this act begins the next part of the hero's life, in which he proves his worth as a human being, accepting the will of the gods while still asserting his own dignity and independence. Thus he cries out to the Chorus (1329–1335):

> Apollo it was, Apollo, who brought to fruition these my evil sufferings. No one struck [my eyes] but I in my misery. Why should I need to see, when there is nothing sweet for me to see?

Oedipus recognizes the power of the god and the impossibility of avoiding the divine will. Yet he also recognizes his own responsibility—he is the one who committed the crimes against the divine law, and he is the one who blinded himself. He is also the one who now, even in his miserable state, gives instructions to Creon (1446: "These are my orders to you. . . .") for the burial of Jocasta, for his own exile from Thebes (where, he commands, he is not to be buried), and for the reunion with his daughters, Antigone and Ismene, who in the last lines of the play are taken from him as he is led back into the palace.

The nobility of Sophocles' interpretation can be seen if we look back to the lines in the tragedy where Jocasta dismisses the prophecies of Apollo, thinking that the details of the killing of Laius, as told by Oedipus, have proved that the oracle was false (857–858):

> I would not in the future look for prophecies on this side or on that.

The Chorus, speaking for ordinary citizens of Thebes (or of any Greek city that honored the gods), is appalled. They (so they affirm) will not resist what is fated, for its laws have been established by Zeus and never die, while human beings grow old and die. The human being who dismisses the laws of Zeus commits hubris (pride, leading to insolent violence) and becomes a tyrant, his world being one in which the proper order of things human and divine is thrown into disorder. Such insolence, so the Chorus sings, they never will display. In famous lines they conclude (893–896):

> What man who lives his life like this [i.e., disregarding the divine law] can protect his soul from the shafts [of Zeus]? If deeds such as his are honored, why should I dance in the Chorus?

In the lines that follow these words, they pray to Zeus to assert his power, for if the prophecies of Apollo are disregarded, then religion (and with it, the power of the gods) no longer has any meaning.

Immediately after this chorus, in a brilliant dramatic stroke, Sophocles brings on Jocasta, the very person who had declared that the prophecies of Apollo were useless. She has kept faith in the god but not in the prophecies she believes were delivered by his false prophets. Jocasta sacrifices at the altar of Apollo but to no avail. In bitter irony, her prayer is answered at once by the arrival of the Corinthian messenger, who sets in motion events leading to her own death. The inexorable progress of Oedipus' discovery continues to its fated climax.

Returning now to the last scene of the tragedy, we see that the power of Zeus is confirmed, but with it comes the potential for the hero to assert his dignity in the face of the worst that the will of Zeus can do to him. In the final lines of the drama, the Chorus, in lines that appear repeatedly in Sophocles (and in Herodotus' story of Croesus, as told in Chapter 6), sing (1528–1530):

> Call no man happy until he reaches the end of his life without suffering.

The will of Zeus, as foretold by Apollo at Delphi, has triumphed, but so also has Oedipus, who has asserted his greatness as a human being and has not given in to despair.

Sophocles' *Oedipus at Colonus*

Sophocles died in 406–405 B.C. at about the age of ninety, and his final drama, *Oedipus at Colonus*, was produced at Athens by his grandson in 401.[4] It is the longest of Sophocles' tragedies, and it is a profound meditation on the wisdom that old age brings after a lifetime of experience—success and failure, suffering and happiness. It develops the themes of the *Oedipus Tyrannus*, produced in about 428, bringing the hero to his mysterious yet glorious end near the village of Colonus, the birthplace of Sophocles himself.

The drama begins with Oedipus, after years of wandering as an exile and beggar, coming to Colonus accompanied by Antigone. A citizen of Colonus tells him that he is on holy ground, sacred to the Eumenides, daughters of Earth and Darkness, ground possessed also by Poseidon and Prometheus. The citizen leaves to find the king of Athens, **Theseus**, and Oedipus prays to the Eumenides that they will bring an end both to his wandering and to his life, as prophesied by Apollo and hinted at in the dialogue with Creon at the end of the *Oedipus Tyrannus*. Thus, in this imposing opening scene, Sophocles sets out the essential plot of the drama, the climax of which is to be the end of the hero's life on earth.

A Chorus of old men, citizens of Colonus, enters and learns the identity of this stranger. Naturally, they think he is a pollution on their land, and in the subsequent scenes Oedipus looks back on his crimes from the perspective of the end of a long life. Thus he says (265–274):

> Neither [the condition of] my body nor my deeds were mine. Know that I was the sufferer in my deeds, not the agent, if I *must* tell you of what happened with my mother and my father. This is why you are afraid of me, I know well. Yet how was I evil in nature if I reacted to what I suffered, so that, if I did what I did with full awareness, I would not have been an evil-doer? Yet, as it is, I have come where I have come not knowing what I did. I suffered and was destroyed by those who knew [i.e., the gods].

So in this play Sophocles discusses the intractable question of Oedipus' guilt or innocence more fully than in the earlier tragedy. By establishing the innocence of Oedipus, he prepares for his transformation to heroic status (in the religious sense) at the end of his life, while he in no way diminishes the horror that we (represented by the citizens of Colonus) feel at his crimes of parricide and incest. The role of the Eumenides in the drama makes Sophocles' solution yet more powerful, for they had been the Erinyes, the terrible goddesses who pursued and punished those who committed crimes against members of their own families.[5] It is in their sacred temenos (enclosure) that the action takes place, and it is to them whom Oedipus first prays before the entry of the Chorus and again following the instructions of the Chorus (486–487):

> Since we call them Eumenides you should pray that they should be the suppliant's saviors, acting with kindly hearts.

The action of the drama is therefore intertwined with the resolution of Oedipus' crimes, so that at the end he is justified and can control the final scene of his life, as he proceeds to his miraculous disappearance from the earth.

Creon, king of Thebes, appears with an armed escort and tries by persuasion and by force to get Oedipus to return to Thebes, even kidnapping Antigone and Ismene in his efforts to overpower him. But Oedipus is secure in the protection of Theseus, which the Athenian king has promised him before the appearance of Creon. Theseus appears just as the young women have been led off, and he sends soldiers to recover them. Meanwhile, Creon attempts to justify himself before Theseus, the Chorus, and Oedipus, whose great speech in response is the most detailed defense of his actions. We translate most of it here (962–1002):

> Murder, marriage, misfortune—you have hurled these charges from your mouth. These things I suffered unwillingly, for they were the will of the gods, who perhaps have been angry with our family for generations past. As for myself alone, you never could reproach me for a crime in doing the deeds I did against myself and members of my family. Then show me this: if you came upon an oracle prophesying that [my] father must be killed by his children, how could you justly call me guilty? My mother had not then been filled with my father's seed, and I had not been conceived. Again, if I, appearing as the victim of an evil fate (as I did appear)—if I fought with my father and killed him, knowing nothing of what I was doing and to whom I was doing it, how could you reasonably find fault with an unwilling deed? (962–977)   10
>
> Then, you wretch, you are not ashamed to force me to speak of my mother's marriage, your own sister! I will speak, I will not be silent. . . . For she bore me— yes, she gave me birth, unhappy man that I am. She did not know, and I, her child, knew not. She gave birth to me and then to her shame bore children to me. One thing I know, that you slander her and me in saying that I did these things willingly.

> Unwillingly did I marry her, and unwillingly do I say these things now. Not even in this marriage can you find me guilty, nor in the murder of my father (which you constantly bring up with your bitter charges). Answer me this one question: if someone came up to you—you righteous man—to kill you, would you ask if your killer were your father? Or would you pay him back immediately? I think, if you love life, you would pay back the criminal and you would not look round for justification. (978–996)   20
>
> Well, these were the evils that I walked into, led by the gods. I do not think even my father's soul, if he were alive again, would disagree. But you, you are not just: you think it good to say anything, things that can be spoken and things that should remain unspoken, and you make these charges in the presence of these men. (997–102)

Oedipus ends by calling on the Eumenides to support him and his protector, Theseus (1010–1013):

> I call upon these goddesses, I beg them with my prayers, to come as my helpers and defenders, so that you [Creon] may know what sort of men are guardians of this city [Athens].

Creon leaves, and Theseus' soldiers return with Antigone and Ismene. But now another threat to Oedipus appears as Polynices, his elder son, comes from Argos to ask his father's blessing and presence as he marches with six heroic allies to claim the throne of Thebes. Before Polynices appears, Theseus promises Oedipus that he will not allow him to leave under compulsion, and we know therefore that Polynices will fail. The scene between Polynices and Oedipus is powerful. Though Oedipus is blind and a wandering beggar, he is still the father who has the authority to bless or curse his son.

Polynices makes a self-serving speech, in which he describes the expedition that he is making against his own city.[6] He knows that the army that has Oedipus with it will be victorious, and he promises to restore Oedipus to Thebes. Oedipus' reply is a masterpiece of reproach and chastisement. He shows who in fact has been guilty of transgressing the unwritten laws of the family, the very charge that he himself had answered in his speech to Creon. He says (1354–1364):

> When you held the power and ruled at Thebes, as now your brother does, yourself you banished your own father; you made me a man without a city and made me wear these rags, which now make you weep to see. Now you suffer the same troubles as I and suffer the same evils. They do not call for tears, but I must endure them all my life, as I remember that you were my destroyer. You made me live with suffering, you thrust me out; you made me a wanderer who must beg his daily life from others.

Oedipus disowns his sons, contrasting them with Antigone and Ismene, who have truly been loyal to him. He foretells the failure of the expedition against Thebes, reminding Polynices that he had cursed him long ago. He curses him once more (1383–1396):

> Go! I spit you out, you are no son of mine. You are the worst of evil men. Take with you these curses which I call down on you—never may you rule your own land by force, and never may you return to the vale of Argos. May you die by your

> brother's hand and may you kill the man [your brother] who drove you out! These
> are my curses. I call on the hateful, dark abyss of Tartarus, where my ancestors
> lie, to keep you from your city. I call on these goddesses [the Eumenides]; I call
> on Ares, who thrust this terrible hatred into your hearts. Hear this and go! Tell all
> the Thebans and tell your loyal allies that Oedipus has bequeathed this legacy to
> his children.

Before he goes, Polynices refuses to listen to Antigone's request that he
give up his expedition. In Antigone's moving words Sophocles foreshadows
her fate: to die upholding the unwritten laws of Zeus that compel her to break
the laws of man in burying her brother. This is the plot of Sophocles' tragedy
Antigone.

The End of the Life of Oedipus

The drama of *Oedipus at Colonus* has looked back at Oedipus' crimes and has
proved him innocent of deliberate intention in his crimes against his family.
It has looked forward to the self-destructive hatred of the sons of Oedipus for
each other, and it has foreshadowed the tragic self-sacrifice of Antigone. It has
brought Oedipus to Colonus, where he is protected by the earthly power of King
Theseus and the divine power of the Eumenides. One thing remains, the final
moments of the hero's life on earth. As Polynices leaves, thunder is heard, and
Oedipus knows that this is the sign for the ending of his life. Theseus reappears,
and the blind Oedipus, with the authority of one who fully knows who he is and
at peace with himself, leads him and the young women toward the place where
his life will end. He blesses Theseus and Athens, asking only that Theseus never
reveal the place of his disappearance.

What happens next is related in the speech of the messenger who was
an eyewitness. We give the passage in full here, since it clearly tells us how
Sophocles viewed the relationship of Oedipus the man to Oedipus the hero.
The poet carefully describes the place, for a hero is associated with a particular locality. He connects Oedipus' passing with the powers beneath the
earth (Zeus is called by his title Chthonius, that is, "Zeus of the Earth");
yet Theseus rightly worships the powers of both earth and heaven after the
miracle, for the hero is part of the array of Greek divinities, those of heaven
as well as the chthonic powers. And Oedipus' passing is miraculous and
without grief, in this symbolizing his benign influence on the place where
he passed from mortal sight and his power as a hero to perform miracles
for those who worship him. Here then is Sophocles' description (*Oedipus at
Colonus* 1587–1665):

> You know how he left this place without any of his friends to guide him, himself
> the leader of us all. When he came to the edge of the ravine, which is rooted in
> the earth by the brazen stairs, he stood in one of the paths which meet there—the
> place is by the hollow basin where the pact of Theseus and Pirithoüs was forever
> made. Around him were the rock of Thoricus, the hollow wild pear tree, and the
> stone tomb. Here he sat and loosened his dust-stained garments. Then he called
> his daughters and bade them bring him water from the running stream to wash

with and make libations. So they went to the hill of Demeter, bringer of green freshness, which overlooks the place, and soon returned bringing what their father had asked for. Thus they washed and clothed him as custom demands. When he was satisfied with all that they were doing and none of his commands had gone unfulfilled, then Zeus of the Earth thundered, and the girls shuddered as they heard. They clasped their father's knees and wept; continuously they beat their breasts and wailed. But he immediately answered their unhappy cry, clasped his arms around them, and said: "My children, today your father ceases to be. All that is mine has come to an end; no more need you labor to support me. Hard was that task, I know, my daughters; yet one word alone relieves all that toil—for of *Love* you never will have more from any man than me. And now you will pass your lives bereft of me." (1587–1619)   10

In this way, they all sobbed and wept, embracing each other. When they came to an end of weeping and were silent, a sudden voice called him and all were afraid and their hair stood on end. It was God who called him repeatedly. "Oedipus, Oedipus," he called, "why wait we to go? Too long have you delayed." Then Oedipus, knowing that God was calling him, called King Theseus to him, and when he drew near said: "Dear friend, give your hand to my children as a solemn pledge, and you, my children, give yours to him. And do you, Theseus, swear never knowingly to betray these girls and always to act for their good?" And Theseus, without complaint, swore on his oath that he would do as his friend asked, for he was a man of generous nature. (1620–1637)   20

When this was done, Oedipus straightway felt his children with unseeing hands and said: "My daughters, you must resolutely leave this place; you may not ask to see what is not right for you to see, nor hear words that you should not hear. Go then; let only King Theseus stay and behold what will be done." (1638–1644)   30

All of us heard his words, and with groans and tears went with the girls. As we began to leave, we turned and saw Oedipus no longer there; the king we saw, shielding his eyes with his hand, as if some dread sight had appeared which he could not bear to look upon. Yet soon after we saw him worship Earth and Olympus, the gods' home above, with the same words. (1645–1655)

How Oedipus died no man can tell except Theseus. No fiery thunderbolt from God consumed him, no whirlwind from the sea. Some divine messenger came for him, or the deep foundations of the earth parted to receive him, kindly and without pain. Without grief he passed from us, without the agony of sickness; his going was more than mortal, a miracle. (1656–1665)   40

So Oedipus became a hero, bringing good to the country in which he lay, and thus Sophocles honors Attica and his own deme of Colonus in this version of the end of Oedipus' life.

Other Versions of the Myth of Oedipus

There were, however, other versions. We have seen (p. 410) that in Homer Jocasta is not the mother of Oedipus' children and that he apparently dies in battle. In the *Oedipus* of Euripides (of which a few lines survive), the servants of Laius boast that they blinded Oedipus. "We pushed the son of Polybus to the ground," they say; "we destroyed his eyes and blinded him" (Euripides, *Oedipus*, fr. 541). At the end of Sophocles' *Oedipus Tyrannus*, he is led into the palace, whereas the playwright had earlier indicated (1446–1454) that Oedipus was to be thrust out of the city to wander and die on Mt. Cithaeron, where he had been exposed as a baby. In the *Phoenissae* of Euripides (produced about a decade before the *Oedipus at Colonus*), Oedipus is still in the palace at the time of the expedition of the Seven against Thebes and Jocasta is still living. After his sons have killed each other and Jocasta has killed herself over their corpses, he emerges for the first time and is sent into exile by Creon. At the end of the play, he leaves Thebes accompanied by Antigone and foretells that he will come to Colonus: in this respect, the version of Euripides harmonizes with that of Sophocles. In his final speech in the *Phoenissae*, Oedipus looks back over his tragic life (1758–1763):

> O citizens of my glorious homeland, look! Here am I, Oedipus, I, who knew the hard riddles; I, once the greatest of men. I alone ended the violence of the murderous Sphinx. Now I, the same man, I am being driven out of my land, a pitiful figure, deprived of my rights. Yet why bewail these things and weep in vain? A mortal must endure what the gods compel him to suffer.

Oedipus the Hero

Oedipus is basically an archetypal Greek hero whose legend is consistent with the criteria given at the beginning of this chapter or with Propp's formulation (see Chapter 1, pp. 13–14). The *Odyssey* version of the story focuses on the kingship of Oedipus—he kills his father, king of Thebes; succeeds him; and inherits his wife. After she commits suicide, he continues to rule and dies, as a king often does, in battle (as may be implied in the *Iliad*'s reference to his death). Kingship, rather than incest, is the focus of Oedipus' myth (as opposed to that of Epicasta/Jocasta) in its early stages. Sophocles seems to have brought the theme of incest into the foreground, and in so doing to have taken the myth beyond the traditional ending of the hero's quest, that is, the winning of a bride. And from Sophocles' great tragedy have descended the psychoanalytical theories in Chapter 1.[7]

Other than kingship and family relations, the myth also focuses on the hero's wisdom and his effect on society. Gustave Moreau (see image on p. 410) commented in preparing his painting that Oedipus was "a man of mature age wrestling with the enigma of life," and for Moreau this was the principal focus of the myth, not parricide and incest. For Lévi-Strauss and the structuralists, the myth mediates between extremes in family relationships that would be intolerable otherwise. Others have adopted the structuralist approach of including all variants of a myth in their context. Jan Bremmer, for example, accepts the Freudian notion of father–son rivalry and sees the Greek myth as a "warning to the younger generation" to respect their fathers, whom they will succeed. Modern fascination with the Freudian interpretation—powerful and satisfying as it may be—should not obscure the origins of the myth in the role of kingship in preclassical Greek society, nor should we ignore the fact that the myth as we have it is made up of many elements from different Greek (and non-Greek) societies.

The Seven against Thebes

The Preliminaries to the Expedition

In his speech cursing Polynices in the *Oedipus at Colonus*, Oedipus refers to an earlier curse that he had laid upon his sons, Eteocles and Polynices (1375). According to early epics, now lost, they had disobeyed Oedipus by using a golden cup and a silver table belonging to Laius in serving a meal to him while he was shut up in the palace, and he cursed them. Later, they served him a less honorable portion of meat than was his due as a king, and he cursed them again. The curses were that they should divide the kingdom of Thebes, that there should "always be war and battle between them," and that they should kill each other.[8] Thus the curse uttered in the *Oedipus at Colonus* is the third one.

The curses were fulfilled after Oedipus' death or (in the version of the *Phoenissae* of Euripides) while he was still alive. Eteocles and Polynices quarreled over the kingship at Thebes. They agreed that each should rule in alternate years, while the other went into exile. Eteocles ruled for the first year, while Polynices went to Argos, taking with him the necklace and robe of Harmonia. At Argos, Polynices and another exile, Tydeus of Arcadia, married the daughters of the king, Adrastus, who promised to restore them to their lands and decided to attack Thebes first. This war and its consequences are the subject of the saga of the Seven against Thebes, which is the title of one of the tragedies of Aeschylus.

Several other dramas deal with the saga, including two with the title *Phoenician Women*, one by Euripides and the other by the Roman author Seneca. The consequences of the war are the subject of *The Suppliant Women* by Euripides and of *Antigone* by Sophocles. The saga is most fully narrated by the Roman poet Statius, whose epic, *Thebaid*, written in about A.D. 90, was widely read in medieval and Renaissance Europe.

The Argive army had seven leaders: besides **Adrastus**, **Polynices**, and **Tydeus**, there were **Capaneus**, **Hippomedon**, **Parthenopaeus**, and **Amphiaraüs**. Amphiaraüs, who had the gift of prophecy, knew that except for Adrastus all seven would be killed and therefore

Capaneus. Campanian red-figure vase, ca. 350 B.C. On the left, Capaneus, holding the torch in his left hand and an axe (grasped horizontally) in his right hand, climbs the ladder. The thunderbolt that will destroy him is painted in the top left panel; to the right of it are two defenders. In the right upper panel is an old man with a scepter. Below him is a winged woman, similar to the Vanth of Etruscan mythology (see the next illustration). At the bottom, a four-horse chariot approaches from the right. (*The J. Paul Getty Museum, Villa Collection, Malibu, California*)

opposed the expedition. But Polynices bribed Amphiaraüs' wife, **Eriphyle**, with the necklace of Harmonia, to persuade her husband to change his mind. As he set out, he ordered his sons to avenge his death on their mother and themselves to make an expedition against Thebes when that of the Seven had failed.

Incidents on the Journey from Argos to Thebes

Before the army reached Thebes, two episodes intervened. At Nemea (not far from the Isthmus of Corinth), they were led to a spring of water by Hypsipyle, nurse of Opheltes, the infant son of the local king, Lycurgus. (See pp. 599–600 for the earlier life of Hypsipyle and her part in the saga of Jason.) She left the baby lying on the ground while she showed the way, and he was killed by a serpent. In Euripides' tragedy *Hypsipyle*, Eurydice, wife of Lycurgus, tries to kill Hypsipyle but is prevented by Amphiaraüs. He entrusts Hypsipyle to her sons by Jason, Thoas and Euneos, who were searching for their mother and arrived at Nemea just then, and they take her back to Lemnos. The Seven killed the serpent and in honor of the dead child celebrated the athletic contests that became the **Nemean Games**. Amphiaraüs changed his name from Opheltes (Snake Child) to Archemorus (Beginner of Death), as an omen of what was yet to come.

In the second episode Tydeus was sent to Thebes as an ambassador to demand the abdication of Eteocles in accordance with his agreement with Polynices. While at Thebes, Tydeus took part in an athletic contest and by winning humiliated the Thebans, who ambushed him as he returned to the army. Tydeus killed all fifty of his attackers, except for one man who took the news to Thebes.

The Failure of the Attack on Thebes

When the army reached Thebes, each leader attacked one of the city's seven gates. The central part of Aeschylus' tragedy *Seven against Thebes* consists of matched speeches in which the herald describes each of the Seven and is answered by Eteocles, who stations a Theban hero at each gate of the city. The herald's speeches give a vivid idea of the qualities of each Argive hero (selections from Aeschylus, *Seven against Thebes* 375–685):[9]

> Tydeus raging . . . shouts out with midday cries like a dragon. . . . Upon his shield he has this proud sign embossed, the heaven blazing beneath the stars. The bright full moon, the oldest of the stars, the eye of night, shines brightly in the middle of the shield. . . .
>
> Capaneus . . . is another giant, greater than the one already named. . . . He threatens to sack the city, whether the god is willing or not. . . . His device is a naked man carrying fire, and the torch with which his hand is equipped blazes, and in golden letters he says, "I will burn the city."
>
> Hippomedon with a war-cry stands before the gates of Athena. . . . It was no mean craftsman who placed this work upon his shield, Typhon, belching fiery smoke through his mouth, and the encircling hollow of the shield is covered with wreathed serpents. . . . [10]
>
> [Parthenopaeus the Arcadian] swears . . . that he will violently sack the city of Cadmeia. . . . Upon his bronze shield he wields the flesh-eating Sphinx, the reproach of the city. . . .

> The sixth I would say is the most virtuous man, the prophet best in might, strong Amphiaraüs. . . . Upon his shield was no sign, for he did not wish to seem, but to be, the best. . . . Against him I advise setting wise and virtuous defenders, for terrible are those whom the gods revere.

Finally, the herald describes Polynices, whose threats against his brother are the most terrible of all. Upon his shield is a double device, a woman leading an armed man:

> She says she is Justice, as the inscription says: "I will bring this man back, and he shall possess his father's city and go about its houses." (646–648)

In these descriptions, Aeschylus has given an impressive picture of the heroic stature of the Seven, whose individual characters are delineated through the devices on their shields. Eteocles refuses to be intimidated and arms himself for battle, denying that Justice is on Polynices' side. He knows that he must kill his brother, and he knows that in so doing he will be the instrument fulfilling the curse of Oedipus. When the Chorus asks him if he wishes to kill his own brother, he replies, "When the gods give evil, you cannot escape their gift."

These were the final words of Eteocles before the Seven attacked the city, and they express the inevitability of the curse on the sons of Oedipus. The failure of the Seven was foretold by the Theban prophet Tiresias, who prophesied that if one of the Spartoi sacrificed himself, the city would have atoned fully for the blood-guilt incurred by the killing of Ares' sacred serpent and so be saved. Here is part of the prophecy of Tiresias, as given by Euripides (*Phoenissae* 931–941):

> This man [i.e., Menoeceus] must be killed at the lair of the earthborn serpent, the guardian of Dirce's fountain, and he must pay the earth with his blood for the water drawn by Cadmus. This is the result of the ancient anger of Ares, who will avenge the death of the earthborn serpent. If you [i.e., Creon and the Thebans] do this, you will have Ares as your ally. If the earth takes your fruit for hers, and for her blood the blood of mortals, she will favor you—she who once put forth the gold-helmeted crop of Sown Men [*Spartoi*]. Of their descendants, one must die, one who is descended from the serpent.

Menoeceus, son of Creon and a descendant of the Spartoi, willingly died for the city: "Dying for the city," says the messenger in Euripides' play (*Phoenissae* 1090–1092), "he plunged the black-bound sword through his throat to save this land, upon the top of the city-walls," and so he fell into the serpent's lair. In the ensuing fight, only Capaneus succeeded in scaling the wall. As he reached the top, he boasted that not even Zeus could keep him out, and for his blasphemy "Zeus," says Sophocles (*Antigone* 131–137), "hurled him with brandished fire as he stood upon the parapet eager to raise the victory cry. Down he fell to the hard earth, hurled through the air, as he breathed out rage and madness in his frenzied assault."

Eteocles and Polynices killed each other in single combat, which Statius describes at great length in Book 11 of his epic, *Thebaid*. Even after death their enmity continued. Statius imagines Antigone, after the battle, trying to burn the corpse of Polynices on the very place where Eteocles had been cremated.

She cries out in horror as the flames split in two with divided tongues, symbols of the brothers' eternal hatred.

Of the other heroes, Hippomedon, Parthenopaeus, and Tydeus fell in battle. (Tydeus, indeed, could have been made immortal by Athena, whose favorite he was, but she revoked her gift when she saw him eating the brains of the man who had fatally wounded him.)

According to Euripides (in his tragedy *The Suppliant Women*), Adrastus and the mothers of the Seven went to Eleusis (in Attica) as suppliants. Helped by Aethra, mother of Theseus, they persuaded Theseus to attack Thebes and obtain an honorable burial for the dead Argives. Theseus returned victorious with the corpses of the heroes (other than Polynices, Amphiaraüs, and Adrastus himself) and conducted their funeral rites. Capaneus was granted a separate pyre, and his widow, Evadne, threw herself into its flames.

Amphiaraüs

Only Amphiaraüs and Adrastus escaped; Adrastus was saved by the speed of his divine horse Arion and returned to Argos; Amphiaraüs was swallowed up in the earth, with his chariot and driver, as he fled along the banks of the river Ismenus, one of the rivers of Thebes. The scene is vividly described by Statius (*Thebaid* 7.816–820):

> The earth parted with a deep, steep-sided chasm, and the stars above and the dead below were both struck with fear. The huge abyss swallowed Amphiaraüs and enveloped the horses as they began to cross. He did not relax his hold on his arms or the reins: just as he was, he drove the chariot straight into Tartarus.

Amphiaraüs became an important hero, and chthonic cults (i.e., cults whose ritual was directed toward the earth and the Underworld) were established in his honor in several places. He was worshiped at the place beside the river Ismenus where he was said to have descended into the earth. His most famous cult was at Oropus (a city in northeastern Attica near the border with Boeotia), where an elaborate shrine, the Amphiaraüm, was developed in the fifth century B.C. (see p. 257). He exemplifies the hero who is associated with the place (or places) where his life was said to have ended. Like Oedipus at Colonus, he experienced a mysterious death and made the place where he disappeared holy.

Antigone

The deaths of Eteocles and Polynices posed difficult religious and political dilemmas, which are presented in Sophocles' tragedy *Antigone*. The four children of Oedipus and Jocasta, as noted earlier, were Antigone, Ismene, Eteocles, and Polynices. Creon, Antigone's uncle, became king of Thebes again on the death of Eteocles. He gave orders that Polynices was not to be buried, on the grounds that he was a traitor who had attacked his own city. To leave the dead unburied was an offense against the gods, for it was the religious duty of the relatives of the dead to give them a pious burial. Antigone, as the sister of both Eteocles and Polynices, owed such a burial to both brothers, even though she would be breaking Creon's edict by burying Polynices. Alone (for Ismene refused to join

Death of Eteocles and Polynices. This Etruscan funerary ash urn (third to second century B.C.) depicts the heroes as they have fallen in mortal combat. Two supporters on each side attend the heroes. Between them flies a winged Vanth, a female demon associated with death. She holds a torch in her right hand. (© *DeA Picture Library/Art Resource, NY*)

in her defiance), she gave him a symbolic burial by throwing three handfuls of dust over his corpse. For this Creon condemned her to be buried alive. Antigone expresses her defiance of Creon in words of unforgettable power (Sophocles, *Antigone* 441–455):

> CREON: Do you admit that you did this or deny it?
> ANTIGONE: I admit it and I do not deny it.
> CREON: Did you know that this was forbidden by my decree?
> ANTIGONE: I knew it for it was clear to all.
> CREON: And yet you dared to break these laws?
> ANTIGONE: Yes, for it was not Zeus who gave me this decree, nor did Justice, the companion of the gods below, define such laws for human beings. Nor did I think that your decrees were so strong that you, a mortal man, could overrule the unwritten and unshaken laws of the gods.

Antigone was right. Creon's order defied the law of the gods, and he was soon punished. His son **Haemon** attempted to save Antigone (to whom he was engaged to be married) and, finding she had hanged herself in her tomb, killed himself with his sword. Creon's wife, **Eurydice**, killed herself when she heard the news of her son's death. Warned by Tiresias, Creon himself relented too late.

The *Antigone* of Sophocles, like his *Oedipus Tyrannus*, shows how human beings cannot ignore the demands of the gods. Antigone is a heroine who is willing to incur a lonely death rather than dishonor the gods by obeying the king's command.[10]

Sophocles' dramatization of eternal political, philosophical, and moral issues is enhanced by his illuminating portrayal of Antigone herself. Some perceive Antigone as a romantic heroine but have difficulty providing evidence from the text.

Antigone Is Brought before Creon. Lucanian (South Italian) *nestoris* by the Dolon painter, ca. 380 B.C. The *nestoris* was a type of large vase developed in southern Italy early in the fourth century B.C., wide in the middle and narrow at the foot and neck, with two pairs of handles, one horizontal and the other vertical, extending from the center to the neck; the base of one of each pair can be seen to the right of this scene. The scene shows the moment when Antigone is brought before Creon, who is seated on a stool to the left, wearing a tiara and an oriental headdress. Two guards escort her, one of whom addresses Creon. Antigone has drawn up her cloak over her head and she keeps her right hand inside the cloak, while with her left she gestures as if about to speak. This painting illustrates a theatrical performance, rather than literally interpreting Sophocles' text. (© *The Trustees of the British Museum*)

Nowhere in the play does she even mention Haemon, her betrothed. After Antigone has been brought as a prisoner to face Creon, she chastises Ismene for her unwillingness to participate in her deed and scornfully rejects Ismene's offer to die with her. Ismene asks Creon (569) if he will kill the woman who is to be the bride of his son. He replies that he will do so because he does not want Haemon to marry an evil wife. At this, Ismene exclaims (571): "O dearest Haemon, how your father dishonors you!" Those who want desperately some direct expression by Antigone of her feelings toward Haemon would assign this line to Antigone, in defiance of our manuscript tradition.

Sophocles deliberately focuses solely on Haemon's love for Antigone. After the confrontation between Haemon and Creon, Haemon leaves in a rage and the Chorus sings about the invincible power of love (Eros and Aphrodite), which has stirred up this bitter quarrel between father and son, and it is a love that has been inspired by the desire aroused by the soft cheeks and beautiful eyes of his betrothed. When the messenger relates the terrifying scene in the tomb, where Antigone by her suicide has cheated Creon of the possibility of saving her and redeeming himself, once again, it is Haemon's love for Antigone that becomes a focal point.

After the tomb is opened, Creon beholds Antigone, hanging by the neck, and Haemon by her side with his arms about her waist, bewailing the death of his bride, her murder by his father, and his marriage lost. Creon calls out to his son to come out of the tomb. Haemon does not answer but only glares at him angrily and spits in his face. Then he draws his sword and makes for his father, who avoids the thrust. Furious with himself, Haemon drives his sword into his side. While still alive, he clasps his beloved and stains her white cheek with red blood. There they lie, corpse embracing corpse, his marriage rites consummated in the realm of Hades.

One will never know how Antigone really feels about marriage to the son of Creon, a man whom she must hate, even before their conflict over the burial of Polynices, because of what she, together with her father, Oedipus, has already suffered at his hands. (One suspects that Creon, as the brother of Jocasta, had encouraged this marriage to affirm his new power in Thebes by strengthening his ties to the family of the Labdacids.) At any rate, for Antigone, Hades is her bridegroom, and her tomb, her bridal chamber. She will not be denied her pious martyrdom, inspired by her passionate devotion to the supremacy of divine over human law and ultimately her love for her brother.

In the first part of the play, Antigone appears as a heroic personality, relentless in her defiance and fierce, just like her father, as the Chorus observes (471–472). As she is led away, however, and faces, all alone, the horrifying reality of the consequences of her actions—to be buried alive—she reveals her inner conflict and remorse. She laments the destiny of her family and that of her father, his incestuous marriage with her ill-fated mother. Her brother Polynices by his death has destroyed her life. To this family she now goes, accursed, unmarried, childless, confident that she has won their loving acceptance in the afterlife. No regret is expressed, however, for the loss of Haemon.

As she is about to be entombed, a distraught Antigone presents a desperate defense of her actions and asks anguished and disturbing questions about justice and the gods and the price she has to pay (905–928):

> O Polynices, to those who are wise, I did right to honor you. If I had children die, of whom I was the mother, or a husband, rotting, unburied, never would I have undertaken this heavy task in defiance of the state. In deference to what law do I say this? If my husband had died, I could have taken another, and borne a child by another man, if I had lost the first, but since my mother and my father are hidden in the realm of Hades, never could another brother live for me. This is the nature of the law, by which I honored you above all, but Creon thought that I dared to commit a terrible crime, my beloved brother. . . . What justice of the gods have I violated? Why must I still look to the gods for help, wretched as I am? Whom can I call upon to be my ally? Although I acted piously, I stand convicted of impiety. If this seems right to the gods, I should forgive them for my suffering because I have indeed done wrong. But if the others are the ones who have done wrong, may they suffer no worse evils than they inflict unjustly upon me.   10

There is no compelling evidence for denying the authenticity of the preceding lines (endlessly disputed), in which Antigone's ultimate rationale is the fact that she could never have another brother.[11] Yet, they are rejected because of the interpretative sensibilities of some critics who will not allow their Antigone to resort to such an argument. But many, especially today, see in her words the complexity of her emotions: her psyche, revealed by the insight of Sophocles, the master of characterization. Her motives are complex, those of a grand, spiritual idealist and a disturbed and frantic human being.

Like Sophocles, Euripides wrote dramas on the Theban saga. Two of them, the *Oedipus* and the *Antigone*, are lost except for about thirty lines of each, but enough is known of them for us to learn that Euripides, writing some time after the production of the two plays of the same name by Sophocles, changed the legend. In the *Oedipus*, the servants of Laius boasted of having blinded Oedipus in the confrontation with Laius on the road (see pp. 417–418). In the *Antigone*, Euripides invented (or transmitted) quite a different legend from Sophocles. Antigone and Argia, the widow of Polynices, placed the corpse of Polynices on Eteocles' pyre. When they were caught, Argia fled, but Antigone was taken to Creon who gave her to Haemon (who was betrothed to her and had already made her pregnant) to be executed. Haemon ignored his father's orders and instead gave Antigone into the keeping of some shepherds but told Creon that he had obeyed his order to kill her. Antigone gave birth to a son, Maeon, who years later came to Thebes and was recognized by Creon, who now realized Haemon's disobedience and, despite the intercession of Heracles, ordered the execution of the lovers. They frustrated him, however, by committing suicide. Some scholars conjecture that Dionysus acts as the deus ex machina. Even from this conjectural reconstruction of the plot of Euripides' tragedy, it is clear that Euripides shared Sophocles' focus on Haemon's love, but that in extending the time between Antigone's "crime" and her death, he chose to dissipate the extraordinary power of Sophocles' presentation of the heroine.

Finally, in Euripides' (extant) *Phoenissae*, Oedipus is still in the palace at the time of the attack of the Seven, and Jocasta is still living. At the end of the play, Antigone defies Creon's order and promises that she will herself bury Polynices and kill Haemon, if Creon forces her to marry him. Creon weakens in the face of her defiance and sends her into exile with Oedipus.

The Epigoni, Sons of the Seven against Thebes

Amphiaraüs had ordered his sons to attack Thebes and to punish their mother, Eriphyle, for her treachery in accepting the necklace of Harmonia from Polynices as a bribe. Alcmaeon, one of his sons, carried out these commands ten years later. He and the sons of the Seven (they are known as the **Epigoni**, "the later generation") made a successful expedition against Thebes and destroyed the city, which the Thebans had abandoned on the advice of Tiresias. At this point, saga touches on history, for the war of the Epigoni took place, it was said, not long before the Trojan War. In the catalog of ships in the *Iliad*, which is certainly historical, only Hypothebae (Lower Thebes) is mentioned, implying that the ancient town and its citadel had been abandoned.

Alcmaeon, Eriphyle, and the Necklace of Harmonia

Alcmaeon, encouraged by an oracle of Apollo, avenged his father by killing Eriphyle. The Furies pursued him as a matricide until he found temporary shelter in Arcadia, where he married the daughter of King Phegeus, giving her the necklace of Harmonia. But the land was soon afflicted with famine, the result of the pollution caused by the presence of the matricide Alcmaeon. Obedient to another oracle, he searched for a land on which the sun had not shone when he killed his mother. In western Greece, he found land at the mouth of the river Acheloüs recently formed by the river's silt. Settling here, he was purified of his guilt by the river-god, whose daughter Callirhoë he married. But he soon was killed by the sons of Phegeus for the crime of stealing the necklace of Harmonia in order to give it to Callirhoë. The necklace eventually was dedicated by the sons of Callirhoë and Alcmaeon at Delphi. Alcmaeon's sons became the founders of Acarnania, a district of western Greece.

Tiresias

A recurring figure in the Theban saga is the blind prophet Tiresias. Descended from one of the Spartoi, he was the son of a nymph, Chariclo, a follower of Athena, and a Theban nobleman, Eueres. He appears in the *Bacchae* of Euripides as a companion of Cadmus in the worship of Dionysus (see pp. 302–305). Pindar (*Nemean Odes* 1.60–69) describes him as "the outstanding prophet of Zeus" and tells how Amphitryon summoned him to interpret the miracle of the strangling of the snakes by the infant Heracles (we translate this passage on pp. 546–547). On this occasion, Tiresias foretold the labors of Heracles and his part in the defeat of the giants by the Olympians (see p. 85). Tiresias, then, was distinguished for his longevity; he lived for seven generations, says Hesiod, and he continued to have the gift of prophecy after his death, for in the Underworld, where the souls of the dead are insubstantial and futile, he alone retained his full mental faculties. Accordingly, Homer makes him Odysseus' informant when he consults with the dead, and he foretells the end of Odysseus' wanderings and the manner of his death.

There are different stories about Tiresias' blindness, an affliction shared by many prophets and poets in Greek literature. Ovid tells the story in full (*Metamorphoses* 3.318–338):

> They say that Jupiter once had driven away his serious worries with nectar and was joking with Juno, saying, "You women have more pleasure than men, I am sure." She disagreed, and they decided to ask the experienced Tiresias for his opinion, since he had known the act of love both as man and as woman. For once he had struck with his staff the bodies of two large serpents copulating in the green forest, and he miraculously passed seven autumn seasons turned from man into woman. In the eighth, he saw the same serpents and said, "If striking you has the power to change the striker to the other sex, then I will strike you again now." He struck the serpents, and his former body returned with his native physique. So, being made the judge of the lighthearted quarrel, he agreed with Jupiter. Juno, they say, was more angry than was just and condemned the arbiter [Tiresias] to eternal blindness. But the all-powerful father [Jupiter] granted him in return for the loss of his sight knowledge of the future.   10

The sight of two large snakes entwined in the act of copulation is mysterious and impressive, and a person who violates the snakes can readily be thought to have offended against a divine power. The idea of the violation of the divine is explicit in the second legend of the blinding of Tiresias, which is similar in this respect to the legend of Actaeon (see pp. 221–223), also a Theban hero. In this version (narrated by the third-century B.C. Alexandrian poet Callimachus), Tiresias came upon Athena and Chariclo as they were bathing in the waters of the fountain Hippocrene, on the slopes of Mt. Helicon. Athena caused him to lose his sight, a punishment for having seen what mortal eyes should not have seen, but gave him the power of prophecy. Callimachus (*Hymn* 5.121–30) has her speak this to Chariclo:

> Do not lament, my companion. For your sake I shall give him many other honors. I will make him a prophet, to be honored in song by future generations, a far greater prophet than any other. He will have knowledge of birds, those that are of good omen as they fly, and those that are ill-omened. He will give many oracles to the Boeotians and to Cadmus, and, last of all, to the family of Labdacus. I will give him, too, a great staff, to guide his feet where he must go, and I will give him a limit to his life after many generations. And he alone when he dies will walk among the dead having intelligence, and he will be honored by the great Gatherer of the People [i.e., Hades].

In the story of Oedipus, Tiresias revealed the truth before Oedipus or the Thebans were ready to understand it (Sophocles, *Oedipus Tyrannus* 350–367):

> TIRESIAS: I bid you obey your own decree, and on this day speak neither to these men here nor to me, for you are the unholy pollution on this land.
> OEDIPUS: Tell me again, that I may better learn.

> TIRESIAS: I say that you are the murderer of Laius. Unwittingly you live most shamefully with those who are dearest to you, and you do not see how far gone you are in evil.

Oedipus still cannot believe Tiresias and goads him into telling him the truth even more terribly (412–419):

> TIRESIAS: These are my words, since you have reproached me with being blind: you see, and you do not see the evil in which you are, nor where you live, nor with whom you dwell. Do you know from whom you are sprung? You do not know that you are hateful to your family below and above upon the earth, and that the double curse from your mother and your father will track you down and drive you from this land, now seeing clear, but then in darkness.

The words of Tiresias powerfully express the horror of Oedipus' crimes. Through the images of seeing and blindness, they bring before us the inevitability of the justice of the gods.

Tiresias, in Sophocles' *Antigone*, also warned Creon of the disastrous mistakes he was making, only to be understood too late. Finally, before the attack of the Epigoni, Tiresias advised the Thebans to abandon the city and migrate to found the city of Hestiaea. He never reached the new city; on the way, he drank from the spring called Telphusa and died on the spot.

Select Bibliography

Bloom, Harold, ed. *Sophocles.* New York: Chelsea House, 2003.

Bremmer, Jan. "Oedipus and the Greek Oedipus Complex," in J. Bremmer, ed., *Interpretations of Greek Mythology.* New York: Routledge, 1988.

Butler, Judith P. *Antigone's Claim: Kinship between Life and Death.* New York: Columbia University Press, 2000. Three lectures explore the ambivalent feminist archetype of Antigone.

Daniels, Charles B., and Sam Scully. *What Really Goes on in Sophocles' Theban Plays.* Lanham, MD: University Press of America, 1996. An examination of the characterization of Oedipus, Antigone, and Creon in the context of the development of the plots of *Oedipus at Colonus* and *Antigone.*

Dawe, R. D., ed. *Sophocles; The Classical Heritage.* New York: Garland, 1996. A selection of writings from Italy, Germany, France, and English-speaking countries that examine the lasting influence of Sophocles.

Edmunds, Lowell. *Oedipus.* Gods and Heroes of the Ancient World Series. New York: Routledge, 2006

———. *Oedipus: The Ancient Legend and Its Later Analogues.* Baltimore, MD: Johns Hopkins University Press, 1985.

Goldhill, Simon. *Reading Greek Tragedy.* New York: Cambridge University Press, 1986. An introduction for the Greekless reader, with advanced and informed critical insights.

Goux, Jean-Joseph. *Oedipus, Philosopher.* Translated from the French by Catherine Porter. Palo Alto, CA: Stanford University Press, 1993. An analysis of Sophocles that focuses on Freud's identification of the Oedipus complex.

Johnson, Allen W., and Douglass Richard Price-Williams. *Oedipus Ubiquitous: The Family Complex in World Literature.* Stanford, CA: Stanford University Press, 1996. One hundred thirty-nine folk tales are included in this study, drawn from Europe and Euro-America.

Loraux, Nicole. *The Experience of Tiresias: The Feminine and the Greek Man.* Translated from the French by Paula Wissing. Princeton, NJ: Princeton University Press, 1998 [1995]. Associations made include a discussion of Socrates, Heracles, Helen, and Athena.

Mullahy, Patrick. *Oedipus, Myth and Complex: A Review of Psychoanalytic Theory.* New York: Grove Press, 1955. An excellent survey.

Steiner, George. *Antigones.* Oxford: Oxford University Press, 1984. A discussion of the many reinterpretations of the legend.

Story, Ian Christopher, and Arlene Allen. *A Guide to Greek Drama.* London: Blackwell, 2005. An introduction to Greek drama and dramatists, helpful to undergraduates.

Trendall, A. D., and T. B. L. Webster. *Illustrations of Greek Drama.* New York: Phaidon Press, 1971. Illustrations and commentary on scenes from Greek plays arranged by genre and author. Especially valuable for fourth-century B.C. south Italian vase paintings.

Primary Sources

Sources in the Chapter

Aeschylus	*Seven against Thebes* 375–685
Callimachus	*On the Bath of Pallas* (Hymn 5) 121–130
Euripides	*Fragment s*, edited by C. Collard and M. Cropp, 2 vols. Cambridge, MA: Harvard University Press, 2008 (Loeb Classical Library, 504, 506). Fragments of the lost plays of Euripides with English translation and informative introductions to each play. A valuable resource for all Greek sagas.
	Phoenissae (The Phoenician Women) 639–675; 931–941; 1758–1763
Ovid	*Metamorphoses* 2.846–3.2; 3.318–338
Sophocles	*Antigone* 441–455; 905–928
	Oedipus at Colonus (selections)
	Oedipus Tyrannus (selections)
Statius	*Thebaid* 7.816–820

Additional Sources

Apollodorus	*Library* 3.5.4–3.7.7: The legend of Thebes from Cadmus and Harmonia to Alcmaeon. For intricate details about the family and legends of Tydeus and Diomedes, read Apollod. 1.8.4–1.8.6
Euripides	*Suppliant Women*
Seneca	*Oedipus*
	The Phoenician Women

Notes

1. One of Laius' retainers escaped: in Sophocles' play, he is the very servant who originally failed to expose Oedipus, and his story brings about the final discovery of Oedipus' identity.
2. There are several variants of the riddle and its answer. The shortest (Apollodorus 3.53–54) is given here.

3. Cf. Lowell Edmunds, *Oedipus: The Ancient Legend and Its Later Analogues* (Baltimore, MD: Johns Hopkins University Press, 1985), a survey of the many versions of the myth. Two modern novels are of merit: *Oedipus on the Road* (1990), originally in French by Henry Bauchau, recounting the journey of Oedipus, blind and bleeding, from Thebes, with his daughter Antigone and a shepherd-bandit named Clius, through an imaginative geographical and spiritual landscape; and *Emmeline* (1980) by Judith Rossner, a powerful retelling of the Oedipus legend, set in the eastern United States in the mid-nineteenth century.

4. In the intervening four years, Athens had surrendered to Sparta and her allies at the end of the Peloponnesian War; the "long walls" between the city and its port had been pulled down. The democracy had been replaced by an oligarchy led by a committee of thirty, itself soon replaced by the restored democracy.

5. The transformation of the Erinyes (Furies) into Eumenides (Kindly Ones) is the climactic theme of Aeschylus' *Oresteia* (see p. 437); Aeschylus brings the goddesses to Athens, where they take up their new home.

6. In lines 1284–1345 of his speech, Polynices names the Seven against Thebes. We translate a similar passage from Aeschylus' *Seven against Thebes* on pp. 420–421. Another catalog is given by Euripides in the *Phoenissae* (1090–1199), where a messenger reports the failure of the attack on Thebes.

7. For a psychoanalytic interpretation, a good place to begin is with *Oedipus: Myth and Complex, A Review of Psychoanalytic Theory*, by Patrick Mullahy (see the Select Bibliography for this chapter). Mullahy discusses Sigmund Freud, Alfred Adler, C. G. Jung, Otto Rank, Karen Horney, Eric Fromm, and Harry Stack Sullivan. Of related interest is a study of the use of myth (with emphasis on psychoanalytic interpretation) in the works of William Butler Yeats, Ezra Pound, T. S. Eliot, and W. H. Auden: Lillian Feder, *Ancient Myth and Modern Poetry* (Princeton, NJ: Princeton University Press, 1971).

8. The legends contained in the lost epics (with the titles of *Oedipodea* and *Thebais*) are discussed by G. A. Huxley, *Greek Epic Poetry* (Cambridge, MA: Harvard University Press, 1969), chap. 3.

9. The herald's description of Eteoclus (son of Iphis), whom Aeschylus names as the third hero in place of Adrastus, is omitted. For other catalogs of the Seven in Euripides and Sophocles, see note 6 in this chapter.

10. Antigone, as the symbol of individual conscience against the unjust laws of the state, has inspired many literary and musical works. See George Steiner, *Antigones* (Oxford: Oxford University Press, 1984).

11. Aristotle (*Rhetoric* 3.16.9) quotes lines from this passage, and so he must have known our text. That Antigone's sentiments are not unique is shown by a story told by Herodotus (3.119) about Intaphernes' wife, who makes the same argument as Antigone: she chooses to save the life of her brother on the grounds that she could never have another. The insightful Karl Reinhardt (*Sophocles*, translated from the German by Hazel and David Harvey [New York: Barnes & Noble, 1979]) deserves the last word in this controversy (p. 84): "Just as Antigone follows divine law, and her own nature, so too she follows the *nomos* [law] of love for her brother. For Sophocles the one embraces the other."

THE MYCENAEAN SAGA

Where will the might of madness [*ate*] rest and end?

—**AESCHYLUS**, *Choephori*, 1075–1076

THE LEGENDS OF MYCENAE are particularly concerned with the House of Atreus and the greatest of its princes, Agamemnon, leader of the Achaeans against Troy. We consider the Trojan War later; in the present chapter, we discuss the fortunes of the house as they developed in Greece itself.

Tantalus and Pelops

The ancestor of the family of Atreus was Pelops, son of Tantalus, who came from Asia Minor as a suitor for the hand of **Hippodamia**, daughter of **Oenomaüs**, king of Pisa, whose territory included Olympia. This fact accounts for the importance of Pelops in the religious cults at Olympia. From the end of the Mycenaean Age, Pisa and Olympia were for most of the time controlled by the Peloponnesian city of Elis.

In the time of Tantalus and Pelops, there was easy intercourse between gods and mortals, and in some way Tantalus abused the privilege of eating with the gods. In the best-known version of the myth, he invited the gods to dine with him and cut up his son Pelops, boiled the parts in a cauldron, and served them at the feast. Pindar is reluctant to believe the story, but he told it nevertheless (Pindar, *Olympian Ode* 1.47–58):

> One of the envious neighbors secretly told the tale that they cut your limbs up with a knife and [put them] into the water boiling over the fire, and at the second course of the meat at the tables they divided you and ate. I cannot say that any of the blessed gods was gluttonous—I stand aside. . . . But if the guardians of Olympus honored a mortal man, that man was this Tantalus. Yet he could not digest great fortune, and in his fullness he brought on himself great madness. Thus the Father [Zeus] balanced above him a mighty rock, and longing always to throw it away from his head, he is an exile from good cheer.

431

The most familiar version of Tantalus' punishment is that he was condemned to suffer everlasting thirst and hunger in the Underworld. We have given Homer's account (*Odyssey* 11.582–592) in Chapter 15. There are two other Greek myths that involve cannibalism, both from places connected with Elis. One is the story of Lycaon, king of Arcadia, told by Ovid (*Metamorphoses* 1.211–243, see pp. 98–99), and the other is the banquet of Thyestes, which we discuss later in this chapter. The existence of these myths is evidence enough that in the distant past some form of cannibalism once underlay sacrificial rituals.[1]

In the usual version of the myth, the gods recognized Tantalus' deception, and all, except for Demeter, refused to eat. She, it was said, ate the flesh from Pelops' shoulder, so that when he was restored to life and wholeness by the gods, an ivory shoulder had to be substituted. Pindar gives a different explanation of the temporary disappearance of Pelops, saying that Poseidon fell in love with him and took him up to Olympus, as Zeus had done with Ganymede. In any case, says Pindar, "the immortal gods sent back the son [of Tantalus] to be among the short-lived race of mortals." It was after this that Pelops traveled to Greece as the suitor of Hippodamia.

Pelops became an important hero with a cult at Olympia, where his shrine, the Pelopion, was next to the temple of Zeus. Pindar says (*Olympian Ode* 1.90–93):

> Now he lies by the crossing of the Alpheus and is present at the blood-drenched festival. He has a busy tomb, close by the altar [of Zeus] visited by multitudes.

Indeed, sacrifices to Zeus and Pelops were central to the ritual of the Olympic festival, and Pelops received a sacrifice (usually a black ram) before each sacrifice to Zeus. Not only did he give his name to the southern part of the Greek mainland, the **Peloponnese (Pelops' Island)**, but also he received honors at the center of the greatest of the Panhellenic festivals. When the great temple of Zeus was built around 460 B.C. to house Pheidias' gold and ivory statue of Zeus seated upon his throne, the sculptures of the west pediment showed the moment before the start of the race between Pelops and Oenomaüs (we have described the temple on pp. 117–119).

This race was the origin of the curse on the descendants of Pelops. To win Hippodamia, a suitor had first to win a chariot race against Oenomaüs from Pisa to the Isthmus of Corinth. He would have a short start and take Hippodamia in his chariot with him; Oenomaüs would follow, and if he caught up, he would kill the suitor. Thirteen suitors had failed before Pelops came, and their heads decorated Oenomaüs' palace.

According to Pindar, Pelops prayed to his lover, Poseidon, before the race. His words give a sense of Pelops' heroic stature (*Olympian Ode* 1.75–89):

> [Pelops said] "If the dear gifts of Love, Poseidon, can be turned to good, shackle the brazen spear of Oenomaüs and bring me upon the swiftest chariot to Elis and set me near to power. For he has killed thirteen suitors and puts off his daughter's marriage. Great danger, however, does not take hold of the coward. Among those who must die, why should a man sitting in darkness pursue old age without glory, to no purpose? Before me, however, lies this contest. May you give me the action dear to me." Thus he spoke, and his words were not without success. Honoring him, the god gave him a golden chariot and tireless winged horses. He overcame the violence of Oenomaüs and took the girl as wife. And she bore him six princes, sons eager in virtue.   10

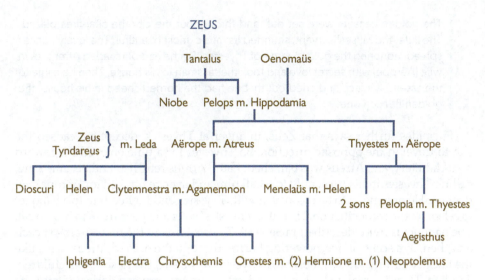

Figure 18.1 The House of Atreus

This version is simpler and probably older than the better-known one, according to which Pelops bribed Oenomaüs' charioteer, **Myrtilus** (son of the god Hermes), to remove the linchpins from Oenomaüs' chariot so that it crashed during the pursuit, killing Oenomaüs.

So Pelops won Hippodamia and drove away with her, accompanied by Myrtilus. Now Myrtilus expected that Pelops would reward him by allowing him to enjoy Hippodamia on the first night. At a resting place on the journey, he attempted to violate her, and when Pelops discovered this, he threw Myrtilus from a cliff into the sea. As Myrtilus fell, he cursed Pelops and his descendants. This curse, and the blood-guilt of the murder of Myrtilus, led to the misfortunes of the House of Atreus. Seneca, however, whose tragedy *Thyestes* is the only classical drama on this theme to survive, connects the murder with the crime of Tantalus (*Thyestes* 138–148):

> Neither right nor shared crimes have prevailed. Betrayed, the master [Oenomaüs] of Myrtilus has perished, and he, meeting with the same loyalty [from Pelops] as he had shown [to Oenomaüs] has given his name to the noble sea [the Myrtoan Sea]. . . . The child Pelops, running to kiss his father, was met with the impious sword and fell, a young victim at the hearth. He was cut up by your hand, Tantalus, so that you might make a feast for your guests, the gods.

Atreus and Thyestes

Pelops returned to Pisa and became king in place of Oenomaüs. His children, Thyestes and Atreus, quarreled over the kingdom of Mycenae, which had been offered to "a son of Pelops" in obedience to an oracle. It was agreed that the possessor of a golden-fleeced ram should become king. According to Euripides (*Electra* 698–725), Pan brought the golden-fleeced ram to Atreus, and the people of Mycenae were celebrating his succession to the throne:

> The golden censers were set out, and throughout the city the altar-fires blazed. The flute, the Muses' servant, sounded its music, most beautiful. The lovely dances spread, honoring the golden ram—of Thyestes. For he had persuaded Atreus' own wife [Aërope] with secret love and took the talisman to his house. Then he came to the assembly-place and cried out that he had the horned sheep in his house, the golden-fleeced one.

Euripides further says that Zeus, in anger at Thyestes' deception, caused the sun to travel in the opposite direction. So Thyestes for a time enjoyed the reward of his adultery, and Atreus was banished. Later, Atreus returned and became king, exiling Thyestes in his turn, only to recall him and avenge himself for Aërope's seduction. He pretended to be reconciled with Thyestes and invited him to a banquet to celebrate the reconciliation. He killed Thyestes' sons and gave them to him to eat. The banquet is twice described in Seneca's *Thyestes*, first in the messenger's speech and then, in a scene of overpowering horror, through the eyes of Atreus, who, like the audience in the theater, observes Thyestes as he eats the flesh of his children. Too late, Thyestes realized what he had eaten. As the heavens darkened and the sun hid from sight of the crime, Thyestes cursed Atreus and went into exile.

Adrastus and Thyestes at Sicyon. Apulian red-figure krater by the Darius painter, ca. 325 B.C.; height 25¼ in. A scene from Sophocles' (lost) tragedy *Thyestes at Sicyon*. Adrastus, king of Sicyon, central figure in the lower register, commands Thyestes (wearing a cap) to give up the baby Aegisthus to the huntsman (extreme lower left) for exposure. On the lower right, the baby's mother, Pelopia, is comforted by the queen of Sicyon, Amphithea. In the top register, Apollo (with a swan and a panther) sits in the middle looking toward a Fury (right center): Apollo had commanded the incest of Thyestes, and the Fury foreshadows the further working out of the curse on the house of Atreus if Aegisthus survives. On the right is the figure of Sicyon, representing the city bearing his name, and on the left Artemis (protectress of the young) orders Pan to see that Aegisthus is saved, perhaps (like Zeus on Crete) through being suckled by a goat. The vase shows that other traditions of the myths of Thyestes and Adrastus existed as well as those known from Aeschylus. Here Adrastus is ruler at Sicyon, having fled from Argos, and Aegisthus is born at Sicyon, where Pelopia had been sent for safety after the "banquet of Thyestes" at Argos. (*Photograph © 2022 Museum of Fine Arts, Boston*)

Agamemnon, Clytemnestra, and Aegisthus

Thus the curse of Myrtilus affected the first generation of Pelops' descendants. The quarrel of Thyestes and Atreus was continued by their sons. In his second exile, Thyestes lay with his daughter Pelopia, as he had been advised to do by an oracle, and became the father of Aegisthus, who continued the vendetta in the next generation. The son of Atreus, Agamemnon, succeeded his father as king of Mycenae. He married Clytemnestra and their children were **Iphigenia**, **Electra**, and **Orestes**; a third daughter, **Chrysothemis**, is important only as a foil for Electra in Sophocles' play (see the Additional Reading at the end of this chapter).

Agamemnon in his turn committed an unspeakable crime against one of his children. He sacrificed his daughter Iphigenia at the start of the Trojan expedition in order to appease Artemis and gain favorable winds to sail from Greece. This is one of the most powerful and pervasive of all Greek myths and was frequently represented in literature and art. It is the central myth with which Aeschylus sets forth the background to the action of his tragedy *Agamemnon* (184–249), and it is the theme of Euripides' final tragedy, *Iphigenia in Aulis* (see the painting by David on p. 477). It was narrated by the Roman poet Lucretius in a moving passage that we translate on page 477.

Agamemnon's crime earned the implacable hatred of his wife, Clytemnestra. During his absence at Troy, she committed adultery with Aegisthus, who had his own reasons to join her in plotting vengeance against Agamemnon. On his return from Troy with his prisoner, the Trojan princess **Cassandra**, Agamemnon was enticed into the palace and murdered by Clytemnestra and Aegisthus. This is the central event (although it takes place off stage) of the *Agamemnon* of Aeschylus. After the murder, Clytemnestra justifies the deed in a speech we translate later in this chapter (Aeschylus, *Agamemnon* 1372–1398). Aegisthus also took full responsibility for the deed, which he welcomed as a just vengeance upon the son of Atreus, the enemy of his father, Thyestes.

In the *Odyssey*, Agamemnon's ghost tells Odysseus how he and Cassandra were murdered (Homer, *Odyssey* 11.408–426):

> It was not brigands who murdered me on land, but Aegisthus, with my cursed wife, who killed me, arranging my death and fate, having called me into the house and given me a feast—killing me like an ox at the manger. Thus I died a most pitiable death, and around me my other companions were being ruthlessly killed, like tusked boars. . . . You have in the past experienced the death of many men, but if you had seen those deaths you would have most of all been grieved to see us lying in the hall amid the wine-bowls and tables full with food, and the whole floor flowing with blood. Most pitiable was the voice of the daughter of Priam that I heard, of Cassandra, whom treacherous Clytemnestra killed with me. But I, lifting my hands [in supplication] let them fall to the earth as I died by the sword, and my shameless wife turned away, nor did she dare, even though I was going down to the House of Hades, to close my eyes or mouth with her hands. 10

In this version, Agamemnon was killed by Aegisthus and Clytemnestra at the banquet celebrating his homecoming. The more widely accepted version is that of Aeschylus, in which Clytemnestra kills him in his bath, trapping him in a robe while she stabs him. Aeschylus has Cassandra foresee the murder and her own death in a dramatic prophecy before she enters the palace. She links

The Death of Agamemnon.
Attic red-figure krater by the Dokimasia painter, ca. 470 B.C.; height 20½ in. Aegisthus holds Agamemnon by his hair, having already thrust his sword into him. Agamemnon, enmeshed in a net, slips to the ground as Clytemnestra (holding an axe) runs in from the left and a woman (perhaps Electra) tries to protect Agamemnon. On the other side of this vase, the death of Aegisthus is painted. (*Photograph © 2022 Museum of Fine Arts, Boston*)

Agamemnon's murder to the banquet of Thyestes, which she describes as if it were before her eyes (*Agamemnon* 1095–1129):

> Yes, I am persuaded by the evidence I see, as I weep for these children murdered, for the cooked flesh eaten by their father. . . . What now is this new sorrow? Great is the evil being plotted in this palace, intolerable to its friends, hard to atone for, and one where defense is far away. . . . Oh, wretched woman, is this your purpose? As you wash your husband, who shares your bed, . . . how shall I describe the end? . . . What is this I see? Some net, the net of Hades? But the net is she who shares the guilt for the murder. . . . Ah! Ah! Keep the bull from the cow! She takes him in the robes and strikes him with the black-horned weapon.[2] He falls in the bath full of water. It is the fate brought by the bath, contriver of treacherous murder, that I describe to you.

The prophetic cries of the inspired victim describe, as vividly as any objective report, the death of Agamemnon, which she shortly is to share. With the corpses of Agamemnon and Cassandra at her feet, Clytemnestra defends the justice of her actions. Her speech ends with the terrifying image of Clytemnestra as the earth mother being renewed by the rain of the sky-god—in this case the blood of her murdered husband. The archetypal Sacred Marriage has never been used with greater poetic effect (Aeschylus, *Agamemnon* 1372–1398):

> I have said many things previously to serve my purpose, all of which I shall now contradict, without any shame. For how else could anyone fulfill hatred for an enemy who pretends to be a friend and string up nets of woe too high for him to overleap? For me this contest in this ancient quarrel has come after long planning—in the fullness of time, I say. I stand here where I struck him, over my deeds. Thus did I act, I shall not deny it, so that he could not escape or ward off his doom. I entrapped him in the fatal richness of the robe, encircling him with the huge net, like fishes. I struck him twice, and with two cries he let his limbs go slack; a third blow did I add as a thank-offering to Zeus below the earth, keeper of the dead. Thus fallen he gasped out his life, and at his dying breath he spattered me with rapid spurts, a dark-red rain of blood, and I rejoiced no less than the sown Earth rejoices in the glory of the rain that Zeus sends for the birth of the swelling buds. Thus my case rests, elders of Argos assembled, and may you too rejoice, if you would like to rejoice. As for me, I exult in my imprecations. If I had poured a libation for the corpse as would be fitting, it would have been of wine and curses—with justice, yes, with more than justice. So great were the accursed evils with which he filled our cup in the house, and now by his homecoming he drinks it to the dregs.

It is notable that of the sons of Atreus only Agamemnon was affected by the curse of Myrtilus. Menelaüs had his own sorrows in the adultery and flight of his wife, Helen, the cause of the Trojan War. Euripides portrays him in a contemptible light in his tragedy *Orestes*, the action of which takes place soon after Orestes has murdered Clytemnestra. He is hardly any more attractive in the *Andromache* (whose action we describe later in this chapter) or in the *Trojan Women*, whose action takes place immediately after the sack of Troy. All the literary versions of the myth portray the working out of the curse on the House of Atreus exclusively in the family of Agamemnon, whose son, Orestes, inherits its consequences.

Orestes and Electra

According to Aeschylus, Orestes was away from Mycenae at the time of Agamemnon's murder. While Clytemnestra and Aegisthus usurped the throne, he grew to manhood in exile at the court of Strophius, king of Phocis. It was now his duty to avenge the murder of his father, even though one of the murderers happened to be his own mother; and Apollo commanded him to carry out his duty. He returned to Mycenae and, with the encouragement of his sister Electra, murdered Clytemnestra and Aegisthus. In the *Odyssey*, Homer makes Zeus praise Orestes for his piety toward his dead father; and Sophocles, of the three Athenian tragedians (each of whom wrote a tragedy on the murder of Clytemnestra), is the most neutral. In both Aeschylus and Euripides, however, the feeling of revulsion at the matricide predominates. In this tradition, Orestes was pursued by the Erinyes, the Furies, the ancient divinities who avenge the victims of murder. At the end of Euripides' *Electra*, the Dioscuri prophesy that Orestes must go into exile, pursued by the Furies. Eventually, they promise, he will appeal to Athena and be acquitted of the charge of matricide by the court of the Areopagus at Athens.

These events are the subject of the *Eumenides*, the third drama in Aeschylus' trilogy *Oresteia*. The play begins at Delphi, where Orestes has come pursued by the Furies. There Apollo orders him to go to Athens, promising to protect him. At Athens Orestes pleads his case before the court of the **Areopagus**, whose members, citizens of Athens, are the jury.[3] Apollo defends him, and Athena presides, while the Erinyes claim the justice of their punishment. The jury's votes are tied, and Athena gives her casting vote in favor of Orestes' acquittal, on the grounds that the killing of a mother does not outweigh the murder of a husband and father and that the son's duty toward a father outweighs all other relationships. Thus the curse on the House of Atreus comes to an end; the **Erinyes** are appeased and given a new name, the **Eumenides** (**Kindly Ones**), and worshiped thereafter at Athens.

This version of the myth focuses on the development of law as the vehicle for justice, as against the ancient system (represented by the Erinyes) of blood-guilt and vengeance. But Athena's arguments are hardly persuasive, and we are left in some doubt as to whether Aeschylus himself believed in their validity. Nor is this so important as the fact that it was Zeus' will that had already determined that Orestes would be acquitted.[4] Indeed, to Aeschylus, as to many authors, playwrights, and poets since his time (including Eugene O'Neill and T. S. Eliot in the twentieth century), the legend of Orestes is important because of the moral and religious principles that it introduces. In its original form, the story of the House of Atreus is one of blood-guilt descending from one generation to another. The murder of Agamemnon is an act of vengeance, which is more fundamental to the myth than the tragic pride (hubris) that precedes the fall of Agamemnon or the jealousy of Clytemnestra against Cassandra. Similarly, Orestes acted with piety in avenging his father's death; his "guilt" is a later—if more humane—interpretation. Indeed, it is illogical, for it ignores the fact that Apollo had ordered him to murder Clytemnestra. It was the genius of Aeschylus that transformed the primitive legend and, in place of the ancient doctrine of blood-guilt and vengeance, substituted the rule of reason and law.

Aeschylus presents his monumental tragic version in his trilogy *Oresteia*, consisting of *Agamemnon*, *Libation Bearers* (*Choephori*), and *Eumenides*. We are fortunate to have dramas of all three tragedians—Aeschylus, Sophocles, and Euripides—that deal with the events of the saga that concern Electra, the return of Orestes, and the murder of Clytemnestra and Aegisthus. These are the subjects of the second play (*Libation Bearers*) in Aeschylus' trilogy, the *Electra* of Sophocles, and the *Electra* of Euripides. Thus we are in the unique position of being able to compare the three great dramatists in their manipulation of the same plot. Each has produced a masterpiece, stamped with an individual conception of motivation, character, and religion. These three plays on an identical theme could not be more different in their personal statements and universal implications.

Electra is the focal point of Sophocles' play. Even while Orestes is killing their mother, it is Electra whom we see outside the palace with her cry, "Strike her again!" And it is Electra who, with exquisite Sophoclean irony, taunts and lures Aegisthus to his death at the hands of Orestes. Sophocles accepts the fact that Orestes has acted justly in his obedience to Apollo's command, and he presents us with a compelling portrait of Electra, passionate in her devotion to her murdered father, consumed by hatred for her mother, Clytemnestra, and her mother's lover, Aegisthus, and kept alive by the hope that Orestes will return to mete out retribution and justice. Among the glories of Sophocles' version are a dramatic confrontation between mother and daughter and a recognition scene between brother and sister of great emotional intensity. Sophocles shows us what anger, frustration, and longing can do to the psyche of a young woman.

Even more brutal, Euripides' portrayal of Electra affords its own kind of pity and fear, tinged as it is by the sordid, realistic, and mundane. Electra's revenge, in particular, is motivated as much by sexual jealousy as by any sublime sense of absolute justice. Her monologue to the head of Aegisthus is a study in horror, and brother and sister join side by side in butchering their mother. Castor, the deus ex machina, with typically Euripidean philosophical ambiguity, tells us that Apollo is wise but that his orders to Orestes were not wise.

For a lengthier analysis of Aeschylus' *Libation Bearers* and the *Electras* of Sophocles and Euripides with pertinent excerpts from the texts, see the Additional Reading at the end of this chapter.

It is not surprising that there are other versions of Orestes' story, which allow him to be purified from the blood-guilt by performing either some ritual or an expiatory deed, without undergoing trial and acquittal. In Euripides' play, *Iphigenia in Tauris*, not all the Erinyes have accepted the judgment of Athena, and some still pursue Orestes. Once again he comes to Delphi, where he is told by

Orestes at Delphi. Apulian red-figure krater, ca. 370 B.C.; height 35½ in. Orestes clings to the omphalos in the temple of Apollo, while Apollo wards off a Fury who flies in from the upper left. The Pythia runs off in horror from her tripod (seen between the legs of Apollo), and Artemis, on the right, with her hunting hounds, scans the heavens for more flying Furies. Various other details reinforce the setting in the temple—the three Ionic columns, the second tripod (to the left), the Pythia's key to the temple, which she is dropping, and the dedications (chariot wheels and helmets) at the top center. (*Scala/Art Resource, NY*)

Transformations of the Legend

The legend of the *Oresteia* has inspired many works of literature. Especially memorable in the twentieth century were Eugene O'Neill's trilogy *Mourning Becomes Electra* (1931), a saga set in nineteenth-century New England, and T. S. Eliot's *The Family Reunion* (1939), where the setting is the house of an English family. John Barton has written a monumental cycle of ten plays entitled *Tantalus: An Ancient Myth for a New Millennium* (2000, an extension of an earlier work, *The Greeks*), which embraces the sagas of Mycenae and the Trojan War. In French there is, for example, Jean Giraudoux's *Electra* (1937), and Jean-Paul Sartre in his play *The Flies* transforms Orestes into a paradigm of existentialism. *The Prodigal* (1960), by the American playwright Jack Richardson, might also be mentioned.

In the ingenious novel *Angel of Light* (2004), by the American Joyce Carol Oates, Orestes and Electra have become students in Washington, D.C., descendants of the abolitionist martyr John Brown. The siblings are convinced that their father, a director in the Ministry of Justice, has been murdered by their mother. In the end, Owen (Orestes) becomes a terrorist.

Apollo to go to the land of the **Tauri** (the modern Crimea) and fetch a wooden statue of Artemis. It was the custom of the Tauri to sacrifice strangers to Artemis in her temple, and Orestes and his companion **Pylades** (now the husband of Electra) are handed over to the priestess of Artemis, none other than Orestes' sister Iphigenia. She questions the Greek strangers about events at Argos and Mycenae and then reveals to Orestes who she is and how she has been miraculously saved at Aulis by Artemis and transported to the land of the Tauri. Once she recognizes Orestes, they deceive Thoas, king of the Tauri, into letting them take the statue of Artemis to the sea, to be cleansed of the pollution caused by Orestes, the matricide. They board Orestes' ship and set sail, but adverse wind and waves drive them back toward the land. Before Thoas can seize them, Athena appears and instructs him to let them go. So Orestes and Iphigenia return to Greece. They dedicate the statue of Taurian Artemis at Halae in Attica. Orestes returns to Mycenae, while Iphigenia stays in Attica as the priestess of Artemis at Brauron for the rest of her life.

Euripides deals with the further events in Orestes' life in two tragedies, both of which were popular in antiquity despite their complex, and sometimes incredible, plots. In the earlier tragedy, *Andromache*, produced in about 425 B.C., Menelaüs, king of Sparta, and his daughter, **Hermione**, are totally unsympathetic figures. The action is set in Phthia, over which Peleus, father of Achilles, reigns. Andromache, given as a slave to Neoptolemus, the son of Achilles, after the sack of Troy, has borne him a son, while Hermione, his wife, is childless. She, helped by Menelaüs, proposes to kill Andromache while Neoptolemus is away at Delphi; unexpectedly, however, Peleus appears and saves her, whereupon Menelaüs shamefully leaves. At this point, Orestes appears and announces that *he* is rightfully betrothed to Hermione, whom he takes away to Argos to be his wife. Orestes has previously arranged for the murder of Neoptolemus at Delphi, and a messenger brings news of his death.

Immediately, the corpse of Neoptolemus is brought back, and as Peleus prepares to bury his grandson, Thetis appears as deus ex machina and announces that Neoptolemus is to be buried in the sanctuary of Apollo at Delphi (where he will be honored as a hero) and that Andromache is to go with her child to Molossia (to the northwest of Greece) and there be united with the Trojan survivor **Helenus**: it is there that Vergil brings Aeneas in the third book of the *Aeneid* to be welcomed by her and to hear the prophecy of Helenus about his own future (see p. 675). Peleus himself is to wait by the sea for the return of Thetis with her fifty Nereids: she will make him immortal, so that he can live with her forever, and he will once more see Achilles, who is not in the Underworld but in the island of Leuke.

Pindar tells rather a different story of the death of Neoptolemus (*Nemean Ode* 7.33–47: cf. *Paean* 6.98–120):

> Neoptolemus came as a defender to the great navel of the broad-bosomed earth, when he had sacked the city of Priam, where the Danaäns had labored. He sailed from Troy past Scyros, and wandering they came to Ephyra [Corinth]. And for a short time he ruled over Molossia, and his descendants always have this honor. But he went to the god [Apollo], bringing the first fruits of the spoils from Troy. And there a man killed him with a dagger fighting over the [sacrificial] meat.

Euripides elaborates the legend of Orestes in his late tragedy *Orestes*, which was produced in 408 B.C.. Its setting is outside the palace at Argos, some time after the murder of Clytemnestra. Orestes, nursed by Electra and tormented by visions of the Furies, lies in front of the palace. That very day he and Electra are to be judged by the assembly of the Argives; if they are found guilty of murder, they will be condemned to death. Menelaüs and Helen appear with Hermione, and Menelaüs refuses to help Orestes, persuaded by Tyndareus (husband of Leda, the mother of Helen and Clytemnestra), who arrives from Sparta. News of the condemnation of Orestes and Electra is brought to Electra (Orestes had defended himself in the assembly), and she and Orestes and Pylades (who has also arrived to share in his friend's fate) plot first to avenge themselves on Menelaüs by killing Helen and Hermione. Helen miraculously escapes, and Orestes and Electra appear on the roof of the palace with Hermione (against whose throat Orestes holds his sword), while Menelaüs, locked out of the palace, rages at them. Orestes now begins to set fire to the palace, and at this moment of total confusion, Apollo, serving as deus ex machina, appears and announces his solution to the tangled plot. Helen, he says, has been carried off to join her brothers (Castor and Polydeuces) as an immortal goddess; Orestes will go to Athens, where he will be tried and acquitted by the Areopagus, and he will marry Hermione (despite having tried to kill her!); Pylades will marry Electra.

In this way, Euripides brings to an end the saga of the House of Atreus and its curse. The younger generation (that of Orestes and Electra) is neatly paired off, and Apollo, the god who had ordered Orestes to avenge his father's murder, restores moral, political, and social order. Yet this is very different from the solutions put forward by Aeschylus and Sophocles, and the lack of heroic dignity in any of the characters is disturbing. The ancient critic Aristophanes of Byzantium commented: "the final scene is closer to comedy. . . . The play's characters are noble in birth but its morality is utterly ignoble. For all the characters (except for Pylades) are mean." As he did in his *Electra*, Euripides, by presenting the mythical figures in an unheroic light, compels us to see how their moral dilemmas are relevant to the sordid realities of ordinary society.

The myth of Orestes ends with his ruling over Argos, Mycenae, and (through Hermione) Sparta. After his death, his bones were buried at Tegea, a city not far from Sparta and its rival in historical times. Herodotus tells how the Spartans recovered the bones and were thereafter always victorious over the Tegeans. The son of Orestes and Hermione, Tisamenus, led the Achaeans against the Heraclidae and died in battle.

Additional Reading: Orestes and the Three Electras

Aeschylus' *Oresteia* was first produced in 458 B.C. The second play of this trilogy, *Libation Bearers* (*Choephori*), tells of the return of Orestes, his reunion with his sister Electra, and the murder of their mother Clytemnestra and her lover and husband Aegisthus. As has been noted in this chapter, Sophocles and Euripides also wrote plays on this same theme, affording us a unique opportunity to compare and contrast the methods and purposes of these three great dramatists. Following are some interpretative observations with translations of pertinent excerpts from each of the three plays.

Aeschylus' *Libation Bearers* (*Choephori*)

The play opens with Orestes, accompanied by his companion Pylades, having returned to Argos. Orestes, with a prayer to Hermes, places two locks of his hair on the tomb of his father Agamemnon. As Electra enters accompanied by a chorus of women bringing offerings to the grave, the two young men withdraw. After libations have been offered, during which Electra reveals her plight, she discovers Orestes' locks of hair and immediately recognizes them because, in texture, they are like her own. Similarly, she is convinced that Orestes has returned because the footprints that he has left match hers exactly. These signs of recognition strike the contemporary reader as dubious and extremely curious, but apparently they were used by primitive people.[5]

At this point, Orestes reveals his identity by showing a woven design on his clothing of wild animals that his sister remembers. Their recognition scene is short, swift, and joyous. To Electra, her brother brings the light and the hope of her salvation; in him alone four lost loves are restored: that of her father, her mother, her sacrificed sister, and her beloved Orestes himself. A lengthy threnody follows in which Orestes, Electra, and the Chorus elaborate on the theme of their just retribution and call upon Agamemnon, with prayers to Zeus and Apollo as well. Orestes, very much in command, reveals his plans for the murders of Aegisthus and Clytemnestra and gives Electra directions for her limited role in his plot. Orestes will be received into the palace and convey to Clytemnestra the false news that Orestes is dead (supposedly learned from Strophius, to whom the child Orestes had been sent).

Orestes has already disclosed the devastating power of Apollo's oracle with its dire predictions. If he does not kill to avenge Agamemnon's murder, his life will become a horror. Pursued relentlessly by the terrifying Furies of his father and covered by boils and a kind of leprosy, he will wander endlessly, an exile and pariah until he dies in misery. Orestes, then, is motivated by fear of these punishments as well as by compassion for his father, by desire to win the inheritance that is his due, and by dismay that heroes who returned from Troy

Electra at the Tomb of Agamemnon. Lucanian *pelike* (a large vase for wine with two handles) by the Choephori painter, ca. 350 B.C. In this scene from Aeschylus' *Choephori*, Electra mourns at the tomb of her murdered father. Seated on the top step of the tomb's base, she is approached by Orestes, who is about to pour a libation, from the viewer's left, while Hermes on the right holds up a wreath. Behind Electra is a column rising from the stepped base of the tomb, with a kalyx-krater on its top. Other vases (hydria on the top step; lekythoi on the second step and beside the bottom step) are evidence of Electra's repeated libations at the tomb, whose lack of success accounts for her dejected appearance. Other objects used in her offerings are shown—an egg and a pomegranate on the middle step, fillets (ribbons) tied to the column and lying on the two lower steps, and a third fillet and a tripod on the column. The vases and other objects are significant reminders of Electra's failures, while Hermes' wreath anticipates the success of Orestes' libation. (© *RMN-Grand Palais/Art Resource, NY*)

with his father are now subjected to the rule of two women, Clytemnestra and the weakling Aegisthus.

Orestes and Pylades are received by Clytemnestra into the palace. She accepts the report of her son's death with intense and mixed emotions. The servant Cilissa is called upon to take the news to Aegisthus, who is away, and we learn that it was this Cilissa who nursed and cared for Orestes when he was a baby and saw to it that he got safely away after the murder of Agamemnon.

Aegisthus returns to confirm the good news and upon entering the palace meets his death at Orestes' hands. Clytemnestra will soon be next. She had sent the women with libations to the tomb of Agamemnon because, in a terrifying dream, she gave birth to a snake and nestled it to sleep in coverlets. She gave the little monster her breast to suck and cried aloud in fright and pain as it fed and tore at her nipple, drawing blood that stained the milk. Now Orestes the serpent has come to fulfill her nightmare.

A servant cries out that Aegisthus has been murdered and rouses Clytemnestra with warnings that she will be next; Clytemnestra realizes that Orestes is not dead but alive and ready to kill her (885–930):

> CLYTEMNESTRA: What is the matter? What is this shouting within the palace? (885)
> SERVANT: I tell you that the dead one is alive and come to strike the living dead.
> CLYTEMNESTRA: Ah! I understand the meaning of your riddle. We die by treachery, just as we killed by treachery. Someone, quickly, give me an axe to kill a man. Let us see whether we win or lose. Now I have reached the critical moment in these terrible events. (887–891)

Orestes is revealed with Pylades at his side and the murdered Aegisthus at his feet (894–930):

> ORESTES: It is you I am looking for. I have dealt well enough with this one here.
> CLYTEMNESTRA: Alas, strong Aegisthus, dearest, are you dead? (894–895)

ORESTES: You love the man, do you? Fine, for you will lie in the same grave. Never will you be unfaithful to him now that he is dead.

CLYTEMNESTRA: Stop, my son, have reverence for this, your mother's breast, my child, from which so many times with toothless gums you drowsily sucked the milk that nourished you.

ORESTES: Pylades, what shall I do? Shouldn't I be in dread of killing my own mother?

PYLADES: What about the future and the sanctity of Apollo's oracles delivered by   10
his holy priestess? What about binding pledges sworn in good faith? Make enemies of mortals rather than the gods. (900–902)

ORESTES: You overcome my fears; your advice is good. Come, mother, I want to slaughter you right next to Aegisthus here. For, when he was alive, you thought him better than my father; now sleep with him in death, since you love him and hate the man you should have loved. (903–907)

CLYTEMNESTRA: I gave life to you and I want to grow old with you.

ORESTES: You killed my father and you want to live with me?

CLYTEMNESTRA: My son, Fate had a part in all that has happened. (910)

ORESTES: Then Fate has determined what is about to happen now.   20

CLYTEMNESTRA: Aren't you afraid of the curses of a mother, my son?

ORESTES: A mother? You bore me and then threw me out to misery.

CLYTEMNESTRA: I did not throw you out but sent you away to friends.

ORESTES: I, free born, was shamefully sold out, my person and my patrimony betrayed. (915)

CLYTEMNESTRA: Where, then, is the price that I received for giving you up?

ORESTES: I blush to enumerate what you got in return, much to your shame.

CLYTEMNESTRA: You should count the sins of your father, not only mine.

ORESTES: Don't malign him, who suffered much, while you stayed safe at home.   30

CLYTEMNESTRA: It is grief for women to be without a husband, my son. (920)

ORESTES: Yet the hardships of the husband ensure the safety of the wife at home.

CLYTEMNESTRA: My son, you are going to kill your mother.

ORESTES: It is you who kill yourself, not I.

CLYTEMNESTRA: Watch out, beware the Furies, hounds of a mother's curse.

ORESTES: How can I escape the curse of my father, if I do not act? (925)

CLYTEMNESTRA: I plead for my life as though to a dead man entombed, all in vain.

ORESTES: The fate of my father brings this fate down upon you.

CLYTEMNESTRA: Ah, this is the snake that I gave birth to and nourished.   40

ORESTES: The terror of your dreams prophesied the truth. You should not have committed murder. Suffer your own murder in retaliation. (930)

A Chorus comments upon the terrifying events and reiterates the themes of vengeance, justice, and the will of god. Then Orestes appears with the corpses of Aegisthus and Clytemnestra at his feet to claim that he has acted with justice. The scene parallels the one in the *Agamemnon* (with its rich and profound imagery of ensnarement, entanglement, and the net), where Clytemnestra after the murders of Cassandra and Agamemnon appears with her victims to claim that her actions have been just (p. 436). Orestes holds in his hands the very robe in which Agamemnon was entangled and butchered (973–1006):

ORESTES: Behold the two of them, tyrants of this land, murderers of my father and despoilers of his estate. Haughtily they once sat on their august thrones, lovers then and even now, as you may infer from what has befallen them. They have remained true to their pledges: together they vowed death for my poor father and swore to die together. All these things that they swore are truly accomplished. (973–979)

As you listen to my litany of their wicked deeds, look at this robe, an entanglement which they devised for my poor father as a fetter for his hands and a shackle for his feet. Spread it out, stand in a circle around it, point out this trap to ensnare her husband for father to see these unholy deeds of my mother, not my father but Helius, the Sun, the one who watches over everything so that he may bear witness 10 for me when the time for judgment comes that I, with justice, was responsible for the fate of my mother. Aegisthus' death I need not mention, for he has received the just deserts of an adulterer according to the law. But she who devised this monstrous crime against her husband became pregnant by him; the children that she bore him she loved once, but now, as it is all too clear, they have become her dire enemy. I'll tell you what she is like. If she had been born a serpent or a viper, she would have been able to infect by touch alone, no need of fangs to bite, because of an inherent, venomous audacity. (980–996)

This robe, what am I to call it? Could I find the proper words? A trap for a wild beast, a snare for a corpse, or a covering for after the bath. One might call it a net to 20 catch fish or one for animals or fabric to entangle the feet. The sort of thing a thief might own in order to make his living by ensnaring wayfarers and robbing them. With such a treacherous device, he could kill many, steal much, and warm his heart in comfort. (997–1004)

May I never get this kind of woman for a wife. By the will of the gods, may I die first, childless.

In the finale of the play, Orestes is driven out by the Furies, frightening, with faces like Gorgons and serpents entwined in their hair. He will find salvation in the third play, the *Eumenides* (as we have seen), through the agency of Apollo and Athena and a civil court of law. The righteous will of Zeus is eventually accomplished.

In Aeschylus' *Libation Bearers*, Orestes maintains center stage, determining the course of the action. True, a stirring and compelling portrait of Electra emerges, delineating characteristics with great potential for further development. Yet she exits from the play before Orestes and Pylades enter the palace, and her presence, therefore, does not dilute the power of a vengeance delivered by Orestes himself at the dictates of Apollo. All is as it should be for the central play of a trilogy entitled *Oresteia*.

Sophocles' *Electra*

How different are the two *Electras* that follow! We do not know for sure whether Sophocles wrote his version before or after that of Euripides; the date for Sophocles' play is unknown, and 416 B.C. for Euripides' is only a conjecture. Because of the nature of the motives and characterizations that are developed and the drastic shift in religious and philosophical sentiment, Euripides' play is best considered last.

Sophocles' *Electra* begins with the return of Orestes to Mycenae, accompanied by both his tutor and his friend Pylades, ready to set in motion his plans to exact vengeance against Aegisthus and Clytemnestra for their murder of his father, Agamemnon. In Sophocles, both are the murderers, not as in Aeschylus, where Clytemnestra did the actual deed herself. Orestes clearly and succinctly emphasizes the justice of his mission, ordained by god (32–37):

> ORESTES: When I went to the Pythian oracle to find out how I should win justice from the murderers of my father, Phoebus Apollo uttered this response, which I will tell you now: I alone, without men in arms, am to steal by treachery their righteous slaughter by my own hand.

The moans of a grieving Electra are heard from within the palace, and at the tutor's urging the three leave to carry out the orders of Apollo. Thus the recognition scene between brother and sister is postponed to later in the play in order to achieve its full effect.

In her lengthy exchange with the chorus of sympathetic women, Electra reveals her misery; she cannot ever forget that her mother and her mother's bed partner split the skull of her father with an axe, much as one would cut down a mighty and regal oak. Her laments for her beloved father are endless and her hatred for his murderers relentless; she lives only in her hope for the return of her brother and vengeance. Unmarried and alone, without children, she has become a slave and a beggar in her father's house. In her helpless isolation, she awaits the return of her brother, her savior and her salvation. She reveals her soul and her psyche in the following summation (254–309):

> ELECTRA: I am ashamed, women, if it seems to you that I am too excessive in my suffering and my many complaints. Forgive me, but I am forced to act this way. How could a woman of noble integrity help but behave as I do, if she sees what I see— calamitous evils in my father's house, never ceasing causes of pain, continually fresh and renewed. (254–260)
>
> First of all, my relationship with the mother who bore me has come to be most hateful. Then, in my own house I live with the murderers of my own father; I am ruled by them, I am dependent on them for what they give and what they take away alike. Furthermore, what kind of day do you think that I spend when I see Aegisthus sitting on the throne of my father and I behold him wearing the same clothes as 10 he did, pouring libations at the very hearth where he killed him, and I witness the ultimate hubris, the murderer in the bed of my father, with my abominable mother— if I should call the woman who sleeps with him my mother. She is so brazen that she lives with the guilty wretch, unafraid of any retribution from any of the Furies. Instead, as though laughing exultantly at her wicked deeds, she has fixed the date on which she killed my father through treachery—and on this day of each month she has established choruses and sacrifices, a holy celebration for the gods who keep her safe. (261–281)
>
> I, however, ill fated, seeing in these halls this evil ceremonial in the name of my father, I, all alone lament, myself to myself, and weep and pine away; but I cannot 20 indulge my grief as much as would fill my heart with joy because this queen of lies shouts wicked renunciations such as these: "Damned and hateful creature, are you the only one for whom a father has died? No other person in the world has ever been in mourning? May you go to hell and may the gods below never release you from your agonies." (282–292)
>
> Thus she wantonly rages, except when she hears some rumor that Orestes has returned. Then, mad with rage, she stands close beside me and yells: "Aren't you the one responsible? Isn't all this your doing, you, the one who stole Orestes safely

> out of my arms? I want you to know that you will pay the just reward that you de- 30
> serve." Such are the words she screams at me; and present by her side, he urges her
> on with the same reproaches, this renowned bridegroom of hers, completely impo-
> tent, an utter disaster, whose battles are only fought behind the skirts of a woman.
> (293–302)
>
> I, poor wretch, waste away, waiting for Orestes to put an end to these miseries,
> for living in the constant expectation that he is about to accomplish this great feat,
> I have lost all possible hope that he will ever return. So, dear women, in such cir-
> cumstances, I cannot behave with pious self-control but in the midst of these evils,
> necessity compels me to pursue an evil course. (303–309)

Sophocles purposefully changes Aeschylus, who has the servant Cilissa nurse the infant Orestes and whisk him away after the murder, in order to depict Electra as mother-figure to her brother.

A scene follows in which Electra encounters her sister Chrysothemis, who, as we learn, has been willing to obey Clytemnestra and Aegisthus and as a result lives freely and normally with them in the palace. Such compromise is incomprehensible and disgusting to Electra. Chrysothemis warns Electra that if she does not change her ways, she is to be sentenced upon Aegisthus' return to spend the rest of her life imprisoned in a dungeon. We learn also that Chrysothemis has been sent to the grave of Agamemnon with libations from Clytemnestra, who has been tormented by an ambiguous dream that could foretell Orestes' vengeance: she saw Agamemnon come to life again. He took back his royal scepter, now held by Aegisthus, and planted it in his own ground; there it burst into luxuriant leaf and quite overshadowed the whole of Mycenae.

Chrysothemis' only importance lies in her role in Sophocles, where she is created as a dramatic foil for Electra, in much the same way as this playwright uses Ismene to illuminate by contrast the character of Antigone. Central to Sophocles' play is a bitter and revealing confrontation between mother and daughter (516–609); there is no such scene in Aeschylus. Clytemnestra argues that Agamemnon should not have sacrificed their daughter Iphigenia. Instead, a child of Menelaüs and Helen should have been the victim at Aulis, since the Greek expedition against Troy was on behalf of Menelaüs, whose wife Helen had been abducted by the Trojan prince Paris. Electra responds with a vehement defense of her father:

> CLYTEMNESTRA: It is obvious that you feel free to leave the palace and without
> any restraint disgrace your family and friends, since Aegisthus is not here to prevent
> you as he always does. But now since he is away you show me no respect. Over and
> over again, for many to hear, you have spoken out that I rule brazenly and unjustly,
> treating you and all that you hold dear outrageously. Bu t I am not guilty of hubris.
> I revile you only because you revile me so often. (516–524)
>
> Your father is always your excuse, and nothing else—that he died by my hand. By
> my hand, I am well aware of that and cannot deny the charge. But Justice killed him,
> not I alone, and you would be on the side of Justice if you had any sense at all. Why?
> Because this father of yours, whom you are always bemoaning, was the only one of 10
> the Greeks to have the effrontery to sacrifice his daughter to the gods, Iphigenia,
> your sister. Of course it was easy enough for him to beget her, with none of the pain
> that I suffered when I gave her birth. So be it! Yet explain this to me. Why and for
> whom did he sacrifice her? Will your answer be, for the Greeks? But they had no

right to kill a daughter of mine. If he killed her on behalf of his brother Menelaüs, didn't he still owe me just retribution for killing what was mine? Menelaüs had two children of his own; since the expedition against Troy was for the sake of their mother and father, wasn't it only right that they should die, instead of my daughter? Did Hades have some sort of longing for the death of a child of mine rather than one of Helen's? Did your accursed father love the children of Menelaüs and feel nothing for those that I bore to him? Isn't this the behavior of an evil, foolish father with no scruples? I think so, even if you do not. Iphigenia who is dead would agree with me, if she could speak. I am not sorry for what I have done. If you think that I am evil for feeling as I do, you had better have justice on your side before you blame others. (525–551)

ELECTRA: This time you cannot claim that I started this painful confrontation and that you were only responding to my reproaches. Yet if you will allow me, I would like to make a righteous defense on behalf of both my dead father and my sister. (552–555)

CLYTEMNESTRA: Yes, I allow you. If you always began your speeches so politely, you would not be such a pain to listen to. (556–557)

ELECTRA: Then I will speak to you. You say that you killed my father. What further admission could be more disgraceful, whether you acted justly or not? I tell you that you killed him not in justice but because you were enticed by the allurement of the evil man with whom you live. Ask the huntress Artemis what ransom she demanded for the release of the many winds which she held fast at Aulis. Since we cannot find out the answer from her, I will tell you what I have been told. Once when my father was hunting in a sacred grove of the goddess, at the sound of his footsteps a dappled stag with antlers started up. He killed it and happened to make some boast or other; at this, the daughter of Leto was enraged and detained the Achaeans until the time he would sacrifice his own daughter in compensation for the animal. Thus it was that Iphigenia was sacrificed; there was nothing else he could do so that the army could sail either homeward or to Troy. It was for this and not for Menelaüs that he sacrificed her, with great reluctance and much against his will. (558–576)

Suppose that he did perform the sacrifice out of a desire to help Menelaüs, as you argue. Did he have to die at your hands because of this? According to what kind of law? Be careful that you do not regret imposing such a law for human beings since you bring punishment down upon yourself. For if we are to commit murder in retaliation for murder, you should be the first to die, in order to satisfy the justice you deserve. But watch out that you are not making an insubstantial excuse to justify your actions. (577–584)

Tell me, if you like, for what reason you are doing the most shameful thing of all, you who sleep with the murderer with whom you once killed my father, and you who have begotten a child by him but have cast out your legitimate children born in holy wedlock.[6] How could I sanction such behavior? Or will you say that these actions too are done in recompense for your daughter? If you do argue so, it is to your shame. For it is not right to marry the enemy, Aegisthus, for the sake of your daughter. Yet it is impossible to give good advice to you, the one who continually berates us with the charge that we speak ill of our mother, and I consider you more a tyrant than a mother toward us, I who live a life of misery, suffering many torments at the hands of you and your bedmate. Your other child far away, poor Orestes, having barely escaped your violence, wastes away his ill-starred life. Many times you have accused me of nurturing him to be your avenger. Know full well that I would have

> done so, if I had the power. For these reasons then denounce me to everyone, whether you proclaim me as evil or loud-mouthed or full of shamelessness. Indeed, if I am so accomplished in such behavior, it only shows that I do not in the least belie a nature and character just like yours. (585–609)   70

In this way mother and daughter argue their case. The scene ends with Clytemnestra calling upon Apollo to grant that her dream might turn out well for her and that she might live a long, safe, and happy life. At the conclusion of her prayer, the tutor arrives to announce the false news of Orestes' death and set in motion the action that will end in death for Clytemnestra and Aegisthus. With similar dramatic irony, Sophocles in *Oedipus the King* marks the beginning of the end for Jocasta when the messenger from Corinth arrives immediately after her invocation to Apollo for salvation.

Belief that Orestes is dead brings Clytemnestra a joyous relief but also a painful sadness. Electra is devastated and in a second clash with Chrysothemis reveals that she is ready, all alone, to kill Aegisthus herself. Sophocles' Electra does not even contemplate the murder of her mother.

When Orestes and Pylades arrive bringing an urn that supposedly contains the ashes of the dead Orestes, Electra receives it into her hands and utters these heartbreaking words (1126–1170):

> ELECTRA: This urn is a memorial of the life of Orestes, to me the most beloved of men. Here is all that is left of him. With what high hopes I sent you away, dear brother, and how far they have fallen now that I have gotten you back. Now I fondle you in my hands but you are no more. You were gloriously alive when I rescued you out of the palace. (1126–1130)
>
> How I wish that I had died before I stole you away with these same hands and delivered you into a foreign land to save you from being murdered; if I had not done so, you could then on that day have died here, and shared death and a grave with your father. But now as it is, you have died miserably, far from home, an exile in a foreign land, separated from your sister. I, wretched me, did not   10 bathe your corpse with loving hands or remove your remains from the blazing pyre as I should have; instead, poor brother, your funeral was in the hands of foreigners and you have come back to me as a handful of ashes in a tiny urn. Alas, unhappy me, all for nothing was the care which long ago I lavished upon you—a sweet burden; you never loved your mother more than you did me, and I was your nurse, not anyone else in the household; in addition to mother and nurse, you could call me your sister. But now with your death, all is over in one day. You have gone and have taken everything away with you, like a whirlwind. Father is gone, you yourself are gone and your death has killed me. Our enemies laugh and our mother is insane with joy, she no mother at all, against whom you were   20 to appear as an avenger, as you so often promised in secret messages. But your unfortunate fate and mine have taken everything away and have sent you back to me thus—ashes, an ineffectual shade instead of the living form of my dear, dear brother. (1159)
>
> Woe is me, O pitiable corpse, alas! You have been sent on a most dread journey. Welcome me to this home of yours, me your sister, whom you have destroyed— nothingness into nothingness—so that I may live with you below for the rest of time. Since I shared equally with you when I was in the upper world, now too in death I long to be given a place with you in your tomb. For I envision an end of suffering for those who are dead. (1160–1170)   30

In the recognition scene that follows, Electra, with an overwhelming joy, rushes into the arms of her brother. It is a signet-seal of his father that Orestes shows as final proof of his identity—proof more realistic, if not irrefutable, than that in Aeschylus! Orestes, her surrogate father and mother, now becomes in a sense her surrogate lover and most certainly her very real savior.

Apollo will grant Electra's prayer for success. She remains center stage while Orestes kills Clytemnestra and Aegisthus. Sophocles reverses the order of the murders with telling effect. Here is the conclusion of his play (1398–1510):

ELECTRA: Dearest women, the men will accomplish their mission at once. Just be silent and wait.

CHORUS: How now? What are they doing? (1400)

ELECTRA: She is preparing the urn for burial and the two are standing beside her.

CHORUS: Why have you hastened out of the palace?

ELECTRA: I must watch so that we may know when Aegisthus returns.

CLYTEMNESTRA: (from within the palace): Alas, the house is bereft of friends but teeming with killers. (1404–1405)

ELECTRA: Someone is crying out from within. Don't you hear, my friends?

CHORUS: I heard a chilling cry that makes me shudder.   10

CLYTEMNESTRA: Woe is me, O Aegisthus, where can you be?

ELECTRA: Listen, someone is calling out again.

CLYTEMNESTRA: My child, my child, pity your mother who bore you! (1409–1410)

ELECTRA: But he received no pity from you, and neither did his father who begat him.

CHORUS: O unfortunate city! O unhappy family! The fate that supported you daily now is waning, waning.

CLYTEMNESTRA: Ah, I am struck!

ELECTRA: Strike her again, and more deeply, if you have the strength. (1415)

CLYTEMNESTRA: Ah, I am struck again!   20

ELECTRA: I only wish Aegisthus were there too!

CHORUS: The curses are being fulfilled. Those who lie beneath the earth are alive, for those once dead are draining the blood of the murderers in retribution. Look, they are before us. A hand drips with blood from a sacrifice to Ares, and I cannot find any fault.

ELECTRA: Orestes, how has it turned out?

ORESTES: It has turned out well in the house, if Apollo prophesied well. (1424–1425)

ELECTRA: Is the wretched woman dead?

ORESTES: No longer be afraid that your mother's arrogance will ever dishonor you again.   30

CHORUS: Be quiet, for I see Aegisthus approaching.

ELECTRA: Orestes and Pylades, get back.

ORESTES: Where do you see the man? (1430–1431)

ELECTRA: He comes towards us from the outskirts of the city, with a smile on his face.

CHORUS: Get back inside as fast as you can so that you may take care of the situation well, as you have just done previously.

ORESTES: Rest assured, we will do it.

ELECTRA: Now hurry within. (1435)

ORESTES: I am gone.   40

ELECTRA: Let me take care of him out here.

CHORUS: It would be a good idea for him to hear from you a few gentle words of assurance so that he may rush unsuspecting into his hidden ordeal with justice.

AEGISTHUS: Which one of you knows the whereabouts of the strangers from Phocis, who they say have brought the news that Orestes has lost his life in the wreckage of a chariot? You, I ask you, yes you, the one always so insolent before, for I believe that his death touches you especially and you especially know about it and can answer. (1442–1447)

ELECTRA: (her responses to Aegisthus are laden with dramatic irony): I know 50 about it. How could I not know about it and remain uninformed about a calamity touching those dearest to me?

AEGISTHUS: Then where might the strangers be? Tell me. (1450)

ELECTRA: Within. They have greeted a loving hostess.

AEGISTHUS: Did they bring the news that he was truly dead—for sure?

ELECTRA: Yes, and not by word alone, but they even offered proof.

AEGISTHUS: Is it possible for us to see this proof clearly?

ELECTRA: We certainly can and it is a very unenviable sight. (1455)

AEGISTHUS: You have said much to please me—how unusual!

ELECTRA: May you be pleased, if this happens to give you pleasure.   60

AEGISTHUS: I order that the doors be opened to display his corpse for all the Mycenaeans and Argives to see, so that if any of them were once elated by vain hopes in this man, now upon beholding him dead they may accept my bridle and learn good sense without my having to chastise them with force. (1458–1463)

ELECTRA: Certainly I have learned this lesson; in time I have come to my senses and now acquiesce with those who are stronger.

AEGISTHUS: (upon the revelation of the corpse): O Zeus, what I behold is a portent that has befallen not without the ill will of the gods. If it entails a just nemesis, I do not say. Remove the covering over the eyes completely so that my relative may receive proper lamentation from me. (1466–1469)   70

ORESTES: Lift the cloth yourself; it is yours to do, not mine—to behold this face and to speak words of affection.

AEGISTHUS: You give good advice and I will follow it. But you, call Clytemnestra, if by any chance she is in the house. (1472–1473)

ORESTES: She is close to you; no need to look elsewhere.

AEGISTHUS: Ah, what do I look upon?

ORESTES: Of whom are you afraid? Whom do you not recognize? (1475)

AEGISTHUS: Into the trap of what men have I fallen? Poor me!

ORESTES: Haven't you been aware that you who are alive have been conversing face to face with the dead?   80

AEGISTHUS: I understand your meaning. It cannot be otherwise; this must be Orestes who is speaking to me. (1479–1480)

ORESTES: You the best of prophets and yet fooled for so long?

AEGISTHUS: Wretched me, I am done for! Yet let me say a word.

ELECTRA: Don't let him say more, brother; don't prolong all this talk, by the gods. When mortals are enmeshed in evil, what advantage is there in delay for the one who is about die? Kill him as quickly as possible, and when he is dead throw his body to scavengers for the burial he deserves, far from our sight, since for me this would be the only deliverance from evil. (1483–1490)

ORESTES: Go inside. Be quick about it. For now the contest is no longer of words 90 but about your life.

> AEGISTHUS: Why do you force me into the palace? If your action is good, how come you need the dark and are not ready to kill me out here?
> ORESTES: Don't give orders to me. Go inside where you killed my father so that you may die in the same place. (1495–1496)
> AEGISTHUS: Is it really necessary that this house witness future as well as the present evils that have fallen upon the family of Pelops?
> ORESTES: It will witness yours, for sure. I am your unerring prophet in this.
> AEGISTHUS: You boast about a skill that you did not inherit from your father. (1500)
> ORESTES: Your replies are too long and our short journey is delayed. Now go.   100
> AEGISTHUS: Lead on.
> ORESTES: You must go first.
> AEGISTHUS: So that I may not escape you?
> ORESTES: No, so that you may not die where it pleases you. I must see to it that this is bitter for you. This swift justice should be meted out to all who desire to act outside of the laws—death, for then there would not be so much crime. (1503–1507)
> CHORUS: O family of Atreus, how much you have suffered to reach freedom amid such adversity, freedom crowned by this present act of daring.

Apollo's will has been accomplished, and the justice of Zeus has been fulfilled. There are no Furies to pursue a guilty Orestes in this masterpiece that explores so profoundly the heart and the soul of a frightening, pitiable, and tragic Electra.

Euripides' *Electra*

By clever manipulation of the plot to create a different emphasis in the interpretation of the characters and their motives, Euripides seriously questions religious and philosophical beliefs about right and wrong action and the nature of justice. The setting for his play is the hut of a peasant, who is the husband of Electra. This peasant provides a prologue that gives the essential background for the plot with its subtle Euripidean twists, only a few of which can be mentioned in this brief summary. Most important is the fact that Aegisthus has married off Electra to this poor but well-meaning man, in the belief that he would have nothing to fear from such a match. Indeed, Electra has remained a virgin, untouched sexually by her husband, whose nature is admirably noble.

Orestes, at the command of Apollo, returns with Pylades and encounters Electra. Eventually, their scene of recognition is confirmed most realistically. The servant who once saved the infant Orestes now, as an old man, points out to Electra a scar that proves the identity of her brother. As Electra makes abundantly clear, similarity in locks of hair and footprints or the design of woven fabric are not enough for certainty.

Now Orestes can make plans for his vengeance. He receives a great deal of assistance from the old servant for his scheme against Aegisthus, and it is Electra who takes a particularly vicious delight in laying the plot herself for the death of her mother, Clytemnestra. Euripides, like Aeschylus, places the murder of Clytemnestra last for his own macabre purposes.

The circumstances and the religious setting of the murder of Aegisthus place him in an ingratiating light. The scene is described by a messenger to a gloating Electra. Aegisthus is approached by Orestes and Pylades while

The Death of Aegisthus. Athenian krater by the Dokimasia painter, ca. 470 B.C. Orestes, armed, holds Aegisthus by his hair and is about to thrust his sword into him again, for Aegisthus is already bleeding from the first blow. Clytemnestra approaches from the left with an axe, and Electra, her right hand held out, runs in from the right. Aegisthus slides from his chair as his lyre drops from his left hand and he tries to beg for mercy with his right. The other side of this vase, shown on p. 436, depicts the death of Agamemnon. (*William Francis Warden Fund/Museum of Fine Arts, Boston*)

he is preparing a sacrifice in honor of the nymphs, and he welcomes the strangers most hospitably as guests and friends. After he has butchered the sacrificial bull and bends over to examine the severed parts of the animal in fear of bad omens, Aegisthus is brutally stabbed in the back by Orestes, who brings his body and his severed head to his sister. Electra, painfully triumphant, addresses the remains of her most bitter enemy with the following apostrophe (907–961):

ELECTRA: Alas, first of all in reproaching you with evils, where will I begin? What sort of ending will I provide? How shall I list all those in between? To be sure, from early dawn I never ceased rehearsing the things that I wanted to say to you face to face if ever I should become free from those former terrors. Well now we are free, and I will repay you with this litany of evils which I wanted to recite to you when you were alive. (907–913)

You destroyed me and you made me and Orestes here bereft of a dear father, even though you were never wronged. You married my mother shamefully and killed her husband, commander-in-chief of the Hellenic forces against Troy, while you stayed at home. You reached such a pinnacle of folly that you expected that,   10 having wronged my father's bed and married my mother, she would do you no wrong. Whenever anyone has corrupted the wife of another in a clandestine affair and then is compelled to marry her, let him know for sure that he is a sorry fool if he thinks that she who has already betrayed one husband will be a chaste wife for him. You lived a most abominable life, not realizing how evil it was. Yet you knew that you had entered into an unholy marriage and my mother knew that she had taken an impious man as her husband. Both of you base, each partaking of each other's evil fate, she of yours and you of hers. And among all the Argives Clytemnestra never was called the wife of Aegisthus; instead you heard yourself denigrated as the husband of Clytemnestra. (914–931)   20

This is a disgrace that the woman and not the man controls the household, and I hate it when in the city children are designated not as the offspring of the male, the father, but of the mother. When a husband has married a conspicuously superior wife, the woman receives all the attention, but no account is taken of the man. But this is what deceived you, what you did not understand. You boasted that you were somebody relying on wealth for your importance. But money is nothing. It is our consort for only a little while. Nature is what remains steadfast, a good character, not money; it stays with us always and lifts away evils. But wealth, dishonest associate of the foolish, flourishes for a short time and then flies out the door. (932–944)   30

As for your affairs with women, I remain silent. Since it is not proper for a virgin to speak out about them, I will only offer discreet hints. You behaved outrageously, possessed as you were of a royal palace and endowed with physical beauty. As for me, may I get a husband who does not look like a girl but is manly, whose children would be like Ares. Good looks alone are merely a pretty adornment for devotees of the dance. (945–951)

Away with you, completely ignorant that you have paid the penalty for your crimes that have in time been found out. Let no one as wicked as you think that, if he has run the first phase of the course well, he is triumphing over Justice, before he approaches the final turn and the end of his life. (952–956)   40

CHORUS: He has done terrible things and he has paid a terrible retribution to you and Orestes because of the power of Justice.

ELECTRA: So be it. Servants, you must carry the body inside and hide it in the darkness so that when my mother arrives she may not see the corpse before she is slaughtered. (959–961)

At this point, Clytemnestra arrives upon the scene. She had been summoned with the false announcement that Electra had recently borne a son, just as Electra had planned, and, as it was with Aegisthus, her entrapment appears particularly sordid. The confrontation between mother and daughter raises similar issues that had been argued in Sophocles' version, but Euripides provides crucial additions with disturbing differences in motivation; so much of their conflict is steeped in sexual rivalry and jealousy and psychological perversity. Clytemnestra is even very much aware of the nature of Electra's complex when she observes that it is ingrained in her daughter's nature to love her father more than her mother.

Here is a much weaker Orestes than we have ever seen, who must be goaded and driven by his sister to murder their mother, and Electra herself, obsessed with a passionate hatred, actually participates in the killing.

ELECTRA: Hold on now, another decision is thrust upon us. (962)

ORESTES: What is it? Do I see an armed force coming from Mycenae?

ELECTRA: No, but the mother who gave birth to me.

ORESTES: Good! She is stepping right into the trap. (965)

ELECTRA: How splendid she looks in her fine chariot and robes.

ORESTES: What are we to do now? Will we murder our mother?

ELECTRA: Are you overcome with pity at the sight of your mother in person?

ORESTES: Ah, how am I to kill her, the one who bore me and nourished me?

ELECTRA: In the same way as she butchered your father and mine. (970)

ORESTES: Oh Phoebus, you prophesied sheer folly.   10

ELECTRA: Where Apollo is a fool, who are wise?

ORESTES: You, Phoebus, who told me to kill my mother, a crime which I should not commit.

ELECTRA: What possible harm is there since you are avenging your own father?

ORESTES: I am guiltless now, but if I do the deed I will be condemned as the killer of my mother. (975)

ELECTRA: But if you do not avenge your father, you will be impious against god.

ORESTES: The murder of my mother—to whom will I pay the penalty?

ELECTRA: To whom will you pay, if you fail to accomplish vengeance for your father?

ORESTES: Did some demon, disguised as god, order me to do this?   20

ELECTRA: A demon sitting on the sacred tripod? I really don't think so. (980)

ORESTES: I cannot be convinced that this divine oracle was right.
ELECTRA: Don't become a coward and a weakling.
ORESTES: Am I to devise the same treachery against her?
ELECTRA: Yes, the same that you used when you killed her husband Aegisthus.
ORESTES: I will go in and undertake a terrible task. I will do a terrible thing—if the gods think it is right, so be it. This ordeal is both bitter and sweet for me. (985–987)
CHORUS: Lady and queen of the land of Argos, daughter of Tyndareus and sister of the noble twins, the sons of Zeus, who live amid the stars in the fiery firmament and are honored by mortals as their saviors in storms at sea. Greetings, I give you honor equal to the gods because of your great wealth and blessed happiness. Now is the right time for your fortunes to be provided for. Hail, O queen! (988–997)
CLYTEMNESTRA: Out of the chariot, Trojan women, take my hand and help me to get down. The temples of the gods are adorned with Trojan spoils, and for my palace I have taken these chosen women from Troy, a small yet lovely gift, in exchange for the daughter whom I lost. (998–1003)
ELECTRA: Shouldn't I, mother, take hold of your royal and blessed hand, for I also am a slave, cast out of my ancestral home and living in a miserable one?
CLYTEMNESTRA: I have these slaves here; don't trouble yourself on my account.
ELECTRA: Well, am I not just like these women, taken prisoner when my palace was captured, driven out of the house, left bereft of my father? (1008–1010)
CLYTEMNESTRA: Such are the results of actions your father devised against those whom he should have loved. I will explain. I know that when a reputation for evil clings to a woman, a bitter sharpness inevitably invests the tone of her argument. So it is with us, and that is not good. But if, upon learning the truth, you have a worthy reason to hate, it is right to hate but if not, why should there be hatred? (1011–1017)

Tyndareus gave me to your father, and the marriage was not intended to bring death to him or me or the children whom I bore. Yet that man, Agamemnon, through the pretext of marriage with Achilles, took my daughter from home and brought her to Aulis, where the fleet was kept from sailing. There he placed Iphigenia high upon the sacrificial altar and slit her white throat. If to avert the capture of his city or to benefit his house or to his other children he killed this one girl on behalf of many, it would be forgivable. No, it was for the sake of Helen, a voracious whore, and because Menelaüs, who married her, did not know how to control his adulterous wife. This was the reason why Agamemnon murdered my daughter. And yet for all that, having been wronged, I would not have become a savage and killed my husband. But he came back to me bringing with him the maiden Cassandra, mad, possessed by god, and he brought her to our marriage bed; now there were two wives in the same household! (1018–1034)

Women really are foolish prey, I do not deny it. This is taken for granted, every time a husband wrongfully rejects his marriage bed for someone else. When his wife at home in her desire to follow his example takes on a lover, then all the blame is blazoned forth upon us women, but the men who are responsible hear not a word of criticism. What if Menelaüs had been secretly abducted from his home? Would it then have been necessary for me to kill Orestes so that I might rescue Menelaüs, the husband of my sister, Helen? How would your father have tolerated that crime? I would have had to suffer death at his hands for killing his son. Should he not have died for killing my daughter? Yes, and so I killed him, turning to his enemies—the only way possible. For any friend of your father would never have conspired with me in his slaughter. Speak your refutation freely, if you like, and explain how your father died unjustly. (1035–1050)

CHORUS: You have made a just argument, but your justice is tainted with shame. A woman who is right-minded should concede to her husband in everything. Any woman who does not think so is not included in my reckoning.

ELECTRA: Remember, mother, your last words which gave me liberty to speak. (1055–1056)

CLYTEMNESTRA: Yes I do, and I stand by them now, my child.

ELECTRA: After you have heard what I have to say, mother, will you treat me badly?

CLYTEMNESTRA: Not at all. I will be sweetly disposed toward you.   80

ELECTRA: I will speak then, and this is how I will begin. I only wish you, O you who gave me birth, were of a better mind and character. You and Helen are sisters, through and through. The physical beauty of you both is worthy of my praise, but the two of you morally are whores, and I do not consider you worthy of your noble brother Castor. Helen was willing in her rape and brought about her own ruin, and you destroyed the best man of Hellas, making up the pretext that you killed your husband because of your daughter. Those who believe you do not know you as well as I do. (1060–1068)

Even before the sacrifice of your daughter and when your husband had scarcely left home, you were primping before a mirror as you adorned your blonde tresses. 90 A wife who decks herself out in beauty while her husband is away, I label a wicked woman. For she should not vaunt her fair features out of doors, unless she is looking for evil. I know for a fact that you alone of all the women of Hellas rejoiced when you heard that the Trojans were doing well, but if they were losing, your eyes would look troubled because you did not want Agamemnon to return from Troy. Yet there was every reason for you to behave properly. You had a husband in no way inferior to Aegisthus, whom Hellas chose as its commander-in-chief. Furthermore, in contrast to Helen, your sister, who did such terrible things, you could have won for yourself great renown for virtue since evil actions present a foil to enhance the good for all to see. (1069–1085)   100

If, as you say, my father killed your daughter, in what way have I or my brother done you wrong? After you killed our father, why didn't you include us in the ancestral estate? Instead, you gave what was not really yours as a dowry for your lover and bought your marriage with him. Your husband Aegisthus is not banished because of your son Orestes, nor has he died on my account, even though he has inflicted a living death upon me, twice as painful as the death of Iphigenia. If slaughter demands slaughter as a just penalty, then I and your son Orestes will kill you to avenge our father. If your actions are just, ours would be too. (1086–1096)

CLYTEMNESTRA: My child, it is ingrained in your nature to love your father always. This is the way things are. Some are attached to the fathers, others love 110 their mothers more than their fathers. I will forgive you, for in truth I am not that exultant at all about the things that I have done, my daughter. But you so unwashed and so unkempt in your dress, have you just recently given birth and become a mother? Alas, poor me and my plots! I drove myself into a fury against my husband, more than I should have. (1102–1110)

ELECTRA: Too late for bewailing when you have no remedy for your plight. My father is dead, so why don't you recall your son who wanders far from home?

CLYTEMNESTRA: I am afraid to. I must look to my own safety, not his, since they say that he is enraged at the murder of his father. (1114–1115)

ELECTRA: Why do you allow your husband Aegisthus to treat me so cruelly?   120

CLYTEMNESTRA: That's the way he is; and you are inherently stubborn.

ELECTRA: I am suffering, yet I will put an end to my fury.

CLYTEMNESTRA: If so, he will persecute you no longer.

ELECTRA: He is arrogant because he lives in my house. (1120)

CLYTEMNESTRA: You see, you are at it again, kindling a fresh inflammatory quarrel.

ELECTRA: I'll be quiet, for I fear him, how I fear him!

CLYTEMNESTRA: Stop such talk. Why did you summon me here, my child?

ELECTRA: You have heard, I know, about the birth of my child. Make the proper sacrifice for me—I don't know how—as it is ordained for a son after he is born.   130 I have no experience in this because until now I have been childless. (1124–1127)

CLYTEMNESTRA: This is not my duty but that of the woman who delivered the child.

ELECTRA: I gave birth alone and delivered the child myself.

CLYTEMNESTRA: Is your home so bereft of friendly neighbors? (1130)

ELECTRA: No one wants to have friends who are poor.

CLYTEMNESTRA: I will go and sacrifice to the gods as is appropriate after the child's birth, and when I have done this favor for you, I will go out to the countryside, where my husband is offering sacrifice to the Nymphs. Servants, take the horses out to pasture and when you think that I have finished this sacrifice to the gods, be back here, for I must also oblige my husband. (1132–1138)   140

ELECTRA: Enter my humble house, but be careful that the soot inside does not defile your robes, for you will make to the gods the sacrifice that you should. All is made ready, the knife that was sharpened has already slaughtered the bull, next to which you will fall after you have been struck down. Even in the house of Hades you will be joined in matrimony with the one whom you slept with in life. I will grant this favor to you and you will grant to me justice for my father. (1139–1146)

CHORUS: Retribution for evils. Changed gales of vengeance blow through the house. Once my king, mine, fell stricken in his bath. The stones and the rooftop shrieked with the cry that he uttered: "O wretched woman, my wife, why will you kill me who have returned to my dear fatherland after ten years?" In retribution,   150 this unhappy woman of an adulterous marriage is brought to justice, she who took up an axe with sharpened blade and by her own hand killed her husband who had returned after many years to his home and its Cyclopean walls that reach to the sky. A poor, suffering husband, whatever evil wrong took hold of his unhappy wife. Like a lioness roaming the woods, who pastures in the mountains, she accomplished her deeds. (1147–1164)

CLYTEMNESTRA: (from inside the house): O my children, by the gods, do not kill your mother.

CHORUS: Do you hear her cry from within?

CLYTEMNESTRA: Ah, woe is me!   160

CHORUS: I pity her, overpowered and undone by her children. God metes out justice, sooner or later. You have suffered a terrible fate, but you, poor wretch, committed an unholy crime against your husband. But here they come out of the house, defiled with freshly shed blood of their mother, triumphal testimony of how they silenced her cries of anguish. No house is more lamentable than that of the family of Tantalus. (1168–1176)

Orestes and Electra appear, the bodies of both Aegisthus and Clytemnestra at their feet. After the horror of murdering their mother, all bravado is gone, and upon full realization of what they have done, they become craven with a remorse that is both sad and repellent. Electra must bear full responsibility for committing the crime along with Orestes; brother and sister have learned to their dismay and regret that the desire for retribution, even when ordained by the command of god, is far different emotionally and psychologically from the real trauma of actually killing their mother.

> ORESTES: O Earth and Zeus, you who witness all that mortals do, behold these bloody, abominable murders, two corpses lying on the ground, struck down by my hand in recompense for my sufferings. (1177–1181)
>
> ELECTRA: Our tears overflow, my brother, and I am the cause. In fiery rage I, poor wretch, came against this mother of mine, who bore me, her daughter.
>
> CHORUS: Alas for misfortune, your misfortune. You, the mother who bore them, have suffered unforgettable misery and more at the hands of your children and you have paid justly for the murder of their father. (1185–1189)
>
> ORESTES: O Phoebus, you prophesied a justice I could not foresee, but all too clear now is the misery that you have wrought. You have bestowed on me the fate 10 of a murderer driven from this land of Hellas. To what other city will I go? What friend, what god-fearing human being will look upon the face of a man who has killed his mother? (1190–1197)
>
> ELECTRA: Alas, woe is me! Where will I go? At what dance will I be accepted? What marriage will be in store for me? What husband will take me to his marriage bed?
>
> CHORUS: Your thoughts have been changed back once again to considerations that are good. Now your thinking is holy; then it was not and you made your brother do a terrible thing, when he did not want to. (1201–1205)
>
> ORESTES: Did you see how the poor woman opened her robe to show me her breast as I slaughtered her, alas for me, and I grabbed at her hair as her body that 20 gave me birth sank to the floor?
>
> CHORUS: I know full well the pain that you went through when you heard the piercing cry of your mother who bore you. (1210–1212)
>
> ORESTES: This was the cry that she uttered as she touched my cheek with her hand: "My child, I beg you," and then she clung to me so closely that my sword fell from my hand.
>
> CHORUS: Poor woman! How did you dare to see with your own eyes your mother breathing out her life? (1218–1220)
>
> ORESTES: I covered my eyes with my cloak as we began the sacrifice, plunging the sword into my mother's flesh. 30
>
> ELECTRA: I ordered you to do it as we took hold of the sword together.
>
> CHORUS: You have done a most terrible deed.
>
> ORESTES: Come, help me cover the limbs of our mother with her garments and close up her wounds. You gave birth to your own murderers.
>
> ELECTRA: See how we cover you, whom we loved and we hated. (1230–1231)

The play ends with the appearance of the Dioscuri, and it is Castor who acts as the deus ex machina. He reaffirms religious and philosophical issues raised by Orestes himself as he hesitates in horror, while his sister is prodding him to join her in murdering their mother. To kill a mother is a terrible crime, with devastating ramifications, whether or not it is decreed by god.

> CHORUS: Thus end great evils for this house. But look! Who are these two who arrive high above the house? Are they divine spirits or gods from the heavens? Mortals do not appear in this way. Why in the world do they come into the clear sight of humans? (1232–1237)

> DIOSCURI (Castor speaks for the two of them):   Listen, son of Agamemnon.
> We, Castor and Polydeuces, address you, we the twin sons of Zeus, brothers of
> your mother. We just now calmed a terrible storm at sea and come to Argos in
> time to witness here the slaughter of our sister and your mother. She received jus-
> tice, but you did not act justly. And Phoebus, O Phoebus—but since he is my lord,
> I keep silent. Being wise, he did not prophesy to you wise things. Yet all this must   10
> be commended and now you have to do what Fate and Zeus have ordained for you.
> (1238–1248)

Castor goes on at some length to predict the future course of events, including the pursuit of Orestes by the Furies and his acquittal by the court of the
Areopagus in Athens. Pylades is to marry Electra.

Select Bibliography

Bloom, Harold, ed. *Aeschylus.* New York: Chelsea House, 2002.

Goldhill, S. *Aeschylus: The Oresteia.* New York: Cambridge University Press,
1992.

Herington, C. J. *Aeschylus.* New Haven, CT: Yale University Press, 1986.

Lloyd-Jones, H. *The Justice of Zeus.* 2d ed. Berkeley: University of California Press,
1983.

Simon, Bennett. *The Tragic Drama and the Family: Psychoanalytic Studies from
Aeschylus to Beckett.* New Haven, CT: Yale University Press, 1988. The Greek plays
included are the *Oresteia* and *Medea.*

Vermeule, Emily. "Baby Aegisthus and the Bronze Age." *Proceedings of the Cambridge
Philological Society* 38 (1987), pp. 122–152.

Primary Sources

Sources in the Chapter

Aeschylus	*Agamemnon* 1095–1129, 1372–1398
	Libation Bearers (*Choephori*) 885–930, 973–1006
Euripides	*Electra* 698–725, 907–1248
Homer	*Odyssey* 11.408–426
Pindar	*Nemean Ode* 7.33–47
	Olympian Ode 1.47–58, 175–193
Seneca	*Thyestes* 138–148
Sophocles	*Electra* (selections)

Additional Sources

Aeschylus	*Eumenides*
Euripides	*Iphigenia at Aulis*
	Iphigenia in Tauris
Herodotus	*History of the Persian Wars* 1.67.1–1.68.6 (the bones of Orestes)
Seneca	*Agamemnon*

Notes

1. These tales are brilliantly discussed by Walter Burkert, *Homo Necans* (Berkeley, CA: University of California Press, 1983), pp. 83–109, in part of his chapter entitled "Werewolves around the Tripod Kettle."
2. The Greek phrase is obscure. Cassandra refers to the instrument of the murder, either a sword or an axe, one or the other of which appears in different poetic accounts and vase paintings of the murder.
3. The Areopagus was the court at Athens that heard homicide cases; its members were former archons, that is, state officials. The court had been a center of political controversy shortly before Aeschylus produced his play.
4. Apollo's argument that the child's begetter is the father and not the mother because the mother is only the nurse of the newly sown seed need not be interpreted as a manifestation of Greek misogyny, as Mary R. Lefkowitz so clearly perceives in *Women in Greek Myth* (Baltimore, MD: Johns Hopkins University Press, 1986), pp. 122–123: "[Apollo] is acting as an advocate for a person accused of matricide; had Orestes been accused of killing his father to avenge his mother, Apollo might well have said what Aeschylus has the Erinyes say about the primacy of maternal blood ties. The role of the female in conception, of course, was not clearly understood; opinions varied about whether the female seed present in the menstrual fluid contributed to the appearance and character of the child. . . . But no Athenian audience would have believed that Apollo's argument was conclusive. . . . In fact, the jury in Aeschylus' drama gives Apollo and the Erinyes equal votes, and it is only because Athena, who was born from her father Zeus without a mother, casts her vote for Apollo that Orestes is acquitted."
5. For comparative examples, see George Thomson, *Aeschylus and Athens*, 3d ed. (London: Lawrence & Wishart, 1996), p. 449.
6. The child of Clytemnestra and Aegisthus was Erigone, the theme of a lost play by Sophocles and mentioned by the early cyclic poet Cinaethon.

THE TROJAN SAGA AND THE *ILIAD*

A shudder in the loins engenders there
The broken wall, the burning roof and tower
And Agamemnon dead.

—**W. B. YEATS**, *Leda and the Swan*

LEDA, WIFE OF TYNDAREUS, king of Sparta, bore four children to Zeus, who visited her in the shape of a swan; the four were born from two eggs—from the one sprang **Polydeuces** and **Helen**, from the other **Castor** and **Clytemnestra**.

The Dioscuri

The legends of the Dioscuri (Sons of Zeus), Castor and Polydeuces (his Roman name is **Pollux**), are not part of the saga of the Trojan War. Castor was renowned as a tamer of horses, and Polydeuces was famous for his skill in boxing. Polydeuces was the immortal son of Zeus, whereas Castor was the mortal son of Tyndareus, who eventually shared in the immortality of his brother. They were perhaps originally mortal heroes, later worshiped as gods. According to Pindar, the Dioscuri quarreled with the two sons of Aphareus, **Idas** and **Lynceus**, over the division of some cattle that the four of them had taken in a raid. In the quarrel, Lynceus and Castor were killed, and Idas was destroyed by Zeus' thunderbolt. As Castor lay dying, Polydeuces prayed to Zeus that he might die with him. Zeus gave him the choice either of immortality for himself and death for Castor or of living with Castor but spending alternate days on Olympus and in Hades. Polydeuces chose the latter, and so the Dioscuri shared both immortality and death.[1]

As gods, Castor and Polydeuces were especially connected with seafarers, to whom they appear as St. Elmo's fire.[2] They were particularly honored at Sparta, and in the early fifth century B.C. their cult spread to Rome.[3] One of the most prominent buildings in the Forum at Rome was the temple of Castor.

In the two *Homeric Hymns to the Dioscuri*, they are addressed as the Tyndaridae because their mother, Leda, was the wife of Tyndareus. Hymn 17 is short and focuses on their conception and birth:

> About Castor and Polydeuces sing, clear-voiced Muse, the Tyndaridae, who are sprung from Olympian Zeus. Beneath the peaks of Mt. Taÿgetus lady Leda bore them, after she had been stealthily seduced by the dark-clouded son of Cronus.

Hymn 33 depicts the Dioscuri in their important role as patron deities of sailors and seafarers:

> O bright-eyed Muses, tell about the sons of Zeus, the Tyndaridae, splendid children of lovely-ankled Leda—Castor, the horse-tamer, and faultless Polydeuces. Leda joined in love with Zeus, the dark-clouded son of Cronus, and she gave birth beneath the summit of the great mountain, Taÿgetus, to these children, saviors of people on earth and of swift-moving ships, when wintry winds rage over a savage sea. Those on the ship go to the highest part of the stern and call on great Zeus with promises of white lambs. The strong wind and swell of the sea put the ship under water, but suddenly the two brothers appear, darting on tawny wings through the air. At once they calm the blasts of the harsh winds and quell the waves on the expanse of the whitecapped sea. Those who have been freed from pain and toil rejoice, since they have seen these two fair signs of deliverance from distress. (1–17)
> Hail, Tyndaridae, riders of swift horses! Yet I shall remember you and another song too.

10

Helen

The daughters of Zeus and Leda were Clytemnestra and Helen. Clytemnestra became the wife of Agamemnon, and we have discussed her part in the Mycenaean saga (Chapter 18). Helen grew up to be the most beautiful of women, and from the many Greek princes (including Theseus and Odysseus) who were her suitors she chose Menelaüs, who became king of Sparta. The rejected suitors swore to respect her choice and help Menelaüs in time of need.

Helen lived for some years at Sparta and bore a daughter, Hermione, to Menelaüs. In time, however, the Trojan prince **Paris** (also called **Alexander**), the son of Priam and Hecuba, visited Sparta while Menelaüs was away in Crete. There he seduced Helen and took her back to Troy with him. To recover her and vindicate the rights of Menelaüs, the Achaean (Mycenaean Greek) expedition, led by Agamemnon, brother of Menelaüs, was raised against Troy.

Another version of Helen's story was invented by the seventh-century poet Stesichorus, who says in his *Palinode*:

> That story is not true; you did not go in the well-benched ships, nor did you go to the towers of Troy.

In Stesichorus' version, Helen got only as far as Egypt, where King Proteus detained her until Menelaüs took her back to Sparta after the Trojan War. It was merely a phantom of Helen who accompanied Paris to Troy, and this was sufficient pretext for the war, which Zeus had determined should occur to reduce the population of the earth.[4]

The Judgment of Paris

The Olympian gods were guests at the wedding feast of Peleus and Thetis. During the feast, **Eris**, goddess of Discord (who was not a guest), threw onto the table an apple inscribed with the words "For the most beautiful." Hera, Athena, and Aphrodite each claimed it, and Zeus decided that the argument should be settled by Paris.

Now Paris had been exposed as an infant because of a dream that came to his mother Hecuba (the Greek form of her name is Hekabe) before his birth. She dreamed that she had given birth to a firebrand that consumed the whole of Troy, and a soothsayer[5] foretold that her baby would be the destruction of the city. The infant was exposed on **Mt. Ida** and suckled by a bear. He was found and brought up by a shepherd. Hermes led the three goddesses to him, and each offered the best gift she could provide in return for his favorable decision. Hera promised him royal power and Athena, victory in war, while Aphrodite promised Helen as his wife. He chose Aphrodite, and so the train of events that led to the Trojan War was set in motion, in which Hera and Athena were hostile to the Trojans.

Lucian (*Dialogues of the Gods* 20; Loeb ed., vol. 3, pp. 383–409, *The Judgment of the Goddesses*) offers a satiric version of the judgment of Paris, in tone not unlike Cranach's painting (p. 464). The sardonic wit of his portrayal illuminates the bitter rivalry, ruthless ambition, and irresponsible passion of the characters, and in so doing they intensify the horror of the tragic events to follow. How bitterly ironic is Paris' response to Athena: "War and battles serve absolutely no purpose to me. As you see, there is peace throughout Phrygia and Lydia and the entire kingdom of my father." The satire begins as Zeus gives the golden apple to Hermes with directions to take it and the three goddesses to Paris, who is tending his flocks on Mt. Ida. Hermes is to tell Paris that he has been chosen to make the decision because he is so handsome and knowledgeable in matters of love. Zeus disqualifies himself as judge by saying that he loves all three equally and that if he gives the apple to one, he will incur the anger of the others. The goddesses agree to Zeus' scheme and fly away to Ida with Hermes as their guide. In the course of the journey, each goddess asks for pertinent information about their judge, Paris. As they approach Mt. Ida, Hermes decides that they had better make a landing and walk up to Paris amiably, rather than frighten him by swooping down from the sky. Hermes explains everything to the bewildered Paris and hands him the golden apple with its inscription (20.7–9):

> PARIS: Well then, look at what it says: "Let the beautiful one take me." Now, lord Hermes, I am a mere mortal and from the country; how am I to become the judge of this marvelous spectacle, too great for a herdsman to handle? To make a decision such as this is a job for a city sophisticate. I could probably judge which is the more beautiful in a contest between two she-goats or two cows, but all these goddesses are equally beautiful. Their beauty surrounds and engulfs me completely. My only regret is that I am not Argus, and so I cannot look at them with eyes all over my body. It seems to me that my best judgment would be to give the apple to all three. For, besides everything else, this one happens to be the sister and wife of Zeus, and these two are his daughters. Doesn't all this make the decision extremely difficult?
>
> HERMES: I don't know. Yet it is impossible to avoid an order given by Zeus.

10

PARIS: Just this one request, Hermes. Persuade them—I mean the two who lose—not to hold their defeat against me and to realize that the fault was in my eyes.

HERMES: They agree that they will not blame you; but now the time has come to go through with the contest.

PARIS: I'll try. What else can a man do? Still, first I want to know if it will be enough to look at them as they are, or will it be necessary for them to undress for a proper examination?   20

HERMES: This would be up to you as the judge. Conduct the proceedings as you desire.

PARIS: As I desire; I'd like to see them naked.

HERMES: You goddesses there, undress! And you, Paris, look them over. I have already turned my back. (7–9)

The goddesses proceed to undress, and Paris is overwhelmed (11–16).

PARIS: O Zeus, god of marvels! What a sight, what beauty, what ecstasy! The virgin Athena is such a vision! How regal and august is the radiance of Hera, truly a wife worthy of Zeus! The gaze of Aphrodite is so sweet and lovely, and she gave me such a seductive smile. Already this rapture is too much, but if it is all right with you, I'd like to see each one separately, since at this moment I am overwhelmed.

APHRODITE: Let's do what he wants.

PARIS: Then the two of you go away, but, Hera, you stay here.

HERA: Here I stay, and after you have looked me over carefully, the time will be right for you to think about whether other considerations are beautiful too—I mean, the gifts that you will get in return for your vote for me. Paris, if you judge me to be   10
the beautiful one, you will be master of all Asia.

PARIS: My vote is not determined by gifts: go on now. Athena, you step forward. (11)

ATHENA: I am right beside you, and if you judge me the beautiful one, Paris, you will never leave a battle in defeat but always victorious. I shall turn you into a warrior and a conquering hero.

PARIS: War and battles serve absolutely no purpose for me. As you see, there is peace throughout Phrygia and Lydia and the entire kingdom of my father. But cheer up! You will not be at a disadvantage, even if my judgment is not to be made on the basis of gifts. Get dressed now and put on your helmet, for I have seen enough. It's time for Aphrodite to step forward. (12)   20

APHRODITE: No rush! Here I am, right beside you. Look at every detail scrupulously. Take your time over every inch of my body, and as you examine me, my beautiful lad, listen to what I have to say. I noticed the moment I saw you how young and handsome you are—I doubt if there is any other fellow in the whole of Troy who is better looking. I congratulate you on your beauty, but it pains me that you do not leave these stony crags for a life in the city. Instead, you are letting your beauty go to waste amid this isolation. What fun do you get out of these mountains? What good is your beauty to the cows? By now you should be married, not to some country bumpkin like the women from Mt. Ida but to someone from Greece—from Argos or Corinth—or to a Spartan like Helen, young and beautiful as I am and, above all,   30
amorous. If she only got a look at you, I know very well that she would leave everything behind, succumb to you completely, follow you home in surrender to live with you as your wife. Of course, you have heard at least something about her? (13)

The Judgment of Paris,
by Lucas Cranach the Elder (1472–1553); oil on panel, ca. 1528, 40⅛ × 28 in. This painting wittily exploits the incongruities of a tale where great goddesses appear naked before a shepherd. Paris is a corpulent Renaissance knight in armor and foppish hat, while an aged Hermes, with stern demeanor, sets off the sensuality of the goddesses. Aphrodite looks fully at the viewer, while Athena looks directly and points at Paris. In the background the towers and spires of Troy can be seen. Cupid draws his bow above, and to the left the horse seems to add his own view of the contest. The horse was omitted in Romare Bearden's *Prologue to Troy No. 2,* which is not included in this edition of *Classical Mythology.* Bearden "transposed Cranach to a black circumstance" (i.e., Paris and the divine figures are black), and he added that "my Paris doesn't need a stud horse in the background." (*Image copyright © The Metropolitan Museum of Art/ Art Resource, NY*)

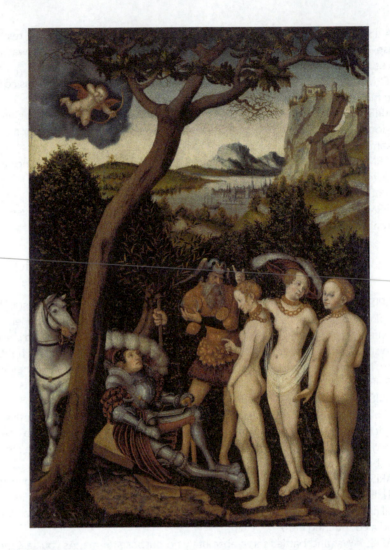

PARIS: Not a thing, Aphrodite, but it would be my pleasure to hear you tell me everything about her.

APHRODITE: She is actually the daughter of beautiful Leda, whom Zeus seduced after flying down to her in the form of a swan.

PARIS: What does she look like?

APHRODITE: As fair as you would expect the daughter of a swan to be, and soft and delicate, since she was hatched from an eggshell, but yet very athletic too—so sought-after, in fact, that even a war has already been waged over her, because Theseus carried her off when she was still quite young. Furthermore, when she reached the peak of her present perfection, all the best of the Achaeans gathered to seek her hand in marriage. Menelaüs, of the family of Pelops, was the one chosen. If you'd like, I'll arrange her marriage to you.

PARIS: What are you saying? Me with a married woman?

APHRODITE: You are young and naive, but I know how this kind of thing must be managed.

PARIS: How? I want to know too. (14)

40

The Judgment of Paris. Mosaic from Antioch, early second century A.D.; 73¼ × 73¼ in. This mosaic was the central panel of an elaborate mosaic floor in a dining room of the Atrium House in Antioch. The three goddesses—Hera enthroned in the center, Athena to the viewer's left, and Aphrodite to the right—appear on a rocky hill, each holding a long scepter. On the left and below, Paris, in Phrygian dress, turns to talk with Hermes. He is guarding a mixed flock of oxen, sheep, and goats, one each of which is shown, the goat drinking from a pool of water. In the center are a tree and a column, on top of which is a golden vase. On the left Psyche (identified by her butterfly wings) stands on a rock, and matching her on the right a winged cupid stands on a column, anticipating the victory of Aphrodite in the contest. Framing the panel is an elaborate vine, populated with birds, reptiles, and insects, with masks of a man and a woman. (© *RMN-Grand Palais/Art Resource, NY*)

APHRODITE: You will take a trip, ostensibly a tour of Greece, and when you come   50
to Sparta, Helen will see you. From then on, it will be up to me to manage how she
will fall in love and follow you home.

PARIS: This is the very thing that seems so incredible to me, that she would want
to leave her husband and sail away with a foreigner she doesn't know.

APHRODITE: Don't fret about it, for I have two beautiful children, Desire (*Himeros*)
and Love (*Eros*). I shall give them to you as guides for your journey. Love will insinuate
himself completely into her very being and compel the woman to love you. Desire
will make you desirable and irresistible by suffusing you with the very essence of his

being. I'll be there myself, too, and I'll ask the Graces to accompany me. In this way, all of us together will persuade her to submit.   60

PARIS: It is not in the least clear to me how this will all turn out, Aphrodite. But I am already in love with Helen. I seem to see her now—I'm sailing straight for Greece—I'm visiting Sparta—I'm returning home holding the woman in my arms! I am very upset that I am not doing all this right now. (15)

APHRODITE: Hold on, Paris! Don't fall in love until you have rewarded me with your decision—me, the one who is fixing the marriage and giving away the bride. It would be only fitting that I, your helper, be the winner of the prize, and that we celebrate at the same time both your marriage and my victory. For it is up to you. You can buy everything—love, beauty, marriage—the cost is this apple.

PARIS: I am afraid that you will forget about me after my decision.   70

APHRODITE: And so you want me to swear an oath?

PARIS: Not at all, only promise me again.

APHRODITE: I promise to give you Helen as your wife and that she herself will follow and come with you to your family in Troy. I shall be at your side myself, and I shall help accomplish everything.

PARIS: And you will bring Love, Desire, and the Graces?

APHRODITE: Never fear, I shall even bring along Passionate Longing and Hymen, the god of Marriage.

HERMES: For these promises, then, I award you the apple. Take it. (16)

Homer never mentions this story; according to him (*Iliad* 24.25–30), Paris once insulted Hera and Athena when they visited him but praised Aphrodite, who gave him the power to attract women irresistibly. This simpler version is certainly older than the more famous literary account of the judgment, but it is the latter that has dominated the tradition and fascinated an endless line of poets and artists.

Troy and Its Leaders

Dardanus

Electra, daughter of Atlas, had two sons by Zeus, Iasion and Dardanus. On the death of Iasion in Samothrace, Dardanus sailed to the Troad, where **Teucer**, son of the river-god Scamander, was king. There Dardanus married the king's daughter and built a city called by his name. On the death of Teucer, the land was called **Dardania** and its inhabitants (as in Homer) **Dardani**. From Dardanus was descended the Trojan royal house.

Laomedon

Apollo and Poseidon (disguised as mortals) built the walls of Troy for its king Laomedon, who then cheated them of their pay.[6] In punishment, Apollo sent a plague and Poseidon a sea monster to harass the Trojans. The oracles advised that the only way to get rid of the monster was to expose Laomedon's daughter **Hesione** and let it devour her. When Heracles came to Troy (see p. 552), he agreed to kill the monster and save Hesione in return for Laomedon's immortal horses, which were the gift of Zeus.[7] Once again Laomedon cheated his

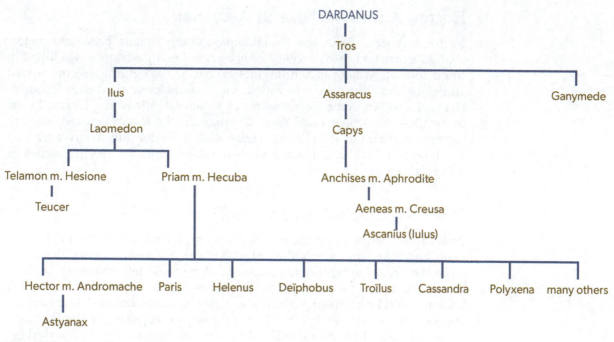

Figure 19.1 The Royal House of Troy

benefactor; Heracles therefore returned with an army, captured Troy, and gave Hesione as wife to his companion, **Telamon**, by whom she became the mother of Teucer. Heracles killed Laomedon but spared his young son Podarces, who became king of the ruined city, changing his name to Priam.

Priam and Hecuba

King Priam was father of fifty sons and twelve (or fifty) daughters, of whom nineteen were children of his second wife, Hecuba (Arisba, his first wife, is not significant in the legend). In the *Iliad*, Hecuba appears as a tragic figure whose sons and husband are doomed; her most famous legend takes place after the fall of Troy (pp. 499–500).

Paris (Alexander)

The most important sons of Priam and Hecuba were Paris and Hector. While Paris was a shepherd on Mt. Ida, he fell in love with a nymph, **Oenone**, who had the gift of healing. He left her for Helen. Years later, when he was wounded by Philoctetes, she refused to heal him, but when he died, she killed herself in remorse. As a young man, Paris had returned to the royal palace and had been recognized by Priam as his son. As we have seen, Paris' actions led to the Trojan War, in which he appears as a brave warrior, though uxorious. He was the favorite of Aphrodite, who saved him from being killed in combat by Menelaüs. His vanity and sensuality contrasted with the dignity and courage of Hector. Paris shot the arrow that fatally wounded Achilles.

Hector, Andromache, and Astyanax

Hector, brother of Paris, was the champion of the Trojans, brave and honorable. As a warrior he was excelled only by Achilles, by whom he was killed in single combat. As long as Achilles took no part in the fighting, Hector carried all before him. When he was killed, the Trojans knew they were doomed. His wife was Andromache, daughter of Eëtion (an ally of the Trojans killed by Achilles), and their child was Astyanax. In the *Iliad*, Homer draws unforgettable portraits of Paris and Helen and of Hector and Andromache, as he juxtaposes their characters and their relationships in moving scenes of universal power.

Helenus, Deïphobus, and Troïlus

Priam's son Helenus had the gift of prophecy, for when he was a child serpents had licked his ears. In the last year of the war, the prophet Calchas advised the Greeks to capture him, since he alone could tell what must be done to end the war. He was caught by Odysseus and honorably treated, so that he alone of Priam's sons survived the war. He eventually married Andromache and became a ruler in Epirus. As a prophet, he appears for the last time in the *Aeneid*, where he foretells the course of Aeneas' future wanderings (p. 675).

Of Priam's many other sons, Deïphobus married Helen after the death of Paris; his ghost spoke with Aeneas in the Underworld; and Troïlus, who was killed by Achilles, became more significant in later times.[8]

Cassandra and Polyxena

Cassandra and Polyxena are Priam's most important daughters. Cassandra had been loved by Apollo, who gave her the gift of prophecy. When she rejected him, he added to the gift the fate that she should never be believed. Thus she foretold the fall of Troy and warned the Trojans against the Trojan horse all in vain. Her fate in the sack of Troy is described later in this chapter; as we have seen, she died in Mycenae, murdered by Clytemnestra.

Polyxena, as we describe later in this chapter, was sacrificed on the tomb of Achilles as his share of the spoils after the sack of Troy.

Aeneas

Of the Trojan leaders outside Priam's immediate family, the most prominent is Aeneas, who belonged to another branch of the royal family. Although he was the son of **Anchises** and **Aphrodite**, he was not the equal of Priam in prestige or of Hector as a warrior. In the *Iliad*, he fights in single combat with Achilles and is saved from death by Poseidon, who transports him miraculously from the fight. Poseidon prophesies that now that Zeus has withdrawn his favor from Priam's family, Aeneas and his descendants will be the future rulers of Troy. We consider his later prominence, as depicted by Vergil, in Chapter 26.

Antenor

Antenor, brother of Hecuba, was conspicuous among those who did not want the war, and he advised returning Helen to the Greeks. When the Greeks first landed, he saved their ambassadors from being treacherously killed by the Trojans. In the last year of the war, he protested the breaking of a truce by the Trojans and still proposed the voluntary return of Helen. The Greeks spared him at the sack, and he and his wife, Theano, the priestess of Athena, were allowed to sail away. They reached Italy, where they founded the city of Patavium (Padua).

Glaucus

Of the allies of Troy, the most prominent in the *Iliad* were the Lycians, led by Glaucus and Sarpedon. When Glaucus and the Greek hero Diomedes were about to fight, they discovered that they were hereditary guest-friends (i.e., their ancestors had entertained one another and exchanged gifts). They exchanged armor instead of fighting and parted amicably. Since Glaucus' armor was made of gold and that of Diomedes of bronze, Diomedes had the better of the exchange, as Homer says (*Iliad* 6.234–236):

> Zeus took away Glaucus' wits, for he exchanged golden armor with Diomedes for bronze, armor that was worth a hundred oxen for armor worth only nine.

Glaucus eventually was killed by Ajax (son of Telamon) in the fight over the corpse of Achilles.

Sarpedon

Sarpedon was the son of Zeus and the Lycian princess Laodamia, daughter of Bellerophon. Zeus foresaw Sarpedon's death but could not change his destiny (*moira*) without upsetting the established order. He therefore had to be content with raining drops of blood on the earth to honor his son before the catastrophe and saving his body after it. Here is Homer's description of the scene (*Iliad* 16.676–683) after Sarpedon has been killed by Patroclus and Zeus has instructed Apollo to save his body:

> Thus [Zeus] spoke, and Apollo did not disobey his father. He went down from the peaks of Ida into the terrible din of battle and straightway lifted godlike Sarpedon out of the way of the missiles and carried him far off. He washed him in the flowing waters of the river and anointed him with ambrosia and clothed him with immortal garments. And he sent him to be carried by two swift escorts, the twins Sleep and Death, who quickly set him down in the fertile land of broad Lycia.

After Hector, Sarpedon is the most noble of the heroes on the Trojan side. In Book 12 of the *Iliad*, when the Trojans are attacking the wall of the Greek camp, he addresses Glaucus in words expressing heroic *arete* (excellence) and nobility as memorable as those of Achilles in Book 9 (translated on pp. 484–485). Unlike Achilles, he speaks as the leader of a community (*Iliad* 12.310–328):

Glaucus, why are we specially honored in Lycia with seats of honor, with meat and more cups of wine, and all people look upon us like gods, and we have been allotted a great domain beside the banks of the Xanthus, fine for the planting of vineyards and for grain-bearing tillage? Therefore now must we stand in the front rank of the Lycians and face the raging battle, so that one of the well-armored Lycians may say: "Indeed not without glory do our kings rule over Lycia and eat the fat lambs and drink choice honey-sweet wine. Noble also is their strength, since they fight among the leaders of the Lycians." My friend, if we were to avoid this war and were to live out our lives ever ageless and deathless, then neither would I myself fight among the leaders, nor would I station you in the battle that destroys men. Now, as it is, let us go, for ten thousand death-bringing fates are close upon us.

10

Rhesus

Other allied contingents who appeared at Troy were those of the Amazons and the Ethiopians, and the Thracians led by Rhesus. Their arrival coincided with a night patrol by Diomedes and Odysseus, during which they caught and killed a Trojan spy, **Dolon**, who first told them of the Thracians. They went on to kill Rhesus and twelve of his men and to capture his white horses. Rhesus, who was a son of one of the Muses, was worshiped as a hero in Thrace.

The Achaean Leaders

The organization of the Greek army was different from that of the Trojans, for Troy was a great city led by a powerful king and helped in war by independent allies. We have seen that Helen's suitors had sworn to help Menelaüs if he called on them, and they assembled for war under the leadership of Agamemnon, king of Mycenae. While Agamemnon's position as leader was unquestioned, each of the Greek princes led his contingent independently and could at any time withdraw, as Achilles did.

The Death of Sarpedon. Athenian red-figure krater by Euphronios, ca. 510 B.C.; height 18 in. The winged gods, Sleep (Hypnos, *left*) and Death (Thanatos, *right*), carry the body from the battlefield under the guidance of Hermes as two Greek warriors look on. The gods wear armor (note the chain mail of Thanatos), but the corpse of Sarpedon has been stripped. The vase is one of the masterpieces of Athenian vase painting. (*Soprintendenza per i Beni Archeologici dell'Etruria Meridionale*)

Agamemnon

Agamemnon was the "lord of men," greatest in prestige among the Greeks, although neither the greatest warrior nor the wisest in council. His stature is shown in the scene in Book 3 of the *Iliad* when Helen names the Greek warrior whom Priam points out to her from their viewpoint on the wall (hence the scene is known as the "viewing from the wall," or *teichoskopia*). Priam begins (*Iliad* 3.166–190):

"Tell me the name of this mighty man, whoever he is of the Greeks, a man valiant and great. . . ."

> Then Helen answered in words, goddess-like
> among women. . . . "This is the son of Atreus,
> Agamemnon, ruler of a broad kingdom, both a
> noble king and a strong warrior. He was my hus-
> band's brother." Thus she spoke, and the old man
> was filled with wonder and said: "O happy son
> of Atreus, favored by Destiny, blest by fortune,
> many sons of the Achaeans are your subjects.
> Long ago I went to Phrygia rich in vineyards, and
> there I saw great numbers of Phrygian warriors
> on their swift horses. . . . But not even they were
> as great as are the quick-eyed Achaeans."

10

In Book 11 (36–40), the terror inspired by
Agamemnon as a warrior is shown in the devices
on his shield and shield-strap, "The grim-looking
Gorgon with her terrifying gaze, and around the
shield Terror and Fear. And on the strap coiled a
dark serpent, and it had three heads turning all
ways, growing from one neck." Yet great warrior
as Agamemnon was, he was a lesser hero than
Achilles.

Menelaüs

We have seen how Menelaüs, king of Sparta,
and his wife Helen were involved in the origin
of the war. In the war itself, he fought Paris in
single combat. Aphrodite saved Paris just as
Menelaüs was on the point of killing him. For
the adventures of Menelaüs after the sack of Troy, see pp. 509–510, and for
Euripides' versions of his part in the stories of Orestes and Neoptolemus, see
pp. 439–440.

Diomedes

Diomedes, king of Argos, was a much greater warrior than Menelaüs. He
was the son of Tydeus and second only to Agamemnon in power and prestige. He was also a wise counselor. He was a favorite of Athena and with her
help could oppose even the gods in battle. He wounded both Ares and
Aphrodite. He was especially associated with Odysseus, with whom he
fetched Achilles from Scyros and later Philoctetes from Lemnos. Odysseus
was also his companion in the night patrol where Dolon and Rhesus were
killed and in the theft of the Palladium from Troy. This **Palladium** (the statue
of Pallas, which Athena had made and Zeus cast down from heaven into
Troy) was worshiped and looked upon as a talisman for the city's survival.
When Odysseus and Diomedes stole it, Troy was doomed. Diomedes' meeting with Glaucus has already been described; his adventures after the war
are discussed on p. 510.

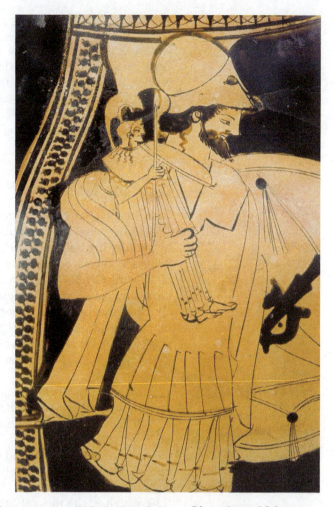

Diomedes and Odysseus Stealing the Palladium from Troy. Detail from an Attic red-figure amphora by the Tyszkiewicz painter, early fifth century B.C. Diomedes holds the Palladium in his right hand. (*Medelhavsmuseet, Stockholm, photographer Ove Kaneberg. Inv. nr. MM 1963:1*)

Nestor

Nestor, king of Pylos and a son of Neleus, was the oldest and wisest of the Greek leaders. Like Priam, he had become king after Heracles sacked his city. In the sack, Neleus and all his sons except Nestor were killed. At Troy, Nestor was a respected counselor, and his speeches, full of reminiscences, contrast with the impetuosity of the younger princes. He himself survived the war, although his son Antilochus was killed by Memnon. There is no tradition of his death.

Ajax the Greater of Salamis, the Son of Telamon

Ajax, son of Telamon, was second only to Achilles as a warrior.[9] He is called the Great (or Greater) to distinguish him from Ajax the Less (or Lesser), son of Oïleus. In the fighting before the Greek ships (Books 13–15), he was the most stalwart defender, always courageous and the last to give ground to the enemy. Again he was the Greek champion in the fight over the body of Patroclus in Book 17, providing cover while Menelaüs and Meriones retreated with the body. At the climax of that battle, he prayed to Zeus to dispel the mist of battle and let him die in the clear sunlight, a striking scene in which the sudden appearance of the sun and clear vision seems especially appropriate for this straightforward warrior. In the *teichoskopia*, Priam asks Helen (*Iliad* 3.226–229):

> "Who is this other Achaean warrior, valiant and great, who stands out from the Achaeans with his head and broad shoulders?" [Helen replies] "This is Ajax, of huge size, the bulwark of the Achaeans."

Ajax is both the foil to and the rival of Odysseus. His gruff and laconic speech in the embassy to Achilles (Book 9), which we discuss later, contrasts with the smooth words of the diplomatic Odysseus. In Book 23, they compete in the wrestling match in the funeral games; Ajax's defeat there foreshadows his far more tragic defeat in the contest with Odysseus for the armor of Achilles, discussed later in this chapter.

Ajax the Less (or Lesser)

Ajax the Less (as Homer calls him), prince of the Locrians and son of Oïleus, is a less attractive character than his namesake. Although he figured prominently in the fighting and was the leader of a large contingent, his sacrilegious violation of Cassandra during the sack of Troy diminished his stature and led to his death on the voyage back to Greece (p. 509).

Idomeneus

Another important fighter with a large contingent was Idomeneus, son of Deucalion and leader of the Cretans. He stood in a different relationship to Agamemnon from most of the other leaders in that he came as a voluntary ally. He had long been a friend of Menelaüs, and Agamemnon showed him great respect. In Book 13 of the *Iliad*, he defends the Greek camp bravely and

Achilles and Ajax Playing a Board Game. Attic amphora signed by Exekias as painter and potter, ca. 535 B.C.; height 24½ in. There is no literary source for this scene, which appears in over 150 vase paintings, sometimes with the addition of Athena in armor. Achilles (to the viewer's left) and Ajax are partly armed, while their shields are propped up behind them along with Ajax's helmet on the right. Bending over the log that serves as a game board, they count their points won, the numbers (four for Achilles, three for Ajax) being written out on the painting. The theme of heroes taking a break from battle is further emphasized by the elaborate decoration of their mantles, hardly the dress for warriors going into battle. (*Scala/Art Resource, NY*)

kills a number of leading Trojan warriors. Good as he was as fighter and counselor at Troy, his most important legend is concerned with his return (p. 510).[10]

Odysseus

When Menelaüs and Agamemnon sent heralds throughout Greece and the islands to summon the Greek leaders and their contingents to the war, not all the Greek heroes came willingly; two of the most important, Odysseus and Achilles, attempted to avoid the war by subterfuge.

Odysseus, king of Ithaca, pretended to be mad. When Agamemnon's envoys came, he yoked an ox and an ass and plowed a field, sowing salt in the furrows. One of the envoys, **Palamedes**, took Odysseus' infant son Telemachus from his mother, Penelope, and put him in the path of the plow. Odysseus was sane enough to avoid him; his pretense was uncovered, and he joined the expedition.[11]

Odysseus was the craftiest and wisest of the Greeks, as well as a brave warrior. He was the best in council, and his powerful speech in Book 2 (284–332) decided the debate in favor of staying before Troy to finish the war. He attacked the unattractive and sardonic **Thersites** for intervening in the debate, when only princes should speak, and for this he was greatly honored by the Greeks. He was the principal speaker in the embassy to Achilles in Book 9, and he undertook the dangerous night mission with Diomedes as well as other missions mentioned earlier. Above all, Odysseus was a skilled speaker, as is brought out in the *teichoskopia* (a viewing from the wall), a designation given to the section of the *Iliad* where Helen identifies for Priam the Greek commanders (*Iliad* 3.191–224):

> Next the old man [Priam] asked about Odysseus. "Come, tell me also about this man, dear child, who he is. He is shorter by a head than Agamemnon, son of Atreus, but I see that he is broader in the shoulders and chest. His arms lie on the fruitful earth, and he like a ram is going up and down the ranks of warriors. I liken him to a thick-fleeced ram which goes through the flocks of white-fleeced sheep." Then Helen, daughter of Zeus, answered: "This is crafty Odysseus, son of Laërtes, who was raised in the land of Ithaca, rocky though it is. He knows all kinds of deceit and clever plans." (191–202)
>
> Then wise Antenor spoke to her and said: "Lady, true indeed are your words. Godlike Odysseus came here once before with Menelaüs, dear to Ares, for news

10

of you. I was their host and welcomed them in my home, and I knew their stature and their wise intelligence. But when they joined in the assembly of the Trojans, Menelaüs was taller when they stood by his [head and] broad shoulders; yet when they both were seated Odysseus was the more noble. But when they began to weave their speeches and proposals before all, then indeed Menelaüs spoke glibly, a few words in a clear voice, since he was not long-winded or irrelevant, and he was younger also. But whenever wise Odysseus rose to speak, he would stand and look down and fix his eyes on the ground, and he would not gesture with the scepter before or behind him, but held it stiffly, like some unskilled man. You would say that he was angry and unintelligent too. But when he sent forth the great voice from his chest and the words that were like falling winter snows, then no other mortal could compete with Odysseus. Indeed, then we were not amazed as we looked at the appearance of Odysseus." (203–224)

20

The double portrait of the wise orator and the glib young king vividly puts before us two sides of the heroic ethos, and it prepares us for the complexity of Odysseus' character in the saga of his return from Troy.

Achilles, His Parents, Peleus and Thetis, and His Son, Neoptolemus (Pyrrhus)

The second chieftain who attempted to avoid the war was Achilles, prince of the **Myrmidons** (a tribe of Phthia, in northern Greece on the southern border of Thessaly) and the greatest of the Greek warriors as well as the swiftest and most handsome. He was the son of Peleus and Thetis; Thetis was a sea-goddess, daughter of Nereus, who was avoided by Zeus when the secret was revealed hitherto known only to Prometheus and Themis—that Thetis' son would be greater than his father.[12] Their son Achilles did indeed become greater than his father.

Peleus was the son of Aeacus, king of Aegina and brother of Telamon. For killing his half-brother Phocus, he had to leave Aegina, whereupon he went to Eurytion of Phthia, who purified him and gave him part of his kingdom. Peleus accompanied Eurytion on the Calydonian boar hunt and accidentally killed him with a javelin intended for the boar. He went into exile again and was purified by Acastus, son of Pelias and king of Iolcus.

Now the wife of Acastus, Astydamia (Pindar calls her Hippolyta), fell in love with Peleus, and when he refused her advances, she accused him before her husband of trying to seduce her.[13] Rather than kill his guest, Acastus took him hunting on Mt. Pelion, where he left him asleep, but not before hiding his sword (a gift from Hephaestus) in a pile of dung. Peleus awoke to find himself surrounded by wild animals and centaurs, who would have killed him had not Chiron protected him and given him back his sword.

When Zeus avoided a union with Thetis, whose son was destined to be greater than his father, she was given to Peleus because of his virtue. The wedding feast was celebrated on Mt. Pelion, and all the gods and goddesses came as guests. As we have seen, with them came Eris (Discord) as an uninvited guest, bringing the apple that eventually led to the judgment of Paris and the Trojan War. Peleus returned to Phthia, where he became the father of Achilles. Thetis soon left Peleus, angry because he interrupted her while she was making Achilles immortal.

Peleus Wrestles with Thetis. Red-figure kylix by the Peithinos painter, ca. 510 B.C. Peleus holds on to the body of Thetis, who transforms herself into wild animals, represented here by a lion and three snakes (respectively on the right forearm and feet of Peleus and the left arm of Thetis). The inscriptions name Peleus and Thetis and include a dedication by Peithinos to his lover, Athenodotus. (*bpk Bildagentur/Staatliche Antikensammlung/Art Resource, NY*)

Thus Thetis was married to a mortal, Peleus, king of the Phthians. Peleus took part in the Argonauts' expedition and the Calydonian boar hunt, but as a mere mortal he was hardly a match for Thetis. It was with difficulty that he married her, for she was able to turn herself into various shapes in attempting to escape from him. Although the gods attended their wedding feast, Thetis left Peleus not long after the birth of Achilles. She tried to make Achilles immortal, either by roasting him in the fire by night and anointing him with ambrosia by day[14] or by dipping him in the waters of the Styx. In the latter story, all parts of Achilles' body that had been submerged were invulnerable. Only his heel, by which Thetis held him, remained vulnerable. It was here that he received the fatal arrow wound.

Once Thetis had left Peleus, Achilles was sent to the centaur **Chiron** for his education. From him he learned the art of music and other skills. While Achilles was with Chiron, Thetis learned that Troy could not be taken without Achilles; she also knew that he could live long and die ingloriously or go to Troy and die young and glorious. To circumvent his early death, she tried to prevent his going by disguising him as a girl and taking him to the island of **Scyros**, where he was brought up with the **daughters of Lycomedes**, king of the island. One of them was **Deïdamia**, with whom Achilles fell in love; their child, born after Achilles left Scyros, was Neoptolemus (also called Pyrrhus, which means "redhead"), who took part in the capture of Troy after his father's death. Odysseus and Diomedes exposed Achilles' disguise at Scyros. They took gifts for the daughters of Lycomedes, among them weapons and armor, in which Achilles alone showed any interest. As the women were looking at the gifts, Odysseus arranged for a trumpet to sound; the women all ran away, thinking it was a battle signal, but Achilles took off his disguise and put on the armor. Here is the description of the scene by the Roman poet Statius (*Achilleid* 1.852–884), after the gifts have been set out by Diomedes:

> The daughters of Lycomedes see the arms and assume that they are a present for their mighty father. But when fierce Achilles saw the shining shield close by, chased with scenes of war and lying next to the spear, he grew violent . . . and Troy filled his heart. . . . When he saw his reflection in the golden shield, he shuddered and blushed. Then observant Odysseus stood close to him and whispered: "Why do you hesitate? We know. You are the pupil of the centaur, Chiron, you are the descendant of [the gods of] sky and sea. The Greek fleet is waiting for you, the Greek army is waiting for you before raising its standards, the walls of Troy itself are ready to fall before you. Hurry, no more delaying!". . . . Already Achilles was beginning to take off his woman's dress when Agyrtes sounded a loud blast on the trumpet, as he had been ordered to do [by Odysseus]. The girls began to run away, scattering the gifts. . . . Achilles' clothing of itself fell from his chest, and he quickly seized the shield and short spear and, miraculously, he seemed to be taller by head and shoulders than Odysseus and Diomedes. . . . Stepping like a hero he stood forth.

So Achilles was discovered and joined the expedition. At Troy, he proved to be the mightiest of the champions on either side and a hero of enormous passions.

Phoenix and Patroclus

Two of Achilles' associates, Phoenix and Patroclus, are important. Phoenix, at the instigation of his mother, lay with his father's mistress. His father cursed him with childlessness, and Phoenix sought refuge from his father's wrath with Peleus, who made him the tutor and companion of Achilles both in Phthia and at Troy.

Patroclus was a great warrior. When very young, he had killed a rival in anger over a dice game. Peleus took him in and brought him up to be the companion of Achilles. Achilles and Patroclus become devoted friends and perhaps lovers, and their relationship provides a major theme for the *Iliad*.[15]

The Gathering of the Expedition at Aulis

Menelaüs and Agamemnon sent heralds throughout Greece and the islands to summon the Greek leaders and contingents to the war; the expedition gathered at **Aulis** (on the coast of Boeotia, opposite Euboea) numbering nearly 1,200 ships with their crews and fighting men.[16]

The Sacrifice of Iphigenia

There were delays before the fleet could sail; for a long time contrary winds blew, and in despair Agamemnon consulted the prophet Calchas. He knew that Artemis had caused the unfavorable weather because Agamemnon had offended

The Anger of Achilles, by J.-L. David (1748–1825); oil on canvas, 1819, 41½ × 57¼ in. Iphigenia has been brought to Aulis on the pretext that she is to be the bride of Achilles. David shows the moment when Agamemnon has revealed his true intention to Achilles, who draws his sword in anger to strike Agamemnon. The anger of the men contrasts with the sadness of Iphigenia, who has learned that she will be sacrificed, and of Clytemnestra, who gazes at Achilles as she puts her hand on her daughter's shoulder. The subject is based on Euripides' tragedy, *Iphigenia at Aulis*. (*Kimbell Art Museum, Fort Worth, Texas/Art Resource, NY*)

her[17] and that she could only be appeased by the sacrifice of Agamemnon's daughter Iphigenia, who therefore was fetched from Mycenae (on the pretext that she was to be married to Achilles) and sacrificed. In another version, Artemis saved her at the last moment, substituted a stag as the victim, and took Iphigenia to the land of the Tauri (the modern Crimea) to be her priestess.[18]

Lucretius, the Roman poet (ca. 55 B.C.), tells the story of Iphigenia with bitter pathos to show to what lengths men will go in the name of religion (*De rerum natura* 1.84–101):

> Look how the chosen leaders of the Greeks, the foremost of men, foully defiled the altar of virgin Artemis at Aulis with the blood of Iphigenia. As they placed around her maiden's hair the headband which hung down evenly by her cheeks, she suddenly caught sight of her father standing sadly before the altar and at his side his ministers hiding the knife, while the people shed tears at the sight of her. Dumb with fear she fell to the ground on her knees. At such a moment little help to her in her misery was it that she had been his first child, that she had first bestowed upon the king the name of father. The hands of men brought her trembling to the altar, not that she might perform the customary ritual of marriage to the clear-ringing songs of Hymen, but that at the very time for her wedding she might fall a sad and sinless victim, sinfully butchered by her own father, all for the happy and auspicious departure of the fleet. Such are the monstrous evils to which religion could lead.   10

Calchas' Prophecy

Calchas the prophet was an important figure in the Greek expedition, especially in times of doubt or perplexity. At Troy, as we shall see later, he gave the reason for Apollo's anger and advised the return of Chryseïs to her father. At Aulis, he interpreted a famous omen. A snake was seen to climb up a tree and devour eight chicks from a nest high in its branches; it then ate the mother and was itself turned into stone by Zeus. Calchas correctly interpreted this to mean that the Greeks would fight unsuccessfully at Troy for nine years before capturing the city in the tenth.[19]

The Arrival at Troy

Philoctetes

The expedition finally sailed from Aulis but did not go straight to Troy. On the way, the Greeks were guided by Philoctetes, son of Poeas, to the island of Chryse to sacrifice to its goddess. There Philoctetes was bitten in the foot by a snake; and as the fleet sailed on, the stench from his wound became so noisome that the Greeks abandoned him on the island of Lemnos, where he remained alone and in agony for nearly ten years. Now Philoctetes' father, Poeas, had lit the funeral pyre of Heracles and had in return been given Heracles' bow and arrows, which Philoctetes later inherited. In the last year of the war, the Greeks captured Priam's son Helenus, who prophesied that only with the aid of Heracles' bow and arrows could Troy be captured. Accordingly, Odysseus and Diomedes fetched Philoctetes from Lemnos. The sons of Asclepius, Podalirius and Machaon, healed his wound, and with the arrows he shot Paris, thus removing the most formidable of the surviving Trojan champions.[20]

Achilles Heals Telephus

On the way to Troy, the Greeks landed in Mysia, a district of Asia Minor. In the battle against the Mysians, Achilles wounded the Mysian Telephus, a son of Heracles. When the wound would not heal, Telephus despairingly asked the Delphic oracle for advice. Learning that "he that wounded shall heal," he went to the Greek army disguised as a beggar and asked Achilles to cure his wound. Achilles said he could not, for he was not a

Philoctetes on Lemnos. Red-figure lekythos, ca. 430 B.C. A lekythos was a type of vase for storing oil or perfume, used primarily in religious contexts, including funerals. Many vases of this type have been found in tombs, and the subject matter is often somber in tone. Illustrations of this tale depict either Philoctetes at the depth of his despair on the island of Lemnos or the expedition of the Greeks to Lemnos to fetch the great hero. Philoctetes sits alone on his deserted isle, his left foot bandaged, resting on a rock, with the unerring bow of Heracles by his side. (*Image copyright © The Metropolitan Museum of Art/Art Resource, NY*)

doctor, but Odysseus pointed out that it was Achilles' spear that had caused the wound. Scrapings from it were applied, and Telephus was healed. The myth of Telephus was prominent in the Great Altar at Pergamum (see p. 84).

Protesilaüs and Laodamia

When the Greeks reached Troy, the first to leap ashore was Protesilaüs, who was immediately killed by Hector. His wife, Laodamia, could not be comforted in her grief. Pitying her, Hermes brought back her husband from Hades for a few hours, and when he was taken away again, she killed herself. This story, with its themes of return from the dead and a wife's love, was developed in Euripides' tragedy *Protesilaus*, now mostly lost. Another person to die in the first skirmish was a Trojan, **Cycnus**, son of Poseidon, who was turned into a swan. The Greeks successfully established a beachhead, made a permanent camp with their ships drawn up on shore, and settled down to besiege Troy.

The *Iliad*

While the events of the first nine years of the war are obscure (since the epic poems in which they were described survive only in prose summaries), those of the tenth are in part brilliantly illuminated by the *Iliad*. The poem, however, deals only with events from the outbreak of the quarrel between Achilles and Agamemnon to the ransoming and burial of Hector.

Nine years were spent in a fruitless siege of Troy, varied only by abortive diplomatic exchanges and raids against cities allied with Troy. The division of the spoil from these cities led to the quarrel between Agamemnon and Achilles. Agamemnon was given in his share **Chryseïs**, daughter of **Chryses**, priest of Apollo—but (as we shall see) he had to send her back. Therefore he took **Briseïs**, who had been given to Achilles and whom Achilles had come to love greatly. The wrath of Achilles, the principal theme of the *Iliad*, is characterized in the poem's opening lines (1.1–7):

> The wrath of Achilles, Peleus' son, sing, O goddess, a ruinous wrath, which put countless woes upon the Achaeans and hurled many mighty souls of heroes to Hades, and made them a feast for dogs and a banquet for birds, and the will of Zeus was being accomplished, from the time when first Agamemnon and Achilles stood opposed in strife.

The passionate theme of "wrath," the very word with which the poem begins, determines the intensity of emotion and the scope and form of its action. In verses of visual and auditory clarity as deceptively simple as they are profound, the story unfolds through scenes of great dramatic power. With Chryseïs in his possession, Agamemnon refused to allow Chryses to ransom his daughter, and Chryses therefore prayed to Apollo to punish the Greeks. Apollo's answer to the prayer is described in these vivid lines (*Iliad* 1.43–52):

> So Chryses prayed, and Phoebus Apollo heard him. Angry at heart, he strode down from the peaks of Olympus, having his bow slung from his shoulder and his hollow quiver. The arrows clashed loudly upon his shoulders as he strode in his anger, and

> like night did he go. Then he sat apart from the ships and shot an arrow; terrible was the twang of his silver bow. First he shot the mules and the swift dogs, and next he shot his sharp arrow at the men. Constantly were the funeral pyres burning in great numbers.

This is the first appearance of a god in the *Iliad*, and it shows how the gods are participants in the saga of Troy, with Apollo constantly favoring the Trojans. Calchas advised that the evil could be ended only by the return, without ransom, of Chryseïs. Accordingly, she was sent back, but this left Agamemnon without his share of the spoils, a humiliating situation for the greatest of the Greek kings. He therefore took Briseïs from Achilles, and Achilles repaid the dishonor by withdrawing his contingent, the Myrmidons, from the war.

Achilles is the embodiment of heroic *arete* (excellence). Important in the concept of *arete* is one's standing in the eyes of others, which is gained not only by words and deeds but also by gifts and spoils relative to those of others. Therefore, Achilles' honor was slighted when Agamemnon took away Briseïs, and he had good cause to withdraw from the fighting, even though the Greeks suffered terribly as a result. Homer describes the mighty quarrel, during the course of which Athena restrains Achilles from attacking Agamemnon. Homer describes the prophecy of Achilles as he withdraws from the war (1.234–246):[21]

> "By this scepter, which will never grow leaves or roots, since it was cut in the mountains . . . and now the sons of the Achaeans bear it in their hands when they administer justice, for they defend Justice in the name of Zeus—and this will be a great oath: In time all the sons of the Achaeans will long for Achilles. Then you [Agamemnon] will not be able to do anything, grieved though you be, while many men fall in death before Hector, slayer of men. And you will tear your heart, angry that you did not honor the best of the Achaeans." So spoke the son of Peleus, and he cast the golden-studded scepter upon the ground, and down he sat.

Angry, hurt, and resentful, Achilles finds comfort and support from his mother, Thetis. Theirs is a sad and touching relationship, tragic in the knowledge that Achilles has chosen to come to Troy to die young and gloriously rather than stay at home to live a long but mundane existence. Thetis agrees to go to Zeus for help, and she obtains from the supreme god an oath that he will honor her son, whom Agamemnon has dishonored, and grant success to the Trojans in his absence, so that the Greeks will come to regret Agamemnon's actions and increase the glory of Achilles.

At the end of Book 1, it is difficult not to condemn Agamemnon as a guilty, arrogant sinner, first against Apollo and his priest and then against Achilles. Achilles' tragic withdrawal, like Apollo's arrows, will cause the deaths of countless of his Greek companions, and he will be condemned for his selfish, cruel, and pitiless behavior. Yet the wrath of Apollo, until properly appeased, has been just as devastating, heartless, and indiscriminate, causing innumerable deaths, in this case, too, because of the arrogance of Agamemnon. Homer juxtaposes the wrath of Achilles and that of Apollo at the beginning of his epic. Are we to judge the actions of the god and those of the mortal demigod by two different standards?

In Book 3, a truce is agreed upon to allow Menelaüs and Paris to fight in individual combat in order to decide the issues and the fate of Helen. In the duel, Menelaüs gets the better of Paris. He takes hold of Paris by the helmet and swings him around so that he is choked by the neck strap. When Aphrodite notices that Paris is lost, she quickly snatches up her favorite with the ease of a goddess and transports him to his fragrant bedchamber. She goes to summon Helen, who has already witnessed the humiliation of her husband from a high tower of Troy. Although Aphrodite is disguised as an old woman, Helen recognizes the beautiful breasts and flashing eyes of her mirror image, and with this recognition of herself she rebels.

As the scene proceeds, through the literal depiction of the goddess Aphrodite, the inner soul (the psyche) of Helen is laid bare. Helen wonders where in the world beauty and passion—Aphrodite—will lead her next, and in indignation she demands that the goddess abandon Olympus and go herself to Paris until he makes her his wife or his slave. Helen is too ashamed before the eyes of the Trojan women to return to his bed. At this, Aphrodite becomes enraged and threatens to turn against Helen. Helen submissively returns to her bedchamber and to Paris, whom Aphrodite has restored from a bedraggled loser into a beautiful dandy. Yet a disillusioned Helen greets her beloved with these demeaning words (3.428–436):

> You have come out of battle? You ought to have died there, beaten by a stronger man, who was my former husband. To be sure you boasted before that you were mightier than warlike Menelaüs in the might of your hands and your sword. So then go now and challenge warlike Menelaüs again to face you in battle. No, I bid you hold on and do not fight in combat against blond Menelaüs in your rashness, lest somehow you will quickly be subdued by his spear.

Paris responds with characteristic nonchalance, and Aphrodite is victorious once again (3.438–447):

> "My wife, do not rebuke me with harsh words; now Menelaüs has won with the help of Athena. At another time I will beat him, for the gods are on our side too. Come on now, let us go to bed and make love. Never at any time has desire so clouded my senses, not even when we first consummated our love on the island of Cranaë, after I had carried you out of lovely Sparta and we sailed away. This is how I love you now and how sweet desire takes hold of me." He spoke, and led her to bed, and his wife followed along.

In Book 6, Hector, the valiant brother of Paris, seeks out his wife, Andromache, to bid her farewell before returning to the battlefield. On his way he looks in on Paris, who is still dallying with Helen in their home. After his defeat by Menelaüs and his lovemaking with Helen, Paris is sullenly polishing his armor. Hector has presumably interrupted another of their quarrels. Paris tells his brother how Helen has just now been urging him to go out to battle, and he agrees with them both that it is time for him to return. Helen speaks to Hector in words fraught with misery and self-reproach (6.344–358):

> My brother-in-law, how I wish that I—cold, evil-scheming bitch that I am—had died on the day when first I was born before all this had happened—that a terrible blast of wind had hurled me into the side of a mountain or into a wave of the resounding sea to be swept away. But since the gods have so ordained these evils, I wish that I

were the wife of a better man, who felt a sense of guilt and shame before the eyes of society. But his character is not rooted in such values and he will never change, and so I think that he will reap the rewards. Now come here and sit down in this chair, brother-in-law, since the battle toil has crushed you the most, all on account of me, a bitch, and retribution for Paris' guilt. Upon us both has Zeus imposed an evil fate, so that we might become for future generations the subjects for poetic songs.   10

Hector tells Helen that he must be on his way. He finds that his wife, their son Astyanax, and the boy's nurse are not at home; they have been anxiously watching from the battlements in concern for his fate. In the sad farewell between husband and wife, Andromache implores Hector not to go to battle and leave her a widow and their child an orphan. Achilles has already killed her father and seven brothers; he captured their mother, and although he accepted a ransom for her return, she has died too. So Hector is father, mother, and brother to her, as well as dear husband. Hector responds with loving conviction (6.441–484):

"To be sure, all these things are of deep concern to me too, but I should feel terrible shame before the Trojan women with their long robes if like a coward I were to shrink from battle. Nor would my spirit allow me to, since I have learned to be brave always and to fight amid the first of the Trojans, winning great glory for myself and for my father. For I know this well in my heart and in my soul. The day will come when Troy will be destroyed and Priam and the people of Priam of the fine ashen spear. The suffering that will follow for the Trojans—for Hecuba herself and king Priam and my many brave brothers who will fall in the dust under the hands of their enemies—is not so much a grief for me as is the pain that you will endure when one of the bronze-clad Achaeans leads you away weeping and takes from you the day of   10 your liberty. In Greece at another's bidding you will work the loom and draw water from a spring in Laconia or Thessaly, much against your will, but heavy necessity will lie upon you. Then someone, seeing you in tears, will say, 'This is the wife of Hector, who was by far the best fighter when the horse-taming Trojans did battle for Ilium.' Thus at some time will someone speak, and your grief will be awakened anew because you are without such a husband to ward off the day of your slavery. But may I die with the earth heaped up over my grave before I hear your cries of anguish as you are dragged away a captive." (6.441–465)

Thus radiant Hector spoke and reached out for his son, but the child clung to the bosom of the fair-girdled nurse, screaming in dismay at the sight of his father,   20 startled as he saw the bronze crest of his helmet and the horsehair plume nodding dreadful from its peak. His dear father laughed aloud, and his lady mother, and immediately Hector took the helmet from his head and placed it all-shining on the ground. Then he kissed his dear son and fondled him in his arms and spoke in prayer to Zeus and the other gods: (6.466–475)

"Zeus and you other gods, grant that this son of mine become outstanding among the Trojans, just as I am, excellent in his might and a strong ruler over Ilium. Some day let someone say that this boy has turned out to be far better than his father, as he comes out of the battle, and when he has killed his enemy may he bring home the gory spoils and may his mother rejoice in her heart." Thus speaking he   30 placed his son in the hands of his dear wife. She took him to her fragrant bosom, laughing amid her tears. (6.476–484)

Hector and Andromache, by Giorgio de Chirico (1888–1978); oil on canvas, 1917, 35½ × 23½ in. Husband and wife, mannequins backed by receding frames, part at the Scaean Gate in an austere, stage-like setting with receding perspective. They are sheathed in geometrically shaped metallic plates, and the baby Astyanax is reduced to a steel wedge with a black disk for his head. De Chirico's images of the intersection of war and the family are a disturbing interpretation of Homer's moving scene. (*Scala/Art Resource, NY*)

On two other occasions, Andromache prophesies her fate and that of her son and of the city, each time addressing Hector's corpse. Here is how she takes her farewell of him (24.725–738):

> My husband, you were young when you were taken from life, and you leave me a widow in the palace. The boy is still just a baby, who is our child, yours and mine, ill-fated that we are. I do not think that he will grow to manhood, for the city will first be utterly sacked now that you, its guardian, are dead, who defended the city, the chaste wives, and the little children. They will soon go away in the hollow ships, and

> I with them. And you, my child, either will go with me, where you will perform demeaning tasks, laboring for a harsh master; or else one of the Achaeans will take you by the hand and hurl you in anger from the tower—a grim death—because Hector once killed his brother or father or son.

Indeed, Andromache became the slave of Neoptolemus after the fall of Troy, and her infant son Astyanax was thrown from the city walls.

A major development in the theme of Achilles' wrath occurs in the ninth book. Should Achilles have relented when Agamemnon offered to restore Briseïs with many valuable gifts? It is a measure of his sensitive and passionate nature that he refused the offer, presented by three envoys, Odysseus, Phoenix, and Ajax, son of Telamon.

Odysseus' speech to Achilles echoes for the most part the directions given by Agamemnon, but it begins and ends with more tactful and artful persuasion. In describing the successes of the Trojans, Odysseus emphasizes the danger to Achilles and the opportunity to destroy Hector. The fury of Hector cannot wait to come down to destroy their ships. Then he lists the gifts to be given to Achilles immediately upon his return: seven tripods, ten talents of gold, twenty shining cauldrons, twelve prize-winning horses, seven women from Lesbos, particularly beautiful and skilled (whom Achilles had picked out for himself when he took Lesbos!), and Briseïs, with a solemn oath that Agamemnon had never slept with her. In addition, if the gods were to grant that Priam's city be sacked, Achilles might heap up his ship with gold and bronze and choose twenty Trojan women for himself, the most beautiful after Helen. Beyond this, if they return safely to Greece, Agamemnon promises to make Achilles his son-in-law, with a dowry larger than any ever given before and a kingdom of seven rich cities over which he might rule like a god.

At the conclusion of his speech, Odysseus is careful not to repeat Agamemnon's final instructions: "Let him be subdued—Hades is the most hateful of gods and mortals because he is inexorable and inflexible. Let him submit to me, inasmuch as I am more royal and assert that I am the elder" (9.158–161). Instead Odysseus, with more tact and wisdom, begs that Achilles, even if his anger and hatred of Agamemnon are too great for forgiveness, should at least have pity on the other Greeks, who are worn out in battle and will upon his return honor him like a god. In conclusion, Odysseus tries to win Achilles over by playing upon his jealousy of Hector's arrogant success, implying that now is his chance to achieve his desire for glory through the defeat of Hector, who thinks that no Greek is his match. By questioning some of these values in his reply, Achilles reveals a sensitivity and introspection that make him unique (9.309–345):

> I must give a direct answer to your speech, telling you honestly what I think and what I will do, so that you ambassadors may not try to wheedle me one after the other. For I hate the man who hides one thing in his heart and says something else as much as I hate Hades and his realm. I will say outright what seems to me best. I do not believe that the son of Atreus, Agamemnon, will persuade me, nor will the other Greeks, since it was no pleasure for me always to fight against the enemy relentlessly. The coward is held in equal honor with the brave man who endures and fights hard, and equal is his fate. The one who does nothing and the one who does much find a similar end in death. It was no advantage to me when I suffered deeply, continually risking my life in battle. As a bird brings food to her unfledged nestlings,

10

> after she has won it with much distress, so I used to spend many sleepless nights and endure days of blood in fighting against enemies belligerent in the defense of their wives. (9.309–327)
>
> Indeed, I say to you, I plundered twelve populated cities by ship and attacked another eleven by land; from all these I took many splendid treasures and brought them back to give to Agamemnon, the son of Atreus. He who had remained behind by his swift ships took them, distributing a few things but keeping much for himself. All that he gave as prizes to the nobles and kings they keep secure; it was from me alone of the Achaeans that he stole. He has a dear wife; let him sleep with her for his pleasure. Why must the Greeks fight with the Trojans? Why did the son of Atreus gather an army to bring here? Was it not on account of Helen with her beautiful hair? Are the sons of Atreus the only ones among mortals who love their wives? To be sure, any decent and responsible man loves and cares for his own, just as I loved Briseïs from the depths of my heart, even though she was won by my spear. As it is now, since he took my prize out of my hands and deceived me, let him not try me, since I know him too well—he will not persuade me. (9.328–345)

20

Achilles' response continues at some length. He makes it clear that he despises gifts from Agamemnon, however grand they may be, and he has no need or desire to be chosen as his son-in-law. Surely Agamemnon could find someone more royal and worthy of respect! The shameless Agamemnon, "dog that he is, would not dare to look me in the face!" The gifts are excessively generous, but Achilles sees through Agamemnon's facade. This is not reconciliation but bribery. Many critics have said, with some justice, that Achilles by his rejection of these gifts has gone too far in his pride and that he is guilty of the sin of hubris. He should understand, they say, that Agamemnon cannot humiliate himself by coming to Achilles with apologies, as if to a god. Is it really too much, however, to ask a good king to admit his error in person? Agamemnon by his royal arrogance may be as guilty as Achilles, if not more so, because he, the commander-in-chief, is ultimately responsible for all the slaughter and suffering that might have been avoided.

So Agamemnon's attempt to win Achilles back has failed. Achilles' old tutor, Phoenix, also tries to persuade Achilles, but to no avail. In the course of his speech, he draws a parallel between Achilles and the hero, Meleager, who foolishly rejected gifts (see the appendix to this chapter). The third envoy, the warrior Ajax, son of Telamon, bluntly concludes the embassy (9.628–638):

> Achilles has put a savage and proud spirit within his breast. Obdurate, he does not care for the love of his friends, with which we honored him above all men beside the ships, unpitying as he is. Yet others have accepted payment for the death of a brother or a son. . . . But the gods have put in your breast a spirit unforgiving and harsh, because of one girl.

Without Achilles, the Greeks were driven back by the Trojans until Hector began to set fire to the ships. All this was done, says Homer, in fulfillment of the will of Zeus (1.5), for Zeus had agreed to honor Achilles in this way after Thetis had prayed to him to avenge the wrong done by Agamemnon.

When Hector broke through to the Greek ships, Achilles finally allowed his friend and companion, Patroclus, to take his armor and fight Hector and the Trojans. For a while, Patroclus carried all before him, even killing Sarpedon, son of Zeus. But he went too far in his fury. Homer (16.786–867) describes how Apollo opposed him in the battle and struck him across the back with his hand. Patroclus was dazed by the blow, and the Trojan Euphorbus wounded him with a spear. It was left for Hector to deal the death blow to the enfeebled and stunned Patroclus.

The death of Patroclus is the turning point of the epic. Achilles is overcome by grief, guilt, and remorse. His anguish is so terrifying that his comrades fear he may take his own life. Yet his mother, Thetis, provides comfort once again as Achilles steadfastly makes the tragic decision to return to battle to avenge Patroclus and so, assuredly, to fix the seal upon his own fate. At the beginning of Book 18, Antilochus, son of Nestor, who brings the tragic news of Patroclus' death, finds Achilles agonized with anxiety and fear that Patroclus has ignored his warning not to fight Hector and is dead. Antilochus, in tears, addresses Achilles (18.18–38):

> "Ah, son of brave Peleus, you must hear my painful message—how I wish this had never happened—Patroclus lies dead and they are fighting over his corpse, which is naked. Hector with the flashing helmet has taken his armor." (18.18–21)
>
> Thus he spoke, and a black cloud of grief enveloped Achilles. He clutched the black dirt with both his hands and poured it over his head, and his handsome face was defiled. The dark filth covered his immortal tunic and he, his mighty self, lay stretched out mightily on the ground, and he tore at his hair and befouled it. (18.22–27)
>
> And the women whom Achilles and Patroclus had taken as captives, stricken to the heart with grief, cried aloud and ran out to surround great Achilles, and they all beat their breasts and the limbs of each of them went limp. Antilochus also by his side, shedding tears and lamenting, restrained the hands of Achilles, whose proud heart was overwhelmed with sorrow, because he feared that he would cut his throat with his sword. Achilles cried out a terrifying scream of woe, and his divine mother heard him, as she sat beside her aged father Nereus in the depths of the sea and in turn she answered with a cry. The goddesses gathered around her, all her sister Nereids who were there in the deep sea. (18.28–38)

10

Homer goes on to name all these Nereids in lines that read very much like a catalog that might have been composed by Hesiod. Homer then continues (18.50–126):

> Together all the Nereids beat their breasts and Thetis began her lament: (50–51)
>
> "Hear me, my sisters, daughters of Nereus, so that all of you, once you have listened, will know well how many sorrows are in my heart. Ah, poor me, unhappy mother of the best of sons born for an evil fate, since I give birth to a child, both blameless and strong, the best of heroes. He shot up like a young sapling, and I nurtured him and he flourished like a tree, growing up strong, the pride of the orchard. But then I sent him forth with the curved ships to battle against the Trojans on Ilium. He will not return home to the house of Peleus, and I will never get him back again. All the while that he lives and looks upon the light of the sun, he suffers in anguish, and when I go to him I am not able to help him at all. Nevertheless, I will go to him in order to see my dear son and I will listen to the sorrow that has come to him as he stays out of the battle." (18.52–64)
>
> Thetis lamented thus and left her cavern and her sisters went with her, in tears, and the swell of the sea broke and gave way. When they reached fertile Troy, they

10

all came to shore in an orderly stream, where the cluster of the Myrmidons' ships were anchored close by swift Achilles. His divine mother stood before him, as she heaved a deep sigh, and uttering a sharp cry she clasped the head of her son and grieving spoke winged words: "My son, why are you weeping? What sorrow has touched your heart? Tell me and don't keep it hidden. These things have been brought to fulfillment through Zeus, just as you once wanted, lifting your hands in prayer that all the sons of the Achaeans be pinned against the prows of their ships and suffer terrible atrocities, all because of their need for you." (18.65–77)

20

Achilles, swift of foot, groaning deeply answered: "Mother, Olympian Zeus has accomplished these things for me but what joy is there in them now, since my dear friend has perished, Patroclus, whom I loved more than my other comrades, loved as much as my own life. I have lost him. Hector has killed him and stripped him of my mighty armor, wondrous to behold. The gods gave it to Peleus, a splendid gift, on the day when they brought you to the bed of a mortal man. How I wish you had continued to live among the immortal goddesses of the sea and Peleus had won a mortal wife! But as it is now there must be endless sorrow in your heart for the death of your son, whom you will never welcome back again, as he returns home. For I have no more heart to go on living, unless Hector first is struck down by my spear and loses his life and pays the price for stripping my armor from Patroclus, son of Menoetius." (18.78–93)

30

Thetis then in turn answered him amid her tears: "My son, your life will soon be over from what you are saying. For right after the death of Hector, your own death is at hand." (18.94–96)

Then in great distress Achilles, swift of foot, answered her: "So may I die at once, since it was never destined to save my comrade from death. He has perished very far from his fatherland because he did not have me, with my prowess in war, as protector. Now then alas I will not return to my fatherland and I did not become any light of salvation for Patroclus or my other comrades, so many of whom were struck down by mighty Hector. But I sit by my ships, useless, a burden on the earth, though I am superior in battle like no other of the bronze-armored Achaeans, even if others are better speakers in counsel. I wish strife would disappear from among both gods and human beings and wrath, which has sent even the most sensible into a rage and which, much more sweet than the dripping of honey, wells up in the breasts of men like smoke. Thus the king of men Agamemnon enraged me, but we will let this be a thing of the past, and even though I am angry I will overcome the anger in my heart because I have to. For now I will go back into battle so that I may seek out Hector, the slayer of my dear friend. I will accept my own death whenever Zeus wishes to bring it about or the other immortal gods. For not even Heracles in his might escaped death, he who was most dear to Zeus the king, son of Cronus, but fate defeated him and the fierce anger of Hera. So I too, if a like fate has been fashioned for me, will lie down in acceptance when death comes. But now may I win goodly renown and compel some one of the Trojan women or deep-girdled Dardanians to wipe away the tears from her tender cheeks with both her hands in her outburst of grief and may they so realize that I have stayed away from the fighting for too long a time. Do not try to keep me away from the battle, however much you love me because you will not persuade me." (18.97–126)

40

50

60

Thetis sadly agrees with Achilles' tragic decision to determine his own death by avenging Patroclus, and she tells him that she will go to Hephaestus to have new armor made for him.

Grief over the death of Patroclus drove Achilles to end his quarrel with Agamemnon and to return to the fighting with one goal, to kill Hector. So Briseïs was returned with costly gifts, and upon her return she lamented over the corpse of Patroclus (19.287–300):

> Patroclus, most dear to my unhappy heart, I left you alive when I was taken from the hut, and now upon my return I find you, leader of the host, dead. Thus for me evil follows upon evil. I saw my husband, to whom my father and lady mother gave me, transfixed by a sharp spear in front of his city, and my dear brothers, all three born to our mother, on that day found their way to ruinous death. You would not let me cry when swift Achilles killed my husband and sacked the city of godlike Mynes, but you said that I would be made the wedded wife of god-like Achilles and that I would be taken back in his ship to Phthia to celebrate our marriage among the Myrmidons. So I lament for you unceasingly, you who were always gentle.   10

Thetis brought new armor, made by Hephaestus, to her son. Homer describes the shield of Achilles in detail, with its portrayal of the human world of the Mycenaeans—cities at war and at peace, scenes of farming and other peaceful activities (a lawsuit, for example, marriage, dancing, and music).

Meanwhile, Hector has spoiled Patroclus' corpse of the armor of Achilles, which he himself put on. As he changes his armor, Zeus watches and foretells his doom (17.194–208):

> He put on the immortal armor of Achilles, son of Peleus, which the gods had given to his father and he in turn in his old age gave to Achilles his son. But the son did not grow old in the armor. And when Zeus the cloud-gatherer saw Hector from afar arming himself with the arms of the godlike son of Peleus, he moved his head and spoke to his own heart: "Ah, wretched man! You do not now think of death that will come close to you. You are putting on the immortal arms of the best of men, before whom others also tremble. That man's friend you have killed, gentle and strong, and you have taken the arms from his head and shoulders, as you should not have done. For now I will give you great strength. In return, Andromache will never take the noble arms of the son of Peleus from you when you return from battle.   10

Achilles returned to the battle and drove the Trojans back to the city, in his rage fighting even the river-god Scamander and filling the river with Trojan corpses. Eventually, the Trojans were driven into the city, and only Hector remained outside the wall. The single combat between Hector and Achilles is the climax of the *Iliad*. Hector is chased by Achilles three times around the walls; "as in a dream the pursuer cannot catch him who is running away, nor can he who runs escape nor the other catch him" (22.199–200). Finally, Zeus agrees to the death of Hector (*Iliad*, 22.209–214):

> Then indeed the Father held up the golden scales, and in them he put two lots of grievous death, the one for Achilles, and the other for Hector, tamer of horses, and he held the scales by the middle. And the fatal day of Hector sank down toward the house of Hades. Then Phoebus Apollo left Hector, and Athena, the gray-eyed goddess, came to the son of Peleus.

Athena helps Achilles by leading Hector to his death through treachery. She takes the form of his brother, Deïphobus, in whom Hector, now rendered defenseless, puts his final trust (22.294–301):

> He called with a great shout to white-shielded Deïphobus and asked for a long spear, but Deïphobus was nowhere near him. And Hector knew the truth in his heart and said, "Alas! Now for sure the gods have summoned me deathward. For I thought that the hero Deïphobus was beside me, but he is inside the walls and Athena has deceived me. Now indeed evil death is not far away but very near, and I have no way out."

Deserted by the gods and deceived by Athena, Hector died at the hands of Achilles, who refused to show any mercy and dragged the corpse back to his hut behind his chariot. Next Achilles celebrated the funeral of Patroclus, on whose pyre he sacrificed twelve Trojan prisoners. He also held athletic games in honor of Patroclus, at which he presided and gave valuable prizes for the winners. Yet his anger against Hector was still unassuaged, and daily for twelve days he dragged Hector's body round the tomb of Patroclus behind his chariot; the mutilated corpse was refreshed and restored by Apollo each day. Only when Thetis

Priam and Achilles. Red-figure skyphos, by the Brygos painter, ca. 490 B.C. This is one of the finest and most striking renderings of the Ransom of Hector. Priam, white haired and holding a walking staff, approaches Achilles from the left. Behind Priam four attendants, two men (shown here) followed by two women, bring the gifts. Achilles reclines on a banquet couch alongside the banquet table still laden with food. The couch, covered with mattress and blanket, is handsomely built and decorated. Achilles is turning to address a serving boy. He holds a piece of meat in his left hand, which rests on two large cushions, and a dagger in his right, which he has brought to his lips. Achilles has not yet noticed Priam's arrival. Hector's wounded body can clearly be seen beneath the couch in full view. While this detail is contrary to Homer's tale, vase painters often included the body of Hector for dramatic effect. Another added feature is the presence of Hector's (formerly Achilles') armor on the wall and a shield with a gorgoneion (a representation of a stylized head of a Gorgon). The artist has also taken liberties with the timing of the scene. In Homer, Achilles has just finished eating when Priam enters. This slight change has resulted in a stark contrast that is particularly gruesome: Achilles eating meat with the corpse beneath, while grease from the food drips onto the bloody body. The horror of the scene is fully realized when one recalls both Achilles' vow to refrain from eating until he has avenged the death of Patroclus and his threat to Hector, just before he kills him, that if he had the heart, he would tear his flesh apart and eat him raw. (*Erich Lessing/Art Resource, NY*)

brought him the message of Zeus was Achilles ready to relent. Priam himself, with the help of Hermes, came to Achilles' hut and ransomed the corpse of his son. The scene where the old man kneels before the killer of so many of his sons is one of the most moving in all Greek saga (24.477–484):

> Great Priam entered, unseen by Achilles' companions, and stood near Achilles. With his hands he took hold of Achilles' knees and kissed his hands, hands terrible and

The Death of Hector, by Peter Paul Rubens (1577–1640); 43 × 50 in. A *modello* is the second stage of preparatory designs for a tapestry, following a smaller oil sketch and preceding a larger cartoon. Rubens designed a series of eight tapestries depicting *The Life of Achilles*, of which *The Death of Hector* was the seventh. Since tapestry weavers worked from the back of the web, the figures in the *modello* are left-handed. The scene depicts the fatal thrust of Achilles' spear (which had been given back to Achilles by Athena after it had first missed its target) into Hector's throat (*Iliad* 22.326–329). Hector, armed only with a sword (for his spear, too, had missed its mark, but there was no goddess to restore it), looks at Achilles, still able to ask for a decent burial. His request will be denied, for his body will be dragged around the walls of Troy (shown in the right background with anxious Trojans gathered before the towers of the gate and on the walls) by the horses that appear in the left background. Athena, accompanied by her owl and with a spear in her left hand, hovers above to give encouragement to Achilles. Prominent in the center is the shield of Achilles, the subject of much of Book 18 of the *Iliad*, and behind it flows the river Scamander. The herm (a column with the head of a divine figure) on the left represents Heracles, who had first sacked Troy (see p. 552): his club rests against the herm. The herm on the right represents Ares, whose head is turned away from Hector. Above two *putti* hold a cartouche, into which a Latin metrical inscription was inserted in the tapestry. At the bottom is an altar, on which lie two cornucopias filled with the victor's palm fronds; in its center are two fighting cocks. (*LAMMERTSE, FRISO AND VERGARA, ALEJANDRO; PETER PAUL RUBENS, THE LIFE OF ACHILLES* © 2003 NAi Publishers Rotterdam)

> man-killing, which had killed many of Priam's sons. . . . Achilles was full of wonder as he looked at godlike Priam, and the others also wondered and they looked at each other.

When Priam has made his appeal to Achilles and they both have had their fill of lamentation, each remembering his sorrows, Achilles explains the ultimate reason for human misery (24.524–532):

> No [human] action is without chilling grief. For thus the gods have spun out for wretched mortals the fate of living in distress, while they live without care. Two jars sit on the doorsill of Zeus, filled with gifts that he bestows, one jar of evils, the other of blessings. When Zeus, who delights in thunder, takes from both and mixes the bad with the good, a human being at one time encounters evil, and at another

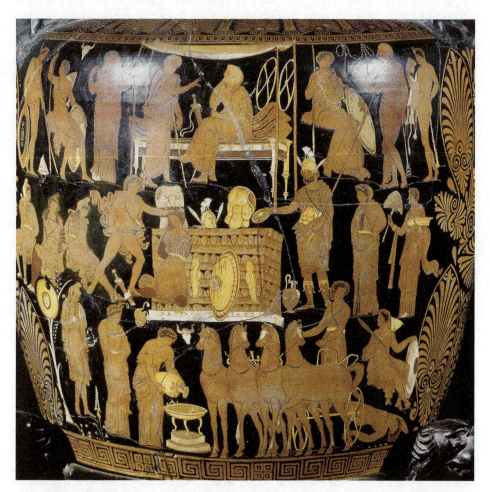

The Funeral of Patroclus. Apulian red-figure krater by the Darius painter, ca. 330 B.C.; height 56 in. In the central panel is the pyre with Hector's spoils (originally Achilles' armor worn by Patroclus) on it. To its left Achilles holds a Trojan prisoner by her hair before running her through with his sword: three other bound prisoners to the left await the same fate. To the right of the pyre, Agamemnon pours a libation. In the lower panel, the charioteer of Achilles, Automedon, prepares to drag the corpse of Hector behind the four-horse chariot around the tomb of Patroclus. In the upper register of the central panel, the old warriors Nestor (seated) and Phoenix converse in a tent. (© *Alinari Archives/Art Resource, NY*)

> good. But the one to whom Zeus gives only troubles from the jar of sorrows, this one he makes an object of abuse, to be driven by cruel misery over the divine earth.

Through suffering, Achilles has finally learned true compassion. His pessimistic view of human existence lies at the core of the Greek tragic view of life. It is a view mirrored with sad beauty by Herodotus, as we have seen in Chapter 6, and echoed again and again by the dramatists, who delight in the splendid fall of those who were once great and blessed. "Never count a person happy until dead."

So Priam ransomed Hector and returned to Troy with the corpse. The *Iliad* ends with the funeral of Hector, over whose body Andromache, Hecuba, and finally Helen had poured out their lamentations. For nine days the people of Troy mourned for Hector, whose death had made inevitable their own fate.

Achilles is not only subject to vehement passions. Alone of the Greek heroes he knows his destiny clearly: to Odysseus' speech in the embassy he replies (9.410–416):

> My mother, Thetis of the silver feet, has told me that two fates are carrying me to the goal of my death. If I stay here and fight before the city of the Trojans, then I lose my homecoming, but my glory will never fade. But if I return home to my own dear land, then gone is my noble glory, and my life will be long.

The character of Achilles is perfectly expressed in these words. When his horse, Xanthus, prophesies his death (19.404–417), Achilles replies:

> Well do I know that my destiny is to die here, far from my dear father and mother. Even so, I shall keep on. I shall not stop until I have harried the Trojans enough with my warfare. (19.421–423)

Again, when the dying Hector foretells Achilles' death, Achilles resolutely accepts his fate. Nor is Achilles always violent. At the funeral games for Patroclus, he presides with princely dignity and even makes peace between the hot-tempered competitors. We have also seen how he gave up his anger against Hector and treated Priam with dignity and generosity. Achilles is a splendid and complex hero, incomparably the greatest figure in the Trojan saga.

The Olympian Gods in Battle

The gods are all-important participants in the Trojan War. We have seen in Chapter 5 (pp. 124–127) how Hephaestus settles the quarrel between Zeus and Hera at the end of the first book of the *Iliad*, an episode that vividly displays the gulf between mortal and immortal emotions. The first book sets forth the quarrel between Agamemnon and Achilles, which (as the poet says in the second line of the poem) ends in the death of so many people. In contrast, the quarrel between Zeus and Hera ends in laughter and lovemaking. We also have seen in Chapter 5 (p. 116) the sacred marriage of Zeus and Hera in Book 14 of the *Iliad*, the union of sky-god and earth-goddess. Usually, the gods are distant observers of human battle, which is nevertheless a direct concern to them. Yet individual gods and goddesses sometimes take part in battle by helping or protecting their mortal favorites.

In two episodes (which are called **theomachies**), however, the gods themselves fight each other on the battlefield. In the first of these, Athena descends to the battle in a chariot with Hera. We translate here the description of her arming (*Iliad* 5.736–747):

> Athena put on a tunic and armed herself for tear-filled battle with the armor of Zeus, the cloud-gatherer. Round her shoulders she put the tasseled aegis, a fearsome sight, ringed all around with Fear. In it is Strife, in it is Might, in it is icy Pursuit, in it is the head of the frightening monster Gorgon—a terrible and grim image, the

The Universality of the *Iliad*

Since the *Iliad*, if not before, war has served as one of the greatest themes in all literature, a universal human experience, one that lays bare the extremes of human character and passion and explores with wrenching intensity the heights and depths of human relationships. What age has not known war, despite all condemnation, a universal and persistent plague? What man and woman do not care about how they are seen by others? Who has never let rage control action? Who has not had to face an encounter and quailed before it in fear? Who has never felt controlled by a greater power that cares little for the lot of humans and has never questioned standards of moral behavior or concluded that we are all victims and that injustice too often motivates human action? The archetypal Trojan War has become a mirror through which we see war forever, not only in all its devastating horror and brutality but also in the lofty grandeur of the achievements it can inspire in the face of life and death: we see men and women, husbands and wives, brothers and sisters challenged by the most harrowing ordeals, which put them to the test and define their bravery or cowardice, their love or betrayal, their selfishness or their patriotism. The great heroes and heroines of the *Iliad*, in their diversity and scope, transcend the mores of their time and place to epitomize us all. It is easy to recognize not only the men as prototypes but also the women from the depth and grandeur of individual depictions: Andromache, the deeply devoted wife of Hector and mother of Astyanax; Hecuba, the powerful and aged queen, loving wife and mother, who sees her Hector killed and will eventually lose her husband and all her children and be reduced to utter desolation; Helen, trapped by her own passion, as she herself admits, between two opposing forces, a woman of grand stature, the focal point of the entire struggle. The reinterpretations of Helen's character since the time of Homer to the present day have been legion, with judgments ranging from guilty whore to guiltless victim.[22] Her beauty has inspired countless poems: Christopher Marlowe made her an object of sensual desire in *Dr. Faustus* with the lines beginning, "Was this the face that launched a thousand ships / and burn't the topless towers of Ilium?" For Goethe, in *Faust* (part 2, act 3), she symbolized all that is beautiful in classical antiquity (see Chapter 27 on the companion website).

The universality of the *Iliad* and the devastating truth of Homer's depiction of war and its hero Achilles find powerful and specific confirmation in a book by Jonathan Shay that illuminates the experiences and sufferings of Vietnam veterans through a study of the *Iliad*, in particular the character and emotions of Achilles.[23] Shay, a psychiatrist who appreciates Homer's contemporary value, finds parallel themes such as these: betrayal of "what's right" by a commander; the shrinkage of social and moral horizons; intense comradeship reduced to a few friends; and the death of one of these special comrades, followed by feelings of grief and guilt culminating in a berserk rage.

sign of Zeus the aegis-carrier. On her head she put the double-crested golden helmet with its four metal plates, decorated with images of defenders of a hundred cities. She climbed into the fiery chariot, she grasped the heavy, long spear, with which she lays low the ranks of men with whom she, daughter of a mighty Father, is angry.

She helps Diomedes and herself takes part in the fighting. Even Aphrodite enters the battle and is wounded by Diomedes—a mortal wounding an immortal. Aphrodite returns to Olympus and is comforted by her mother, Dione (*Iliad* 5.382–384):

Be patient, my child, and endure, even though you are in pain. For many of us who dwell in the palaces of Olympus have endured suffering caused by men, causing harsh pain to each other.

Dione goes on to name gods who have been wounded by mortals. Finally, Zeus, alerted by Athena and Hera, says to Aphrodite (*Iliad* 5.428–430):

Battle is not your gift, my child. You should busy yourself with the work of desire and love. Leave all this business to swift Ares and Athena.

Diomedes wounds even the god of war himself, Ares, who complains to Zeus and finds little sympathy (see pp. 129–130).

The second theomachy is in Books 20 and 21. In the Council of the Gods at the beginning of Book 20, Zeus gives the gods permission to fight on the field of battle, while he remains above it all (*Iliad* 20.22–25):

I will stay here in a fold of Olympus: I will watch from my seat and delight my mind. You other gods may go to the Trojans and Achaeans and give help to both sides, wherever you decide.

Thus the battle becomes more violent, as the gods inspire the heroes with fighting spirit and themselves take part. Once again the contrast is drawn between the reality of human suffering and the triviality of the gods' injuries. Mortals must fight and die: the wounds of the immortals are soon healed.

Not all the gods who are on the battlefield fight. Poseidon challenges Apollo, who replies (*Iliad* 21.462–467):

Earth-shaker, you would not say I was prudent if I were to fight you for the sake of wretched mortals. They are like leaves that flourish with fiery colors, for a little while eating the fruits of the earth. Then they fade away and perish, lifeless. Let us, however, stop fighting now, and let mortals fight.

The theomachies help us see the unbridgeable gap between the mortal and the divine. They show that it *is* ridiculous for gods to fight like mortals, yet they also show that human warfare is a concern of the Olympians. The theomachies, by recognizing the triviality of divine pain, serve to illuminate human suffering. Nor should we take them too seriously: we end this discussion with the description of Hera's attack on Artemis (*Iliad* 21.489–496):

> Hera spoke and with her left hand seized Artemis by her wrists. With her right hand she stripped the bow and arrows from her shoulder, and with a smile she boxed her ears and stunned her. Out fell the arrows from the quiver. In tears the goddess [Artemis] fled like a pigeon that flies into a hole in a rock chased by a hawk (for it was not fated that the pigeon should be caught)—even so did Artemis run away in tears and left her bow and arrows there.

The Fall of Troy

The brilliance of the *Iliad* makes the rest of the saga of the Trojan War pale by comparison. Episodes are recorded in summaries of lost epics, in drama, in many vase paintings, and in Vergil's *Aeneid*, so that we can tell the story of the rest of the war.

Achilles and Penthesilea

After the funeral of Hector, the fighting resumed, and Achilles killed the leaders of two contingents that came from the ends of the earth to help the Trojans. From the north came the Amazons—the legendary warrior women—led by Penthesilea. Achilles killed her; in some versions, just as Achilles was about to deal the fatal thrust, their eyes met and he fell in love with her.[24] Achilles mourned over her death and her beauty and killed Thersites, who taunted him.[25] For this murder Achilles had to withdraw for a time to Lesbos, where he was purified by Odysseus.

Achilles and Memnon

A second foreign contingent was that of the Ethiopians, from the south. They were led by Memnon, son of Eos (Aurora), goddess of the dawn, and of Tithonus (a brother of Priam). After Memnon's death, his followers were turned into birds that fought around his tomb. Achilles did not long survive these victories.

The Death of Achilles

As he pursued the Trojans toward the city, Achilles was fatally wounded in the heel by an arrow shot by Paris with the help of Apollo. After a fierce fight, his corpse was recovered by Ajax, son of Telamon, and buried at Sigeum, the promontory near Troy. Agamemnon's ghost tells the ghost of Achilles about the battle over his corpse and his splendid funeral. The Greeks prepared the corpse for cremation and shaved their heads. Thetis herself came from the sea accompanied by her sea-nymphs, and, with the Muses, they mourned with wailing and dirges, while the Greeks wept (*Odyssey* 24.63–70):

> For seventeen days and nights, immortal gods and mortal men, we wept for you. On the eighteenth we gave you to burning fire, and we sacrificed flocks of fat sheep. You were burned in the clothing of the gods, anointed with oil and sweet honey. Many of the Achaean heroes paraded in armor around the burning pyre, men on foot and horseback, and a loud roar arose.

Agamemnon describes how Achilles' bones were put in a golden urn by Thetis, mixed with those of Patroclus. Then the great tomb was raised, and Thetis gave funeral games in honor of her dead son. Thus Achilles, the greatest of Greek heroes, was given a funeral and burial that would ensure his fame for posterity.[26] (See *The Funeral of Patroclus*, p. 491.)

The ghost of Achilles appeared to the Greeks after the sack of Troy and demanded that Polyxena, the daughter of Priam and Hecuba, be sacrificed at his tomb. The sacrifice of Polyxena is one of the principal themes of Euripides' tragedy *Hecuba*, in which the dignity and virtue of Polyxena are a striking contrast to the violence of the young Greeks and their leaders. Thus the aftermath of the war involved the sacrifice of a maiden before the Greek army just as it had been preceded by the sacrifice of Iphigenia. In a version especially popular in medieval legend, Polyxena had been loved by Achilles, and it was while he was meeting her that he was ambushed and killed by Paris.

Odysseus and Ajax Compete for the Armor of Achilles

Achilles' armor was claimed by both Odysseus and Ajax, son of Telamon, as the leading warriors surviving on the Greek side. Each made a speech before an assembly of the Greeks, presided over by Athena. Trojan prisoners gave evidence that Odysseus had done them more harm than Ajax, and the arms were awarded to Odysseus. The disgrace of losing sent Ajax mad; he slaughtered a flock of sheep (which he believed were his enemies) and on becoming sane again killed himself for shame by falling on his sword. From his blood sprang a flower (perhaps a type of hyacinth) with the initials of his name (AI-AI) on its petals.[27]

This legend is the subject of Sophocles' tragedy *Ajax*, in which the hostility of Athena toward Ajax contrasts with Odysseus' appreciation of the human predicament. Athena asks Odysseus if he knows of a hero who was greater than Ajax, and his reply is a final commentary on the heroic tragedy of the *Iliad* (Sophocles, *Ajax* 121–133):

> ODYSSEUS: I do not know [of a greater hero]. I pity him in his misery, nevertheless, although he is my enemy. Because he is yoked to evil madness [*ate*], I look at this man's troubles no more than at my own. For I see that we who live are nothing more than ghosts and weightless shadows. (121–126)
> ATHENA: Therefore when you see such things, say nothing yourself against the gods and swear no boastful oath if your hand is heavy [with success] or with deep and enduring wealth. For time lays low and brings back again all human things. The gods love those who are moderate [*sophrones*] and hate those who are evil. (127–133)

We can hardly find a better expression of the way in which the Greeks used mythology to express their deepest understanding of human life.

The Roman poet Ovid tells the story of Ajax and the armor of Achilles at length. Here is how he describes its end (*Metamorphoses* 13.382–398):

> The Greek leaders were impressed [i.e., by the speech of Odysseus], and the power of eloquence was made clear in the consequences. The eloquent man took away the armor of the brave warrior. Ajax, who alone so many times had resisted Hector, who had opposed iron missiles and fire and the will of Jupiter, could not resist one

thing, anger. Shame conquered the unconquered hero. He seized the sword and thrust the lethal blade into his breast, never before wounded. The ground reddened with his blood and put forth a purple flower from the green grass, the flower which earlier had sprung from the wound of Hyacinthus. The same letters were written on the petals for hero and youth, for the one signifying his name, for the other the mourning cry.

10

The Deaths of Paris and Priam

After Achilles' death, Odysseus captured Helenus, who told the Greeks of a number of conditions that must be fulfilled before they could capture the city. Among these conditions was the summoning of two absent heroes, Neoptolemus (Pyrrhus) and Philoctetes. As we have mentioned, Philoctetes was brought from Lemnos, cured of his snakebite, and with his indispensable bow and arrows shot Paris. Neoptolemus (his name means "new recruit"), the son of Achilles, proved himself to be a brutal warrior; his butchering of Priam at the altar during the sack of Troy is one of the most moving scenes in the *Aeneid*. Vergil's description of Priam's remains echoes a familiar theme: the once mighty king now "lies, a great and mutilated body, head torn from the shoulders, a nameless corpse on the seashore" (2.557–558).

The Wooden Horse

The Greeks finally took the city by deception. One of them, **Epeus,** built an enormous hollow wooden horse, in which the leading warriors were concealed. The *Iliad* does not mention the Trojan horse, which is repeatedly mentioned in the *Odyssey*. In Book 8 the bard, **Demodocus,** sings a second song at the request of Odysseus, whose identity has not yet been revealed (*Odyssey* 8.487–495):

[Odysseus speaks:] "Demodocus, I honor you above all mortals. A Muse, daughter of Zeus, was your teacher, or Apollo, for well do you sing in proper order of the sorrows of the Greeks—their deeds and sufferings and labors—as if you yourself had been there or had heard them from another. Come now, and change your song: sing of the wooden horse, which Epeus made with the help of Athena. Odysseus brought it as a deception into the acropolis [of Troy], when he had filled it with men who sacked Troy."

Demodocus then tells the story of the horse, in which Odysseus has the most prominent role (*Odyssey* 8.502–515):

They [i.e., the Greek heroes] sat around glorious Odysseus in the center of Troy, concealed in the horse, for the Trojans themselves had dragged it up to the acropolis. Thus it stood there, and the Trojans sat and debated around it. They favored three plans: either to drive a sharp bronze [spear] through its hollow belly, or to drag it to the edge of the precipice and throw it down the rocks, or to let it be a great dedication to placate the gods. This was the course which they would choose, for it was fated that they would be destroyed once the city held the great wooden horse, where sat all the noblest of the Argives, bringing slaughter and fate to the Trojans. He sang, too, how the sons of Achaeans sacked the city when they poured out of the horse, leaving their hollow place of ambush.

10

The Building of the Trojan Horse, by Giovanni Domenico Tiepolo (1727–1804); oil on canvas, 1773, 76 × 141 in. This huge painting is the only survivor of three final versions of a series on the Fall of Troy, for which all three preparatory oil sketches exist. The massive horse dominates the composition, as workmen with their tools and ladders swarm over it. To the left, two figures stand on a rock outside the walls of Troy, probably Epeus (gesturing) and, behind him, Odysseus disguised with a turban and ill-fitting cloak. In the background are the walls of Troy, in front of which a warrior, a woman with a baby, and a servant (possibly, if improbably, Hector and his family) observe the building, while other Trojans look down from the tower on the left. (© *National Gallery, London/Art Resource, NY*)

"This was the bard's song," says Homer, and Odysseus wept when he heard it, even as a woman weeps whose husband has been killed in battle—the very suffering that Odysseus himself had inflicted on the Trojans. The song of Demodocus is the basis for Vergil's detailed account of the sack of Troy in the second book of the *Aeneid*. Odysseus himself tells the story of the horse to the ghost of Achilles in the Underworld, narrating how only Achilles' son, Neoptolemus, had been fearless and eager to fight as he sat waiting in the horse, whereas the other Greek heroes had wept and their knees were weak with fear. Odysseus is shown in both of these accounts to be the leader of the Greeks in the horse.

The horse was left outside the city walls, while the other Greeks sailed off to the island of Tenedos, leaving behind one man, **Sinon**. The Trojans, thinking that their troubles were over, came out of the city and captured Sinon, who pretended to be the bitter enemy of Odysseus and the other Greeks. He told the Trojans that the horse was an offering to Athena, purposely made too big to pass through the city walls; if it were brought inside, the city would never be captured. Not all the Trojans believed him; Cassandra, the prophetic daughter of Priam, foretold the truth, and **Laocoön**, son of Antenor and priest of Apollo, hurled his spear into the horse's flank and said that it should be destroyed. Yet the Trojans ignored Cassandra and failed to hear the clash of armor as Laocoön's spear struck the horse. Their judgment appeared to be vindicated when two huge serpents swam over the sea from Tenedos as Laocoön was sacrificing to Apollo and throttled him and his two sons.

The Sack of Troy

The Trojans pulled down part of the city walls and dragged the horse in. Helen walked round it calling to the Greek leaders, imitating the voice of each one's wife, but they were restrained from answering by Odysseus.[28] So the horse achieved its purpose; that night, as the Trojans slept after celebrating the end of the war, Sinon opened the horse and released the Greeks. The other Greeks sailed back from Tenedos and entered the city; the Trojans were put to the sword and the city was burned.

Antenor was spared, and of the other Trojan leaders only Aeneas escaped, along with his son, Ascanius, and his father, Anchises. Priam and the others were killed; Hector's infant son, Astyanax, was thrown from the walls, and his widow, Andromache, along with Hecuba and the other Trojan women, were made slaves of the Greek leaders. Neoptolemus' share of the spoils included Andromache, but eventually she married Helenus and founded the dynasty of the Molossian kings. In Book 3 of the *Aeneid*, she and Helenus figure prominently. She is the only one of the Trojan women to regain some sort of independent status after the fall of Troy.

During the sack of the city, Cassandra took refuge in the temple of Athena. She was dragged from this asylum by Ajax the Locrian, son of Oïleus, and for this he was killed by the gods on his way home.[29] Cassandra became the slave and concubine of Agamemnon, who took her back to Mycenae, where she was murdered with him by Clytemnestra. In Aeschylus' play *Agamemnon*, she foresees her own death in a moving scene (see p. 436); yet her audience, the Chorus in the play, does not believe her. The curse of Apollo remained with her to the end.

As Hecuba sailed back to Greece with Odysseus (to whom she had been given as part of the spoils), she landed in Thrace and there recognized the corpse of her son Polydorus when it washed up on the seashore. He had been murdered by the local king Polymestor (to whom he had been sent for safety during the war) because

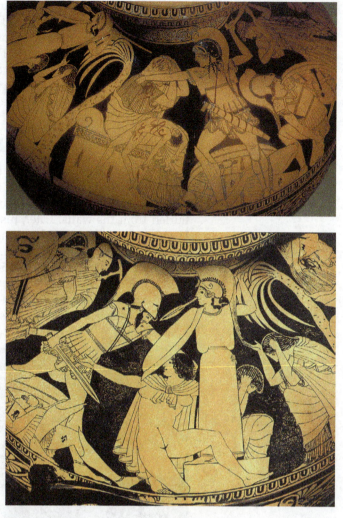

The Sack of Troy. Attic red-figure hydria by the Kleophrades painter, ca. 480 B.C.; height of vase 16½ in., height of painting 6½ in. In the upper picture, Priam sits on the altar with the dead and mutilated Astyanax across his knees, as Neoptolemus rushes forward to kill him. Behind Neoptolemus a Trojan woman attacks with a club-like implement. In the lower image, Ascanius, on the left (helmeted), leads the way for Aeneas, who carries Anchises on his back (Anchises looks back toward the central scene). In the center, Ajax Oïleus brutally drags Cassandra from the statue of Athena, whose threatening stance foreshadows his fate. Between the statue and a palm tree, Trojan women grieve for their coming fate. (*INTERFOTO/Alamy Stock Photo*)

of the treasure that had been sent with him. Taking advantage of Polymestor's avarice, Hecuba enticed him and his children into her tent, pretending that she knew the whereabouts in Troy of some hidden treasure, while she appeared to know nothing of the murder of Polydorus. Once they were in the tent, Hecuba's women murdered the children before Polymestor's eyes, then blinded him with their brooches. After this, Hecuba was turned into a bitch; when she died, the place of her burial (in Thrace) was called Cynossema, which means the "dog's tomb."

The Trojan Women of Euripides

In Euripides' tragedy the *Trojan Women*, the results of the fall are seen through the eyes of Hecuba, Cassandra, and Andromache. The death of Astyanax is a central part of the tragedy, in which he is torn from his mother's embrace to be hurled from the walls. Later, his body is brought back on stage and placed by Hecuba on the shield of Hector, a symbol of the defenselessness of Troy once her champion had been killed. The Chorus of Trojan captives recalls the entry of the wooden horse (*Trojan Women* 515–541):

> Now I shall sing of Troy, how I was destroyed by the four-wheeled contrivance of the Greeks and made their prisoner, when they left the horse at the gates, echoing

The Flight of Aeneas from Troy, by Federico Barocci (1535–1612); oil on canvas, 1598, 17½ × 101 in. Barocci faithfully represents Vergil's narrative. The central group of Aeneas, Ascanius, and Anchises (who is clutching the household gods of Troy) is separated from Creusa, who falls behind. In the foreground are Aeneas' shield and spear, now useless, while in the background is a round temple, the *Tempietto* of the Roman church of San Pietro in Montorio, in the portico and gallery of which men are fighting. Beside the temple is the column of Marcus Aurelius, and in the flames behind are the figures of the gods hostile to Troy. Barocci's signature is on the base of the newel post on the left. (© *Alinari Archives/Mauro Magliani/ Art Resource, NY*)

to the skies with the clash of armor and caparisoned with gold. And the Trojan people shouted as it stood on the rock of Troy: "Come, the labor of war is over! Bring in this wooden horse as a holy offering to the daughter of Zeus, guardian of Troy!" Who of the young women did not go, who of the old men stayed at home? Charmed by music, they took hold of the treacherous means of their destruction. All the Phrygian people gathered at the gates, and with ropes of flax they dragged it, like the dark hull of a ship, to the stone temple's floor, bringing death to their city—the temple of the goddess Pallas.

The Sack of Troy in the *Aeneid*

The principal source for the fall of Troy is the second book of the *Aeneid*. Here is how Vergil describes the horror of the end of a city deserted by its divine protectors in Aeneas' vision at the climactic moment of the sack, as his mother, Venus, allows him a moment of divine insight (*Aeneid* 2.602–606, 608–625):[30]

> [Aeneas recalls the words of Venus:] "It is the pitiless gods, the gods who are destroying the wealth of Troy and laying the city low from top to bottom. Look—for I will remove the cloud that now dulls your mortal sight. . . . Here, where you see the shattered towers and huge stones torn up, where dust and smoke are billowing, Neptune is convulsing the walls, shaking the foundations with his trident as he uproots the city. Here Juno, most cruel, leads the others in seizing the Scaean gates: raging and clad in iron armor she calls the Greeks from the ships. Look over here—even now Tritonian Pallas has taken up her place upon the height of Troy's citadel: see how she is lit with the lurid storm-cloud and the ferocious Gorgon! The Father of the gods himself renews the courage and violence of the Greeks, himself he urges them on to fight. . . ."
>
> I saw the fatal vision and the mighty power of the gods hostile to Troy. Then, indeed, I saw all Ilium collapse into the flames and Troy, built by Neptune, overturned from its foundations.

Yet Aeneas escaped, taking with him his father, Anchises (who carried the images of the city's gods in his hands), and his son, Ascanius (also called Iulus). His wife, **Creusa**, started with him and was lost to Aeneas' sight. Only her ghost appeared to him, foretelling his destiny and encouraging him to travel to a new world. The scene of Aeneas leaving Troy is heavy with symbolism, and it is with hope for the future that Aeneas, burdened with the past, leaves the doomed city (*Aeneid* 2.707–711, 721–724):

> "Then come, dear father, sit on my shoulders; I will carry you, the load will not weigh me down. Whatever chance may fall, we will share a common danger and a

Flight from Troy (1618–1619). Detail of a marble statue by Gian-Lorenzo Bernini (1598–1680); height 86½ in. This is Bernini's first major work, executed when he was twenty years old. Unlike Barocci, he focuses exclusively on the central figures of the flight—Aeneas, solemn, young, and strong; Anchises, clutching his son and, in his wide-eyed gaze, recognizing the implications of the destruction of Troy; finally, the city's household gods, whose preservation will lead eventually to the foundation of a new Troy in another land. Not seen in this detail is Ascanius (Iulus), who stumbles along beside the left leg of Aeneas. (*Scala/ Art Resource, NY*)

> common salvation. Let little Iulus walk beside me and let my wife follow. . . ." With these words I spread my cloak and the skin of a tawny lion across my shoulders and neck and lifted the burden. Little Iulus took my right hand and, hardly able to keep up, walked beside his father.

Appendix: Meleager and the Calydonian Boar Hunt

In the *Iliad*, as we have seen, Agamemnon sends Phoenix as one of the three envoys to Achilles in an attempt to assuage him. Phoenix, tutor, friend, and surrogate father at Troy, addresses Achilles at length, urging him to conquer his stubborn pride and give up his wrath. At the core of his speech (9.524–599), he offers as a warning the story of Meleager.

After the famous Calydonian boar hunt, in a quarrel over the slain animal, Meleager killed the brother (or brothers) of his mother **Althaea**. In her terrible grief, she prayed for her son's death. In the war between the Aetolians, who were defending their city of Calydon, and the Curetes, who were laying siege to the city, as long as Meleager fought with the Aetolians, things went well for them. Yet, when Meleager was overwhelmed by passion because of blind rage against his mother Althaea, he withdrew from battle.

The Curetes reached the gates of Calydon, and the Aetolians in desperation appealed to Meleager to return to battle, offering him splendid gifts. But he refused. As the Curetes were pillaging the city, Meleager's wife **Cleopatra** begged him in tears to come to their rescue. He was moved by her appeals. Compelled by his own conscience, he saved the city and the people but got none of the rich rewards that they had offered him for returning.

And so, Phoenix admonished Achilles not to behave like Meleager, but to accept the generous gifts promised by Agamemnon now and return to battle.

The legend of Meleager and the Calydonian boar hunt is an important one but difficult to present as a single, coherent narrative because of conflicting versions, as the summary that follows will make clear. The text of Homer itself offers its own confusion.

The François vase is an appropriate final illustration for this chapter. It depicts not only the Calydonian boar hunt, with Meleager and Peleus, the father of Achilles, but also scenes from the Trojan War.

Among the descendants of Aeolus was Oeneus, king of Calydon and father of Heracles' wife Deïanira; his son was Meleager. Shortly after the birth of Meleager, the Fates (Moirai) appeared before his mother, Althaea, and told her that Meleager would die when a log, which was burning on the hearth, had burned out. Althaea snatched up the log, extinguished it, and kept it in a chest. Years later, when Meleager was a young man, Oeneus offended Artemis by failing to sacrifice her share of the first fruits, and the goddess sent a huge boar to ravage Calydon.

Meleager gathered many of the noblest Greek heroes to hunt the boar, and with them came **Atalanta**, daughter of the Boeotian king Schoeneus.[31] In the hunt, after several heroes had been killed, Atalanta was the first to wound the boar. Meleager gave it the coup de grâce and therefore received the boar's skin, which he presented to Atalanta. His uncles, the brothers of Althaea, were insulted at being given less honor than Atalanta, and in the ensuing quarrel Meleager killed them. In grief and anger at their deaths, Althaea took the unburned log

The François Vase. Attic black-figure krater by the potter Ergotimos and the painter Kleitias, ca. 575 B.C.; height 30 in. There are four bands of mythological scenes and a fifth band with plants and animals, a battle of pygmies and cranes on the foot, and more figures, including Ajax carrying the corpse of Achilles, on the handles. The detail (below the image of the whole vase) shows the top bands on one side: Meleager and Peleus thrust at the Calydonian boar with their spears, with Atalanta and Milanion behind them. A dead hound and hunter lie on the ground, and other hunters (all named) attack or prepare to attack the beast. The band below shows the chariot race from the funeral games for Patroclus: Diomedes leads Damasippus, and the prize, a tripod, is shown below to the left. The third band on the full vase shows the wedding procession of Peleus and Thetis, who are on the chariot to the left. The band below shows Achilles pursuing Troilus: on the left is the fountain house where Polyxena (sister of Troilus) had been drawing water. To its right a Trojan woman gesticulates in alarm, and next to her (in order) are Thetis, Hermes, and Athena, the latter urging on Achilles (the top half of whose body is missing). Troilus rides a horse beside a second riderless horse, and beneath lies Polyxena's amphora, which she has dropped in her flight. She runs in front of Troilus (her top half is missing) toward the walls of Troy, from which two armed warriors, Hector and Polites, are emerging. In front of Troy sits Priam, who is receiving a report from Antenor about the danger to Troilus. (*Top: Nimatallah/Art Resource, NY; Bottom: Scala/Art Resource, NY*)

from its chest and cast it on the fire. As it burned to ashes, Meleager's life ebbed away. Both Althaea and Meleager's wife Cleopatra hanged themselves, while the women who mourned for him at his funeral became guinea fowl, which the Greeks called *meleagrides*.

This is Ovid's version of the Calydonian boar hunt. Homer, however (*Iliad* 9.553–572), says that Artemis sent the boar to ravage the land during a war between the Calydonians and the Curetes. Meleager killed it and led the Calydonians in the battle against the Curetes over the boar's body. But Althaea cursed her son Meleager "because of the murder of her brother" and called on

Hades to kill him. Meleager withdrew in anger. Then he relented, went back into battle, and saved Calydon. Homer says that the Calydonians did not reward him as they had promised, and he implies that Meleager died as a result of Althaea's curse.

In the Underworld, Meleager's ghost talked with Heracles, and in Bacchylides' fifth *Epinician Ode* (93–154) he tells Heracles his story, in which the Homeric details of the boar and the battle with the Curetes are combined with the burning log:

> There [i.e., in the battle with the Curetes] I killed with many others Iphiclus and Aphares, my mother's swift brothers; for bold Ares does not distinguish a friend in war, but blind are the weapons hurled from one's hands. My mother, ill-fated and unfearing woman, planned my death. She burned the log that brought me a speedy death, taking it from the cunningly made chest. It had the *Moira* [i.e., allotted portion] fated to be the limit of my life. And my sweet life ebbed, and I knew that I was losing my strength—alas!—and unhappily I wept as I breathed my last, leaving lovely youth.

In this version, although Meleager accidentally kills his uncles in battle, their sister still avenges their death, her ties to her father's family being even stronger than those to her son. As Bacchylides also tells us, Heracles responded to Meleager's story with a promise to marry Deïanira, Meleager's sister, when he returned to the world of the living (see p. 556).

Nowhere in Homer or Bacchylides is there any mention of Atalanta, nor is there any complete account of her part in the legend earlier than Ovid. She appears in the François vase, which was made in about 575 B.C., a century before Bacchylides' poem. About 165 years later, in 411–410 B.C., Euripides says in his play *Phoenissae* (1104–1109) that Atalanta's son, Parthenopaeus, one of the seven heroes who attacked Thebes, had the device on his shield of "Atalanta subduing the Aetolian boar with her arrows shot from afar," whereas in the François vase she brandishes a hunting spear and marches in the second rank, behind Meleager and Peleus. Finally, her companion on the vase is named Milanion, who wins the Arcadian Atalanta as his bride in yet another tale.

From all this, we can conclude that several legends have been conflated around Meleager and Atalanta, whose myths were originally separate. Ovid created a unified narrative from these different elements.

Select Bibliography

Anderson, M. J. *The Fall of Troy in Early Greek Art.* Oxford: Clarendon Press, 1997.

Bothmer, D. von. *Amazons in Greek Art.* New York: Oxford University Press, 1957.

Burgess, Jonathan S. *The Death and Afterlife of Achilles.* Baltimore, MD: Johns Hopkins University Press, 2009. The story of Achilles told on the basis of literary, iconographical, and archaeological sources.

———. *Tradition of the Trojan War in Homer and the Epic Cycle.* Baltimore, MD: Johns Hopkins University Press, 2004. The authority of the *Iliad* and *Odyssey* is challenged in a study of the wider context of epic poetry in the archaic period.

Dalby, Andrew. *Rediscovering Homer: Inside the Origins of the Epic.* New York: Norton, 2006. The growth of the saga of Troy, the various versions, and the transition from oral recitation to written text.

Griffin, Jasper. *Homer.* New York: Hill & Wang, 1980.

———. *Homer on Life and Death.* New York: Oxford University Press, 1980.

Gumpert, Matthew. *Grafting Helen: The Abduction of the Classical Past*. Madison: University of Wisconsin Press, 2002. Traces the myth of Helen from ancient to modern times.

Louden, Bruce. *"The Iliad": Structure, Myth, and Meaning*. Baltimore, MD: Johns Hopkins University Press, 2006. An analysis of how the epic is related to Near Eastern mythologies.

Lowenstam, Steven. *As Witnessed by Images: The Trojan War Tradition in Greek and Etruscan Art*. Baltimore, MD: Johns Hopkins University Press, 2008. An investigation of visual depictions from ca. 650 B.C. to 300 B.C.

Maguire, Laurie. *Helen of Troy: From Homer to Hollywood*. New York: Wiley–Blackwell, 2009. Not only about the transformation of Helen in film but also an extensive and valuable exploration of her literary afterlife.

Manguel, Alberto. *Homer's "The Iliad" and "The Odyssey": A Biography*. New York: Atlantic Monthly Press, 2007. A survey of the afterlife of the poems.

McAuslan, Ian, and Peter Walcott, eds. *Homer*. Greece and Rome Studies, Vol. 1V. New York: Oxford University Press, 1998. A collection of scholarly essays.

McCarty, Nick. *The Myth and Reality behind the Epic Legend*. New York: Barnes & Noble, 2004. How the legend has been reflected in plays, poems, and films.

Powell, B. B., and I. Morris, eds. *A New Companion to Homer*. Leiden: Mnemosyne, Bibliotheca Classica Batava. Supplementum 163, 1997.

Redfield, James M. *Nature and Culture in "The Iliad": The Tragedy of Hector*. Chapel Hill, NC: Duke University Press, 1993 [1975].

Rutherford, Richard. *Homer*. Greece and Rome. New Surveys in the Classics, 26. New York: Oxford University Press, 1996. Excellent survey with bibliography.

Schein, S. *The Mortal Hero: An Introduction to Homer's* Iliad. Berkeley, CA: University of California Press, 1984.

Shay, Jonathan. *Achilles in Vietnam*. New York: Atheneum, 1994.

Silver, Vernon. *The Lost Chalice: The Epic Hunt for a Priceless Masterpiece*. New York: HarperCollins, 2009. An account of the amazing history of the famous red-figure krater by Euphronios, *The Death of Sarpedon*, which turned up in the collection of a Hollywood producer, eventually was purchased by the Metropolitan Museum of Art and now resides in Italy.

Tyrrell, W. B. *Amazons: A Study in Athenian Mythmaking*. Baltimore, MD: Johns Hopkins University Press, 1984.

Wilde, Lyn Webster. *On the Trail of the Women Warriors, the Amazons in Myth and History*. New York: St. Martin's Press, 2000. Evidence is sifted and analyzed to prove the historical reality of the Amazons.

Winkler, Martin M., ed. *Troy: From Homer's "Iliad" to Film Epic*. Malden, MA: Blackwell, 2006. Includes an annotated list of films (including TV) on the Trojan War, with illustrations.

Woodford, Susan. *The Trojan War in Ancient Art*. Ithaca, NY: Cornell University Press, 1993. A useful survey.

Zanker, Graham. *The Heart of Achilles: Characterization and Personal Ethics in the Iliad*. Ann Arbor: University of Michigan Press, 1994.

Primary Sources

Sources in the Chapter

Bacchylides	*Epinician Ode* 5.93–154
Euripides	*Trojan Women* 515–541
Homer	*Iliad* (selections)
	Odyssey 8.487–495, 502–515; 24.63–70
Homeric Hymn 17	*To the Dioscuri*

Homeric Hymn 33	*To the Dioscuri* (see p. 461)
Lucian	*Dialogues of the Gods: The Judgment of the Goddesses* 7–16
Lucretius	*De rerum natura* 1.84–101 (sacrifice of Iphigenia)
Ovid	*Metamorphoses* 13.382–398
Sophocles	*Ajax* 121–133
Statius	1.852–884
Vergil	*Aeneid* 2.602–606, 608–625, 707–711, 721–724

Additional Sources

Euripides	*Andromache*
	Hecuba
	Helen
	Rhesus
Ovid	*Heroides*
Plato	*Lesser Hippias* (Hippias Minor) 363a–365c (the *Iliad* and *Odyssey* compared), 369a–372e (Achilles and Odysseus compared)
Seneca	*Trojan Women*
Sophocles	*Philoctetes*

Notes

1. Pindar, *Nemean Ode* 10. In Theocritus, *Idyll* 22, the quarrel begins when the Dioscuri carry off the daughters of Leucippus from their intended husbands, Idas and Lynceus. The "rape of the Leucippides" was a common subject in ancient art. Another version has one of the divine twins in heaven and the other in Hades on alternate days.

2. Euripides brings them on dramatically at the end of his *Electra*, not only as the protectors of sailors but also as champions of a better morality than that represented by Apollo (see p. 457).

3. Their appearance as horsemen on white steeds at the battle of Lake Regillus in 496 B.C. led to a great Roman victory.

4. Aphrodite is said (also by Stesichorus) to have made Helen unfaithful as punishment for Helen's father, Tyndareus, who had once omitted to sacrifice to the goddess. For Helen in Egypt, see Herodotus 2.112–120 and Euripides, *Helen*.

5. Hecuba's stepson, Aesacus.

6. For the historical facts about Troy and the Trojan War, see pp. 46–54.

7. Laomedon was a nephew of Ganymede, whom Zeus had snatched up to Olympus to become the cupbearer of the gods (pp. 122–123). In compensation, Zeus gave Tros (father of Ganymede) the divine horses that Laomedon inherited and failed to give to Heracles.

8. The story of Troïlus' love for Cressida (daughter, in this version, of Calchas) is an invention of the Middle Ages; Boccaccio and Chaucer took the story from the *Roman de Troie* of Benôit de Ste. Maure. Shakespeare's play is a further variation.

9. Although the contingents supplied by Odysseus, king of Ithaca, and Ajax, prince of Salamis, were among the smallest (only twelve ships each), their personal prowess gave them preeminence.

10. The comparative importance of the Greek leaders may be gauged from the size of their contingents in the *Catalogue* in Book 2 of the *Iliad*: Agamemnon, one hundred ships; Nestor, ninety; Diomedes and Idomeneus, eighty each; Menelaüs, sixty; Achilles, sixty; Ajax the Less, forty; Ajax, son of Telamon, and Odysseus, twelve each.

11. Palamedes, son of Nauplius, was, after Odysseus, the cleverest of the Greeks; he was credited with a number of inventions. His unmasking of the "madness" earned him the hostility of Odysseus, who eventually contrived his death.

12. For the role of this secret in the story of Prometheus, p. 95; for Thetis' supplication to Zeus on behalf of Achilles, see p. 125.

13. Similar stories are those of Phaedra and Hippolytus, Bellerophon and Stheneboea, and the biblical Joseph and Potiphar's wife (Gen. 39).

14. Similar magic was practiced by Demeter at Eleusis on the child Demophoön (see p. 334).

15. Nowhere does Homer mention a physical relationship between Achilles and Patroclus. In Plato's *Symposium*, Pausanias, probably not speaking in purely spiritual terms, identifies Patroclus as older and less beautiful than Achilles and his lover, contradicting Aeschylus, who (in a play no longer extant) made Achilles the lover rather than the beloved of Patroclus.

16. The figure is given in the *Catalogue* in Book 2 of the *Iliad*. Ancient as this document is and historically of the greatest importance, its numbers are inflated.

17. The most common version of his offense is that he had killed a stag sacred to the goddess. Some say that Artemis caused no winds to blow at all.

18. This version underlies Euripides' tragedy *Iphigenia in Tauris* (see pp. 438–440).

19. After the Trojan War, Calchas challenged the seer Mopsus to a contest by asking him how many unripe figs there were on a nearby tree. When Mopsus gave the correct answer, Calchas died, for he was fated to do so if he met a more clever prophet than himself.

20. Some versions have Calchas make the prophecy and Neoptolemus accompany Odysseus to Lemnos. Aeschylus, Sophocles, and Euripides all wrote tragedies on Philoctetes; that of Sophocles is extant.

21. Pope's translation of this passage is given in Chapter 27 on the companion website.

22. Today Helen is often defended as the guiltless victim; for example, see Mihoko Suzuki, *Metamorphoses of Helen* (Ithaca, NY: Cornell University Press, 1989). Helen is studied in the depictions by Homer, Vergil, Spenser (*The Faerie Queene*), and Shakespeare (*Troilus and Cressida*), using theories of sacrifice and scapegoating and the conflict between patriarchal attitudes and victimized women.

23. Jonathan Shay, *Achilles in Vietnam* (New York: Atheneum, 1994).

24. Of great interest is *Penthesilea*, by the renowned German playwright Heinrich von Kleist, translated into English by Joel Agee, with pictures by Maurice Sendak (New York: HarperCollins, 1998).

25. This is the same Thersites who spoke out of turn in the assembly of the Greeks in Book 2 of the *Iliad*.

26. In another version, Thetis takes the corpse of Achilles to the island of Leuce (in the Black Sea), where she restores it to life. In Book 11 of the *Odyssey*, the ghost of Achilles talks with Odysseus and complains bitterly of his fate in the Underworld.

27. Ajax is the Latin form of the Greek Aias. For the metamorphosis of Hyacinthus, see p. 256.

28. Menelaüs narrates this episode in Book 4 of the *Odyssey* to Odysseus' son, Telemachus.

29. His sacrilege had a strange historical consequence; for a thousand years, the Locrians annually sent two daughters of noble families to serve as temple servants of Athena at Troy (i.e., the later foundations after the fall of Priam's city) as a penance for Ajax's crime. If any of these girls was caught by the Trojans before she reached the temple, she was put to death. This penance was ended not long before A.D. 100. There is a connection between the name Oïleus and the Greek name for Troy, Ilium.

30. The gods are here called by their Latin names.

31. Atalanta, daughter of Schoeneus, is easily confused with Atalanta of Arcadia. The latter also is a virgin huntress, who joined in the Calydonian boar hunt. She attempted to join the Argonauts' expedition, but Jason refused to accept her because he was concerned about a beautiful woman amid a crew of all men. The most famous story about the Arcadian Atalanta revolves around her race with Milanion, who was also named Hippomenes (see p. 650).

For additional digital learning resources please go to
www.oup.com/he/morford12e

THE RETURNS AND THE *ODYSSEY*

I am a part of all that I have met.

—TENNYSON, *Ulysses*

Legends of the Returns

The returns of the Greek leaders from Troy were narrated in an epic called **Nostoi** (**Returns**), of which only a brief prose summary and three lines of verse are extant.[1] It omits the return of Odysseus, which is the subject of Homer's *Odyssey*.

Agamemnon, Menelaüs, and Nestor

Agamemnon and Menelaüs quarreled over the departure and so parted company. Agamemnon sailed for Greece with part of the fleet, including the contingent of the Locrians. Near the island of Mykonos, Athena, angered by the sacrilege committed at Troy by the Locrian leader **Ajax** (p. 472), caused a storm to wreck many of the ships. Ajax swam to a nearby rock, where he boasted that not even the gods could prevent his escape from the dangers of the sea. For this blasphemy, Poseidon struck the rock with his trident, and Ajax was hurled into the sea and drowned.

During a second storm, which struck Agamemnon's fleet at Cape Caphareus in Euboea, Nauplius avenged the death of his son Palamedes by luring many ships onto the rocks with a false beacon. Agamemnon finally reached Mycenae, only to be murdered by Aegisthus and Clytemnestra.

Meanwhile, Menelaüs, Nestor, and Diomedes set sail together from Troy. Nestor returned to Pylos safely. In the *Odyssey*, he tells Telemachus how Menelaüs lost all of his fleet except for five ships in a storm off Crete and eventually reached Egypt. On the advice of the sea-nymph **Eidothea**, Menelaüs forced her father, **Proteus**, to tell him how to appease the gods and secure a safe voyage home. Thus after seven years Menelaüs and Helen returned to Sparta, where they resumed their rule.[2] Euripides, perhaps to appeal to the anti-Spartan prejudices of Athenian audiences during the Peloponnesian War (432–404), makes Menelaüs a bombastic and ineffectual character in his tragedies *Andromache* (produced in 425) and *Orestes* (408). In the *Orestes*, Helen miraculously escapes being killed by Orestes and Electra, and Apollo announces that Helen has become a goddess, joining her brothers (Castor and Polydeuces) as protectors of seafarers (p. 440). At the end of his life, Menelaüs was transported to the Elysian Fields, avoiding the usual fate of going to Hades because he was the husband of Helen and the son-in-law of Zeus.

Diomedes

Diomedes reached Argos quickly, but there he found that his wife, Aegialia (daughter of Adrastus), had been unfaithful. Her adulteries were caused by Aphrodite, angry because Diomedes had wounded her at Troy. Diomedes left Argos and came to Italy, where the Apulian king, Daunus, gave him land. Diomedes founded several cities in Italy, but he declined to help King Latinus against Aeneas. After his death, Diomedes was worshiped as a hero in many places in Italy; in one story, Athena made him an immortal god.[3] His followers were turned into birds.[4]

Idomeneus

Idomeneus returned to Crete to find that his wife, Meda, had committed adultery with Leucus, who had then murdered her and her daughter and made himself king over ten cities of Crete. Idomeneus was driven out by Leucus and came to Calabria in southern Italy, where he was worshiped as a hero after his death.[5]

Servius, the ancient commentator on Vergil, tells a legend that is similar to the biblical story of Jephthah's vow (*Judges* 11:30–11:40). Idomeneus was caught in a storm during the voyage home and vowed, if he were saved, to sacrifice to Poseidon the first living thing that met him. When he returned home, his son came out first to meet him. After Idomeneus had fulfilled his vow, a pestilence attacked the Cretans, who took it to be a divine punishment for Idomeneus' act and drove him into exile.

Philoctetes

Philoctetes returned to Thessaly but was driven out by his people. He came to southern Italy, where he founded a number of cities and after his death was worshiped as a hero.

The stories of Diomedes, Idomeneus, and Philoctetes seem to reflect the founding of Greek colonies in southern Italy from the eighth century onward. All three were worshiped as heroes after their death.

Neoptolemus

Achilles' son, Neoptolemus, warned by Thetis not to return by sea, took the land route back to Greece, accompanied by Helenus and Andromache. With them and his wife, **Hermione** (daughter of Menelaüs), he left his home in Phthia and came to Molossia in Epirus, where he ruled over the Molossi. He was killed at Delphi, and there became a hero with his own cult (see pp. 439–440).

The Return of Odysseus

The return of Odysseus forms a saga in itself, to which many folk tale elements have accrued. Here is the summary of the *Odyssey* given by Aristotle in his *Poetics* (17.10):

> The story of the *Odyssey* is not long; a man is away from home for many years; Poseidon constantly is on the watch to destroy him, and he is alone; at home his property is being wasted by suitors, and his son is the intended victim of a plot. He reaches home, tempest-tossed; he makes himself known, attacks his enemies and destroys them, and is himself saved. This is the heart of the matter: the rest is episodes.

The adventures of Odysseus have been taken as symbolic (e.g., Odysseus conquers death in his visit to the Underworld) or as connected with real places that had become known to the Greeks as their trade and colonization expanded. For the most part, however, they are romantic legends and folk tales set in imaginary places and grafted onto the saga of a historical prince's return from a long absence.[6]

During the Trojan War, Odysseus was the wisest of the Greek heroes and a brave warrior. After Achilles' death, Odysseus inherited his divine armor. In the *Odyssey* he experiences many adventures, usually escaping from danger through his intelligence and courage. He meets with many men, women, goddesses, and monsters, and he remains faithful to **Penelope**, the wife whom he left in Ithaca with his son, **Telemachus**.[7] Homer, with his customary perception and art, frames just the right introduction to establish our good faith in Odysseus. In Book 5, we first meet our hero, who has been marooned for seven years on the island of Ogygia, captive of the beautiful and divine nymph, Calypso. She comes down to the shore to find her unhappy victim Odysseus, pining for home (151–158):

> Calypso found Odysseus sitting on the shore. His eyes were always wet with tears. His sweet life was ebbing away, while he bemoaned the impossibility of his homecoming, since the nymph no longer gave him any pleasure. The nights he was forced to spend lying with her in her grotto; certainly he did not want to, but she did. The days he spent amid the rocks on the shore, his heart racked by tears and groans and misery, as he looked out across the barren sea, weeping.

Story of the *Odyssey*

At the time the poem begins, Odysseus is in the middle of his adventures. Books 1–4 relate the situation in Ithaca, where in Odysseus' absence Penelope is besieged by suitors who want her hand in marriage and with it her kingdom. As we have just seen, we first meet Odysseus in Book 5, detained on Ogygia, the island of the divine nymph Calypso. After he has sailed away from this island and his raft has been wrecked, Odysseus relates to his rescuers the events preceding his arrival on Ogygia. The poem then continues with the arrival of Odysseus on Ithaca, his revenge on the suitors for the hand of Penelope, and his eventual recognition by and reunion with Penelope.

The resourceful character of Odysseus dominates the story, but the gods also play a significant part, especially Poseidon, who is hostile to the hero, and Athena, who protects him. Homer introduces Odysseus in the opening lines (1.1–21) of the *Odyssey*:

> Of the man tell me, O Muse, the man of many ways,[8] who traveled afar after he had sacked the holy city of Troy. He experienced the cities and the thoughts of many men, and his spirit suffered many sorrows on the sea, as he labored for his own life

Calypso and Ulysses, by Emily Marshall; watercolor on paper, 1820–1835; 19 × 24 in. Calypso, in the dress of a woman of the early nineteenth century, tries to comfort Odysseus as he looks over the ocean and thinks of Penelope. Her left hand rests on his shoulder, and behind is a river landscape with a palm tree to give a suitably exotic air. Nothing is known of the artist, whose deceptively naive style has caught the pathos of the situation in which the goddess and the hero find themselves. (*Abby Aldrich Rockefeller Folk Art Museum, Colonial Williamsburg Foundation, Williamsburg, VA*)

and for the homecoming of his companions. Yet even so he could not protect his companions, much though he wished it, for they perished by their own folly, when thoughtlessly they had eaten the cattle of Helius, Hyperion the sun-god. And the god took away the day of their homecoming. From some point in these things, O goddess, daughter of Zeus, begin to tell me also the tale. (1.1–10)

Then all the others, who had escaped sheer destruction, were at home, safe from the sea and the war. But this man alone, longing for his homecoming and his wife, did the nymph, the lady Calypso, keep in her hollow cave, desiring him as her husband. But when, as the years rolled round, that year came in which the gods had destined his return home to Ithaca, not even then did he escape from his labors nor was he with his friends. Yet the gods pitied him, all except Poseidon, and he unrelentingly was hostile to godlike Odysseus, until he returned to his own land. (1.11–21)

10

The Cicones and the Lotus Eaters

It took Odysseus ten years to reach home. When he and his contingent left Troy, they came to the Thracian city of Ismarus, home of the Cicones, which they sacked before being driven off. They had spared **Maron**, priest of Apollo, in their attack, and he in return gave them twelve jars of fragrant red wine, which was to prove its value later. They were driven southward by a storm to the land of the lotus eaters. Here their reception was friendly but no less dangerous, for whoever ate of the fruit of the lotus forgot everything and wanted only to stay where he was, eating lotus fruit. Odysseus got his men away, even those who had tasted the fruit, and sailed to the land of the Cyclopes.

The Cyclopes

The Cyclopes were one-eyed giants, herdsmen, living each in his own cave. One of them was **Polyphemus**, son of Poseidon, whose cave Odysseus and twelve picked companions entered. In the cave were sheep and lambs, cheeses, and other provisions, to which they helped themselves while waiting for the return of the cave's owner. When Polyphemus returned with his flocks, he shut the entrance of the cave with a huge stone and then caught sight of the visitors, two of whom he ate for his supper. He breakfasted on two more the next day and another two when he returned the second evening.

Now Odysseus had with him some of the wine of Maron, and with this he made Polyphemus drunk; he told him his name was **Nobody (Outis)**, and the giant, in return for the excellent wine, promised that he would reward Nobody by eating him last. He then fell asleep. Odysseus sharpened a wooden stake and heated it in the fire; then he and his surviving men drove it into the solitary eye of the sleeping giant. As he cried out in agony, the other Cyclopes came running to the cave's entrance, only to hear the cry "Nobody is killing me," so that they assumed that not much was wrong and left Polyphemus alone.

The next morning Polyphemus, now blind, removed the stone at the entrance and let his flocks out, feeling each animal as it passed. But Odysseus had tied his men each to the undersides of three sheep, and himself clung to the belly of the biggest ram; so he and his men escaped. As Odysseus sailed away, he shouted his real name to the Cyclops, who hurled the top of a mountain at him and nearly wrecked the ship. Polyphemus had long before been warned of Odysseus, and as he recognized the name, he prayed to his father Poseidon (*Odyssey* 9.530–536):

> Grant that Odysseus may not return home, but if it is fated for him once more to see those he loves and reach his home and country, then let him arrive after many years, in distress, without his companions, upon another's ship, and may he find trouble in his house. . . . The prayer was heard.

The story of the one-eyed giant is one of the most frequently recurring folk tales in the world. A particularly close parallel to Homer's version is found in the Voyages of Sinbad, related in *The Arabian Nights*.

Aeolus and the Laestrygonians

Odysseus, reunited with the rest of his fleet, next reached the floating island of Aeolus, keeper of the winds, who lived with his six sons, who were married to his six daughters.[9] After he had entertained Odysseus, Aeolus gave him as a parting gift a leather bag containing all the winds and showed him which one to release so as to reach home. Thus he sailed back to Ithaca and was within reach of land when he fell asleep. His men, believing that the bag contained gold that Odysseus was keeping for himself, opened it, and all the winds rushed out and blew the ships back to Aeolus' island. Aeolus refused to help them anymore, reasoning that the gods must hate them. Odysseus and his men sailed on to the land of the Laestrygonians who sank all Odysseus' ships except his own and ate up the crews. So Polyphemus' curse was already working, and Odysseus sailed away with his solitary ship.

Circe

Odysseus reached the island of **Aeaea**, the home of the witch Circe, daughter of the Sun. Odysseus divided his men into two groups; he stayed behind with the one, while the other, twenty-three men in all, went to visit the ruler of the island. They

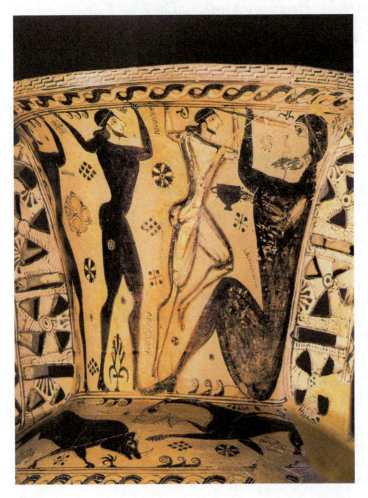

The Blinding of Polyphemus. Proto-Attic vase from Eleusis, mid-seventh century B.C.; height of vase 56 in., of neck 15 in. Odysseus (painted in white) and his companions drive a long pole into the eye of the Cyclops, who holds the cup of wine that has made him drunk. This brutal scene is one of the earliest "free" vase paintings after the Geometric period. (*Erich Lessing/Art Resource, NY*)

found Circe with various animals around her, and they themselves (except for Eurylochus, who brought the news back to Odysseus) became pigs when they ate her food, swine in appearance and sound, but still having human minds.[10] As Odysseus went to rescue his men, he encountered the god Hermes, who told him how to counter Circe's charms and gave him as an antidote the magic herb **moly**, whose "root is black and flower as white as milk." So he ate Circe's food unharmed and threatened her with his sword when she tried to turn him into a pig. She recognized him and instead made love to him. She then set a feast before him, which he would not touch before he had made her change his men back into their human shape. Odysseus lived with Circe for a year and by her begot a son, **Telegonus**. At the end of a year Odysseus, urged on by his men, asked Circe to send him on his way home. She agreed but told him that he first had to go to the Underworld where he would learn the way home from the prophet Tiresias.

The *Nekuia*

Book 11 of the *Odyssey*, which tells of Odysseus' experiences in the Underworld, is generally referred to as the Book of the Dead or the *Nekuia*, the name of the rite by which ghosts were summoned and questioned. Odysseus' visit to the Underworld is a conquest of death, the most formidable struggle a hero has to face. The hero who can return from the house of Hades alive has achieved all that a mortal can achieve. The *Nekuia* of Odysseus is different from its most famous imitation in one important respect: in the *Aeneid*, Aeneas actually descends to the Underworld and himself passes through it, whereas Odysseus goes to the entrance and there performs the ritual sacrifice that summons up the spirits of the dead. Passages that tell of Odysseus' journey from Aeaea to the Underworld, his performance of the rite, and his conversations with a number of the ghosts are translated at length at the beginning of Chapter 15; here we provide a summary of his visit.

Following Circe's directions, Odysseus sailed with his men to the western limit of the world.

Odysseus Threatens Circe, Attic red-figure kalyx krater by the Persephone painter, 440 B.C. In the upper panel, Circe has risen from her chair and runs away from Odysseus, dressed as a traveler and threatening her with his sword. She drops her wand and the bowl in which she had mixed her drugs. To the left, two of Odysseus' men approach with agitated gestures, one transformed into a boar and the other a donkey, but both still with human legs and arms. In the lower panel there is a pursuit with a young man and two women, but whether it illustrates a scene from myth is uncertain. (*The Metropolitan Museum of Art Gift of Amelia E. White, 1941*)

As he performed the ritual sacrifice at the entrance to the world of the dead, many ghosts came, among them **Tiresias**, who foretold the disasters that yet awaited Odysseus on his journey. He would reach home, but alone and after many years. At Ithaca he would find the arrogant suitors pressing Penelope hard and wasting his substance. But he would kill them all, and he would have still more travels ahead of him before death came.

From Tiresias, Odysseus also learned that the spirits with whom he wished to speak must be allowed to drink the blood of the sacrificial victim; the others he kept away by threatening them with his sword. Among the ghosts who appeared and spoke were those of Odysseus' mother, **Anticlea**, and of Agamemnon, Achilles, and Ajax, son of Telamon. Achilles said that "he would rather be a slave to a poor man on earth than be king over all the souls of the dead." Ajax would not answer Odysseus a word, for he still was grieved by losing the contest for Achilles' arms.

Eventually, Odysseus left the house of Hades for fear that the Gorgon's head (which turns all whom it beholds to stone) might appear. He rejoined his men and sailed back to Aeaea.

The Sirens, the Planctae, Charybdis, and Scylla

Circe sent Odysseus on his way after warning him of the dangers that lay ahead. First were the Sirens (said by Homer to be two in number, but by other authors to be more). To Homer they were human in form, but in popular tradition they were birdlike, with women's heads. From their island meadow they would lure passing sailors onto the rocks; all around them were the whitened bones of their victims. Odysseus sailed by them unharmed, stopping his men's ears with wax, while he had himself bound to the ship's mast so that he could not yield to the irresistible allurement of the Sirens' song, which tempted Odysseus, the cleverest of men, with the gift of further knowledge (*Odyssey* 12.184–191):

> Come hither, famous Odysseus, great glory of the Achaeans! Halt your ship so that you may hear our voice. For no one yet has sailed past this place in a black ship before hearing our sweet song. Then he sails on joyfully and endowed with greater knowledge. For we know all that the Argives and the Trojans endured in the broad plain of Troy through the will of the gods. And we know everything that happens upon the fertile earth.

The next danger was the two wandering rocks (Planctae) between which one ship only, the *Argo*, had ever safely passed. Odysseus avoided them by sailing close to two high cliffs; in the lower of these lived Charybdis (she is not described by Homer), who three times a day sucked in the water of the strait and spouted it upward again. To sail near that cliff was certain destruction, and Odysseus chose as the lesser evil the higher cliff where was the cave of Scylla, daughter of the sea deity Phorcys. Originally a sea-nymph, she had been changed through the jealousy of Poseidon's wife Amphitrite into a monster with a girdle of six dogs' heads and with twelve feet, by means of which she would snatch sailors from passing ships. From Odysseus' ship she snatched six men, whom she ate in her cave. Odysseus and the rest of the crew were unharmed.

Odysseus and the Sirens. Athenian red-figure stamnos, ca. 450 B.C.; height 13¾ in. Odysseus, lashed to the mast, safely hears the song of the Sirens as his men row by, their ears plugged with wax. Two Sirens (winged creatures with human heads) stand on cliffs, while a third plunges headlong into the sea. The artist, by the dramatic angle of Odysseus' head, expresses the hero's longing to be free of his bonds, and the turned head of the oarsman on the right and the helmsman's gesture add further tension to the scene. (© *The Trustees of the British Museum*)

The Cattle of the Sun

Last, Circe told Odysseus of the island of **Thrinacia**, where Helius (the Sun) pastured his herds of cattle and sheep; she strictly warned Odysseus not to touch a single one of the animals if he and his men wished ever to return to Ithaca. But Odysseus' men could not show such restraint after weeks of being detained by adverse winds, and while he was sleeping they killed some of the cattle for food. Helius complained to Zeus, and as a punishment for the sacrilege of killing the god's cattle, Zeus raised a storm when the ship set sail and hurled a thunderbolt at it. The ship sank, and all the men were drowned except for Odysseus, who escaped, floating on the mast and part of the keel.

After the wreck, Odysseus drifted back to Charybdis, where he avoided death by clinging to a tree growing on the cliff until the whirlpool propelled his mast to the surface after sucking it down.

Calypso

Odysseus drifted over the sea to **Ogygia**, the island home of Calypso, daughter of Atlas, with whom he lived for seven years. Although she loved him and offered to make him immortal, he could not forget Penelope. Finally, after Hermes brought her Zeus' express orders, Calypso helped Odysseus build a raft and sail away.

The Phaeacians

Even now Odysseus was not free from disaster; Poseidon saw him as he approached **Scheria** (the island of the Phaeacians) and shattered the raft with a storm. After two days and two nights, helped by the sea-goddess **Leucothea** (formerly the mortal Ino, daughter of Cadmus) and by Athena, he reached land, naked, exhausted, and alone.

The king of the Phaeacians was **Alcinoüs**, and his daughter was **Nausicaä**. The day after Odysseus landed, Nausicaä went to wash clothes near the seashore and came face to face with Odysseus. She gave him her protection and brought

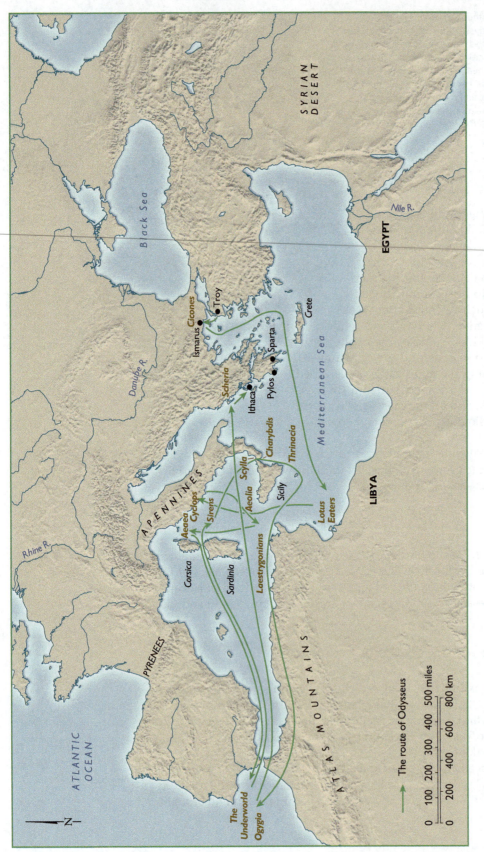

Map 20.1 The Return of Odysseus. It is difficult to overlay a legendary landscape upon a real geography, and the map indicates the uncertainty of precise identification. Most of the places Odysseus visits are impossible to locate, though the attempt has not stopped ingenious speculation. Even in antiquity, many believed that the western Mediterranean was the focus of Odysseus' wandering, whereas the most famous of the adventures of Jason, which may in fact be older than those of Odysseus' voyage, take place in and around the Black Sea region. The first chapters of the Geography of Strabo, a first-century A.D. geographer, are particularly illuminating on the subject of Homeric geography and the ideas current in Strabo's time.

Odysseus and Nausicaä. Red-figure amphora, ca. 440 B.C. On the left, Odysseus holds two olive branches (signaling that he is a suppliant), while Athena, her head turned toward him, stands between him and Nausicaä (seen on the right). Encouraged by Athena, Nausicaä stops running away and turns toward Odysseus. Behind Odysseus, clothes hang on a tree to dry. (*Amphora, red-figure pottery, detail showing Ulysses, Athena and Nausicaa, Greek Civilization, 6th–4th Century BC/ De Agostini Picture Library/The Bridgeman Art Library*)

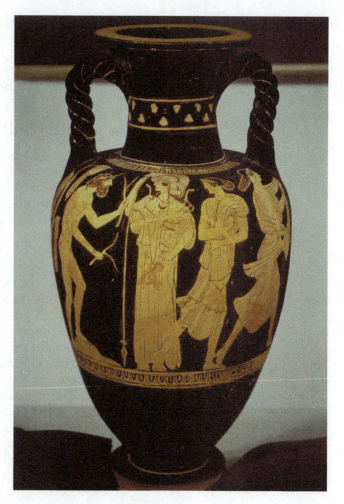

him back to the palace. Here he was warmly entertained by Alcinoüs and his queen, **Arete**, and related the story of his adventures to them. The Phaeacians gave him rich gifts, and a day later they brought him back to Ithaca on one of their ships, in a deep sleep. So Odysseus reached Ithaca ten years after the fall of Troy, alone and on another's ship, as Polyphemus had prayed. Yet even now Poseidon did not relax his hostility. As the Phaeacians' ship was entering the harbor of Scheria on its return, Poseidon turned the ship and its crew to stone as a punishment of the Phaeacians for conveying strangers over the seas, especially those who were the objects of Poseidon's hatred.

Ithaca

In Ithaca, more than one hundred suitors (young noblemen from Ithaca and the nearby islands) were courting Penelope in the hope of taking Odysseus' place as her husband and as king of Ithaca (for Telemachus, Odysseus' son by Penelope, was considered still too young to succeed). They spent their days feasting at Odysseus' palace, wasting his possessions. Penelope, however, remained faithful to Odysseus, even though he seemed to be dead. She put the suitors off by promising to choose one of them when she finished weaving a magnificent cloak intended as a burial garment for Odysseus' father, Laertes. For three years she wove the robe by day and undid her work by night, but in the fourth year her deception was uncovered, and a decision was now unavoidable.

At this stage Odysseus returned. Helped by Athena, he gained entrance at the palace disguised as a beggar, after finding refuge in the hut of his faithful old swineherd, **Eumaeus**, and revealing his identity to his son, Telemachus. Telemachus had been on a journey to Pylos and Sparta and had learned from Nestor and Menelaüs that his father was still alive. Outside the palace, Odysseus' old hound, **Argus**, recognized his master after nineteen years' absence and died.

At the palace, Odysseus was insulted by the suitors and by another beggar, Irus, whom he knocked out in a fight. Still in disguise, he gave Penelope an exact description of Odysseus and of a curious brooch he had worn. As a result, she confided in him her plan to give herself next day to the suitor who succeeded in stringing Odysseus' great bow and shooting an arrow straight through a row of twelve axe heads. Also at this time, Odysseus was recognized by his old nurse, **Euryclea**, who knew him from a scar on his thigh, which he had received when hunting a boar with his grandfather, Autolycus. Thus the scene was set for Odysseus' triumphant return; his son and his faithful retainers knew the truth, and Penelope had fresh encouragement to prepare her for the eventual recognition.

The Bow and the Killing of the Suitors

The trial of the bow took place the next day. When none of the suitors could even so much as string it, Odysseus asked to be allowed to try. Effortlessly, he achieved the task and shot the arrow through the axes. Next he shot the leading suitor, **Antinoüs**, and in the ensuing fight he and Telemachus and their two faithful servants killed all the other suitors. The scene where Odysseus strings the bow and reveals himself to the suitors is one of the most dramatic in all epic poetry (*Odyssey* 21.404–423; 22.1–8):

> But crafty Odysseus straightway took the great bow in his hands and looked at it on all sides, just as a man who is skilled at the lyre and at song easily stretches a string round a new peg, fitting the well-turned sheep's gut around the peg—even so without effort did he string the great bow, did Odysseus. He took it in his right hand and made trial of the string, and it sang sweetly under his hand, in sound like a swallow. Then great sorrow seized the suitors, and in all of them their skin changed color. Zeus, giving a sign, thundered loudly. Then godlike, patient Odysseus rejoiced that the son of wily Cronus had sent him a sign. Then he chose a swift arrow, one that lay on the table beside him uncovered, while the others lay in the hollow quiver—and these the Achaeans would soon feel. This arrow, then, he took, and he drew back 10 the string and the notched arrow, sitting where he was on his stool. And he shot the arrow aiming straight ahead, and of the hafted axes he missed none from the first to the last, and the arrow weighted with bronze sped straight through to the end.
> . . . (21.404–423)
>
> Then wily Odysseus stripped off his rags, and he leaped to the great threshold holding the bow and the quiver full of arrows, and he poured out the arrows in front of his feet. Then he spoke to the suitors: "This my labor inexorable has been completed. Now I shall aim at another target which no man has yet struck, if I can hit it and Apollo grants my prayer." He spoke and shot a death-dealing arrow straight at Antinoüs. (22.1–8)   20

All the suitors were killed; only the herald, Medon, and the bard, Phemius, were spared. Odysseus called Euryclea to identify the twelve servant women who had insulted him and had been the lovers of the suitors. They were forced to cleanse the hall, and then they were mercilessly hanged, while the disloyal goatherd, Melanthius, was mutilated and killed. The consequences of the battle in the hall were grisly, a reminder that Odysseus was a warrior who had taken part in the sack of Troy and was merciless to his enemies.

The Father of Odysseus

Laertes is usually identified as the father of Odysseus, and in the last book of the *Odyssey*, Odysseus after his return to Ithaca reveals his identity to his father, Laertes, in a moving scene.

One story, however, makes **Sisyphus**, the son of Aeolus, the father of Odysseus, whose mother, Anticlea, he seduced before she married Laertes. Anticlea's father was the master thief **Autolycus**, son of Hermes, who gave him the power to steal whatever he wished undetected. For a long time he was in the habit of stealing Sisyphus' cattle until Sisyphus branded the animals on their hooves and so easily recognized and recovered those that Autolycus had stolen. The two heroes became friends, and Autolycus allowed Sisyphus to lie with Anticlea. Thus (in this version) the trickster Sisyphus, a sinner in Hades (see p. 355), was really the father of Odysseus, who inherited his devious nature.

Telemachus

The *Odyssey's* portrait of Telemachus, the son of Odysseus and Penelope, is a masterful depiction of the hero as a young man. His introduction in Book 1 establishes his character with sure and subtle brevity. Athena has come down from Olympus to inspire courage and action in Telemachus, still a boy at heart. We first meet him in the palace, helplessly witnessing the abusive arrogance of the suitors. He sits sad and despondent, daydreaming that his father had already returned and driven out the suitors and saved him from their insolence and disrespect. Amid their drunken revels, he is the only one to notice Athena disguised as Mentes waiting at the threshold. He alone rises and greets her with the courtesy demanded by the sacred bond of guest-friendship. In a few lines, we know that Telemachus is a worthy son of his heroic father and we are prepared for his gratifying development. By the end of Book 1, he will have stood up to his mother, who is surprised by his manly effort to break loose from her. He will go on to have an odyssey of his own (appropriately a mini-odyssey, to be sure, in Books 3 and 4) to Pylos and Sparta to obtain news of Odysseus from Nestor and Menelaüs and Helen. When Odysseus does return, it is Telemachus who can almost, but not quite yet, string his father's bow, although he would have done so if his father had allowed him a fourth try. At the climax of the poem, it is father and son, side by side, who kill the suitors.

Penelope

We have said earlier that Odysseus "remained faithful to Penelope," and the reunion with his wife is the goal of the epic. Penelope is not a passive figure: she is the equal of Odysseus in intelligence and loyalty, and she is resourceful in fending off the suitors and, equally significant, in choosing her time and method for recognition of Odysseus. When she finally does recognize him, the poet describes her "as fitting his heart" (*thymares*); that is, she is a perfect match for the man who is the "man of many twists and turns" (*polytropos*, an epithet given him in the first line of the poem), the cleverest of the Greeks.

Penelope's usual epithet is *periphron* (circumspect); that is, she is wary and resourceful, able to keep the suitors at bay by her intelligence. In her first meeting with Odysseus (in Book 19), she says: "I spin out my stratagems," and she tells him of the weaving and unraveling of the burial garment for Laertes. She used her sexual power to weaken the suitors. When she appears before them, she is repeatedly likened to Aphrodite and Artemis, and "the suitors' knees went slack; she bewitched their spirits with lust, and all longed to lie beside her in

TWO RETURNS OF ODYSSEUS

Bernardino di Betto, nicknamed Pinturicchio (Little Painter) because of his small stature, was born in Perugia around 1454 and died in Siena in 1513. Though details of his early life are scant, it is known that he worked with Perugino on frescoes for the Sistine Chapel. Pinturicchio achieved fame for many of his frescoes, including those decorating the Vatican apartments commissioned by Pope Alexander VI and those decorating the Piccolomini Library in the cathedral of Siena. The National Gallery in London houses Pinturicchio's famous fresco, later transferred to canvas, entitled *Penelope and the Suitors*, commissioned by Pandolfo Petrucci. Pinturicchio's fresco was painted to celebrate Petrucci's wedding in 1509. In 1512, Petrucci became ruler of Siena.

During this period, Italy was made up of small principalities and states that were continually vying for dominance over one another. Siena itself witnessed bloody conflict between various factions within the city. The story of Odysseus' return, his killing of the suitors, and his reunion with his wife were intended to underscore the calculation and brutality necessary to keep and maintain power in the state. Even so, there is some debate regarding who the central figure in the fresco is meant to be. As stated in the caption, it may indeed be Telemachus, bursting into the room to tell his mother Penelope that his father has returned and the suitors are dead. But if so, Pinturicchio is taking liberties with the narrative. In the *Odyssey*, the nurse Euryclea rushes upstairs to rouse Penelope from her slumber and tell her that her husband is home and the suitors are killed. Penelope rather poignantly says that she has not slept so well since the

The Return of Odysseus, by Pintoricchio (Bernardo Betti, 1454–1513); fresco transferred to canvas, 1509, 60 × 50 in. To the left sits Penelope at her loom, with Euryclea beside her; above her head are the bow and quiver of Odysseus. Telemachus runs to greet his mother, and behind him are a young suitor (note the falcon on his wrist), the seer Theoclymenus, and Eumaeus. Odysseus, disguised as a beggar, is coming through the door on the right. In the background is the ship of the Phaeacians; to its left is Odysseus' boat being shattered by Poseidon, and, in the wooded landscape beyond, Odysseus meets Circe, while his men root around as pigs. This fresco was originally painted for a wall in a room of the Ducal Palace in Siena. (© *National Gallery, London/Art Resource, NY*)

day Odysseus sailed away, but at first she does not believe the nurse's news. Penelope goes downstairs to find out for herself what has happened and discovers Odysseus sitting against a great column staring at the ground, waiting for her to speak. Penelope is wary. Telemachus is also present and begins to chastise her for her stubbornness, but Odysseus sends him out on an errand so that she can question her husband. Another interpretation is that the central figure is simply one of the suitors. The scene may represent Penelope's trick of the loom at the moment it is exposed.

Romare Bearden (1911–1988) is one of the most acclaimed artists of the twentieth century. He was born in Charlotte, North Carolina, but eventually settled in New York. The Harlem Renaissance, an efflorescence of African American culture in the 1920s, had an important influence on him in his youth. Throughout his career, Bearden worked in a variety of media and had many cultural influences. He is perhaps best known for his collages. He found inspiration in some of the greatest artists of the European tradition, including Giotto, Picasso, and, of course, Pinturicchio. Collage became a way for Bearden to express his sensitivity to collaborative work and to art that reflected the harmonious unity one can achieve through the creative joining of discrete elements. The collage, in form and content, was a method for integrating his art with his concerns for racial equality; the medium also reflected the African American experience in its angularity, broken pieces, fractured perspective, and sharp juxtapositions.

In 1977, Bearden produced a series of collages entitled *Black Odyssey*, based on episodes from Homer's *Odyssey*. In his collage *The Return of Odysseus* (*Homage to Pintoricchio and Benin*), Bearden deliberately juxtaposes this contemporary art form with the classical story, relating the myth of Odysseus, his suffering, and his ultimate triumph directly to the African American experience. He also celebrates the influence of European and African traditions. The European influence is evident in his debt to Pinturicchio's fresco, and the African influence is seen in his use of black figures reminiscent of the sculpture of the African kingdom of Benin from the fourteenth through the seventeenth centuries.

The Return of Odysseus. Watercolor, gouache, and ink on paper (1977) by Romare Bearden (1912–1988): 12¾ × 15½ in. Bearden twice expressed his "Homage to Pintoricchio," first in a collage of 1969 with this title. Bearden's mythological figures are black, for, as he remarked, "if a child in Benin or in Louisiana . . . sees my paintings of Odysseus, he can understand the myth better." The figures are the same as in Pintoricchio's painting, with a simpler version of the Phaeacians' ship in the background and Odysseus, in green and yellow, hardly visible as he enters in the top right corner. (*Art © Romare Bearden Foundation/Licensed by VAGA, New York, NY*)

bed" (*Odyssey* 18.212–214). She gets them to give her gifts (observed with joy by Odysseus himself, who is in the hall disguised as a beggar), and, when it appears inevitable that she must choose one of them, she devises the test of the bow. Finally, she insists that the stranger (i.e., Odysseus, with whom, as we have seen earlier, she had conversed) be allowed to take part in the test. But before Odysseus actually strings the bow, she is told by Telemachus (now for the first time asserting himself as his father's heir apparent and head of the household) to go upstairs. Thus she is absent during Odysseus' successful stringing of the bow, the battle in the hall and its cleansing, and the killing of the servants. The stage is set, as it were, for the climactic scene between Penelope and Odysseus, leading to recognition and reunion.

At their first meeting (in Book 19), she had asked the stranger who he was, and he had begun his reply by likening her to a king who rules over a just and prosperous city—in other words, he likens his wife to himself as king of Ithaca. Later (still not revealing how much she knows of his identity), she shares with him a dream in which an eagle kills her flock of twenty geese, and he agrees with her that it is an omen of Odysseus' return. Penelope's words are fraught with psychological import. She begins with confidences about how her nights are filled with anxiety. She lies awake, miserable with indecision (525–534):

> Should I stay here by the side of my son and keep all my possessions safe, my property, my slaves, and my grand and lofty palace, respecting the bed of my husband and what people might say, or should I go off with the best one of the Achaeans here who court me and offer lavish gifts? As for my son, as long as he was still young and immature, he would not allow me to leave the palace and marry a new husband, but now that he is grown up and has reached maturity, he beseeches me to go away, so upset is he about his estate, which these Achaeans are swallowing up.

Penelope goes on to relate her dream (535–553):

> Now I want you to listen to a dream of mine and interpret it for me. At my home there are twenty geese who come to eat corn from a water-trough, and I love watching them. But down from a mountain swoops a huge eagle with hooked beak, and he breaks their necks and kills them all. They lie strewn together about the house, but he flies aloft into the divine upper air. I weep and wail, although it is only a dream and the Achaean women with lovely hair gather round me as I grieve bitterly because the eagle has killed my geese. He comes back and perched on a beam jutting from the roof speaks in a human voice and restrains my tears. "Take heart, daughter of renowned Icarius. This is not a dream but a reality, a good deed that will be accomplished. The geese are your suitors and I who am the eagle in your dream will come back as your husband, who will bring a sorry fate down upon all your suitors." Thus he spoke and honeyed sleep left me. Looking around, I saw my geese in the courtyard by the trough, pecking at the grain, exactly where they were before.

The stranger in a brief answer assures Penelope that there is only one possible interpretation of her dream. Certain death lies in store for each and every suitor. We wonder how Odysseus feels about Penelope's avowed affection for her geese and marvel at Homer's subtle portrait of a complex woman, devoted to her husband but wary about her own future and not unflattered and unmoved by the attention and the gifts of a flock of suitors. Could she knowingly be leading this stranger on?

The Washing of Odysseus' Feet. Attic red-figure skyphos, ca. 440 B.C.; height 8 in., diameter 6.2 in. Euryclea (named Antiphata on the vase) looks up at Odysseus with her mouth open, as she recognizes him from the scar. To the right is the hand of Eumaeus, evidently offering a gift to Odysseus, who wears the traveler's cap and carries the beggar's basket and stick. On the other side, Penelope sits sadly at her loom, while Telemachus talks with her. (*akg-images/André Held*)

After the battle in the hall, Penelope is wakened by Euryclea and refuses to admit that the stranger is Odysseus (we are not told whether she thinks he is). She comes down, and she and Odysseus sit opposite each other. When Telemachus reproves her for not embracing Odysseus she replies that if the stranger truly is Odysseus then "we will know it from each other even better, for we have signs which we know, hidden from others." Then she orders Euryclea to move the bed, which Odysseus himself had made, out of the marriage chamber for him to sleep on outside.

Odysseus is furious that anyone would move his bed, for he had built it using a living olive tree as one of its supports and building the marriage chamber around it. Thus he revealed the secret, and Penelope knew now that it was he.[11] Then, and only then, did she give way and embrace the husband who had been away for twenty years. The poet again uses a simile for Penelope that identifies her with Odysseus (*Odyssey* 23.232–240):

> He wept as he held the wife who matched his heart (*thymares*). Just as land is a welcome sight to shipwrecked sailors whose well-made ship Poseidon has shattered on the sea, battering it with wind and wave: few escape from the gray sea to reach land, and their skin is caked with brine, but they escape destruction and stand on land with joy—even so with joy did she look upon her husband, and her white arms would not let go of his neck.

In a sense, Penelope *is* Odysseus, the sailor wrecked by Poseidon who reaches land. Thus by the similes of the king and the sailor, and by her resourceful patience and deliberate testing of the stranger, she gets him to reveal himself and proves herself to be his match.

The poet describes the end of Odysseus' labors with tact and delicacy. At the same time, he allows Odysseus to recall his adventures (*Odyssey* 23.300–343):

> So when they (Odysseus and Penelope) had taken their delight in the joys of love, they took delight in words and spoke to each other. She, goddess-like among women, told of all she had endured in the hall as she watched the unseemly mob of suitors, who to win her slaughtered many oxen and fine sheep and drank many casks of wine. In his turn godlike Odysseus told all, the cares he had brought upon men and the grievous sufferings that he had endured. She delighted in his tale, and sleep did not fall upon her eyes until he had finished his tale. (23.300–309)

Naming Odysseus

After Euryclea has recognized Odysseus from the scar on his thigh, Homer tells the story of the naming of Odysseus. His grandfather, Autolycus (father of Anticlea, the mother of Odysseus), was asked to name the infant, whom Euryclea had placed on his knees. "I shall call him *Odysseus*," he said, "because I have come being hateful [Greek, *odyssamenos*] to many men and women all over the fruitful earth." The Greek word is in the middle voice; that is, its subject can be either "an agent of rage or hatred but also its sufferer" (B. Knox's phrase). George Dimock suggests "man of pain," implying both the hero's sufferings and the suffering that he caused to others.

The anonymity or naming of Odysseus is an essential element in his story. In the first line of the *Odyssey*, he is simply "*[the] man*": contrast the first line of the *Iliad*, where the hero, Achilles, is named. The conventions of heroic hospitality allowed hosts to ask their guest's name after he had eaten at their table: so Antinoüs asks, "Tell me the name that your mother and father call you by [at home]," and only then does Odysseus reply (*Odyssey* 9.19), "I am Odysseus, son of Laertes." Odysseus controls the revelation of his name: for example, urged on by Athena, he chooses when to reveal himself to Telemachus in Book 16. Euryclea's discovery caught him by surprise, and his reaction was to threaten to kill her if she revealed it to others. The Cyclops asks his name and is told that it is *Outis* ("Nobody"). Arrived on Ithaca, Odysseus tells Athena that he is a Cretan. Penelope's first question at their first interview (19.105) is, "Tell me, what people do you come from? Where are your city and your parents?" and Odysseus replies that he is a Cretan named *Aethon* [shining, an epithet like that of the Cretan queen, *Phaedra*, bright]. Only after outwitting him with the test of the bed does Penelope finally achieve the self-revelation of the hero. Odysseus, "man of pain," is indeed both "Nobody" and the universal hero.[12]

[*Note*: The Latin name for Odysseus is *Ulixes* or *Ulysses*, etymologically the same as the Greek name, with *Od-* shifting to *Ul-*, possibly (it has been suggested) influenced by a local dialect in Sicily or southern Italy.]

He told first how he had subdued the Cicones and how he had come to the fertile land of the lotus-eating men. He told of the Cyclops' deeds and how he avenged   10 his valiant companions, whom the Cyclops had pitilessly devoured. He told how he came to Aeolus, who received him kindly and sent him onward, yet it was not yet destined for him to come to his own dear land, for a storm again snatched him and bore him over the fish-full sea, groaning deeply. He told how he came to Telepylus and the Laestrygonians, who destroyed his ships and his well-greaved companions. He told of the deceit and wiles of Circe, and he told how he came to the dank house of Hades to consult the soul of Theban Tiresias, sailing on his well-benched ship. There he saw his companions and his mother, who bore him and nourished him when he was a baby. (23. 310–325)   20

He told how he heard the song of the clear-voiced Sirens and how he came to the wandering rocks of the Planctae, and to terrible Charybdis and Scylla, whom no man before had escaped alive. He told how his companions had slain the cattle of Helius, and how Zeus, who thunders in the high heavens, had struck his swift ship with a smoky thunderbolt and killed all his companions, and only he escaped evil death. He told how he came to the island Ogygia and the nymph Calypso, who kept him there in her hollow cave, desiring him to be her husband. She fed him and promised to make him immortal and ageless all his days, yet she did not persuade the heart in his breast. He told how, after many sufferings, he reached the Phaeacians, who honored him like a god and sent him with a ship to his own   30 dear homeland with ample gifts of bronze and gold and clothing. (23.326–340)

This was the last tale he told, when sweet sleep came upon him, sleep that relaxes the limbs and releases the cares of the spirit.

The End of the *Odyssey*

The last book of the *Odyssey* begins with Hermes escorting the souls of the dead suitors to the House of Hades, where they converse with the souls of Agamemnon and Achilles. The ghost of Amphimedon (one of the leading suitors) tells Agamemnon's ghost of Penelope's weaving and the test of the bow and the slaughter of the suitors. Agamemnon's ghost replies (*Odyssey* 24.192–200):

Happy son of Laertes, wily Odysseus! You married a wife of great excellence (*arete*)! How virtuous was the mind of peerless Penelope, daughter of Icarius! How well she kept the memory of Odysseus, her wedded husband! Therefore the fame of her virtue will never fade, and the immortals will fashion a lovely song for mortals to sing in honor of Penelope, the wife who kept her counsel. She did not contrive crimes like the daughter of Tyndareus, who murdered her wedded husband.

Penelope is repeatedly contrasted with Clytemnestra in the *Odyssey*, most eloquently by Agamemnon himself.[13] Meanwhile, Odysseus leaves the palace to find his father, Laertes, who is living as a farmer, away from the city. At first he conceals his identity from the old man, but soon he reveals himself. As they are sharing a meal in Laertes' farmhouse, news comes that the relatives of the suitors are approaching to avenge their deaths. Once again Odysseus must fight, helped by Athena, and Laertes, miraculously energized by the goddess, kills Eupeithes, father of Antinoüs. At this point Athena orders the men to stop fighting, and Zeus casts a thunderbolt at her feet to confirm her command. She makes peace between Odysseus and the suitors' families, and so the epic ends.

Odysseus and Athena

Odysseus was especially helped by the goddess Athena, whose own attributes of wisdom and courage complement his gifts. The relationship of goddess and hero is brilliantly depicted by the poet in a scene after Odysseus, asleep, has been put ashore on Ithaca by the Phaeacians and wakes up, not knowing where he is. Athena, disguised as a young shepherd, has told him that he is on Ithaca (*Odyssey* 13.250–255, 287–301):

> Thus she spoke, and patient godlike Odysseus was glad, rejoicing in his own fatherland, as Pallas Athena had told him, the daughter of Zeus, bearer of the aegis. And he replied to her with winged words. He did not tell her the truth, but he held it back, always directing his mind in his breast for every advantage. [Odysseus then makes up a story which, however, does not fool the goddess.] (250–255)
>
> Thus he spoke, and the goddess, gray-eyed Athena, smiled and stroked him with her hand. In form she was like to a beautiful and tall woman, one who is expert in fine handiwork. She addressed him with these winged words: (287–290)
>
> "Crafty and wily would he be who could surpass you in every trick, even if a god were to compete with you. You rogue, deviser of tricks, never satisfied with deceit, even in your own land you were not going to abandon your deceit and your deceiving words, which are dear to you from your inmost heart. Still, come now, let us no longer talk like this, since we both know how to get the advantage. For you are by far the best of all mortals in counsel and in words, and I am famous among all the gods for wisdom and cunning. Yet you did not recognize Pallas Athena, daughter of Zeus, who stands beside you in every labor and protects you." (291–301)

10

The End of Odysseus' Life

Homer tells the subsequent history of Odysseus in the words of Tiresias' prophecy (*Odyssey* 11.119–137):

> When you have killed the suitors in your palace . . . then you must go, carrying a well-made oar, until you come to men who know not the sea nor eat food flavored with salt; nor know they of red-painted ships nor of shapely oars, which are the wings of ships. This shall be a clear sign that you shall not miss: when another traveler meets you and says that you have a winnowing-fan upon your fine shoulder, then plant the well-turned oar in the ground and sacrifice to Poseidon . . . and to all the immortal gods. And death shall come to you easily, from the sea, such as will end your life when you are weary after a comfortable old age, and around you shall be a prosperous people.

Odysseus appeased Poseidon in the manner foretold by Tiresias, founding a shrine to Poseidon where he planted the oar. He returned to Ithaca. Years later, Telegonus, who had grown up on his mother Circe's island, sailed to Ithaca in search of his father. He was plundering the island and killed Odysseus, who was defending his possessions, not knowing who he was.[14]

The Universality of the *Odyssey*

The *Odyssey* is a splendid intermingling of true myth (tales about the gods), legend (stories ultimately reflecting the history of real heroes and heroines), and folk tales, fairy tales, and the like, which both amuse and edify. It is, perhaps, the finest example of the persistent mythological theme of the legendary Quest. In the case of Odysseus, his personal quest brings him back home, surmounting all obstacles on his journey to punish the wicked and regain his wife, his son, and his kingdom. In subsequent literature, he has become a kind of Everyman. Certainly, to the Romans Odysseus (Ulysses) was a symbol of virtuous patience, and his endurance of adversity made him an example, especially for the Stoics. Plato, in the myth of Er that ends the *Republic*, shows Odysseus in the Underworld choosing for his next life an inconspicuous existence because of his memory of adversity (see p. 361).

Odysseus, then, perhaps more than any other, is the archetypal hero, just as Penelope is par excellence the archetypal heroine, each beautifully illustrating aspects of an exemplary human and heroic *arete* (excellence). Recently, special attention has been given to the character and motives of Penelope. She has been seen as the peer of Odysseus in intelligence and in patience, qualities shown in her resistance to the long siege by the suitors and in her restraint on declaring her recognition of Odysseus. Penelope's reluctance to recognize Odysseus has increasingly been interpreted as a manifestation of her wisdom and self-control, leading attributes of her husband. The final reunion of husband and wife is consummated through the incident concerning their shared knowledge about the solid construction of their immovable marriage bed, with the olive tree forming one leg, a powerful symbol of the strength and persistence of their physical and spiritual love.

Homer's great epic has a unique, universal appeal to both young and old—and to the child and philosopher in us all. It can be read solely as a most entertaining story of travel and adventure, full of exciting episodes of delightful variety, a tale of abiding love that ends happily, with the just triumph of good over evil, or it can reveal to the artist and the sage the most profound insights about men and women, the gods and fate, and the meaning of human existence. The word "odyssey" itself has come into our language as synonymous with a journey and a quest, and never has the word "homecoming" found a more joyous resonance or deeper meaning than in the final books of the poem.[15]

Select Bibliography

Boitani, Piero. *The Shadow of Ulysses: Figures of a Myth*. Translated by Anita Weston. Oxford: Clarendon Press, 1994.

Buitron, Diana. *The Odyssey in Ancient Art: An Epic in Word and Image*. New York: David Brown, 1992. Fourteen essays explore the impact of the poem on literature and art (pottery, sculpture, and jewelry).

Clay, Jenny Strauss. *The Wrath of Athena: Gods and Men in the Odyssey*. Princeton, NJ: Princeton University Press, 1983.

Cohen, B., ed. *The Distaff Side: Representing the Female in Homer's Odyssey*. New York: Oxford University Press, 1995.

Dimock, G. *The Unity of the Odyssey*. Amherst: University of Massachusetts Press, 1989.

Doherty, L. E. *Siren Songs: Gender, Audience, and Narrators in the Odyssey*. Ann Arbor, MI: University of Michigan Press, 1995.

Griffin, Jasper. *Homer: The Odyssey*. New York: Cambridge University Press, 1987.

Hall, Edith. *The Return of Ulysses: A Cultural History of Homer's Odyssey*. Baltimore, MD: Johns Hopkins University Press, 2008.

Louden, Bruce. *"The Odyssey": Structure, Narration, and Meaning*. Baltimore, MD: Johns Hopkins University Press, 1999.

Malkin, I. *The Returns of Odysseus: Colonization and Ethnicity*. Berkeley, CA: University of California Press, 1998.

Murnaghan, S. *Disguise and Recognition in the Odyssey*. Ewing, NJ: Princeton University Press, 1987.

Page, Denys. *Folktales in Homer's Odyssey*. Cambridge, MA: Harvard University Press, 1973.

Peradotto, J. J. *Man in the Middle Voice: Name and Narration in the Odyssey*. Princeton, NJ: Princeton University Press, 1990, especially Chapters 5 and 6.

Schein, Seth L., ed. *Reading the Odyssey: Selected Interpretive Essays*. Princeton, NJ: Princeton University Press, 1996. Ten essays by important critics, including Pierre Vidal-Naquet, Jean-Pierre Vernant, Pietro Pucci, and Charles P. Segal.

Shay, Jonathan. *Odysseus in America*: *Combat Trauma and the Trials of Homecoming*. New York: Scribner, 2002. The author of *Achilles in Vietnam* now turns to the *Odyssey*, which can be read as a metaphor, illuminating the problems of veterans returning from combat. The brief foreword is by Senator John McCain and former Senator Max Cleland.

Stanford, W. B. *The Ulysses Theme: A Study in the Adaptability of a Traditional Hero*. Ann Arbor, MI: University of Michigan Press, 1968.

Tracy, Stephen V. *The Story of the Odyssey*. Princeton, NJ: Princeton University Press, 1990.

Primary Sources

Sources in the Chapter

Aristotle	*Poetics* 17.10
Homer	*Odyssey* (selections)

Additional Sources

Apollodorus	*Library*, Epitome 1–6.29 (the returns of the heroes); 7.1–7.40 (the return of Odysseus)
Epic Cycle	*Nostoi* (*Returns*)
Euripides	*Cyclops*

Notes

1. The summary is ascribed to the fifth-century A.D. scholar Proclus, who names Agias of Troezen as the author of the *Nostoi*. For a useful discussion, see G. L. Huxley, *Greek Epic Poetry* (Cambridge, MA: Harvard University Press, 1969), Chapter 12.
2. For the story that Helen was in Egypt during the Trojan War, see p. 461.
3. Pindar, *Nemean Odes* 10.7. Among the many narratives of the legend of Diomedes are those of Vergil (*Aeneid* 11.243–295) and Ovid (*Metamorphoses* 14.460–511).
4. Said by Ovid to be "next in shape to swans." What these birds were can only be surmised.
5. He is also associated with Colophon in Asia Minor.
6. Many attempts have been made to follow the route of Odysseus. See T. Severin, *The Ulysses Voyage: Sea Search for the Odyssey* (London: Hutchinson, 1987). Compare T. Severin, *The Jason Voyage: The Quest for the Golden Fleece* (New York: Simon & Schuster, 1985).
7. According to the conventions of Homeric society, the liaisons with Calypso and Circe did not make Odysseus unfaithful. Cf. Mary R. Lefkowitz, *Women in Greek Myth* (London: Duckworth, 1986), p. 64: "[Penelope] does not demand strict fidelity; neither she nor Helen object to their husbands' liaisons with other women, so long as they are

temporary." The same point is made by Sarah Pomeroy, *Goddesses, Whores, Wives, and Slaves* (New York: Schocken, 1975), pp. 26–27, and by Marilyn Katz, *Penelope's Renown* (Princeton, NJ: Princeton University Press, 1991), p. 13.

8. The Greek word *polytropos* (of many ways) means a combination of complexity, intelligence, and being widely traveled.

9. On the island of Lesbos lived Macareus, a son of Aeolus, whose story was told by Euripides in his lost play *Aeolus*. He fell in love with his sister Canace and by her became father of a child. When Aeolus discovered the truth, he sent Canace a sword with which to kill herself, and Macareus also committed suicide.

10. A powerful adaptation of this legend is the Circe episode in James Joyce's *Ulysses*.

11. The living olive tree and the bed are powerful sexual symbols for a psychoanalytical interpretation.

12. See G. Dimock, "The Name of Odysseus." *Hudson Review* 9 (1956), pp. 52–70.

13. The soul of Agamemnon describes his murder in the first Underworld scene (*Odyssey* 11.405–456). The *Odyssey* focuses on Clytemnestra's deed, not on Agamemnon's killing of his own daughter, Iphigenia, which motivated Clytemnestra's revenge.

14. The adventures of Odysseus subsequent to the *Odyssey* were narrated in the lost epic *Telegonia* by Eugammon of Cyrene. It ends with Telegonus conveying Odysseus' body with Penelope and Telemachus to Circe, who makes them immortal. Telegonus then marries Penelope, and Circe marries Telemachus.

15. The most powerful adaptation of the myth of Odysseus is that of Dante, discussed in Chapter 27 on the companion website. For the many uses of Odysseus made by authors in medieval, Renaissance, and modern times, see the books by Boitani and Stanford listed in the bibliography for this chapter.

For additional digital learning resources please go to
www.oup.com/he/morford12e

21

PERSEUS AND THE LEGENDS OF ARGOS

At that time Argos excelled all the cities in the land that is now called Hellas.

—HERODOTUS, *Histories* 1.1

Argive Hera

Argos was connected in history and in legend with Corinth and Thebes, and the Argive sagas demonstrate the many contacts of Argos with the eastern Mediterranean, notably the Levant and Egypt. While some of the legendary heroes are associated with a particular city of the Mycenaean Argolid (e.g., Heracles with Tiryns, Diomedes with Argos, and Perseus with Mycenae), it is often hard to distinguish between the separate cities. We shall generally use "Argos" to cover the whole Argolid and its cities.

Argos was the greatest center in Greece for the worship of Hera, and the **Heraeum**, the hill where Hera's sanctuary stood, was the religious center of the whole area. In the Argive saga, the first of men was Phoroneus, who established the kingdom of Argos and decided in favor of Hera in the contest for the land between Poseidon and Hera. In anger, Poseidon dried up the Argive rivers, one of which, Inachus, was the father of Phoroneus. Ever after, the Argive rivers have been short of water.

The richness of the Argive saga can be seen from the opening lines of Pindar's tenth *Nemean Ode*:

> Sing, O Graces, of the city of Danaüs and his fifty daughters on their shining thrones, of Argos, dwelling of Hera, a home fit for the gods; bright is the flame of her brave deeds unnumbered in their excellence. Long is the tale of Perseus and the Gorgon, Medusa; many are the cities of Egypt founded by the wisdom of Epaphus; Hypermnestra kept to the path of virtue and alone did not draw the dagger from its sheath. Fair Athena once made Diomedes divine; in Thebes the earth, struck by Zeus' thunderbolts, received the seer Amphiaraüs, the storm cloud of war. Ancient is Argos' excellence in beautiful women; Zeus revealed this truth when he came to Alcmena and to Danaë. (1–11)   10

The Legend of Perseus

Danaë and Acrisius

Of the heroes of Argos, first in importance, though not in time, is Perseus. His great-grandfather Abas had twin sons, **Proetus** and Acrisius, who quarreled even before their birth.[1] Acrisius, who became king of Argos itself while Proetus ruled Tiryns, had no sons and only one daughter, Danaë; an oracle foretold that her son would kill Acrisius. To keep her from having children, Acrisius shut Danaë up in a brazen underground chamber in his palace, but Zeus loved her and entered the chamber in the form of a shower of gold and lay with her.[2] Their child was Perseus, and Danaë kept him in the chamber for four years, unknown to Acrisius, until he was discovered from the noise he made while playing. Acrisius refused to believe that Zeus was the child's father and put mother and child into a chest which he set afloat on the sea. The chest floated to the island of **Seriphos**, where the fisherman **Dictys** (whose name means "net") found it and rescued Danaë and Perseus, giving them shelter in his own home.

Polydectes

Now Polydectes, brother of Dictys, was king of Seriphos, and as Perseus grew to manhood, Polydectes fell in love with Danaë, who refused him. He then summoned the leading men of the island to a banquet at which each man had to present him with the gift of a horse. Perseus boasted that he could just as easily give Polydectes the Gorgon's head. Polydectes, eager to get Perseus out of the way, took him at his word and ordered him to perform the task. In despair, Perseus wandered to a lonely part of Seriphos, where Hermes and Athena came to his help with advice. That two gods should assist him is remarkable; Hermes belongs more to the Peloponnese than Athena, and it is very likely he was originally the hero's only supernatural helper. Since the Gorgon's head was an attribute of Athena's aegis, she may very early have been associated with the saga, for much of the literary tradition was in the hands of Athenians.[3] Pindar, writing in the first half of the fifth century B.C., makes Athena the sole helper: "Breathing courage, Danaë's son joined the company of blessed men, and Athena was his guide" (*Pythian Odes* 10.44–46).

Danaë and the Brazen Tower, by Edward Burne-Jones (1833–1898); oil on canvas, 1888, 94 × 44½ in. Danaë, in the foreground, watches the raising of her future prison, a solitary and beautiful figure contrasted with the small figures of the distant workmen and the soldier and courtiers speaking with Acrisius. The tragedy of her coming immurement is heightened by the tension between the two regions of the painting, the garden with its exquisite flowers and the palace courtyard, through whose iron-studded gate she must soon be taken to a life bereft of freedom and human company. (*Pictures Now/Alamy Stock Photo*)

The Graeae

Advised by Hermes and Athena, Perseus made his way to the three daughters of Phorcys, sisters of the Gorgons and old women (in Greek, the *Graiai*) from their birth. They alone could tell Perseus the way to some nymphs who possessed

Two Romantic Idealists

Gustave Moreau (1826–1898) and Edward Burne-Jones (1833–1898) were profoundly inspired by classical mythology, and their art goes far beyond the morality and symbolism of many of their contemporaries. Moreau's great paintings *Prometheus*, *Oedipus*, and *Heracles* probe the meaning of the classical texts and express a heroic humanism appropriate for the challenges of his time. In England, Burne-Jones, who shared with William Morris the ideals of the Pre-Raphaelite movement, returned again and again to the classical myths to support his search for purity and beauty in the past. In *Danaë and the Brazen Tower* (1888), he focuses on Danaë's feelings as the tower is built, not on the lust of Zeus and the anger of Acrisius. In the *Pygmalion Series* (1878) and the *Perseus Series* (1887), Burne-Jones turns from the anger of the gods and the violence of the hero to the ideals of piety, chivalry, and chaste love. These very ideals involve the psychological and sexual tensions that Freud (1856–1939) at the same time was beginning to explore.

the magic objects he would need for his task, but they would part with their information only under duress. Among them they had one eye and one tooth, which they passed to one another in turn. Perseus got hold of both eye and tooth and gave them back only when the Graeae had told him the way to the nymphs. From the nymphs he received three objects: a **Cap of Invisibility**, a pair of **winged sandals**, and a **wallet** or **kibisis**.[4] From Hermes he received a **scimitar**, the only object given directly by Hermes.[5]

The Gorgons

Perseus now flew to the Gorgons, whose home was somewhere on the edge of the world, usually situated in North Africa.[6] Pindar, who makes Perseus go to the far north, gives a beautiful description of the perfect life lived by the Hyperboreans. His account is one of the few continuous passages in extant classical Greek literature that deals with the legend of Perseus (*Pythian Odes* 10.29–48):

> Not with ships nor on foot would you find the marvelous road to the assembly of the Hyperboreans. Once did Prince Perseus feast among them when he entered their palace; he found them solemnly sacrificing one hundred donkeys to their god. In their feasts continually and in their hymns Apollo especially takes delight, and he laughs as he sees the pride of the animals rearing up. The Muse is always with them and is a part of their customs: everywhere are the maidens' dances, the music of lyres and of the deep-sounding flutes. They bind their hair with golden laurel-wreaths, feasting with joy. Neither disease nor wasting old age has any part in their holy nation. Without labor, without battles, they live, escaping the severe justice of Nemesis. Breathing courage, Danaë's son joined the company of blessed men, and Athena was his guide. And he slew the Gorgon and came bearing the head with hair of writhing snakes, for the islanders a stony death.

10

The three Gorgons, of whom only **Medusa** was mortal, were of terrifying aspect, and those who looked upon their faces were turned to stone.[7] They were asleep when Perseus came, guided by Athena. Looking only at the Gorgon's reflection in his brazen shield, he beheaded Medusa and put the head in the *kibisis.* As she was beheaded, **Chrysaor (He of the Golden Sword)** and **Pegasus**, the winged horse, sprang from her body. Their father was Poseidon; Chrysaor became father of the monster Geryon, and Pegasus was prominent in the legend of Bellerophon. According to Ovid, his hoof struck Mt. Helicon and caused the fountain Hippocrene (Horse's Fountain) to gush forth, which from then on was loved by the Muses and associated with poetic inspiration.

This is not the only association of the legend of Medusa with music and poetry. Pindar, praising Midas of Akragas, winner in the competition for flute-playing at the Pythian Games, tells how Athena invented the music of the flute in imitation of the Gorgons' lament for the death of Medusa (*Pythian Odes* 12.5–23):

> Receive this garland from Delphi for glorious Midas who is the best in Greece in the art that Pallas Athena wove from the deadly lament of the impetuous Gorgons, which Perseus heard pouring from the snaky heads that could not be approached. Grievously he labored when he killed the third part of the sisters, bringing death to sea-girt Seriphos and its people. Indeed, he brought the darkness of death to the Gorgons, god-born children of Phorcys;
> 10 and grievous did the son of Danaë make the banquet of Polydectes, and the long servitude of his mother and her forced love. His spoil was the head of fair-cheeked Medusa. And he, we say, was born from the shower of gold. But when the virgin Athena had delivered the hero dear to her from these labors, she made the music of the flutes with its many notes, so that with instruments she might imitate the loud-sounding lamentation that was forced from the hungry jaws of Euryale.[8] This was the goddess's invention, but she gave it to mortals and called it "the music of many heads."

Medusa, by Caravaggio (1571–1610); oil on a wooden shield covered with canvas, ca. 1598. The biographer Vasari relates that a young Leonardo da Vinci had once painted a monster upon a shield. That work has been lost, but this painting, commissioned by Cardinal Francesco Maria del Monte, has been seen as Caravaggio's attempt to compete with the legacy of the great Leonardo. It is a tour de force. Though painted on a convex shield, the image itself seems to construct a concave space. The fantastical image is rendered with a startling realism. The Gorgon Medusa has just been decapitated by the hero Perseus. The wound gushes with blood. The snakes are finely drawn. The face of Medusa seems frozen in the moment of recognition of what has happened. The horror of her gaze is double-edged: both instilling petrifying terror and yet itself trapped in a horrifying realization, as her eyes look down at her missing body. (*Scala/Ministero per i Beni e le Attività culturali/Art Resource, NY*)

Perseus was able to fly away from Medusa's sisters unharmed, since he was wearing the Cap of Invisibility. In the original version of the saga, he probably returned directly to Seriphos and dealt with Polydectes.

Andromeda

At a very early stage, the legend of Andromeda was added to the story of Perseus' return. Andromeda was the daughter of King **Cepheus** and his queen, **Cassiepea**. Their kingdom is variously placed in **Ethiopia** or in the Levant.[9]

Danaë and the Chest. Attic red-figure lekythos, ca. 470 B.C.; height 16 in. The infant Perseus, already in the chest, reaches up to his reluctant mother. Acrisius gestures impatiently to her to get in. In her left hand Danaë holds a perfume jar. (*The Providence Painter, Red Figure Lekythos, about 470 B.C., slip-decorated earthenware, Toledo Museum of Art, Purchased with funds from the Libbey Endowment, Gift of Edward Drummond Libbey, 1969.369. Photo Credit: Toni Marie Gonzalez, Toledo Museum of Art*)

Cassiepea boasted that she was more beautiful than the Nereids. As a punishment, Poseidon flooded Cepheus' kingdom and sent a sea-monster to ravage the land. Cepheus consulted the oracle of Zeus Ammon and learned that the monster could be appeased only if Andromeda were offered to it, chained to a rock. Cepheus obeyed, but at this point, Perseus came on the scene and undertook to kill the monster if he could marry Andromeda. Making use of his sandals and cap, Perseus killed the beast with Hermes' scimitar and released Andromeda, whom he married, using the Gorgon's head to deal with the opposition of Cepheus' brother **Phineus**, to whom Andromeda had previously been betrothed. After their son Perses was born, Perseus and Andromeda flew back to Seriphos, leaving Perses behind as heir to Cepheus' kingdom.

The Origin of Libyan Snakes, the Atlas Range, and Coral

A number of other details have been added to the original account of Perseus' flight with the Gorgon's head. The Gorgon's blood is said to have dripped through the *kibisis* as Perseus flew over Libya, and

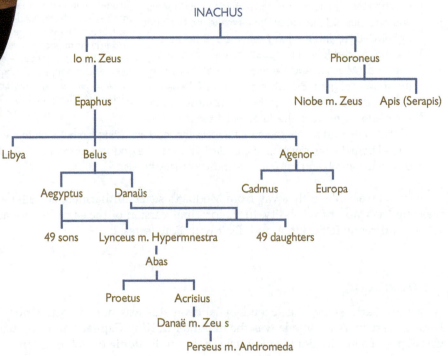

Figure 21.1 The Ancestry of Perseus

from the drops sprang the infinite number of poisonous snakes that (according to the belief of the ancients) infested the Libyan desert. The giant Atlas, supporter of the heavens, refused to show Perseus any hospitality, and Perseus turned him into stone with the Gorgon's head. His head and body became a mountain range, his hair the forests upon the mountains. As an example of these ingenious additions to the legend, we give Ovid's description of the creation of coral (*Metamorphoses* 4.740–752):

> Perseus washed his hands, bloody from his victory over the monster, in the sea. So that the hard sand should not damage the snake-bearing head, he made the ground soft with leaves and branches that grow beneath the sea's surface, and on these he placed the head of Medusa, daughter of Phorcys. The branch that a few moments before had been fresh and filled with living
> 10 pith absorbed the monster's power; and touched by the head, its leaves and stems took on a new hardness. But the sea-nymphs tested the miraculous change on other branches and rejoiced to see the same thing happen. Now coral still retains its same nature: it grows hard in contact with air, and what in the sea was flexible becomes stone out of the water.

Perseus Beheads Medusa. Limestone metope from Selinus, ca. 540 B.C.; height 58 in. To the left stands Athena, wearing a peplos. The winged horse, Pegasus, springs from the body of Medusa. The frontality of the figures compels the viewer to confront the horror of Medusa's face and the necessity for Perseus of avoiding her gaze. (*Scala/Art Resource, NY*)

Polydectes and Perseus' Return to Argos

When Perseus and Andromeda reached Seriphos, they found that Danaë and Dictys had taken refuge at an altar from the violence of Polydectes. Perseus displayed the Gorgon's head before Polydectes and his assembled followers, who were all turned to stone. Thus Danaë was released and returned to Argos with Perseus and Andromeda. Perseus made Dictys king of Seriphos and returned the magic objects to the gods—the sandals, *kibisis*, and cap to Hermes (who returned them to the nymphs) and the Gorgon's head to Athena, who set it in the middle of her shield.

The Death of Acrisius

When Acrisius heard that Danaë's son was indeed alive and returning to Argos, he left the city and went to the city of Larissa, in Thessaly, where Perseus followed him. Here Acrisius met his long-foretold death. Competing in the athletic games

Perseus and Andromeda, by Titian (ca. 1487–1576); oil on canvas, 1554–1556, 70½ × 77¾ in. For six centuries, the subject of Andromeda has been a favorite vehicle for painters' interpretations of the theme of "Beauty and the Beast." Titian correctly gives Perseus winged sandals and *harpe*. In many versions Perseus is confused with Bellerophon and rides on the winged horse, Pegasus. (*Bridgeman Art Library International—New York*)

that the king of Larissa was celebrating in honor of his dead father, Perseus threw a discus that accidentally killed Acrisius. He was buried outside Larissa and honored there as a hero. Perseus, having shed kindred blood, returned not to Argos but to Tiryns, whose king Megapenthes, son of Proetus, exchanged kingdoms with him. As king of Tiryns, Perseus founded Mycenae, where in historical times he was honored as a hero. The children of Perseus and Andromeda became kings of Mycenae, and from them descended Heracles and Eurystheus.

Saga and Folk Tale

An interesting feature of the saga of Perseus is its number of folk tale motifs, more than in any other Greek saga. These include the magic conception of the hero by the princess, his mother; the discovery of the hero as a child by the noise of his playing; the villainous king and his good and humble brother; the rash promise of the hero, which he performs with the aid of supernatural helpers and magic objects; the three old women from whom advice must be sought; the Gorgons, imaginary monsters of ferocious ugliness; and, finally, the vindication of the hero and the punishment of the villain. Nevertheless, Euripides found material in these tales for two tragedies, *Danaë* and *Dictys*, both of which are now largely lost.

Other Legends of Argos

The Family of Inachus

Among the earliest legends of Argos are those of the family of Inachus. The daughter of Inachus was **Io**, much of whose story is told on pages 96–98 in connection with Aeschylus' *Prometheus Bound*. Beloved by Zeus, Io was changed into a white cow by jealous Hera and guarded by all-seeing Argus until Hermes, sent by Zeus to rescue her, cut off Argus' head. Next Hera sent a gadfly to madden her; but after wandering the earth, Io came at last to Egypt, where Zeus restored her human form. There she gave birth to a son, Epaphus, destined to be the ancestor of the hero Heracles.

From other sources we learn that the Egyptians identified **Epaphus** with **Apis**, the sacred bull. His birth did not bring an end to Io's wanderings. Hera had Epaphus kidnapped, and Io set out in search of him, eventually finding him in Syria. She now returned to Egypt, where she came to be worshiped as **Isis**.

The story of Io has many confusing elements. An Apis was said to have been a son of Phoroneus and to have given the Peloponnese its ancient name of Apia; after his death he was identified with **Serapis**, who is the same as the Egyptian bull-god Apis. Io was originally a goddess; she may have been a form of Hera herself. Herodotus, who himself visited Egypt, said that Isis was identified there with Demeter, whose image Io had first brought there, and that Isis was always represented as a woman with cow's horns (in this detail being similar to the great Phoenician moon-goddess, Astarte). The versions of Io's legend vary considerably, and Aeschylus, in his two plays, the *Supplices* and *Prometheus Bound*, gives different reasons for her departure from home and her transformation. She was originally a divine being rather than a human heroine, and through Greek contacts with the East (especially Egypt), she was assimilated into Egyptian mythology.

Perseus, by Benvenuto Cellini (1545–1553). Cellini was a Florentine goldsmith and sculptor. This work, which stood (as it still does today) in the Loggia dei Lanzi looking out upon the Piazza della Signoria, the heart of the Florentine republic, was the product of the artist's maturity and is considered his masterpiece. It was commissioned by Cosimo de' Medici, the Duke of Florence between 1537 and 1574. Prior to this the Medici had been expelled from Florence by the republican government, but they would eventually return to power. In this work Cosimo sought to celebrate the triumph of the Medici and to underscore the threat of what would happen to their enemies. Perseus stands as the invincible hero who has just decapitated Medusa. He carries the curved sword or scimitar that he received from Hermes and the winged sandals and cap of invisibility (also winged perhaps to resemble Hermes' own cap) that he received from the Graeae. The heroic figure is exalted in triumph, yet his head and eyes are turned down, both to prevent his looking upon the head and to suggest a modesty at the apex of victory. The modeling of Perseus' body and the decorations of the plinth, which is an exquisitely wrought work of art in itself, display the perfection of the bronzesmith's art. (*vvoe/Shutterstock*)

The Descendants of Io

Through Epaphus, Io was the founder of the royal families of Egypt and Argos, as well as those of Phoenicia, Thebes, and Crete. Epaphus himself was said to have founded many cities in Egypt, including the royal city of Memphis. His daughter was Libya, who gave her name to part of North Africa; he also had twin sons, Agenor and Belus. Agenor became the Phoenician king, father of Cadmus (founder of Thebes) and Europa (mother of the Cretan king Minos). Belus stayed in Egypt and also became the father of twin sons, Aegyptus and Danaüs, who, like their descendants Proetus and Acrisius, were bitter enemies.

The Daughters of Danaüs

Aegyptus and Danaüs quarreled over the kingdom, so that Danaüs was compelled to leave Egypt. Sailing with his fifty daughters (the **Danaïds**) via Rhodes, he came to Argos, where he peaceably established himself as king. (His subjects were called after him **Danaï**—the term by which Homer generally refers to the Greeks.) Now Aegyptus had fifty sons, who claimed as next of kin the right to marry their cousins and pursued them to Argos. Danaüs gave his daughters in marriage, but to each he gave a dagger with orders to kill her husband on the wedding night. All obeyed, save one only, **Hypermnestra**, who spared her husband, Lynceus, and hid him. As to the sequel, accounts vary. According to the most popular version, the forty-nine Danaïds who obeyed their father were punished in the Underworld by eternally having to fill water jars, through which the water leaked away. According to Pindar, however, Danaüs gave them as wives to the winners of an athletic contest. After a period of imprisonment by Danaüs, Hypermnestra was reunited with Lynceus and became the mother of Abas, father of Proetus and Acrisius. Thus the line of descent of the Argive kings from Inachus to Heracles remained unbroken.

Amymone

The Danaïd Amymone was sent by her father to search for water and came upon a satyr who attempted to seduce her. She was saved by Poseidon, who then himself lay with her and as a reward caused a spring to burst from a rock with a stroke of his trident. In historical times, the spring Amymone was still shown near Argos.

Other Argive Heroes

Important Argive heroes were the seer Melampus (p. 121) and the heroes who took part in the expedition of the Seven against Thebes. Among these heroes was Tydeus, whose son Diomedes, a leading Greek hero in the Trojan War and the last great mythical prince of Argos, was widely worshiped as a hero after his death. Pindar says that Athena gave him the immortality that she denied Tydeus.

The Baleful Head, by Edward Burne-Jones (1833–1898); oil on canvas, 1887, 60½ × 50¾ in. This is the final painting in Burne-Jones' Perseus cycle, undertaken for Arthur Balfour in 1875 and based on William Morris' poem "The Doom of Acrisius" in *The Earthly Paradise*. Ten full-scale watercolor cartoons (now in Southampton, England) and four oil paintings (now in Stuttgart, Germany) were completed. Burne-Jones sets the lovers in an enclosed garden. They look at the reflection of the Gorgon's head, held up by Perseus, in the surface of a marble-sided well. The bright, open eyes of Andromeda provide a dramatic contrast to the reflection of Medusa's closed eyes. The scene is an intense yet peaceful close to the turbulent adventures of Perseus, who still must face the battle with Phineus. (*Staatsgalerie Stuttgart © Foto: Staatsgalerie Stuttgart*)

Appendix: Bellerophon and the Chimera

The famous mythological horse Pegasus is sometimes given to Perseus, but he really belongs to Bellerophon. Here is his legend, which tells how he received, harnessed, and mounted Pegasus and performed mighty deeds.

Bellerophon, grandson of Sisyphus, was the greatest of Corinthian heroes. His legend is told in Homer by the Lycian leader Glaucus, when he meets Diomedes in battle. It is set both in the Argolid and in Asia Minor. Bellerophon may even have been introduced into Greek legend from the East.

Bellerophon was only one of several significant heroes associated with the important city-state of **Corinth**. The Corinthian poet Eumelos identified the Homeric "Ephyra" with Corinth. Homer (*Iliad* 6.152–159) says:

> There is a city, Ephyra, in a corner of horse-rearing Argos, and there lived Sisyphus, who was the most cunning of men, Sisyphus, son of Aeolus. He was father to Glaucus, and Glaucus was father to virtuous Bellerophon, to whom the gods gave beauty and lovely manliness. But Proetus devised evil against him in his heart and drove him out from the people of Argos, since Bellerophon was a better man than he. For Zeus had made him subject to Proetus.

Originally, Ephyra was no more than a minor city in the kingdom of Argos (which includes Tiryns, normally given as the city ruled by Proetus), and its rulers, Sisyphus and his grandson Bellerophon, were minor chieftains subject to the king of Argos. By identifying Ephyra with Corinth, Eumelos magnified the status of the city and its rulers. According to Eumelos, Sisyphvus became the king of Corinth (which had been founded by the son of Helius, Aeëtes) after Medea left. Others make Sisyphus the founder of Corinth. In this way, the hero Bellerophon and his exploits became famous.

Born in Corinth, he left home, perhaps because of blood-guilt after unintentionally killing a brother, and went to the court of Proetus, king of Tiryns, who purified him. There Proetus' wife **Stheneboea** (or Antea, as Homer calls her) fell in love with him. When he rejected her, she accused him before Proetus of trying to seduce her. Proetus therefore sent Bellerophon to his wife's father Iobates, king of Lycia, with a sealed letter that told of Stheneboea's accusation and asked Iobates to destroy Bellerophon. Accordingly, Iobates sent the hero on a number of dangerous expeditions (Homer, *Iliad* 6.179–193):

> First, he bid him kill the fearsome Chimera, which was of divine, not mortal, breed—a lion in its forepart with a serpent's tail and in the middle a goat, and it breathed fire. He killed it, trusting in the gods' signs. Next, he fought the mighty Solymi, and this was his most violent battle with men. Third, he slew the warrior Amazons. And as he returned, the king devised another plot against him; he chose the most valiant men in all Lycia and set them in ambush. Not one of them returned home, for gallant Bellerophon killed them all.
>
> So when the king realized that he was truly of divine descent, he kept him there in Lycia and gave him his daughter and the half of his kingdom.

Bellerophon became the father of Hippolochus (Glaucus' father) and of Isandrus, who was killed fighting the Solymi, and of a daughter, Laodamia. She was loved by Zeus and by him became the mother

Bellerophon and the Chimera. Byzantine ivory plaque, fifth century; 8½ × 3½ in. Bellerophon rides on Pegasus to the right and thrusts his lance into the lion's mouth, as the monster collapses on its front paws. Its serpent-tail twines round one of the three trees that represent the landscape setting, and the goat's head melds with another. (© *The Trustees of the British Museum*)

of Sarpedon, whom Patroclus killed at Troy. Laodamia was "killed by Artemis in anger," and Bellerophon ended his days in sorrow; "hated by the gods, he wandered over the Alean plain alone, eating out his heart and avoiding the paths of men" (Homer, *Iliad* 6.200–202).

In Homer, Bellerophon is the hero who performs certain tasks and wins the prize of a kingdom and a princess. His tragic end, to which Homer refers in vague terms, is the theme of Euripides' tragedy *Bellerophon*, in which Bellerophon tries to mount to heaven itself and fails.

Both Euripides and Pindar introduce the winged horse **Pegasus** into the myth of Bellerophon. Poseidon gave it to him, but he could not master it, as it stood by the Corinthian spring Pirene, until Athena appeared to him in a dream and gave him a magic bridle with golden trappings (Pindar, *Olympian Odes* 13.63–92):

> Much did he labor beside the spring in his desire to harness the offspring of the snake-girdled Gorgon, until the maiden Pallas brought him the gold-accoutred bridle, and quickly his dream became reality. "Are you sleeping," said she, "King, descendant of Aeolus? Come, take this charm to soothe the horse and sacrifice a white bull to your forefather Poseidon, the Tamer of Horses."
>
> These were the words which the maiden with the dark aegis seemed to speak as he slept; he leaped to his feet and took the divine object that lay beside him. And strong Bellerophon, after all his efforts, caught the winged horse by putting the gentle charm around its mouth. Mounting it straightway, he brandished his arms, himself in armor of bronze. With it he slew the archer army of women, the Amazons, shooting them from the unpeopled bosom of the cold upper air, and he slew the fire-breathing Chimera and the Solymi. His fate I shall not mention; the ancient stalls of Zeus' stable in Olympus shelter the horse.

Bellerophon, then, met his end in attempting to rise too high. This theme of Euripides' *Bellerophon* is also expressed in Pindar's words (*Isthmian Odes* 7.60–68):

> If any man sets his eye on a distant target, he is too short to reach the brass-paved home of the gods. For winged Pegasus hurled his rider Bellerophon, who wished to enter the palaces of Heaven and join Zeus' company.

Euripides wrote two tragedies on Bellerophon's saga. His *Bellerophon* included the hero's fall from the heavens and ended with the announcement that Pegasus had been "harnessed to the chariot of Zeus, carrying his lightning."[10] He also wrote a *Stheneboea* (now mostly lost), in which Bellerophon returned to Tiryns after his labors in Lycia and killed Stheneboea by luring her onto Pegasus and throwing her down as they flew high over the sea. For Euripides, Bellerophon's end is that of a human being who fails in a high endeavor, but originally, he must have been punished, like Tantalus and Ixion, because he abused the friendship of the gods.

Select Bibliography

Dobrov, Gregory W. *Figures of Play: Greek Drama and Metafictional Poetics.* New York: Oxford University Press, 2001.

Ogden, Daniel. *Perseus.* Gods and Heroes of the Ancient World Series. New York: Routledge, 2008.

Wilk, Stephen R. *Solving the Mystery of the Gorgon*. New York: Oxford University Press, 2000. An exploration with illustrations of various facets of the legacy of the Gorgon and her imagery from ancient to modern times.

Woodward, Jocelyn. *Perseus: A Study in Greek Art and Legend*. New York: Cambridge University Press, 1976 [1937].

Primary Sources

Sources in the Chapter

Homer	*Iliad* 6.152–159, 179–193 (Bellerophon)
Pindar	*Isthmian* 7.60–68
	Nemean Ode 10.1–11
	Olympian Ode 13.63–92
	Pythian Ode 10.29–48; 12.5–23
Ovid	*Metamorphoses* 4.740–752

Additional Sources

Aeschylus	*Suppliant Women* (legend of the daughters of Danaüs)
Apollodorus	*Library* 2.4.1–2.4.5
Herodotus	*History of the Persian Wars* 2.91

Notes

1. For Proetus and Bellerophon, see the appendix to this chapter.
2. The Roman poet Horace (*Odes* 3.16) changed Danaë's prison to a brazen tower, which has become the traditional version.
3. The Athenian historian Pherecydes (early fifth century B.C.) is an early authority for the saga.
4. The word *kibisis* is not Greek and in antiquity was believed to be Cypriote.
5. Hermes wears the Cap of Darkness in the Gigantomachy and is regularly portrayed with winged sandals. Athena wore the Cap of Invisibility at Troy (*Iliad* 5.844–845).
6. It is also placed by others in the far north, among the Hyperboreans, or in the far south, among the Ethiopians.
7. For their origin, see p. 170.
8. The Gorgon Euryale is mourning for her dead sister, Medusa.
9. In the first century A.D. the marks of Andromeda's fetters were still being shown on the rocks near the city of Joppa.
10. Euripides is following Hesiod, *Theogony* 285–286.

HERACLES

Hercules' harsh labors assure his fame.

—**BOETHIUS**, *Consolation of Philosophy*, 4.7.13

HERACLES IS THE GREATEST of the Greek heroes. His legends include elements of saga and folk tale,[1] while his status as man, hero, and god is controversial. In Greece, he was particularly associated with the area around Argos, with Thebes (the city of his birth), and with Trachis and **Mt. Oeta** in southern Thessaly (the place of his death and apotheosis).

Amphitryon and Alcmena

The father of Heracles was Amphitryon, son of Alcaeus and brother of the king of Mycenae, **Electryon**, whose daughter, Alcmena, became his wife. After Amphitryon accidentally killed Electryon, as punishment Amphitryon was exiled from Mycenae and came to Thebes, taking Alcmena with him. There he was purified by the Theban king, Creon, and set out to campaign against the Teleboans, a people of western Greece, who had attacked Electryon in Mycenae and killed all but one of his sons.[2] The expedition was successful through the treachery of Comaetho, daughter of the Teleboan king Pterelaüs. Out of love for Amphitryon she pulled from Pterelaüs' head the golden hair that guaranteed him immortality and made the Teleboans invincible. Thus Pterelaüs died and Amphitryon was victorious. Amphitryon killed Comaetho and returned to Thebes.[3]

Amphitryon expected to lie with Alcmena, and he did not know that Zeus, disguised as Amphitryon, had visited her the previous night, which extended to three times its proper length, and had told her the full story of the Teleboan expedition. Alcmena only accepted Amphitryon after Tiresias had revealed the truth. Thus Amphitryon lay "all night long with his chaste wife, delighting in the gifts of golden Aphrodite" (Hesiod, *Shield of Heracles*, 46–47). Alcmena conceived twins (it was said); the elder by one night was Heracles, son of Zeus, and the younger was Iphicles, son of Amphitryon.

In the *Amphitruo* of the Roman dramatist Plautus, Jupiter (Zeus) and Mercury (Hermes) disguise themselves as Amphitryon and Amphitryon's servant Sosia, respectively. Amphitryon returns just after Jupiter has left Alcmena, who is thoroughly confused. She gives birth to twins, one of whom is stronger than the other and immediately strangles two serpents sent by Juno (Hera) to kill him. Just as

545

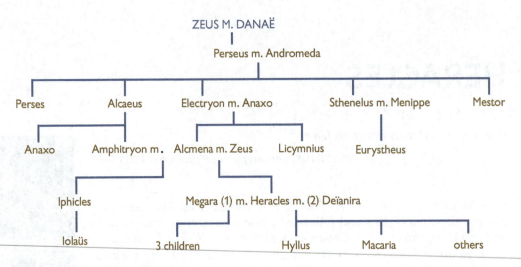

Figure 22.1 The Ancestry of Heracles

Alcmena's servant Bromia is describing the scene, Jupiter himself appears and reveals the truth to Amphitryon. This is the only one of Plautus' surviving plays whose plot is taken from mythology.

The Birth of Heracles and His Early Exploits

The birth of Heracles introduces a constant feature of his story: the hostility of Hera. On the day when Heracles was to be born, Zeus had boasted on Olympus (Homer, *Iliad* 19.103–105):

> Today Eileithyia, helper in childbirth, will bring to the light a man who shall rule over all that dwell around him; he shall be of the race that is of my blood.

Hera deceived Zeus by hastening the birth of the child of Sthenelus (king of Mycenae), whose wife was seven months pregnant, and sending Eileithyia to delay the birth of Alcmena's sons.[4] Sthenelus was the grandson of Zeus, and so his son rather than Alcmena's fulfilled the terms of Zeus' boast. He was **Eurystheus**, for whom Heracles performed the Labors.

Pindar tells the story (mentioned earlier in connection with the *Amphitruo* of Plautus) that Hera also sent a pair of snakes to kill the infant Heracles, whose birth she had not been able to prevent. The passage ends with the prophet Tiresias foretelling the hero's part in the battle of the gods against the Giants and his eventual deification (*Nemean Odes* 1.33–72):

> Willingly do I take hold of Heracles upon the high peaks of Virtue as I retell an ancient tale. When the son of Zeus had escaped from the birth pangs with his twin and had come into the bright light, he was wrapped in the yellow swaddling bands, and Hera of the golden throne saw him. Straightway in hasty anger, the queen of the gods sent snakes, which passed through the open doors into the farthest part of the wide room, eager to coil their quick jaws around the children. But Heracles lifted up his head and for the first time made trial of battle; with his two hands, from

which there was no escape, he seized by their necks the two serpents, and his grip squeezed the life out of the huge monsters, strangling them. (33–47)

Then fear unbearable struck the women who were helping Alcmena at the birth. Alcmena, too, leaped to her feet from the bedclothes, unclothed as she was, as if to protect her babies from the attack of the beasts. Then the Theban leaders quickly ran and assembled with their bronze weapons, and Amphitryon came, smitten with the bitter pangs of anxiety and brandishing his sword unsheathed. . . . He stood with amazement hard to bear mixed with joy, for he saw the immeasurable spirit and power of his son. The immortals indeed had made the words of the messengers untrue. Then he summoned Tiresias, his neighbor, excellent mouthpiece of Zeus the most high. To Amphitryon and to all his armed men he foretold with what fortunes Heracles would meet, how many lawless wild beasts he would kill on the sea, how many on land. He foretold how Heracles would give to his fate the man who walks with crooked insolence, most hateful of men. For, he foretold, when the gods should do battle with the giants on the plain of Phlegra, beneath the onrush of his missiles, bright hair would be soiled in the dust. But Heracles himself, in peace for all time without end, would win rest as the choice reward for his great labors, and in the palaces of the blessed he would take Hebe to be his youthful bride. Feasting at his wedding beside Zeus, son of Cronus, he would praise the holy customs of the gods. (48–72)

Thus Heracles survived. In his education, he was taught chariot driving by Amphitryon, wrestling by Autolycus, archery by Eurytus, and music by Linus.[5] Heracles killed Linus, who was a son of Apollo, by striking him with his lyre, and for this was sent away to the Theban pastures on Mt. Cithaeron, where he performed a number of exploits. He killed a lion that was preying on the cattle of Amphitryon and of Thespius, king of the Boeotian town of Thespiae. During the hunt for the lion, Heracles was entertained for fifty days by Thespius and lay with one of his fifty daughters each night (or with all fifty in the same night). He also freed the Thebans from paying tribute to the Minyans of Orchomenus, leading the Theban army himself into battle. In gratitude, Creon gave him his daughter Megara as wife, and by her he had three children.

The Madness of Heracles

Some time later, Hera brought about a fit of madness in which Heracles killed **Megara** and her children. When he recovered his sanity, he left Thebes and went first to Thespiae, where Thespius purified him, and then to Delphi, where he sought further advice. Here the priestess of Apollo called him Heracles for the first time (until then he had been known as Alcides) and told him to go to Tiryns and there, for twelve years, serve Eurystheus, performing the labors that he would impose. If he did them, she said, he would become immortal.

This is the simplest story of the origin of the Labors; there is, however, great confusion over the chronology of Heracles' legends. Euripides in his *Heracles* puts the murder of Megara and her children after the Labors. Sophocles in his *Trachiniae* has Heracles marry his second wife Deïanira before the Labors, whereas Apollodorus places the marriage after them. All are agreed that for a number of years Heracles served Eurystheus. Heracles' ghost says to Odysseus: "I was a son of Zeus, but infinite was my suffering; for I was slave to a far inferior mortal, and heavy were the labors he laid upon me" (Homer, *Odyssey* 11.620–622).

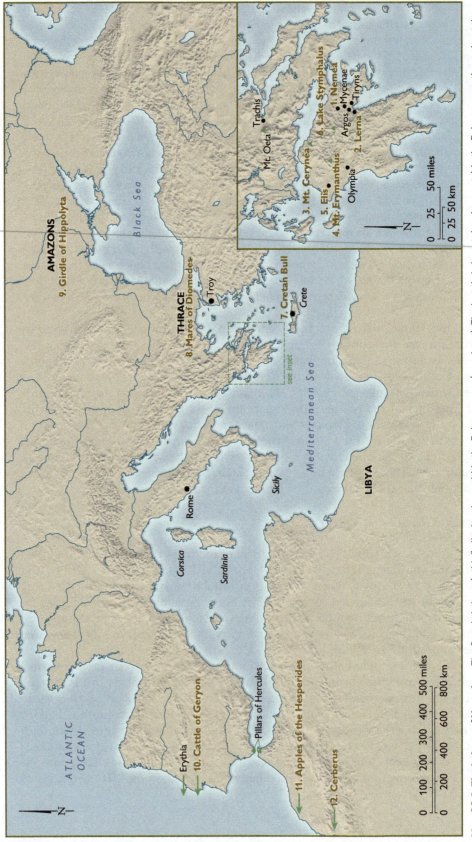

Map 22.1 The Labors of Heracles. The first six Labors (*athloi*) all take place within the Peloponnese (map inset). The last six Labors take place outside the Peloponnese throughout the Mediterranean; of these, the last three occur in the farthest western reaches of the known world.

The Twelve Labors

The Greek word for labors is **athloi**, which really means contests undertaken for a prize. In Heracles' case, the prize was immortality, and at least three of his Labors are really conquests of death.[6] Heracles did not always perform the Labors unaided; sometimes Athena helped him, sometimes his nephew, **Iolaüs**. The first six Labors all take place in the northern Peloponnese and the remaining six in different parts of the world. In these last six Labors, Heracles has changed from a local hero into the benefactor of all humankind. The list of the Labors varies, but the twelve given are traditional and were represented on the metopes of the temple of Zeus at Olympia (see pp. 554–555).

The Peloponnesian Labors

1. The Nemean Lion   Heracles was required to bring the skin of this beast to Eurystheus. Heracles killed it with a club that he had himself cut. Theocritus (in his twenty-fifth *Idyll*) makes the lion invulnerable, and Heracles has to strangle it and then flay it by using its own claws to cut its hide. The club and lion skin henceforth were Heracles' weapon and clothing and are his attributes in art and literature.

2. The Lernaean Hydra   This serpent lived in the swamps of Lerna, near Argos. It had nine heads, eight of which were mortal, and the ninth was immortal. Each time Heracles clubbed a head off, two grew in its place. The labor was made the more difficult by a huge crab, which Hera sent to aid the Hydra. First, Heracles killed this monster, and then he killed the Hydra, helped by his nephew, Iolaüs, son of Iphicles. Each time he removed one of the heads, Iolaüs cauterized the stump with a burning brand so that another could not grow. Heracles buried the immortal head under a huge rock. He then dipped his arrows in the Hydra's poison. As for the crab, Hera took it and made it into the constellation Cancer.

3. The Cerynean Hind   The hind had golden horns and was sacred to Artemis; it took its name from Mt. Cerynea in Arcadia.[7] It was harmless, and it could not be harmed without incurring Artemis' wrath. After pursuing it for a year, Heracles caught it by the river Ladon and carried it back to Eurystheus. On the way, Artemis met him and claimed her sacred animal, but she was appeased when Heracles laid the blame on Eurystheus.

This version of the story is entirely set in the Peloponnese. A different account, however, is given by Pindar in his beautiful third *Olympian Ode*. In this version, Heracles went to the land of the Hyperboreans in the far north in search of the hind, on whose golden horns the nymph Taÿgete, a daughter of Atlas, had stamped the name of Artemis.[8] Pindar's narrative allows us to connect this labor with that of the Apples of the Hesperides, for in the latter story Heracles goes to the limits of the world in search of a miraculous golden object, and again Ladon (in the form of a dragon) and Atlas appear.[9] The labor of the Apples of the Hesperides is a conquest of death, and apparently the story of the Cerynean stag is another version of the same theme.

4. The Erymanthian Boar   This destructive animal had to be brought back alive from Mt. Erymanthus. Heracles chased the boar into deep snow and there trapped it with nets. He brought it back to Eurystheus, who cowered in terror in a large jar.

This labor resulted in a side adventure (or *parergon*).[10] On his way to the chase, Heracles was entertained by the centaur Pholus, who set before him a jar of wine that belonged to all the centaurs in common. When it was opened, the

Hercules and the Lernaean Hydra, by Gustave Moreau (1826–1898); oil on canvas, 1869–1876, 70½ × 60¼ in. Moreau, who painted several of Hercules' Labors, devoted enormous effort to this painting. Hercules is young and of normal human size and anatomy. He stands in the attitude (legs reversed) of the *Apollo Belvedere* (p. 264), with his attributes of lion skin, bow (also Apollo's weapon), and club. The seven-headed Hydra towers over the hero, and in front of it lie the remains of its victims. The rocky cliffs heighten the drama, a suitable setting for the fearless hero. The conquest of the Hydra had long been a parable for the triumph of good government over disorder, but Moreau focuses on the moral stature of the hero rather than on political allegory. (*The Art Institute of Chicago/Art Resource, NY*)

other centaurs, attracted by its fragrance, attacked Heracles, who repelled and pursued them. Most of them were scattered all over Greece, but Chiron was wounded by one of Heracles' poisoned arrows. Since he was immortal and could not die, he suffered incurable agonies until Prometheus interceded with Zeus and took upon himself the immortality of Chiron. Pholus also met his death when he accidentally dropped a poisoned arrow on his foot.

5. The Augean Stables Augeas, son of Helius (the Sun) and king of Elis, owned vast herds of cattle whose stables had never been cleaned out. Heracles was commanded by Eurystheus to perform the task and successfully completed it within one day by diverting the rivers Alpheus and Peneus so that they flowed through the stables. Augeas agreed to give Heracles one-tenth of his herds as a reward but then refused to keep his promise and expelled both Heracles and his own son Phyleus (who had taken Heracles' part in the quarrel). Heracles was received by a nearby prince, Dexamenus (whose name, indeed, means "the receiver"), whose daughter he saved from the centaur Eurytion. After he had finished the Labors, Heracles returned to Elis at the head of an army, took the city, and killed Augeas, making Phyleus king in his place.

It was after this expedition that Heracles was said to have instituted the Olympic Games, the greatest of Greek festivals, held every four years in honor of Zeus. He marked out the stadium by pacing it out himself, and he fetched an olive tree from the land of the Hyperboreans to be, as Pindar described it, "a shade for the sacred precinct and a crown of glory for men" (*Olympian Odes* 3.16–18), for at that time there were no trees at Olympia, and at the games the victors were awarded a garland of olive leaves.[11]

6. The Stymphalian Birds Heracles was required to shoot these creatures, which flocked together in a wood by the Arcadian lake Stymphalus. He flushed them out by clashing brazen castanets that Athena had given him, and then he shot them.[12]

The Non-Peloponnesian Labors

7. The Cretan Bull   This bull was one that Minos had refused to sacrifice to Poseidon. Heracles caught it and brought it back alive to Eurystheus. It was then turned loose and eventually came to Marathon, where in time Theseus caught and sacrificed it.

8. The Mares of Diomedes Diomedes, son of Ares, was a Thracian king who owned a herd of mares that were fed human flesh. Heracles, either alone or with an army, gained possession of them and tamed them by feeding them Diomedes himself. He took them back to Argos, where Eurystheus set them free and dedicated them to Hera. On his way to Thrace, Heracles was entertained by **Admetus**, king of Pherae, who disguised his grief at the recent death of his wife, **Alcestis**. Heracles discovered the truth and himself wrestled with Thanatos (Death), forcing Thanatos to give up Alcestis, whom he restored to her husband (see p. 262).

9. The Girdle of Hippolyta Hippolyta was queen of the Amazons, the warrior women who lived at the northern limits of the world. Heracles was sent to fetch her girdle, which had magical powers. He killed Hippolyta in battle and took the girdle. In historical times, it was displayed at Argos.

While returning from this labor, Heracles came to Troy and there rescued Hesione from the sea-monster (see p. 466). Cheated by King Laomedon of his reward, Heracles returned later (after his time as the servant of Omphale) with an armed force and sacked the city, giving Hesione to his ally Telamon and leaving Podarces (Priam) on the throne of the ruined city.

10. The Cattle of Geryon The last three labors are most clearly conquests of death, with the abduction of Cerberus as their climax. Geryon lived on the island of Erythia, far away to the west. Geryon was a three-bodied monster, offspring of the Oceanid Callirhoë and Chrysaor; he tended a herd of cattle, helped by a giant herdsman, Eurytion, and a two-headed hound, Orthus (or Orthrus). Heracles' labor was to bring the cattle back to Eurystheus. To reach Erythia, Heracles was helped by Helius (the Sun), who gave him a golden cup in which to sail upon the River of Ocean, which girdles the world. He killed Orthus, Eurytion, and Geryon and then sailed back in the cup to Tartessus (i.e., Spain) with the cattle. He returned the cup to Helius and then began to drive the cattle back to Greece.

As a monument of his journey to the western edge of the world, he set up the Pillars of Heracles at the Atlantic entrance to the Mediterranean. They are sometimes identified with the rocks of Calpe (Gibraltar) and Abyla (Ceuta), which flank the Straits of Gibraltar. In the sixteenth and seventeenth centuries these Pillars became a significant part of the political imagery of the Spanish monarchy, symbolizing the crossing of the Atlantic Ocean by Spanish explorers and traders, who returned with the wealth of the Americas to the greater glory of

Melampus and the Cattle of Phylacus

The myth of Melampus is like the tenth Labor of Heracles. He must bring back cattle from a distant place guarded, like Geryon's Erythia or Hades itself, by a dog. Like Heracles, Melampus is the bringer of cattle and even the conqueror of death itself.[13]

Bias, the son of Amythaon, was a suitor for the hand of Pero, the daughter of Neleus, for whom the bride-price was the cattle of Phylacus, the king of Phylace (in Phthia). He appealed to his brother Melampus for help, and Melampus agreed to get the cattle, even though he knew he would have to spend a year in prison at Phylace. The cattle were guarded by a monstrous dog, and Melampus was caught in the act of stealing them and so was imprisoned. After nearly a year, he heard two woodworms saying to each other that they had very nearly finished gnawing through the roofbeams of the cell. He insisted on being moved to another cell, and shortly afterward the first cell collapsed. Phylacus then set Melampus free and asked him how to cure the impotence of his son Iphiclus. Melampus agreed to tell him on condition that he be given the cattle. He sacrificed a pair of bulls, and from a vulture that was feeding on their flesh, he learned that Iphiclus' debility was the result of being frightened as a child while watching his father gelding some rams. On that occasion, Phylacus had stuck the knife, still bloody, into an oak tree, and the tree's bark by now covered it over. If it could be found and the rust from its blade scraped off and put in Iphiclus' drink for ten days, his impotence would cease. All this came to pass and Iphiclus became the father of two sons, Podarces and Protesilaüs. Melampus was given the cattle, which he drove back to Pylos and handed over to Neleus. In return, he got Pero and gave her to Bias. See also the box on p. 121.

the monarchy. Thus, as early as 1526, Charles V had adopted the Pillars as his symbol, with the motto *Plus Ultra* ("further beyond"), and on his triumphal entry into Seville that year he was greeted as "the new Hercules, who has established the limits of the new world, just as Hercules established those of the ancient world." The imagery of the Pillars continued well into the seventeenth century, when, for example, they were prominent in the Arch of the Mint designed by Peter Paul Rubens for the Joyful Entry of the Spanish Archduke Ferdinand into Antwerp in 1535.[14]

Heracles' journey back to Greece has many *parerga*. While crossing the south of France, he was attacked by the tribe of the Ligurians and exhausted his supply of arrows defending himself. He prayed for help from Zeus, who sent a rain of stones that gave Heracles the ammunition he needed to drive off the attackers. He then crossed the Alps and traversed Italy, where he was said to have founded several cities.[15] While Heracles was in Italy, the Italian fire god **Cacus** stole the cattle of Geryon. He killed the thief and recovered the cattle. (See p. 661 for Vergil's version of this story, which he locates in Rome.)

Heracles' wanderings in Italy also took him across the strait to Sicily. There he wrestled with Eryx (king of the mountain of the same name at the western end of the island), whom he killed. He returned to Greece by traveling around the head of the Adriatic and through Dalmatia. At the Isthmus of Corinth, he killed the giant and brigand, Alcyoneus. As for the cattle, Eurystheus sacrificed them to Hera.

Herodotus tells quite a different version of the legend of Geryon. In this narrative, Heracles journeyed to the cold lands beyond the Danube, and there lay with Echidna (Snake Woman), a monster who was half woman and half serpent, who bore him three sons, Agathyrsus, Gelonus, and Scythes. When the three grew up, only Scythes was able to draw a bow and put on a belt that Heracles had left behind. The other two were driven away by Echidna, and Scythes became king and ancestor of the Scythians.[16]

11. The Apples of the Hesperides The Hesperides were the three daughters of Night, living far away to the west; they guarded a tree on which grew golden apples. The Hesperides were helped by the serpent **Ladon**, who was coiled around the tree. The apples had originally been a wedding gift from Ge to Hera when she married Zeus, and Ge put them in the garden of the Hesperides. Heracles first had to find the sea-god Nereus and learn from him the whereabouts of the garden. Nereus would tell him only after he had turned himself into many different shapes, being held all the while by Heracles. At the garden, in Euripides' version, Heracles killed Ladon and plucked the apples himself. In the tradition represented by the metopes at Olympia, however, he had the help of the Titan **Atlas**, who held up the heavens. Heracles, helped by Athena, took the heavens on his own shoulders while Atlas fetched the apples. He then returned the load to Atlas' shoulders and brought the apples back to Eurystheus. Athena is then said to have taken the apples back to the garden of the Hesperides.

This labor is a conquest of death. The apples are symbols of immortality, and the tree in the garden of the Hesperides is a kind of Tree of Life. As in the labor of Geryon, the journey to a mysterious place in the far west is really a journey to the realm of death.

On his journey to the garden of the Hesperides, Heracles killed the king of Egypt, Busiris, who would sacrifice all strangers to Zeus.[17] In Libya he conquered the giant **Antaeus**, son of Ge and Poseidon, who would wrestle with those who

THE TEMPLE OF ZEUS AT OLYMPIA AND ITS SCULPTURAL PROGRAM

By the time the Olympic Games were reorganized in 776 B.C., it was commonly believed that Heracles had been their original founder in the legendary past. Construction on the Doric temple of Zeus at Olympia was begun ca. 472 and completed ca. 456 B.C. (See pp. 117–119 for a fuller discussion of the temple and its decorative program.) It is significant that this temple represents one of the first major building programs since the invasion of the Persians earlier in the century. Pausanias, the second-century A.D. travel writer, in his *Description of Greece* (5.7 ff.), describes the sanctuary and the temple, including its decoration. According to Pausanias, on the eastern and western facades, the Doric frieze included twelve metopes detailing the twelve *athloi* (labors) of Heracles that he completed in service to King Eurystheus. Pausanias describes them in the order he saw them: on the front of the temple (the eastern side), arranged from left to right: the Erymanthian Boar (7), the Mares of Diomedes (8), the Cattle of Geryon (9), the Apples of the Hesperides (10), and the Augean Stables (12); on the back (western side), apparently to be read from right to left: the Nemean Lion (1), the Lernaean Hydra (2), the Stymphalian Birds (3), the Cretan Bull (4), the Cerynean Hind (5), and the Girdle of Hippolyta (6). The omission of Cerberus (11) in Pausanias' account seems an accident; it most likely should be included among the metopes on the front, between the Apples of the Hesperides and the Augean Stables. The order of the Labors does not strictly follow the arrangement of Peloponnesian and non-Peloponnesian Labors as we present it in this chapter. Some scholarly debate has arisen about the artistic logic of the ordering or whether this represents the original arrangement, but most scholars accept it.

Heracles, Assisted by Athena, Cleans the Augean Stables. Marble metope over the east porch of the temple of Zeus at Olympia, ca. 460 B.C.; height 63 in. This local legend is given the place of honor as the final one of the series of the Labors of Heracles in the metopes of the temple of Zeus. Athena is helmeted and clothed in the Doric *peplos*, her left hand resting on her shield. With her spear (now missing), she directs Heracles as he labors to open (with a crowbar) the stables so that the river Alpheus can flush them clean. (*Erin Babnik/Alamy Stock Photo*)

Athena, Heracles, and Atlas. Metope no. 10, high relief in marble, ca. 460 B.C.; height: 1.63 m. The original is in the Olympia Archaeological Museum. The artist has chosen to represent the moment that Atlas returns to Heracles, bringing the Apples of the Hesperides. Heracles had taken up the burden of the vault of the sky while Atlas was away. A folded cushion helps Heracles support the weight. Athena, who customarily gives assistance to the greatest heroes, appears here in simple dress and not in her more usual battle garb. She offers gentle and unobtrusive aid with a supporting hand. It is a brilliant artistic stroke that the panel in its original placement beneath the pediment suggests Heracles is burdened by the weight of the temple roof. (*Erich Lessing/ Art Resource, NY*)

W 1. Nemean Lion W 2. Lemean Hydra W 3. Stymphalian Birds W 4. Cretan Bull

 E 5. Kerynian Hind  E 6. Amazon 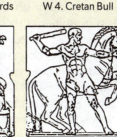 E 7. Erymanthian Boar E 8. Mares of Diomedes

E 9. Geryon E 10. Apples of the Hesperides E 11. Cerberus E 12. Augean Stables

Figure 22.2 Diagram of Olympia Metopes. The diagram shows the arrangement of the metopes and the composition of the individual panels, though they are now in a fragmentary state. The depiction of Heracles performing his twelve Labors is completely appropriate for the temple of Zeus and the Olympic sanctuary: Heracles is a son of Zeus and the founder of the Olympic Games. He is seen here as the heroic competitor who eventually wins both immortality and immortal glory. If read correctly, the Nemean Lion is the first scene and the capture of Cerberus the last but one. It has been suggested that the Cleansing of the Augean Stables was placed last to give prominence to a local Labor. The individual panels are composed of few figures and with a simplicity of design, and they vary in the precise, dramatic moment they choose to illustrate. According to scholars, it may be an aesthetic consideration that Athena in the present arrangement is depicted in the first, third, tenth, and twelfth panels.

Heracles Shows Cerberus to Eurystheus. Etruscan hydria from Caere, ca. 530 B.C.; height 17 in. The terrified Eurystheus leaps into a storage jar to escape from the Hound of Hades, which bares its three sets of teeth while its snakes furiously hiss at him. Heracles, with club and lion skin, strides forward confidently, guiding Cerberus with a leash. The humor in this splendid vase is remarkable. Compare Blake's *Cerberus* on p. 366. (© RMN-Grand Palais/Art Resource, NY)

came to his kingdom. Antaeus was invincible: every time an opponent threw him, he came in contact with his mother (Earth) and rose with renewed strength. Thus Antaeus had killed all comers and used their skulls in building a temple to his father, Poseidon. Heracles held him aloft and crushed him to death.

Some versions of this story take Heracles to the Caucasus Mountains. There he found Prometheus chained to his rock and released him after killing the eagle that tormented him (see p. 98). Prometheus advised him to use Atlas in getting the apples and foretold the battle against the Ligurians. On this occasion, too, Prometheus took over the immortality of Chiron and satisfied Zeus by letting Chiron die in his place.

12. Cerberus The final labor was to fetch Cerberus, the three-headed hound of Hades. This labor is most clearly a conquest of death, and Heracles himself (in the *Odyssey* 11.617–626) said that it was the most difficult of the Labors and that he could not have achieved it without the aid of Hermes and Athena. In the Underworld, Heracles wrestled with Cerberus, brought him back to Eurystheus, and then returned him to Hades.

In Hades, Heracles saw Theseus and Pirithoüs, chained fast because of their attempt to carry off Persephone. He was able to release Theseus, who out of gratitude sheltered him after his madness and the murder of Megara. He also saw the ghost of Meleager, whose sister, if he still had one living, he offered to marry. Meleager named Deïanira, "upon whose neck was still the green of youth, nor did she know yet of the ways of Aphrodite, charmer of men" (Bacchylides, *Epinician Ode* 5.172–175). Thus the train of events that eventually led to the death of Heracles was set in motion.

In conclusion, we translate a chorus from Euripides' *Heracles*, which tells of the great hero's Labors. This choral ode also reveals the nature of our sources for Greek legends, where the dry facts are enlivened by poetic expression (Euripides, *Heracles* 352–427):

> I wish to offer a glorious crown for labors done, by singing the praises of him who descended into the darkness of earth's realm of shades—whether I am to call him the son of Zeus or of Amphitryon. For the renown of noble deeds is a joy to those who have died. First, he cleared Zeus' grove of the lion; and he wore its tawny skin upon his back, with the fearful jaws of the beast framing his fair head. (352–363)
>
> He laid low the mountain race of savage Centaurs with his deadly arrows, slaughtering them with his winged shafts. The beautiful stream of Peneus was a witness and the vast extent of the plains without crops and the vales of Mt. Pelion and the places on the green glens of Homole—all haunts where they filled their hands with weapons of pine and, galloping as horses, brought fear to the land of the Thessalians. (364–374)

10

He slew the dappled hind with golden horns and dedicated this ravaging plunderer to the huntress Artemis of Oenoë.

He mounted the chariot of Diomedes and mastered with the bit the four mares, who ranged wild in stables drenched in blood and reveled in their horrid feasts of human flesh with ravenous jaws. (380–385)

In his labors for the king of Mycenae, he crossed over the banks of the silver-flowing Hebrus; and along the sea-cliff of Pelion, by the waters of the Amaurus, he killed with his bow Cycnus, the guest-murderer who lived alone near Amphanaea. (386–393)   20

He came to the western home of the singing maidens, to pluck from amid the golden leaves the fruit of the apple, and the fiery dragon who kept guard coiled around the tree, hard even to approach, him he killed.

He made his way into the farthest corners of the sea and made them safe for men who ply the oar. (400–402)

Having come to the abode of Atlas, he extended his hand to support the vault of heaven in its midst, and by his manly strength held up the starry homes of the gods.

He crossed the swell of the Euxine Sea to the land of the Amazons, who rode in force where many rivers flow into Lake Maeotis. Mustering a band of friends from   30
Hellas, he sought to win the gold-encrusted adornment of the warrior maid—the deadly booty of her girdle—and Hellas captured the renowned prize of the foreign queen, which is kept safe in Mycenae. (408–418)

He seared the many heads of the deadly monster, the Lernaean Hydra, and dipped his arrows in its venom; with that he killed three-bodied Geryon, the herdsman of Erythia.

He won the glorious crown for these and other labors; and he sailed to the tearful realm of Hades—the final task of all. (425–427)

Other Deeds of Heracles

Cycnus, Syleus, and the Cercopes

Heracles fought and killed a number of harmful beings. Cycnus, son of Ares, used to rob men passing on their way through Thessaly to Delphi. Heracles, helped by Athena and with Iolaüs as charioteer, killed Cycnus and wounded Ares.[18] Another robber was Syleus, who lived by the Straits of Euboea. Heracles destroyed his vineyard, in which Syleus compelled passers-by to work, and then killed Syleus himself.

More folk tale than myth is Heracles' encounter with the Cercopes, whose home is placed in various parts of Greece or Asia Minor. They were a pair of dwarfs who spent their time playing tricks on people. They had been warned by their mother "to beware of the black-bottomed man." Now as Heracles was asleep under a tree, they attempted to steal his weapons, but he caught them and slung them from a pole across his shoulders upside down. They thus had an uninterrupted view of his backside which, since the lion skin did not cover it, had been burned black by the sun. They joked about the sight so much that Heracles, himself amused, let them go. Later they tried to trick Zeus and were punished by being turned into either apes or stones.

Hylas

Heracles was among the heroes who sailed on the *Argo*. But he was too important to be subordinate to other heroes in the saga, and so he soon dropped out of the expedition. In one version, he went looking for the boy Hylas, whom he loved. When the *Argo* put in at Cios (in Asia Minor), Hylas went to a nearby spring to draw water, and the water-nymphs were so entranced by his beauty that they pulled him into the water, to remain with them forever. Heracles spent so long searching for him that the rest of the Argonauts sailed away without him, and he returned on his own to Argos after establishing a cult of Hylas at Cios. In late antiquity, the people still searched for him annually, calling out his name.[19]

Hylas and the Nymphs, by J. W. Waterhouse (1849–1917); oil on canvas, 1896, 38 × 63 in. The young Hylas is lured to his fate by seven water-nymphs. The artist brilliantly combines English Victorian ideals of female beauty and landscape (the latter in colors of great beauty) with psychological insight that anticipates Freud. (© *Manchester Art Gallery/ Bridgeman Images*)

Military Expeditions

Heracles took part in Zeus' battle against the giants, during which he slew the terrible Alcyoneus. He attacked Laomedon, king of Troy, and Augeas, king of Elis, who had both cheated him. He made an expedition against Neleus, king of Pylos, who had refused to purify Heracles after the murder of Iphitus. He killed eleven of the twelve sons of Neleus; the twelfth, Nestor, eventually became king of Pylos and took part in the Trojan War. According to Hesiod, one of the sons of Neleus was Periclymenus, to whom Poseidon had given the ability to transform himself into every sort of bird, beast, or insect. With the help of Athena, Heracles recognized him in the form of a bee settled upon the yoke of his horse-drawn chariot and shot him with an arrow.

In this expedition also, says Homer, Heracles wounded the god Hades, "in Pylos among the corpses" (*Iliad* 5.395–397), as if the expedition were another conquest of death. Homer also mentions that Heracles wounded Hera and says that this was another example of Heracles' violence—"brutal and violent man, who did not scruple to do evil and wounded the Olympian gods with his arrows" (*Iliad* 5.403–404). This is an older view of Heracles and more likely represents the character of the original mythical hero than that of Pindar, who makes the following protest (*Olympian Odes* 9.29–36):

> How would Heracles have brandished his club with his hands against the trident, when, in defense of Pylos Poseidon pushed him back, and Apollo shook him and drove him back with his silver bow, nor did Hades keep his staff unmoved, with which he drives mortal bodies to the hollow ways of the dead? Hurl this story, my mouth, far away!

We can see that by Pindar's time (the first half of the fifth century B.C.) the transformation of Heracles was already well advanced, from the primitive strongman into a paragon of virtue. Heracles also made an expedition against Hippocoön, king of Sparta, and his sons, who had given assistance to Neleus. Iphicles was killed in this campaign. While returning home from Sparta, Heracles lay at Tegea with Auge, whose father, fearing an oracle that Auge's son would kill her brothers, had made her priestess of Athena. The son she conceived was Telephus, and mother and baby crossed the sea to Asia Minor floating in a chest. There Telephus eventually became king of the Mysians.[20]

In Thessaly, Heracles appeared as an ally of Aegimius, king of the Dorians, against the attacks of his neighbors, the Lapiths and the Dryopes. This legend brings Heracles back to central Greece, where the legends of the last part of his life are placed.

Heracles, Deïanira, and Iole

Marriage to Deïanira

Some time after the completion of the Labors, Heracles fulfilled the promise he had made to the soul of Meleager to marry his sister Deïanira, daughter of Oeneus, king of Calydon. To win her, Heracles had to wrestle with the river-god **Acheloüs**, who was horned like a bull and had the power to change himself into different shapes. This is how Sophocles describes the scene (*Trachiniae* 513–525):

> They came together desiring marriage; alone between them as umpire was Aphrodite, maker of marriages. Then was there confusion of sounds, the beating of fists, the twang of bow, the clash of bull's horns. There were the wrestling holds, the painful collision of heads, and the groans of both. But she, the prize, fair and delicate, sat afar upon a hill, waiting for him who was to be her husband.

In the struggle, Heracles broke off one of Acheloüs' horns; after his victory, he gave it back, receiving in return the miraculous horn of Amalthea, which could supply its owner with as much food and drink as he wished.[21] Heracles returned with Deïanira to Tiryns. On the way, the centaur **Nessus** carried Deïanira across the river Evenus. When he attempted to violate her, Heracles shot him with his bow. As Nessus was dying, he advised Deïanira to gather some of the blood that flowed from his wound, which had been caused by an arrow that had been dipped in the Hydra's poison. It would, he said, prevent Heracles from loving any other woman more than he loved Deïanira. She therefore kept the blood, and for a number of years she and Heracles lived at Tiryns, where she bore him children, including a son, Hyllus, and a daughter, Macaria.

Iole

But Heracles fell in love with Iole, daughter of Eurytus, king of Oechalia, who had once taught Heracles archery. Eurytus refused to let him have Iole, even though he won an archery contest that was to decide whose wife Iole should be. Heracles returned to Tiryns, bitter at the insult, and when Iphitus, brother of Iole, came to Tiryns in search of some lost mares, Heracles threw him from the citadel to his death. For this murder, he had to leave Tiryns, going first to Pylos, where Neleus refused to purify him. Having obtained purification at Amyclae, he went to Delphi to find out what more he should do to be cured of the madness that had caused him to kill Iphitus. When the Pythia would not reply, he attempted to carry off the sacred tripod, intending to establish an oracle of his own (see illustration on p. 562). Apollo himself wrestled with him to prevent this theft, and their fight ended when Zeus threw a thunderbolt between them. Finally, Heracles obtained the advice he had asked for, which was that he must be sold as a slave and serve for one year.

Omphale

Accordingly, Hermes auctioned Heracles, and he was bought by Omphale, queen of the Lydians; he served her for a year and performed various tasks for her in keeping with his heroic character. Later versions, however, make Heracles perform women's work for the queen and picture him dressed as a woman and spinning wool. At the end of his year, he mounted the expedition against Troy and then returned to Greece, determined to punish Eurytus and to win Iole.

The Death of Heracles

Deïanira, meanwhile, was living in Trachis, where King Ceyx had received her and Heracles after they left the Peloponnese. According to Sophocles, whose *Trachiniae* is the most important source for the last part of Heracles' life, she knew nothing of Oechalia and Iole until the herald Lichas brought news of the sack of the city. She had not seen Heracles for fifteen months, before his servitude to Omphale. In this account, Heracles killed Eurytus and sacked Oechalia on his way back from Asia, sending Iole and the other captive women back to Trachis with Lichas. When she realized that Heracles loved Iole, Deïanira, hoping to win him back, dipped a robe in the blood of Nessus and sent it to Heracles by Lichas' hand for him to wear at his thanksgiving sacrifice to Zeus.

As the flames of the sacrificial fire warmed the poisoned blood, the robe clung to Heracles and burned him with unendurable torment. In his agony, he hurled Lichas to his death in the sea and had himself carried back to Trachis, where a huge funeral pyre was made for him upon Mt. Oeta. Deïanira killed herself with a sword when she realized what she had done, while Hyllus went with his father to Oeta. There Heracles instructed Hyllus to marry Iole after his death and gave his bow to the shepherd Poeas (father of Philoctetes), since he alone had dared to light the pyre. So the mortal part of Heracles was burned away and he gained immortality, ascending to Olympus, there to be reconciled with Hera and to marry her daughter Hebe. This is Pindar's version (*Isthmian Odes* 4.61–67):

> To Olympus went Alcmena's son, when he had explored every land and the cliff-girt levels of the foaming sea, to tame the straits for seafarers. Now beside Zeus he enjoys a perfect happiness; he is loved and honored by the immortals; Hebe is his wife, and he is lord of a golden palace, the husband of Hera's daughter.

Nessus and Deïanira, by Guido Reni (1575–1642); oil on canvas, 1623, 104 × 77 in. Reni painted a series of four scenes from the life and death of Heracles for Ferdinando Gonzaga, Duke of Mantua, in 1621. When the original *Nessus and Deïaneira* was removed to Prague (where it still is) during the sack of Mantua by the troops of Charles V, Reni replaced it with this splendid and romantic interpretation of the myth. The young centaur, triumphant in his conquest, bears off Deïanira, who twists away as she realizes the fate that has overtaken her, while Heracles in the background takes an arrow from his quiver. Thus Reni focuses on the joy of the centaur, soon to be turned to tragedy for himself, Deïanira, and Heracles. The contrast with the stark realism of the Attic artist's painting on the seventh-century B.C. vase on p. 563 is a remarkable example of the way in which the same myth can inspire different emotions. (*Erich Lessing/ Art Resource, NY*)

Heracles and Apollo Struggle for the Pythian Tripod. Attic red-figure amphora by the Andocides painter, ca. 520 B.C.; height of vase 22½ in. Athena is armed with helmet, spear, and shield, and her aegis is tasseled with snakes, with a Gorgon's head at the center. She stands at the left watching Heracles and Apollo struggling for the Pythian tripod. (*bpk Bildagentur/ Staatliche Antikensammlung/ Jürgen Liepe/Art Resource, NY*)

Sophocles' *Trachiniae* ends with Heracles, in torment, being carried from his palace to the pyre on Mt. Oeta. In this scene, Hyllus says: "No one foresees what is to come" (1270), thus leaving the destiny of Heracles shrouded in ambiguity. Ovid's description is explicit (*Metamorphoses* 9.239–272):

> And now . . . the flames were attacking the limbs that did not fear them and him who despised them. The gods were anxious for earth's champion [Hercules] and them did Jupiter . . . in happiness thus address: "Your fear is my joy, O gods . . . let not your hearts tremble with empty fear, despite Oeta's flames! He who conquered all will conquer the flames which you see, and only his mother's part will feel the power of Vulcan [i.e., fire]. That part which he inherited from me is immortal, immune to death, impervious to fire, and it will I receive in the heavens when its time 10 on earth is done. . . ." The gods approved. Meanwhile, Vulcan had consumed all that fire could consume, and the recognizable form of Hercules was no longer to be seen. He kept no part of himself that came from his mother, and he kept only the features drawn from Jupiter. . . . So, when the hero of Tiryns had put off his mortal body, his better part kept its vigor. He began to seem greater in size and awe-inspiring with august dignity. The almighty Father received him as he ascended into the surrounding clouds in a four-horse chariot and placed him among the shining 20 constellations.

Heracles: Man, Hero, and God

Odysseus describes his meeting with the ghost of Heracles in this way (Homer, *Odyssey* 11.601–603):

> Then saw I mighty Heracles—his ghost, but he himself delights in feasting among the immortal gods, with fair-ankled Hebe for his wife.

In this very early passage, the ambiguity of Heracles' status as man and god is evident. That he was a man before he became a god is shown by his name (which means "glory of Hera"), since Greek gods do not form their names from compounds of other gods' names. Certainly Euripides, in his tragedies *Alcestis* and *Heracles*, portrays him more as a mortal than a god, as can be seen, for example, in the scene from the *Heracles* in which Lyssa, the goddess of madness, is sent by Hera to torment Heracles.

Since his legend is particularly associated with Argos, Mycenae, and Tiryns, Heracles' saga may have had its origin in a prince of Tiryns who was vassal to the lord of Mycenae. This fits with the theme of subservience to Eurystheus. But other areas with which Heracles is especially associated are Boeotia (the traditional setting of his birth and of a group of his exploits) and Trachis, the scene of his final exploits and death.

The Death of Nessus. Detail of an Attic black-figure amphora, ca. 620 B.C.; height of vase 48 in., of painting 14 in. The scene is painted on the neck of the vase, with owls, a swan, and a pigeon on the handles. The names of Heracles (written right to left) and Nessus (spelled "Netos") are given. Heracles finishes Nessus off with a sword, grasping his hair and violently thrusting his left foot into the Centaur's back. He ignores Nessus' pleas for mercy, shown by the gesture of touching the chin. The hero does not wear the lion skin, nor does he carry his club and bow. (© *Cooper Hewitt, Smithsonian Design Museum/Art Resource, NY*)

This leads to one of two possibilities: either legends of the hero of Tiryns spread to Boeotia and other parts of Greece, where his fame attracted local legends, or else he was brought into Greece by early settlers from the north and his fame spread all over Greece. The latter explanation seems the more acceptable, but it has led many people to believe wrongly that Heracles was a Dorian hero, brought in by invaders who entered Greece at the end of the Mycenaean Age. It is better to suppose that Heracles is an older hero common to all the Greek peoples but associated more with certain areas (Argos, Thebes, Trachis) than with others. Thus we find his exploits covering the whole of the Greek world and his legends and cult flourishing in areas of Greek colonization, such as Asia Minor and Italy (where as Hercules he passed into the Roman state religion).

Many people have thought of Heracles primarily as a god. Herodotus believed that Heracles the god was quite distinct from Heracles the man and that the god was one of the twelve ancient gods of Egypt. He himself even traveled to the Phoenician city of Tyre, whose chief god, Melkart, was identified with Heracles, to find support for his theory. Since the mythology of Melkart is virtually unknown, the similarities between him and Heracles remain unclear; nor can we establish the exact relationship between Heracles and other oriental figures with whom he shares many similarities, for example, the Israelite hero Samson, the Mesopotamian Gilgamesh, and the Cilician god Sandas. These figures may have contributed elements to the Greek hero's legend. In general, it is safe to reject Herodotus' theory and accept the nearly unanimous view of the ancients that Heracles the man became a god.

Still, the origins of Heracles are a subject of great interest. The similarities to the Eastern figures mentioned are undeniable, as are similarities to the Indian hero Indra, who killed the three-headed monster Visvarupa and released the cattle penned in his cave. The monsters that Heracles overcame, such as the lion and the many-headed Hydra, belong more to Eastern mythology, yet Heracles is very definitely a Greek hero, and his myths are Greek traditional tales. Many different tales, then, have become attached to the hero called Heracles. The process can be seen in the large number of *parerga* that cluster around several of the Labors. Some of the myths have a structure consistent with Propp's Quest (see pp. 13–14), and in these the basic structure of the myth remains, despite its varied appearances. The primitive origins of much of Heracles' mythology are apparent from his violence and brutality. His association with many different types of animals has led some scholars to see in him a kind of "Master of Animals," not least because of his association with cattle, the chief source of food in a pastoral society. There is much that is persuasive in Walter Burkert's conclusion:

> *Heracles is, basically, not a heroic figure in the Homeric sense: he is not a warrior fighting warriors, he is mainly concerned with animals, just as he is a savage clad in a skin; and his main job is to tame and bring back the animals which are eaten by man.*[22]

The Greek hero, son of Zeus and exemplar of strength and patience, is also the man wielding the primitive weapon of the club and wearing the lion skin, whose origins lie perhaps far from Greece and certainly in a time long before the development even of Mycenaean culture.

The Apotheosis of Hercules, by Peter Paul Rubens (1577–1640); oil on panel, 1636, 11 × 12¾ in. In this oil sketch for Philip IV's hunting lodge near Madrid, Rubens represents Ovid's narrative at the moment when Hercules ascends from the pyre to Olympus. The flames can be seen at the bottom left, and the bulky hero (Ovid says that "he began to seem greater in size") climbs on the chariot provided by Jupiter. A flying putto puts the victor's wreath on his head, and a second guides the chariot. Rubens does not show Jupiter, so as not to detract from the focus on the triumphant hero. (*Musée Royaux des Beaux-Arts de Belgique, Brussels, Belgium*)

The Choice of Heracles, by Annibale Carracci (1560–1609); oil on canvas, 1596, 65¾ × 93¼ in. Formerly the central painting in the ceiling of the *camerino* (private office) of the Farnese Palace, Carracci's painting is a lucid interpretation of Prodicus' parable. Heracles, identified by his club and lion skin, ponders the choice of Pleasure (to the viewer's right), whose attributes include an actor's mask and a musical instrument. On the other side, Virtue, holding a sheathed sword, points to the rocky upward path, at the top of which stands Pegasus. At the bottom left a poet sits ready to record the deeds of the hero, whose eyes indicate that he has already made his choice of Virtue. In the central background is a palm tree, source of the future victor's wreath. (© *Alinari Archives/Luciano Pedicini/Art Resource, NY*)

So diverse a character attracted a variety of interpretations and uses. Indeed, as Aristotle pointed out in the *Poetics* (8), his very diversity made it impossible for a unified epic or tragedy to be written about him. Only three extant Greek tragedies deal with his legend—Sophocles' *Trachiniae* and Euripides' *Heracles* and *Alcestis*. To the comic poets like Aristophanes, he is good material for slapstick; in the *Frogs*, for example, he is largely motivated by gluttony and lust. Several Greek vases portray him as drinking (and losing) in contests with Dionysus, and in the *Alcestis* he is entertained by Admetus and given plenty to drink before he learns the truth about Alcestis.[23]

More significant was the use made of his virtues by the moralists and philosophers, to whom Heracles became a model of unselfish fortitude, laboring for the good of humankind and achieving immortality by his virtue. This process is best typified by the famous parable told by Prodicus of Ceos:[24] As a young man, Heracles was faced with the choice between two women, representing Pleasure (with ease) and Virtue (with hardship), and chose the latter. Heracles was especially important as a paradigm of virtue in Roman Stoicism, whose doctrines set high value on the Heraclean qualities of endurance and self-reliance. In a modern setting, the character of Harcourt-Reilly in T. S. Eliot's *The Cocktail Party* (1949) combines the Heracles of the myth of Alcestis with the virtues of a Christlike hero.

Perhaps we would do better to leave Heracles by returning to the ancient invocation to him in the *Homeric Hymn to Heracles, the Lion-Hearted* (15). Here we may focus on the man who after a lifetime of toil became a hero and a god:

> Of Heracles will I sing, son of Zeus, whom Alcmena bore in Thebes, city of delightful dances, when she had lain with the son of Cronus, lord of the dark clouds, to be by far the greatest of men on earth. He traversed long ago vast distances of land

and sea at the order of King Eurystheus; many were the bold deeds he did, many were the things he endured. Now he dwells in joy in the beautiful palace of snowy Olympus and has for wife slender-ankled Hebe.

Hail, lord, son of Zeus. Grant [me] both excellence and wealth.[25]

The Heraclidae

Alcmena, Eurystheus, and the Children of Heracles

After the death of Heracles, his mother Alcmena and his children were persecuted by Eurystheus. King Ceyx was unable to protect them, and so they fled to Athens. The Athenians fought Eurystheus, who died in battle with his five sons. His head was brought to Alcmena, who gouged out the eyes with brooches.

According to Euripides, however, in his drama *Heraclidae*, Alcmena and her grandchildren were received at Athens by King Demophon, son of Theseus. Demophon was ordered "by all the oracles to sacrifice a virgin, daughter of a noble father, to the daughter of Demeter [Persephone], to be the defeat of our enemies and the salvation of the city" (*Heraclidae* 407–409, 402). Macaria, daughter of Heracles, voluntarily offered herself for the sacrifice and so brought victory to the Athenians. In the battle, Iolaüs, the nephew of Heracles, was miraculously rejuvenated by Heracles and Hebe and pursued Eurystheus, whom he captured and brought back to Alcmena. The play ends with Alcmena gloating over her prisoner and ordering him off to be executed. With his last words Eurystheus prophesies that his body, if it were buried in Attica, would protect the land from invaders.

Yet another version was given by Pindar (*Pythian Odes* 9.79–83):

> Seven-gated Thebes knew that the Right Time (*Kairos*) favored Iolaüs. Him they buried, after he had cut off the head of Eurystheus with his sword, deep in the earth in the tomb of Amphitryon the charioteer. His grandfather [Amphitryon] lay there, guest of the Spartoi, who lived as a foreigner in Cadmeia, city of white horses.

In this version, Iolaüs killed Eurystheus, and his body, rather than that of Eurystheus, protected the foreign land that had welcomed him—in this case, Thebes (which was Pindar's own city).

Alcmena herself also became associated with a cult. In one version, she died in Thebes and was transported by Hermes to the Elysian Fields, where she married Rhadamanthys, brother of Minos. In the version of Apollodorus, she married Rhadamanthys in Thebes after the death of Amphitryon, but was reunited with Amphitryon in the Underworld. As she was being carried out to burial in a coffin, Hermes, at the command of Zeus, substituted for her body a large stone, which the sons of Heracles discovered (for the coffin had suddenly become very heavy) and set up in a shrine sacred to her.[26]

The Farnese Hercules. Marble copy by Glycon, early third century A.D., of an original by Lysippus, mid-fourth century B.C.; height 125 in. This huge statue was found in the Baths of Caracalla at Rome, for which it had been specially copied. The weary hero leans on his club, which rests on a stump over which the lion skin is draped. His vast body is bursting with mountainous muscles. It has been suggested (by M. Robertson) that he is "an athlete in decay"; more likely, his stance is one of weariness after his labors. (© Alinari Archives/Luciano Pedicini/Art Resource, NY)

The Return of the Heraclidae

The saga of the descendants of Heracles (the Heraclidae) explains the occupation of a large part of the Peloponnese by Dorian tribes in the period after the end of the Mycenaean Age. Hyllus married Iole as his father had commanded and consulted Delphi about his return to the Peloponnese. He was advised to wait "until the third fruit" and was told that victory would come "from the Narrows." After waiting two more years, Hyllus attacked by way of the Isthmus of Corinth. He himself was killed in single combat by Echemus, king of Tegea; his army withdrew, and a truce of one hundred years was agreed upon. At the end of that time, the Heraclid Temenus again consulted the oracle, who told him that the "third fruit" meant not the third harvest but the third generation, and that "the Narrows" meant the entrance to the Gulf of Corinth. Temenus therefore invaded the northwest Peloponnese, crossing over near Patrae and taking as a guide a "three-eyed man" in accordance with the advice of the oracle; this was an Aetolian exile named Oxylus, whom Temenus found riding a one-eyed horse. With his help, the Heraclids defeated the Peloponnesian defenders, who were led by Tisamenus, son of Orestes. Thucydides (1.12) relates these events to the disruptions in Greece that followed the Trojan War and the return of the Greek leaders. He says that "the Dorians with the Heraclidae took possession of the Peloponnese in the eightieth year [after the fall of Troy]."

Thus the "Return of the Heraclidae" took place. The leaders divided up the three principal areas that they had conquered. Lacedaemon (Sparta) was given to Procles and Eurysthenes, sons of the lately dead leader Aristodemus, and they became founders of the two royal houses of Sparta. Argos fell to Temenus and Messene to Cresphontes. Temenus was killed by his sons, whom he had passed over in the succession to his throne. Cresphontes was also murdered, along with two of his sons, by a rival Heraclid, Polyphontes. His widow, Merope, was forced to become Polyphontes' queen, but she succeeded in getting her surviving son Aepytus out of the kingdom to Aetolia, where he grew up. Later, Aepytus secretly returned to Messene and was recognized by Merope, with whose connivance he killed Polyphontes and recovered his father's throne. Of the three Dorian kingdoms, Sparta and Argos flourished for many centuries, but Messene was subjugated by the Spartans within a comparatively short time.

Some Later Survivals of the Myth of Heracles

Besides the Pillars of Heracles mentioned here in connection with the tenth Labor, there were many other examples, ancient and more modern, of the desire of political leaders to identify themselves with Heracles. Thus, for example, the Roman emperor Augustus was identified with Heracles on his return from campaigning in Spain in 24 B.C. by the poet Horace (*Odes* 3.14). Horace was thinking of Heracles as the hero who made the world a better place by ridding it of monsters and other threats to civilization. More trivial—indeed ridiculous—was the emperor Nero (d. 68 A.D.), who, it was said at the time of his death, was preparing to fight, in the guise of Heracles, a specially prepared Nemean lion in the amphitheater. More than a century later, the emperor Commodus (d. A.D. 192) gave

Hercules Victor (The Farnese Hercules), by Hendrik Goltzius (1558–1617). Engraving 1589; published 1617. Goltzius' engraving shows the overmuscled body of the hero from the rear, clutching the Apples of the Hesperides in his right hand. The two contemporary observers emphasize the vastness of his body silhouetted against the sky. The Latin iambic lines (to the left and right of the caption) say: "I, Hercules, terror of the world, rest, weary after subduing the three-formed king [Geryon] of further Spain and after taking the apples from the turning-point of Hesperus, where the never-sleeping serpent had guarded them in gardens of gold." (*V&A Images, London/Art Resource, NY*)

himself the title of *Hercules Romanus* and was portrayed clothed in Heracles' lion skin and holding the Apples of the Hesperides (see p. 631).

In Europe, the image of the "Gallic" Heracles was well known in the sixteenth and seventeenth centuries. This Heracles had his origin in the *Herakles* of Lucian, a Greek author of the second century A.D. According to Lucian, this "Celtic" Heracles was an old man, with the traditional emblems of the lion skin, the club, and the bow, but was also an orator who drew people to himself by the power of his rhetoric. Renaissance handbooks show him as an old man from whose tongue chains extend to his audience, who follow him willingly, overcome by his rhetoric. The Gallic Heracles was used especially in French political imagery: For example, King Henri IV was welcomed into Avignon in 1600 as "L'Hercule Gaulois," and seven arches decorating the processional route celebrated his Labors.

Select Bibliography

Brommer, Frank. *Heracles: The Twelve Labors of the Hero in Ancient Art and Literature.* Translated by Shirley Schwartz. New Rochelle, NY: Caratzas, 1986.

Galinsky, G. Karl. *The Herakles Theme: The Adaptation of the Hero in Literature from Homer to the Twentieth Century.* Oxford: Blackwell, 1972.

For further material see notes 25 and 26.

Primary Sources

Sources in the Chapter

Euripides	*Heracles* 352–427
Homer	*Iliad* 19.103–105
	Odyssey 11.601–603, 620–633
Homeric Hymn 15	*To Heracles, the Lion-Hearted*
Ovid	*Metamorphoses* 9.239–272
Pindar	*Isthmian Ode* 4.61–67
	Nemean Ode 1.33–72
	Pythian Ode 9.79–83
Sophocles	*Trachiniae (Women of Trachis)* 513–525

Additional Sources

Apollodorus	*Library* 2.4.5–2.8.5
Apollonius of Rhodes	*Argonautica* 1.1153–1357
Euripides	*Heraclidae* (Children of Heracles)
Herodotus	2.43.1–2.45.3 (the Egyptian Heracles)
Plautus	*Amphitryon*
Seneca	*Hercules Furens (The Madness of Hercules)*
	Hercules Oetaeus (Hercules on Mt. Oeta)
Xenophon	*Memorabilia* 2.1.21–2.1.34 (Heracles at the crossroads)

Notes

1. The Greek form of his name, which means "glory of Hera," is used here. Its Latin form is Hercules. He is also called Alcides (i.e., descendant of Alcaeus) and sometimes Amphitryoniades (i.e., son of Amphitryon).
2. Licymnius, surviving son of Electryon, was later killed by a son of Heracles.
3. According to Apollodorus, Amphitryon was helped by Creon after ridding Thebes of a monstrous fox with the aid of Cephalus and his magic hound (see pp. 574–576).
4. Eileithyia sat outside Alcmena's door with her hands clasped around her knees in a gesture of sympathetic magic. Alcmena's servant Galanthis broke the spell by rushing out crying, "My mistress has borne a son!" Eileithyia leaped up and unclasped her hands, and the birth took place. She punished Galanthis by turning her into a weasel.
5. Eurytus was grandson of Apollo and king of the Euboean city of Oechalia. See p. 560 for his death at the hands of Heracles.
6. The Cattle of Geryon, the Apples of the Hesperides, and Cerberus.
7. Although the hind is female, it is always shown with horns. Euripides makes the hind destructive, and some authors call it the Cerynitian hind, from the Achaean river Cerynites.
8. Atlas was the name of a mountain in Arcadia as well as of the more famous range in North Africa.
9. The hind is shown beside the tree of the Hesperides in a vase painting.
10. *Parerga* are adventures incidental to the Labors.
11. Pausanias attributes the founding of the games to "Heracles the Dactyl," an attendant of the great Cretan goddess. He had nothing to do with the Greek hero Heracles.
12. The attributes of the birds vary with the imagination of individual authors. See D'Arcy W. Thompson, *Glossary of Greek Birds*, 2d ed. (New York: Oxford University Press, 1936), p. 273. The birds are later encountered by the Argonauts on the Island of Ares (see pp. 601–602).

13. There are many folk tale elements in the legend, for example, the bridegroom's task, the magician who can understand the speech of animals, and the cure of disease by sympathetic magic (cf. Telephus, pp. 478–479).

14. The Spanish painter Francesco Zurbarán (1598–1664) painted a series of ten canvasses for Philip IV of Spain to be placed in the Palace of Buen Retiro in Madrid (they are all now in the Prado), thus continuing the theme of Heracles' importance to the Spanish monarchy.

15. The killing of Cacus is one of the *parerga* to this labor (see p. 661).

16. The Agathyrsi and Geloni were tribes to the north of Scythia, which was the area between the Danube and the Don.

17. His name means "the house of Osiris." Herodotus points out that the Egyptians did not practice human sacrifice.

18. The combat is described in the pseudo-Hesiodic poem, *The Shield of Heracles*. This Cycnus (whose name in Greek means "swan") is one of several mentioned in various poems.

19. Vergil describes this in the sixth *Eclogue* (6.44): *ut litus Hyla, Hyla omne sonaret* ("so that the shore echoed to the cries of 'Hylas, Hylas'").

20. There are many variants of the legend of Telephus, about whom both Sophocles and Euripides wrote tragedies.

21. This is the *cornu copiae* (horn of plenty). Amalthea is the name of a goddess of Plenty and of the goat that suckled the infant Zeus. Ovid says that the horn of Acheloüs became the cornucopia when the Naiads picked it up and filled it with fruit and flowers.

22. Walter Burkert, *Structure and History in Greek Mythology and Ritual* (Berkeley, CA: University of California Press, 1979), p. 94.

23. The "comic" Heracles is well described by Galinsky, Chapter 4.

24. Xenophon, *Memorabilia* 2.21–34; Cicero, *De Officiis* 1.118. The parable has been very important in Western art: see E. Panofsky, *Hercules am Scheideweg* (Leipzig, 1930).

25. For further discussion, see L. R. Farnell, *Greek Hero-Cults and Ideas of Immortality* (New York: Oxford University Press, 1921), Chapters 5–7, and G. Karl Galinsky, *The Herakles Theme* (Oxford: Blackwell, 1972). The best discussion is that of Burkert, *Structure and History*. For Heracles in art, see Frank Brommer, *Herakles*, 2 vols. (Darmstadt: Wissenschaftliche Buchgesellschaft, 1972–1984); vol. 1 has been translated by Shirley J. Schwarz as *Heracles: The Twelve Labors of the Hero in Ancient Art and Literature* (New Rochelle, NY: Caratzas, 1984). See also Jane Henle, *Greek Myths: A Vase Painter's Notebook* (Bloomington: Indiana University Press, 1973), pp. 231–238.

26. For the different versions of her myth, see J. G. Frazer's notes on pp. 181–182 and 303 in vol. 1 of his edition of *Apollodorus* (Cambridge, MA: Loeb Classical Library, Harvard University Press, 1961 [1921]).

THESEUS AND THE LEGENDS OF ATTICA

Descendants of Erechtheus, fortunate from of old and children of the blessed
gods, dwelling in a land that has never been ravaged, feeding on most
famous wisdom. . .

—EURIPIDES, *Medea*, 824–829

The Early Kings and Their Legends

Cecrops, Erichthonius, and Erechtheus

The Athenians boasted that they were **autochthonous** (literally,
"sprung from the earth"), that is, that they were not descended from
any invaders of Attica. They said that Cecrops, their earliest king, had
sprung from the earth and was serpent-shaped in the lower half of
his body. He has little importance in legend except as the founder of
Attica, which he called Cecropia after himself. It was in his time that
the contest between Poseidon and Athena for the possession of Attica
took place (see p. 174). Poseidon continued to be an important divinity
at Athens, and his worship on the Acropolis was closely connected
with that of Athena.

Another early figure in Attic mythology is Erichthonius, who
was also partly serpent-shaped and (as the element *-chthon-* in his
name implies) sprung from the earth. When Hephaestus attempted
to violate Athena, his semen fell on the ground, and from it sprang
Erichthonius. Athena took him up and put him in a chest, which she
gave to the daughters of Cecrops, Pandrosos, Auglauros, and Herse
(or only to Pandrosos), forbidding them to look inside. The sisters
disobeyed: driven mad by what they saw (either a pair of snakes or
Erichthonius with his snake-like body), they hurled themselves off the
Acropolis.[1] After this, Athena took Erichthonius back and brought him
up herself. As king of Athens, he was credited with instituting the
great annual festival of the Panathenaea and setting up the wooden
statue of Athena on the Acropolis.

Erichthonius' myth focuses on his birth, the most important feature of which is that he was "sprung from the earth." He is to some
extent confused with his grandson and successor as king of Athens,

The Discovery of the Infant Erichthonius, by Peter Paul Rubens (1577–1640); oil on canvas, ca. 1616, 85 × 125 in. Rubens has painted the moment when Aglauros has opened the basket containing Erichthonius and shows him to her sisters, Pandrosos (on the right) and Herse (on the left) with a brilliant red robe. Cupid gestures toward her as the future bride of Mercury. Behind is a fountain of the many-breasted Artemis, whose fertility is echoed by the herm of the lascivious god Pan, on the left. The identity of the old woman is not known. (*Liechtenstein Museum/Alamy Stock Photo*)

Erechtheus. Both are in fact forms of Poseidon. Athena prophesied that after his death Erechtheus would be worshiped at Athens with his own cult-site, "ringed around with stones," and that under the title of "**Poseidon-Erechtheus** he will be offered sacrifices of bulls."[2]

Toward the end of the fifth century B.C., the beautiful temple on the Acropolis known as the **Erechtheum** was dedicated jointly to **Athena Polias** (i.e., Athena as Guardian of the City) and Erechtheus.[3] In it were sacred objects associated with the earliest stages of Athenian religion, including the wooden statue of Athena, the tomb of Erechtheus, and the salt spring produced by the blow of Poseidon's trident in his contest with Athena, which was known as "the sea of Erechtheus." In this "sea" were the marks of Poseidon's trident where he struck the earth, and linked to the sanctuary was the olive tree produced by Athena. The temple took the name by which it is generally known, Erechtheum, from Erechtheus-Poseidon; but in antiquity it was known officially as "the temple in which is the ancient statue."

Thus the Erechtheum and its neighboring shrines were closely bound up with the most ancient myths of Athens. It was built upon the Acropolis, the site of the Mycenaean fortress of Athens, and so it linked Athenians to the earliest stages of their city's history. Athena, the great Olympian protectress of the city, here was associated with both her rival Poseidon and her predecessor, the chthonic divinity Erechtheus. Her triumph in the struggle for the honor of protecting the city was visible nearby in the sculptures of the west pediment of the Parthenon.

Erechtheus was important in the mythology of Athens. He successfully defended Athens in her earliest war, the attack of the Eleusinians led by the Thracian Eumolpus, who was a son of Poseidon and ancestor of the hereditary priests of Eleusis. With the approval of his wife, Praxithea, Erechtheus sacrificed one (or all three) of his daughters to secure the victory for Athens.[4] In the battle he killed Eumolpus, and for this deed was himself killed by Poseidon, who thrust him into the earth with his trident. The sacrifice of the daughter was a central theme in Euripides' tragedy *Erechtheus*, in which Praxithea played a prominent part.[5]

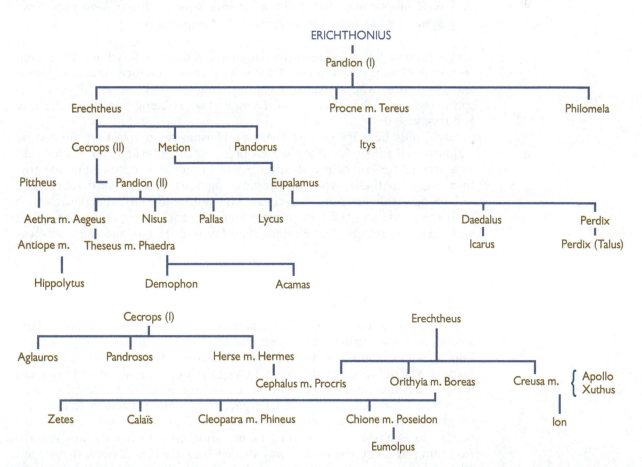

Figure 23.1. The Royal Families of Athens

In Euripides' tragedy *Ion*, Ion's mother, **Creusa**, one of Erechtheus' daughters, gives a different version, in which all the daughters of Erechtheus were sacrificed except for herself (*Ion* 277–282):

> ION: Did your father Erechtheus sacrifice your sisters?
> CREUSA: He hardened himself to kill the maidens as a sacrificial offering for the earth.
> ION: How then were you saved alone among your sisters?
> CREUSA: I was a newborn baby in my mother's arms.
> ION: And does a chasm in the earth truly hide your father?
> CREUSA: Yes—blows from the ocean-god's trident killed him.

As a final reminder of Erechtheus' importance in Athenian mythology and the pride of the Athenians in being autochthonous, we quote from the opening lines (824–830) of the beautiful chorus in praise of Athens that Euripides composed for his tragedy *Medea*:[6]

> The descendants of Erechtheus are fortunate from of old and children of the blessed gods, [dwelling in] a holy land that has never been conquered, feeding on most famous wisdom and walking lightly through the shining air.

We have earlier mentioned the daughters of Cecrops to whom Athena entrusted the infant Erichthonius. They were three in number, Aglauros, Herse, and Pandrosos, whose names, meaning "bright," "dew," and "all-dew," respectively, show that they are truly mythological beings, in origin fertility goddesses.[7]

Ovid tells how Herse was loved by Hermes, who was first noticed by Aglauros as he flew down to the Acropolis. Aglauros asked Hermes for gold as a reward for her help in bringing him to Herse. For this Aglauros further angered Athena, who was already angry because of her disobedience in looking inside Erichthonius' chest. Athena therefore filled Aglauros with such envy that she tried to prevent Hermes from going in to Herse and he turned her into a rock. Hermes then lay with Herse, and their son was Cephalus.

Cephalus and Procris

Cephalus was loved by **Eos (Dawn)** and was an ally of Amphitryon. In later legend, he is the husband of Procris, daughter of Erechtheus. In Ovid's story, Cephalus was tempted by **Aurora** (the Latin form of Eos), who also loved him, to make trial of Procris' faithfulness. In disguise Cephalus attempted to seduce her, and when he was on the point of succeeding, revealed himself. In shame Procris fled and joined Artemis, who gave her a hound, **Laelaps**, that always caught its quarry and a javelin that never missed its mark. Later, she was reconciled to Cephalus and returned home, bringing with her the magic gifts. According to Ovid, the hound was turned into marble, along with its prey, when Cephalus was hunting near Thebes. The javelin had a longer and more tragic history. Here is part of Ovid's story (*Metamorphoses* 7.804–859; Cephalus is the speaker):

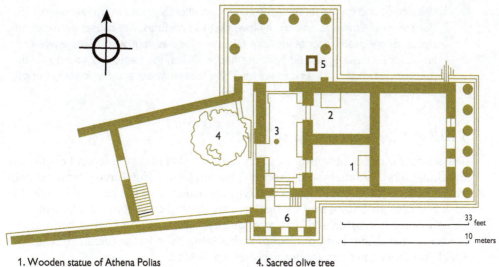

1. Wooden statue of Athena Polias
2. Tomb of Erechtheus
3. Salt spring
4. Sacred olive tree
5. Zeus' thunderbolt
6. Porch of the maidens (caryatids)

Figure 23.2. Plan of the Erechtheum (after W. B. Dinsmoor)

When the sun's first rays had just begun to touch the topmost peaks, I used to go, like the young man I was, to the forest to hunt. No servants went with me, nor horses, nor keen-scented dogs trained to follow the knotted hunting nets—all I relied upon was the javelin. When my right hand had had enough of killing wild beasts, I would look for the cool shade and the breeze (*aura*) that came from the cold valleys. The gentle breeze would I call for in the midday heat; the breeze would I wait for, refreshment after my labors. "Come, Aura" (for I remember my words), would I sing, "assist me and most pleasing, enter my bosom; be willing to relieve as you do, the heat with which I burn."[8] Perhaps I would add (for this way tended my fate) more endearments and would say, "You are my great pleasure; you restore and   10 refresh me, you make me love the forest and solitary places; may your breath always be caught by my mouth." (804–820)

Someone listening to my words with their double meaning was deceived; thinking the name of *aura* that I called upon so often was the name of a nymph, she believed that it was a nymph I loved. Soon a rash informer falsely charged me before Procris and repeated the murmurings she had heard. Love is credulous, yet often Procris hesitated and refused to believe the informer; she would not condemn her husband's crime unless she saw it herself. (821–834)

The next dawn's light had driven the night away: I went to the forest and, successful in the hunt, lay on the grass and said, "Come, Aura, and give relief to my   20 labor." Suddenly I thought I heard a sob as I spoke, yet still as I was saying, "Come, most excellent Aura," a fallen leaf rustled; and, thinking it was a wild animal, I hurled my javelin through the air. It was Procris; and as she held her wounded breast, she groaned "Ah, me." When I recognized the voice of my faithful wife, headlong I ran to her in dismay. I found her half dead, her blood staining her torn clothes, and plucking her own gift, alas, from the wound. Gently I lifted her body, dearer to me than my own. . . and implored her not to leave me, guilty of her death. (835–850)

> Weakened and on the point of death, with an effort she said these few words: "By our marriage vows. . . and by my love that still endures, the cause, even as I am dying, of my death, do not let Aura take my place as your wife." Those were her words; then finally I realized how she had mistaken the name and told her of the mistake. Yet what use was it to tell her? She fainted away, and her feeble strength failed as her blood flowed out.[9] (851–859)

Philomela, Procne, and Tereus

The successor of Erichthonius was Pandion, who is famous in legend chiefly for his daughters Philomela and Procne. The Thracian king Tereus came to help Pandion in a war against Thebes and was rewarded with the hand of Procne. He took her back to Thrace and by her became the father of **Itys**. Later, Philomela came to visit her sister and was attacked by Tereus, who violated her, cut out her tongue, and shut her up in a remote building deep in the forest. Here is how Ovid continues the story (*Metamorphoses* 6.572–600):

> What could Philomela do? Her prison, with its walls of unyielding stone, kept her from flight. Her mouth, dumb, could not tell of the crime. Yet sorrow is inventive, and cunning is an ally in distress. Skillfully she hung the threads from the barbarian loom and interwove purple scenes with the white threads, telling of the crime.

Cephalus and Aurora, by Nicolas Poussin (1594–1665); oil on canvas, ca. 1630, 38 × 51½ in. Cephalus gazes at a portrait of Procris, held up to him by a cupid, as he resists the advances of Aurora. In the background, Pegasus waits to pull the chariot of the Dawn. The sleeping god with the urn is a river-god used by Poussin to signify a mythological landscape. (© *National Gallery, London/Art Resource, NY*)

> She gave the finished embroidery to a servant and by signs asked her to take it to her mistress. The servant, not knowing what she was bringing, obeyed and took the embroidery to Procne. The cruel tyrant's wife unrolled the tapestry and read the unhappy saga of her own misfortunes. She held her peace (a miracle that she could!); sorrow restrained her words. . . . (572–583)
>
> Now came the time when the Thracian matrons celebrated Bacchus' triennial feast; Night accompanied their rites. Queen Procne left her palace, garbed in the god's ritual dress and holding the instruments of his ecstasy. . . . In a frenzy, with threatening looks, Procne rushed through the forest with a crowd of followers; driven by the madness of sorrow she pretended, Bacchus, that it was your madness. At length she reached the lonely prison and raised the Bacchic cry, *Evoe*; she broke down the doors, seized her sister, and put on her the Bacchic vestments, veiling her face with leaves of ivy. Dragging the stunned Philomela, Procne brought her sister to the palace. (587–600)

10

Ovid then tells how Procne decides to revenge herself upon Tereus by murdering their son Itys (636–645):

> Without delay, Procne seized Itys. . . . In a distant part of the lofty palace, as he stretched out his hands (for he saw his fate before him) and cried, "Mother, mother," trying to embrace her, she struck him with a sword, where the chest meets the body's flank, and she did not look away. One wound was enough to kill him, but Philomela cut his throat with a knife. They tore apart his body, while it still retained vestiges of life.

Ovid describes, in considerable detail, how the sisters cooked Itys and served him up to Tereus, who recognized too late what he had eaten. The tale continues (666–674):

> Now Tereus drew his sword and pursued the daughters of Pandion: you would think that their bodies were clothed with feathers, and indeed they were. One flew to the forest; the other to the roof, and still the murder marked her breast and her feathers were stained with blood. Tereus, rushing swiftly in sorrow and in eagerness for revenge, turned into a bird with crested head; a long beak projects in place of his sword; the bird's name is Epops (Hoopoe), and its face seems armed.

In the Greek version of the story, it is the nightingale (Procne) that mourns for her dead son, while the tongueless swallow (Philomela) tries to tell her story by her incoherent chatter. The Latin authors, however, changed the names, making Philomela the nightingale and Procne the swallow.

The *Ion* of Euripides

Pandion was said to have been succeeded as king by Erechtheus, whose myths we discussed earlier. Among his daughters was Creusa, the heroine of Euripides' play *Ion*. Creusa was the only one of the daughters not to have been sacrificed by her father before the battle against Eumolpus. She was loved by Apollo and bore him a son, Ion, whom she exposed out of fear of her father. Ion was saved

The Banquet of Tereus, by Peter Paul Rubens (1577–1640); oil on canvas, 1636–1638, 77 × 105 in. Procne, wearing a Maenad's animal skin, shows the head of their son to Tereus. Behind her follows Philomela, her mouth open as if trying to speak, wreathed with ivy and carrying the Maenad's thyrsus. Tereus has kicked over the table, and he reaches for his sword with which to kill Procne. In the background, a servant watches from a half-opened door, and a putto looks on from above. (*Erich Lessing/Art Resource, NY*)

by Hermes at Apollo's request and taken by Apollo to Delphi, where he was brought up as a temple servant and became treasurer of the sanctuary. Creusa, meanwhile, was given as wife to Xuthus as a reward for helping Erechtheus defeat the Chalcodontids of Euboea. After years of childlessness, Xuthus and Creusa consulted the Delphic oracle as to how they might have children; Xuthus was told to greet as his son the first person he met on going out of the temple.[10] This person was Ion, but Creusa, who did not know that he was her own son, took him for a bastard son of Xuthus and attempted to kill him. The attempt miscarried, and with the intervention of Athena, mother and son recognized each other. Xuthus, Creusa, and Ion returned together to Athens, where Ion became the ancestor of the four Ionic tribes (which were the main units of the early Athenian political structure). His descendants colonized part of the coast of Asia Minor and the islands, thereafter called Ionia.[11]

Orithyia and Boreas and Their Children

Another daughter of Erechtheus, Orithyia, was loved by the North Wind, Boreas. He carried her off to Thrace as she was playing by the river Ilissus.[12] In Thrace, she became the mother of the winged heroes **Zetes** and **Calaïs**, and of two daughters, Cleopatra and Chione. Zetes and Calaïs were prominent in the Argonauts' expedition (see pp. 600–601). Phineus was married to Cleopatra, who was said to have caused the blindness of her stepsons (born to Phineus from another woman) by falsely accusing them of attempting to seduce her. Chione became the mother, by Poseidon, of Eumolpus, whose expedition against Athens we discussed earlier.

The Confused Genealogy of the Kings of Athens

According to Apollodorus, Erechtheus was succeeded by his son Cecrops, and Cecrops by his son Pandion; Cecrops and Pandion thus repeat the names of earlier kings. Pandion was driven out of Attica by his uncle Metion and fled to Megara, where he became the father of four sons: Aegeus, Pallas, Nisus, and Lycus. After Pandion's death, the four brothers recovered the throne at Athens and shared the power; Aegeus, however, as the oldest, was in effect the sovereign, while Nisus returned to Megara as its king.

Theseus

Aegeus, like Erechtheus, is another form of the god Poseidon. This is indicated by his connection with the **Aegean Sea** and by the tradition that Poseidon rather than Aegeus was Theseus' father.[13] As king of Athens, Aegeus was threatened by the opposition of his brother **Pallas**. Being childless, Aegeus was told by the Delphic oracle "not to undo the wineskin's mouth" until he had returned home. Perplexed by this riddle, he asked the advice of **Pittheus**, king of **Troezen**, his host on the journey. Pittheus, who understood the oracle, made Aegeus drunk and gave him his daughter **Aethra** to lie with.[14] When Aegeus left Troezen, he told Aethra that if their child were a boy she must bring him up without saying who his father was. She was to send him to Athens when he was old enough to lift a rock by himself, under which Aegeus would leave a sword and a pair of sandals as tokens by which he could recognize his son. In due time, Aethra bore a son, Theseus, who grew up and set out for Athens after securing the tokens.

Theseus is the great national hero of Attica, and Athens came to be the focal point of his legends. His earlier links with Marathon and Troezen were weakened. He is associated with Heracles in some of his adventures, and his deeds are similar to those of Heracles—for example, his ridding the land of brigands

Mary Renault's Theseus

An entertaining novel retelling the life of Theseus in a very compelling fashion is *The King Must Die* (1958) by Mary Renault, who is exceptional in her ability to make classical mythology and legend come alive. Robert Graves is another so gifted, for example, in his novel *Hercules, My Shipmate* (1945).

Renault has a firm grasp of both the ancient sources and modern archaeology, and by her sensitive art she has re-created the civilization and the characters in a most credible and exciting manner. Dominant among the many political and religious issues in her novel is the overriding motif of Theseus caught in the archetypal battle between matriarchy and patriarchy. This young, inspiring hero could never fall victim to the horrifying, archaic ritual by which the king must die to ensure the dominance and fertility of the earth mother. Renault's sequel, *The Bull from the Sea* (1962), depicts the life of the Amazons, one of whom becomes the mother of Hippolytus.

and monsters and his expedition against the Amazons. Some of the characters in his saga were themselves heroes with cults of their own, for example, Sciron and Hippolytus. The legends of Theseus have become famous largely through the genius of Athenian writers.[15]

Theseus' Six Labors on His Journey from Troezen to Athens

The adventures of Theseus fall into fairly well-defined groups,[16] of which the first contains six deeds he performed while traveling to Athens from Troezen. To expose himself to the challenge of more dangerous adventures, Theseus chose the land route.

At Epidaurus he killed the brigand **Periphetes**, a son of Hephaestus, who was armed with a club and generally called **Corynetes (Club Man)**. Theseus took the club for himself, and it plays no further part in his legend (except in artistic representations).

At the Isthmus of Corinth, Theseus killed the robber **Sinis**, called **Pityocamptes (Pine Bender)** from the way in which he killed his victims. He would bend two pine tree saplings to the ground, tie one end of his victim to each of the two trees, and then release the trees. Theseus killed him in this way.

On the border of the Isthmus and the Megarid, Theseus killed a **monstrous sow** near the village of **Crommyon**. Next he found the brigand **Sciron** barring his way at the so-called Cliffs of Sciron. Sciron, originally a local hero of

The Labors of Theseus. Attic red-figure kylix, ca. 475 B.C.; height of kylix 5 in., diameter 12¾ in. The cycle of Theseus' labors was often painted on Athenian vases, especially drinking cups (*kylikes*), in the fifth century. This cup is unusual in that the cycle is painted (almost identically, except for the Minotaur) on both the exterior and the interior. The interior, with the Minotaur at the center, is shown here. Starting at the top and going in a clockwise direction, the labors are: (1) Cercyon; (2) Procrustes; (3) Sciron (note the turtle); (4) the bull of Marathon; (5) Sinis (Pityocamptes); and (6) the sow of Crommyon. At the center Theseus drags the dying Minotaur out of the Labyrinth to dispatch him with his sword. Periphetes does not appear, since this labor does not enter the cycle until after 475 B.C. (© *The Trustees of the British Museum*)

neighboring areas,[17] blocked the path along which travelers through the Megarid must go to pass the cliffs and compelled all comers to stoop and wash his feet. He would then kick his victims into the sea, where a gigantic turtle ate them up. Theseus killed him by his own methods.

Drawing closer to Athens, Theseus met **Cercyon** at Eleusis. Like Sciron, Cercyon was originally a local hero. He compelled travelers to wrestle with him to the death. Theseus defeated him in wrestling, held him high in the air, and then dashed him to his death upon the ground.

Finally, between Eleusis and Athens, Theseus met the brigand **Procrustes** (his name means "**the stretcher**"),[18] who possessed a hammer, a saw, and a bed. He compelled travelers to lie on the bed, and those who were too long for it he would cut down to size; those who were too short he would hammer out until they fit it exactly. He, too, perished at Theseus' hands in the way in which he had killed his victims.

Theseus Is Recognized by Aegeus

Theseus' arrival at Athens is dramatically described by the lyric poet Bacchylides of Ceos. In reply to the citizens' questions, Aegeus speaks (Bacchylides, *Dithyramb* 18.16–60):

> "A messenger has come, traversing the long road from the Isthmus; incredible are the deeds of a mighty man that he relates. This man killed violent Sinis, strongest of mortals. He killed the man-slaying sow in the glens of Crommyon and killed the cruel Sciron. The wrestling ring of Cercyon has he suppressed; Procoptes [Slicer, i.e., Procrustes] has dropped the mighty hammer of Polypemon [Troubler, i.e., Procrustes' father?], for he has met a more valiant man. I fear what this news portends." "Who is this man?" [ask the citizens, and Aegeus continues]: "Two companions only come with him, says the messenger; upon his shoulders he wears an ivory-hilted sword, and in his hand he carries two polished spears; upon his red-haired head is set a Spartan cap, well-made; around his body he has cast a purple tunic and over it a woolen cloak from Thessaly. From his eyes darts blood-red flame, as from Lemnos' volcano. Yet he is but a youth in his first prime, whose skill is in the delight of war and the brazen blows of battle. In quest of shining Athens does he come." 10

Theseus' arrival was hedged with further danger. Aegeus was married to **Medea**, who expected their son Medus to succeed as king of Athens. Medea, immediately recognizing Theseus as Aegeus' son and a rival to Medus, attempted to have Theseus poisoned before Aegeus could recognize him. She advised Aegeus that the newcomer would be a threat to his power. He should entertain Theseus at a banquet where he would drink poisoned wine, for which Medea would provide the poison. Theseus at the banquet carved his meat with the sword that he had recovered from under the rock at Troezen; Aegeus recognized the sword, dashed the cup of poison out of Theseus' hand, and publicly recognized him as his son and successor.

Pallas, brother of Aegeus, and his sons had hoped and plotted to take over Aegeus' power and resorted to violence upon Theseus' recognition. Theseus killed all the members of one of the two groups into which they had divided, and Pallas himself and his surviving sons ceased to be a threat.

The Bull of Marathon

Theseus' next labor was to catch the bull of Marathon, which was said to have been the one that Heracles had brought from Crete. He mastered the bull and drove it back to Athens, where he sacrificed it to Apollo Delphinius. On his way to Marathon an old woman, **Hecale**, entertained Theseus. She promised she would sacrifice to Zeus if Theseus returned successful, but on his return he found her already dead and ordered that she share the honors henceforth paid to Zeus Hecalus at a local annual festival.

The Minotaur

Androgeos, son of the Cretan king **Minos**, had been killed in Attica because of the jealousy he aroused by winning all the contests at the Panathenaic games. In revenge, Minos mounted an expedition against Athens and her ally, Megara, where Nisus, brother of Aegeus, was king. Megara was attacked first, and some time after its fall Athens made a treaty with Minos, with the provision that at intervals (of one or nine years) seven Athenian youths and seven girls, children of noble families, should be sent to Crete as tribute, there to be shut up in the Labyrinth and devoured by the Minotaur. The victims were chosen by lot, and Theseus volunteered to go.[19]

On the voyage to Crete, Minos attacked one of the maidens, Eriboea, who called on Theseus for help. When Theseus intervened, Minos prayed to Zeus for a sign that he was indeed Minos' father (and therefore that his son need be under no restraint in dealing with other men). Zeus sent lightning, and Minos

Theseus and Amphitrite. Attic red-figure cup by the painter Onesimos and signed by the potter Euphronios, ca. 500 B.C.; diameter 15¾ in. The boyish figure of Theseus is held up underwater by a tiny Triton, as dolphins cavort to the left. Amphitrite, seated on a stool, holds the wreath in her left hand, as Athena (with helmet, spear, and aegis) looks toward her. This scene anticipates the narrative of Bacchylides by some twenty-five years. (© RMN-Grand Palais/Art Resource, NY)

then challenged Theseus' claim to be the son of Poseidon by throwing a ring overboard, which Theseus was to recover. A beautiful poem by Bacchylides describes the sequel (*Dithyramb* 17.92–116):

> The Athenian youths trembled as the hero leaped into the sea, and tears poured from their lily-like eyes as they awaited the sorrow of what had to be. Yet the dolphins, dwellers in the sea, swiftly brought great Theseus to the palace of his father, the ruler of horses. There with awe he saw the noble daughters of rich Nereus, and in the lovely palace he saw his father's own wife, the beauteous Amphitrite, in all her majesty. Round him she cast a purple robe, and upon his thick hair the unwithered wreath, dark with roses, which subtle Aphrodite had given her at her own marriage.

With these gifts (the poet does not mention the ring), Theseus returned miraculously to the ship and so came to Crete. There the daughter of Minos, **Ariadne**, fell in love with him and gave him a thread with which he could trace his way back out of the **Labyrinth**. With this aid he entered the Labyrinth, killed the **Minotaur**, and emerged unharmed. He then sailed from Crete with his thirteen Athenian companions, taking Ariadne with him.

Ariadne on Naxos

Another tradition, however, makes Ariadne give Theseus a wreath that lights up the darkness of the Labyrinth and so helps him escape. In the poem of Bacchylides, this wreath is made the gift not of Ariadne but of Amphitrite, so that Theseus himself brings it to Crete. Ariadne wore the wreath on her flight with Theseus until he deserted her on Naxos and she was found by **Dionysus**. The god took the wreath and set it in the heavens, where it became the constellation Corona.

Here is Ovid's version of the metamorphosis (*Metamorphoses* 8.174–181):

> Quickly the son of Aegeus sailed to Dia after seizing Minos' daughter and cruelly left his companion deserted on that shore. Alone and bitterly complaining, Ariadne found comfort in the embraces of Bacchus, who took the wreath from her brow and placed it in the heavens so that Ariadne might be made famous by a constellation. The wreath flies through the thin air, and as it flies its jewels are turned into fires and become fixed in their place, still with the appearance of a wreath (*corona*).

Ariadne is originally a divine person, perhaps another form of Aphrodite. Hesiod (*Theogony* 947–949) describes her as the "wife of Dionysus, whom Zeus made immortal." Later versions of the Theseus legend make her a forlorn heroine, deserted by her lover Theseus upon the island of Dia (the early name for Naxos) during the voyage back to Athens. Here is the narrative of Catullus (64. 52–59):

> Ariadne, with uncontrolled passion in her heart, looking out from the shore of Dia with its sounding waves, saw Theseus receding into the distance with his fleet at full speed. Not yet could she believe her eyes, for she had only just been wakened from deceitful sleep and saw that she was alone, unhappy, upon the shore. But the young man, forgetful, parted the waves with his oars in flight, leaving his promises unfulfilled to the gusts of wind.

Death of a Monster, by Pablo Picasso (1881–1973); pencil on paper, 1937, 15 × 22¼ in. The contorted and dying Minotaur sees himself in a mirror held up by a sea-goddess, perhaps Amphitrite herself. Picasso used the violence and horror of the Minotaur to express his anger at the atrocities of the Spanish Civil War; this drawing is dated December 6, 1937, eight months after the bombing of Guernica. (© *Succession Picasso. DACS, London 2021. National Galleries Scotland. Purchased with the support of the Heritage Lottery Fund and the Art Fund 1995*)

Ovid, who related this legend three times,[20] describes the arrival of Dionysus and his companions (*Ars amatoria* 1.535–564):

> And now Ariadne beat her soft breast again and again: "My faithless lover has gone," cried she. "What will become of me?" "What will become of me?" she cried; the shore reechoed to the sound of cymbals and the frenzied beating of drums. She swooned in fear, and her words trailed away; no blood remained in her fainting body. Look! here are the maenads, their hair streaming down their backs. Look! here come the dancing satyrs, forerunners of the god. Look! here is old Silenus, hardly able to keep his seat upon the swaybacked donkey. . . . And now came the god in his chariot decked to the top with vines, driving yoked tigers with golden reins. Ariadne lost her color, her voice, her thoughts of Theseus; thrice she tried to run away, and thrice fear held her rooted. . . . Then said the god: "Behold I am here, a more faithful object of your love. Away with fear! You shall be the Cretan wife of Bacchus. Take the heavens as my gift; you shall be observed in the heavens as a constellation. Often as the Cretan Crown (Corona) will you guide lost sailors." So he spoke and jumped down from the chariot, lest she be alarmed by the tigers, and took her up in his arms, for she could not resist; all things are easy for a god. Some of his followers chant the marriage cry, "O Hymen," and others cry, "*Evoe, evoe;*" so the god and his bride lay together in the sacred bed.

10

Homer says that Ariadne was killed by Artemis upon Naxos as a punishment for eloping with Theseus when she was already betrothed to Dionysus. Yet another story has her die in Cyprus in giving birth to Theseus' child. When Theseus returned, he instituted a ritual in her honor. In historical times, she was honored under the title of Ariadne Aphrodite, part of the ritual being for a young man to lie down and imitate a woman in childbirth. In all these conflicting stories, it is clear that Ariadne is no ordinary mortal and that her partner was not a man, Theseus, but a god.

Theseus Becomes King of Athens

After leaving Dia (Naxos), Theseus went to Delos, where he sacrificed to Apollo and danced the **Crane dance** with his companions. The dance became traditional at Delos, and its intricate movements were said to imitate the windings of the Labyrinth.[21] From Delos Theseus sailed home to Athens. Now he had arranged with Aegeus that he should change the black sail of his ship for white if he had been successful. This he forgot to do, and as Aegeus saw the black-sailed ship approaching, he threw himself from a cliff into the sea, which thereafter was called the **Aegean Sea**.

So Theseus became king of Athens. He was credited with a number of historical reforms and institutions, including the **synoecism** of Attica (i.e., the union of the different villages into one political unit with Athens as its center) and the refounding of the **Isthmian Games**.[22]

The Amazons

Theseus joined with Heracles in his expedition against the Amazons, and as his share of the spoil received the Amazon, **Antiope**, by whom he became the father of **Hippolytus**. The Amazons in revenge invaded Attica and were defeated by Theseus. During the Amazon attack, Antiope died. The battle between Theseus and the Amazons became a favorite theme in Athenian art after the Persian Wars, when the Amazons were seen as symbols of the barbarians, who, like the Persians, had been defeated by the Greeks.[23]

Theseus and Pirithoüs

Pirithoüs, king of the Thessalian tribe of the **Lapiths** and son of Ixion, was Theseus' friend. Theseus was among the guests at the marriage of Pirithoüs and took part in the fight against the **centaurs**, which became an important theme in Greek art.

Theseus and Pirithoüs vowed to help each other in securing a wife. Theseus attempted to take **Helen**, and Pirithoüs, **Persephone**. Helen, who at the time was only a child, was kidnapped from Sparta and brought back to Attica, where she was put in the care of Theseus' mother, Aethra, in the Attic village of Aphidnae. While Theseus and Pirithoüs were away on their attempt against Persephone, the **Dioscuri** invaded Attica and recovered their sister. The Dioscuri were favorably received in Athens itself, where the regent Menestheus instituted a cult in their honor.[24] Aethra was taken back to Sparta as Helen's servant and went with her to Troy.

Dionysus and Ariadne. Marble sarcophagus, ca. A.D. 180; width 77 in., height (without lid) 20½ in., height of lid 11 in. Dionysus approaches from the left riding on a chariot drawn by a lyre-playing centaur, in front of and to the right of whom a centauress blows on a kind of trumpet. Before him go Pan and a silenus, and a silenus mask lies on the ground in the left center. A cupid hovers near the god. In the center the god stands, now clothed in a long robe, holding a reversed thyrsus in his left hand, his right hand resting on the leading silenus. He looks toward the sleeping Ariadne, whose robe is being drawn aside by a cupid, while two maenads look back at the god. To the right two maenads are about to attack Pentheus. On the lid are reliefs of the god's thiasos, and a deer (far right) is being sacrificed. The waking of Ariadne to the coming of the god of new life was popular in the funerary art of late antiquity as a parable of the waking of the soul to eternal life after death. This sarcophagus is in a tomb in the cemetery under St. Peter's Basilica in the Vatican. It is not known whether its occupant was pagan or Christian. (*Photo courtesy of the Fabbrica di San Pietro in Vaticano*)

Pirithoüs met his end in attempting to abduct Persephone. He and Theseus descended to the Underworld where they were held fast in magic chairs. In the Athenian tradition, **Heracles** interceded for Theseus' release, while Pirithoüs stayed in Hades forever. Thus the Athenian hero was again associated with Heracles, in this case in his last and greatest labor, the conquest of death.

Theseus, Phaedra, and Hippolytus

Theseus was also married to Phaedra, another daughter of Minos, and she bore him two sons, Demophon and Acamas. Phaedra (whose name means "bright") may originally have been a Cretan goddess like Ariadne. As we learned in Chapter 10, she fell passionately in love with Hippolytus, Theseus' son by Antiope, but did not tell him of her desire. During an absence of Theseus, her old nurse found out the secret and told Hippolytus. In shame at the discovery of her secret, Phaedra hanged herself and left behind a letter falsely accusing Hippolytus of attempting to seduce her. When Theseus returned, saw Phaedra's corpse, and read the letter, he banished Hippolytus and called on Poseidon to destroy him.[25] As Hippolytus was driving his chariot along the seashore on his way into exile, Poseidon sent a bull from the sea, which so frightened the horses that they bolted, threw Hippolytus from the chariot, and dragged him almost to his death. He was carried back to Theseus and died after a reconciliation with his father, assured by Artemis of his future honor as a hero with a cult.

The legend of Hippolytus owes its fame largely to Euripides, who wrote two tragedies on the subject (one of which is extant), and to Seneca, whose *Phaedra* was the model for Racine's *Phèdre*.[26] In Euripides' *Hippolytus*, the drama is set at Troezen; but most other authors make Athens the scene. Hippolytus himself was honored with a cult at Troezen and was closely connected with Artemis, in whose honor he avoided all women. At Athens he was connected with Aphrodite, whose temple on the south side of the Acropolis was called "Aphrodite by Hippolytus." Hippolytus himself was said to have been brought to life by Asclepius, and in his resurrected form he was absorbed by the Italians with the name of Virbius. His legend is of the greatest literary importance: it connects Attica and Troezen and links Theseus to the great goddesses worshiped in Crete, Troezen, and Athens.

Theseus as Champion of the Oppressed

In the fifth century B.C., a number of legends were developed in which kings of Athens were portrayed as protectors of victims of tyranny who had been driven from their homes. In Euripides' *Medea*, Aegeus, father of Theseus, promises to protect Medea, who has been exiled from Corinth. Theseus was especially popular in these legends. He generously gave refuge to the exiled Oedipus (see pp. 413–417), and in the *Suppliant Women* of Euripides he champions the mothers of the dead heroes of the Seven against Thebes. Led by Adrastus, the sole

Dionysus and Ariadne. Bronze krater (the Derveni Krater), second half of the fourth century B.C.; height 35½ in. The krater, which held the ashes of a Thessalian nobleman, was discovered at Derveni, not far from Thessaloniki, in 1962. The reliefs on the central panel show Dionysus, naked, seated on a rock with his leg over Ariadne's thigh. She draws her veil aside, the gesture of a bride accepting her husband. Behind Dionysus is a panther, and birds, animals, vines, and ivy ornament the neck and body of the krater. Figures of maenads flank the divine pair, and in the upper register the seated Dionysus gestures toward a sleeping maenad. The handles, in the form of serpents, frame the head of a horned god to the left and of Heracles (with lion skin over his head) to the right. (*Top: Archaeological Museum, Thessaloniki, Greece, © Vanni/ Art Resource, NY; Bottom: The Art Archive/ Archaeological Museum Salonica/Gianni Dagli Orti*)

survivor of the expedition, they come to Eleusis, where Aethra has come to sacrifice to Demeter. She takes pity on the women and appeals to Theseus to protect them and help them persuade the Theban king Creon to allow them to bury the dead Argive princes. Theseus is at first unpersuaded by her pleas and those of Adrastus, but eventually he relents and attacks Thebes with an Athenian army. He returns victorious, bringing the bodies of the dead Argive leaders, over whom Adrastus makes a funeral oration. The bodies are then cremated, although the pyre of Capaneus is separate from the others because he was killed by the thunderbolt of Zeus and therefore is sacred to the god. In the climactic scene of the tragedy, Evadne, the widow of Capaneus, hurls herself into the flames of his pyre (see p. 422).

The figure of Theseus as the noble king has frequently been portrayed in later literature. He is the compassionate champion of the Argive women in the twelfth book of Statius' *Thebaid*, in which he actually kills Creon. In Chaucer's *Canterbury Tales* he is, in "The Knight's Tale," the protector of the Argive women and the wise king. He is rather less loftily called "Duke Theseus" in Shakespeare's *Midsummer Night's Dream*.

Other Adventures of Theseus

Theseus was not originally a member of the great expeditions of saga, but this important national hero naturally came to be included in the roster of heroic adventurers, so that he was said to have been an Argonaut and one of those present on the Calydonian boar hunt. Indeed, "not without Theseus" became an Athenian proverb, and he was called "a second Heracles." His life was said to have ended in failure. He was driven out of Athens, his power usurped by Menestheus, who is mentioned in the *Iliad*'s catalog of ships as the Athenian

Theseus in Greek Tragedy

In a meticulous and lucid study, Sophie Mills distinguishes Theseus in the *Hippolytus* of Euripides as individual and quite different from his depiction in other plays and explains why this is the case.[27] Basic elements in the legend of Theseus—for example, his abduction of Helen, his ill-fated journey to the Underworld, his Cretan adventure, and the Centauromachy—were developed in Greece long before the fifth century B.C.. In Attica, however, with the emergence of democracy and the establishment of the Athenian Empire, an idealized portrait of Theseus was deliberately created to exemplify and glorify the character of the individual, the state, and the empire. The legend of Theseus was cleansed of any dubious traits, and Theseus himself, thus purified, was artfully transformed into an ideological paradigm, an honorable hero, brave and just, representing Athenian intelligence and virtue. This is the Theseus in Euripides' *Suppliants* and *Heracles* and Sophocles' *Oedipus at Colonus*. The depiction of Theseus in Euripides' *Hippolytus* offers a striking contrast. He is not represented in this play as the heroic king of Athens, noble model for his city and its citizens; instead he is most realistically portrayed as a vulnerable human being, a tragically flawed individual, whose character and actions are integral to the drama.[28]

leader at Troy. Theseus went to the island of Scyros and was there killed by Lycomedes, the local king. Menestheus continued to reign at Athens but died at Troy. The sons of Theseus then recovered their father's throne. After the Persian Wars, the Greek allies, led by the Athenian Cimon, captured Scyros in the years 476–475 B.C. There Cimon, obedient to a command of the Delphic oracle, searched for the bones of Theseus. He found the bones of a very large man with a bronze spearhead and sword and brought them back to Athens. So Theseus returned, a symbol of Athens' connection with the heroic age and of her claim to lead the Ionian Greeks.

Demophon

Theseus' son Demophon helped the children of Heracles (see p. 566), and he has a number of other legends.[29] He loved the Thracian princess Phyllis, and on leaving her in Thrace, he swore to return soon. When he never came back, she hanged herself and became an almond tree. Too late he returned and embraced the tree, which then burst into leaf.

Codrus

The last king of Athens was Codrus, who sacrificed himself for his city. The Peloponnesians invaded Attica, assured by the Delphic oracle that the side would win whose king was killed. When Codrus learned of the oracle, he disguised himself as a peasant and provoked a quarrel with some enemy soldiers, who killed him; the Peloponnesians were defeated.

Minos

Daedalus and Minos

Daedalus was the son or grandson of Metion, the younger brother of Cecrops, and therefore a member of the Athenian royal house. He was a skilled craftsman and inventor; his assistant was his nephew **Perdix**.[30] One day Perdix invented the saw, getting the idea from a fish's backbone. In a fit of jealousy, Daedalus hurled him from a rock. As he fell, he was turned into a partridge, which still bears the name *perdix*. Being now guilty of homicide, Daedalus had to leave Athens. He went to Crete, where Minos and Pasiphaë employed his skills.

Now Minos had prayed to Poseidon to send him a bull from the sea for sacrifice; when Poseidon answered his prayer, Minos was so covetous that he sacrificed another, less beautiful bull, keeping Poseidon's animal for himself. As a punishment, Poseidon caused his wife, **Pasiphaë**, to fall in love with the bull. To satisfy her passion, Daedalus constructed a lifelike hollow cow in which Pasiphaë was shut up to mate with the bull. Her offspring was the Minotaur. It had a man's body and the head of a bull and was held captive in the Labyrinth, a mazelike prison of Daedalus' devising. We have already seen how Theseus destroyed it. The famous discoveries at Cnossus in Crete (pp. 40–41) have shown that the bull played a significant part in Cretan ritual and that a common sacred object was the *labrys*, or double-headed ax, which is certainly connected with

The Fall of Icarus, by Pieter Brueghel the Elder (1525–1569); oil on canvas, 30 × 44 in. Only the legs of Icarus are visible in the sea near the galleon. The ploughman, the fisherman, and the shepherd, observers in Ovid's narrative, here mind their own business. The partridge (Latin name, *perdix*), too, is Ovidian, a reference to Daedalus' rival and victim Perdix: in Ovid it gloats over the burial of Icarus. (*Scala/Art Resource, NY*)

the word *labyrinth*. The idea of the maze has plausibly been thought to have its origin in the huge and complex palace of Cnossus, with its many passageways and endless series of rooms. Minos and Pasiphaë, like their daughters Ariadne and Phaedra, are probably divine figures; Minos was son and friend of Zeus,[31] while Pasiphaë was the daughter of Helius.

The Flight of Icarus

Daedalus eventually tired of his life in Crete, but Minos would not let him go. Daedalus therefore contrived feathered wings, held together by wax, by means of which he and his son Icarus could escape. As they flew high above the sea, Icarus ignored his father's warning not to fly too close to the sun, and as the wax on his wings melted he fell into the sea, which thereafter was called *Mare Icarium*. The story is told by Ovid (*Metamorphoses* 8.200–230):

> When Daedalus the craftsman had finished [making the wings], he balanced his body between the twin wings and by moving them hung suspended in air. He also gave instructions to his son, saying: "Icarus, I advise you to take a middle course. If you fly too low, the sea will soak the wings; if you fly too high, the sun's

*un moment
di libes.
Ne devrait=on
pas faire ac.
complir un
grand voyage
en avion aux
jeunes gens
ayant-terminé
leurs études.*

54

Icarus, by Henri Matisse (1869–1954); stencil print of a paper cutout, 1947, 16½ × 25½ in. This is Plate 8 (p. 54) in Matisse's *Jazz* (Paris: Tériade, 1947). The plates were printed from paper cutouts pasted on and painted through stencils. The artist wrote the text in his own firm handwriting, and opposite *Icarus* is the last of seven pages titled *L'Avion* (*The Airplane*). Matisse reflects on the freedom in space experienced by air travelers; then he concludes: "Ought one not to make young people who have finished their studies take a long journey in an airplane." The red heart of Icarus—symbol of his courage and creativity—stands out in the black silhouette against the sky and stars that he tried, and failed, to reach. (*Artwork © 2022 Succession H. Matisse/Artists Rights Society (ARS), New York. Image from Museum of Modern Art/Licensed by SCALA/Art Resource, NY*)

heat will burn them. Fly between sea and sun! Take the course along which I shall lead you." (200–208)

As he gave the instructions for flying, he fitted the novel wings to Icarus' shoulders. While he worked and gave his advice, the old man's face was wet with tears, and his hands trembled with a father's anxiety. For the last time, he kissed his son and rose into the air upon his wings. He led the way in flight and was anxious for his companion, like a bird that leads its young from the nest into the air. He encouraged Icarus to follow and showed him the skills that were to destroy him; he moved his wings and looked back at those of his son. Some fisherman with trembling rod, or shepherd leaning on his crook, or farmer resting on his plow saw them and was amazed, and believed that those who could travel through the air were gods. (208–220)

Now Juno's Samos was on the left (they had already passed Delos and Paros), and Lebinthos and Calymne, rich in honey, were on the right, when the boy began to exult in his bold flight. He left his guide and, drawn by a desire to reach the heavens, took his course too high. The burning heat of the nearby sun softened the scented wax that fastened the wings. The wax melted; Icarus moved his arms, now uncovered, and without the wings to drive him on, vainly beat the air. Even as he called upon his father's name the sea received him and from him took its name. (220–230)

Daedalus himself reached Sicily, where **Cocalus**, king of the city of Camicus, received him.[32] Here he was pursued by Minos, who discovered him by the ruse of carrying round a spiral shell, which he asked Cocalus to have threaded. Cocalus gave the shell to Daedalus, who alone of men was ingenious enough to succeed. Minos knew that Daedalus was there when Cocalus gave him back the threaded shell. However, Daedalus still stayed out of Minos' reach, for the daughters of Cocalus drowned Minos in boiling water. There is no reliable legend about the further history or death of Daedalus.

The Family of Minos

Several of the children of Minos and Pasiphaë have their own legends; there were four sons—Catreus, Deucalion, Glaucus, and Androgeos—and four daughters, of whom only Ariadne and Phaedra have important legends.

Catreus, who became the Cretan king, had a son Althaemenes, of whom an oracle foretold that he would kill his father. Althaemenes tried to avoid his fate by leaving Crete and going to Rhodes with his sister Apemosyne.[33] She was seduced by Hermes and killed by Althaemenes as a punishment for her apparent unchastity. Catreus later came to Rhodes in search of his son; he and his party were taken for pirates, and in the ensuing skirmish Catreus was killed by his son. When Althaemenes learned how the oracle had been fulfilled, he avoided the company of other men and was eventually swallowed up by the earth. The Rhodians honored him as a hero.

Of the other sons of Minos, Deucalion (not to be confused with Deucalion of the flood legend) became the father of Idomeneus, the Cretan leader at Troy. As a boy, **Glaucus** fell into a vat of honey and drowned. Minos could not find him and was told by the oracle that the person who could find an exact simile for a magic calf in the herds of Minos would be able both to find Glaucus and to restore him to life. This calf changed color every four hours, from white to red to black; but the seer **Polyidus** most fittingly likened it to a mulberry, which changes from white to red to black as it ripens. With the help of various birds, Polyidus found Glaucus' corpse in the vat. It was placed in a tomb, and Polyidus was then shut up in the tomb and ordered to bring Glaucus back to life. While he was wondering what to do, a snake came. Polyidus killed it with his sword, whereupon another snake came, looked at the dead snake, and went away, returning with an herb, which it put on the dead snake's body. The dead snake then came to life again, and Polyidus took the herb and used it on Glaucus, who likewise came to life. Even now, Minos was not satisfied; he compelled Polyidus to teach Glaucus the seer's art before he would let him return home to Argos. Polyidus obeyed, but as he left, he told Glaucus to spit into his mouth, whereupon Glaucus forgot all that he had learned.[34]

Androgeos was killed in Attica, and his death led to Minos' expedition and the attack on **Megara**. The king of Megara, **Nisus**, had a purple lock of hair, which was the city's talisman, for the city would fall if the lock were cut off. Now **Scylla**, daughter of Nisus, fell in love with Minos (whom she could see from the city walls). To please him she cut off her father's purple lock and brought it to Minos. When the city fell, Minos rejected Scylla and sailed away; she clung to the stern of his ship and was turned into a sea bird called *ciris*,[35] while Nisus turned into a sea eagle, forever pursuing her.

Select Bibliography

Barr-Sharrar, Beryl. *The Derveni Krater: Masterpiece of Classical Greek Metalwork.* Princeton, NJ: American School of Classical Studies, 2008. A much wider discussion of Greek and Macedonian culture than its title suggests.

Mills, Sophie. *Theseus, Tragedy and the Athenian Empire.* New York: Oxford University Press, 1997. An examination of how Theseus became the embodiment of the ideals of Periclean Athens.

Morris, Sarah. *Daedalus and the Origins of Greek Art.* Princeton, NJ: Princeton University Press, 1992. The myth of Daedalus analyzed to show artistic and literary influence on Greece from the Near East.

Walker, Henry J. *Theseus and Athens.* New York: Oxford University Press, 1995. A study that explores the image of Theseus in the early period and then in the fifth century B.C. through major literary works.

Ward, Anne G., ed. *The Quest for Theseus.* New York: Praeger, 1970. A useful collection of essays on the saga of Theseus.

Primary Sources

Sources in the Chapter

Bacchylides	*Dithyramb* 17.92–116
	Dithyramb 18.16–60
Catullus	Poem 64.52–59
Euripides	*Ion* 277–282
	Medea 824–830
Ovid	*Ars amatoria* 1.535–564
	Metamorphoses 6.572–674; 7.804–859; 8.174–181, 200–230

Additional Sources

Apollodorus	*Library* 3.14.5–3.16.2
Isocrates	*Speech* 10.14–10.69 (encomium of Helen with a lengthy digression on Theseus [10.22–10.37])
	Speech 12.119–12.131 (encomium of early Athens and Theseus)
Plutarch	*Theseus*

Notes

1. According to Ovid, only Aglauros disobeyed Athena.
2. Euripides, *Erechtheus*, frag. 18, 94–98.
3. For the Erechtheum, one might begin by consulting John Travlos, *Pictorial Dictionary of Ancient Athens* (New York: Praeger, 1971): entry for "Erechtheum." See also G. P. Stevens and J. M. Paton, *The Erechtheum* (Cambridge, MA: Harvard University Press, 1927).
4. The sacrifice of a virgin was the original form of the legend. Later versions give her the name of Chthonia (which means "earth woman") and have her sisters take an oath to kill themselves so as to die with her. According to others, the names of the daughters of Erechtheus were Pandora, Protogeneia, and Orithyia.
5. Euripides' *Erechtheus* survives only in fragments; its ending (including a long speech from Athena), first published in 1967, has helped fill out many of the missing details of the relationship between the myth of Erechtheus and his cult. Erechtheus took the title of the god who caused his death (i.e., he became Poseidon-Erechtheus).

His original status as a hero, with a cult located at the place of his burial, was later confused with that of the god. His daughters had become goddesses with the title Hyacinthides, to be worshiped with annual sacrifices and dances.

6. The lines are sung just after Medea has secured the promise of protection from Aegeus.

7. Pandrosos had her own shrine and cult on the Acropolis, close to the Erechtheum. She was the one of the three daughters of Cecrops, to whom, in some versions, Athena had entrusted Erichthonius. Aglauros was worshiped in a cave on the north side of the Acropolis, while the name *Herse* had been connected etymologically with the festival of the *Arrephoria*, in which two specially chosen young girls carried mysterious objects from the Acropolis by night down to the sanctuary of Aphrodite and Eros, which was also on the north side of the Acropolis.

8. Ovid plays on words with a double meaning, literal and erotic, for which English has no adequate equivalent.

9. In another version, Procris was discovered by Cephalus with a lover. She fled to Minos, king of Crete, who himself fell in love with her. He had been bewitched by his wife, Pasiphaë, so that whenever he lay with a woman he discharged snakes and other creatures. Procris cured him and then lay with him, being rewarded with the gift of the hound and the javelin. Later, she returned to Athens and was reconciled with Cephalus.

10. There is a pun here on Ion's name, which is also the Greek word meaning "going."

11. The legend of Ion stems almost entirely from Euripides' play. It explains the historical fact of the colonization of Ionia by mainland Greeks (principally from Athens) during the unsettled period after the collapse of the Mycenaean civilization.

12. The chief source is Plato's *Phaedrus* 229, where Socrates rationalizes the legend: "I would say that the North Wind pushed her, as she was playing, down from the nearby rocks. She died in this way; but her death was described as her being ravished by Boreas."

13. And by his link with the cult of Apollo Delphinius, that is, Apollo as a god of spring, when the sea becomes navigable and the dolphins appear as portents of good sailing weather. See pp. 247 and 269.

14. The oracle is difficult to reconcile with this story if the "home" referred to should be Athens. Euripides has Medea cure Aegeus of his sterility after she has joined him in Athens.

15. Theseus was idealized in the latter part of the sixth century B.C. when Pisistratus was tyrant of Athens, and again immediately after the Persian Wars (ca. 475).

16. The most complete source for the legend of Theseus is Plutarch's *Life of Theseus* (early second century A.D.). This biography blurs the lines between mythology, history, and philosophy.

17. Sciron originally had his own legend and cult at Megara, on the island of Salamis, and in Attica where there were limestone outcrops (his name means "limestone").

18. Procrustes is also called Damastes (Subduer), Procoptes (Slicer), and Polypemon (Troubler). Polypemon may also be the name of his father.

19. According to the fifth-century B.C. historian Hellanicus, Minos himself chose the victims and took them on his ship back to Crete.

20. Respectively, in the tenth letter of the *Heroides*; in *Ars amatoria* 1.527–564; and in *Metamorphoses* 8.174–192.

21. This dance was represented on the François vase (ca. 575 B.C.). At Athens, Theseus instituted the *Oschophoria* in which two boys disguised as girls carried vine branches in a procession to honor Bacchus and Ariadne.

22. Sisyphus, a son of Aeolus and brother of Salmoneus, Cretheus, and Athamas, came from Thessaly to Ephyra. Ino, the wife of his brother Athamas, leaped into the sea with her child Melicertes and became the sea-goddess Leucothea, while her child became the god Palaemon. Melicertes' body was brought ashore on the Isthmus of

Corinth by a dolphin. Sisyphus found and buried it, instituting the Isthmian Games in the child's honor. At first, the games were mainly religious and ritualistic; Theseus is said to have founded them a second time and thus gave them the athletic character that they acquired in historical times.

23. In Athens, the battle with the Amazons was depicted in the Hephaesteum and in the Stoa Poecile (Painted Colonnade); it was one of the subjects of the metopes of the Parthenon and was depicted on the shield of Pheidias' statue of Athena Parthenos. It also appeared on the pedestal of the statue of Zeus at Olympia.

24. They were referred to by the title of *Anakes* or *Anaktes* (Kings), and their temple was called the *Anakeion*.

25. Poseidon was said to have granted Theseus three wishes, of which this was the third. The others were to escape from the Labyrinth and to return from Hades.

26. Twentieth-century dramatic adaptations of the myth include *The Cretan Woman* by Robinson Jeffers and *Desire under the Elms* by Eugene O'Neill.

27. Sophie Mills, *Theseus, Tragedy and the Athenian Empire* (New York: Oxford University Press, 1997).

28. The surviving tragedy of *Hippolytus* was Euripides' second to present this myth: the first, *Hippolytus Veiled* (now mostly lost), did not, apparently, present Theseus more favorably. Euripides presented five other tragedies (now mostly lost) on Athenian mythical subjects: *Aegeus, Antiope, Erechtheus, Theseus* (focusing on Theseus' killing of the Minotaur and his abandonment of Ariadne), and *Cretans* (focusing on Minos and Pasiphae). He also presented a satyr-play, *Sciron*, in which a band of satyrs was released from servitude to Sciron after Theseus had killed him.

29. He was said to have succeeded Menestheus as Athenian leader at Troy and to have brought his grandmother Aethra back to Athens.

30. The boy is also called Talus, and his mother, Daedalus' sister, Perdix.

31. Homer (*Odyssey* 19.178–179) describes him as the intimate friend of Zeus; and Hesiod (frag. 103) calls him "the most kingly of mortal kings, who ruled over most subjects and held his scepter from Zeus."

32. In the opening lines of the sixth book of Vergil's *Aeneid*, Daedalus comes to Cumae in Italy.

33. Two other sisters are mentioned: Aërope, who became the wife of a Mycenaean prince (either Pleisthenes or Atreus); and Clymene, who became the wife of Nauplius and the mother of Palamedes.

34. Forgetfulness induced by spitting is a folk tale motif, as is also the seer who can understand the ways of birds and snakes.

35. Its identification is unknown. According to Aeschylus, Scylla was bribed by Minos with a golden necklace to betray Nisus.

For additional digital learning resources please go to
www.oup.com/he/morford12e

JASON, MEDEA, AND THE ARGONAUTS

And now is all that ancient story told
Of him who won the guarded fleece of gold.

—**WILLIAM MORRIS**, *The Life and Death of Jason*

The Minyae

The saga of the Argonauts covers much of the Greek world in its geographical scope and includes many of the leading Greek heroes of the age before the Trojan War. The crew of the **Argo** included the flower of Greece, descendants of gods and ancestors of Greek nobles. They are often referred to as **Minyae**, and among cities that claimed Minyan descent were **Iolcus** in Thessaly and Miletus in Ionia. Jason belonged to the ruling family of Iolcus, and the Euxine Sea (i.e., the Black Sea), where the main part of the saga takes place, was an area particularly colonized by the Milesians.

The name *Minyae* therefore tells us something about the origin of the saga. Homer calls the *Argo* "all men's concern," reflecting the adventures of the seamen of Mycenaean Greece. Later additions reflect the expansion of the Greeks into the Black Sea area from the eighth century B.C. onward. Folk tale elements can be seen in the name **Aea** (which means no more than "land") that Homer uses for the country to which the *Argo* sailed, and its king, **Aeëtes** (Man of the Land). It is a mysterious land on the edge of the world, a suitable setting for a story in which magic and miracle play a big part. The folk tale element can further be distinguished in the formal outline of the legend, where a hero is set a number of impossible tasks that he performs unscathed, helped by the local princess, whom he then marries.[1]

Jason and the Golden Fleece

The saga concerns the quest for the Golden Fleece by Jason and the crew of the *Argo*. The Boeotian king **Athamas** took as his first wife **Nephele**, whose name means "cloud." After bearing Athamas two children, **Phrixus** and **Helle**, she returned to the sky. Athamas then married **Ino**, one of the daughters of Cadmus, who attempted to destroy her stepchildren. She also persuaded the Boeotian women to parch the seed grain so that when it was sown nothing grew. In the ensuing famine, Athamas sent to Delphi for advice, but Ino suborned the envoys to report that the god advised Athamas to sacrifice Phrixus if he wanted the famine to end. As he was about to perform the sacrifice, Nephele snatched Phrixus and Helle up into the sky and set them on a golden-fleeced ram that Hermes had given her. The ram carried them eastward through the heavens. Above the straits between Europe and Asia (the **Dardanelles**), Helle fell off and drowned, and the straits were called the **Hellespont** after her. Phrixus continued his flight and came to Colchis, at the eastern end of the Black Sea, where King Aeëtes (son of Helius and brother of Circe and Pasiphaë) received him with kindness and gave him his elder daughter, Chalciope, as his wife. Phrixus sacrificed the ram to Zeus Phyxius (i.e., Zeus as god of escape) and gave the Golden Fleece to Aeëtes, who hung it up on an oak tree in a grove sacred to Ares, where it was guarded by a never-sleeping serpent. Phrixus himself lived on at Colchis, where he finally died; his four sons by Chalciope—Argus, Melas, Phrontis, and Cytisorus—play a minor part in the Argonauts' saga. The fleece, a golden treasure guarded by a dragon, became a goal for a hero's quest.

The Building of the Argo. Terra cotta relief from Campania, mid-first century A.D. Athena sits on the left; her shield rests against her stool, while her owl perches on a column behind her. She helps a workman (or possibly an Argonaut) place a sail on the yard-arm. To the right Argus works on the stern with a hammer and chisel. In the background is a city wall with a closed gate and a tree. (*Jastrow/Wikimedia Commons (CC BY 2.5)*)

Cretheus, brother of Athamas, was king of Iolcus. At his death, his stepson Pelias (son of Poseidon and Tyro, wife of Cretheus) usurped the throne and deposed the rightful heir, **Aeson**, son of Cretheus and Tyro and father of Jason. Jason's mother, Polymede,[2] sent the boy away to the hills to be educated by the centaur **Chiron** and cared for by Chiron's mother, Philyra. After twenty years, Jason returned to Iolcus to claim the throne that rightly belonged to his family. Pelias knew that he was fated to be killed by a descendant of Aeolus, and the Delphic oracle had warned him to "beware of the man with one sandal." He realized his fate was approaching when Jason appeared wearing one sandal.

On the way down from the hills, Jason had carried an old woman across the river Anaurus in full spate, losing one sandal as he tried to get a foothold in the mud. The old woman was the goddess **Hera**, who thereafter favored him, just as she remained hostile to Pelias, who had neglected to sacrifice to her. Pelias promised to yield the throne as soon as Jason brought him the Golden Fleece, which Phrixus, appearing to him in a dream, had ordered him to obtain. Whether for this reason or for some other, Jason readily undertook the task.

The Argonauts

In preparation for the expedition, the *Argo* was built, "which . . . first through the Euxine seas bore all the flower of Greece" (Spenser, *Faerie Queen* 2.12.44). Its name means "swift," and it was built by Argus, son of Arestor, with the help of Athena. In its bows Athena put a piece of wood made from an oak of Dodona (where there was an oracle of Zeus), which had the power of speech.

The crew came from all over Greece, motivated by the heroic quality of *arete* (Pindar, *Pythian Odes* 4.184–187):

> Hera kindled all-persuading sweet desire in the sons of gods for the ship *Argo*, so that none should be left behind to nurse a life without danger at his mother's side, but rather that he should find even against death the fairest antidote in his own courage along with others of his age.

Lists of the names of the Argonauts vary, since the Greeks of later ages were eager to claim an Argonaut for an ancestor. Two heroes who figure prominently in all the lists, **Orpheus** and **Heracles**, have no place in the original story. Orpheus is a post-Homeric figure, and Heracles, as the most important of the Greek heroes, could hardly be left out of a saga that occurred in his own lifetime. He refused to accept the leadership, in favor of Jason, and he disappeared from the expedition before the *Argo* had even reached the Black Sea.

Of the fifty or so names included among the Argonauts, certain groups stand out. These are the heroes from Thessaly, such as Jason, and those from the Peloponnese, such as Augeas, king of Elis; a third group consists of Meleager and other heroes who took part in the Calydonian boar hunt; a fourth includes the parents of Trojan War heroes, such as Peleus (father of Achilles), Telamon (father of Ajax Telamonius), Oïleus (father of Ajax the Less), and Nauplius (father of Palamedes).

Some of the Argonauts had special gifts. These were the seers Idmon and Mopsus; Castor and Polydeuces, excellent as horseman and boxer, respectively, with their later enemies, Idas and Lynceus, the latter of whom had such keen sight that he could see even beneath the earth; Periclymenus, son of Neleus,

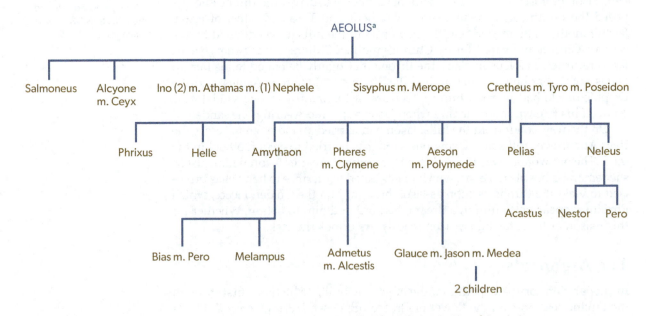

ᵃThis Aeolus was the son of Hellen and is to be distinguished from Aeolus, the king of the winds.

Figure 24.1. The Ancestry of Jason

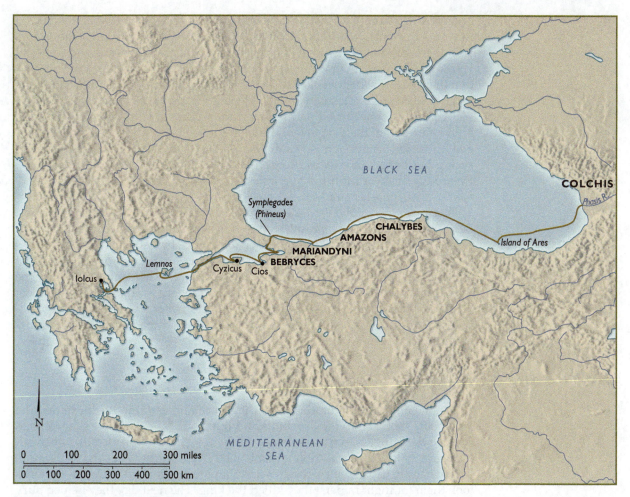

Map 24.1. The Voyage of the Argo to Colchis. Jason's voyage to Colchis is simpler to trace geographically. The return voyage to Iolcus is confused and takes the Argonauts around Italy in the north to Libya on the coast of North Africa.

who could take whatever shape he liked in battle (this was Poseidon's gift); Euphemus, son of Poseidon, who could run so fast over the waves of the sea that his feet stayed dry; Zetes and Calaïs, the winged sons of Boreas; Argus, the skilled shipwright; and finally, the helmsman, Tiphys. Of these, only Polydeuces, Zetes, Calaïs, Argus, and Tiphys have any significant part in the legend as we now have it. Originally, the individual Argonauts must have used their gifts to help Jason perform his otherwise impossible tasks.

The Voyage to Colchis

Hypsipyle and the Lemnian Women

After leaving Iolcus, the Argonauts sailed to the island of Lemnos, where they found only women, led by their queen, Hypsipyle. Aphrodite had punished them for neglecting her worship and had made them unattractive to their husbands.

The men therefore had taken Thracian concubines whom they had captured in war. In revenge, the Lemnian women murdered every male on the island, with the exception of the king, **Thoas**, who was son of Dionysus and father of Hypsipyle. Hypsipyle first hid Thoas in the temple of Dionysus and then put him in a chest in which he floated to the land of the Tauri (i.e., southern Russia) and there became a priest of Artemis. Meanwhile, the Lemnian women received the Argonauts, who stayed on the island for a year. Among the many children born as a result of their stay were the twin sons of Jason and Hypsipyle, Euneos and Thoas (or Nebrophonus). After Jason's departure, Hypsipyle's deception in saving her father Thoas was discovered, and she was driven from the island. Eventually, she was captured by pirates and sold into slavery, becoming the servant of Lycurgus, king of Nemea.

In Greece, Hypsipyle became the nurse of the child of Lycurgus, **Opheltes**. Euripides presented this part of Hypsipyle's story in the tragedy *Hypsipyle* (see p. 420). She was eventually brought back to Lemnos by her sons. As a mythological figure, Hypsipyle is significant because she was the queen of a society from which males have been driven out and also because of her connection with the founding of the Nemean Games in honor of Opheltes. The Roman epic poet Statius devoted a long episode of his *Thebaid* to her story, as did his contemporary Valerius Flaccus, in his epic *Argonautica*. Ovid made her a romantically deserted heroine in his *Heroides*.

Cyzicus and Cios

After touching at Samothrace, where they were initiated into the mysteries, the Argonauts sailed on to the Propontis and put in at Cyzicus, where the Doliones lived under King Cyzicus, who received them well. In return for this hospitality, Heracles killed the earthborn giants who lived nearby. The Argonauts were driven back to Cyzicus by contrary winds, and in a night battle (for the Doliones took them for night raiders) they killed the king. The next day they helped bury Cyzicus before sailing off again.

Their next port of call was Cios, farther eastward along the Asiatic shore of the Propontis, where they landed so that **Heracles** could replace his broken oar. Here **Hylas** was lost and Heracles left the expedition (see p. 458).

Amycus

Next, the Argonauts passed into the Euxine (the Black Sea) and came to the land of the Bebryces, a Bithynian tribe whose custom was to compel strangers to box with their king, Amycus, a son of Poseidon, who had never lost a boxing match. **Polydeuces** fought Amycus and killed him.

Phineus and the Harpies and the Symplegades

Next they came to Salmydessus on the Euxine shore of Thrace, where they were received by King Phineus, a blind prophet.[3] Phineus was tormented by the Harpies, two winged monsters (their name means "**the snatchers**") who, every time a meal was set before him, swooped down upon it, snatched away most of the food, and fouled the rest. When the Harpies next appeared, **Zetes** and **Calaïs**, the winged sons of Boreas, pursued them with drawn swords to the Strophades Islands, where Iris put an end to the chase by making the sons of Boreas return and the Harpies swear never to go near Phineus again. Phineus foretold the rest of the voyage to the Argonauts and forewarned them of its dangers. He told them of the Symplegades (Clashing Rocks), two huge rocks near the western end of the Black Sea that clashed together driven by the force of the winds. Nothing had ever yet passed between them, and it was fated that they should remain fixed once a ship had made the passage. Phineus advised the Argonauts to release a dove, and if it succeeded in flying between the rocks, then they themselves were to row hard between them as they recoiled. If it failed, they were to turn back. In the event the dove was successful, and the Argonauts, with the help of Athena (or Hera), got through before the rocks clashed for the last time, losing part of the ship's stern ornament. The Symplegades remained fixed, never to threaten seafarers again.[4]

The Voyage through the Euxine Sea

Not far along the Asiatic coast of the Euxine lived the Mariandyni, whose king, Lycus, received the Argonauts hospitably. Here Idmon was killed by a boar, and the helmsman, Tiphys, died. Nevertheless, with the Arcadian hero Ancaeus, son of Lycurgus, as the new helmsman, they sailed on past the land of the Amazons and that of the iron-working Chalybes and came to the Island of Ares, where the Stymphalian Birds (frightened away from Greece by Heracles in his sixth

Jason Is Disgorged by the Dragon That Guards the Golden Fleece. Athenian red-figure cup by Douris, ca. 470 B.C.; diameter 11¾ in. Athena (not Medea) watches the bearded dragon disgorge Jason. She holds an owl and wears the aegis. The fleece hangs on the tree in the background. There are no literary sources for this version of the myth. (© Album/Art Resource, NY)

Labor) now lived. These they kept at bay by clashing their shields together. Here they also found Phrixus' four sons, shipwrecked during an attempted voyage from Colchis to Boeotia. They took them on board the *Argo* and found them of no little help when they reached Colchis. Finally, they sailed up the river Phasis to Colchis.

Jason at Colchis

At Colchis, Aeëtes was prepared to let Jason take the fleece only if he first performed a series of impossible tasks. These were to yoke a pair of brazen-footed, fire-breathing bulls, the gift of Hephaestus to Aeëtes, and with them plow a large field and sow it with dragon's teeth, from which would spring up armed men, whom he would then have to kill.[5]

Medea

Medea, Aeëtes' younger daughter, now enters the saga and brings to it elements of magic and folk tale. Through the agency of Hera and Aphrodite, she fell in love with Jason and agreed to help him at the request of Chalciope, mother of Argus (who had returned to Colchis with the Argonauts). She was herself priestess of **Hecate**, as skilled in magic as her aunt **Circe**. She gave Jason a magic ointment that would protect him from harm by fire or iron for the space of a day. So he plowed the field with the fire-breathing bulls, and he threw a stone among the armed men who sprang from the dragon's teeth to set them fighting one another. Then he took the fleece, with Medea's help, drugging the serpent with herbs that she had provided.

Euripides, however, in his tragedy *Medea*, gives Medea a larger part in performing the tasks and gaining the fleece. She, rather than Jason, is the dragon slayer, as she reminds Jason (*Medea* 476–482):

> I saved you, as all the Greeks know who embarked with you on the ship *Argo*, when you were sent to master the fire-breathing bulls with yokes and sow the death-bringing field. I killed the serpent, which unsleeping guarded the golden fleece, twining its many coils around it, and I brought you the light of salvation.

In the red-figure cup pictured here, Jason's part is even less heroic, as he hangs limply from the jaws of the serpent while Athena (not Medea) stands before him.

Ovid's Narrative

Ovid's account restores Jason's heroic stature. His narrative begins the day after Medea's meeting with Jason at the shrine of Hecate (*Metamorphoses* 7.100–158):

> The next dawn had put to flight the gleaming stars when the people assembled in Mars' sacred field and took their place on the higher ground. The king himself sat enthroned among his army, conspicuous by his purple robe and ivory scepter. The brazen-footed bulls puffed forth fire from their adamantine nostrils, and the grass burned at the touch of their breath. . . Yet Jason faced them; with threatening look,

Jason Takes the Golden Fleece, by Peter Paul Rubens (1577–1640); oil on panel, 1636, 10½ × 11¼ in. Jason jauntily passes by the statue of Mars (Ares), with the fleece draped over his left arm. He is dressed as a Roman soldier. Rubens follows the narrative of Hyginus, who said that Phrixus dedicated the fleece in the temple of Mars, rather than the narrative given here. Note the absence of Medea or Athena as Jason's helpers. (*Royal Museums of Fine Arts of Belgium, Brussels/photo: F. Maes (MRBAB)*)

they turned their awesome faces toward him as he came, their horns tipped with iron; with their cloven hooves they pounded the dusty earth and filled the place with their bellowing and clouds of smoke. The Argonauts were petrified with fear. On came Jason and felt not their fiery breath, so great was the power of [Medea's] drugs. He stroked their deep dewlaps with fearless hand and compelled them, driven beneath the yoke, to draw the plow's heavy weight and tear open the soil as yet unplowed. The Colchians were amazed, while the Argonauts shouted encouragement and strengthened Jason's spirits. (100–121)

Next he took the serpent's teeth in a bronze helmet and sowed them in the plowed field. The soil softened the seed, which had been smeared with strong poison, and the teeth grew and became new bodies. Just as a baby takes on human form in its mother's womb and inside its whole body grows in due proportion, only to issue into the outside world when it is fully formed, so, when the forms of men had been made in the womb of the pregnant earth, they rose from the mother-furrows, and, yet more miraculously, at their birth clashed their weapons. (121–130)

When the Greeks saw these warriors preparing to hurl their sharp spears at the head of the young Thessalian, their eyes and spirits were lowered by fear. Medea, too, who had made him safe from attack, grew pale when she saw so many enemies attacking the solitary young hero. . . Jason threw a heavy rock into the middle of the enemy and turned their attack from himself to them: the earthborn brothers killed each other and fell in civil war. The Greeks applauded and eagerly embraced the victor. . . (131–143)

It remained yet to put to sleep with drugs the wakeful serpent. It was the fearsome guardian of the golden tree, a monster with a crest, three tongues, and curved teeth. This serpent Aeson's heroic son fed with a soporific herb and repeated thrice a charm that brought peaceful sleep. When sleep came upon those eyes that it had not visited before, Jason took the gold, and in the pride of his spoils, took her who had made possible his success, a second prize. Victorious, he returned to the harbor of Iolcus with his wife. (149–158)

30

The Return of the Argonauts

Pindar's Narrative

Ovid's narrative focuses on Jason the hero, winner not only of the fleece, the prize of his quest, but also of the princess Medea. He set sail with her, pursued by the Colchians under the leadership of Medea's brother, **Apsyrtus**, whom he killed in an ambush near the mouth of the Danube.[6] Pindar gives the earliest continuous account of the capture of the fleece and the return journey. The poem is addressed to Arcesilas, king of Cyrene and winner of the chariot race at Delphi in 462 B.C.[7] Pindar's narrative begins after Jason has successfully completed ploughing with the fire-breathing bulls (*Pythian Odes* 4.239–254):

His companions stretched out their welcoming hands to the valiant hero, and they crowned him with garlands of grass and congratulated him with honeyed words. Then [Aeëtes] the wonderful child of the Sun told him of the shining fleece, where the knives of Phrixus had stretched it out. And he did not expect that Jason would complete that labor. For the fleece lay in a thicket, the lair of a serpent, held in its fearsome jaws, and the serpent in thickness and length was greater than a fifty-oared ship which the blows of iron have built. . . . (239–246)

He killed the gray-eyed spotted serpent, O Arcesilas, and he stole Medea with her connivance, and she caused the death of Pelias. And they came to the waves of Oceanus and the Red Sea and the nation of the women of Lemnos, who had killed their men. And there they showed their strength in physical contests with clothing for the prize, and there they lay together. (249–254)

10

Pindar's narrative is brief and clear. Jason, as befits the hero of the quest, himself performed the final labor, took the prize, and returned home with the princess. Their journey took them to the ends of the earth (for the River of Ocean encircles the earth; see the map on p. 607) and to the mysterious but unspecified "Red Sea," which in Pindar's time usually meant the Indian Ocean. Earlier in the poem, Medea had referred to the journey during which "relying on my counsel we carried the sea-ship on our shoulders for twelve days, hauling it up from Ocean, across the desert lands" (4.26–28). Although the twelve-day portage appears to have taken place in Africa, Pindar seems rather to be describing a voyage whose details are set in a mythological landscape (indicated by the River of Ocean beyond the boundaries of the world) than in any particular lands. Lemnos is a recognizable place in the Greek world, and Pindar places the

Lemnian episode during the return. He adds the celebration of the **Lemnian Games**, which evidently were part of the funerary ritual in honor of the dead men of Lemnos, with a cloak as the appropriate prize for a festival that also marked the resumption of marriage.

Apollonius' Narrative and the Marriage of Jason and Medea

Apollonius of Rhodes took the Argonauts up the Danube, across to the head of the Adriatic, then up the mythical Eridanus River and across to the Rhone, down which they sailed to the Mediterranean Sea. Here they sailed to the western coast of Italy, where they visited Circe (the aunt of Medea), who purified Jason and Medea from the pollution caused by Jason's murder of Apsyrtus. After this, they encountered many of the same dangers described by Odysseus—the Planctae, Scylla and Charybdis, and the Sirens.

Next they came to the land of the Phaeacians, still pursued by the Colchians. Medea appealed to Queen Arete for protection, and she and the king, Alcinoüs, agreed not to give Medea up if she were already married to Jason. That night they celebrated the marriage, and the Colchians gave up their pursuit. Resuming their journey, the Argonauts sailed to Libya, where they were stranded on the shoals of the Syrtes. They carried the *Argo* on their shoulders to Lake Tritonis (a twelve-day journey), past the garden of the Hesperides. On the way Mopsus was killed by a snake. From the lake, they made their way back to the Mediterranean, guided by the sea-god Triton.[8]

Talus

Another adventure took place off the coast of Crete. The island was guarded by the bronze giant Talus, who walked around it three times a day and kept strangers from landing by throwing rocks at them. His life depended on a membrane (or bronze nail) that closed the entrance to a vein above one ankle. If this were opened, the ichor (the divine equivalent of human blood) would flow out and he would die. The Argonauts caused this to happen and thus Talus perished.[9]

The End of the Journey

Finally, the Argonauts reached Iolcus, and there the saga (like the epic of Apollonius) ends. Jason handed the fleece over to Pelias, and he dedicated the *Argo* to Poseidon at the Isthmus of Corinth. Years later, Jason was struck on the head and killed by a piece of timber from its stern that fell upon him.

The geographical details of the return of the Argonauts are confused and largely fanciful. The time when the saga was taking its final form (i.e., in the archaic period, before the sixth century) was one of expansion and discovery in the Greek world, when the Greeks traveled far to the east and west for trade and colonization, venturing as far as Russia and North Africa. The voyage of the *Argo* perhaps recalls actual voyages, but it is impossible to attempt to match details from Pindar and Apollonius with actual places.[10]

Jason and Medea in Greece

Iolcus

At Iolcus, Pelias refused to honor his pact with Jason, and Medea therefore contrived to cause his death. Making a display of her magic arts, Medea rejuvenated Jason's father, Aeson, by cutting him up and boiling him in a cauldron along with magic herbs, and then rejuvenated an old ram as well. Persuaded by these examples, the daughters of Pelias tried to rejuvenate their father in the same way. But Medea did not give them the magic herbs, and their attempt led only to Pelias' death.

Corinth

Thus, Jason was revenged on Pelias, but he did not gain the throne of Iolcus; for being defiled by the murder of Pelias, he and Medea were driven out of the city by Acastus, son of Pelias. They went to Corinth, the setting for Euripides' tragedy *Medea.* The connection between Medea and Corinth was made as early as the eighth century B.C. by the Corinthian poet Eumelos. In his version, Aeëtes and his brother Aloeus were the sons of Helius and Antiope. Helius divided his lands between the brothers, so that Aloeus inherited Arcadia and Aeëtes received "Ephyra," which Eumelos identified with Corinth. Aeëtes then went to Colchis, leaving Corinth in the hands of a regent. Later, the Corinthians summoned Medea from Iolcus to be their queen. Thus Jason became king of Corinth through his marriage with Medea, who meanwhile had resisted the advances of Zeus out of respect for Hera (who was especially worshiped at Corinth). As a reward, Hera promised to make Medea's children immortal. Medea therefore concealed her children in the sanctuary of Hera, believing that in this way she

---

Geography and Myth

It is tempting to try to trace the journeys of the heroes of saga: Odysseus and Jason are prime "tempters." The map on p. 607 shows diagrammatically how Pindar's contemporaries saw their world. Neither Pindar nor Apollonius can be used as a source for geographical identification: their world is one of the literary imagination, even though real places are named in their poems. Archaeologists, however, have shown that there is some basis for identifying Colchis with an area in modern Georgia, the territory that lies to the east of the Black Sea, occupied in antiquity by farmers and metalworkers at least since the third millennium B.C. (see map on p. XXX). Greek trading settlements have been found dating from about 550 B.C., that is, about a century before Pindar's poem. The mythological river Phasis is safely identified with the modern river Rioni, and the modern town of Vani was the most prosperous ancient city, corresponding to the mythical Colchis. Beyond these facts, and the fact that the area in Greek times was rich in gold, copper, and iron, there can be no certainty in making geographical identifications. The modern equivalent of gold is perhaps oil, for an oil pipeline has been built across Georgia from the Caspian coast of Azerbaijan to the Black Sea coast.

would make them immortal, but they died and were honored with a cult. Medea refers to this in her final speech to Jason in Euripides' tragedy (*Medea* 1378–1383):

> I shall bury them with my hand, carrying them into the sanctuary of Hera Akraia [Hera of the Acropolis], so that none of my enemies can violate them by digging up their graves. And I shall impose upon this land of Sisyphus [Corinth] a solemn feast and ritual for the future, in return for this impious murder.

The death of the children of Jason and Medea therefore was a central feature in the original myth.

Another variant, however, named **Creon** as king of Corinth and the enemy of Medea, who killed him and left her children in the sanctuary of Hera when she fled to Athens. The boys were killed by Creon's family, who said that Medea had killed them. This version was the foundation of Euripides' powerful drama, in which Jason and Medea lived in Corinth as exiles from Iolcus. Jason divorced Medea to marry **Glauce** (also called **Creusa**), the daughter of King Creon. In

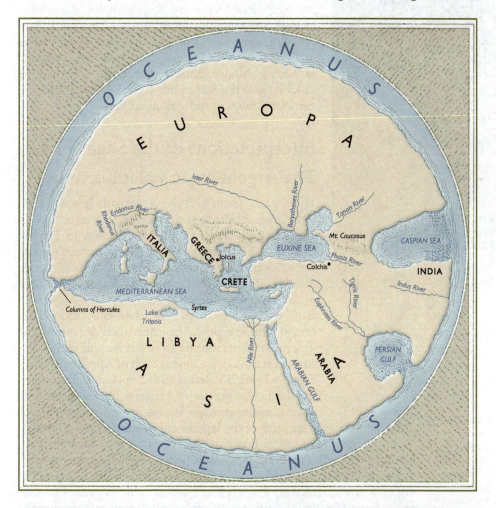

Map 24.2 Map of the World according to the Ideas of Hecataeus of Miletus (ca. 500 B.C.). The River of Ocean is assumed to run around the edge of the inhabited world, which is divided into Europe and Asia. (© *Laszlo Kubinji, 1994*)

revenge, Medea sent her two children with a robe and a crown as wedding gifts to Glauce. The magic ointment with which Medea had smeared the gifts burned Glauce and Creon to death. After this, Medea killed her children as a final act of vengeance against Jason and escaped to Athens in a chariot drawn by winged dragons provided by her grandfather Helius. In the final scene of the drama, Medea appears in the chariot high above the stage holding the bodies of her murdered children, triumphing over Jason and foretelling his miserable end. Jason lived on at Corinth, and Medea was given asylum at Athens by King Aegeus. In the Additional Reading to this chapter, we have added a summary of translations of important episodes from Euripides' *Medea* and commentary. From these, readers will be able to see for themselves how complex is the drama of Euripides and how disturbing are the issues that he raises.

Athens

While at Athens, Medea was said to have become the mother of Medus by Aegeus. Later, she nearly caused Aegeus to poison his son Theseus (see p. 581). Failing in this scheme, she fled from Athens to Persia, where Medus established the kingdom of Media. Medea herself eventually returned to Colchis, and the rest of her legend is lost in the ingenious fancies of individual authors.

Interpretations of the Saga

The Argonauts in Later Literature

The saga of Jason and the Argonauts has been filtered through literary interpretations as much as any other Greek saga.[11] It was known to Homer (who does not mention Medea), and it formed part of the epics of the eighth-century B.C. Corinthian poet Eumelos. In the third century B.C., it was the subject of the epic *Argonautica* of Apollonius of Rhodes, a work that was translated or adapted by more than one Roman epic poet. The unfinished *Argonautica* of Valerius Flaccus, dating from the second half of the first century A.D., includes much of Apollonius' narrative, to which Valerius added episodes of his own, including the rescue of Hesione by Hercules and Telamon (see p. 466). Statius, as we noted earlier, included a lengthy account of the legend of Hypsipyle in his *Thebaid*.

In drama, the *Medea* of Euripides has been a powerful influence, inspiring tragedies by Ovid (now lost), Seneca (which survives), and, in the twentieth century, Robinson Jeffers (*Medea*, 1946), to say nothing of many versions by French and German playwrights. It is one of the most frequently performed Greek tragedies in our contemporary theater. The saga appealed especially to the Victorians. William Morris' long narrative poem, *The Life and Death of Jason*, was published

Medea, by Eduardo Paolozzi (1924–2005); welded aluminum, 1964, height 81 in. The machine parts threateningly imply the destructive power of the barbarian princess. The mythological title suggests an allegorical meaning for the work without precise narrative content. Paolozzi's use of mechanical parts can also be interpreted as a satire on the modern age of machines. (© *Kröller-Müller Museum, Otterlo, The Netherlands*)

in 1867 and soon became popular. Its seventeen books cover the whole of Jason's saga, including the events in Corinth and his death. It owes as much, however, to Morris' feeling for medieval chivalry as to the classical epics, and Jason is a less ambiguous hero than he is in Apollonius or Euripides. Episodes from the saga were brilliantly narrated in Nathaniel Hawthorne's *Tanglewood Tales* (1853) and Charles Kingsley's *The Heroes* (1855). These versions were written with a strong moral bias toward courage and adventure, and they are, as Michael Grant has happily described them, "brisk, antiseptic narratives . . . jolly good hero-worshipping yarns, without esoteric overtones or significances."[12]

The Hero's Quest

Jason's legend is better seen as a Quest using Propp's model. This view makes many of the folk tale elements fall into a coherent structure. At the same time, much of the saga goes back to the earliest stages of Greek mythology, not excepting Medea, whose status as the granddaughter of the Sun must once have been more important than her functions as a magician. By far the most powerful interpretation of her part in the saga is the tragedy of Euripides, produced at Athens in 431 B.C. While Euripides concentrates on the psychology of Medea and explores the tensions in her relations with Jason, he also makes Medea into a quasi-divine being in the final scene, as she leaves in the chariot of the Sun. Medea is older (in terms of the development of the myth) and grander than the romantic heroine of Apollonius and Valerius Flaccus, and more formal than the driven, deserted, and clever heroine of Euripides. She and many of the other leading characters in the saga have attributes that point to elements in the myth that are both earlier and more significant than the quasi-historical tale of adventure that it has become.

Additional Reading: Jason and Medea in Euripides

This summary of Euripides' *Medea* with commentary centers on a translation of the three scenes in which Jason and Medea appear together. Euripides begins with one of his typical prologues (cf. the *Hippolytus* and the *Bacchae* in Chapters 10 and 13)—a monologue that provides essential background and sets the scene for the tragedy to follow. The very first line that the Nurse utters is fraught with foreboding: "How I wish that the ship *Argo* had never winged its way between the dark Clashing Rocks into the land of the Colchians." After they had come to Corinth, Jason and Medea and their two sons led a happy life, but now all is enmity between husband and wife. Jason has abandoned Medea and their children and has married Creusa (also called Glauce), daughter of Creon, king of Corinth. Medea is beside herself with anguish and rage, and the Nurse is terrified at the thought of what Medea might do; she even fears for the safety of the children, whom Medea has come to loathe because of their father. In the following scene between the Nurse and the Tutor, we learn further that Creon is about to exile both Medea and her children from the city. Medea enters, lamenting, crying out that she wants to die and eventually winning over the Chorus, women of Corinth, to her side by appealing to their common plight as women, which includes the virtual impossibility of finding a good husband. Her appeal, beginning with the words (215) "Women of Corinth," is reminiscent of Phaedra's to the women of Troezen in the *Hippolytus* and is equally laden with issues that belong to fifth-century B.C. Athens as much as to Mycenaean Greece.

Medea Leaves Corinth in a Chariot Drawn by Dragons. Medea, wearing oriental cap and dress, drives a chariot sent by the Sun, whose rays encircle her. Winged Furies look down on the human figures below—on the left, Jason railing at Medea, and on the right the children's tutor and Medea's nurse mourning over the bodies of the two children, which are draped across an altar. A spotted feline reacts energetically to the dragons. The painting represents the final scene of Euripides' *Medea*. (*Attributed to the Policoro Painter [South Italy, active 420–380 B.C.]. Lucanian Calyx-Krater, c. 400 B.C. Red-figure earthenware with added white, red, yellow, and brown wash; H. 50.5 cm. The Cleveland Museum of Art, Leonard C. Hanna Jr., Fund 1991.1*)

Creon enters, and his first outcry is to order Medea and her children to leave Corinth at once and go into exile. He is afraid of Medea's rage and her dire threats of terrible retaliation against the royal family, and, since he knows about her notorious skill in evil arts, he wants to ensure, in particular, the safety of his daughter. In the exchange that follows, we witness Medea's subtle guile, as she cleverly manipulates Creon to soften, with assurances of his safety; having been made sympathetic to her plight, he yields to her plea that she remain for only one day. In Robinson Jeffers' paraphrase, Medea begs, "lend me this inch of time. . . ."[13] What possible harm could this unfortunate woman do in such a brief period?

When Creon leaves, Medea confides in the Chorus with brutal frankness. She tells them that she would never have fawned upon this man, unless she were plotting revenge, and that he is a fool to have given her this one day to accomplish her revenge. She openly reveals some possible courses her actions might take to murder with impunity Creon himself, his daughter, and her husband.

The next scene presents the first encounter between Medea and Jason (446–626):

JASON: Now is not the first time but many times before I have seen your fierce temper and how it is an evil, impossible to cope with. You could have stayed in

Corinth and kept your home, if only you had easily submitted to the decisions of those in power, but instead, because of your unreasonable arguments you will be exiled from this land. It doesn't matter to me. Go on forever, if you like, telling everyone that Jason is the vilest of men. But for what you have said against the ruling family, consider it pure luck that you are being punished only with exile. I, to be sure, have always tried to assuage the fury of the outraged king, but you never give up your stupidity, with your continual abuse of the royal family. And so you will be thrown out of this land. (446–458)   10

Nevertheless, even after all this, I have not disowned those dear to me, and I have come to provide for your well-being, woman, so that you will not go into exile with the children, penniless and in need of anything. Exile brings in its train many hardships, and indeed even if you hate me, I would not be able to think badly of you, ever. (459–464)

MEDEA: O most vile human being in every way. These are the worst words that I can find with which to accost you verbally for your lack of manliness. You have come to me, you have come, even though you are most hateful to the gods, and not only to me and the entire human race. This is not courage nor even audacity to do wrong to dear ones and then look them in the face—this is shamelessness, a   20 disease, the greatest of all the vices among human beings. Yet you did well to come here, for after I have told you how evil you are, my soul will be lightened and you will suffer pain because of what you hear. (465–474)

From first things first I will begin what I have to say. I saved you, as all the Greeks know who embarked with you on the ship *Argo*, when you were sent to master the fire-breathing bulls with yokes and sow the death-bringing field. I killed the serpent, which unsleeping guarded the golden fleece, twining its many coils around it, and brought you the light of salvation. I myself betrayed my father and my home and came to Iolcus, below Mt. Pelion, with you, I too much in love but not too wise.   30 And I murdered Pelias at the hands of his own daughters, in a most dreadful way to die, and ruined his home. After benefiting from all these things that I did, you, vilest of men, have betrayed me. You have taken a new wife, although children had been born to us. Indeed, if you were still childless, you might have been forgiven for desiring this second marriage. No more is there trust in your oaths to me. I am not able to discern whether you think the gods you swore by then no longer still rule or that new divine ordinances are now to be followed among human beings, since you know full well that you have not been true to what you swore to me. Oh, my poor right hand, which you clasped so many times and my poor knees, how   40 they were clutched for nothing by a base man, and how I have been cheated of my hopes. (475–498)

Still I will share my dilemma with you as though you were a friend. What helpful solution can I expect from you? Nevertheless, I will do so, for having been asked what I should do, you will appear all the more vile. Where can I turn now? To the house of my father which I betrayed for you by coming to your fatherland or to the wretched daughters of Pelias? A fine reception I would receive in their home, I who killed their father. And so this is my predicament. I have made my loved ones at home hate me and, because of what I did for you, I have made enemies of those   50 whom I should never have wronged. As a reward for these services, you have made me so happy, I am sure, in the eyes of many women. In you I possess an amazing and trustworthy husband, if I am thrown out of this land and wander an exile bereft of friends, with my children, alone and abandoned. A fine reproach for a newly married bridegroom that his children wander as beggars and I do too, the one who saved you. (499–515)

O Zeus, who gave to human beings sure signs for gold that is counterfeit, why is there no birthmark stamped on the skin by which one must recognize the man who is base?

CHORUS: Terrible is the rage and very difficult to heal, when loved ones battle it out. (520–521)   60

JASON: I must, as it seems, not be a bad speaker but just like a trusty captain of a ship reef up the sails and ride out from under the stormy verbiage of your busy tongue. While you exaggerate excessively your kindness to me, I consider Aphrodite alone of gods and mortals to be the savior of my expedition. You do have a clever mind, but it would be invidious to go through the story of how Eros with his unerring arrows compelled you to save my life. But I will not go into the many details. Where you did help me, however, you got more in return for my safety than you gave, as I will explain. First, you dwell in the land of Hellas instead of a barbarian country and you experience justice and the exercise of laws, without the mere gratification of force. All Hellenes have come to know that you are wise and you have gained a reputation. But if you were still living at the very end of the earth, you would be of no account. I would rather have the good fortune of an outstanding reputation than a house full of gold or the power to sing a more beautiful song than Orpheus. (522–544)

So much then I say to you about my labors. After all, you started this contest of words. With respect to your reproaches against me concerning my marriage into royalty, I will prove to you that in this first of all I was wise, next that I was not driven   80
by sex, and finally that I acted as a great friend to you and to my sons.

Now, now, Medea, be quiet. (550)

After I moved here from the land of Iolcus, bringing with me the burden of many hopeless misfortunes, what luckier find could I have come upon than this: to marry the daughter of the king, even though I was an exile. It was not that I loathed your bed, your accusation that so galls you, and I was not anxious to outrival those who have many children. The ones I have are enough and I have no complaint. But my purpose was to ensure that we should live well, this is of the greatest importance, and not be in want, knowing full well that every one takes pains to avoid a friend who is poor. Also I wanted to bring up my children in a manner that was worthy of my house and to father brothers and sisters for the children born of you. I wanted to   90
treat them all alike and, having established one unified family, I would be blessed with happiness. For you, why is there need of children? For me, it is profitable to benefit the ones I already have by means of those whom I hope will be born. I haven't planned badly, have I? Even you would agree, if only the marriage and matter of sex did not gall you so. You women think everything depends on sex! If any trouble happens on that score, you turn the best laid, finest plans into causes for hostility. Men ought to be able to beget children from some other source and the female gender should not exist. Then evil would not exist for human beings.   100
(551–575)

CHORUS: Jason, you have made your arguments look good but, nevertheless, to me, even if I am speaking against your point of view, you seem not to act justly in betraying your wife.

MEDEA: To be sure, I am at odds with many people about many things. For to me the man who is unjust and born a clever speaker incurs the heaviest retribution, because overly confident that he can cover up his wrongs beautifully, he stops at nothing in his tongue-wagging arguments. But he is not as clever as all that. And so it is with you. Do not now become a specious liar and a devastating talker against me, for one word will lay you out. If you were not a coward, you should have persuaded me to agree before making this marriage, but not without saying a thing to your loved ones. (579–587)   110

JASON: You would have given me splendid support, I imagine, if I had told you about the marriage, you, who not even now can bring yourself to abandon your overwhelming rage.

MEDEA: It was not this consideration that controlled your behavior, but rather you thought that as you grew older a foreign marriage was likely to end badly.

JASON: You can be sure of this: it was not on account of a woman that I made this marriage with the daughter of a king, to which I am committed but, just as I said before, it was because of my wish to save you and to beget royal children as brothers and sisters to my own children, a bulwark for our family.

MEDEA: I do not wish to have a life of good fortune that causes pain nor a prosperity that galls my heart. (598–599)   120

JASON: Do you not know how you must change your wish to show yourself the wiser? Wish that your best interests not appear painful and that you do not think that you are unfortunate when you are fortunate.

MEDEA: Continue with your hubris, since there is a refuge for you, but I will go from this land, an abandoned exile.

JASON: You choose this yourself. Don't blame anyone else. (605)

MEDEA: What did I do? I didn't take a wife and betray you.   130

JASON: You uttered unholy curses against the royal house.

MEDEA: Yes, and I am a curse to your house too.

JASON: I will not debate the matter any further, but if you want to accept any financial help for the children and yourself in your exile, say so. Know that I am ready to give with an ungrudging hand and to send introductions to my friends who will treat you well. You are crazy not to want to accept these offers, woman. If you forget your rage, you will have the more to gain. (609–615)

MEDEA: I would never use the help of your friends, and I would not accept anything from you, so don't give me anything. For gifts from an evil man hold no benefit.   140

JASON: Well then, I call the gods as witnesses that I want to do everything for you and the children. What is good for you isn't to your liking but you push away your friends by your audacity. Therefore you suffer all the more. (619–622)

MEDEA: Go, for you must be possessed by longing for your newly won girl, being so long away from the palace. Play your role as bridegroom; perhaps—and with god's help I will say this—you have made such a marriage that will end up to your grief. (623–629)

Within the framework of a heroic myth, we witness a mundane and frighteningly real confrontation between a man and a woman, husband and wife, once a marriage is over. It is difficult to sympathize with Jason, arrogant and cold, who immediately takes the stance of the tolerant and benevolent provider, even though it is Medea, he claims, who is in the wrong. It is true, as we have learned from Creon himself, that Medea's rage and deadly threats against the royal family have been the reasons for her exile, but, in Medea's view, no other recourse is possible except vengeance against her enemies. When Medea lists her services to Jason, including betrayal of her family and country, murder, and even the slaying of the dragon, the eternal question immediately arises: should the continuation of a marriage be based upon debts from the past? Her appeal to earlier pledges and oaths perhaps has a greater religious and moral authority.

It seems that her foreign marriage with Jason holds no legal validity for Jason in Corinth.

When Jason lists the blessings that he has conferred upon Medea in return, he presents us with one of the many fascinating issues raised by the play. He boasts that he has brought Medea to a system of justice in an enlightened land, far superior to that of her own barbarian country, where brute force is the rule. For Medea, no justice at all exists in a land where she can be treated with such injustice, and vengeful violence represents to her an earlier and better standard of morality.

One of the most heartless responses to Medea is Jason's claim that she had no choice in her actions; all that she did for him she did under the compulsion of an overwhelming love, inspired by Aphrodite and Eros. He never mentions any kind of affection that he might have once held for her. It is most rewarding to read the *Argonautica* of Apollonius of Rhodes for his version of the events in Colchis and the beginnings of the relationship between Jason and Medea. In Book 3, Apollonius draws a justly admired portrait of Medea as a woman smitten by love, and he seems to take his cue from these lines of Jason in Euripides. When Medea, at the court of Aeëtes, first set eyes on Jason, an invisible Eros, crouched low at Jason's feet, shoots an arrow directly at Medea, and she is consumed with the flame of passion. Eventually, though, Jason too is touched by feelings of love.

In Euripides, Jason's rhetoric is that of the exemplary sophist, one who by clever and devious arguments can make or try to make the worse cause seem the better. To Medea, all his words are specious and insincere, designed to disguise the fact that he is a base and cowardly man and his actions are despicable. But at least some of his arguments may be true and very understandable, however morally dubious and unforgivable. Despite all of Medea's help, Jason did not realize his ultimate goal, to become the king of Iolcus. The murder of Pelias, orchestrated by Medea, failed in its purpose, and Jason had to flee with Medea to Corinth. Now with his days of glory past, his shattered hopes inspire a desperate ambition. As he explains, his marriage into the royal family is calculated and pragmatic, his golden opportunity, a last chance for power and success. Less credible may be his contentions that his actions are not motivated by passion (the beautiful young princess holds no sexual attraction for him) and that his plans were designed to help Medea and the children; yet, apparently he had not expected them to be exiled, and perhaps he did have in mind a prosperous future in which they might be included. Medea is not above sophistry herself: she claims that Jason has left them destitute, while at the same time refusing to accept the liberal help that he offers.

To continue with Euripides, Aegeus, the king of Athens, arrives in Corinth (a lucky coincidence that does not seem too contrived in the momentum of performance). He has been to the oracle of Apollo at Delphi to inquire about a cure for his inability to beget children and is on his way to consult with Pittheus, king of Troezen, about the response before he returns home. Medea tells Aegeus about her husband's cruel betrayal and her imminent exile and makes him feel pity toward her plight and critical of Jason's behavior. She begs Aegeus to receive her into his house in Athens as a suppliant, never to give her over to her enemies in pursuit, and she in return will, through her knowledge of medicines, cure him of his childlessness.[14] Aegeus agrees to this exchange of favors first because of the gods (her salvation is a just cause) and then because of her benefit to him.

Medea, however, must leave Corinth by her own devices because Aegeus as a guest there does not want to offend his hosts by interfering. If Medea does reach Athens, Aegeus promises to protect her, since he is a just king. At Medea's insistence, he swears a solemn oath by Earth, the sacred light of Helius, and all the gods that he will do what he has promised.

Once again Medea has duped a king. Now she has made her escape secure, eliciting a safe refuge from Aegeus, who is ignorant of what she is planning to do. It may be that Euripides ironically depicts his Athens, so renowned in myth and drama for being a righteous champion of the oppressed, as the deceived protector of a murderer, whose victims include her own children.

Medea now exults before the Chorus, calling upon Zeus, the justice of Zeus, and the light of the Sun in her victory over her enemies. She goes on boldly to reveal fully the exact details of her plans for what she in actual fact will accomplish. The laughter of one's enemies is intolerable; they must pay. We learn as well, amid her anguished groans, of her chilling decision to kill her children. Has the realization of Aegeus' desperation over his childlessness steeled her for the decision to commit this atrocity? Jason, with god's help, will never see alive his children born by her, and he will never have other children by his new bride. Medea claims she would never want to be considered weak, passive, or base. No, just the opposite, she, like those whose life is most renowned, is hurtful to enemies and kindly to friends. Among her enemies now, it seems, are her children by Jason. And so she begins her plans for destruction by sending the Nurse to summon Jason, and she artfully feigns reconciliation in this second scene between the two of them (866–975):

> JASON: I have come at your command. For even though you bear ill will, I would still not fail to come, but I will hear you out. What is it now that you want from me, woman? (866–868)
>
> MEDEA: Jason, I beg you to forgive what I have said. It is only fair that you bear with my rages now, since many have been the acts of love between us in the past. I have argued the case with myself and am full of self-reproach. "Stubborn fool, why am I so insane and hostile to those who are making good plans, and why do I persist in my enmity against the rulers of this land and against my husband, who is doing for us what is most advantageous by marrying a princess and begetting children who will be as brothers and sisters to my own? Will I not cease from my anger? What is   10 wrong with me? The gods are providing for me well. I have children and I know that we are being exiled from this land and are in need of friends." I mulled over these considerations and realized my great lack of foresight and my useless rage. And so now I applaud and think that you are most wise and reasonable to take on this marriage for us. I am the foolish one. I ought to share in your plans, join you in carrying them out, stand by our nuptial bed, and take joy in my support of your marriage. But we women are what we are, I don't say evil, but just women. You should not imitate our nature or respond to our childishness with childishness. I give in and admit that I was not thinking right then, but now I have come to a better understanding of this situation. (869–893)   20
>
> O children, children, here, come out of the house, come out. Embrace your father, greet your father with me, and along with your mother be reconciled and turn from our former enmity against a loved one. We have made peace and our anger has given way. Take his right hand. Alas for me when I think about any of the possible hidden misfortunes in store. O my children, will you stretch out your dear

hands so, throughout a long life? Poor me, how prone to weep and full of fear. Now that I have at long last ended the quarrel with your father, I have drenched your tender faces with my tears. (894–905)

CHORUS: Fresh tears have started in my eyes too. May the present evil not proceed any further and increase.   30

JASON: I approve, woman, of all this and I do not blame your former hostility. It is to be expected that women become enraged when a husband secretly makes a deal for a marriage of a different sort. But your heart has changed for the better, and you have come to recognize the winning plan. This is the behavior of a reasonable woman. (908–913)

For you, children, your father, thoughtful and concerned, has provided great security, with the help of the gods. For I believe that you with your new brothers and sisters will be foremost in this land of Corinth in time to come. Only you must grow to manhood. Both your father and whatever god is kindly will take care of   40
the rest. May I see you coming to young manhood, strong and victorious over my enemies.

You there, Medea, moist with fresh tears. Why do you turn away, so pale? Why are you not happy to hear what I have been saying?

MEDEA: It is nothing. I was thinking about these children here. (925)

JASON: Bear up now, for I will take care of them.

MEDEA: I will bear up. I will not distrust your words, but a woman is by nature feminine and prone to tears.

JASON: Why, then, do you cry over these children too much?

MEDEA: I gave birth to them. When you prayed that the children might live, I wondered if this would happen and pity overwhelmed me. (930–931)   50

But I have told you only some of the reasons for you having to come to talk to me, and now I will mention the others. Since the rulers of this land have decided to banish me, this is the best thing for me too, I know full well, not to live here and be in your way or theirs since I seem to be a menace to the royal house. I, for my part, am resigned to go into exile, but the children, beg Creon that they not be exiled too so that they may be brought up by your hand. (932–940)

JASON: I don't know if I can persuade him, but I will try.

MEDEA: Then you beg your wife to ask her father not to exile the children.   60

JASON: Certainly, I'll do it and I think I will persuade her. (944)

MEDEA: If she is a woman like the rest, you will, and I will help you in this. I will send her gifts, which I know are by far the most beautiful of any on this earth today, an exquisite robe and a diadem of gold, and the children will bring them. But one of the servants here must bring them out as quickly as possible. Your bride will be blessed by happiness forever, since she has found you, the best of men, to be her husband and been given this treasure, which Helius, father of my father, gave to his descendants. (945–955)

Take these bridal gifts, children, into your hands, carry them, and give them to the princess, the happy bride. Certainly she will accept these gifts with which she   70
can find no fault.

JASON: O foolish woman, why do you empty your hands of these things? Do you think the royal household is in need of fine robes, or gold; do you really think so? Keep these things; do not give them away. For if my wife prizes me at all, she will prefer to oblige me rather than accept treasures, I am quite sure. (959–963)

MEDEA: No, you must not dissuade me. They say gifts persuade even the gods and for mortals gold is more powerful than a thousand words. Divine luck is hers;

> now god blesses her good fortune. She is young and a princess. I would give my 80
> life and not only gold to repeal the exile of my children. (964–968)
>
> But children, when you both have entered the rich palace, entreat the new bride
> of your father, my mistress, and beg her that you not be banished from this land.
> Give her these treasures and, most important of all, she must accept these gifts into
> her own hand. (909–973)
>
> So go quickly as possible! May you succeed and come back to your mother,
> good messengers of what she is longing to hear.

Pompous Jason is fooled by obsequious flattery into believing Medea has accepted the wisdom of his actions. She fully understands how to play upon the foibles of his character and make him completely blind to the treachery in hers, which he fails even to suspect despite his knowledge of their past. The scene confirms Jason's love for his sons, and there is an ominous irony in Medea's tears, which he does not understand.

There follows a terrifying scene between Medea and her blameless children, exposing her pain and agonized indecision in the face of their loving tenderness. Then comes the return of the messenger from the palace who describes for an

Medea Murders Her Son. Campanian red-figure amphora by the Ixion painter, ca. 325 B.C. Only one of Medea's sons is shown in this scene, as she thrusts her sword a second time into his body, which is already bleeding. He stretches out his arm, pleading for mercy in vain. The scene is set in a temple; on the right, on a column above the altar, is a small statue of a god, perhaps Apollo. (*Erich Lessing/ Art Resource, NY*)

exultant Medea, relishing every exquisite detail, the horrifying deaths of the bride Creusa and her father Creon. Convinced by Jason, the princess accepted the beautiful gifts from the children. As the poisoned robe and diadem consumed her, her father rushed to save her but he became fused in her struggles to escape and they died in agony together. With this news of her success, Medea decides with finality that her children (who will be killed anyway, she assumes, because of what she has done) must die by her own hand. We hear their piteous cries from within, as Medea kills them with a sword.

Upon the deaths of Creusa and Creon, Jason rushes to confront Medea and the play ends with this final confrontation (1293–1414):

JASON: You women standing near the door, is she still inside the house, Medea, the one who has done such terrible things, or has she made her escape in flight? To be sure, she will have to hide in the depths of the earth or soar aloft on wings to the heavens above, if she is to avoid paying retribution to the royal house. Does she imagine that she will flee from here unpunished for having killed the sovereigns of this land? Still I am not as concerned about her as I am about my children. Those whom she has wronged will take care of her punishment, but I have come to save the life of my sons so that the next of kin may do them no harm by exacting vengeance for the unholy crime committed by their mother. (1293–1305)   10

CHORUS: Jason, poor man, if you knew the depths of your misfortune, you would not have spoken these words.

JASON: What do you mean? Can it be that she wants to kill me too?

CHORUS: Your children are dead, murdered by their mother.

JASON: Woe is me! What are you saying? Woman, how you have destroyed me. (1310)

CHORUS: You must understand that your children are no longer alive.

JASON: Where has she killed them, within the house or outside?

CHORUS: Open the doors and you will see the slaughter of your sons.

JASON: Quickly, servants, unlock the doors and open them up so that I may see   20 this twofold evil, my dead sons and her, their killer, whom I will kill in just retribution. (1314–1316)

MEDEA: Why do you rush at the doors and attempt to unlock them in order to find the corpses and their murderer? Stop your efforts. If there is anything you want of me, say what it is that you wish, but you will never be able to touch me. Helius, the father of my father, has given me this chariot, a defense against the hand of an enemy. (1317–1322)

JASON: O hatred personified, most detestable abomination to the gods, to me, and to the whole race of human beings. You who gave them birth brought yourself to drive a sword into your own children and kill them and destroy me too by   30 making me childless. Having done this, you still look upon the sun and the earth, even though you dared this most impious deed. May you die! Now I am sane; but then I was insane when I brought you out of a barbarian land from your house to a home among the Hellenes, you, a great evil, the betrayer of your father and the country that nourished you. The gods have brought down upon me the avenging spirit that should have been meant for you, for it was you who killed your brother at the hearth before you even set foot on the *Argo*, my ship with its beautiful prow. You began with actions like these. Now after you had married a man like me and borne me children, you murdered them because of sex and jealousy. There are no women in Hellas who would ever dare such a thing. Instead of one of them, I preferred to   40 marry you, a hateful union and ruinous for me, you, a lioness, not a woman, more savage in nature than Scylla in her Tuscan waters. But I would not be able to sting you, however endless my reproaches, since you have such an inbred brazen hostility. Go to perdition, evil-doer, child-killer! All I have left is to bewail my ill-fate. (1323–1347)

From my new bride and marriage I will not derive any joy and benefit, and as for my boys whom I raised, I will not be able to speak to them again alive but I have lost them.

MEDEA: I would have gone on at length to respond to these words of yours, if Zeus, the father, did not understand what I did for you and what you did to me. You 50 were not about to spend a happy life laughing at me after you had dishonored our bed, nor were the princess and Creon, who gave her to you in marriage, about to throw me out of this land, with impunity. And so call me a lioness if you wish and Scylla who lives in the Tuscan sea. I have stung you in the heart, as I had to do. (1351–1360)

JASON: You yourself also feel the pain and share in my misfortune.

MEDEA: Only too true, but the pain is soothed if you cannot laugh at me.

JASON: O my children, fated with such a wicked mother!

MEDEA: O my sons, you were destroyed by your father's sick treachery!

JASON: Now then, it was not my hand that killed them. (1365)   60

MEDEA: No, it was your hubris and your newly arranged marriage.

JASON: Do you really believe it right to kill them, just because of a marriage?

MEDEA: Do you really think that this painful insult is trivial to your wife?

JASON: To a wife who is sensible, but to you everything is vile.

MEDEA: These children are no more. This will sting you. (1370)

JASON: These children are alive, alas, spirits of vengeance down upon your head.

MEDEA: The gods know who began this suffering.

JASON: They know, to be sure, your hateful mind and heart.

MEDEA: Go ahead and hate! I loathe your bitter, barking voice.   70

JASON: As I do yours. Our separation is only too easy. (1375)

MEDEA: How so? What shall I do? For I too want it desperately.

JASON: Let me bury these corpses and mourn over them.

MEDEA: Certainly not! I will bury them by my own hand, bringing them to the sanctuary of Hera Akraia in Corinth, so that no one of my enemies will violate their graves by tearing them up. In this Corinthian land of Sisyphus, I will institute a holy festival and religious rites forevermore, in expiation for this impious murder. I myself will go to Athens in the land of Erechtheus to live with Aegeus, son of Pandion. But you, as is fitting for a base coward, will die an unheroic death, struck on the head by a piece of your *Argo*, having witnessed the bitter end of my marriage to you.   80 (1378–1388)

JASON: May the avenging Fury of the murdered children destroy you, and also Justice, avenger of blood-guilt.

MEDEA: What god or divine spirit will hear you, false liar, and betrayer of oaths.

JASON: Oh, alas, you polluted murderess of children!

MEDEA: Go home and bury your wife.

JASON: I am going, bereft of my two sons. (1395)

MEDEA: Your mourning has not really begun yet; old age is left for you to grieve.

JASON: O children, so very dear!

> MEDEA: To their mother, not you.
> JASON: And yet you killed them.
> MEDEA: Yes, to cause you pain.
> JASON: Oh, poor wretch that I am, how I long to embrace my children and kiss their dear lips. (1399–1400)
> MEDEA: Now you speak to them, now you greet them with love, before you rejected them.
> JASON: By the gods, let me touch the soft and gentle bodies of my sons.
> MEDEA: That is impossible. You ask in vain.
> JASON: Zeus, do you hear all this? How I am driven away, the treatment I suffer from this polluted, child-slaying lioness. But insofar as I have the power and am able, I offer up my lament and call upon the gods to witness how you killed my sons and prevented me from touching them and burying their bodies. How I wish that I had never begotten them to see them dead by your hand. (1405–1414)

90

Jason approved when Medea killed more than once on his behalf; now true recognition has come at last (but too late) that she is a murderess. For Medea, her hatred of Jason and the compulsion to cause him the ultimate pain are more powerful than her love for her children and her own suffering wrought by their murder. How unbearable for us is the slaughter of sweet, young innocence to satisfy cruel, selfish, and ruthless passions. Both Medea and Jason are responsible for the tragedy, but Medea's claim that Jason, not she, is the real perpetrator must surely be the ultimate sophistry of all! In this horrifying denouement, Euripides' masterful use of the deus ex machina illuminates the profundity of his art. It is Medea herself who acts as the deus ex machina, the protagonist integral to the whole plot who provides its resolution from without (not unlike Dionysus in the *Bacchae*). When Medea appears untouchable, above Jason in the chariot sent by her grandfather Helius, she becomes transformed and takes on the attributes of a primordial deity who has with divine impunity meted out the cruel and terrible vendetta of an older order of justice.

No other play illustrates more succinctly how our reactions to a work of art are inevitably determined by who we are, what we believe, and what we have experienced. Its ruthless delineation of character and motivation and the relentless power of its emotional and cathartic impact never fail to elicit the most conflicting judgments and vehement interpretations; the arguments will surely go on forever.

Select Bibliography

Apollonius Rhodius. *Jason and the Golden Fleece*, ed. **Richard Hunter.** New York: Oxford University Press, 2009. A prose translation with commentary of the *Argonautica*.

Bloom, Harold. *Euripides.* New York: Chelsea House, 2003.

Clauss, James J., and **Sara Iles Johnston,** eds. *Medea: Essays on Medea in Myth, Literature, Philosophy, and Art.* Princeton, NJ: Princeton University Press, 1997.

Griffiths, Emma. *Medea.* Gods and Heroes of the Ancient World Series. New York: Routledge, 2006.

Pucci, Pietro. *The Violence of Pity in Euripides' Medea.* Ithaca, NY: Cornell University Press, 1980.

Romey, K. M. "Land of the Golden Fleece." *Archaeology* 54, no. 2 (2001), pp. 28–31.

Primary Sources

Sources in the Chapter

Euripides	*Medea* (selections)
Ovid	*Metamorphoses* 7.100–158
Pindar	*Pythian Ode* 4.184–187, 239–254

Additional Sources

Apollonius of Rhodes	*Argonautica*
Seneca	*Medea*
Valerius Flaccus	*Argonautica*

Notes

1. Sources for the saga are the Greek epic *Argonautica* by Apollonius of Rhodes (third century B.C.) and the Latin epic *Argonautica* by Valerius Flaccus (late first century A.D.). Pindar's complex fourth *Nemean Ode* (ca. 460 B.C.) is the most poetic account, and Ovid (early first century A.D.) has a brief narrative in Book 7 of the *Metamorphoses*. Graham Anderson, *Fairytale in the Ancient World* (London: Routledge, 2000), pp. 72–82, analyzes the fairy tale motifs in the story.
2. Her name is also given as Alcimede or Amphinome.
3. He was the son of Poseidon and the husband of Cleopatra, daughter of Boreas. Different reasons are given for his blindness.
4. Clashing rocks called *Planctae* (Wanderers) appear in the Argonauts' return voyage and in the *Odyssey*. Herodotus calls them *Cyaneae* (Dark-rocks).
5. The teeth came from the Theban serpent killed by Cadmus and had been given to Aeëtes by Athena.
6. Apollodorus has Medea take Apsyrtus on the *Argo* and delay the pursuers by cutting him up and throwing his limbs piecemeal into the sea.
7. The earliest epic narratives of the saga were part of the *Corinthiaka* and *Naupaktika* of the Corinthian poet Eumelos (ca. 730 B.C.). Only a few lines survive.
8. Triton gave a clod of earth to the Argonaut Euphemus as a token that his descendants would rule in Libya. From it grew the island of Thera, from which eventually the Greek colony of Cyrene was founded in Libya by the descendants of Euphemus.
9. There are many different accounts of the origin, functions, and death of Talus.
10. See Janet R. Bacon, *The Voyage of the Argo* (London: Methuen, 1925), Chapter 9. For yet another attempt to retrace the journey, see T. Severin, *The Jason Voyage: The Quest for the Golden Fleece* (New York: Simon & Schuster, 1985).
11. For a discussion of some literary and artistic interpretations, see James J. Clauss and Sarah Iles Johnston, eds., *Medea: Essays on Medea in Myth, Literature, Philosophy, and Art* (Princeton, NJ: Princeton University Press, 1997).
12. Michael Grant, *Myths of the Greeks and Romans* (London: Weidenfeld & Nicolson, 1962; New York: Mentor Books, 1964), p. 302 of the London edition. A modern verse epic is by John Gardner, *Jason and Medeia* (New York: Knopf, 1973).
13. Robinson Jeffers, *Medea* (New York: Random House, 1946), p. 25.
14. For the problem in reconciling the oracle received by Aegeus with Medea's promise to cure him of childlessness, see p. 579 with note 14, on p. 605.

The Nature of Roman Mythology

Jacques-Louis David, *The Oath of the Horatii*

PART THREE
The Nature of Roman Mythology

GREEK MYTHOLOGY IN THE ROMAN WORLD

Graecia capta ferum victorem cepit et artis intulit agresti Latio.

—HORACE, *Epist.* II.1.156–157

Captured Greece took her untamed victor captive, and brought her arts to the peasants of Latium.

—JACQUES-LOUIS DAVID, *The Oath of the Horatii*

The Spread of Greek Influence in Italy

Greece is a mountainous country with relatively small areas of arable land and a very lengthy coastline. Once the turbulence of the Dorian invasions had settled, it was inevitable that the Greeks would emigrate to acquire better land and to engage in trade and piracy. The most stable system of Greek emigration was sending out colonies (*apoikiai*), that is, groups of settlers sent by a "mother" city to sites that had no doubt been chosen by advance surveys and approved by Apollo at Delphi, which had a good store of useful information. The first great period of Greek emigration occurred in the eighth century B.C., primarily in the region of the Aegean Sea, but also into the regions of the Black Sea, Illyria, and northwest Greece and (most important for this chapter) into southern Italy and Sicily. A group of colonists (mostly men and predominantly warriors) would leave their mother city and found their *apoikia* quite independent of the mother city. With them they would take their religious rituals and, presumably, the stories of their gods and heroes. Thus Roman contacts with these Greek settlers would have included awareness of their myths.

Southern Italy and Sicily

Two areas of southern Italy in particular (see map, p. 656) attracted Greek settlers. The earliest was around the shores of the Bay of Naples, where the earliest Greek settlement was founded on the island of Ischia early in the eighth century B.C. This settlement was transferred to the mainland in 757 B.C. and became the Greek city of **Cumae**. Later in the century, several Greek colonies were established in the toe and heel of Italy and around the gulf of Taranto. Among these colonies, the Spartan *apoikia* of Taras (Latin Tarentum, modern Taranto), sent out in 706 B.C., with its fine harbor, was especially important. (It should be noted that the distances in the south of Italy are considerable—about 300 miles as the crow flies and many more on land lie between Tarentum and Rhegium.) The Greeks crossed into Sicily and founded colonies on the northern and eastern coasts of the island. Of these colonies, by far the most successful was Syracuse, founded by Corinthians in 720 B.C. Thus, at exactly the period when Rome became a town (traditionally dated to 753 B.C.), the Greeks were establishing themselves in southern Italy. A small tribe from Boeotia, the Graioi, was among the emigrants. Its name was transmitted by the Romans as **Graeci**, while the Greek settlements in the boot of Italy and the eastern coast of Sicily were called **Magna Graecia**, perhaps meaning "Greece enlarged" rather than "great Greece." The Greeks then and to this day call themselves **Hellenes** and their country **Hellas**. Although this wave of emigration occurred nearly five centuries before Rome finally controlled all of peninsular Italy south of the Arno and Rubicon rivers, we can assume that there was plenty of intercourse between the Romans and the Greeks.

The Etruscans

To the northwest of Rome were the Etruscans. Their origin is much debated, but we do know that they controlled the area up to the Arno River and along the right bank of the Tiber. Their political system was based on a network of separate cities, each with its own defenses, religious buildings, and rituals, and their surrounding lands. Particularly important for Rome were the cities of **Veii** (a close neighbor), Tarquinii, and Caere (modern Cerveteri). The Etruscans traded as far to the east as Asia Minor and over the western Mediterranean, and although they suffered naval defeats at the hands of the Greek Phocaeans in 535 B.C. and the Cumaeans in 474 B.C., they remained economically powerful while Rome was an emerging city, engaged militarily in fighting its neighbors in the Sabine hills and the Latins to the southeast of Rome. Rome maintained friendly relations with Caere and made two forty-year treaties with Tarquinii (beginning in 351 B.C.) but was hostile for the most part to Veii. Two of the last three kings of Rome (and probably all three, if the sixth king, Servius Tullius, was Etruscan) were Etruscans, so the Etruscan influence was intertwined with the development of early Rome and certainly continued into the fifth century, after the establishment of the Roman Republic, traditionally dated to 509 B.C. The defeat and destruction of Veii in 396 B.C. was an important turning point in Roman relations with Etruria, and the Romans established colonies (which were primarily military) throughout Etruria within the next two centuries. To the south, in Campania, the Etruscans founded Capua in the seventh century B.C. and several other cities in the following century. But they failed to subdue Cumae, and the naval battle of 474 B.C. effectively ended their Campanian empire.

The Romans characteristically allowed the religious institutions and practices of the people whom they conquered to merge with their own (with the best-known exceptions being the Druids and the Christians). The identification of Italian gods with Greek gods is explained in Chapter 26, but the same kind of syncretism seems to have taken place with the Etruscans. The Etruscan gods **Tin**, **Uni**, and **Menvra** were assimilated, respectively, with Zeus/Jupiter, Hera/Juno, and Athena/Minerva. It is easy to see how the great temple of Jupiter Optimus Maximus on the Capitol, traditionally dated to 509 B.C., with its three inner chambers (*cellae*), one for each god, was dedicated to Jupiter, Juno, and Minerva instead of Tin, Uni, and Menvra. Other Etruscan divinities whose names are known were Fufluns, assimilated with Dionysus/Bacchus, and Sethlans, assimilated with Hephaestus/Vulcan. Thus a ready framework existed in Etruscan/Roman religion for the adoption of Greek traditional stories. One god whose name remained the same in Etruscan, Greek, and Roman religions was Apollo. A large statue of Apollo was found near Veii that originally had been placed on the ridgepole of a temple dedicated to Menvra. It was made in about 500 B.C.

The Etruscans possessed an enormous number of Greek vases, whether imported from Greece or made in Etruria by Greek artisans. We illustrated two examples earlier on pages 281 and 556, both of which were made in Etruria. It is obvious that the Romans would have become familiar with Greek legends through such artifacts. Nevertheless, Roman energies in the early centuries of the republic were devoted to agricultural and military action, as Horace's epigraph to this chapter indicates: Rome was *ferum*, that is, it was "fierce" in military action, and Latium (including Rome) was *agresti*, that is, its citizens were largely peasant farmers far removed from the *artes* of the cultivated Greeks.

Apollo of Veii. Height 74.5 in. This terra cotta statue of Apollo was made by the Etruscans in about 500 B.C., within a decade of the traditional date of the start of the Roman Republic. The god strides forward from the peak of the temple's roof, and his hands would have held his traditional objects, the lyre and the bow. The smile on his face is typical of Etruscan sculpture, while his swirling mantle is similar to Greek sculpture of the late sixth century. (*Scala/Ministero per i Beni e le Attività culturali/Art Resource, NY*)

Rome

This, then, was the state of affairs in general during the first two centuries of the Roman Republic. In the later part of the fourth century and the early third century B.C., however, the Romans successfully conquered, with much difficulty, the Greek cities of Campania, the fierce Italic tribes of southern Italy, and finally the cities of Magna Graecia, culminating in the capture of Tarentum in 272 B.C.[1] The most important result of this expansion, for the purposes of this chapter, was the bringing of the Greek Livius Andronicus to Rome as a captive slave, as we will discuss later. Roman military victories continued to spread the republic's holdings throughout the Mediterranean, not least in Greece itself, where **Flamininus** defeated the forces of Philip V of Macedon at Cynoscephalae in 197 B.C. This brought Rome firmly into the heart of the Greek world, even though Flamininus decided not to let Rome become too closely involved in Greek affairs. About thirty years later, in 168 B.C., the Romans defeated Perseus, the son and successor of Philip V of Macedon, at Pydna in northern Greece. This time there were cultural consequences, for Scipio Aemilianus, the son of the victorious

Roman commander Aemilius Paullus, brought back to Rome the Greek library of Perseus. The final collapse of Greek independence from Rome occurred with the destruction of Corinth by the Roman general **Lucius Mummius** in 146 B.C. The southern part of Greece was loosely attached to the province of Macedonia, which had been formed in 147 B.C. and was made into the province of Achaea by Augustus in 27 B.C. While Rome expanded her power in Asia Minor during the second century, these conquests did not materially affect the involvement of the Romans with Greek legends.

Greek Mythology and Roman Architecture

Roman Temples

The first and greatest of the Roman temples, the **temple of Jupiter Optimus Maximus** on the Capitoline Hill, did not include any mythological legends in its sculptural program, not even in the reconstructions that followed its destruction by fire in 83 B.C., A.D. 69, and A.D. 80, before its final destruction by Stilicho and Narses in the fifth and sixth centuries A.D., respectively. It had an Etruscan foundation, said to have been planned and built by Tarquinius Superbus (the last of the Etruscan kings of Rome), and its dedication coincided with the establishment of the Roman Republic in 509 B.C. The cult figures of Jupiter, Juno, and Minerva each occupied their separate *cellae*, but the decorations on the roof were not drawn from Greek mythology. Jupiter in his four-horse chariot occupied the peak of the roof, above the pediment. This rigorously nonmythological program was maintained in subsequent reconstructions. We know little about the decorations of the many other temples in Rome.[2] The only temple dedicated to Apollo before the great temple dedicated by Augustus on the Palatine was called the **temple of Apollo Sosianus**, built and dedicated in 431 B.C. and restored by the consul Sosius in 32 B.C. On its frieze were reliefs of a battle between Greeks and Amazons. From the archaeological remains of Roman temples, as well as from coins and other illustrations, it seems safe to say that (at least for the most part) they did not include reliefs and freestanding sculptures drawn from Greek mythology. Little remains of the great **temple of Mars Ultor (Mars the Avenger)**, which Augustus vowed to build on the field of Philippi in 42 B.C. and dedicated in 2 B.C. in the Forum of Augustus. It had little in the way of mythological ornamentation, beyond some figures of Pegasus as architectural elements in the interior. Its pediment, known from a relief on an altar elsewhere in Rome that was dedicated by Claudius in A.D. 43, contained a relief of Mars in the center, flanked by Venus and Fortuna, beside whom were seated, respectively, figures of Romulus and Roma. In the restricted space of the corners were figures usually identified as the Palatine Hill and Father Tiber. In other words, the decoration of this great Augustan temple was uncompromisingly Roman (for Venus was the ancestress of Augustus).

While this temple, like that of Apollo Sosianus, was the depository of many works of art (including those with mythological subjects), we can safely assume that Greek mythology played very little part in the decoration of Roman temples. A prominent and surprising exception is the great temple of Apollo dedicated by Augustus on the Palatine Hill in 28 B.C. Little of this construction remains today, but the Augustan poet Propertius left a detailed description of the dedication (Propertius 2.31.1–16):

> You ask why I have been late in coming to you. The golden Portico of Apollo had been opened by mighty Caesar [Augustus]. So great was the sight of the columns of African marble, and in between them were the daughters of old Danaus. Here I thought that the marble statue of Apollo was more beautiful than the god himself as he opened his mouth for song above his silent lyre. And around the altar stood the sculptor Myron's cattle, four bulls, lifelike figures. Then in brilliant marble rose the temple in the middle, more dear to Apollo than Ortygia, his homeland. On it, above the highest point, was the chariot of the Sun. And there were doors, noble work of Libyan ivory. The one showed the Gauls [Celts] thrown down from the heights of Parnassus, while the other showed the sad scene of the deaths of the Niobids. Then Apollo himself, between his mother [Latona] and his sister [Diana], sang his song dressed in a long robe.

10

Why did Augustus choose the Greek mythological figures of the Danaïds and Niobids? The Danaïds were the fifty daughters of Danaus of Argos, who (with the exception of Hypermestra) murdered their husbands, sons of Aegyptus.[3] That their legend was significant to Augustus was proved by Vergil (who died nine years after the dedication described by Propertius), who twice described the sword-belt of Pallas, the son of King Evander, who had welcomed Aeneas to his home at the future site of Rome. When the Rutulian hero Turnus killed Pallas, he stripped him of the sword-belt, which was decorated with "the band of young men killed together on their marriage night." Turnus fatefully wore the sword-belt in his final duel with Aeneas, and it was the sight of it, "the reminder of cruel grief" (*saevi monimenta doloris*), that filled Aeneas with anger and drove him to kill Turnus in the final lines of the *Aeneid*. The Danaïds, then, were reminders of the emotions that are the accompaniment of war, and Augustus boasted that he had put an end to the civil wars that Rome had endured for decades. Moreover, his final enemy, Mark Antony, had allied himself with the Egyptian queen Cleopatra, and it was in Egypt that they had ended their lives, leading to Egypt becoming a Roman province personally governed by Augustus.[4]

The reliefs of the doors, made of ivory (a very expensive material), conspicuously contrasted with each other, for one was historical and the other mythical. The Celts had attacked Apollo's most sacred sanctuary, Delphi, in 278 B.C. and were repelled by unexpectedly disastrous weather, which was ascribed by the Greeks (and Augustus) to Apollo. Niobe was an example of arrogance and pride, as Horace pointed out in a poem written in 17 B.C. and as we have earlier related.[5] The relevance of these two stories to the recent victory of Augustus at Actium in 31 B.C. over Antony and Cleopatra was obvious.

Roman Public Buildings

Later Roman emperors built fora, arches, and other public monuments to celebrate their successes and decorated them with historical reliefs without mythological representations. There were exceptions: Gaius (Caligula, who reigned from A.D. 37 to 41) was said to have appeared in public dressed as Zeus/Jupiter and holding the god's thunderbolt. Domitian planned a forum dedicated to Minerva, which was completed by Nerva in A.D. 97. In it was a frieze showing the arts and crafts that Minerva protected, including a relief, still extant, of Arachne weaving, a story we related earlier.[6]

Greek Mythology and the Imperial Regime

Augustus was deified after his death, and the deification of his successors (excepting Tiberius, Gaius, and Nero) weakened the distinction between human and divine that is a basic feature of Greek religion and its related legends. While individual Greek gods appear in later Roman sculpture and art, Greek mythological legends were subordinated to Roman historical records or, not surprisingly, Roman entertainments. The Roman poet Martial (writing in about A.D. 80) mentions a live performance of Pasiphaë's union with a bull, and he and Suetonius (writing in about A.D. 120) refer to an enactment of the flight of Daedalus and Icarus: the wires suspending them were so arranged that Icarus would fall to his death (in one case splattering Nero with his blood), while Daedalus, who landed safely, would be torn apart by a bear. Such was the Roman people's taste for Greek mythology.[7]

Tiberius, the successor to Augustus (he reigned from A.D. 14 to 37), possessed a villa on the coast about 75 miles to the southeast of Rome, between the modern towns of Tarracina and Gaeta. Nearby were large caves, in one of which, at **Sperlonga** (a modern corruption of the Latin word *spelunca*, a cave), Tiberius liked to dine; it was here that he was saved by his senior minister Sejanus during a landslide and, literally, a cave-in. This cave was ornamented with large marble representations of some of the adventures of Ulysses, most notably the episode with Scylla, who was traditionally believed to have inhabited a large cave (mentioned by Homer) in this neighborhood. Fragments of Ulysses' ship and its crew are extant, and some of the work has been reconstructed.[8] This is another example of the Roman taste for literal representations of Greek myths.

Hercules

The most enduring figure from Greek mythology was Heracles, called Hercules by the Romans, whom we discuss in the next chapter.[9] The moneychangers of Rome, who were under the protection of Hercules, erected an arch in A.D. 204 known as the *Arcus Argentariorum*, on which there were reliefs of Hercules (in addition to those of the emperor Septimius Severus and his family). Suetonius tells us that Nero had intended to imitate the deeds of Hercules and had prepared to kill a lion, either with a club or by strangling, in an arena watched by the Roman crowd.[10] Equally deluded was the emperor Commodus, who reigned from A.D. 180 until 192. In this bust, Commodus is portrayed as Hercules. The Arch of Constantine (A.D. 315) had reliefs taken from buildings erected in Hadrian's time (about A.D. 130) that showed sacrifices to Apollo and to Hercules. Far from Rome, in the basilica at Leptis in North Africa, birthplace of the emperor Septimius, were floral reliefs of pilasters (famous as "peopled scrolls") that included Hercules and other mythological figures.

Commodus as Hercules. Height 49 in. The jaws of the Nemean lion are over the emperor's head, and its paws are knotted over his chest. In his right hand he holds the knotted club of Hercules and in his left the Apples of the Hesperides. The symbolic figures below the sun—Roma (headless) with a prisoner, and the globe—cannot, like the attributes of Hercules, make this emperor any less arrogant, cruel, and self-indulgent than he was in real life. His cruelty and self-delusion led to his assassination in 192. (*Erich Lessing/Art Resource, NY*)

Mercury

Not far behind Hercules in popularity was Mercury, the Roman equivalent of Hermes. He, too, was the protector of commerce and profit, as we explain in the next chapter.[11] The Augustan poet Horace fully described his functions at Rome in the first book of his *Odes* (the poem is translated in the next chapter), all of them the same as his traditional powers in Greek mythology. Since Mercury was a musician, playing the lyre, Horace revered him as the protector of *lyric* poets like himself, even referring to himself as *homo mercurialis*. Mercury is found in reliefs and other types of art all over the Roman Empire. A beautiful amethyst from a ring, only half an inch in size, was found at the Roman palace of Fishbourne in Sussex, England.[12] Exquisitely carved, it shows Mercury with his winged hat and *caduceus* leaning against a pillar and holding a moneybag in his right hand; at his feet are a cock (symbol of the god's wakefulness) and a ram (symbol of his protection of flocks and herds). It was probably made in about A.D. 100, that is, about sixty years after the conquest of Britain in A.D. 43. This is a perfect example of the spread of Roman mythology (itself derived from the Greeks) through appropriation by wealthy provincials following military conquest or trade.

Roman Military Power

In the Greek world, the survival of Greek mythology after the Roman conquest was general but politically constrained by the need to acknowledge Roman supremacy. Thus the Greek gods and their myths were often associated with Roman military successes. The best example of this process can be seen in the Greek city of Aphrodisias in southwestern Turkey. As its name shows, the city was under the protection of Aphrodite, whose Roman equivalent was Venus and from whom Julius Caesar and Augustus were descended, thus giving the city a special relationship with its Roman masters. In the middle of the first century A.D., two wealthy families built and dedicated a **Sebasteion**, that is, a temple complex dedicated to Aphrodite, the **theoi sebastoi** (gods who should be worshiped), and the *demos* (people). Among the *theoi sebastoi* were the Roman emperors and their families, and they were portrayed in large relief sculptures that were displayed in a long portico built as an approach to the temple of Aphrodite. In the Greek-speaking eastern half of the Roman Empire, *sebastos* (reverend or venerable) became the standard Greek translation of the Roman title *Augustus*, which would be adopted by all later Roman emperors. The Roman emperors Augustus, Tiberius, Claudius, and Nero were portrayed heroically naked and victorious over various barbarian peoples such as Britons and Armenians; it was appropriate for the Greeks, who had been conquered by the Romans two centuries earlier, to align themselves with the Romans and be on their side in the conquest of contemporary barbarians. Among the ninety marble relief panels were allegorical and mythological reliefs, including those depicting Leda and the swan, Demeter and Triptolemus, Bellerophon and Pegasus, and many others. As the scholar who first published these panels observed, "this was part of the international *koine* (common language) of myth . . . that was part of the basic cultural minimum for educated Greeks and Romans under the empire."[13]

Greek Mythology and Roman Art

Mosaic

Greek mythology was widely used in mosaics throughout the Roman world.[14] Mosaics might be portable, made in a tray inserted into the decorative scheme of the floor of a building; such mosaics are called *emblemata*. Mosaics of a second kind, "carpet" mosaics, occupy the whole floor of a room. These usually have decorative geometrical borders with central areas containing a large and often mythological representation. In the Roman world, one could not go to a carpet shop in some bazaar and choose a carpet; instead, one would engage craftsmen (often Greek) to make a mosaic that demonstrated the owner's wealth, education, and taste. Finally, some mosaics were placed vertically, often as the decorations of fountains and other sources of water. The Greek world extends as far east as modern Syria, and at Antioch and nearby there were many mosaics with mythological subjects. One example is the Judgment of Paris (see p. 465), which was the centerpiece of a large carpet mosaic in the house of a wealthy family. Many carpet mosaics could be found in Italy, especially at Ostia (the port of Rome near the mouth of the Tiber), in Campania, and in Magna Graecia. Often these were black and white, a style developed in Italy. A common subject was Neptune, sometimes with Amphitrite and often with sea-monsters and marine horses drawing his chariot. A splendid example can be seen in the so-called Baths of Neptune in Ostia, dating from the time of Hadrian, about A.D. 140. In Sicily, at the villa of Piazza Armerina, there are colored mosaics from the fourth century A.D. showing the labors of Hercules and Ulysses in the cave of Polyphemus.

But the richest source of Roman mythological mosaics is the province of Africa Proconsularis, which covered much of modern Tunisia and Algeria. Over 2,000 mosaics in this region are known. The great scene of Odysseus and the Sirens dates from the third century A.D. Much of the Roman province had Greek cities that dated from before the Roman conquest; therefore Greek mythology was familiar. Although many carpet mosaics took the activities of contemporary life as their subjects, many also were mythological. In these mosaics, Dionysus, Hercules, Neptune, and Amphitrite were especially popular subjects.

Mosaics were widely used in the northern parts of the Roman Empire as well, especially Britain and Germany. In Britain at Corinium (modern Cirencester) were mosaics depicting Orpheus, and elsewhere there were mosaics of Venus, including one in Yorkshire from about A.D. 350 showing a strangely bulbous Venus with animals in the side panels, including a bull called *Omicida* (Man-killer).

Common also were carpet mosaics with the heads of a sea-god or Medusa in the center. In Germany, there were large mosaics of the nine Muses at Trier and of Dionysus at Cologne, both from the fourth century.

Finally, mosaics were placed on vaults and vertical walls. We have shown an example of the former in the *Christus Apollo* on p. 262, and there are many Dionysian derivatives in the vault mosaics of the fourth-century church of Santa Constanza in Rome. A good example of a fountain mosaic is one of Neptune and Amphitrite in the house called by their names at Herculaneum, dating from a few years before the eruption of Vesuvius in A.D. 79.

Painting

Many mosaics were derived from Roman paintings, a genre that has been damaged far more than mosaics over the centuries. Best known are the wall paintings from the private houses in Pompeii and Herculaneum, all dating from before the eruption of Vesuvius, and some paintings in Rome. Among the latter is a wall painting of Apollo as a musician, found on the Palatine Hill not far from the house of Augustus, which stood close to the complex of the temple of Apollo on the Palatine Hill.[15] Holding his lyre, the god is seated against a bright blue background, reminding us that Greek and Roman temples, sculpture, and painting were full of color. To people not used to the brilliant light of the Mediterranean basin, the bright colors of, for example, pediment sculpture on Greek and Roman temples would appear garish, whereas they were appropriate for the bright southern sunlight. In a house on the Esquiline Hill in Rome is a long, painted frieze depicting scenes from Books 10 and 11 of the *Odyssey*.

Odysseus (or Roman Ulysses) and the Sirens. Third-century A.D. mosaic from Dougga in Algeria. Odysseus, tied to the mast, turns to gaze upon the Sirens, seduced by their alluring song. His comrades, whose ears have been stopped with wax to prevent them from hearing and becoming bewitched, face the opposite direction, intent on rowing past the danger that the Sirens represent. According to Homer, the Sirens (depicted here with birds' feet and wings) know all that happens upon earth, and sailors who are tempted by this knowledge row too close and are dashed upon the rocks. This mosaic, from North Africa and dated to the Roman imperial period, testifies to the widespread and abiding appeal of Homer's epics. (*Erich Lessing/Art Resource, NY*)

The events are set in a continuous landscape, so that the human figures are but one contributing element in the larger scene. These paintings date from around the middle of the first century B.C.

Mythological subjects are very common in the surviving wall paintings from Pompeii and other sites in Campania. Some are religious, such as the continuous painting of the initiation into the mysteries of Dionysus in the **Villa of the Mysteries**, contemporary with the *Odyssey* paintings in Rome. Some wealthy owners could afford to fill every wall of a room in their house with mythological scenes. This was the case in Pompeii with the **House of the Vettii**, who were probably two successful merchants who redecorated their house after the earthquake of A.D. 62, not long before the disaster of 79. In one room there were large paintings with mythological subjects on each wall, the principal one being Theseus after killing the Minotaur (nine other versions of this subject from Roman houses and public buildings have survived). Elsewhere in the same house were paintings of the infant Hercules strangling two snakes and of Pirithoüs and the centaurs. Other houses at Pompeii held many other mythological paintings depicting scenes such as the rescue of Andromeda, the fall of Icarus, Polyphemus and Galatea, and Pyramus and Thisbe. A painting of Pan discovering both sexual attributes of Hermaphroditus and reacting with horrified surprise is unique. From nearby Herculaneum, also buried in the disaster of A.D. 79, is a large painting of Phaedra and Hippolytus in which the Nurse is revealing Phaedra's love to Hippolytus; this painting derives ultimately from Euripides' tragedy *Hippolytus*. A painting in Pompeii of Dionysus robed in grapes, with a stylized Vesuvius in the background and vineyards growing on its slopes, shows how religion, mythology, and the local economy all intersected.

There were also plenty of erotic paintings and small sculptured figures, usually showing Venus with either Cupid or Priapus, while the latter with his enormous phallus was found in gardens and frequently in *tintinnabula* (decorated hanging chimes). In general, then, Greek mythology flourished in the decoration of Roman houses, reflecting the education and tastes of their owners, as well as their religious beliefs and superstitions. Whether or not the paintings and other objects were the work of Greek artists is a subject that excites art historians. What is important for us is that the patrons of the artists were Romans and that their houses and public buildings were Roman.

Other Media

Greek mythology also was quite common in the luxury arts, that is, articles made of precious materials such as silver or gold, engraved glassware, or painted pottery.[16] Besides the Fishbourne amethyst mentioned previously, we show here the Corbridge *lanx* (dish), a silver dish made in the third century A.D. and found by the river Tyne in northern Britain in the eighteenth century. Its decoration is religious in nature, showing Apollo, Artemis (Diana), and their mother Leto (Latona), along with other figures. Who owned it or where it came from is not known, but it is evidence for the continued patronage of mythological subjects in a distant Roman province.

An exceptional, indeed unique, example of the Roman luxury arts is the glass cage cup, now in the British Museum, depicting the punishment of Lycurgus, king of Thrace. In the version of the myth on the cup, Lycurgus tried to attack

The Corbridge Lanx. 15 × 21 in.; late fourth century A.D. A lanx is a dish or platter; this one, made of an expensive metal (silver), was intended for display rather than use, unlike the lanx that holds the fruit and other offerings on the round altar below the seated figure. Apollo is shown on the right standing in front of his shrine and holding his bow in his left hand, while his lyre lies beside his left foot. On the left Diana enters dressed as a huntress, her bow unstrung. Facing her, with a gesture indicating that she intends to speak, is Minerva, next to whom is Latona. The seated figure, who seems to be holding a distaff, may be Latona's sister Ortygia or perhaps the Pythia. (It is also possible that Latona is the seated figure and Ortygia is the standing one.) In the lower register, Diana's hound is to the left, and a wounded stag appears in the center. To the right is a gryphon, a mythical animal said by Herodotus to guard the gold of the peoples of Scythia (Russia) and described by Aeschylus as "the sharp-beaked silent dogs of Zeus." The edges are decorated with alternating bunches of grapes and leaves. This lanx is perhaps the most important witness to the continued interest in Greek mythology in the late Roman Empire. It was made in a Mediterranean city, perhaps Alexandria, and we can only guess who brought it to Corstopitum (Corbridge), a garrison town on Hadrian's Wall in Britain. (© *The Trustees of the British Museum/Art Resource, NY*)

the maenad Ambrosia, who was changed into a vine that twined itself around the king. On the viewer's left is the figure of Ambrosia, and on the right a satyr who is about to throw a rock at Lycurgus.

Greek Mythology and Roman Literature

Greek Phlyakes and Atellane Farces

One of the most frequent features of the art of Pompeii are tragic and comic masks and little terra cotta masks (*oscilla*, "little mouths") made to swing in the wind, as well as tragic or comic actors preparing to perform, and occasionally representations of scenes from Greek tragedy or comedy, such as the scene from Euripides' *Hippolytus*. Theatrical performances were a common feature of

Roman culture, not only in large urban theaters but also in less formal performances in villages and country towns. Tacitus mentions Nero's anger that his
prominent critic Thrasea Paetus had refused to flatter the emperor in Rome and
"had performed, dressed in tragic clothes, at his home town, Patavium."[17] The
popularity of the theater in the Roman world had its origin in the Greek cities of
Magna Graecia. Many Greek vases from southern Italy and Campania, particularly those from the fourth and third centuries B.C., depicted scenes from Greek
tragedy, one of which (from Campania) is illustrated on p. 617. Tragedy, however,
developed quite differently in Magna Graecia in the early third century B.C.,

The Lycurgus Cup. Height 6¼ in.; ca. A.D. 300. Made of glass heavily undercut to leave the figures of
Lycurgus and the other actors in high relief as a "cage" around the cup. The glass is "dichroic," that is, of
two colors: green in normal light and red when illuminated from behind. The narrative is different from
the one described in this chapter (see p. 316): Lycurgus resists Dionysus and attacks his followers, including the nymph Ambrosia, who appears just to the left of Lycurgus in this view. Either she is transformed
into a vine, which traps him, or the god makes the vine spring up and Lycurgus tries to cut it down with an
axe, which lies useless beside his left foot. Other figures (not visible in this view) are a satyr, Pan, a panther, and, on the other side, Dionysus holding his thyrsus. The gilt-bronze rim and the foot were added in
about 1800. Like the Corbridge lanx, this cup was probably made by specialist artisans available only in a
major center such as Alexandria. (© *The Trustees of the British Museum/Art Resource, NY*)

when "hilarious tragedy" (*hilarotragoedia*), that is, parodies of tragic subjects, began to be produced. These works and their actors were called *phlyakes*, a word meaning "farces" (of the works) and "comics" (of the actors). The works themselves have been almost entirely lost, but they are well known from scenes painted on the many surviving vases from Magna Graecia.[18] The actors typically wore grotesque masks and padded clothes, sometimes with a phallus attached. These phlyakes often involved musicians, dancers, and acrobats. Many of them had mythological subjects, and not even Zeus himself was spared from parody—in one scene from a representative play, he is seated helplessly on his throne while a grotesque Hercules insults him and Iolaüs pours a libation at an altar. Hercules was a very common character in phlyakes, which is not surprising given his reputation in Greek comedy for gluttony and other vices.

The phlyakes were written in Greek, and their native Italian equivalents were written in Oscan, the language of the indigenous people of southern Italy. Oscan farces, usually called **Atellane farces**, were less inventive in their subjects, and they had stock characters—the old man, the braggart, the buffoon, the glutton, and so on.[19] Even so, some Atellanes did include Greek mythological characters, including Dionysus and Hercules, and characters from Trojan saga such as Agamemnon and Andromache. Nevertheless, it was the jokes and comic action of the Atellanes, as with the phlyakes, that appealed to Roman audiences. Both kinds of farces were performed by traveling troupes of actors, who would set up a simple stage with wooden materials that they brought with them. Such a stage consisted of no more than a platform supported on wooden posts like modern four-by-fours. More elaborate stages might involve simple curtains and drapery, a flight of steps, or even a temporary stone construction. Thus the farces could be performed in small towns and rural areas, so that dramatic performances became available to a wider public than urban and relatively literate audiences. By the late fourth and early third centuries B.C., the Atellanes were being performed in Latin, and they reached Rome just as the Roman Republic was coming into close and continuous contact with Greek culture, as we have described earlier in this chapter.

Livius Andronicus

There was nothing as sophisticated as the Greek phlyakes or Oscan Atellanes in Roman Latin dramas in the early republic. They could hardly be called plays, for they were so-called Fescennine verses, which consisted, so it seems, very largely of improvised jokes and satirical comments on individuals, without any mythological content. Margaret Bieber has rightly remarked: "All later Roman plays were taken over from foreign peoples and adapted to Roman taste."[20] So Greek mythology continued to exert its influence through literary tragedies, which began to be written and produced in Latin in the mid-third century B.C., and, to a lesser extent, through Roman comedy. Only one of the twenty surviving plays of Plautus has a mythological subject—the *Amphitruo*.[21] We have mentioned earlier the capture of Tarentum in 272 B.C. and the capture there of **Livius Andronicus**, who would have been about twelve years old at the time. He was brought to Rome as a slave in one of the families of the *gens* (clan) of the Livii, which gave him his first name (his original name, Andronicus, was Greek). He was given his freedom, and in 240 B.C. he produced the first performances of a Latin tragedy and a Latin comedy, in which he himself acted. Few fragments remain of his tragedies, but the titles of eight are known, all derived from Greek saga.[22] At some point, perhaps earlier, Livius made a rough translation, or rather adaptation, of the *Odyssey* into Latin using the native Saturnian meter rather than attempting to reproduce Homeric hexameters.[23] He also translated into Latin the plays of Sophocles and Euripides. Thus he was crucial in the spread of knowledge of Greek mythology in the Roman world.

Naevius

Four early Roman poets followed Livius in composing Latin tragedies about subjects drawn from Greek mythology. Naevius was about ten or twenty years younger than Livius, and he fought in the first Punic war (i.e., war against the Carthaginians), which lasted from 264 to 241 B.C. He was a Roman citizen and wrote many comedies (of which the titles of thirty-four are known) that involved satirical attacks on prominent Romans who saw to it that he spent some time in prison and was eventually exiled, dying in Africa in 200 B.C. He wrote six tragedies on subjects drawn from several fields of Greek mythology, including a *Danaë* and a *Lycurgus*. Perhaps his most important achievement was the invention of a national epic on a subject from Roman history, the first Punic war. Like Livius, he used the Saturnian meter; the early part of the epic was to some extent mythological and divine, culminating in the capture of Troy and the departure of Aeneas and the Trojan survivors.

Ennius

The second and greatest of the four poets was **Ennius**, who lived from 239 to 169 B.C. He came from Calabria (the "heel" of Italy) and fought in the second Punic war (218–202 B.C.), coming permanently to Rome in 204 B.C. and becoming a full Roman citizen in 184 B.C. He once said that he had three hearts: an Oscan (his first language), a Greek (the language of Magna Graecia), and a Latin, the language in which he wrote his plays, lesser poems, and epic. His greatest work, written in hexameters, was his *Annals*, eighteen books narrating the second Punic war. It began with Ennius' invocation of the Muses and his dream of Homer appearing to him and telling him that he had migrated to Ennius' body. In other words, Ennius placed himself firmly in the Greek mythological tradition that derived from Homer's *Iliad*. He was the first Roman poet to write a national epic in the Homeric meter, hexameter, and the first line of his epic was an invocation to the Greek Muses, not the Latin Camenae.[24] Livius had appealed to Camena in the first line of his *Odyssey*, and Naevius said in his own epitaph that the Camenae would mourn at his death.

Ennius wrote in many genres, and fragments of twenty tragedies with subjects drawn from Greek saga are extant. Many of these fragments appear as quotations in Cicero's works, an indication that they were still known (and sometimes acted) a century after Ennius' death. Many of his subjects are drawn from the Trojan saga, but his last tragedy, produced in the last year of his life, was *Thyestes*, a significant choice, since at least two distinguished Roman plays on the same subject were produced in later times. The first was by the Augustan poet Varius, a friend of Vergil, Horace, and Maecenas. It was produced in A.D. 29, at the celebrations of Augustus' (Octavian's) victory over Antonius at Actium in A.D. 31. Despite its great success, the tragedy has been lost. Still surviving is the *Thyestes* of the younger Seneca (d. A.D. 65), showing that the saga of Atreus and

Thyestes had not lost its attraction for Roman readers and audiences more than two centuries after Ennius' production.

Finally, Ennius translated into Latin (or paraphrased) the *Sacred History* of Euhemerus.[25] Although Euhemerus of Messene (ca. 300 B.C.) was concerned with disproving the traditional views of the gods, saying that they were originally mortal heroes, he (and Ennius) needed to narrate their myths in order to disprove them. Particularly striking is his description of the death and burial of Jupiter in Crete.

Pacuvius and Accius

Pacuvius, the third of the four early poets, lived from 220 until about 130 B.C. He was a painter as well as a poet; born at Brundisium (the modern Brindisi in Puglia), he was both Oscan and Roman. At least one of his paintings was famous, included in the temple of Hercules in the Forum Boarium in Rome.[26] The titles of thirteen of his tragedies are known, and they, like those of Naevius, covered a wide range of Greek saga.

The fourth and last of the early poets, Accius (170–ca. 86 B.C.), was, like Pacuvius, much admired by Cicero, who actually met him. Like his predecessors, Accius came to Rome as an adult, for he was born at Pisaurum, a town on the Adriatic coast of Italy, and his parents were freedmen, that is, former slaves. He was producing tragedies there by 140 B.C., when he and Pacuvius (who was his friend, despite the fifty years' difference in their ages) produced plays at the same festival. Forty titles of his tragedies are known, apparently ranging over the whole of Greek saga. Horace said that Pacuvius was more of a scholar, but Accius was more lofty in style.[27]

Greek Tragedy in Rome

Thus Greek tragedy brought Greek mythology to the Romans in the Latin language. Following the epigraph to this chapter, Horace wrote: "[The untamed victorious Roman] was late in applying his intelligence to Greek manuscripts, and being at peace after the Punic wars he began to enquire what Sophocles and Thespis and Aeschylus had that was useful."[28] He goes on to describe the decline of tragedy as public entertainment in his own time (he was writing in 14 B.C.), when the "uneducated and stolid" public, in the middle of the performance of a play, demanded "a bear-show or boxers." Thus the taste for serious drama was lost, replaced by triumphal processions with their display of captive kings, treasures, and vast numbers of wild elephants displayed in the arena. If someone tried to write a serious play, "the public would think that he was telling his story to a donkey."[29] Augustus' own boast (see note 29) proves how right Horace was. It is small wonder that Ovid's tragedy *Medea* was never performed; it was much admired by its readers in antiquity and is now completely lost.

Public and Private Performance

Greek mythological performances nevertheless did continue in Rome in three forms: as private performances; as public staged entertainments; and, in the reign of Nero (A.D. 54–68), as the public performances for Nero himself (which was especially a feature of the plays of **Seneca**, which were possibly written for performance at Nero's court). As evidence of the first of these performances is the epitaph of Eucharis, a fourteen-year-old freedwoman, who died in the mid-50s: "I graced the entertainments of the nobles with my dancing, and I was the first to appear before the people in a Greek play."[30] She was an actress and a dancer, acting in mimes, the stage presentations that displaced the tragedies of the second century A.D. These could be serious in their subject matter, especially when staged as private performances before an educated audience, but the popular mime was a public staged entertainment closer in its cruelty and vulgarity to the entertainments that Augustus enjoyed and Horace criticized. We have described previously (p. 590) the fate of Icarus at such an entertainment, and plenty of executions, crucifixions, and mutilations of condemned criminals were presented as mimes of stories from Greek myths. Perhaps the most detailed account of such a myth is related toward the end of the *Metamorphoses* (better known as the *Golden Ass*) of Apuleius, written in about A.D. 160.[31] Lucius, in the form of a donkey, is about to be forced to copulate on stage at Corinth with a criminal woman in a parody of the story of Pasiphaë, which we have related previously (p. 589). By this time, the mimes were very elaborate in their scenery and accompanying music and dancing. The scenery included a wooden mountain like the Homeric Ida; waterfalls and flowing streams; grass meadows with goats grazing like those in the Phrygian Paris' flock; and dancers impersonating Greek gods (with their Latin names) such as Mercury, Jupiter, Minerva, and, above all, Venus, naked except for a diaphanous skirt. Such was the fate of Greek mythology in the Roman world.

One public and two private performances of myth illustrate the extremes to which Roman taste could go, even among the aristocratic classes. Lucius Munatius Plancus, who became consul in 42 B.C. and censor in 22 B.C. during the reign of Augustus, "painted in blue and naked, his head bound with a garland of reeds and dragging a fish-tail, danced the role of Glaucus at a banquet."[32] In 41 B.C., Antony summoned Cleopatra from Egypt to Tarsus (in Cilicia). In a scene famously described by Plutarch and Shakespeare, Antony sat enthroned in the city as Dionysus, while Cleopatra, decked out as Aphrodite, sailed to meet him in her barge.[33] Finally, Messalina, the young wife of the emperor Claudius, privately went through a kind of *hieros gamos* (sacred marriage) with Silius, the young man who was about to become consul, while Claudius was away from Rome. She performed as Ariadne and her ladies-in-waiting as maenads, while Silius was Dionysus. When they realized that Claudius was returning, the orgy ended, and both Messalina and Silius were soon executed.[34]

Catullus and the New Poets

The change in the tastes and behavior of the Roman upper classes from the old-fashioned virtues of dignity, hard work, and strict discipline took place in the last years of the Roman Republic, at the time when Epicharis was dancing and Plancus was acting as Glaucus. Whether those virtues ever were as strictly observed as conservative critics like Cicero claim is debatable. What is certain is that at this time a new type of poetry began to be written that was derived from the third-century B.C. poets of Alexandria, a Greek city despite its location in Egypt. Cicero in the 80s B.C. had translated into Latin hexameters the poem of the Alexandrian Aratus called *Phaenomena*, but his pedestrian poetry was soon eclipsed by the truly inspired poetry of Catullus, Calvus, and their friends. Cicero scornfully called these men New Poets (*poetae novi*, among other epithets), and new they were. Catullus, however, achieved a much more powerful re-creation of Greek myth in his sixty-fourth poem, ostensibly about the wedding of Peleus and Thetis, but containing the brilliant narrative of the myth of Ariadne and Theseus (see pp. 583–585).

Ovid

Catullus, then, was a necessary step in the literary development of Greek myths at Rome, preparing the way for the greatest poet in this field, Ovid (43 B.C.–A.D. 17).[35] Ovid is by far the most important classical author for the transmission of Greek, Roman, and Near Eastern legends. His imaginative and narrative powers combined with his (often unappreciated) rhetorical skill are unique. Furthermore, he is set apart from other ancient poets (approached perhaps only by Euripides) in his deep sympathy with the emotions and suffering of his characters, especially young women who are raped by stronger males, human and divine. Thus, except for the *Iliad* and the *Odyssey*, his poems have been dominant in transmitting the classical legends to the medieval, Renaissance, and modern worlds. Indeed, there was a period in the later Middle Ages, between the thirteenth and fifteenth centuries, that has been described as an *aetas Ovidiana*, an age when Ovid was supreme among the ancient poets.

In his early poetry (particularly in the elegiac poems known as the **Amores (Loves)**, Ovid used mythological legends more for decorative or allusive purposes. Here is part of his description of watching the races as he sits in the stands with his girlfriend (*Amores* 3.2.27–32):

> Your cloak has dropped close to the ground: pick it up—or (look!) I'm picking it up with my own hands! Oh, you jealous cloak, to cloak such lovely legs. And the closer one looks—oh, what a jealous cloak! These legs are like those of speedy Atalanta which Milanion longed to lift with his own hands. These legs are like those of Diana in pictures where she is pursuing powerful animals, herself more powerful.

Later Ovid composed the **Heroides**, fifteen letters from mythological heroines to their absent lovers, to which he added three pairs of letters in which the lovers replied. In these poems, Ovid displayed his understanding of women in love and of the hardships of separation. Some of the heroines, like Penelope or Helen, were already well known from epic and drama. Others, such as Oenone, loved by Paris before he fell in love with Helen, owe their survival in later literature to the *Heroides* (e.g., Tennyson's poem *Oenone*). In a later revision of the *Amores*, Ovid tells how writing about the unhappy loves of these heroines was an alternative to being a teacher of the arts of love (*Amores* 2.18.19–25):

> I write what I am allowed [by my girlfriend] to write. Either I teach the arts of tender Love (alas, I suffer from my own precepts!), or I compose Penelope's letter to Ulysses, or I write of your tears, deserted Phyllis, or words that Paris and Macareus and ungrateful Jason and Hippolytus and his father [Theseus] may read, or words to be spoken by unhappy Dido as she holds the drawn sword.

Here is one story that comes from the Aegean island of Ceos (*Heroides* 20 and 21). **Cydippe**, a Cean girl, was loved by **Acontius**, who was not her social equal. Unable to approach her and declare his love, he left in her path an apple, on which were inscribed the words, "I swear before Artemis to marry only Acontius." She picked it up and read the words out loud, thus binding herself by the vow. Each time her parents found a suitable husband for her, she fell so ill that she could not be married. Eventually the truth was revealed, and she and Acontius were united.

In A.D. 8, Ovid was exiled by Augustus to Tomis (the modern city of Costanza in Romania), and he spent the rest of his life there. When he left Rome, he had almost completed work on the *Metamorphoses*, and he had completed the first six books of the *Fasti* (**Calendar**), a poem on the festivals and customs in the Roman calendar, which he organized by months, one book to each month. Ovid allowed the mythological characters to speak for themselves, often in response to an inquiry from the poet. Here, for example, is his conversation with **Flora**, the Italian fertility goddess of flowering. Her festival, the Floralia, lasted from April 28 until May 3 and was full of cheerful festivities and indecent mimes in the theater at Rome. Ovid speaks to her (*Fasti* 5.191–195):

> "Tell me yourself who you are. What men say is unreliable: you will be the best authority to tell of your name." That is what I said, and this is the reply of the goddess to my request (and while she spoke her mouth breathed springtime roses). "I used to be called Chloris, but my name now is Flora."

She tells the story of her rape by and marriage to **Zephyrus** (god of the west wind) and describes her garden and the flowers that grow there, which are mythological figures who were turned into flowers (*Fasti* 5.209–230):

> I have a fertile garden in the lands that are my wedding gift, filled with noble flowers by my husband, who said, "Be ruler, O goddess, over flowers." As soon as the dewy frost is shaken from the leaves . . . the Hours come together clothed in many colors and gather my flowers in light baskets. Then come the Graces twining flowers into garlands. . . . I was the first to make a flower from the blood of the boy from Therapnae [Hyacinthus]. . . . You too, Narcissus, keep your name in my well-tended garden. . . . And need I tell of Crocus and Attis and Adonis, the son of Cinyras, from whose wounds I caused the flowers to spring that honor them?

Cydippe, by Paulus Bor (ca. 1600–1669); ca. 1640. Cydippe holds the apple with its fateful inscription. True to Ovid's narrative, the artist represents Cydippe as a well-to-do young woman. The identification with Cydippe (which is certain) was not made until 1981: before then, a number of scholars made wild guesses, the least unlikely of which was "Mythological Figure, perhaps Pomona." The errors are an example of what can happen when readers neglect the painter's literary source, in this case, Ovid's Heroides. (*Rijksmuseum, Amsterdam (CC0 1.0)*)

The Kingdom of Flora, by Nicolas Poussin (1594–1665); oil on canvas, 1631, 52½ × 72½ in. Ovid's description in the Fasti (translated previously) is the basis of Poussin's exquisite evocation of Spring and the regenerative power of flowers (symbolized by the floral cornucopia in the left foreground). In the center Flora dances, clothed in a green chiton and accompanied by four putti (a fifth lies in the lower right corner), as she pours dew over her garden. In the heavens above, Apollo drives the chariot of the sun, and on the left is a herm of Priapus, god of gardens. The other figures are of mortals (other than the nymph opposite Narcissus) who were turned into flowers: from the left, Ajax falling on his sword, Clytie looking up to Apollo, Narcissus with a nymph holding the urn of water in which he sees his reflection, the overeager lovers Crocus and Smilax, and (behind them) Adonis and his hounds, showing the wound in his thigh, and, to his left, Hyacinthus, whose left hand points to the fatal wound in his head. The garden is set in a landscape bounded on the left by rocks and an urn from which water overflows, and in the center and right by a pergola wreathed in flowers. (*Erich Lessing/Art Resource, NY*)

Here Ovid uses Greek mythology to give substance to the Italian fertility goddess. The Greek figures of the Hours (*Horae,* or "Seasons"), the Graces (*Charites*), and the youths who were changed into flowers give a narrative element to Flora, creating a Roman mythology from Greek stories. Ovid's description of the garden of Flora was the inspiration for Nicolas Poussin's famous painting *The Kingdom of Flora*, in which he has gathered six of the young men and women who were changed into flowers.

The *Metamorphoses*

Ovid's *Metamorphoses* was an epic written in the epic meter, hexameters. Ovid had before him Vergil's *Aeneid* (Vergil had died in 19 B.C.), and he clearly sets forth his intention to create an epic to rival Vergil's. These are the opening four lines:[36]

> I am moved to tell of forms changed into new bodies. Gods, inspire the work I have begun (for you have changed this too), and finely weave my continuous poem from the very beginning of the world to my own times!

The words "continuous poem" (*perpetuum carmen*) mean that he is composing an epic. However, he also alludes to the desire, under the influence of the Hellenistic scholar-poet Callimachus, that poetry should be finely wrought. He intends this poem to be a different kind of epic from those of his predecessors (Vergil's being the most recent and most distinguished). Thus, at the very beginning of this remarkable work, Ovid has displayed a metamorphosis of his own. Ovid will create a new kind of poem by joining together epic form and the more congenial amatory themes of his earlier poetry. Ovid's epic contains about 250 metamorphoses, several of which we have related earlier, such as those of Apollo and Daphne (pp. 253–255) and Artemis and Actaeon (pp. 221–223). More than in his earlier poems, his psychological sensitivity in the *Metamorphoses* is exquisite. The poem is distinguished also by its visual quality—its descriptions of forests, pools, mountains, and other features—which are of great beauty in themselves but are also the setting for violent and tragic events. The metamorphoses, usually into a tree, a bird, a stone, a river, or some other natural object, do little to diminish Ovid's basic humanity. The final metamorphosis is that of the poet himself, in the last nine lines of the poem (15.871–879):

> Now I have completed a work which neither the anger of Jupiter nor fire nor gnawing age can destroy. When it wants to, let that day, which only has power over my body, put an end to the uncertain period of my life. With the better part of myself I shall rise above the stars, eternal, and my name will never be erased. Wherever Roman power is spread over conquered peoples, I shall be read by the people, and with fame for all ages, if the prophecies of bards have any truth, I shall live.

In the 130 lines before this passage, Ovid speaks at length of the deification of Julius Caesar and the future deification of Augustus—but it is clear who he believes most deserves to be deified! Similarly, Apollo is, as it were, reduced to size in the first extended narrative of metamorphosis, the story of Daphne. What was Augustus to think, after his magnification of Apollo on the Palatine?

Ovid gathered his stories from many Greek, Italian, and Near Eastern sources, few of which can now be identified. From his 250 stories we tell two here as illustrations of local legends that he wove into the tapestry of his universal poem.

> ***Pomona and Vertumnus.*** Pomona was an Italian fertility goddess, the goddess of fruit that can be picked from trees. She, like Flora, had no myths of her own, so Ovid linked her to an Etruscan god, Vertumnus, whose name is connected with the Latin word *vortere*, meaning both "to turn" and "to change." Pomona had a garden from which she excluded her lovers, among them Vertumnus, who could

Vertumnus and Pomona, by Jan Tengnagel (1584–1635); oil on copper, 1617, 8½ × 11½ in. In this tiny painting, Pomona is a working gardener, seated on a wheelbarrow with her tools beside her, as she listens to Vertumnus quite skeptically. The gates of her walled garden (hortus inclusus) are closed, a symbol of virginity. But her sickle is reversed (in many paintings of the story, the sickle points threateningly at Vertumnus), and the broken pot in the foreground, with the peacock and dolphin in the background, hint that Vertumnus' speech is having some effect. He gestures to the elm tree and vine behind him, the final parable that will persuade Pomona. Even the hem of Pomona's skirt, which shows the zodiacal signs of spring and summer, indicates that she, like her garden, will be fruitful. (*Rijksmuseum, Amsterdam (CC0 1.0)*)

> change himself into different shapes. Disguised as an old woman, he approached her and advised her to marry Vertumnus. His advice included the cautionary tale of Iphis and Anaxarete (which we narrate in "Additional Reading: Stories from Ovid's Metamorphoses"), and he was so successful that he resumed his natural appearance as a young man and won Pomona's love (Metamorphoses 14.623–771).

Pyramus and Thisbe.   Although Ovid makes Babylon the setting for the story of Pyramus and Thisbe, its origin was probably Cilicia in southern Asia Minor, since the river Pyramus was there and the name Thisbe was variously associated with springs in Cilicia or Cyprus. Pyramus and Thisbe were next-door neighbors in Babylon, forbidden by their parents to marry or even to meet each other. They conversed through a crack in the common wall of their houses and arranged to meet at the tomb of Ninus outside the city. Thisbe arrived first, only to be frightened by a lioness that had come to drink at a nearby fountain. As she fled, she dropped her veil, which the lioness mangled with her jaws, bloodstained from a recent kill. Pyramus came and found the footprints of the lioness and the bloodstained veil. He concluded that the lioness had eaten Thisbe and fell on his sword. As he lay dying, Thisbe returned and in grief killed herself with the same sword. They lay together in death beneath a mulberry tree, whose

Pyramus and Thisbe. Mosaic from the House of Dionysus in Nea Paphos, Cyprus; end of third century A.D. Pyramus (whose name, like Thisbe's, is given in Greek capital letters) is clearly a river-god, shown by his reclining position, the wreath of reeds round his head, and the water flowing out of the jar under his left arm. In his right hand he holds a cornucopia and in his left a reed. On the other side, Thisbe is running away, while a lioness (said also to be a leopardess) in the center is mauling part of a garment, presumably Thisbe's. This mosaic is a remarkable conflation of the two versions of the legend. (*HIP/Art Resource, NY*)

fruit, which before had been white, henceforth was black, in answer to Thisbe's dying prayer that it be a memorial of the tragedy (*Metamorphoses* 4.55–166).

This is one of Ovid's most beautifully told stories, of which a paraphrase is at best a pale reflection. Shakespeare used the structure of the tale for the main plot of *A Midsummer Night's Dream*, with its meetings outside the city and lovers' errors. Countless people have enjoyed Shakespeare's hilarious yet pathetic burlesque of the tale, presented by the "rude mechanicals" in the last act of the play.

After Ovid

The zenith of Roman literary interaction with Greek mythology was reached in Ovid. Greek mythology certainly continued to be prominent in epic but was less so (as far as can be known) in other types of poetry. **Quintilian**, in his *Institutio Oratoria* (*Education of the Orator*, written in the early 90s A.D.), sets out the necessary reading for the future orator in both Greek and Roman authors, beginning with Homer (*Institutio Oratoria* 10.1.46). He makes it clear that knowledge of mythology was necessary for the educated speaker—"part of the basic cultural minimum for educated Greeks and Romans under the empire." Even **Lucan** (A.D. 38–65), the only major poet to avoid the gods and other trappings of mythology, inserted a long digression on Hercules and Antaeus in his epic *Bellum Civile*.[37] Other writers of epic, however, inspired particularly by Vergil, continued to make mythology an essential part of their poems.

The most important of these writers is **Statius** (ca. A.D. 50–96), who produced two epic poems, *Thebaid* and the unfinished *Achilleid*, on mythological subjects.[38] The *Thebaid* is especially important, since it is the most complete narrative incorporating the many legends concerning Thebes, and it was widely read and admired in the Middle Ages. Statius himself was diffident about his poetic powers: in the final lines of the poem (12.810–819), he acknowledges that he "follows far behind the divine *Aeneid*." He does not do himself justice, for his style and his way of incorporating the gods into his complex narrative are different, as Dante knew when he made Statius, as an *anima naturaliter Christiana*, succeed Vergil as his guide through Purgatorio and Paradiso. Besides the obvious battle scenes of the Seven against Thebes, Statius brings out the distress of Antigone after the battle, in this following Sophocles. We have noted (p. 422) the scene in which Antigone adds the corpse of Polynices (which Creon had ordered to be left on the battlefield) to the still-warm pyre on which Eteocles had been burned. Here is some of that scene (*Thebaid* 12.429–443):

> Here again are the brothers! As soon as the consuming fire touched the limbs [of Polynices] the pyre shook and tried to drive away the newly added body. The flames swell up divided, and the two tongues of flame flash with intermittent light. . . . Antigone, appalled, cried out: "I have failed, and I have increased their anger [i.e., of Eteocles and Polynices], which used my hands as its agent! He [Polynices] was my brother. . . . Their hateful enmity lives on, it lives! War has achieved nothing. Unhappy [brothers], as you fight, so Creon is the victor!"

None of this is in Sophocles, who has Antigone throw dust over the corpse as a symbolic burial and then perish in the cave. Moreover, Creon, who in Sophocles acts as a tyrant in his palace, only to repent too late, in Statius is killed by Theseus.

Lucan and Statius are the most important poets to succeed Vergil. Far behind them in power are their near-contemporaries **Valerius Flaccus** and Silius Italicus. Valerius, who died sometime between the eruption of Vesuvius in A.D. 79 and the death of Domitian in A.D. 96, composed an epic *Argonautica*, that is, the story of Jason and the Golden Fleece. It breaks off with Medea's passionate appeal to Jason not to hand her over to her brother Apsyrtus.[39] Valerius certainly was following the Greek epic *Argonautica* of Apollonius of Rhodes, but not slavishly. We cannot know how far he was influenced by the earlier translation into Latin of Apollonius by Varro of Atax, an author from the Roman province of Gallia Narbonensis born in 82 B.C., whose *Argonautae* is almost entirely lost. In the opening lines, Valerius focuses on the *Argo*, which was the first ship to open up the world to future sailors (*Argonautica* 1.1–4):

> My poem is about the narrow seas first traveled by the heroic sons of gods and the prophetic ship, which dared to sail to the land of Scythian Phasis, and speedily made its course between high rocks.

This is important for Valerius' view of the significance of the first sea voyage ever made, for it made possible the discovery of new lands, new trade, and new wealth. This is confirmed by the prophecy of Jupiter at *Argonautica* 1.533–560, imitating Jupiter's prophecy in the *Aeneid*, part of which we translate later (p. 677). Jupiter foresees the coming of war following the spread of humankind over the seas, but also the attainment of wealth and empire. He concludes that he himself will find out "which empire I shall wish to rule most widely over all peoples," a clear reference to the Roman empire of Valerius' own time.

Silius Italicus was the only Roman epic poet to have had a distinguished public career. He was made consul in A.D. 68 and proconsul of Asia nine years

Hercules Killing the Hydra. The Via Latina catacomb, discovered in 1955, contained both pagan and Christian burials. Hercules could have belonged to either category, as the pagan hero who achieved immortality or as a parable for Christians of virtuous struggles in life leading to life eternal. (*Scala/Art Resource, NY*)

later. His epic **Punica** is the longest Roman poem ever written, at over 12,000 lines spread over seventeen books. Unlike Lucan, he includes the gods, especially Juno, who in the very first lines of the poem recalls Dido's curse (which we translate on p. 679) invoking undying hostility between Carthage and Rome. Her words inflame Hannibal, and so the second Punic war begins. Critics have not been kind to Silius' divine interventions; especially feeble is Jupiter, despite being *pater omnipotens* (omnipotent father, 3.163), who first appears in Book 3, when he sends Mercury to incite Hannibal in a dream. Vergil had succeeded in the difficult task of involving the gods in a historical epic, but Silius was not equal to the challenge. So let us conclude, as he does, with a double mythological simile for Scipio Africanus as he enjoys his Triumph, the colorful procession of the victorious general, dressed as a god, through the heart of Rome, ending at the temple of Jupiter Optimus Maximus on the Capitoline Hill (*Punica* 17.646–651):

> He [Scipio], standing in his chariot and decorated in gold and purple showed his martial face for the Roman people to see. He was like Liber [Dionysus] when he comes from India, driving his chariot decorated with vine-leaves and drawn by tigers. Or he was like the Tirynthian [Hercules] marching over the Phlegraean plains when he had finished the huge task of killing the giants, his head touching the stars.[40]

With Silius we end our survey of Greek mythology in the Roman world. This mythology continued to be used after the end of the Roman Empire, enduring through the early Middle Ages (although in a much-attenuated form), revived in the Italian Renaissance, and transmitted, still vital, to our own time. The early Christians made use of it, and the sarcophagus illustrated on page 298 (which possibly could have been Christian, since there were Christian sarcophagi in the same tomb) is decorated with the myths of Dionysus. In the catacomb by the Via Latina outside Rome, there is a painting of Hercules clubbing the Hydra. Hercules could easily be transmitted to Christian art as a symbol of virtue triumphing over evil or of the human soul attaining immortality, just as Hercules became divine after his labors. Then there is the extraordinary conjunction of Christian and pagan narratives in the mosaic of Christus Apollo (see p. 262). Boethius, imprisoned for treason in A.D. 523–524, used classical mythology in his *Consolation of Philosophy* to encourage himself and attain the ability to reason in the face of adversity.

Additional Reading: Stories from Ovid's *Metamorphoses*

Ovid tells more than 200 legends in his epic *Metamorphoses*. We have chosen 7 to summarize here, adding translations of Ovid's texts on the accompanying website [www.oup.com/us/morford].

Crocus and Smilax

Ovid gives only one line (*Metamorphoses* 4.283) to Crocus and Smilax, having named Crocus briefly in Flora's speech (mentioned previously) in the *Fasti*. He says that they were turned into "tiny flowers," and the encyclopedic Pliny the Elder said that Smilax could not win the love of Crocus and was turned into the plant *smilax*. George Sandys, whose translation of Ovid's *Metamorphoses* was published in 1632, one year after Poussin's painting of *The Kingdom of Flora*, gives the story that was Poussin's inspiration: "*Crocus* and *Smilax*, mutually beloued of each other, when they could not inioy their affections were turned into flowers which preserue their names." Sandys then quotes a passage from an obscure Latin poet, Sabaeus, telling how Smilax could have replaced Hebe, and Crocus Ganymede, as cupbearers to Zeus and Hera. However, they were turned into flowers "as fragrant now as their desires were flagrant." In fact, the *crocus* was the source of saffron, an important herb for gourmet cooking in Rome (as it still is to this day), and the *smilax* was a thorny vine often confused with ivy but in fact useless for garlands (here Poussin bends the facts to give Smilax an ivy wreath).

Ceyx and Alcyone

Ceyx was king of Trachis (in central Greece) and son of Eosphoros (Lucifer, the Morning Star), and his wife was Alcyone, daughter of Aeolus. They called themselves Zeus and Hera and were punished by being turned into sea-birds. Ovid made them into romantic lovers (*Metamorphoses* 11.270–748). Ceyx left Trachis

Landscape for Philemon and Baucis, by David Ligare (b. 1945); oil on canvas, 1984, 32 × 48 in. The cottage of Baucis and Philemon has become a temple, while the two spouses have been transformed into the intertwined trees on the right. The lake conceals the homes of the villagers who were so inhospitable to Zeus and Hermes. The size of the trees and the ruinous state of the temple indicate that the metamorphosis took place long ago. (*Wadsworth Atheneum Museum of Art/Art Resource, NY*)

on a sea voyage and drowned during a storm. Alcyone, left behind in Trachis, learned of her husband's death in a dream. She found his corpse washed up on the shore, and in her grief she became a sea-bird. As she flew by the corpse and touched it, it came to life and became a bird. For seven days each winter Aeolus forbids the winds to blow while the halcyon (*alcyone*) sits on the eggs in her nest as it floats upon the waves.

Atalanta and Milanion

Atalanta was daughter of the Arcadian Iasus. She was a virgin huntress who as a baby was exposed by her father and nurtured by a bear that suckled her until some hunters found her and brought her up. Once grown, she was recognized by her father, but she refused to let him give her away in marriage unless her suitor could beat her in a footrace. Those who lost were executed. After many young men had died in the attempt, Milanion (also called Hippomenes) raced her. He had three golden apples given him by Aphrodite. These he dropped one by one during the race to delay Atalanta. So he won the race and his wife, but in their impatience, they made love in a sacred place (a precinct of either Zeus or Cybele), and for this sacrilege, they were turned into a lion and a lioness (*Metamorphoses* 10.560–707).[41]

Anaxarete and Iphis

In the Cypriot city of Salamis lived Anaxarete, who scorned her lover Iphis. In despair, he hanged himself at the door of her house, yet she still showed no pity. As she was watching his funeral procession pass her house, she was turned into stone. Ovid says that her stone figure became the cult statue of Venus at Salamis, with the title of *Venus Prospiciens* (Venus the Beholder). This was the story told by Vertumnus to Pomona that persuaded her to yield to him (*Metamorphoses* 14.698–761).

Iphis and Ianthe

Crete is the setting for the story of Iphis, daughter of Ligdus (and different from the boy Iphis who loved Anaxarete). Ligdus ordered her mother, Telethusa, to expose the baby if it proved to be a girl. Encouraged by a vision of the goddess Isis, Telethusa kept the baby girl, giving her a name suitable for either a boy or a girl and dressing her like a boy. Thus deceived, Ligdus betrothed Iphis to another girl, Ianthe, whom Iphis did indeed come to love. On the night before they were to be married, Telethusa prayed to Isis to pity Iphis and Ianthe (for Ianthe did not yet know the real sex of her lover), and the goddess in answer turned Iphis into a boy, who next day married his Ianthe (*Metamorphoses* 8.666–797).

Baucis and Philemon

From Phrygia comes the legend of Baucis and Philemon, a poor and pious old couple who unwittingly entertained Zeus and Hermes in their cottage. The gods, who had not been received kindly by anyone else on their visit to the earth, saved Baucis and Philemon from the flood with which they punished the rest of Phrygia, and their cottage became the gods' temple. Being granted one wish each, they prayed that they might together be priest and priestess of the shrine and die together. And so it happened: full of years, they simultaneously turned into trees, an oak and a linden (*Metamorphoses* 8.617–724).

Byblis and Caunus

Byblis, daughter of Miletus, fell in love with her brother Caunus. Unable either to forget her love or to declare it, she wrote a letter to Caunus confessing it. In horror, Caunus left Miletus (the city named after their father), and Byblis followed him. Still unable to fulfill her desire, she sank to the ground in exhaustion and became a fountain that was called by her name (*Metamorphoses* 9.454–665).

Select Bibliography

Buxton, Richard. *Forms of Astonishment: Greek Myths of Metamorphosis*. New York: Oxford University Press, 2009.

Fantham, Elaine. *Ovid's Metamorphoses*. New York: Oxford University Press, 2004.

Feeney, D. C. The Gods in Epic. Oxford: Clarendon Press, 1991.

Galinsky, G. Karl. *Ovid's Metamorphoses: An Introduction to the Basic Aspects*. Berkeley, CA: University of California Press, 1975.

Henig, Martin, ed. *A Handbook of Roman Art*. Ithaca, NY: Cornell University Press, 1983.

Hulley, Karl K., and Stanley T. Vandersall. *Ovid's Metamorphosis*. Lincoln, NE: University of Nebraska Press, 1970.

Martindale, Charles, ed. *Ovid Renewed: Ovidian Influences on Literature and Art from the Middle Ages to the Twentieth Century*. New York: Cambridge University Press, 1988. A collection of essays on different aspects of Ovid's afterlife.

Sandys, George. *Ovid's Metamorphosis*. Oxford, 1632. Online version, edited by Daniel Kinney, available from the University of Virginia's e-text program, *The Renaissance Reception of Ovid in Image and Text*.

Wilkinson, L. P. *Ovid Recalled*. Cambridge: Cambridge University Press, 1955. Abridged paperback, *Ovid Surveyed*. After fifty years, this is still the most urbane discussion of Ovid's poetry in any language.

Primary Sources

Sources in the Chapter

Horace	*Epistles* 2.1.161–163
Ovid	*Amores* 2.18.19–26; 3.2.27–32
	Fasti 5.191–195, 209–230
	Metamorphoses 1.1–4 (Proem); 4.55–166 (Pyramus and Thisbe); 14.623–771 (Pomona and Vertumnus); 15.871–879 (Ovid and his survival)
Propertius	*Elegies* 2.31.1–16
Silius Italicus	*Punica* 17.646–651
Statius	*Thebaid* 12.429–443
Valerius Flaccus	*Argonautica* 1.1–4

Additional Sources

Apollodorus	*Library* 1.7.4 (Ceyx); 3.9.2 (Atalanta)
Apuleius	*Metamorphoses* or *The Golden Ass*
Catullus	Poem 64
Lucan	*Bellum Civile*
Ovid	*Amores*
	Heroides
	Fasti
	Metamorphoses
Seneca	Tragedies: *Hercules Furens, Hercules Oetaeus, Medea,*
	Oedipus, Phaedra, Phoenissae, Thyestes, Troades
Statius	*Thebaid*
Valerius Flaccus	*Argonautica*

Notes

1. Since Tarentum was captured a second time by the Romans in 209 B.C. (from the Carthaginians), some people have wrongly dated the arrival of Livius Andronicus in Rome to 209 B.C.
2. Seventy-three temples are listed in Filippo Coarelli's standard *Guida Archaeologica di Roma* of 1974. Augustus himself boasted that he had restored eighty-two temples in Rome (*Res Gestae*, 20.4).
3. See p. 540.
4. Vergil, *Aeneid*, 10.496–500, 12.941–952. *Res Gestae* 3 and 25 (for the war against Antony and Cleopatra), 13 (for the end of wars), and 27 (for Egypt).
5. Horace, *Odes* 4.6.1–2; see pp. 220–221.
6. See pp. 177–182.
7. See pp. 589–592; Martial, 1.5 and 1.8; Suetonius, *Nero* 12.
8. Homer, *Odyssey* 12.73–126. Suetonius, *Tiberius* 39; and Tacitus, *Annals* 4.59 for the cave-in. The sculptures were said by Pliny the Elder to have been made by the same artists as those who carved the *Laocoon*.
9. See p. 671.
10. Suetonius, *Nero* 53. Nero already believed that he was the equal of Apollo in song and of the Sun as a charioteer. Emulating Hercules was to be his climactic triumph.
11. See p. 668, where Horace, *Odes* 1.10, is translated.
12. Described in Barry Cunliffe, *Fishbourne* (London: Thames & Hudson, 1971), p. 208 and plate 67.
13. R. R. R. Smith, in the *Journal of Roman Studies* 77 (1987): 88–138, with plates III–XXVI, p. 97 quoted. A selection of the many publications about Aphrodisias is given in the article *Aphrodisias* in the *Oxford Classical Dictionary*, 4th ed. (Oxford: Oxford University Press, 2012), p. 116.
14. A good survey of Roman art is Martin Henig (ed.), *A Handbook of Roman Art* (Ithaca, NY: Cornell University Press, 1983); David Smith reviews Roman mosaics on pp. 116–138.
15. Plate 5b in G. Karl Galinsky, *Augustan Culture* (Princeton, NJ: Princeton University Press, 1996). His assertion that the painting is from the house of Augustus is not supported by the archaeological evidence.
16. Discussed by Martin Henig in Chapter 6 of Henig (see note 14), pp. 138–165.
17. Tacitus, *Annals* 15.21. Patavium is the modern Padua. Horace's *Ars Poetica* is full of references to tragedy and comedy as part of Roman entertainment, for example, lines 51–58 and 141–156.

18. There are two excellent sources for phlyakes: Margaret Bieber, *The History of the Greek and Roman Theater* (Princeton, NJ: Princeton University Press, 1971 [1939]), Chapter 10, pp. 129–146; A. D. Trendall, *Red Figure Vases of South Italy and Sicily* (London: Thames & Hudson, 1989), especially Chapter 8 ("Myth and Reality"), pp. 255–268. Both are copiously illustrated.

19. Respectively, *Pappus, Bucco, Maccus, Dossennus*. Plautus took Maccus as his middle name. The Oscans did not use the phallus.

20. Bieber (see note 18), p. 147.

21. See p. 545.

22. Collected in E. H. Warmington, ed., *Remains of Old Latin*, Vol. 2 (Cambridge, MA: Harvard University Press, 1935).

23. Saturnians were distinguished by strong accents, as opposed to the metrical feet of hexameters. Livius, for example, described Circe's transformation of Odysseus' men back into human form as follows: *tópper fécit hómones út priús fuérunt* ("quickly she made them into men as they were before"); cf. Homer, *Odyssey* 10.395.

24. For the Camenae, see p. 666.

25. For Euhemerism, see p. 7 and Chapter 27 on the companion website.

26. See p. 671 for the significance of this.

27. Horace, *Epistles* 2.1.55–56: *"aufert / Pacuvius docti famam senis, Accius alti"* ("Pacuvius has the reputation of being a learned old man, Accius of being a lofty one").

28. Horace, *Epistles* 2.1.161–163. Thespis was said to have been the founder of Greek tragedy—hence the modern word for an actor, "thespian."

29. Horace, *Epistles* 2.1.182–200: 184–186 and 199–200 quoted. Suetonius said that Augustus "was an intense fan of boxers." In his *Res Gestae* 22, Augustus boasted that he gave eight gladiatorial shows involving a total of 10,000 fighters; five times he presented athletes from all over the world; and he presented twenty-six wild beast hunts in which about 3,500 African wild beasts were killed.

30. The epitaph is reproduced and discussed by T. P. Wiseman in *Catullus and His World* (Cambridge: Cambridge University Press), 1985), pp. 30–33.

31. Apuleius, *Metamorphoses* 10.29–34. Many more myths are described, and Lucius managed to escape his fate.

32. Related by Velleius Paterculus 2.83.2, written in about A.D. 30. Plancus must have behaved in this way before his consulship, and certainly before he was pardoned by Octavian after he changed sides.

33. Plutarch, *Life of Antony*, 26; Shakespeare, *Antony and Cleopatra*, Act 2, Scene 2.

34. Related by Tacitus, *Annals*, 11.31–32. Memorably staged in the BBC production of *I, Claudius* (1976), episode 11.

35. Peter Wiseman in *The Myths of Rome* (Exeter: University of Exeter Press, 2004), p. 236, justly calls his *Metamorphoses* "the western world's mythological encyclopaedia from Chaucer to Ted Hughes."

36. Translation taken from Mark Morford, *The Roman Philosophers* (London: Routledge/Taylor & Francis, 2002), p. 153.

37. Lucan, *Bellum Civile* 4.593–655. See pp. 553–556.

38. We have translated passages from the *Thebaid* on p. 422 and from the *Achilleid* on p. 476.

39. See p. 604.

40. The mythical Phlegraean plains were said to be in Campania. The future apotheosis of Hercules is meant by "his head touching the stars." For the Gigantomachy, see pp. 83–85.

41. *Metamorphoses* 10.560–707. For the story of the other Atalanta, daughter of Schoeneus, see p. 508, note 31.

ROMAN MYTHOLOGY AND SAGA

Our city was founded with proper auspices and augury: every place in it is full of religious awe and gods.

—LIVY, *Ab urbe condita* 5. 52

THE FUNDAMENTAL DIFFERENCES BETWEEN Greek and Roman mythology account for the dominant influence of Greek myths over native Italian myths and Roman legends. The Italian gods were not as generally anthropomorphic as the Olympian gods, about whom the Greeks developed legends that they expressed in poetry and art of great power. The Roman gods were originally associated more with cult than with myth, and such traditional tales as were told about them did not have the power of Greek legends. In the third century B.C., when the first historians and epic poets began to write in Latin, the influence of Greek literature was already dominant. Many of the early authors were themselves Greeks and were familiar with Greek mythology. Thus many Roman legends are adaptations of Greek legends, and to a varying extent they owe their present form to sophisticated authors such as Vergil and Ovid.

Roman mythology nevertheless had an independent existence in the cults of Roman religion and the legends of early Roman history. The roots of Roman religion lay in the traditions of pre-Roman Italic peoples such as the Sabines and Etruscans. The native Italian gods, however, became identified with the Greek gods—Saturnus with Cronus, Jupiter with Zeus, and so on. The poet Ennius (239–169 B.C.) came from southern Italy and spoke Greek, Oscan, and Latin. He equated the twelve principal Roman gods with the twelve Olympians as follows:[1]

> Iuno (Hera), Vesta (Hestia), Minerva (Athena), Ceres (Demeter), Diana (Artemis), Venus (Aphrodite), Mars (Ares), Mercurius (Hermes), Iovis (Zeus), Neptunus (Poseidon), Vulcanus (Hephaestus), Apollo.

Of these, only Apollo is identical with his Greek counterpart. Of the others, the Italian fertility spirit, Venus, becomes the great goddess underlying the fertility of nature and human love. In contrast, the great Italian agricultural and war deity, Mars, is identified with Ares, one of the less important Olympians. The others more or less retain their relative importance.

654

As a result of these identifications, Greek myths were transferred to Roman gods. In **Ovid**'s *Metamorphoses*, for example, most of the myths of the Olympians are Greek, although the names of the gods are Roman. Some genuinely Roman or Italic legends, however, have been preserved in the poetry of Ovid, **Vergil**, and **Propertius** (to name the three most important poets in this respect) and in the prose writers **Cicero, Varro** (a polymath and antiquarian who died at the age of eighty-nine in 27 B.C.), and **Livy**. The outline of other legends can be recovered from what is known of the cults and rituals of Roman divinities. Especially important in this respect is Ovid's *Fasti*, in which he describes the festivals of the first six months of the Roman calendar. He tells many legends of the gods, while describing their cults and explaining the origins of their rituals.

Legends attached to the early history of Rome are the Roman equivalent of saga. A few of these are associated with specific local heroes, of whom the most important are Aeneas and Romulus. A large group of legends associated with the early history of Rome idealized the past, and their central figures exemplify Roman virtues. Such idealizing was especially practiced in the time of Augustus (who reigned from 27 B.C. to A.D. 14), a period of reconstruction and revival of the supposed principles of the early Romans. All the authors named here as sources for Roman mythology were contemporaries of Augustus, and of them, only Varro (fifty-three years older than Augustus) and Cicero (forty-three years older) died before the Augustan reconstruction had begun. Thus the definition of myth as a "traditional tale" has a special coloring in Roman mythology. Livy justifies the process of idealization in the "Preface" to his history (sects. 6–10):

> I do not intend to accept or deny the truth of traditional legends about events before and during the founding of the city. These are more suitable for poetic fables than for reliable historical records. But one can excuse ancient legends because they make the origins of the city more august by uniting human and divine actions. If any nation has the right to consider its origins sacred and to ascribe them to the gods, it is the Roman people, for they claim that Mars is their ancestor and the father of the founder [Romulus].

The Italian Gods

Janus, Mars, and Bellona

Among the gods of the Roman state, Janus takes first place; in formal prayers to the gods, he was named first. He is a very ancient deity, and he may have had an equivalent in the Etruscan god, Culsans, who was worshiped at the Etruscan city of Cortona. He is the god who presides over beginnings, and in this connection we preserve his name in the month that begins our year. It is likely, however, that in his earliest form he was connected with water, especially with crossing places and bridges. Thus in the city of Rome, there were five shrines to Janus, all placed near crossings over the river or watercourses, and he was intimately connected with the boundaries of the earliest settlements at Rome, the approaches to which required crossing the Tiber or one of its tributary brooks. As the city expanded, these early crossing places lost their importance, and Janus' original functions were obscured. Yet they can be detected in later times; the gates of his shrine near the Argiletum entrance to the Forum were open in time of war and closed in time of peace. They were closed by Augustus with great ceremony, for example, to mark the end of the protracted civil wars that brought him to power. In the early days of Rome, the bridges would have been broken when the city was threatened by an enemy; an analogy for opening the gates of Janus in time of war would be raising a drawbridge over a moat.

In later times, "Janus" was used not only as the name of a deity but also as a common noun (a janus), which Cicero (*De natura deorum* 2.67) defined as "a crossing-place with a roadway," in this recalling the god's early functions. While

Map 26.1 Roman Italy and Sicily.

Janus' significance as a god of bridges waned, he attracted to himself other functions; he was the god of going in and coming out, and therefore of doors, entrances, and archways, as well as of beginnings. In another form, as the youthful god **Portunus**, he was god of harbors (which are the entrances to lands from overseas) and ferries. Portunus helped the winners of the boat race in the *Aeneid*.

There are few legends of Janus; it was said that after the Sabines, under Titus Tatius, had captured the Capitol, they were kept from entering the Forum by jets of boiling water that Janus caused to gush forth. The only ancient statues of Janus surviving are two four-faced marble "herms" on the parapet of the Pons Fabricius in Rome; on coins he is portrayed with two faces, for as a god of entrances and exits he could look both before and behind.

The Italian deity Mars (or Mavors) was much more important than Ares, his Greek equivalent. In origin, he was an agricultural deity worshiped by many Italian tribes. His association with spring, the time of regeneration and growth, is shown by the use of his name for the month of March, which began the Roman year in the pre-Julian calendar. As an agricultural god, he is associated with a number of rural deities like Silvanus and Flora; the latter supposedly provided Juno with a magical flower whose touch enabled her to conceive Mars without any father. Mars sometimes has as his consort the Sabine fertility goddess **Nerio**, who is often identified with Minerva. Ovid tells how Mars asked **Anna Perenna** (the ancient goddess of the year) to act as his go-between with Nerio. After he had made love to Nerio, he found on unveiling her that his bride was none other than Anna, who was old and wrinkled and thoroughly enjoyed her deception. This, says Ovid, was the origin of jokes and obscenities at marriage parties.

Just as the Roman people turned from farming to war, so Mars became a war god, and this aspect became more important than his agricultural character. Sacrifices were offered to him before and after a battle, and a portion of the spoils was dedicated to him. The most famous of his temples at Rome was that of **Mars Ultor (Mars the Avenger)**, vowed by Augustus at the battle of Philippi (42 B.C.) and dedicated forty years later. The **Campus Martius (Field of Mars)** was the open space outside the gates of the ancient city where the people assembled under arms and practiced their military skills. As the god of war, Mars often had the title **Gradivus** (perhaps meaning "**the Marcher**"); he was also closely associated with the Sabine war deity **Quirinus**, with whom Romulus was later identified. In battle, Mars was generally accompanied by a number of lesser deities and personifications, of whom the war goddess Bellona is the best known. Bellona herself was often identified with the Greek personification of war, **Enyo** (connected with the title of Ares, *Enyalios*), and a temple was first dedicated to her in Rome in 296 B.C.

Mars is particularly associated with two animals, the wolf and the woodpecker. A she-wolf suckled his sons, the infants Romulus and Remus. The woodpecker, *picus*, was said in one legend to have been a Latin king **Picus**, whose wife was the nymph **Canens (Singer)**. Circe, the magician, tried to seduce him, and when he rejected her, she turned him into a woodpecker. After searching in vain for him for six days and six nights, Canens wasted away into nothing more than a voice.

Jupiter

The great Italian sky-god was Jupiter, the forms of whose name are etymologically connected with those of other Indo-European sky-gods, including Zeus. At the end of the regal period (509 B.C.), the temple of **Jupiter Optimus Maximus** was built on the **Capitoline Hill** and the great sky-god became localized in a temple with a statue like a Greek city god. He shared the temple with **Juno**, the chief Italian goddess of women, and **Minerva**, an Italian fertility and war goddess who at Rome was worshiped principally as the patroness of handicrafts and wisdom. These three deities formed the "**Capitoline triad**."

Jupiter was called by many titles. In his temple on the Capitol, he was worshiped as Jupiter Optimus Maximus (Best and Greatest). The great ceremonial procession of the Triumph wound its way through the Forum up to this temple. The triumphing general was robed as if he were a god, proceeding in his chariot amid the cheering crowds, with his soldiers around him and his prisoners before him. On the Capitoline Hill he sacrificed to Jupiter, acknowledging by this ritual that Jupiter was the source of Roman greatness and military might.

As sky-god, Jupiter directly influenced Roman public life, in which the weather omens of thunder and lightning, his special weapons, played an important role. After lightning had struck, a ritual purification or expiatory rite was required, and Jupiter himself was said to have given **King Numa** the original instructions for the sacrifice. Advised by the nymph **Egeria**, Numa captured the two forest divinities, Picus and Faunus, on the Aventine Hill and compelled them to tell him how to summon Jupiter. When Jupiter himself came, Numa asked what objects were necessary for the expiatory rite. "A head," the god replied, and Numa interrupted with "of an onion." "Of a man," Jupiter went on, and Numa added "a hair"; finally Jupiter demanded "a life." "Of a fish," said Numa, and Jupiter good-naturedly agreed to accept these objects (the head of an onion, a human hair, and a fish) as part of the expiatory ritual. Ovid's narrative (*Fasti* 3.285–346), which is summarized here, explains why these objects were offered instead of a human sacrifice, almost certainly the original form of expiation.

Jupiter also promised to give Numa a sign to support Rome's claim to exercise power over other communities. In full view of the people of Rome, Jupiter caused a **shield** (*ancile*) to fall miraculously from heaven. This *ancile* was of the archaic figure-eight shape; since it was a talisman of Roman power, Numa had eleven others made exactly like it, so that it would be hard to steal the genuine *ancile*. The twelve *ancilia* were kept in the Regia (the office of the **Pontifex Maximus**, the official head of the hierarchy of the state religion)[2] and were used by the priests of Mars, **the Salii**, in the sacred war dance they performed each spring. As they danced, they sang an ancient hymn containing the words *mamuri veturi*, whose meaning had long since been forgotten. According to tradition, the craftsman who made the eleven false *ancilia* was named Mamurius, and he had asked for his name to be included in the hymn as a reward.

Jupiter's many titles indicate his supreme importance in all matters of the state's life in war and peace. As **Jupiter Latiaris**, he was the chief god of the Latins, worshiped by the Romans in an annual ceremony upon the Mons Albanus (the modern Monte Cavo) 20 miles from Rome. As the god before whom the most solemn oaths were sworn, he was closely associated with the goddess **Fides** (**Good Faith**) and identified with the old Sabine god Dius Fidius. Oaths sworn by Dius Fidius had to be sworn under the open sky (Jupiter's realm). The Latin deity Semo Sancus (the name comes from the same root as *sancire*, the Latin word for ratifying an oath) is also identified with Dius Fidius and Jupiter.

Another of Jupiter's titles is **Indiges**, by which he was worshiped near the river Numicus. The word *Indiges* has never been explained. It evidently refers to a state god, and the Di Indigetes were a well-known group of gods whose exact role remains unknown. Livy believed that Aeneas was worshiped as Jupiter Indiges after his death beside the river Numicus. Ovid tells the story (*Metamorphoses* 14.598–608):

> [Venus] came to the shore at Laurentum, where the waters of the river Numicus, concealed by reeds, wind into the nearby sea. She commanded the river to wash away from Aeneas all that was mortal and to carry it away silently into the sea. The horned river-god performed the commands of Venus and purified all that was mortal of Aeneas and cleansed it with his waters. The best part of Aeneas remained. His mother [Venus] anointed the purified body with divine perfume; she touched his face with ambrosia and sweet nectar and made him a god. Him the people of Quirinus [i.e., the Romans] hailed as "Indiges," and received him with a temple and altars.

Juno

Juno, the second member of the Capitoline triad, was originally an independent Italian deity who presided over every aspect of the life of women. She was especially associated with marriage and (as **Juno Lucina**) childbirth. The festival of Juno Lucina, the **Matronalia**, was celebrated in March as a spring festival, when all nature was being renewed. Juno was also worshiped as **Juno Moneta** on the **Arx (Citadel)**, the northern peak of the Capitoline Hill. Moneta means "adviser" (from the same root as the Latin word *monere*), but the word survives in the English word "mint": Juno's temple on the Arx was next to the Roman Mint, which was known as *ad Monetam*.

Another of Juno's titles was **Juno Regina (Queen Juno)**. Livy (5.21) describes how the Romans invited Juno to leave the Etruscan city of Veii after its defeat in 396 B.C. At Rome, Camillus dedicated a temple in her honor on the Aventine Hill. The ritual of persuading an enemy's gods to leave their city was called **evocatio (calling out)**. By accepting the invitation, the goddess was believed to have come willingly to her new home in Rome, while the Etruscans were deprived of her protection.

Under the influence of Greek literature, Juno, the great Italian goddess of the life of women, became the wife and sister of Jupiter. In the *Aeneid*, she has a prominent role in opposing the fated success of Aeneas, but eventually Jupiter and Fate are superior and she accepts the union of the Trojan newcomers and the indigenous Italian tribes.

Minerva

Minerva, the third member of the Capitoline triad, was also an Italian deity, introduced to Rome by the Etruscans. She became identified with Athena and Athena's legends, so it is hard to distinguish her original functions. She may have been a war goddess, for she shared her great festival, the **Quinquatrus**, with Mars, whose consort, the Sabine goddess Nerio, was often identified with her. Her chief importance for the Romans, however, was as the goddess of all activities involving mental skill. She was the patroness of craftspeople and skilled workers, among whom Ovid (in his invocation to Minerva in the *Fasti*) includes

Jupiter, Juno, and Minerva. Marble panel relief from the attic of the west side of the Arch of Trajan at Benevento, ca. A.D. 115; height of panel, 90½ in. Jupiter, the central figure in the Capitoline triad, hands his thunderbolt, symbol of power, to Trajan, who appears in the corresponding panel on the other side of the central inscription on the attic. The arch was erected to celebrate the completion of the Via Traiana, the road from Rome to Brindisi, where it left the old Appian Way. In the background are other Olympian gods: Hercules to the left (behind Minerva), Apollo, Venus, and Mercury (with his winged cap). (*Vanni/Art Resource, NY*)

authors and painters.[3] She was also the goddess of schoolchildren, and Quinquatrus was the time both of school holidays and the payment of school fees.

Divinities of Fire: Vesta, Vulcan, and Cacus

The most important of the other Roman state gods who were of Italian origin were the two concerned with fire, Vesta and Vulcan (Volcanus). Vesta (whose name is etymologically identical with the Greek Hestia) was the goddess of the hearth, the center of family life. Since the state was a community of families, it had a hearth with an ever-burning fire as the symbolic center of its life. The fire was kept alight in the round temple of Vesta in the Roman Forum and was tended by the six **Vestal Virgins**. These were daughters of noble families who entered the service of Vesta before their tenth birthday and remained until their fortieth year, or even longer. Their life was hedged with many taboos and rituals, and their vow of chastity was strictly observed. The Vestals were treated with the highest honor and were some of the most important persons in the hierarchy of Roman state religion. Their offices and living quarters were in the Forum, next to the Regia.

The second Roman king, Numa, was said to have founded the cult of Vesta. The myths of Vesta are few and uninteresting. Ovid (*Fasti* 6.319–338) tells how the fertility god **Priapus** tried to seduce her and was prevented by the braying of a donkey. He gives another version of the story (see p. 665), in which the nymph Lotis is Priapus' intended victim.

Closely associated with Vesta were the household spirits of the Romans, the **Penates**, whose name derives from the *penus*, or store cupboard, source of food and therefore symbol of the continuing life of the family. Originally the spirits on whom the life and food of the individual family depended, they became an essential part of the life of the state. The Romans were vague about their number or identity, and a useful definition is that of Servius (fourth century A.D.), "all the gods who are worshiped in the home." The Penates were originally Italian and were especially worshiped at the Latin town of Lavinium. It was said that when an attempt was made to remove them from Lavinium to Alba Longa, they miraculously returned to their original home. At Rome, they became identified with the Trojan gods entrusted by Hector to Aeneas on the night of Troy's destruction and brought by him to Italy. Among the sacred objects kept in the *penus Vestae* (i.e., the sacred repository in the temple of Vesta) was the **Palladium**, the statue of the Trojan Athena given by Diomedes to one of Aeneas' followers. When the temple of Vesta was burned in 241 B.C., the consul L. Caecilius Metellus earned great glory by saving the Palladium with his own hands. Yet he was blinded for the act because he had looked upon a sacred object that it was not lawful for a man to see.

Vulcan (Volcanus) was the chief Italian fire-god and was more important than his Greek equivalent, Hephaestus. The Greek god was the god of industrial, creative fire, whereas Vulcan was the god of destructive fire and a potent power to be worshiped in a city frequently ravaged by conflagrations.[4] Through his identification with Hephaestus, Vulcan acquired creative attributes shown by his other name, **Mulciber** (**He who tempers**). Vergil has a fine description of Vulcan's smithy deep below Mt. Aetna (*Aeneid* 8.424–438):

> The Cyclopes were working the iron in the vast cave, Brontes and Steropes and naked Pyracmon. In their hands was a thunderbolt, partly finished and partly yet to be finished, one of very many which the Father [i.e., Jupiter] hurls to the earth from all over the sky. They had put onto it three rays of twisted rainstorms, three of watery clouds, three of red fire and the winged south wind. Just then they were adding the terrifying lightning to the weapon and the penetrating flames of [Jupiter's] anger. In another part they were working on the chariot of Mars and its winged wheels, with which he stirs up men and cities. They were busily polishing the fearsome aegis, the weapon of aroused Minerva, with serpents' scales and gold. It had entwined snakes and the Gorgon's head itself turning its gaze.   10

The Italian fire-god, Cacus, was associated with Vulcan. Vergil narrates how he was killed by **Hercules** (*Aeneid* 190–267). Cacus had stolen the **Cattle of Geryon** from Hercules and had hidden them in his cave on the Aventine Hill. Here is the climax of the fight, when Hercules has broken open the cave of Cacus (*Aeneid* 8.247–261):

> Hercules overwhelmed Cacus from above with missiles, Cacus who had been suddenly trapped by the unexpected daylight, shut in his rocky cave and bellowing as he was not used to do. Hercules summoned up all his weapons and attacked him with branches and huge boulders. But Cacus (who had no escape from the danger) belched forth (a miracle to narrate) clouds of smoke, enveloping his cave in blind darkness and taking away the sight from Hercules' eyes. He filled the cave with the smoky blackness of night and darkness mixed with fire. Brave Hercules did not put up with this: he leaped headlong through the fire, where the waves of smoke were the thickest and the black clouds billowed through the cave. Here he held Cacus knotted in his grip, as he vainly belched forth fire in the darkness. Clinging tight he throttled him, so that his eyes burst out and no blood was left in his throat. Then the doors of the black cave were wrenched off and it was suddenly thrown open. Displayed to the sky were the stolen cattle and the theft that Cacus had denied, and the monstrous corpse was dragged out by its feet. The people could not have enough of gazing on the terrible eyes of the monster, on the face and the chest with its bristling hair and the throat with fire extinct.   10

Vergil's narrative ostensibly explains the origin of the worship of Hercules at the **Ara Maxima**, an ancient cult site in the low-lying ground (called the Forum Boarium) between the Aventine and the Tiber. But he makes a monster of the ancient Italian fire-god, whose name survived in the *Scalae Caci* (**Steps of Cacus**), a pathway leading up onto the corner of the Palatine Hill that was associated with the earliest settlement on the site of Rome.

Agricultural and Fertility Divinities

Saturn, Ceres, and Their Associates

Saturn was an ancient god, perhaps of Etruscan origin. His temple dated from the early days of the Republic, and beneath it was the state treasury. His origins are obscure; he was an agricultural deity, and his festival, the **Saturnalia**, celebrated on December 17, was perhaps originally connected with the winter grain sowing. Like many other country festivals, it was accompanied by a relaxation of the normal social inhibitions. This was a prominent feature of the Saturnalia in historical times, when slaves were allowed freedom of speech. The Saturnalia came to be linked with the festival of **Ops**, which was celebrated two days later, and eventually the festival period lasted for a week.

Saturn was very soon identified with the Greek Cronus and like him was believed to have ruled over a golden age. Rhea, the Greek consort of Cronus, was likewise identified with Ops, the Italian goddess of plenty, who was the partner of Saturn in popular mythology. His partner in cult, however, was the obscure Italian deity Lua. In the cult of Ops, her partner was **Consus**, an Italian harvest deity, whose festival, the **Consualia**, was celebrated in both August and December. Livy tells us that the seizure of the Sabine women took place at the games held during the Consualia.

Agricultural deities were very prominent in early Roman religion, and others besides Mars, Saturn, and their associates were connected with the fertility of the land. The cult of Ceres at Rome went back to the earliest days of the Roman Republic, when in 493 B.C. a temple on the Aventine was dedicated to Ceres, **Liber**, and **Libera**. Ceres was identified with Demeter, Liber with Dionysus, and Libera with Kore (i.e., Persephone, Demeter's daughter). Thus the Eleusinian triad of Demeter, Kore, and Iacchus/Bacchus had its exact counterpart at Rome. The mythology of Ceres and Liber is entirely Hellenized, and the ritual of worship in their temple was Greek, even the prayers being spoken in Greek. The wine-god Liber, however, did not share in the ecstatic aspects of Dionysus.

The Aventine temple of Ceres, Liber, and Libera was also important as a political and commercial center. It was a center of plebeian activity and was especially connected with the plebeian aediles and tribunes. In front of it was the headquarters of the state-subsidized grain supply (*statio annonae*).

Also associated with Ceres was the Italian earth-goddess **Tellus Mater**, with whom she shared the festival of the sowing of the seed (*feriae sementivae*) in January. Thus the grain was watched over from seed to granary by three divinities—Ceres before it was sown, Tellus Mater when it was put in the earth, Consus when it was harvested and stored.

The deities who presided over the livestock of the farm were called **Pales**. Originally a pair, their name was later used for one deity, either male or female. The festival of Pales, the **Parilia** (or **Palilia**), was celebrated in April and was also considered to be the anniversary of the founding of Rome.

Forest Divinities: Silvanus and Faunus

Silvanus (Forester) and Faunus (Favorer) were gods of the woods and forests. Silvanus had to be propitiated when a forest was being cleared or trees felled. In the *Aeneid*, Faunus is the son of Picus and grandson of Saturn, and the father of Latinus by an Italian birth-goddess, **Marica**. Originally, he was a woodland spirit, occasionally mischievous but generally favorable to the farmer who worshiped him. His consort (or daughter) was **Fauna**, who was identified with the **Bona Dea** (**Good Goddess**), a divinity worshiped only by women. Both Faunus and Silvanus were identified with the Arcadian pastoral god Pan. Faunus and Fauna were further identified with minor gods of woodland sounds because they were considered responsible for strange and sudden forest noises. Thus (according to Livy), the night after a closely fought battle against the Etruscans, the Romans heard Silvanus (whom Livy here confuses with Faunus) cry out from a nearby forest that they had won the victory, with the result that the Etruscans acknowledged defeat and returned home. Faunus also had oracular powers; Latinus consulted him about the prodigies that accompanied the arrival of Aeneas in Italy, and Numa received advice from him in a time of famine.

Faunus was officially worshiped at Rome and had a temple on the Tiber island. His festival was in December, but he was closely connected with the more famous festival of the **Lupercalia**, which took place in February. The Arcadian king Evander was said to have come to Rome and there to have founded the first settlement on the Palatine Hill. On the side of the hill is a cave, the **Lupercal**, where the she-wolf (*lupa*) was later believed to have suckled Romulus and Remus. Here Evander worshiped his Arcadian god Pan, who was the equivalent of Faunus. Thus Faunus was connected with the Lupercalia, whose central ritual was a sacrifice in the Lupercal, at which two young noblemen were smeared with the victims' blood. They were called the **Luperci**, and after the sacrifice they ran nearly naked around the boundary of the Palatine, striking the women they met with leather straps. Barren women, it was believed, became fertile by this act.

Ovid relates a folk tale explaining the nudity of the Luperci. Hercules and the Lydian queen Omphale came once to a cave where they exchanged clothes while supper was being prepared. After the meal they went to sleep, still each in the other's clothes. Meanwhile, Faunus had determined to seduce Omphale. He entered the cave and lay with the person dressed as a girl. His reception was far from warm, and ever after he ordered his followers (i.e., the Luperci) to be naked at his cult, to prevent the repetition of so painful a mistake.

Garden Divinities: Venus and Priapus

Venus was an Italian fertility goddess whose original functions are not known. She was worshiped in a number of places under titles that indicate that she had as much to do with luck and the favor of the gods as with beauty and fertility, and she was apparently particularly the protectress of gardens. A temple to her was dedicated at Rome in 295 B.C. with the title **Venus Obsequens** (**Venus who is favorable**), the same title as in Plautus' comedy *Rudens*, which takes place in front of her temple by the seashore in Libya. During the fourth century B.C., contact with the Greek world led to identification of Venus with the Greek goddess of love, Aphrodite.

In 217 B.C., after the Roman defeat at the battle of Lake Trasimene, the dictator Quintus Fabius Maximus Cunctator consulted the Sibylline books, which ordered him to dedicate a temple on the Capitoline Hill to **Venus**

Erycina. Eryx, at the western end of Sicily, was the site of a great temple to the Phoenician fertility goddess Astarte, who later became identified with Aphrodite and then with Venus. The dedication of the temple of Venus Erycina in 215 was significant in the development of the worship of Venus at Rome. In that year, a *lectisternium* was also conducted, a festival at which the statues of the gods were laid out on couches, two to a couch, and offered a banquet while supplication was made to them. The ceremony had first been conducted at Rome in 399 for six gods. The ceremony of 215 was the first in which the twelve great gods were so honored, and Ennius' lines naming them (see p. 654) described this event. In the *lectisternium* Venus was paired with Mars. Thus she gained in status, since Mars was acknowledged as the ancestor of the Romans.

In about 55 B.C., Lucretius began his poem with an eloquent invocation to Venus as the creative principle of life. The opening lines of the poem transfer the majesty and creative power of the Greek Aphrodite to a Roman context (*De rerum natura* 1.1–13):

> Mother of the descendants of Aeneas, bringer of pleasure to gods and men, nurturing Venus, beneath the gliding constellations of heaven you fill the ship-bearing sea and the fruitful lands. Through you all living things are conceived and at birth see the light of the sun. Before you, O goddess, the winds withdraw, and at your coming, the clouds in heaven retreat. For you the variegated earth puts forth her lovely flowers, for you the waters of the sea laugh and the sky at peace shines, overspread with light. For you the West Wind, creator of life, is unbarred. You first, O goddess, and your coming do the birds of the air salute, their hearts struck by your power.

At about the time that Lucretius was writing his poem, the Roman general Pompey dedicated a temple in his theater (the first permanent stone theater at Rome) to **Venus Victrix** (**Bringer of Victory**). The family of Julius Caesar traced its ancestry back to her, and he dedicated a temple to her in his forum (which was completed by Augustus). Her connection with Troy led to her importance in the *Aeneid* as the mother of Aeneas. More than a century later, Hadrian dedicated one of Rome's most magnificent temples to the two goddesses, **Venus Felix** (**Bringer of Success**) and Roma Aeterna, thus uniting the personification of the city with its divine ancestress.

The shrine of **Venus Cloacina** stood in the Forum Romanum. Cloacina was presumably the goddess of the **Cloaca**, the Etruscan drainage system that drained the Forum area and allowed the city of Rome to develop in the low-lying ground from the sixth century B.C. onward. How this goddess was identified with Venus is unknown. Among Italian divinities connected with the success of agriculture was **Robigo**, the goddess of blight, whose festival, the **Robigalia**, was celebrated in April. She was offered the gruesome sacrifice of a dog and a sheep so that the growing crops would not be attacked by mildew. Naming a divinity after a natural feature (good or ill) is typical of Roman religion.

The protector of gardens, Priapus, was originally Greek. He was represented by a wooden statue, painted red, with an enormous erect phallus. His principal cult in the Greek world was at Lampsacus (a city overlooking the Hellespont), where he was offered the sacrifice of a donkey. Ovid explains the choice of this victim in this story (*Fasti* 1.415–440):[5]

The Feast of the Gods, by Giovanni Bellini (1430–1516), with additions by Titian; oil on canvas, 1514, 67 × 74 in. Painted when the artist was eighty-four years old, this painting has been called "both mysterious and comic." Its subject is the attempt of Priapus to rape the nymph Lotis (cf. Ovid, *Fasti* 1.391–440 and 6.319–346, where the intended victim is Vesta), shown on the right. The gods appear as young Renaissance men and women: Jupiter (drinking from a cup) is in the center, Mercury (wearing a helmet) reclines in the left center foreground, and a group consisting of a satyr, Silenus, and Dionysus (kneeling on one knee) is on the left. Between Dionysus and Silenus is the donkey whose braying woke Lotis. (*Widener Collection, Image courtesy of the Board of Trustees, National Gallery of Art, Washington*)

Red Priapus, the ornament and guardian of gardens, loved Lotis, above all the Naiads. She laughed at him scornfully. It was night, and [the Naiads], made drowsy by wine, lay in different places overcome with sleep. Lotis, just as she was, tired by play, slept farthest away on the grassy ground beneath the branches of a maple. Up rose her lover, and holding his breath he silently made his way on tiptoe to the nymph's resting place. Even now he was balancing [on tiptoe] on the distant grass, yet she still was sleeping soundly. He rejoiced; and lifting her dress from her feet, he had happily begun to reach his longed-for goal. But look! The donkey, Silenus' mount, began ill-timed braying. Up leaped the terrified nymph and pushed Priapus away, arousing the whole wood as she fled. But the god, all too ready with his obscene member, was an object of ridicule to all by the light of the moon. The source of the noise paid the penalty with his life, and this is the victim that is pleasing to the god of the Hellespont.   10

Water Gods: Portunus and the Gods of Rivers and Springs

Water gods were important to the Italian farmer. Each river and spring had its deity, who needed to be propitiated by offerings. **Tiberinus**, god of the river **Tiber**, was propitiated each May when twenty-seven straw dummies, called *Argei*, were thrown into the river from the Pons Sublicius, the wooden bridge of the early city. This ceremony was attended by the *pontifices* (priests of the state religion) and the Vestal Virgins, but even the Romans did not know its origin. Propitiation of a potentially damaging god by means of dummies (substitutes for human sacrifice) is as likely an explanation as any.

Neptunus, later identified with Poseidon, was originally a freshwater divinity whose festival occurred in July, when the hot Italian summer was at its driest. Portunus also was an old Italian god, originally the god of gates (*portae*), but later the god of harbors (*portus*), whose temple was near the Aemilian Bridge in Rome. Vergil makes him help Cloanthus to victory in the boat race in the *Aeneid* (5.241–243). He was also identified with the Greek sea-god Palaemon, originally Melicertes (see note 3, p. 328). Both of the Roman sea-gods, therefore, were originally freshwater divinities who acquired their attributes as sea-gods from Greek mythology.

Of the river-gods, the most important was Tiberinus, and bridging his river was a significant religious matter. The Pons Sublicius (mentioned earlier) was administered by the *pontifices* (whose title may originally have meant "bridge builders"), and there were various religious taboos involved in its construction and administration. Tiberinus himself plays an important role in Book 8 of the *Aeneid* when he appears to Aeneas in a dream and tells him that he has arrived at his final home. He shows Aeneas the sign of the sow and her thirty piglets, and he calms his waters so that Aeneas' boat can move smoothly upstream to Pallanteum (*Aeneid* 8.31–96).

Springs of running water were under the protection of the nymphs. In the Forum at Rome was the spring of **Juturna**, who in Vergil appears as the sister of Turnus and the victim of Jupiter's lust. She was worshiped in the Forum and the Campus Martius, and the headquarters of the city's water administration lay in her precinct. Her festival was the **Juturnalia**. After the battle of Lake Regillus in 496 B.C. the Dioscuri (Castor and Pollux) watered their horses at her spring in the Forum. Their temple was next to her precinct.

Outside the Porta Capena at Rome were a spring and a small park dedicated to the **Camenae**, water-nymphs of great antiquity but unknown origin. Later, they were identified with the Greek Muses. The Vestals drew water from the fountain of the Camenae for purification of the temple of Vesta. Closely associated with the spring of the Camenae was the nymph Egeria, said to have been the counselor and consort of Numa, to whom so much of Roman religious custom was ascribed. Egeria is also found in the precinct of Diana at Aricia, and her spring was one of those that fed Lake Nemi. She was the helper of pregnant women and may indeed have once been a birth-goddess. Another nymph associated with the Camenae is **Carmentis** (or **Carmenta**), who also has the double association with water and with birth. As a water-nymph, she shared the festival of Juturna, and she is sometimes named as the mother of Evander, the king of Pallanteum, an earlier city on the site of Rome. Like the

Parcae (the Roman birth-goddesses identified with the three Fates), she had prophetic powers, as is indicated by her name, for *carmen* means a song or prophetic utterance.

Diana

The Italian goddess Diana was worshiped at **Aricia** with a cult established by members of the Latin League. Aricia is near **Lake Nemi**, which was known as "Diana's mirror," perhaps indicating her association with the moon, reflected in the waters of the lake. This cult was the starting point for Sir James Frazer's *The Golden Bough*. The priest of Diana at Aricia was a fugitive slave, who had the title of **"King of the Grove"** (*Rex Nemorensis*). He became priest by killing his predecessor in single combat, having challenged him by plucking a bough from a sacred tree. As priest he always went armed, watching for the successor who would kill him. It is likely that the sacred grove was originally an asylum for runaway slaves and the sacred bough was the branch carried by suppliants at an altar.

Diana was concerned with the life of women (especially in childbirth). She was often identified with the Italian goddess **Lucina**, who brought babies into the light (Latin, *lux, lucis*), although Lucina was more commonly a title of Juno.

Diana was also worshiped at Mt. Tifata near Capua. It is possible that this is where she began to be identified with Artemis. Through Artemis she acquired her powers as goddess of the hunt and (as Hecate) her association with the Underworld. At Rome she was worshiped upon the Aventine Hill, and her cult was established by Servius Tullius. Like her cult at Aricia, it was originally shared by members of the Latin League, being situated outside the early city's walls. Under Augustus, her status as sister of Apollo was emphasized and was dramatically expressed in Horace's *Carmen Saeculare*, sung at the celebration of the Secular Games in 17 B.C. by antiphonal choirs of boys and girls, standing, respectively, upon the Palatine and Aventine hills.

Horace embodies the triple functions of Diana (as Artemis, mistress of animals; Lucina, goddess of childbirth; and Hecate, goddess of the Underworld) in the following hymn, in which he dedicates a pine tree to her (*Odes* 3.22):

> Guardian of mountains and woods, virgin, you who, when called upon three times, hear women laboring in childbirth, three-formed goddess, let the pine that overshadows my villa be yours, to which I will gladly sacrifice at the end of each year the blood of a boar as it prepares the sideways slash [of its tusk].

At Aricia the resurrected **Hippolytus** was identified with the minor Italian divinity, **Virbius**, and associated with Diana. Both Vergil and Ovid tell his story, in which he is put under the protection of the nymph Egeria, and Vergil suggests that it was because of his violent death in a chariot crash that horses were excluded from Diana's shrine.

Mercury

In early Rome, the god Mercury (Mercurius) was worshiped as a god of trading and profit (the Latin word *merces* means **"merchandise"**), and his temple stood by the **Circus Maximus** in the busiest commercial center of Rome. As a character in Plautus' play *Amphitruo*, he describes himself still as the god of commerce and gain. As he came to be identified with the Greek Hermes, however, he acquired Hermes' other functions—musician, messenger of Jupiter, and escort of the dead. Horace, who elsewhere called himself *mercurialis*—that is, a lyric poet under the special protection of Mercury, inventor of the lyre—addressed a hymn to Mercury that elegantly combines his functions (*Odes* 1.10):

> Mercury, eloquent grandson of Atlas, who with language and the rules of the well-mannered gymnasium cleverly fashioned the crude manners of new-made humankind, of you shall I sing, messenger of great Jupiter and the gods, inventor of the curved lyre, clever at concealing with light-hearted theft whatever you like. Apollo laughed at you when he found his quiver missing as he threatened you, a child, unless you returned his stolen cattle. Indeed, with you as guide rich Priam left Troy and unnoticed passed by the proud sons of Atreus, the watch-fires of the Thessalians, and the enemy camp. You bring back the souls of the good to the blessed fields; and with your golden wand you restrain the weightless crowd [of ghosts of the dead], welcome to the gods on high and in the Underworld.   10

Thus the Roman Mercury adopts the functions that were described in the *Homeric Hymn to Hermes*, in Priam's journey to the tent of Achilles in Book 24 of the *Iliad*, and in escorting the dead suitors to the Underworld in the opening lines of Book 24 of the *Odyssey* (where the "golden wand" of Hermes is described).

Divinities of Death and the Underworld

We have already seen (in Chapter 15) something of the Roman idea of the Underworld and its system of rewards and punishments. This conception, which is found principally in Vergil, is literary and sophisticated, derived from different philosophical, religious, and literary sources, most of them Greek. The native Italian ideas of the Underworld and its spirits originated in the simple religion of the early agricultural communities. The spirits of dead ancestors were propitiated at the festival of the **Parentalia** that took place from February 13 to 21 (which in the old Roman calendar was the last month of the year). During this period, no one got married, the temples were closed, and offerings were made to the spirits by the head of the family as a guarantee of their friendliness to the family in the ensuing year. The Parentalia was a family celebration. Its gods were simply **"gods of the ancestors"** (*divi parentum*), without names and without mythology.

The festival of the **Lemuria** was celebrated in May. The head of the family would propitiate the **Lemures**, spirits who could do great harm to the household. The ceremony was conducted by night with a magic ritual—the paterfamilias was barefoot, his fingers and thumb forming an "O," his hands ritually washed before he threw behind him black beans for the Lemures to pick up, while uttering nine times a formula intended to drive the spirits from the house.

Ovid identifies the Lemures with the **Manes**, who were synonymous with the dead. Each person has his or her Manes, and epitaphs conventionally began with *Dis manibus sacrum*, "sacred to the divine Manes of … ," followed by the person's name.

The Manes, the Parentalia, and the Lemuria, which involve no mythology or legend, are far removed from Vergil's elaborate Underworld, which was derived mostly from Greek sources. From the Etruscans the Romans learned to propitiate the dead by offering human blood spilled on the earth. This is the origin of the gladiatorial games, which were first celebrated at Rome in 264 B.C. at the funeral games for Decimus Junius Brutus. The Etruscans shared with the Greeks many Underworld divinities, such as Charon and Persephone, and added some of their own, such as the demon **Tuculcha**. The Underworld itself in Roman literature is commonly called **Orcus** (sometimes personalized as a god), and its ruler was **Dis Pater**, whose name (Dis 5 *dives*, or wealth) is the equivalent of the Greek Pluto. The worship of Dis Pater was established at Rome in 249, although he was certainly known there long before. He and Proserpine shared a cult at an underground altar in the Campus Martius, whose precinct was called Tarentum (the etymology of the name is still unexplained), and its cult was associated with the festival of the Secular Games.

The burial goddess, **Libitina**, was Italian; but her name, origin, and associations have never been satisfactorily explained. Her name was used by the later poets as synonymous with Death, and undertakers were known as *libitinarii*.

Lares and Genius

The Lares were divinities often linked with the Penates. The origin and etymology of their name are unknown. Although they have been identified with spirits of the dead, particularly of ancestors, the Lares were probably household spirits in origin who could bring prosperity and happiness to the farmer and his farm.

François Tomb Fresco. The François tomb (4th century B.C.), near the Etruscan town of Vulci, was unearthed in 1857. The tomb was entered by a long passageway and contained a number of chambers, which were decorated with wall paintings illustrating various historical and mythological narratives. The atrium, the main chamber of the tomb, included this scene, drawn from the *Iliad*. Achilles is sacrificing Trojan prisoners at the funeral of Patroclus. To the left of Achilles is the mysterious Vanth, sometimes described as a winged demon or an Etruscan version of an Erinys (Fury). To the right of the sitting prisoner is Charun, the Etruscan version of the Greek Charon. He is an escort to the Underworld and is usually depicted with a blue complexion, perhaps representing the pallor of a corpse, and a hammer, which is a symbol of this power. (*The Picture Art Collection/Alamy Stock Photo*)

This agricultural origin survived in the *Compitalia* (**Crossroads Festival**), a winter feast celebrated when work on the farm had been completed. A crossroads in primitive communities was regularly the meeting point of the boundaries of four farms, and the Lares honored at the Compitalia were the protecting spirits of the farms. At each crossroads was a shrine, with one opening for each of the four properties. The farmer would hang a doll in the shrine for each free member of his household and a ball of wool for each slave. This seems to have been a purification ritual at the end of the farmer's labor, when substitutes for the human beings were hung up to be purified by the air.

The Lares are basically kindly spirits, protecting the household. Transferred from farm to city, they kept this function, and each house had its *Lar familiaris* to whom offerings of incense, wine, and garlands were made. In Plautus' play *Aulularia*, the *Lar familiaris* speaks the prologue and describes how he can bring happiness and prosperity if he is duly worshiped; if he is neglected, the household will not prosper. Just as each household had its Lar, so the city had its Lares (called the *Lares praestites* or **"guardian Lares"**), who were worshiped on May 1. Augustus revived the celebration of the Compitalia in the city by instituting shrines of the *Lares Compitales* in each of the 265 *vici* or subdivisions of the city. In this function, according to Ovid, the Lares "protect the crossroads and are constantly on guard in our city" (*Fasti* 2.616). At the city Compitalia, the Lares were worshiped together with the Genius of Augustus himself.

The Lares were also protectors of travelers by land (*Lares viales*) and by sea (*Lares permarini*). In 179 B.C., a temple was dedicated to the *Lares Permarini* to commemorate a naval victory over King Antiochus eleven years earlier.

The Genius represented the creative power of a man, seen most especially in the *lectus genialis*, or marriage bed, symbol of the continuing life of the family. It was associated more generally with the continued well-being of the family. Slaves swore oaths by the Genius of the head of the family, and offerings were made to it on his birthday. For women, the equivalent of the male Genius was her Juno.

Lararium. This wall shrine dedicated to the household gods or Lares was found at Pompeii in the atrium of the House of the Vettii. The shrine to the Lares is in the form of a temple or *aedicula* in Latin (aedicule). In the center is the Genius of the paterfamilias, who is holding in his right hand a *patera* (shallow libation vessel) between two Lares, holding rhytons (vessels for pouring libations). Below is a serpent, an *agathodaemon*, a protective spirit that can attend an individual or home. (*PRISMA ARCHIVO/ Alamy Stock Photo, Image supplied by DEA/G. DAGLI ORTI/Contributor via Getty Images*)

Non-Italian Gods

Hercules

Several foreign deities had an important place in Roman religion. In most cases, they came from Greece or the East, and their arrival can often be dated.

The earliest newcomer was the Greek Heracles, called Hercules at Rome. Livy says that when Romulus founded the city, the cult of Hercules was the only foreign one that he accepted. We have seen how Hercules visited Rome with the Cattle of Geryon and there killed the monster Cacus (p. 553). To commemorate the event, his cult was established, either by Hercules himself or by Evander, in the **Forum Boarium** (the cattle market between the Circus Maximus and the Tiber). His precinct there was the Ara Maxima (Greatest Altar), and the cult was in the hands of two noble families until 312 B.C., when it was taken over by the state. The Forum Boarium area was a natural landing place on the Tiber, and it was among the earliest commercial quarters of the city. Since Hercules was the patron of traders, this area was appropriate for his worship. Like Mercury, Hercules brought luck (including chance finds) and profit, and successful traders dedicated a tithe of their profits to him. Besides the Ara Maxima, at least twelve shrines or temples were dedicated to him in the city.

The Dioscuri

The Dioscuri, **Castor** and **Pollux**, were worshiped from the time of the early republic. After they appeared at the battle of **Lake Regillus** (probably in 496 B.C.), a temple in the Forum was dedicated to them both, although its official name was the **Temple of Castor**. In the battle, the Romans were being hard pressed by the Latins, when the Dioscuri appeared before them on horseback and led them to victory. They then appeared in the Roman Forum and announced the victory. After watering their horses at the fountain of Juturna, they vanished. The appearance of the Dioscuri in battle is fairly common in ancient legend, and they were said to have appeared at other battles in later Roman history. They came to Rome from the Greek cities of southern Italy (perhaps from Tarentum) after a period as important deities at Tusculum, a Latin city near Lake Regillus. At Rome, they were especially the patrons of horsemen and of the knights (i.e., the economic and social class below the senators). Only women swore by them, using the oath *ecastor*.

The Sibylline Oracles

An even older arrival in Rome than the Dioscuri were the Sibylline oracles, which were traditionally associated with the Greek colony of Cumae. Collections of oracles written in Greek hexameters were common throughout the Greek world; they were especially associated with the **Sibyls**, prophetesses said to be inspired by Apollo. The **Cumaean Sibyl** was said to have been granted a life of 1,000 years by Apollo, who withheld the compensation of eternal youth (see pp. 251–252). She was Aeneas' guide in the Underworld.

A well-known legend tells how the Sibylline books came to Rome. The Sibyl mysteriously appeared before the last Roman king, **Tarquinius Superbus**, and offered to sell him nine books of oracles for a high price. When he refused, she burned three of the books and offered the remaining six at the same price. Again he refused, and again she burned three books and offered the last three at the same price. This time, acting on the advice of the augurs (an important group of priests), Tarquin bought the books. The Sibyl handed them over and promptly disappeared. The books were stored in the Capitoline temple of Jupiter, to be consulted only on the orders of the senate, for guidance in times of calamity and perplexity or during a pestilence, or after the appearance of disturbing prodigies. The priests who had charge of them were prominent citizens. The books were considered so important that after they were destroyed in the Capitoline fire of 83 B.C., a new collection was made, which Augustus later deposited in the base of the statue of Apollo in his new temple on the Palatine Hill. The Sibylline books are an example of early Greek influence at Rome. They also were influential in bringing new cults to Rome. For example, they advised the introduction of the cults of Ceres, Liber, and Libera in 496 B.C. and of Apollo in 433.

Apollo and Aesculapius

Apollo—the only one of the great Greek gods not to change his name at Rome—arrived as the result of a pestilence, and his temple was dedicated in 431 B.C., two years after the Sibylline books had been consulted. Until the time of Augustus, this remained his only temple at Rome. Except for his cult under Augustus and, to a lesser extent, under Nero, he was never as prominent at Rome as he was in the Greek world. He was worshiped originally as **Apollo Medicus** (corresponding to his Greek title of Paean, the Healer). Later, his other attributes and interests were introduced, and in 212 the **Ludi Apollinares (Games of Apollo,** an annual festival) were instituted. Augustus had a special regard for Apollo, and in 28 B.C. he dedicated a magnificent new temple to him on the Palatine Hill.

In 293 B.C., during an epidemic, the Sibylline books counseled bringing Asclepius, the Greek god of healing, to Rome from Epidaurus. He came in the form of a sacred serpent; when the ship bringing him came up the Tiber to Rome, the serpent slipped onto the island that is in the middle of the present-day city and there made its home. A temple to Aesculapius (his Latin name) was built on the island, and his cult was established.

Cybele

In 205 B.C., during another period of public distress, the Sibylline books advised the Romans to bring in the Phrygian mother-goddess Cybele, known also at Rome as the **Magna Mater (Great Mother)**. After a visit to Delphi, a solemn embassy went to the city of Pessinus in Phrygia, where it received a **black stone** that was said to be the goddess. It was brought to Rome with much ceremony; a temple was built on the Palatine Hill, and the festival of the **Megalensia** was instituted in honor of Cybele. The ecstatic nature of her worship was exceptional at Rome. Her priests (known as **Galli**) practiced self-castration, and until the reign of Claudius, Roman citizens were forbidden to become Galli. The Megalensia, however, and its processions, celebrated in April, were a colorful and popular feature of the Roman religious calendar. Lucretius (2.614–624) and Ovid (*Fasti*

4.181–186) have left vivid descriptions of the Galli with their wild music, and Catullus (Poem 63) has brilliantly told the myth of **Attis** (see pp. 197–198).

Other Eastern gods made their way to Rome, especially in the time of the empire. The Egyptian Isis, the Asiatic Ma, the Syrian Baal, and the Persian Mithras were widely worshiped (see pp. 389–390).

Legends of the Founding of Rome

Aeneas and Romulus

The origins of Rome traditionally went back to Aeneas, whose son **Iulus** (also called **Ascanius**) was ancestor of the *gens Iulia,* the family of Augustus.[6] But Aeneas left Troy some 475 years before the traditional date for the founding of Rome in 753 B.C. The gap between the two dates was filled by a line of kings at the Latin city of Alba Longa. Aeneas succeeded in establishing a foothold in Latium but died soon after. Iulus then founded Alba Longa, and from there Romulus came eventually to found Rome itself. The earliest settlement at Rome may indeed date from the eighth century B.C., and it is also known that early Rome was an alliance of villages on the different hills by the Tiber, which in time were unified. As Rome became a city, it was sometimes under the control of neighboring peoples (the Tarquins, the fifth and seventh kings of Rome, were Etruscans, and the sixth king, Servius Tullius, may have been Etruscan), but by the early part of the fifth century, the city was strong enough to assert its independence. Then it extended its control over the Etruscan cities and the Sabine and Latin tribes, whose customs and gods it often absorbed. The legendary connection between Rome and Alba Longa is historically likely; that between Rome and Troy is more doubtful.

Aeneas: The Tradition before Vergil

In the foundation myth that connects Rome with Troy, the central figure is Aeneas, son of **Aphrodite** and **Anchises**. In the *Iliad*, he was an important warrior but inferior to the Trojan champion Hector. When he meets Achilles in single combat (*Iliad* 20.158–352), he is saved from death by Poseidon, who makes this prophecy (*Iliad* 20.300–308):

> Come, let us lead him away from imminent death, lest Zeus be angry if Achilles kill him. For he is fated to escape, so that the race of Dardanus may not perish without seed and invisible. For Zeus loved Dardanus most of all his children whom mortal women bear to him. Already Zeus is angry with the family of Priam. Now indeed strong Aeneas and his children's children will rule over the Trojans.

Thus there was Homeric authority for the development of Aeneas' saga after the fall of Troy. There are many irreconcilable variations in his legend before Vergil, but his wanderings over the Aegean and Mediterranean and his arrival in Italy seem to have become traditional quite early, and he was associated with a number of shrines of Aphrodite in the areas to which he was said to have traveled. The fifth-century Greek historian Hellanicus recorded his arrival in Italy, and he was well known to the Etruscans. At Veii, for example, a number of statuettes have been found, dating from about 500 B.C., showing Aeneas carrying Anchises from Troy. The same scene appears on seventeen Greek vases from the same period found in Etruria. His travels were narrated in the epics on the Punic wars by Naevius (who died shortly before 200) and Ennius, and it is possible that Naevius introduced his meeting with Dido into the tradition.

The early Roman historians also developed the legend of Aeneas. Around 200 B.C. Fabius Pictor, who wrote in Greek, described his arrival in Italy and the founding of **Alba Longa** by **Ascanius (Iulus)** thirty years later. In his *Origines*, the founder of Latin historiography, Cato the Elder (who died in 149), brought Aeneas to Italy, where he married **Lavinia** and founded the city of **Laurolavinium** (which is evidently the same as **Lavinium**) in an area called the *Ager Laurens.* In this version, Latinus fought against Aeneas, while both Turnus and Aeneas perished in a later battle, and the Etruscan warrior Mezentius was killed by Ascanius in a third battle. Ascanius then left Laurolavinium to found Alba. Finally, Cato calculated that there were 432 years between the fall of Troy and the founding of Rome by Romulus.

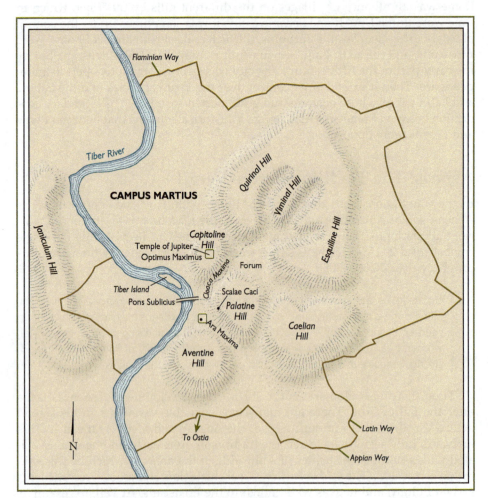

Map 26.2 Map of Early Rome. (© *Laszlo Kubinji, 1994*)

This is the basic version of Aeneas' myth, which is also told with some variations by Livy, Vergil's contemporary. All these stories make Aeneas fight with the indigenous inhabitants (called *Aborigines* by Cato and Livy), marry a local princess (Lavinia), found a city (Lavinium), die, become a god, and leave Ascanius, now called Iulus, as his successor. Ascanius then founds Alba, and some 400 years later Romulus founds Rome itself from Alba.

Vergil's *Aeneid*

This was the material from which Vergil created his epic, the great national poem of Rome, combining Homeric conventions, Greek mythology, and Roman ethical and historical insights. It records the events of a distant mythological past, yet it has reference to the events and hopes of Vergil's own day, when Augustus was rebuilding the Roman state after decades of civil war and instability. In the prologue, Vergil links Roman history to the mythological tradition and focuses on the hero Aeneas, survivor of the fall of Troy and ancestor of Rome's leaders (*Aeneid* 1.1–7):

> Of war and a man I sing, who first from Troy's shores, an exile by the decree of fate, came to Italy and Lavinium's shores. Much was he tossed on sea and land by the violence of the gods, because of cruel Juno's unforgetting anger. Much, too, did he endure in war as he sought to found a city and bring his gods to Latium. From him are descended the Latin people, the elders of Alba, and the walls of lofty Rome.

According to Vergil, Aeneas sailed by way of Thrace and Delos to Crete, where he stayed a year, believing that this was the place from which **Dardanus** came and that therefore it was the future home foretold him by the oracle at Delos. But a pestilence and a vision of the Penates led him to sail in search of Italy, which proved to be Dardanus' original home. He sailed to Epirus, where Helenus and Andromache had settled. Here **Helenus** foretold some of his future wanderings and in particular told of their ending, which Aeneas would know had come when he saw a white sow with thirty piglets on a river bank in Italy. This prophecy complemented one that Aeneas received from the Harpy **Celaeno**, who foretold that he would reach Italy and would found his new city only when hunger had compelled the Trojans to eat the tables on which their food lay.

Leaving Helenus, Aeneas reached Sicily, sailing past the shore of southern Italy and avoiding the perils of Charybdis. A direct link with Odysseus was provided by the appearance of one of his men, **Achaemenides**, a survivor of the adventure with the Cyclopes, who warned Aeneas of Polyphemus and other dangers. It was in Sicily, too, that Anchises died and was buried.

The fall of Troy and Aeneas' wanderings to this point are narrated by him to Dido in Books 2 and 3 of the *Aeneid*. The poem begins with a storm that scatters Aeneas' fleet after setting sail from Sicily. The survivors were reunited in northern Africa, where **Dido**, queen of Carthage, hospitably received them. She fell deeply in love with Aeneas, who would himself have been content to stay with her had not Mercury appeared to him and transmitted Jupiter's orders to sail away to fulfill his destiny in Italy. As he left,

Dido laid a curse on Aeneas and his descendants that they should always be the enemies of Carthage and then killed herself with the sword that Aeneas had given her.

Aeneas sailed back to Sicily and was welcomed by the king of Egesta, the Trojan Acestes. Here he celebrated funeral games in honor of Anchises, during which the Trojan women, incited by Juno, set fire to some of the ships, the rest being saved by Jupiter in a miraculous rainstorm.[7] Aeneas left some of his followers behind in Sicily and now sailed on to Italy, where he reached **Cumae**. Here the Sibyl foretold the wars he must fight in the new land and escorted him to the Underworld, where he talked with many of the dead whom he had known in his past life. The climax of his visit to the Underworld was his meeting with Anchises, who foretold the greatness of Rome and showed him a pageant of future Romans. The visit to the Underworld is the turning point in Aeneas' saga; after it, he is sure of his destiny and determined to settle in Italy, whatever obstacles have to be surmounted.

From Cumae, Aeneas sailed to the mouth of the Tiber, where the prophecy of Celaeno was fulfilled; as the Trojans ate the flat cakes upon which their food was placed, Iulus said, "Why, we are even eating our tables!" In **Latium**, **King Latinus** had betrothed his daughter **Lavinia** to the prince of the tribe of the Rutuli, **Turnus**. Worried by prodigies, Latinus consulted the oracle of Faunus, who advised him to give Lavinia to a foreigner instead. Latinus attempted to obey this advice by giving Lavinia to Aeneas, but Juno sent the Fury **Allecto** to madden Turnus and Lavinia's mother **Amata**, so that they violently opposed Aeneas.

War became inevitable, and Latinus was powerless to prevent it. Turnus and the Latins, with other Italian leaders (notably the Etruscan exile **Mezentius**), opposed the Trojans, who had for allies the Etruscans under Tarchon and the men of **Pallanteum**, Evander's city on the future site of Rome. Aeneas' visit to **Evander** had been preceded by the vision of the river-god Tiberinus. Evander himself showed Aeneas the city that was to become Rome and sent back with him his own son, **Pallas**, who later was killed by Turnus. After ferocious battles between the Latin allies and the Trojans, Aeneas killed Turnus in single combat. At this point the *Aeneid* ends.

This bald outline hardly reveals the extraordinary power of Vergil's poem. Writing in the epic tradition of Homer, he created a new kind of Roman epic. We illustrate three of his innovations—his use of Jupiter and prophecy to combine myth and Roman history; his creation of a different kind of hero, in some ways like Achilles and Odysseus, but differing completely in the Roman nature of his *pietas* (a virtue that includes a sense of duty and service); and finally, the prominent role he gives to Dido.

Jupiter in the *Aeneid*

In the *Aeneid*, the traditional Olympian figure of Zeus–Jupiter becomes identified with destiny or fate. Therefore his prophecies are especially important, and through them Vergil links mythology and Roman history to make the destiny of Rome both noble and inevitable.

In Book 1, Aeneas is driven to land near Carthage by a storm raised by **Juno** and **Aeolus**, and Venus complains to Jupiter of the sufferings of her son. In reply, Jupiter foretells his glorious destiny and that of his Roman descendants. Here are a few lines from this prophecy (*Aeneid* 1.267–279):

> But young Ascanius, who now has assumed the additional name of Iulus … will complete thirty mighty cycles of the rolling months as king, and he will transfer his kingdom from its place at Lavinium and will found with much force Alba Longa. Here the family of Hector will rule for 300 whole years, until the royal priestess Ilia, pregnant by Mars, will bear twin children. Then Romulus, rejoicing in the tawny covering of the skin of the wolf (his nurse), will succeed as ruler of the race and will found the city of Mars and call its people Romans after his own name. For them I give no limits of events or time: I have given them empire without end.

This sense of high destiny, in which the traditional myths serve a historical purpose, is repeatedly emphasized by Vergil in Aeneas' visit to the Underworld in Book 6 (see Chapter 15), in the description of his shield at the end of Book 8, and in the final prophecy of Jupiter in Book 12 (830–840). By these means, Vergil preserves the Homeric figures of the Olympian gods, but Jupiter is a more powerful figure than Zeus, while the other gods play their traditional roles, favoring one side or the other. Juno is hostile to Aeneas and favors those who would divert him from his destiny, notably Dido and Turnus, while Venus consistently favors her son and intercedes with Jupiter for him.

Aeneas: A New Epic Hero

Aeneas is motivated by *pietas*, which leads him to leave ease and comfort to pursue a destiny of which he does not become fully aware until after his visit to the Underworld. He is a wanderer, like Odysseus, in search of a home; and he is the son of a goddess, like Achilles, terrible in single combat. But he is also an exile, who has been defeated in a great war and has seen his city destroyed. His character is epitomized in the scene where he leaves Troy with Anchises, symbol of the past, on his shoulders, while holding the hand of Ascanius, hope of the future (see p. 501). When we first meet Aeneas in the storm in Book 1, he wishes he were dead and his "limbs were loosened with cold fear" (1.92–96). Yet on coming to land, he speaks to his followers words that show his patience, courage, and hope (*Aeneid* 1.198–207):

> My companions—for we are not inexperienced in adversity—O friends who have suffered worse, the god will bring an end to these things also. You came to the fury of Scylla and the sounding rocks, you experienced the cave of the Cyclops. Recall your courage and dismiss dejected fear. Perhaps we shall be glad to remember these things also in the future. Through varied fortunes,

Dido and Aeneas in the Storm. Fifth-century Vergilius Romanus manuscript written on parchment; 13 × 12¾ in. This manuscript is one of two illustrated manuscripts of Vergil's works from the fifth century. It includes nineteen full-page miniatures, each enclosed in a painted "frame." Here the artist depicts the storm that drove Aeneas and Dido to the same cave during their hunt. The lovers are shown frontally, Dido embracing Aeneas with both arms, while their shields (of different shapes) and hunting spears are propped beside them. Outside, their horses and guards endure the rain: one guard is protected in part by a tree, and the other uses his shield as an umbrella. The details are carefully rendered, such as the red saddle of Dido's horse and the hose of the guards, one matching that of Dido and the other that of Aeneas. (*Art Collection 3/Alamy Stock Photo*)

through so many dangers, we go to Latium, where fate shows us a peaceful home. There the kingdom of Troy is destined to rise again. Endure, and keep yourselves for prosperous times!

Yet Aeneas' path is never simple. In Carthage he loves and is loved by Dido, and in a last interview with her he tells her that he must obey Jupiter, whose messenger Mercury has appeared to him, however unwillingly (4.356–361):

Now also the messenger of the gods sent from Jupiter himself has brought his orders flying swiftly through the air. I myself saw the god in the clear light entering the city and with my own ears I heard him speak. Do not inflame me and yourself with your complaints. I go to Italy not of my own will.

In the last part of the poem, Aeneas must fight a terrible war against the Rutulians, led by Turnus, and their allies. In the final scene of the poem, Aeneas and Turnus meet in single combat, and the poem ends with the death of Turnus, who has pleaded with Aeneas for his life. Turnus had earlier killed Pallas, son of Evander, Aeneas' host at Pallanteum, and put on his victim's sword-belt. Here are the last fifteen lines of the poem (12.938–952):

Dido in Resolve, by David Ligare (b. 1945); 1989, 116 × 80 in. Dido, dressed in a white robe, confirms her resolution to die. She has sent her sister, Anna, to build a pyre and now sits, alone, high in her palace, where she can see Aeneas' fleet sailing out of the harbor. (*Museum of Art and Archaeology, University of Missouri. Gift of the Student Fee Capital Improvement Committee*)

Aeneas stood armed eager to attack, surveying [Turnus], and he kept his hand from striking. Even now more and more Turnus' appeal had begun to deflect him as he hesitated, while the ill-starred belt came into his view high on [Turnus'] shoulder and the well-known studs glittered on the boy Pallas' strap. Turnus had felled him with a [fatal] wound and wore his enemy's fittings on his shoulders. Aeneas gazed profoundly at the reminder of his savage grief and at the spoils; and on fire with rage and terrible in his anger, he spoke: "Will you, wearing the spoils taken from my friends, be snatched from me? Pallas with this blow sacrifices you and exacts payment from your sinful blood."

With these words in hot anger he sank the sword in Turnus' chest. His limbs collapsed in the coldness [of death] and his life fled with a groan complaining to the Underworld.

10

Thus, at the end, Aeneas is overcome by anger mixed with devotion to his dead friend. Vergil leaves us in doubt—is the *pietas* of Aeneas weaker than his passion? Is he after all a hero motivated by passion like Achilles, rather than the Roman hero inspired by *pietas*? Vergil leaves his readers to decide.

Dido

The greatest obstacle to Aeneas' success is Dido, queen of Carthage and favorite of Juno. In the tradition before Vergil, she was called **Elissa**, a princess of Tyre, married to **Sychaeus**, who was murdered by her brother, **Pygmalion**. She escaped from **Tyre** (taking with her Pygmalion's treasure) and came to north Africa where, as Dido (which in Punic means "Virgin"), she founded **Carthage**, whose territory she was given by the local prince, Iarbas. Vergil makes her a gracious queen, a leader whom he likens to the goddess Diana. She welcomed the Trojan survivors of the storm, and Aeneas is moved as he sees the history of his own sufferings at Troy portrayed on the city's temple. When Dido first appears, she is likened to Diana herself; all is light and activity. She graciously invites the Trojans to her palace, for, she says, "I also was tossed about with many sufferings and Fortune finally wished me to settle in this land. Not without experience of evil, I know how to help the unfortunate" (*Aeneid* 1.628–630).

But destiny is against Dido; Venus and Juno conspire to make her fall in love with Aeneas; and after he has recounted to her the fall of Troy and his wanderings, she is stricken with love, likened by Vergil to a wounded deer. Her passion is described in Book 4, along with the hunt and her union with Aeneas, the complaint of her rejected suitor Iarbas to his father, Jupiter (who had seduced Iarbas' mother), the appearances of Mercury urging Aeneas to leave, the final confrontation of Dido and Aeneas, Aeneas' departure, and Dido's decision to die. Before she dies, Dido utters a curse on Aeneas and his descendants (4.607–629):

> O Sun, you who traverse all earth's works with your flames, and you, O Juno, mediator in these troubles and witness, and Hecate, called on with weird cries by night at the crossways in the cities, and dire avenging goddesses (*Dirae*), and gods of dying Elissa [i.e., Dido], accept my words and hear my prayer! If it is necessary for his cursed head to reach harbor and come to land, and if Jupiter's fate so demands and this ending is fixed, then let him beg for help, harried by war with a brave and well-armed people, an exile with no home, torn from the embrace of Iulus, and let him see the untimely death of his companions. And when he has yielded himself to the terms of an unfair peace, then may he not enjoy his kingdom nor the light he longed for. Let him fall before his time and lie unburied on the shore. This is my prayer, this is my final word as I shed my blood. Then may you, O my Tyrians, harass his family and all his future descendants with hatred and send this offering to my ashes. Let there be no love, no treaty between our peoples. May you arise, some avenger, from my bones, and may you pursue the Trojan settlers with fire and sword, now, in the future, whenever time gives you strength. This is my curse—shore with opposing shore, sea with sea, arms with arms, let them and their descendants fight!

10

Vergil has again united myth and history, for Dido's curse vividly reminds the reader of Rome's times of greatest danger, the wars against Carthage. But in Dido, Vergil also created a character who has always aroused the sympathy of his readers—we are reminded of Augustine, who confessed that he shed tears for Dido before he did for Christ. As with Aeneas and his legend, Vergil took the traditional story of the founding of Carthage by the Phoenician queen Elissa and transformed the saga into profoundly moving tragedy.

Other Characters in the *Aeneid*

The *Aeneid* is full of characters and scenes that have become part of traditional Roman legend. Besides the fall of Troy, Vergil takes Aeneas to the future site of Rome, where he is welcomed by the Arcadian king Evander and hears the story of Hercules and Cacus. We have seen in Chapter 15 how Aeneas visits the

Underworld. In Book 7, we see how Juno rouses the malevolent powers of the Underworld in her attempt to thwart the fulfillment of destiny. Aeneas' enemy Turnus is, like Dido, a victim of destiny, both a cruel warrior and a gallant champion of his people. Mythical Italian characters are vividly portrayed: the warrior maiden **Camilla**, leader of the Volscians, who could run over the fields of ripe grain without bruising the crops and over the waves of the sea without her feet touching the water (7.808–811), and Mezentius, "despiser of the gods," the Etruscan leader who in other versions of the saga survived the war and was later killed by Ascanius. In the *Aeneid*, both he and his son, **Lausus**, are killed by Aeneas. Camilla is killed by the Etruscan Arruns, who is himself killed by Diana's follower Opis in punishment for killing her favorite. Finally, Vergil's tragic narrative of the Trojan warriors Nisus and Euryalus (*Aeneid* 9.176–449) invests a night patrol with the emotions of a dangerous military adventure and the love of Nisus for his younger companion Euryalus. Nisus avenges the death of Euryalus and then kills himself, falling upon his friend's body. In a moving apostrophe Vergil concludes (9.446–449):

> Fortunate pair! If my poem has any power, never in all future history will you be forgotten, so long as the descendants of Aeneas dwell on the immovable rock of the Capitol and the Roman father [Jupiter] holds his power.

The Death of Aeneas

The *Aeneid* ends with the death of Turnus. The saga continues with Aeneas' marriage to Lavinia and his founding of Lavinium. He died in battle after only three more years and became a god, being worshiped with the divine title *Indiges*.[8]

Anna and Anna Perenna

The myth of Anna, Dido's sister, is related by Ovid (*Fasti* 3.523–656) in connection with the New Year's festival (celebrated in March, originally the first month of the Roman calendar) in honor of Anna Perenna. Anna fled from Carthage, which had been occupied by Iarbas, and came to Melita (Malta). Here her brother Pygmalion, who had killed Dido's husband, Sychaeus, and driven her from Tyre, found her and demanded that she be handed over. Fleeing again, she was shipwrecked off the coast of Latium, reaching land in Aeneas' territory in the *ager Laurens*. Aeneas found her and gave her a refuge in his palace, but Lavinia out of jealousy plotted to kill her. Warned by Dido in a dream, Anna fled once more and came to the banks of the river Numicus, where Aeneas' followers searched for her. Here is how the story ends (*Fasti* 3.651–656):

> They came to the banks [of the Numicus], where her footsteps were. The river, which knew [what had happened], stopped the flow of his silent waters. Anna herself seemed to speak: "I am a nymph of the peaceful Numicus. I hide in the river that flows year round (*perenne*) and my name is Anna Perenna." Immediately they feasted in the meadows where they had wandered in their search and celebrated the day and themselves with copious wine.

Thus Ovid identified Anna, sister of Dido, with Anna Perenna, the Italian goddess of the New Year, whose festival was marked by feasting in the open air, drinking, and lovemaking.

Romulus and the Earliest Legends of Rome

Romulus and Remus

The last king of Alba Longa was **Amulius**, who had usurped the throne from his brother **Numitor**. Numitor's daughter was **Rhea Silvia**, also called **Ilia**, whom Amulius attempted to keep from marriage by making her a Vestal Virgin. Mars loved her, however, and she bore him twin sons, Romulus and Remus, whom Amulius ordered to be thrown into the Tiber. But the servants pitied them and left them by the edge of the river, which was in flood. When the waters receded, the twins were safe on dry ground, where they were found by a she-wolf, who suckled them. The place was marked by the **Ficus (fig tree) Ruminalis**, a name that is related to the word *rumis*, a teat. It grew near the Lupercal cave below the Palatine Hill, which was the site of Evander's city, Pallanteum.

The babies were found by one of Amulius' shepherds, **Faustulus**, who brought them to his home, where he and his wife **Acca Larentia** brought them up. When they were grown up, they made their living, it was said, by attacking brigands and relieving them of their spoils. Eventually, Remus was arrested and brought before Numitor, but his punishment was prevented by the appearance of Romulus, who related the story told to him by Faustulus of the twins' rescue. So grandfather and grandsons recognized each other, and together they brought about the death of Amulius and the restoration of Numitor to the throne of Alba. Romulus and Remus then left Alba and founded their own city at the site of their miraculous rescue from the Tiber.

The theme of fraternal rivalry now appears in the story of Romulus and Remus, and it led to the death of Remus. To decide which should give his name to the city, Romulus and Remus resorted to augury, that is, taking omens from the flight of birds. Here is how Ennius describes the scene (*Annales* 1, frag. 47):

> Then caring with great care and desiring to rule they give their attention to auspices and augury. Remus takes his place on the hill and alone watches for a favorable bird. But handsome Romulus watches from the heights of the Aventine, observing the race of high-flying birds. Their contest was whether to name the city Roma or Remora. All [the people] were in suspense as to who would be their leader. Straightway the bright light came forth, struck by the rays [of the sun], and at the same time high up a bird flew on the left, by far the most beautiful bird of augury. At the same time the golden sun rose, and thrice four sacred bodies of birds flew from the heavens and settled in the lucky places of good omen. Then Romulus saw that the throne and land of the kingdom had been given to him as his own by augury.

In Ennius' account, Romulus and Remus watch from different parts of the Aventine, and the birds appear only to Romulus. In later versions, Romulus watched from the Palatine Hill, Remus from the Aventine. The first omen, six vultures, appeared to Remus, and then twelve appeared to Romulus. In the ensuing quarrel as to whether the winner was he who saw more birds or he who saw the omen first, Remus was killed. Romulus gave his name to the new city of Rome and became its king.

Ennius, however, gave a different version of Remus' death, which was followed by Livy and Ovid. Romulus began to build his city on the Palatine, and when the walls had risen a little way, Remus scornfully leaped over them and was killed by his brother because he had acted as an enemy, for a friend enters a city by the gate.

Romulus and the Sabines

Romulus now set about establishing his kingdom and laying the foundations of Rome's political structure. In order to increase the population, he declared the area between the two parts of the Capitoline Hill an *asylum* (i.e., a sanctuary where any man could be assured of freedom from violence or persecution). To this place men came from many directions to become Rome's future citizens. There was a shortage of women, however, and attempts to remedy this situation led to a long series of incidents involving the Romans and the Sabines.

In the first place, the surrounding tribes refused requests from Roman embassies for young women to be wives for Roman men. Romulus decided therefore to use deceit and force. Men and women from the Sabine tribes were invited to attend the festival games of the Consualia. At a given signal, the Roman men seized the young Sabine women, whose relatives fled. Such an act could not go unavenged, and the Sabines, under the leadership of **Titus Tatius**, organized themselves for war on the Romans. In the first encounter, Romulus killed the king of the Sabine town of Caenina and dedicated his armor to **Jupiter Feretrius** (perhaps Jupiter "to whom one brings"). This was the first of only three occasions in the history of the Roman Republic that a Roman commander dedicated the armor of an enemy commander whom he had personally slain. Such dedications were known as the *spolia opima* (**the most glorious trophy**). In the second battle, when Romulus was again victorious, **Hersilia**, the wife of Romulus, acted as conciliator and persuaded her husband to accept the defeated Sabines as Roman citizens.

Mars and Rhea Silvia, by Peter Paul Rubens (1577–1640); oil sketch on canvas, 1616–1617; 21½ × 29¼ in. Mars, in armor, rushes impetuously toward the Vestal Virgin. Already a cupid has removed his helmet, and another (with a quiver of arrows) is unbuckling his breastplate. Rhea looks at him with mixed emotions. The setting is the temple of Vesta, whose sacred fire burns on the altar in front of the Palladium. The sketch may have been intended for a tapestry, since Athena's spear and shield are reversed (her shield would normally be on the left arm) and Mars' sword is on his right side. (*LIECHTENSTEIN, The Princely Collections, Vaduz-Vienna/SCALA, Florence*)

Finally the Sabines attacked Rome itself and through the treachery of **Tarpeia** captured the Capitoline Hill. In the legend, Tarpeia was the daughter of the Roman commander upon the Capitol; greedy for gold, she agreed to let the Sabines in if they would give her "what they had upon their left arms"— meaning their gold bracelets. After the capture, they crushed her to death under their shields, for the left arm is the shield arm. Although they were masters of the citadel, the Sabines could not capture the Forum—its entrance was barred by miraculous jets of boiling water emitted by Janus. In the low ground where the Forum lay, fierce fighting took place, and the Sabines were successful until Romulus turned the tide of battle by vowing a temple to **Jupiter Stator (Jupiter the Stayer)**.

The next stage of the battle is associated with a cavity in the Roman Forum called the **Lacus Curtius**. The fiercest of the Sabine soldiers was Mettus Curtius, who rode on his horse into the marshy ground and miraculously escaped from his pursuers. The low-lying depression was named after him. Livy also gives another (more patriotic) account of the Lacus Curtius, which has proved more popular. In 362 B.C., a chasm mysteriously opened up in the Forum, and the soothsayers announced that it could be closed only by putting into it that which was most valuable to Rome; if it were so filled, the Roman state would endure forever. A young Roman, **Marcus Curtius**, realized that military courage was Rome's greatest treasure, and in full panoply and before the assembled people he prayed to the gods and rode into the chasm. Thus it was closed, and the place took its name from the hero who had been swallowed up by the earth.

The battle between Romulus and the Sabines was brought to an end by the Sabine women themselves, wives (and now mothers) of Romans and daughters of Sabines. They ran into the middle of the battle and by their direct appeals brought about a truce. Peace was made, and the Sabines and Romans agreed to live together at Rome, with Titus Tatius becoming Romulus' colleague in the kingship, while the Sabines provided the name by which the Roman citizens were addressed, *Quirites*.[9]

Thus the unification of the two peoples was achieved. Titus Tatius was killed some years later by the people of Lavinium. Romulus himself, after a long reign, disappeared while reviewing his army in the Campus Martius, amid thunder and lightning. He became the god **Quirinus** and appeared to a farmer, Proculus Julius, who reported his final words. They eloquently embody the ideals that later Romans attributed to the founder of their state (Livy 1.16):

> "Go," said he, "and tell the Romans that it is the gods' will that my city of Rome should be the capital of the world. Let them exercise their military skill and let them know—and let them tell their descendants—that no mortal power can resist the Romans."

Some of the saga of Romulus is rooted in fact, as has been proved by recent archaeological discoveries. Much of his legend, however, is literary invention. Romulus himself is the eponym of Rome, to whom many features of the Roman constitution are ascribed. His deification is problematic, since Quirinus was a Sabine god with whom Mars was associated. Sometimes his

The Capitoline Wolf. Etruscan bronze statue, ca. 480 B.C.; 30 × 46 in. The two babies were added late in the fifteenth century. The history of this iconic figure is not fully known, beyond that it has been placed in various places in Rome, even after it was given by Pope Sixtus IV in 1471 to the conservators of Rome, whose palace is on the Capitoline Hill. Recent analysis has suggested that it may actually be a thirteenth-century copy—a suggestion that is not accepted here. The contrast between the smooth fur of the wolf's body and the elaborate curls of her neck is remarkable. *(Scala/Art Resource, NY)*

name stands by itself; sometimes it is attached to Mars (Mars Quirinus) or to Janus, Jupiter, or even Hercules. One ancient Roman scholar (Servius on *Aeneid* 1.292) described Quirinus as "Mars when he presides in peacetime." The idea of a god of a military state when it is not at war is particularly suitable for Romulus, organizer of the peaceful state and successful leader in its first wars. Quirinus, moreover, being Sabine, is suitably fused with the Roman Romulus; there were separate communities with different cultures upon the Palatine, Oppian, and Quirinal hills in the eighth century B.C., and the legend of a fusion, symbolized by the god Romulus-Quirinus, is supported by archaeological evidence.

Other Characters in the Legend of Romulus

Several other characters in the Romulus legend are divine. Faustulus, the shepherd who reared the twins, may have some connection with Faunus, since the root of his name is the same and has the connotation of "favoring" or "bringing increase." Cato and Varro, followed by Ovid, connected Acca Larentia, Faustulus' wife, with the festival of the **Larentalia** on December 23, at which offerings were made to the dead, but her exact divine function is unknown. It has been suggested that her name, Acca, is the same as the Sanskrit word for "mother" and that she was therefore the *mater Larum*, mother of the Lares (although the first *a* of *Larentia* is long and that of *Larum* is short). All that can be said with certainty is that both Acca and Faustulus are old divinities whose precise attributes and functions had been forgotten by the time of the early Roman writers.

Hersilia, the wife of Romulus, became **Hora Quirini**, the consort of the deified Romulus. Almost certainly her name, Hora, meant "the power" or "the will" of Quirinus, and this was her original function, before the myth made her the wife of the mortal Romulus.

The treacherous Tarpeia gave her name to the **Tarpeian Rock**, from which condemned criminals were thrown to their deaths. She, too, was divine, for libations were offered at her tomb. Although Livy makes her a Sabine, her name is Etruscan.

Some of the elements in the legend explain features of the Roman constitution. The dual kingship of Romulus and the colorless Titus Tatius foreshadows the collegiate principle of republican magistracies, in particular the dual consulship.

Legends of the Regal Period

The period of the kings (which traditionally ended in 509 B.C.) and of the early republic is full of stories that are more myth than history. We give a few examples here.

The Horatii

In the reign of the third king, **Tullus Hostilius**, there was war between Rome and Alba Longa, which ended in the destruction of Alba. At an earlier stage, the two sides agreed to decide the issue by a battle between champions, three brothers on each side; the Alban champions were the **Curiatii**, and the Romans were the Horatii. Two Romans were quickly killed, but the third, who was unwounded, separated and dispatched singly his wounded opponents. Now his sister had been betrothed to one of the Curiatii; and as her brother was triumphantly entering Rome, bearing the spoils of the dead Curiatii, she cried out in grief. **Horatius** killed her immediately for her inopportune and unpatriotic gesture. As a murderer, he was condemned to death, but on appeal to the people, he gained a reversal of the verdict because of his popularity as a courageous soldier. He underwent a ritual purification by offering a sacrifice and passing with veiled head beneath a kind of yoke or crossbar (i.e., a horizontal beam supported by two upright poles). The crossbar was called the *tigillum sororium* and was flanked by two altars, one dedicated to **Janus Curiatius**, the other to **Juno Sororia**.

The association of Horatius with the *tigillum sororium* was the result of confusing the archaic title of Juno Sororia with the Latin word *soror*, a sister. Passing under the yoke was indeed a ceremony of purification, but, as the titles of the two divinities prove, the purification in this case was of boys and girls reaching the age of puberty. The boys, initiated at the altar of Janus Curiatius, went out to their first battle, and on their return they were purified from blood-guilt by passing beneath the *tigillum*. Juno Sororia likewise presided over the initiation of girls into adult life. Other details of the legend are etiological. The appeal of Horatius explains the Roman citizen's right of appeal to the people. The legend of the Horatii and Curiatii may have derived from five ancient mound tombs, in two groups of two and three, respectively, outside Rome in the direction of Alba. Another ancient stone tomb stood near the place where Horatia was said to have been killed by her brother.

THE RAPE OF LUCRETIA

Kings ruled Rome before the fifth century B.C.; by the fifth century, Rome had become a republic. The historical causes for this change are complex and multifarious, but by the first century B.C., the Romans had crystallized their understanding of the political revolution in terms of a symbolic legend of sexual violence perpetrated by the son of the king upon a noblewoman. This story is known as the Rape of Lucretia. The tale is preserved in two authors: Dionysius of Halicarnassus (late first century B.C.), a Greek who wrote a history of Rome in Greek entitled *Roman Antiquities*; and Livy (59 B.C.–A.D. 17), a Roman historian who wrote a history of Rome in Latin from its foundation to his own day, entitled *Ab Urbe Condita* (*From the Foundation of the City*). Though the accounts differ in some important ways and a comparison of the two tales would be fruitful, it is Livy's story that has become the standard version.

As the story opens, the last king of Rome, Tarquin the Proud, has decided to lay siege to the city of Ardea, whose wealth he hopes will soften some of the growing resentment among the people for his high-handed treatment. The siege is prolonged, and during a respite from the fighting, the royal princes spend time drinking in the tent of Sextus Tarquinius, the eldest son of the king. With them is a noble named Collatinus, from a town near Rome called Collatia. As the evening wears on, the men begin to discuss their wives, each one praising the exceptional virtues of his own wife. The discussion becomes heated, and Collatinus suggests that the surest way to resolve the dispute will be for them to return to their homes and see what their wives are doing at that very moment. Since the men are all intoxicated, they agree to the proposal. And so they all ride off.

When they arrive, the princes discover their wives enjoying the company of friends, eating and drinking, and generally living the high life. But when they come to the house of Collatinus late at night, they find his wife, Lucretia, spinning by candlelight along with her maidservants. As soon as she realizes the house has visitors, she rises and welcomes everyone, and Collatinus suggests they all stay for dinner. It is while they are enjoying the hospitality of the house that Sextus Tarquinius begins to lust after Lucretia. After dinner, the soldiers return to camp.

Tarquin and Lucretia (1571), by Titian (ca. 1485–1576); oil on canvas: 37½ × 29 in. Titian painted two versions of this subject (the earlier one is now in Vienna). Here, in the close confines of Lucretia's bedroom, Tarquin, dressed in red and with his right knee thrust between Lucretia's legs, threatens her with his dagger, while she tries to push him away with her free arm (for the other is held by Tarquin). Though naked, she still wears the jewels and hair ornaments of a wealthy aristocrat. In the left background the servant, whom Tarquin will kill and place beside the body of Lucretia if she does not give in to his lust, draws the bed curtain aside. (*Fitzwilliam Museum, University of Cambridge, UK/The Bridgeman Art Library*)

Some days later, Sextus returns with a companion to the home of Lucretia, unbidden and without the knowledge of Collatinus. Again she welcomes him graciously and offers him dinner. She also invites him to stay the night in one of the guest bedrooms. There, he waits until everyone has gone to bed and the house is quiet. With his sword drawn, he steals into Lucretia's bedchamber, intending to rape her. Lucretia is asleep, but she awakes in terror when he lays a hand on her breast. He silences her with threats of death and thereupon tries to persuade, threaten, and even plead with her that she willingly submit to his lust. She refuses. Then he tells her that he will shame her into submission. If she does not agree to sleep with him, first he will kill her and then he will kill a slave of the house and place his body next to hers. When Collatinus returns, he will be told that his wife has been killed in the act of adultery with a slave. Lucretia submits to his lust.

Rape of Lucrece, by Reuben Nakian (1897–1986); steel, 1953–1958, height 144 in. Nakian has transformed conventional representations of the scene into a violent confrontation of abstract forms constructed from steel plates and pipes. The intimidating figure on the right, topped by a helmet-like shape, threatens the slighter figure on the left, who starts back from the attacker, while she leaps (we can imagine) to the ground from her bed. Nakian's disjointed shapes starkly express the breakdown of moral and social order represented by the crime of Tarquinius. (*Courtesy of the Hirshhorn Museum and Sculpture Garden and Reuben Nakian Estate*)

When Sextus finally leaves, Lucretia writes a letter to her father in Rome and her husband at the siege of Ardea. She urges them to return at once with trusted friends (*amici*) but does not commit to the letter what has happened. Her father comes with a friend named Valerius; her husband, Collatinus, is joined by Brutus. When they arrive, they find Lucretia sitting in her room weeping. To her husband's tender question about her welfare she responds that her body (*corpus*) has been violated by another man, but that her mind (*animus*) is innocent. She has them swear an oath that they will punish the man who did this to her and then names Sextus as the perpetrator. They give their solemn word and try to comfort her in her distress, saying that it is the mind that sins, not the body. Without intention there can be no fault. Lucretia understands that there is no fault in her, and yet to prevent her experience from being used as a pretext for other women to commit adultery, she takes a knife and stabs herself. Her husband and father cry out in horror. Brutus removes the knife from her body and vows that with that same knife he will punish Tarquin the Proud, his wife, and all his children.

Livy's story of the rape of Lucretia crystallizes a great many Roman values, including the idea that the personal and the political, the public and the private, are inextricably linked; a revolution in the state is stirred by what happens in a single home. Lucretia kills herself rather than allow herself to be used as an excuse for immorality in others; communal responsibility is more important than individual desires. A tyrant suffers no equals; Livy has Sextus accompanied by a "companion" and Collatinus by a trusted "friend."

The Oath of the Horatii, by Jacques-Louis David (1748–1825); oil on canvas, 1785, 128¼ × 168 in. David moved from Paris to Rome in order to imbibe the classical inspiration necessary for this huge and heroic painting. The scene is based not on Livy, but on Corneille's tragedy *Horace* (1640) and Noverre's ballet (1782) on the same theme. The elder Horatius, holding the brothers' swords, administers the oath to the brothers, who salute with military precision, which indicates (for David's patrons) patriotic self-sacrifice but bears more ominous associations for modern viewers. On the right, in the background, the mother of the three brothers comforts her grandchildren, and, in front, Sabina (wife of one of the brothers and sister of the Curiatii) and Camilla (sister of the Horatii and engaged to one of the Curiatii) mourn for their coming bereavement. (© *RMN-Grand Palais/Art Resource, NY*)

The Tarquins and Servius Tullius

The last three kings of Rome were Tarquinius Priscus, Servius Tullius, and Tarquinius Superbus. The two Tarquins were Etruscans, and Servius probably was Etruscan, although his name is Latin. Servius was a founder and organizer of Roman institutions second only to Romulus, and a number of legends gathered round him. His mother, Ocrisia, was a slave who had been captured in war and assigned to the household of Tarquinius Priscus. She was of the royal house at Corniculum. According to the legend, Servius' father was the son of Vulcan, who miraculously appeared in phallic form to Ocrisia as she was sitting by the fire in the palace. When Servius was a baby, Vulcan showed his favor by causing a miraculous flame to play around the child's head without harming him. Favored by such portents, Servius was assured of special treatment in the palace; he was brought up in the king's family and married to his daughter. When Tarquin was murdered, his widow, **Tanaquil**, skillfully arranged for the transfer of power to Servius.

Apart from his political and military reforms, Servius is credited with introducing the cult of Diana to Rome. Like King Numa, he is said to have had a divine counselor and consort, in this case the goddess Fortuna. His death was said to have been caused by his daughter, called Tullia the Younger, who was married to Arruns, the son of Tarquinius Priscus, while her sister (called Tullia the Elder) was married to his brother Tarquinius. Tullia the Younger had her husband and her sister murdered and then married Tarquinius, whom she urged to usurp the throne and murder Servius. The corpse of Servius lay in the street called the Clivus Urbius, where Tullia drove her coach over her father's body. Because of the crime, the name of the street was changed to Vicus Sceleratus (Crime Street).

Lucretia and the End of the Monarchy

Thus **Tarquinius Superbus** (the proud) became king; in the historical tradition, he is a tyrant, and his expulsion led to the establishment of the Roman Republic. The crime that caused his removal became one of the most famous of Roman legends. In the Roman army during the siege of the Rutulian capital of Ardea were a number of young nobles, including **Tarquinius Collatinus** and **Sextus Tarquinius**, the son of the Roman king. Full of wine one evening, they rode off to pay surprise visits to their wives in order to see who was the most virtuous and faithful. Alone of all whom they visited, the wife of Collatinus, Lucretia, was acting in a chaste and matronly way; they all judged her to be the best and returned to camp. Now Sextus Tarquinius was so taken by Lucretia's beauty that he returned alone to Collatia some nights later and surprised and raped her. Next day she sent for both her father and her husband, who came together with **Lucius Junius Brutus**. She told them what had happened and made them promise to avenge themselves on her attacker. Then she plunged a dagger into her heart.

Lucretia's martyrdom led to the end of the monarchy. Tarquinius Superbus was driven into exile with two of his sons. Sextus Tarquinius went to the Latin town of Gabii, where he was murdered. Rome became a republic, the chief power being exercised by two praetors elected annually (the title was changed to "consuls" some sixty years later). One of the original praetors was Brutus.

The early centuries of the Roman Republic were idealized by historians and poets. As early as the fourth century B.C. , legends were created about Roman leaders to express heroic and moral ideals. In the view of Georges Dumézil, the legends of the monarchy and early Republic reflect the tripartite organization of Indo-European society (for there were three tribes in early Rome), which he classifies by function: priest-kings, warriors, and food producers. He believes that the traditional tales enshrined in the histories (most notably the early books of Livy) were the genuine myths of this society. This view is controversial, but it does recognize the Romans' peculiar ability to make national heroes of their historical figures, as Livy saw. Nevertheless, the stories of these early Roman heroes belong more to the realm of history than to that of pure myth, and we end our survey of Roman mythology with the end of the Roman monarchy.[10]

Select Bibliography

Banta, Louisa. *The Etruscan Cities and Their Culture.* London: Batsford, 1973. Especially valuable for its illustrations and Chapter 6, on Etruscan religion.

Beard, Mary, John North, and Simon Price. *Religions of Ancient Rome,* vol. 1: *A History;* vol. 2: *A Sourcebook.* New York: Cambridge University Press, 1998. A survey of religious life in Rome from the foundations of the city to its conversion into Christianity, with visual evidence and pertinent texts in translation.

Bremmer, J. N., and Horsfall, N. M. *Roman Myth and Mythography.* London: University of London, Institute of Classical Studies, 1987.

Donaldson, Ian. *The Rapes of Lucretia: A Myth and Its Transformations.* New York: Oxford University Press, 1982.

Feeney, D. *Literature and Religion at Rome: Cultures, Contexts, and Beliefs.* New York: Cambridge University Press, 1998.

Galinsky, Karl G. *Aeneas, Sicily, and Rome.* Princeton, NJ: Princeton University Press, 1969.

Grant, Michael. *Roman Myths.* New York: Dorset, 1984 [1971].

Green C. M. C. *Roman Religion and the Cult of Diana at Aricia.* New York: Cambridge University Press, 2007. A study of the cult of Diana and its bearing on Roman religion.

Griffin, Jasper. *Virgil.* New York: Oxford University Press, 1986. A brief but perceptive introduction to the poet.

Hardie, P. *Vergil (Greece & Rome New Surveys in the Classics, No. 28).* New York: Oxford University Press, 1998. A valuable survey of every aspect of Vergil's work.

Harrison, S. J., ed. *Oxford Readings in Virgil's Aeneid.* New York: Oxford University Press, 1990. An important collection of essays by leading scholars.

McAuslan, I., and P. Walcot. *Vergil (Greece and Rome Studies).* New York: Oxford University Press, 1990. The most helpful collection of essays on its subject.

Quinn, Stephanie, ed. *Why Vergil? A Collection of Interpretations.* Wauconda, IL: Bolchazy-Carducci Publishers, 1999. Part 2 includes "Some 20th Century Heirs: Poetry and Power," among whom are Robert Frost, C. Day Lewis, and W. H. Auden, as well as an excerpt from Hermann Broch's acclaimed novel *The Death of Virgil* (translated by Jean Starr Untermeyer).

Richardson, L. *A New Topographical Dictionary of Ancient Rome.* Baltimore, MD: Johns Hopkins University Press, 1992. This work gives much valuable information about the religious significance of places and buildings in the city.

Scheid, John. *An Introduction to Roman Religion.* Translated by Janet Lloyd. Bloomington, IN: Indiana University Press, 2003.

Warrior, Valerie M. *Roman Religion: A Source Book.* New York: Cambridge University Press, 2006 [2002]. Accessible translations of short excerpts about a wide variety of subjects on Roman religion and religious practices.

Wiseman, T. P. *The Myths of Rome.* Exeter: University of Exeter Press, 2004. Written by the leading authority on early Roman mythology; the first three chapters are very helpful. The notes, giving the author's sources, are an unparalleled resource.

———. *Remus: A Roman Myth.* New York: Cambridge University Press, 1995. A historical analysis of the origins and development of the foundation legend of Rome.

———. *Unwritten Rome.* Exeter: University of Exeter Press, 2008. Essays on Rome's earliest times for which the written evidence is thin.

Vout, Caroline. *The Hills of Rome.* New York: Cambridge University Press, 2016.

Wildfang, Robin Lorsch. *Rome's Vestal Virgins*. New York: Routledge, 2006. A comprehensive and new analysis.

Ziolkowski, Theodore. *Virgil and the Moderns*. Princeton, NJ: Princeton University Press, 1993. Discusses the ideological biographical tradition and the influence of Vergil on the Continent, in Britain, and in the New World.

Primary Sources

Sources in the Chapter

Ennius	*Annales* 1, frag. 47
Homer	*Iliad* 20.300–308
Horace	*Odes* 1.10; 3.22
Livy	*Ab urbe condita* Preface 1.6–10, 16
Lucretius	*De rerum natura* 1.1–13
Ovid	*Fasti* 1.415–440; 3.651–656
	Metamorphoses 14.598–608
Vergil	*Aeneid* 1.1–7, 198–207, 267–279; 4.607–629; 8.247–261, 424–438; 12.938–952

Additional Sources

Livy	*Ab urbe condita*, Book 1
	Livy's history of Rome, *Ab urbe condita (From the Founding of the City)*, was a massive work that commenced with the arrival of Aeneas in Italy and was brought to completion with the reign of Augustus. The work has not survived intact, but the first five books—a unit sometimes referred to as the first pentad—are among the existing portions and contain a wealth of information from the foundation to the sack of Rome by the Gauls.
Ovid	*Fasti*
	Ovid's poetical treatment of the Roman calendar contains a wealth of material on religious and mythological matters.
Vergil	*Aeneid*

Notes

1. Because of the demands of the Latin hexameter, the gods are not named in order of importance. Ennius' forms are given, but we refer to Mercury and Jupiter (for Mercurius and Iovis).
2. Augustus continued to live on the Palatine Hill after he became Pontifex Maximus in 12 B.C.
3. Her name seems to be connected with the Latin words for mind (*mens*) and remembering (*meminisse*).
4. Some years after the great fire of A.D. 64, the emperor Domitian set up altars to Vulcan in every one of the fourteen districts of Rome.
5. Ovid tells the same story of Priapus and Vesta at *Fasti* 6.319–346. The story of Lotis is the subject of Bellini's painting *The Feast of the Gods* on p. 665.
6. R. Ross Holloway, *The Archaeology of Early Rome and Latium* (New York: Routledge, 1996). An overview that includes the recent archaeological discoveries relating to early Rome, such as the shrine of Aeneas at Lavinium and the walls of the Romulan city on the Palatine.

7. These ships reached Italy and were turned into sea-nymphs by Cybele, who, as the Phrygian goddess, protected ships made from Phrygian trees (*Aeneid* 10.220–231).

8. See pp. 658–659 for Ovid's account of Aeneas' death and his epithet. The meaning of the title *Indiges* is not certain. A group of gods were called the *Di Indigetes*, and certain gods (e.g., Jupiter and Sol) were sometimes worshiped with this epithet. Aeneas was sometimes called *Pater Indiges*.

9. The etymology of *Quirites* is unknown. It has the same root as the god Quirinus and the Quirinal Hill. The Romans wrongly connected it with the Sabine town Cures.

10. See Georges Dumézil, *Archaic Roman Religion*. Translated by P. Knapp, 2 vols. (Baltimore, MD: Johns Hopkins University Press, 2003 [1970]). For further reading in Roman mythology, we particularly recommend T. P. Wiseman, *The Myths of Rome* (Exeter: Exeter University Press, 2005).

Glossary of Mythological Words and Phrases in English

MANY OF US TALK the language of myth without even realizing it. Myth encompasses a tradition, a repository of images, themes, motifs, and archetypes that can serve to give human speech resonance beyond its immediate context. When Hamlet says his murdered father was to his uncle as Hyperion was to a satyr, he speaks a powerful shorthand; the images conveyed by these two personages do more to express his inner state than if he were simply to speak admiringly of the one and disparagingly of the other. Often we use mythological references in our everyday speech, blissfully unaware that many of our common everyday expressions find their origin in the mythic traditions of Greece and Rome; one can use the word *chaotic* without knowing its ultimate source. The following list briefly explains the original mythological meaning of some of the more common terms that have entered our language.

Achillean/Achilles' heel/Achilles tendon Achilles was the son of the mortal Peleus and the nymph Thetis. A warrior of legendary prowess in battle and the hero of Homer's *Iliad*, he was essential to the Greek war effort against Troy. To describe someone as *Achillean* is to mark that person as invincible or invulnerable, or nearly so. Achilles himself had one vulnerable spot. His mother dipped the infant Achilles in the magical waters of the river Styx in a vain attempt to render him immortal; she grasped him by the heel in order to submerge him in the stream, thereby leaving one spot on his body susceptible to injury. Paris took advantage of this weakness and with Apollo's help delivered the fatal arrow to Achilles' heel. An *Achilles heel* refers to the one assailable feature or weakness a person may have; in anatomy, the *Achilles' tendon* stretches from the heel bone to the calf muscle.

Adonis Adonis was such a handsome youth that Aphrodite herself found him irresistible. A capable hunter, he disregarded the warnings of the goddess to retreat in the face of a ferocious boar and sustained a fatal injury from a charging boar's tusk. A grieving Aphrodite sprinkled nectar on the blood-soaked ground, and the anemone blossomed forth. To call a man an *Adonis* is to draw attention to his beauty.

aegis The aegis is the shield of Zeus (originally a goatskin), which thunders when he shakes it. Athena also bore the aegis, often tasseled and with the head of Medusa affixed, its petrifying power still intact. This divine shield afforded safety and security, and so to be under the *aegis* of an individual or of an institution is to be favored with protection, sponsorship, or patronage.

Aeolian harp or lyre Aeolus was put in charge of the winds by Zeus. He kept watch over his subjects in a cave on the island of Aeolia. An *Aeolian harp* is a box-shaped musical instrument across which strings are strung; the strings vibrate when wind passes across them.

Amazon The Amazons were a warrior-race of women from the North who joined battle with a terrifying war cry. They were the equal of men in the field. They came to be seen as haters of men, women who sought foreign husbands, only to kill their sons and raise their daughters as Amazons. Later tradition has it that they cut off their right breasts to become better archers. A vigorous and aggressive woman today might be deemed an *amazon*, with enormous physical stature perhaps implied as well. Often it is a derogatory term. The *Amazon ant* is a species of red ant that captures the offspring of other species and turns them into slaves.

ambrosia/ambrosial The Greek gods on Olympus took food and drink as mortals do. But since the gods are of a different order from mortals, so too is their sustenance. Ambrosia, culled from the regions beyond the Wandering Rocks, served variously as food for the gods, as unguent or perfume, or as fodder for horses. It is often coupled with nectar, which provided drink for the Olympians. Both words derive from roots that indicate their power to bestow immortality and stave off death. Today *ambrosia* can refer to a dessert of fruit and whipped cream or, especially when joined with nectar, any gourmet masterpiece. Generally, *ambrosial* has come to indicate anything fit for the gods or of divine provenance, or anything delicious or fragrant. See **nectar**.

aphrodisiac According to Hesiod, Aphrodite was born of the foam around the severed genitals of Uranus, a fitting beginning for a divinity whose concern is the sexual. From her name comes the noun *aphrodisiac*, denoting anything that has the power to excite the sexual passions.

apollonian Apollo had as his purview the arts, prophecy, and healing. At his chief shrine at Delphi the watchword was "Know thyself," the beginning and principal aim of human understanding. He is the god of rationality, harmony, and balance, known by the epithet Phoebus, "bright" or "shining," by which he is equated with the Sun and more broadly the order of the cosmos. The adjective *apollonian* describes that which partakes of the rational and is marked by a sense of order and harmony. Its opposite is dionysian, which describes unbridled nature, the frenzied and the irrational. These polarities, the apollonian and the dionysian, were recognized by the Greeks as twin aspects of the human psyche. See also **bacchanal**.

Apple of Discord All the gods and goddesses were invited to the wedding of Peleus and Thetis, save one, Eris ("strife"). To avenge this slight, this goddess of discord tossed into the wedding hall a golden apple with the inscription "For the Fairest." It was immediately claimed by three rival goddesses: Hera, Athena, and Aphrodite. Zeus refused to decide the issue, but instead gave it to Paris, the son of Priam, king of Troy, to settle. The Judgment of Paris, as the decision has come to be known, bestowed the apple on Aphrodite, who had promised to Paris the most beautiful woman in the world, namely, Helen, wife of Menelaüs, king of Sparta. The abduction of Helen by Paris was the cause of the ten-year siege and destruction of Troy under the onslaught of the Greek forces, pledged to wreak vengeance on the seducer. "Apple of Discord" describes any action or situation that causes dissension and turmoil and is more trouble than it is worth.

arachnid Arachne was a common girl with a remarkable skill in weaving. She won such fame that Athena, slighted and envious, challenged Arachne to a contest. Athena wove themes, including the fate of foolish mortals who dared to vie with the gods. Arachne depicted the gods' compromising love affairs. Outraged, Athena struck the girl with her shuttle and, after Arachne hanged herself, in remorse transformed Arachne into a spider, so that she and her species might practice her art of weaving forever. An *arachnid* is any of the various arthropods of the class Arachnida, including the spider.

Arcadia/arcadian Arcadia is the central mountainous region of the Peloponnese. Often it is described in idyllic terms: the ideal land of rustic simplicity, especially dear to Hermes, the home of Callisto (the favorite of Artemis), the usual playground of Pan; for the bucolic poets, Arcadia is a place where life is easy, where shepherds leisurely tend their flocks and pursue romantic dalliances. Thus *Arcadia* becomes that imagined primeval terrain, where human beings lived in contentment and harmony with the natural world. The word *arcadian* refers to any place or time signifying the simple, rustic, pastoral life of a golden age lost.

Argus/argus-eyed One of Zeus' sexual escapades involved the maiden Io. In an attempt to keep Hera from discovering the truth of his dalliance, Zeus transformed Io into a cow. Hera, not easily thrown off the scent of her husband's affairs, prevailed upon Zeus to give her the cow as a present and an assurance of his good faith, after which Hera enlisted the aid of Argus, a giant with one hundred eyes, to keep a close watch over the poor girl. In English, one who is ever vigilant or watchful can be called an *argus* or be described as *argus-eyed*.

Atlas/Atlantic/atlantes/Atlantis Atlas was a titan who opposed Zeus in the battle between the Olympians and the earlier generation of Titans. The defeated Titans were condemned to Tartarus, but Atlas was punished with the task of supporting upon his shoulders the vault of the heavens, thereby keeping the earth and sky separate. Through a mistaken notion that this vault, sometimes depicted as a sphere, was actually the earth, Atlas has given his name to that particular kind of book which contains a collection of geographical maps. It was not until the Flemish cartographer Gerhardus Mercator (1512–1594) depicted on the frontispiece of his *atlas* the Titan carrying the earth that the association became fixed. The plural of atlas has given us the architectural term *atlantes*, which refers to support columns formed in the shape of men, corresponding to the maiden columns known as caryatids. Atlas endured his torment at the western edge of the world and so has given his name to the ocean beyond the straits of Gibraltar, the *Atlantic*, as well as to the *Atlas Mountains* in northwest Africa. The mythical island of *Atlantis* was located, according to Plato, in the western ocean.

Augean stables/Augean One of Heracles' labors, performed in service to King Eurystheus, was to clean the stables of King Augeas of Elis. King Augeas had not cleaned his stalls for some years, and the filth and stench had become unbearable. Heracles agreed to the task and succeeded in diverting the course of two rivers to achieve his aim. *Augean stables* has since become a byword for squalor. *Augean* describes anything that is extremely filthy or squalid.

aurora australis/borealis Aurora was the Roman goddess of the dawn (the Greek Eos). The sons of Aurora and the titan Astraeus were the four winds: Boreas, who blows from the north; Notus, the southwest; Eurus, the east; and Zephyrus, the west. The spectacular streaks of light that appear in the sky at night are a result of the effect of the particles of the sun's rays on the upper atmosphere. Seen especially at the poles, in the Northern Hemisphere they are called the northern lights or the *aurora borealis*; in the South, they are the *aurora australis*, Auster being the Roman name of the southwest wind.

bacchanal/bacchanalia/bacchanalian/bacchant/bacchante/bacchic Dionysus, the Roman Bacchus, was the god of wine, frenzied music and dance, and the irrational. He presided over ecstatic, sometimes orgiastic rites, which involved initiation and drove the participants into another plane of perception as they became possessed by the deity. He is usually represented in the midst of a retinue of female worshipers, known as maenads, *bacchae*, or *bacchantes* (the feminine singular is *bacchante*; a male follower is a *bacchant*, plural *bacchants*); he is also attended by male satyrs, mischievous and lecherous creatures, half-human and half-animal. Wine proved a powerful conduit to the ineffable, amid rituals that included the rending of a sacrificial victim and the eating of its raw flesh. Dionysiac rites among the Romans became known as Bacchanalia, and the sometimes extreme behavior of the initiates provoked the Roman Senate to outlaw them in 186 B.C. Thus we derive the words *bacchanal* and *bacchanalia* to refer to any debauched party or celebration. *Bacchanal*, *bacchant*, *bacchante*, and *bacchae* can be used to characterize an overzealous partygoer. The adjectives *bacchanalian* and *bacchic* describe any exuberant, drunken revelry. See also **dionysian** and **apollonian**.

Beware of Greeks bearing gifts/I fear Greeks even when they bear gifts The fall of Troy was finally accomplished by a ruse of the Greeks. They constructed an enormous hollow wooden horse in which they hid some of their best fighters. The horse was left behind as the rest of the Greek host sailed off to the nearby island of Tenedos and waited. The treacherous Sinon convinced the Trojans to drag the gift into the city, despite the warnings of Laocoön, a priest of Poseidon. In Vergil's account, Laocoön implored his countrymen not to bring the treacherous horse into Troy, crying, "I fear Greeks even when they bear gifts" (*Timeo Danaos et dona ferentis*). Two serpents emerged from the sea to strangle Laocoön and his two sons. The Trojans were convinced that they should accept the horse, and thus they wrought their own destruction. Laocoön's utterance has become a warning to beware of treachery and look for the hidden motives behind even the most fair-seeming generosity.

boreal Boreas, the north wind, has given us this adjective, which refers to the region of the world from which his blasts come. See also **aurora**.

by Jupiter/by Jove/jovian/jovial Jupiter was the Roman counterpart of Zeus, the supreme god and father. He was a god of the sky, and his name is derived from Indo-European roots *dyaus/pitr*, which literally mean god/father. In Latin, the common oath "by Jupiter" would be rendered "pro Jove" (Jove being a different form of his name). In the Christian tradition, there is no religious significance to this exclamation, but English writers, by using it as an expression of surprise or pleasure, avoided taking God's name in vain; thus "by Jupiter" or "by Jove" was used to replace the offensive "by God." To describe someone or something as *jovian* imputes some of that awe-inspiring majesty that is particular to a supreme god. Many mythological names also found a new existence in the field of astrology. Since it was felt that the heavenly bodies influence the life of humans on earth, celestial bodies were given appellations drawn from mythology. For example, Jupiter became the name not only of a god but also of a planet. Those who were born under the influence of the planet Jupiter were said to be of a cheerful disposition, hence the meaning of the adjective *jovial*.

Cadmean victory Cadmus was informed by the oracle at Delphi that he would establish a great city. When he eventually found the site of the future Thebes, he prepared to sacrifice to the gods in thanksgiving. He soon discovered that the local spring from which he needed to draw water for a proper sacrifice was guarded by a serpent. He sent his men to dispatch the monster and bring back the ritual water. All of his men failed in the attempt, and Cadmus eventually took it upon himself to kill the serpent. Though Cadmus was ultimately victorious, he now found himself bereft of his comrades and despaired of establishing his realm. A *Cadmean victory* has come to mean a victory won at great loss to the victor.

caduceus In Latin, the herald's staff was known as the caduceum, derived from the Greek word *keryx*, or herald, and his staff, the *kerykeion*. Hermes, as divine messenger, was invariably depicted with the caduceus, which was represented as a staff with white ribbons or intertwined snakes. The white ribbons may have indicated the inviolability of his office. The image of intertwined snakes may have been drawn from the Near Eastern use of copulating snakes as a symbol of fertility, for Hermes was a fertility god. The staff of Hermes became confused with the staff of Asclepius, the renowned mythic physician and son of Apollo, because some stories about Asclepius involved snakes and the reptile has the ability to slough its old skin and seemingly be "reborn," and so had associations with healing.

calliope Calliope was one of the nine Muses, who gives her name to the musical instrument, made up of tuned steam whistles and played like an organ. Calliope is also the name for the California hummingbird. See also **muse**.

Calypso/calypso music Calypso ("she who hides or conceals") was the daughter of Thetis and either Atlas, Nereus, or Oceanus. Odysseus was detained on her island home of Ogygia for seven years with the promise that she would make him immortal. Though he enjoyed her bed, each day he would weep and look longingly over the sea to his homeland, Ithaca. Eventually, Zeus sent Hermes to inform Calypso that she must give up Odysseus. *Calypso music*, derived from the name of the nymph, originated on the islands of the West Indies and features topical or amusing themes.

Cassandra Trojan Cassandra, daughter of Priam and Hecuba, was amorously pursued by the god Apollo. Having at first agreed to succumb to his advances, she was awarded the gift of prophecy, but later, when she changed her mind and refused him, Apollo punished her. She would remain a prophetess, but she would never be believed. Cassandra's predictions were invariably of disaster, for example, foretelling the murder of Agamemnon by Clytemnestra or the destruction of Troy through the ruse of the Trojan horse. A *Cassandra* today is anyone who utters dire warnings of the future, regardless of their truth that people prefer to ignore.

catamite Zeus was so impressed with the beauty of the Trojan youth Ganymede that he took the form of an eagle and brought him to Olympus to become the cupbearer of the gods. The Latin rendering of Ganymede's name was Catamitus, and his relationship with Zeus (or Jupiter) was interpreted by some as overtly homosexual to lend divine authority to ancient pederastic practices. Today a *catamite* is still the designation for a boy used for pederastic purposes.

Cerberus Cerberus, the hound of the Underworld, stood guard at the gates of Hades and prevented those not permitted from entering. He is usually described as a beast with three heads and the tail of a dragon. When Aeneas journeyed to the lower regions under the guidance of the Sibyl, he brought along a medicated cake to drug the animal and ensure their safe passage. To "throw a sop to Cerberus" means to give a bribe and thereby ward off an unpleasant situation.

cereal Ceres (the Roman counterpart of Demeter) was goddess of grain and the fertility of the earth. From her name is derived the Latin adjective *Cerealis* (having to do with Ceres and the grain), from which comes our English word *cereal*.

chaos/chaotic Whether Chaos is to be understood as a void or a primordial, formless, undifferentiated, and seething mass out of which the order of the universe is created, it is the starting point of creation. This unformed beginning is contrasted with later creation, a universe called the cosmos, a designation meaning, literally, harmony or order. The sky and the stars, the earth and its creatures, and the laws and cycles that direct and control creation seem to exhibit the balance, order, and reason that the mind discerns in the natural world. For us *chaos*, together with its adjective *chaotic*, simply means a state of confusion. See also **cosmos**.

Chimera/chimerical/chimeric A wild, hybrid creature, the Chimera had the head of a lion, the body of a goat, and the tail of a serpent, and it breathed fire. It was killed by the Corinthian hero Bellerophon on one of his journeys. Today a *chimera* is a fantastic delusion, an illusory creation of the mind, or a hybrid organism, usually a plant. *Chimerical* and *chimeric* designate something as unreal, imaginary, or fantastic. These adjectives can also signify that one is given to fantasy.

cornucopia The Latin *cornucopia* means "horn of plenty." There are two stories about this horn, which bestows upon the owner an endless bounty. Zeus, in his secluded infancy on Crete, was nursed by a goat named Amalthea, which was also the name of the goddess of plenty. One of the horns of this goat was broken off and became the first cornucopia. The horn of plenty is also associated with Hercules. In order to win Deïanira as his bride, he had to defeat the horned river-god Acheloüs. In the struggle, Hercules broke off one of the horns of the river-god, but after his victory he returned the horn and received as recompense the horn of Amalthea. Ovid, however, relates that the horn of Acheloüs became a second horn of plenty. Today the *cornucopia* is a sign of nature's abundance, and the word has come to mean a plenteous bounty.

cosmos/cosmic/cosmology/cosmetic/cosmetician *Cosmos* refers to the universe and all that is ordered and harmonious. *Cosmology* is the study of the origin and structure of the universe. The adjective *cosmic* may designate the universe beyond and apart from the earth itself, or it may in a generalized sense describe something of vast significance or implication. Akin to the word cosmos are various English words derived from the Greek adjective *cosmeticos*. Cosmos means not only order and harmony, but also arrangement and decoration; thus a *cosmetic* is a substance that adorns or decorates the body, and a *cosmetician* is the person involved with cosmetics. See also **chaos**.

cupidity The Latin word *cupidus* ("desirous" or "greedy") gave rise to Cupido, Cupid, the Roman equivalent of the Greek god of love, Eros. In early representations, he is a handsome youth, but he becomes increasingly younger and develops his familiar attributes of bow and arrow (with which he rouses passion in both gods and mortals) and wings, until he finally evolves into the Italian *putti* or decorative cherubs frequently seen in Renaissance art. From the same Latin root comes *cupiditas* to denote any intense passion or desire, from which we derive *cupidity* (avarice or greed). See also **erotic**.

cyclopean There were two distinct groups of giants called the Cyclopes, whose name means circle-eyed and indicates their principal distinguishing feature, one round eye in the center of the forehead. The first, offspring of Uranus and Ge, were the smiths who labored with Hephaestus at his forge to create the thunderbolt for Zeus, among other masterpieces. The second group of Cyclopes were a tribe of giants, the most important of whom was Polyphemus, a son of Poseidon encountered by Odysseus. The word *cyclopean* refers to anything that pertains to the Cyclopes or partakes of their gigantic and powerful nature. Thus the Cyclopes were said to be responsible for the massive stone walls that surround the palace-fortresses of the Mycenaean period. And so *cyclopean* is used generally to describe a primitive building style, which uses immense, irregular, stone blocks, held together by their sheer weight without mortar.

cynosure The constellation Ursa Minor ("little bear") was called Kunos-oura ("the dog's tail") by the astronomer Aratus, who saw in it one of the nymphs who raised the infant Zeus. Long a guiding star for seafarers, it has given us the word *cynosure*, which can describe anything that serves to focus attention or give guidance.

demon/demoniac/demonic/demonology In Greek, *daimon* was a word of rather fluid definition. In Homer, the Olympians are referred to as either gods (*theoi*) or *daimones* ("divine powers"). In later literature, the *daimones* became intermediate beings between gods and men, or often the spirits of the dead came to be called *daimones*, especially among the Romans. *Daimon* could also denote that particular spirit granted to each mortal at birth to watch over its charge. This corresponds to the Roman *Genius*, a vital force behind each individual, originally associated with male fertility and particularly with the male head of a household. Later, it became a tutelary spirit assigned to guide and shape each person's life. With the triumph of Christianity, all pagan deities were suspect, and *daimon*, viewed solely as a power sprung from the devil, became our *demon* (any evil or satanic spirit). The adjectives *demonic* and *demoniac* suggest possession by an evil spirit and can mean simply fiendish. As a noun, *demoniac* refers to one who is or seems possessed by a demon. *Demonology* is the study of evil spirits. As for genius, it has come to denote a remarkable, innate intellectual or creative ability, or a person possessed of such ability. Through French we have the word *genie*, which had served as a translation of Jinni, spirits (as in the *Arabian Nights*) that have the power to assume human or animal form and supernaturally influence human life.

dionysian The *dionysiac* or *dionysian* experience is the antithesis of the *apollonian*, characterized by moderation, symmetry, and reason. See also **apollonian** and **bacchanal**.

echo There are two major myths that tell how the acoustic phenomenon of the echo arose. According to one, Echo was originally a nymph who rejected the lusty advances of the god Pan. In her flight, she was torn apart by shepherds, who had been driven into a panic by the spurned god, Pan. The second version involves the mortal Narcissus. Echo had been condemned by Hera to repeat the last utterance she heard and no more. It was in this state that Echo caught sight of the handsome Narcissus. Narcissus, a youth cold to all love, rejected the amorous advances of Echo, who could now only mimic Narcissus' words. Stung deeply by this rebuff, she hid herself in woods and caves and pined for her love, until all that remained of the nymph was her voice. As for Narcissus, too proud in his beauty, he inevitably called down upon himself the curse of a spurned lover. Narcissus was doomed to be so captivated by his own reflection in a pool that he could not turn away his gaze, even to take food and drink. He wasted away and died. From the spot where he died sprang the narcissus flower. Narcissism has come to mean an obsessive love of oneself. As used in psychoanalysis, it is an arrested development at an infantile stage characterized by erotic attachment to oneself. One so afflicted with such narcissistic characteristics is a narcissist. See also **panic** and **narcissism**.

Electra complex Comparable to the Oedipus complex in the development of the female is the Electra complex, a psychotic attachment to the father and hostility toward the mother, a designation also drawn from myth. Electra was the daughter of Agamemnon and Clytemnestra, a young woman obsessed by her grief over the murder of her beloved father and tormented by unrelenting hatred for her mother who killed him. See also **Oedipus**.

Elysian Fields/elysian/Elysium In Vergil's conception of the Underworld, there is a place in the realm of Hades reserved for mortals who, through their surpassing deeds and virtuous life, have won a blessed afterlife. It is named the Elysian Fields or Elysium, and the souls who inhabit this paradise live a purer, more carefree, and pleasant existence. The adjective *elysian* has come to mean blissful.

enthusiasm In cultic ritual, particularly Dionysiac, the initiate was often thought to become possessed by the god and transported to a state of ecstatic union with the divine. The Greeks described a person so exalted as being *entheos* ("filled with the god"), which gave rise to the verb *enthousiazein*. Thus we have the English word *enthusiasm*, meaning an excited interest, passion, or zeal. See also **bacchanal**.

eristic Eris was the goddess of "strife" or "discord," responsible for all the dissension arising from the Apple of Discord, which she threw among the guests at the wedding banquet of Peleus and Thetis. Thus is derived the term *eristic*, which as an adjective means pertaining to argument or dispute; as a noun, it refers to rhetoric or the art of debate. See also **Apple of Discord**.

erotic/erotica/eratomania To the Greeks, Eros was one of the first generation of divinities born from Chaos; he was also said to be the son of Aphrodite and Ares. From the Greek adjective *eroticos*, we derive *erotic*, which describes anyone or anything characterized by the amatory or sexual passions. *Erotica* is a branch of literature or art whose main function is the arousal of sexual desire. *Eratomania* is an obsessive desire for sex. See also **cupidity**.

Europe Europa was the daughter of Agenor, king of Tyre in Phoenicia. Zeus, disguised as a white bull, enticed the girl to sit on his back and then rushed into the sea and made his way toward Greece. When they reached Crete, Zeus seduced Europa, who bore a son named Minos and gave her name to a foreign continent. The word *Europe* may be of Semitic origin, meaning "land of the setting sun."

Faunus/faun/fauna/flora Faunus, whose name means "one who shows favor, " was a Roman woodland deity. He was thought to bring prosperity to farmers and shepherds and was often depicted with horns, ears, tail, and sometimes legs of a goat; therefore he was associated with the Greek god Pan and also Dionysiac satyrs. A *faun* came to be another name for a satyr. Faunus' consort was Fauna, a female deity like him in nature. Flora was another, though minor, agricultural deity, a goddess of flowers, grain, and the grapevine. When we talk of *flora* and *fauna*, we refer, respectively, to flowers and animals collectively.

Furies/furious/furioso The Erinyes (Furies) were avenging spirits. They sprang from the severed genitals of Uranus when drops of his blood fell to the earth. The Furies pursued those who had unlawfully shed blood, particularly within a family. They were said to rise up to avenge the blood of the slain and pursue the murderer, driving the guilty to madness. As chthonic deities, they are associated with the Underworld and are charged with punishing sinners; they are usually depicted as winged goddesses with snaky locks. In English, *fury* can refer to a fit of violent rage or a person in the grip of such a passion, especially a woman. The Latin adjective *furiosus* has given us our adjective *furious* as well as the musical term *furioso*, which is a direction to play a piece in a turbulent, rushing manner.

Gaia hypothesis Gaia (Gaea or Ge), sprung from Chaos, is the personification of the earth. Her name has been employed in a recent coinage called the *Gaia hypothesis*, a theory that views the earth as a complete living organism, all of its parts working in concert for its own continued existence.

genius The Latin word *Genius* designated the creative power of an individual that was worshiped as a mythological and religious concept. See also **demon**.

gorgon/gorgoneion/gorgonian/gorgonize The Gorgons were three sisters who had snakes for hair and a gaze so terrifying that a mortal who looked into their eyes was turned to stone. Medusa, the most famous of the three, was beheaded by Perseus, aided by Athena and Hermes. Perseus gave the head to Athena, who affixed it to her shield (see **aegis**). The head of the Gorgon was often depicted in Greek art in a highly stylized manner; this formalized depiction is called a *gorgoneion*. Today, *gorgon* can mean a terrifying or ugly woman. There is also a species of coral known as gorgonian with an intricate network of branching parts. The verb "to gorgonize" means to paralyze by fear.

halcyon/halcyon days The mythical bird called the halcyon is identified with the kingfisher. Ceyx and Alcyone were lovers. Ceyx, the king of Trachis, was drowned at sea. Hera sent word to Alcyone in her sleep through Morpheus, the god of dreams, that her husband was dead. Alcyone in her grief was transformed into the kingfisher; as she tried to drag Ceyx's lifeless body to shore, he too was changed into a bird. The lovers still traverse the waves, and in winter she broods her young in a nest that floats upon the surface of the water. During this time, Alcyone's father, Aeolus, king of the winds, keeps the winds from disturbing the serene and tranquil sea. Today, *halcyon days* are a period of calm weather during the winter solstice, especially the seven days preceding and following it. The phrase "halcyon days" can also describe any time of tranquility.

harpy The Harpies ("snatchers"), daughters of Thaumas and Electra, were originally conceived of as winds, but eventually they came to be depicted as birdlike women who tormented mortals. The Argonauts rescued Phineus, the blind king and prophet of Salmydessus, whose food was "snatched" away by these ravenous monsters. Today when we call someone a *harpy*, we evoke images of these vile, foul-smelling, predatory creatures. *Harpy* can also simply mean a shrewish woman.

hector Hector was the greatest warrior of the Trojans, who was defeated by his counterpart on the Greek side, Achilles. *To hector* means to bluster and bully. The noun *hector* denotes a bully. The connection between the noble Hector and this later conception originated in the Middle Ages, when Hector was portrayed as a braggart and bully.

heliotrope/heliotropism, etc. Helius was god of the sun. The Greek root *trop-* refers to a turning in a certain direction. *Heliotropism* is the biological term for the growth or movement of an organism toward or away from sunlight. A *heliotrope* is a genus of plant that behaves in that manner. Several scientific or technical words derive from the name of the sun-god; for example, a *heliostat* is an instrument that uses a mirror to reflect sunlight; *heliotherapy* is treatment by means of the sun's rays; *heliotype* is a photomechanical process of printing a plate, or the printing plate itself produced in this fashion; a *heliograph* is an instrument used to photograph the sun; and *heliocentric* refers to anything that has the sun as a center or is relative to the sun.

Hercules/herculean/Hercules' club Hercules, in Greek Heracles, was the greatest hero in the ancient world, who wore a lion skin and brandished a club. He achieved countless remarkable exploits and is most famous for twelve canonical Labors. To describe someone as *herculean* is to liken him to Hercules in strength and stature. Herculean effort requires a tremendous exertion or spirit of heroic endurance. *Hercules* is a constellation in the Northern Hemisphere near Lyra and Corona Borealis. A shrub indigenous to the southeastern United States and characterized by prickly leaves and large clusters of white blossoms is known as *Hercules' club*.

hermetic/hermeneutic/hermeneutics/hermaphrodite The god Hermes became associated with the Egyptian god Thoth and received the appellation Trismegistus ("thrice-greatest"). A number of works on occult matters, known as the Hermetic Corpus, were attributed to Hermes Trismegistus; today *hermetic* refers to occult knowledge, particularly alchemy, astrology, and magic. From this notion of secret or sealed knowledge *hermetic* comes to mean completely sealed; a *hermetic jar* is one closed against outside contamination. From Hermes' primary function as a bearer of messages came the Greek *hermeneus* ("interpreter") and the phrase *hermeneutike techne* ("the art of interpretation"). *Hermeneutics* is the science of interpretation, and *hermeneutic*, as adjective or noun, connotes an interpretive or explanatory function. Hermaphroditus, the beautiful son of Hermes and Aphrodite, was bathing in a pool when the nymph Salmacis caught sight of him and was filled with desire. She plunged into the water and entwined her limbs around him. He fought her efforts to seduce him, but her prayer to the gods that they might become united into one being was granted. A *hermaphrodite* has both male and female genitalia and secondary sexual characteristics.

hydra Heracles' second Labor was to encounter the Hydra, a nine-headed serpent that would grow back two heads for every one that was severed. Every time he clubbed off one of the heads, he cauterized the stump so that another could not grow. In marine biology, a *hydra* is a polyp with a cylindrical body and tentacles surrounding an oral cavity, and it has the ability to regrow itself from cut-off parts. A *hydra* can also be a destructive force that does not succumb to a single effort. *Hydra* is a constellation in the equatorial region of the southern sky near the constellation Cancer.

hymen/hymeneal Hymen was the god of marriage who was invoked during the wedding ceremony with the chant "O Hymen, Hymenaeus"; thus he was the overseer of *hymeneal* or marriage rites. Originally, the Greek word *hymen* referred to any membrane, but today the *hymen* is a membranous fold of tissue that covers the outer orifice of the vagina.

hyperborean The Hyperboreans were a mythical race that inhabited a paradise in the far north, at the edge of the world, "beyond" (hyper) the reach of the north wind (Boreas) and his arctic blasts. In English, *hyperborean* merely means arctic or frigid.

hypnosis/hypnotic, etc. Hypnos, son of Nyx ("night") and brother of Thanatos ("death"), was the god of sleep and father of Morpheus, the god of dreams. *Hypnosis* is a sleep-like condition in which one becomes susceptible to suggestion. *Hypnotic*, as an adjective, means to pertain to or induce hypnosis. As a noun, it refers to the person *hypnotized*, something that promotes *hypnotism*, or simply a soporific, that which induces sleep. *Hypnogogic* refers to a drug that produces sleep or describes the state immediately preceding sleep, while *hypnopompic* refers to the state immediately preceding awakening; both states may be marked by visual or auditory hallucination as well as sleep-induced paralysis. *Hypnophobia* is a pathological fear of sleep.

Icarian/Icarian Sea Daedalus had crafted out of wax and feathers two pairs of wings to escape from the imprisonment imposed by King Minos of Crete, one pair for himself and one for his young son, Icarus. Heedless of his father's advice, the young Icarus flew too close to the sun. The wax of the wings melted and the boy fell into the sea. That part of the Mediterranean along the coast of Asia Minor into which he fell ever after was known as the *Icarian Sea*. *Icarian* denotes acts that are reckless and impetuous and lead to ruin.

ichor Gods, though immortal, can suffer wounds. Human blood does not flow from those wounds but rather a clear, rarefied liquid—divine ichor. In English, *ichor* can refer to a fluid, like blood, or, in pathological terms, a watery substance discharged from wounds or ulcers.

iris/iridescent Iris was the goddess of the rainbow (the meaning of her name). The adjective *iridescent* describes anything that gleams with the colors of the rainbow. The *iris* is the colored portion of the eye that contracts when exposed to light. *Iris* also is a genus of plant that has narrow leaves and multicolored blossoms.

junoesque Juno was the mighty and majestic queen of the Roman Pantheon, wife and sister of Jupiter, identified with the Greek Hera. To describe someone as *junoesque* is to liken her to the goddess in stature and stately bearing.

labyrinth/labyrinthine In Crete, King Minos had Daedalus construct a maze in which to imprison the monstrous Minotaur. Theseus' greatest achievement was to kill the Minotaur and, with the help of Ariadne's thread, find his way out of the maze, which was known as the Labyrinth. Excavations of the complex and vast palace of Cnossus in Crete with its network of rooms seem to substantiate elements of this legend. A *labyrinth* is a maze, and the adjective *labyrinthine* describes something winding, complicated, and intricate. *Labyrinth* can also denote anatomical features marked by connecting passages, in particular the structures of the internal ear.

Lethe/lethargy/lethargic/Lethean Lethe was the river of "forgetfulness" in the Underworld. Souls would drink from it and thereby forget their experiences upon being reincarnated. *Lethe* now refers to a state of oblivion or forgetfulness; *lethargy* and *lethargic* denote a state of persistent drowsiness or sluggishness; *Lethean* characterizes anything that causes forgetfulness of the past.

lotus/lotus-eater Odysseus was driven to North Africa and the land of the Lotus Eaters, who consumed the fruit of the lotus and lived in a continual state of dreamy forgetfulness and happy irresponsibility. Today a *lotus-eater* is anyone who succumbs to indolent pleasure. The *lotus*, a small tree of the Mediterranean, produces the fruit supposedly consumed by the Lotus Eaters; it is also an aquatic plant indigenous to southern Asia.

maenad A maenad is a female worshiper of Dionysus. See also **bacchanal**.

March/martial/martial law Mars was the Roman god of war, equated with the Greek Ares. He personified the conflict of battle in all its brutality and bloodshed. The adjective *martial* means of or pertaining to battle; when the military authority usurps the power of civil authority, the population is said to be under *martial law*. Also, the name of the month March is derived from Mars.

matinee/matins Matuta was a minor Roman deity, the goddess of the dawn (in Latin dawn is *tempus matutinum*). Through French, we have *matinee*, a theatrical or cinematic performance given in the daytime, and *matins* (also called Morning Prayer), the first division of the day in the system of canonical hours of the monastic tradition.

mentor In Book 1 of Homer's *Odyssey*, Odysseus' palace is ravaged by suitors for the hand of his wife, Penelope. His son Telemachus, daydreaming of his father's return, is incapable of action. Athena, in the guise of Odysseus' trusted counselor, Mentor, comes to Ithaca to rouse Telemachus and give him advice and hope. Thus *mentor* means a trusted guardian and teacher.

mercury/mercurial Mercury was the Roman equivalent of the Greek Hermes. This fleet-footed messenger of the gods has given us the word *mercury*, a silver metallic element that at room temperature is in liquid form, also called "quicksilver" because of the nature of its movement. In astrology, *Mercury* is the name given to the planet closest to the sun, around which it completes one revolution in eighty-eight days. *Mercurialis* is a genus of weedy plants. To describe someone as *mercurial* is to impart the individual craftiness, eloquence, cunning, and swiftness, all attributes of the god. The term can also simply mean quick or changeable in temperament, either from the nature of the god or from the influence of the planet.

Midas'/ass's ears/Midas touch/the golden touch Apollo and Pan entered into a musical contest. When Apollo was judged victorious by the mountain-god Tmolus, Midas, the king of Phrygia, disagreed. For his lack of perception, Apollo transformed Midas' offending ears into those of an ass. To have *ass's ears* means to lack true musical judgment and taste. On another occasion, the god Dionysus granted Midas' wish that whatever he might touch be turned into gold. To his despair, Midas found that even as he put food or drink to his mouth it was transmuted into gold. Dionysus granted him relief by telling him to bathe in the river Pactolus, whose bed became golden. To have *the golden touch* or *Midas' touch* means to be successful in any endeavor.

money/monetary In the Temple of Juno Moneta ("money," "mint") was housed the Roman mint. The epithet Moneta means "the warner" and refers to an important legend regarding this temple. When Rome was threatened in 390 B.C. by an invasion of Gauls, the sacred geese in Juno's temple began to squawk, rousing the Romans to battle. Moneta, through the Old French *moneie*, has given us the word *money*; the adjective *monetary* (pertaining to money) comes from the stem *monet-*.

morphine Morpheus was the god of dreams, or more particularly the shapes (*morphai*) that come to one in dreams. Later, he became confused with the god of sleep, and it is from this confusion that the English word *morphine* comes. Morphine, an addictive compound of the opium plant, is used as an anesthetic or sedative. Words that include the stem *morph-*, such as *metamorphosis* (a transformation into another shape or state of being), are drawn from the Greek word *morphe* ("shape" or "form") and not the god Morpheus.

muse/music/museum/mosaic The nine Muses were the daughters of Zeus and Mnemosyne ("memory"), whose province was inspiration in the arts, particularly poetry and music; from Muse we derive the word *music*. The Greek word *mouseion* ("place of the Muses"), in Latin *museum*, has given us *museum*, a place for displaying works of artistic, historical, or scientific interest. From the adjective *mousaicos* ("pertaining to the Muses") comes *mosaic*, a picture or design made up of small colored tiles or stones.

narcissism/narcissist/narcissistic/narcissus *Narcissism* refers to the psychological state of a person who has a pathological attachment to himself or herself. See also **echo**.

nectar Nectar is the special drink of the gods, usually paired with their food, ambrosia. *Nectar* has come to mean any refreshing drink, the pure juice of a fruit, or the liquid gathered by bees from the blossoms of flowers, used in making honey. See **ambrosia**.

nemesis Nemesis is the goddess of vengeance who brings retribution to those who have sinned, especially through *hubris* ("overweening pride"). The word *nemesis* denotes the following: the abstract idea of retributive vengeance; the agent of retribution; an invincible rival in a contest or battle; or a necessary or inevitable consequence.

nestor Nestor, the oldest and wisest of the Greek kings at Troy, lived to see three generations of heroes. A brave and strong warrior when young, in old age he was prized for his good counsel and his oratory. Homer tells us that his speech flowed more sweetly than honey. When a politician or statesman today is called a *nestor*, it is these qualities of wisdom, good counsel, and oratory that are emphasized.

nymph/nymphomania/nympholepsy Nymphs are beautiful, idyllic goddesses of wood and stream and nature, often the objects of love and desire. A *nymph* today may simply mean a remarkably attractive young woman, but if she were to suffer from *nymphomania* ("nymph-madness"), she would be showing sexual promiscuity. *Nympholepsy* (from *lepsis*, "a seizing") refers to the madness that assails one who has glimpsed a nymph. It can also denote a strong desire for what is unattainable (cf. **satyr/satyriasis**).

ocean In mythology, the world is a disc circled by a stream of water, the god Oceanus, who is the father of the Oceanids—that is, all the lesser rivers, streams, brooks, and rills that flow over the earth. Today *ocean* can refer to the entire body of seawater or any of its major divisions covering the globe.

odyssey Homer's *Odyssey* recounts the return of Odysseus to Ithaca, his wife, Penelope, and his son, Telemachus. After ten years of war at Troy, Odysseus found the day of his return postponed for another ten years by the god Poseidon. On his extended travels, he overcame many challenges before winning his homecoming. *Odyssey* has come to mean a long, tortuous period of wandering, travel, and adventure, often in search of a quest, both literally and spiritually.

Oedipus/Oedipal complex King Laius of Thebes was given a prophecy that his wife, Jocasta, would bear a son who would kill his father and marry his mother. They did have a son, whose name was Oedipus, and when he grew up he killed his father and married his mother, despite all that was done to avert the prophecy and destiny. Sophocles' masterpiece, *Oedipus the King*, inspired Sigmund Freud to crystalize one of his major, defining ideas on the nature of the human psyche and infantile sexual development. *Oedipus complex* is the term he used to describe the natural progression of psychosexual development in which the child has libidinal feelings for the parent of the opposite sex and hostility for the parent of the same sex. The term may be applied to a male child. See also **Electra complex**.

Olympic Games/olympian The Greek gods had their homes on the heights of Mt. Olympus in northern Greece and so were called the Olympians. The term *olympian* carries with it notions of the new order ushered in by Zeus and his family and distinguishes these gods in their sunlit heights from the chthonic ("of the earth") deities, who have associations with the gloom of the Underworld. Therefore, olympian means "towering," "awesome," and "majestic," akin to the gods of Olympus. The adjective can also refer to one who competes in or has won a contest in the Olympic Games, but this designation is derived from the ancient Olympic Games, celebrated at Olympia, which was a major sanctuary of Zeus in the Peloponnese.

paean Paean was an epithet of the god Apollo, invoked in a cry for victory in battle or for deliverance from sickness. A *paean* thus became a song of thanksgiving. Today it refers to a song of joy or praise, whether to a god or to a human being.

palladium As a child, Athena had a special girlfriend named Pallas, with whom she used to play at war. During one of their skirmishes, Athena inadvertently killed Pallas, and in her memory she built a wooden statue of the girl. This statue was thrown down to earth by Zeus, where it came to be known as the *Palladium* and became for the Trojans a talisman for their city; as long as they had possession of it, the city would stand. Thus in English *palladium* means a protection from harm for a people or state, a lucky charm.

Pandora's box Pandora was the first woman, given to men as punishment for Prometheus' theft of fire. Sent with her was a jar, which, when opened, released all the ills that now plague human beings. Later this jar became a box, and now *Pandora's box* refers to something that should be left unexamined lest it breed disaster.

panic *Panic* describes a state of great fear and anxiety with an attendant desire for flight, which was believed to be inspired by the god Pan. See also **echo**.

phaëton Helius, the sun-god, assured Phaëthon that he was truly his father and swore an oath that his son could have anything he desired. Phaëthon asked that he be allowed to drive his father's chariot across the sky. Helius could not dissuade the boy, and Phaëthon could not control the horses and so drove to his death. *Phaëton* has come into English as a four-wheeled chariot drawn by two horses or an earlier type of convertible automobile.

priapism/priapic Priapus was the ithyphallic son of Aphrodite. He is most often depicted with an enormous and fully erect penis. *Priapic* is an adjective referring to priapian characteristics. *Priapism* is a pathological condition in which the penis is persistently erect.

procrustean/procrustean bed Procrustes ("one who stretches") was encountered by Theseus. He would make unwitting travelers lie down on a bed. If they did not fit it exactly, he would either cut them down or stretch them out to size. The adjective *procrustean* refers to someone or something that aims at conformity through extreme methods. *Procrustean bed* describes a terrible, arbitrary standard against which things are measured.

Prometheus/promethean The god Prometheus, whose name means "forethought," was a son of the Titan Iapetus and the creator and benefactor of humanity. He bestowed upon mortals many gifts that lifted them from savagery to civilization. One of his most potent benefactions was fire, which he stole from heaven in a fennel stalk to give to humankind, a boon expressly forbidden by Zeus. As a punishment for his championship of human beings in opposition to Zeus, Prometheus was bound to a rocky crag and a vulture ate at his liver, which would grow back again for each day's repast. Thus the name Prometheus has become synonymous with the archetypal champion, with fire his symbol of defiance and progress. The adjective *promethean* means "courageous," "creative," "original," and "life-sustaining." Beethoven's music may be called promethean, and Mary Shelley called her gothic horror novel *Frankenstein, A Modern Prometheus*.

protean Proteus was a sea-god who could change shape and possessed knowledge of the future. To obtain information, one had to grapple with the god until his metamorphoses ceased. The word *protean* means of changeable or variable form, or having the ability to change form.

psyche/psychology, etc. The Greek word for the soul was psyche. The myth of Cupid and Psyche can be interpreted as the soul's longing for an eventual reunification with the divine through love. For Freudians, psyche means mind, and psychic refers to mental activity; many English derivatives describe the study of the mind and the healing of its disorders (psychology, psychiatry, etc.). In psychoanalytic terms, the soul is the mind, the seat of thoughts and feelings, our true self, which seeks to orient our lives to our surroundings.

python Apollo established the major sanctuary for his worship and his oracle at Delphi, but to do so he had to kill the serpent that guarded the site. He named his new sanctuary Pytho, from the rotting of the serpent after it had been killed (the Greek verb *pythein* means "to rot"); or the serpent's name was Python. Zoologically, pythons belong to a particular family of nonvenomous Old World snakes.

Rhadamanthus/Rhadamanthine or Rhadamantine Rhadamanthus, along with Minos and Aeacus, is one of the judges in the Underworld. *Rhadamanthus* and *Rhadamanthine* describe a rigidly just and strict person.

rich as Croesus Croesus was the king of Lydia who possessed great wealth that became legendary. Thus to emphasize the possession of extreme riches, we describe a person as being *rich as Croesus*.

saturnalia/saturnian/saturnine/saturnism The titan Saturn (equated with the Greek Cronus) castrated his father, hated his children, devoured them, and was in turn castrated and overthrown by his son Zeus. After his defeat, Saturn ruled over the Golden Age of the world; according to Roman mythology, he fled to the west and brought a new golden age to Italy. Originally, Saturn was an old Italic deity of the harvest; the Romans built a temple to Saturn on the Capitoline Hill and each December celebrated the winter planting with the Saturnalia, a time of revelry and the giving of presents. *Saturnalia* today denotes a period of unrestrained or orgiastic revelry. *Saturn* gives his name to the sixth planet from the sun, the third largest planet in the solar system, after Jupiter. One born under the influence of Saturn may have a *saturnine temperament*, that is, a gloomy or melancholy disposition like that of the god who castrated his father and was overthrown. *Saturnian* simply means pertaining to the god or the planet Saturn. The planet Saturn was also associated with the element lead, and the term for lead poisoning is *saturnism*.

satyr/satyriasis Satyrs were male woodland deities with the ears and legs of a goat who worshiped Dionysus (Bacchus), god of wine, often in a state of sexual excitement. A *satyr* today is nothing more than a lecher. A man who has an excessive and uncontrollable sexual drive suffers from *satyriasis*. See also **nymph/nymphomania/nympholepsy**.

Scylla and Charybdis Scylla, once a beautiful maiden, was transformed into a hideous creature with the heads of yapping dogs protruding from her midriff. Charybdis was a terrible whirlpool. Both of these dangers were said to lurk in the Strait of Messina between southern Italy and Sicily, bringing terror to sailors who endeavored to navigate these waters. The phrase "between Scylla and Charybdis" is much like "between a rock and a hard place"; it denotes a precarious position between two equally destructive dangers.

siren/siren song The Sirens were nymphs (encountered by Odysseus) often depicted with birdlike bodies, who sang such enticing songs that seafarers were lured to their death. A *siren* has come to mean a seductive woman, or a device that uses compressed steam or air to produce a high, piercing sound as a warning. *Siren song* refers to bewitching or alluring temptation that also may be treacherous.

sisyphean Sisyphus was a famous resident of Hades who was condemned to roll an enormous rock up a hill only to have it fall back down, a punishment for revealing the secret of one of Zeus' love affairs. *Sisyphean task* has become a term for work that is difficult, laborious, almost impossible to complete. See also **tantalize** and **tartarean**.

sphinx The Sphinx terrorized Thebes before the arrival of Oedipus (see **Oedipal complex**). She was a hybrid creature with the head of a woman, body of a lion, wings of an eagle, and the tail of a serpent. She punished those who failed to answer her riddle with strangulation (the Greek verb *sphingein* means "to strangle"). At some point, the Greek Sphinx became associated with Egyptian iconography, in which the creature had a lion's body and a hawk's or man's head. When we liken someone to a Sphinx, we have in mind the great riddler of the Greeks and not the Egyptian conception. A *sphinx* is an inscrutable person given to enigmatic utterances (the Greek word *ainigma* means "riddle").

stentorian Stentor, the herald of the Greek army at Troy, could speak with the power of fifty men. Today we may liken a powerful orator to Stentor and designate the effect of his voice as *stentorian*.

structuralism highly influential theory of myth interpretation.

stygian Across the river Styx, the "hateful" river that circles the realm of the Underworld, the ferryman Charon transports human souls to Hades. The gods swear their most dread and unbreakable oaths by invoking the name of the river Styx. *Stygian* describes something to be linked with the infernal regions of Hell, something gloomy or inviolable.

syringe Syrinx ("pan-pipes") rejected the god Pan and was turned into a bed of reeds from which he fashioned his pan-pipes. A *syringe* is a device made up of a pipe or tube, used for injecting and ejecting liquids. *Syringa* is a genus of plants used for making pipes or pipestems.

tantalize Tantalus, who through hubris tried to feed the gods human flesh, is punished by being in a state of perpetual thirst and hunger, food and drink always just beyond his reach. *To tantalize* is therefore to tease and tempt without satisfaction. See also **sisyphean** and **tartarean**.

tartarean Tartarus is the region in the realm of Hades reserved for the punishment of sinners, among whom are those who have committed the most heinous crimes and suffer the most terrible punishments. The adjective *tartarean* refers to those infernal regions. See also **sisyphean** and **tantalize**.

terpsichorean From Terpsichore, one of the nine Muses, comes the adjective *terpsichorean*, which refers to her special area of expertise, dancing. See also **muse**.

titan/titanic The twelve Titans, the second generation of gods, born of Ge and Uranus, were of gigantic stature, most of them conceived of as natural forces, and although defeated and punished by Zeus, virtually invincible. Their massive strength is preserved in the adjective *titanic*, which was also the name given to the ocean vessel thought to be unsinkable. To call someone a *titan* is to emphasize the person's enormous mastery and ability in any field or endeavor.

Trojan horse The Trojans foolishly dragged into their city a large, wooden horse, which deceptively contained in its belly enemy Greek soldiers; the result was the utter destruction of Troy. In computer terminology, a *Trojan horse* is a piece of software, disguised as harmless but in fact bearing a destructive application, which also may be downloaded from a website or as an email attachment. It is different from a computer virus because it does not replicate itself.

typhoon Zeus' struggle with the dragon Typhon (also named Typhaon or Typhoeus) was the most serious battle that he had before finally consolidating his rule. Typhon had one hundred heads and tongues, fire shot out of his eyes, and terrible cries bellowed from his throats. The word *typhoon*, meaning a severe tropical hurricane that arises in the China Sea or the western Pacific Ocean, comes from the Chinese *ta* ("great") and *feng* ("wind"), but the form of the word is influenced by the name Typhon.

venereal/venery/veneration Venus was the powerful Roman goddess of love, equated with the Greek Aphrodite, who was born from the foam around Uranus' castrated genitals. Her dominant sexual aspect is made clear by the nature of her origin. The adjective *venereal* denotes a sexually transmitted disease, and the noun *venery* is indulgence in sexual license. *Veneration*, however, is the act of showing respectful love, adoration, or reverence.

volcanic/volcano/volcanism/volcanize/volcanology, etc. (each of these words may also be spelled with vul-) The Roman god Vulcan, identified with the Greek Hephaestus, was the supreme craftsman of the gods. His helpers were three Cyclopes, and his forge was located in various places, but most often under Mt. Aetna in Sicily, or similar volcanic regions, which betray its presence. A volcano is a vent in the earth's crust that spews forth molten material and thereby forms a mountain. *Volcanism/vulcanism* refers to any volcanic force or activity. *To vulcanize* is to subject a substance, especially rubber, to such extremes of heat that it undergoes a change and thereby becomes strengthened. *Volcanology* is the scientific study of volcanic phenomena.

wheel of fortune Fors or Fortuna was an Italic fertility goddess who controlled the cycles of the seasons and became associated with the Greek conception of good or bad fortune (*tyche*). She is often represented holding the cornucopia in one hand and a wheel in the other, to signify the rising and falling of an individual's prospects. From that iconography comes *wheel of fortune*, a device used in a game of chance. See also **cornucopia**.

zephyr Zephyrus is the west wind (see **aurora borealis**), which signals the return of spring. Today a *zephyr* is a pleasant, gentle breeze, as well as a reference to any insignificant or passing thing.

The Greek Spelling of Names

IN THE TRANSLITERATION of Greek into English, the letter upsilon (υ) usually appears as y. The letter chi (χ) usually becomes ch but sometimes kh; both forms are given. The following changes are to be noted in the Latin and English spelling of Greek words*:

k = c:	Kastor = Castor
ai = ae, or e:	Graiai = Graeae; Klytaimnestra = Clytaemnestra, Clytemnestra
ei = e or i:	Medeia = Medea; Kleio = Clio
ou = u:	Medousa = Medusa
oi = oe:	Kroisos = Croesus
oi = i:	Delphoi = Delphi
final e = a:	Athene = Athena
final on = um:	Ilion = Ilium
final os = us:	Hyllos = Hyllus

Achaia, Akhaia = Achaea
Acheloos, Akheloos = Acheloüs
Acheron, Akheron = Acheron
Achilleus, Akhilleus = Achilles
Admetos = Admetus
Adrastos = Adrastus
Agathyrsos = Agathyrsus
Agaue = Agave
Aglaia = Aglaea
Aglauros = Aglaurus
Akamas = Acamas
Akarnania = Acarnania
Akastos = Acastus
Akestes = Acestes
Akis = Acis
Akontios = Acontius
Akrisios = Acrisius
Aktaion = Actaeon
Aia = Aea
Aiaia = Aeaea
Aiakos = Aeacus
Aias = Ajax
Aietes = Aeëtes
Aigeus = Aegeus
Aigialeia = Aegialia

Aigimios = Aegimius
Aigina = Aegina
Aigis = Aegis
Aigisthos = Aegisthus
Aigyptos = Aegyptus
Aineias = Aeneas
Aiolos = Aeolus
Aipytos = Aepytus
Aisakos = Aesacus
Aison = Aeson
Aithra = Aethra
Aitolia = Aetolia
Alekto = Alecto
Alexandros = Alexander
Alkestis = Alcestis
Alkibiades = Alcibiades
Alkeides = Alcides
Alkinoos = Alcinoüs
Alkmaion = Alcmaeon
Alkmene = Alcmena
Alkyone = Alcyone
Alkyoneus = Alcyoneus
Alpheios = Alpheus
Althaia = Althaea
Althaimenes = Althaemenes

Amaltheia = Amalthea
Amphiaraos = Amphiaraüs
Amyklai = Amyclae
Amykos = Amycus
Anios = Anius
Ankaios = Ancaeus
Antaios = Antaeus
Anteia = Antea
Antikleia = Anticlea
Antilochos, Antilokhos = Antilochus
Antinoos = Antinoüs
Apsyrtos = Apsyrtus
Arachne, Arakhne = Arachne
Areion = Arion
Areiopagos = Areopagus
Arethousa = Arethusa
Argos = Argus
Aristaios = Aristaeus
Arkadia = Arcadia
Arkas = Arcas
Askanios = Ascanius
Asklepios = Asclepius
Asopos = Asopus
Atalante = Atalanta
Athene = Athena

Augeias = Augeas
Autolykos = Autolycus
Bakchos, Bakkhos = Bacchus
Boiotia = Boeotia
Briareos = Briareus
C, see K
Chairephon, Khairephon = Chaerephon
Chalkiope, Khalkiope = Chalciope
Chariklo, Khariklo = Chariclo
Cheiron, Kheiron = Chiron
Chimaira, Khimaira = Chimaera
Chronos, Khronos = Chronus
Chrysippos, Khrysippos = Chrysippus
Chthonios, Khthonios = Chthonius
Daidalos = Daedalus
Danaos = Danaüs
Dardanos = Dardanus
Deïaneira = Deïanira, Dejanira
Deidameia = Deïdamia
Delphoi = Delphi
Deukalion = Deucalion
Dikte = Dicte
Dionysos = Dionysus
Dioskouroi = Dioscuri
Dirke = Dirce
Echemos, Ekhemos = Echemus
Elektra = Electra
Elysion = Elysium
Epeios = Epeus
Epigonoi = Epigoni
Epikaste = Epicasta
Erebos = Erebus
Erytheia = Erythia
Eteokles = Eteocles
Euadne = Evadne
Euboia = Euboea
Eumaios = Eumaeus
Euneos = Euneus
Europe = Europa
Eurykleia = Euryclea
Eurydike = Eurydice
Gaia = Gaea
Galateia = Galatea
Ganymedes = Ganymede
Glauke = Glauce
Glaukos = Glaucus
Graiai = Graeae
Haides = Hades
Haimon = Haemon
Hekabe = Hecabe, Hecuba
Hekate = Hecate
Hekatoncheires, Hekatonkheires = Hecatonchires
Hektor = Hector
Helenos = Helenus
Helios = Helius

Hephaistos = Hephaestus
Herakles = Heracles, Hercules
Hippodameia = Hippodamia
Hippolyte = Hippolyta
Hippolytos = Hippolytus
Horai = Horae
Hyakinthos = Hyacinthus
Hyllos = Hyllus
Iakchos, Iakkhos = Iacchus
Iason = Jason
Ikarios = Icarius
Ikaros = Icarus
Ilion = Ilium
Inachos, Inakhos = Inachus
Iokaste = Jocasta
Iolaos = Iolaüs
Iolkos = Iolcus
Iphigeneia = Iphigenia
Iphikles = Iphicles
Iphiklos = Iphiclus
Iphimedeia = Iphimedia
Iphitos = Iphitus
Ithaka = Ithaca
J, see I
Kadmos = Cadmus
Kaineus = Caeneus
Kalchas, Kalkhas = Calchas
Kallidike = Callidice
Kalliope = Calliope
Kallisto = Callisto
Kalypso = Calypso
Kanake = Canace
Kapaneus = Capaneus
Kassandra = Cassandra
Kassiepeia = Cassiepea
Kastor = Castor
Kerkops = Cercops
Kelaino = Celaeno
Keleus = Celeus
Kentauros = Centaurus, Centaur
Kephalos = Cephalus
Kerberos = Cerberus
Kerkopes = Cercopes
Kerkyon = Cercyon
Keto = Ceto
Keyx = Ceyx
Kirke = Circe
Kithairon = Cithaeron
Kleio = Clio
Klymene = Clymene
Klytaimnestra = Clytaemnestra, Clytemnestra
Knossos = Cnossus
Kodros = Codrus
Koios = Coeus
Kokytos = Cocytus
Kolchis, Kolkhis = Colchis

Kolonos = Colonus
Komaitho = Comaetho
Korinthos = Corinthus, Corinth
Koronis = Coronis
Kreon = Creon
Kreousa = Creusa
Kroisos = Croesus
Kronos = Cronus
Kybele = Cybele
Kyklops = Cyclops
Kyknos = Cycnus
Kyparissos = Cyparissus
Kypros = Cyprus
Kythera = Cythera
Kytisoros = Cytisorus
Kyzikos = Cyzicus
Labdakos = Labdacus
Laios = Laius
Lakedaimon = Lacedaemon
Laodameia = Laodamia
Learchos, Learkhos = Learchus
Leukippe = Leucippe
Leukippos = Leucippus
Leukothea = Leucothea
Leukothoe = Leucothoë
Likymnios = Licymnius
Linos = Linus
Lykaon = Lycaon
Lykia = Lycia
Lykomedes = Lycomedes
Lykurgos = Lycurgus
Lykos = Lycus
Lynkeus = Lynceus
Makareus = Macareus
Makaria = Macaria
Machaon, Makhaon = Machaon
Mainas = Maenas, Maenad
Medeia = Medea
Medousa = Medusa
Meleagros = Meleager
Meliai = Meliae
Melikertes = Melicertes
Menelaos = Menelaüs
Menoikeus = Menoeceus
Minotauros = Minotaurus, Minotaur
Musaios = Musaeus
Mousa, Mousai = Musa, Musae, Muse, Muses
Mykenai = Mycenae, Mycene
Myrtilos = Myrtilus
Narkissos = Narcissus
Nausikaä = Nausicaä
Neoptolemos = Neoptolemus
Nessos = Nessus
Nykteus = Nycteus
Oidipous = Oedipus
Oinomaos = Oenomaüs

Okeanos = Oceanus
Olympos = Olympus
Orchomenos, Orkhomenos =
    Orchomenus
Oreithyia = Orithyia
Orthros = Orthrus
Ourania = Urania
Ouranos = Uranus
Palaimon = Palaemon
Palladion = Palladium
Panathenaia = Panathenaea
Parnassos = Parnassus
Parthenopaios = Parthenopaeus
Patroklos = Patroclus
Pegasos = Pegasus
Peisistratos = Pisistratus
Peneios = Peneus
Penthesileia = Penthesilea
Peloponnesos = Peloponnesus,
    Peloponnese
Periklymenos = Periclymenus
Persephone = Proserpina

Perikles = Pericles
Phaiakes = Phaeaces, Phaeacians
Philoktetes = Philoctetes
Phoibe = Phoebe
Phoibos = Phoebus
Plouton = Pluton, Pluto
Ploutos = Plutus
Podaleirios = Podalirius
Poias = Poeas
Polybos = Polybus
Polydeukos = Polydeuces
Polyneikes = Polynices
Polyphemos = Polyphemus
Priamos = Priamus, Priam
Prokne = Procne
Prokris = Procris
Prokrustes = Procrustes
Rheia = Rhea
Rhesos = Rhesus
Salmakis = Salmacis
Satyros = Satyrus, Satyr
Schoineus, Skhoineus = Schoeneus

Seilenos = Silenus
Seirenes = Sirenes, Sirens
Sibylla = Sibylla, Sibyl
Sisyphos = Sisyphus
Skeiron = Sciron
Skylla = Scylla
Stheneboia = Stheneboea
Tantalos = Tantalus
Tartaros = Tartarus
Telemachos, Telemakhos =
    Telemachus
Teukros = Teucer
Thaleia = Thalia
Thorikos = Thoricus
Thrinakie = Thrinacia
Tityos = Tityus
Troizen = Troezen
U, *see* Ou
Xanthos = Xanthus
Xouthos = Xuthus
Zephyros = Zephyrus, Zephyr
Zethos = Zethus

Indexes

Index of Authors, Artists, Composers, and Titles

GLOSSARY/INDEX OF MYTHOLOGICAL AND HISTORICAL PERSONS, PLACES, AND SUBJECTS

A simple guide to pronunciation follows words in this index. The long vowels are to be pronounced as follows: ā (cape), ē (bee), ī (ice), ō (boat), and ū (too). Syllabication is marked by a prime mark (') and a hyphen (-). Syllables that precede the prime are stressed. **Note**: pictorial representations are in **bold** type.

Tiresias (ti-rē' si-as), Theban priest and prophet, 121, 155, 229, 302–5, 312, 323, 326, 351–53, 421, 423, 426–28, 515, 516, 527–28, 545, 546

Tiryns (ti' rinz), Mycenaean citadel in the Argolid, associated with Heracles and excavated by Schliemann, 39, 44, 315, 400, 401, 532

Tisamenus (ti-sam' en-us), son of Orestes and Hermione and leader against the Heraclidae, 441, 567

Tisiphone (ti-sif' ō-nē), a Fury, 368, 375

Titan, Titans (tī' tanz), twelve children of Uranus and Ge, 27, 59, 63, 65–70, 318, 369, 374, 385; Titanomachy (tī-tan-o' ma-kē), battle in which Zeus and the Olympians defeat Cronus and the Titans, 81–83, 85, **90**, 94, 95, 102

Tithonus (ti-thō' nus), brother of Priam, beloved of Eos, and turned into a grasshopper, 21, 69–70, 202–3, 495

Titus Tatius (tī' tus tā' shi-us or ta' ti-us), Sabine leader who became Romulus' colleague, 657, 682, 683, 685

Tityus (tit' i-us), killed by Apollo for his attempt to rape Leto, and punished in the Underworld by vultures devouring his liver forever, 262, 369, 374, 375

Tragedy, 639

Trajan, Roman emperor (98–117 A.D.), **660**

Trial of the Bow, 520

Trickster: archetypal, 288; divine or heroic, 93

Trier (trī' er), an important Roman town in Germany, 633

Triptolemus (trip-tol' e-mus), prince in Eleusis and Demeter's messenger, 341, **341**

Triton (trī' ton), son of Poseidon and Amphitrite, merman, trumpeter of the sea, 100, 165, 169, **171**, 177, 181, 605

Troezen (trē' zen), city in the Argolid associated with the saga of Theseus, 230, 231, 240, 579–81

Troïlus (troy' lus), Priam's son, killed by Achilles, 467, 468, **503**

Trojan horse, 497, **498**

Trophonius (tro-fō' ni-us), "He who fosters growth," builder, brother of Agamedes, and chthonic hero or god with an oracle, 121

Tros (trō s), son of Dardanus, king of Troy, and father of Ganymede, 122, 467

Troy, situated near the Dardanelles and first excavated by Schliemann there were nine settlements on the site, including that of Priam and the Trojan War, Trojan(s), Trojan War, 28, 39, 46–54, 48, 50, 87; Achaean leaders, 470–76; arrival of Greek expedition at, 485–86; fall of, 28, 494–502; leaders of, 470–76; sack of, 499–500, **500**, 501–502; saga of, 460–504; Troy I, 46; Troy II, 46–47; Troy III-V, 47; Troy VI, 47–49, **49**; Troy VII (Troy VIIa), 47–49

Tuculcha (tu-kul' ka), Etruscan divinity or the Underworld, 669

Tullia (tul' li-a), wicked daughter of Servius Tullius, 689

Tullus Hostilius (tul' lus hosti' li-us), third king of Rome, 685

Turnus (tur' nus), leader of the Rutuli in Italy and bitter opponent of Aeneas, by whom he is killed, 629, 666, 674, 676, 677, 678, 680

Tyche (tī' kē), Fortune or Chance, 131

Tydeus (tī' de-us), one of the Seven against Thebes and father of Diomedes, 368, 419, 420, 422, 471, 540

Tyndareus (tin-dar' e-us), king of Sparta, husband of Leda, 433, 440, 460

Typhaon (tī-fa' on), Typhoeus (tī-fē' us), or Typhon (tī' fon), name of monstrous dragons, one killed by Zeus, another by Apollo, 83–85, 102–3, 170, 268–71

Tyre (tī r), original home of Dido, 679

Tyro (tī' rō), daughter of Salmoneus, wife of Cretheus, loved by Poseidon, and mother of Neleus and Pelias, 165, 597, 598

Ullikummis (ul-li-kū m' mis), giant created by Kumarbi as a threat to the gods, 108

Ulysses (ū-lis' sē z), **512**, 529, 630, 632, **633**. *See also* Odysseus

Underworld, 21, 28, 48, 108, 113, 214, 226, 288, 290, **340**, 341, 343, 348, 351, 351–76, **354**, 556; in *Aeneid*, 363–76; depictions of, 357; Descent to (myth), 103, 108; in myth of Er, 358–63; in *Odyssey*, 351–56; Orpheus' descent to, 379–84; Roman divinities of, 667 (*See also* Hades)

Uni, Etruscan goddess, assimilated into the Roman goddess Juno, 627

Urania (ū-ra' ni-a), Muse of astronomy, 131

Uranus (ū' ra-nus), sky-god, husband of Ge, castrated by his son Cronus; from his genitals, Aphrodite Urania, Celestial Aphrodite, was born, 59, 61, 62–65, 68, 70–71, 74, 78, 81, 83, 95, 102, 108, 187, 372, 375, 387

Urizen (u-rī z' en), Blake's creator of the world, **78**

Ursa Major (ur' sa mā' jor), the constellation of the Great Bear, which Callisto became, 224

Ursa Minor, the constellation of the Little Bear, which Arcas became, 224

Uruk (ur' uk), Sumerian city, 103, 105

Ut-napishtim, 104, 105

Veii (vā y' ē), an important Etruscan town, 626, 673

Venus (vē' nus), Italian fertility goddess whom the Romans equated with Aphrodite, 70, 113, 169, 188–91, **189**, **191**, **194**, **199**, 213–15, 501, 650, 654, 659, 663–665; Venus Felix, 664; Venus Obsequens, 663; Venus the Beholder (Prospiciens), a statue at Cypriot Salamis, 650; Venus Victrix, 664

Vertumnus (ver-tum' nus), Etruscan god who won Pomona's love, 644, 645, 650

Vesta (ves' ta), Roman goddess of the hearth, equated with Hestia, 113, 654, 660–61, 666; Vestal Virgin(s), 660, 666, 681, **682**

Vesuvius, volcano in Campania that erupted in 79 A.D., destroying the cities of Herculaneum and Pompeii, 633, 634, 647

Vicus Sceleratus (vi' cus sce-le-rā' tus), "Crime Street," named after Tullia's crime, 689

Villa of the Mysteries, villa at Pompeii with sequence of paintings depicting initiation into Dionysiac mysteries, 634

Virbius (vir' bi-us), an Italian divinity identified with Hippolytus, 587, 667

Virgin Mary, 200

Vulcan (vul' kan), Vulcanus (vul-ka' nus), chief Italian fire-god, whom the Romans equated with Hephaestus, 67, 113, **126**, 627, 657, 660–61, 688

Winged sandals, 534, **538**, **539**

Women, in Greek society, 19–20

Xanthus (zan' thus), horse of Achilles, who prophesied his death, 492

Xerxes (zer' ksē z), Persian king who visited Troy and invaded Greece, 51, 148

Xuthus (zū' thus), son of Hellen, husband of Creusa, and father of Achaeus, 82, 573, 578

Zagreus (zag' re-us), another name for Dionysus as god of the mysteries, 318, 346, 386

Zephyrus (ze' fi-rus), West Wind, 642

Zetes (zē' tē z), he and his brother Calaïs were winged sons of Boreas and Orithyia, and Argonauts, 573, 578, 599, 600–1

Zethus (zē' thus), herdsman, king of Thebes, son of Zeus and Antiope, brother of Amphion, and husband of Thebe, 404, 405, 408

Zeus (zū s), son of Cronus and Rhea and supreme god of the Greeks, 6, 7, 21, 22, 27, 42, 44, 45, 59, 60, 63–65, 67–69, 74–77, **83**, 81–119, **89**, **117**, 121–131, **120**, **123**, 135–38, 140, 146, 148, 151, 153, 156, 159, 163, 165–67, 173–74, **174**, 177, 180, 184, 187–89, 196–202, 203, 206–7, 219, 243, 247, 248, 252, 259, 262, 277–78, **281**, 283–84, 286, 288, 296, **297**, 298, 299, 301, 304, 316–18, 330–32, 336–40, 348, 355, 369, 372, 376, 384, 387, 390, 403, 404, 405, 408, 412–13, 416, 421, 432, 433, 434, 437, 441, 444, 451, 460, 461, 463, 464, 466, 468, 469, 471, 474, 478, 480, 485–86, 488–90, 492, 494, 510, 517, 527, 533, 434, 536, 539, 542, 543, 545–46, 549, 551, 553, 556, 557, 558, 560, 564–66, 582, 583, 584, 588, 597, 606, 615, 627, 629, 637, 649–650, 654, 657, 676, 677; birth of, 74–78; children of Hera and, 121–30; children of Leda and, 460; defeat of Cronus, 81–83; Dictaean, 75; diverse character of, 115–16; in Gigantomachy, 83–85; Hecalus, 582; and Lycaon, 98–99; monotheism and, 137–38; other children of, 130–31; Phyxius, 597; and Prometheus, 90–91; sacred marriage with Hera, 116–17; temple of, 117–20, 174, 175, 260, 262, 549, 554–55

Ziusudra (zius-ū' dra), Sumerian equivalent of Ut-napishtim, survivor of the Flood, 104